T0220786

Lecture Notes in Computer Science   11363

Commenced Publication in 1973
Founding and Former Series Editors:
Gerhard Goos, Juris Hartmanis, and Jan van Leeuwen

More information about this series at http://www.springer.com/series/7412

C. V. Jawahar · Hongdong Li ·
Greg Mori · Konrad Schindler (Eds.)

Computer Vision – ACCV 2018

14th Asian Conference on Computer Vision
Perth, Australia, December 2–6, 2018
Revised Selected Papers, Part III

 Springer

Editors
C. V. Jawahar
IIIT Hyderabad
Hyderabad, India

Greg Mori
Simon Fraser University
Burnaby, BC, Canada

Hongdong Li
ANU
Canberra, ACT, Australia

Konrad Schindler (ID)
ETH Zurich
Zurich, Zürich, Switzerland

ISSN 0302-9743 ISSN 1611-3349 (electronic)
Lecture Notes in Computer Science
ISBN 978-3-030-20892-9 ISBN 978-3-030-20893-6 (eBook)
https://doi.org/10.1007/978-3-030-20893-6

LNCS Sublibrary: SL6 – Image Processing, Computer Vision, Pattern Recognition, and Graphics

This Springer imprint is published by the registered company Springer Nature Switzerland AG
The registered company address is: Gewerbestrasse 11, 6330 Cham, Switzerland

Preface

The Asian Conference on Computer Vision (ACCV) 2018 took place in Perth, Australia, during December 2–6, 2018. The conference featured novel research contributions from almost all sub-areas of computer vision.

This year we received a record number of conference submissions. After removing the desk rejects, 979 valid, complete manuscripts were submitted for review. A pool of 34 area chairs and 1,063 reviewers was recruited to conduct paper reviews. Like previous editions of ACCV, we adopted a double-blind review process to determine which of these papers to accept. Identities of authors were not visible to reviewers and area chairs; nor were the identities of the assigned reviewers and area chairs visible to authors. The program chairs did not submit papers to the conference.

Each paper was reviewed by at least three reviewers. Authors were permitted to respond to the initial reviews during a rebuttal period. After this, the area chairs led discussions among reviewers. Finally, a physical area chairs was held in Singapore, during which panels of three area chairs deliberated to decide on acceptance decisions for each paper. At the end of this process, 274 papers were accepted for publication in the ACCV 2018 conference proceedings, of which five were later withdrawn by their authors.

In addition to the main conference, ACCV 2018 featured 11 workshops and six tutorials.

We would like to thank all the organizers, sponsors, area chairs, reviewers, and authors. Special thanks go to Prof. Guosheng Lin from Nanyang Technological University, Singapore, for hosting the area chair meeting. We acknowledge the support of Microsoft's Conference Management Toolkit (CMT) team for providing the software used to manage the review process.

We greatly appreciate the efforts of all those who contributed to making the conference a success.

December 2018

C. V. Jawahar
Hongdong Li
Greg Mori
Konrad Schindler

Organization

General Chairs

Kyoung-mu Lee   Seoul National University, South Korea
Ajmal Mian   University of Western Australia, Australia
Ian Reid   University of Adelaide, Australia
Yoichi Sato   University of Tokyo, Japan

Program Chairs

C. V. Jawahar   IIIT Hyderabad, India
Hongdong Li   Australian National University, Australia
Greg Mori   Simon Fraser University and Borealis AI, Canada
Konrad Schindler   ETH Zurich, Switzerland

Advisor

Richard Hartley   Australian National University, Australia

Publication Chair

Hamid Rezatofighi   University of Adelaide, Australia

Local Arrangements Chairs

Guosheng Lin   Nanyang Technological University, Singapore
Ajmal Mian   University of Western Australia, Australia

Area Chairs

Lourdes Agapito   University College London, UK
Xiang Bai   Huazhong University of Science and Technology, China
Vineeth N. Balasubramanian   IIT Hyderabad, India
Gustavo Carneiro   University of Adelaide, Australia
Tat-Jun Chin   University of Adelaide, Australia
Minsu Cho   POSTECH, South Korea
Bohyung Han   Seoul National University, South Korea
Junwei Han   Northwestern Polytechnical University, China
Mehrtash Harandi   Monash University, Australia
Gang Hua   Microsoft Research, Asia

Rei Kawakami	University of Tokyo, Japan
Tae-Kyun Kim	Imperial College London, UK
Junseok Kwon	Chung-Ang University, South Korea
Florent Lafarge	Inria, France
Laura Leal-Taixé	TU Munich, Germany
Zhouchen Lin	Peking University, China
Yanxi Liu	Penn State University, USA
Oisin Mac Aodha	Caltech, USA
Anurag Mittal	IIT Madras, India
Vinay Namboodiri	IIT Kanpur, India
P. J. Narayanan	IIIT Hyderabad, India
Carl Olsson	Lund University, Sweden
Imari Sato	National Institute of Informatics
Shiguang Shan	Chinese Academy of Sciences, China
Chunhua Shen	University of Adelaide, Australia
Boxin Shi	Peking University, China
Terence Sim	National University of Singapore, Singapore
Yusuke Sugano	Osaka University, Japan
Min Sun	National Tsing Hua University, Taiwan
Robby Tan	Yale-NUS College, USA
Siyu Tang	MPI for Intelligent Systems
Radu Timofte	ETH Zurich, Switzerland
Jingyi Yu	University of Delaware, USA
Junsong Yuan	State University of New York at Buffalo, USA

Additional Reviewers

Ehsan Abbasnejad
Akash Abdu Jyothi
Abrar Abdulnabi
Nagesh Adluru
Antonio Agudo
Unaiza Ahsan
Hai-zhou Ai
Alexandre Alahi
Xavier Alameda-Pineda
Andrea Albarelli
Mohsen Ali
Saad Ali
Mitsuru Ambai
Cosmin Ancuti
Vijay Rengarajan Angarai
    Pichaikuppan
Michel Antunes
Djamila Aouada

Ognjen Arandjelovic
Anil Armagan
Chetan Arora
Mathieu Aubry
Hossein Azizpour
Seung-Hwan Baek
Aijun Bai
Peter Bajcsy
Amr Bakry
Vassileios Balntas
Yutong Ban
Arunava Banerjee
Monami Banerjee
Atsuhiko Banno
Aayush Bansal
Dániel Baráth
Lorenzo Baraldi
Adrian Barbu

Nick Barnes
Peter Barnum
Joe Bartels
Paul Beardsley
Sima Behpour
Vasileios Belagiannis
Boulbaba Ben Amor
Archith Bency
Ryad Benosman
Gedas Bertasius
Ross Beveridge
Binod Bhattarai
Arnav Bhavsar
Simone Bianco
Oliver Bimber
Tolga Birdal
Horst Bischof
Arijit Biswas

Soma Biswas

Henryk Blasinski

Vishnu Boddeti

Federica Bogo

Tolga Bolukbasi

Terrance Boult

Thierry Bouwmans

Abdesselam Bouzerdoum

Ernesto Brau

Mathieu Bredif

Stefan Breuers

Marcus Brubaker

Anders Buch

Shyamal Buch

Pradeep Buddharaju

Adrian Bulat

Darius Burschka

Andrei Bursuc

Zoya Bylinskii

Weidong Cai

Necati Cihan Camgoz

Shaun Canavan

Joao Carreira

Dan Casas

M. Emre Celebi

Hakan Cevikalp

François Chadebecq

Menglei Chai

Rudrasis Chakraborty

Tat-Jen Cham

Kwok-Ping Chan

Sharat Chandran

Chehan Chang

Hyun Sung Chang

Yi Chang

Wei-Lun Chao

Visesh Chari

Gaurav Chaurasia

Rama Chellappa

Chen Chen

Chu-Song Chen

Dongdong Chen

Guangyong Chen

Hsin-I Chen

Huaijin Chen

Hwann-Tzong Chen

Jiacheng Chen

Jianhui Chen

Jiansheng Chen

Jiaxin Chen

Jie Chen

Kan Chen

Longbin Chen

Ting Chen

Tseng-Hung Chen

Wei Chen

Xi'ai Chen

Xiaozhi Chen

Xilin Chen

Xinlei Chen

Yunjin Chen

Erkang Cheng

Hong Cheng

Hui Cheng

Jingchun Cheng

Ming-Ming Cheng

Wen-Huang Cheng

Yuan Cheng

Zhi-Qi Cheng

Loong Fah Cheong

Anoop Cherian

Liang-Tien Chia

Chao-Kai Chiang

Shao-Yi Chien

Han-Pang Chiu

Wei-Chen Chiu

Donghyeon Cho

Nam Ik Cho

Sunghyun Cho

Yeong-Jun Cho

Gyeongmin Choe

Chiho Choi

Jonghyun Choi

Jongmoo Choi

Jongwon Choi

Hisham Cholakkal

Biswarup Choudhury

Xiao Chu

Yung-Yu Chuang

Andrea Cohen

Toby Collins

Marco Cristani

James Crowley

Jinshi Cui

Zhaopeng Cui

Bo Dai

Hang Dai

Xiyang Dai

Yuchao Dai

Carlo Dal Mutto

Zachary Daniels

Mohamed Daoudi

Abir Das

Raoul De Charette

Teofilo Decampos

Koichiro Deguchi

Stefanie Demirci

Girum Demisse

Patrick Dendorfer

Zhiwei Deng

Joachim Denzler

Aditya Deshpande

Frédéric Devernay

Abhinav Dhall

Anthony Dick

Zhengming Ding

Cosimo Distante

Ajay Divakaran

Mandar Dixit

Thanh-Toan Do

Jose Dolz

Bo Dong

Chao Dong

Jingming Dong

Ming Dong

Weisheng Dong

Simon Donne

Gianfranco Doretto

Bruce Draper

Bertram Drost

Liang Du

Shichuan Du

Jean-Luc Dugelay

Enrique Dunn

Thibaut Durand

Zoran Duric

Ionut Cosmin Duta

Samyak Dutta

Pinar Duygulu
Ady Ecker
Hazim Ekenel
Sabu Emmanuel
Ian Endres
Ertunc Erdil
Hugo Jair Escalante
Sergio Escalera
Francisco Escolano Ruiz
Bin Fan
Shaojing Fan
Yi Fang
Aly Farag
Giovanni Farinella
Rafael Felix
Michele Fenzi
Bob Fisher
David Fofi
Gian Luca Foresti
Victor Fragoso
Bernd Freisleben
Jason Fritts
Cheng-Yang Fu
Chi-Wing Fu
Huazhu Fu
Jianlong Fu
Xueyang Fu
Ying Fu
Yun Fu
Olac Fuentes
Jan Funke
Ryo Furukawa
Yasutaka Furukawa
Manuel Günther
Raghudeep Gadde
Matheus Gadelha
Jürgen Gall
Silvano Galliani
Chuang Gan
Zhe Gan
Vineet Gandhi
Arvind Ganesh
Bin-Bin Gao
Jin Gao
Jiyang Gao
Junbin Gao

Ravi Garg
Jochen Gast
Utkarsh Gaur
Xin Geng
David Geronimno
Michael Gharbi
Amir Ghodrati
Behnam Gholami
Andrew Gilbert
Rohit Girdhar
Ioannis Gkioulekas
Guy Godin
Nuno Goncalves
Yu Gong
Stephen Gould
Venu Govindu
Oleg Grinchuk
Jiuxiang Gu
Shuhang Gu
Paul Guerrero
Anupam Guha
Guodong Guo
Yanwen Guo
Ankit Gupta
Mithun Gupta
Saurabh Gupta
Hossein Hajimirsadeghi
Maciej Halber
Xiaoguang Han
Yahong Han
Zhi Han
Kenji Hara
Tatsuya Harada
Ali Harakeh
Adam Harley
Ben Harwood
Mahmudul Hasan
Kenji Hata
Michal Havlena
Munawar Hayat
Zeeshan Hayder
Jiawei He
Kun He
Lei He
Lifang He
Pan He

Yang He
Zhenliang He
Zhihai He
Felix Heide
Samitha Herath
Luis Herranz
Anders Heyden
Je Hyeong Hong
Seunghoon Hong
Wei Hong
Le Hou
Chiou-Ting Hsu
Kuang-Jui Hsu
Di Hu
Hexiang Hu
Ping Hu
Xu Hu
Yinlin Hu
Zhiting Hu
De-An Huang
Gao Huang
Gary Huang
Haibin Huang
Haifei Huang
Haozhi Huang
Jia-Bin Huang
Shaoli Huang
Sheng Huang
Xinyu Huang
Xun Huang
Yan Huang
Yawen Huang
Yinghao Huang
Yizhen Huang
Wei-Chih Hung
Junhwa Hur
Mohamed Hussein
Jyh-Jing Hwang
Ichiro Ide
Satoshi Ikehata
Radu Tudor Ionescu
Go Irie
Ahmet Iscen
Vamsi Ithapu
Daisuke Iwai
Won-Dong Jang

Dinesh Jayaraman
Sadeep Jayasumana
Suren Jayasuriya
Hueihan Jhuang
Dinghuang Ji
Mengqi Ji
Hongjun Jia
Jiayan Jiang
Qing-Yuan Jiang
Tingting Jiang
Xiaoyi Jiang
Zhuolin Jiang
Zequn Jie
Xiaojie Jin
Younghyun Jo
Ole Johannsen
Hanbyul Joo
Jungseock Joo
Kyungdon Joo
Shantanu Joshi
Amin Jourabloo
Deunsol Jung
Anis Kacem
Ioannis Kakadiaris
Zdenek Kalal
Nima Kalantari
Mahdi Kalayeh
Sinan Kalkan
Vicky Kalogeiton
Joni-Kristian Kamarainen
Martin Kampel
Meina Kan
Kenichi Kanatani
Atsushi Kanehira
Takuhiro Kaneko
Zhuoliang Kang
Mohan Kankanhalli
Vadim Kantorov
Nikolaos Karianakis
Leonid Karlinsky
Zoltan Kato
Hiroshi Kawasaki
Wei Ke
Wadim Kehl
Sameh Khamis
Naeemullah Khan

Salman Khan
Rawal Khirodkar
Mehran Khodabandeh
Anna Khoreva
Parmeshwar Khurd
Hadi Kiapour
Joe Kileel
Edward Kim
Gunhee Kim
Hansung Kim
Hyunwoo Kim
Junsik Kim
Seon Joo Kim
Vladimir Kim
Akisato Kimura
Ravi Kiran
Roman Klokov
Takumi Kobayashi
Amir Kolaman
Naejin Kong
Piotr Koniusz
Hyung Il Koo
Dimitrios Kosmopoulos
Gregory Kramida
Praveen Krishnan
Ravi Krishnan
Hiroyuki Kubo
Hilde Kuehne
Jason Kuen
Arjan Kuijper
Kuldeep Kulkarni
Shiro Kumano
Avinash Kumar
Soumava Roy Kumar
Kaustav Kundu
Sebastian Kurtek
Yevhen Kuznietsov
Heeseung Kwon
Alexander Ladikos
Kevin Lai
Wei-Sheng Lai
Shang-Hong Lai
Michael Lam
Zhenzhong Lan
Dong Lao
Katrin Lasinger

Yasir Latif
Huu Le
Herve Le Borgne
Chun-Yi Lee
Gim Hee Lee
Seungyong Lee
Teng-Yok Lee
Seungkyu Lee
Andreas Lehrmann
Na Lei
Spyridon Leonardos
Marius Leordeanu
Matt Leotta
Gil Levi
Evgeny Levinkov
Jose Lezama
Ang Li
Chen Li
Chunyuan Li
Dangwei Li
Dingzeyu Li
Dong Li
Hai Li
Jianguo Li
Stan Li
Wanqing Li
Wei Li
Xi Li
Xirong Li
Xiu Li
Xuelong Li
Yanghao Li
Yin Li
Yingwei Li
Yongjie Li
Yu Li
Yuncheng Li
Zechao Li
Zhengqi Li
Zhengqin Li
Zhuwen Li
Zhouhui Lian
Jie Liang
Zicheng Liao
Jongwoo Lim
Ser-Nam Lim

Kaimo Lin
Shih-Yao Lin
Tsung-Yi Lin
Weiyao Lin
Yuewei Lin
Venice Liong
Giuseppe Lisanti
Roee Litman
Jim Little
Anan Liu
Chao Liu
Chen Liu
Eryun Liu
Fayao Liu
Huaping Liu
Jingen Liu
Lingqiao Liu
Miaomiao Liu
Qingshan Liu
Risheng Liu
Sifei Liu
Tyng-Luh Liu
Weiyang Liu
Xialei Liu
Xianglong Liu
Xiao Liu
Yebin Liu
Yi Liu
Yu Liu
Yun Liu
Ziwei Liu
Stephan Liwicki
Liliana Lo Presti
Fotios Logothetis
Javier Lorenzo
Manolis Lourakis
Brian Lovell
Chen Change Loy
Chaochao Lu
Feng Lu
Huchuan Lu
Jiajun Lu
Kaiyue Lu
Xin Lu
Yijuan Lu
Yongxi Lu

Fujun Luan
Jian-Hao Luo
Jiebo Luo
Weixin Luo
Khoa Luu
Chao Ma
Huimin Ma
Kede Ma
Lin Ma
Shugao Ma
Wei-Chiu Ma
Will Maddern
Ludovic Magerand
Luca Magri
Behrooz Mahasseni
Tahmida Mahmud
Robert Maier
Subhransu Maji
Yasushi Makihara
Clement Mallet
Abed Malti
Devraj Mandal
Fabian Manhardt
Gian Luca Marcialis
Julio Marco
Diego Marcos
Ricardo Martin
Tanya Marwah
Marc Masana
Jonathan Masci
Takeshi Masuda
Yusuke Matsui
Tetsu Matsukawa
Gellert Mattyus
Thomas Mauthner
Bruce Maxwell
Steve Maybank
Amir Mazaheri
Scott Mccloskey
Mason Mcgill
Nazanin Mehrasa
Ishit Mehta
Xue Mei
Heydi Mendez-Vazquez
Gaofeng Meng
Bjoern Menze

Domingo Mery
Pascal Mettes
Jan Hendrik Metzen
Gregor Miller
Cai Minjie
Ikuhisa Mitsugami
Daisuke Miyazaki
Davide Modolo
Pritish Mohapatra
Pascal Monasse
Sandino Morales
Pietro Morerio
Saeid Motiian
Arsalan Mousavian
Mikhail Mozerov
Yasuhiro Mukaigawa
Yusuke Mukuta
Mario Munich
Srikanth Muralidharan
Ana Murillo
Vittorio Murino
Armin Mustafa
Hajime Nagahara
Shruti Nagpal
Mahyar Najibi
Katsuyuki Nakamura
Seonghyeon Nam
Loris Nanni
Manjunath Narayana
Lakshmanan Nataraj
Neda Nategh
Lukáš Neumann
Shawn Newsam
Joe Yue-Hei Ng
Thuyen Ngo
David Nilsson
Ji-feng Ning
Mark Nixon
Shohei Nobuhara
Hyeonwoo Noh
Mehdi Noroozi
Erfan Noury
Eyal Ofek
Seong Joon Oh
Seoung Wug Oh
Katsunori Ohnishi

Iason Oikonomidis
Takeshi Oishi
Takahiro Okabe
Takayuki Okatani
Gustavo Olague
Kyle Olszewski
Mohamed Omran
Roy Or-El
Ivan Oseledets
Martin R. Oswald
Tomas Pajdla
Dipan Pal
Kalman Palagyi
Manohar Paluri
Gang Pan
Jinshan Pan
Yannis Panagakis
Rameswar Panda
Hsing-Kuo Pao
Dim Papadopoulos
Konstantinos Papoutsakis
Shaifali Parashar
Hyun Soo Park
Jinsun Park
Taesung Park
Wonpyo Park
Alvaro Parra Bustos
Geoffrey Pascoe
Ioannis Patras
Genevieve Patterson
Georgios Pavlakos
Ioannis Pavlidis
Nick Pears
Pieter Peers
Selen Pehlivan
Xi Peng
Xingchao Peng
Janez Perš
Talita Perciano
Adrian Peter
Lars Petersson
Stavros Petridis
Patrick Peursum
Trung Pham
Sang Phan
Marco Piccirilli

Sudeep Pillai
Wong Ya Ping
Lerrel Pinto
Fiora Pirri
Matteo Poggi
Georg Poier
Marius Popescu
Ronald Poppe
Dilip Prasad
Andrea Prati
Maria Priisalu
Véronique Prinet
Victor Prisacariu
Hugo Proenca
Jan Prokaj
Daniel Prusa
Yunchen Pu
Guo-Jun Qi
Xiaojuan Qi
Zhen Qian
Yu Qiao
Jie Qin
Lei Qin
Chao Qu
Faisal Qureshi
Petia Radeva
Venkatesh Babu
   Radhakrishnan
Ilija Radosavovic
Bogdan Raducanu
Hossein Rahmani
Swaminathan Rahul
Ajit Rajwade
Kandan Ramakrishnan
Visvanathan Ramesh
Yongming Rao
Sathya Ravi
Michael Reale
Adria Recasens
Konstantinos Rematas
Haibing Ren
Jimmy Ren
Wenqi Ren
Zhile Ren
Edel Garcia Reyes
Hamid Rezatofighi

Hamed Rezazadegan
   Tavakoli
Rafael Rezende
Helge Rhodin
Alexander Richard
Stephan Richter
Gernot Riegler
Christian Riess
Ergys Ristani
Tobias Ritschel
Mariano Rivera
Antonio Robles-Kelly
Emanuele Rodola
Andres Rodriguez
Mikel Rodriguez
Matteo Ruggero Ronchi
Xuejian Rong
Bodo Rosenhahn
Arun Ross
Peter Roth
Michel Roux
Ryusuke Sagawa
Hideo Saito
Shunsuke Saito
Parikshit Sakurikar
Albert Ali Salah
Jorge Sanchez
Conrad Sanderson
Aswin Sankaranarayanan
Swami Sankaranarayanan
Archana Sapkota
Michele Sasdelli
Jun Sato
Shin'ichi Satoh
Torsten Sattler
Manolis Savva
Tanner Schmidt
Dirk Schnieders
Samuel Schulter
Rajvi Shah
Shishir Shah
Sohil Shah
Moein Shakeri
Nataliya Shapovalova
Aidean Sharghi
Gaurav Sharma

Pramod Sharma
Li Shen
Shuhan Shen
Wei Shen
Xiaoyong Shen
Zhiqiang Shen
Lu Sheng
Baoguang Shi
Guangming Shi
Miaojing Shi
Zhiyuan Shi
Takashi Shibata
Huang-Chia Shih
Meng-Li Shih
Sheng-Wen Shih
Atsushi Shimada
Nobutaka Shimada
Daeyun Shin
Young Min Shin
Koichi Shinoda
Tianmin Shu
Zhixin Shu
Bing Shuai
Karan Sikka
Jack Sim
Marcel Simon
Tomas Simon
Vishwanath Sindagi
Gurkirt Singh
Maneet Singh
Praveer Singh
Ayan Sinha
Sudipta Sinha
Vladimir Smutny
Francesco Solera
Amir Arsalan Soltani
Eric Sommerlade
Andy Song
Shiyu Song
Yibing Song
Humberto Sossa
Concetto Spampinato
Filip Šroubek
Ioannis Stamos
Jan Stuehmer
Jingyong Su

Jong-Chyi Su
Shuochen Su
Yu-Chuan Su
Zhixun Su
Ramanathan Subramanian
Akihiro Sugimoto
Waqas Sultani
Jiande Sun
Jin Sun
Ju Sun
Lin Sun
Min Sun
Yao Sun
Zhaohui Sun
David Suter
Tanveer Syeda-Mahmood
Yuichi Taguchi
Jun Takamatsu
Takafumi Taketomi
Hugues Talbot
Youssef Tamaazousti
Toru Tamak
Robert Tamburo
Chaowei Tan
David Joseph Tan
Ping Tan
Xiaoyang Tan
Kenichiro Tanaka
Masayuki Tanaka
Jinhui Tang
Meng Tang
Peng Tang
Wei Tang
Yuxing Tang
Junli Tao
Xin Tao
Makarand Tapaswi
Jean-Philippe Tarel
Keisuke Tateno
Joao Tavares
Bugra Tekin
Mariano Tepper
Ali Thabet
Spiros Thermos
Shangxuan Tian
Yingli Tian

Kinh Tieu
Massimo Tistarelli
Henning Tjaden
Matthew Toews
Chetan Tonde
Akihiko Torii
Andrea Torsello
Toan Tran
Leonardo Trujillo
Tomasz Trzcinski
Sam Tsai
Yi-Hsuan Tsai
Ivor Tsang
Vagia Tsiminaki
Aggeliki Tsoli
Wei-Chih Tu
Shubham Tulsiani
Sergey Tulyakov
Tony Tung
Matt Turek
Seiichi Uchida
Oytun Ulutan
Martin Urschler
Mikhail Usvyatsov
Alexander Vakhitov
Julien Valentin
Ernest Valveny
Ian Van Der Linde
Kiran Varanasi
Gul Varol
Francisco Vasconcelos
Pascal Vasseur
Javier Vazquez-Corral
Ashok Veeraraghavan
Andreas Velten
Raviteja Vemulapalli
Jonathan Ventura
Subhashini Venugopalan
Yashaswi Verma
Matthias Vestner
Minh Vo
Jayakorn Vongkulbhisal
Toshikazu Wada
Chengde Wan
Jun Wan
Renjie Wan

Baoyuan Wang
Chaohui Wang
Chaoyang Wang
Chunyu Wang
De Wang
Dong Wang
Fang Wang
Faqiang Wang
Hongsong Wang
Hongxing Wang
Hua Wang
Jialei Wang
Jianyu Wang
Jinglu Wang
Jinqiao Wang
Keze Wang
Le Wang
Lei Wang
Lezi Wang
Lijun Wang
Limin Wang
Linwei Wang
Pichao Wang
Qi Wang
Qian Wang
Qilong Wang
Qing Wang
Ruiping Wang
Shangfei Wang
Shuhui Wang
Song Wang
Tao Wang
Tsun-Hsuang Wang
Weiyue Wang
Wenguan Wang
Xiaoyu Wang
Xinchao Wang
Xinggang Wang
Yang Wang
Yin Wang
Yu-Chiang Frank Wang
Yufei Wang
Yunhong Wang
Zhangyang Wang
Zilei Wang
Jan Dirk Wegner

Ping Wei
Shih-En Wei
Wei Wei
Xiu-Shen Wei
Zijun Wei
Bihan Wen
Longyin Wen
Xinshuo Weng
Tom Whelan
Patrick Wieschollek
Maggie Wigness
Jerome Williams
Kwan-Yee Wong
Chao-Yuan Wu
Chunpeng Wu
Dijia Wu
Jiajun Wu
Jianxin Wu
Xiao Wu
Xiaohe Wu
Xiaomeng Wu
Xinxiao Wu
Yi Wu
Ying Nian Wu
Yue Wu
Zheng Wu
Zhirong Wu
Jonas Wulff
Yin Xia
Yongqin Xian
Yu Xiang
Fanyi Xiao
Yang Xiao
Dan Xie
Jianwen Xie
Jin Xie
Fuyong Xing
Jun Xing
Junliang Xing
Xuehan Xiong
Yuanjun Xiong
Changsheng Xu
Chenliang Xu
Haotian Xu
Huazhe Xu
Huijuan Xu

Jun Xu
Ning Xu
Tao Xu
Weipeng Xu
Xiangmin Xu
Xiangyu Xu
Yong Xu
Yuanlu Xu
Jia Xue
Xiangyang Xue
Toshihiko Yamasaki
Junchi Yan
Luxin Yan
Wang Yan
Keiji Yanai
Bin Yang
Chih-Yuan Yang
Dong Yang
Herb Yang
Jianwei Yang
Jie Yang
Jin-feng Yang
Jufeng Yang
Meng Yang
Ming Yang
Ming-Hsuan Yang
Tien-Ju Yang
Wei Yang
Wenhan Yang
Yanchao Yang
Yingzhen Yang
Yongxin Yang
Zhenheng Yang
Angela Yao
Bangpeng Yao
Cong Yao
Jian Yao
Jiawen Yao
Yasushi Yagi
Mang Ye
Mao Ye
Qixiang Ye
Mei-Chen Yeh
Sai-Kit Yeung
Kwang Moo Yi
Alper Yilmaz

Contents – Part III

Oral Session O3: Face, Gesture and Text

RankGAN: A Maximum Margin Ranking GAN for Generating Faces

Felix Juefei-Xu[1], Rahul Dey[2][✉], Vishnu Naresh Boddeti[2],
and Marios Savvides[1]

[1] Carnegie Mellon University, Pittsburgh, PA 15213, USA
[2] Michigan State University, East Lansing, MI 48824, USA
deyrahul@msu.edu

Abstract. We present a new stage-wise learning paradigm for training generative adversarial networks (GANs). The goal of our work is to progressively strengthen the discriminator and thus, the generators, with each subsequent stage without changing the network architecture. We call this proposed method the RankGAN. We first propose a margin-based loss for the GAN discriminator. We then extend it to a margin-based ranking loss to train the multiple stages of RankGAN. We focus on face images from the CelebA dataset in our work and show visual as well as quantitative improvements in face generation and completion tasks over other GAN approaches, including WGAN and LSGAN.

Keywords: Generative adversarial networks ·
Maximum margin ranking · Face generation

1 Introduction

Generative modeling approaches can learn from the tremendous amount of data around us to obtain a compact description of the data distribution. Generative models can provide meaningful insight about the physical world that human beings can perceive, insight that can be valuable for machine learning systems. Take visual perception for instance, in order to generate new instances, the generative models must search for intrinsic patterns in the vast amount of visual data and distill its essence. Such systems in turn can be leveraged by machines to improve their ability to understand, describe, and model the visual world.

Recently, three classes of algorithms have emerged as successful generative approaches to model the visual data in an unsupervised manner. *Variational*

F. Juefei-Xu and R. Dey—Contribute equally and should be considered co-first authors.

Electronic supplementary material The online version of this chapter (https://doi.org/10.1007/978-3-030-20893-6_1) contains supplementary material, which is available to authorized users.

© Springer Nature Switzerland AG 2019
C. V. Jawahar et al. (Eds.): ACCV 2018, LNCS 11363, pp. 3–18, 2019.
https://doi.org/10.1007/978-3-030-20893-6_1

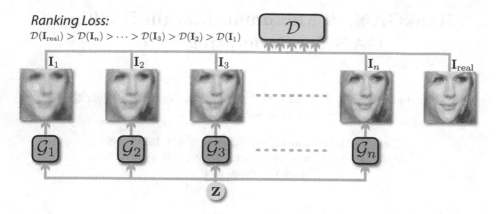

Fig. 1. The RankGAN framework consists of a discriminator that ranks the quality of the generated images from several stages of generators. The ranker guides the generators to learn the subtle nuances in the training data and progressively improve with each stage.

autoencoders (VAEs) [20] formalize the generative problem as a maximum log-likelihood based learning objective in the framework of probabilistic graphical models with latent variables. The learned latent space allows for efficient reconstruction of new instances. The VAEs are straightforward to train but at the cost of introducing potentially restrictive assumptions about the approximate posterior distribution. Also, their generated samples tend to be slightly blurry.

Autoregressive models such as PixelRNN [24] and PixelCNN [27] get rid of the latent variables and instead directly model the conditional distribution of every individual pixel given the previous starting pixels. PixelRNN/CNN have a stable training process via softmax loss and currently give the best log likelihoods on the generated data, indicating high plausibility. However, they lack a latent code and are relatively inefficient during sampling.

Generative adversarial networks bypass maximum-likelihood learning by training a generator using adversarial feedback from a discriminator. Using a latent code, the generator tries to generate realistic-looking data in order to fool the discriminator, while the discriminator learns to classify them apart from the real training instances. This two-player minimax game is played until the Nash equilibrium where the discriminator is no longer able to distinguish real data from the fake ones. The GAN loss is based on a measure of distance between the two distributions as observed by the discriminator. GANs are known to generate highest quality of visual data by far in terms of sharpness and semantics.

Because of the nature of GAN training, the strength (or quality) of the generator, which is the desired end-product, depends directly on the strength of the discriminator. The stronger the discriminator is, the better the generator has to become in generating realistic looking images, and vice-versa. Although a lot of GAN variants have been proposed that try to achieve this by exploring different divergence measures between the real and fake distributions, there has not been much work dedicated to self-improvement of GAN, *i.e.*, progressively improving the GAN based on self-play with the previous versions of itself. One way to achieve this is by making the discriminator not just compare the real and fake samples, but also rank fake samples from various stages of the GAN, thus forcing it to get better in attending to the finer details of images. In this work, we propose a progressive training paradigm to train a GAN based on a maximum margin ranking criterion that improves GANs at later stages keeping the network capacity same. Thus, our proposed approach is orthogonal to other progressive paradigms such as [18] which increase the network capacity to improve the GAN and the resolution of generated images in a stage-wise manner. We call our proposed method RankGAN.

Our contributions include (1) a margin-based loss function for training the discriminator in a GAN; (2) a self-improving training paradigm where GANs at later stages improve upon their earlier versions using a maximum-margin ranking loss (see Fig. 1); and (3) a new way of measuring GAN quality based on image completion tasks.

1.1 Related Work

Since the introduction of Generative Adversarial Networks (GANs) [7], numerous variants of GAN have been proposed to improve upon it. The original GAN formulation suffers from practical problems such as vanishing gradients, mode collapse and training instability. To strive for a more stable GAN training, Zhao *et al.* proposed an energy-based GAN (EBGAN) [31] which views the discriminator as an energy function that assigns low energy to the regions near the data manifold and higher energy to other regions. The authors have shown one instantiation of EBGAN using an autoencoder architecture, with the energy being the reconstruction error. The boundary-seeking GAN (BGAN) [10] extended GANs for discrete data while improving training stability for continuous data. BGAN aims at generating samples that lie on the decision boundary of a current discriminator in training at each update. The hope is that a generator can be trained in this way to match a target distribution at the limit of a perfect discriminator. Nowozin *et al.* [23] showed that the generative-adversarial approach in GAN is a special case of an existing more general variational divergence estimation approach, and that any f-divergence can be used for training generative neural samplers. On these lines, least squares GAN (LSGAN) [22] adopts a least squares loss function for the discriminator, which is equivalent to minimizing the Pearson χ^2 divergence between the real and fake distributions, thus providing smoother gradients to the generator.

Perhaps the most seminal GAN-related work since the inception of the original GAN [7] idea is the Wasserstein GAN (WGAN) [3]. Efforts have been made to fully understand the training dynamics of GANs through theoretical analysis in [2] and [3], which leads to the creation of WGAN. By incorporating the smoother Wasserstein distance metric as the objective, as opposed to the KL or JS divergences, WGAN is able to overcome the problems of vanishing gradient and mode collapse. WGAN also made it possible to first train the discriminator till optimality and then gradually improve the generator making the training and balancing between the generator and the discriminator much easier. Moreover, the new loss function also correlates well with the visual quality of generated images, thus providing a good indicator for training progression.

On the other hand, numerous efforts have been made to improve the training and performance of GANs architecturally. Radford *et al.* proposed the DCGAN [25] architecture that utilized strided convolution and transposed-convolution to improve the training stability and performance of GANs. The Laplacian GAN (LAPGAN) [5] is a sequential variant of the GAN model that generates images in a coarse-to-fine manner by generating and upsampling in multiple steps. Built upon the idea of sequential generation of images, the recurrent adversarial networks [12] has been proposed to let the recurrent network learn the optimal generation procedure by itself, as opposed to imposing a coarse-to-fine structure on the procedure. The stacked GAN [11] consists of a top-down stack of GANs, each trained to generate plausible lower-level representations, conditioned on higher-level representations. Discriminators are attached to each feature hierarchy to provide intermediate supervision. Each GAN of the stack is first trained independently, and then the stack is trained end-to-end. The generative multi-adversarial networks (GMAN) [6] extends the GANs to multiple discriminators that collectively scrutinize a fixed generator, thus forcing the generator to generate high fidelity samples. Layered recursive generative adversarial networks (LR-GAN) [29] generates images in a recursive fashion. First a background is generated, conditioned on which, the foreground is generated, along with a mask and an affine transformation that together define how the background and foreground should be composed to obtain a complete image.

The introspective adversarial networks (IAN) [4] proposes to hybridize the VAE and the GAN by leveraging the power of the adversarial objective while maintaining the efficient inference mechanism of the VAE.

Among the latest progress in GANs, Karras *et al.* [18] has the most impressive image generation results in terms of resolution and image quality. The key idea is to grow both the generator and discriminator progressively: starting from a low resolution, new layers that model increasingly fine details are added as the training progresses. This both speeds the training up and greatly stabilizes it, allowing us to produce images of unprecedented quality. On the contrary, we focus on improving the performance of GANs without increasing model capacity, making our work orthogonal to [18]. In the following sections, we will first discuss the background and motivation behind our work, followed by details of the proposed approach.

2   Background

We first provide a brief background of a few variants of GAN to motivate the maximum margin ranking based GAN proposed in this paper.

2.1   GAN and WGAN

The GAN framework [7] consists of two components, a Generator $\mathcal{G}_\theta(\mathbf{z}) : \mathbf{z} \to \mathbf{x}$ that maps a latent vector $\mathbf{z}$ drawn from a known prior $p_\mathbf{z}(\mathbf{z})$ to the data space and a Discriminator $\mathcal{D}_\omega(\mathbf{x}) : \mathbf{x} \to [0, 1]$ that maps a data sample (real or generated) to a likelihood value in $[0, 1]$. The generator $\mathcal{G}$ and the discriminator $\mathcal{D}$ play adversary to each other in a two-player minimax game while optimizing the following GAN objective:

$$\min_{\mathcal{G}} \max_{\mathcal{D}} V(\mathcal{G}, \mathcal{D}) = \mathbb{E}_{\mathbf{x} \sim p_{\text{data}}(\mathbf{x})} [\log(\mathcal{D}(\mathbf{x}))] + \mathbb{E}_{\mathbf{z} \sim p_{\mathbf{z}}(\mathbf{z})} [\log(1 - \mathcal{D}(\mathcal{G}(\mathbf{z}))] \qquad (1)$$

where $\mathbf{x}$ is a sample from the data distribution p_{data}. This objective function is designed to learn a generator $\mathcal{G}$ that minimizes the Jensen-Shannon divergence between the real and generated data distributions.

Many of the variants of GAN described in Sect. 1.1 differ in the objective function that is optimized to minimize the divergence between the real and generated data distributions. Wasserstein GAN [2,3] has been proposed with the goal of addressing the problems of vanishing gradients and mode collapse in the original GAN. Instead of minimizing the cross-entropy loss, the discriminator in WGAN is optimized to minimize the Wasserstein-1 (Earth Movers') distance $W(\mathbb{P}_r, \mathbb{P}_g)$ between the real and generated distributions.

$$W(\mathbb{P}_r, \mathbb{P}_g) = \inf_{\gamma \in \Gamma(\mathbb{P}_r, \mathbb{P}_g)} \mathbb{E}_{(x, y) \sim \gamma} [\|x - y\|] \qquad (2)$$

where $\Gamma(\mathbb{P}_r, \mathbb{P}_g)$ is the set of all joint distributions $\gamma(x, y)$ whose marginals are $\mathbb{P}_r$ and $\mathbb{P}_g$ respectively. Given the intractability of finding the infimum in Eq. (2), WGAN optimizes the dual objective given by the Kantorovich-Rubinstein duality [28] instead, which also constraints the discriminator to be a 1-Lipshichtz function.

2.2 Limitations with GANs and Its Variants

An essential part of the adversarial game being played in a GAN is the discriminator, which is modeled as a two-class classifier. Thus, intuitively, the stronger the discriminator, the stronger (better) should be the generator. In the original GAN, stronger discriminator led to problems like vanishing gradients [2]. Variants like WGAN and LSGAN attempt to solve this problem by proposing new loss functions that represent different divergence measures. We illustrate this effect in Fig. 2. The scores of the standard GAN model saturate and thus provide no useful gradients to the discriminator. The WGAN model has a constant gradient of one while RankGAN model (described in the next section) has a gradient that depends on the slope of the linear decision boundary. Therefore, from a classification loss perspective, RankGAN generalizes the loss of the WGAN critic. In practice, these variants don't easily reach convergence, partially because of limited network capacity and finite sample size of datasets. Loss functions for optimizing the discriminator are typically averaged over the entire dataset or a mini-batch of samples. As a result, the discriminator often keeps on increasing the margin between well-separated real and fake samples while struggling to classify the more difficult cases. Furthermore, we argue that a margin-based loss, as in the case of support vector machines, enables the discriminator to focus on the difficult cases once the easier ones have been well classified, making it a more effective classifier. Going one step further, by ranking several versions of

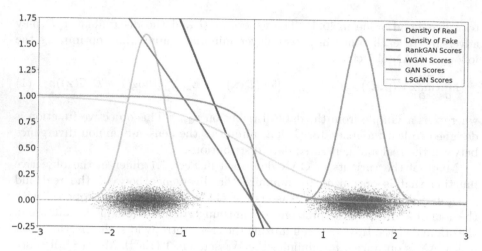

Fig. 2. Scores of the optimal discriminator for GAN, WGAN, LSGAN and RankGAN when learning to differentiate between two normal distributions. The GAN scores are saturated and hence results in vanishing gradients. The WGAN and RankGAN models do not suffer from this problem. See text for more details.

the generator, the discriminator would more effectively learn the subtle nuances in the training data. The supervision from such a strong discriminator would progressively improve the generators. This intuition forms the basic motivation behind our proposed approach.

3 Proposed Method: RankGAN

In this section, we describe our proposed GAN training framework - RankGAN. This model is designed to address some of the limitations of traditional GAN variants. RankGAN is a stage-wise GAN training paradigm which aims at improving the GAN convergence at each stage by ranking one version of GAN against previous versions without changing the network architecture (see Fig. 3). The two basic aspects of our proposed approach are the following:

- We first adopt a margin based loss for the discriminator of the GAN, as opposed to the cross-entropy loss of the original GAN and the WGAN loss. We refer to this model as MarginGAN.
- We extend the margin-based loss into a margin-based ranking loss. This enables the discriminator to rank multiple stages of generators by comparing the scores of the generated samples to those of the real samples (see Fig. 4 for an illustration).

  By applying certain constraints on the discriminator, which we will describe later, we can use this mechanism to steadily improve the discriminator at each stage, thereby improving the quality of generated samples.

The complete RankGAN training flow is shown in Algorithm 1. We now describe the various novelties in our approach.

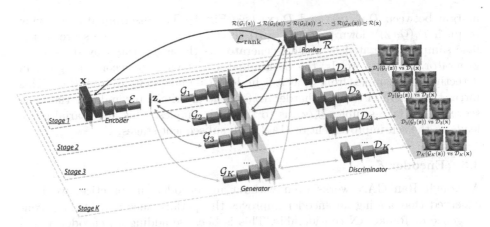

Fig. 3. Overall flowchart of the proposed RankGAN method. Our model consists of (1) An encoder that maps an image to a latent representation. (2) A series of generators that are learned in a stage-wise manner. (3) A series of discriminators that are learned to differentiate between the real and the generated data. (4) A ranker that ranks the real face image and the corresponding generated face images at each stage. In practice the discriminator and the ranker are combined into a single model.

3.1 Margin Loss

The intuition behind the MarginGAN loss is as follows. WGAN loss treats a gap of 10 or 1 equally and it tries to increase the gap even further. The MarginGAN loss will focus on increasing separation of examples with gap 1 and leave the samples with separation 10, which ensures a better discriminator, hence a better generator. The ϵ-margin loss is given by:

$$\mathcal{L}_{\text{margin}} = [\mathcal{D}_w(\mathcal{G}_\theta(\mathbf{z})) + \epsilon - \mathcal{D}_w(\mathbf{x})]_+ \tag{3}$$

where $[x]_+ = \max(0, x)$ is the hinge loss. The margin loss becomes equal to the WGAN loss when the margin $\epsilon \to \infty$, hence the generalization.

3.2 Ranking Loss

The ranking loss uses margin loss to train the generator of our GAN by ranking it against previous version of itself. For stage i discriminator $\mathcal{D}_i$ and generator $\mathcal{G}_i$, the ranking loss is given by:

$$\begin{aligned}
\mathcal{L}_{\text{disc\_rank}} &= [\mathcal{D}_i\left(\mathcal{G}_i(\mathbf{z})\right) - \mathcal{D}_i\left(\mathcal{G}_{i-1}(\mathbf{z})\right)]_+ \\
\mathcal{L}_{\text{gen\_rank}} &= [\mathcal{D}_i\left(\mathbf{x}\right) - \mathcal{D}_i\left(\mathcal{G}_i(\mathbf{z})\right)]_+
\end{aligned} \tag{4}$$

The ranking losses for the discriminator and the generator are thus zero margin loss functions ($\epsilon \to 0$) where the discriminator $\mathcal{D}_i$ is trying to have a zero margin between $\mathcal{D}_i(\mathcal{G}_i(\mathbf{z}))$ and $\mathcal{D}_i(\mathcal{G}_{i-1}(\mathbf{z}))$, while the generator is trying to have zero margin between $\mathcal{D}_i(\mathcal{G}_i(\mathbf{z}))$ and $\mathcal{D}_i(\mathbf{x})$ (see Fig. 4). The discriminator is trying to push $\mathcal{D}_i(\mathcal{G}_i(\mathbf{z}))$ down to $\mathcal{D}_i(\mathcal{G}_{i-1}(\mathbf{z}))$ so that it gives the same score to the fake samples generated by stage i generator as those generated by stage $i-1$ generator. In other words, the discriminator is trying to become as good in detecting fake samples from $\mathcal{G}_i$ as it is in detecting fake samples from $\mathcal{G}_{i-1}$. This forces the generator to 'work harder' to fool the discriminator and give the same score to the fake samples $\mathcal{G}_i(\mathbf{z})$ as to the real samples. This adversarial game leads to the self-improvement of GAN with subsequent stages.

3.3 Encoder $\mathcal{E}$

Although RankGAN works even without an encoder, in practice, we have observed that adding an encoder improves the performance and training convergence of RankGAN considerably. This is because adding an encoder allows the discriminator to rank generated and real samples based on image quality and realisticity rather than identity. To obtain the encoder, we first train a VAE [20] in the zeroth stage. After the VAE is trained, the encoder is frozen and forms the first component of the RankGAN architecture (see Fig. 3). During RankGAN training, the encoder takes the real image $\mathbf{x}$ and outputs a mean $\mu(\mathbf{x})$ and variance $\Sigma(\mathbf{x})$ to sample the latent vector as $\mathbf{z} \sim \mathcal{N}(\mu(\mathbf{x}), \Sigma(\mathbf{x}))$ which is used by the subsequent stage generators to generate fake samples for training. The VAE decoder can also be used as the zeroth stage generator.

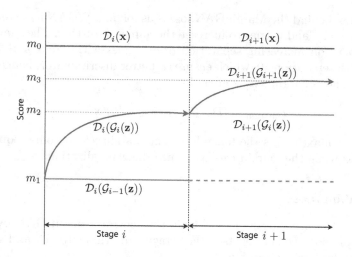

Fig. 4. RankGAN stage-wise training progression following $\mathcal{D}_i(\mathbf{x}) > \mathcal{D}_i(\mathcal{G}_i(\mathbf{z})) > \mathcal{D}_i(\mathcal{G}_{i-1}(\mathbf{z}))$. At stage i, $\mathcal{D}_i(\mathbf{x})$ and $\mathcal{D}_i(\mathcal{G}_{i-1}(\mathbf{z}))$ are clamped at the initial margins m_0 and m_1, respectively while $\mathcal{D}_i(\mathcal{G}_i(\mathbf{z}))$ slowly increases from m_1 to m_2 (point of Nash equilibrium) at the end of stage i. The same is repeated at stage $i+1$, where $\mathcal{D}_{i+1}(\mathbf{x})$ and $\mathcal{D}_{i+1}(\mathcal{G}_i(\mathbf{z}))$ are clamped at margins m_0 and m_2 respectively while $\mathcal{D}_{i+1}(\mathcal{G}_{i+1}(\mathbf{z}))$ slowly increases from m_2 to m_3 till convergence. (Color figure online)

3.4 Discriminator Penalties

We enforce Lipschitz constrain on the discriminator using gradient penalty (GP) as proposed by Gulrajani *et al.* [8]. GP penalizes the norm of the gradient of the discriminator w.r.t. its input $\hat{\mathbf{x}} \sim \mathbb{P}_{\hat{\mathbf{x}}}$, which enforces a soft version of the constraint. The GP loss is given by:

$$\mathcal{L}_{\text{gp}} = \mathbb{E}_{\hat{\mathbf{x}} \sim \mathbb{P}_{\hat{\mathbf{x}}}} \left[\left(\| \nabla_{\hat{\mathbf{x}}} \mathcal{D}(\hat{\mathbf{x}}) \|_2 - 1 \right)^2 \right] \tag{5}$$

In addition, Eq. (4) does not prevent the discriminator from cheating by letting $\mathcal{D}_i(\mathbf{x})$ and $\mathcal{D}_i(\mathcal{G}_{i-1}(\mathbf{z}))$ to simultaneously converge to the level of $\mathcal{D}_i(\mathcal{G}_i(\mathbf{z}))$ (blue and green curves converging towards the red curve in Fig. 4), thereby defeating the purpose of training. To prevent this, we add a penalty term to the overall ranking loss given by:

$$\mathcal{L}_{\text{clamp}} = \left[m_i^{\text{high}} - \mathcal{D}_i(\mathbf{x}) \right]_+ + \left[\mathcal{D}_i(\mathcal{G}_{i-1}(\mathbf{z})) - m_i^{\text{low}} \right]_+ \tag{6}$$

where m_i^{high} and m_i^{low} are the high and low margins for stage-i RankGAN respectively. Thus, the clamping loss constraints the discriminator so as not to let $\mathcal{D}_i(\mathbf{x})$ go below m_i^{high} and $\mathcal{D}_{i-1}(\mathcal{G}_i(\mathbf{z}))$ go above m_i^{low}. We call this **Discriminator Clamping**. The overall discriminator loss thus becomes:

$$\mathcal{L}_{\text{disc}} = \mathcal{L}_{\text{disc\_rank}} + \lambda_{\text{gp}} \mathcal{L}_{\text{gp}} + \lambda_{\text{clamp}} \mathcal{L}_{\text{clamp}} \tag{7}$$

In our experiments, we find $\lambda_{\text{gp}} = 10$ and $\lambda_{\text{clamp}} = 1000$ to give good results.

4 Experiments

In this section, we describe our experiments evaluating the effectiveness of the RankGAN against traditional GAN variants *i.e.*, WGAN and LSGAN. For this purpose, we trained the RankGAN, WGAN and LSGAN models on face images and evaluated their performance on face generation and face completion tasks. Due to space limit, we will omit some implementation details in the paper. Full implementation details will be made publicly available.

4.1 Database and Metrics

We use the **CelebA** dataset [21] which is a large-scale face attributes dataset with more than 200K celebrity images covering large pose variations and background clutter. The face images are pre-processed and aligned into an image size of 64 × 64 while keeping a 90-10 training-testing split.

To compare the performance of RankGAN and other GAN variants quantitatively, we computed several metrices including Inception Score [26] and Fréchet Inception distance (FID) [9]. Although, Inception score has rarely been used to evaluate face generation models before, we argue that since it is based on sample entropy, it will favor sharper and more feature-full images. The FID, on the other hand, captures the similarity of the generated images to the real ones, thus capturing their realisticity and fidelity.

Algorithm 1. RankGAN Training

$\alpha_{\mathcal{D}}, \alpha_{\mathcal{G}} \leftarrow 5e - 5, \alpha_{\mathcal{E}} \leftarrow 1e - 4;$
for $i = 1 \dots nstages$ **do**
    if $i = 1$ **then**
        train **VAE** with **Encoder** $\mathcal{E}$ and **Decoder** $\mathcal{G}_1$;
        train **Discriminator** $\mathcal{D}_1$ for 1 epoch using WGAN loss of Eqn. 5;
    else
        $j, k \leftarrow 0, 0;$
        initialize $\mathcal{D}_i \leftarrow \mathcal{D}_{i-1}$ and $\mathcal{G}_i \leftarrow \mathcal{G}_{i-1}$;
        freeze $\mathcal{D}_{i-1}$ and $\mathcal{G}_{i-1}$;
        compute $m_i^{\text{high}} = \mathbb{E}[\mathcal{D}_{i-1}(\mathbf{x}_{\text{val}})]$ and $m_i^{\text{low}} = \mathbb{E}[\mathcal{D}_{i-1}(\mathcal{G}_{i-1}(\mathbf{z}))]$;
        while $j < nepochs$ **do**
            while $k < 5$ **do**
                obtain real samples $\mathbf{x}$ and latent vectors $\mathbf{z} \sim \mathcal{E}(\mathbf{x})$;
                compute $\mathcal{L}_{\text{disc}}$ using Eqn. 7;
                optimize $\mathcal{D}_i$ using $AdamOptimizer(\alpha_{\mathcal{D}}, \beta_1 = 0, \beta_2 = 0.99)$;
                $j \leftarrow j + 1, k \leftarrow k + 1$
            end
            compute $\mathcal{L}_{\text{gen}}$ using Eqn. 4;
            optimize $\mathcal{G}_i$ using $AdamOptimizer(\alpha_{\mathcal{G}}, \beta_1 = 0, \beta_2 = 0.99)$;
            $k \leftarrow 0$
        end
    end
end

4.2 Evaluations on Face Generation Tasks

For all the experiments presented in this paper, we use the same network architecture based on the one used in [18]. Both the discriminators and generators are optimized using the Adam optimizer [19] with $\beta_1 = 0.0$ and $\beta_2 = 0.99$ and a learning rate of $5e - 5$. The criterion to end a stage is based on the convergence of that particular stage and is determined empirically. In practice, we terminate a stage when either the discriminator gap stabilizes for 10–20 epochs or at least 200 stage-epochs are finished, whichever is earlier. Lastly, no data augmentation was used for any of our experiments.

Figure 5 shows the visual progression of Open-Set face generation results from various stages in RankGAN when the latent vector $\mathbf{z}$ is obtained by passing the input faces through the encoder $\mathcal{E}$. Figure 6 shows the visual progression of face generation results when the latent vectors $\mathbf{z}$'s are randomly generated without the encoder $\mathcal{E}$. In both the cases, we can clearly see that as the stage progresses, RankGAN is able to generate sharper face images which are visually more appealing.

Quantitative results are consolidated in Table 1 with FID (the lower the better) and Inception score (the higher the better). As can be seen, as the training progresses from stage-1 to stage-3, the trend conforms with the visual results where stage-3 yields the highest Inception score and the lowest FID.

Table 1. Quantitative results for face image generation with and without the encoder.

	With encoder		Without encoder	
	FID	Inception score	FID	Inception score
Real	N/A	2.51	N/A	2.51
Stage-1	122.17	1.54	140.45	1.54
Stage-2	60.45	1.78	75.53	1.75
Stage-3	**46.01**	**1.89**	**63.34**	**1.91**

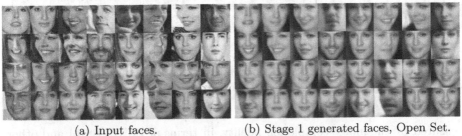

(a) Input faces.   (b) Stage 1 generated faces, Open Set.

(c) Stage 2 generated faces, Open Set.   (d) Stage 3 generated faces, Open Set.

Fig. 5. Face generation with RankGAN. Latent vectors z's are obtained by passing the input faces through the encoder $\mathcal{E}$.

(a) Stage 1, Open Set.   (b) Stage 2, Open Set.   (c) Stage 3, Open Set.

Fig. 6. Face generation with RankGAN. Latent vectors z's are randomly generated w/o encoder $\mathcal{E}$.

4.3   Evaluations on Face Completion Tasks

A good generative model should perform well on missing data problems. Motivated by this argument, we propose to use image completion as a quality measure for GAN models. In short, the quality of the GAN models can be quantitatively

Fig. 7. Interpolation between two latent vectors which are obtained by passing the input faces through the encoder $\mathcal{E}$. The 3 rows within each montage correspond to Stage 1, 2, and 3 in RankGAN.

Fig. 8. Interpolation between two latent vectors that are randomly selected (without the encoder $\mathcal{E}$) from a unit normal distribution. The 3 rows within each montage correspond to Stage 1, 2, and 3 in RankGAN.

measured by the image completion fidelity, in terms of PSNR, SSIM and other metrics. Traditional shallow methods [16,17] have shown some promising results but still struggle when dealing with face variations. Deep learning methods based on GANs are expected to handle image variations much more effectively. To take on the image completion task, we need to utilize both the $\mathcal{G}$ and $\mathcal{D}$ from the RankGAN and the baselines WGAN and LSGAN, pre-trained with uncorrupted data. After training, $\mathcal{G}$ is able to embed the images from p_{data} onto some non-linear manifold of $\mathbf{z}$. An image that is not from p_{data} (*e.g.*, with missing pixels) should not lie on the learned manifold. We seek to recover the image $\hat{\mathbf{y}}$ on the manifold "closest" to the corrupted image $\mathbf{y}$ as the image completion result. To quantify the "closest" mapping from $\mathbf{y}$ to the reconstruction, we define a function consisting of contextual and perceptual losses [30]. The **contextual loss** measures the fidelity between the reconstructed image portion and the uncorrupted image portion, and is defined as (Figs. 7 and 8):

$$\mathcal{L}_{\text{contextual}}(\mathbf{z}) = \|\mathbf{M} \odot \mathcal{G}(\mathbf{z}) - \mathbf{M} \odot \mathbf{y}\|_1 \tag{8}$$

where $\mathbf{M}$ is the binary mask of the uncorrupted region and $\odot$ denotes the Hadamard product. The **perceptual loss** encourages the reconstructed image to be similar to the samples drawn from the training set (true distribution p_{data}). This is achieved by updating $\mathbf{z}$ to fool $\mathcal{D}$, or equivalently by maximizing $\mathcal{D}(\mathcal{G}(\mathbf{z}))$. As a result, $\mathcal{D}$ will predict $\mathcal{G}(\mathbf{z})$ to be from the real data with a high probability.

$$\mathcal{L}_{\text{perceptual}}(\mathbf{z}) = -\mathcal{D}(\mathcal{G}(\mathbf{z})) \tag{9}$$

Thus, $\mathbf{z}$ can be updated, using backpropagation, to lie closest to the corrupted image in the latent representation space by optimizing the objective function:

$$\hat{\mathbf{z}} = \arg\min_{\mathbf{z}}(\mathcal{L}_{\text{contextual}}(\mathbf{z}) + \lambda \mathcal{L}_{\text{perceptual}}(\mathbf{z})) \tag{10}$$

Table 2. Data: CelebA, Mask: Center Large

	FID	Inception	PSNR	SSIM	OpenFace (AUC)	PittPatt (AUC)
Original	N/A	2.3286	N/A	N/A	1.0000 (0.9965)	19.6092 (0.9109)
Stage-1	27.09	2.1524	22.76	0.7405	0.6726 (0.9724)	10.2502 (0.7134)
Stage-2	23.69	2.1949	21.87	0.7267	0.6771 (0.9573)	9.9718 (0.8214)
Stage-3	27.31	**2.2846**	**23.30**	**0.7493**	**0.6789 (0.9749)**	**10.4102 (0.7922)**
WGAN	**17.03**	2.2771	23.26	0.7362	0.5554 (0.9156)	8.1031 (0.7373)
LSGAN	23.93	2.2636	23.11	0.7361	0.6676 (0.9659)	10.1482 (0.7154)

where λ (set to 10 in our experiments) is a weighting parameter. After finding the optimal solution $\hat{z}$, the reconstructed image $y_{completed}$ can be obtained by:

$$y_{completed} = \mathbf{M} \odot \mathbf{y} + (1 - \mathbf{M}) \odot \mathcal{G}(\hat{z}) \qquad (11)$$

Metrics: In addition to the FID and Inception Score, we used metrics such as PSNR [14], SSIM, OpenFace [1] feature distance under normalized cosine similarity (NCS) [13] and PittPatt face matching score [15] to measure fidelity between the original and reconstructed face images. The last two are off-the-shelf face matchers that can be used to examine the similarity between pairs of face images. For these two matchers, we also obtain the area under the ROC curves (AUC) score as an auxiliary metric.

Occlusion Masks: We carried out face completion experiments on four types of facial masks, which we termed as: 'Center Small', 'Center Large', 'Periocular Small', and 'Periocular Large'.

Open-Set: It is important to note that all of our experiments are carried out in an Open-Set fashion, *i.e.*, none of the images and subjects were seen during training. This is of course a more challenging setting than Closed-Set and reflects the generalization performance of these models.

Discussion: Due to lack of space, we only show results based on the Center Large mask in the main paper (more qualitative and quantitative results can be found in the supplementary). These results have been summarized in Table 2 and can be visualized in Fig. 9. As can be seen in Table 2, RankGAN Stage-3 outperforms all other baselines in all metrics except FID. The lower FID value for WGAN can be attributed to the fact that FID captures distance between two curves and is, in a way, similar to the Wasserstein distance that is minimized in the case of WGAN. The Stage-3 images appear to be both sharp (as measured by the Inception Score) as well as fidelity-preserving as compared to the original images (as measured by identity matching metrics). All the four identity-based metrics, PSNR, SSIM, OpenFace scores, and PittPatt scores are higher for Stage-3 of RankGAN. This is due to the fact that our formulation enforces identity-preservation through the encoder and the ranking loss.

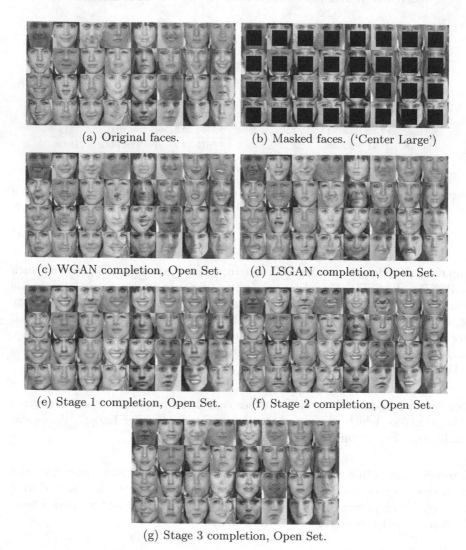

(a) Original faces.   (b) Masked faces. ('Center Large')

(c) WGAN completion, Open Set.   (d) LSGAN completion, Open Set.

(e) Stage 1 completion, Open Set.   (f) Stage 2 completion, Open Set.

(g) Stage 3 completion, Open Set.

Fig. 9. Best completion results with RankGAN on CelebA, 'Center Large' mask.

5   Conclusions

In this work, we introduced a new loss function to train GANs - the margin loss, that leads to a better discriminator and in turn a better generator. We then extended the margin loss to a margin-based ranking loss and evolved a new multi-stage GAN training paradigm that progressively strengthens both the discriminator and the generator. We also proposed a new way of measuring GAN quality based on image completion tasks. We have seen both visual and quantitative improvements over the baselines WGAN and LS-GAN on face generation and completion tasks.

References

1. Amos, B., Bartosz, L., Satyanarayanan, M.: OpenFace: a general-purpose face recognition library with mobile applications. Technical report, CMU-CS-16-118, CMU School of Computer Science (2016)
2. Arjovsky, M., Bottou, L.: Towards principled methods for training generative adversarial networks. In: ICLR (2017)
3. Arjovsky, M., Chintala, S., Bottou, L.: Wasserstein GAN. arXiv preprint arXiv:1701.07875 (2017)
4. Brock, A., Lim, T., Ritchie, J., Weston, N.: Neural photo editing with introspective adversarial networks. arXiv preprint arXiv:1609.07093 (2016)
5. Denton, E.L., Chintala, S., Fergus, R., et al.: Deep generative image models using a Laplacian pyramid of adversarial networks. In: NIPS, pp. 1486–1494 (2015)
6. Durugkar, I., Gemp, I., Mahadevan, S.: Generative multi-adversarial networks. arXiv preprint arXiv:1611.01673 (2016)
7. Goodfellow, I., et al.: Generative adversarial nets. In: NIPS, pp. 2672–2680 (2014)
8. Gulrajani, I., Ahmed, F., Arjovsky, M., Dumoulin, V., Courville, A.C.: Improved training of Wasserstein GANs. In: NIPS, pp. 5769–5779 (2017)
9. Heusel, M., Ramsauer, H., Unterthiner, T., Nessler, B., Klambauer, G., Hochreiter, S.: GANs trained by a two time-scale update rule converge to a nash equilibrium. arXiv preprint arXiv:1706.08500 (2017)
10. Hjelm, R.D., Jacob, A.P., Che, T., Cho, K., Bengio, Y.: Boundary-seeking generative adversarial networks. arXiv preprint arXiv:1702.08431 (2017)
11. Huang, X., Li, Y., Poursaeed, O., Hopcroft, J., Belongie, S.: Stacked generative adversarial networks. arXiv preprint arXiv:1612.04357 (2016)
12. Im, D.J., Kim, C.D., Jiang, H., Memisevic, R.: Generating images with recurrent adversarial networks. arXiv preprint arXiv:1602.05110 (2016)
13. Juefei-Xu, F., Luu, K., Savvides, M.: Spartans: single-sample periocular-based alignment-robust recognition technique applied to non-frontal scenarios. IEEE TIP 24(12), 4780–4795 (2015)
14. Juefei-Xu, F., Pal, D.K., Savvides, M.: NIR-VIS heterogeneous face recognition via cross-spectral joint dictionary learning and reconstruction. In: CVPRW, pp. 141–150, June 2015
15. Juefei-Xu, F., Pal, D.K., Singh, K., Savvides, M.: A preliminary investigation on the sensitivity of COTS face recognition systems to forensic analyst-style face processing for occlusions. In: CVPRW, pp. 25–33, June 2015
16. Juefei-Xu, F., Pal, D.K., Savvides, M.: Hallucinating the full face from the periocular region via dimensionally weighted K-SVD. In: CVPRW, pp. 1–8, June 2014
17. Juefei-Xu, F., Savvides, M.: Fastfood dictionary learning for periocular-based full face hallucination. In: BTAS, pp. 1–8, September 2016
18. Karras, T., Aila, T., Laine, S., Lehtinen, J.: Progressive growing of GANs for improved quality, stability, and variation. arXiv preprint arXiv:1710.10196 (2017)
19. Kingma, D., Ba, J.: Adam: a method for stochastic optimization. arXiv preprint arXiv:1412.6980 (2014)
20. Kingma, D.P., Welling, M.: Auto-encoding variational bayes. arXiv preprint arXiv:1312.6114 (2013)
21. Liu, Z., Luo, P., Wang, X., Tang, X.: Deep learning face attributes in the wild. In: ICCV, December 2015
22. Mao, X., Li, Q., Xie, H., Lau, R.Y., Wang, Z.: Least squares generative adversarial networks. arXiv preprint arXiv:1611.04076 (2017)

23. Nowozin, S., Cseke, B., Tomioka, R.: f-GAN: training generative neural samplers using variational divergence minimization. arXiv preprint arXiv:1606.00709 (2016)
24. van den Oord, A., Kalchbrenner, N., Kavukcuoglu, K.: Pixel recurrent neural networks. arXiv preprint arXiv:1601.06759 (2016)
25. Radford, A., Metz, L., Chintala, S.: Unsupervised representation learning with DCGAN. arXiv preprint arXiv:1511.06434 (2015)
26. Salimans, T., Goodfellow, I., Zaremba, W., Cheung, V., Radford, A., Chen, X.: Improved techniques for training GANs. In: NIPS, pp. 2226–2234 (2016)
27. van den Oord, A., Kalchbrenner, N., Vinyals, O., Espeholt, L., Graves, A., Kavukcuoglu, K.: Conditional image generation with PixelCNN decoders. arXiv preprint arXiv:1606.05328 (2016)
28. Villani, C.: Optimal Transport: Old and New, vol. 338. Springer, Heidelberg (2008)
29. Yang, J., Kannan, A., Batra, B., Parikh, D.: LR-GAN - layered recursive generative adversarial networks for image generation. In: ICLR (2017)
30. Yeh, R., Chen, C., Lim, T.Y., Hasegawa-Johnson, M., Do, M.N.: Semantic image inpainting with perceptual and contextual losses. arXiv preprint arXiv:1607.07539 (2016)
31. Zhao, J., Mathieu, M., LeCun, Y.: Energy-based generative adversarial network. arXiv preprint arXiv:1609.03126 (2016)

Zero-Shot Facial Expression Recognition with Multi-label Label Propagation

Zijia Lu[1,2], Jiabei Zeng[1(✉)], Shiguang Shan[1,3,4], and Xilin Chen[1,3]

[1] Key Lab of Intelligent Information Processing of Chinese Academy of Sciences (CAS), Institute of Computing Technology, CAS, Beijing 100190, China
{luzijia,jiabei.zeng,sgshan,xlchen}@ict.ac.cn
[2] NYU Shanghai, Shanghai, China
[3] University of Chinese Academy of Sciences, Beijing 100190, China
[4] CAS Center for Excellence in Brain Science and Intelligence Technology, Shanghai 200031, China

Abstract. Facial expression recognition classifies a face image into one of several discrete emotional categories. We have a lot of exclusive or non-exclusive emotional classes to describe the varied and nuancing meaning conveyed by facial expression. However, it is almost impossible to enumerate all the emotional categories and collect adequate annotated samples for each category. To this end, we propose a zero-shot learning framework with multi-label label propagation (Z-ML^{2}P). Z-ML^{2}P is built on existing multi-class datasets annotated with several basic emotions and it can infer the existence of other new emotion labels via a learned semantic space. To evaluate the proposed method, we collect a multi-label FER dataset FaceME. Experimental results on FaceME and two other FER datasets demonstrate that Z-ML^{2}P framework improves the state-of-the-art zero-shot learning methods in recognizing both seen or unseen emotions.

Keywords: Zero-shot learning · Facial expression recognition · Multi-label classification

1 Introduction

Facial expression is an important part of human communication. Automatic facial expression recognition (FER) is a long-standing problem in computer

This work is done by Zijia Lu during his internship in Institute of Computing Technology, Chinese Academy of Sciences. We gratefully acknowledge the supports from National Key R&D Program of China (grant 2017YFA0700800), National Natural Science Foundation of China (grant 61702481), and External Cooperation Program of CAS (grant GJHZ1843). We also thank Yong Li for his help in adapting the annotation tool to Windows OS.

Electronic supplementary material The online version of this chapter (https://doi.org/10.1007/978-3-030-20893-6_2) contains supplementary material, which is available to authorized users.

C. V. Jawahar et al. (Eds.): ACCV 2018, LNCS 11363, pp. 19–34, 2019.
https://doi.org/10.1007/978-3-030-20893-6_2

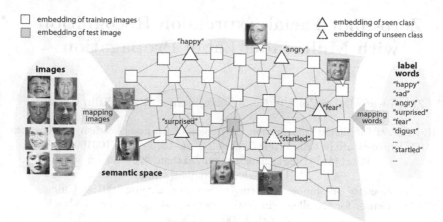

Fig. 1. The main idea of the proposed Z-ML²P framework. Z-ML²P embeds the facial images and all the emotion classes into a shared semantic space. Then, given a test image, we infer its labels by the proposed multi-label label propagation mechanism.

vision and human-machine interaction. The FER problem is always defined as a multi-class classification that divides the facial expressions into several discrete emotional categories. Ekman Paul [8] has proposed six basic emotions: anger, disgust, fear, happiness, sadness, and surprise. However, they are insufficient to describe all the facial expressions. Some works extend the list with neutral [28], contempt [24], fatigue [20], engagement [20]. Other works annotate the facial expressions as mixtures of the basic emotions [7,22], such as "happily surprise" and "sadly fear". Unfortunately, there exist innumerable complex and subtle words to describe the nuanced emotions. It is prohibitive to gather a complete list of all emotion classes or collect adequate training samples for each emotion.

To address the issue, we propose a Zero-shot framework with Multi-Label Label Propagation on semantic space (Z-ML²P). Z-ML²P is built on existing multi-class datasets annotated with several basic emotions and can generalize to new emotions according to their relations with the basic emotions. Figure 1 shows the main idea of our Z-ML²P framework. It embeds the images and emotion classes into a shared semantic space. The class embeddings are mapped from the word vectors of the emotions' names, which implicitly encode the relation information between the emotions. The image embeddings are forced to be close to the embeddings of their belonging classes and similar images. In the end, a graph is built upon the embeddings to capture the manifold structure of the semantic space and propagate labels from class embeddings to the image embeddings via a proposed Multi-Label Label Propagation (ML²P) mechanism. Our contributions are summarized as the following.

1. We build a Z-ML²P framework to recognize the unseen emotion categories of facial images. To our knowledge, it is the first work to address facial expression recognition with emotions that are unseen during the training.
2. We construct a shared semantic space for facial images and the emotion classes, and then propose a novel multi-label label propagation (ML²P)

schema that can efficiently infer the seen or unseen emotions of a query image. Previous label propagation methods require a unlabelled dataset of new, unseen classes. We successfully remove the requirement.

3. We collect a *Facial* expression dataset with *Multiple Emotions* (FaceME) to evaluate the Z-ML^{2}P framework. Experimental results on FaceME and two other multi-label facial expression datasets demonstrate that our Z-ML^{2}P framework improves the state-of-the-art zero-shot learning methods in recognizing both seen or unseen emotions.

2   Related Work

This section firstly reviews the recent work in facial expression recognition. Then, we briefly review zero-shot learning, multi-label learning, and label propagation. The three fields are technically relevant to the proposed Z-ML^{2}P.

Facial Expression Recognition(FER). Efforts have been made during the last decades in recognizing facial expressions [5,6,10,11,23,33]. Most existing methods classify the facial expressions into several discrete emotion categories, either based on hand-crafted features [18,41] or using end-to-end deep learning frameworks [37,38]. Ekman and Friesen proposed 6 basic emotions [8]. Du et al. [7] proposed 21 emotions as different combinations of the basic emotions. With these combined emotions, the FER can be solved as either a multi-class [24] or multi-label [42] classification problem. Meanwhile, some works employ Facial Action Coding System [9]. It uses a set of specific localized movements of the face, called Action Units, to encode the facial expression [31,40,43]. Some other works use three contiguous numerical dimensions to encode emotions [26,34].

Zero-Shot Learning (ZSL). ZSL methods are capable of correctly classify data of new, never-seen classes. Class embedding is the key component to connect seen classes and unseen classes. One type of representations are human-crafted attribute [30]. Yet those attributes are hard to obtain for new class as it requires expert knowledge. An alternative is using the word vectors of the class names, such as pretrained word vectors via GloVe [32] and Skip-Gram [27] methods, or learning new word vectors from textual corpus [15,35]. To compare images with class embeddings, most ZSL methods introduce a semantic space [14,19,39] where images and classes are mapped according to their semantic meanings.

Multi-label (ML) Learning. In multi-label learning, each instance can be assigned with multiple labels simultaneously. Typically, it is addressed from two approaches: *binary relevance* and *label ranking* [16]. *Binary relevance* splits a multi-label task into multiple binary classification problems. Its deficit is failure to capture class correlation and interdependence. *Label ranking* is frequently employed as an alternative, especially in large scale problems [39]. Its objective is to rank relevant labels ahead of the irrelevant ones thus requires the model to understand class relations. Thus It has been used in many multi-class ZSL models [1,13,19,36]. In this paper, we also employ label ranking method to bridge multi-class task and multi-label task.

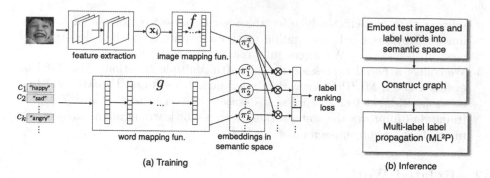

Fig. 2. (a) The network architecture to learn the semantic space during the training stage. (b) Diagram of the inference stage in the Z-ML^{2}P framework.

Label Propagation (LP). Label Propagation is a graph-based semi-supervised algorithm [44]. It builds graphs to model the manifold structure in data and utilize the structure to propagate label from labelled data to the unlabelled ones. Recent works [14,21] introduce it into ZSL to propagate label from class representations to test images. However, these works require an axillary unlabelled dataset of the new, unseen classes. It violates with the essential ZSL assumption that unseen classes are unknown in advance and have no available data.

3   Learning the Semantic Space

Figure 2 shows the training stage (Fig. 2(a)) and the inference stage (Fig. 2(b)) of the proposed zero-shot learning framework with multi-label label propagation on semantic space (Z-ML^{2}P). At training stage, Z-ML^{2}P learns to embed the emotion classes and images into a shared semantic space. In the semantic space, the embeddings of classes must preserve their syntactic and semantic structure. The embeddings of images must surround those of their relevant classes. During inference, Z-ML^{2}P projects the seen and unseen classes as well as the training and test images into the semantic space. It then constructs a graph upon the embeddings to perform multi-label label propagation(ML^{2}P).

In the rest part of this section, we introduce the details of learning the semantic space. In Sects. 4 and 5, we present the inference procedure for unseen classes and seen classes, respectively.

3.1   Problem Setup

Let $\mathcal{C} = \{\text{"happy", "sad",} \ldots\}$ denote the name set of all the classes that are seen or unseen. Without losing generality, we assume the first s elements are the seen classes and the rest u elements are unseen classes. c_k represents the k-th class in $\mathcal{C}$. $\mathcal{S} = \{1, 2, \ldots, s\}$ and $\mathcal{U} = \{s+1, \ldots, s+u\}$ are the index sets of seen and unseen classes respectively.

The training dataset $\{\mathbf{x}_i, \mathcal{Y}_i\}_{i=1}^n$ contains n images labelled with seen classes $\mathcal{C}_{\mathcal{S}}$. $\mathbf{x}_i \in \mathbb{R}^h$ is the h-dimensional feature of the i-th image. $\mathcal{Y}_i \subset \mathcal{S}$ is the index set of the i-th image's relevant classes. The test dataset $\{\mathbf{x}_i^t, \mathcal{Y}_i^t\}_{i=1}^{n_t}$ contains n_t images of both seen and unseen classes. $\mathbf{x}_i^t$ is the feature of the i-th test image. $\mathcal{Y}_i^t \subset \mathcal{S} \cup \mathcal{U}$ is the index set of the i-th test image's relevant classes. The proposed method is expected to predict whether a test image is relevant to each of the seen and unseen classes.

3.2   The Learning Architecture

In this section, we introduce the general network structure to learn a shared semantic space for images and emotion classes. As shown in Fig. 2a, there are four important components: feature extraction unit, image mapping function f, word mapping function g and the ranking loss.

The network takes images and the class names $\{c_1, c_2, \ldots, c_s\}$ as inputs. The feature extraction unit is a CNN network (e.g., residual CNN [17]) and extracts feature $\mathbf{x}_i$ of a given input image. f and g learns to embed the visual feature $\mathbf{x}_i$ and the class names into the semantic space. We use $\pi_i^x = f(x_i)$ to denote the embedding of the i-th image and $\pi_k^c = g(c_k)$ to denote the embedding of the k-th class. To ensure $\{\pi_k^c\}$ capturing the class relations, they are taken as the pretrained word vectors of the class names, or transformed word vectors but with constraints to maintain their original structure.

The ranking loss ensures the image embeddings are close to its relevant classes and far from its irrelevant classes. It requires that, for every relevant-irrelevant label pair, a image is embedded closer to its relevant class than the irrelevant one. The ranking loss is proved to have advantages in capturing class interdependence [3]. Moreover, ranking loss is applicable to multi-class problems and enables us to train a multi-label network on the existing multi-class datasets. There exist many variants of the label ranking loss. Here we present two of the widely-used formulas: max margin loss $\mathcal{L}_{\max}$ and soft margin loss $\mathcal{L}_{\text{soft}}$:

$$\mathcal{L}_{\max}(\mathbf{x}_i, \mathcal{Y}_i) = \alpha_i \sum_{k_+ \in \mathcal{Y}_i} \sum_{k_- \in \mathcal{S} - \mathcal{Y}_i} \max\left(0, \Delta_{k_+ k_-} + S_{ik_-} - S_{ik_+}\right), \tag{1}$$

$$\mathcal{L}_{\text{soft}}(\mathbf{x}_i, \mathcal{Y}_i) = \alpha_i \sum_{k_+ \in \mathcal{Y}_i} \sum_{k_- \in \mathcal{S} - \mathcal{Y}_i} \log\left(1 + \exp\left(S_{ik_-} - S_{ik_+}\right)\right), \tag{2}$$

where k_+ and k_- are the indices of the image's relevant and irrelevant classes, respectively. S_{ik} is the similarity between the π_i^x and π_k^c, such as the result of inner product $\langle \pi_i^x, \pi_k^c \rangle$. $\Delta_{k_+ k_-}$ in Eq. (1) is the margin between class k_+ and k_-. It is either predefined or set to 1 for all class pairs. α_i is a weight term. By varying it from 1, weighted loss can be formed. Both the losses force the image embedding to be closer to its relevant class k_+ than its irrelevant class k_- for every (k_+, k_-) pair.

4 Inference with ML^2P for Unseen Classes

During the test stage, we are given some new classes that are unseen during the training. Our goal is to predict whether a test image belongs to the unseen classes or not. Typical zero-shot learning methods [1,2,4,13,36,39] classify the image to its nearest classes in the semantic space. However, the nearest neighbor method is likely to fail when the embeddings are lying on a non-linear manifold. In the multi-label label propagation (ML^2P) mechanism, we construct a graph to model the manifold structure of each class.

To fully capture the manifold structure, we need large amount of images to build the graph. Yet, in zero-shot learning, we have no access to the images labelled with unseen classes. In ML^2P, the training images are used to estimate the unseen classes' manifolds. There are two reasons supporting our method. Firstly, although un-annotated, the unseen emotions or its resembling expressions are probable to occur in the training images because emotions are no-exclusive and highly correlated. Secondly, ML^2P benefits from the manifolds of seen classes revealed by the training images. The manifold structure of related seen emotions embodies valuable information to the unseen classes. If an unseen emotion is not related to any training images, ML^2P has a better estimation of the manifold shape than the methods with nearest neighbor mechanism.

4.1 Graph Construction

To predict whether a test image $\mathbf{x}$ belongs to an unseen class c, a directed graph $\mathcal{G}(\mathbf{x}, c) = \{V, E, \mathbf{W}, \mathbf{r}\}$ is constructed. V is the set of vertices, including the embeddings of the test image, training images and a subset of classes. Each vertex has a score indicating its relevance to class c. Thus the score of class c is 1 and those of the other classes are 0. The scores of the test image and training images are unknown and to be inferred. We denote the vertices scores as $\mathbf{r} \in [0,1]^{|V|} = \begin{bmatrix} \mathbf{r}_l \\ \mathbf{r}_u \end{bmatrix}$, where $\mathbf{r}_l$ denotes the known scores and $\mathbf{r}_u$ denotes the to-be-learned scores. E is the edge set. The weight on a edge indicates the similarity of vertices on the two ends. A larger weight indicates two more similar vertices. $\mathbf{W} \in \mathbb{R}^{|V| \times |V|}$ denotes the weight matrix. The weight of edge from vertex j to i is computed as:

$$w_{ij} = \frac{\exp(\alpha_{ij}/\tau)}{\sum_{p=1}^{|V|} \exp(\alpha_{jp}/\tau)} \tag{3}$$

where α_{ij} is the similarity of the i-th and j-th vertices, measured by inner product or negative euclidean distance and τ is a length-scale hyper-parameter.

Vertices of Class Embeddings. It is straightforward to include all class embeddings in the graph and set the label score of class c to 1 and the other scores to 0. However, if a synonymous or related class of c is present, setting its score to 0 will misguide label propagation. To address the issue, we employ a

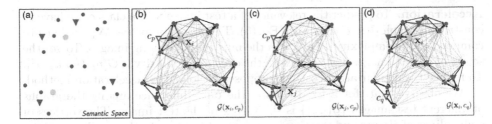

Fig. 3. Illustration of ML^{2}P Graphs. (a) is an example of embeddings in the semantic space. Triangles are class embeddings. Small blue dots are training image embeddings and large yellow dots are test images embeddings. (b), (c), (d) demonstrate three graphs created for different test images and classes. The edge widths represent the magnitude of edge weights. (Color figure online)

simple yet effective method: exclude classes from $\mathcal{G}(\mathbf{x}, c)$ that are semantically-close to class c. However, for a large class set, identifying those classes itself is cumbersome. Therefore, we first divide embeddings of all seen and unseen classes into a few groups via KNN then a selected representative class embedding for each group, which can either be a real class embedding or an average of all embeddings in the group. This set of representative class, $\mathcal{C}^r$, are expected to cover the semantic meaning of most of the classes and it is much easier to find the semantically-close classes on this smaller set. Finally, class embeddings in $\mathcal{G}(\mathbf{x}, c)$ is $\{\pi_c\} \cup \{\pi_k | k \in \mathcal{C}^r; k, c \text{ is not semantically-close}\}$ and the label of class c is 1 and the others' are 0. Figure 3 illustrates three example graphs created for different class c and test image $\mathbf{x}$.

4.2 Multi-label Label Propagation

The multi-label label propagation (ML^{2}P) mechanism propagates labels from labelled vertices (e.g., vertices of classes) to unlabelled vertices (vertices of unlabelled images). To achieve it, on graph $\mathcal{G}(\mathbf{x}, c)$, ML^{2}P estimates the unlabelled vertices' scores $\mathbf{r}_u$ by minimizing

$$\min_{r_i \in \mathbf{r}_u} \frac{1}{2} \sum_{ij} w_{ij}(r_i - r_j)^2 \tag{4}$$

where r_i is i-th element of the $\mathbf{r} = [\mathbf{r}_l; \mathbf{r}_u]$, denoting the score of i-th vertex belonging to class c. Equation (4) has a close-form solution

$$\mathbf{r}_u = (I - \mathbf{W}_{uu})^{-1} \mathbf{W}_{ul} \mathbf{r}_l \tag{5}$$

where $\mathbf{r}_l$ is the scores of labelled vertices. $\mathbf{W}_{uu}$ are the weights of edges between two unlabeled vertices and $\mathbf{W}_{ul}$ are those of edges from labelled ones to unlabelled ones. The weight matrix can be rewritten as $\mathbf{W} = \begin{bmatrix} \mathbf{W}_{ll} & \mathbf{W}_{lu} \\ \mathbf{W}_{ul} & \mathbf{W}_{uu} \end{bmatrix}$.

Acceleration. To predict the relevance of a test image $\mathbf{x}$ to a class c, we have to construct a graph $\mathcal{G}(\mathbf{x}, c)$ and solve Eq. (5). The inversion of $I - \mathbf{W}_{uu}$ is hard to compute, with complexity $\mathcal{O}(n^3)$. n is the number of training images. To get the scores of all test images and all classes, the overall complexity is $\mathcal{O}[n_t \cdot (s+u) \cdot n^3]$. To reduce the computation cost, we propose the following acceleration method.

We observe that, for a fixed class c, the only difference among the graphs of different test images $\{\mathcal{G}(\cdot, c)\}$ is the vertex of the test image. The vertices of embeddings of classes and training images are the same. As the number of those shared vertices is much larger than 1 (the number of test image vertex), it is safe to assume the scores of training images have little change when the test image changes. Therefore, we decompose the matrix $I - \mathbf{W}_{uu}$ to $\begin{bmatrix} I - \mathbf{W}_{tr,tr} & -\mathbf{w}_{tr,i} \\ -\mathbf{w}_{i,tr}^{\top} & 1 - w_{i,i} \end{bmatrix}$ and set $\mathbf{w}_{tr,i} = 0$, meaning that the label score of test image does not influence those of training images. $\mathbf{W}_{tr,tr}$ denotes the edge weights between training images and $\mathbf{w}_{tr,i}$ denotes the edge weights between training images and the test image i. When the test image changes, $I - \mathbf{W}_{tr,tr}$ remains the same and only the last row of $I - \mathbf{W}_{uu}$ is updated. With this property, the score of the test image can be efficiently obtained by Eq. (6) using Bordering Method [12].

$$r_i = (1 - w_{ii})^{-1} \left[\mathbf{w}_{i,l}^{\top}, \mathbf{w}_{i,tr}^{\top} \right] \begin{bmatrix} \mathbf{r}_l \\ \mathbf{r}_{tr} \end{bmatrix} \tag{6}$$

where $\mathbf{r}_l$ is the scores of labelled vertices. $\mathbf{W}_{ul} = \begin{bmatrix} \mathbf{W}_{tr,l} \\ \mathbf{w}_{i,l}^{\top} \end{bmatrix}$ is the edge weights between unlabelled and labelled vertices. $\mathbf{r}_{tr} = (\mathbf{I} - \mathbf{W}_{tr,tr})^{-1} \mathbf{W}_{tr,l} \mathbf{r}_l$ is the label scores of training images. It is the same for all graphs $\{\mathcal{G}(\cdot, c)\}$. Therefore, for a given class c, we only need to compute matrix inversion once to obtain $\mathbf{r}_{tr}$ with complexity $\mathcal{O}(n^3)$ and share it in all graphs. Given $\mathbf{r}_{tr}$, computing r_i only requires vector product with complexity $\mathcal{O}(n + s + u)$. The overall complexity is reduced to $\mathcal{O}[(s+u) \cdot n^3 + (s+u) \cdot n_t \cdot (n+s+u)]$.

Beta Normalization. ML^{2}P propagates the label scores with respect to multiple classes. The score distributions $w.r.t.$ different classes are often skewed and of different scales. Therefore, scores $w.r.t.$ different classes are not comparable. We propose Beta Normalization (BN) to align the ranges of the distributions and remove the skewness. For each class, we estimate the score distribution as a Generalized Beta Distribution. Then the test images' scores are converted from absolute values to the percentile ranks by the cumulative distribution function.

Mathematically speaking, let r_{ik} denote the score of the i-th test image $w.r.t.$ class k. $\mathbf{R}^u \in \mathbb{R}^{n_t \times u} = [r_{ik}]$ is the score matrix for all the test images and unseen classes. $\mathbf{r}_{*k}$ is $\mathbf{R}^u$'s k-th column, representing all test images' scores of belonging to class c_k. We assume r_{ik} follows Generalized Beta Distribution [25] with parameter $\boldsymbol{\theta}_k$ as $r_{ik} \sim GB(\boldsymbol{\theta}_k)$. The normalized score $\mathbf{r}'_{*k}$ is computed as

$$\mathbf{r}'_{*k} = F(\mathbf{r}_{*k}; \boldsymbol{\theta}_k) \tag{7}$$

where F is the cumulative distribution function. It converts $\mathbf{r}_{*k}$ as absolute values to $\mathbf{r}'_{*k}$ as percentile ranks. After the normalization, the distributions of $\mathbf{r}'_{*k}$ for all the classes are of same range with little skewness.

To estimate score distribution, adequate amount of data are required. In our settings of zero-shot learning, only one test image is available at inference time. Thus we are not able to directly estimate the score distributions of test data. Instead, we take the score distributions of training images as an approximation and learn an approximated $\hat{\theta}_k$ on training images then use it in Eq. (7).

5   Inference with ML^2P for Seen Classes

Similar to unseen classes, given a test image $\mathbf{x}$ and a seen class c, a graph $\mathcal{G}(\mathbf{x}, c) = \{V, E, \mathbf{W}, \mathbf{r}\}$ is built. V includes the embeddings of all training images, the test image and all seen classes. In contrast to the case of unseen classes, vertices of classes and training images are all labelled and the test image is the only unlabelled vertex. As labelled vertices are rich, class exclusion mentioned in Sect. 4.1 is no longer needed. Then the new close-form solution is

$$r_u = (1 - w_{uu})^{-1} \mathbf{w}_{ul} \mathbf{r}_l \tag{8}$$

which does not involve matrix inversion so the acceleration step is omitted as well. Collecting r_u for all test images and seen classes, we have $\mathbf{R}^s$ as the score matrix for seen classes.

In terms of beta normalization, the distribution parameter $\hat{\theta}$ cannot be directly approximated from training images as they are labelled vertices with discrete scores, 0 or 1. To address this issue, we use K-fold method: we divide training images into K folds and first pretend the images in the first fold are unlabeled while the others are still labelled, then perform LP to get the label scores for the first fold. Repeating this process to other folds, we get the label scores for all training images as if they are unlabeled. In the end, these scores are utilized to learn $\hat{\theta}$.

After beta normalization, the normalized score of seen classes, $\mathbf{R}^{s'}$, is obtained. The final output for all classes $\mathbf{R}' = \left[\mathbf{R}^{s'}, \mathbf{R}^{u'}\right] \in \mathbb{R}^{n_t \times (s+u)}$.

6   Experiments

6.1   Datasets

We chose AffectNet Dataset as our training dataset and evaluated our model on RAF, Emotic and FaceME datasets. The latter is a multi-label dataset collected by ourselves. **AffectNet** [28] is a multi-class dataset with 287,618 training images and 8 basic emotion classes: {*neutrality, happiness, sadness, anger, surprise, fear, disgust, contempt*}. These 8 emotions are our seen classes. Please note we did not have large amount of multi-labelled images for training. Each AffectNet image only has one of the 8 emotion labels.

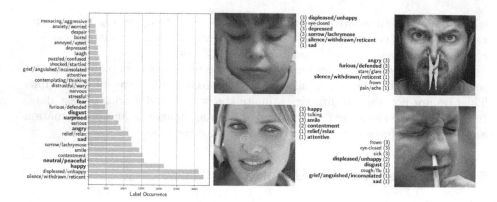

Fig. 4. FaceME dataset sample images and label occurrence of the selected 30 labels. Texts aside the images are their labels. The numbers in the parenthesis denote how many annotators choose that label.

RAF [22] is a multi-class dataset containing of a 7-class basic emotion part and a 12-class compound emotion part. We used the compound label part in our experiments, where the labels are formed by combining 2 of the 6 *Seen* classes: {*happy, sad, anger, surprise, fear, disgust*}. We regarded the compound emotion classification problems as a multi-label problem. There are 3956 images with compound labels.

Emotic [20] is a multi-label dataset with 26 emotion labels and images of people in real environments. Emotions have to be inferred from the context and in many of the images, faces are covered or invisible. To evaluate our model, we used a face detector to crop out the faces and got 7134 cropped images in the end. 20 of the 26 labels are unseen classes and 6 of them are seen classes: {*peace*(correspondent to *neutral*), *anger, fear, happiness, sadness, surprise*}. It represents a hard scenario with noisy label.

FaceME is a multi-label facial expression dataset collected by ourselves. It has 10062 images and 85 labels. The labels not only include emotions, but also labels about action, health and inward thoughts. Each image is labelled by 3 annotators. In the experiments, we discarded the labels annotated by only one person. From the 85 labels, we selected out 30 labels for evaluation that are emotion-related and have adequate amount of images and 7 of them are seen classes (not including *"contempt"*). Excluding the images not having the selected 30 labels, there are 9687 images left. In Fig. 4, the label occurrence distribution and sample images are shown.

6.2   Evaluation Protocol

We evaluated the models from three different aspects: discriminative separation of relevant and irrelevant labels, intra-class ranking and inter-class ranking.

Separation of Relevant and Irrelevant Labels: It is evaluated by **F1**. Given the ground truth labels of a class and predictions for test images, we computed the Precision rate and Recall rate and the class's F1 score was the harmonic average of the two rates. The final F1 was the average of each class's F1. Since label ranking models only predict rank scores, we estimated two additional thresholds for each model to separate relevant and irrelevant classes, one for seen classes and one for unseen classes. We choose F1 instead of accuracy because the amounts of relevant and irrelevant labels are imbalanced.

Intra-class Ranking: It is evaluated by **Mean Average Precision** (mAP). Given a ranked list of images for a certain class, mAP measures the area under precision-recall curve.

Inter-class Ranking: We propose a new metric **Ranking F1** (rF1) to normalize the ranking accuracy according to the label imbalance. As the sample quantities of some frequent labels are much larger than the infrequent ones, if the accuracy score is not normalized, a model always ranking the frequent labels on the top of the list can reach a very high score.

Given a image with l relevant labels, we define a class c as positive if it is a relevant label and the prediction of c is positive if it is ranked as one of top l relevant labels. With these two definitions, the true positive rate and false positive rate of the rank result can be computed, so as a F1 score, which we name as Ranking F1. The final rF1 was the average of each class's rF1.

For each metrics, we reported results under three experiment setups: prediction results for the seen classes only (**S**), for the unseen classes only (**U**) and for all classes (**A**).

6.3   Implementation of Z-ML^{2}P framework

We implemented three configurations of the framework's four components introduced in Sect. 3.2. They correspond to three state-of-art ZSL models. In all of configurations, the feature extraction unit and f is the same. g and ranking loss follow the set-up in the original papers. We briefly introduce them below.

(1) **Fast0Tag(F0T)** [39]: It uses Soft Margin Loss and g is a lookup function which maps the class names to their word vectors.
(2) **ALE** [1]: It uses Weighted Max Margin Loss with the same g as F0T.
(3) **SYNC** [4]: It uses Structured Max Margin Loss in which margins are predefined according to class relations and g first maps the class names to the word vectors then embed them into semantic space (Model Space in [4]) via phantom classes.

The feature extraction part is an 80-layer residual CNN. It is pretrained on AffectNet by minimizing cross-entropy loss. The image features $\{x_i\}$ are its last Conv layer's output. f is implemented as a single FC layer. It differs from the set-up in [1,4,39] only in the number of layers. GloVe vectors used in g are 300 dimension vectors pretrained on Wikipedia corpus. During training,

Table 1. Results on RAF dataset.

	SYNC	SYNC+LP	SYNC+ML^{2}P	F0T	F0T+LP	F0T+ML^{2}P	ALE	ALE+LP	ALE+ML^{2}P
mAP	71.8	73.1	**73.1**	74.3	75.5	**75.5**	73.4	75.8	**75.8**
rF1	62.1	63.6	**63.6**	64.4	63.1	63.9	64.3	63.3	64.0
F1	61.9	64.3	**64.3**	64.2	63.5	**65.0**	63.7	64.8	**65.8**

the CNN and GloVe vectors are freezed. The other parts of the framework are optimized w.r.t the ranking losses via SGD on AffectNet. In AffectNet, each image is assigned to only one class. In ranking loss, this class is treated as a relevant label and the other classes as irrelevant ones.

For the representative class set of label propagation model, we found using the 8 basic seen classes is good enough. To estimate the hyperparameters, since the three datasets are relatively small and many classes have low occurrences, we did not divide validation and test set. Instead, for seen classes, we split the data via KFold and tuned the hyperparameters on one fold then applied them onto the others and for unseen classes, we split classes via KFold.

For each configuration, we evaluated the prediction results by network only, by network and label propagation without beta normalization and by network and ML^{2}P.

6.4 Experimental Results

The results on RAF, Emotic and FaceME datasets are summarized in Tables 1, 2, 3, respectively. In the tables, X denotes the result of network of certain configuration. $X+LP$ denotes the result of network and our label propagation method without beta normalization. $X + ML^2P$ denotes the result of network and ML^{2}P. It can be observed that our ML^{2}P model gives impressive results on intra-class, inter-class ranking and relevant-irrelevant label separations and on both seen and unseen classes.

It is worth noting that our Z-ML^{2}P framework is an efficient method to address multi-label zero-shot learning and applicable to various real-world tasks such as image annotation and image retrieval. With our acceleration method, the inference time is short. On an Intel i7 CPU, computing r_{tr} in Eq. (6) takes 0.3 s for a seen class and 0.5 s for a unseen class. Then it takes only 100 μs to infer the labels of a test image.

Evaluations on Seen Classes. For seen classes, the ML^{2}P models shows improvements on almost all evaluation metrics against their network baselines, especially on FaceME dataset. It shows, although the networks are directly optimized on seen classes, there still exists information that is missed by the network yet captured in the data manifold structure. In terms of rF1 score on RAF dataset, ML^{2}P is slightly worse than the network baseline. It is caused by incomparability of the scores of different classes mentioned in Sect. 4.2. Compared to LP method, ML^{2}P mitigates the issue although a small gap remains. The improvement in mAP and F1 still proves the effectiveness of our algorithm.

Table 2. Results on FaceME dataset

		SYNC	SYNC+LP	SYNC+ML^{2}P	F0T	F0T+LP	F0T+ML^{2}P	ALE	ALE+LP	ALE+ML^{2}P
mAP	S	46.9	57.3	**57.3**	50.1	57.2	**57.2**	49.3	59.0	**59.0**
	U	12.1	17.5	**17.5**	13.0	19.5	**19.5**	12.5	19.3	**19.3**
	A	20.2	26.8	**26.8**	21.6	28.3	**28.3**	21.1	28.6	**28.6**
rF1	S	48.8	58.1	**65.3**	54.8	62.4	**67.1**	55.4	64.5	**67.6**
	U	9.7	3.6	**20.4**	11.4	3.3	**19.5**	11.2	2.8	**20.2**
	A	14.1	13.1	**27.8**	17.4	12.8	**27.4**	17.3	12.9	**28.2**
F1	S	39.1	47.7	**53.1**	46.5	49.4	**53.6**	45.9	51.5	**53.6**
	U	13.1	10.6	**19.3**	15.0	12.4	**21.2**	13.6	12.2	**19.9**
	A	19.2	19.3	**27.3**	22.3	21.0	**28.8**	21.1	21.4	**27.8**

Table 3. Results on emotic dataset

		SYNC	SYNC+LP	SYNC+ML^{2}P	F0T	F0T+LP	F0T+ML^{2}P	ALE	ALE+LP	ALE+ML^{2}P
mAP	S	20.5	21.5	**21.5**	22.0	22.4	**22.4**	20.4	21.6	**21.6**
	U	10.7	11.5	**11.5**	11.3	12.5	**12.5**	11.1	12.4	**12.4**
	A	12.9	13.8	**13.8**	13.8	14.8	**14.8**	13.2	13.6	**14.6**
rF1	S	26.5	33.1	**37.9**	32.4	37.4	**39.0**	33.2	37.5	**38.0**
	U	14.0	4.0	**15.5**	16.3	4.1	**18.1**	16.3	4.0	**17.5**
	A	13.7	8.3	**16.9**	15.7	9.1	**18.6**	15.4	8.6	**18.1**
F1	S	17.3	22.7	**22.9**	18.4	23.2	**23.2**	18.4	22.4	**22.6**
	U	13.0	12.9	**14.4**	11.3	11.7	**15.1**	13.2	9.5	**15.5**
	A	14.0	15.1	**16.3**	13.0	14.4	**16.9**	14.4	12.5	**17.1**

Evaluations on Unseen Classes. The performance on unseen classes is the most important aspect of ZSL methods. ML^{2}P substantially outperforms the network baseline on both FaceME and Emotic datasets and on all metrics. The improvement in mAP confirms that, without the need of auxiliary data of unseen classes, the manifold structure of training images indeed facilitates label propagation. mAP of LP and ML^{2}P are the same because Beta Normalization does not change the results of intra-class ranking. rF1 score shows the increase in inter-class ranking accuracy. ML^{2}P successfully addresses the score incomparability issue of unseen classes.

Effectiveness of Beta Normalization. Comparing the results of LP and ML^{2}P, we can observe the effectiveness of beta normalization. Although LP has higher mAP than the network baseline, its rF1 degrades seriously. It shows the score incomparability issue again. For the network baseline, the incomparability exists between seen classes and unseen classes. On Emotic dataset, the rF1 of networks' predictions for all classes is lower than either the score of seen classes only or unseen classes only. Beta normalization resolves the issue by correctly aligning the score distributions, as shown in the result of ML^{2}P. Moreover, it helps F1 score as well. Since all unseen classes or seen classes share the same threshold to separate relevant and irrelevant labels, if the scores are not aligned, there exists no good universal threshold.

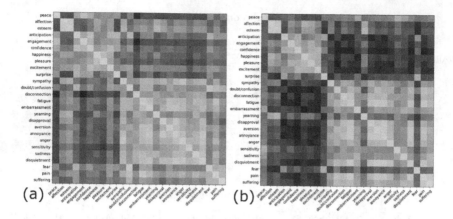

Fig. 5. Label Score Correlation Coefficient Matrix of ALE configuration on Emotic Dataset. (a) and (b) plot the matrix of network baseline and ML²P. Darker in color means lower correlation. (Color figure online)

6.5   Detailed Analysis

In this section, we first measured how well a model captures the relations among classes. We plotted the correlation coefficient of predicted scores between different classes in Fig. 5a and b of ALE configuration on Emotic dataset. On the correlation matrix of network baseline (Fig. 5a), two bright blocks can be weakly identified, one for positive emotions and the other for the negative ones. In contrast, this structure is much more obvious on ML²P's matrix (Fig. 5b). It shows our method have strong capacity for learning class relations and is suitable for multi-label learning problems.

Due to space limitation, matrix of other configurations and the per-class mAP scores are presented in supplement. In addition, we showed the framework is robust to the feature extraction unit by replacing the residual CNN with VGG-Face network [29]. The results are also included in the supplement.

7   Conclusion

We proposed a novel Zero-shot learning framework with Multi-Label Label Propagation (Z-ML²P) and collect a new *Fac*ial *e*xpression dataset with *M*ultiple *E*motions (FaceME). Our framework for the first time addresses multi-label zero-shot FER problem using existing multi-class emotion dataset only and successfully adopts label propagation to multi-label task and shows impressive improvement on both seen classes and unseen classes.

References

1. Akata, Z., Perronnin, F., Harchaoui, Z., Schmid, C.: Label-embedding for image classification. IEEE T-PAMI **38**(7), 1425–1438 (2016)
2. Akata, Z., Reed, S., Walter, D., Lee, H., Schiele, B.: Evaluation of output embeddings for fine-grained image classification. In: Proceedings of CVPR (2015)
3. Bucak, S.S., Mallapragada, P.K., Jin, R., Jain, A.K.: Efficient multi-label ranking for multi-class learning: application to object recognition. In: Proceedings of ICCV (2009)
4. Changpinyo, S., Chao, W.L., Gong, B., Sha, F.: Synthesized classifiers for zero-shot learning. In: Proceedings of CVPR (2016)
5. Cohn, J.F., De la Torre, F.: Automated face analysis for affective computing. In: The Oxford Handbook of Affective Computing (2014)
6. De la Torre, F., Cohn, J.F.: Facial expression analysis. In: Moeslund, T., Hilton, A., Krüger, V., Sigal, L. (eds.) Visual Analysis of Humans, pp. 377–409. Springer, London (2011). https://doi.org/10.1007/978-0-85729-997-0_19
7. Du, S., Tao, Y., Martinez, A.M.: Compound facial expressions of emotion. Proc. Nat. Acad. Sci. **111**(15), E1454–E1462 (2014)
8. Ekman, P., Friesen, W.V.: Constants across cultures in the face and emotion. J. Pers. Soc. Psychol. **17**(2), 124–9 (1971)
9. Ekman, P., Rosenberg, E.L.: What the Face Reveals: Basic and Applied Studies of Spontaneous Expression Using the Facial Action Coding System (FACS). Oxford University Press, Oxford (1997)
10. Eleftheriadis, S., Rudovic, O., Pantic, M.: Discriminative shared gaussian processes for multiview and view-invariant facial expression recognition. IEEE Trans. Image Process. **24**(1), 189–204 (2015)
11. Fabian Benitez-Quiroz, C., Srinivasan, R., Martinez, A.M.: Emotionet: an accurate, real-time algorithm for the automatic annotation of a million facial expressions in the wild. In: Proceedings of CVPR (2016)
12. Faddeev, D.K., Faddeeva, V.N.: Computational methods of linear algebra. J. Sov. Math. **15**(5), 531–650 (1981)
13. Frome, A., Corrado, G., Shlens, J.: Devise: a deep visual-semantic embedding model. In: Proceedings of NIPS (2013)
14. Fu, Y., Hospedales, T.M., Xiang, T., Gong, S.: Transductive multi-view zero-shot learning. IEEE T-PAMI **37**(11), 2332–2345 (2015)
15. Gaure, A., Gupta, A., Verma, V.K., Rai, P.: A probabilistic framework for zero-shot multi-label learning. In: Proceedings of UAI (2017)
16. Gibaja, E., Ventura, S.: A tutorial on multilabel learning. ACM Comput. Surv. **47**(3), 52:1–52:38 (2015)
17. He, K., Zhang, X., Ren, S., Sun, J.: Deep residual learning for image recognition. In: Proceedings of CVPR (2015)
18. Kacem, A., Daoudi, M., Amor, B.B., Alvarez-Paiva, J.C.: A novel space-time representation on the positive semidefinite cone for facial expression recognition. In: Proceedings of ICCV (2017)
19. Kodirov, E., Xiang, T., Gong, S.: Semantic autoencoder for zero-shot learning. In: Proceedings of CVPR (2017)
20. Kosti, R., Alvarez, J.M., Recasens, A., Lapedriza, A.: Emotion recognition in context. In: Proceedings of CVPR (2017)
21. Li, A., Lu, Z., Wang, L., Xiang, T., Li, X., Wen, J.R.: Zero-Shot Fine-Grained Classification by Deep Feature Learning with Semantics. CoRR abs/1707.00785, pp. 1–10 (2017)

22. Li, S., Deng, W., Du, J.: Reliable crowdsourcing and deep locality-preserving learning for expression recognition in the wild. In: Proceedings of CVPR (2017)
23. Liu, M., Shan, S., Wang, R., Chen, X.: Learning expressionlets via universal manifold model for dynamic facial expression recognition. IEEE Trans. Image Process. **25**(12), 5920–5932 (2016)
24. Lucey, P., Cohn, J.F., Kanade, T., Saragih, J., Ambadar, Z., Matthews, I.: The extended Cohn-Kanade dataset (CK+): a complete dataset for action unit and emotion-specified expression. In: Proceedings of CVPR (2010)
25. McDonald, J.B., Xu, Y.J.: A generalization of the beta distribution with applications. J. Econometrics **66**(1), 133–152 (1995)
26. Mehrabian, A.: Framework for a comprehensive description and measurement of emotional states. Genet. Soc. Gen. Psychol. Monogr. **121**(3), 339–361 (1995)
27. Mikolov, T., Corrado, G., Chen, K., Dean, J.: Efficient estimation of word representations in vector space. In: Proceedings of ICLR (2013)
28. Mollahosseini, A., Hasani, B., Mahoor, M.H.: Affectnet: a database for facial expression, valence, and arousal computing in the wild. IEEE Trans. Affect. Comput. (2017)
29. Parkhi, O.M., Vedaldi, A., Zisserman, A.: Deep face recognition. In: Proceedings of BMVC (2015)
30. Patterson, G., Hays, J.: Sun attribute database: discovering, annotating, and recognizing scene attributes. In: Proceedings of CVPR (2012)
31. Peng, G., Wang, S.: Weakly supervised facial action unit recognition through adversarial training. In: Proceedings of CVPR (2018)
32. Pennington, J., Socher, R., Manning, C.D.: GloVe: global vectors for word representation. In: Proceedings of EMNLP (2014)
33. Sang, D.V., Dat, N.V., Thuan, D.P.: Facial expression recognition using deep convolutional neural networks. In: Proceedings of KSE (2017)
34. Soleymani, M., Asghari-Esfeden, S., Fu, Y., Pantic, M.: Analysis of eeg signals and facial expressions for continuous emotion detection. IEEE Trans. Affect. Comput. **7**(1), 17–28 (2016)
35. Wang, P., Liu, L., Shen, C.: Multi-attention network for one shot learning. In: Proceedings of CVPR (2017)
36. Xian, Y., Akata, Z., Sharma, G., Nguyen, Q., Hein, M., Schiele, B.: Latent embeddings for zero-shot classification. In: Proceedings of CVPR (2016)
37. Yang, H., Ciftci, U., Yin, L.: Facial expression recognition by de-expression residue learning. In: Proceedings of CVPR (2018)
38. Zhang, F., Zhang, T., Mao, Q., Xu, C.: Joint pose and expression modeling for facial expression recognition. In: Proceedings of CVPR (2018)
39. Zhang, Y., Gong, B., Shah, M.: Fast zero-shot image tagging. In: Proceedings of CVPR (2016)
40. Zhang, Y., Dong, W., Hu, B.G., Ji, Q.: Classifier learning with prior probabilities for facial action unit recognition. In: Proceedings of CVPR (2018)
41. Zhao, G., Pietikainen, M.: Dynamic texture recognition using local binary patterns with an application to facial expressions. IEEE T-PAMI **29**(6), 915–928 (2007)
42. Zhao, K., Chu, W., la Torre, F.D., Cohn, J.F., Zhang, H.: Joint patch and multi-label learning for facial action unit and holistic expression recognition. IEEE Trans. Image Process. **25**(8), 3931–3946 (2016)
43. Zhao, K., Chu, W.S., Martinez, A.M.: Learning facial action units from web images with scalable weakly supervised clustering. In: Proceedings of CVPR (2018)
44. Zhu, X., Ghahramani, Z., Lafferty, J.: Semi-supervised learning using Gaussian fields and harmonic functions. In: Proceedings of ICML (2003)

Believe It or Not, We Know What You Are Looking At!

Dongze Lian[ID], Zehao Yu[ID], and Shenghua Gao[✉][ID]

School of Information Science and Technology, ShanghaiTech University,
Shanghai, China
{liandz,yuzh,gaoshh}@shanghaitech.edu.cn

Abstract. By borrowing the wisdom of human in gaze following, we propose a two-stage solution for gaze point prediction of the target persons in a scene. Specifically, in the first stage, both head image and its position are fed into a gaze direction pathway to predict the gaze direction, and then multi-scale gaze direction fields are generated to characterize the distribution of gaze points without considering the scene contents. In the second stage, the multi-scale gaze direction fields are concatenated with the image contents and fed into a heatmap pathway for heatmap regression. There are two merits for our two-stage solution based gaze following: (i) our solution mimics the behavior of human in gaze following, therefore it is more psychological plausible; (ii) besides using heatmap to supervise the output of our network, we can also leverage gaze direction to facilitate the training of gaze direction pathway, therefore our network can be more robustly trained. Considering that existing gaze following dataset is annotated by the third-view persons, we build a video gaze following dataset, where the ground truth is annotated by the observers in the videos. Therefore it is more reliable. The evaluation with such a dataset reflects the capacity of different methods in real scenarios better. Extensive experiments on both datasets show that our method significantly outperforms existing methods, which validates the effectiveness of our solution for gaze following. Our dataset and codes are released in https://github.com/svip-lab/GazeFollowing.

Keywords: Gaze following · Saliency · Multi-scale gaze direction fields

1 Introduction

Gaze following is a task of following other people's gaze in a scene and inferring where they are looking [22]. It is important for understanding the behavior of

---

D. Lian and Z. Yu—Contribute equally.

Electronic supplementary material The online version of this chapter (https://doi.org/10.1007/978-3-030-20893-6_3) contains supplementary material, which is available to authorized users.

© Springer Nature Switzerland AG 2019
C. V. Jawahar et al. (Eds.): ACCV 2018, LNCS 11363, pp. 35–50, 2019.
https://doi.org/10.1007/978-3-030-20893-6_3

human in human-human interaction and human-object interaction. For example, we can infer the intention of persons based on their gaze points in human-human interaction. In new retailing scenario, we can infer the interest of the consumers in different products based on their eyes contact with those products (as shown in Fig. 1(a) (b)), and infer what kind of information (ingredients of the food, the price, expire data, *etc.*) attracts the consumers' attention most. Although gaze following is of vital importance, it is extremely challenging because of the reasons below: firstly, actually inferring the gaze point requires the depth information of the scene, head pose and eyeball movement [27,31], nevertheless it is hard to infer the depth of scene with a monocular image. Further, head pose and eyeball movements are not easy to be estimated because of occlusion (usually self-occlusion), as shown in Fig. 1(c); secondly, ambiguity exists for gaze point estimated by different third-view observers with a single view image, as shown in Fig. 1(d); thirdly, the gaze following involves the geometric relationship understanding between target person and other objects/persons in the scene as well as scene contents understanding, which is a difficult task.

(a)   (b)   (c)   (d)

Fig. 1. (a) and (b) show the application of gaze following in supermarket scenario. (c) and (d) show the challenges in gaze following (The self-occluded head and ambiguity of gaze point).

To tackle these problems, early works usually simplify the setting to avoid the handicaps for general gaze following, for example, making assumption that face is available for better head pose estimation [32], with multiple inputs for depth inference [18], with eye tracker for ground truth annotation or restricting the application scenario to people looking at each other for disambiguation. However, these simplifications restrict the applications of general gaze following. Recently, Recasens *et al.* propose to study general gaze following under most of general settings [22]. Specifically, they propose a two-pathway method (a gaze pathway and a saliency pathway) based deep neural networks for gaze following. However, in their solution, the saliency pathway and gaze pathway are independent of each other. For a third-view person, when he/she infers the gaze point of a target person, he/she infers the gaze direction first based on head pose, and then estimates the gaze point from the scene contents along the gaze direction, where gaze point denotes the position that one person is looking at in the image, and gaze direction means the direction from head position to gaze point in this paper. In other words, the saliency pathway relies on gaze direction estimation, which is neglected in [22].

In this paper, we propose a two-stage solution to mimic the behavior of a third-view person for gaze following. Specifically, in the first stage, we leverage a gaze direction pathway to predict the gaze direction based on the head image and head position of target person. There are two motivations for such gaze direction pathway: firstly, it is more natural to infer the gaze direction rather than gaze point merely based on head image and head position; secondly, since the gaze direction can be inferred in the training phase, thus we can introduce a loss w.r.t. gaze direction to facilitate the learning of this gaze direction pathway. Next, we encode the predicted gaze direction as the multi-scale gaze direction fields. In the second stage, based on the gaze direction and the context information of the objects along the gaze direction, we can estimate a heatmap through a heatmap pathway. In this stage, we concatenate the multi-scale gaze direction fields with the original image as the input of the heatmap pathway for heatmap estimation.

A proper dataset is important for the evaluation of gaze following. The only existing gaze following dataset (GazeFollow dataset [22]) is annotated by the third-view persons. In this paper, to evaluate the performance for real problem, we build a video-based gaze following dataset, named Daily Life Gaze dataset (DL Gaze). Particularly, we have 16 volunteers to freely move in 4 different indoor scenes, including working office, laboratory, library, corridor in the building. During the period, they can talk, read books, use their mobile phones, or freely look at other places in the scene. We record the video for them and ask the volunteer to annotate where they look later. There are 95,000 frames in total. Compared with GazeFollow, the ground truth annotated by the persons in the video is more reliable than that annotated by third-view workers. Further, it is a video-based gaze following dataset and records the gaze following for real scenes. Therefore the evaluation of gaze following on this dataset reflects the performance of different methods for real problem.

The main contributions of our paper are summarized as follows: (i) we propose a two-stage solution for gaze following task. Our network architecture is inspired by the behavior of human in gaze following, therefore it is more psychological plausible; (ii) we use ground truth to supervise the learning of both stages, consequently facilitates the network training. In addition, we introduce multi-scale gaze direction fields for attention prediction, which further improves the performance of gaze following; (iii) we collect a video-based gaze following dataset (DL Gaze), with the ground truth annotated by the persons in the video. Therefore the evaluation on this dataset reflects the real performance for gaze following in real problem; (iv) Extensive experiments on both datasets validate the effectiveness of our solution for gaze following.

2   Related Work

Gaze Following. Previous work about gaze following paid attention to restricted scenes, which added some priors for specific applications. In [32], a face detector was employed to extract face, which was limited for the people looking away from the camera. [17] detected whether people were looking at each other in a movie, which was helpful for interaction. Eye tracker was utilized to predict the next object in order to improve action recognition in [3]. [20] only estimated the gaze direction from head position, but not the specific gaze point. These methods were applied to a particular scene. Recent works [18,22,23] focused on general gaze following, which had wider applications. Given a single picture containing one or more people, the gaze points of some people in the image were estimated, without any restrictions in [22]. Some extensive works [18,23] focused on multi-modality image or predicted gaze point in videos. The RGB-D image was introduced to predict gaze in images and videos [18] because the multi-modality data provided 3D head pose information in order to find more accurate gaze point. In [23], the cross-frame gaze point in videos could be predicted for the people in a frame.

Eye Tracking. Eye tracking is strongly related to gaze following. Different from gaze following, eye tracking technology inferred which direction or which point on the screen one person was looking at [29]. Previous work [6,33] built the geometry model to infer the gaze point on the screen target. Recently, many appearance-based methods [11,31] solved the problem by learning a complex function from the eye images to gaze point, which needed large-scale dataset. These methods took the eye images and face image as inputs because gaze direction could be determined according to the eye movement and head pose [31]. However, the eye images could not be utilized to predict gaze point because they were occluded or very noisy in gaze following. Thus, gaze following direction is almost obtained from the head image.

Saliency. Saliency detection and gaze following are two different tasks [22,23] even though they were closely related. Saliency detection predicts fixation map from observers out of the original images [7,9,14]. Gaze following in image predicts the position that people in a scene were looking at. Previous works about saliency prediction considered the low-level features and saliency maps at different scales [8]. Subsequently, the features from different levels were combined to model a bottom-up, top-down architecture [9]. Recently, deep neural networks have been applied to saliency prediction and achieve great success [13,19]. However, the object in the gaze point region may be not salient, which reveals that it is hard to find the gaze point through a saliency algorithm directly.

3   Approach

Inspired by the behavior of human in gaze following, we propose a two-stage solution. Specifically, when a third-view person estimates the gaze of the target person, he/she first estimates the gaze direction of the target based on the head image, then the gaze point is predicted based on the scene content along the gaze direction. Similarly, we feed the head image and its position in the image into a gaze direction pathway for gaze direction prediction in the first stage, and then the multi-scale gaze direction fields are encoded. In the second stage, the gaze direction fields are concatenated with the original image as the input of heatmap pathway for heatmap regression. It is worth noting that all components in our network are differentiable and the whole network can be trained with an end-to-end learning. The network architecture is shown in Fig. 2.

3.1 Gaze Direction Pathway

Gaze direction pathway takes head image and head position as inputs for gaze direction prediction. We feed the head image into a ResNet-50 for feature extraction, and then concatenate head features with head position features encoded by a network with three fully connected layers for gaze direction prediction. Different from work of Recasens *et al.* [22], which takes head image and head position for gaze mask prediction, our network only estimates the gaze direction. There are two reasons accounting for our solution. Firstly, it is easier to infer the gaze direction than gaze mask merely based on head image and its position. Secondly, we can use gaze direction to supervise the learning of gaze direction pathway to make it more robustly trained. It is also worth noting that the predicted gaze direction would be used to generate gaze direction fields, which is further used for heatmap regression in the heatmap pathway, and the optimization of heatmap would also update the parameters in the gaze direction pathway.

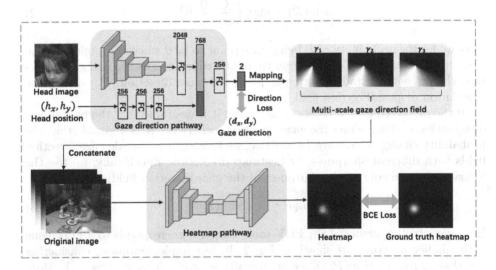

Fig. 2. The network architecture for gaze following. There are two modules in this network: gaze direction pathway and heatmap pathway. In the first stage, a coarse gaze direction is predicted through gaze direction pathway, and then it is encoded as multi-scale gaze direction fields. We concatenate the multi-scale fields and the original image to regress heatmap of final gaze point through heatmap pathway.

3.2 Gaze Direction Field

Once the gaze direction is estimated, the gaze point is likely to be along the gaze direction. Usually, the field of view (FOV) of the target person is simplified as a cone with the head position as the apex of the cone. So given a point $P = (p_x, p_y)$, if we do not consider the scene contents, then the probability of the point P being the gaze point should be proportional to the angle θ between line L_{HP} and predicted gaze direction, here $H = (h_x, h_y)$ is the head position, as shown in Fig. 3(a). If θ is small, then the probability of the point being gaze point is high, otherwise, the probability is low. We utilize the cosine function to describe the mapping from the angle to the probability value. We denote the probability distribution of the points being gaze point without considering the scene contents as the **gaze direction field**. Thus, gaze direction field is a probability map, where intensity value of each point shows the probability that this point is the gaze point. Its size is the same as the scene image.

Particularly, the line direction of L_{HP} can be calculated as follows:

$$G = (p_x - h_x, p_y - h_y) \tag{1}$$

Given an image with size $W \times H$ (here W and H are the width and height of image, respectively), we denote the predicted gaze direction as $\hat{d} = (\hat{d}_x, \hat{d}_y)$, then the probability of the point P being the gaze point can be calculated as follows:

$$Sim(P) = \max\left(\frac{\langle G, \hat{d} \rangle}{|G||\hat{d}|}, 0\right) \tag{2}$$

Here we let the probability of P being gaze point to be 0 when the angle between gaze direction and line L_{HP} is larger than 90°, which means the real gaze direction should not contradict with the predicted gaze direction. We depict the calculation of gaze direction field.

If the predicted gaze direction is accurate, it is desirable that the probability distribution is sharp along the gaze direction, otherwise, it is desirable that the probability changes smoothly. In practice, we leverage multi-scale gaze direction fields with different sharpness for heatmap prediction. Specifically, we use the following way to control the sharpness of the gaze direction field:

$$Sim(P, \gamma) = [Sim(P)]^\gamma \tag{3}$$

Here γ controls aperture of the FOV cone. Larger γ corresponds to a FOV cone with smaller aperture, as shown in Fig. 2. In our implementation, considering the change rate of $Sim(P, \gamma)$, we empirically set $\gamma_1 = 5, \gamma_2 = 2, \gamma_3 = 1$. More details about γ can be found in the supplementary material.

It also worth noting that the gaze direction fields are differentiable w.r.t. the network parameters of gaze direction pathway, so that the whole architecture can be trained with an end-to-end learning strategy.

3.3   Heatmap Pathway

Gaze direction fields encode the distribution of gaze points inferred from gaze direction, together with scene contents, we can infer the gaze point. Specifically, we concatenate the original image and the multi-scale gaze direction fields, and

(a)   (b)

Fig. 3. (a) The original image: the blue line shows gaze direction of the left girl inside the image, and the green dot shows the head position. Gaze direction field, which measures the probability of each point being gaze point with cosine function between the line direction of L_{HP} and predicted gaze direction $\hat{d}$. (b) Our DL Gaze dataset. (Color figure online)

feed them into a heatmap pathway for heatmap regression. The point corresponding to the maximum value of the heatmap is considered as the final gaze point. In practice, we leverage a feature pyramid network (FPN) [15] for the heatmap pathway in light of its success in object detection. The last layer of heatmap pathway is followed with a Sigmoid activation function, which guarantees the probability of each pixel falls into $[0, 1]$.

There are two reasons to predict probability heatmap instead of a direct gaze point coordinate:

- As pointed in [25], mapping from image to the coordinates of gaze point directly is a highly non-linear function. Compared with gaze point estimation, heatmap prediction is more robust, which means even some entries of heatmap are not accurately predicted, the gaze point prediction based on heatmap can still be correct. Thus heatmap regression is more commonly used in many applications, including pose estimation [21] and face alignment. The experimental results in Sect. 4 also validate the advantage of heatmap regression over gaze point regression.
- Gaze following in an image is sometimes ambiguous [22] due to the lack of the ground truth. Different workers may vote for different gaze points, especially when the eye images are invisible, the head image is low-resolution or occluded. Thus, the gaze point is usually multimodal, and the output of network is expected to support the multimodal prediction. Heatmap regression satisfies such requirement.

Following [21], the heatmap of ground truth gaze point is generated by centering a Gaussian kernel at the position of gaze point as follows:

$$H(i,j) = \frac{1}{\sqrt{2\pi}\sigma}e^{-\frac{(i-g_x)^2 + (j-g_y)^2}{2\sigma^2}} \qquad (4)$$

where $g = (g_x, g_y)$ and $H(i,j)$ are the ground truth gaze point and its heatmap, respectively. σ is the variance of Gaussian kernel. We empirically set $\sigma = 3$ in our implementation.

3.4   Network Training

The inputs of our network consist of three parts: head image, head position and the original image. The head and original image are resized to 224×224, and the head position is the coordinate when the original image size is normalized to 1×1. The outputs of network consist of two parts: gaze direction and visual attention. The gaze direction is the normalized vector from the head position to gaze point and the visual attention is a heatmap with size 56×56, whose values indicate the probability that the gaze point falls here.

Specifically, the gaze direction loss is:

$$\ell_d = 1 - \frac{\langle d, \hat{d} \rangle}{|d||\hat{d}|} \tag{5}$$

where d and $\hat{d}$ are the ground truth and predicted gaze direction, respectively.

We employ the binary cross entropy loss (BCE Loss) for heatmap regression, which is written as follows:

$$\ell_h = -\frac{1}{N} \sum_{i=1}^{N} H_i \log(\hat{H}_i) + (1 - H_i) \log(1 - \hat{H}_i) \tag{6}$$

where H_i and $\hat{H}_i$ are the i-th entry of ground truth heatmap and predicted visual heatmap, respectively. N is with the size 56×56.

The whole loss function consists of gaze direction loss and heatmap loss:

$$\ell = \ell_d + \lambda \ell_h \tag{7}$$

where λ is the weight to balance ℓ_d and ℓ_h. We set $\lambda = 0.5$ in our experiments.

4   Experiments

4.1   Dataset and Evaluation Metric

Dataset. The GazeFollow dataset [22] is employed to evaluate our proposed method. The images of this dataset are from different source datasets, including SUN [26], MS COCO [16], Actions 40 [28], PASCAL [2], ImageNet [24] and Places [30], which is challenging due to variety of scenarios and amounts of people. The whole dataset contains 130,339 people and 122,143 images. The gaze points of people are inside the image. There are 4,782 people of dataset used for testing and the rest for training. To keep the evaluation consistency with existing work, we follow the standard training/testing split in [22].

To validate the performance of different gaze following algorithms for real scenarios, we also build a video-based Daily Life Gaze following dataset (DL Gaze). Specifically, DL Gaze contains the activities of 16 volunteers in 4 scenes, and these scenes include working office, laboratory, library and corridor in the building. They can freely talk, read books, use their mobile phones, and look at other places in the scene, as shown in Fig. 3(b). We record the video for these volunteers with an iPhone 6 s. Then we ask each volunteer to annotate what he/she looks at. Two frames are annotated per second. So the ground truth annotation is more reliable. It worth noting the occlusion also exists and there is severe change of illumination. Therefore our dataset is very challenging. The performance of gaze following in our dataset reflects the capability of gaze following in real scenarios. There are 86 videos, 95,000 frames (30 fps) in total. We test the model trained on GazeFollow with our dataset directly.

Evaluation Metric. Following [22], we employ these metrics (**AUC, Dist, MDist, Ang**) to evaluate the difference between the predicted gaze points and their corresponding ground truth. Details can be found in the supplementary material. In addition, we also introduce **Minimum angular error (MAng)**, which measures the minimum angle between the predicted gaze direction and all ground truth annotations:

4.2   Implementation Details

We implement the proposed method based on the PyTorch framework. In the training stage, We employ a ResNet-50 to extract head image feature and encode the original image feature. The network is initialized with the model pretrained with ImageNet [1]. When the first stage of training converges, we train the heatmap pathway and finally we finetune the whole network with an end-to-end learning strategy. The hyper-parameters of our network are listed as follows: batch size (128), learning rate ($1e^{-4}$), weight decay (0.0005). Adaptive moment estimation (Adam) algorithm [10] is employed to train the whole network.

4.3   Performance Evaluation

We compare our proposed method with the following state-of-the-art gaze following methods:

- Judd *et al.* [9]: Such a method uses a saliency model as a predictor of gaze and the position with maximum saliency value is used as predicted gaze point inside the image.
- SalGAN [19]: SalGAN [19] is the latest saliency method, and it takes the original image as input to generate visual heatmap. The position of maximum in visual attention is regarded as gaze point.
- SalGAN for heatmap: We replace the FPN with SalGAN in heatmap pathway, and all the rest components are the same with our method.
- Recasens *et al.* [22]: The gaze pathway and saliency pathway are introduced to extract the image and head feature, and both features are fused to get the final gaze point. The supervision is introduced in the last layer.
- Recasens *et al.**: For a fair comparison, we modify the backbone of Recasens *et al.* [22] from the AlexNet [12] to ResNet-50 [5] to extract head feature and image feature. All other parts remain the same as Recasens *et al.* [22].

– One human [22]: A third-view observer is employed to predict gaze points on the testing set in [22]. It is desirable that machine can achieve the human level performance.

Table 1. Performance comparison with existing methods on the GazeFollow dataset. One-scale and multi-scale correspond to the number of gaze direction fields in our model. For one-scale model, $\gamma = 1$.

Methods	AUC	Dist	MDist	Ang	MAng
Center [22]	0.633	0.313	0.230	49.0°	-
Random [22]	0.504	0.484	0.391	69.0°	-
Fixed bias [22]	0.674	0.306	0.219	48.0°	-
SVM + one grid [22]	0.758	0.276	0.193	43.0°	-
SVM + shift grid [22]	0.788	0.268	0.186	40.0°	-
Judd *et al.* [9]	0.711	0.337	0.250	54.0°	-
SalGAN [19]	0.848	0.238	0.192	36.7°	22.4°
SalGAN for heatmap	0.890	0.181	0.107	19.6°	9.9°
Recasens *et al.* [22]	0.878	0.190	0.113	24.0°	-
Recasens *et al.** [22]	0.881	0.175	0.101	22.5°	11.6°
One human [22]	0.924	0.096	0.040	11.0°	-
Ours (one-scale)	0.903	0.156	0.088	18.2°	9.2°
Ours (multi-scale)	**0.906**	**0.145**	**0.081**	**17.6°**	**8.8°**

The experiment results in Tables 1 and 2 show that our model outperforms all baselines in terms of all evaluation metrics. We also have the following findings: (1) Recasens *et al.** outperforms Recasens *et al.* shows the importance of the basic network. (2) SalGAN has the better performance than Judd *et al.*, which shows that better saliency detection method agrees with visual attention better. (3) Although employing the same basic network (ResNet-50), our method (one-scale) still achieve the better performance than Recasens *et al.**, which proves the soundness of our human behavior inspired a two-stage solution for gaze following. (4) The multi-scale model achieves better performance than that of one-scale, which validates the importance of multi-scale fields fusion. (5) Performance on our dataset is worse than that on GazeFollow, which shows the challenge of gaze following in real applications. (6) The improvement of our method over SalGAN for heatmap validates the effectiveness of FPN for heatmap regression.

We further compare our method with Recasens *et al.* using accumulative error curve and the results are shown in Fig. 4. We can see that our method usually achieves better prediction than the work of Recasens *et al.* [22].

Ablation Study. In order to evaluate the effectiveness of every component of different inputs and network. We design the following baselines:

– original image: We directly feed the original image into heatmap pathway for heatmap regression.

Table 2. Performance comparison with existing methods on our dataset. Each frame only contains one gaze point, so only Dist and Ang are used for performance evaluation.

Methods	Dist	Ang
Recasens *et al.* [22]	0.203	26.9°
Recasens *et al.** [22]	0.169	21.4°
Ours (multi-scale)	0.157	18.7°

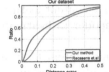 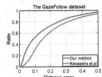 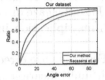 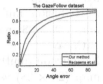

Fig. 4. Accumulative error curves of different methods on both datasets.

- original image + ROI head: We directly feed the original image into heatmap pathway for heatmap regression. Further, we directly extract the features corresponding to Region of Interest (ROI, the region of head) from the heatmap pathway and use it for gaze direction regression. Then we train the whole network with multi-task learning.
- w/o mid-layer supervision: The gaze direction supervision is removed, and both pathways are trained with an end-to-end learning strategy. Only one-scale gaze direction field is concatenated to the original image.

Table 3. The results of ablation study.

Methods	AUC	Dist	MDist	Ang	MAng
Original image	0.839	0.212	0.146	32.6°	21.6°
Original image + ROI head	0.887	0.182	0.118	22.9°	10.7°
W/O mid-layer supervision	0.875	0.178	0.101	24.4°	12.5°
Ours (one-scale)	**0.903**	**0.156**	**0.088**	**18.2°**	**9.2°**

The experiment results are listed in Table 3. We can see that predicting heatmap merely based on the scene image is not easy, even the head and its position are already included in the image. With gaze direction as supervision (original image+ ROI head) to aid the heatmap pathway learning, the performance can be boosted. With a gaze direction pathway to predict gaze direction, our method greatly outperforms original image-based solution for gaze following, which further validates the importance of two-stage solution. Further the improvement of our method (one scale) over w/o mid-layer supervision validates the importance of gaze direction prediction, which is an advantage of our solution, *i.e.*, our two-stage method benefits from gaze direction prediction.

The Information Fusion. In the second stage, we combine the gaze direction field and image content information. However, how to choose the position (early, middle, late fusion) and way (multiplication or concatenation) of fusing? Here we compare our method with the following information fusion strategies:

- Middle fusion (mul): Fuse the gaze direction field and the image content feature map (7×7) with multiplication in the middle layer.
- Middle fusion (concat): Fuse the gaze direction field and the image content feature map (7×7) with concatenation in the middle layer.
- Early fusion (mul): Fuse the gaze direction field and the image content feature map (28×28) with multiplication in the early layer of encoder in heatmap pathway.
- Late fusion (mul): Fuse the gaze direction field and the image content feature map (28×28) with multiplication in the last layer of decoder in heatmap pathway.
- Image fusion (mul): Directly multiply the original image with gaze direction field.

Table 4. Different information fusion strategies.

Methods	AUC	Dist	MDist	Ang	MAng
Middle fusion (mul)	0.882	0.183	0.118	21.7°	10.7°
Middle fusion (concat)	0.884	0.177	0.105	21.0°	10.5°
Early fusion (mul)	0.898	0.160	0.098	18.7°	9.6°
Late fusion (mul)	0.888	0.176	0.102	20.1°	10.1°
Image fusion (mul)	0.895	0.163	0.096	19.3°	9.7°
Ours (concat)	**0.903**	**0.156**	**0.088**	**18.2°**	**9.2°**

Table 4 shows the results of different information fusion strategies. We can find that early fusion usually obtains higher performance than middle and late fusion, which implies early suppression of useless scene contents is important for gaze following. Furthermore, we find that usually concatenating the gaze direction field with image or feature achieves slightly better results than the multiplication. The possible reason is that the predicted gaze direction may not be very accurate, and the multiplication between image and the gaze direction field would lead to the change of intensities of pixels and cause information loss. While for concatenation, the information is still there and the heatmap pathway can tackle the heatmap prediction, even the gaze direction fields are not accurate.

Objective. Since the predicted gaze point may be multimodal, we introduce heatmap as the ground truth. Here, we also compare our method with networks based on other types of outputs, including:

- Point: We employ two ResNet-50 to extract features for both original image and head image. Such a comparison is fair because the encoder part of FPN is also ResNet-50. In this baseline, we only predict gaze point.

Table 5. The evaluation of different objectives.

Methods	AUC	Dist	MDist	Ang	MAng
Point	0.892	0.173	0.103	21.9°	10.5°
Multi-task point	0.900	0.165	0.097	20.4°	10.1°
Shifted grid [22]	0.899	0.171	0.096	21.4°	10.3°
Heatmap (our)	**0.903**	**0.156**	**0.088**	**18.2°**	**9.2°**

- Multi-task regression: The network architecture is the same as point regression, but it predicts both gaze direction and gaze point simultaneously.
- Shifted grid: Based on our network architecture, shifted grid (10 × 10) [22] is utilized to classify the gaze point into different grids.

Fig. 5. Some prediction results on the testing set, the red lines indicate the ground truth gaze and the yellow ones are the predicted gaze. (Color figure online)

The comparison results of different objectives are listed in Table 5. In our network architecture, heatmap regression achieves the best results than both point and shifted grid based objectives. As aforementioned, heatmap regression is more robust than directly point prediction because even a portion of heatmap values is incorrect, it is still possible to correctly predict the gaze point. Thus such a heatmap regression strategy is commonly used for human pose estimation [4]. Our experiments also validate its effectiveness for gaze following.

4.4 Visualization of Predicted Results

We show the predicted gaze points and their ground truth in Fig. 5, and predicted heatmaps in Fig. 6(a). We can see that for most of points, our method can

(a) Some accurate preditions.   (b) Some failures.

Fig. 6. The first row: ground truth (red lines) and predicted gaze (yellow lines). The second row: predicted heatmaps. (Please zoom in for details.) (Color figure online)

predict gaze points accurately (As shown in Fig. 4, when the distance error is 0.1, the portions of correctly predicted points is 50% and 45% on the GazeFollow dataset and DL Gaze, respectively). There are two reasons contribute the good performance of our method: (i) our two-stage solution agrees with the behavior of human, and gaze direction field would help suppress the regions falling out of gaze direction, which consequently improves the heatmap regression; (ii) the supervision on gaze direction helps train a more robust network for gaze following. We also show some failures in Fig. 6(b). The first three columns of examples show that our predictions can be multimodal. Although the position of heatmap maximum is not right, some others peaks can also predict the gaze point. Regarding the last three columns of failures, we can see that the predicted heatmap is inaccurate. This probably caused by the small head or head occlusion, which makes gaze direction and gaze point prediction extremely difficult, even for us human.

5 Conclusion

In this paper, we proposed a two-stage solution for gaze tracking. In stage I, we feed the head image and its position for gaze direction prediction. Then we use gaze direction field to characterize the distribution of gaze points without considering the scene contents. In stage II, the gaze direction fields are concatenated with original image, and fed into a heatmap pathway for heatmap regression. The advantages of our solution are two-fold: (i) our solution mimics the behavior of human in gaze following, therefore it is more psychological plausible; (ii) besides leverage heatmap to supervise the training of our network, we can also leverage gaze direction to facilitate the training of gaze direction pathway, therefore our network can be more robustly trained. We further build a new DL Gaze dataset to validate the performance of different gaze following methods in real scenarios. Comprehensive experiments show that our method significantly outperforms existing methods, which validates the effectiveness of our solution.

Acknowledgement. This project is supported by NSFC (No. 61502304).

References

1. Deng, J., Dong, W., Socher, R., Li, L.J., Li, K., Fei-Fei, L.: ImageNet: a large-scale hierarchical image database. In: 2009 IEEE Conference on Computer Vision and Pattern Recognition, CVPR 2009, pp. 248–255. IEEE (2009)
2. Everingham, M., Van Gool, L., Williams, C.K., Winn, J., Zisserman, A.: The Pascal visual object classes (VOC) challenge. Int. J. Comput. Vis. **88**(2), 303–338 (2010)
3. Fathi, A., Li, Y., Rehg, J.M.: Learning to recognize daily actions using gaze. In: Fitzgibbon, A., Lazebnik, S., Perona, P., Sato, Y., Schmid, C. (eds.) ECCV 2012. LNCS, vol. 7572, pp. 314–327. Springer, Heidelberg (2012). https://doi.org/10.1007/978-3-642-33718-5_23
4. Fragkiadaki, K., Levine, S., Felsen, P., Malik, J.: Recurrent network models for human dynamics. In: 2015 IEEE International Conference on Computer Vision (ICCV), pp. 4346–4354. IEEE (2015)
5. He, K., Zhang, X., Ren, S., Sun, J.: Deep residual learning for image recognition. In: Proceedings of the IEEE Conference on Computer Vision and Pattern Recognition, pp. 770–778 (2016)
6. Hennessey, C., Noureddin, B., Lawrence, P.: A single camera eye-gaze tracking system with free head motion. In: Proceedings of the 2006 Symposium on Eye Tracking Research & Applications, pp. 87–94. ACM (2006)
7. Itti, L., Koch, C.: Computational modelling of visual attention. Nat. Rev. Neurosci. **2**(3), 194 (2001)
8. Itti, L., Koch, C., Niebur, E.: A model of saliency-based visual attention for rapid scene analysis. IEEE Trans. Pattern Anal. Mach. Intell. **20**(11), 1254–1259 (1998)
9. Judd, T., Ehinger, K., Durand, F., Torralba, A.: Learning to predict where humans look. In: 2009 IEEE 12th International Conference on Computer Vision, pp. 2106–2113. IEEE (2009)
10. Kingma, D.P., Ba, J.: Adam: a method for stochastic optimization. arXiv preprint arXiv:1412.6980 (2014)
11. Krafka, K., et al.: Eye tracking for everyone. arXiv preprint arXiv:1606.05814 (2016)
12. Krizhevsky, A., Sutskever, I., Hinton, G.E.: Imagenet classification with deep convolutional neural networks. In: Advances in Neural Information Processing Systems, pp. 1097–1105 (2012)
13. Kümmerer, M., Theis, L., Bethge, M.: Deep gaze I: boosting saliency prediction with feature maps trained on imagenet. arXiv preprint arXiv:1411.1045 (2014)
14. Leifman, G., Rudoy, D., Swedish, T., Bayro-Corrochano, E., Raskar, R.: Learning gaze transitions from depth to improve video saliency estimation. In: Proceedings of IEEE International Conference on Computer Vision, vol. 3 (2017)
15. Lin, T.Y., Dollár, P., Girshick, R., He, K., Hariharan, B., Belongie, S.: Feature pyramid networks for object detection. In: CVPR, vol. 1, p. 4 (2017)
16. Lin, T.-Y., et al.: Microsoft COCO: common objects in context. In: Fleet, D., Pajdla, T., Schiele, B., Tuytelaars, T. (eds.) ECCV 2014. LNCS, vol. 8693, pp. 740–755. Springer, Cham (2014). https://doi.org/10.1007/978-3-319-10602-1_48
17. Marín-Jiménez, M.J., Zisserman, A., Eichner, M., Ferrari, V.: Detecting people looking at each other in videos. Int. J. Comput. Vis. **106**(3), 282–296 (2014)
18. Mukherjee, S.S., Robertson, N.M.: Deep head pose: gaze-direction estimation in multimodal video. IEEE Trans. Multimed. **17**(11), 2094–2107 (2015)
19. Pan, J., et al.: SaLGAN: visual saliency prediction with generative adversarial networks. arXiv preprint arXiv:1701.01081 (2017)

20. Parks, D., Borji, A., Itti, L.: Augmented saliency model using automatic 3d head pose detection and learned gaze following in natural scenes. Vis. Res. **116**, 113–126 (2015)
21. Pfister, T., Charles, J., Zisserman, A.: Flowing convnets for human pose estimation in videos. In: Proceedings of the IEEE International Conference on Computer Vision, pp. 1913–1921 (2015)
22. Recasens*, A., Khosla*, A., Vondrick, C., Torralba, A.: Where are they looking? In: Advances in Neural Information Processing Systems (NIPS) (2015). * indicates equal contribution
23. Recasens, A., Vondrick, C., Khosla, A., Torralba, A.: Following gaze in video. In: Proceedings of the IEEE Conference on Computer Vision and Pattern Recognition, pp. 1435–1443 (2017)
24. Russakovsky, O., et al.: Imagenet large scale visual recognition challenge. Int. J. Comput. Vis. **115**(3), 211–252 (2015)
25. Tompson, J.J., Jain, A., LeCun, Y., Bregler, C.: Joint training of a convolutional network and a graphical model for human pose estimation. In: Advances in Neural Information Processing Systems, pp. 1799–1807 (2014)
26. Xiao, J., Hays, J., Ehinger, K.A., Oliva, A., Torralba, A.: Sun database: large-scale scene recognition from abbey to zoo. In: 2010 IEEE Conference on Computer Vision and Pattern Recognition (CVPR), pp. 3485–3492. IEEE (2010)
27. Xiong, X., Liu, Z., Cai, Q., Zhang, Z.: Eye gaze tracking using an RGBD camera: a comparison with a RGB solution. In: Proceedings of the 2014 ACM International Joint Conference on Pervasive and Ubiquitous Computing: Adjunct Publication, pp. 1113–1121. ACM (2014)
28. Yao, B., Jiang, X., Khosla, A., Lin, A.L., Guibas, L., Fei-Fei, L.: Human action recognition by learning bases of action attributes and parts. In: 2011 IEEE International Conference on Computer Vision (ICCV), pp. 1331–1338. IEEE (2011)
29. Zhang, X., Sugano, Y., Fritz, M., Bulling, A.: Appearance-based gaze estimation in the wild. In: Proceedings of the IEEE Conference on Computer Vision and Pattern Recognition, pp. 4511–4520 (2015)
30. Zhou, B., Lapedriza, A., Xiao, J., Torralba, A., Oliva, A.: Learning deep features for scene recognition using places database. In: Advances in Neural Information Processing Systems, pp. 487–495 (2014)
31. Zhu, W., Deng, H.: Monocular free-head 3D gaze tracking with deep learning and geometry constraints. In: The IEEE International Conference on Computer Vision (ICCV), October 2017
32. Zhu, X., Ramanan, D.: Face detection, pose estimation, and landmark localization in the wild. In: 2012 IEEE Conference on Computer Vision and Pattern Recognition (CVPR), pp. 2879–2886. IEEE (2012)
33. Zhu, Z., Ji, Q.: Eye gaze tracking under natural head movements. In: 2005 IEEE Computer Society Conference on Computer Vision and Pattern Recognition, CVPR 2005, vol. 1, pp. 918–923. IEEE (2005)

COSONet: Compact Second-Order Network for Video Face Recognition

Yirong Mao[1,2], Ruiping Wang[1,2(✉)], Shiguang Shan[1,2],
and Xilin Chen[1,2]

[1] Key Laboratory of Intelligent Information Processing of Chinese Academy of
Sciences (CAS), Institute of Computing Technology, CAS, Beijing 100190, China
yirong.mao@vipl.ict.ac.cn, {wangruiping,sgshan,xlchen}@ict.ac.cn
[2] University of Chinese Academy of Sciences, Beijing 100049, China

Abstract. In this paper, we study the task of video face recognition. The face images in the video typically cover large variations in expression, lighting, or pose, and also suffer from video-type noises such as motion blur, out-of-focus blur and low resolution. To tackle these two types of challenges, we propose an extensive framework which contains three aspects: neural network design, training data augmentation, and loss function. First, we devise an expressive COmpact Second-Order network (COSONet) to extract features from faces with large variations. The network manages to encode the correlation (*e.g.* sample covariance matrix) of local features in a spatial invariant way, which is useful to model the global texture and appearance of face images. To further handle the curse of high-dimensional problem in the sample covariance matrix, we apply a layer named 2D fully connected (2D-FC) layer with few parameters to reduce the dimension. Second, due to no video-type noises in still face datasets and small inter-frame variation in video face datasets, we augment a large dataset with both large face variations and video-type noises from existing still face dataset. Finally, to get a discriminative face descriptor while balancing the effect of images with various quality, a mixture loss function which encourages the discriminability and simultaneously regularizes the feature is elaborately designed. Detailed experiments show that the proposed framework can achieve very competitive accuracy over state-of-the-art approaches on IJB-A and PaSC datasets.

Keywords: Video face recognition · Second-order network · Data augmentation

---

Electronic supplementary material The online version of this chapter (https://doi.org/10.1007/978-3-030-20893-6_4) contains supplementary material, which is available to authorized users.

© Springer Nature Switzerland AG 2019
C. V. Jawahar et al. (Eds.): ACCV 2018, LNCS 11363, pp. 51–67, 2019.
https://doi.org/10.1007/978-3-030-20893-6_4

1   Introduction

As tremendous video data are being created from real-word application scenarios such as video surveillance, movies, or daily photo albums, video face recognition (VFR) has caught much more attention nowadays.

To solve this task, many approaches have been proposed [5,6,8,9,15,16,31, 32,36,37,39]. As shown in the left of Fig. 1, a VFR model generally consists of two important parts: an image-level feature extractor to get the face descriptor (*e.g.* deep or hand-crafted feature) of each face image and a video modeling module to aggregate face descriptors within a video into a compact video representation. Lots of prior work focus on the latter [5,6,8,15,16,31,36,37,39], whereas, few efforts are made in the former, except [9,32]. In this paper, we focus on the former (image-level feature extractor) based on convolutional neural networks (CNNs). Since subjects in videos are often in movement, video faces suffer from large variations (*e.g.* expression, lighting or pose variations), and they also have video-type noises such as motion blur, out-of-focus blur and low resolution. Therefore, to devise an image-level feature extractor, two intuitions should be kept in mind: (1) the network should be qualified for handling large variations, and (2) the extracted face descriptor should be robust against both video-type noises and large face variations.

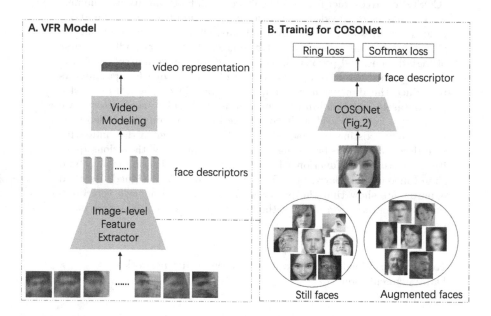

Fig. 1. Left is the general VFR model composed of two parts: image-level feature extractor and video modeling module. Right is the pipeline of training COSONet. Each training image in a batch is either picked from still faces or video-like augmented ones. The COSONet is trained with two losses: softmax loss and ring loss.

To address the problem of large face variations, CNNs used for image-level feature extractors have been developed into deeper or wider. CASIANet [40] (10 layers), VGGFace [27] (16 layers), ResNet [35] (64 layers), and GoogleNet [39] (wider) are typical network structures among them. These networks are all based on first-order feature statistics while rarely consider second-order or higher-order feature statistics. Recently, networks based on second-order feature have gained impressive performance in numerous vision tasks [18,20–23]. The second-order feature (*e.g.* sample covariance matrix) encodes the correlation of local features in a translationally invariant way, which is useful to model the texture and appearance of images or regions [34]. In light of the strong modeling capacity and promising performance of the second-order based networks, we aim to obtain a superior network to extract image-level face descriptor based on this technique. After local feature extraction, we perform second-order pooling to compute the sample covariance matrix as the second-order feature.

The sample covariance matrix is a structured representation which has two distinctive attributes: (1) it is a Symmetric Positive Definite (SPD) matrix lying on a specific Riemannian manifold, and (2) it is a high-dimensional matrix (size of $d \times d$ if local features are d-dimension). For the first aspect, it is shown that normalizing the sample covariance matrix is essential to achieve better performance [18,20,22]. We resort to a stable and fast matrix operation: approximate matrix square root [20] to normalize it. Due to the second attribute, it's necessary to get a compact representation. A straightforward scheme is to flatten the sample covariance matrix into a 1D vector and transform it into lower-dimensional vector by an FC layer. However, there will be plenty of parameters. Instead, we extend the traditional FC layer applied for 1D vectors into 2D matrices, similarly in 2D-PCA [38] and [10,14], then propose a layer dubbed 2D fully connected (2D-FC) layer with few parameters to obtain a lower-dimensional matrix as the final second-order feature.

Fig. 2 describes the overall network structure, which is composed of four blocks: convolution layers for local feature extraction, second-order pooling for sample covariance matrix estimation, approximate matrix square root for normalization and 2D-FC for a compact representation. We name the network as COmpact Second-Order network (COSONet).

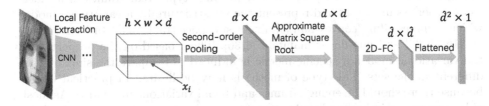

Fig. 2. The network structure of COSONet.

For training the COSONet robust against large face variations and video-type noises, face images in training dataset should possess these two types of characteristics. Large still face datasets have large facial variations, but lack of video-type noises. Though large video face datasets have some video-type noises, their face images are redundant and their actual scales are smaller than those still face datasets. Considering the drawbacks of these two types of datasets, we augment video-like faces from large still face dataset by degenerating still faces with video-type noises. Such augmented dataset will be characterized with both large face variations and video-type noises. On the other hand, the dataset will cover face images with varying quality. However, it is found that the L_2-norm of low-quality face images' features tends to be smaller than that of high-quality face images', when the widely used softmax loss is the training loss function [29]. As a result, the network is likely to be biased to high-quality images and fails to deal with low-quality ones. To handle such problem, we design our final loss with two terms, where one is the typical softmax loss for encouraging discriminative face descriptors, and the other is the newly developed ring loss [42] for regularizing all face descriptors with equal L_2-norm regardless of image qualities.

Right part of Fig. 1 shows our training pipeline. In summary, this paper contributes to the following two aspects:

- For the neural network, we propose COSONet to get a compact second-order image-level face descriptor, which performs better than first-order networks.
- For a well-trained COSONet, we augment video-like face images from large still face datasets and a mixtured loss is used to train the network.

2   Related Work

Our method mainly covers two aspects: video face recognition and second-order networks. We will briefly review the works related to these two aspects.

Video Face Recognition. Existing video face recognition methods can be roughly divided into two classes. One type of them tries to model facial variations in a video. The other type of them attempts to tackle the low-quality problem in video frames. Approaches of the first type treat frames in a video as an orderless image set and represent the set structure by a variational model which includes affine/convex hull [5], linear subspace [13,15,33], statistical models [16,25,37] and non-linear manifold [6,36]. Then, based on the properties of the variational model, a specific metric is induced to compare the similarity of different image sets. This type of methods may be limited in practical usage, because there should be enough frames and facial variations in a video. As most video frames are in low quality due to existing video-type noises, methods of the second type focus on addressing these noises. For instance, [30] generated more discriminative images from multiple degenerating video frames. [24,39] adopted attention-based pooling to filter out low-quality frames. They first estimated the quality of each frame as its weight and then weakened the effect of low-quality frames by weighted average pooling. In case that all frames in a video are of poor quality, quality scores will be all equally low. As a result, the attention-based pooling will degenerate into average pooling. However, the low-quality problem is not yet solved. Instead, [9,32] extracted discriminative feature from video frames regardless of their qualities.

These two types of methods all need an image-level feature extractor to get the feature of each frame. In this work, we propose an elaborate network based on second-order networks to fulfill this.

Second-Order Networks. Second-order networks recently have gained more and more attention. These networks mainly perform second-order pooling after convolution layers. For example, a pioneer work [23] proposed bilinear pooling to model pairwise feature interaction for fine-grained classification and found normalization was essential to improve the performance. Then several normalization methods were proposed. One such method is the matrix-logarithm operation. It maps the second-order representation (*e.g.* the sample covariance matrices) from Symmetric Positive Definite (SPD) matrices manifold to Euclidean space [18]. Later, both [22] and [21] found that matrix power normalization especially matrix square root was more stable and robust than matrix-logarithm. [20] and [22] further accelerated matrix square root by approximate solution. Since the second-order features are high dimensional, [11] adopted two low-dimensional kernel approximation methods to mitigate this problem.

3   Approach

In this section, we first introduce our COSONet structure. Then we describe the details of data augmentation and loss functions.

3.1   COSONet Structure

The overview of our COSONet is depicted in Fig. 2. For a face image, after convolution layers for local feature extraction, we perform second-order pooling to compute the sample covariance matrix of local features, then the sample covariance matrix is normalized by approximate matrix square root. 2D-FC is further applied to get a compact second order representation. Finally, the 2D matrix is flattened into a vector as the face descriptor. Next, we will introduce each block in details.

Second-Order Pooling. Networks that encode second-order statistics information for local features have shown promising results on various vision tasks including fine-grained classification [22,23], large-scale visual recognition [20,21], semantic segmentation [18] and face recognition [7]. We exploit it as our image-level feature extractor. Given a face image, let the output of the last convolution layer to be a $h \times w \times d$ tensor with spatial height h, spatial width w, channel d. We reshape it into a matrix $\mathbf{X}$ with size of $n \times d$, where $n = h \times w$, each row of

$\mathbf{X}$ is a d-dimension local feature $\mathbf{x_i}$. We then perform second-order pooling by estimating the sample covariance matrix as

$$\mathbf{C} = \frac{1}{n-1}\sum_{i=1}^{n}(\mathbf{x_i} - \bar{\mathbf{x}})(\mathbf{x_i} - \bar{\mathbf{x}})^{\top} \tag{1}$$

where $\mathbf{x_i}$ represents the local feature across location $i = 1, 2, \ldots n$. $\bar{\mathbf{x}}$ represents the mean of local features, which is given by $\bar{\mathbf{x}} = \frac{1}{n}\sum_{i=1}^{n}\mathbf{x_i}$. The diagonal elements of $\mathbf{C}$ represent the variance of each feature channel, the off-diagonal elements represent the correlation between different feature channels. The variance or correlation statistics information is useful to model global texture and appearance of a face image.

Approximate Matrix Square Root Normalization. The sample covariance matrix $\mathbf{C}$ is an SPD matrix lying on a specific Riemannian manifold, directly operating on it is non-trivial. Moreover, to achieve a good performance, it's necessary to normalize it [18,21,22]. Currently, there are two normalization strategies: (1) Matrix-logarithm is applied to map the SPD matrices from Riemannian manifold to Euclidean space, specifically, through $\log(\mathbf{C}) = \mathbf{U}\log(\mathbf{S})\mathbf{U}^{\top}$ with $\mathbf{C} = \mathbf{USU}^{\top}$ (the SVD for $\mathbf{C}$). (2) Matrix power normalization, especially matrix square root, concretely, through $\mathbf{C}^{\frac{1}{2}} = \mathbf{US}^{\frac{1}{2}}\mathbf{U}^{\top}$. As stated in [21], a more robust sample covariance matrix could be estimated by matrix square root and this normalization was shown to have better performance than matrix logarithm in [21,22]. Thus it's better to choose matrix square root for normalization. However, matrix square root requires SVD which is numerical unstable during gradient back propagation, and is also time-consuming as it is usually difficult to be accelerated by GPUs.

Instead of accurately calculating matrix square root, we try to find the solution of equation $\mathbf{F}(\mathbf{\Sigma}) = \mathbf{\Sigma}^2 - \mathbf{C} = 0$, as advocated in [20]. This equation can be solved by Newton-Schulz iteration efficiently. Specifically, given initial states: $\mathbf{Y}_0 = \mathbf{C}$ and $\mathbf{Z}_0 = \mathbf{I}$, where $\mathbf{I}$ is the identity matrix, the iterative update rule is:

$$\mathbf{Y}_k = \frac{1}{2}\mathbf{Y}_{k-1}(3\mathbf{I} - \mathbf{Z}_{k-1}\mathbf{Y}_{k-1}), \mathbf{Z}_k = \frac{1}{2}(3\mathbf{I} - \mathbf{Z}_{k-1}\mathbf{Y}_{k-1})\mathbf{Z}_{k-1} \tag{2}$$

SVD isn't required, instead, only matrix product is involved which is stable and fast on GPUs. Since the matrices $\mathbf{Y}_k$ can converge to $\mathbf{C}^{\frac{1}{2}}$ quadratically only if $\mathbf{C}$ is in the region of $||\mathbf{C} - \mathbf{I}|| < 1$, to transform any $\mathbf{C}$ into the convergence region, we should first pre-normalize it. Thus, the final approximate matrix square root normalization has three steps:

1. Pre-normalization by the trace as:

$$\hat{\mathbf{C}} = \frac{1}{tr(\mathbf{C})}\mathbf{C} \tag{3}$$

2. Newton-Schulz iteration with N times (a hyper-parameter) through Eq. 2, where the initial states accordingly are $\mathbf{Y}_0 = \hat{\mathbf{C}}$ and $\mathbf{Z}_0 = \mathbf{I}$.

3. Post-normalization to recover the magnitudes and get the matrix square root of $\mathbf{C}$ as:

$$\Sigma = \sqrt{tr(\mathbf{C})}\mathbf{Y}_N \qquad (4)$$

2D Fully Connected Layer. After normalization, the second-order representation Σ is a matrix with size of $d \times d$. If it is flattened into a vector as the face descriptor and directly sent into the last FC layer of softmax loss function while training, there will be $d \times d \times k$ parameters, where k is the number of classes in the training set. However in large scale face datasets, k may be up to 10,000 (*e.g.* 10,575 subjects in WebFace [40]), if d is 256, there will be 655M parameters! Besides, each face descriptor will be a d^2-dimension vector which is too large to store. Considering these problems, it is necessary to get a compact representation. A naive way is to first flatten Σ into a d^2-dimension vector and transform it into a lower-dimensional one by traditional FC layer. On the contrary, we apply a more efficient way. We treat Σ as a matrix and extend traditional FC layer applied for 1D vectors into 2D matrice, similarly in [10,14]. Our specific transformation is given by:

$$\mathbf{H} = \mathbf{W}^\top \Sigma \mathbf{W} \qquad (5)$$

where $\mathbf{W} \in \mathbb{R}^{d \times \widehat{d}}$ is a learnable parameter matrix and $\widehat{d}$ is much smaller than d. We name this transformation as 2D fully connected layer (2D-FC) as in [10]. After 2D-FC, $\mathbf{H}$ is flattened into a vector ($\mathbf{f} = \mathbf{H}(:)$) to get a $\widehat{d}^2$-dimension face descriptor. It can be seen that the 2D-FC layer has much fewer parameters, compared to the naive way (FC layer operated on the flattened $\Sigma(:)$). FC layer would have $d^2 \times \widehat{d}^2$ parameters to get the same dimensional face descriptor, whereas, 2D-FC layer merely needs $d \times \widehat{d}$ parameters.

3.2 Data Augmentation

For COSONet automatically extracting robust feature against large face variations and video-type noises, the training datasets should have these two types of data characteristics. Large still face datasets such as WebFace [40] and VGGFace2 [4] have large face variations but no video-type noises. Large video face datasets such as UMDFaces-Video [1] have video-type noises, but face images contain some redundancy because nearby faces are similar for some videos. The actual scale of video face datasets is smaller than those still face datasets with similar number of face images. Considering the shortcoming of these two kinds of existing datasets, we propose to augment video-like faces from the given large still face dataset for training. Such augmented dataset will be characterized with both large face variations and video-type noises. Concretely, we apply three types of augmentation strategies as similarly done in [9,32]:

- Motion blur: we generate motion blur-like images with linear kernels whose length and angle are randomly chosen from {11, 15, 19} and {0, 45, 90, 135} respectively.

- Out-of-focus blur: we simulate out-of-focus blur by Gaussian kernels whose size and width are randomly chosen from {9, 11, 15} and {1.5, 3.0, 4.5}.
- Low resolution: we resize images with scales randomly chosen from $\{\frac{1}{2}, \frac{1}{4}, \frac{1}{6}\}$.

Three types of transformations are employed sequentially into a face image with probability of 0.5. The first two strategies are inspired by the generally explored principles in deblurring works where the blur effects can be modeled as some convolution operations between the original image and blur filter kernels. Figure 3 shows some augmented images. The COSONet is trained on the mixtured face datasets containing still faces and augmented faces with video-type noises.

Fig. 3. Augmented video-like images. Upper row is the original still faces. Left, middle and right section of the lower row are augmented faces with motion blur, out-of-focus blur and low resolution respectively.

3.3   Loss Function

We use softmax loss function to train our COSONet, as it can converge much fast, and at the same time it can get impressive performance. But another problem should be also noticed. After data augmentation, face images in the dataset are in various quality. As noted in [29], features for low-quality face images tend to have smaller L_2-norm comparted to high-quality ones if only softmax loss is used. In such situation, low-quality face images are more likely to be ignored while training. To alleviate this issue, we should balance features' L_2-norm regardless of image qualities. Specifically, we utilize the lately proposed ring loss [42] to regularize the features, which is given by:

$$L_r = (\|\mathbf{f}\|_2 - R)^2 \tag{6}$$

where R is a learnable scale parameter. Through ring loss, the network can learn to normalize the feature on a hypersphere with the same L_2-norm. Finally, our loss function becomes:

$$L_s = -\log \frac{e^{\mathbf{W}_k^\top \mathbf{f} + b_k}}{\sum_{i=1}^K e^{\mathbf{W}_i^\top \mathbf{f} + b_i}} + \lambda L_r \tag{7}$$

where k is the ground-truth label and K is the total number of subjects. L_s contains two terms, the former is softmax loss to get discriminative face descriptors, and the latter is ring loss to constrain the L_2-norm of face descriptors. A scalar λ is used for balancing the two loss functions.

4   Experiments

We divide our experiments into several sections. In the first section, we introduce our datasets and evaluation protocols. In the second section, we present our implementation details. In the third section, we conduct component analysis for each technique of the proposed method. In the fourth section, we compare with state-of-the-art methods. Then we visualize what are learned by the networks. Finally, we provide a further discussion.

4.1   Datasets and Evaluation Protocols

We have two training datasets, one is WebFace [40] with about 0.5M images of 10,575 subjects, and the other one is the recent published VGGFace2 [4] with 3.1M images of 8,631 subjects. Since WebFace is small, we train on it for our later detailed component analysis (in Sect. 4.3). VGGFace2 is quite large, we train on it to get comparable performance with the state-of-the art methods (in Sect. 4.4). We evaluate our method on two datasets: IARPA Janus Benchmark A (IJB-A) [19] and Point-and-Shoot Challenge (PaSC) [2].

IJB-A dataset contains 5,712 still images and 20,414 video frames of 500 subjects. All images and frames are captured in unconstrained conditions and cover large variations in pose and image quality. Each sample or instance in IJB-A is called a 'template' which consists of the mixture between still images and video frames. IJB-A provides two protocols: 1:1 face verification and 1: N face identification. We only focus on the former protocols where 10-fold testing is conducted. PaSC dataset includes 2,802 videos of 265 subjects. Half of its videos are captured by hand held camera (denoted as PaSC-H), the rest are captured by controlled camera (denoted as PaSC-C). Subjects in the dataset are asked to do predesigned actions. Thus, faces cover large pose variations and serious video-type noises. We test on PaSC dataset with the provided face verification protocol.

We report the true acceptance rate (TAR) at different false acceptance rates (FARs).

4.2   Implementation Details

Preprocessing. We use MTCNN [41] algorithm to detect faces in both training and testing datasets. The bounding box is extended by a factor of 0.3 to include some context. The shorter side of each image is resized into 256 and the other side is resized accordingly to keep the original ratio. While training, a region of 224×224 is randomly cropped from an image or its horizontal flip, with the per-pixel mean subtracted. While testing, a region of 224×224 is cropped from the center of each image.

Detailed Network Configurations. We implement our method with PyTorch[1] [28]. The local feature extraction block of our COSONet is based

---

[1] The source code is available at http://vipl.ict.ac.cn/resources/codes.

Table 1. The network structure of plain ResNet-type networks and our COSONet structure. SO_normed: second order pooling and approximate matrix square root normalization. conv_co: $1 \times 1 \times 256$ convolution layer for compressing the channels.

Plain ResNet-18 or ResNet-34				
Layer name	conv(1-4)	conv5	Average pooling	Flattened
Output size	$14 \times 14 \times 256$	$7 \times 7 \times 512$	$1 \times 1 \times 512$	512-d
Our COSONet				
Layer name	conv(1-4)	conv5	conv_co	SO_normed	2D-FC	Flattened
Output size	$14 \times 14 \times 256$	$14 \times 14 \times 512$	$14 \times 14 \times 256$	256×256	64×64	4096-d

on two ResNet-type networks: ResNet-18 and ResNet-34. We slightly change the CNN structure to obtain 196 local features after the last convolution layers. ResNet-type networks have five convolution blocks. We keep the first 4 convolution blocks the same. A convolution layer for down sampling in the 5th convolution block is canceled. The details of network structure are given in Table 1. We empirically run Newton-Schulz iteration 5 times ($N = 5$), following [20] and set the output size of 2D-FC to be 64×64. Compared with ResNet, COSONet only brings extra 256×64 parameters in 2D-FC layer ($\mathbf{W}$ in Eq. 5). More detailed settings are provided in the supplemental material.

Detailed Settings in Testing. For face images in a template (in IJB-A) or video (in PaSC), each face image is forwarded into the network to get its face descriptor. Since we focus on the image-level feature extractors rather than video modeling modules, we just apply simple video aggregation method, average pooling across face descriptors in the template or video to get a compact video representation. Finally, the similarity between two video representations is computed by the cosine similarity.

4.3   Component Analysis

Effect of the COSONet Structure. In this part, we mainly study the effect of COSONet structure. We implement our COSONet based on two ResNet-type

Table 2. Performance comparison for plain network and COSONet on IJB-A and PaSC. '–' and '✓' represent plain network and COSONet respectively. 10^{-3} and 10^{-2} indicate different FARs.

Method		IJB-A		PaSC-H		PaSC-C	
CNN	COSO	10^{-3}	10^{-2}	10^{-3}	10^{-2}	10^{-3}	10^{-2}
ResNet-18	–	0.567 ± 0.058	0.788 ± 0.025	0.029	0.266	0.352	0.749
ResNet-18	✓	$\mathbf{0.616 \pm 0.043}$	$\mathbf{0.811 \pm 0.024}$	**0.088**	**0.400**	**0.613**	**0.873**
ResNet-34	–	0.591 ± 0.056	0.813 ± 0.025	0.080	0.381	0.506	0.844
ResNet-34	✓	$\mathbf{0.682 \pm 0.045}$	$\mathbf{0.858 \pm 0.019}$	**0.185**	**0.581**	**0.730**	**0.927**

Table 3. Performance comparison for without or with effect of data augmentation on IJB-A and PaSC. '–' and '✓' represent without and with data augmentation respectively. 10^{-3} and 10^{-2} indicate different FARs. The ROC curve is shown in supplemental material.

Method		IJB-A		PaSC-H		PaSC-C	
Model	Aug	10^{-3}	10^{-2}	10^{-3}	10^{-2}	10^{-3}	10^{-2}
A	–	0.591 ± 0.056	0.813 ± 0.025	0.080	0.381	0.506	0.844
B	✓	$\mathbf{0.644 \pm 0.057}$	$\mathbf{0.841 \pm 0.019}$	**0.182**	**0.478**	**0.536**	**0.845**

networks: ResNet-18 and ResNet-34 as mentioned above. These two networks and their COSONet are trained from scratch on WebFace. The initial learning rate is 0.2 and decreased by a factor of 0.5 for every 3 epochs. The batch size is 256. For fair comparison, we only use softmax loss as the loss function. Table 2 shows that our COSONet can improve the performance by a large margin no matter what type of networks is used. It indicates that our COSONet has stronger modeling capacity than plain fisrt-order networks to deal with large face variations in videos.

Effect of Data Augmentation. In this part, we fix the network structure as ResNet-34 and loss function as softmax loss to study the effect of data augmentation. For WebFace (0.5M), we augment the same number of images with the original data. ResNet-34 is first trained on WebFace dataset (0.5M) and then is finetuned on the augmented WebFace dataset (total 1.0M). Table 3 presents the comparison results. Notably, the base network trained on WebFace performs badly on PaSC hand held mode but after it is finetuned on the augmented Web-Face, they can get much improvement. This is mainly because faces in PaSC hand held mode are in serious capture condition and have a large domain gap with still faces in WebFace. Through augmentation, the gap could be narrowed. On other hand, compared to the hand held mode, the improvement on controlled mode is slightly small, which demonstrates that faces in controlled mode are similar to still faces. Overall, data augmentation can improve the performance. We

Table 4. Performance comparison for the impact of ring loss. '–' and '✓' represent without or with the corresponding technique. The ROC curve is shown in supplemental material.

Model	COSO	Aug	Ring loss	IJB-A		PaSC-H		PaSC-C	
				10^{-3}	10^{-2}	10^{-3}	10^{-2}	10^{-3}	10^{-2}
I	✓	–	–	0.682 ± 0.045	0.858 ± 0.019	0.185	0.581	0.730	0.927
II	✓	–	✓	0.735 ± 0.042	0.885 ± 0.014	0.320	0.693	0.794	0.935
III	✓	✓	✓	0.758 ± 0.037	0.894 ± 0.014	0.470	0.805	0.829	0.951

Table 5. Comparative performance on IJB-A dataset. The network of model $D^\dagger$ and D' are the same as model D, but their pooling schemes are different in test stage. $D^\dagger$ utilizes media-pooling where images in each media are first aggregated separately by average pooling according to the media id, as in [39]. D' adopts the SoftMax score pooling which is also applied in [26,42]. *: Ring loss [42] didn't provide the result at FAR=10^{-2} and the standard deviation in its paper.

Method				10^{-3}	10^{-2}
Existing methods					
Ring loss [42]				0.915*	–
VGGFace2 [4]				**0.921 ± 0.014**	**0.968 ± 0.006**
Quality aware network [24]				0.893 ± 0.392	0.942 ± 0.153
Neural aggregation network [39]				0.881 ± 0.011	0.941 ± 0.008
DREAM [3]				0.868 ± 0.015	0.944 ± 0.009
Template adaptation [8]				0.836 ± 0.027	0.939 ± 0.013
Data augmentation + Video pooling [26]				0.725 ± 0.044	0.886 ± 0.017
Unsupervised domain adaptation [32]				0.649 ± 0.022	0.864 ± 0.007
Our approach					
Model	COSO	Aug	Ring loss		
A	–	–	–	0.854 ± 0.032	0.949 ± 0.010
B	✓	–	–	0.881 ± 0.023	0.957 ± 0.006
C	✓	✓	–	0.883 ± 0.024	0.952 ± 0.006
D	✓	✓	✓	0.902 ± 0.022	0.958 ± 0.005
$D^\dagger$	✓	✓	✓	0.915 ± 0.015	0.962 ± 0.005
D'	✓	✓	✓	0.913 ± 0.014	0.963 ± 0.004

attribute this to the fact that the network can automatically learn robust feature against video-type noises from the augmented data.

Effect of Ring Loss for Our Proposed Method. As the effectiveness of ring loss has been validated in [42] with only first-order CNNs, in this part, we verify its influence for our COSONet and data augmentation strategy. The local feature extraction block of COSONet is based on ResNet-34. Training data are the same as the last part. Table 4 displays the result. For Model I (COSONet only with softmax loss) and Model II (COSONet with softmax loss and ring loss), we can see that ring loss also takes effects on our COSONet. For Model II and Model III (with data augmentation), data augmentation gets similar improvement as the last part.

4.4   Comparison with State-of-the-Art Methods

In this section, we compare our whole approach with the state-of-the-art methods. To get a more powerful COSONet, we train the network on VGGFace2

Table 6. Comparative performance on PaSC dataset.

Method				PaSC-H		PaSC-C	
				10^{-3}	10^{-2}	10^{-3}	10^{-2}
Existing methods							
Trunk-branch ensemble CNN [9]				–	**0.962**	–	0.958
Attention-aware [31]				–	0.937	–	0.956
DAN [30]				–	0.803	–	0.920
CERML [16]				–	0.773	–	0.801
SPDNet [14]				–	0.728	–	0.801
GrassmannNet [17]				–	0.727	–	0.805
Our approach							
Model	COSO	Aug	Ring loss				
A	–	–	–	0.429	0.811	0.858	0.955
B	✓	–	–	0.596	0.879	0.884	0.962
C	✓	✓	–	0.765	0.934	0.902	0.966
D	✓	✓	✓	0.852	0.960	0.927	**0.974**

and its augmented data where we augment 1.0M video-like images. For the local feature extraction of COSONet, we implement it based on ResNet-34.

Tables 5 and 6 present our best performance on IJB-A and PaSC, as well as previously reported results by state-of-the-art methods. We also gradually add each technique to evaluate its influence. The results of other works are directly copied from their original papers.

First, in view of Model A and Model B, Model A is trained with soft-max loss as a baseline. When we change the network to our COSONet (Model B), we observe consistent improvement. On IJB-A dataset, for example, TAR@FAR = 10^{-3} increases from 0.854 to 0.881 and even a larger gain on PaSC hand held mode, from 0.429 to 0.596.

Second, for Model B and Model C, we finetune Model C from Model B on the augmented dataset with our generated 1.0M video-like images. Although there is no improvement on IJB-A, on PaSC hand held mode the improvement is prominent, from 0.596 to 0.765 when TAR@FAR = 10^{-3}. This is mainly because faces in PaSC hand held mode are in serious captured condition as mentioned earlier.

Finally, we finetune Model D from Model C with softmax loss and ring loss to get the ultimate model. On IJB-A dataset, we apply different pooling schemes other than the average feature pooling, during testing. Model $D^{\dagger}$ and Model D' explore media pooling [39] and SoftMax score pooling [26] respectively. We get comparable performance against other works. Ring loss [42] utilized the same loss function and the same pooling scheme (SoftMax score pooling) in test stage with our Model D'. Its network (ResNet-64) is deeper than ours but the performance

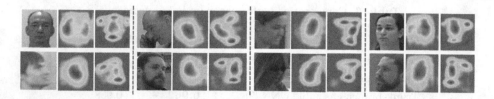

Fig. 4. In each group, the first is the inputed face image, the second and the third are the corresponding averaged feature maps along the channel dimension of the plain first-order network and our COSONet. The two feature maps are respectively from the output of the fourth block convolution layer of Model A and Model B (in Sect. 4.4).

is similar. The network of VGGFace2 [4] is trained on VGGFace2 dataset and then finetuned on MS-Celeb-1M [12]. Their datasets are larger than ours but the performance is also similar. On PaSC dataset, we get comparable and even better performance than other works on hand held and controlled mode respectively. The method of Trunk-Branch Ensemble CNN [9] finetuned their network on PaSC, whereas, we didn't.

4.5 Feature Visualization

To further investigate the effectiveness of our COSONet, we compare its feature response with the plain first-order network in Fig. 4. It can be seen that our COSONet can automatically focus on discriminative face regions, which has illustrated its effective modeling capacity to mitigate the pose variation problem.

4.6 Discussion

As for media pooling on IJB-A dataset (Model $D^\dagger$ in Table 5), there are two types of media images in a template, video frames and still images. As [39], we first aggregate images in each media by average pooling and then combine these two media features by averaging. The exact equation is given by

$$\mathbf{v} = \frac{1}{2|\mathcal{S}|} \sum_{\mathbf{f} \in \mathcal{S}} \mathbf{f} + \frac{1}{2|\mathcal{V}|} \sum_{\mathbf{f} \in \mathcal{V}} \mathbf{f} \qquad (8)$$

where $\mathcal{S}$ and $\mathcal{V}$ represent the set of face descriptors for still images and video frames within a template, respectively. $|\cdot|$ is the size of a set. $\mathbf{v}$ is the video representation. We observe media pooling can get some enhancement in our paper and other papers [8,39]. We dig slightly deeper into this. We find the average ratio between the number of video frames ($|\mathcal{V}|$) and the number of still images ($|\mathcal{S}|$) in each template is 7.36 : 1. This means that media pooling is actually a weighted average pooling. Weights for video frames are smaller than those for still images. However, this pooling scheme is biased to IJB-A dataset.

5   Conclusions

We propose a whole framework for extracting robust image-level face descriptors for VFR. Extensive experiments have validated the superiority of each technique and the proposed method. Existing video modeling methods can be integrated into the framework to further refine the video representation. Nevertheless, we attribute the good performance of our method to three aspects: (1) COSONet is superior to first-order network to handle large face variations. In future we will fuse multiple order information to encode local features. (2) data augmentation can upgrade the robustness of the face descriptors, and (3) an elaborate mixture loss function is adopted to the data characteristics.

Acknowledgements. This work is partially supported by Natural Science Foundation of China under contracts Nos. 61390511, 61772500, 973 Program under contract No. 2015CB351802, Frontier Science Key Research Project CAS No. QYZDJ-SSW-JSC009, and Youth Innovation Promotion Association CAS No. 2015085.

References

1. Bansal, A., Castillo, C., Ranjan, R., Chellappa, R.: The do's and don'ts for CNN-Based face verification. In: ICCV Workshop, pp. 2545–2554 (2017)
2. Beveridge, J.R., Phillips, P.J., Bolme, D.S., Draper, B.A.: The challenge of face recognition from digital point-and-shoot cameras. In: ICB, pp. 1–8 (2013)
3. Cao, K., Rong, Y., Li, C., Tang, X., Loy, C.C.: Pose-robust face recognition via deep residual equivariant mapping. In: CVPR, pp. 5187–5196 (2018)
4. Cao, Q., Shen, L., Xie, W., Parkhi, O.M., Zisserman, A.: VGGFace2: a dataset for recognising faces across pose and age. arXiv:1710.08092 (2017)
5. Cevikalp, H., Triggs, B.: Face recognition based on image sets. In: CVPR, pp. 2567–2573 (2010)
6. Chen, S., Sanderson, C., Harandi, M.T., Lovell, B.C.: Improved image set classification via joint sparse approximated nearest subspaces. In: CVPR, pp. 452–459 (2013)
7. Chowdhury, A.R., Lin, T.Y., Maji, S., Learnedmiller, E.: One-to-many face recognition with bilinear CNNs. In: WACV, pp. 1–9 (2016)
8. Crosswhite, N., Byrne, J., Stauffer, C., Parkhi, O., Cao, Q., Zisserman, A.: Template adaptation for face verification and identification. In: FG, pp. 1–8 (2017)
9. Ding, C., Tao, D.: Trunk-branch ensemble convolutional neural networks for video-based face recognition. In: IEEE TPAMI, pp. 1002–1014 (2018)
10. Dong, Z., Jia, S., Zhang, C., Pei, M., Wu, Y.: Deep manifold learning of symmetric positive definite matrices with application to face recognition. In: AAAI, pp. 4009–4015 (2018)
11. Gao, Y., Beijbom, O., Zhang, N., Darrell, T.: Compact bilinear pooling. In: CVPR, pp. 317–326 (2016)
12. Guo, Y., Zhang, L., Hu, Y., He, X., Gao, J.: MS-Celeb-1M: a dataset and benchmark for large-scale face recognition. In: Leibe, B., Matas, J., Sebe, N., Welling, M. (eds.) ECCV 2016. LNCS, vol. 9907, pp. 87–102. Springer, Cham (2016). https://doi.org/10.1007/978-3-319-46487-9_6

13. Hamm, J., Lee, D.D.: Grassmann discriminant analysis: a unifying view on subspace-based learning. In: ICML, pp. 376–383 (2008)
14. Huang, Z., Gool, L.V.: A riemannian network for SPD matrix learning. In: AAAI, pp. 2036–2042 (2017)
15. Huang, Z., Wang, R., Shan, S., Chen, X.: Projection metric learning on grassmann manifold with application to video based face recognition. In: CVPR, pp. 140–149 (2015)
16. Huang, Z., Wang, R., Shan, S., Gool, L.V., Chen, X.: Cross euclidean-to-riemannian metric learning with application to face recognition from video. In: IEEE TPAMI (2018). https://doi.org/10.1109/TPAMI.2017.2776154
17. Huang, Z., Wu, J., Gool, L.V.: Building deep networks on grassmann manifolds. In: AAAI, pp. 3279–3286 (2018)
18. Ionescu, C., Vantzos, O., Sminchisescu, C.: Matrix backpropagation for deep networks with structured layers. In: ICCV, pp. 2965–2973 (2015)
19. Klare, B.F., et al.: Pushing the frontiers of unconstrained face detection and recognition: IARPA Janus Benchmark A. In: CVPR, pp. 1931–1939 (2015)
20. Li, P., Xie, J., Wang, Q., Gao, Z.: Towards faster training of global covariance pooling networks by iterative matrix square root normalization. In: CVPR, pp. 947–955 (2018)
21. Li, P., Xie, J., Wang, Q., Zuo, W.: Is second-order information helpful for large-scale visual recognition? In: ICCV, pp. 2089–2097 (2017)
22. Lin, T.Y., Maji, S.: Improved bilinear pooling with CNNs. In: BMVC (2017). CoRRabs/1707.06772
23. Lin, T.Y., Roychowdhury, A., Maji, S.: Bilinear CNN models for fine-grained visual recognition. In: ICCV, pp. 1449–1457 (2015)
24. Liu, Y., Yan, J., Ouyang, W.: Quality aware network for set to set recognition. In: CVPR, pp. 4694–4703 (2017)
25. Lu, J., Wang, G., Moulin, P.: Image set classification using holistic multiple order statistics features and localized multi-kernel metric learning. In: ICCV, pp. 329–336 (2013)
26. Masi, I., Trán, A.T., Hassner, T., Leksut, J.T., Medioni, G.: Do we really need to collect millions of faces for effective face recognition? In: Leibe, B., Matas, J., Sebe, N., Welling, M. (eds.) ECCV 2016. LNCS, vol. 9909, pp. 579–596. Springer, Cham (2016). https://doi.org/10.1007/978-3-319-46454-1_35
27. Parkhi, O.M., Vedaldi, A., Zisserman, A.: Deep face recognition. In: BMVC, pp. 1–12 (2015)
28. Paszke, A., et al.: Automatic differentiation in pytorch. In: NIPS Workshop (2017)
29. Ranjan, R., Castillo, C.D., Chellappa, R.: L2-constrained softmax loss for discriminative face verification. arXiv:1703.09507 (2017)
30. Rao, Y., Lin, J., Lu, J., Zhou, J.: Learning discriminative aggregation network for video-based face recognition. In: ICCV, pp. 3801–3810 (2017)
31. Rao, Y., Lu, J., Zhou, J.: Attention-aware deep reinforcement learning for video face recognition. In: ICCV, pp. 3951–3960 (2017)
32. Sohn, K., Liu, S., Zhong, G., Yu, X., Yang, M.H., Chandraker, M.: Unsupervised domain adaptation for face recognition in unlabeled videos. In: ICCV, pp. 5917–5925 (2017)
33. Tae-Kyun, K., Josef, K., Roberto, C.: Discriminative learning and recognition of image set classes using canonical correlations. In: IEEE TPAMI, pp. 1005–1018 (2007)

34. Tuzel, O., Porikli, F., Meer, P.: Region covariance: a fast descriptor for detection and classification. In: Leonardis, A., Bischof, H., Pinz, A. (eds.) ECCV 2006. LNCS, vol. 3952, pp. 589–600. Springer, Heidelberg (2006). https://doi.org/10.1007/11744047_45

35. Wang, H., et al.: CosFace: large margin cosine loss for deep face recognition. In: CVPR, pp. 5265–5274 (2018)

36. Wang, R., Chen, X.: Manifold discriminant analysis. In: CVPR, pp. 429–436 (2009)

37. Wang, W., Wang, R., Shan, S., Chen, X.: Discriminative covariance oriented representation learning for face recognition with image sets. In: CVPR, pp. 5749–5758 (2017)

38. Yang, J., Zhang, D., Frangi, A.F., Yang, J.Y.: Two-dimensional PCA: a new approach to appearance-based face representation and recognition. In: IEEE TPAMI, pp. 131–137 (2004)

39. Yang, J., Ren, P., Chen, D., Wen, F., Li, H., Hua, G.: Neural aggregation network for video face recognition. In: CVPR, pp. 5216–5225 (2017)

40. Yi, D., Lei, Z., Liao, S., Li, S.Z.: Learning face representation from scratch. arXiv:1411.7923 (2014)

41. Zhang, K., Zhang, Z., Li, Z., Qiao, Y.: Joint face detection and alignment using multitask cascaded convolutional networks. In: IEEE SPL, pp. 1499–1503 (2016)

42. Zheng, Y., Pal, D.K., Savvides, M.: Ring loss: convex feature normalization for face recognition. In: CVPR, pp. 5089–5097 (2018)

Visual Re-ranking with Natural Language Understanding for Text Spotting

Ahmed Sabir[1]([✉]), Francesc Moreno-Noguer[2], and Lluís Padró[1]

[1] TALP Research Center, Universitat Politècnica de Catalunya, Barcelona, Spain
{asabir,padro}@cs.upc.edu
[2] Institut de Robòtica i Informàtica Industrial (CSIC-UPC), Barcelona, Spain
fmoreno@iri.upc.edu

Abstract. Many scene text recognition approaches are based on purely visual information and ignore the semantic relation between scene and text. In this paper, we tackle this problem from natural language processing perspective to fill the gap between language and vision. We propose a post-processing approach to improve scene text recognition accuracy by using occurrence probabilities of words (unigram language model), and the semantic correlation between scene and text. For this, we initially rely on an off-the-shelf deep neural network, already trained with large amount of data, which provides a series of text hypotheses per input image. These hypotheses are then re-ranked using word frequencies and semantic relatedness with objects or scenes in the image. As a result of this combination, the performance of the original network is boosted with almost no additional cost. We validate our approach on ICDAR'17 dataset.

1 Introduction

Machine reading has shown a remarkable progress in Optical Character Recognition systems (OCR). However, the success of most OCR systems is restricted to simple-background and properly aligned documents, while text in many real images is affected by a number of artifacts including partial occlusion, distorted perspective and complex backgrounds. In short, developing OCR systems able to read text in the wild is still an open problem. In the computer vision community, this problem is known as *Text Spotting*. However, while state-of-the-art computer vision algorithms have shown remarkable results in recognizing object instances in these images, understanding and recognizing the included text in a robust manner is far from being considered a solved problem.

Text spotting pipelines address the end-to-end problem of detecting and recognizing text in unrestricted images (traffic signs, advertisements, brands in clothing, etc.). The problem is usually split in two phases: (1) *text detection stage*, to estimate the bounding box around the candidate word in the image and (2) *text recognition stage*, to identify the text inside the bounding boxes. In this work we focus on the second stage, an introduce a simple but efficient post-processing approach based on Natural Language Processing (NLP) techniques.

© Springer Nature Switzerland AG 2019
C. V. Jawahar et al. (Eds.): ACCV 2018, LNCS 11363, pp. 68–82, 2019.
https://doi.org/10.1007/978-3-030-20893-6_5

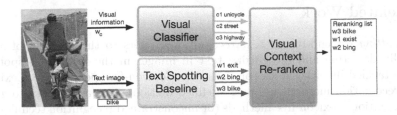

Fig. 1. Overview of the system pipeline. A re-ranking post-process using visual context information to re-rank the potential candidate word based on the semantic relatedness with the context in the image (where the text is located). In the example of the figure, the word *bike* has been re-ranked thanks to the detected visuals (w_c) *unicycle, street, highway*.

There exist two main approaches to perform text recognition in the wild. First, lexicon-based methods, where the system learns to recognize words in a pre-defined dictionary. Second, lexicon-free, unconstrained recognition methods, that aim at predicting character sequences.

In this paper, we propose an approach that intends to fill the gap between language and vision for the scene text recognition problem. Most recent state-of-the-art works focus on automatically detecting and recognizing text in unrestricted images from a purely computer vision perspective. In this work, we tackle the same problem but also leveraging on NLP techniques. Our approach seeks to integrate prior information to the text spotting pipeline. This prior information biases the initial ranking of candidate words suggested by a deep neural network, either lexicon based or not. The final re-ranking is based on the word frequency and on the semantic relatedness between the candidate words and the information in the image.

Figure 1 shows an example where the candidate word *bike* is re-ranked thanks to the visual context information *unicycle, street, highway* detected by a visual classifier. This is a clear example that illustrates the main idea of our approach.

Our main contributions include several post-processing methods based on NLP techniques such as word frequencies and semantic relatedness which are typically exploited in NLP problems but less common in computer vision ones. We show that by introducing a candidate re-ranker based on word frequencies and semantic distance between candidate words and objects in the image, the performance of an off-the-shelf deep neural network can be improved without the need to perform additional training or tuning. In addition, thanks to the inclusion of the unigram probabilities, we overcome the baseline limitation of false detection of short words of [1,2].

The rest of the paper is organized as follows: Sects. 2 and 3 describe related work and our proposed pipeline. Sections 4 and 5 introduce the external prior knowledge we use, and how it is combined. Section 6 presents experimental validation of our approach on a publicly available standard dataset. Finally, Sects. 7 and 8 summarize the result and specifies future work.

2   Related Work

Text spotting (or end-to-end text recognition), refers to the problem of automatically detecting and recognizing text in images in the wild. Text spotting may be tackled by either a lexicon-based or a lexicon-free perspective. Lexicon-based recognition methods use a pre-defined dictionary as a reference to guide the recognition. Lexicon-free methods (or unconstrained recognition techniques), predict character sequences without relying on any dictionary. The first lexicon-free text spotting system was proposed by [3]. The system extracted character candidates via maximally stable extremal regions (MSER) and eliminated non-textual ones through a trained classifier. The remaining candidates were fed into a character recognition module, trained using a large amount of synthetic data. More recently, several deep learning alternatives have been proposed. For instance, PhotoOCR [4] uses a Deep Neural Network (DNN) that performs end-to-end text spotting using histograms of oriented gradients as input of the network. It is a lexicon-free system able to read characters in uncontrolled conditions. The final word re-ranking is performed by means of two language models, namely a character and an N-gram language model. This approach combined two language models, a character based bi-gram model with compact 8-gram and 4-gram word-level model. Another approach employed language model for final word re-ranking [5]. The top-down integration can tolerate the error in text detection or mis-recognition.

Another DNN based approach is introduced by [1], which applies a sliding window over Convolutional Neural Network (CNN) features that use a fixed-lexicon based dictionary. This is further extended in [6], through a deep architecture that allows feature sharing. In [7] the problem is addressed using a Recurrent CNN, a novel lexicon-free neural network architecture that integrates Convolutional and Recurrent Neural Networks for image based sequence recognition. Another sequence recognition approach [2] that uses LSTM with visual attention mechanism for character prediction. Although this method is lexicon-free, it includes a language model to improve the accuracy. Finally most recently, [8] introduced a CNN with connectionist temporal classification (CTC) [9] to generate the final label sequence without a sequence model such as LSTM. This approach use stacked convolutional to capture the dependencies of the input sequence. This algorithm can be integrated with either lexicon-based or lexicon-free recognition.

However, deep learning methods –either lexicon-based or lexicon-free– have drawbacks: Lexicon-based approaches need a large dictionary to perform the final recognition. Thus, their accuracy will depend on the quality and coverage of this lexicon, which makes this approach unpractical for real world applications where the domain may be different to that the system was trained on. On the other hand, lexicon-free recognition methods rely on sequence models to predict character sequences, and thus they may generate likely sentences that do not correspond to actual language words. In both cases, these techniques rely on the availability of large datasets to train and validate, which may not be always available for the target domain.

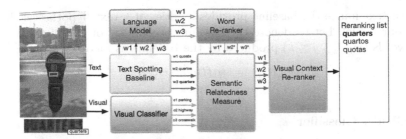

Fig. 2. Scheme of the proposed visual context information pipeline integration into the text spotting system. Our approach uses the language model and a semantic relatedness measure to re-rank the word hypothesis. The re-ranked word *quarters* is semantically related with the top ranked visual *parking*. See more examples in Fig. 3.

The work of [10] also uses visual prior information to improve the text spotting task, through a new lexicon built with Latent Dirichlet Allocation (LDA) [11]. The topic modeling learns the relation between text and images. However, this approach relies on captions describing the images rather than using the main key words semantically related to the images to generate the lexicon re-ranking. Thus, the lexicon generation can be inaccurate in some cases due to the short length of captions. In this work, we consider a direct semantic relation between scene text and its visual information. Also, unlike [10] that only uses visual information over word frequency count to re-rank the most probable word, our approach combines both methods by leveraging also on a frequency count based language model.

3 General Description of Our Approach

Text recognition approaches can be divided in two categories: (a) character based methods that rely on a single character classifier plus some kind of sequence modeling (e.g. n-gram models or LSTMs), and (b) lexicon-based approaches that intend to classify the image as a whole word.

In both cases, the system can be configured to predict the k most likely words given the input image. Our approach focuses on re-ranking that list using language information such as word frequencies, or semantic relatedness with objects in the image (or `visual context`) in which the text was located.

3.1 Baseline Systems

We used two different off-the-shelf baseline models: First, a CNN [1] with fixed lexicon based recognition. It uses a fixed dictionary containing around 90 K word forms. Second, we considered a LSTM architecture with a visual attention model [2]. The LSTM generates the final output words as character sequences, without relying on any lexicon. Both models are trained on a synthetic dataset [12]. The output of both models is a vector of softmax probabilities for candidate words.

For each text image the baseline provides a series of k text hypotheses, that is fed to our model. Let us denote the baseline probability of any of the k most likely words $(w_j, 1 \le j \le k)$ produced by the baseline as follows:

$$P_{BL}(w_j) = softmax(w_j, BL) \tag{1}$$

3.2 Object Classifier

Next, we will use out-of-the-box state-of-the-art visual object classifiers to extract the image context information that will be used to re-rank candidate words according to their semantic relatedness with the context.

We considered three pre-trained CNN classifiers: ResNet [13], GoogLeNet [14] and Inception-Resnet-v2 [15]. The output of these classifiers is a 1000-dimensional vector with the probabilities of 1000 object instances. In this work we consider a threshold of most likely objects of the context predicted by the classifier. Additionally, we use a threshold to filter out the probability predictions when the object classifier is not confident enough.

3.3 Scene Classifier

Additionally, we considered a scene classifier [16] to extract scene information from each image. We used a pre-trained scene classifier *Places365-ResNet*[1] to extract scene categories.

According to the authors of *Places365-ResNet* the network achieved good result in *top-5 accuracy*, which make it ideal for multiple visual context extraction. The output from this classifier is a 365 scene categories. Also, we consider a threshold to extract most likely classes in the images, and eliminate low confidence predictions.

3.4 Semantic Similarity

We aim to re-rank the baseline output using the visual context information, i.e. the semantic relation between the candidate words and the objects in the image. We use a pre-trained visual classifier to detect objects-scenes in the image and devise a strategy to reward candidate words that are semantically related to them. As shown in the example of Fig. 2 the top position of the re-ranking yields *quarters* as the most semantically related with the top position re-ranked object in the image *parking*.

Once the objects-scene in the image have been detected, we compute their semantic relatedness with the candidate words based on their word-embeddings [17]. Specifically, let us denote by $\boldsymbol{w}$ and $\boldsymbol{c}$ the word-embeddings of a candidate word w and the most likely object c detected in the image. We then compute their similarity using the cosine of the embeddings:

$$sim(w, c) = \frac{\boldsymbol{w} \cdot \boldsymbol{c}}{|\boldsymbol{w}| \cdot |\boldsymbol{c}|} \tag{2}$$

---

[1] http://places2.csail.mit.edu/.

4 Re-ranking Word Hypothesis

In this section we describe the different re-rankers we devised for the list of candidate words produced by the baseline DNN of Sect. 3.1.

4.1 Unigram Language Model (ULM)

The first and simpler re-ranker we introduce is based on a word Unigram Language Model (ULM). The probabilities of the unigram model computed from *Opensubtitles*[2] [18] and *Google book n-gram*[3] text corpora. The main goal of ULM is to increase the probability of the most common words proposed by the baseline.

$$P_{ULM}(w) = \frac{count(w_j)}{\sum_{w \in C} count(w)} \tag{3}$$

It is worth mentioning that the language model is very simple to build, train, and adapt to new domains, which opens the possibility of improving baseline performance for specific applications.

4.2 Semantic Relatedness with Word Embedding (SWE)

This re-ranker relies on the similarity between the candidate word and objects-scenes detected in the image. We compute (SWE) in the following steps: First, we use a threshold β to eliminate lower probabilities from the visual classifier (objects, scenes). Secondly, we compute the similarity of each visual with the candidate word. Thirdly, we take the max-highest similarity score, most semantically related, to the candidate word C_{max} as:

$$C_{max} = \operatorname*{argmax}_{\substack{c_i \in Image \\ P(c_i) \geq \beta}} sim(w, c_i) \tag{4}$$

Finally, following [19] with confirmation assumption $p(w|c) \geqslant p(w)$, we compute the conditional probability from similarity as:

$$P_{SWE}(w|c_{max}) = P(w)^{\alpha} \quad \text{where } \alpha = \left(\frac{1 - sim(w, c_{max})}{1 + sim(w, c_{max})}\right)^{1 - P(c_{max})} \tag{5}$$

where $P(w)$ is the probability of the word in general language (obtained from the unigram model), and $P(c_{max})$ is the probability of the most semantically related context object or places to the spotted text (obtained from the visual classifier).

Note that Eq. 5 already includes frequency information from the ULM, therefore it is taking into account not only the semantic relatedness, but also the word frequency information used in the ULM re-ranker above. Also, the ULM act alone in case there is no visual context information.

---

[2] https://opensubtitles.org.
[3] https://books.google.com/ngrams.

4.3 Estimating Relatedness from Training Data Probabilities (TDP)

A second possibility to compute semantic relatedness is to estimate it from training data. This should overcome the word embedding limitation when the candidate word and the image objects are not semantically related in general text, but are in the real world. For instance, as shown in the top-left example of Fig. 3, the sports TV channel *kt* and the object *racket* have no semantic relation according to the word embedding model, but they are found paired multiple times in the training dataset, which implies they do have a relation. For this, we use training data to estimate the conditional probability $P_{TDP}(w|c)$ of a word w given that object c appears in the image:

$$P_{TDP}(w|c) = \frac{count(w,c)}{count(c)} \tag{6}$$

Where $count(w,c)$ is the number of training images where w appears as the gold standard annotation for recognized text, and the object classifier detects object c in the image. Similarly, $count(c)$ is the number of training images where the object classifier detects object c.

4.4 Semantic Relatedness with Word Embedding (revisited) (TWE)

This re-ranker builds upon a word embedding, as the SWE re-ranker above, but the embeddings are learnt from the training dataset (considering two-word "sentences": the target word and the object in the image). The embeddings can be computed from scratch, using only the training dataset information (TWE) or initialized with a general embeddings model that is then biased using the training data (TWE*).

In this case, we convert the similarity produced by the embeddings to probabilities using:

$$P_{TWE}(w|c) = \frac{\tanh(sim(w,c)) + 1}{2P(c)} \tag{7}$$

Note that this re-ranker does not take into account word frequency information as in the case of the SWE re-ranker.

5 Combining Re-rankers

Our re-ranking approach consists in taking the softmax probabilities computed by the baseline DNN and combine them with the probabilities produced by the re-ranker methods described in Sect. 4. We combine them by simple multiplication, which allows us to combine any number of re-rankers in cascade. We evaluated the following combinations:

1. The baseline output is re-ranked by the unigram language model:

$$P_1(w) = P_{BL}(w) \times P_{ULM}(w) \tag{8}$$

2. The baseline output is re-ranked by the general word-embedding model (SWE). Note that this reranker also includes the ULM information.

$$P_2(w, c) = P_{BL}(w) \times P_{SWE}(w|c) \tag{9}$$

3. The baseline output is re-ranked by the relatedness estimated from the training dataset as conditional probabilities (TDP).

$$P_3(w, c) = P_{BL}(w) \times P_{TDP}(w|c) \tag{10}$$

4. The baseline output is re-ranked by the word-embedding model trained entirely on training data (TWE) or a general model tuned using the training data (TWE*):

$$P_4(w, c) = P_{BL}(w) \times P_{TWE}(w|c) \tag{11}$$

5. We also apply SWE and TDP re-rankers combined:

$$P_5(w, c) = P_{BL}(w) \times P_{SWE}(w|c) \times P_{TDP}(w|c) \tag{12}$$

6. The combination of TDP and TWE:

$$P_6(w, c) = P_{BL}(w) \times P_{TDP}(w|c) \times P_{TWE}(w|c) \tag{13}$$

7. Finally, we combine all re-rankers together:

$$P_7(w, c) = P_{BL}(w) \times P_{SWE}(w|c) \times P_{TDP}(w|c) \times P_{TWE}(w|c) \tag{14}$$

6   Experiments and Results

In this section we evaluate the performance of the proposed approaches in the **ICDAR-2017-Task3 (end-to-end)** [20] dataset. This dataset is based on Microsoft COCO [21] (Common Objects in Context), which consists of 63,686 images, and 173,589 text instances (annotations of the images). COCO-Text was not collected with text recognition in mind, therefore, not all images contain textual annotations. The *ICDAR-2017 Task3* aims for end-to-end text spotting (i.e. both detection and recognition). Thus, this dataset includes whole images, and the texts in them may appear rotated, distorted, or partially occluded. Since we focus only on text recognition, we use the ground truth detection as a golden detector to extract the bounding boxes from the full image. The dataset consists of 43,686 full images with 145,859 text instances, and for training 10,000 images and 27,550 instances for validation. We evaluate our approach on a subset[4] of the validation containing 10,000 images with associated bounding boxes.

---

[4] https://github.com/ahmedssabir/dataset/.

6.1   Preliminaries

For evaluation, we used a more restrictive protocol than the standard proposed by [22] and adopted in most state-of-the-art benchmarks, which does not consider words with less than three characters or with non-alphanumerical characters. This protocol was introduced to overcome the false positives on short words that most current state-of-the-art struggle with, including our Baselines. However, we overcome this limitation by introducing the language model re-ranker. Thus, we consider all cases in the dataset, and words with less than three characters are also evaluated.

In all cases, we use two pre-trained deep models, CNN [1] and LSTM [2] as a baseline (BL) to extract the initial list of word hypotheses. Since these BLs need to be fed with the cropped words, when evaluating on the ICDAR-2017-Task3 dataset we will use the ground truth bounding boxes of the words.

6.2   Experiments with Language Model

As a proof of concept, we trained our unigram language model on two different copora. The first ULM was trained on *Opensubtitles*, a large database of subtitles for movies containing around 3 million word types, including numbers and other alphanumeric combinations that make it well suited for our task. Secondly, we trained another model with *Google book n-gram*, that contains 5 million word types from American-British literature books. However, since the test dataset contains numbers, the accuracy was lower than that obtained using the *Opensubtitles* corpus. We also evaluate a model trained on the union of both corpora, that contains around 7 million word types.

In this experiment, we extract the $k = 2, \ldots, 9$ most likely words –and their probabilities– from the baselines. Although the sequential nature of the LSTM baseline captures a character-based language model, our post-process uses word-level probabilities to re-rank the word as a whole. Note that since our baselines work on cropped words, we do not evaluate the whole end-to-end but only the influence of adding external knowledge.

The first baseline is a CNN [1] with fixed-lexicon recognition, which is not able to recognize any word outside its dictionary. The results are reported in Table 1. We present three different accuracy metrics: (1) *full* columns correspond to the accuracy on the whole dataset, while (2) *dictionary* columns correspond to the accuracy over the solvable cases (i.e. those where the target word is among the 90K-words of the CNN dictionary, which correspond to 43.3% of the whole dataset), and finally (3) *list* shows the accuracy over the cases where the right word was in the k-best list output by the baseline. We also provide the results using different numbers of k-best candidates. Table 1 top row shows the performance of the CNN baseline, and the second row reports the influence of the ULM. The best result is obtained with $k = 3$, which improved the baseline model in 0.9%, up to 22% *full*, and 2.7%, up to 61.3% *dictionary*.

The second baseline we consider is an LSTM [2] with visual soft-attention mechanism, performing unconstrained text recognition without relying on a lexicon. The first row in Table 2 reports the LSTM baseline result on this dataset,

Table 1. Results of re-ranking the k-best ($k = 2 \ldots 9$) hypotheses of the CNN baseline on ICDAR-2017-Task3 dataset (%)

Model	$k = 2$			$k = 3$			$k = 5$			$k = 9$		
	full	dict	list	full	dict	list	full	dict	list	full	dict	list
$CNN\,baseline_1$	full: 21.1 dictionary: 58.6											
CNN+ULM$_{7M}$	21.8	60.6	90.0	22.0	61.3	84.2	21.6	60.1	77.7	21.0	58.5	68.7
CNN+SWE$_{object}$	22.3	62.1	92.3	22.6	63.0	86.5	22.8	63.4	81.9	22.6	62.9	73.9
CNN+SWE$_{place}$	22.1	61.4	91.2	22.5	62.5	85.8	22.6	62.6	80.8	22.6	62.8	73.8
CNN+TDP	22.2	61.7	91.6	22.7	63.3	86.9	22.7	63.2	81.6	22.6	62.8	73.8
CNN+SWE$_{object}$+TDP	22.4	62.2	92.4	22.9	63.6	87.4	**23.0**	**64.0**	**82.6**	22.9	63.7	74.8
CNN+SWE$_{place}$+TDP	22.1	61.6	91.5	22.6	62.7	86.1	22.8	63.4	81.9	22.8	63.4	74.5
CNN+TWE	22.3	61.9	92.0	22.6	62.9	86.4	22.6	62.8	81.1	22.7	63.0	74.0
CNN+TDP+TWE*	22.3	62.1	92.3	22.8	63.4	87.0	22.9	63.8	82.4	**23.0**	**64.0**	**75.2**
CNN+All$_{object}$	22.3	62.1	92.3	22.7	63.2	86.7	22.9	63.6	82.1	22.7	63.3	74.3
CNN+All$_{place}$	22.2	61.8	91.9	22.7	63.1	86.6	22.8	63.4	81.9	22.6	63.0	74.0

and the second row shows the results after the ULM re-ranking. The best results are obtained by considering $k = 3$ which improves the baseline in 0.7%, from 18.72% to 19.42%.

In summary, the lexicon-based baseline CNN performs better than the unconstrained approach LSTM, since the character sequences prediction generation that may lead up to random words, which the ULM may be unable to re-rank.

6.3 Experiments with Visual Context Information

The main contribution of this paper consists in re-ranking the k most likely hypotheses candidate word using the visual context information. Thus, we use ICDAR-2017-Task3 dataset to evaluate our approach, re-ranking the baseline output using the semantic relation between the spotted text in the image and its visual context. As in the language model experiment, we used ground-truth bounding boxes as input to the BL. However, in this case, the whole image is used as input to the visual classifier.

In order to extract the visual context information we considered two different pre-trained state-of-the-art visual classifiers: object and scene classifiers. For image classification we rely on three pre-traind network: ResNet [13], GoogLeNet [14] and Inception-ResNet-v2 [15], all of them able to detect pre-defined list of 1,000 object classes. However, for testing we considered only Inception-ResNet-v2 due to better *top-5 accuracy*. For scene classification we use places classifier *Place365-ResNet152* [16] that able to detect 365 scene categories.

Although the visual classifiers use a softmax to produces only one probable object hypotheses per image, we use *threshold* to extract a number of object-scene hypotheses, and eliminate low-confidence results. Then, we compute the

Table 2. Results of re-ranking the k-best ($k = 2 \ldots 9$) hypotheses of the LSTM baseline on ICDAR-2017-Task3 dataset (%)

Model	$k = 2$		$k = 3$		$k = 5$		$k = 9$	
	full	list	full	list	full	list	full	list
LSTM baseline$_2$				18.7				
LSTM+ULM$_{7M}$	19.3	87.7	19.4	79.3	19.1	69.5	18.7	60.7
LSTM+SWE$_{object}$	19.3	88.0	19.8	80.7	20.0	73.0	20.1	66.2
LSTM+SWE$_{place}$	19.3	87.9	19.7	80.5	20.1	73.6	20.0	65.5
LSTM+TDP	19.0	86.6	19.3	78.8	19.5	71.3	20.0	65.6
LSTM+SWE$_{object}$+TDP	19.4	88.6	20.0	81.6	20.3	74.3	20.6	67.4
LSTM+SWE$_{place}$+TDP	19.4	88.5	19.9	81.1	20.3	74.2	20.4	66.8
LSTM+TWE	19.5	88.7	20.0	81.5	20.1	73.6	20.3	66.6
LSTM+TDP+TWE*	19.5	88.9	20.0	81.8	20.3	74.3	**20.8**	**68.3**
LSTM+All$_{object}$	19.4	88.3	19.8	80.9	20.3	74.2	20.4	67.0
LSTM+All$_{place}$	19.4	88.2	20.0	81.5	20.3	74.1	20.3	66.7

semantic relatedness for each object-scene hypotheses with the spotted text. Finally, we take the most related visual context.

In this experiment we re-rank the baseline k-best hypotheses based on their relatedness with the objects in the image. We try two approaches for that: (1) semantic similarity computed using word embeddings [17] and (2) correlation based on co-ocurrence of text and image object in the training data.

First, we re-rank the words based on their word embedding: semantic relatedness with multiple visual context from general text: (1) object (SWE$_{object}$) and (2) scene (SWE$_{place}$). For instance, the top-right example in Fig. 3 shows that the strong semantic similarity between scene information *parking* and *pay* re-ranked that word from 3rd to 1st position. We tested three pre-trained models trained on general text as baseline (1) word2vec model with 100 billion tokens (2) glove model with 840 billion tokens [23] and (3) fastText with 600 billion tokens [24]. However, we adopt glove as baseline, due to a better similarity score.

Secondly, we use the training data to compute the conditional probabilities between text image and object in the image happen together (TDP). We also combined both relatedness measures as described in Eq. 12, obtaining a higher accuracy improvement on both baselines, as can be seen in Tables 1 and 2, (SWE+TDP) boosted the accuracy for both baseline. The LSTM accuracy improved up to 1.9%. In other hand, the CNN, with 90k fixed lexicon, accuracy is boosted up to 1.9% on *full* dataset and 5.4% *dictionary*. For example, as shown in Fig. 3 top-left example, text image *kt* (sport channel) happens often with visual context *racket*, something that can not be captured by general word embedding models. Also, scene classifier SWE$_{place}$+TDP boost the baseline 1.7% *full* and 4.8% *dictionary*. The scene classifier SWE$_{place}$ perform better than the object classifier in instance outdoor. For instance, the spotted text in a signboard *way*

Table 3. Examples of $P(word|object)$ for each re-ranker. TDP and TWE capture relevant information to improve the baseline for pairs word-object/scene that appear in the training dataset. The TPD overcome word-embedding limitation in samples happen in training datasets.

Word	Visual	SWE	TDP	TWE	TWE*
delta	airliner	0.0028	**0.0398**	0.0003	0.00029
kt	racket	0.0004	**0.0187**	0.0002	0.00006
plate	moving	0.0129	0.00050	**0.326**	0.00098
way	street	0.1740	0.02165	**0.177**	0.17493

is more semantically related with *downtown* than a man holding *an umbrella* in the image.

Finally, we trained a word embedding model using the training dataset (TWE). Due to the dataset is too small, we train skip-gram model with one window, and without any word filtering. In addition, we initialized the model weight with the baseline (SWE) that trained on general text, we call it TWE*. The result is 300-dimension vector for about 10K words. Also, we initialized the weight randomly but when we combined the re-rankers the pre-trained initialized model is slightly better. The result in both Tables 1 and 2 button two rows shows that (TWE) outperform the accuracy of SWE model that trained on general text.

The result in Table 1 CNN shows that the combination model TDP+TWE also significantly boost the accuracy up to 5.4% *dictionary* and 1.9% *full*. Also, in Table 2, the second baseline LSTM accuracy boosted up to 2.1%. Not to mention that TDP+TWE model only rely on the visual context information, computed by Eq. 7.

7 Discussion

The visual context information re-ranks potential candidate words based on the semantic relatedness with its visual information (SWE). However, there are some cases when there is no direct semantic correlation between the visual context and the potential word. Thus we proposed TDP to address this limitation by learning correlations from the training dataset. However, there are still cases unseen in the training dataset, for instance, as shown in Fig. 3 bottom-left text image *copyrighting* and its visual context *ski slop, snowfield* have neither semantic correlation nor were seen in the training dataset. There are also cases where is no relation at all, as in Fig. 3 the brand name *zara* and the visual context *crosswalk* or *plaza*.

The results we have presented show that our approach is a simple way to boost accuracy of text recognition deep learning models, or to adapt them to particular domains, with a very low re-training/tuning cost. The proposed post-processing approach can be used as a drop-in complement for any text-spotting

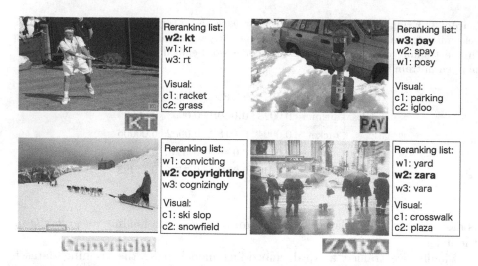

Fig. 3. Some examples of visual context re-ranker. The top-two examples are successful results of the visual context re-ranker. The top-left example is a re-ranking result based on the relation between text and its visuals happen together in the training dataset. The top-right example is a re-ranking result based on semantic relatedness between the text image and its visual. The two cases in the bottom are examples of words either have no semantic correlation with the visual or exist in the training dataset. Not to mention that the top ranking visual c_1 is the most semantically related visual context to the spotted text. (Bold font words indicate the ground truth)

algorithm (either deep-learning based or not) that outputs a ranking of word hypotheses. In addition, our approach overcomes some of the limitations that current state-of-the-art deep model struggle to solve in complex background text spotting scenarios, such as short words.

One limitation of this approach is that when the language model re-ranker is strong, the visual context re-ranker is unable to re-rank the correct candidate word. For instance, the word *ohh* has a large frequency count in general text. This problem can be tackled by adjusting the weight of uncommon short words in the language model.

8   Conclusion

In this paper we have proposed a simple post-processing approach, a hypothesis re-ranker based on visual context information, to improve the accuracy of any pre-trained text spotting system. We also show that by integrating a language model re-ranker as a prior to the visual re-ranker, the performance of the visual context re-ranker can be improved. We have shown that the accuracy of two state-of-the-art deep network architectures, a lexicon-based and lexicon-free recognition, can be boosted up to 2 percentage-points on standard benchmarks. In the future work, we plan to explore end-to-end based fusion schemes that can automatically discover more proper priors in one shot deep model fusion architecture.

Acknowledgments. We would like to thank Ernest Valveny and Suman K. Ghosh for useful discussions on the second baseline. This work was supported by the KASP Scholarship Program and by the MINECO project HuMoUR TIN2017-90086-R.

References

1. Jaderberg, M., Simonyan, K., Vedaldi, A., Zisserman, A.: Reading text in the wild with convolutional neural networks. Int. J. Comput. Vis. **116**(1), 1–20 (2016)
2. Ghosh, S.K., Valveny, E., Bagdanov, A.D.: Visual attention models for scene text recognition. arXiv preprint arXiv:1706.01487 (2017)
3. Neumann, L., Matas, J.: A method for text localization and recognition in real-world images. In: Kimmel, R., Klette, R., Sugimoto, A. (eds.) ACCV 2010. LNCS, vol. 6494, pp. 770–783. Springer, Heidelberg (2011). https://doi.org/10.1007/978-3-642-19318-7_60
4. Bissacco, A., Cummins, M., Netzer, Y., Neven, H.: Photoocr: reading text in uncontrolled conditions. In: Proceedings of the IEEE International Conference on Computer Vision (2013)
5. Mishra, A., Alahari, K., Jawahar, C.: Top-down and bottom-up cues for scene text recognition. In: CVPR-IEEE Conference on Computer Vision and Pattern Recognition. IEEE (2012)
6. Jaderberg, M., Vedaldi, A., Zisserman, A.: Deep features for text spotting. In: Fleet, D., Pajdla, T., Schiele, B., Tuytelaars, T. (eds.) ECCV 2014. LNCS, vol. 8692, pp. 512–528. Springer, Cham (2014). https://doi.org/10.1007/978-3-319-10593-2_34
7. Shi, B., Bai, X., Yao, C.: An end-to-end trainable neural network for image-based sequence recognition and its application to scene text recognition. IEEE Trans. Pattern Anal. Mach. Intell. **39**(11), 2298–2304 (2016)
8. Gao, Y., Chen, Y., Wang, J., Lu, H.: Reading scene text with attention convolutional sequence modeling. arXiv preprint arXiv:1709.04303 (2017)
9. Graves, A., Fernández, S., Gomez, F., Schmidhuber, J.: Connectionist temporal classification: labelling unsegmented sequence data with recurrent neural networks. In: Proceedings of the 23rd International Conference on Machine Learning. ACM (2006)
10. Patel, Y., Gomez, L., Rusiñol, M., Karatzas, D.: Dynamic lexicon generation for natural scene images. In: Hua, G., Jégou, H. (eds.) ECCV 2016. LNCS, vol. 9913, pp. 395–410. Springer, Cham (2016). https://doi.org/10.1007/978-3-319-46604-0_29
11. Blei, D.M., Ng, A.Y., Jordan, M.I.: Latent dirichlet allocation. J. Mach. Learn. Res. **3**, 993–1022 (2003)
12. Jaderberg, M., Simonyan, K., Vedaldi, A., Zisserman, A.: Synthetic data and artificial neural networks for natural scene text recognition. arXiv preprint arXiv:1406.2227 (2014)
13. He, K., Zhang, X., Ren, S., Sun, J.: Deep residual learning for image recognition. In: Proceedings of the IEEE Conference on Computer Vision and Pattern Recognition (2016)

14. Szegedy, C., et al.: Going deeper with convolutions. In: Proceedings of the IEEE Conference on Computer Vision and Pattern Recognition (2015)
15. Szegedy, C., Ioffe, S., Vanhoucke, V., Alemi, A.A.: Inception-v4, inception-resnet and the impact of residual connections on learning. In: AAAI (2017)
16. Zhou, B., Lapedriza, A., Khosla, A., Oliva, A., Torralba, A.: Places: a 10 million image database for scene recognition. IEEE Trans. Pattern Anal. Mach. Intell. **40**(6), 1452–1464 (2017)
17. Mikolov, T., Sutskever, I., Chen, K., Corrado, G.S., Dean, J.: Distributed representations of words and phrases and their compositionality. In: Advances in Neural Information Processing Systems (2013)
18. Tiedemann, J.: News from OPUS-A collection of multilingual parallel corpora with tools and interfaces. In: Recent Advances in Natural Language Processing (2009)
19. Blok, S., Medin, D., Osherson, D.: Probability from similarity. In: AAAI Spring Symposium on Logical Formalization of Commonsense Reasoning (2003)
20. Veit, A., Matera, T., Neumann, L., Matas, J., Belongie, S.: Coco-text: dataset and benchmark for text detection and recognition in natural images. arXiv preprint arXiv:1601.07140 (2016)
21. Lin, T.-Y., et al.: Microsoft COCO: common objects in context. In: Fleet, D., Pajdla, T., Schiele, B., Tuytelaars, T. (eds.) ECCV 2014. LNCS, vol. 8693, pp. 740–755. Springer, Cham (2014). https://doi.org/10.1007/978-3-319-10602-1_48
22. Wang, K., Babenko, B., Belongie, S.: End-to-end scene text recognition. In: 2011 IEEE International Conference on Computer Vision (ICCV). IEEE (2011)
23. Pennington, J., Socher, R., Manning, C.: Glove: global vectors for word representation. In: Proceedings of the 2014 Conference on Empirical Methods in Natural Language Processing (EMNLP) (2014)
24. Bojanowski, P., Grave, E., Joulin, A., Mikolov, T.: Enriching word vectors with subword information. Trans. Assoc. Comput. Linguist. **5**, 135–146 (2017)

TextNet: Irregular Text Reading from Images with an End-to-End Trainable Network

Yipeng Sun[✉], Chengquan Zhang[✉], Zuming Huang, Jiaming Liu,
Junyu Han, and Errui Ding

Baidu Inc, Beijing, China
{sunyipeng,zhangchengquan,huangzuming,
liujiaming03,hanjunyu,dingerrui}@baidu.com

Abstract. Reading text from images remains challenging due to multi-orientation, perspective distortion and especially the curved nature of irregular text. Most of existing approaches attempt to solve the problem in two or multiple stages, which is considered to be the bottleneck to optimize the overall performance. To address this issue, we propose an end-to-end trainable network architecture, named *TextNet*, which is able to simultaneously localize and recognize irregular text from images. Specifically, we develop a scale-aware attention mechanism to learn multi-scale image features as a backbone network, sharing fully convolutional features and computation for localization and recognition. In text detection branch, we directly generate text proposals in quadrangles, covering oriented, perspective and curved text regions. To preserve text features for recognition, we introduce a perspective RoI transform layer, which can align quadrangle proposals into small feature maps. Furthermore, in order to extract effective features for recognition, we propose to encode the aligned RoI features by RNN into context information, combining spatial attention mechanism to generate text sequences. This overall pipeline is capable of handling both regular and irregular cases. Finally, text localization and recognition tasks can be jointly trained in an end-to-end fashion with designed multi-task loss. Experiments on standard benchmarks show that the proposed *TextNet* can achieve state-of-the-art performance, and outperform existing approaches on irregular datasets by a large margin.

Keywords: Text reading · Irregular text · End-to-end ·
Text recognition · Spatial attention · Deep neural network

1 Introduction

Reading text from images is one of the most classical and elemental problems in pattern recognition and machine intelligence. This problem has received much attention due to its profound impact and valuable applications in both research

© Springer Nature Switzerland AG 2019
C. V. Jawahar et al. (Eds.): ACCV 2018, LNCS 11363, pp. 83–99, 2019.
https://doi.org/10.1007/978-3-030-20893-6_6

and industrial communities. End-to-end text reading is to tell the locations and content of text from images, combining text detection and recognition. Benefiting from the deep learning paradigm for generic object detection [9,19,29,35] and sequence-to-sequence recognition [1,10,43], recent advances have witnessed dramatic improvement in terms of both recognition accuracy and model simplicity for text localization [18,31,45] and recognition [24,38,39]. Regarded as the ultimate goal of text reading, end-to-end task can be tackled by integrating text detection and recognition algorithms into an end-to-end framework (Fig. 1).

Fig. 1. End-to-end results of irregular text: (a) existing approaches (b) the proposed TextNet results.

Conventional end-to-end text reading paradigm typically works as a two-stage or multi-stage system, integrating detection and recognition modules into an overall pipeline [20,41]. Recent text detection approaches are able to generate text locations in an end-to-end trained model [31,45]. The state-of-the-art text recognition methods can be formulated as an end-to-end "translation" problem from a cropped text image to text sequence [24,38]. More recently, in contrast to multi-stage text reading systems, fully trainable models to tackle end-to-end text reading task have been proposed in [5,16,25]. These approaches are capable of predicting locations and content of regular text in one model. However, these state-of-the-art approaches face difficulties in handling irregular text with perspective distortion, and fail to tackle curved text cases. Therefore, it is still challenging to localize and recognize irregular text in an end-to-end framework, and it is an open issue to read both regular and irregular text in a unified model.

Towards this end, we propose an end-to-end trainable text reading network, named *TextNet*, which is able to read irregular text from images, especially for perspective and curved cases. Taking a full image as the input, the proposed network can generate word proposals by directly regressing quadrangles to cover both oriented and curved text regions. To preserve text features for recognition, we develop a perspective RoI transform layer to align these proposals into small feature maps. To extract more effective features from text proposals, we propose to encode the aligned RoI (Region-of-Interest) features in RNN (Recurrent Neural Network), and utilize the spatial attention mechanism to recognize both regular and irregular text sequences. Text localization and recognition tasks are designed as an end-to-end trainable network by multi-task learning. The contributions of this paper are listed as follows:

- We propose an end-to-end trainable network that can simultaneously localize and recognize irregular text in one model.
- To cover perspective and curved text regions, we directly predict quadrangle text proposals, and develop a perspective RoI transform layer to align these proposals into small feature maps, keeping invariance in aspect ratio.
- To extract effective text features for recognition, we propose to encode the aligned features using RNN in both vertical and horizontal directions, and utilize spatial attention mechanism to decode each character despite of imprecise predicted locations.
- Experiments on datasets demonstrate that the proposed *TextNet* can achieve comparable or state-of-the-art performance on the standard benchmarks, and outperform the existing approaches on irregular datasets by a large margin.

To our best knowledge, it is the first end-to-end trainable text reading network, which is able to handle oriented, perspective and curved text in a unified model.

2 Related Work

In this section, we will summarize the existing literatures on text localization and text recognition, respectively. As the combination of both text localization and recognition, recent advances in end-to-end text reading and spotting will also be discussed.

Text localization aims to tell the locations of words or text-lines from images. Conventional approaches can be roughly classified as components-based [33,40] and character-based methods [18]. These methods first attempt to find local elements, such as components, windows, or characters, and then group them into words to generate the final bounding boxes. In recent years, most of these approaches utilize deep convolutional neural network to learn text features, which has shown significant performance improvement. Inspired by recent advances in generic object detection [19,29,35], the state-of-the-art text detection approaches [31,45] are designed to directly predict word-level bounding boxes, which simplifies the previous multi-stage pipeline into an end-to-end trainable model. These approaches can be further classified as proposed-based or single-shot models. To tackle multi-scale and orientation problems in text detection, Liao et al. [27] employ SSD framework with specifically designed anchor boxes to cover text regions. Liu et al. [31] develop a rotational proposal network to localize text rotational bounding boxes. Following the general design of DenseBox [19], Zhou et al. [45] and He et al. [17] propose to directly regress multi-oriented text in quadrangle representation.

Text recognition aims to assign text labels to each character, taking a cropped word or a text-line as input. Traditional text recognition methods are generally considered as character-based [2], or word-based classification [12] problems. These paradigms are either composed of multiple steps or difficult to generalize to non-Latin script languages. In recent years, the success of recurrent neural network has inspired the text recognition approaches to be formulated as a variable-length sequence-to-sequence problem. Following the paradigms of speech recognition [11] and handwritten recognition, He et al. [15] and Shi et al. [38] propose to extract convolutional features, reshape to an one-dimensional sequence and encode context in RNN for recognition. The whole model can be trained as a sequence labeling problem with CTC (Connectionist Temporal Classification) [10] loss. These approaches make it possible to train word-level and line-level text recognition in an end-to-end trainable framework. Most recently, with the neural machine translation break-through by attention mechanism [1], several attention-based text recognition models [24,39] are developed to encode convolutional image features into sequence context with RNN, and predict each character using attention-based decoder.

End-to-end text reading is typically recognized as the ultimate evaluation of text recognition from images. Building upon both text detection and recognition algorithms, traditional approaches are mostly composed of multiple steps to achieve end-to-end results [20,26,41]. Jaderberg et al. [20] first generate text proposals in high recall, and then refine the bounding boxes to estimate more precisely. Finally, cropped word images are recognized by a CNN-based word classifier. In contrast to traditional methods in multiple steps, recently, there are a number of approaches designed in a fully end-to-end trainable framework. Li et al. [25] propose an end-to-end trainable text reading model, using RPN (Region Proposal Network) to estimate proposals and LSTM with attention to decode each words. To address the multi-orientation problem of text, Busta et al. [5] utilize YOLOv2 [34] framework to generate rotational proposals, and train RoI sampled features with CTC loss. Other approaches are designed to further speed up computation for inference [30]. All these approaches are trainable in an end-to-end fashion, which can improve the overall performance and save computation overhead by alleviating multiple processing steps. However, it is still challenging to handle both horizontal, oriented and perspective, especially curved text in an end-to-end framework. As one of the ultimate goals for end-to-end text reading, this problem has not been investigated yet in the existing literatures.

3   Model Architecture

TextNet is an end-to-end trained network capable of localizing and recognizing both regular and irregular text simultaneously. As shown in Fig. 2, the overall network architecture consists of four building blocks, i.e., the backbone network, quadrangle text proposal, perspective RoI transform and spatial-aware text recognition. To enable the joint training of text detection and recognition tasks, we derive a backbone network to share deep convolution features, and aggregate the multi-scale features into $\frac{1}{4}$ resolution of the input image. In our work, we utilize ResNet-50 [14] as the backbone network for its ease-of-use. To learn multi-scale text features, we develop a scale-aware attention mechanism to fuse multi-scale features to generate the final feature map. To cover oriented, perspective and curved text regions, text proposal network can directly predict the locations of text in quadrangles. Furthermore, in order to preserve information from quadrangle proposals for recognition, we develop a perspective RoI transform layer to convert the features of quadrangle proposals into fixed-height features with variable-size width. Finally, as the recognition network, we propose to use RNN as feature context encoder and combine spatial attention-based RNN decoder, thus improving the recognition performance despite of imperfect detection as well as perspective and curved text distortion. The overall architecture containing both detection and recognition branches can be jointly trained in an end-to-end manner. In this section, we will describe each part of the model in detail, respectively.

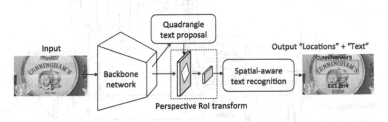

Fig. 2. The overall architecture of *TextNet*.

3.1 Backbone Network

Using ResNet-50 as a shared feature extractor, we manage to make use of features in 4-scales to generate the final feature map. Since visual objects usually vary in size, it becomes difficult to detect multi-scale objects. In recent deep learning paradigm, it has shown its effectiveness to aggregate multi-scale features to localize objects. Existing literatures have introduced a U-shape network [36] to merge multi-scale features, build a feature pyramid to boost the object detection performance [28], and fuse multi-scale convolutional features by attention mechanism to improve image segmentation accuracy [6]. Since the scales of text usually vary in much a wider range than generic objects, feature maps from low to high resolutions have different responses corresponding to the scale of text. Therefore, there exists an optimal feature map scale for each text to maximize its response.

Towards this end, inspired by the multi-scale attention mechanism in image segmentation [6], we come up with the idea of learning to fuse features by adaptively weighting multi-scale feature maps. In our work, we develop a scale-aware attention mechanism to fuse features at different scales, adaptively merging them into one feature map. This can help to improve the recall and precision of both large and small characters. As shown in Fig. 3, the developed backbone network takes four scales of features from ResNet-50 as its input, transform these features into the same scale at 1/4 by upsampling, and predict attention maps corresponding to features at different scales. The final feature map is the element-wise addition of 4-scale features, which are spatially weighted by attention mechanism. In this network, Conv-Block-1, 2, 3, 4 are standard convolutional operations of (conv 3×3, 256) + (conv 1×1, 128), and Conv-Fuse is a feature fusion block by (conv 1×1, 4) operation, generating attention weights in 4 scales. With the developed structure, the backbone network can learn multi-scale features of text, thus improving the detection and recognition performance.

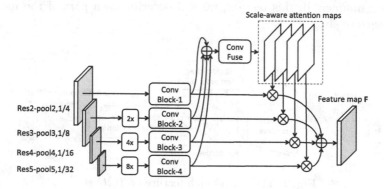

Fig. 3. Scale-aware attention mechanism for multi-scale features aggregation.

3.2   Quadrangle Text Proposal

To improve the recall of text regions, we utilize the quadrangle representation to define a text proposal, following the design of EAST [45]. The text detection branch can directly generate a score map $\mathbf{S} = \{p_{ij}|i, j \in \Omega\}$, where Ω is defined as the feature region. The score map is used to distinguish between text and non-text with probability p_{ij} as being text. Besides, 4-point coordinate offsets are estimated for every position to form quadrangle representation, which can be defined as $\mathbf{Q} = \{(\Delta x_k, \Delta y_k)_{k=1,2,3,4}\}$. Taking the finally aggregated feature map $\mathbf{F}$ as input, the output channels in text detection branch are predicted in fully convolutional operations by $\mathbf{Q} = \mathrm{conv}_{3 \times 3,8}(\mathbf{F})$ and $\mathbf{S} = \mathrm{conv}_{3 \times 3,1}(\mathbf{F})$. Finally, the text proposals in quadrangles are calculated by NMS (Non-Maximum Suppression) in the predicting stage, following state-of-the-art object detection pipeline.

During the training stage, the text detection loss L_{det} is composed of two parts, which can be defined as $L_{det} = L_{quad} + \lambda L_{cls}$. In this equation, L_{cls} measures the difference between the predicted and ground-truth score maps by cross-entropy loss. L_{quad} is defined as the smooth L_1 loss to measure the distance between the predicted coordinates and ground-truth locations, and λ is the regularization parameter that can control the trade-off between two loss functions.

3.3 Perspective RoI Transform

The conventional RoI-pooling [9] extracts a small fixed-size feature map from each RoI (e.g., 8×8). To improve image segmentation accuracy, RoI-Align introduced by Mask R-CNN [13] aims to solve the misalignment between input and output features. To better design for text regions, the varying-size RoI pooling [25] has been developed to keep the aspect ratio unchanged for text recognition. Moreover, to handle oriented text regions, rotational text proposal [5] and RoI-Rotate [30] have been developed to address this issue using affine transformation, motivated by the idea of Spatial Transformer Network [21] to learn a transformation matrix.

By contrast, following the generated quadrangle proposals, we develop perspective RoI transform to convert an arbitrary-size quadrangle into a small variable-width and fixed-height feature map, which can be regarded as the generalization of the existing methods. Our proposed RoI transform can warp each RoI by perspective transformation and bilinear sampling. The perspective transformation T_θ can be calculated between the coordinates of a text proposal and the transformed width and height. Each RoI from the feature map can be transformed to axis-aligned feature maps by perspective transformation. The perspective transformation is denoted as $T_\theta = [\theta_{11}, \theta_{12}, \theta_{13}; \theta_{21}, \theta_{22}, \theta_{23}; \theta_{31}, \theta_{32}, 1]$, and w^t, h^t denote the width and height of a transformed feature map, respectively. The parameters of T_θ can be calculated using the source and destination coordinates, following the principle of perspective transformation. Using these parameters, the transformed feature map can be obtained by perspective transformation as

$$
\begin{pmatrix} u \\ v \\ w \end{pmatrix} = T_\theta \begin{pmatrix} x_k^t \\ y_k^t \\ 1 \end{pmatrix},
\tag{1}
$$

where (x_k^t, y_k^t) are the target coordinates from the transformed feature map with pixel index k for $\forall k = 1, 2, ..., h^t w^t$, and u, v, and w are auxiliary variables. The source coordinates (x_k^s, y_k^s) from the input are defined as $x_k^s = u/w$ and $y_k^s = v/w$, respectively. The pixel value of (x_k^t, y_k^t) can be computed by bilinear sampling from the input feature map as $V_k = \sum_n^{h^s} \sum_m^{w^s} U_{nm} K(x_k^s - m) K(y_k^s - n)$, where V_k is the output value of pixel k, h^s and w^s are the height and width of the input. In this equation, U_{nm} denotes the value at location (n, m) from the input, and the kernel function is defined as $K(\cdot) = \max(0, 1 - |\cdot|)$. Note that the bilinear sampling operates on each channel, respectively.

3.4 Spatial-Aware Text Recognition

To handle irregular cases, the proposed text detection network attempts to cover text regions by quadrangle proposals, improving the performance in terms of recall. In an end-to-end text reading task, it is crucial to design a concatenation module between text detection and recognition to achieve better accuracy. The detected text regions may not be precise enough for text recognition approaches, especially in irregular text cases. The conventional text recognition approaches [24,38] assume that the input words or text lines have been well cropped and aligned. Therefore, in perspective and curved text cases, it is difficult to capture effective features in these approaches to recognize characters, which leads to failure cases. Recent studies have paid attention to irregular text recognition problem [39,44]. These approaches utilize cropped words provided by the datasets. From the perspective of end-to-end task, however, it has not been investigated yet for irregular text recognition. The spatial attention mechanism has been applied in road name recognition [42] and handwritten recognition [3,4], however, it is still limited to specific applications and has not shown effective yet for general scene text recognition.

Taking aligned RoI features as input, we propose to encode convolutional features by RNN to extract spatial context, and combine spatial attention mechanism [43], forming an encoder-decoder architecture with attention mechanism to sequentially decode each character. This approach aims to attend to features-of-interest to cover both horizontal, oriented, perspective, and curved cases, extracting effective character features at each time step. As illustrated in Fig. 4, the proposed text recognition network takes each RoI aligned feature map as the input, and predicts each character label y_t as the output.

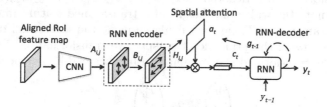

Fig. 4. Spatial-aware text recognition network

Encoder. The encoder part consists of stacked convolutional operations and two layers of RNN. The convolutional operations are 4-layer of (conv 3×3, 128) followed by batch normalization and ReLU. The first layer of RNN encodes each columns of the feature map $A \in R^{h_A \times w_A \times c_A}$ as

$$h_i^c = RNN(A_{i,j}, h_{i-1}^c), \forall j = 1, 2, \cdots, w_A, \tag{2}$$

where h_i^c is the hidden state in the i-th row. The second layer of RNN encoder takes the output $B \in R^{h_B \times w_B \times c_B}$ of the first layer, and encodes each row of the feature map as

$$h_j^r = RNN(B_{i,j}, h_{j-1}^r), \forall i = 1, 2, \cdots, h_B, \tag{3}$$

where h_j^r is the hidden state in the j-th column. In our work, we use GRU (Gated Recurrent Unit) as RNN encoder for its ease-of-use. After two layers of RNN operations, the final generated feature map $H \in R^{h_H \times w_H \times c_H}$ contains context information in both horizontal and vertical directions.

Decoder. In the decoder part, spatial attention is to calculate the similarity between encoder feature map $H_{i,j}$ and RNN decoder state g_{t-1}, which is to learn the spatial alignment

$$e_{i,j,t} = Attention(H_{i,j}, g_{t-1}) \tag{4}$$

to weight the importance of feature $H_{i,j}$ at time t. In Eq. 4, we utilize a feed forward neural network as $Attention(\cdot)$ function following [1], and normalize the alignment as

$$\alpha_{i,j,t} = \frac{\exp(e_{i,j,t})}{\sum_{i,j} \exp(e_{i,j,t})}. \tag{5}$$

With the predicted spatial attention weights $\alpha_{i,j,t}$, the context vector c_t at time t is calculated as

$$c_t = \sum_{i,j,t} \alpha_{i,j,t} H_{i,j}. \tag{6}$$

Feeding c_t and the former output y_{t-1} as input, the RNN decoder can directly update its hidden state g_t and predict the output label y_t by fully connected weights and softmax classification. The final output is to achieve the character that can maximize the posterior probability as $\hat{y}_t = \arg\max_{y_t \in \mathcal{D}} p(y_t|g_t, y_{t-1})$, where $\mathcal{D}$ is the set of labels. During the training stage, the recognition loss for sequences is derived as the average uncertainty, which can be defined as

$$L_{reg} = -\frac{1}{NT} \sum_{n=1}^{N} \sum_{t=1}^{T} \log p(y_t|y_{t-1}, g_{t-1}, c_t). \tag{7}$$

Training this objective function is to minimize L_{reg} over all training samples and time steps. In this equation, N and T denote the number of training samples and the count of time steps, respectively.

3.5 Joint Localization and Recognition

Benefiting from the developed modules above, we are able to unify the quadrangle text detection, perspective RoI transform, and spatial-aware text recognition network in one model. To train localization and recognition networks simultaneously, we utilize a multi-task loss defined as

$$L = L_{det} + \beta L_{reg}, \tag{8}$$

where β is the regularization parameter that can balance between two network branches. During the joint training stage, the input of the model consists of image samples, ground-truth labels of locations and the corresponding text. Text locations in quadrangles can be converted to geometry and score maps $\mathbf{G} = \{\mathbf{Q}_n, \mathbf{S}_n\}_{n=1,...,N}$. With the provided table of characters, the ground-truth text labels can be mapped to the corresponding class labels. During training and testing, the $START$ and EOS (End-of-Sequence) symbols are added to tell the RNN decoder when to start and end in text sequence recognition.

To jointly train text localization and recognition network, the overall training procedure is divided into two stages. To overcome the shortage of small datasets, we utilize the vgg-synthetic data [12], i.e., VGG-Synth 800k, to train the base network using ImageNet pretrained model. Specifically, one training strategy is to train the detection branch until it almost converges to a steady point, and jointly train detection and recognition branches simultaneously. Another training strategy is to train the recognition branch at first instead, and then jointly train the whole network. These two training procedures are equal to achieve the final convergence in our attempts. To evaluate the performance on benchmarks, we finetune the VGG-Synth trained model on ICDAR-13, ICDAR-15, and Total-Text, respectively. To ease training and improve generalization by data argumentation, we randomly crop samples from images, resize the long-side to 512 pixels with mean value paddings. In experiments, we use multi-GPU clusters to train the model. The batch-size is 16 per GPU, and the number of RoIs in a batch is set to 32 per GPU for the recognition branch. The optimization algorithm is Adam, and the initial learning rate is set to 1×10^{-4}.

4   Experiments

To validate the performance of the proposed model, we conduct experiments on standard benchmarks, e.g., ICDAR-13, ICDAR-15, as the regular datasets, and the curved dataset, e.g., Total-Text, as the irregular dataset. We evaluate and compare the performance of the proposed model on end-to-end and word spotting tasks with other competitive approaches.

4.1   Datasets

ICDAR-13 and ICDAR-15. The widely used benchmarks for text reading include ICDAR-13 and ICDAR-15 [23] datasets. These datasets come from ICDAR 2013 and ICDAR 2015 Robust Reading Competitions, respectively. ICDAR-13 mainly includes horizontal text as focused scene text with word-level bounding box annotations and text labels. There are 229 images for training and 233 images for testing. Images from the ICDAR-15 dataset are captured in an incidental way with Google Glass, and word-level quadrangle annotations and text labels are available. There are 1000 images for training and 500 for testing.

VGG Synth. We also utilize the VGG synthetic dataset [12], which consists of 800, 000 images. Synthetic text strings are well rendered and blended with background images. The dataset provides detailed character-level, word-level and line-level annotations, which can be used for model pre-training.

Total-Text. The Total-Text dataset [7] released in ICDAR 2017 is a collection of irregular text. Unlike the previous ICDAR datasets, there are a number of curved text cases with multiple orientations. There are 1255 images in the training set, and 300 images in the test set with word-level polygon and text annotations.

4.2   Quantitative Comparisons with Separate Models

To validate the effectiveness of end-to-end training, we compare the text detection results of TextNet with the proposed detection branch only as a baseline. The evaluation protocols of text detection exactly follow the public criterion of ICDAR competitions, including the ICDAR-13, and ICDAR-13 DetEval and ICDAR-15. The IoU (intersection-of-union) threshold is 0.5 as the default value to decide whether it is a true positive sample or not. As shown in Table 1, our proposed TextNet achieves 91.28%, 91.35% and 87.37% in F-measure under ICDAR-13, ICDAR-13 DetEval and ICDAR-15 criterion, respectively. The end-to-end trained model can achieve +6.66%, +6.65% and +4.13% absolute F-measure improvement, compared with the detection model without recognition branch. Different from conventional text detectors, the joint trainable model with text recognition branch can help improve the representation power using shared backbone features, and improve both recall and precision during the detection stage.

For irregular cases, we conduct ablation experiments on Total-Text dataset, and compare the end-to-end trained results with the two-stage approach, which is developed using separately trained detection and recognition models. As shown in Table 4, the proposed TextNet can obtain substantial improvement over the two-stage approach in detection and end-to-end tasks in terms of F-measure. Different from previous two-stage and end-to-end training methods, the proposed approach can tackle irregular cases in a unified framework, especially curved text, which further demonstrate the effectiveness of TexNet.

4.3   Quantitative Comparisons with State-of-the-Art Results

Detection Results. To validate the text detection performance, we compare the proposed TextNet with other state-of-the-art text detection methods. Quantitative results on ICDAR-13 and ICDAR-15 in terms of recall, precision and F-measure are listed in Table 1, respectively. From the table, we find that the proposed algorithm can achieve state-of-the art results with at least +3% improvement in F-measure on ICDAR-13 and ICDAR-15 datasets. Note that * indicates the corresponding results have not been released in the original paper. The proposed jointly trainable model can improve the representation and generalization of text features in a shared backbone network by modeling detection and recognition in a unified network. To tackle regular and irregular cases with a two-directional RNN encoder, the spatial attention-based recognition branch can not only improve detection precision compared to other competitive results, but also increase the detection accuracy in terms of recall.

End-to-End Results. We conduct experiments on ICDAR-13, ICDAR-15, and Total-Text datasets, evaluating the results on regular and irregular benchmarks. For fair comparisons, the quantitative results of TextNet on ICDAR-13 and ICDAR-15 are shown in Tables 2 and 3 in terms of F-measure for end-to-end

Table 1. Text detection results on ICDAR-13 and ICDAR-15 for comparisons. Note that R, P and F in this table are short for recall, precision, and F-measure, respectively. In the table, 'TextNet-detection only' indicates that the model is trained for text detection without the help of recognition branch, and 'TextNet' is the end-to-end trainable model to localize and recognize results simultaneously.

Method	ICDAR-13			ICDAR-13 DetEval			ICDAR-15		
	R	P	F	R	P	F	R	P	F
TextBoxes [27]	83	88	85	89	83	86	*	*	*
CTPN [40]	*	*	*	83	93	88	52	74	61
Liu et al. [31]	*	*	*	*	*	*	68.22	73.23	70.64
SegLink [37]	*	*	*	83.0	87.7	85.3	76.8	73.1	75.0
SSTD [5]	86	88	87	86	89	88	73.86	80.23	76.91
WordSup [18]	*	*	*	87.53	93.34	90.34	77.03	79.33	78.16
RRPN [32]	*	*	*	88	**95**	91	77.13	83.52	80.20
EAST [45]	*	*	*	*	*	*	78.33	83.27	80.72
He et al. [17]	81	92	86	*	*	*	82	80	81
R2CNN [22]	*	*	*	82.59	93.55	87.73	79.68	85.62	82.54
FTSN [8]	81	92	86	*	*	*	80.07	88.65	84.14
Li et al. [25]	80.5	91.4	85.6	*	*	*	*	*	*
TextNet-detection only	82.01	83.40	84.62	82.15	87.40	84.70	80.83	85.79	83.24
TextNet	**89.39**	**93.26**	**91.28**	**89.19**	93.62	**91.35**	**85.41**	**89.42**	**87.37**

Table 2. End-to-end text reading and word spotting results on ICDAR-13. Note that S, W and G are short for strong, weakly and generic conditions, and TextNet indicates the multi-scale testing of the proposed model.

Method	End-to-end			Word spotting		
	S	W	G	S	W	G
Deep2Text II+	81.81	79.49	76.99	84.84	83.43	78.90
TextBoxes [27]	**91.57**	89.65	83.89	93.90	91.95	85.92
Li et al. [25]	91.08	**89.81**	**84.59**	94.16	92.42	**88.20**
TextSpotter [5]	89.0	86.0	77.0	92.0	89.0	81.0
TextNet	89.77	88.80	82.96	**94.59**	**93.48**	86.99

and word spotting tasks, following the evaluation protocols in ICDAR competitions under strong, weakly and generic conditions. These results demonstrate its superior performance over state-of-the-art approaches on ICDAR benchmarks, especially on ICDAR-15 dataset. On ICDAR-13 dataset, the end-to-end trainable model proposed by Li et al. [25] shows better performance for horizontal cases, but fails to cover cases in multi-orientations on ICDAR-15 dataset. For irregular cases, experimental results on Total-Text is illustrated in Table 4. We report the text localization and end-to-end results in terms of recall, precision

Table 3. End-to-end text reading and word spotting results on ICDAR-15 for comparison. Note that * indicates that the corresponding results have not been reported in the original paper.

Method	End-to-end			Word spotting		
	S	W	G	S	W	G
HUST MCLAB [38]	67.86	*	*	70.57	*	*
TextProposals+DictNet	53.30	49.61	47.18	56.00	52.26	49.73
TextSpotter [5]	54.0	51.0	47.0	58.0	53.0	51.0
TextNet	**78.66**	**74.90**	**60.45**	**82.38**	**78.43**	**62.36**

Table 4. Text detection and end-to-end recognition performance on irregular dataset, i.e., Total-Text. The detection results exactly follows the evaluation rules of Total-Text [7]. Note that * indicates that the corresponding results have not been reported yet in the original paper.

Method	Detection			End-to-end		
	Recall	Precision	F-measure	Recall	Precision	F-measure
DeconvNet [7]	33	40	36	*	*	*
Two-stage approach	**59.80**	61.05	60.42	43.10	47.12	45.02
TextNet	59.45	**68.21**	**63.53**	**56.39**	**51.85**	**54.02**

and F-measure. In the end-to-end task, the score of F-measure on Total-text is to evaluate the raw model output according to ground-truth labels without any vocabularies and language models. The results on irregular text demonstrate that the proposed TextNet have shown dramatic improvement over the baseline algorithm, which validates the effectiveness of the attention mechanism to tackle irregular text, especially for curve cases. Note that the most recent approaches [30] are designed for regular text and are difficult to cover curve cases.

4.4 Qualitative Results

Qualitative results of TextNet on ICDAR-13, ICDAR-15 and Total-Text datasets are shown in Figs. 5, 6, and 7, respectively. The localization quadrangles and the corresponding predicted text are drawn in figures. From these visual results, we can see that the proposed approach is able to tackle regular and irregular cases. The proposed algorithm can accurately localize and recognize these samples in an end-to-end fashion, which validates its effectiveness of the proposed approach.

4.5 Speed and Model Size

To evaluate the speed of TextNet, we calculate the average time cost during the testing stage. On the ICDAR-13 dataset, we can achieve 370.6 ms in terms of

Fig. 5. End-to-end visualized results of TextNet on ICDAR-13 dataset.

Fig. 6. End-to-end visualized results of TextNet on ICDAR-15 dataset.

average time cost using ResNet-50 without any model compression and acceleration. Note that the long-side length of testing images is normalized to 920, and
the time cost is evaluated using a single Tesla P40 GPU. The total number of

Fig. 7. End-to-end visualized results of TextNet on Total-Text dataset.

parameters of TextNet is 30M including ResNet-50, which includes 23M coefficients taking the most of parameters in the proposed model. By sharing backbone network, the jointly trained model not only reduces the time cost during predicting stage but also saves almost half of parameters compared with separately trained models.

5   Conclusions

In this paper, we have proposed a fully end-to-end trainable network, i.e., *TextNet*, which is capable of simultaneously localizing and recognizing regular and irregular text. The proposed network can extract multi-scale image features by scale-aware attention mechanism, and generate word proposals by direct regression of quadrangles to cover regular and irregular text regions. To further extract features-of-interest from text proposals, we have proposed to encode the well aligned feature maps in RNN, and utilize the spatial attention mechanism to generate text sequences. The experimental results on benchmark datasets have shown that the proposed *TextNet* can achieve superior performance on ICDAR regular datasets, and outperform existing approaches for irregular cases by a large margin.

References

1. Bahdanau, D., Cho, K., Bengio, Y.: Neural machine translation by jointly learning to align and translate. arXiv preprint arXiv:1409.0473 (2014)
2. Bissacco, A., Cummins, M., Netzer, Y., Neven, H.: Photo-OCR: reading text in uncontrolled conditions. In: Proceedings of ICCV, pp. 785–792 (2013)
3. Bluche, T.: Joint line segmentation and transcription for end-to-end handwritten paragraph recognition. In: Proceedings of NIPS, pp. 838–846 (2016)
4. Bluche, T., Louradour, J., Messina, R.: Scan, attend and read: end-to-end handwritten paragraph recognition with mdlstm attention. arXiv preprint arXiv:1604.03286 (2016)

5. Bušta, M., Neumann, L., Matas, J.: Deep textspotter: an end-to-end trainable scene text localization and recognition framework. In: Proceedings of ICCV (2017)
6. Chen, L.C., Yang, Y., Wang, J., Xu, W., Yuille, A.L.: Attention to scale: scale-aware semantic image segmentation. In: Proceedings of CVPR, pp. 3640–3649 (2016)
7. Chng, C.K., Chan, C.S.: Total-text: a comprehensive dataset for scene text detection and recognition. In: Proceedings of ICDAR (2017)
8. Dai, Y., Huang, Z., Gao, Y., Chen, K.: Fused text segmentation networks for multi-oriented scene text detection. arXiv preprint arXiv:1709.03272 (2017)
9. Girshick, R.: Fast R-CNN. arXiv preprint arXiv:1504.08083 (2015)
10. Graves, A., Fernández, S., Gomez, F., Schmidhuber, J.: Connectionist temporal classification: labelling unsegmented sequence data with recurrent neural networks. In: Proceedings of ICML, pp. 369–376. ACM (2006)
11. Graves, A., Mohamed, A.R., Hinton, G.: Speech recognition with deep recurrent neural networks. In: Proceedings of ICASSP, pp. 6645–6649 (2013)
12. Gupta, A., Vedaldi, A., Zisserman, A.: Synthetic data for text localisation in natural images. In: Proceedings of CVPR, pp. 2315–2324 (2016)
13. He, K., Gkioxari, G., Dollár, P., Girshick, R.: Mask R-CNN. In: Proceedings of ICCV, pp. 2980–2988 (2017)
14. He, K., Zhang, X., Ren, S., Sun, J.: Deep residual learning for image recognition. In: Proceedings of CVPR, pp. 770–778 (2016)
15. He, P., Huang, W., Qiao, Y., Loy, C.C., Tang, X.: Reading scene text in deep convolutional sequences. In: Proceedings of AAAI, vol. 16, pp. 3501–3508 (2016)
16. He, T., Tian, Z., Huang, W., Shen, C., Qiao, Y., Sun, C.: An end-to-end textspotter with explicit alignment and attention. CoRR abs/1803.03474 (2018)
17. He, W., Zhang, X.Y., Yin, F., Liu, C.L.: Deep direct regression for multi-oriented scene text detection. In: Proceedings of ICCV (2017)
18. Hu, H., Zhang, C., Luo, Y., Wang, Y., Han, J., Ding, E.: Wordsup: exploiting word annotations for character based text detection. In: Proceedings of ICCV (2017)
19. Huang, L., Yang, Y., Deng, Y., Yu, Y.: Densebox: unifying landmark localization with end to end object detection. arXiv preprint arXiv:1509.04874 (2015)
20. Jaderberg, M., Simonyan, K., Vedaldi, A., Zisserman, A.: Reading text in the wild with convolutional neural networks. Int. J. Comput. Vis. 116(1), 1–20 (2016)
21. Jaderberg, M., Simonyan, K., Zisserman, A., et al.: Spatial transformer networks. In: Proceedings of NIPS, pp. 2017–2025 (2015)
22. Jiang, Y., et al.: R2CNN: rotational region CNN for orientation robust scene text detection. arXiv preprint arXiv:1706.09579 (2017)
23. Karatzas, D., et al.: ICDAR 2015 competition on robust reading. In: Proceedings of ICDAR, pp. 1156–1160. IEEE (2015)
24. Lee, C.Y., Osindero, S.: Recursive recurrent nets with attention modeling for OCR in the wild. In: Proceedings of CVPR, pp. 2231–2239 (2016)
25. Li, H., Wang, P., Shen, C.: Towards end-to-end text spotting with convolutional recurrent neural networks. In: Proceedings of ICCV (2017)
26. Liao, M., Shi, B., Bai, X.: Textboxes++: a single-shot oriented scene text detector. arXiv preprint arXiv:1801.02765 (2018)
27. Liao, M., Shi, B., Bai, X., Wang, X., Liu, W.: TextBoxes: a fast text detector with a single deep neural network. In: Proceedings of AAAI, pp. 4161–4167 (2017)
28. Lin, T.Y., Dollár, P., Girshick, R., He, K., Hariharan, B., Belongie, S.: Feature pyramid networks for object detection. In: Proceedings of CVPR (2017)

29. Liu, W., et al.: SSD: single shot MultiBox detector. In: Leibe, B., Matas, J., Sebe, N., Welling, M. (eds.) ECCV 2016. LNCS, vol. 9905, pp. 21–37. Springer, Cham (2016). https://doi.org/10.1007/978-3-319-46448-0_2

30. Liu, X., Liang, D., Yan, S., Chen, D., Qiao, Y., Yan, J.: FOTS: fast oriented text spotting with a unified network. arXiv preprint arXiv:1801.01671 (2018)

31. Liu, Y., Jin, L.: Deep matching prior network: toward tighter multi-oriented text detection. In: Proceedings of CVPR (2017)

32. Ma, J., et al.: Arbitrary-oriented scene text detection via rotation proposals. arXiv preprint arXiv:1703.01086 (2017)

33. Neumann, L., Matas, J.: Real-time scene text localization and recognition. In: Proceedings of CVPR, pp. 3538–3545 (2012)

34. Redmon, J., Farhadi, A.: Yolo9000: better, faster, stronger. arXiv preprint 1612 (2016)

35. Ren, S., He, K., Girshick, R., Sun, J.: Faster R-CNN: towards real-time object detection with region proposal networks. In: Proceedings of NIPS, pp. 91–99 (2015)

36. Ronneberger, O., Fischer, P., Brox, T.: U-net: convolutional networks for biomedical image segmentation. In: Navab, N., Hornegger, J., Wells, W.M., Frangi, A.F. (eds.) MICCAI 2015. LNCS, vol. 9351, pp. 234–241. Springer, Cham (2015). https://doi.org/10.1007/978-3-319-24574-4_28

37. Shi, B., Bai, X., Belongie, S.: Detecting oriented text in natural images by linking segments. In: Proceedings of CVPR (2017)

38. Shi, B., Bai, X., Yao, C.: An end-to-end trainable neural network for image-based sequence recognition and its application to scene text recognition. IEEE Trans. Pattern Anal. Mach. Intell. **39**(11), 2298–2304 (2017)

39. Shi, B., Wang, X., Lyu, P., Yao, C., Bai, X.: Robust scene text recognition with automatic rectification. In: Proceedings of CVPR, pp. 4168–4176 (2016)

40. Tian, Z., Huang, W., He, T., He, P., Qiao, Y.: Detecting text in natural image with connectionist text proposal network. In: Leibe, B., Matas, J., Sebe, N., Welling, M. (eds.) ECCV 2016. LNCS, vol. 9912, pp. 56–72. Springer, Cham (2016). https://doi.org/10.1007/978-3-319-46484-8_4

41. Wang, T., Wu, D.J., Coates, A., Ng, A.Y.: End-to-end text recognition with convolutional neural networks. In: Proceedings of ICPR, pp. 3304–3308 (2012)

42. Wojna, Z., et al.: Attention-based extraction of structured information from street view imagery. In: Proceedings of ICDAR (2017)

43. Xu, K., et al.: Show, attend and tell: Neural image caption generation with visual attention. In: Proceedings of ICML, pp. 2048–2057 (2015)

44. Yang, X., He, D., Zhou, Z., Kifer, D., Giles, C.L.: Learning to read irregular text with attention mechanisms. In: Proceedings of IJCAI (2017)

45. Zhou, X., et al.: EAST: an efficient and accurate scene text detector. In: Proceedings of CVPR (2017)

Text2Shape: Generating Shapes from Natural Language by Learning Joint Embeddings

Kevin Chen[1](✉), Christopher B. Choy[1], Manolis Savva[2,3], Angel X. Chang[2,4],
Thomas Funkhouser[5], and Silvio Savarese[1]

[1] Stanford University, Stanford, USA
kevin.chen@cs.stanford.edu
[2] Simon Fraser University, Burnaby, Canada
[3] Facebook AI Research, Menlo Park, USA
[4] Eloquent Labs, Redwood City, USA
[5] Princeton University, Princeton, USA

Abstract. We present a method for generating colored 3D shapes from natural language. To this end, we first learn joint embeddings of freeform text descriptions and colored 3D shapes. Our model combines and extends learning by association and metric learning approaches to learn implicit cross-modal connections, and produces a joint representation that captures the many-to-many relations between language and physical properties of 3D shapes such as color and shape. To evaluate our approach, we collect a large dataset of natural language descriptions for physical 3D objects in the ShapeNet dataset. With this learned joint embedding we demonstrate text-to-shape retrieval that outperforms baseline approaches. Using our embeddings with a novel conditional Wasserstein GAN framework, we generate colored 3D shapes from text. Our method is the first to connect natural language text with realistic 3D objects exhibiting rich variations in color, texture, and shape detail.

1 Introduction

Language allows people to communicate thoughts, feelings, and ideas. Research in artificial intelligence has long sought to mimic this component of human cognition. One such goal is to bridge the natural language and visual modalities through tasks such as captioning, visual question answering (VQA), or image generation. However, one unexplored area between language and vision is how to connect language with full visual 3D shape structures and attributes. Imagine describing a "round glass coffee table with four wooden legs", and having a matching colored 3D shape be retrieved or generated. We refer to these tasks as (i) *text-to-shape retrieval* and (ii) *text-to-shape generation*.

Electronic supplementary material The online version of this chapter (https://doi.org/10.1007/978-3-030-20893-6_7) contains supplementary material, which is available to authorized users.

Systems with such capabilities have applications in computational design, fabrication, and augmented/virtual reality (AR/VR). Text-to-shape retrieval systems can be useful for querying 3D shape databases (TurboSquid, 3D Warehouse, Yobi3D, etc.) without reliance on human annotation of individual shapes. Likewise, text-to-shape generation can facilitate 3D design, circumventing our dependence on expensive modeling software (e.g., Maya, 3DS Max, Blender) with steep learning curves and time-consuming manual design. A text-to-shape generation system can initialize shapes with basic attributes defined using natural language descriptions. Such a technology can save time and money, and allow inexperienced users to design shapes for fabrication, AR, or VR.

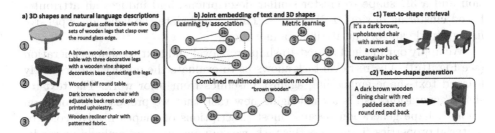

Fig. 1. By leveraging our dataset of natural language descriptions paired with colored 3D shapes (a), our method extends learning by association and metric learning to jointly learn text and 3D shape embeddings which cluster similar shapes and descriptions, establishing implicit semantic connections (dashed lines) (b). We apply our learned embedding to two tasks: text-to-shape retrieval (c1), and the challenging new task of text-to-shape generation (c2).

To achieve this goal, we need a system that understands natural language and 3D shapes. One way to connect language with shapes is to use a joint embedding space for text and shapes. While there has been prior work on text to image embedding [12,13,20,30,33] and image to shape embedding [15], there has been no prior work on text to 3D shape embedding to the best of our knowledge. Moreover, prior approaches in learning text-image representations rely on fine-grained, category-level class or attribute labels [20,21,23,35]. Such annotations are not only expensive, but also ill-defined: should we classify objects by color, material, or style? Ideally, we would like to learn a joint embedding of text and 3D shapes directly from natural language descriptions, without relying on fine-grained category or attribute annotations. However, connecting natural language to 3D shapes is challenging because there is no simple one-to-one mapping between text and 3D shapes (e.g., both "round table" and "circular table" can describe similar real objects). Given a shape there are many ways to describe it, and given a natural language description there are many possible shapes that match the description.

In this paper, we first present a method for learning a joint text and shape representation space directly from natural language descriptions of 3D shape instances, followed by our text-to-shape generation framework. Unlike related work in text-to-image synthesis [20, 22, 35], we do not rely on fine-grained category-level class labels or pre-training on large datasets. Furthermore, we train the text and shape encoding components jointly in an end-to-end fashion, associating similar points in our data both within a modality (text-to-text or shape-to-shape) and between the two modalities (text-to-shape).

To do this, we take inspiration from recent work on learning by association [10] to establish implicit cross-modal links between similar descriptions and shape instances, and combine this with a metric learning scheme [27] which strengthens links between similar instances in each modality (see Fig. 1(b)). Our approach leverages only instance-level correspondences between a text description and a 3D shape to cluster similar descriptions, and induces an attribute-based clustering of similar 3D shapes. Thus, we obviate the need for expensive fine-grained category or attribute annotations.

We apply our method to text-to-shape retrieval and text-to-shape generation (see Fig. 1(c)). The retrieval task allows us to evaluate the quality of our jointly learned text-shape embedding against baselines from prior work. The text-to-shape generation task is a challenging new task that we propose. We focus on colored shape generation because most descriptions of shapes involve color or material properties. To address this task, we combine our joint embedding model with a novel conditional Wasserstein GAN framework, providing greater output quality and diversity compared to a conditional GAN formulation. Lastly, we use vector embedding arithmetic and our generator to manipulate shape attributes.

For realistic and challenging evaluation, we collect 75K natural language descriptions for 15K chair and table shapes in the ShapeNet [2] dataset. To facilitate controlled evaluation, we also introduce a dataset of procedurally generated colored primitives (spheres, pyramids, boxes, etc.) with synthetic text captions. Our experimental results on these datasets show that our model outperforms the baselines by a large margin for both the retrieval and generation tasks. In summary, our contributions are as follows:

- We propose an end-to-end instance-level association learning framework for cross-modal associations (text and 3D shapes).
- We demonstrate that our joint embedding of text and 3D shapes can be used for text-to-shape retrieval, outperforming baseline methods.
- We introduce the task of text to colored shape generation and address it with our learned joint embeddings and a novel Conditional Wasserstein GAN.
- We assemble two datasets of 3D shape color voxelizations and corresponding text: (i) ShapeNet objects with natural language descriptions, and (ii) procedurally generated geometric primitives with synthetic text descriptions.

2   Related Work

We review work in related areas such as multimodal representation learning, text-to-image synthesis, and 3D shape generation.

Learning Representations for Visual Descriptions. Reed et al. [20] learn text embeddings which capture visual information. This work was the basis for several text-to-image synthesis works [21,22,35]. While this method [20] was applied to the text-to-image problem [21,22,35], it utilizes pre-training on large image datasets. More importantly, it relies on fine-grained category-level labels for each image (e.g. bird species), which are expensive to collect and not always well-defined (e.g., should 3D chairs be classified by color, material, or style?). In contrast, we do not rely on fine-grained category or attribute labels and use no pre-training.

Other works which also attempt to learn multimodal representations include Ngiam et al. [18], in which they present a stacked multimodal autoencoder to learn joint audio and video representations. Srivastava and Salakhutdinov [28] train a deep Boltzmann machine to model images and text tags. More recent work in text-image joint embeddings [12,29] focuses on other aspects such as decoding distributed representations and using unsupervised learning.

Metric Learning. Metric learning using deep neural networks has gained significant attention in recent years. Common methods include using a contrastive loss [3], triplet loss [25,31], or N-pair loss [26]. We extend the method of Song et al. [27] in our joint representation learning approach. Since our problem is learning a joint metric space across different modalities, our framework is similar in spirit to prior cross-modal metric learning formulations [30] in that we compute distances both within modality (text-text) and across modalities (text-shape). However, we use a smoothed, triplet-based similarity loss.

Generative Models and Generative Adversarial Networks (GANs). Generative models are particularly relevant to our text-to-shape generation task. Recent works have shown the capability of neural networks to understand semantics [5] and generate realistic images [7,19]. Reed et al. [22] explored the challenging problem of text to image synthesis using GANs. They separately train a text embedding [20], and then use GANs to generate images. More recent work has improved text-to-image generation [21,35]. StackGAN [35] and related works [34,36], for example, focuses on an orthogonal aspect of the problem and can in fact be combined with our approach. Unlike these works, we do not use fine-grained labels, making our method more scalable. Lastly, Xu et al. [33] also propose an interesting method for image generation by attending to words in text descriptions.

3D Voxel Generation. Common approaches for 3D voxel generation using deep learning rely on losses such as voxel-wise cross entropy [4,6]. GANs have also been used to generate 3D shape voxelizations from noise or shape inputs [14,32]. Our framework builds upon 3D GANs but performs colored voxel generation from *freeform text* and uses a Wasserstein GAN formulation [1]. To our knowledge, we are the first to address *text to colored voxel* generation.

| A large red sphere | A large short wide green box | The blue cone is large tall | A cushioned chair which is grey in color. The legs are small. | A rectangular wooden coffee table with an iron base | White square table with four legs that curve out from the base |

Fig. 2. Our proposed 3D voxel – text datasets. Left: Procedurally generated primitives dataset with associated generated text descriptions. Right: Voxelizations of ShapeNet 3D CAD models with natural language descriptions.

3 Datasets

We address the problem of learning joint representations for freeform text descriptions and 3D shapes (CAD models). To train and evaluate methods on this task, we introduce two new datasets: a dataset of human-designed 3D CAD objects from ShapeNet [2], augmented with natural language descriptions, and a controlled, procedurally generated dataset of 3D geometric primitives (Fig. 2).

Data Representation. Our datasets consist of text description – 3D shape voxel grid pairs (x, s) where x is the textual description of a shape $s \in [0, 1]^{v^3 \cdot c}$. Here, x is an arbitrary length vector of word indices where each word index corresponds to a word in the vocabulary, v is the maximum number of voxels along any single dimension, and c is the number of channels per voxel (4 for RGB + occupancy).

ShapeNet Objects and Natural Language Descriptions. To create a realistic dataset with real 3D objects and natural language descriptions, we use the ShapeNet [2] table and chair object categories (with 8,447 and 6,591 instances, respectively). These 3D shapes were created by human designers to accurately represent real objects. We choose the table and chair categories because they contain many instances with fine-grained attribute variations in geometry, color and material. We augment this shape dataset with 75,344 natural language descriptions (5 descriptions on average per shape) provided by people on the Amazon Mechanical Turk crowdsourcing platform (see Fig. 1(a)). We then produce color voxelizations of the CAD 3D meshes using a hybrid view-based and surface sampling method, followed by downsampling with a low-pass filter in voxel space. The process for collecting natural language descriptions, the algorithm for producing color voxelizations, and the overall dataset construction are described in more detail in the supplemental material. This large-scale dataset provides many challenging natural language descriptions paired with realistic 3D shapes.

Primitive Shapes. To enable systematic quantitative evaluation of our model, we create a dataset of 3D geometric primitives with corresponding text descriptions. This data is generated by voxelizing 6 types of primitives (cuboids, ellipsoids, cylinders, cones, pyramids, and tori) in 14 color variations and 9 size variations.

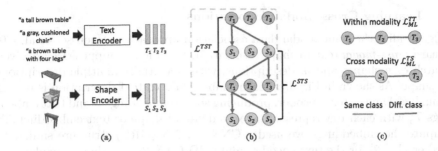

Fig. 3. Our joint representation learning approach. Text and shape encoders compute embeddings (a). Instances of each modality make round trips back to similar instances of the same modality, establishing cross-modal associations (b). Metric learning is applied within and across modalities (c).

The color and size variations are subjected to random perturbations generating 10 samples from each of 756 possible primitive configurations, thus creating 7560 voxelized shapes. We then create corresponding text descriptions with a template-based approach that fills in attribute words for shape, size, and color in several orderings to produce sentences such as *"a large red cylinder is narrow and tall"* (see supplemental material for more details). In total, we generate 192,602 descriptions, for an average of about 255 descriptions per primitive configuration. Such synthetic text does not match natural language but it does allow for an easy benchmark with a clear mapping to the attributes of each primitive shape.

4   Joint Text–3D Shape Representation Learning

Figure 1(b) shows an illustration of the components of our approach, with explicit text-shape links in solid lines and implicit similarity links in dashed lines. We would like our joint embedding to: (i) cluster similar text together and similar shapes together, (ii) keep text descriptions close to their associated shape instance, and (iii) separate text from shapes that are not similar. To address (i), we generalize the learning by association approach [10] to handle multiple modalities (Sect. 4.1) and to use instance-level associations between a description and a shape (Sect. 4.2). By using text-shape-text round trips we establish implicit connections between separate text and shape instances that are semantically similar (e.g. "round table" pulling shapes 1 and 2 together in Fig. 1). To enforce properties (ii) and (iii) in the embedding space, we jointly optimize an association learning objective with metric learning (Sect. 4.3). Our combined multimodal association model anchors text to associated shape instances while allowing latent similarities between different shapes and text to emerge.

4.1   Learning Cross-Modal Associations

We generalize the same-modal data association approach of Haeusser et al. [10] to learn *cross-modal* text-to-shape associations (see Fig. 3). Suppose we are given a batch of n shapes and m descriptions, with potentially multiple descriptions per shape. As shown in Fig. 3(a), each shape and each text description is passed through a shape or text encoder, producing shape embeddings S and text embeddings T, with each row representing an individual shape or text embedding. To compute the embeddings, we used a CNN + RNN (GRU) structure similar to Reed et al. [22] for the text encoder, and a 3D-CNN for the shape encoder.

We define the text-shape similarity matrix $M_{ij} = T_i \cdot S_j$ where T_i and S_j are the ith and jth rows of the corresponding matrices. To convert this into the probability of description i associating with shape j (as opposed to another shape in S), we pass these through a softmax layer: $P_{ij}^{TS} = e^{M_{ij}}/\sum_{j'} e^{M_{ij'}}$. Similarly, we can compute the probability of associating shape i to description j by replacing M with $M^\top$. The round-trip probability for associating description i with certain shapes and then associating those shapes with description j in T is then: $P_{ij}^{TST} = (P^{TS} P^{ST})_{ij}$. We abbreviate this text-shape-text round trip as TST (see Fig. 3(b) dashed box). For a given description i, our goal is to have P_{ij}^{TST} be uniform over the descriptions j which are similar to description i. Thus, we define the round-trip loss $\mathcal{L}_R^{TST}$ as the cross-entropy between the distribution P^{TST} and the target uniform distribution.

To associate text descriptions with all possible matching shapes, we also impose a loss on the probability of associating each shape with any description: $P_j^{\text{visit}} = \sum_i P_{ij}^{TS}/m$. We maximize the entropy on this distribution P^H, using an entropy loss $\mathcal{L}_H^{TST}$ computed from the cross entropy between the P_j^{visit} and the uniform distribution over the shapes. Thus, our cross-modal association loss is:

$$\mathcal{L}^{TST} = \mathcal{L}_R^{TST} + \lambda \mathcal{L}_H^{TST} \tag{1}$$

4.2   Instance-Level Associations

The approach described in Sect. 4.1 relies on fine-grained category-level classification labels for each text description (e.g. a label for all brown chairs and a different label for all blue chairs). These fine-grained annotations are expensive to obtain and are not necessarily well-defined for 3D shapes from ShapeNet [2] where descriptions can contain multiple colors or materials. Thus, we extend the above approach to work without such fine-grained *category-level* annotations, making the method more scalable and practical.

We assume each shape belongs to its own *instance-level* class containing its corresponding descriptions. These instance-level labels are appropriate for the association learning approach (Sect. 4.1) since it does not explicitly separate descriptions and shapes not labeled to correspond to each other. Thus, our cross-modal association learning is more relaxed than previous approaches [20,30] that use direct supervision over cross-modal relationships, allowing us to learn cross-modal associations between descriptions and shapes that were not labeled as corresponding (e.g. two similar chairs, each with its own text descriptions).

Moreover, we extend the association learning approach with additional round trips as shown in Fig. 3(b). Our experiments show this greatly improves the performance of our model for the multimodal problem. In addition to enforcing a loss over the text-shape-text (TST) round trip, we impose a shape-text-shape (STS) loss $\mathcal{L}^{STS}$ which takes a form similar to Eq. (1). This ensures that the shapes are associated with all of the text descriptions and provides additional supervision, which is beneficial when our dataset has only instance-level labels.

4.3 Multimodal Metric Learning

To facilitate learning cross-modal associations, we impose metric learning losses. This serves as a bootstrapping method which improves the cross-modal associations significantly compared to using either association learning [9] or metric learning [27] (ML) alone.

As in Sect. 4.1, we define similarity between embeddings with the dot product. Given a triplet (x_i, x_j, x_k) of text description embeddings in which (x_i, x_j) belong to the same instance class (positive pair) and (x_i, x_k) belong to different instance classes (negative pair), our metric learning constraint is: $F(x_i; \theta) \cdot F(x_j; \theta) > F(x_i; \theta) \cdot F(x_k; \theta) + \alpha$, where F maps to the metric space and α is the margin. We use a variation of metric learning that uses a soft max to approximate hard negative mining [27] and combine it with the similarity constraint above in our text-to-text loss:

$$\mathcal{L}_{ML}^{TT} = \frac{1}{2|\mathcal{P}|} \sum_{(i,j)\in\mathcal{P}} [\log(V_i + V_j) - m_{i,j}]_+^2 \qquad (2)$$

where $m_{i,j}$ denotes the similarity between x_i and x_j, and $V_l = \sum_{k\in\mathcal{N}_l} \exp\{\alpha + m_{l,k}\}$. Here, $\mathcal{N}_l$ is a negative set, defined as the set of indices that belong to an instance class other than the class l is in, and $\mathcal{P}$ is a positive set in which both indices i and j belong to the same instance class.

The above approach can cluster similar text descriptions together and separate dissimilar text descriptions. To extend this for cross-modal similarities, we define cross-modal constraints with anchors from each modality (see Fig. 3(c)): $F(x_i; \theta) \cdot F(y_j; \theta) > F(x_i; \theta) \cdot F(y_k; \theta) + \alpha$, where x represents text embeddings and y represents shape embeddings. The corresponding text-to-shape loss $\mathcal{L}_{ML}^{TS}$ can be derived similarly to Eq. (2).

4.4 Full Multimodal Loss

We combine the association losses with the metric learning losses to form the final loss function used to train the text and shape encoders:

$$\mathcal{L}_{total} = \mathcal{L}^{TST} + \mathcal{L}^{STS} + \gamma(\mathcal{L}_{ML}^{TT} + \mathcal{L}_{ML}^{TS}) \qquad (3)$$

5   Generating Colored 3D Shapes from Text

We apply our joint representation learning approach to text-to-shape generation using generative adversarial networks. The model is comprised of three main components: the text encoder, the generator, and the critic. The text encoder maps the text into latent representations. The latent vectors are concatenated with a noise vector and then passed to the generator, which constructs the output shapes. Lastly, the critic determines both how realistic the generated outputs look and how closely they match with the corresponding text descriptions. Details for the architecture are in the supplemental material.

GANs are ideal for text-to-shape generation because they encourage the model to generate outputs with the correct properties while avoiding the use of per-voxel constraints. This is crucial because the same description should be able to generate different shapes which all capture the specified attributes. Penalizing the model for generating shapes which capture the correct attributes but do not match a specific model instance would be incorrect. Thus, the conditional GAN plays a key role in our text-to-shape framework.

Our formulation is based on the Wasserstein GAN [1,8] which improves output diversity while avoiding mode collapse issues with traditional GANs. To our knowledge, we present the first conditional Wasserstein GAN. Rather than using the traditional conditional GAN [17] approach, we sample batches of matching and mismatching text descriptions and shapes, in line with Reed et al. [22]. In particular, we sample matching text-shape pairs, mismatching text-shape pairs, and text for the generator from the marginal distribution p_T. The critic evaluates not only how realistic the shapes look but also how well they correspond to the descriptions. Thus, our objective is the following:

$$\mathcal{L}_{\text{CWGAN}} = \mathbb{E}_{t \sim p_T}[D(t, G(t))] + \mathbb{E}_{(\tilde{t}, \tilde{s}) \sim p_{\text{mis}}}[D(\tilde{t}, \tilde{s})]$$
$$- 2\mathbb{E}_{(\hat{t}, \hat{s}) \sim p_{\text{mat}}}[D(\hat{t}, \hat{s})] + \lambda_{GP}\mathcal{L}_{GP} \tag{4}$$

$$\mathcal{L}_{GP} = \mathbb{E}_{(\bar{t}, \bar{s}) \sim p_{GP}}[(\|\nabla_{\bar{t}}D(\bar{t}, \bar{s})\|_2 - 1)^2 + (\|\nabla_{\bar{s}}D(\bar{t}, \bar{s})\|_2 - 1)^2] \tag{5}$$

where D is the critic, G is the generator, and p_{mat} and p_{mis} are matching text-shape and mismatching text-shape pairs, respectively. For enforcing the gradient penalty, rather than sampling along straight lines as in Guljarani et al. [8], we randomly choose samples (p_{GP}) from the real distribution p_{mat} (with probability 0.5) or from the generated fake voxelizations. Note that t refers to text embeddings (Sect. 4) concatenated with randomly sampled noise vectors.

6   Experiments

We evaluate our learned joint representation through retrieval and generation experiments. In Sect. 6.1 we quantitatively evaluate the representations on the primitives dataset for text-to-shape retrieval, and show qualitative results on the ShapeNet dataset. In Sect. 6.2 we compare our text-to-shape generation results with baselines for a voxel resolution of 32. Lastly, we visualize different dimensions of the learned embeddings and show generation results using vector arithmetic in Sect. 6.3.

6.1 Retrieval Task

We evaluate on the text-to-shape retrieval task, where we are given a sentence and we retrieve the nearest shapes in the joint embedding space. Ideally, we would like to see that the retrieved shapes closely correspond with the query sentence. Here, we show results for the text-to-shape retrieval task. Additional experiments for text-to-text, shape-to-shape, and shape-to-text retrieval are in the supplemental material. Our goal in these experiments is to verify that our method produces reasonable embeddings that cluster semantically similar descriptions and shapes using only text-shape instance-level correspondences.

The primitives dataset is constructed such that each shape-color-size configuration is a single class with text describing only that class and no others. This admits a quantitative retrieval evaluation where the goal is to retrieve descriptions and shapes belonging to the same configuration. For the ShapeNet dataset it is possible that a description could apply to multiple shapes (e.g. "brown chair"), but we only have ground truth association for one shape. Thus, we show quantitative results for the retrieval task on the primitives dataset (Table 1) and qualitative results for the ShapeNet dataset (Fig. 4). Quantitative and qualitative ShapeNet retrieval results comparing our method with baselines are included in the supplemental material.

Table 1. Text-to-shape retrieval evaluation on primitives dataset. Our approach significantly outperforms baselines from prior work.

Metric	Random	DS-SJE [20]	LBA-TST [10]	ML	LBA-MM	Full-TST	Full-MM
RR@1	0.24	81.77	5.06	25.93	91.13	94.24	**95.07**
RR@5	0.76	90.70	15.29	57.24	98.27	97.55	**99.08**
NDCG@5	0.27	81.29	5.92	25.00	91.90	95.20	**95.51**

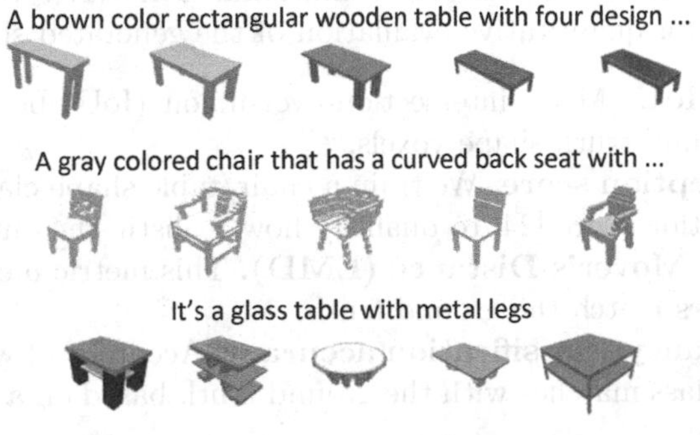

A brown color rectangular wooden table with four design ...

A gray colored chair that has a curved back seat with ...

It's a glass table with metal legs

Fig. 4. Text-to-shape retrieval. Each row shows the five nearest neighbors to the text in our learned embedding, which match in category, color, and shape. (Color figure online)

We compare our model with the deep symmetric structured joint embedding (DS-SJE) by Reed et al. [20] and the original formulation of learning by association [10] with only TST round trips (LBA-TST). We also decompose our full model into the following: association learning only with both round trips (LBA-MM), metric learning (ML) only, combined LBA and ML with TST round trip only (Full-TST), and the full combined model (Full-MM). MM for "multimodal" denotes using both TST and STS losses. We measure retrieval performance using normalized discounted cumulative gain (NDCG) [11], a commonly used information retrieval metric, and recall rate (RR@k) [27], which considers a retrieval successful if at least one sample in the top k retrievals is of the correct class.

Table 1 shows that our full model achieves the best performance. We see that the DS-SJE method [20], which requires a pre-trained model, works well, as it directly optimizes for this objective. Our association learning–only approach with additional round trips (LBA-MM) performs significantly better, largely due to the simplistic nature of the primitives dataset. We found that for the ShapeNet dataset, the LBA-MM model struggled to learn a joint embedding space of text and shapes (see the supplemental material for more details). Our full model (Full-MM) performs the best on both the primitives and ShapeNet dataset. Figure 4 shows that the retrieved shapes generally match the query sentence. These examples show that our encoders cluster together similar descriptions and similar shapes despite the fact that retrieved neighbors come from different instances.

6.2   Text-to-Shape Generation Task

Can our learned joint representation be used for shape synthesis? To answer this question, we apply our learned embedding to the novel task of text-to-shape generation. We compare our representation learning and Wasserstein GAN approach (CWGAN) with the GAN-INT-CLS text-to-image synthesis method [22], which uses DS-SJE [20] with the coarse chair/table labels for learning embeddings. We also compare with using our joint embeddings in conjunction with GAN-CLS [22] (using the sampling method described in Sect. 5), which we abbreviate as CGAN since it is a variant of the conditional GAN [17]. We introduce the following metrics for quantitative evaluation of the generated shapes:

- **Occupancy: IoU.** Mean intersection-over-union (IoU) between generated voxels and ground truth shape voxels.
- **Realism: inception score.** We train a chair/table shape classifier and compute the inception score [24] to quantify how realistic the outputs look.
- **Color: Earth Mover's Distance (EMD).** This metric measures how well generated colors match the ground truth.
- **Color/occupancy: classification accuracy.** Accuracy of whether the generated shape class matches with the ground truth based on a shape classifier.

Table 2 shows that the CGAN model trained with our embedding outperforms the GAN-INT-CLS on all metrics. The CWGAN model further improves on all

Table 2. Text-to-shape generation evaluation on ShapeNet dataset.

Method	IoU↑	Inception↑	EMD↓	Class Acc.↑
GAN-INT-CLS [22]	9.51	1.95	0.5039	95.57
Ours (CGAN)	6.06	1.95	0.4768	**97.48**
Ours (CWGAN)	**9.64**	**1.96**	**0.4443**	97.37

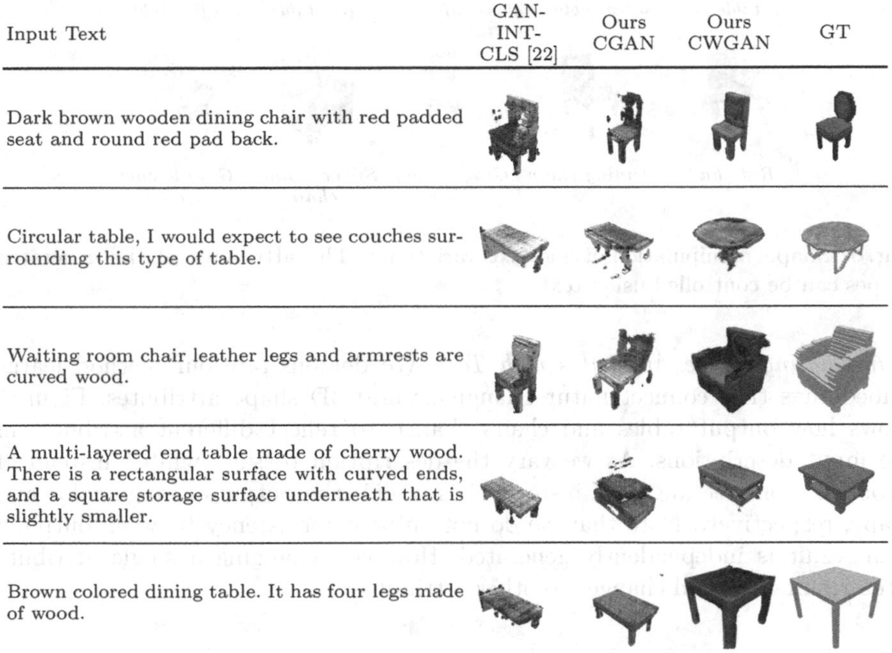

Input Text	GAN-INT-CLS [22]	Ours CGAN	Ours CWGAN	GT
Dark brown wooden dining chair with red padded seat and round red pad back.				
Circular table, I would expect to see couches surrounding this type of table.				
Waiting room chair leather legs and armrests are curved wood.				
A multi-layered end table made of cherry wood. There is a rectangular surface with curved ends, and a square storage surface underneath that is slightly smaller.				
Brown colored dining table. It has four legs made of wood.				

Fig. 5. Example text-to-shape generations. Our CWGAN approach is correctly conditioned by the input text, generating shapes that match the described attributes. The baseline approach struggles to generate plausible shapes. Additional results can be found in the supplementary material.

metrics except class accuracy. Qualitatively, Fig. 5 shows that the GAN-INT-CLS text-to-image synthesis method [22] struggles to generate color and occupancy distributions which correspond with the text. This is largely attributed to poor embeddings learned using coarse chair/table labels. Our CGAN achieves comparable conditioning and generation results without relying on additional class labels, but there are still significant structural and color artifacts. Lastly, our CWGAN generates the most realistic shapes with more natural color distributions and better conditioning on the text compared to the baselines. For example, our model correctly generates a chair with red padding on the seat and backrest in Fig. 5 (first row). Likewise, the table in the 4th row has multiple layers as desired. However, there is room for improvement: the table is not fully supported by its legs, and the circular table (row 2) has erratic coloring.

| White coffee table | Wooden coffee table | Rectangular glass coffee table | Glass round coffee table | Red round coffee table |

| Red chair | Dining chair | Gray dining chair | Silver leather chair | Gray leather chair |

Fig. 6. Shape manipulation using text variations. The attributes of the generated shapes can be controlled using text.

Manipulating Shape Attributes with Text. We demonstrate our method learns embeddings that connect natural language and 3D shape attributes. Figure 6 shows how output tables and chairs change to reflect different attributes in the input descriptions. As we vary the description to say "white" instead of "wooden", or "rectangular" instead of "round", the outputs change color and shape, respectively. Note that we do not enforce consistency between outputs; each result is independently generated. However, changing a single attribute often results in small changes to other attributes.

6.3   Analysis of Learned Representation

Activation Visualization. We visualize the representations learned by our model to demonstrate that they capture shape attributes. Using the text and shape encoders, we compute embeddings for ShapeNet test set objects to show that individual dimensions in our representation correlate with semantic attributes such as category, color, and shape.

Figure 7 shows a saturated bar in each row representing activation in a given dimension of the text embedding for the shape above. In the top-left, one dimension is sensitive to the shape category (chair vs. table). In the subsequent rows, other dimensions are sensitive to physical shape (rectangular vs. round tables) and color (white vs. brown vs. red). Further research in this direction to disentangle representations could enable generating shapes by composing attributes.

Vector Arithmetic. Mikolov et al. [16] demonstrated vector arithmetic on text embeddings (e.g., 'King' − 'Man' + 'Woman' ≈ 'Queen'). Following this, work on GANs (such as Radford et al. [19]) evaluated their models by vector arithmetic to show a meaningful representation space was learned. We similarly show vector

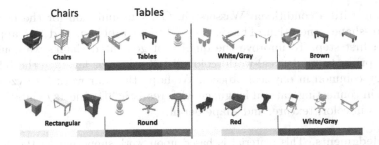

Fig. 7. Visualizing learned representations. Each of the 4 examples above visualizes the activation for a specific dimension, with darker colors indicating higher values. Individual dimensions correlate with category (top-left: chair vs. table), shape (bottom-left: rectangular vs. round), and color (top-right: white vs. brown, bottom-right: red vs. white/gray). (Color figure online)

Fig. 8. Vector arithmetic on joint text-shape embeddings. Our embeddings admit composition and transfer of attributes to control shape generation.

arithmetic results in Fig. 8. The generator interprets the manipulated embeddings to produce shapes with the desired properties. For example, "round" is expressed by subtracting a rectangular object from a round one, and adding it to an existing rectangular shape (of a different color) produces a round version of the shape. We can also perform arithmetic on a mixture of shape and text embeddings. This shows that our representation encodes shape attributes in a structured manner. Our model connects descriptions and shapes based on semantic attributes without labeling of attribute relations between shape instances.

7   Conclusion

We presented a method for bridging the natural language and 3D shape modalities by learning joint embeddings of text and 3D shapes, trained end-to-end using only instance-level natural language descriptions of 3D shapes. To evaluate our method, we introduced new datasets which connect the two modalities. We showed that the learned embeddings enable retrieval between the text and shape modalities, outperforming approaches from prior work. We then combined our embedding with a conditional Wasserstein GAN formulation for the new task of text-to-shape generation. This is a challenging problem, and our approach is only a first step. To improve the quality of generated shapes we could use stronger priors to model real-world color distributions or leverage the bilateral symmetry common in physical objects. We hope that our work catalyzes more research in connecting natural language with realistic 3D objects exhibiting rich variations in color, texture, and shape detail.

Acknowledgments. This material is based upon work supported by the National Science Foundation Graduate Research Fellowship Program under Grant No. DGE – 1147470. Any opinions, findings, and conclusions or recommendations expressed in this material are those of the author(s) and do not necessarily reflect the views of the National Science Foundation. This work is supported by Google, Intel, and with the support of the Technical University of Munich–Institute for Advanced Study, funded by the German Excellence Initiative and the European Union Seventh Framework Programme under grant agreement no. 291763.

References

1. Arjovsky, M., Chintala, S., Bottou, L.: Wasserstein GAN. arXiv:1701.07875 (2017)
2. Chang, A.X., et al.: ShapeNet: an information-rich 3D model repository. Technical report arXiv:1512.03012 [cs.GR], Stanford University – Princeton University – Toyota Technological Institute at Chicago (2015)
3. Chopra, S., Hadsell, R., LeCun, Y.: Learning a similarity metric discriminatively, with application to face verification. In: IEEE Computer Society Conference on Computer Vision and Pattern Recognition, CVPR 2005, vol. 1, pp. 539–546. IEEE (2005)
4. Choy, C.B., Xu, D., Gwak, J.Y., Chen, K., Savarese, S.: 3D-R2N2: a unified approach for single and multi-view 3D object reconstruction. In: Leibe, B., Matas, J., Sebe, N., Welling, M. (eds.) ECCV 2016. LNCS, vol. 9912, pp. 628–644. Springer, Cham (2016). https://doi.org/10.1007/978-3-319-46484-8_38
5. Dosovitskiy, A., Tobias Springenberg, J., Brox, T.: Learning to generate chairs with convolutional neural networks. In: Proceedings of the IEEE Conference on Computer Vision and Pattern Recognition, pp. 1538–1546 (2015)
6. Girdhar, R., Fouhey, D.F., Rodriguez, M., Gupta, A.: Learning a predictable and generative vector representation for objects. In: Leibe, B., Matas, J., Sebe, N., Welling, M. (eds.) ECCV 2016. LNCS, vol. 9910, pp. 484–499. Springer, Cham (2016). https://doi.org/10.1007/978-3-319-46466-4_29
7. Goodfellow, I., et al.: Generative adversarial nets. In: Advances in Neural Information Processing Systems, pp. 2672–2680 (2014)
8. Gulrajani, I., Ahmed, F., Arjovsky, M., Dumoulin, V., Courville, A.: Improved training of Wasserstein GANs. arXiv:1704.00028 (2017)
9. Haeusser, P., Frerix, T., Mordvintsev, A., Cremers, D.: Associative domain adaptation. arXiv:1708.00938 (2017)
10. Haeusser, P., Mordvintsev, A., Cremers, D.: Learning by association-a versatile semi-supervised training method for neural networks. arXiv:1706.00909 (2017)
11. Järvelin, K., Kekäläinen, J.: Cumulated gain-based evaluation of IR techniques. ACM Trans. Inf. Syst. (TOIS) **20**(4), 422–446 (2002)

12. Kiros, R., Salakhutdinov, R., Zemel, R.S.: Unifying visual-semantic embeddings with multimodal neural language models. arXiv:1411.2539 (2014)
13. Klein, B., Lev, G., Sadeh, G., Wolf, L.: Associating neural word embeddings with deep image representations using Fisher vectors. In: Proceedings of the IEEE Conference on Computer Vision and Pattern Recognition, pp. 4437–4446 (2015)
14. Li, J., Xu, K., Chaudhuri, S., Yumer, E., Zhang, H., Guibas, L.: GRASS: generative recursive autoencoders for shape structures. ACM Trans. Graph. (TOG) **36**(4), 52 (2017)
15. Li, Y., Su, H., Qi, C.R., Fish, N., Cohen-Or, D., Guibas, L.J.: Joint embeddings of shapes and images via CNN image purification. ACM Trans. Graph. **34**(6), 234:1 (2015)
16. Mikolov, T., Sutskever, I., Chen, K., Corrado, G.S., Dean, J.: Distributed representations of words and phrases and their compositionality. In: Advances in Neural Information Processing Systems, pp. 3111–3119 (2013)
17. Mirza, M., Osindero, S.: Conditional generative adversarial nets. arXiv:1411.1784 (2014)
18. Ngiam, J., Khosla, A., Kim, M., Nam, J., Lee, H., Ng, A.Y.: Multimodal deep learning. In: Proceedings of the 28th International Conference on Machine Learning (ICML 2011), pp. 689–696 (2011)
19. Radford, A., Metz, L., Chintala, S.: Unsupervised representation learning with deep convolutional generative adversarial networks. arXiv:1511.06434 (2015)
20. Reed, S., Akata, Z., Lee, H., Schiele, B.: Learning deep representations of fine-grained visual descriptions. In: Proceedings of the IEEE Conference on Computer Vision and Pattern Recognition, pp. 49–58 (2016)
21. Reed, S., Akata, Z., Mohan, S., Tenka, S., Schiele, B., Lee, H.: Learning what and where to draw. In: NIPS (2016)
22. Reed, S., Akata, Z., Yan, X., Logeswaran, L., Schiele, B., Lee, H.: Generative adversarial text-to-image synthesis. In: Proceedings of the 33rd International Conference on Machine Learning (2016)
23. Reed, S., van den Oord, A., Kalchbrenner, N., Bapst, V., Botvinick, M., de Freitas, N.: Generating interpretable images with controllable structure. Technical report, Google DeepMind (2016)
24. Salimans, T., Goodfellow, I., Zaremba, W., Cheung, V., Radford, A., Chen, X.: Improved techniques for training GANs. In: Advances in Neural Information Processing Systems, pp. 2234–2242 (2016)
25. Schroff, F., Kalenichenko, D., Philbin, J.: FaceNet: a unified embedding for face recognition and clustering. In: Proceedings of the IEEE Conference on Computer Vision and Pattern Recognition, pp. 815–823 (2015)
26. Sohn, K.: Improved deep metric learning with multi-class n-pair loss objective. In: Advances in Neural Information Processing Systems, pp. 1857–1865 (2016)
27. Song, H.O., Xiang, Y., Jegelka, S., Savarese, S.: Deep metric learning via lifted structured feature embedding. In: CVPR (2016)
28. Srivastava, N., Salakhutdinov, R.R.: Multimodal learning with deep Boltzmann machines. In: Advances in Neural Information Processing Systems (2012)
29. Tsai, Y.H.H., Huang, L.K., Salakhutdinov, R.: Learning robust visual-semantic embeddings. In: ICCV (2017)
30. Wang, L., Li, Y., Lazebnik, S.: Learning deep structure-preserving image-text embeddings. In: Proceedings of the IEEE Conference on Computer Vision and Pattern Recognition, pp. 5005–5013 (2016)

31. Weinberger, K.Q., Blitzer, J., Saul, L.K.: Distance metric learning for large margin nearest neighbor classification. In: Advances in Neural Information Processing Systems, pp. 1473–1480 (2006)
32. Wu, J., Zhang, C., Xue, T., Freeman, W.T., Tenenbaum, J.B.: Learning a probabilistic latent space of object shapes via 3D generative-adversarial modeling. In: Advances in Neural Information Processing Systems, pp. 82–90 (2016)
33. Xu, T., et al.: Attngan: fine-grained text to image generation with attentional generative adversarial networks. In: CVPR (2018)
34. Zhang, H., et al.: Stackgan++: realistic image synthesis with stacked generative adversarial networks. arXiv:1710.10916 (2017)
35. Zhang, H., et al.: Stackgan: text to photo-realistic image synthesis with stacked generative adversarial networks. In: ICCV (2017)
36. Zhang, Z., Xie, Y., Yang, L.: Photographic text-to-image synthesis with a hierarchically-nested adversarial network. In: CVPR (2018)

Poster Session P2

Understanding Individual Decisions of CNNs via Contrastive Backpropagation

Jindong Gu[1,2]($\boxtimes$), Yinchong Yang[2]($\boxtimes$), and Volker Tresp[1,2]($\boxtimes$)

[1] The University of Munich, Munich, Germany
[2] Siemens AG, Corporate Technology, Munich, Germany
{jindong.gu,yinchong.yang,volker.tresp}@siemens.com

Abstract. A number of backpropagation-based approaches such as DeConvNets, vanilla Gradient Visualization and Guided Backpropagation have been proposed to better understand individual decisions of deep convolutional neural networks. The saliency maps produced by them are proven to be non-discriminative. Recently, the Layer-wise Relevance Propagation (LRP) approach was proposed to explain the classification decisions of rectifier neural networks. In this work, we evaluate the discriminativeness of the generated explanations and analyze the theoretical foundation of LRP, i.e. Deep Taylor Decomposition. The experiments and analysis conclude that the explanations generated by LRP are not class-discriminative. Based on LRP, we propose Contrastive Layer-wise Relevance Propagation (CLRP), which is capable of producing instance-specific, class-discriminative, pixel-wise explanations. In the experiments, we use the CLRP to explain the decisions and understand the difference between neurons in individual classification decisions. We also evaluate the explanations quantitatively with a Pointing Game and an ablation study. Both qualitative and quantitative evaluations show that the CLRP generates better explanations than the LRP.

Keywords: Explainable deep learning · LRP · Discriminative saliency maps

1 Introduction

Deep convolutional neural networks (DCNNs) achieve start-of-the-art performance on many tasks, such as visual object recognition [10,26,29], and object detection [7,18]. However, since they lack transparency, they are considered as "black box" solutions. Recently, research on explainable deep learning has received increased attention: Many approaches have been proposed to crack the "black box". Some of them aim to interpret the components of a deep-architecture model and understand the image representations extracted from

Electronic supplementary material The online version of this chapter (https://doi.org/10.1007/978-3-030-20893-6_8) contains supplementary material, which is available to authorized users.

© Springer Nature Switzerland AG 2019
C. V. Jawahar et al. (Eds.): ACCV 2018, LNCS 11363, pp. 119–134, 2019.
https://doi.org/10.1007/978-3-030-20893-6_8

deep convolutional architectures [5,12,14]. Examples are Activation Maximization [6,25], DeConvNets Visualization [32]. Others focus on explaining the individual classification decisions. Examples are Prediction Difference Analysis [21,24], Guided Backpropagation [25,27], Layer-wise Relevance Propagation (LRP) [3,15], Class Activation Mapping [23,36] and Local Interpretable Model-agnostic Explanations [19,20].

More concretely, the models in [17,36] were originally proposed to detect object only using category labels. They work by producing saliency maps of objects corresponding to the category labels. Their produced saliency maps can also explain the classification decisions to some degree. However, the approaches can only work on the model with a specific architecture. For instance, they might require a fully convolutional layer followed by a max-pooling layer, a global average pooling layer or an aggregation layer, before a final softmax output layer. The requirement is not held in most off-the-shelf models e.g., in [10,26]. The perturbation methods [19–21] require no specific architecture. For a single input image, however, they require many instances of forward inference to find the corresponding classification explanation, which is computationally expensive.

The backpropagation-based approaches [3,25,27] propagate a signal from the output neuron backward through the layers to the input space in a single pass, which is computationally efficient compared to the perturbation methods. They can also be applied to the off-the-shelf models. In this paper, we focus on the backpropagation approaches. The outputs of the backpropagation approaches are instance-specific because these approaches leverage the instance-specific structure information (ISSInfo). The ISSInfo, equivalent to *bottleneck* information in [13], consist of selected information extracted by the forward inference, i.e., the Pooling switches and ReLU masks. With the ISSInfo, the backpropagation approaches can generate instance-specific explanations. A note on terminology: although the terms "sensitivity map", "saliency map", "pixel attribution map" and "explanation heatmap" may have different meanings in different contexts, in this paper, we do not distinguish them and use the term "saliency map" and "explanation" interchangeably.

The primal backpropagation-based approaches, e.g., the vanilla Gradient Visualization [25] and the Guided Backpropagation [27] are proven to be inappropriate to study the neurons of networks because they produce non-discriminative saliency maps [13]. The saliency maps generated by them mainly depend on ISSInfo instead of the neuron-specific information. In other words, the generated saliency maps are not class-discriminative with respect to class-specific neurons in output layer. The saliency maps are selective of any recognizable foreground object in the image [13]. Furthermore, the approaches cannot be applied to understand neurons in intermediate layers of DCNNs, either. In [8,32], the differences between neurons of an intermediate layer are demonstrated by a large dataset. The neurons are often activated by certain specific patterns. However, the difference between single neurons in an individual classification decision has not been explored yet. In this paper, we will also shed new light on this topic.

The recently proposed Layer-wise Relevance Propagation (LRP) approach is proven to outperform the gradient-based approaches [15]. Apart from explaining image classifications [11,15], the LRP is also applied to explain the classifications and predictions in other tasks [2,28]. However, the explanations generated by the approach has not been fully verified. We summarise our three-fold contributions as follows:

1. We first evaluate the explanations generated by LRP for individual classification decisions. Then, we analyze the theoretical foundation of LRP, i.e., Deep Taylor Decomposition and shed new insight on LRP.
2. We propose Contrastive Layer-wise Relevance Propagation (CLRP). To generate class-discriminative explanations, we propose two ways to model the contrastive signal (i.e., an opposite visual concept). For individual classification decisions, we illustrate explanations of the decisions and the difference between neuron activations using the proposed approach.
3. We build a GPU implementation of LRP and CLRP using Pytorch Framework, which alleviates the inefficiency problem addressed in [24,34].

Related work is reviewed in the next section. Section 3 analyzes LRP theoretically and experimentally. In Sect. 4, the proposed approach CLRP is introduced. Section 5 shows experimental results to evaluate the CLRP qualitatively and quantitatively on two tasks, namely, explaining the image classification decisions and understanding the difference of neuron activations in single forward inference. The last section contains conclusions and discusses future work.

2   Related Work

The DeConvNets were originally proposed for unsupervised feature learning tasks [33]. Later they were applied to visualize units in convolutional networks [32]. The DeConvNets maps the feature activity to input space using ISSInfo and the weight parameters of the forward pass. [25] proposed identifying the vanilla gradients of the output with respect to input variables are their relevance. The work also showed its relation to the DeConvNets. They use the ISSInfo in the same way except for the handling of rectified linear units (ReLUs) activation function. The Guided Backpropagation [27] combine the two approaches to visualize the units in higher layers.

The paper [3] propose LRP to generate the explanations for classification decisions. The LRP propagates the class-specific score layer by layer until to input space. The different propagation rules are applied according to the domain of the activation values. [15] proved that the Taylor Expansions of the function at the different points result in the different propagation rules. Recently, one of the propagation rules in LRP, z-rule, has been proven to be equivalent to the vanilla gradients (saliency map in [25]) multiplied elementwise with the input [9]. The vanilla Gradient Visualization and the Guided Backpropagation are shown to be not class-discriminative in [13]. This paper rethinks the LRP and evaluates the explanations generated by the approach.

Existing work that is based on discriminative and pixel-wise explanations are [4,23,34]. The work Guided-CAM [23] combines the low-resolution map of CAM and the pixel-wise map of Guided Backpropagation to generate a pixel-wise and class-discriminative explanation. To localize the most relevant neurons in the network, a biologically inspired attention model is proposed in [31]. The work uses a top-down (from the output layer to the intermediate layers) Winner-Take-All process to generate binary attention maps. The work [34] formulate the top-down attention of a CNN classifier as a probabilistic Winner-Take-All process. The work also uses a contrastive top-down attention formulation to enhance the discriminativeness of the attention maps. Based on their work and the LRP, we propose Contrastive Layer-wise Relevance Propagation (CLRP) to produce class-discriminative and pixel-wise explanations. Another publication related to our approach is [4], which is able to produce class-discriminative attention maps. While the work [4] requires modifying the traditional CNNs by adding extra feedback layers and optimizing the layers during the backpropagation, our proposed methods can be applied to all exiting CNNs without any modification and further optimization.

3   Rethinking Layer-Wise Relevance Propagation

Each neuron in DCNNs represents a nonliear function $X_i^{L+1} = \phi(\boldsymbol{X}^L \boldsymbol{W}_i^L + \boldsymbol{b}_i^L)$, where ϕ is an activation function and $\boldsymbol{b}_i^L$ is a bias for the neuron X_i^{L+1}. The inputs of the nonliear function corresponding to a neuron are the activation values of the previous layer $\boldsymbol{X}_i$ or the raw input of the network. The output of the function are the activation values of the neuron X_i^{L+1}. The whole network are composed of the nested nonlinear functions.

To identify the relevance of each input variables, the LRP propagates the activation value from a single class-specific neuron back into the input space, layer by layer. The logit before softmax normalization is taken, as explained in [3,25]. In each layer of the backward pass, given the relevance score $\boldsymbol{R}^{L+1}$ of the neurons $\boldsymbol{X}^{L+1}$, the relevance R_i^L of the neuron X_i^L are computed by redistributing the relevance score using local redistribution rules. The most often used rules are the z^+-rule and the z^β-rule, which are defined as follows:

$$
z^+\text{-rule: } R_i^L = \sum_j \frac{x_i w_{ij}^+}{\sum_{i'} x_{i'} w_{i'j}^+} R_j^{L+1}
$$

$$
z^\beta\text{-rule: } R_i^L = \sum_j \frac{x_i w_{ij} - l_i w_{ij}^+ - h_i w_{ij}^-}{\sum_{i'} x_{i'} w_{i'j} - l_i w_{i'j}^+ - h_{i'} w_{i'j}^-} R_j^{L+1}
\tag{1}
$$

where w_{ij} connecting X_i^L and X_j^{L+1} is a parameter in L-th layer, $w_{ij}^+ = w_{ij} * 1_{w_{ij}>0}$ and $w_{ij}^- = w_{ij} * 1_{w_{ij}<0}$, and the interval $[l,h]$ is the domain of the activation value x_i.

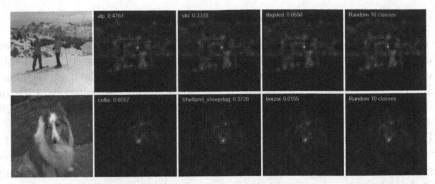

(a) The explanations generated by LRP on AlexNet.

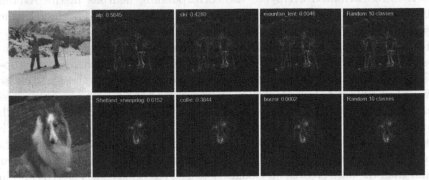

(b) The explanations generated by LRP on VGG16 Network.

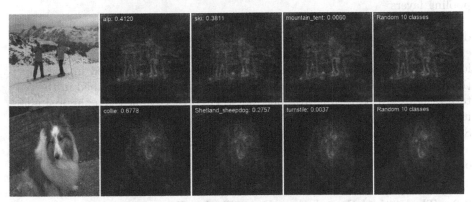

(c) The explanations generated by LRP on GoogLeNet.

Fig. 1. The images from validation datasets of ImageNet are classified using the off-the-shelf models pre-trained on the ImageNet. The classifications of the images are explained by the LRP approach. For each image, we generate four explanations that correspond to the top-3 predicted classes and a randomly chosen multiple-classes.

3.1   Evaluation of the Explanations Generated by the LRP

The explanations generated by LRP are known to be instance-specific. However, the discriminativeness of the explanations has not been evaluated yet. Ideally, the visualized objects in the explanation should correspond to the class the class-specific neuron represents. We evaluate the explanations generated by LRP on the off-the-shelf models from *torchvision*, specifically, AlexNet [10], VGG16 [26] and GoogLeNet [29] pre-trained on the ImageNet dataset [22].

The experiment settings are similar to [15]. The z^β-rule is applied to the first convolution layer. For all higher convolutional layers and fully-connected layers, the z^+-rule is applied. In the MaxPooling layers, the relevance is only redistributed to the neuron with the maximal value inside the pooling region, while it is redistributed evenly to the corresponding neurons in the Average Pooling layers. The biases and normalization layers are bypassed in the relevance propagation pass.

The results are shown in Fig. 1. For each test image, we create four saliency maps as explanations. The first three explanation maps are generated for top-3 predictions, respectively. The fourth one is created for randomly chosen 10 classes from the top-100 predicted classes (which ensure that the score to be propagated is positive). The white text in each explanation map indicates the class the output neuron represents and the corresponding classification probability. The explanations generated by AlexNet are blurry due to incomplete learning (due to the limited expressive power). The explanations of VGG16 classifications are sharper than the ones created on GoogLenet. The reason is that VGG16 contains only MaxPooling layers and GoogLenet, by contrast, contains a few average pooling layers.

The generated explanations are instance-specific, but not class-discriminative. In other words, they are independent of class information. The explanations for different target classes, even randomly chosen classes, are almost identical. The conclusion is consistent with the one summarised in the paper [1,5], namely, almost all information about input image is contained in the pattern of non-zero pattern activations, not their precise values. The high similarity of those explanations resulted from the leverage of the same ISSInfo (see Sect. 3.2). In summary, the explanations are not class-discriminative. The generated maps recognize the same foreground objects instead of a class-discriminative one.

3.2   Theoretical Foundation: Deep Taylor Decomposition

Motivated by the divide-and-conquer paradigm, Deep Taylor Decomposition decomposes a deep neural network (i.e. the nested nonliear functions) iteratively [15]. The propagation rules of LRP are derivated from Deep Taylor Decomposition of rectifier neuron network. The function represented by a single neuron is $X_j^{L+1} = max(0, \boldsymbol{X}^L \boldsymbol{W}_j^L + b_j^{L+1})$. The relevance R_j^{L+1} of the neurons X_j^{L+1} is given. The Deep Taylor Decomposition assumes $R_j^{L+1} = max(0, \boldsymbol{X}^L \boldsymbol{W}_j^L + b_j^{L+1})$. The function is expanded with Taylor Series at a point $\boldsymbol{X}_i^r$ subjective to

$max(0, \boldsymbol{X}^{r\,L}\boldsymbol{W}_j^L + b_j^{L+1}) = 0$. The LRP propagation rules are resulted from the first degree terms of the expansion.

One may hypothesize that the non-discriminativeness of LRP is caused by the first-order approximation error in Deep Taylor Decomposition. We proved that, under the given assumption, the same propagation rules are derived, even though all higher-order terms are taken into consideration (see the proof in the supplementary material). Furthermore, we found that the theoretical foundation provided by the Deep Taylor Decomposition is inappropriate. The assumption $R_j^{L+1} = max(0, \boldsymbol{X}^L\boldsymbol{W}_j^L + b_j^{L+1}) = X_j^{L+1}$ is not held at all the layers except for the last layer. The assumption indicates that the relevance value is equal to the activation value for all the neurons, which, we argue, is not true.

In our opinion, the explanations generated by the LRP result from the ISS-Info (ReLU masks and Pooling Switches). The activation values of neurons are required to create explanations using LRP. In the forward pass, the network output a vector $(y_1, y_2, \cdots, y_m)$. In the backward pass, the activation value of the class y_1 is layer-wise backpropagated into input space. In fully connected layers, only the activated neurons can receive the relevance according to any LRP propagation rule. In the Maxpooling layers, the backpropagation conducts an unpooling process, where only the neuron with maximal activations inside the corresponding pooling region can receive relevance. In the convolutional layer, only specific part of neurons R_{conv1} in feature map have non-zero relevance in the backward pass. The part of input pixels P_{input} live in the convolutional regions of those neurons (R_{conv1}). Only the pixels P_{input} will receive the propagated relevance. The pattern of the P_{input} is the explanation generated by LRP.

The backward pass for the class y_2 is similar to that of y_1. The neurons that receive non-zero relevance are the same as in case of y_1, even though their absolute values may be slightly different. Regardless of the class chosen for the backpropagation, the neurons of each layer that receive non-zero relevance stay always the same. In other words, the explanations generated by LRP are independent of the class category information, i.e., not class-discriminative.

In summary, in deep convolutional rectifier neuron network, the ReLU masks and Pooling Switches decide the pattern visualized in the explanation, which is independent of class information. That is the reason why the explanations generated by LRP on DCNNs are not class-discriminative. The analysis also explains the non-discriminative explanations generated by other backpropagation approaches, such as the DeConvNets Visualization [32], The vanilla Gradient Visualization [25] and the Guided Backpropagation [27].

4   Contrastive Layer-Wise Relevance Propagation

Before introducing our CLRP, we first discuss the conservative property in the LRP. In a DNN, given the input $\boldsymbol{X} = \{x_1, x_2, x_3, \cdots, x_n\}$, the output $\boldsymbol{Y} = \{y_1, y_2, y_3, \cdots, y_m\}$, the score S_{y_j} (activation value) of the neuron y_j before softmax layer, the LRP generate an explanation for the class y_j by redistributing the score S_{y_j} layer-wise back to the input space. The assigned relevance values

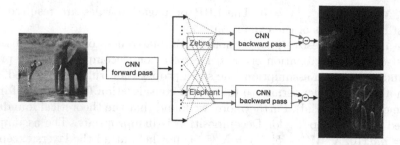

Fig. 2. The figure shows an overview of our CLRP. For each predicted class, the app-roach generates a class-discriminative explanation by comparing two signals. The blue line means the signal that the predicted class represents. The red line models a dual concept opposite to the predicted class. The final explanation is the difference between the two saliency maps that the two signal generate. (Color figure online)

of the input neurons are $R = \{r_1, r_2, r_3, \cdots, r_n\}$. The conservative property is defined as follows:

Definition 1. *The generated saliency map is conservative if the sum of assigned relevance values of the input neurons is equal to the score of the class-specific neuron, $\sum_{i=1}^{n} r_i = S_{y_j}$.*

In this section, we consider redistributing the same score from different class-specific neurons respectively. The assigned relevance R are different due to different weight connections. However, the non-zero patterns of those relevance vectors are almost identical, which is why LRP generate almost the same expla-nations for different classes. The sum of each relevance vector is equal to the redistributed score according to the conservative property. The input variables that are discriminative to each target class are a subset of input neurons, i.e., $X_{dis} \subset X$. The challenge of producing the explanation is to identify the dis-criminative pixels X_{dis} for the corresponding class.

In the explanations of image classification, the pixels on salient edges always receive higher relevance value than other pixels including all or part of X_{dis}. Those pixels with high relevance values are not necessary discriminative to the corresponding target class. We observe that X_{dis} receive higher relevance values than that of the same pixels in explanations for other classes. In other words, we can identify X_{dis} by comparing two explanations of two classes. One of the classes is the target class to be explained. The other class is selected as an auxiliary to identify X_{dis} of the target class. To identify X_{dis} more accurately, we construct a virtual class instead of selecting another class from the output layer. We propose two ways to construct the virtual class.

The overview of the CLRP are shown in Fig. 2. We describe the CLRP for-mally as follows. The j−th class-specific neuron y_j is connected to input variables by the weights $W = \{W^1, W^2, \cdots, W^{L-1}, W_j^L\}$ of layers between them, where W^L means the weights connecting the $(L-1)$−th layer and the L−th layer, and

W_j^L means the weights connecting the $(L-1)$-th layer and the j-th neuron in the L-th layer. The neuron y_j models a visual concept O. For an input example X, the LRP maps the score S_{y_j} of the neuron back into the input space to get relevance vector $R = f_{LRP}(X, W, S_{y_j})$.

We construct a dual virtual concept $\overline{O}$, which models the opposite visual concept to the concept O. For instance, the concept O models the **zebra**, and the constructed dual concept $\overline{O}$ models the **non-zebra**. One way to model the $\overline{O}$ is to select all classes except for the target class representing O. The concept $\overline{O}$ is represented by the selected classes with weights $\overline{W} = \{W^1, W^2, \cdots, W^{L-1}, W_{\{-j\}}^L\}$, where $W_{\{-j\}}$ means the weights connected to the output layer excluding the j-th neuron. E.g. the dashed red lines in Fig. 2 are connected to all classes except for the target class **zebra**. Next, the score S_{y_j} of target class is uniformly redistributted to other classes. Given the same input example X, the LRP generates an explanation $R_{dual} = f_{LRP}(X, \overline{W}, S_{y_j})$ for the dual concept. The Contrastive Layer-wise Relevance Propagation is defined as follows:

$$R_{CLRP} = \max(0, (R - R_{dual})) \qquad (2)$$

where the function $\max(0, X)$ means replacing the negative elements of X with zeros. The difference between the two saliency maps cancels the common parts. Without the dominant common parts, the non-zero elements in R_{CLRP} are the most relevant pixels X_{dis}. If the neuron y_j lives in an intermediate layer of a neural network, the constructed R_{CLRP} can be used to understand the role of the neuron.

Similar to [34], the other way to model the concept $\overline{O}$ is to negate the weights W_j^L. The concept $\overline{O}$ can be represented by the weights $\overline{W} = \{W^1, W^2, \cdots, W^{L-1}, -1 * W_j^L\}$. All the weights are same as in the concept O except that the weights of the last layer W_j^L are negated. In the experiments section, we call the first modeling method CLRP1 and the second one CLRP2. The contrastive formulation in [34] can be applied to other backpropagation approaches by normalizing and subtracting two generated saliency maps. However, the normalization strongly depends on the maximal value that could be caused by a noisy pixel. Based on the conservative property of LRP, the normalization is avoided in the proposed CLRP.

5   Experiments and Analysis

In this section, we conduct experiments to evaluate our proposed approach. The first experiment aims to generate class-discriminative explanations for individual classification decisions. The second experiment evaluates the generated explanations quantitatively on the ILSVRC2012 validation dataset. The discriminativeness of the generated explanations is evaluated via a Pointing Game and an ablation study. The last experiment aims to understand the difference between neurons in a single classification forward pass.

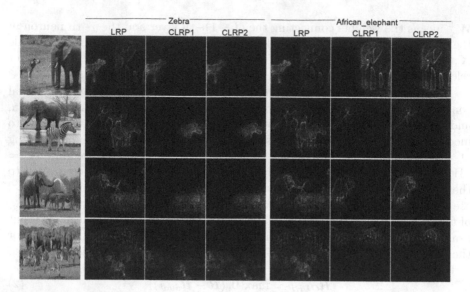

Fig. 3. The images of multiple objects are classified using VGG16 network pre-trained on ImageNet. The explanations for the two relevant classes are generated by LRP and CLRP. The CLRP generates class-discriminative explanations, while LRP generates almost same explanations.

5.1 Explaining Classification Decisions of DNNs

In this experiment, the LRP, the CLRP1 and the CLRP2 are applied to generate explanations for different classes. The experiments are conducted on a pre-trained VGG16 Network [26]. The propagation rules used in each layer are the same as in the Sect. 3.1. We classify the images of multiple objects. The explanations are generated for the two most relevant predicted classes, respectively. The Fig. 3 shows the explanations for the two classes (i.e., *Zebra* and *African_elephant*). The explanations generated by the LRP are same for the two classes. Each generated explanation visualizes both *Zebra* and *African_elephant*, which is not class-discriminative. By contrast, both CLRP1 and CLRP2 only identify the discriminative pixels related to the corresponding class. For the target class *Zebra*, only the pixels on the zebra object are visualized. Even for the complicated images where a zebra herd and an elephant herd co-exist, the CLRP methods are still able to find the class-discriminative pixels.

We evaluate the approach with a large number of images with multiple objects. The explanations generated by CLRP are always class-discriminative, but not necessarily semantically meaningful for every class. One of the reasons is that the VGG16 Network is not trained for multi-label classification. Other reasons could be the incomplete learning and bias in the training dataset [30].

The implementation of the LRP is not trivial. The one provided by their authors only supports CPU computation. For the VGG16 network, it takes the 30 s to generate one explanation on an Intel Xeon 2.90 GHz × 6 machine.

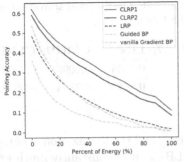 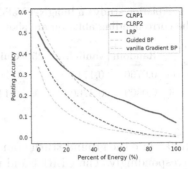

(a) Pointing Accuracy On the AlexNet   (b) Pointing Accuracy On the VGG16

Fig. 4. The figure shows the localization ability of the saliency maps generated by the LRP, the CLRP1, the CLRP2, the vanilla Gradient Visualization and the Guided Backpropagation. On the pre-trained models, AlexNet and VGG16, the localization ability is evaluated at different thresholds. The x-axis corresponds to the threshold that keeps a certain percentage of energy left, and the y-axis corresponds to the pointing accuracy.

The computational expense makes the evaluation of LRP impossible on a large dataset [34]. We implement a GPU version of the LRP approach, which reduces the 30 s to 0.1824 s to generate one explanation on a single NVIDIA Telsa K80 GPU. The implementation alleviates the inefficiency problem addressed in [24,34] and makes the quantitative evaluation of LRP on a largét dataset possible.

5.2 Evaluating the Explanations

In this experiments, we quantitatively evaluate the generated explanations on the ILSVRC2012 validation dataset containing 50, 000 images. A Pointing Game and an ablation study are used to evaluate the proposed approach.

Pointing Game: To evaluate the discriminativeness of saliency maps, the paper [34] proposes a pointing game. The maximum point on the saliency map is extracted and evaluated. In case of images with a single object, a hit is counted if the maximum point lies in the bounding box of the target object, otherwise a miss is counted. The localization accuracy is measured by $Acc = \frac{\#Hits}{\#Hits+\#Misses}$. In case of ILSVRC2012 dataset, the naive pointing at the center of the image shows surprisingly high accuracy. Based on the reason, we extend the pointing game into a difficult setting. In the new setting, the first step is to preprocess the saliency map by simply thresholding so that the foreground area covers p percent energy out of the whole saliency map (where the energy is the sum of all pixel values in saliency map). A hit is counted if the remaining foreground area lies in the bounding box of the target object, otherwise a miss is counted.

The Fig. 4 show that the localization accuracy of different approaches in case of different thresholds. With more energy kept, the remained pixels are less

Table 1. Ablation study on ImagNet Validation dataset. The dropped activation values after the corresponding ablation are shown in the table.

	Random	vanilGrad [25]	GuidedBP [27]	**LRP** [3]	**CLRP1**	**CLRP2**
AlexNet	0.0766	0.1716	0.1843	0.1624	0.2093	0.2030
VGG16	0.0809	0.3760	0.4480	0.3713	0.3844	0.3913

likely to fall into the ground-truth bounding box, and the localization accuracy is low correspondingly. The CLRP1 and the CLRP2 show constantly much better pointing accuracy than that of the LRP. The positive results indicate that the pixels that the contrastive backpropagation cancels are on the cluttered background or non-target objects. The CLRP can focus on the class-discriminative part, which improves the LRP. The CLRP is also better than other primal backpropagation-based approaches. One exception is that the Guided Backpropagation shows a better localization accuracy in VGG16 network in case of high thresholds. In addition, the localization accuracy of the CLRP1 and the CLRP2 is similar in the deep VGG16 network, which indicates the equivalence of the two methods to model the opposite visual concept.

Ablation Study: In the Pointing Game above, we evaluate the discriminativeness of the explanations according to the localization ability. In this ablation study, we evaluate the discriminativeness from another perspective. We observe the changes of activation in case of ablating the found discriminative pixels. The activation value of the class-specific neuron will drop if the ablated pixels are discriminative to the corresponding class.

For an individual image classification decision, we first generate a saliency map for the ground-truth class. We identify the maximum point in the generated saliency map as the most discriminative position. Then, we ablate the pixel of the input image at the identified position with a 9×9 image patch. The pixel values of the image patch are the mean value of all the pixel values at the same position across the whole dataset. We classify the perturbated image and observe the activation value of the neuron corresponding to the ground-truth class. The dropped activation value is computed as the difference between the activations of the neuron before and after the perturbation. The dropped score is averaged on all the images in the dataset.

The experimental results of different approaches are shown in the Table 1. For the comparison, we also ablate the image with a randomly chosen position. The random ablation has hardly impact on the output. The saliency maps corresponding to all other approaches find the relevant pixel because the activations of the class-specific neurons dropped a lot after the corresponding ablation. In both networks, CLRP1 and CLRP2 show the better scores, which means the discriminativeness of explanations generated by CLRP is better than that of the LRP. Again, the Guided Backpropagation shows better score than CLRP. This ablation study only considers the discriminative of the pixel with maximal relevance value, which corresponds to a special case in the Pointing Game, namely, only one pixel with maximal relevance is left after the thresholding. The two experiments show the consistent result that the Guided Backpropagation is better than LRP in the special case. We do not report the performance of the GoogLeNet in the experiments. Our approach shows that the zero-padding operations of convolutional layers have a big impact on the output of the GoogLeNet model in *torchvision* module of Pytorch. The impact leads to a problematic saliency map (see supplementary material).

5.3   Understanding the Difference Between Neurons

The neurons of DNNs have been studying with their activation values. The DeConvNets [32] visualize the patterns and collect the images that maximally activate the neurons, given an image set. The activation maximization method [6,16] aims to generate an image in input space that maximally activates a single neuron or a group of neurons. Furthermore, the work [8,35] understand the semantic concepts of the neurons with an annotated dataset. In this experiment, we aim to study the difference among neurons in a single classification decision.

The neurons of low layers may have different local receptive fields. The difference between them could be caused by the different input stimuli. We visualize high-level concepts learned by the neurons that have the same receptive fields, e.g., a single neuron in a fully connected layer. For a single test image, the LRP and the CLRP2 are applied to visualize the stimuli that activate a specific neuron. We do not use CLRP1 because the opposite visual concept cannot be modeled by the remaining neurons in the same layer.

In VGG16 network, we visualize 8 activated neurons x_{1-8} from the $fc1$ layer. The visualized maps are shown in Fig. 5. The image is classified as a *toyshop* by the VGG16 network. The receptive field (the input image) is shown in the center, and the 8 explanation maps are shown around it. While the LRP produces almost identical saliency map for the 8 neurons (in Fig. 5a), the CLRP2 gains a meaningful insight about their difference, which shows that different neurons focus on different parts of images. By comparison (see Fig. 5b), the neurons x_1, x_2, x_3 in the first row are activated more by the *lion*, the *gorilla*, and the *monkey* respectively. The neurons x_4, x_5 in the second row by the eye of the *elephant* and the *bird* respectively. The right-down one x_6 by the *panda*. The last two neurons x_7 and x_8 focus on the similar patterns (i.e., the *tiger*).

To our knowledge, there is no known work on the difference between neurons in an individual classification decision and also no evaluation metric. We evaluate the found difference by an ablation study. More concretely, we first find the discriminative patch for each neuron (e.g., x_{1-8}) using CLRP2. Then, we ablate the patch and observe the changes of neuron activations in the forward pass. The discriminative patch of a neuron is identified by the point with maximal value in its explanation map created by CLRP2. The 9×9 neighboring pixels around the maximum point are replaced with the values that are mean of pixel values in the same positions across the whole dataset.

The ablation study results are shown in the Fig. 5c. The positive value in the grid of the figure means the decreased activation value, and the negative

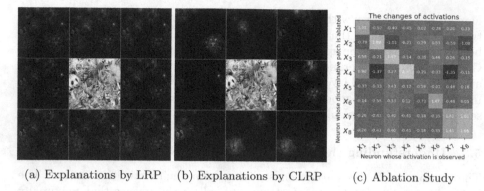

(a) Explanations by LRP   (b) Explanations by CLRP   (c) Ablation Study

Fig. 5. The figures show explanation maps of neurons in $fc1$ layers. The explanations generated by LRP are not discriminative. By contrast, the ones generated by CLRP explain the difference between the neurons.

ones mean the activations increase after the corresponding ablation. In case of the ablation corresponding to neuron x_i, we see that the activation of x_i is significantly dropped (could become not-activated). The maximal droped values of each row often occur on the diagonal axis. We also try with other ablation sizes and other neurons, which shows the similar results. The ablations for the last two neurons x_7 and x_8 are same because their explanation maps are similar. The changes of activations of all other neurons are also the same for the same ablation. We found that many activated neurons correspond to same explanation maps.

6   Conclusion

The explanations generated by LRP are evaluated. We find that the explanations are not class-discriminative. We discuss the theoretical foundation and provide our justification for the non-discriminativeness. To improve discriminativeness of the generated explanations, we propose the Contrastive Layer-wise Relevance Propagation. The qualitative and quantitative evaluations confirm that the CLRP is better than the LRP. We also use the CLRP to shed light on the role of neurons in DCNNs.

We propose two ways to model the opposite visual concept the class-specific neuron represents. However, there could be other more appropriate modeling methods. Even though our approach produces a pixel-wise explanation for the individual classification decisions, the explanations for similar classes are similar. The fine-grained discriminativeness are needed to explain the classifications of the intra-classes. We leave the further exploration in future work.

References

1. Agrawal, P., Girshick, R., Malik, J.: Analyzing the performance of multilayer neural networks for object recognition. In: Fleet, D., Pajdla, T., Schiele, B., Tuytelaars, T. (eds.) ECCV 2014. LNCS, vol. 8695, pp. 329–344. Springer, Cham (2014). https://doi.org/10.1007/978-3-319-10584-0_22
2. Arras, L., Montavon, G., Müller, K.R., Samek, W.: Explaining recurrent neural network predictions in sentiment analysis. arXiv preprint arXiv:1706.07206 (2017)
3. Bach, S., Binder, A., Montavon, G., Klauschen, F., Müller, K.R., Samek, W.: On pixel-wise explanations for non-linear classifier decisions by layer-wise relevance propagation. PLoS ONE **10**(7), e0130140 (2015)
4. Cao, C., et al.: Look and think twice: capturing top-down visual attention with feedback convolutional neural networks. In: Proceedings of the IEEE International Conference on Computer Vision, pp. 2956–2964 (2015)
5. Dosovitskiy, A., Brox, T.: Inverting visual representations with convolutional networks. In: Proceedings of the IEEE Conference on Computer Vision and Pattern Recognition, pp. 4829–4837 (2016)
6. Erhan, D., Bengio, Y., Courville, A., Vincent, P.: Visualizing higher-layer features of a deep network. Univ. Montreal **1341**(3), 1 (2009)
7. Girshick, R., Donahue, J., Darrell, T., Malik, J.: Rich feature hierarchies for accurate object detection and semantic segmentation. In: Proceedings of the IEEE Conference on Computer Vision and Pattern Recognition, pp. 580–587 (2014)
8. Gonzalez-Garcia, A., Modolo, D., Ferrari, V.: Do semantic parts emerge in convolutional neural networks? Int. J. Comput. Vis. **126**(5), 476–494 (2018)
9. Kindermans, P.J., Schütt, K., Müller, K.R., Dähne, S.: Investigating the influence of noise and distractors on the interpretation of neural networks. arXiv preprint arXiv:1611.07270 (2016)
10. Krizhevsky, A., Sutskever, I., Hinton, G.E.: Imagenet classification with deep convolutional neural networks. In: Advances in Neural Information Processing Systems, pp. 1097–1105 (2012)
11. Lapuschkin, S., Binder, A., Müller, K.R., Samek, W.: Understanding and comparing deep neural networks for age and gender classification. arXiv preprint arXiv:1708.07689 (2017)
12. Mahendran, A., Vedaldi, A.: Understanding deep image representations by inverting them. CoRR abs/1412.0035 (2014)
13. Mahendran, A., Vedaldi, A.: Salient deconvolutional networks. In: Leibe, B., Matas, J., Sebe, N., Welling, M. (eds.) ECCV 2016. LNCS, vol. 9910, pp. 120–135. Springer, Cham (2016). https://doi.org/10.1007/978-3-319-46466-4_8
14. Mahendran, A., Vedaldi, A.: Visualizing deep convolutional neural networks using natural pre-images. Int. J. Comput. Vis. **120**(3), 233–255 (2016)
15. Montavon, G., Lapuschkin, S., Binder, A., Samek, W., Müller, K.R.: Explaining nonlinear classification decisions with deep taylor decomposition. Pattern Recogn. **65**, 211–222 (2017)
16. Nguyen, A., Dosovitskiy, A., Yosinski, J., Brox, T., Clune, J.: Synthesizing the preferred inputs for neurons in neural networks via deep generator networks. In: Advances in Neural Information Processing Systems, pp. 3387–3395 (2016)
17. Oquab, M., Bottou, L., Laptev, I., Sivic, J.: Is object localization for free?-weakly-supervised learning with convolutional neural networks. In: Proceedings of the IEEE Conference on Computer Vision and Pattern Recognition, pp. 685–694 (2015)
18. Redmon, J., Divvala, S., Girshick, R., Farhadi, A.: You only look once: unified, real-time object detection. In: Proceedings of the IEEE Conference on Computer Vision and Pattern Recognition, pp. 779–788 (2016)

19. Ribeiro, M.T., Singh, S., Guestrin, C.: Nothing else matters: model-agnostic explanations by identifying prediction invariance. arXiv preprint arXiv:1611.05817 (2016)
20. Ribeiro, M.T., Singh, S., Guestrin, C.: Why should i trust you?: explaining the predictions of any classifier. In: Proceedings of the 22nd ACM SIGKDD International Conference on Knowledge Discovery and Data Mining, pp. 1135–1144. ACM (2016)
21. Robnik-Šikonja, M., Kononenko, I.: Explaining classifications for individual instances. IEEE Trans. Knowl. Data Eng. **20**(5), 589–600 (2008)
22. Russakovsky, O., et al.: Imagenet large scale visual recognition challenge. IJCV **115**, 211–252 (2015)
23. Selvaraju, R.R., Cogswell, M., Das, A., Vedantam, R., Parikh, D., Batra, D.: Grad-CAM: visual explanations from deep networks via gradient-based localization. arXiv:1610.02391v3, vol. 7, no. 8 (2016)
24. Shrikumar, A., Greenside, P., Kundaje, A.: Learning important features through propagating activation differences. arXiv preprint arXiv:1704.02685 (2017)
25. Simonyan, K., Vedaldi, A., Zisserman, A.: Deep inside convolutional networks: visualising image classification models and saliency maps. arXiv preprint arXiv:1312.6034 (2013)
26. Simonyan, K., Zisserman, A.: Very deep convolutional networks for large-scale image recognition. arXiv preprint arXiv:1409.1556 (2014)
27. Springenberg, J.T., Dosovitskiy, A., Brox, T., Riedmiller, M.: Striving for simplicity: the all convolutional net. arXiv preprint arXiv:1412.6806 (2014)
28. Srinivasan, V., Lapuschkin, S., Hellge, C., Müller, K.R., Samek, W.: Interpretable human action recognition in compressed domain. In: 2017 IEEE International Conference on Acoustics, Speech and Signal Processing, pp. 1692–1696. IEEE (2017)
29. Szegedy, C., et al.: Going deeper with convolutions. In: 2015 IEEE Conference on Computer Vision and Pattern Recognition (CVPR), pp. 1–9, June 2015
30. Torralba, A., Efros, A.A.: Unbiased look at dataset bias. In: 2011 IEEE Conference on Computer Vision and Pattern Recognition (CVPR), pp. 1521–1528. IEEE (2011)
31. Tsotsos, J.K., Culhane, S.M., Wai, W.Y.K., Lai, Y., Davis, N., Nuflo, F.: Modeling visual attention via selective tuning. Artif. Intell. **78**(1–2), 507–545 (1995)
32. Zeiler, M.D., Fergus, R.: Visualizing and understanding convolutional networks. In: Fleet, D., Pajdla, T., Schiele, B., Tuytelaars, T. (eds.) ECCV 2014. LNCS, vol. 8689, pp. 818–833. Springer, Cham (2014). https://doi.org/10.1007/978-3-319-10590-1_53
33. Zeiler, M.D., Krishnan, D., Taylor, G.W., Fergus, R.: Deconvolutional networks. In: 2010 IEEE Conference on Computer Vision and Pattern Recognition (CVPR), pp. 2528–2535. IEEE (2010)
34. Zhang, J., Lin, Z., Brandt, J., Shen, X., Sclaroff, S.: Top-down neural attention by excitation backprop. In: Leibe, B., Matas, J., Sebe, N., Welling, M. (eds.) ECCV 2016. LNCS, vol. 9908, pp. 543–559. Springer, Cham (2016). https://doi.org/10.1007/978-3-319-46493-0_33
35. Zhou, B., Khosla, A., Lapedriza, A., Oliva, A., Torralba, A.: Object detectors emerge in deep scene CNNs. arXiv preprint arXiv:1412.6856 (2014)
36. Zhou, B., Khosla, A., Lapedriza, A., Oliva, A., Torralba, A.: Learning deep features for discriminative localization. In: 2016 IEEE Conference on Computer Vision and Pattern Recognition (CVPR), pp. 2921–2929. IEEE (2016)

Say Yes to the Dress: Shape and Style Transfer Using Conditional GANs

Michael A. Hobley$^{(\boxtimes)}$ and Victor A. Prisacariu

University of Oxford, Oxford, UK
{mahobley,victor}@robots.ox.ac.uk

Abstract. Objects are defined by their shape and visual style. Previous work into image manipulation has generally altered the stylistic appearance of a whole image, while maintaining the image content and object shapes. In this paper we transfer both the shape and style of chosen objects between images, leaving the remaining areas unaltered. To tackle this problem, we propose a two stage method, where each stage contains a generative adversarial network, that will alter the shape and style of objects in a subject image to reflect a donor image. We demonstrate the effectiveness of our method by transferring clothing between images.

Keywords: Generative adversarial network · Conditional GAN · Style transfer · Shape transfer · Fashion · Clothing · Machine learning

1 Introduction

There are countless applications where altering the appearance of specific objects in an image is needed and, due to the visual nature of image manipulation, example images are often more useful than textual descriptions or tags. An object is defined by both its shape and visual style, which includes its colour, texture and pattern. Therefore to produce compelling object alterations from image examples, we must reproduce the shape and style from the example in the subject image. Several researchers have addressed simple image translation and style transfer tasks [4,6,19,21]. The alterations are generally applied to the whole image [4,6,19], or a simply masked area [21]. All of these methods have focused on the style of an image, maintaining the shape and location of component objects. However, to realistically transfer the appearance of an object between images, both the shape and style must be transferred (Fig. 1).

An ideal example of a selective object transfer task is swapping clothing between photos, as clothing is characterised by its distinctive shapes and styles. To convincingly swap garments between images, one must generate realistic clothes that reflect the donor garments, while still maintaining the pose, body shape and appearance of the subject. Garment shape transfer has previously been addressed using three dimensional methods, requiring anthropomorphic data [11,27]. We make no assumptions about the three dimensional geometry,

© Springer Nature Switzerland AG 2019
C. V. Jawahar et al. (Eds.): ACCV 2018, LNCS 11363, pp. 135–149, 2019.
https://doi.org/10.1007/978-3-030-20893-6_9

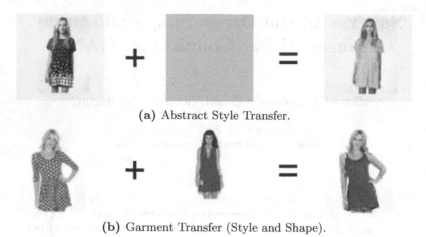

(a) Abstract Style Transfer.

(b) Garment Transfer (Style and Shape).

Fig. 1. Generated examples using the proposed system for garment style transfer and full garment transfer. The subject (*left*) and a donor (*middle*) are used to create an image with chosen features of the donor image while keeping the subject the same. For the full effect view in colour. (Color figure online)

instead we only use a single subject image to capture the appearance and pose of the person, and a single donor image to define the style and type of the generated garment.

To transfer the visual appearance of garments in two dimensions using single images, we propose a two-stage method. Each stage is comprised of an encoder and a conditional generative adversarial network [10]. Our first stage alters the shape of the chosen garments in a subject image to match a donor image. Our second stage selectively transfers the style of chosen garments of a donor image to the appropriate areas in the updated subject image.

The main contributions of this paper are: (i) we transfer style between certain selected objects in images, agnostic to their original appearance, as discussed in Subsect. 3.3; (ii) we manipulation the shape of objects based on their shape in a second image while maintaining their pose, as discussed in Subsect. 3.4; (iii) we create a complete method for compelling object transfer between images, demonstrated in Sect. 4.

2 Related Work

We discuss previous work related to the broad area of image generation, the use of images as an input to generative models, the previous methods that have been applied to garment related generation and how our approach differs from previous work.

2.1 Image Generation

Image generation is a classic problem in computer vision, with the goal of creating realistic, high resolution images that match a set of user constraints.

The most popular current approach to image generation is the Generative Adversarial Network (GAN) [9]. GANs improve upon traditional convolution neural networks by learning a representation of a dataset rather than using a simple loss function. Promising research has been conducted into generating images in stages by using multiple GANs [2,6,20,28]. These approaches first generate the coarse structure of an object in the form of surface normals [20] or a low resolution image [28], then use this as the input to a GAN that generates a final, detailed image. These coarse-to-fine schemes are generally more stable during training, allowing for more detailed, complex, and higher resolution results [8].

2.2 Image Conditioning

Conditional networks use a conditioning variable as the network's input array rather than a random set of values. Once trained, the user can control the generated result by manipulating this variable. The generated result should be reflective of the conditioning variable as well as representative of the training dataset.

Early conditioning methods used relatively simple labels [15,16,24], or basic textual descriptions [17,28], but more recently entire images have been used as the conditioning variable in image generation [4,6,12,18,29,30]. Image conditioning has mainly been used for simple photo editing [18], full image style transfer [4], supervised domain transfer [6,30], and unsupervised domain transfer [12,29].

Domain transfer or image translation aims to alter the style of an image while maintaining the shape or location of individual objects. Basic image translation tasks include colourising greyscale images and converting a semantic map to a textured image. Traditionally, image translations alter the domain or style of an entire image indiscriminately, however work has recently been conducted into guiding the transfer using semantic channels as masks [14]. Image translation suffers from the same instability as GANs in unconditioned fields.

Wang et al. [19] combined methods of multi-stage GAN stabilisation [8,28] with work on image translation to create a high resolution domain invariant architecture. They also developed a method for varying the style of single instances in an image, however their results were simple and had minimal user control, limited to choosing from a discrete number of the most common styles found in the dataset.

2.3 Fashion

Clothing related computer vision has generally been focused on the discriminative tasks of classification and recognition [1,3,26] to generate textual descriptions, labels, or tags from an image.

Generative tasks related to clothing have traditionally involved generating a three dimensional representation of the subject and their clothing using body measurements [11, 27]. The three dimensional clothing can then be mapped between subjects. Processing and generating three dimensional models is computationally intensive, and gathering the data for each instance is time consuming and expensive. Yang et al. [25] generated three dimensional models from a single photograph of a subject. However, this method still required the use of anthropometric data and accurate three dimensional human body models.

Purely two dimensional fashion manipulation was recently addressed by Zhu et al. [31], who created a framework to generate clothing for a subject, based on a textual description. Zhu et al. [31] generated garment shape to match the pose and body shape from a subject image, then applied the desired style. This framework was able to implement generation of simple changes to garment shape and could generate images with plain clothes. No complex or abstract pattern results were shown. Xian et al. [23] recently developed TextureGAN, a method for generating images from a sketch and a simple texture samples. The results from TextureGAN are simple, repeating the same pattern, and are generally independent of any image context or variation that may come with shape.

In this paper, in contrast to previous image translation work [6, 12, 29, 30], we recognise the importance of shape, as well as style, to the visual appearance of an object. We aim to capture the shape and style of chosen garments from a complex image, and transfer this representation onto a second image, leaving the remaining areas untouched. We divide the generation into two sections, shape and style. Our method treats the style and shape of each garment between images independently, allowing for complete flexibility at generation time. In contrast to previous work into texture generation, for example TextureGAN [23], our style generation alters texture based on context and shape, creating accurate features like creases in the correct garments and places. We deconstruct the object shapes into the garment shapes and the wearers pose, we can then alter the garment shapes while maintaining the appearance of the subject. We enable transfer of styles between multiple sections independently by combining feature-wise style encodings of the subject and donor images.

3   Training and Generation Methodology

In order to represent a complete garment we separate its visual appearance into its shape, and its style, described by colour, pattern and texture. We use a dataset of fashion images and their associated garment segmentations. The segmentations divide the image into their component classes: background, hair, face, upper-body clothes, lower-body clothes, legs, and arms. We use the segmentation to define the shape of each garment.

We capture the representation of the shape and style independently and generate them separately in two separate networks, as in Fig. 2. We can utilise the style generation stage alone to alter the style of garments in an image while maintaining the shape for *Garment Style Transfer* or alter both the shape and style of garments for *Complete Garment Transfer*. We condition the generators on the shape and style separately to ensure their independence.

In the following section, we train two encoder-generator pairs to generate realistic clothing and realistic part segmentations. We then manipulate the encodings to alter the style of the garments and the shape of the segmentations to reflect another image.

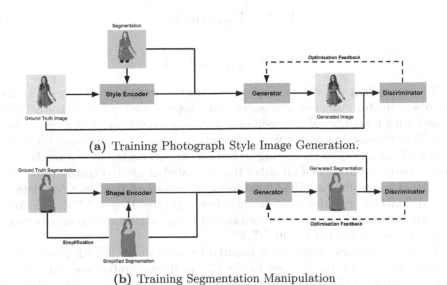

(a) Training Photograph Style Image Generation.

(b) Training Segmentation Manipulation

Fig. 2. Training models for the Image Generation stage and the Segmentation Manipulation Stage. The generated image and segmentation are both evaluated on the likelihood they were from the input dataset and on their similarity to the original input.

3.1   Style Training

Our method is a development of conditional GANs [10] which are themselves a development of the GAN [9]. In a GAN, two adversarial networks, a generator and discriminator, are trained simultaneously. The discriminator is trained to distinguish ground truth images from generated results, while the generator attempts to trick the discriminator by generating ever more realistic results. The discriminator learns a more complex and nuanced set of rules about what defines a realistic looking image, and what the conditioning variables represent, than could be specified manually. This complex set of rules in turn encourages the generator to learn to generate more realistic results.

In our method we incorporate a style encoder to condition the generator on the style of the input image, seen in Fig. 2a. The style encoder generates a style encoding, $\mathbf{e}_i^{img}$, for each class, $\mathbf{s}_i$, in the segmenation, $\mathbf{S}_0$, $1 \leq i \leq N$, where N is the number of classes in $\mathbf{S}_0$. To ensure coherence within each class, we take the mean value of $\mathbf{e}_i^{img}$. The style encodings are then grouped into a feature-wise encoding, $\mathbf{E}^{img}$, that represents the style of each garment. The encoder is trained with the generator and discriminator to encourage meaningful and specific encodings.

The image generator, G_{image}, uses the shape and style from the original image, represented by $\mathbf{S}_0$ and $\mathbf{E}^{img}$ respectively, to create its estimate, $\mathbf{I}^*$, of the ground truth image $\mathbf{I}_0$.

$$\mathbf{E}^{img} \leftarrow E_{image}(\mathbf{I}_0, \mathbf{S}_0) \tag{1}$$

$$\mathbf{I}^* \leftarrow G_{image}(\mathbf{S}_0, \mathbf{E}^{img}) \tag{2}$$

The image discriminator only appears in the training phase, shown in Fig. 2a. The discriminator evaluates how realistic and representative $\mathbf{I}^*$ is of the original dataset with a traditional unconditional GAN loss function. A perceptual loss term [7] in the discriminator gives a broader evaluation of texture and the wider context of the image by comparing activations at various layers in a pre-trained image classifier conditioned on either the generated or ground truth image. Our perceptual loss utilises a VGG-19 network, pretrained on the ImageNet dataset A conditional loss function also evaluates how reflective $\mathbf{I}^*$ is of $\mathbf{E}^{img}$. This form of conditional discrimination has been shown to incentivise consistency between conditions and generated results [17,31].

We use a network architecture inspired by Isola et al. [6], with two down-sampling layers and nine ResNet blocks [22] in the generator, and use a three value encoding for the style of each garment. The networks were trained for 50 epochs. These training conditions create a generator that can alter the style of clothing while maintaining the shape of the garments, allowing generation of realistic clothing with a given style.

3.2 Shape Training

As the style generation stage strictly maintains the shape of each garment, a segmentation stage is needed to alter garment shapes while maintain pose of the original subject. The generated segmentation can then be used as a conditioning input for the style generation.

The segmentation generation stage is a simplified version of the image generation stage. Both stages are trained in similar ways, depicted in Fig. 2. Whereas in the style stage the input is an image of a person and a part segmentation, in this stage we use the part segmentation and another 'simplified segmentation'. In our application, the 'simplified segmentation' contains four classes: background, hair, face, and potential clothing. Where potential clothing refers to areas that could be classified as garments in the generated segmentation, including garment classes, arms, and legs from the original image.

During training the segmentation encoder, $E_{segmentation}$, finds $\mathbf{E}^{seg}$, a set of segmentation feature encodings $\mathbf{e}_i^{seg}$, $1 \leq i \leq N^-$, where N^- is the number of classes in the simplified segmentation, $\mathbf{S}^-$. The segmentation generator then hallucinates $\mathbf{S}^*$, its attempt to reconstruct $\mathbf{S}_0$, as shown in Fig. 2b.

$$\mathbf{E}^{seg} \leftarrow E_{segmentation}(\mathbf{S}_0, \mathbf{S}^-) \tag{3}$$

$$\mathbf{S}^* \leftarrow G_{segmentation}(\mathbf{S}^-, \mathbf{E}^{seg}) \tag{4}$$

The segmentation discriminator is identical to that in the image generation stage. The discriminator incentivises the generator to replicate the pose of the original image present in the simplified segmentation and shape of each garment given by the complete segmentation encoding.

While more complex methods of discretisation could be used to insure class constraints, for example mean fields or CRFs, we are able to generate quality results by using a continuous spectrum while training and only later applying the class constraints.

The segmentation stage has a simpler architecture than the style stage to avoid modal collapse. The segmentation generator contains a single downsampling layer and three ResNet blocks. The smaller model and less complex problem meant the segmentation generation stage needed considerably less training than the image generation stage, achieving consistently high-quality results after only two epochs of training.

3.3   Style Transfer

Once trained, G_{image} can be used to transfer the style of garments from a donor image. During style transfer, a translated encoding is created as the combination of the subject and donor encodings as

$$\mathbf{e}_{trans,\,i}^{img} = \begin{cases} \mathbf{e}_{don,\,i}^{img} & \text{if } i \in T \\ \mathbf{e}_{sub,\,i}^{img} & \text{elsewhere} \end{cases} \tag{5}$$

where $1 \le i \le N_{trans}$, and N_{trans} is the number of classes in the segmentation, and T is the set of garments to transfer. These encodings are combined to create, $\mathbf{E}_{trans}^{img}$, where each class reflects the style of the subject or donor image. $\mathbf{E}_{trans}^{img}$ and the original segmentation are then used as the conditioning variables for the image generator, which generates a realistic representation of the subject with garments that reflect the donor's.

3.4   Complete Garment Transfer

We can combine the two stages to create the complete garment transfer method shown in Fig. 3. To transfer garments between images, we first generate the translated segmentation, $\mathbf{S}_{trans}$, from the simplified subject segmentation, $\mathbf{S}_{sub}^-$, as well as the donor segmentation encoding, $\mathbf{E}_{don}^{seg}$. As above, we combine the image style encodings to create $\mathbf{E}_{trans}^{img}$. Finally we generate the translated image, $\mathbf{I}_{trans}$, using $\mathbf{S}_{trans}$ and $\mathbf{E}_{trans}^{img}$.

$$\mathbf{E}_{don}^{seg} \leftarrow E_{segmentation}(\mathbf{S}_{don}, \mathbf{S}_{don}^{-}) \tag{6}$$

$$\mathbf{E}_{sub}^{img} \leftarrow E_{image}(\mathbf{I}_{sub}, \mathbf{S}_{sub}) \quad \text{and} \quad \mathbf{E}_{don}^{img} \leftarrow E_{image}(\mathbf{I}_{don}, \mathbf{S}_{don}) \tag{7}$$

$$\mathbf{S}_{trans} \leftarrow G_{segmentation}(\mathbf{S}_{sub}^{-}, \mathbf{E}_{don}^{seg}) \tag{8}$$

$$\mathbf{E}_{trans}^{img} \leftarrow Combine(\mathbf{S}_{trans}, \mathbf{E}_{sub}^{img}, \mathbf{E}_{don}^{img}) \tag{9}$$

$$\mathbf{I}_{trans} \leftarrow G_{image}(\mathbf{S}_{trans}, \mathbf{E}_{trans}^{img}) \tag{10}$$

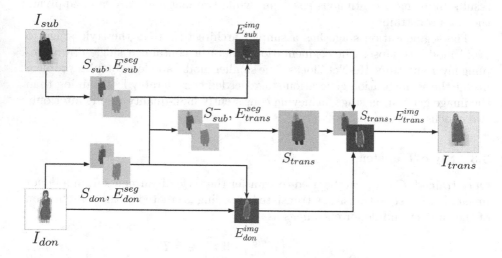

Fig. 3. Complete Garment Transfer schematic.

4   Evaluation and Results

After training the two stages independently on replication tasks, they were then both applied to transfer tasks. In this section we evaluate the style and shape transfer stages alone, before then evaluating the performance of the stages together. The first characterisation of performance is to replicate ground truth images by using the same image as both the subject and the donor. This was done with both stages independently, and later together. After this, we evaluate the method's ability to transfer style and shape as intended by replacing the garments in the subject image with those captured from the donor image.

It should be noted that a better representation of the subject would be achieved if the background, face and hair pixels were replaced with their original values. However, all the data presented is from the generator to demonstrate the ability to reproduce these features.

4.1 Dataset

While our method could be applied to any image domain we chose to generate clothing due to its complexity and diversity. We used the DeepFashion dataset [13], a large dataset of low resolution (128 × 128 pixels) fashion images and their associated segmentations from Zhu et al. [31]. We used the same 70,000 training images as Zhu et al. [31].

4.2 Garment Style Transfer

As the two stages are independent it is possible to evaluate the quality of the style transfer stage alone. We evaluate the style transfer stage in two ways: we attempt to replicate a ground truth image by using the same image as both subject and donor, as in Fig. 4, we also attempt to transfer styles of various sections of a single donor image onto the associated sections on a subject image, as demonstrated by Fig. 5.

Our method is able to generate realistic and representative results, as can be seen by the results from replicating of ground truth images in Fig. 4. The model is also able to transfer styles from both example images of garments and abstract style samples to create consistent and realistic images, as in Fig. 5. The abstract style transfer pipeline is identical to that used for garment transfer, the only difference being that an entire abstract image is encoded instead of a selected area from a garment segmentation. Abstract style transfer would allow users to design and alter clothing without requiring an exact subject image matching their requirements.

With only three encoder values defining the style of each garment, the style encoding can produce complex patterns, as can be seen in the bottom row of Fig. 5. These patterns and textures are significantly more complex than demonstrated in previous two dimensional garment generation work [31].

Complex garment features, such as creases, are convincingly generated in the correct garments and locations. The accurate location of creases in appropriate clothing shows that folds in clothing are correctly taken to be a function of garment shape and are ignored by the style encoder, this also explains the presence of realistic creases in loose garments generated using an abstract style as in Fig. 5.

We have compared our method to the neural style transfer method of Gatys et al. [5] both qualitatively as shown in Fig. 6 and quantitatively as is discussed further below. The traditional style transfer method is only able to extract a single style from the whole donor image, meaning we could only compare the results for abstract style transfer. Gatys et al. [5] also focused on transfer of image texture, so could not transfer a single, flat colour. Their method is also unable to selectively apply this style to a subject image, so in order to evaluate their method for clothing, we masked the results and only perform numerical evaluation on the pixels in the areas of interest in the final image.

The traditional approach is unable to separate garment shape and pattern, so some of the original garment pattern is present in the final image. Our method, on the other hand is agnostic to the original garment style and presents no artifacts of the original pattern. Since the traditional style transfer method has not been trained to specifically generate realistic clothing it is unable to generate any realistic creases or similar features.

We compare the two methods quantitatively by translating the style of an image twice, first to an abstract style, then back to the original images style to generate an approximation of the original, ground truth image. We find both the average pixel difference between the original and ground truth images and the percentage of pixels within certain absolute pixel difference tolerances. These results are shown in Table 1.

Due to the nature of GANs and our goal, to create novel images of people in different outfits while maintaining their pose, complex analysis and evaluation is difficult, since we are creating an image that has not existed before. Comparison to other work is also difficult as we are unaware of any similar work on semantic style transfer. While the comparison above is not perfect, as it does not measure global perceptual appearance, we believe it sufficient to objectively show our method is superior to a standard approach. We also believe that because this evaluation only values pixel similarity it puts our more nuanced results at a disadvantage to a more similar pattern generation tool, as, for example, a crease may be generated in a different place which would be perceived as realistic but evaluated as a large error.

The poor quality of the DeepFashion dataset creates simple errors in our style transfer results. The dataset's segmentations contains a significant number of misclassification errors. The effect of which can be seen in the hands in Fig. 4. The dataset also has very limited classes, excluding less common clothing items such as jewellery, hats and belts so this information has to be captured in the style encoding.

4.3   Segmentation Transfer

Despite the poor quality and errors in the dataset, our segmentation generation model generates well defined, acceptable results. The garment shape is altered while the subject pose and body shape are maintained. This is clearly demonstrated in Fig. 7a, where the sleeve length of a dress is dramatically changed.

This challenging shape alteration is achieved even when the original segmentation is in an obstructive pose, here the person with arms against their sides is wearing long sleeves.

Table 1. Quantiative evaluation of our method and traditional style transfer [5]. Values refer to absolute pixel value differences

	Mean difference	% within 15	% within 25	% within 50
Ours	24.5	45.93	64.59	86.548
Masked NST	92.64	10.75	17.92	33.84

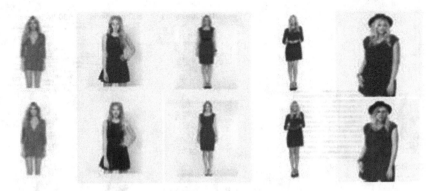

Fig. 4. Style replication results. The same input image (*top*) is used as the subject and donor for style transfer. The ideal result would be for the generated image to be identical to the input image.

Fig. 5. Style transfer results. The style of a donor image (*left*) is transferred to chosen sections of subject images. The style of the dresses are transferred in all cases, the hair colour is also transferred in the case of the top row. Notice how the creases look natural and realistic in the first two rows. For full effect view in colour. (Color figure online)

4.4   Complete Garment Transfer

We combine the two stages to create a single garment generation method, which we evaluate similarly to the style transfer stage, first by replicating ground truth images, as seen in the leading diagonal of Fig. 7b, then by evaluating true garment transfers between images as demonstrated by the remainder of Figs. 7b and 8.

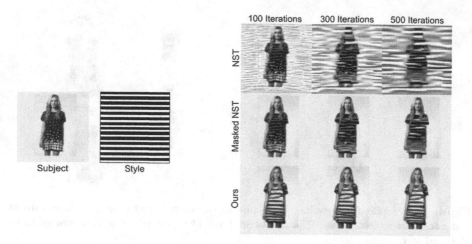

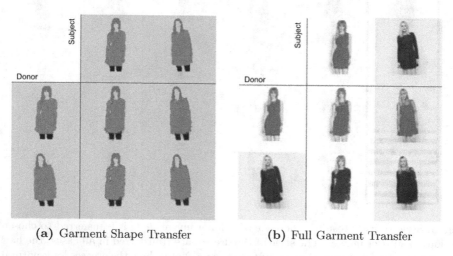

Fig. 6. Comparison between our method and Neural Style Transfer Gatys et al. [5].

(a) Garment Shape Transfer   (b) Full Garment Transfer

Fig. 7. Full garment swap. The replicated ground truth images (leading diagonal) are accurate, even with somewhat flawed segmentations.

We found the generated results were realistic and reflected the shape and style of donor garments well. The bottom row of Fig. 8 further demonstrates the encoder's ability to capture, as well as replicate, the main colours and repetitive nature of a complex pattern with only three values in the style encoding.

Fig. 8. Garment transfer results. The dress from a donor image (*left*) is transferred to various subject images.

5   Conclusion and Discussion

We present a method which enables the transfer of object shape and style between images. Our method includes two separate GANs to alter the shape and style of an object independently. The shape alteration stage can maintain the original subject pose while being invariant to the original shape. The style of the generated object is only dependent on the style extracted from the donor image. The remainder of the image is unaffected by the object transfer. This method could be applied to a variety of two dimensional object transfer tasks. We apply this method to complex garment transfer tasks and achieve impressive, realistic clothing transfer.

Our current work has been limited by the lack of variation in the dataset we used. It would be valuable to explore a more diverse dataset containing more poses and body shapes. Here we used three values to define each garments shape. While this encoding has demonstrated the quality of the method experimentally, a more diverse dataset would likely require the use of a wider shape encoding to capture the full variation of the available data. It is likely too that the loss function in shape stage could be optimised to encourage low frequency results.

References

1. Bossard, L., Dantone, M., Leistner, C., Wengert, C., Quack, T., Van Gool, L.: Apparel classification with style. In: Lee, K.M., Matsushita, Y., Rehg, J.M., Hu, Z. (eds.) ACCV 2012. LNCS, vol. 7727, pp. 321–335. Springer, Heidelberg (2013). https://doi.org/10.1007/978-3-642-37447-0_25
2. Denton, E., Chintala, S., Szlam, A., Fergus, R.: Deep Generative Image Models using a Laplacian Pyramid of Adversarial Networks. CoRR, June 2015
3. Fitzgibbon, A., Lazebnik, S., Perona, P., Sato, Y., Schmid, C. (eds.): ECCV 2012. LNCS, vol. 7577. Springer, Heidelberg (2012). https://doi.org/10.1007/978-3-642-33783-3
4. Gatys, L.A., Ecker, A.S., Bethge, M.: A Neural Algorithm of Artistic Style (2015). https://doi.org/10.1167/16.12.326. http://arxiv.org/abs/1508.06576

5. Gatys, L.A., Ecker, A.S., Bethge, M.: Texture synthesis using convolutional neural networks. In: The IEEE Conference on Computer Vision and Pattern Recognition, pp. 2414–2423 (2015). https://doi.org/10.1109/CVPR.2016.265
6. Isola, P., Zhu, J.Y., Zhou, T., Efros, A.A.: Image-to-image translation with conditional adversarial networks. In: Proceedings - 30th IEEE Conference on Computer Vision and Pattern Recognition, CVPR 2017, January 2017, pp. 5967–5976, November 2017. https://doi.org/10.1109/CVPR.2017.632. http://arxiv.org/abs/1611.07004
7. Johnson, J., Alahi, A., Fei-Fei, L.: Perceptual losses for real-time style transfer and super-resolution. In: Leibe, B., Matas, J., Sebe, N., Welling, M. (eds.) ECCV 2016. LNCS, vol. 9906, pp. 694–711. Springer, Cham (2016). https://doi.org/10.1007/978-3-319-46475-6_43
8. Karras, T., Aila, T., Laine, S., Lehtinen, J.: Progressive Growing of GANs for Improved Quality, Stability, and Variation, October 2017
9. Kinoshita, S., Ogawa, T., Haseyama, M.: LDA-based music recommendation with CF-based similar user selection. In: 2015 IEEE 4th Global Conference on Consumer Electronics, GCCE 2015, pp. 215–216, June 2016. https://doi.org/10.1109/GCCE.2015.7398561
10. Larsen, A.B.L., Sønderby, S.K., Larochelle, H., Winther, O.: Autoencoding beyond pixels using a learned similarity metric. Class Project for Stanford CS231N: Convolutional Neural Networks for Visual Recognition, Winter semester 2014, vol. 5, p. 2 (2015)
11. Lassner, C., Pons-Moll, G., Gehler, P.V.: A generative model of people in clothing. In: Proceedings of the IEEE International Conference on Computer Vision, October 2017, pp. 853–862 (2017). https://doi.org/10.1109/ICCV.2017.98
12. Liu, M.Y., Breuel, T., Kautz, J.: Unsupervised Image-to-Image Translation Networks, March 2017
13. Liu, Z., Luo, P., Qiu, S., Wang, X., Tang, X.: DeepFashion: powering robust clothes recognition and retrieval with rich annotations. In: 2016 IEEE Conference on Computer Vision and Pattern Recognition (CVPR), pp. 1096–1104. IEEE, June 2016. https://doi.org/10.1109/CVPR.2016.124
14. Men, Y., Lian, Z., Tang, Y., Xiao, J.: A common framework for interactive texture transfer. In: CVPR (2018)
15. Odena, A., Olah, C., Shlens, J.: Conditional Image Synthesis With Auxiliary Classifier GANs, October 2016
16. van den Oord, A., Kalchbrenner, N., Vinyals, O., Espeholt, L., Graves, A., Kavukcuoglu, K.: Conditional Image Generation with PixelCNN Decoders, June 2016
17. Reed, S., Akata, Z., Yan, X., Logeswaran, L., Schiele, B., Lee, H.: Generative Adversarial Text to Image Synthesis, May 2016
18. Stroud, M.L., Stilgoe, S., Stott, V.E., Alhabian, O., Salman, K.: Vitamin D - a review. Aust. Fam. Physician 37(12), 1002–1005 (2008). https://doi.org/10.1177/1470320311410924
19. Wang, T.C., Liu, M.Y., Zhu, J.Y., Tao, A., Kautz, J., Catanzaro, B.: High-Resolution Image Synthesis and Semantic Manipulation with Conditional GANs, November 2017
20. Wang, X., Gupta, A.: Generative image modeling using style and structure adversarial networks. In: Leibe, B., Matas, J., Sebe, N., Welling, M. (eds.) ECCV 2016. LNCS, vol. 9908, pp. 318–335. Springer, Cham (2016). https://doi.org/10.1007/978-3-319-46493-0_20

21. Wells, A., Wood, J., Xiao, M.: Localized Style Transfer With Semantic Segmentation, p. 2015 (2016)
22. Wu, S., Zhong, S., Liu, Y.: Deep residual learning for image steganalysis. Multimedia Tools Appl. **77**(9), 1–17 (2018). https://doi.org/10.1007/s11042-017-4440-4
23. Xian, W., et al.: TextureGAN: Controlling Deep Image Synthesis with Texture Patches, June 2017
24. Yan, X., Yang, J., Sohn, K., Lee, H.: Attribute2Image: conditional image generation from visual attributes. In: Leibe, B., Matas, J., Sebe, N., Welling, M. (eds.) ECCV 2016. LNCS, vol. 9908, pp. 776–791. Springer, Cham (2016). https://doi.org/10.1007/978-3-319-46493-0_47
25. Yang, S., et al.: Detailed garment recovery from a single-view image. CoRR abs/1608.01250 (2016)
26. Yang, W., Luo, P., Lin, L.: Clothing co-parsing by joint image segmentation and labeling. In: Proceedings of the IEEE Computer Society Conference on Computer Vision and Pattern Recognition, pp. 3182–3189, February 2014. https://doi.org/10.1109/CVPR.2014.407
27. Zhang, C., Pujades, S., Black, M., Pons-Moll, G.: Detailed, accurate, human shape estimation from clothed 3D scan sequences. In: Proceedings - 30th IEEE Conference on Computer Vision and Pattern Recognition, CVPR 2017, January 2017, pp. 5484–5493, March 2017. https://doi.org/10.1109/CVPR.2017.582
28. Zhang, H., et al.: StackGAN: text to photo-realistic image synthesis with stacked generative adversarial networks. In: Proceedings of the IEEE International Conference on Computer Vision, October 2017, pp. 5908–5916, December 2017. https://doi.org/10.1109/ICCV.2017.629
29. Zhu, J.Y., Park, T., Isola, P., Efros, A.A.: Unpaired image-to-image translation using cycle-consistent adversarial networks. In: Proceedings of the IEEE International Conference on Computer Vision, October 2017, pp. 2242–2251 (2017). https://doi.org/10.1109/ICCV.2017.244
30. Zhu, J.Y., et al.: Toward Multimodal Image-to-Image Translation, November 2017
31. Zhu, S., Fidler, S., Urtasun, R., Lin, D., Loy, C.C.: Be your own prada: fashion synthesis with structural coherence. In: Proceedings of the IEEE International Conference on Computer Vision, October 2017, pp. 1689–1697, October 2017. https://doi.org/10.1109/ICCV.2017.186

Towards Multi-class Object Detection in Unconstrained Remote Sensing Imagery

Seyed Majid Azimi[1,2]([✉]) [iD], Eleonora Vig[1] [iD], Reza Bahmanyar[1] [iD],
Marco Körner[2] [iD], and Peter Reinartz[1] [iD]

[1] German Aerospace Center, Remote Sensing Technology Institute,
Wessling, Germany
seyedmajid.azimi@dlr.de

[2] Technical University of Munich, Chair of Remote Sensing, Munich, Germany

Abstract. Automatic multi-class object detection in remote sensing images in unconstrained scenarios is of high interest for several applications including traffic monitoring and disaster management. The huge variation in object scale, orientation, category, and complex backgrounds, as well as the different camera sensors pose great challenges for current algorithms. In this work, we propose a new method consisting of a novel joint image cascade and feature pyramid network with multi-size convolution kernels to extract multi-scale strong and weak semantic features. These features are fed into rotation-based region proposal and region of interest networks to produce object detections. Finally, rotational non-maximum suppression is applied to remove redundant detections. During training, we minimize joint horizontal and oriented bounding box loss functions, as well as a novel loss that enforces oriented boxes to be rectangular. Our method achieves 68.16% mAP on horizontal and 72.45% mAP on oriented bounding box detection tasks on the challenging DOTA dataset, outperforming all published methods by a large margin (+6% and +12% absolute improvement, respectively). Furthermore, it generalizes to two other datasets, NWPU VHR-10 and UCAS-AOD, and achieves competitive results with the baselines even when trained on DOTA. Our method can be deployed in multi-class object detection applications, regardless of the image and object scales and orientations, making it a great choice for unconstrained aerial and satellite imagery.

Keywords: Object detection · Remote sensing · CNN

1 Introduction

The recent advances in *remote sensing (RS)* technologies have eased the acquisition of very high-resolution multi-spectral satellite and aerial images. Automatic RS data analysis can provide an insightful understanding over large areas in a short time. In this analysis, multi-class object detection (*e.g.*, vehicles, ships, airplanes, etc.) plays a major role. It is a key component of many applications

© Springer Nature Switzerland AG 2019
C. V. Jawahar et al. (Eds.): ACCV 2018, LNCS 11363, pp. 150–165, 2019.
https://doi.org/10.1007/978-3-030-20893-6_10

such as traffic monitoring, parking lot utilization, disaster management, urban management, search and rescue missions, maritime traffic monitoring and so on. Object detection in RS images is a big challenge as the images can be acquired with different modalities (*e.g.*, panchromatic, multi- and hyper-spectral, and Radar) with a wide range of *ground sampling distance (GSD) e.g.*, from 10 cm to 30 m. Furthermore, the objects can largely vary in scale, size, and orientation.

In recent years, deep learning methods have achieved promising object detection results for ground imagery and outperformed traditional methods. Among them, *deep convolutional neural networks (DCNNs)* have been widely used [10,13,26]. In the RS domain, newly introduced large-scale multi-class image datasets such as DOTA [30] have provided the opportunity to leverage the applications of deep learning methods. The majority of current deep learning-based methods detect objects based on *horizontal bounding boxes (HBBs)*, which are appropriate for ground-level images. However, in the RS scenarios, objects can be arbitrarily oriented. Therefore, utilizing *oriented bounding boxes (OBBs)* is highly recommended, especially when multiple objects are located tightly close to each other (*e.g.*, cars in parking lots).

Region-based convolutional neural networks (RCNNs) such as (Fast(er))-RCNN [8,23,24] and Mask-RCNN [9] have achieved state-of-the-art object detection results in large-scale ground imagery datasets [6,15]. Fast-RCNN [24] improves the detection accuracy of RCNN [8] by using a multi-task loss function for the simultaneous region proposal regression and classification tasks. As an improvement, Faster-RCNN integrates an end-to-end trainable network, called *region proposal network (RPN)*, to learn the region proposals for increasing the localization accuracy of Fast-RCNN. To further improve Faster-RCNN, one could perform multi-scale training and testing to learn feature maps in multiple levels; however, this will increase the memory usage and inference time.

Another alternative is image or feature pyramids [7,12,14,20,21,31]. Recently, Lin et al. [14] proposed the *feature pyramid network (FPN)* which extracts feature maps through a feature pyramid, thus facilitating object detection in different scales, at a marginal extra cost. Although joint image and feature pyramids may further improve results, this is avoided due to its computation cost.

Object detection in RS images has been investigated by a number of works in the recent years. The majority of the proposed algorithms focus on object detection with a small number of classes and a limited range of GSDs. Liu and Mattyus [16] proposed *histogram of oriented gradients (HOG)* features and the AdaBoost method for feature classification to detect multi-class oriented vehicles. Although this approach achieves a fast inference time, it does not have high detection accuracy as it lacks high-level feature extraction. Sommer et al. [27] and Tang et al. [29] proposed RCNN-based methods using hard-negative mining together with concatenated and deconvolutional feature maps. They showed that these methods achieve high accuracies in single-class vehicle detection in aerial images for HBBs task. Liu et al. [17] proposed rotated region proposals to predict object orientation using *single shot detector (SSD)* [18] improving the localization of the OBBs task. Yang et al. [32] improved [17] by integrating FPNs.

In this paper, we focus on improving the object localization of region-based methods applied to aerial and satellite images. We propose a new end-to-end CNN to address the aforementioned challenges of multi-class object detection in RS images. The proposed method is able to handle images with a wide range of scales, aspect ratios, GSDs, and complex backgrounds. In addition, our proposed method achieves accurate object localization by using OBBs. More specifically, the method is composed of the following consecutive modules: *image cascade network (ICN), deformable inception network (DIN)*, FPN, *multiscale rotational region-proposal network (R-RPN), multi-scale rotational region of interest network (R-ROI)*, and *rotational non-maximum suppression (RNMS)*. The main contributions of our work are the following:

- We propose a new joint image cascade and feature pyramid network (ICN and FPN) which allows extracting information on a wide range of scales and significantly improves the detection results.
- We design a DIN module as a domain adaptation module for adapting the pre-trained networks to the RS domain using deformable convolutions and multi-size convolution kernels.
- We propose a new loss function to enforce the detection coordinates, forming quadrilaterals, to shape rectangles by constraining the angles between the edges to be 90°. This augments object localization.
- We achieve significant improvements on three challenging datasets in comparison with the state of the art.

In addition, we employ rotational region proposals to capture object locations more accurately in RS images. Finally, in order to select the best localized regions and to remove redundant detections, we apply R-NMS which is the rotational variant of the conventional NMS. Furthermore, we initialize anchor sizes in R-RPNs with clustered data from rotated ground truth bounding boxes proposed by Redmon and Farhadi [22] rather than manual initialization used in Faster-RCNN. In order to evaluate the proposed method, we applied it to the DOTA [30] dataset, a recent large-scale satellite and aerial image dataset, as well as the UCAS-AOD and NWPU VHR-10 datasets. Results show that the proposed method achieves a significantly higher accuracy in comparison with state-of-the-art object detection methods.

2   Proposed Method

Figure 1 gives a high-level overview of our joint horizontal and oriented bounding box prediction pipeline for multi-class object detection. Given an input image, combined image cascade and feature pyramid networks (ICN and FPN) extract rich semantic feature maps tuned for objects of substantially varying sizes. Following the feature extraction, a R-RPN returns category-agnostic rotated regions, which are then classified and regressed to bounding-box locations with a R-ROI. During training, we minimize a multi-task loss both for R-RPN and R-ROI. To obtain rectangular predictions, we further refine the output quadrilaterals by computing their minimum bounding rectangles. Finally, R-NMS is applied as a post-processing.

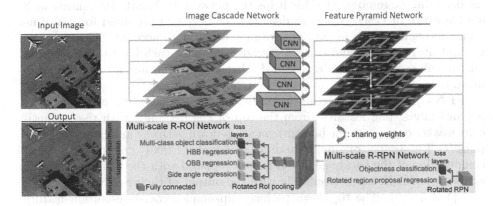

Fig. 1. Overview of our algorithm for (non-)rotated multi-class object detection.

2.1 Image Cascade, Feature Pyramid, and Deformable Inception Subnetworks

In order to extract strong semantic information from different scales, this work aims at leveraging the pyramidal feature hierarchy of *convolutional neural networks (CNNs)*. Until recently, feature extraction was typically performed on a single scale [23]. Lately, however, multi-scale approaches became feasible through FPN [14]. As argued in [14], the use of pyramids both at the image and the feature level is computationally prohibitive. Nevertheless, here we show that by an appropriate weight sharing, the combination of ICN (Fig. 2) and FPN (Fig. 3) becomes feasible and outputs proportionally-sized features at different levels/scales in a fully-convolutional manner. This pipeline is independent of the backbone CNN (*e.g.*, AlexNet [13], VGG [26], or ResNet [10]). Here, we use ResNet [10]. In the **ICN**, as illustrated in Fig. 2, we use ResNet to compute a feature hierarchy C_1, C_2, C_3, C_4, C_5, which correspond to the outputs of the residual blocks: conv1, conv2, conv3, conv4, and conv5 (blue boxes in Fig. 2). The pixel strides for different residual boxes are 2, 4, 8, 16, and 32 pixels with respect to the input image.

To build our image cascade network, we resize the input image by bilinear interpolation to obtain four scaled versions ($1.5\times$, $1\times$, $0.75\times$, $0.5\times$) and extract the feature hierarchy using ResNet subnetworks. For example, while all five residual blocks are used for the upsampled input ($1.5\times$), for the half-resolution version ($0.5\times$), only C_4 and C_5 are used. The cascade network is thus composed of different subnetworks of the ResNet sharing their weights with each other. Therefore, apart from resizing the input image, this step does not add further computation costs with respect to the single resolution baseline. ICN allows combining the low-level semantic features form higher resolutions (used for detecting small objects) with the high-level semantic features from low resolutions (used for detecting large objects). This helps the network to handle RS images with a wide range of GSD. A similar definition of ICN was proposed for real-time semantic segmentation in [33], but without taking into account different scales in the feature domain and using a cascaded label for each level to compensate for the sub-sampling. Such a cascaded label is more suitable for semantic segmentation.

FPNs [14] allow extracting features at different scales by combining the semantically strong features (from the top of the pyramid) with the semantically weaker ones (from the bottom) via a top-down pathway and lateral connections (cf. Fig. 3). The original bottom-up pathway of FPN (*i.e.*, the feed-forward computation of the backbone CNN) is here replaced with the feature hierarchy extraction of ICN, more specifically with the output of their residual blocks C_i, $i \in \{1,2,3,4,5\}$. The top-down pathway upsamples coarse-resolution feature maps (M_i) by a factor of 2 and merges them with the corresponding bottom-up maps C_{i-1} (*i.e.*, the lateral connections). The final set of feature maps P_i, $i \in \{1,2,3,4,5\}$, is obtained by appending 3×3 convolutions to M_i to reduce the aliasing effect of upsampling. We refer the reader to the work of Lin et al. [14] for more details on FPNs.

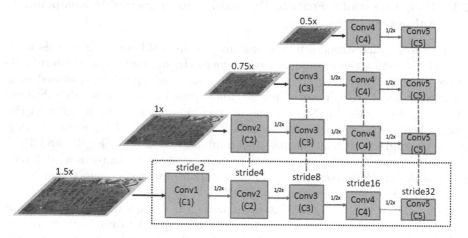

Fig. 2. Illustration of the image cascade network (ICN). Input images are first up- and down-sampled. Then they are fed into different CNN cascade levels. (Color figure online)

In the original FPN, the output of each C_i goes through a 1×1 convolution to reduce the number of feature maps in M_i. Here, we replace the 1×1 convolution with a **DIN** (Deformable Inception Network, cf. Fig. 3) to enhance the localization properties of CNNs, especially for small objects which are ubiquitous in

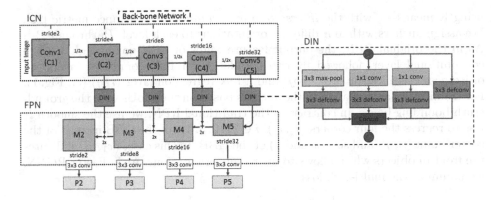

Fig. 3. Illustration of the ICN and FPN subnetworks with deformable inception network (DIN). DIN is the modified Inception block to learn features of objects including geometrical features in flexible kernel sizes with stride 1. "defconv" stands for deformable convolution.

RS datasets. Although Inception modules [28] have shown promising results in various tasks such as object recognition, their effectiveness for detection has not been extensively studied. While most current state-of-the-art methods, such as Faster-RCNN, R-FCN [3], YOLOv3 [22], and SSD [18], focus on increasing the network depth, the benefit of Inception blocks lies in capturing details at varied scales which is highly desirable for RS imagery.

Deformable networks aim at overcoming the limitations of CNNs in modeling geometric transformations due to their fixed-size convolution kernels. When applying the models pretrained on ground imagery (such as our ResNet backbone) to RS images, the parameters of traditional convolution layers cannot adapt effectively to the new views of objects leading to degradations in localization performance. Using deformable convolutions in DIN helps accommodating such geometric transformations [4]. Furthermore, the offset regression property of deformable convolution layers helps localizing the objects even outside the kernel range. Here, we train the added offset layer from scratch to let the network adjust to the new domain. 1×1 convolution layers reduce dimensions by half for the next deformable convolution (def-conv) layers. The channel input to DIN is divided equally among the four DIN branches. In our experiments, we did not observe an improvement by using 5×5 def-conv layers, hence the use of 3×3 layers.

2.2 Rotation Region Proposal Network (R-RPN)

The output of each P_i block in the FPN module is processed by multi-scale rotated region proposal networks (R-RPN) in order to provide rotated proposals, inspired by [19]. More precisely, we modify RPN to propose rotated regions with 0, 45, 90, and 135° rotation, not differentiating between the front and back of objects. For initializing the anchors, we cluster the scales and aspect ratios using K-means++ with the *intersection over union (IoU)* distance metric [22]. We assign anchors with four different orientations to each level, P_2 through P_6[1]. As in the original RPN, the output feature maps of FPN go through a 3×3 convolutional layer, followed by two parallel 1×1 fully-connected layers: an objectness classification layer (*obj*) and a box-regression layer (*reg*) (cf. Fig. 1). For training, we assign labels to the anchors based on their IoUs with the ground-truth bounding boxes. In contrast to the traditional RPN, we use the smooth l_1 loss to regress the four corners (x_i, y_i), $i \in \{1, 2, 3, 4\}$, of the OBB instead of the center point (x, y), and size (w and h) of the HBB. In this case, (x_1, y_1) indicates the front of objects which allows to infer their orientations. As in Faster-RCNN, we minimize the multi-task loss

$$L\left(\{p_i\}, \{t_i\}\right) = \frac{1}{N_{obj}} \sum_i L_{obj}(p_i, p_i^*) + \lambda \frac{1}{N_{reg}} \sum_i p_i^* L_{reg}\left(t_i, t_i^*\right), \quad (1)$$

where, for an anchor i in a mini-batch, p_i is its predicted probability of being an object and p_i^* is its ground-truth binary label. For classification (object/not-object), the log-loss $L_{obj}(p_i, p_i^*) = -p_i^* \log p_i$ is used, while we employ the smooth l_1 loss

$$L_{reg}(t_i, t_i^*) = l_1^{smooth}(t_i - t_i^*) \quad \text{with } l_1^{smooth}(x) = \begin{cases} 0.5x^2 & \text{if } |x| < 1 \\ |x| - 0.5 & \text{otherwise} \end{cases} \quad (2)$$

for the bounding box regression. Here,

$$t_{xi} = (x_i - x_{i,a})/w_a, \qquad\qquad t_{yi} = (y_i - y_{i,a})/h_a \qquad (3)$$
$$t_{xi}^* = (x_i^* - x_{i,a})/w_a, \qquad\qquad t_{yi}^* = (y_i^* - y_{i,a})/h_a \qquad (4)$$

are the four parameterized coordinates of the predicted and ground-truth anchors with x_i, $x_{i,a}$, and x_i^* denoting the predicted, anchor, and ground-truth, respectively (the same goes for y); and w_a and h_a are width and height of the anchor. N_{obj} and N_{reg} are normalizing hyper-parameters (the mini-batch size and number of anchor locations); and λ is the balancing hyper-parameter between the two losses which is set to 10.

2.3   Rotated Region of Interest Network (R-ROI)

Similar to [14], we use a multi-scale ROI pooling layer to process the regions proposed by R-RPN. Because the generated proposals are rotated, we rotate them to be axis-aligned. The resulting fixed-length feature vectors are fed into sequential fully-connected (*fc*) layers, and are finally sent through four sibling *fc* layers, which – for each object proposal – output the class prediction, refined HBB and OBB positions, as well as the angles of OBBs.

---

[1] P_6 is a stride 2 sub-sampling of P_5 used to propose regions for large objects. P_1 is not computed due to its large memory footprint.

As seen for R-RPNs, OBBs are not restricted to be rectangular: R-RPN predicts the four corners of quadrilaterals without any constraint on the corners or edges. However, we observed that annotators tend to label rotated objects in RS images with quadrilaterals that are close to rotated rectangles. In order to enforce a rectangular shape of OBBs, we propose a new loss that considers the angles between adjacent edges, *i.e.*, we penalize angles that are not 90°.

Let us consider P_{ij} a quadrilateral side connecting the corners i to j, where $i, j \in \{1, 2, 3, 4\}$ and $i \neq j$. Then, using the cosine rule, we calculate the angle between adjacent sides (*e.g.*, θ_1 between P_{12} and P_{13}) as:

$$\theta_1 = \arccos((|P_{12}|^2 + |P_{13}|^2 - |P_{23}|^2)/(2 * |P_{12}| * |P_{13}|)), \tag{5}$$

where $|P_{ij}|$ is the length of the side P_{ij}. There are multiple ways to constrain $\theta_l, l \in \{1, 2, 3\}$ to be right angles. (Note that θ_4 can be computed from the other three angles). We experimented with the following three angle-losses:

$$\text{Tangent L1} : L_{angle-OBB}(\theta) = \sum_{l=1}^{3} (|tan(\theta_l - 90)|)$$

$$\text{Smooth L1} : L_{angle-OBB}(\theta) = \sum_{l=1}^{3} smooth_{L1}(|\theta_l - 90|) \tag{6}$$

$$\text{L2} : L_{angle-OBB}(\theta) = \sum_{l=1}^{3} \|(\theta_l - 90)\|^2.$$

Our final loss function is a multi-task loss composed of four losses that simultaneously predict the object category (L_{cls}), regress both HBB and OBB coordinates ($L_{loc-HBB}$ and $L_{loc-OBB}$), and enforce OBBs to be rectangular ($L_{angle-OBB}$):

$$L(p, u, t^u, v) = L_{cls}(p, u) + \lambda[u \geq 1]L_{loc-HBB}(t^u, v) + \\ \lambda[u \geq 1]L_{loc-OBB}(t^u, v) + \lambda[u \geq 1]L_{angle-OBB}(\theta), \tag{7}$$

where $L_{cls}(p, u) = -u \log p$ and $L_{loc-OBB}(t^u, v)$ is defined similar to L_{reg} as in R-RPN above. u is the true class and p is the discrete probability distribution for the predicted classes, defined over $K+1$ categories as $p = (p_0, ..., p_K)$ in which "1" is for the background category. $t^u = (t^u_{xi}, t^u_{yi})$ is the predicted OBB regression offset for class u and $v = (v_{xi}, v_{yi})$ is the true OBB ($i \in \{1, 2, 3, 4\}$). $L_{loc-HBB}(t^u, v)$ is defined similar to L_{reg} in Faster-RCNN in which instead of OBB coordinates, $\{xmin, ymin, w, h\}$ (the upper-left coordinates, width and height) of t^u and v for the corresponding HBB coordinates are utilized. In case the object is classified as background, $[u \geq 1]$ ignores the offset regression. The balancing hyper-parameter λ is set to 1. To obtain the final detections, we compute the minimum bounding rectangles of the predicted quadrilaterals. As the final post-processing, we apply R-NMS in which the overlap between rotated detections is computed to select the best localized regions and to remove redundant regions.

3 Experiments and Discussion

In this section, we present and discuss the evaluation results of the proposed method on three RS image datasets. All experiments were conducted using NVIDIA Titan X GPUs. The backbone network's weights were initialized using the ResNet-50/101 and ResNeXt-101 models pretrained on ImageNet [5]. Images were preprocessed as described in baseline [30]. Furthermore, the learning rate was 0.0005 for 60 epochs with the batch size of 1 using flipped images as the data augmentation. Additionally, during training, we applied *online hard example mining (OHEM)* [25] to reduce false positives and we use Soft-NMS [1] as a more accurate non-maximum suppression approach only for the HBB benchmark.

3.1 Datasets

The experiments were conducted on the DOTA [30], UCAS-AOD [34], and NWPU VHR-10 [2] datasets which all have multi-class object annotations.

DOTA is the largest and most diverse published dataset for multi-class object detection in aerial and satellite images. It contains 2,806 images from different camera sensors, GSDs (10 cm to 1 m), and sizes to reflect real-world scenarios and decrease the dataset bias. The images are mainly acquired from Google Earth, and the rest from the JL-1 and GF-2 satellites of the China Center for Resources Satellite Data and Application. Image sizes vary from 288 to 8,115 pixels in width, and from 211 to 13,383 pixels in height. There are 15 object categories: plane, baseball diamond (BD), bridge, ground field track (GTF), small vehicle (SV), large vehicle (LV), tennis court (TC), basketball court (BC), storage tank (SC), soccer ball field (SBF), roundabout (RA), swimming pool (SP), helicopter (HC), and harbor. DOTA is split into training (1/2), validation (1/6), and test (1/3) sets.

UCAS-AOD contains 1,510 satellite images ($\approx 700 \times 1300$ px) with 14,595 objects annotated by OBBs for two categories: vehicles and planes. The dataset was randomly split into 1,110 training and 400 testing images.

NWPU VHR-10 contains 800 satellite images ($\approx 500 \times 1000$ px) with 3,651 objects were annotated with HBBs. There are 10 object categories: plane, ship, storage tank, baseball diamond, tennis court, basketball court, ground track field, harbor, bridge, and small vehicle. For training, we used non-rotated RPN and *region of interest (ROI)* networks only for the HBBs detection task.

3.2 Evaluation

In order to assess the accuracy of our detection and the quality of region proposals, we adopted the same *mean average precision (mAP)* and *average recall (AR)* calculations as for DOTA [30]. We conducted ablation experiments on the validation set of DOTA. Furthermore, we compare our method to the ones in [30] for HBB and OBB prediction tasks as well as Yang et al. [32] for OBB task based on the test set whose ground-truth labels are undisclosed (Fig. 4). The results reported here were obtained by submitting our predictions to the official DOTA evaluation server[2]. We used 0.1 threshold for R-NMS and 0.3 for Soft-NMS.

The Impact of ICN: Table 1 shows the evaluation results of ICN. According to the table, adding OHEM to ResNet-50 improved the accuracy by a narrow margin. Using a deeper network such as ResNet-101 further improved the accuracy. As a next step, adding a 1.5× cascade level increased mAP by around 2% indicating that the up-sampled input can have a significant impact. Based on this, we added smaller cascade levels such as 0.75× and 0.5×, which however, increased the accuracy to a lesser extent. This could be due to the fact that the majority of objects within this dataset are small, so reducing resolution is not always optimal. Further increasing the cascade levels (*e.g.*, 1.75× and 2×) degraded the accuracy, which is due to the lack of annotations for very small objects such as small vehicles. We argue that extracting ResNet features on upsampled images (1.5×) is beneficial for the small objects in the DOTA dataset, whereas doing this on the downsampled input (0.75×, 0.5×) brings smaller improvements because of the lower number of large objects in the dataset. We observed that replacing ResNet-101 with ResNeXt-101 causes a small drop in accuracy which could be due to the shallower architecture of ResNeXt-101. Results indicated that using a higher number of proposals (2000) increases the accuracy to a small degree, which however came with an increased computation cost; thus, we considered 300 proposals for the rest of our experiments.

Table 1. Evaluation of (1) the impact of ICN with different cascade levels, (2) the effect of the backbone network (ResNet50/101, ResNeXt101), and (3) the influence of the number of proposals for the OBB prediction task. The models were trained on the DOTA training set and results are on the validation set.

Cascade level	Proposals	Backbone	OHEM	mAP (%)
1	300	ResNet-50	—	63.35
1	300	ResNet-50	✓	64.61
1	300	ResNet-101	✓	65.37
[1.5, 1]	300	ResNet-101	✓	67.32
[1.5, 1, 0.75]	300	ResNet-101	✓	68.06
[1.5, 1, 0.75, 0.5]	300	ResNet-101	✓	68.17
[1.5, 1, 0.75, 0.5]	300	ResNeXt-101	✓	68.09
[1.5, 1, 0.75, 0.5]	2000	ResNet-101	✓	**68.29**
[1.75, 1.5, 1, 0.75]	2000	ResNet-101	✓	67.36
[2, 1.5, 1.5, 1, 0.75]	2000	ResNet-101	✓	66.86

The Impact of DIN: From Table 2 we see that replacing the 1×1 convolution after the residual blocks C_i by DIN can augment mAP by more than 2%. More

---

specifically, using DIN after lower level C_is resulted in slightly higher accuracy than using it after higher levels (*e.g.*, mAP for C4 > mAP for C5). In addition, employing DIN after multiple C_is can further improve model performance (*e.g.*, mAP for C4 < mAP for C4—C5 < mAP for C3—C5). Kernel size strongly affects the high resolution (semantically weak) features. Thus, applying DIN to the low-level C_is enriched the features and adapts them to the new data domain. Comparing the last two rows of Table 2, we see that deformable convolutions also have a positive impact; however, the improvement is smaller.

Table 2. Evaluation of employing DIN after certain residual blocks C_i with and without deformable convolutions on the validation set of DOTA.

DIN	Def. conv.	mAP (%)
-	-	65.97
C4	-	66.24
C5	-	66.28
C4—C5	-	66.41
C3—C5	-	66.75
C2—C5	-	67.47
C2—C5	✓	**68.17**

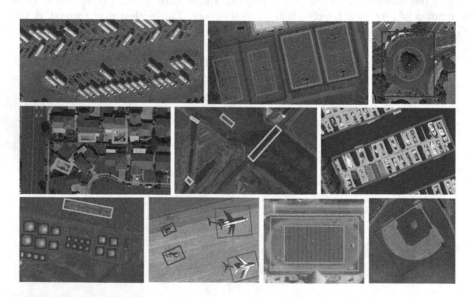

Fig. 4. Sample OBB predictions in the DOTA test set.

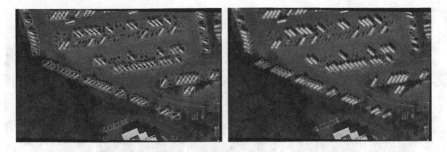

Fig. 5. Outputs of HBB (left) and OBB (right) prediction on an image of DOTA.

Table 3. Evaluation of (1) the impact of rotated RPN and RoI and (2) the effect of the loss functions enforcing the rectangularity of the bounding boxes.

Angle Loss functions	Rotated BBs in RPN & RoI	mAP (%)
-	-	64.27
-	✓	65.67
Tangent L1	✓	66.91
Smooth L1	✓	67.41
L2	✓	**68.17**

Rotated RPN and ROI Modules: Using clustered initialized anchors with rotation, we obtained an additional 0.7% mAP. To initialize anchors, we selected 18 anchors compared to 15 in Faster-RCNN in clustering ground-truth OBBs. We observed no significant increase in IoU with higher number for anchors. Furthermore, we considered each anchor at four different angles (0, 45, 90, 135° rotation). The total number of anchors is thus 18 × 4. Table 3 shows that using rotated proposals in the R-RPN/ R-ROI layers improves mAP by 1.4%, indicating that these proposals are more appropriate for RS images (Fig. 5).

In addition, we see that using a joint loss function (for HBB and OBB prediction) can increase the prediction of OBBs by 0.81% mAP. We believe that HBBs provide useful "hints" on the position of the object for regressing OBBs more accurately. This is not the case for HBB prediction: here, using only the HBB regression loss achieves 3.98% higher mAP as compared to the joint loss. This could be due to the complexity that OBB imposes on the optimization problem. Thus, we apply our algorithm on the HBB benchmark without the OBB loss.

Enforcing Rectangular Bounding Boxes: We investigated three different loss functions to enforce the rectangularity of the quadrilateral bounding boxes. Results in Table 3 show that all three angle losses improve the output accuracy and angle L2 performs the best. The reason behind the lower performance of angle tangent L1 could be the property of the *tangent* function: it leads to very high loss values when the deviation from the right angle is large. Angle smooth

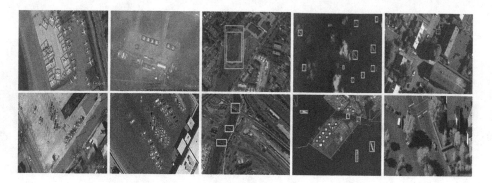

Fig. 6. Sample outputs of our algorithm on the NWPU VHR-10 (three right columns – different camera sensors) and UCAS-AOD (two left columns – different weather conditions, camera angles, and GSDs) datasets.

Table 4. Quantitative comparison of the baseline and our method on the HBB task in test set of DOTA dataset. FR-H stands for Faster R-CNN [23] trained on HBB. TV stands for 'trainval' and T for 'train' subsets.

method	data	mAP	plane	BD	bridge	GTF	SV	LV	ship	TC	BC	ST	SBF	RA	harbor	SP	HC
Yolov2-[22]	TV	39.20	76.90	33.87	22.73	34.88	38.73	32.02	52.37	61.65	48.54	33.91	29.27	36.83	36.44	38.26	11.61
R-FCN[3]	TV	52.58	81.01	58.96	31.64	58.97	49.77	45.04	49.29	68.99	52.07	67.42	41.83	51.44	45.15	53.3	33.89
SSD[18]	TV	29.86	57.85	32.79	16.14	18.67	0.05	36.93	24.74	81.16	25.1	47.47	11.22	31.53	14.12	9.09	0.0
FR-H[23]	TV	60.64	80.32	77.55	32.86	68.13	53.66	52.49	50.04	90.41	75.05	59.59	57.00	49.81	61.69	56.46	41.85
ours	T	70.54	89.54	73.48	51.96	70.33	73.39	67.91	78.15	90.39	78.73	78.48	51.02	59.41	73.81	69.00	52.59
ours	TV	**72.45**	**89.97**	**77.71**	**53.38**	**73.26**	**73.46**	**65.02**	**78.22**	**90.79**	**79.05**	**84.81**	**57.20**	**62.11**	**73.45**	**70.22**	**58.08**

L1 performs marginally worse than angle L2 which could be due to its equal penalization for deviations larger than 1° from the right angle.

By studying the recall-IoU curve, we noticed that very small and very large objects (*e.g.*, small vehicles and very large bridges) have the lowest localization recall and medium-size objects have the highest recall. Overall AR for the proposals on DOTA is 61.25%. A similar trend is observed for prec-recall curves.

On False Positives: To investigate false positives, we used the object detection analysis tool from [11]. For the sake of brevity, we merge the bridge and harbor as the long objects class, and the LV, SV, and ship classes as the vehicles class. Similar observations were made for the rest of the classes. The large blue area in Fig. 7 indicates that our method detects object categories with a high accuracy. Moreover, recall is around 80% (the red line) and is even higher with "weak" (10% overlap with the ground truth) localization criteria (dashed red line). The majority of confusions are with the background (the green area) while the confusion with similar object classes is much smaller (yellow area). This issue is more severe for long objects. Although using only down-sampled levels in the image cascade alleviates this issue, it lowers the performance for small objects. Since the proposals are not able to capture long objects effectively, they cause a large localization error. Additionally, the false positives for similar-classes often occur for vehicles: small and large vehicles are mistaken for each other.

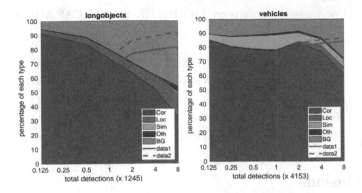

Fig. 7. False positive trends. Stacked area plots show the fraction of each type of false positive by increasing the number of detections; line plots show recall for the weak localization with more than 10% overlap with ground truth (dashed line) and the strong one with more than 50% overlap (solid line). Cor: correct, Loc: localization, Sim: similar classes, Oth: other reasons, BG: background. (Color figure online)

Table 5. Quantitative comparison of the baselines and our method on the OBB prediction task in test set of DOTA dataset. Abbreviations are the same as in Table 4. Note that only FR-O [23] is trained with OBB.

method	data	mAP	plane	BD	bridge	GTF	SV	LV	ship	TC	BC	ST	SBF	RA	harbor	SP	HC
Yolov2-[22]	TV	25.49	52.75	24.24	10.6	35.5	14.36	2.41	7.37	51.79	43.98	31.35	22.3	36.68	14.61	22.55	11.89
R-FCN[3]	TV	30.84	39.57	46.13	3.03	38.46	9.1	3.66	7.45	41.97	50.43	66.98	40.34	51.28	11.14	35.59	17.45
SSD[18]	TV	17.84	41.06	24.31	4.55	17.1	15.93	7.72	13.21	39.96	12.05	46.88	9.09	30.82	1.36	3.5	0.0
FR-H[23]	TV	39.95	49.74	64.22	9.38	56.66	19.18	14.17	9.51	61.61	65.47	57.52	51.36	49.41	20.8	45.84	24.38
FR-O[23]	TV	54.13	79.42	**77.13**	17.7	64.05	35.3	38.02	37.16	89.41	69.64	59.28	50.3	52.91	47.89	47.4	46.3
R-DFPN[31]	TV	57.94	80.92	65.82	33.77	58.94	55.77	50.94	54.78	90.33	66.34	68.66	48.73	51.76	55.10	51.32	35.88
Yang et al.[32]	TV	62.29	81.25	71.41	36.53	67.44	61.16	50.91	56.60	90.67	68.09	72.39	55.06	55.60	62.44	53.35	**51.47**
ours	T	64.98	81.24	68.74	43.36	61.07	**65.25**	67.72	69.20	90.66	71.47	70.21	**55.41**	57.28	66.49	61.3	45.27
ours	TV	**68.16**	**81.36**	74.30	**47.70**	**70.32**	64.89	**67.82**	69.98	90.76	79.06	78.20	53.64	**62.90**	67.02	**64.17**	50.23

Comparison with the State of the Art: Tables 4 and 5 show the performance of our algorithm on the HBB and OBB prediction tasks DOTA, based on the official evaluation of the methods on the test set with non-disclosed ground-truth. We evaluate our method in two scenarios: training only on the 'train' subset, and training on the training and validation sets ('trainval'). Our method significantly outperforms all the published methods evaluated on this benchmark, and training on 'trainval' brings an additional 2–4% in mAP over training only on 'train'. Looking at individual class predictions, only the mAPs of the helicopter, bridge, and SBF classes are lower than the baseline, possibly due to their large (and unique) size, complex features, and low occurrence in the dataset.

Generalization on the NWPU VHR-10 and UCAS-AOD Datasets: As shown in Table 6, our algorithm significantly improves upon the baseline also on these two additional datasets. This demonstrates the good generalization capability of our approach (Fig. 6). Results are competitive even when we trained our algorithm only on DOTA dataset.

Table 6. Comparison of results on NWUH VHR-10 and UCAS-AOD datasets.

Method	Train data	Test data	mAP
Cheng et al. [2]	NWUH VHR-10	NWUH VHR-10	72.63
Ours	NWUH VHR-10	NWUH VHR-10	95.01
Ours	DOTA	NWUH VHR-10	82.23
Xia et al. [30]	UCAS-AOD	UCAS-AOD	89.41
Ours	UCAS-AOD	UCAS-AOD	95.67
Ours	DOTA	UCAS-AOD	86.13

4 Conclusions

In this work, we presented a new algorithm for multi-class object detection in unconstrained RS imagery evaluated on three challenging datasets. Our algorithm uses a combination of image cascade and feature pyramids together with rotation proposals. We enhance our model by applying a novel loss function for geometric shape enforcement using quadrilateral coordinates. Our method outperforms other published algorithms [30,32] on the DOTA dataset by a large margin. Our approach is also robust to differences in spatial resolution of the image data acquired by various platforms (airborne and space-borne).

References

1. Bodla, N., Singh, B., Chellappa, R., Davis, L.S.: Improving object detection with one line of code. In: ICCV (2017)
2. Cheng, G., Zhou, P., Han, J.: Learning rotation-invariant convolutional neural networks for object detection in VHR optical remote sensing images. IEEE TGRS **54**, 7405–7415 (2016)
3. Dai, J., Li, Y., He, K., Sun, J.: R-FCN: Object detection via region-based fully convolutional networks. In: NIPS (2016)
4. Dai, J., et al.: Deformable convolutional networks. In: ICCV (2017)
5. Deng, J., Dong, W., Socher, R., Li, L., Li, K., Fei-Fei, L.: Imagenet: a large-scale hierarchical image database. In: CVPR (2009)
6. Everingham, M., Gool, L.V., Williams, C.K.I., Winn, J., Zisserman, A.: The PASCAL Visual Object classes (VOC) challenge. IJCV **88**, 303–338 (2010)
7. Ghiasi, G., Fowlkes, C.C.: Laplacian pyramid reconstruction and refinement for semantic segmentation. In: Leibe, B., Matas, J., Sebe, N., Welling, M. (eds.) ECCV 2016. LNCS, vol. 9907, pp. 519–534. Springer, Cham (2016). https://doi.org/10.1007/978-3-319-46487-9_32
8. Girshick, R., Donahue, J., Darrell, T., Malik, J.: Rich feature hierarchies for accurate object detection and semantic segmentation. In: CVPR (2014)
9. He, K., Gkioxari, G., Dollár, P., Girshick, R.: Mask R-CNN. In: ICCV (2017)
10. He, K., Zhang, X., Ren, S., Sun, J.: Deep residual learning for image recognition. In: CVPR (2016)
11. Hoiem, D., Chodpathumwan, Y., Dai, Q.: Diagnosing error in object detectors. In: Fitzgibbon, A., Lazebnik, S., Perona, P., Sato, Y., Schmid, C. (eds.) ECCV 2012. LNCS, vol. 7574, pp. 340–353. Springer, Heidelberg (2012). https://doi.org/10.1007/978-3-642-33712-3_25

12. Honari, S., Yosinski, J., Vincent, P., Pal, C.: Recombinator networks: learning coarse-to-fine feature aggregation. In: CVPR (2016)
13. Krizhevsky, A., Sutskever, I., Hinton, G.E.: Imagenet classification with deep convolutional neural networks. In: NIPS (2012)
14. Lin, T., Dollár, P., Girshick, R.B., He, K., Hariharan, B., Belongie, S.J.: Feature pyramid networks for object detection. In: CVPR (2017)
15. Lin, T.Y., et al.: Microsoft COCO: common objects in context. In: Fleet, D., Pajdla, T., Schiele, B., Tuytelaars, T. (eds.) ECCV 2014. LNCS, vol. 8693, pp. 740–755. Springer, Cham (2014). https://doi.org/10.1007/978-3-319-10602-1_48
16. Liu, K., Mattyus, G.: Fast multiclass vehicle detection on aerial images. IEEE TGRS Lett. **12**, 1938–1942 (2015)
17. Liu, L., Pan, Z., Lei, B.: Learning a rotation invariant detector with rotatable bounding box. arXiv preprint arXiv:1711.09405 (2017)
18. Liu, W., et al.: SSD: single shot multibox detector. In: Leibe, B., Matas, J., Sebe, N., Welling, M. (eds.) ECCV 2016. LNCS, vol. 9905, pp. 21–37. Springer, Cham (2016). https://doi.org/10.1007/978-3-319-46448-0_2
19. Ma, J., et al.: Arbitrary-oriented scene text detection via rotation proposals. IEEE Trans. Multimedia **20**, 3111–3122 (2018)
20. Newell, A., Yang, K., Deng, J.: Stacked hourglass networks for human pose estimation. In: Leibe, B., Matas, J., Sebe, N., Welling, M. (eds.) ECCV 2016. LNCS, vol. 9912, pp. 483–499. Springer, Cham (2016). https://doi.org/10.1007/978-3-319-46484-8_29
21. Pinheiro, P.O., Lin, T.-Y., Collobert, R., Dollár, P.: Learning to refine object segments. In: Leibe, B., Matas, J., Sebe, N., Welling, M. (eds.) ECCV 2016. LNCS, vol. 9905, pp. 75–91. Springer, Cham (2016). https://doi.org/10.1007/978-3-319-46448-0_5
22. Redmon, J., Farhadi, A.: YOLO9000: better, faster, stronger. In: CVPR (2017)
23. Ren, S., He, K., Girshick, R., Sun, J.: Faster R-CNN: towards real-time object detection with region proposal networks. In: NIPS (2015)
24. Ross, G.: Fast R-CNN. In: CVPR (2015)
25. Shrivastava, A., Gupta, A., Girshick, R.: Training region-based object detectors with online hard example mining. In: CVPR (2016)
26. Simonyan, K., Zisserman, A.: Very deep convolutional networks for large-scale image recognition. In: ICRL (2015)
27. Sommer, L.W., Schuchert, T., Beyerer, J.: Deep learning based multi-category object detection in aerial images. In: SPIE Defense and Security (2017)
28. Szegedy, C., et al.: Going deeper with convolutions. In: CVPR (2015)
29. Tang, T., Zhou, S., Deng, Z., Zou, H., Lei, L.: Vehicle detection in aerial images based on region convolutional neural networks and hard negative example mining. Remote Sens. **17**(2), 336 (2017)
30. Xia, G., et al.: DOTA: a large-scale dataset for object detection in aerial images. In: CVPR (2018)
31. Yang, X., et al.: Automatic ship detection in remote sensing images from Google earth of complex scenes based on multiscale rotation dense feature pyramid networks. Remote Sens. **10**, 132 (2018)
32. Yang, X., Sun, H., Sun, X., Yan, M., Guo, Z., Fu, K.: Position detection and direction prediction for arbitrary-oriented ships via multiscale rotation region convolutional neural network. arXiv preprint arXiv:1806.04828 (2018)
33. Zhao, H., Qi, X., Shen, X., Shi, J., Jia, J.: ICNet for real-time semantic segmentation on high-resolution images. arXiv preprint arXiv:1704.08545 (2017)
34. Zhu, H., Chen, X., Dai, W., Fu, K., Ye, Q., Ji, X.: Orientation robust object detection in aerial images using deep convolutional neural network. In: ICIP (2015)

Panorama from Representative Frames of Unconstrained Videos Using DiffeoMeshes

Geethu Miriam Jacob$^{(\boxtimes)}$ ⓘ and Sukhendu Das ⓘ

Visualization and Perception Lab, Department of Computer Science and Engineering,
Indian Institute of Technology, Madras, Chennai, India
geethumj@cse.iitm.ac.in, sdas@iitm.ac.in

Abstract. Panorama creation from unconstrained hand-held videos is
a challenging task due to the presence of large parallax, moving objects
and motion blur. Alignment of the frames taken from a hand-held video
is often very difficult to perform. The method proposed here aims to
generate a panorama view of the video shot given as input. The proposed framework for panorama creation consists of four stages: The first
stage performs a sparse frame selection based on alignment and blur
score. A global order for aligning the selected frames is generated by
computing a Minimum Spanning Tree with the most connected frame as
the root of the MST. The third stage performs frame alignment using a
novel warping model termed as DiffeoMeshes, a demon-based diffeomorphic registration process for mesh deformation, whereas the fourth stage
renders the panorama. For evaluating the alignment performance, experiments were first performed on a standard dataset consisting of pairs of
images. We have also created and experimented on a dataset of 20 video
shots for generating panorama. Our proposed method performs better
than the existing state-of-the-art methods in terms of alignment error
and panorama rendering quality.

1 Introduction

Panorama creation has become a popular photography application with the
advent of hand-held digital devices. In many of the real-time panorama applications, much constraints are forced on the users while providing input images,
to obtain a clear and high quality panorama. However, many of the state-of-
the-art techniques (softwares), such as Hugin, AutoStitch and Adobe Photoshop
fail when images/frames are obtained from an unconstrained video shot using
a hand-held device. The unconstrained and shaky (jittery) videos occur due to

Partially supported by TCS Foundation, India.

Electronic supplementary material The online version of this chapter (https://
doi.org/10.1007/978-3-030-20893-6_11) contains supplementary material, which is
available to authorized users.

ⓒ Springer Nature Switzerland AG 2019
C. V. Jawahar et al. (Eds.): ACCV 2018, LNCS 11363, pp. 166–182, 2019.
https://doi.org/10.1007/978-3-030-20893-6_11

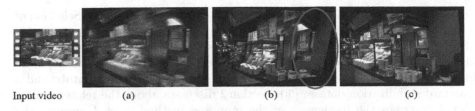

Input video   (a)   (b)   (c)

Fig. 1. Panorama creation from unconstrained videos: outputs of: (a) AutoStitch [1], (b) Adobe Photoshop, (c) Our proposed work.

unstable camera platform, moving objects and motion blur, which make it difficult to generate a clear and high quality panorama. Moreover, the frames of an unconstrained video have large parallax error.

In this paper, we propose a method to create panoramas from an unconstrained video by selecting and aligning only high quality frames of the video, which are best suited for alignment among each other accurately. Many previous methods [2–4] assume that the motion should follow a smooth camera motion model. This assumption causes most methods to fail. The unconstrained videos also have low resolution, which makes the task of panorama creation even more challenging. Figure 1 shows an example of an unconstrained video for which the popular panorama technique of AutoStitch [1] fails to generate the full panorama (Fig. 1(a)), and the commercial software Adobe Photoshop distorts the panorama at the right. Our method generates a panorama without any elongation, blur and ghosting effects. Our method follows the same pipeline of existing works [1,3,4] for panorama generation: Collect the frames/images for panorama creation, align the frames, blend (stitch) and render the frames to obtain a panorama. However, the proposed method selects a best subset of frames and discards others based on the blur and alignment scores. The frames that have less blur and those that are possible to align well are selected by minimizing a novel sparse frame selection function (matrix). This reduces the number of frames necessary to process for generating the final panorama. A global and optimal order of aligning the frames, by creation of a Minimum Spanning Tree (MST) based on the alignment score is adopted. The root (central) frame of the MST is selected based on the centrality score [5], which decides the connectedness of each frame with the rest of the frames.

To overcome the issue of large parallax error, we have proposed a new mesh-based warping technique termed as "DiffeoMeshes". DiffeoMeshes performs meshwise diffeomorphic registration along with the similarity transformation of the vertices. A demon-based diffeomorphic registration gives a per-pixel movement of the frame such that it aligns accurately with the reference frame. The per-pixel movement, when adopted in the mesh warping model, helps in reducing the parallax error while aligning the frames.

The main contributions of the proposed work are: (i) Design of a novel inter-frame dissimilarity score based on alignment and blur for reducing the number of representative frames to be processed, (ii) Alignment of the frames using a novel diffeomorphic mesh based model, known as DiffeoMeshes, (iii) Selection of a reference frame for constructing an MST representing the frame at the center of the panorama using Closeness Centrality score and obtaining a global order of stitching, (iv) Experimentation on a dataset, formed by us, consisting of 20 unconstrained videos collected from publicly available domains (Youtube and a standard stabilization dataset [6]). Section 2 discusses about the related works, Sect. 3 describes the framework of the proposed method, Sect. 4 presents the experimental results and Sect. 5 concludes the paper.

2   Related Works

Inspite of being a matured topic in computer vision, stitching images with large parallax, occlusions and moving objects are yet to be thoroughly explored. We propose a demon-based diffeomorphic mesh warping model and seam stitching technique to overcome the challenges. An overview of the various warping models, panorama creation methods and demon-based registration methods follow.

2.1   Warping Models

Several warping models have been proposed in the past few decades. Richard Szeliski has given a comprehensive study on the various image stitching methods and the different warping models used for warping in [7].

Homography-Based Warps: The traditional methods [8,9] use a single homography to warp images. These methods produce artifacts for images with large parallax. Gao *et al.* [10] proposed dual homography warps, generated for dominant planes in the image. This method gives good results when there are 2 dominant planes in the frame but fails in presence of large parallax.

Spatially Varying Warps: Spatially varying warps were introduced to handle parallax errors. Many methods, such as Smoothly Varying Affine warps (SVA) [11], Content Preserving Warps (CPW) [12], Adaptive As Natural As Possible (AANAP) [13] and As Projective As Possible (APAP) [14] have been proposed in the past. These methods deform the warps mesh-wise thus eliminating parallax error. However, when images have large parallax, artifacts such as wobbles are introduced. In Shape Preserving Half Preserving (SPHP) [15], the projective and similarity models are combined. The NIS method [16] adds a global similarity prior to the local warping models. Recently, Lin *et al.* [17] adopted photometric alignment [18] for mesh deformation.

Parallax Tolerant Warping Models: Some methods [19,20] provide a solution for large parallax by combining homography and CPW, followed by seam-cuts and blending. Lin *et al.* in [21] proposed multiple alignment hypotheses to locate a good seam for stitching. These methods aim at obtaining good stitching results by computing optimal seams, rather than aligning the images accurately, yielding unsatisfactory results. Our method aligns the frames using demon-based diffeomorphic registration for mesh deformation resulting in panoramas with less distortions, and also performs seam cutting to overcome large parallax errors.

2.2   Panorama Creation

The focus of panorama creation has recently shifted towards the need for accurate alignment of images. The method in [22] transforms images using Mellin transform and segments the moving objects completely to disjoint regions to avoid ghosting effects. Some traditional methods create mosaics from video sequences by performing an iterative motion compensation using affine transformation [23] or by 8-point homographies and bundled block adjustments [24]. An edge-based stitching method [25] estimates and refines the camera parameters. Panoramas are extracted from web videos in [2] by finding a series of mosaicable video segments which have good quality. Brown and Lowe [1] generated panoramas by matching SIFT features, performing bundle adjustment and rendering the panoramas using multi-band blending. The method in [26] attempts to solve the challenges of parallax and object motion by taking advantage of depth cues, whereas in [4] the challenges of limited space and texture in an indoor environment are considered. Furthermore, a combined SIFT and dynamic programming algorithm is proposed in [27], where an optimal seam searching criterion that protects the moving objects from being split is used. Our proposed method aims at generating panoramas from unconstrained videos, where no motion model and constraints are assumed while shooting the videos. These are mostly not dealt in prior work published in literature.

2.3   Demons-Based Diffeomorphic Registration

Thirion [28] proposed a diffusion model to perform image-to-image matching on medical images based on Maxwell's demons. The main idea was to consider one image (moving image) to be a deformable grid model which deforms to match the other image (fixed image). Diffeomorphic demons [29] was an extension to the Thirion's demons where the demons were adapted to the space of diffeomorphic transformations. It is shown that diffeomorphic demons algorithm is able to register the images faster and does it with a smooth invertible transformation. We adopt diffeomorphic demons to register/align the images in the mesh warping model, which produces better results.

3   Proposed Framework

Figure 2 illustrates the stages of the proposed framework for panorama creation from unconstrained videos. The four main modules of the framework are:

1. *Sparse Frame Selection*: Fewer frames are selected from the entire set of video frames based on blur score and ability to inter-transform relatively with respect to another, rather than the naive methods of frame selection used previously.
2. *Estimation of Reference Frame and MST*: MST is constructed to get the global order for alignment of frames with root frame indicating the central frame with highest Closeness Centrality score. This module ensures that videos with any pattern of motion can be combined to a panorama.

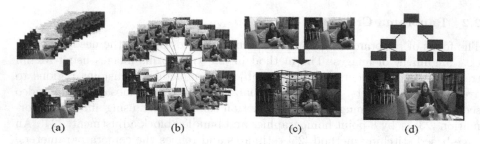

(a)   (b)   (c)   (d)

Fig. 2. Proposed framework: (a) Sparse frame selection, (b) Reference frame and MST estimation, (c) Alignment by DiffeoMeshes, (d) Panorama rendering.

3. *Pairwise alignment of frames*: The frames are aligned according to the global order of alignment, formulated with the help of our proposed "DiffeoMesh" objective function. This alignment helps in aligning images with large parallax error accurately.
4. *Render the panorama*: Once the transformations are estimated, the transformed frames are blended along the ends and the panorama is rendered.

The main contribution lies in the first, second and the third modules. Each module is explained with details elaborated in subsections below.

3.1 Sparse Selection of Frames

Processing on all the frames of the video is computationally expensive. Previous methods [8,30–32] follow naive methods of selecting the frames for panorama generation, where the amount of overlap between frames or geo-spatial information is being utilized for the selection. Several key-frame selection strategies have been proposed in the area of video summarization, video compression and video representation. We propose to adapt a subset selection strategy to model our application. Our sparse frame selection strategy is similar to the sparse subset selection method introduced in [33]. The aim of the module is to select frames with low blur which best align another, among all frames of the unconstrained video, i.e. select M frames from N frames ($M << N$). We first sample every third frame of the video and then perform the frame selection strategy. Consider a pair of frames U_i and U_j. Let $F_j^i = H_{ij}U_j$ be the frame obtained by aligning the frame U_j to the frame U_i using a global homography matrix, H_{ij}, and $\mathcal{O}$ be the overlapping region in the aligned images. We propose a dissimilarity matrix, D, of dimensions $N \times N$, for the purpose of selecting of the frames based on 'interframe-transformation score' (IFTS) and 'interframe-blur score for Alignment' (IBSA). In effect, an entry in the dissimilarity matrix depicts how dissimilar any two frames are after pairwise global homography is performed. An element d_{ij} in the dissimilarity matrix, D, is defined as $d_{ij} = T_{ij} + \alpha B_{ij}$, where

$$T_{ij} = \frac{1}{|\mathcal{O}|} \sum_{k \in \mathcal{O}} ||U_i(k) - F_j^i(k)||^2, \quad B_{ij} = max\left\{B_{ij}^x, B_{ij}^y\right\} \tag{1}$$

$$B_{ij}^x = \frac{\sum_{k \in \mathcal{O}} |G_x(U_i(k)) - G_x(F_j^i(k))|}{max\{\sum_{k \in \mathcal{O}} G_x(U_i(k)), \sum_{k \in \mathcal{O}} G_x(F_j^i(k))\}}$$

$$B_{ij}^y = \frac{\sum_{k \in \mathcal{O}} |G_y(U_i(k)) - G_y(F_j^i(k))|}{max\{\sum_{k \in \mathcal{O}} G_y(U_i(k)), \sum_{k \in \mathcal{O}} G_y(F_j^i(k))\}} \tag{2}$$

where, α is the balancing factor for the two measures, typically set to 0.8, G_x and G_y are the gradients along the x and y directions.

IFTS (T_{ij}) measures how related the two frames (U_i and U_j) are after a global homography transformation. As described in [34], a blur measure of an image is estimated using the sharpness of the gradient image. IBSA (B_{ij}) is obtained by comparing the gradients of the aligned images in both x and y direction. If the gradient difference between frames is high it is less likely that one gets selected as a representative frame of the other using IBSA score. Considering all pairs of frames, a blurred frame will have high IBSA score, thus reducing its chances of being selected. The dissimilarity scores (d_{ij}) are estimated for every pair of frames sampled and this gives a measure of how well one frame represent the other. The lower the score, the better the frames are related.

An optimization function, similar to that in [33], is utilized based on our proposed dissimilarity matrix, to select a smaller set of frames. The function finds a representative frame for a subset of adjacent frames in input video, thus reducing the number of frames finally selected. Considering a matrix $Z = [z_1 \ z_2 \ \cdots \ z_N]$, where z_i is of $N \times 1$ dimension, with z_{ij} as an element of the matrix Z. The optimization function for sparse frame selection is:

$$min_{\{z_{ij}\}}\left\{\sum_{i=1}^{N}\sum_{j=1}^{N} d_{ij}z_{ij} + \lambda \sum_{i=1}^{N} ||z_i||_\infty\right\} \quad s.t. \quad \sum_{i=1}^{N} z_{ij} = 1, \forall j, z_{ij} \geq 0 \tag{3}$$

The first term of the function penalizes the cost of replacing a frame with a representative frame and the second term helps in introducing sparsity to the model. The sparsity regularization parameter λ is empirically assigned an optimal value of 0.3. The constraints ensure that only one frame is taken as the representative and the infinity norm sparsity provides a hard assignment of 0 or 1. Thus, a set of fewer frames representing the entire video is obtained by minimizing the optimization function (Eq. 3) (see [35] for statistics of frame selection on our dataset).

3.2   Estimation of Reference Frame and Optimal Order of Stitching

A naive method of stitching the selected frames in the time order sequentially as per the input video need not be optimal and may often cause ghosting and alignment artifacts. This module aims to find an optimal and global order of stitching the frames resulting in least stitching artifacts. For this purpose, a graph with M nodes depicting the M frames and the edge weights assigned with

IFTS is constructed. There exists an edge between i^{th} and j^{th} nodes in the graph, if a minimum number of matching (corresponding) feature points exists between the frames U_i and U_j. A Minimum Spanning Tree (MST) is generated from the graph, where the root of the MST is selected using the closeness centrality (CC) score. The closeness centrality (CC) score is defined as the total graph-theoretic distance of a given node from all other nodes [5]. It is always desired to get an MST which reduces the accumulated alignment errors. Also, for unconstrained videos with arbitrary camera motion, the middle frame of the video may not be the central frame (in the panorama generated), which if used as root, results in a skewed MST structure equivalent to performing a sequential processing. Hence, we estimate a reference frame, which has the most number of connections (edges) with the least interframe-transformation score (IFTS). The frame with the highest CC score is taken as the reference frame or root of the MST. The closeness centrality score (CC) and the reference frame (R) are estimated as:

$$CC(i) = \frac{M}{\sum_{j=1}^{M} T_{ij}}; \quad R = argmax_i(CC(i)) \tag{4}$$

In many applications such as social networks [36] and text summarization with page ranking [37], the CC score is often used to determine the importance of a node in the graph structure. Similarly here, the frame which has the largest connectedness, i.e. largest IFTS value, is selected as the reference frame. This selection of the reference frame is critical in case of non-uniform motion velocity of the camera. The frame with maximum CC score ensures that the reference frame is central to the panorama, thus being robust to arbitrary camera motions.

3.3   Frame Alignment by DiffeoMeshes

The main challenges faced while generating a panorama from an unconstrained video are large parallax error, occlusion and presence of moving objects. Given two images U_i and U_j, we first perform a global homography transformation, H_{ij}, to get the transformed image, $F_j^i = H_{ij}U_j$. Let the overlapping regions in the aligned images, U_i and F_j^i, be M_i and M_j. The proposed method minimizes the parallax error by performing mesh deformation based on similarity transformation and diffeomorphic registration only over the overlapping region.

Diffeomorphic registration provides per-pixel spatial transformation and helps in reducing the alignment errors not captured by other transformations. Similar to the Content Preserving Warps method [12], we propose a warping model known as "DiffeoMeshes" where the data term is based on demon-based diffeomorphic registration along with the similarity transformation term for generating the deformed mesh. As described in [12], the method aims at estimating the deformed mesh grid vertices $\hat{V}_p^k$, given the initial vertices V_p^k, surrounding any pixel point p, such that the pixel can be represented as the bilinear interpolation of the vertices, $p = \sum_{k=1}^{4} c_k V_p^k$. Thus, we minimize the optimization function for DiffeoMeshes defined as:

$$E(\hat{V}) = E_d(\hat{V}) + \mu E_s(\hat{V}) \tag{5}$$

where, $\hat{V}$ are the vertices of the deformed mesh, E_d is the data term based on demon-based diffeomorphic registration and E_s is the similarity transformation term for mesh deformation. The diffeomorphic registration term in the minimization function estimates 2-D spatial transformation for each pixel. A previous work for alignment [17] (MPA) using mesh deformation utilized photometric alignment, where the formulation exploits the spatial optical flow. Our proposed demon-based diffeomorphic registration term varies from optical flow based term for alignment in two aspects: (i) An edge preserving Total Variation (TV) based regularization term is associated in the cost function for generating the motion vectors, such that the edges of the images are preserved while warping, whereas the optical flow vectors does not guarantee any such preservation of structure of the images and (ii) in general, diffeomorphic transformations preserve the topology of objects and the transformations are smoother and invertible, unlike optical flow vectors.

Data Term Based on Demon-Based Diffeomorphic Registration: This term estimates the diffeomorphic transformation s, using the following registration error [29]:

$$E_{diff}(s) = Sim(M_i, M_j \circ s) + Reg(s) \tag{6}$$

Here, for a pixel p, $s(p) = \hat{p} - p$, where $\hat{p} = \sum_{k=1}^{4} c_k \hat{V}_p^k$. The similarity (correspondence) term is $Sim(M_i, M_j \circ s) = \sum_{p=1}^{L} ||M_i - M_j \circ s(p)||_2^2$, and the second regularization term is defined as $\sum_{p=1}^{L} ||\nabla s(p)||_2$, where, $\circ$ indicates the per-pixel spatial warping function and $L = |M_i| = |M_j|$, where $|.|$ is the cardinality function. All the demon-based diffeomorphic registrations [28,29,38] uses Gaussian smoothing for the purpose of regularization. Our proposed method utilizes TV-based regularization [39] and this helps in preserving the edges while updating the transformation. For the purpose of ease in optimization, the function is rewritten in terms of the 'demon forces' (u) and diffeomorphic transformation (s) as follows:

$$E_{diff}(u, s) = ||M_i - (M_j \circ (s + u))||^2 + \sigma_1 ||u||^2 + \sigma_2 \sum_{p=1}^{L} ||\nabla s(p)||_2 \tag{7}$$

An iterative alternating minimization of the corresponding energy $(E_{corr} = ||M_i - (M_j \circ (s+u))||^2 + \sigma_1 ||u||^2)$ and the regularization energy $(E_{reg} = \sigma_1 ||u||^2 + \sigma_2 \sum_{p=1}^{L} ||\nabla s(p)||_2)$ is performed to obtain u and s. The demon forces for each pixel is obtained from the correspondence energy (E_{corr}) using second order minimization techniques [38]. The following closed form solution for Eq. 7, is used to update/estimate the demon forces:

$$u(p) = \frac{M_i(p) - M_j \circ s(p)}{||J^p||^2 + \sigma_1^2 (M_i(p) - M_j \circ s(p))^2} J^p \tag{8}$$

where $J^p = \nabla M_i(p) + \nabla M_j \circ s(p)$. The demon forces are updated as an exponential map to provide diffeomorphic properties [29]. The updated demon forces

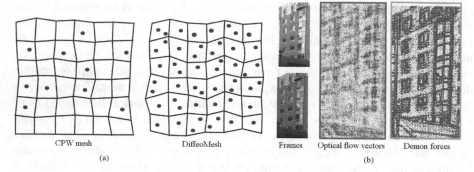

CPW mesh   DiffeoMesh   Frames   Optical flow vectors   Demon forces

(a)   (b)

Fig. 3. (a) Comparison of mesh deformation in CPW and DiffeoMeshes. DiffeoMeshes takes semi-dense points for deformation, whereas CPW takes sparse points. (b) Comparison of the optical flow vectors (MPA [17]) and the demon forces. The demon forces follow the edges of the image more accurately than optical flow vectors.

are used to estimate the diffeomorphic transformation by minimizing the regularization energy function (E_{reg}). FASTA [40] implementation of the forward-backward splitting algorithm is employed for minimizing the regularization function. The process of estimating the deformation transformation is an iterative process (50 for our method). Empirically, for all our experiments, we have used the values 0.3 and 0.7 for the parameters σ_1 and σ_2 in Eq. 7. The edge-preserving property of the TV-based diffeomorphic registration can be seen in Fig. 3(b), where a comparison between the demon forces and the optical flow vectors (used in MPA [17]) are shown. Optical flow vectors and the demon forces are illustrated for an image patch. The demon forces update according to the edges of the image patch, whereas the optical flow is less accurate in the movement along the edges.

We utilize the deformation transformation (s) estimated from Eq. 7 to formulate the data term. The data term of the DiffeoMeshes is given as:

$$E_d(\hat{V}) = \sum_{p=1}^{N_d} || \sum_{p=1}^{4} c_k \hat{V}_p^k - p||_2^2 = \sum_{p=1}^{N_d} ||s(p)||_2^2 \qquad (9)$$

Here, N_d is the number of pixels sampled from the overlap region of the image. Only those pixels belonging to the edges of the image are taken for minimizing the cost function. This is because of the fact that the accuracy of the transformation will be accurate in the edges than in the plain regions and also due to computational considerations.

Similarity Transformation. We adopt the similarity transformation term, E_s (Eq. 5) used in [12] which penalizes the deviation of each deformed mesh grid with the input cell, if the grid cells have not undergone a similarity transformation. The method by [41] is used for preserving the rigidity of the deformed cells. This term avoids unwanted deformation of the meshes.

The optimization of the function in Eq. 5 is performed using linear solvers, since both the diffeomorphic data and the smoothness terms are quadratic (for more details, refer [12]). The demon-based diffeomorphic registration is performed by alternating minimization of the demon forces and the diffeomorphic transformation. We have experimented with a 16×16 mesh grid and performed optimization on those sampled points which belong to the perfectly aligned edges in the overlapping regions. The solution to the optimization function provides the deformed mesh grid and each pixel of the warp is interpolated using a bilinear interpolation to obtain the final warp. An illustration of the difference between CPW and DiffeoMeshes are shown in Fig. 3(a). Sparse set of CPW feature points are used for the deformation of the mesh, whereas in DiffeoMeshes dense points are obtained for the deformation, which makes the mesh more flexible across the grids. The parameter μ in Eq. 5, which determines the amount of deformation of the mesh, is set empirically as 0.8 for best performance.

3.4   Panorama Rendering

The final panorama is rendered from bottom to top with sub-panoramas generated at intermediate nodes. At each intermediate node with two child nodes, a sub-panorama is generated by stitching the parent and the child frames. With moving objects and occlusions, the DiffeoMeshes will not produce perfectly aligned frames. Hence, we adopt a blending process with more weightage given to the parent frame. Our process is similar to the multi-band blending method of [42], where only regions on either side of an edge from both parent and child frames are blended. The order of stitching of the parent-child frames is again based on the IFTS score. For example, considering 3 images with P as the parent frames, C1 and C2, the child frames (with $IFTS$ of $[P, C1]$ pair $> IFTS$ of $[P, C2]$ pair), the frames P and $C1$ are first stitched to obtain $[P, C1]$ sub-panorama, followed by the stitching of $C2$ to $[P, C1]$. This ensures that the pair with higher alignment capability is stitched later to generate a sub-panorama with less artifacts. The above order of stitching gives more importance to the frames at the higher levels of the MST, thus generating the optimal panorama at the root node.

4   Experimental Results

Experiments were performed on two datasets, one for evaluating the quality of alignment and the other for evaluating the quality of panorama generated. The dataset used by [21] (SEAGULL dataset) is used for evaluating the quality of the proposed DiffeoMesh alignment. The dataset has 2 images in each example with large parallax error. Quantitatively, we have compared our output with the state-of-the-art methods, [12,14,15]. We have also compared the performance of the proposed method with of the Mesh-based Photometric Alignment (MPA) method [17]. The semi-dense correspondences for spatial optical flow (as in MPA) are utilized in a mesh framework (with no code available from the authors, we

Fig. 4. Comparison of the proposed method with (a) SPHP [15], (b) SEAGULL [21], (c) APAP [14], (d) Parallax tolerant stitching [19] method. In each subfigure, the first column shows the input images, the second shows the output of the method being compared with and the third shows the output of the proposed method. The image pairs are taken from SEAGULL dataset [21] and Parallax-tolerant dataset [19].

Fig. 5. Comparison of the proposed method with (a) MPA [17] and (b) CPW [12] using two examples. Linear blending is applied to the aligned images of both the examples. First column shows the input images (from the dataset in [19]), second column shows the output of (a) MPA and (b) CPW and the third shows the output of our proposed method. Red boxes indicate regions with alignment error in MPA/CPW and the green boxes indicate the corresponding regions in our method. (Color figure online)

partially implemented this) for comparison, in contrast to the diffeomorphic transformation used in our approach.

For evaluating the quality of the panoramas generated from videos, we generated a dataset consisting of 20 videos, most of them collected from publicly available datasets. Out of the 20 videos, 10 are collected from the stabilization dataset [6] and 10 are video snippets collected from videos publicly available in youtube. The videos in the dataset have the following challenges: (i) they do not have a constrained pattern of movement of camera, (ii) many of them are low-textured and jittery (shaky) in nature, which causes motion blur in many frames, (iii) large parallax error, with depth differences and viewpoint changes, (iv) camera movement is mostly present, which makes the process of panorama generation more challenging. The panorama quality is evaluated by comparing our method qualitatively and quantitatively with the existing commercial softwares, AutoStitch [8] and Adobe Photoshop.

4.1 Alignment Results

Quantitative evaluation of the performance of our warping model, DiffeoMeshes, is done using the correlation error (E_{corr}) and the mean geometric error (E_{mg}). The correlation error is one minus the average normalized correlation coefficient of a 5×5 window around the pixels in the overlapping portion of the aligned frames. The mean geometric error measures how far the feature points are located after the alignment. Mathematically, for the pair of frames, U_i and U_j:

$$E_{corr}(U_i, f(U_j)) = \sqrt{\frac{1}{L} \sum_{p \in \mathcal{O}} (1 - NCC(p, p'))^2},$$

$$E_{mg} = \frac{1}{K} \sum_{i=1}^{K} \|f(c_i) - c_i'\|^2$$

(10)

where, p and p' are the corresponding points in the overlapping region, $\mathcal{O}$, of the two frames aligned using the warping model f. Also, c_i and c_i' are the corresponding feature points and K is the total number of feature points. Smaller values of E_{corr} and E_{mg}, indicate better alignment quality. Table 1 shows the quantitative results of the proposed method with the competing methods [12,14,15] and our implementation of the method [17]. On an average, our method performs the best for both the error metrics and MPA performs the second best. The main reasons for the superior performance of our method are: (i) utilizing semi-dense correspondences instead of sparse correspondences in [12,14,15]

Table 1. Comparison of the performances for aligning/warping using dataset [21]. *-Average over 24 imagesets. +-Our implementation. Metrics are defined in Eq. 10 (lower, the better.)

E_{mg}						E_{corr}					
ImSet	[12]	[14]	[15]	[17]+	Ours	ImSet	[12]	[14]	[15]	[17]+	Ours
IM02	2.99	2.72	3.57	2.01	**1.61**	IM02	0.23	0.28	0.24	0.25	**0.19**
IM03	4.71	2.47	4.22	2.40	**1.54**	IM03	0.37	0.34	0.35	0.36	**0.30**
IM04	5.53	4.75	4.69	4.80	**3.41**	IM04	0.35	0.35	0.33	0.34	**0.32**
IM07	4.72	3.38	6.67	3.56	**1.72**	IM07	0.41	0.43	0.41	0.41	**0.37**
IM10	3.12	2.56	2.60	2.52	**1.06**	IM10	0.37	0.37	0.37	0.36	**0.34**
IM12	9.73	4.49	2.62	3.05	**2.01**	IM12	0.40	0.39	0.38	0.38	**0.37**
IM14	3.31	3.03	1.98	2.01	**1.31**	IM14	0.36	0.40	0.37	0.37	**0.33**
IM15	7.10	3.39	21.69	4.56	**2.05**	IM15	0.33	0.34	0.32	0.32	**0.31**
IM16	5.02	3.59	3.7	2.76	**2.01**	IM16	0.34	0.36	0.35	0.30	**0.28**
IM18	59.90	26.02	8.17	5.89	**2.61**	IM18	0.49	0.52	0.48	0.42	**0.40**
IM19	4.09	3.30	12.96	4.01	**3.11**	IM19	0.33	0.32	0.34	0.33	**0.30**
IM20	4.96	2.66	16.65	4.01	**1.82**	IM20	0.34	0.34	0.32	0.33	**0.31**
Avg*	6.98	4.83	4.88	3.05	**2.40**	**Avg***	0.35	0.36	0.33	0.33	**0.32**

and (ii) mesh deformation based on more accurate diffeomorphic transformation vectors, in contrast to the spatial optical flow vectors used in [17]. Thus, our method combines the advantages of semi-dense correspondences and accuracy of the per-pixel displacement of the diffeomorphic transformation.

Some qualitative results comparing the performance of alignments of 2 frames in SEAGULL dataset is shown in Fig. 4, for the methods [14,15,19,21]. For each example, the 1st column shows the input images to be aligned and stitched, the 2nd column shows the output of the comparing method and the 3rd column shows the output of the proposed method. SPHP fails miserably for the example in the 2nd column of Fig. 4(a), whereas APAP show distortion while alignment at the left top region marked by red oval shape in the 2nd column of Fig. 4(c). The examples in Fig. 4(b) and (d) show the outputs of the methods [21] and [19] respectively in the 2nd column, exhibiting undesired elongation. In all the cases, our method provides the desired perceptually pleasing outputs. The proposed method provides results superior to the CPW [12] and MPA [17], since our method uses semi-dense diffeomorphic correspondence points for finding the warp. Figure 5 illustrates the improvement added to the MPA and CPW by our method. The two aligned images are linearly blended in both the methods for illustration purpose. In Fig. 5, the 1st column shows the input images, the 2nd column shows the output of MPA and CPW and the 3rd shows the output of the proposed method. The red boxes shows the regions for results of MPA and CPW

Fig. 6. Qualitative comparison of the proposed method with AutoStitch [1]. (a), (c) AutoStitch outputs, (b), (d) Outputs of the proposed method. Video samples taken from publicly available Youtube videos. (Color figure online)

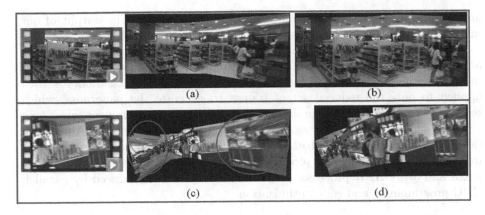

Fig. 7. Qualitative comparison of the proposed method with Adobe Photoshop. (a), (c) Outputs of Adobe Photoshop, (b), (d) Corresponding outputs of the proposed method. The red oval shapes show the distortion produced in the panorama. Video sample of (a) is a snippet taken from a publicly available Youtube video, whereas that of (b) is taken from stabilization dataset [6]. (Color figure online)

Fig. 8. Comparison of our method with Autostitch and Photoshop on representative frames with the MST chain of ordering.

with ghosting artifacts. The green boxes show the same regions in our output, which are distortion free.

4.2 Panorama Creation

The aim of our method is to create panoramas from unconstrained videos for which we have experimented on 20 videos. Some qualitative results are shown in Fig. 6. We have compared the performance with commercial stitching softwares, AutoStitch [1] and Adobe Photoshop (Figs. 7 and 8). Both the methods follow a process of sequential stitching of the frames. The comparison of our method with AutoStitch is shown in Fig. 6. The red oval shapes show the distortion produced in the panorama. AutoStitch generates ghosting artifacts as shown in Fig. 6(a) and (c), since they utilize a blending process for stitching. The output of our method as in Fig. 6(b) and (d), is sharper and clearer.

The frame selection method reduces the number of frames to be processed by at least half (reduces further when more frames provide scope of higher alignment, see Table S1 of supplementary document). The warping model is then applied to only the reduced set of frames to generate the panorama, which reduces the running time. The difference in time is more prominent when long videos are given as input. For example, for a video of 30 s duration, AutoStitch takes 53 min and Adobe Photoshop takes >60 min. Our method selects frames from the video and the whole pipeline takes 20–25 min in a machine with 32 GB RAM and 3.40 GHz i7 processor. This time can further be reduced by parallel, GPU programming and code optimization.

5   Conclusion

We presented a framework for panorama creation from unconstrained videos. The novel frame selection strategy first selects good quality frames based on the IFTS and IBSA scores for alignment. Also, a warping method termed as DiffeoMeshes, based on demon-based diffeomorphic registration and TV - regularization for mesh deformation has been proposed. A global order of stitching algorithm is adopted with a reference frame selected using the closeness centrality score. Quantitative and qualitative results show that our method performs superior to the state-of-the-art methods.

References

1. Brown, M., Lowe, D.G., et al.: Recognising panoramas. In: ICCV (2003)
2. Liu, F., Hu, Y.H., Gleicher, M.L.: Discovering panoramas in web videos. In: ACMMM, pp. 329–338 (2008)
3. Li, Y., Kang, S.B., Joshi, N., Seitz, S.M., Huttenlocher, D.P.: Generating sharp panoramas from motion-blurred videos. In: CVPR (2010)
4. Hu, J., Zhang, D.Q., Yu, H., Chen, C.W.: Long scene panorama generation for indoor environment. In: ICIP (2014)
5. Freeman, S.C., Freeman, L.C.: The networkers network: a study of the impact of a new communications medium on sociometric structure (1979)
6. Liu, S., Yuan, L., Tan, P., Sun, J.: Bundled camera paths for video stabilization. ACM Trans. Graph. (TOG) 32, 78 (2013)
7. Szeliski, R.: Image alignment and stitching: a tutorial. Found. Trends® Comput. Graph. Vis. 2, 1–104 (2006)
8. Brown, M., Lowe, D.G.: Automatic panoramic image stitching using invariant features. Int. J. Comput. Vis. 74, 59–73 (2007)
9. Szeliski, R., Shum, H.Y.: Creating full view panoramic image mosaics and environment maps. In: SIGGRAPH (1997)
10. Gao, J., Kim, S.J., Brown, M.S.: Constructing image panoramas using dual-homography warping. In: CVPR (2011)
11. Lin, W.Y., Liu, S., Matsushita, Y., Ng, T.T., Cheong, L.F.: Smoothly varying affine stitching. In: CVPR (2011)

12. Liu, F., Gleicher, M., Jin, H., Agarwala, A.: Content-preserving warps for 3D video stabilization. ACM Trans. Graph. (TOG) **28**, 44 (2009)
13. Lin, C.C., Pankanti, S.U., Natesan Ramamurthy, K., Aravkin, A.Y.: Adaptive as-natural-as-possible image stitching. In: CVPR (2015)
14. Zaragoza, J., Chin, T.J., Brown, M.S., Suter, D.: As-projective-as-possible image stitching with moving DLT. In: CVPR (2013)
15. Chang, C.H., Sato, Y., Chuang, Y.Y.: Shape-preserving half-projective warps for image stitching. In: CVPR (2014)
16. Chen, Y.-S., Chuang, Y.-Y.: Natural image stitching with the global similarity prior. In: Leibe, B., Matas, J., Sebe, N., Welling, M. (eds.) ECCV 2016. LNCS, vol. 9909, pp. 186–201. Springer, Cham (2016). https://doi.org/10.1007/978-3-319-46454-1_12
17. Lin, K., Jiang, N., Liu, S., Cheong, L.F., Lu, J., Do, M.: Direct photometric alignment by mesh deformation. In: CVPR (2017)
18. Bartoli, A.: Groupwise geometric and photometric direct image registration. IEEE Trans. Pattern Anal. Mach. Intell. **30**, 2098–2108 (2008)
19. Zhang, F., Liu, F.: Parallax-tolerant image stitching. In: CVPR (2014)
20. Jacob, G.M., Das, S.: Large parallax image stitching using an edge-preserving Diffeomorphic warping process. In: Blanc-Talon, J., Helbert, D., Philips, W., Popescu, D., Scheunders, P. (eds.) ACIVS 2018. LNCS, vol. 11182, pp. 521–533. Springer, Cham (2018). https://doi.org/10.1007/978-3-030-01449-0_44
21. Lin, K., Jiang, N., Cheong, L.-F., Do, M., Lu, J.: SEAGULL: seam-guided local alignment for parallax-tolerant image stitching. In: Leibe, B., Matas, J., Sebe, N., Welling, M. (eds.) ECCV 2016. LNCS, vol. 9907, pp. 370–385. Springer, Cham (2016). https://doi.org/10.1007/978-3-319-46487-9_23
22. Davis, J.: Mosaics of scenes with moving objects. In: CVPR (1998)
23. Kourogi, M., Kurata, T., Hoshino, J., Muraoka, Y.: Real-time image mosaicing from a video sequence. In: ICIP (1999)
24. Shum, H.Y., Szeliski, R.: Construction and refinement of panoramic mosaics with global and local alignment. In: ICCV (1998)
25. Hsieh, J.W.: Fast stitching algorithm for moving object detection and mosaic construction. Image Vis. Comput. **22**, 291–306 (2004)
26. Zhi, Q., Cooperstock, J.R.: Toward dynamic image mosaic generation with robustness to parallax. IEEE Trans. Image Process. **21**, 366–378 (2012)
27. Zeng, L., Zhang, S., Zhang, J., Zhang, Y.: Dynamic image mosaic via sift and dynamic programming. Mach. Vis. Appl. **25**, 1271–1282 (2014)
28. Thirion, J.P.: Image matching as a diffusion process: an analogy with Maxwell's demons. Med. Image Anal. **2**, 243–260 (1998)
29. Vercauteren, T., Pennec, X., Perchant, A., Ayache, N.: Diffeomorphic demons: efficient non-parametric image registration. NeuroImage **45**, S61–S72 (2009)
30. Fadaeieslam, M.J., Soryani, M., Fathy, M.: Efficient key frames selection for panorama generation from video. J. Electron. Imaging **20**, 023015 (2011)
31. Steedly, D., Pal, C., Szeliski, R.: Efficiently registering video into panoramic mosaics. In: ICCV (2005)
32. Kim, S.H., et al.: Key frame selection algorithms for automatic generation of panoramic images from crowdsourced geo-tagged videos. In: Pfoser, D., Li, K.-J. (eds.) W2GIS 2013. LNCS, vol. 8470, pp. 67–84. Springer, Heidelberg (2014). https://doi.org/10.1007/978-3-642-55334-9_5
33. Elhamifar, E., Sapiro, G., Sastry, S.S.: Dissimilarity-based sparse subset selection. IEEE Trans. Pattern Anal. Mach. Intell. **38**, 2182–2197 (2016)

34. Crete, F., Dolmiere, T., Ladret, P., Nicolas, M.: The blur effect: perception and estimation with a new no-reference perceptual blur metric. In: Human Vision and Electronic Imaging XII, vol. 6492, p. 64920I (2007)
35. Supplementary Document. http://www.cse.iitm.ac.in/~vplab/ACCV_18/Supplem entary.pdf
36. Opsahl, T., Agneessens, F., Skvoretz, J.: Node centrality in weighted networks: generalizing degree and shortest paths. Soc. Netw. **32**, 245–251 (2010)
37. Erkan, G., Radev, D.R.: LexPageRank: Prestige in multi-document text summarization. In: Proceedings of the 2004 Conference on Empirical Methods in Natural Language Processing (2004)
38. Santos-Ribeiro, A., Nutt, D.J., McGonigle, J.: Inertial demons: a momentum-based Diffeomorphic registration framework. In: Ourselin, S., Joskowicz, L., Sabuncu, M.R., Unal, G., Wells, W. (eds.) MICCAI 2016. LNCS, vol. 9902, pp. 37–45. Springer, Cham (2016). https://doi.org/10.1007/978-3-319-46726-9_5
39. Chambolle, A.: An algorithm for total variation minimization and applications. J. Math. Imaging Vis. **20**, 89–97 (2004)
40. Goldstein, T., Studer, C., Baraniuk, R.: A field guide to forward-backward splitting with a FASTA implementation. arXiv eprint abs/1411.3406 (2014)
41. Igarashi, T., Moscovich, T., Hughes, J.F.: As-rigid-as-possible shape manipulation. ACM Trans. Graph. (TOG) **24**, 1134–1141 (2005)
42. Burt, P.J., Adelson, E.H.: A multiresolution spline with application to image mosaics. ACM Trans. Graph. (TOG) **2**, 217–236 (1983)

Robust and Efficient Ellipse Fitting Using Tangent Chord Distance

Jiarong Ou[1], Jin-Gang Yu[1(✉)], Changxin Gao[2], Lichao Xiao[1], and Zhifeng Liu[1]

[1] South China University of Technology, Guangzhou, China
jingangyu@scut.edu.cn
[2] Huazhong University of Science and Technology, Wuhan, China

Abstract. Ellipse fitting is a fundamental problem in computer vision which has been extensively studied during the past decades. However, this problem still remains unresolved due to many practical challenges such as occlusion, background clutter, noise and outlier, and so forth. In this paper, we introduce a novel geometric distance, called Tangent Chord Distance (TCD), to formulate the ellipse fitting problem. Under the least squares framework, TCD is used as the measure to quantify the fitting error, based on which a nonlinear objective function is established and minimized via the Gauss-Newton method. Compared to existing geometric distance based methods, a key merit of our approach is that, the very time-consuming iterative procedure of finding the counterparts of the given points has a simple closed-form solution in our TCD-based formulation, which can thereby significantly reduce the computational load without sacrificing the performance. Experimental results on both synthetic data and public image datasets have demonstrated the superiority of our method over other compared methods in terms of robustness and efficiency.

1 Introduction

Fitting of elliptical shapes from images is a longstanding fundamental problem in computer vision [1,11,13,17,39]. Given a set of points (typically edge pixels in images), ellipse fitting aims to estimate the parameters of the desired ellipse. The significance of this problem lies in that, quite a large variety of visual objects in images can be reasonably represented by the use of ellipses, which can facilitate the solutions to many vision tasks, such as object recognition [9], visual tracking [23], 3D structure reasoning [12], *etc.* As a consequence, ellipse fitting can be widely used in real-world applications, like biological image analysis [4], traffic sign recognition [32], machine vision [7], just to name a few.

Fundamental Research Funds for the Central Universities, SCUT under Grant 2018MS72.
Guangzhou Science and Technology Program under the Grant 201904010299.

Ellipse fitting is by no means a trivial task in practice due to several aspects of factors. First, the given points are usually incomplete, covering only a portion of the true ellipse [6]. This may stem from occlusion among visual objects which makes the contours of occluded objects partially invisible, or the fragmentation of object contours into disconnected fragments because of the low quality of images or the ineffectiveness of edge detector. Second, the shape of the ground-truth ellipse may greatly influence the fitting in that elongated ellipses are more difficult to fit than round ones. Third, the presence of noise or outlier imposes high requirements on the robustness of ellipse fitting algorithms [29].

Numerous efforts have been made to address the ellipse detection problem during the past decades. Early works were mostly based on the well-known *Hough Transform (HT)* [24,37], which takes voting elements to vote for candidate ellipses in the parameter space, and the fitting result is determined by finding the local maxima in the accumulated vote map. Some variants were later proposed to improve the performance of the original HT method. To accelerate the voting procedure in a 5-dimensional space, Kiryati *et al.* presented the Probabilistic Hough Transform [21], which performs voting on only a portion of edge pixels selected. Xu *et al.* suggested the Randomized Hough Transform [36] which randomly chooses n-tuples of points as the voting elements. Some authors exploited the properties of ellipse to decouple the original 5-dimensional parameter space into lower dimensional subspaces for speedup [8,40]. Other extensions of HT include [15,25,27]. A key merit of these HT-based approaches is that, they do not require the connectivity of voting elements, and thereby can flexibly handle fragmented elliptical contours caused by occlusion or deteriorated edge detection. However, they commonly suffer from the sensitivity of parameter space quantization, and also the difficulty with mode seeking in the vote map.

Another important paradigm for ellipse detection is *least squares fitting* [1, 13]. In this type of methods, an objective function is first established, usually by summing up the fitting errors of the input points, and ellipse fitting can then be achieved by optimizing this objective function possibly under certain constraints. Very important to these methods is the definition of fitting error, which is essentially a measure of the distance from a point to an ellipse. Earlier works mostly relied on algebraic distances, called *algebraic fitting* [5,30]. One representative approach is the direct least squares fitting contributed by Fitzgibbon *et al.* [13]. The authors formulated the ellipse detection problem by means of a generalized eigenvalue system with a quadratic constraint, which turns out to have a simple closed-form solution. Some other methods [16,26] were proposed to further enhance the performance of [13]. Despite of their simplicity and efficiency, these algebraic fitting methods have some inherent weakness. The geometric meaning of algebraic error is uninterpretable, and the fitting results are usually biased to smaller and more elongated ellipses [18,30]. Kanatani [19,20] introduced a series of methods that decrease the bias greatly, but the resulting estimate can be not only ellipses, but also hyperbolas or parabolas.

To tackle the weaknesses of algebraic fitting, *geometric fitting* was developed which alternatively uses geometric distances as the fitting error to define the objective function in least squares fitting. As a milestone work along this line, Anh *et al.* [1] proposed a general orthogonal distance fitting framework for conics, where the orthogonal distance is defined by the minimum distance from a given point to all the points on a given ellipse. While being effective and robust, the optimization in this method requires a extremely time-consuming iterative procedure, which largely limits its practical use. To reduce the computational load, Al-Subaihi and Watson used the ℓ_∞ and ℓ_1 distances instead of the orthogonal distance in [2,3,35]. Rosin and West [31] suggested to replace the orthogonal distance with its first-order approximation. In [38], the authors resorted to the geometric definition of ellipse for measuring the fitting error. In [29], Prasad *et al.* presented an unconstrained and non-iterative ellipse fitting by approximating the time-consuming procedure of finding for a given data point the counterpart on ellipse. In [33], the Sampson distance, which can be considered as the approximation of orthogonal distance, is used as the data-parameter discrepancy measure. Nevertheless, these methods usually improve the computational efficiency at the cost of deterioration of performance and robustness undesirably.

In this paper, we present a novel geometric distance based approach for ellipse fitting. The key contribution of our work is that, we introduce a novel geometric distance, called *Tangent Chord Distance (TCD)*, for measuring the distance between a point and an ellipse. A significant merit of TCD is that, by taking TCD as the fitting error under the least squares fitting framework, the task of finding the counterpart on ellipse for any given point has a closed-form solution, which can greatly simplify the overall optimization procedure and thereby improve the computational efficiency (see Sect. 2.2 for details). Based on TCD, we construct the algorithm for fitting a single ellipse from a given set of points, and also apply the algorithm to multiple ellipse detection from real images. Intensive experiments on both synthetic data and real images demonstrate that, in terms of effectiveness and the robustness to typical challenging factors (including incompleteness, eccentricity and noise), our TCD-based method performs comparably with the most representative geometry fitting method [1] and significantly better than other state-of-the-art methods compared, while being more computationally efficient than [1]. In summary, the main contributions of our work are two-fold:

- We conceptually introduce a novel geometric distance, *i.e.,* the Tangent Chord Distance.
- Based on TCD, we propose a method for ellipse fitting, which performs comparably or better than the state-of-art in terms of both robustness and efficiency.

In the remainder of the paper, we will introduce the basic concept of TCD and detail the proposed TCD-based ellipse fitting approach in Sect. 2. In Sect. 3, we focus on experiments and related analysis. In Sect. 4, the paper ends up with a conclusion.

2 Our Approach

In this section, we will describe our proposed approach for ellipse fitting in detail. Firstly, we introduce the basic concepts and the mathematical definition of TCD. Then, by the use of the newly introduced TCD, we propose the method of single ellipse fitting from a given set of edge pixels, where our formulation basically follows the least squares fitting framework. Finally, we focus on the exploitation of our TCD-based method to real-world images which usually contain multiple ellipses.

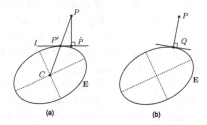

Fig. 1. Illustration of (a) the definition of the Tangent Chord Distance. For comparison, we also include (b) the definition of the well-known orthogonal distance [1].

2.1 Tangent Chord Distance

As state previously, at the core of our work is the Tangent Chord Distance, a geometric measure of how distant a point is from an ellipse. More rigorously, the mathematical definition of Tangent Chord Distance is given as below:

Definition 1. *In the $\mathbb{R}^2$ space, given a point P and an ellipse $\mathbf{E}$ centered at the point C. Let P' be the nearest point at which the line going through P and C intersects the ellipse $\mathbf{E}$, and l be the line tangent to P'. Further, let $\hat{P}$ be the foot of the perpendicular to the line l through the point P. Then, the Tangent Chord Distance between the point P and the ellipse $\mathbf{E}$ is defined by the distance from P to the line l, that is, the length of $|P\hat{P}|$. And we call $\hat{P}$ the counterpart of P on the ellipse $\mathbf{E}$.*

An illustration of the definition above is presented in Fig. 1(a), where we also include the very popular orthogonal distance [1] in Fig. 1(b). The orthogonal distance between the point P and the ellipse $\mathbf{E}$ is quantified by $|PQ|$ where Q denotes the point nearest to P on the ellipse. What motivates us to introduce TCD is that, under the orthogonal distance based ellipse fitting framework, the iterative optimization procedure requires finding, at each iteration and for each given point P, its counterpart Q on the ellipse. This in turn has to be solved in an iterative fashion through another inner loop. As a result, the computational load of the method is extremely high, which largely limits its applications. By contrast, an inherent advantage of TCD is that, the counterpart $\hat{P}$ corresponding to P can be solved very efficiently in close-form. Therefore, it will be much more computationally efficient to take TCD as the fitting error to formulate ellipse fitting. More importantly, the reduce of computational load will not lead to any loss of effectiveness and robustness (see Sect. 3 for experimental analysis).

2.2 TCD-Based Ellipse Fitting

We now focus on the use of TCD to ellipse fitting, where we start with the problem formulation, followed by the optimization method.

Problem Formulation: We firstly introduce some notations. Let $\mathcal{X} = \{\mathbf{x}_i\}_{i=1}^n$ be a given set of points with each $\mathbf{x}_i = (x_i, y_i)^\mathsf{T}$ being a point in $\mathbb{R}^2$ space. An ellipse in $\mathbb{R}^2$ can be represented by five parameters, denoted by a 5-tuple $\boldsymbol{\theta} = (x_c, y_c, \varphi, a, b)^\mathsf{T}$, where $\mathbf{x}_c = (x_c, y_c)^\mathsf{T}$ stands for the ellipse center, a and b the lengths of the semi-major axis and the semi-minor axis respectively, and $\varphi \in (-\pi/2, \pi/2]$ the orientation angle. The task of ellipse fitting can be generally stated as to estimate the elliptical parameters $\boldsymbol{\theta}$ from the given points $\mathcal{X}$ according to a certain objective. The challenges of this task arise from the facts that, the given points are usually incomplete, or corrupted by noise and outlier in practice.

We basically follow the least squares fitting framework to formulate ellipse fitting in this paper. Nevertheless, our work essentially distinguishes from previous works [1,13,29] in that, we use the newly introduced TCD above as the fitting error in our formulation. Let us denote by $\hat{\mathbf{x}}_i = (\hat{x}_i, \hat{y}_i)^\mathsf{T}$ the counterpart of $\mathbf{x}_i$ (see Definition 1), which can be determined by the ellipse parameters $\boldsymbol{\theta}$ and explicitly expressed as $\hat{\mathbf{x}}_i(\boldsymbol{\theta}) = (\hat{x}_i(\boldsymbol{\theta}), \hat{y}_i(\boldsymbol{\theta}))^\mathsf{T}$. According to Definition 1, the TCD between the point $\mathbf{x}_i$ and the ellipse, denoted as σ_i, can be given by $\sigma_i^2 = \|\mathbf{x}_i - \hat{\mathbf{x}}_i(\boldsymbol{\theta})\|_\mathrm{F}^2$. Given all these, our task of ellipse fitting can be further stated as to estimate the optimal parameters $\boldsymbol{\theta}^*$ which minimizes the sum of squared TCD over all the given points, that is,

$$\operatorname*{minimize}_{\boldsymbol{\theta}} f(\boldsymbol{\theta}) = \sum_{i=1}^n \sigma_i^2 = \sum_{i=1}^n \|\mathbf{x}_i - \hat{\mathbf{x}}_i(\boldsymbol{\theta})\|_\mathrm{F}^2. \tag{1}$$

To facilitate subsequent optimization, by introducing the notations $\mathbf{z} = (x_1, y_1, ..., x_n, y_n)^\mathsf{T} \in \mathbb{R}^{2n \times 1}$ and

$$\hat{\mathbf{z}}(\boldsymbol{\theta}) = [\hat{x}_1(\boldsymbol{\theta}), \hat{y}_1(\boldsymbol{\theta}), ..., \hat{x}_n(\boldsymbol{\theta}), \hat{y}_n(\boldsymbol{\theta})]^\mathsf{T} \in \mathbb{R}^{2n \times 1}, \tag{2}$$

we rewrite Eq. (1) as

$$\operatorname*{minimize}_{\boldsymbol{\theta}} f(\boldsymbol{\theta}) = \|\mathbf{z} - \hat{\mathbf{z}}(\boldsymbol{\theta})\|_\mathrm{F}^2 = \sum_{j=1}^{2n} [z_j - \hat{z}_j(\boldsymbol{\theta})]^2. \tag{3}$$

The optimization in Eq. (3) is a nonlinear least squares fitting problem, for which we adopt the Gauss-Newton method as described below.

Optimization by the Gauss-Newton Method: Starting from an initialization $\theta^{(0)}$, the s-th iteration of the Gauss-Newton method for solving Eq. (3) is given by

$$\theta^{(s+1)} = \theta^{(s)} - \lambda(\mathbf{J}^\mathsf{T}\mathbf{J})^{-1}\mathbf{J}^\mathsf{T}\left[\mathbf{z} - \hat{\mathbf{z}}(\theta^{(s)})\right], \tag{4}$$

where λ is the step size, and $\mathbf{J} \in \mathbb{R}^{2n \times 5}$ is the Jacobian matrix defined by

$$\mathbf{J}_{kl} = \left.\frac{\partial \hat{z}_k(\theta)}{\partial \theta_l}\right|_{\theta=\theta^{(s)}}. \tag{5}$$

One can notice that, the key to the iteration in Eq. (4) is the calculation of $\hat{\mathbf{z}}(\theta^{(s)})$ and $\mathbf{J}$, which will be detailed respectively as below.

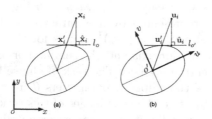

Fig. 2. Illustration of (a) the original coordinate system o-xy, and (b) the intermediate coordinate system o'-uv.

Calculation of $\hat{\mathbf{z}}(\theta^{(s)})$: The calculation of $\hat{\mathbf{z}}(\theta^{(s)}) = \hat{\mathbf{z}}(\theta)|_{\theta=\theta^{(s)}} = (\hat{x}_1(\theta), \hat{y}_1(\theta), ..., \hat{x}_n(\theta), \hat{y}_n(\theta))^\mathsf{T}|_{\theta=\theta^{(s)}}$ is actually to calculate, for each given point $\mathbf{x}_i = (x_i, y_i)^\mathsf{T}$, its counterpart $\hat{\mathbf{x}}_i = (\hat{x}_i, \hat{y}_i)^\mathsf{T}$ on the ellipse parameterized by $\theta = (x_c, y_c, \varphi, a, b)^\mathsf{T}$. As shown in Fig. 2, to facilitate solving the problem, we introduce an intermediate coordinate system o'-uv, which originates at the center of the ellipse, with the u- and v- axes coinciding with the major-axis and the minor-axis respectively. Given these two coordinate systems o-xy and o'-uv as well as the ellipse parameters θ, the counterpart $\hat{\mathbf{x}}_i$ of $\mathbf{x}_i$ can be obtained in the following way:

(1) Transform the given point $\mathbf{x}_i = (x_i, y_i)^\mathsf{T}$ under o-xy into $\mathbf{u}_i = (u_i, v_i)^\mathsf{T}$ under o'-uv by

$$\mathbf{u}_i = \mathbf{R}(\mathbf{x}_i - \mathbf{x}_c), \tag{6}$$

where $\mathbf{x}_c = (x_c, y_c)^\mathsf{T}$ and $\mathbf{R} = \begin{pmatrix} \cos\varphi & \sin\varphi \\ -\sin\varphi & \cos\varphi \end{pmatrix}$.

(2) Under the o'-uv system, compute the counterpart $\hat{\mathbf{u}}_i = (\hat{u}_i, \hat{v}_i)^\mathsf{T}$ of the point $\mathbf{u}_i = (u_i, v_i)^\mathsf{T}$, which can be achieved by first solving the intersection point $\mathbf{u}_i'$, followed by solving the tangent line $l_{o'}$ and the point $\hat{\mathbf{u}}_i$. Since $\mathbf{u}_i'$ is the intersection of an ellipse (quadratic curve) and a line, it simply has a closed-form solution. Consequently, the counterpart $\hat{\mathbf{u}}_i$ can also be solved in close-form solution. More precisely, after some mathematical derivation, we obtain

$$\begin{cases} h_1(\theta) = b^2 u_i \hat{u}_i + a^2 v_i \hat{v}_i - ab\sqrt{b^2 u_i^2 + a^2 v_i^2} = 0, \\ h_2(\theta) = a^2 v_i \hat{u}_i - b^2 u_i \hat{v}_i - (a^2 - b^2)u_i v_i = 0. \end{cases} \tag{7}$$

Denoting $\eta = a^2 - b^2$, $\phi = \sqrt{b^2 u_i^2 + a^2 v_i^2}$, $\gamma = b^4 u_i^2 + a^4 v_i^2$ and solving the equations above, we further have

$$\begin{cases} \hat{u}_i = \dfrac{a^2 u_i v_i^2 \eta + a b^3 u_i \phi}{\gamma}, \\[3mm] \hat{v}_i = \dfrac{-b^2 u_i^2 v_i \eta + a^3 b v_i \phi}{\gamma}. \end{cases} \tag{8}$$

(3) Inversely transform the point $\hat{u}_i$ into the o-xy coordinate system through

$$\hat{\mathbf{x}}_i = \mathbf{R}^{-1} \hat{\mathbf{u}}_i + \mathbf{x}_c, \tag{9}$$

which gives the counterpart $\hat{\mathbf{x}}_i$ to be solved.

Calculation of $\mathbf{J}$: According to the definition in Eq. (5), $\mathbf{J}$ can be rewritten in its matrix form as

$$\mathbf{J} = \left. \frac{\partial \hat{\mathbf{z}}(\boldsymbol{\theta})}{\partial \boldsymbol{\theta}} \right|_{\boldsymbol{\theta} = \boldsymbol{\theta}^{(s)}} = \left[\frac{\partial \hat{\mathbf{x}}_1(\boldsymbol{\theta})}{\partial \boldsymbol{\theta}}, ..., \frac{\partial \hat{\mathbf{x}}_n(\boldsymbol{\theta})}{\partial \boldsymbol{\theta}} \right] \Bigg|_{\boldsymbol{\theta} = \boldsymbol{\theta}^{(s)}}, \tag{10}$$

where the calculation of $\mathbf{J}$ is equivalent to calculating $\frac{\partial \hat{\mathbf{x}}_i(\boldsymbol{\theta})}{\partial \boldsymbol{\theta}}$. From Eq. (9), we have

$$\frac{\partial \hat{\mathbf{x}}_i(\boldsymbol{\theta})}{\partial \boldsymbol{\theta}} = \frac{\partial \mathbf{R}^{-1}}{\partial \boldsymbol{\theta}} \hat{\mathbf{u}}_i(\boldsymbol{\theta}) + \mathbf{R}^{-1} \frac{\partial \hat{\mathbf{u}}_i(\boldsymbol{\theta})}{\partial \boldsymbol{\theta}} + \frac{\partial \mathbf{x}_c}{\partial \boldsymbol{\theta}}. \tag{11}$$

In the above, $\hat{\mathbf{u}}_i(\boldsymbol{\theta})$ can be obtained by Eq. (8), and the terms of $\frac{\partial \mathbf{R}^{-1}}{\partial \boldsymbol{\theta}}$, $\mathbf{R}^{-1}$ and $\frac{\partial \mathbf{x}_c}{\partial \boldsymbol{\theta}}$ are trivial. Here the key is to calculate the term $\frac{\partial \hat{\mathbf{u}}_i(\boldsymbol{\theta})}{\partial \boldsymbol{\theta}}$. Considering $\hat{\mathbf{u}}_i(\boldsymbol{\theta})$ is determined by solving $\mathbf{h}(\mathbf{u}_i, \hat{\mathbf{u}}_i, \boldsymbol{\theta}) = \mathbf{0}$ where $\mathbf{h} = (h_1, h_2)^\mathsf{T}$ (see Eq. (7)), we have

$$\frac{\partial \mathbf{h}}{\partial \mathbf{u}_i} \frac{\partial \mathbf{u}_i}{\partial \boldsymbol{\theta}} + \frac{\partial \mathbf{h}}{\partial \hat{\mathbf{u}}_i} \frac{\partial \hat{\mathbf{u}}_i}{\partial \boldsymbol{\theta}} + \frac{\partial \mathbf{h}}{\partial \boldsymbol{\theta}} = \mathbf{0}, \tag{12}$$

where all the terms can be explicitly derived from Eq. (7) except for the unknown $\frac{\partial \hat{\mathbf{u}}_i}{\partial \boldsymbol{\theta}}$ to be solved, leading to

$$\frac{\partial \hat{\mathbf{u}}_i(\boldsymbol{\theta})}{\partial \boldsymbol{\theta}} = -\left(\frac{\partial \mathbf{h}}{\partial \hat{\mathbf{u}}_i} \right)^{-1} \left(\frac{\partial \mathbf{h}}{\partial \mathbf{u}_i} \frac{\partial \mathbf{u}_i}{\partial \boldsymbol{\theta}} + \frac{\partial \mathbf{h}}{\partial \boldsymbol{\theta}} \right). \tag{13}$$

Substituting Eq. (13) into Eq. (12), we can get

$$\frac{\partial \hat{\mathbf{x}}_i(\boldsymbol{\theta})}{\partial \boldsymbol{\theta}} = -\mathbf{R}^{-1} \mathbf{Q}^{-1} (\mathbf{A}\mathbf{B} + \mathbf{C}) + \mathbf{D}, \tag{14}$$

with

$$\mathbf{Q} = \frac{\partial \mathbf{h}}{\partial \hat{\mathbf{u}}_i} = \begin{pmatrix} \frac{\partial h_1}{\partial \hat{u}_i} & \frac{\partial h_1}{\partial \hat{v}_i} \\[2mm] \frac{\partial h_2}{\partial \hat{u}_i} & \frac{\partial h_2}{\partial \hat{v}_i} \end{pmatrix} = \begin{pmatrix} b^2 u_i & a^2 v_i \\[2mm] a^2 v_i & -b^2 u_i \end{pmatrix},$$

$$A = \frac{\partial h}{\partial u_i} = \begin{pmatrix} b^2 \hat{u}_i - \frac{ab^3 u_i}{\phi} & a^2 \hat{v}_i - \frac{a^3 bv_i}{\phi} \\ -b^2 \hat{v}_i - v_i \eta & a^2 \hat{u}_i - u_i \eta \end{pmatrix},$$

$$B = \frac{\partial u_i}{\partial \theta} = \begin{pmatrix} -\cos\varphi & -\sin\varphi & 0 & 0 & v_i \\ \sin\varphi & -\cos\varphi & 0 & 0 & -u_i \end{pmatrix},$$

$$C = \frac{\partial h}{\partial \theta} = \begin{pmatrix} 0 & 0 & 2av_i \hat{v}_i - b\phi - \frac{a^2 bv_i^2}{\phi} & 2bu_i \hat{u}_i - a\phi - \frac{ab^2 u_i^2}{\phi} & 0 \\ 0 & 0 & 2av_i(\hat{u}_i - u_i) & -2bu_i(\hat{v}_i - v_i) & 0 \end{pmatrix},$$

$$D = \frac{\partial R^{-1}}{\partial \theta} \hat{u}_i(\theta) + \frac{\partial x_c}{\partial \theta} = \begin{pmatrix} 1 & 0 & 0 & 0 & -\hat{u}_i \sin\varphi - \hat{v}_i \cos\varphi \\ 0 & 1 & 0 & 0 & \hat{u}_i \cos\varphi - \hat{v}_i \sin\varphi \end{pmatrix}.$$

For clarity, the procedure of the TCD-base ellipse fitting approach described above is summarized in Algorithm 1.

Algorithm 1. Ellipse Fitting Using Tangent Chord Distance

Input: A set of points $\mathcal{X} = \{x_i\}_{i=1}^n$, the stop condition $\epsilon = 10^{-8}$.
Output: The parameters of the ellipse $\theta^* = (x_c^*, y_c^*, \varphi^*, a^*, b^*)^\mathsf{T}$.
1: Initialize $\theta^{(0)}$ by running the direct least squares fitting algorithm [13], $s = 0$;
2: **while** true **do**
3:     **for** $i = 1$ to n **do**
4:         Calculate for each point x_i the counterpart $\hat{x}_i(\theta^{(s)})$ according to Eqs. (6), (8) and (9);
5:         Calculate $\frac{\partial \hat{x}_i(\theta)}{\partial \theta}\big|_{\theta=\theta^{(s)}}$ according to Eq. (14);
6:     **end for**
7:     Calculate J by Eq. (10) and $\hat{z}(\theta^{(s)})$ by Eq. (2);
8:     Update $\theta^{(s+1)}$ according to Eq. (4);
9:     **if** $\|\theta^{(s+1)} - \theta^{(s)}\| < \epsilon$ or $f(\theta^{(s)}) < \epsilon$ **then**
10:         break;
11:     **end if**
12:     $s = s + 1$;
13: **end while**
14: **return** parameter vector θ of the ellipse

2.3   Multiple Ellipse Detection

In the above, we have clearly described our algorithm for fitting a single ellipse from a given set of points. We focus on some practical issues in applying the algorithm to real images which usually contain multiple ellipses.

Edge Fragment Extraction: The first issue to how to acquire the sets of edge pixels from the input image, to which our TCD-based ellipse fitting algorithm is applied. We adopt the following method: (1) The input image is converted into the L*a*b color space, and the Canny edge detector is used to extract edges over the L channel, resulting in an edge map; (2) The edge-link operation [22] is deployed to the edge map to obtain a list of chained edges; (3) The chained edges are fragmented into edge fragments at inflection points or sharp-turn points, following [17,28]; (4) Post-processing steps are performed to remove those edge fragments which are straight or too short. This procedure finally generates a list of candidate edge fragments (each being a set of chained edge pixels).

Handling Multiple Ellipses: Real images may contain multiple ellipses, and the number is unknown in advance. To this end, we first apply Algorithm 1 to all the candidate edge fragments to get candidate ellipses. Then, we assign a confidence value τ to each candidate ellipse, defined by

$$\tau = \frac{\ell}{r} \exp\left(-d_m\right), \tag{15}$$

where ℓ represents the length of the edge fragment used to fit the ellipse (the number of edge pixels), r the perimeter of the ellipse, and d_m the mean tangent chord distance over the edge pixels. As can be seen, this confidence measure favours complete and faithful ellipse fitting results. Finally, the candidate ellipses with confidence over a threshold τ_0 are selected as the final ellipse detection results.

3   Experiments and Results

In this section, we perform experiments to evaluate the effectiveness of our proposed method. Both synthetic data and a publicly available real image dataset are used for our experiments. By the former, we intend to demonstrate the robustness of our method against several challenges commonly encountered in ellipse fitting, including incomplete data, noise and elongated ellipses, and the superiority in comparison with previous methods. And by the latter, our purpose is to verify that, our method is able to effectively cope with real images with complex scenes. All the experiments in this paper were executed on a desktop with Intel Core(TM) i5-5200 2.2 GHz CPU, 8 GB RAM and Windows 10 OS.

3.1   Experimental Settings

Datasets: The synthetic data are generated by ourselves according to different challenging conditions as detailed below. For real images, we adopt three public datasets [14] which are available on-line[1]. These three datasets, named as Dataset Prasad [28], Dataset #1 and Dataset #2, consist of 198, 400 and 629 images, respectively. Each image contains at least one ellipse and covers various

---

[1] http://imagelab.ing.unimore.it/imagelab/ellipse/ellipse_dataset.zip.

challenging factors like occlusion, background clutter, incomplete data, deformation, and so forth.

Performance Metrics: We adopt *overlap ratio* r_o and *F-measure* as the metrics to quantitatively evaluate and compare the performance of the methods. Given the binary mask corresponding to the detected ellipse M_d and that corresponding to the ground truth M_g, their overlap ratio is given by

$$r_o = \frac{\mathrm{card}(M_d \cap M_g)}{\mathrm{card}(M_d \cup M_g)}, \tag{16}$$

where $\mathrm{card}(\cdot)$ stands for counting the number of non-zero pixels. An ellipse detected is regarded as a correct detection if its overlap ratio with the ground truth is larger than 0.8, as did in [17,34]. We follow [10,17,28] for the definition of *F-measure*.

Methods for Comparison: We consider four representative works for comparative study, which are referred to as Fitzgibbon [13], Ahn [1], Prasad [29] and Szpak [33]. Fitzgibbon [13] is a well-known algebraic fitting method, and Ahn [1] may be the most representative geometric distance based method. Prasad [29] is a recent work which aims to simplify the expensive computation in geometric fitting. Szpak [33] is based on the Sampson distance and strikes a balance between accuracy and efficiency. All methods were implemented in Matlab. For Fitzgibbon[2] [13], Prasad[3] [29] and Szpak[4] [33], we use the source code released by the authors, and for Ahn we use the implementation provided by Sebastian Dingler[5].

3.2   Results on Synthetic Data

Synthetic data are very widely used for evaluating ellipse fitting algorithms in the literature. Following the protocols in previous works [1,29], we intend to compare the performance of the various approaches under three challenging factors: (1) *Completeness*, which means the input points cover only a portion of the true ellipse to be fitted; (2) *Noise*, which is noise and outlier corruption in real images; (3) *Roundness*, which means elongated ellipses (having large eccentricity). More precisely, we generate a ground-truth ellipse and vary the points according to the three factors respectively, and then run the various approaches over the data. The overlap ratio r_o defined in Eq. (16) is adopted as the metric for quantitative comparison, larger r_o indicating better results.

Completeness: We generate the ground truth ellipse with the parameters ($x_c = 320, y_c = 240, \varphi = -\pi/4, a = 250, b = 120$). Only a portion, denoted by a percentage p, of the points on the ellipse are taken as input to perform ellipse fitting,

---

[2] http://homepages.inf.ed.ac.uk/rbf/CVonline/LOCAL_COPIES/PILU1/demo.html.
[3] https://sites.google.com/site/dilipprasad/Source-codes.
[4] http://www.users.on.net/~zygmunt.szpak/.
[5] https://github.com/sebdi/ellipse-fitting.

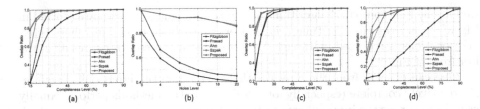

Fig. 3. Quantitative comparison in terms of overlap ratio r_o on synthetic dataset, under varying (a) completeness, (b) noise and (c–d) two different settings of the roundness, with $(a = 250, b = 210)$ for (c) and $(a = 250, b = 30)$ for (d).

Table 1. Average running time on the synthetic dataset

Methods	Fitzgibbon [13]	Prasad [29]	Ahn [1]	Szpak [33]	Proposed
CPU time (ms)	0.48	0.42	14654.45	95.80	28.64

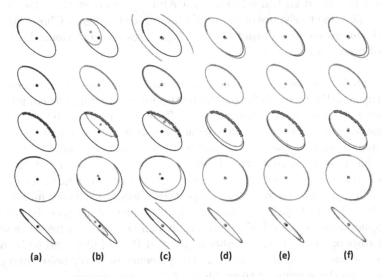

Fig. 4. Representative results obtained by the various methods under different conditions. From top to bottom are low completeness level (the first row), varying noise levels with $\sigma^2 = 0$ (the second row) and $\sigma^2 = 20$ (the third row), two different settings of the roundness, with $(a = 250, b = 210)$ (the fourth row) and $(a = 250, b = 30)$ (the fifth row), respectively. In each row, from left to right are (a) the ground-truth ellipse (black) and the input incomplete contour fragments (blue), and the results (red) obtained by (b) Fitzgibbon [13], (c) Prasad [29], (d) Ahn [1], (e) Szpak [33] and (f) the proposed method, respectively. (Color figure online)

for which we vary the completeness level (p) from 15% to 90%. At each completeness level, we take the points at different locations on the ellipse and calculate their average performance. The average r_o obtained by our proposed method as well as the four compared algorithms as the completeness p varies are plotted in Fig. 3(a), and the running time averaged over the different completeness levels and locations is reported in Table 1. We also show a representative result in the first row of Fig. 4.

One can observe from these results that: (1) When the input elliptic curves are relatively complete (especially for $p > 60\%$), all the methods perform equally well. However, as the input elliptic curves become more incomplete, our method, Ahn [1] and Szpak [33] perform significantly better than Fitzgibbon [13] (one of the most well-known algebraic fitting methods), which might suggest the superiority of geometric fitting over algebraic fitting in dealing with incompleteness. Meanwhile, it is worth noticing that, while Prasad [29] is also a geometric fitting method, it evidently underperforms Fitzgibbon [13], which is probably because that this method makes rather crude approximation to the orthogonal distance so as to acquire high computational efficiency; (2) While the proposed method is comparable or just slightly better than Ahn [1] and Szpak [33] in performance, it runs over five hundred times faster than Ahn [1] and over three times faster than Szpak [33] due to the use of the newly introduced Tangent Chord Distance. This is advantageous over Prasad [29] which reduces computational load at the sacrifice of performance.

Noise: We further assess the robustness of the various methods in the presence of noise corruption. We basically follow the methodology used for the completeness factor above to generate the testing data. The difference is that, we fix the completeness level to be a moderate value of $p = 35\%$ and add varying zero-mean Gaussian random noise to the points taken from the ground-truth ellipse. We vary the noise level by setting its variance to be $\sigma^2 = \{0, 4, 8, 12, 16, 20\}$ respectively, and at each noise level we average the performance over different locations. The quantitative results are reported in Fig. 3(b), which indicates our method, Ahn [1] and Szpak [33] are remarkably more robust to noise than the other two methods compared. Furthermore, it can be observed from the second and third rows of Fig. 4 that, Fitzgibbon [13] and Prasad [29] tend to be biased to smaller and more elongated ellipses in the presence of heavy noise corruption, which might be the reason for their inferiority in performance.

Roundness: Another common challenge for ellipse fitting lies in the shape of the ground-truth ellipse to be fitted, that is, existing approaches are more likely to fail on elongated ellipses than on round ones. Hence, the purpose of this experiment is to inspect the ability of the various methods in fitting ellipses with different roundness. For this purpose, we consider two settings of the ground-truth ellipses, *i.e.*, $(a = 250, b = 210)$ and $(a = 250, b = 30)$, and for each configuration, we follow exactly the same experimental protocol as that used for the completeness factor above. The quantitative performance in terms of overlap ratio r_o are reported in Fig. 3(c–d), and some exemplar results are shown in the fourth and fifth rows of Fig. 4. As can be seen, generally the performance of all the methods degrades to some extent when the ground-truth becomes more elongated. Nevertheless, our method, Ahn [1] and Szpak [33] deteriorate much less than the other two methods (particularly Prasad [29]), which reveals their robustness to ellipse shapes. It can be further observed from the fourth and fifth rows of Fig. 4 that, Fitzgibbon [13] tends to fit smaller ellipses and Prasad [29] often fails in the case of elongated ellipses.

3.3   Results on Real Images

In this experiment, we evaluate the performance of our proposed method on real images and compare with the other four methods. As aforementioned, we make experiments on three publicly available datasets [14]. These datasets cover several practical challenges including incomplete elliptic contours caused by occlusion or incapable edge detection, background clutter, unknown ellipse number, *etc.* Dataset Prasad [28] is the most well-known dataset for ellipse fitting, containing more small ellipses compared to the other two datasets. In Dataset #1, there are some low resolution images with many objects and complex scene. Images in Dataset #2, which is taken from the videos, are challenging due to varying lighting conditions and motion blur. For fair comparison, we follow, for all the methods, the procedure described in Sect. 2.3 except for the core algorithm of single ellipse fitting. The performance in terms of *F-measure* score is comparatively reported in Table 2, and the running time of core fitting algorithm per image, averaged over 198 images of Dataset Prasad, is reported in Table 3. While our method, Ahn [1], Szpak [33] are comparable in performance, our method runs almost 60 times faster than Ahn [1] and slightly faster than Szpak [33]. Note the running time on real images may vary heavily depending on the number of ellipses and the length of edge fragments. Compared to Fitzgibbon [13] and Prasad [29], the proposed method performs significantly better.

Some representative results are shown in Fig. 5. One can observe that, it is quite common for real images that the contours extracted by edge detectors are incomplete, possibly due to the low contrast between the foreground objects and the background (the first row), complexly textured objects (the second), or occlusion (the third row). In these cases, our method, Ahn [1] and Szpak [33] can obtain more favorable results. It can also be seen that our method, Ahn [1] and Szpak [33] are better at detecting elongated ellipses (the fourth row).

Table 2. Quantitative comparison on three datasets.

Methods		Fitzgibbon [13]	Prasad [29]	Ahn [1]	Szpak [33]	Proposed
F-measure	Dataset Prasad	0.379	0.403	0.429	0.434	0.434
	Dataset #1	0.385	0.402	0.432	0.429	0.432
	Dataset #2	0.406	0.405	0.433	0.430	0.431

Table 3. Running time of core fitting algorithm per image on Dataset Prasad.

Methods	Fitzgibbon [13]	Prasad [29]	Ahn [1]	Szpak [33]	Proposed
CPU time (ms)	2.98	1.01	18745.81	363.24	326.28

(a)   (b)   (c)   (d)   (e)   (f)   (g)

Fig. 5. Exemplary results on the Prasad dataset. From left to right are (a) the original images with ground truth labels (red), (b) the selected edge contours fed into the algorithms, and the results (green) obtained by (c) Fitzgibbon [13], (d) Ahn [1], (e) Prasad [29], (f) Szpak [33] and (e) the proposed method, respectively. (Color figure online)

3.4   Limitations

Despite of the superiority, there are still some limitations of our TCD fitting algorithm. The performance may obviously deteriorate in case of (1) incomplete data (completeness < 25 particularly); (2) elongated ellipses ($a : b > 6$ particularly); (3) heavy noise, even though it shows somewhat better tolerance to these challenges than other compared methods. Another limitation is that, the method used to build the multiple ellipse detection method for real images on top of the TCD fitting is limited (like handing multiple detections), since we mainly focus on introducing TCD in this paper.

4   Conclusion and Future Work

In this paper, we have introduced a novel geometric distance, called Tangent Chord Distance, based on which we have developed a method for ellipse fitting from images. Extensive experiments have been conducted on both synthetic data and three publicly available image dataset. The results suggest that, our method is comparable or better than traditional geometric distance based methods in terms of robustness to practical challenges including incomplete contours, noise and elongated ellipses, while it is much more computationally efficient. And it can outperform the compared algebraic fitting method in performance and robustness. In our future work, we will add some discussion on the limitations mentioned above. And we will also apply our method to real-world applications like plant image analysis.

Acknowledgment. This work is supported by National Natural Science Foundation of China under the Grant 61703166.

References

1. Ahn, S.J., Rauh, W., Warnecke, H.J.: Least-squares orthogonal distances fitting of circle, sphere, ellipse, hyperbola, and parabola. Pattern Recogn. **34**(12), 2283–2303 (2001)
2. Al-Subaihi, I., Watson, G.: The use of the l_1 and l_∞ norms in fitting parametric curves and surfaces to data. Appl. Numer. Anal. Comput. Math. **1**(2), 363–376 (2004)
3. Al-Subaihi, I., Watson, G.: Fitting parametric curves and surfaces by l_∞ distance regression. BIT Numer. Math. **45**(3), 443–461 (2005)
4. Bai, X., Sun, C., Zhou, F.: Splitting touching cells based on concave points and ellipse fitting. Pattern Recogn. **42**(11), 2434–2446 (2009)
5. Bookstein, F.L.: Fitting conic sections to scattered data. Comput. Graph. Image Process. **9**(1), 56–71 (1979)
6. Cakir, H.I., Topal, C., Akinlar, C.: An occlusion-resistant ellipse detection method by joining coelliptic arcs. In: Leibe, B., Matas, J., Sebe, N., Welling, M. (eds.) ECCV 2016. LNCS, vol. 9906, pp. 492–507. Springer, Cham (2016). https://doi.org/10.1007/978-3-319-46475-6_31
7. Chen, S., Xia, R., Zhao, J., Chen, Y., Hu, M.: A hybrid method for ellipse detection in industrial images. Pattern Recogn. **68**, 82–98 (2017)
8. Chia, A.Y.S., Leung, M.K., Eng, H.L., Rahardja, S.: Ellipse detection with Hough transform in one dimensional parametric space. In: IEEE International Conference on Image Processing, pp. V–333. IEEE (2007)
9. Chia, A.Y.S., Rajan, D., Leung, M.K., Rahardja, S.: Object recognition by discriminative combinations of line segments, ellipses, and appearance features. IEEE Trans. Pattern Anal. Mach. Intell. **34**(9), 1758–1772 (2012)
10. Dong, H., Prasad, D.K., Chen, I.M.: Accurate detection of ellipses with false detection control at video rates using a gradient analysis. Pattern Recogn. **81**, 112–130 (2018)
11. Duda, R.O., Hart, P.E.: Use of the Hough transformation to detect lines and curves in pictures. Commun. ACM **15**(1), 11–15 (1972)
12. Ellis, T., Abbood, A., Brillault, B.: Ellipse detection and matching with uncertainty. In: Mowforth, P. (ed.) British Machine Vision Conference, pp. 136–144. Springer, London (1991). https://doi.org/10.1007/978-1-4471-1921-0_18
13. Fitzgibbon, A., Pilu, M., Fisher, R.B.: Direct least square fitting of ellipses. IEEE Trans. Pattern Anal. Mach. Intell. **21**(5), 476–480 (1999)
14. Fornaciari, M., Prati, A., Cucchiara, R.: A fast and effective ellipse detector for embedded vision applications. Pattern Recogn. **47**(11), 3693–3708 (2014)

15. Han, J.H., Kóczy, L.T., Poston, T.: Fuzzy Hough transform. In: Second IEEE International Conference on Fuzzy Systems, pp. 803–808. IEEE (1993)
16. Harker, M., O'Leary, P., Zsombor-Murray, P.: Direct type-specific conic fitting and eigenvalue bias correction. Image Vis. Comput. **26**(3), 372–381 (2008)
17. Jia, Q., Fan, X., Luo, Z., Song, L., Qiu, T.: A fast ellipse detector using projective invariant pruning. IEEE Trans. Image Process. **26**(8), 3665–3679 (2017)
18. Kanatani, K.: Statistical bias of conic fitting and renormalization. IEEE Trans. Pattern Anal. Mach. Intell. **16**(3), 320–326 (1994)
19. Kanatani, K.: Ellipse fitting with hyperaccuracy. IEICE Trans. Inf. Syst. **89**(10), 2653–2660 (2006)
20. Kanatani, K., Rangarajan, P.: Hyper least squares fitting of circles and ellipses. Comput. Stat. Data Anal. **55**(6), 2197–2208 (2011)
21. Kiryati, N., Eldar, Y., Bruckstein, A.M.: A probabilistic hough transform. Pattern Recogn. **24**(4), 303–316 (1991)
22. Kovesi, P.D.: MATLAB and Octave functions for computer vision and image processing (2000). http://www.peterkovesi.com/matlabfns/
23. Kwolek, B.: Stereovision-based head tracking using color and ellipse fitting in a particle filter. In: Pajdla, T., Matas, J. (eds.) ECCV 2004. LNCS, vol. 3024, pp. 192–204. Springer, Heidelberg (2004). https://doi.org/10.1007/978-3-540-24673-2_16
24. Leavers, V.F.: Shape Detection in Computer Vision using the Hough Transform. Springer, Heidelberg (1992). https://doi.org/10.1007/978-1-4471-1940-1
25. Lu, W., Tan, J.: Detection of incomplete ellipse in images with strong noise by iterative randomized Hough transform (IRHT). Pattern Recogn. **41**(4), 1268–1279 (2008)
26. Maini, E.S.: Enhanced direct least square fitting of ellipses. Int. J. Pattern Recogn. Artif. Intell. **20**(06), 939–953 (2006)
27. McLaughlin, R.A.: Randomized hough transform: improved ellipse detection with comparison. Pattern Recogn. Lett. **19**(3–4), 299–305 (1998)
28. Prasad, D.K., Leung, M.K., Cho, S.Y.: Edge curvature and convexity based ellipse detection method. Pattern Recogn. **45**(9), 3204–3221 (2012)
29. Prasad, D.K., Leung, M.K., Quek, C.: Ellifit: an unconstrained, non-iterative, least squares based geometric ellipse fitting method. Pattern Recogn. **46**(5), 1449–1465 (2013)
30. Rosin, P.L.: A note on the least squares fitting of ellipses. Pattern Recogn. Lett. **14**(10), 799–808 (1993)
31. Rosin, P.L., West, G.A.W.: Nonparametric segmentation of curves into various representations. IEEE Trans. Pattern Anal. Mach. Intell. **17**(12), 1140–1153 (1995)
32. Soetedjo, A., Yamada, K.: Fast and robust traffic sign detection. In: IEEE International Conference on Systems, Man and Cybernetics, pp. 1341–1346. IEEE (2005)
33. Szpak, Z.L., Chojnacki, W., van den Hengel, A.: Guaranteed ellipse fitting with the Sampson distance. In: Fitzgibbon, A., Lazebnik, S., Perona, P., Sato, Y., Schmid, C. (eds.) ECCV 2012. LNCS, vol. 7576, pp. 87–100. Springer, Heidelberg (2012). https://doi.org/10.1007/978-3-642-33715-4_7
34. Wang, Y., He, Z., Liu, X., Tang, Z., Li, L.: A fast and robust ellipse detector based on top-down least-square fitting. In: British Machine Vision Conference, pp. 156.1–156.12. BMVA Press (2015)
35. Watson, G.: On the Gauss-Newton method for l_1 orthogonal distance regression. IMA J. Numer. Anal. **22**(3), 345–357 (2002)
36. Xu, L., Oja, E., Kultanen, P.: A new curve detection method: randomized Hough transform (RHT). Pattern Recogn. Lett. **11**(5), 331–338 (1990)

37. Yip, R.K., Tam, P.K., Leung, D.N.: Modification of Hough transform for circles and ellipses detection using a 2-dimensional array. Pattern Recogn. **25**(9), 1007–1022 (1992)
38. Yu, J., Kulkarni, S.R., Poor, H.V.: Robust ellipse and spheroid fitting. Pattern Recogn. Lett. **33**(5), 492–499 (2012)
39. Yuen, H., Illingworth, J., Kittler, J.: Detecting partially occluded ellipses using the Hough transform. Image Vis. Comput. **7**(1), 31–37 (1989)
40. Zhang, S.C., Liu, Z.Q.: A robust, real-time ellipse detector. Pattern Recogn. **38**(2), 273–287 (2005)

Knowledge Distillation with Feature Maps for Image Classification

Wei-Chun Chen[✉], Chia-Che Chang, and Che-Rung Lee

National Tsing Hua University, Hsinchu, Taiwan
meatybobby@gmail.com, chang810249@gmail.com, cherung@cs.nthu.edu.tw

Abstract. The model reduction problem that eases the computation costs and latency of complex deep learning architectures has received an increasing number of investigations owing to its importance in model deployment. One promising method is knowledge distillation (KD), which creates a fast-to-execute student model to mimic a large teacher network. In this paper, we propose a method, called KDFM (Knowledge Distillation with Feature Maps), which improves the effectiveness of KD by learning the feature maps from the teacher network. Two major techniques used in KDFM are shared classifier and generative adversarial network. Experimental results show that KDFM can use a four layers CNN to mimic DenseNet-40 and use MobileNet to mimic DenseNet-100. Both student networks have less than 1% accuracy loss comparing to their teacher models for CIFAR-100 datasets. The student networks are 2–6 times faster than their teacher models for inference, and the model size of MobileNet is less than half of DenseNet-100's.

Keywords: Knowledge distillation · Model compression · Generative adversarial network

1 Introduction

Deep learning has shown its capability of solving various computer vision problems, such as image classification [18] and object detection [5]. Its success also enables many related applications, such as self-driving cars [2], medical diagnosis [22], and intelligent manufacturing [32].

However, the state-of-the-art deep learning models usually have large memory footprints and require intensive computational power. For instance, VGGNet [31] requires more than 100 million parameters and more than 15 giga floating-point-operations (GFLOPs) to inference an image of 224×224 resolution. It is difficult to deploy these models on some platforms with limited resources, such as mobile devices, or Internet of Things (IOT) devices. In addition, the inference time may be too long to satisfy the real-time requests of tasks.

Many methods have been proposed to reduce the computational costs of deep learning models during the inference time. For instance, the weight quantization method [14] reduces the network size by quantizing the network parameters. Structure pruning [7] is another example that removes the unnecessary

© Springer Nature Switzerland AG 2019
C. V. Jawahar et al. (Eds.): ACCV 2018, LNCS 11363, pp. 200–215, 2019.
https://doi.org/10.1007/978-3-030-20893-6_13

parameters or channels of a trained convolutional neural network (CNN), and then fine-tunes the model to gain higher accuracy. These methods have achieved competitive accuracy with less model size comparing to those of original models. Although they can effectively reduce the model sizes and inference time, their operations are usually not matching the instructions of commodity acceleration hardware, such as GPU or TPU. As a result, the real performance gain of those methods may not be significant comparing to the original models with hardware acceleration.

Another promising directions of model reduction is Knowledge Distillation (KD) [10], whose idea is to train a student network to mimic the ability of a teacher model. The student model is usually smaller or faster-to-execute than the teacher model. Hinton and Dean [10] coined the name of Knowledge Distillation (KD). They trained student networks by the "soft target", a modify softmax function which can provide more information than the traditional softmax function. The experiment shows KD can improve the performance of a single shallow network by distilling the knowledge in an ensemble model. Romero and Bengio [27] extended the idea of KD and proposed FITNET. They trained thinner and deeper student networks by the "intermediate-level hint", which is from the hidden layers of the teacher network, and the "soft target" to learn the teacher network. The results show that FITNET can use fewer parameters to mimic the teacher network. In [34], Xu and Huang proposed the method that uses conditional adversarial networks to make student networks learn the logits of the teacher networks. Their experiments showed that it can further improve the performance of student models trained by traditional KD.

However, those KD methods only learn the logits of teacher models. They are usually not powerful enough to make student models mimic all kinds of teacher models well. They often need to customize the student models for specific architectures. In addition, as the deep models become more and more complicated, the effectiveness of previous methods for knowledge distillation decreases. One example is DenseNet [12], which connects all layers directly with each other, and requires more computation in inference time. In our experiments, the simple CNN student models learned from previous methods cannot achieve the similar accuracy as the teacher model.

In this paper, we propose a method, called KDFM (Knowledge Distillation with Feature Maps), which learns the feature maps from the teacher model. For the application of image classification, feature maps often provide more information than logits. The feature maps in the last layer are used because they possess the high level features of the input images, which are the most informative for classification. KDFM utilizes two techniques to distill the knowledge of feature maps. First, it lets the teacher model and the student model share the classifier. Through the training of the shared classifier, the student model can learn the feature maps from the teacher. Second, the idea of generative adversarial networks (GANs) [6] is used to improve the learning process. The feature map in CNN is a special type of images. During the learning process, the discriminator is forcing the student model (generator) to generate similar feature maps to those of the teacher model (inputs of GANs).

Although the method could be generally applied to other types of networks, we employ the DenseNets as the teacher models to illustrate the idea and to demonstrate its effectiveness in the experiments. Unlike FITNET [27] whose student models are thin and deep, we let the student models be shallow and fat, because such kind of networks are easier to be parallelized on modern accelerators, such as GPU.

We validated the effectiveness of KDFM using CIFAR-100 datasets [17] and ImageNet datasets [4]. The first experiment uses a simple student network which only contains 4 convolutional layers and a fully-connected layer to mimic DenseNet-40 (DenseNet with 40 layers) on CIFAR-100. The result shows the student model generated by KDFM has less than 1% accuracy loss and 2 times faster inference time comparing to DenseNet-40, which is better than other methods. The second experiment trains the model of MobileNet [11], a state-of-the-art network for mobile and embedded platforms, to mimic DenseNet-100 (DenseNet with 100 layers) on CIFAR-100. The results show that the student model is more than 6 times faster than DenseNet-100 in terms of inference time, with only half model size and less than 1% accuracy loss. The third experiment uses MobileNet v2 [29] to mimic ResNet-152 [9] on ImageNet, and the accuracy of KDFM is better than other KD methods.

The rest of paper is organized as follows. Section 2 gives a brief illustration of knowledge distillation (KD) and generative adversarial networks (GANs). Section 3 introduces the design of KDFM to construct a student model. Section 4 shows the experimental results and the performance comparison with other methods. The conclusion and future work are presented in the last section.

2   Related Work

2.1   Knowledge Distillation

In [1], Ba and Caruana asked an interesting question, "Do Deep Nets Really Need to be Deep?" Their answer is that shallow nets can be trained to perform similarly to complex, well-engineered, deeper convolutional models. The method they used to train shallow networks is mimicking the teacher networks' logits, the value before the softmax activation. In 2017, authors presented more experimental results in [33].

Hinton and Dean [10] generalized this idea as Knowledge Distillation (KD). The concept of knowledge distillation is to train a student network by a hard target P_H and a soft target P_S:

$$P_H(x) = softmax(x) \tag{1}$$

$$P_S(x, t) = softmax\left(\frac{x}{t}\right) \tag{2}$$

where x are logits in a neural network, and t is a hyper-parameter, $t > 1$, to soften the probability distribution over classes. A higher value of t could provide more information.

Let x_T be the logits of the teacher network and x_S be the logits of the student network. The goal of student network is to optimize the loss function

$$L_{KD} = \lambda L_H + (1 - \lambda)L_S, \tag{3}$$

where

$$L_H = \boldsymbol{H}(P_H(x_S), y)) \text{ and} \tag{4}$$
$$L_S = \boldsymbol{H}(P_S(x_S, t), P_S(x_T, t)) \tag{5}$$

and y is ground-truth label. They trained shallow networks by the "soft target" of teacher networks. KD softens the output of the softmax function, providing more information than traditional softmax functions. The experiment in this paper shows KD can improve the performance of a model by distilling the knowledge in an ensemble model into a single model.

Romero and Bengio [27] proposed FITNET, which extends the idea of KD by using "intermediate-level hints" from the hidden layers of the teacher network to guide the student networks. They train thinner and deeper student networks to learn the intermediate representations and the soft target of the teacher network. The results show that the student network of FITNET can perform comparable or even better than the teacher network with fewer parameters.

2.2 Generative Adversarial Networks

Generative Adversarial Networks (GANs) have shown impressive results for unsupervised learning tasks, such as image generation [6], image synthesis [26], and image super-resolution [19]. A GAN usually consists of two modules: a generator (G) and a discriminator (D). In a typical GAN model, the discriminator learns to distinguish real samples and fake results produced by the generator, and the generator learns to create samples which can be judged as real ones by the discriminator.

Mirza and Osindero [21] extended GANs to a conditional model by feeding extra information, such as class labels, to the generator and discriminator. Chen and Abbeel [3] proposed InfoGAN, an information-theoretic extension to GANs, which is able to learn disentangle representation. Some studies [24, 25, 28] modify the discriminator to contain an auxiliary decoder network that can output class labels for training data.

2.3 DenseNet

Huang and Weinberger [12] proposed a new architecture, DenseNet, which connects all layers directly with each other. This idea is extended from ResNet [8] which aggregates previous feature maps and feeds the summation into a layer.

Different from ResNet, DenseNet concatenates the feature maps from all preceding layers. It requires fewer parameters than traditional convolutional networks, because it doesn't need to relearn redundant feature maps. It performs state-of-the-art results on most classification benchmark tasks.

2.4 MobileNet

Howard and Kalenichenko [11] proposed MobileNet for mobile and embedded platforms. MobileNet uses depth-wise separable convolutions to reduce the computation and build a light-weight network. MobileNet allows to build the model on resource and accuracy trade-offs by using width multiplier and resolution multiplier. The effectiveness of MobileNet has been demonstrated across a wide range of applications.

3   The Design of KDFM

KDFM use a GAN with an auxiliary decoder network that can output class labels for training data. More specifically, it consists of three components, a generator G, a discriminator D, and a classifier C. The generator G is a feature extractor who produces the feature maps from the input images. The discriminator D distinguishes the real feature map, generated by the teacher network, and the fake feature map, generated by G. The classifier C is a feature decoder, whose inputs are also feature maps, and outputs are the hard target and the soft target, as defined in (1) and (2).

The goal of KDFM is to make G learn the feature map from the teacher network, and to train C to classify the images based on the feature maps. Two objective functions, adversarial loss and knowledge distillation loss, are designed to achieve the goal. The adversarial loss of KDFM is adopted from the objective function of LSGAN [20],

$$L_{advD} = \frac{1}{2}[D(G(X))]^2 + \frac{1}{2}[D(T(X)) - 1]^2 \tag{6}$$

$$L_{advG} = \frac{1}{2}[D(G(X)) - 1]^2 \tag{7}$$

where X denotes the input images, $G(X)$ is the feature maps generated by G, and $T(X)$ is the feature maps generated by the teacher model. The function D is designed to discriminate between the real feature map $T(X)$ and the fake feature map $G(X)$. We chose LSGAN because it is the state-of-the-art GAN model and the range of its loss function can be easily combined with the knowledge distillation loss.

The knowledge distillation loss in KDFM is defined as below:

$$L_{KD} = \lambda L_H + (1 - \lambda)L_S \tag{8}$$

where

$$L_H = \boldsymbol{H}(P_H(C(G(X))), P_H(z)) + \boldsymbol{H}(P_H(C(T(X))), P_H(z)) \qquad (9)$$
$$L_S = \boldsymbol{H}(P_S(C(G(X)), t), P_S(z, t)) + \boldsymbol{H}(P_S(C(T(X)), t), P_S(z, t)) \qquad (10)$$

the value z is the logits from the teacher network, $\boldsymbol{H}$ refers to cross-entropy, and λ is a hyper-parameter, $0 < \lambda < 1$, controlling the ratio of L_H and L_S. If the student model is similar to the teacher model, λ need not be large. Besides, we change the ground-truth label to the label of the teacher network in (9). The experiment also shows that it achieves better accuracy.

Unlike traditional GAN, the loss function of G in KDFM combines the adversarial loss and the knowledge distillation loss,

$$L_G = L_{advG} + \alpha L_{KD} \qquad (11)$$

where α is a hyper-parameter to balance the scale of the adversarial loss and the knowledge distillation loss.

The training of KDFM is to minimize the loss functions of three components simultaneously. For the generator G, the loss function is L_G, as defined in (11); for the discriminator D, the loss function is L_{advD}, as defined in (6); and for the classifier C, the loss function is L_{KD}, defined in (8).

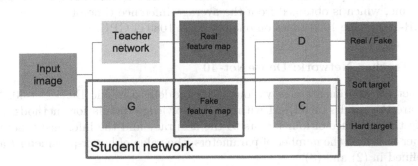

Fig. 1. Overview of KDFM, consisting of three module, a discriminator D, a generator G, and a classifier C. G and C compose a student network. The student network outputs the hard target for the inference.

Figure 1 shows the network architecture of KDFM. The student network consists of two parts, the feature extractor G and the feature decoder C. The feature extractor generates the feature map, and the feature decoder classifies the feature map to probability distribution over classes. After each components are well-trained, the student network is constructed from G and C. In our design, C only has a pooling layer and one fully connected layer.

The training process works like the alternative least square (ALS) method. Let's use L_H to illustrate the idea, since L_S has the same structure. To minimize $\boldsymbol{H}(P_H(C(T(X))), P_H(z))$, the classifier C needs to learn teacher network's hard target $P_H(z)$. Meanwhile, the term L_{KD} is also added to the loss function of the student network. To minimize the $H(P_H(C(G(X))), P_H(z))$, the student model must output feature maps $G(X)$ similar to $T(X)$, so that $P_H(C(G(X)))$ can approximate $P_H(z)$.

4 Experiments

We validated the effectiveness of KDFM using CIFAR-100 and ImageNet datasets. We used DenseNet and ResNet as the teacher models, whose implementations [16] are in TensorFlow, and followed the standard training process with data augmentation. Two types of student models are used in the experiments. The first kind of student models are simple convolutional neural networks (CNNs) that consist of several convolutional layers and one fully-connected layer, with ReLU activation [23], batch normalization [15], and max-pooling layers. The convolutional layers are with 3×3 kernel size, and 64 to 1024 channels, depending on the parameter sizes. The second student model is MobileNet, which has a Tensorflow implementation [30] on Github. We modified the student models so that the dimension of student model's feature maps equal to the teacher model's. Without further specification, the hyper-parameter t and λ, as defined in (2) and (8), are set to 10 and 0.1 respectively. The hyper-parameters α, defined in (11), is set to 10. The performance metrics of models are the accuracy and the inference time, which is obtained from the average inference time of predicting one CIFAR-100 image 1000 times on one NVIDIA 1080Ti GPU.

4.1 Teacher Network: DenseNet-40

This set of experiments uses various CNN models to mimic DenseNet-40. We compare the results of KDFM with other knowledge distillation methods, and justify the influence of four factors to the accuracy and the inference time: the number of layers, the number of parameters, the value of hyper-parameter t and λ, defined in (2) and (8).

Comparison with Other Methods. We compared the accuracy of the student network generated by KDFM and other two knowledge distillation methods: logits mimic learning [1] and KD [10]. We also included the results of the model trained without any KD process as the baseline. The teacher model is DenseNet-40 and the student model has 8 convolutional layers and 8 million trainable parameters. Table 1 shows the results of different training methods. The result indicates that the student model trained by KDFM can achieve similar accuracy as the teacher model's. Logits mimic learning performs poorly. Its accuracy is even lower than that of the baseline in this case.

Different Number of Layers. Table 2 summarizes setting of student and teacher models, and their experimental results. There are four student models

Table 1. Testing accuracy for training the student networks with 8 convolutional layers and 8M parameters by Baseline (typical training process), Logits Mimic Learning, KD, and KDFM.

Method	Accuracy
Baseline	68.53%
Logits Mimic Learning	50.95%
KD	69.14%
KDFM	74.10%
Teacher (DenseNet-40)	74.23%

which have 2, 4, 6, 8 convolutional layers respectively. We fixed the number of parameters to 8 millions. As can be seen, when the number of convolution layers is larger than 4, the student models achieve similar accuracy as the teacher model. Although the model size is not small, the inference time of student models is much shorter than that of the teach network. Particularly, the student network with 4 convolution layers has better accuracy than the teacher model, and its inference time is only half of the teacher model's.

Figure 2 plots the accuracy of student networks for different number of layers. A clear trend is that when the number of layers is larger than 4, the student model can achieve similar accuracy as the teacher model. However, when the number of layers is small, even with a large number of parameters, the student model cannot learn well as the teacher model. This result matches the conclusion made in [33].

Table 2. Testing accuracy and inference time for the student networks with 2, 4, 6, and 8 convolutional layers mimicking DenseNet-40 by KDFM.

Model	No. parameters	Accuracy	Inference time
2 conv	~8M	59.19%	3.65 ms
4 conv	~8M	74.77%	2.46 ms
6 conv	~8M	74.08%	2.59 ms
8 conv	~8M	74.10%	2.75 ms
DenseNet-40 (Teacher)	1.1M	74.23%	5.28 ms

Different Number of Parameters. Table 3 lists the setting and the results of six student models with different number of parameters. The number of layers of CNNs is fixed at 4, and the number of parameters are varied from 0.5M, 1M, 2M, 4M, 6M, to 8M. As can be seen, the more parameters, the better accuracy of the model. When the number of parameters is larger than or equal to 4M, the

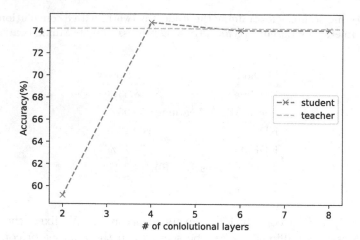

Fig. 2. Accuracy of student networks with different convolution layers and 8 million parameters, the horizontal line is the accuracy of the teacher network, DenseNet-40.

accuracy of student model is similar to that of the teacher model. The difference is less than 1%. Figure 3 shows this trend.

However, the inference time of student models is also increasing as the number of parameter increases. Nevertheless, even when the number of parameter is 8M, the inference time is still less than half of the teacher model's. The trade-off between accuracy and the inference time can be used to adjust the student models to fit the requirements of deployments.

Table 3. Testing accuracy and inference time for the student networks with 4 convolutional layers and different numbers of parameters mimicking DenseNet-40 by KDFM.

Model	No. parameters	Accuracy	Inference time
4conv-0.5M	~0.5M	65.76%	1.61 ms
4conv-1M	~1M	67.83%	1.65 ms
4conv-2M	~2M	71.12%	1.73 ms
4conv-4M	~4M	73.77%	2.01 ms
4conv-6M	~6M	73.84%	2.32 ms
4conv-8M	~8M	74.77%	2.46 ms
DenseNet-40 (Teacher)	1.1M	74.23%	5.28 ms

Different Hyper-Parameter t. We validated the influence of hyper-parameter t, defined in (2), to the accuracy of student models. Tables 4 and 5 show the results for two models, one is a 4 layer CNNs with 2M parameters (small model), and the other is a 4 layer CNNs with 8M parameters (large model). As can be

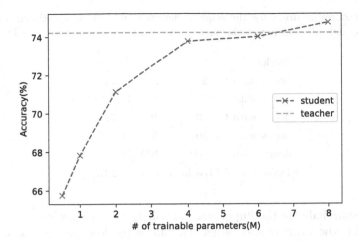

Fig. 3. Accuracy of student networks with 4 convolution layers and different number of parameters, the horizontal line is the accuracy of the teacher network, DenseNet-40.

seen, the best result occurs at $t = 5$ for the small model and at $t = 10$ for the large model. This phenomenon can be reasoned as follows. When t is small, the soft target does not have enough relaxation to encourage student networks learning the teacher model. On the other hand, when t is too large, the teacher model losses the disciplines to coach the student models. For weaker models, smaller t can usually give better accuracy, because they need clearer guidelines to learn.

Table 4. Testing accuracy for the student networks with 4 convolutional layers, 2M parameters, and different hyper-parameter t mimicking DenseNet-40 by KDFM.

Model	t	Accuracy
4conv with $t = 2$	2	70.14%
4conv with $t = 5$	5	71.48%
4conv with $t = 10$	10	71.12%
4conv with $t = 50$	50	67.35%
4conv with $t = 100$	100	67.51%
DenseNet-40 (Teacher)	-	74.23%

Different Hyper-Parameter λ. This experiment compares the accuracy of student models for different hyper-parameter λ, defined in (8). Tables 11 and 7 show the results for two models, one is a 4 layer CNNs with 2M parameters (small model), and the other is a 4 layer CNNs with 8M parameters (large model). For both models, the best result occurs at $\lambda = 0.1$.

Table 5. Testing accuracy for the student networks with 4 convolutional layers, 8M parameters, and different hyper-parameter t mimicking DenseNet-40 by KDFM.

Model	t	Accuracy
4conv with $t = 2$	2	73.11%
4conv with $t = 5$	5	74.07%
4conv with $t = 10$	10	74.77%
4conv with $t = 50$	50	71.44%
4conv with $t = 100$	100	70.72%
DenseNet-40 (Teacher)	-	74.23%

The results indicate the importance of soft target in knowledge distillation. For $\lambda = 0.1$, the value of soft target dominates the loss function of KD. This shows that with more information, student models can learn better. However, if λ is set to 0, the information of hard target totally disappears, and the student model cannot learn the best results from the teacher model (Tables 6 and 7).

Table 6. Testing accuracy for the student networks with 4 convolutional layers, 2M parameters, and different hyper-parameter λ mimicking DenseNet-40 by KDFM.

Model	λ	Accuracy
4conv with $\lambda = 0$	0	70.87%
4conv with $\lambda = 0.1$	0.1	71.12%
4conv with $\lambda = 0.4$	0.4	67.30%
4conv with $\lambda = 0.7$	0.7	66.96%
DenseNet-40 (Teacher)	-	74.23%

Table 7. Testing accuracy for the student networks with 4 convolutional layers, 8M parameters, and different hyper-parameter λ mimicking DenseNet-40 by KDFM.

Model	λ	Accuracy
4conv with $\lambda = 0$	0	74.11%
4conv with $\lambda = 0.1$	0.1	74.77%
4conv with $\lambda = 0.4$	0.4	73.18%
4conv with $\lambda = 0.7$	0.7	71.68%
DenseNet-40 (Teacher)	-	74.23%

Different Hyper-Parameter α. The hyper-parameter α controls the ratio of GAN and KD in generator's loss function, $L_G = L_{advG} + \alpha L_{KD}$. Table 8 lists the achieved accuracy of student model for different α. The best result occurs at $\alpha = 10$ in our experiments. If we take off GAN L_{advG}, as shown in the third line, the accuracy also declines.

Table 8. Testing accuracy for the student networks with 4 convolutional layers, 6M parameters, and different hyper-parameter α mimicking DenseNet-40 by KDFM.

Model	α	Accuracy
4conv with $\alpha = 1$	1	69.58%
4conv with $\alpha = 10$	10	70.62%
4conv without L_{advG}	$L_G = L_{KD}$	69.57%
DenseNet-40 (Teacher)	-	74.23%

4.2   Teacher Network: DenseNet-100

Since one of the goals for knowledge distillation is to create models easy to deploy on small devices, in this experiment, we used MobileNet (student network) to mimic DenseNet-100 (teacher network). For comparison, we included the results of two other CNNs trained by KDFM. Both CNNs have 8 convolutional layers, and one has 20.2M parameters; the other has 28.1M parameters. In addition, the result of MobileNet, trained directly without KDFM, is also included as the baseline.

Table 9 summarizes the results. The first three rows are the networks trained by KDFM, the fourth row is the result for MobileNet without KD, and the last row is the result of DenseNet-100. As shown in the first two rows, simple CNNs, even with large amount of parameters, cannot achieve good accuracy as the teacher model. But their inference times (4.56 ms and 5.7 ms) are much shorter than that of the original DenseNet-100 (18.02 ms).

The MobileNet trained by KDFM, as shown in the third row, has the best result in terms of model size, accuracy, and inference time. The number of parameters of MobileNet (3.5M) is less than half of DenseNet-100's (7.2M), and the inference time (2.79 ms) is about 6 times faster than the original DenseNet-100 (18.02 ms). Comparing to the baseline, MobileNet without KD, the MobileNet trained by KDFM can achieve 77.20% accuracy, which is close to that of DenseNet-100 (77.94%).

4.3   Teacher Network: CondenseNet

We use CondenseNet-86 [13] (with stages [14, 14, 14] and growth [8, 16, 32]) as the teacher network and a smaller CondenseNet-86 (with stages [14, 14, 14] and growth [8, 16, 16]) as the student network using CIFAR-100 dataset. The results are shown in Table 10. The model trained by KDFM is improved.

Table 9. Testing accuracy and inference time for training simple CNNs with 8 convolutional layers and 20.2M, 28.1M parameters, and MobileNet as student networks by KDFM.

Model	No. parameters	Accuracy	Inference time
8 conv-20M (KDFM)	20.2M	74.36%	4.56 ms
8 conv-28M (KDFM)	28.1M	75.25%	5.7 ms
MobileNet (KDFM)	3.5M	77.20%	2.79 ms
MobileNet (Baseline)	3.5M	72.99%	2.79 ms
DenseNet-100 (Teacher)	7.2M	77.94%	18.02 ms

Table 10. Testing accuracy for the smaller CondenseNet-86 mimicking CondenseNet-86 by KDFM and Baseline (typical training process) on CIFAR-100 dataset.

Model	No. parameters	FLOPs	Accuracy
Smaller CondenseNet-86 (Baseline)	0.29M	49.95M	74.13%
Smaller CondenseNet-86 (KDFM)	0.29M	49.95M	75.01%
CondenseNet-86 (Teacher)	0.55M	65.85M	76.02%

4.4 ImageNet Dataset

We used MobileNet v2 as the student model to mimic the pre-trained ResNet-152 using ImageNet dataset. Table 11 shows the experimental results of the testing accuracy using different training methods for the student model. As can be seen, the baseline method (without KD) can only achieve 68.41% accuracy. The KDFM model has the best result, 71.82%.

Table 11. Testing accuracy for MobileNet v2 as the student networks, trained by KDFM, KD, KDFM without L_{advG}, and MobileNet v2 (baseline), to mimic ResNet-152 by KDFM.

Model	Accuracy	Inference time	FLOPs
MobileNet v2 (KDFM)	71.82%	6 ms	300M
MobileNet v2 (KD)	70.16%	6 ms	300M
MobileNet v2 (KDFM without L_{advG} & $L_G = L_{KD}$)	71.32%	6 ms	300M
MobileNet v2 (Baseline)	68.01%	6 ms	300M
ResNet-152 (Pre-trained teacher)	78.31%	21 ms	11G

5   Conclusion and Future Work

We presented a novel architecture, KDFM, which utilizes generative adversarial networks to achieve knowledge distillation. The experiments demonstrate that

KDFM can use simple convolutional neural networks with shallower layers and larger number of trainable parameters to mimic state-of-the-art complicated networks with comparable accuracy and faster inference time.

The idea of using generative adversarial networks for knowledge distillation is not limited to the DenseNet or image classification tasks, but can be generalized to other types of networks for different applications. It is also orthogonal to other model compression methods, which means one can use KDFM to generate a student model and apply model pruning or other compression techniques to further reduce the model size and improve the performance. Last, what is the best student models to be used in KDFM still requires more investigations. One good feature of KDFM is that other objectives, such as model size, inference speed, power consumption, fitting specific hardware, can be incorporated into the student model design.

References

1. Ba, J., Caruana, R.: Do deep nets really need to be deep? In: Ghahramani, Z., Welling, M., Cortes, C., Lawrence, N.D., Weinberger, K.Q. (eds.) Advances in Neural Information Processing Systems 27, pp. 2654–2662. Curran Associates, Inc. (2014). http://papers.nips.cc/paper/5484-do-deep-nets-really-need-to-be-deep.pdf
2. Bojarski, M., et al.: End to end learning for self-driving cars. CoRR abs/1604.07316 (2016). http://arxiv.org/abs/1604.07316
3. Chen, X., Duan, Y., Houthooft, R., Schulman, J., Sutskever, I., Abbeel, P.: InfoGAN: interpretable representation learning by information maximizing generative adversarial nets. CoRR abs/1606.03657 (2016). http://arxiv.org/abs/1606.03657
4. Deng, J., Dong, W., Socher, R., Li, L.J., Li, K., Fei-Fei, L.: ImageNet: a large-scale hierarchical image database. In: CVPR 2009 (2009)
5. Girshick, R.B., Donahue, J., Darrell, T., Malik, J.: Rich feature hierarchies for accurate object detection and semantic segmentation. CoRR abs/1311.2524 (2013). http://arxiv.org/abs/1311.2524
6. Goodfellow, I., et al.: Generative adversarial nets. In: Ghahramani, Z., Welling, M., Cortes, C., Lawrence, N.D., Weinberger, K.Q. (eds.) Advances in Neural Information Processing Systems 27, pp. 2672–2680. Curran Associates, Inc. (2014). http://papers.nips.cc/paper/5423-generative-adversarial-nets.pdf
7. Hassibi, B., Stork, D.G.: Second order derivatives for network pruning: optimal brain surgeon. In: Hanson, S.J., Cowan, J.D., Giles, C.L. (eds.) Advances in Neural Information Processing Systems 5, pp. 164–171. Morgan-Kaufmann (1993). http://papers.nips.cc/paper/647-second-order-derivatives-for-network-pruning-optimal-brain-surgeon.pdf
8. He, K., Zhang, X., Ren, S., Sun, J.: Deep residual learning for image recognition. In: 2016 IEEE Conference on Computer Vision and Pattern Recognition (CVPR), pp. 770–778, June 2016. https://doi.org/10.1109/CVPR.2016.90
9. He, K., Zhang, X., Ren, S., Sun, J.: Deep residual learning for image recognition. CoRR abs/1512.03385 (2015). http://arxiv.org/abs/1512.03385
10. Hinton, G., Vinyals, O., Dean, J.: Distilling the knowledge in a neural network. arXiv e-prints, March 2015

11. Howard, A.G., et al.: MobileNets: efficient convolutional neural networks for mobile vision applications. CoRR abs/1704.04861 (2017). http://arxiv.org/abs/1704.04861

12. Huang, G., Liu, Z., van der Maaten, L., Weinberger, K.Q.: Densely connected convolutional networks. In: 2017 IEEE Conference on Computer Vision and Pattern Recognition (CVPR), pp. 2261–2269, July 2017. https://doi.org/10.1109/CVPR.2017.243

13. Huang, G., Liu, S., van der Maaten, L., Weinberger, K.Q.: Condensenet: an efficient densenet using learned group convolutions. In: The IEEE Conference on Computer Vision and Pattern Recognition (CVPR), June 2018

14. Hubara, I., Courbariaux, M., Soudry, D., El-Yaniv, R., Bengio, Y.: Quantized neural networks: training neural networks with low precision weights and activations. CoRR abs/1609.07061 (2016). http://arxiv.org/abs/1609.07061

15. Ioffe, S., Szegedy, C.: Batch normalization: accelerating deep network training by reducing internal covariate shift. CoRR abs/1502.03167 (2015). http://arxiv.org/abs/1502.03167

16. Khlestov, I.: vision_networks (2017). https://github.com/ikhlestov/vision_networks

17. Krizhevsky, A., Hinton, G.: Learning multiple layers of features from tiny images, vol. 1, January 2009

18. Krizhevsky, A., Sutskever, I., Hinton, G.E.: ImageNet classification with deep convolutional neural networks. In: Proceedings of the 25th International Conference on Neural Information Processing Systems, NIPS 2012, vol. 1, pp. 1097–1105. Curran Associates Inc., USA (2012). http://dl.acm.org/citation.cfm?id=2999134.2999257

19. Ledig, C., et al.: Photo-realistic single image super-resolution using a generative adversarial network. In: 2017 IEEE Conference on Computer Vision and Pattern Recognition (CVPR), pp. 105–114, July 2017. https://doi.org/10.1109/CVPR.2017.19

20. Mao, X., Li, Q., Xie, H., Lau, R.Y.K., Wang, Z., Smolley, S.P.: Least squares generative adversarial networks. In: 2017 IEEE International Conference on Computer Vision (ICCV), pp. 2813–2821, October 2017. https://doi.org/10.1109/ICCV.2017.304

21. Mirza, M., Osindero, S.: Conditional generative adversarial nets. CoRR abs/1411.1784 (2014). http://arxiv.org/abs/1411.1784

22. Mizotin, M., Benois-Pineau, J., Allard, M., Catheline, G.: Feature-based brain MRI retrieval for Alzheimer disease diagnosis. In: 2012 19th IEEE International Conference on Image Processing, pp. 1241–1244, September 2012. https://doi.org/10.1109/ICIP.2012.6467091

23. Nair, V., Hinton, G.E.: Rectified linear units improve restricted Boltzmann machines. In: Proceedings of the 27th International Conference on International Conference on Machine Learning, ICML 2010, pp. 807–814. Omnipress, USA (2010). http://dl.acm.org/citation.cfm?id=3104322.3104425

24. Odena, A.: Semi-supervised learning with generative adversarial networks. arXiv e-prints, June 2016

25. Odena, A., Olah, C., Shlens, J.: Conditional image synthesis with auxiliary classifier GANs. In: Precup, D., Teh, Y.W. (eds.) Proceedings of the 34th International Conference on Machine Learning. Proceedings of Machine Learning Research, vol. 70, pp. 2642–2651. PMLR, International Convention Centre, Sydney, Australia, 06–11 August 2017. http://proceedings.mlr.press/v70/odena17a.html

26. Reed, S., Akata, Z., Yan, X., Logeswaran, L., Schiele, B., Lee, H.: Generative adversarial text to image synthesis. In: Balcan, M.F., Weinberger, K.Q. (eds.) Proceedings of The 33rd International Conference on Machine Learning. Proceedings of Machine Learning Research, vol. 48, pp. 1060–1069. PMLR, New York, New York, USA, 20–22 June 2016. http://proceedings.mlr.press/v48/reed16.html

27. Romero, A., Ballas, N., Kahou, S.E., Chassang, A., Gatta, C., Bengio, Y.: FitNets: hints for thin deep nets. In: Proceedings of ICLR (2015)

28. Salimans, T., et al.: Improved techniques for training gans. In: Lee, D.D., Sugiyama, M., Luxburg, U.V., Guyon, I., Garnett, R. (eds.) Advances in Neural Information Processing Systems 29, pp. 2234–2242. Curran Associates, Inc. (2016). http://papers.nips.cc/paper/6125-improved-techniques-for-training-gans.pdf

29. Sandler, M., Howard, A.G., Zhu, M., Zhmoginov, A., Chen, L.: Inverted residuals and linear bottlenecks: mobile networks for classification, detection and segmentation. CoRR abs/1801.04381 (2018). http://arxiv.org/abs/1801.04381

30. Shi, Z.: MobileNet (2017). https://github.com/Zehaos/MobileNet

31. Simonyan, K., Zisserman, A.: Very deep convolutional networks for large-scale image recognition. CoRR abs/1409.1556 (2014). http://arxiv.org/abs/1409.1556

32. Teti, R., Kumara, S.R.T.: Intelligent computing methods for manufacturing systems. CIRP Ann. 46(2), 629–652 (1997). ISSN 0007-8506

33. Urban, G., et al.: Do deep convolutional nets really need to be deep and convolutional? arXiv e-prints, March 2016

34. Xu, Z., Hsu, Y.C., Huang, J.: Training shallow and thin networks for acceleration via knowledge distillation with conditional adversarial networks (2018). https://openreview.net/forum?id=BJbtuRRLM

Bidirectional Conditional Generative Adversarial Networks

Ayush Jaiswal[✉], Wael AbdAlmageed, Yue Wu, and Premkumar Natarajan

USC Information Sciences Institute, Marina del Rey, CA, USA
{ajaiswal,wamageed,yue_wu,pnataraj}@isi.edu

Abstract. Conditional Generative Adversarial Networks (cGANs) are generative models that can produce data samples (x) conditioned on both latent variables (z) and known auxiliary information (c). We propose the Bidirectional cGAN (BiCoGAN), which effectively disentangles z and c in the generation process and provides an encoder that learns inverse mappings from x to both z and c, trained jointly with the generator and the discriminator. We present crucial techniques for training BiCo-GANs, which involve an extrinsic factor loss along with an associated dynamically-tuned importance weight. As compared to other encoder-based cGANs, BiCoGANs encode c more accurately, and utilize z and c more effectively and in a more disentangled way to generate samples.

1 Introduction

Generative Adversarial Networks (GAN) [6] have recently gained immense popularity in generative modeling of data from complex distributions for a variety of applications such as image editing [24], image synthesis from text descriptions [25], image super-resolution [15], video summarization [18], and others [3,9,11,12,16,27,29–31]. GANs essentially learn a mapping from a latent distribution to a higher dimensional, more complex data distribution. Many variants of the GAN framework have been recently developed to augment GANs with more functionality and to improve their performance in both data modeling and target applications [4,5,7,10,19–22,24,33]. Conditional GAN (cGAN) [22] is a variant of standard GANs that was introduced to augment GANs with the capability of conditional generation of data samples based on both latent variables (or intrinsic factors) and known auxiliary information (or extrinsic factors) such as class information or associated data from other modalities. Desired properties of cGANs include the ability to disentangle the intrinsic and extrinsic factors, and also disentangle the components of extrinsic factors from each other, in the generation process, such that the incorporation of a factor minimally influences that of the others. Inversion of such a cGAN provides a disentangled information-rich representation of data, which can be used for downstream tasks (such as classification) instead of raw data. Therefore, an optimal framework would be one that ensures that the generation process uses factors in a disentangled manner *and* provides an encoder to invert the generation process, giving us a disentangled encoding. The existing equivalent of such a framework is the Invertible

© Springer Nature Switzerland AG 2019
C. V. Jawahar et al. (Eds.): ACCV 2018, LNCS 11363, pp. 216–232, 2019.
https://doi.org/10.1007/978-3-030-20893-6_14

cGAN (IcGAN) [24], which learns inverse mappings to intrinsic and extrinsic factors for *pretrained* cGANs. The limitations of post-hoc training of encoders in IcGANs are that it prevents them from (1) influencing the disentanglement of factors during generation, and (2) learning the inverse mapping to intrinsic factors effectively, as noted for GANs in [5]. Other encoder-based cGAN models either do not encode extrinsic factors [19] or encode them in fixed-length continuous vectors that do not have an explicit form [20], which prevents the generation of data with arbitrary combinations of extrinsic attributes.

We propose the Bidirectional Conditional GAN (BiCoGAN), which overcomes the deficiencies of the aforementioned encoder-based cGANs. The encoder in the proposed BiCoGAN is trained *simultaneously* with the generator and the discriminator, and learns inverse mappings of data samples to *both intrinsic and extrinsic factors*. Hence, our model exhibits implicit regularization, mode coverage and robustness against mode collapse similar to Bidirectional GANs (BiGANs) [4,5]. However, training BiCoGANs naïvely does not produce good results in practice, because the encoder fails to model the inverse mapping to extrinsic attributes and the generator fails to incorporate the extrinsic factors while producing data samples. We present crucial techniques for training BiCoGANs, which address both of these problems. BiCoGANs outperform IcGANs on both encoding and generation tasks, and have the added advantages of end-to-end training, robustness to mode collapse and fewer model parameters. Additionally, the BiCoGAN-encoder outperforms IcGAN and the state-of-the-art methods on facial attribute prediction on cropped and aligned CelebA [17] images. Furthermore, state-of-the-art performance can be achieved at predicting previously unseen facial attributes using features learned by our model instead of images. The proposed model is significantly different from the conditional extension of the ALI model (cALIM) [5]. cALIM does not encode extrinsic attributes from data samples. It requires both data samples and extrinsic attributes as inputs to encode the intrinsic features. Thus, their extension is a conditional BiGAN, which is functionally different from the proposed bidirectional cGAN.

This paper has the following contributions. It (1) introduces the new BiCoGAN framework, (2) provides crucial techniques for training BiCoGANs, and (3) presents a thorough comparison of BiCoGANs with other encoder-based GANs, showing that our method achieves the state-of-the-art performance on several metrics. The rest of the paper is organized as follows. Section 2 discusses related work. In Sect. 3 we review the building blocks underlying the design of our model: GANs, cGANs and BiGANs. Section 4 describes our BiCoGAN framework and techniques for training BiCoGANs. Qualitative and quantitative analyses of our model are presented in Sect. 5. Section 6 concludes the paper and provides directions for future research.

2   Related Work

Perarnau et al. [24] developed the IcGAN model to learn inverse mappings of a *pretrained* cGAN from data samples to intrinsic and extrinsic attributes using two independent encoders trained *post-hoc*, one for each task. In their experiments they showed that using a common encoder did not perform well. In contrast, the proposed BiCoGAN model incorporates a single encoder to embed both intrinsic and extrinsic factors, which is trained jointly with the generator and the discriminator from scratch.

BiGANs are related to autoencoders [8], which also encode data samples and reconstruct data from compact embeddings. Donahue et al. [4] show a detailed mathematical relationship between the two frameworks. Makhzani et al. [19] introduced an adversarial variant of autoencoders (AAE) that constrains the latent embedding to be close to a simple prior distribution (e.g., a multivariate Gaussian). Their model consists of an encoder Enc, a decoder Dec and a discriminator. While the encoder and the decoder are trained with the reconstruction loss $\|x - Dec(Enc(x))\|_2^2$ (where x represents real data samples), the discriminator decides whether a latent vector comes from the prior distribution or from the encoder's output distribution. In their paper, they presented unsupervised, semi-supervised and supervised variants of AAEs. Supervised AAEs (SAAEs) have a similar setting as BiCoGANs. Both SAAE decoders and BiCoGAN generators transform intrinsic and extrinsic factors into data samples. However, SAAE encoders learn only intrinsic factors while encoders of the proposed BiCoGAN model learn both. While the structure of data samples is learned explicitly through the reconstruction loss in SAAE, it is learned implicitly in BiCoGANs.

Variational Autoencoders (VAE) [13] have also been trained adversarially in both unconditional and conditional settings [20,21]. The conditional adversarial VAE of [20] (cAVAE) encodes extrinsic factors of data into a fixed-length continuous vector s. This vector along with encoded latent attributes can be used to reconstruct images. However, s is not interpretable and comes from encoding a real data sample. Hence, generating a new sample with certain desired extrinsic properties from a cAVAE requires first encoding a similar real data sample (with exactly those properties) to get its s. In comparison, such attributes can be explicitly provided to BiCoGANs for data generation.

3 Preliminaries

In this section, we introduce the mathematical notation and a brief description of the fundamental building blocks underlying the design of BiCoGANs including GANs, cGANs and BiGANs.

3.1 Generative Adversarial Networks

The working principle of the GAN framework is learning a mapping from a simple latent (or prior) distribution to the more complex data distribution. A GAN is composed of a generator and a discriminator. The goal of the generator is to produce samples that resemble real data samples, while the discriminator's objective is to differentiate between real samples and those generated by the generator. The data x comes from the distribution p_d and the latent vector z

is drawn from a prior distribution p_z. Therefore, the generator is a mapping $G(z; \theta_G)$ from p_z to the generator's distribution p_G with the goal of bringing p_G as close as possible to p_d. On the other hand, the discriminator $D(x; \theta_D)$ is simply a classifier that produces a scalar value $y \in [0, 1]$ indicating whether x is from p_G or from p_d. The generator and the discriminator play the minimax game (with the networks trained through backpropagation) as shown in Eq. 1.

$$\min_{G} \max_{D} V(D, G) = \mathbb{E}_{x \sim p_d(x)} \left[\log D(x) \right] + \mathbb{E}_{z \sim p_z(z)} \left[\log(1 - D(G(z))) \right] \quad (1)$$

3.2 Conditional Generative Adversarial Networks

Mirza et al. [22] introduced conditional GAN (cGAN), which extends the GAN framework to the conditional setting where data can be generated conditioned on known auxiliary information such as class labels, object attributes, and associated data from different modalities. cGANs thus provide more control over the data generation process with an explicit way to communicate desired attributes of the data to be generated to the GAN. This can be thought of as using a new prior vector $\tilde{z}$ with two components $\tilde{z} = [z \; c]$, where z represents latent *intrinsic* factors and c represents auxiliary *extrinsic* factors. Hence, the generator is a mapping $G(\tilde{z}; \theta_G)$ from $p_{\tilde{z}}$ to p_G and the discriminator models $D(x, c; \theta_D)$ that gives $y \in [0, 1]$. The cGAN discriminator also utilizes the knowledge of c to determine if x is real or fake. Thus, the generator must incorporate c while producing x in order to fool the discriminator. The model is trained with a similar minimax objective as the original GAN formulation, as shown in Eq. 2.

$$\min_{G} \max_{D} V(D, G) = \mathbb{E}_{x \sim p_d(x)} \left[\log D(x, c) \right] + \mathbb{E}_{z \sim p_{\tilde{z}}(\tilde{z})} \left[\log(1 - D(G(\tilde{z}), c)) \right] \quad (2)$$

3.3 Bidirectional Generative Adversarial Networks

The GAN framework provides a mapping from z to x, but not another from x to z. Such a mapping is highly useful as it provides an information-rich representation of x, which can be used as input for downstream tasks (such as classification) instead of the original data in simple yet effective ways [4,5]. Donahue et al. [4] and Dumoulin et al. [5] independently developed the BiGAN (or ALI) model that adds an encoder to the original generator-discriminator framework. The generator models the same mapping as the original GAN generator while the encoder is a mapping $E(x; \theta_E)$ from p_d to p_E with the goal of bringing p_E close to p_z. The discriminator is modified to incorporate both z and $G(z)$ or both x and $E(x)$ to make real/fake decisions as $D(z, G(z); \theta_D)$ or $D(E(x), x; \theta_D)$, respectively. Donahue et al. [4] provide a detailed proof to show that under optimality, G and E must be inverses of each other to successfully fool the discriminator. The model is trained with the new minimax objective as shown in Eq. 3.

$$\min_{G,E} \max_{D} V(D, G, E) = \mathbb{E}_{x \sim p_d(x)} \left[\log D(E(x), x) \right]$$
$$+ \mathbb{E}_{z \sim p_z(z)} \left[\log(1 - D(z, G(z))) \right] \quad (3)$$

4   Proposed Model—Bidirectional Conditional GAN

An optimal cGAN framework would be one in which (1) the extrinsic factors can be explicitly specified so as to enable data generation conditioned on arbitrary combinations of factors, (2) the generation process uses intrinsic and extrinsic factors in a disentangled manner, (3) the components of the extrinsic factors minimally affect each other while generating data, and (4) the generation process can be inverted, giving us a disentangled information-rich embedding of data. However, existing models fail to simultaneously fulfill all of these desired properties. Moreover, formulating and training such a cGAN model is difficult given the inherent complexity of training GANs and the added constraints required to achieve the said goals.

We design the proposed Bidirectional Conditional GAN (BiCoGAN) framework with the aforementioned properties as our foundational guidelines. While goal (1) is fulfilled by explicitly providing the extrinsic factors as inputs to the BiCoGAN generator, in order to accomplish goals (2) and (3), we design the BiCoGAN discriminator to check the consistency of the input data with the associated intrinsic and extrinsic factors. Thus, the BiCoGAN generator must effectively incorporate both the sets of factors into the generation process to successfully fool the discriminator. Finally, in order to achieve goal (4), we incorporate an encoder in the BiCoGAN framework that learns the inverse mapping of data samples to *both* intrinsic and extrinsic factors. We train the encoder *jointly* with the generator and discriminator to ascertain that it effectively learns the inverse mappings and improves the generation process through implicit regularization, better mode coverage and robustness against mode collapse (like BiGANs [4,5]). Thus, BiCoGANs generate samples conditioned on desired extrinsic factors and *effectively* encode real data samples into disentangled representations comprising *both* intrinsic and extrinsic attributes. This provides an information-rich representation of data for auxiliary supervised semantic tasks [4], as well as a way for conditional data augmentation [27,28] to aid their learning. Figure 1 illustrates the proposed BiCoGAN framework.

The generator learns a mapping $G(\tilde{z}; \theta_G)$ from the distribution $p_{\tilde{z}}$ (where $\tilde{z} = [z\ c]$) to p_G with the goal of bringing p_G close to p_{data} while the encoder models $E(x; \theta_E)$ from p_{data} to p_E with the goal of bringing p_E close to $p_{\tilde{z}}$. The discriminator makes real/fake decisions as $D(\tilde{z}, G(\tilde{z}); \theta_D)$ or $D(E(x), x; \theta_D)$. It is important to note that the proposed BiCoGAN encoder must learn the inverse mapping of x to z *and* c just like the generator must learn to incorporate *both* into the generation of data samples in order to fool the discriminator, following from the invertibility under optimality theorem of BiGANs [4,5]. However, in practice, such optimality is difficult to achieve, especially when the prior vector contains structured information or has a complex distribution. While the intrinsic factors are sampled randomly from a simple latent distribution, the extrinsic factors are much more specialized and model specific forms of high-level information, such as class labels or object attributes, making their underlying distribution significantly more difficult to model. To address this challenge, we introduce the **extrinsic factor loss** (EFL) as an explicit mechanism that helps guide

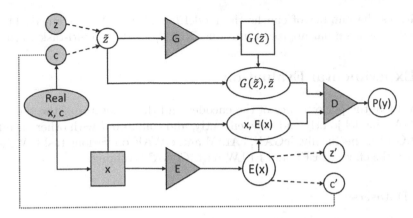

Fig. 1. Bidirectional Conditional Generative Adversarial Network. The dotted line indicates that E is trained to predict the c part of $E(x)$ with supervision.

BiCoGANs to better encode extrinsic factors. This is built on the fact that the c associated with each real data sample is known during training, and can, thus, be used to improve the learning of inverse mappings from x to c. *We do not give an explicit form to EFL in the BiCoGAN objective because the choice of the loss function depends on the nature of c, and hence, on the dataset/domain.*

Adding EFL to the BiCoGAN objective is not sufficient to achieve the best results for both encoding c and generating x that incorporates the knowledge of c. This is justified by the fact that the training process has no information about the inherent difficulty of encoding c (specific to the domain). Thus, it is possible that the backpropagated gradients of the EFL (to the encoder) are distorted by those from the discriminator in the BiCoGAN framework. Therefore, we multiply EFL with an importance weight, which we denote by γ and refer to as the EFL weight (EFLW), in the BiCoGAN objective as shown in Eq. 4.

$$\min_{G,E} \max_{D} V(D, G, E) = \mathbb{E}_{x \sim p_{data}(x)} \left[\log D(E(x), x) \right]$$
$$+ \gamma \, \mathbb{E}_{(x,c) \sim p_{data}(x,c)} \left[\mathrm{EFL}(c, E_c(x)) \right] + \mathbb{E}_{z \sim p_{\tilde{z}}(\tilde{z})} \left[\log(1 - D(\tilde{z}, G(\tilde{z}))) \right] \quad (4)$$

The importance weight γ can be chosen as a constant value or a dynamic parameter that keeps changing during training to control the focus of the training between the naïve adversarial objective and the EFL. While the former option is straightforward, the latter requires some understanding of the dynamics between the original generator-discriminator setup of cGANs and the additional encoder as introduced in the proposed BiCoGAN model. It can be seen that the objective of the generator is significantly more difficult than that of the encoder, making the former more vulnerable to instability during training. Thus, in the dynamic setting, we design γ as a *clipped* exponentially increasing variable that starts with a small initial value, i.e., $\gamma = \min(\alpha e^{\rho t}, \phi)$, where α is the initial value for γ, ϕ is its maximum value, ρ controls the rate of exponential increase and

t indicates the number of epochs the model has already been trained. This is motivated by a similar approach introduced in [2] for deep multi-task learning.

5   Experimental Evaluation

We evaluate the performance of the encoder and the generator of the proposed BiCoGAN model jointly and independently, and compare it with other encoder-based GANs, specifically, IcGAN, cALIM and cAVAE on various tasks. We also evaluate the effect of EFL and EFLW on BiCoGAN training.

5.1   Datasets

All models are evaluated on the MNIST [14] handwritten digits dataset and the CelebA [17] dataset of celebrity faces with annotated facial attributes. We consider the class labels in the MNIST dataset as extrinsic factors and components of writing styles as intrinsic factors. We select the same 18 visually impactful facial attributes of the CelebA dataset as [24] as extrinsic factors and all other factors of variation as intrinsic features. We did not evaluate the other GAN models on datasets for which their official implementations were not available. Therefore, we compare BiCoGAN with IcGAN and cAVAE on MNIST, and with IcGAN and cALIM on CelebA. We also present qualitative results of the proposed BiCoGAN model on the Chairs dataset [1]. Each chair is rendered at 31 different yaw angles, and cropped and downsampled to 32×32 dimensions. We use the yaw angle, a continuous value, as the extrinsic attribute for this dataset and all other factors of variation as intrinsic variables.

5.2   Metrics

We quantify the performance of encoding the extrinsic factors, c, using both mean accuracy (A_c) and mean F_1-score (F_c). We follow the approach in [26] of using an external discriminative model to assess the quality of generated images. The core idea behind this approach is that the performance of an external model trained on real data samples should be similar when evaluated on both real and GAN-generated test samples. We trained a digit classifier using a simple convolutional neural network for MNIST[1] and the attribute predictor Anet [17] model for CelebA. Thus, in our experimental settings, this metric also measures the ability of the generator in incorporating c in the generation of x. We use both accuracy (A_{gen}^{Ext}) and F_1-score (F_{gen}^{Ext}) to quantify the performance of the external model. We show the accuracy and the F_1-score of these external models on real test datasets for reference as A_{real}^{Ext} and F_{real}^{Ext}. We also calculate the adversarial accuracy (AA) as proposed in [33]. AA is calculated by training the external classifier on samples generated by a GAN and testing on real data. If the generator generalizes well and produces good quality images, the AA score should be

---

[1] https://github.com/fchollet/keras/blob/master/examples/mnist_cnn.py.

similar to the A_{gen}^{Ext} score. In order to calculate A_{gen}^{Ext}, F_{gen}^{Ext} and AA, we use each GAN to generate a set of images X_{gen}. Denoting the real training dataset as $\langle X_{train}, C_{train} \rangle$, each image in X_{gen} is created using a $c \in C_{train}$ combined with a randomly sampled z. X_{gen} is then used as the testing set for calculating A_{gen}^{Ext} and F_{gen}^{Ext}, and as the training set for calculating AA. Furthermore, we evaluate the ability of the GAN models to disentangle intrinsic factors from extrinsic attributes in the data generation process on the CelebA dataset using an identity-matching score (IMS). The motivation behind this metric is that the identity of generated faces should not change when identity-independent attributes (like hair color or the presence of eyeglasses) change. We first randomly generate 1000 faces with "male" and "black hair" attributes and another 1000 with "female" and "black hair" attributes. We then generate eight variations of these base images with the attributes: "bangs", "receding hairline", "blond hair", "brown hair", "gray hair", "heavy makeup", "eyeglasses" and "smiling" respectively. We encode all the generated images using a pretrained VGG-Face [23] model. IMS is then calculated as the mean cosine similarity of the base images with their variations. We provide results on MNIST and CelebA for two settings of BiCoGANs; one where we prioritize the performance of the generator (BiCoGAN-gen) and another for that of the encoder (BiCoGAN-enc), which gives us an empirical upper bound on the performance of BiCoGAN encoders.

5.3   Importance of Extrinsic Factor Loss

We analyze the importance of incorporating EFL for training BiCoGAN and the influence of EFLW on its performance. Figures 2d and 3d show some examples of images randomly generated using a BiCoGAN trained without EFL on both MNIST and CelebA, respectively. We see that BiCoGANs are not able to incorporate c into the data generation process when trained without EFL. The metrics discussed in Sect. 5.2 are calculated for BiCoGANs trained with $\gamma \in \{0, 1, 5, 10\}$ on MNIST, with $\gamma \in \{0, 5, 10, 20\}$ on CelebA, and with the dynamic setting of $\gamma = \min(\alpha e^{\rho t}, \phi)$, for $\alpha = 5$, $\rho = 0.25$ and $\phi = 10$, on both. Figure 4 summarizes our results. As before, we see that BiCoGANs are unable to learn the inverse mapping of x to c with $\gamma = 0$. The results show that increasing γ up until a tipping point helps train BiCoGANs better. However, beyond that point, the EFL term starts dominating the overall objective, leading to degrading performance in the quality of generated images (as reflected by A_{gen}^{Ext} and F_{gen}^{Ext} scores). Meanwhile, the dynamic setting of γ achieves the best results on both the datasets on almost all metrics, establishing its effectiveness at training BiCoGANs. It is also important to note that a dynamic γ saves significant time and effort involved in selecting a constant γ through manual optimization, which also depends on the complexity of the dataset. Therefore, we use BiCoGANs trained with dynamic γ for the comparative results in the following sections.

Fig. 2. Randomly generated (MNIST) digits using (a) BiCoGAN with EFL, (b) IcGAN, (c) cAVAE and (d) BiCoGAN without EFL.

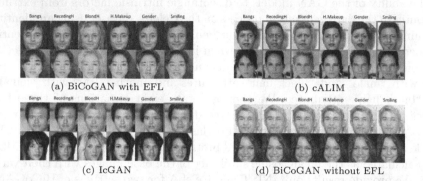

(a) BiCoGAN with EFL   (b) cALIM

(c) IcGAN   (d) BiCoGAN without EFL

Fig. 3. Randomly generated (CelebA) faces. Base images are generated with black hair and gender as male (first row) and female (second row). "Gender" column indicates gender change. Red boxes show cases where unspecified attributes or latent factors are *mistakenly* changed during generation. (Color figure online)

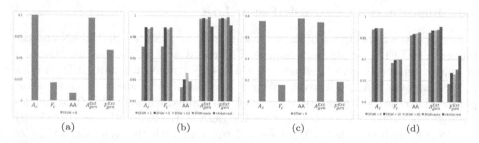

Fig. 4. Influence of γ for BiCoGANs trained on (a & b) MNIST and on (c & d) CelebA. A_c & F_c show the performance of encoding c while A_{gen}^{Ext} & F_{gen}^{Ext} show that of data generation. "EFLW = auto" denotes the dynamic-γ setting. The A_{real}^{Ext} and F_{real}^{Ext} values are shown as "$\langle X \rangle$Ext-real" values. The Y-axes of the plots have been scaled to easily observe differences.

5.4   Conditional Generation

In this section, we evaluate the ability of the BiCoGAN generator to (1) generalize over the prior distribution of intrinsic factors, i.e., be able to generate images with random intrinsic factors, (2) incorporate extrinsic factors while producing images, and (3) disentangle intrinsic and extrinsic factors during generation.

Figures 2a, b and c show some generated MNIST images with BiCoGAN, IcGAN and cAVAE, respectively. For each of these, we sampled z vectors from the latent distribution (fixed along rows) and combined them with the digit class c (fixed along columns). In order to vary c for cAVAE, we picked a random

image from each class and passed it through the cAVAE s-encoder to get its
s-representation. This is required because s in cAVAE does not have an explicit
form and is instead a fixed-length continuous vector. The visual quality of the
generated digits is similar for all the models with cAVAE producing slightly
unrealistic images. Figures 3a, b, and c show some generated CelebA images
with BiCoGAN, cALIM and IcGAN respectively. For each row, we sampled z
from the latent distribution. We set c to male and black-hair for the first row
and female and black-hair for the second row. We then generate each image in
the grids based on the combination of these with the new feature specified as the
column header. The figures show that BiCoGANs perform the best at preserving
intrinsic (like subject identity and lighting) and extrinsic factors (besides the
specified new attribute). Hence, BiCoGAN outperforms the other models in
disentangling the influence of z and the components of c in data generation.

Table 1. Encoding and generation performance - MNIST

Model	A_c	F_c	AA	A_{gen}^{Ext} (0.9897)	F_{gen}^{Ext} (0.9910)
cAVAE	–	–	**0.9614**	0.8880	0.9910
IcGAN	0.9871	0.9853	0.9360	0.9976	**0.9986**
BiCoGAN-gen	0.9888	0.9888	0.9384	**0.9986**	**0.9986**
BiCoGAN-enc	**0.9902**	**0.9906**	0.9351	0.9933	0.9937

Table 2. Encoding and generation performance - CelebA

Model	A_c	F_c	AA	A_{gen}^{Ext} (0.9279)	F_{gen}^{Ext} (0.7253)	IMS
cALIM	–	–	0.9138	**0.9139**	**0.6423**	0.9085
IcGAN	0.9127	0.5593	0.8760	0.9030	0.5969	0.8522
BiCoGAN-gen	0.9166	0.6978	**0.9174**	0.9072	0.6289	**0.9336**
BiCoGAN-enc	**0.9274**	**0.7338**	0.8747	0.8849	0.5443	0.9286

We quantify the generation performance using A_{gen}^{Ext}, F_{gen}^{Ext}, AA and IMS.
Table 1 shows results on MNIST for BiCoGAN, IcGAN and cAVAE. We show
A_{real}^{Ext} and F_{real}^{Ext} for reference within parentheses in the A_{gen}^{Ext} and F_{gen}^{Ext} column
headings, respectively. While BiCoGAN performs the best on A_{gen}^{Ext} and F_{gen}^{Ext}
scores, cAVAE performs better on AA. This indicates that cAVAE is more prone
to producing digits of wrong but easily confusable classes. Table 2 shows results
on CelebA for BiCoGAN, IcGAN and cALIM. BiCoGAN outperforms IcGAN
on almost all metrics. However, cALIM performs the best on A_{gen}^{Ext} and F_{gen}^{Ext}.
While this indicates that cALIM is better able to incorporate extrinsic factors
for generating images, IMS indicates that cALIM does this at the cost of intrinsic
factors. cALIM fails to effectively use the identity information contained in the

intrinsic factors and disentangling it from the extrinsic attributes while generating images. BiCoGAN performs the best on IMS. BiCoGAN also performs the best on AA, indicating that it successfully generates diverse but realistic images.

5.5 Encoding Extrinsic Factors

We assess the performance of the models at encoding the extrinsic factors from data samples using the A_c and F_c metrics. We calculate these scores directly on the testing split of each dataset. Tables 1 and 2 show the performance of IcGAN and BiCoGAN in encoding c on MNIST and CelebA, respectively. We note here that we cannot calculate A_c and F_c scores for cALIM because it does not encode c from x and for cAVAE because the s it encodes does not have an explicit form. BiCoGAN consistently outperforms IcGAN at encoding extrinsic factors from data. Furthermore, we provide an attribute-level breakdown of accuracies for the CelebA dataset in Table 3 and compare it with two state-of-the-art methods for cropped and aligned CelebA facial attribute prediction as reported in [32], namely, LNet+Anet [17] and WalkLearn [32]. BiCoGAN outperforms the state-of-the-art methods even though the EFL directly responsible for it is only one part of the entire adversarial objective. This indicates that supervised tasks (like attribute prediction) can benefit from training the predictor with a generator and a discriminator in an adversarial framework like ours.

Table 3. Attribute-level breakdown of encoder accuracy - CelebA

Attribute	LNet+ANet	WalkLearn	IcGAN	Ours
Bald	0.98	0.92	**0.98**	**0.98**
Bangs	0.95	**0.96**	0.92	0.95
Black_Hair	**0.88**	0.84	0.83	**0.88**
Blond_Hair	**0.95**	0.92	0.93	**0.95**
Brown_Hair	0.8	0.81	**0.87**	**0.87**
Bushy_Eyebrows	0.9	**0.93**	0.91	0.92
Eyeglasses	**0.99**	0.97	0.98	**0.99**
Gray_Hair	0.97	0.95	**0.98**	**0.98**
Heavy_Makeup	0.9	**0.96**	0.88	0.90
Male	**0.98**	0.96	0.96	0.97
Mouth_Slightly_Open	0.93	**0.97**	0.90	0.93
Mustache	0.95	0.90	**0.96**	**0.96**
Pale_Skin	0.91	0.85	0.96	**0.97**
Receding_Hairline	0.89	0.84	0.92	**0.93**
Smiling	0.92	**0.98**	0.90	0.92
Straight_Hair	0.73	0.75	**0.80**	**0.80**
Wavy_Hair	0.8	**0.85**	0.76	0.79
Wearing_Hat	**0.99**	0.96	0.98	0.98
MEAN	0.91	0.91	0.91	**0.93**

5.6   Image Reconstruction with Variations

We assess the performance of the generator and the encoder in the BiCoGAN framework jointly by comparing our model with IcGAN and cAVAE on the ability to reconstruct images with varied extrinsic factors on the MNIST dataset, and with IcGAN on the CelebA dataset. We do not compare against cALIM since it does not encode c. In order to vary c while generating images with cAVAE, we first calculate the s-embedding for each class as we did in Sect. 5.4. Figures 5 and 6 show our results on MNIST and CelebA, respectively. We see that intrinsic factors (such as writing style for MNIST and subject identity, lighting and pose for CelebA) are better preserved in variations of images reconstructed with BiCoGANs compared to other models. On CelebA we also see that for BiCo-GAN, changing an attribute has less effect on the incorporation of other extrinsic factors as well as the intrinsic features in the generation process, compared to IcGAN. This reinforces similar results that we observed in Sect. 5.4.

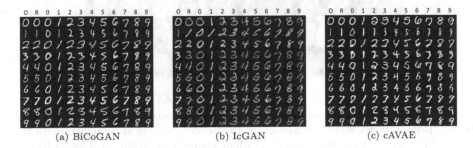

(a) BiCoGAN   (b) IcGAN   (c) cAVAE

Fig. 5. MNIST images reconstructed with varied class information. Column "O" shows the real image; "R" shows the reconstruction. The following columns show images with same z but varied c.

5.7   Continuous Extrinsic Factors

In previous subsections, we have provided results on datasets where c is categorical or a vector of binary attributes. We evaluate the ability of the BiCoGAN to model data distributions when c is continuous, on the Chairs dataset [1] with c denoting the yaw angle. Figure 7a shows chairs generated at eight different angles using our model, with z fixed along rows. The results show that the model is able to generate chairs for different c while preserving the information contained in z. We also assess the ability of BiCoGAN to learn the underlying manifold by interpolating between pairs of chairs. Figure 7b shows results of our experiments. Each row in the grid shows results of interpolation between the leftmost and the rightmost images. We see that the proposed BiCoGAN model shows smooth transitions while traversing the underlying latent space of chairs.

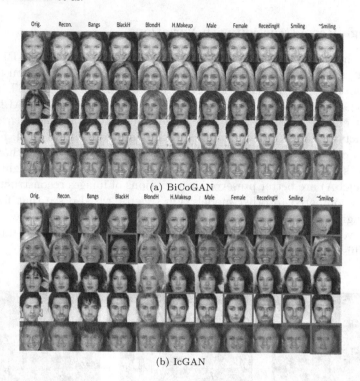

Fig. 6. CelebA images reconstructed with varied attributes. "Orig" shows the real image, "Recon" shows its reconstruction and the other columns show images with the same z but varied c. Red boxes show cases where unspecified attributes or latent factors are *mistakenly* modified during generation. (Color figure online)

Fig. 7. BiCoGAN results on Chairs dataset with continuous extrinsic attributes.

5.8   Using the Learned Representation

Finally, we quantitatively evaluate the encoding learned by the proposed BiCo-GAN model on the CelebA dataset by using the inferred z and c, i.e., the intrinsic factors and the 18 extrinsic attributes on which the model is trained, to predict the other 22 features annotated in the dataset. We train a simple feed-forward neural network for this task. Table 4 shows the results of our experiment with the attribute-level breakdown of prediction accuracies. We show results of the state-of-the-art methods, LNet+ANet [17] and WalkLearn [32], for reference. The results show that it is possible to achieve state-of-the-art results on predicting these attributes by using the z and c encoded by the proposed BiCoGAN model, instead of original images. This not only shows that information about

Table 4. Accuracies of predicting additional factors using encoding - CelebA

Attribute	LNet+ANet	WalkLearn	Ours
5_o_Clock_Shadow	0.91	0.84	**0.92**
Arched_Eyebrows	0.79	**0.87**	0.79
Attractive	0.81	**0.84**	0.79
Bags_Under_Eyes	0.79	**0.87**	0.83
Big_Lips	0.68	**0.78**	0.70
Big_Nose	0.78	**0.91**	0.83
Blurry	0.84	0.91	**0.95**
Chubby	0.91	0.89	**0.95**
Double_Chin	0.92	0.93	**0.96**
Goatee	0.95	0.92	**0.96**
High_Cheekbones	0.87	**0.95**	0.85
Narrow_Eyes	0.81	0.79	**0.86**
No_Beard	**0.95**	0.90	0.92
Oval_Face	0.66	**0.79**	0.74
Pointy_Nose	0.72	**0.77**	0.75
Rosy_Cheeks	0.90	**0.96**	0.94
Sideburns	**0.96**	0.92	**0.96**
Wearing_Earrings	0.82	**0.91**	0.84
Wearing_Lipstick	**0.93**	0.92	**0.93**
Wearing_Necklace	0.71	0.77	**0.86**
Wearing_Necktie	**0.93**	0.84	**0.93**
Young	**0.87**	0.86	0.85
MEAN	0.84	**0.87**	**0.87**

these attributes is captured in the encoded z but also presents a successful use-case of the disentangled embedding learned by the BiCoGAN encoder.

6   Conclusions

We presented the bidirectional conditional GAN framework that effectively generates data conditioned on intrinsic and extrinsic factors in a disentangled manner and provides a jointly trained encoder to encode data into *both* intrinsic and extrinsic factors underlying the data distribution. We presented necessary techniques for training BiCoGANs that incorporate an extrinsic factor loss with an associated importance weight. We showed that BiCoGAN exhibits state-of-the-art performance at encoding extrinsic factors of data and at disentangling intrinsic and extrinsic factors during generation on MNIST and CelebA. We provided results on the Chairs dataset to show that it works well with continuous extrinsic factors also. Finally, we showed that state-of-the-art performance can be achieved at predicting previously unseen attributes using BiCoGAN embeddings, demonstrating that the encodings can be used for downstream tasks.

Acknowledgements. This work is based on research sponsored by the Defense Advanced Research Projects Agency under agreement number FA8750-16-2-0204. The U.S. Government is authorized to reproduce and distribute reprints for governmental purposes notwithstanding any copyright notation thereon. The views and conclusions contained herein are those of the authors and should not be interpreted as necessarily representing the official policies or endorsements, either expressed or implied, of the Defense Advanced Research Projects Agency or the U.S. Government.

References

1. Aubry, M., Maturana, D., Efros, A., Russell, B.C., Sivic, J.: Seeing 3D chairs: exemplar part-based 2D–3D alignment using a large dataset of CAD models, June 2014
2. Belharbi, S., Hérault, R., Chatelain, C., Adam, S.: Deep multi-task learning with evolving weights. In: European Symposium on Artificial Neural Networks (ESANN) (2016)
3. Bousmalis, K., Silberman, N., Dohan, D., Erhan, D., Krishnan, D.: Unsupervised pixel-level domain adaptation with generative adversarial networks. In: The IEEE Conference on Computer Vision and Pattern Recognition (CVPR), July 2017
4. Donahue, J., Krähenbühl, P., Darrell, T.: Adversarial feature learning. In: International Conference on Learning Representations (2017)
5. Dumoulin, V., et al.: Adversarially learned inference. In: International Conference on Learning Representations (2017)
6. Goodfellow, I., et al.: Generative adversarial nets. In: Advances in Neural Information Processing Systems, pp. 2672–2680 (2014)
7. Gurumurthy, S., Kiran Sarvadevabhatla, R., Venkatesh Babu, R.: DeLiGAN : generative adversarial networks for diverse and limited data. In: The IEEE Conference on Computer Vision and Pattern Recognition (CVPR), July 2017
8. Hinton, G.E., Salakhutdinov, R.R.: Reducing the dimensionality of data with neural networks. Science **313**(5786), 504–507 (2006)
9. Huang, S., Ramanan, D.: Expecting the unexpected: training detectors for unusual pedestrians with adversarial imposters. In: The IEEE Conference on Computer Vision and Pattern Recognition (CVPR), July 2017
10. Huang, X., Li, Y., Poursaeed, O., Hopcroft, J., Belongie, S.: Stacked generative adversarial networks. In: The IEEE Conference on Computer Vision and Pattern Recognition (CVPR), July 2017
11. Isola, P., Zhu, J.Y., Zhou, T., Efros, A.A.: Image-to-image translation with conditional adversarial networks. In: The IEEE Conference on Computer Vision and Pattern Recognition (CVPR), July 2017
12. Kaneko, T., Hiramatsu, K., Kashino, K.: Generative attribute controller with conditional filtered generative adversarial networks. In: The IEEE Conference on Computer Vision and Pattern Recognition (CVPR), July 2017
13. Kingma, D.P., Welling, M.: Auto-encoding variational Bayes. In: International Conference on Learning Representations (2014)

14. LeCun, Y., Bottou, L., Bengio, Y., Haffner, P.: Gradient-based learning applied to document recognition. Proc. IEEE **86**(11), 2278–2324 (1998)
15. Ledig, C., et al.: Photo-realistic single image super-resolution using a generative adversarial network. In: The IEEE Conference on Computer Vision and Pattern Recognition (CVPR), July 2017
16. Li, J., Liang, X., Wei, Y., Xu, T., Feng, J., Yan, S.: Perceptual generative adversarial networks for small object detection. In: The IEEE Conference on Computer Vision and Pattern Recognition (CVPR), July 2017
17. Liu, Z., Luo, P., Wang, X., Tang, X.: Deep learning face attributes in the wild. In: Proceedings of International Conference on Computer Vision (ICCV), December 2015
18. Mahasseni, B., Lam, M., Todorovic, S.: Unsupervised video summarization with adversarial LSTM networks. In: The IEEE Conference on Computer Vision and Pattern Recognition (CVPR), July 2017
19. Makhzani, A., Shlens, J., Jaitly, N., Goodfellow, I.: Adversarial autoencoders. In: International Conference on Learning Representations (2016). http://arxiv.org/abs/1511.05644
20. Mathieu, M.F., Zhao, J.J., Zhao, J., Ramesh, A., Sprechmann, P., LeCun, Y.: Disentangling factors of variation in deep representation using adversarial training. In: Advances in Neural Information Processing Systems, pp. 5040–5048 (2016)
21. Mescheder, L., Nowozin, S., Geiger, A.: Adversarial variational Bayes: unifying variational autoencoders and generative adversarial networks. In: International Conference on Machine Learning (ICML) (2017)
22. Mirza, M., Osindero, S.: Conditional generative adversarial nets. arXiv preprint arXiv:1411.1784 (2014)
23. Parkhi, O.M., Vedaldi, A., Zisserman, A.: Deep face recognition. In: British Machine Vision Conference (2015)
24. Perarnau, G., van de Weijer, J., Raducanu, B., Álvarez, J.M.: Invertible conditional GANs for image editing. In: NIPS Workshop on Adversarial Training (2016)
25. Reed, S., Akata, Z., Yan, X., Logeswaran, L., Schiele, B., Lee, H.: Generative adversarial text-to-image synthesis. In: Proceedings of The 33rd International Conference on Machine Learning (2016)
26. Salimans, T., Goodfellow, I., Zaremba, W., Cheung, V., Radford, A., Chen, X.: Improved techniques for Training GANs. In: Advances in Neural Information Processing Systems, pp. 2234–2242 (2016)
27. Shrivastava, A., Pfister, T., Tuzel, O., Susskind, J., Wang, W., Webb, R.: Learning from simulated and unsupervised images through adversarial training. In: The IEEE Conference on Computer Vision and Pattern Recognition (CVPR), July 2017
28. Sixt, L., Wild, B., Landgraf, T.: RenderGAN: generating realistic labeled data. arXiv preprint arXiv:1611.01331 (2016)
29. Tzeng, E., Hoffman, J., Saenko, K., Darrell, T.: Adversarial discriminative domain adaptation. In: The IEEE Conference on Computer Vision and Pattern Recognition (CVPR), July 2017
30. Vondrick, C., Torralba, A.: Generating the future with adversarial transformers. In: The IEEE Conference on Computer Vision and Pattern Recognition (CVPR), July 2017
31. Wan, C., Probst, T., Van Gool, L., Yao, A.: Crossing Nets: combining GANs and VAEs with a shared latent space for hand pose estimation. In: The IEEE Conference on Computer Vision and Pattern Recognition (CVPR), July 2017

32. Wang, J., Cheng, Y., Feris, R.S.: Walk and learn: facial attribute representation learning from egocentric video and contextual data. In: 2016 IEEE Conference on Computer Vision and Pattern Recognition (CVPR), pp. 2295–2304 (2016)
33. Yang, J., Kannan, A., Batra, D., Parikh, D.: LR-GAN: layered recursive generative adversarial networks for image generation. In: International Conference on Learning Representations (2017)

Cross-Resolution Person Re-identification with Deep Antithetical Learning

Zijie Zhuang[✉], Haizhou Ai, Long Chen, and Chong Shang

Tsinghua National Lab for Information Science and Technology (TNList),
Department of Computer Science and Technology, Tsinghua University,
Beijing 100084, People's Republic of China
jayzhuang42@gmail.com, ahz@mail.tsinghua.edu.cn

Abstract. Images with different resolutions are ubiquitous in public person re-identification (ReID) datasets and real-world scenes, it is thus crucial for a person ReID model to handle the image resolution variations for improving its generalization ability. However, most existing person ReID methods pay little attention to this resolution discrepancy problem. One paradigm to deal with this problem is to use some complicated methods for mapping all images into an artificial image space, which however will disrupt the natural image distribution and requires heavy image preprocessing. In this paper, we analyze the deficiencies of several widely-used objective functions handling image resolution discrepancies and propose a new framework called deep antithetical learning that directly learns from the natural image space rather than creating an arbitrary one. We first quantify and categorize original training images according to their resolutions. Then we create an antithetical training set and make sure that original training images have counterparts with antithetical resolutions in this new set. At last, a novel Contrastive Center Loss (CCL) is proposed to learn from images with different resolutions without being interfered by their resolution discrepancies. Extensive experimental analyses and evaluations indicate that the proposed framework, even using a vanilla deep ReID network, exhibits remarkable performance improvements. Without bells and whistles, our approach outperforms previous state-of-the-art methods by a large margin.

Keywords: Person re-identification ·
Image resolution discrepancies · Deep antithetical learning

1 Introduction

Person re-identification (ReID) aims at identifying pedestrian identities across disjoint camera views. It suffers from various difficulties such as large variations of pose, viewpoint, and illumination conditions. Despite that person ReID tasks have been receiving increasing popularity, it remains a very challenging problem, especially in real-world application scenarios.

Recently, many inspiring works [1,15,32,33,36] have been proposed to tackle issues such as part misalignment and viewpoint changes. However, despite that

© Springer Nature Switzerland AG 2019
C. V. Jawahar et al. (Eds.): ACCV 2018, LNCS 11363, pp. 233–248, 2019.
https://doi.org/10.1007/978-3-030-20893-6_15

(a) High resolution images   (b) Low resolution images

Fig. 1. Examples of images with different resolution in public datasets.

these models have achieved remarkable performance on several person ReID benchmarks, two obvious, but as yet, unanswered questions are seldom valued by these approaches: (1) does the image resolution discrepancies in the training set affect the performance of person ReID? and (2) how to prevent a model from being prone to certain resolution combinations when the training data reflects the natural image distribution partially. As shown in Fig. 1, the image resolution discrepancy problem is common in both public datasets and real-world applications. We argue that these discrepancies are caused by arbitrarily rescaling training images with different resolutions to a uniform size. The original resolutions of pedestrian image patches are diverse due to three reasons. First, the graphical perspective leads to various sizes of pedestrians in images. Second, configurations of surveillance cameras are different in both public datasets and real-world applications. Some old surveillance cameras can only produce low-resolution images while other modern cameras generate high-resolution images. Third, to the best of our knowledge, almost all deeply-learned ReID models require rescaling image patches to a uniform size in both training and testing. This procedure will inevitably lead to the image resolution discrepancy problem.

For a person ReID model, sufficient training data with different resolutions is vital for improving its generalization ability. For each image in the training set, if we get all its antithetical counterparts that have the same content but with different resolutions, it will help a ReID model to gain a better generalization ability. However, there is almost no chance of finding a pair of images in which the image from the low-resolution camera has a higher image resolution than the one from the high-resolution camera. It means that the resolution discrepancies in the actual training set are biased since certain resolution combinations are missing. Previous methods cover up this problem with carefully designed training hyperparameters [10,17,36,37,39] or sophisticated image preprocessing method [2]. Unlike these methods, we propose a generic and straightforward framework called deep antithetical learning that directly tackles the resolution discrepancy problem. The first step is the image quality assessment. Since the resolution changes of training images are mostly caused by manually rescaling images into a uniform size, we adopt the No-reference Image Quality assessment (NR-IQA) [29] and measure the image resolution in the frequency domain. In the second step, we generate an antithetical training set in which the resolution of images is antithetical to their counterparts in the original training set. Image counterparts of lower resolutions can be easily generated by randomly downsampling, while approaches for enhancing the image resolution are limited. Generative adversarial networks (GANs) provide a practical approach for that purpose. However, neither CycleGAN [38] nor SRGAN [34] has the ability to enhance the image resolution to a specific level. Despite that we can split the original training set into multiple subsets, we cannot guarantee that every image has counterparts in every subset. Therefore, we roughly split the entire training set into two subsets: one with high-resolution (HR) images and another with low-resolution (LR) images. We then generate an antithetical training set in which the resolution of images is antithetical to their counterparts in the original training set. Specifically, for those HR images in the original set, we generate their LR counterparts by downsampling them randomly. And for those LR images in the original set, a GAN-based model is utilized for recovering fine texture details from them. These recovered images, along with the aforementioned manually blurred images, form the antithetical training set.

Apart from generating a new training set for better representing the natural image distribution, training the ReID model with proper objective functions is also crucial. We analyze the widely-used identification+verification paradigm [6] and find that the triplet loss with online hard negative mining (OHM) has a tendency to select training triplets of certain resolution combinations. This selection bias makes the ReID model suffer from resolution discrepancies and severely damages the performance. We address this problem by proposing a novel Contrastive Center Loss (CCL). The intuition behind is that rather than designing a sophisticated strategy for handling resolution differences between positive image pairs and negative ones, it is much easier to consider positive samples and negative samples separately. During the training procedure, the proposed CCL simultaneously clusters images of same identities and pushes the centers of different clusters away. To summarize, our contribution is three-fold:

- We focus on the image resolution discrepancy problem, which is seldom valued by previous methods as far as we know. We propose a training framework that produces antithetical images from the original training set and utilizes these images to eliminate biased discrepancies during the training phase.
- Unlike the previous super-resolution based ReID method [2], the goal of the proposed framework is to accommodate actual images whose resolution is naturally various. The proposed method does not require arbitrarily enhancing LR images during the test phase. Therefore, it has a potential to serve as a practical method for boosting many existing ReID methods.
- We go deep into the training procedure and investigate how the resolution discrepancies interfere with the triplet selection. The proposed Contrastive Center Loss shows an ability to learn discriminative features from images regardless of their various resolutions.

In conclusion, we present a high-performance person ReID system. Extensive experimental analyses and evaluations are conducted to demonstrate its effectiveness. Without bells and whistles, the proposed approach outperforms previous state-of-the-art methods on three large benchmarks by a large margin.

2 Related Work

Image Quality Assessment. Image quality assessment (IQA) is an important research area. It can be accomplished in three ways: full reference image quality assessment (FR-IQA), reduced reference image quality assessment (RR-IQA), and no reference image quality assessment (NR-IQA). NR-IQA algorithms measure the quality of an image without the need for any reference image or its features. Recently, various strategies have been proposed to measure image quality, including edge detection [40], natural scene statistics [44], wavelet decomposition [42,43], and human visual system model [41]. In this work, since the rescaling procedure is the major source of visual degradation, we evaluate the resolution of images with their sharpness.

Generative Adversarial Network. Generative adversarial network (GAN) contains two sub-networks: a generator and a discriminator. The framework of GANs is first proposed by Goodfellow *et al.* [19]. After that, many researchers focus on improving the stability and visual quality of GANs [20,35,38]. In the field of computer vision, GANs are widely used in applications ranging from motion deblurring (DeblurGAN) [35] to texture recovering (SRGAN) [34]. To generate the antithetical training set, we adopt SRGAN [34] for recovering the fine texture details from low-quality images.

Person Re-identification. Person re-identification (ReID) can be split into two subproblems: feature representations and distance metric learning. Over the past decades, many studies focus on designing discriminative features [18,21,30,31], while others focus on constructing more robust metric learning algorithms [24,26, 28]. With the rise of deep learning, deeply-learned models have dominated person ReID tasks. Several early works [1,3] take advantage of the two-stream siamese network and perform the pair-wise comparison in three steps: (1) extracting features from a given pair of images, (2) splitting feature cubes manually and comparing corresponding fractions across images, (3) determining whether these two images belong to the same identity. Attention-based methods [32,33] provide a more adaptive way for locating different human parts. Unlike these methods which focus on handling the variations of human pose and viewpoint changes, the proposed method tackles another common but crucial problem: the biased image resolution discrepancies in the training data.

3 Our Approach

3.1 Framework

In person ReID tasks, the resolution of training images is naturally various. However, previous methods seldom value these resolution discrepancies. They probably learn biased mappings from these images. Besides, due to the fact that these discrepancies have significant impacts on distances between training images, some aggressive mining strategies such as online hard negative mining (OHM) will make the discrepancy problem even worse. To deal with these issues, we propose an approach to train the person ReID model directly from

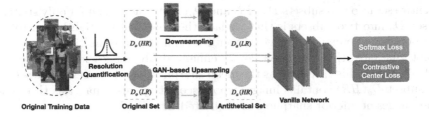

Fig. 2. The proposed training pipeline.

these images by deep antithetical learning. The motivations of the proposed deep antithetical learning are (1) producing antithetical training samples for balancing resolution discrepancies in the training set and (2) proposing a resolution-invariant objective function that produces better estimations of the image space. As demonstrated in Fig. 2, our approach mainly contains three steps. First, we measure the resolution of each image in training set with the sharpness metric. Second, we generate an antithetical training set by augmenting original low-resolution (LR) images with GANs and randomly downsampling original high-resolution (HR) images. In this antithetical training set, the resolution of each image is antithetical to that of its counterpart in the original training set. Third, after getting training samples from both the original training set and the antithetical set, we propose a novel Contrastive Center Loss (CCL) for learning relations between these images with various resolutions.

3.2 Evaluation of Original Training Set

The first step of generating the antithetical training set is to measure the resolution of images in the original training set. Person ReID tasks have two significant characteristics. (1) The standard image preprocessing pipeline does not change the brightness or hue of images but only their resolutions. (2) Images in ReID tasks are cropped image patches with tight bounding boxes, so the human body usually occupies a large portion of the entire image. The abundant texture information from the identity appearance provides rich evidence for measuring the image blurriness. We take advantage of the fact that sharper edges increase the high-frequency components and measure the resolution in the frequency domain.

We follow a simple sharpness metric proposed by De *et al.* [29]. Given an image I of size $h \times w$, we first compute its Fourier transform representation F. Then we calculate the centered Fourier transform F_c of image I by shifting the origin of F to center. The threshold τ is defined as the maximum absolute value of F_c. Now, we define the sharpness of an image I as:

$$\vartheta(I) = \frac{1}{h \times w} \sum_{i=1}^{h} \sum_{j=1}^{w} \mathbb{1}_{F_{i,j} \geq (\tau/1000)},$$ (1)

where $\mathbb{1}_{(condition)}$ represents the indicator function. After we obtain the sharpness of each image in the original training set D_o, we set up a threshold to split the entire set into two subsets $D_o(HR)$ and $D_o(LR)$. The reason for only splitting the set D_o into two subsets is that we lack the approach for tightly controlling the resolution of enhanced images. Even if we split D_o into multiple subsets, we cannot guarantee that the resolution of enhanced LR images reaches a specific level. We define this threshold as the mean sharpness of all images in the set D_o. The subset $D_o(HR)$ contains images whose score is greater than this threshold, while images of inferior sharpness are collected into $D_o(LR)$.

3.3   Antithetical Training Set

As we mentioned above, images in the original training set D_o are different not only in pose, viewpoint, illumination conditions but also in the image resolution. Therefore, we propose to generate an antithetical training set D_a for counteracting the biased resolution discrepancies. In the previous section, we described how to quantify the image resolution and split the original training set into two subsets: $D_o(HR)$ and $D_o(LR)$. Correspondingly, the antithetical training set D_a also contains two subsets: $D_a(LR)$ and $D_a(HR)$.

For high-resolution images in the original subset $D_o(HR)$, the strategy for producing their antithetical low-resolution counterparts is straightforward. For each image, we first downsample this image by a factor which is randomly chosen from a uniform distribution $\mathcal{U}(0.5, 0.8)$, and then we rescale this image to its original size. These manually blurred images are denoted as $D_a(LR)$.

For low-resolution images in the original training set $D_o(LR)$, we adopt SRGAN [34], a GAN-based image super-resolution method, for recovering fine texture details from low-resolution images. For each image of size $h \times w$ in $D_o(LR)$, SRGAN first upsamples it by a factor of 4 and then rescales this image to its original size. This rescaling procedure is necessary for eliminating random noises caused by SRGAN. In this way, we obtain the antithetical high-resolution subset $D_a(HR)$. For each low-resolution image in $D_o(LR)$, there is a corresponding high-resolution image in $D_a(HR)$. We will give a detailed evaluation in Sect. 4.3.

3.4   Contrastive Center Loss and Deep Antithetical Learning

Contrastive Center Loss. The proposed Contrastive Center Loss (CCL) aims at estimating the distance between different images without being interfered by their resolution discrepancies. The softmax loss + triplet loss with online hard negative mining (trihard) approach is widely used in recent works. This paradigm prefers positive images with the maximum distance to the anchor and negative images with the minimum distance to the anchor. However, this paradigm neglects the fact that the resolution discrepancies have a salient influence on these distances (Fig. 3a). We find that in the actual training procedure, trihard tends to select positive image pairs of which the resolution is most different, and negative image pairs of which the resolution is most similar. This biased tendency keeps a ReID model trapped into the local optima and damages its generalization ability. We will give a more detailed analysis in Sect. 4.5.

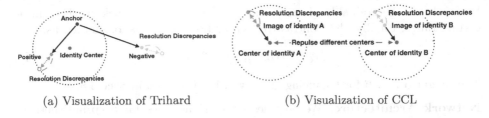

(a) Visualization of Trihard   (b) Visualization of CCL

Fig. 3. Differences between trihard and the proposed CCL.

Figure 3 shows the difference between the proposed CCL and the trihard loss. The trihard loss and the proposed CCL are both based on measuring distances between training samples. As we mentioned before, resolution discrepancies have a significant impact on these distances. For the trihard loss, resolution discrepancies in both positive samples and negative samples will affect the results of the loss function. To reduce the negative influence of resolution discrepancies, the proposed CCL measures intra-identity distances and inter-identity distances separately. For images of the same identity, we first estimate the center of each identity iteratively and minimize the distances between its center and corresponding image features:

$$\mathcal{L}_{intra} = \frac{1}{N} \sum_{i=1}^{N} \left(1 - \cos\left(f_i, C_{y_i}\right)\right), \tag{2}$$

where f_i denotes the feature extracted from the ith image and C_{y_i} stands for the corresponding center. In this way, all features only connect to their corresponding identity centers, so that resolution discrepancies will not spread across different identities. For inter-identity distances, to make the most of negative images and avoid perturbations caused by resolution variations, we use negative samples indirectly. The relations of images of different identities are measured by the cosine distance of their corresponding centers. Since maximizing cosine distances is equivalent to minimizing their cosine similarities, the loss for repulsing different centers is defined as:

$$\mathcal{L}_{inter} = \frac{1}{N} \sum_{i=1}^{N} \sum_{j=1}^{N} \left|\cos\left(C_{y_i}, C_{y_j}\right)\right|, \tag{3}$$

where $|\cdot|$ stands for the absolute value symbol. The reason for using the absolute value is that the orthogonality relation between identity centers is more discriminative than the positive/negative correlation. Note that both the intra-identity losses and the inter-identity losses are measured with cosine distances. An advantage of the cosine metric is that its range is certain. As shown in Table 5, inter-identity Euclidean distances are much greater than intra-identity distances. And during the training procedure, these two kinds of distances change at different speeds, and their corresponding losses change as well. Since these two losses both rely on the trainable identity centers, it is important to keep them in a certain range. Finally, the Contrastive Center Loss (CCL) is formulated as:

$$\mathcal{L}_{LCC} = \alpha\mathcal{L}_{intra} + \beta\mathcal{L}_{inter}. \tag{4}$$

The weight α and β for balancing losses will be discussed in Sect. 4.5.

Network Architecture. We now describe the network for deep antithetical learning. With the help of the antithetical training set and the Contrastive Center Loss, even a vanilla deep network can achieve remarkable performance. We denote this deep network as "VanillaNet" in following sections. VanillaNet contains two basic components: (1) a convolutional network backbone with a global average pooling layer for extracting features, (2) two successive fully-connected layers denoted as FC_0 and FC_1, where FC_1 is used for ID classification. We use the standard Identification+Verification framework for training the VanillaNet. The cross entropy loss of ID classification can be formulated as follow:

$$\mathcal{L}_s\left(p, g\right) = -\sum_{k=1}^{K} \log(p_k)\mathbb{1}_{k=g}, \tag{5}$$

where $\mathbb{1}_{(condition)}$ is the indicator function. p represents the prediction and g stands for the ground truth ID. The proposed CCL is connected to the last ReLU layer of the CNN backbone and the overall objective function for the proposed framework is formulated as:

$$\mathcal{L} = \mathcal{L}_s + \alpha\mathcal{L}_{intra} + \beta\mathcal{L}_{inter}. \tag{6}$$

During the training phase, we simply feed images from both original and antithetical training set into the network. In the testing phase, features from the last ReLU layer are used for ranking.

4   Experiments

4.1   Datasets

To evaluate the proposed framework, we select three public datasets: Market-1501 [13], Duke-MTMC-reID [12], and CUHK03 [1].

CUHK03. The CUHK03 dataset contains 14096 images of 1467 identities. There are at most ten images for each identity shot by two disjoint cameras. Unlike previous testing protocol which only adopts 100 identities for testing, we follow the new protocol presented by Zhong *et al.* [27]. This new protocol adopts 767 identities for training and the rest 700 identities for testing. Under this protocol, each identity has more than one ground truth image in the gallery, which is more consistent with the real-world applications.

Market-1501. The Market-1501 dataset is a large ReID dataset which contains 32643 annotated boxes of 1501 different identities. We divide this dataset into a training set of 750 identities and a testing set of 751. Since images in this dataset are collected by the pedestrian detector, it involves several detector failures. Besides, the quality of images shot by one particular camera is significantly lower than the quality of other images. These two characteristics make this dataset suitable for quantifying the effectiveness of the proposed method.

Duke-MTMC-reID. Duke-MTMC-reID is a newly published dataset. It contains 36411 bounding boxes shot by 8 different cameras. We use 16522 training images of 702 identities, leaving 2228 query images of the other 702 identities and 17661 gallery images for the testing procedure. Unlike Market-1501, the quality of images in this dataset is much higher and more consistent.

4.2   Implementation Details

For the SRGAN, we use the same training parameters provided in its original paper [34]. We first train the model on the DIV2K dataset and then fine-tune it on HR images from the ReID training set. In the training phase, rather than cropping training images randomly, we directly pad HR training images with zeros and resize them to the target scale.

For the VanillaNet, we adopt the ResNet-50 [5] backbone in all experiments. The batch size is set to 60. Both the weight α and β are set to 0.1 and the output dimension of the CNN backbone is 2048. In both training and testing phase, all images are resized to the size of 256×128. The data augmentation includes RandomErasing [25] and random horizontal flipping. To train the model, we adopt stochastic gradient descent (SGD) [23] optimizer with an initial learning rate of 0.01 and weight decay of 5×10^{-4}. In all experiments, the training phase lasts for 60 epochs. And the learning rate starts to decay exponentially at 20th epoch with the base of 0.1. The overall time cost of training the proposed model is minor. For the Market-1501, it takes about 130 min for the training procedure on a single GTX-Titan-Xp GPU.

4.3   Quantifying Image Resolution

In this section, we analyze image resolution distributations of all datasets. Since two subsets of CUHK03 are similar in human pose, viewpoint, and illumination conditions, we only present histograms of the "detected" subset. As shown in Fig. 4, diagrams in each column correspond to Market-1501, Duke-MTMC-reID, and CUHK03 (detected), respectively. Histograms in the first row represent the resolution distributation of the original training set D_o. And the red dashed line in each of them is the threshold for splitting the original set. In the second row, we compare the resolution of images in the original LR set $D_o(LR)$ and its corresponding antithetical set $D_a(HR)$. The blue histogram in each diagram corresponds to $D_o(LR)$, and the orange one corresponds to $D_a(HR)$. We also present the statistical analyses in Table 1 and some examples in Fig. 5.

In summary, for Market-1501, Duke-MTMC-reID, and CUHK03 (labeled), SRGAN can significantly augment low-resolution images in the original training set, especially under low light conditions.

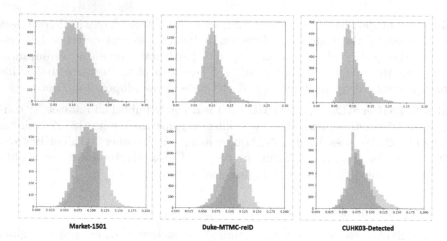

Fig. 4. Visualizations of the image resolution in different datasets. (Color figure online)

Table 1. Quantifying the mean and median of image sharpness scores before and after enhancements. Both the mean and median sharpness scores of low-resolution images are improved.

Datasets	Original set $D_o(LR)$			Antithetical set $D_a(HR)$		
	Num	Mean	Median	Num	Mean	Median
Market-1501	6906	0.087	0.091	6906	0.100	0.102
Duke-MTMC-reID	9121	0.093	0.075	9121	0.111	0.089
CUHK03 (labeled)	4661	0.075	0.088	4661	0.085	0.101
CUHK03 (detected)	4444	0.076	0.066	4444	0.086	0.070

4.4   Analyzing Different Data Fusion Strategies

The antithetical training set D_a is produced by two different approaches: enhancing LR images with SRGAN and downscaling HR images randomly. This specific strategy seems unsymmetrical. In this section, we demonstrate that both strategies are crucial for better estimating the real-world distribution. All following experiments are conducted on the test set of Market-1501. We first evaluate whether the antithetical training set improves the ReID performance. Only softmax identification loss is applied to VanillaNet in these experiments. As shown in Table 2, both the enhanced set $D_a(HR)$ and the decayed set $D_a(LR)$ are beneficial to the ReID performance. When combining $D_a(HR)$, $D_a(LR)$, and D_o together, VanillaNet reaches the highest performance.

Following the same criterion for splitting the training set, we further divide all query images into high-resolution probes and low-resolution probes. As shown in Table 3, the performance of querying with LR probes is much lower than that of querying with HR probes. Furthermore, we notice significant improvements in both LR queries and HR queries when adopting the antithetical training set.

(a) Original LR images

(b) Antithetical HR images

Fig. 5. Examples of low-resolution images in the original training set and their counterparts in the antithetical set.

Table 2. Comparing training data.

Datasets	Rank-1	mAP
D_o	88.63	72.47
$D_o + D_a(LR)$	89.16	73.98
$D_o + D_a(HR)$	89.84	73.75
$D_o + D_a$	**90.11**	**74.33**

Table 3. Comparing query probe.

Probe	D_o		$D_o + D_a$	
	Rank-1	mAP	Rank-1	mAP
LR	85.48	68.95	87.25	70.86
HR	92.26	76.54	93.41	78.33
ALL	88.63	72.47	90.11	74.33

These results indicate that the ReID model benefits from not only the SRGAN but also the random downsampling procedure. To further prove this conclusion, we compare the performance of our data augmentation approach with the other two approaches: (1) enhancing all images in D_o and (2) downsampling all these images. Table 4 demonstrates the performance of these approaches and internal differences on image distances. Note that these experiments are conducted with both the softmax loss and the proposed CCL for clustering images and tracking the identity centers. D_{intra} and D_{inter} stand for the average distance between images of the same identity, images of different identities on the test set. $D_{centers}$ represents the average distance between all identity centers on the training set. We adopt $D_{centers}$ for measuring the separation of different identity clusters.

Compared to other two fusion strategies, VanillaNet with the proposed CCL and antithetical set obtains the smallest intra-identity distances and the largest center distances. These results indicate that VanillaNet gains a better generalization ability on the test set with the proposed CCL and antithetical images.

Table 4. Comparing fusion strategies ($\alpha = 0.1$, $\beta = 0.1$).

Data fusion strategy	Rank-1	mAP	D_{intra}	D_{inter}	$D_{centers}$
Original+All SRGAN	89.85	74.66	0.4559	0.8075	0.6100
Original+All Downscale	87.14	72.47	0.4590	**0.8257**	0.6085
Original+Our Approach	**90.83**	**76.63**	**0.4548**	0.8127	**0.6122**

4.5   Comparing CCL with Other Objective Functions

In this section, we will discuss the differences between triplet loss with OHM (trihard), Center Loss, and the proposed Contrast Center Loss (CCL).

For trihard, our experiments indicate that the resolution of training images has biased influences on the triplet-picking procedure. Given a probe image, trihard expects the farthest image of the same identity and the nearest image of a different identity. As shown in Table 5, when the probe is with low-resolution, it is more likely for trihard to pick a positive HR image and a negative LR image at the same time. We also track all selected triplets during the training phase. Histograms in Fig. 6 show the possibility of picking image pairs with certain resolution combinations. The selected positive images tend to have a most different resolution than that of probe images, while the resolution of picked negative images tends to be the same as that of probe images. In a word, trihard suffers from resolution discrepancies and fails to learn all possible image combinations.

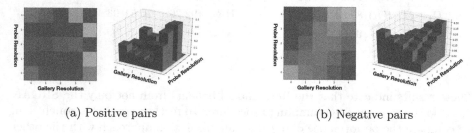

(a) Positive pairs   (b) Negative pairs

Fig. 6. The selection tendency of TriHard. Picked positive image pairs usually have the biggest difference in resolution, while the negative pairs have the most similar resolution. These histograms are normalized along the gallery axis.

Table 5. Distances between images with different resolutions (Training Set).

Distance between selected image pairs	Intra-identity	Inter-identity
(sharp, sharp)	0.2580	0.7306
(blur, blur)	0.2475	0.7182
(sharp, blur) and (blur, sharp)	0.2754	0.7255

For the Center Loss, the resolution discrepancy problem is much less severe. Images are only used for estimating their corresponding identity centers, so the discrepancies will not spread across different identities. However, it is at the cost of ignoring all negative images. Unlike Center Loss, the proposed CCL manages to learn from negative samples indirectly. When updating identity centers, the proposed CCL not only reduces the distance between image features and their corresponding center but also pushes different centers away. In this way, images are connected to their relevant centers directly and irrelevant centers indirectly. As shown in Table 6, the proposed CCL significantly increases the distances between different centers and distances between images of different identity. At the same time, the average intra-identity distance is slightly larger.

Table 6. Compare Center Loss and the proposed CCL.

Data fusion strategy	Rank-1	mAP	D_{intra}	D_{inter}	$D_{centers}$
Softmax	90.11	74.33	0.4110	0.6880	-
Softmax+Center Loss	90.29	75.00	**0.3295**	0.547	0.3893
Softmax+Contrastive Center Loss	**90.83**	**76.63**	0.4548	**0.8127**	**0.6122**

Table 7. Effect of different parameters on Market-1501.

Alpha	Beta	Rank-1	mAP	D_{intra}	D_{inter}
1	1	83.49	61.7	0.4729	1.1591
1	0.1	90.2	75.56	0.2294	0.413
0.1	0.1	**90.83**	**76.63**	0.4548	0.8127
0.1	0.01	90.44	75.36	0.3806	0.6525
0.01	0.01	90.38	76.07	0.4168	0.7093

4.6   Comparing with State-of-the-Art

According to Table 7, we set $\alpha = 0.1$ and $\beta = 0.1$ in all following experiments. We now compare our results with other state-of-the-art methods in Tables 8 and 9. With the single-query settings, our model achieves 90.8% rank-1 accuracy and 76.6% mAP on Market-1501. On Duke-MTMC-reID, compared to the

Table 8. Results on Market1501 and Duke-MTMC-reID in single query mode.

Methods	Market-1501				Duke			
	Rank-1	Rank-5	Rank-10	mAP	Rank-1	Rank-5	Rank-10	mAP
Re-rank [27]	77.1	-	-	63.6	-	-	-	-
LSRO [11]	84.0	-	-	66.1	67.7	-	-	47.1
TriNet [10]	84.9	94.2	-	69.1	-	-	-	-
SVDNet [17]	82.3	92.3	95.2	62.1	76.7	86.4	89.9	56.8
DPFL [15]	88.6	-	-	72.6	79.2	-	-	60.6
Ours (ResNet50)	90.8	**96.9**	**98.0**	76.6	82.9	91.9	93.8	67.3
Ours+Rerank	**92.7**	95.8	97.2	**89.1**	**87.4**	**92.5**	**94.6**	**83.2**
Ours (ResNet101)	91.5	96.8	97.7	79.5	84.5	92.6	94.3	70.1

previous best model, we achieve an absolute improvement of 3.7% in rank-1 and 6.7% in mAP. On CUHK03, the proposed model achieves 62.5% rank-1 accuracy/62.7% mAP on CUHK03 (labeled), and 55.9% rank-1 accuracy/55.0% mAP on CUHK03 (detected). Another observation is that the performance on all datasets can be boosted by simply adopting a more powerful network, such as ResNet-101. Therefore, it has a potential to serve as a practical method for boosting many existing ReID methods.

Table 9. Results on CUHK03 (labeled) and CUHK03 (detected).

Methods	CUHK03 (labeled)		CUHK03 (detected)	
	Rank-1	mAP	Rank-1	mAP
IDE+DaF [8]	27.5	31.5	26.4	30.0
PAN [14]	36.9	35.0	36.3	34.0
DPFL [15]	43.0	40.5	40.7	37.0
SVDNet [17]	40.9	37.8	41.5	37.3
TriNet [10]	58.1	53.8	55.5	50.7
Ours (ResNet50)	62.5	62.7	55.9	55.0
Ours+Rerank	**68.3**	**69.5**	**59.6**	**61.6**
Ours (ResNet101)	68.9	68.7	58.6	59.0

5   Conclusions

In this paper, we analyze the ubiquitous image resolution discrepancy problem in person ReID tasks. Extensive experiments indicate that these discrepancies have a negative impact on the ReID performance, and some mining strategies such as OHM will make this problem even worse. In this paper, we propose a novel training framework called deep antithetical learning and address this issue in two steps. First, an additional antithetical training set is generated for balancing biased resolution discrepancies. Second, we propose a resolution-invariant objective function called Contrastive Center Loss. Experiments demonstrate that even using a vanilla ReID network, the proposed framework outperforms previous state-of-the-art methods by a large margin.

Acknowledgments. This work was supported in part by the Natural Science Foundation of China (Project Number 61521002).

References

1. Li, W., Zhao, R., Xiao, T., Wang, X.: DeepReID: deep filter pairing neural network for person re-identification. In: CVPR (2014)
2. Jiao, J., Zheng, W.S., Wu, A., Zhu, X., Gong, S.: Deep low-resolution person re-identification. In: AAAI (2018)

3. Ahmed, E., Jones, M., Marks, T.K.: An improved deep learning architecture for person re-identification. In: CVPR (2015)
4. Hadsell, R., Chopra, S., LeCun, Y.: Dimensionality reduction by learning an invariant mapping. In: CVPR (2006)
5. He, K., Zhang, X., Ren, S., Sun, J.: Deep residual learning for image recognition. In: CVPR (2016)
6. Zheng, Z., Zheng, L., Yang, Y.: A discriminatively learned CNN embedding for person reidentification. ACM TOMM **14**, 13 (2017)
7. Wen, Y., Zhang, K., Li, Z., Qiao, Y.: A discriminative feature learning approach for deep face recognition. In: Leibe, B., Matas, J., Sebe, N., Welling, M. (eds.) ECCV 2016. LNCS, vol. 9911, pp. 499–515. Springer, Cham (2016). https://doi.org/10.1007/978-3-319-46478-7_31
8. Yu, R., Zhou, Z., Bai, S., Bai, X.: Divide and fuse: a re-ranking approach for person re-identification. arXiv preprint arXiv:1708.04169 (2017)
9. Xie, S., Girshick, R., Dollár, P., Tu, Z., He, K.: Aggregated residual transformations for deep neural networks. In: CVPR (2017)
10. Hermans, A., Beyer, L., Leibe, B.: In defense of the triplet loss for person re-identification. arXiv preprint arXiv:1703.07737 (2017)
11. Zheng, Z., Zheng, L., Yang, Y.: Unlabeled samples generated by GAN improve the person re-identification baseline in vitro. arXiv preprint arXiv:1701.07717 3 (2017)
12. Zheng, Z., Zheng, L., Yang, Y.: Unlabeled samples generated by GAN improve the person re-identification baseline in vitro. In: ICCV (2017)
13. Zheng, L., Shen, L., Tian, L., Wang, S., Wang, J., Tian, Q.: Scalable person re-identification: a benchmark. In: ICCV (2015)
14. Zheng, Z., Zheng, L., Yang, Y.: Pedestrian alignment network for large-scale person re-identification. arXiv preprint arXiv:1707.00408 (2017)
15. Chen, Y., Zhu, X., Gong, S.: Person re-identification by deep learning multi-scale representations. In: CVPR (2017)
16. Liao, S., Hu, Y., Zhu, X., Li, S.Z.: Person re-identification by local maximal occurrence representation and metric learning. In: CVPR (2015)
17. Sun, Y., Zheng, L., Deng, W., Wang, S.: SVDNet for pedestrian retrieval. In: CVPR (2017)
18. Ojala, T., Pietikainen, M., Maenpaa, T.: Multiresolution gray-scale and rotation invariant texture classification with local binary patterns. PAMI **24**, 971–987 (2002)
19. Goodfellow, I., et al.: Generative adversarial nets. In: NIPS (2014)
20. Radford, A., Metz, L., Chintala, S.: Unsupervised representation learning with deep convolutional generative adversarial networks. arXiv preprint arXiv:1511.06434 (2015)
21. Farenzena, M., Bazzani, L., Perina, A., Murino, V., Cristani, M.: Person re-identification by symmetry-driven accumulation of local features. In: CVPR (2010)
22. Li, D., Chen, X., Zhang, Z., Huang, K.: Learning deep context-aware features over body and latent parts for person re-identification. In: CVPR (2017)
23. Bottou, L.: Large-scale machine learning with stochastic gradient descent. In: COMPSTAT (2010)
24. Koestinger, M., Hirzer, M., Wohlhart, P., Roth, P.M., Bischof, H.: Large scale metric learning from equivalence constraints. In: CVPR (2012)
25. Zhong, Z., Zheng, L., Kang, G., Li, S., Yang, Y.: Random erasing data augmentation. arXiv preprint arXiv:1708.04896 (2017)
26. Yi, D., Lei, Z., Liao, S., Li, S.Z.: Deep metric learning for person re-identification. In: ICPR (2014)

27. Zhong, Z., Zheng, L., Cao, D., Li, S.: Re-ranking person re-identification with k-reciprocal encoding. In: CVPR (2017)
28. Davis, J.V., Kulis, B., Jain, P., Sra, S., Dhillon, I.S.: Information-theoretic metric learning. In: ICML (2007)
29. De, K., Masilamani, V.: Image sharpness measure for blurred images in frequency domain. Procedia Eng. **64**, 149–158 (2013)
30. Zhao, R., Ouyang, W., Wang, X.: Unsupervised salience learning for person re-identification. In: CVPR (2013)
31. Yang, Y., Yang, J., Yan, J., Liao, S., Yi, D., Li, S.Z.: Salient color names for person re-identification. In: Fleet, D., Pajdla, T., Schiele, B., Tuytelaars, T. (eds.) ECCV 2014. LNCS, vol. 8689, pp. 536–551. Springer, Cham (2014). https://doi.org/10.1007/978-3-319-10590-1_35
32. Liu, H., et al.: Neural person search machines. In: ICCV (2017)
33. Zhao, L., Li, X., Zhuang, Y., Wang, J.: Deeply-learned part-aligned representations for person re-identification. In: CVPR (2017)
34. Ledig, C., et al.: Photo-realistic single image super-resolution using a generative adversarial network. In: CVPR (2017)
35. Kupyn, O., Budzan, V., Mykhailych, M., Mishkin, D., Matas, J.: DeblurGAN: blind motion deblurring using conditional adversarial networks. arXiv preprint arXiv:1711.07064 (2017)
36. Sun, Y., Zheng, L., Yang, Y., Tian, Q., Wang, S.: Beyond part models: person retrieval with refined part pooling. arXiv preprint arXiv:1711.09349 (2017)
37. Zhang, X., et al.: AlignedReID: surpassing human-level performance in person re-identification. arXiv preprint arXiv:1711.08184 (2017)
38. Zhu, J.Y., Park, T., Isola, P., Efros, A.A.: Unpaired image-to-image translation using cycle-consistent adversarial networks. In: CVPR (2017)
39. Xiao, Q., Luo, H., Zhang, C.: Margin sample mining loss: a deep learning based method for person re-identification. arXiv preprint arXiv:1710.00478 (2017)
40. Marziliano, P., Dufaux, F., Winkler, S., Ebrahimi, T.: Perceptual blur and ringing metrics: application to JPEG2000. Signal Process. Image Commun. **19**, 163–172 (2004)
41. Du, J., Yu, Y., Xie, S.: A new image quality assessment based on HVS. J. Electron. (China) **22**, 315–320 (2005)
42. Sheikh, H.R., Bovik, A.C., Cormack, L.: No-reference quality assessment using natural scene statistics: JPEG 2000. TIP **14**, 1918–1927 (2005)
43. Chen, M.J., Bovik, A.C.: No-reference image blur assessment using multiscale gradient. EURASIP J. Image Video Process. **2011**, 3 (2011)
44. Brandão, T., Queluz, M.P.: No-reference image quality assessment based on DCT domain statistics. Signal Process. **88**, 822–833 (2008)

A Temporally-Aware Interpolation Network for Video Frame Inpainting

Ximeng Sun[✉], Ryan Szeto, and Jason J. Corso

University of Michigan, Ann Arbor, USA
{sunxm,szetor,jjcorso}@umich.edu

Abstract. We propose the first deep learning solution to video frame inpainting, a more challenging but less ambiguous task than related problems such as general video inpainting, frame interpolation, and video prediction. We devise a pipeline composed of two modules: a bidirectional video prediction module and a temporally-aware frame interpolation module. The prediction module makes two intermediate predictions of the missing frames, each conditioned on the preceding and following frames respectively, using a shared convolutional LSTM-based encoder-decoder. The interpolation module blends the intermediate predictions, using time information and hidden activations from the video prediction module to resolve disagreements between the predictions. Our experiments demonstrate that our approach produces more accurate and qualitatively satisfying results than a state-of-the-art video prediction method and many strong frame inpainting baselines. Our code is available at https://github.com/sunxm2357/TAI_video_frame_inpainting.

Keywords: Video inpainting · Video prediction · Frame interpolation

1 Introduction

In this work, we explore the video frame inpainting problem, i.e. the task of reconstructing a missing sequence of frames given both a sequence of *preceding* frames and a sequence of *following* frames. For example, given a clip of someone winding up a baseball pitch and a clip of that person after he/she has released the ball, we would predict the clip of that person throwing the ball. This task is more challenging than general video inpainting because we aim to fill in whole, temporally-contiguous frames rather than small spatio-temporal regions. It is also less ambiguous—and therefore more well-defined and easier to evaluate—than frame interpolation and video prediction, where methods cannot access the contextual information required to rule out many plausible predictions.

X. Sun and R. Szeto—Equal contribution.

Electronic supplementary material The online version of this chapter (https://doi.org/10.1007/978-3-030-20893-6_16) contains supplementary material, which is available to authorized users.

© Springer Nature Switzerland AG 2019
C. V. Jawahar et al. (Eds.): ACCV 2018, LNCS 11363, pp. 249–264, 2019.
https://doi.org/10.1007/978-3-030-20893-6_16

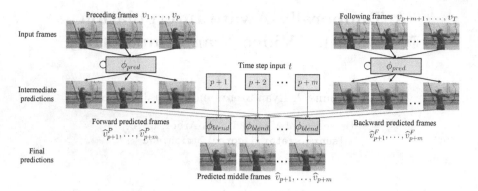

Fig. 1. We predict middle frames by blending forward and backward intermediate video predictions with a Temporally-Aware Interpolation (TAI) network

We present the first deep neural network for video frame inpainting, which approaches the problem in two steps as shown in Fig. 1. First, we use a video prediction subnetwork to generate two intermediate predictions of the middle frames: the "forward prediction" conditioned on the preceding frames, and the "backward prediction" conditioned on the following frames. Then, we blend each pair of corresponding frames together to obtain the final prediction.

Our blending strategy exploits three characteristics of our intermediate prediction process. First, a pair of intermediate prediction frames for the same time step might be inconsistent, e.g. an actor might appear in two different locations. To address this, we introduce a blending neural network that can cleanly merge a given pair of predictions by reconciling the differences between them. Second, for any given time step, the forward and backward predictions are not equally reliable: the former is more accurate for earlier time steps, and the latter is more accurate for later time steps. Hence, we feed time step information directly into the blending network, making it *temporally-aware* by allowing it to blend differently depending on which time step it is operating at. Finally, the intermediate predictions come from a neural network whose hidden features may be useful for blending. To leverage these features, we feed them to the blending network as additional inputs. We call our blending module the **Temporally-Aware Interpolation Network** (or TAI network for short). As we show in our experiments, our approach yields the most visually satisfying predictions among several strong baselines and across multiple human action video datasets.

In summary, we make the following contributions. First, we propose a deep neural network for video frame inpainting that generates two intermediate predictions and blends them with our novel TAI network. Second, we propose and compare against several baselines that leverage the information provided by the preceding and following frames, but do not utilize our TAI blending approach. Finally, we demonstrate that our approach is quantitatively and qualitatively superior to the proposed baselines across three human action video datasets.

2   Related Work

In the *general video inpainting problem* (of which our video frame inpainting task is a challenging instance), we are given a video that is missing arbitrary voxels (spatio-temporal pixels), and the goal is to fill each voxel with the correct value. Existing methods generally fall into one of three categories: *patch-based* methods that search for complete spatio-temporal patches to copy into the missing area [8,16,21,27]; *object-based* methods that separate spatial content into layers (e.g. foreground and background), repair them individually, and stitch them back together [7,18]; and *probabilistic model-based* methods that assign values that maximize the likelihood under some probabilistic model [3–5]. Many of these approaches make strong assumptions about the video content, such as constrained camera pose/motion [7,18,21] or static backgrounds [5,7,18]. In addition, they are designed for the case in which "holes" in the video are localized to small spatio-temporal regions, and may therefore perform poorly when whole, contiguous frames are missing. Finally, to the best of our knowledge, no existing solution has leveraged deep neural networks, which can potentially outperform prior work thanks to the vast amounts of video data available online.

In the *frame interpolation task*, the goal is to predict one or more frames in between two (typically subsequent) input frames. While most classical approaches linearly interpolate a dense optical flow field to an arbitrary number of intermediate time steps [1,2,26], recent approaches train deep neural networks to predict one intermediate frame [11,12,17]. However, all of these approaches require input frames that occur within a miniscule window of time (i.e. no more than 0.05 seconds apart), whereas we are interested in predicting on larger time scales. Furthermore, the task is ambiguous because a pair of individual frames without temporal context cannot sufficiently constrain the appearance of the intermediate frames (for instance, if we observed two frames of a swinging pendulum, we would need its period of oscillation to rule out several plausible appearances). As a result, it is hard to evaluate plausible predictions that deviate from the actual data.

Video prediction, where the goal is to generate the future frames that follow a given sequence of video frames, is yet another actively-studied area with an important limitation. The earliest approaches draw heavily from language modeling literature by extending simple recurrent sequence-to-sequence models to predict patches of video [19,23]; more recent methods utilize structured models that decompose the input data and/or the learned representations in order to facilitate training [9,13,24]. As with frame interpolation, video prediction is inherently underconstrained since the past can diverge into multiple plausible futures.

3   Approach

3.1   Problem Statement

We define the video frame inpainting problem as follows. Let $V = \{v_1, v_2, \ldots, v_T\}$ be a sequence of frames from a real video, p, m, and f be the number of

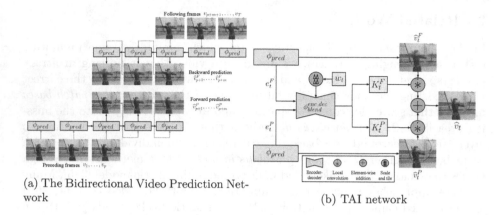

(a) The Bidirectional Video Prediction Network

(b) TAI network

Fig. 2. Architectures of two modules in our model

"preceding", "middle", and "following" frames such that $p + m + f = T$, and $P_V = \{v_1, \ldots, v_p\}, M_V = \{v_{p+1}, \ldots, v_{p+m}\}, F_V = \{v_{p+m+1}, \ldots, v_T\}$ be the sequences of preceding, middle, and following frames from V respectively. We seek a function ϕ that satisfies $M_V = \phi(P_V, F_V)$ for all V.

3.2   Model Overview

We propose a novel deep neural network to approximate the video inpainting function ϕ (see Fig. 1). Instead of learning a direct mapping from the preceding and following sequences to the middle sequence, our model decomposes the problem into two sub-problems and tackles each one sequentially with two tractable modules: the Bidirectional Video Prediction Network (Sect. 3.3) and the Temporally-Aware Interpolation Network (Sect. 3.4).

- The **Bidirectional Video Prediction Network** generates two intermediate predictions of the middle sequence M_V, where each prediction is conditioned solely on the preceding sequence P_V and the following sequence F_V respectively.
- The **Temporally-Aware Interpolation Network** blends corresponding frames from the predictions made by the Bidirectional Video Prediction Network, thereby producing the final prediction $\widehat{M_V}$. It accomplishes this by leveraging intermediate activations from the Bidirectional Video Prediction Network, as well as scaled time steps that explicitly indicate the relative temporal location of each frame in the final prediction.

Even though our model factorizes the video frame inpainting process into two steps, it is optimized in an end-to-end manner.

3.3   Bidirectional Video Prediction Network ϕ_{pred}

We first use the Bidirectional Video Prediction Network ϕ_{pred}, shown in Fig. 2a, to produce two intermediate predictions—a "forward prediction" $\widehat{M}_V^P =$

$\{\widehat{v}_{p+1}^P, \ldots, \widehat{v}_{p+m}^P\}$ and a "backward prediction" $\widehat{M}_V^F = \{\widehat{v}_{p+1}^F, \ldots, \widehat{v}_{p+m}^F\}$—by conditioning on the preceding sequence P_V and the following sequence F_V respectively:

$$\widehat{M}_V^P = \phi_{pred}(P_V), \tag{1}$$

$$\widehat{M}_V^F = \left[\phi_{pred}((F_V)^R)\right]^R, \tag{2}$$

where $(\cdot)^R$ is an operation that reverses the input sequence. Note that the same parameters are used to generate the forward and backward predictions.

In particular, the Bidirectional Video Prediction Network recurrently generates one frame at a time by conditioning on all previously generated frames. For example, in the case of the forward prediction:

$$\widehat{v}_{k+1}^P = \phi_{pred}(\{\widetilde{v}_1^P, \widetilde{v}_2^P, \ldots, \widetilde{v}_k^P\}), \tag{3}$$

where for a given t, $\widetilde{v}_t^P$ is either v_t (an input frame) if $t \in \{1, \ldots, p\}$ or $\widehat{v}_t^P$ (an intermediate predicted frame) if $t \in \{p+1, \ldots, p+m\}$. We also store intermediate activations from the Bidirectional Video Prediction Network (denoted as e_t^P), which serve as inputs to the Temporally-Aware Interpolation Network. We apply an analogous procedure to obtain the backward prediction and its corresponding intermediate activations.

3.4 Temporally-Aware Interpolation Network ϕ_{blend}

Following the Bidirectional Video Prediction Network, the Temporally-Aware Interpolation Network ϕ_{blend} takes corresponding pairs of frames from $\widehat{M}_V^P$ and $\widehat{M}_V^F$ with the same time step, i.e. $(\widehat{v}_t^P, \widehat{v}_t^F)$ for each time step $t \in \{p+1, \ldots, p+m\}$, and blends them into the frames that make up the final prediction $\widehat{M}_V$:

$$\widehat{v}_t = \phi_{blend}(\widehat{v}_t^P, \widehat{v}_t^F), \tag{4}$$

$$\widehat{M}_V = \{\widehat{v}_t \mid t = p+1, \ldots, p+m\}. \tag{5}$$

Blending $\widehat{v}_t^P$ and $\widehat{v}_t^F$ is difficult because (i) they often contain mismatched content (e.g. between the pair of frames, objects might be in different locations), and (ii) they are not equally reliable (e.g. $\widehat{v}_t^P$ is more reliable for earlier time steps). As we show in Sect. 4, equally averaging $\widehat{v}_t^P$ and $\widehat{v}_t^F$ predictably results in ghosting artifacts (e.g. multiple faded limbs in human action videos), but remarkably, replacing a simple average with a state-of-the-art interpolation network also exhibits the same problem.

In order to blend corresponding frames more accurately, our Temporally-Aware Interpolation (TAI) Network utilizes two additional sources of information. Aside from the pair of frames to blend, it receives the scaled time step to predict—defined as $w_t = (t - p)/(m + 1)$—and the intermediate activations from the Bidirectional Video Prediction Network e_t^P and e_t^F. We feed w_t to our interpolation network so it can learn how to incorporate the unequal reliability of $\widehat{v}_t^P$ and $\widehat{v}_t^F$ into its final prediction; we feed e_t^P and e_t^F to leverage the high-level semantics that the Bidirectional Video Prediction Network has learned. We contrast standard interpolation with TAI algebraically:

$$\widehat{v}_t = \phi_{interp}\left(\widehat{v}_t^P, \widehat{v}_t^F\right), \tag{6}$$

$$\widehat{v}_t = \phi_{TAI}\left(\widehat{v}_t^P, e_t^P, \widehat{v}_t^F, e_t^F, w_t\right). \tag{7}$$

TAI blends pairs of intermediate frames $(\widehat{v}_t^P, \widehat{v}_t^F)$ by first applying a unique, adaptive 2D kernel to each patch in the two input frames, and then summing the resulting images pixel-wise à la Niklaus et al. [17]. To generate the set of adaptive kernels, we use an encoder-decoder model, shown in Fig. 2b, that takes in the intermediate activations from the Bidirectional Video Prediction Network, e_t^P and e_t^F, and the scaled time step w_t:

$$K_t^P, K_t^F = \phi_{blend}^{enc\_dec}\left(e_t^P, e_t^F, w_t\right), \tag{8}$$

where K_t^P and K_t^F are 3D tensors whose height and width match the frame resolution and whose depth equals the number of parameters in each adaptive kernel. Note that we inject the scaled time step by replicating it spatially and concatenating it to the output of one of the decoder's hidden layers as an additional channel. Afterwards, we apply the adaptive kernels to each input frame and sum the resulting images pixel-wise:

$$\widehat{v}_t(x,y) = K_t^P(x,y) * \mathcal{P}_P(x,y) + K_t^F(x,y) * \mathcal{P}_F(x,y), \tag{9}$$

where $\widehat{v}_t(x,y)$ is the pixel value of the final prediction at (x,y), $K_t^{(\cdot)}(x,y)$ is the 2D kernel parameterized by the depth column of $K_t^{(\cdot)}$ at (x,y), $*$ is the convolution operator, and $\mathcal{P}_{(\cdot)}(x,y)$ is the patch centered at (x,y) in $\widehat{v}_t^{(\cdot)}$.

3.5   Training Strategy

To train our complete video frame inpainting model, we use both reconstruction-based and adversarial objective functions, the latter of which has been shown by Mathieu et al. [14] to improve the sharpness of predictions. In our case, we train a discriminator D, which is a binary classification CNN, to distinguish between clips from the dataset and clips generated by our model. Meanwhile, we train our model—the "generator"—to not only fool the discriminator, but also generate predictions that resemble the ground truth.

We update the generator and the discriminator in an alternating fashion. In the generator update step, we update our model by minimizing the following structured loss:

$$\mathcal{L}_g = \alpha \left[\mathcal{L}_{img} \left(\widehat{M}_V^P, M_V \right) + \mathcal{L}_{img} \left(\widehat{M}_V^F, M_V \right) + \mathcal{L}_{img} \left(\widehat{M}_V, M_V \right) \right]$$
$$+ \beta \mathcal{L}_{GAN} \left(\widehat{M}_V \right), \tag{10}$$

$$\mathcal{L}_{GAN} \left(\widehat{M}_V \right) = - \log D \left(\left[P_V, \widehat{M}_V, F_V \right] \right), \tag{11}$$

where α and β are hyperparameters to balance the contribution of the reconstruction-based loss $\mathcal{L}_{img}$ and the adversarial loss $\mathcal{L}_{GAN}$. Note that we supervise the final prediction $\widehat{M}_V$ as well as the intermediate predictions $\widehat{M}_V^P$ and $\widehat{M}_V^F$ simultaneously. The loss $\mathcal{L}_{img}$ consists of the squared-error loss $\mathcal{L}_2$ and the image gradient difference loss $\mathcal{L}_{gdl}$ [14], which encourages sharper predictions by penalizing differences along the edges in the image:

$$\mathcal{L}_{img} \left(\widehat{M}_V^{(\cdot)}, M_V \right) = \mathcal{L}_2 \left(\widehat{M}_V^{(\cdot)}, M_V \right) + \mathcal{L}_{gdl} \left(\widehat{M}_V^{(\cdot)}, M_V \right), \tag{12}$$

$$\mathcal{L}_2 \left(\widehat{M}_V^{(\cdot)}, M_V \right) = \sum_{t=p+1}^{p+m} \left\| v_t - \widehat{v}_t^{(\cdot)} \right\|_2^2, \tag{13}$$

$$\mathcal{L}_{gdl} \left(\widehat{M}_V^{(\cdot)}, M_V \right) = \sum_{t=p+1}^{p+m} \sum_{i,j}^{h,w} \left(\left| \left| v_t(i,j) - v_t(i-1,j) \right| - \left| \widehat{v}_t^{(\cdot)}(i,j) - \widehat{v}_t^{(\cdot)}(i-1,j) \right| \right| \right.$$
$$\left. + \left| \left| v_t(i,j-1) - v_t(i,j) \right| - \left| \widehat{v}_t^{(\cdot)}(i,j-1) - \widehat{v}_t^{(\cdot)}(i,j) \right| \right| \right). \tag{14}$$

'Here, $\widehat{M}_V^{(\cdot)}$ can be one of the intermediate predictions $\left\{ \widehat{M}_V^P, \widehat{M}_V^F \right\}$ or the final prediction $\widehat{M}_V$. In the discriminator update step, we update the discriminator by minimizing the cross-entropy error:

$$\mathcal{L}_d = - \log D \left(\left[P_V, M_V, F_V \right] \right) - \log \left(1 - D \left(\left[P_V, \widehat{M}_V, F_V \right] \right) \right). \tag{15}$$

We use the same discriminator as Villegas et al. [24], but replace each layer that is followed by batch normalization [6] with a spectral normalization layer [15], which we have found results in more accurate predictions.

4 Experiments

4.1 Experimental Setup

Our high-level approach to video frame inpainting places few constraints on the network architectures that can be used to implement each module (Sect. 3.2). We instantiate the Bidirectional Video Prediction Network with MC-Net [24]. As for the Temporally-Aware Interpolation Network, we modify the Separable Adaptive Kernel Network [17] to take as input intermediate activations and scaled time steps (refer to the supplementary materials for architectural details).

These choices afford us two benefits: (i) the chosen networks are, to the best of our knowledge, the best-performing models in their original tasks, enabling us to demonstrate the full potential of our approach; and (ii) both networks are fully-convolutional, allowing us to modify the video resolution at test time.

We compare our video frame inpainting model to several baselines (Sect. 4.2) on videos from three human action datasets: KTH Actions [20], HMDB-51 [10], and UCF-101 [22]. KTH Actions contains a total of 2,391 grayscale videos with resolution 120 × 160 (height × width) across six action classes; it also provides a standard training and testing set. We divide the standard training set into a smaller training set and a validation set, which are used for training and hyperparameter search respectively. Following Villegas et al. [24], we reduce the resolution to 128 × 128. We train each model to predict five middle frames from five preceding and five following frames; at inference time, we evaluate each model on its ability to predict ten middle frames from five preceding and five following frames. We double the number of frames to predict at test time in order to evaluate generalization performance (following Villegas et al. [24]).

HMDB-51 contains 6,849 RGB videos across 51 action classes; each video has a fixed height of 240 pixels. The dataset provides three cross-validation folds (each including a training and a test set); we take the test videos from the first fold as our test set and separate the remaining videos into our training and validation sets. During training, we reduce the resolution of each video to 160 × 208, and train each model to predict three middle frames from four preceding and four following frames. At test time, we scale all videos to 240 × 320 resolution (following Villegas et al. [24]) and take in the same number of preceding/following frames, but predict five frames in the middle.

UCF-101 contains 13,320 RGB videos with resolution 240 × 320 across 101 action classes. It provides three cross-validation folds for action recognition; we take the test videos from the first fold as our test set and divide the remaining videos into our training and validation sets. The remainder of our experimental setup for UCF-101 matches our setup for HMDB-51.

4.2   Baselines

The first baseline we compare our method to is MC-Net [24]—we re-implement and train their model to predict the middle frames conditioned only on the preceding frames. We also introduce two classes of baselines specifically designed for the video frame inpainting problem. In the first class, instead of learning a function ϕ, we hand-craft several ϕ's that can perform well on certain video prediction tasks, particularly on videos with little movement or periodic motion. The baselines described by Eqs. 16–18 copy or take a simple average of the last preceding frame v_p and the first following frame v_{p+m+1}:

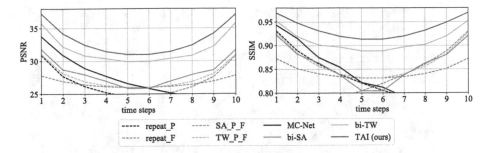

Fig. 3. Quantitative results on the KTH Actions dataset (for both PSNR and SSIM, higher is better). We compare our full model (TAI) to the baselines described in Sect. 4.2

$$\phi_{\text{repeat\_P}}\left(P_V, F_V\right) = \{v_p, v_p, \ldots, v_p\},\tag{16}$$

$$\phi_{\text{repeat\_F}}\left(P_V, F_V\right) = \{v_{p+m+1}, v_{p+m+1}, \ldots, v_{p+m+1}\},\tag{17}$$

$$\phi_{\text{SA\_P\_F}}\left(P_V, F_V\right) = \{\widehat{v}, \widehat{v}, \ldots, \widehat{v}\}, \text{where } \widehat{v} = \frac{v_p + v_{p+m+1}}{2}.\tag{18}$$

Also, we try incorporating the scaled time step of the predicted frame $w_t = (t - p)/(m + 1)$ by computing a time-weighted average of v_p and v_{p+m+1}:

$$\phi_{\text{TW\_P\_F}}\left(P_V, F_V\right) = \{\widehat{v}_{p+1}, \widehat{v}_{p+2}, \ldots, \widehat{v}_{p+m}\},\tag{19}$$

$$\widehat{v}_t = (1 - w_t)\, v_p + w_t v_{p+m+1}.\tag{20}$$

In the second class of baselines, we highlight the value of our TAI module by proposing two bidirectional prediction models that use the same Bidirectional Video Prediction Network architecture as our full model, but blend the forward and backward predictions without an interpolation network. Instead, they blend by computing either a simple average (bi-SA, Eq. 21) or a weighted average based on the scaled time step w_t (bi-TW, Eq. 22):

$$\widehat{v}_t = \left(\widehat{v}_t^P + \widehat{v}_t^F\right)/2,\tag{21}$$

$$\widehat{v}_t = (1 - w_t)\, \widehat{v}_t^P + w_t \widehat{v}_t^F.\tag{22}$$

All baselines are trained independently from scratch.

4.3 KTH Actions

To evaluate the performance of the proposed baselines and our full model with the TAI network (we refer to this full model as TAI for brevity), we follow existing video prediction literature [14,24] by reporting the Structural Similarity (SSIM) [25] and Peak Signal-Noise Ratio (PSNR) between each predicted frame and the ground truth. We draw a series of conclusions from the quantitative comparison shown in Fig. 3. First, the low performance of the hand-crafted

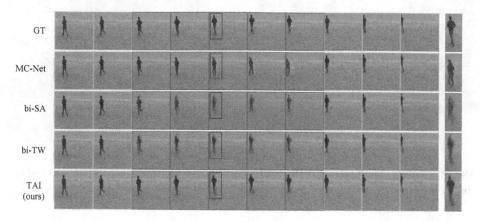

Fig. 4. Comparison of predictions from our TAI model to baseline methods on KTH Actions. We visualize every other frame of the input and predicted sequences. Refer to the supplementary materials for more results

baselines (the dashed curves in Fig. 3) indicate that our task is challenging, and requires a model that generates a *non-trivial* prediction from *multiple* preceding and following frames. Second, the performance of MC-Net drops quickly over time due to its lack of guidance from the following frames. Third, between the bidirectional prediction baselines, bi-TW does a better job than bi-SA since it incorporates the scaled time step w_t via a hand-crafted, time-weighted average. Finally, TAI outperforms bi-TW because it learns a complex blending function that leverages both time step information and intermediate activations from the Bidirectional Video Prediction Network.

In Fig. 4, we visualize the predictions made by MC-Net, bi-SA, bi-TW, and TAI (we encourage the reader to view additional results in the supplementary materials). MC-Net generates blob-like poses that fail to preserve the proper shape of the body and are inconsistent with the following frames. Meanwhile, bi-SA and bi-TW generate frames with a noticeable "ghosting" effect (e.g. both predictions contain two torsos overlapping with each other), leading to a drop in PSNR and SSIM scores. On the other hand, TAI overcomes these challenges: its predictions are consistent with both the preceding and following frames, and they contain one unified, well-shaped torso. We have found that SSIM drops more drastically than PSNR when ghosting occurs, suggesting that it correlates better with human-perceived quality than PSNR.

4.4   Qualitative Analysis of Blending Methods

Next, we visualize the forward, backward, and final predictions of bi-SA, bi-TW, and TAI in order to highlight the benefit of a learned blending function over a hand-crafted one. Across all three models, the forward prediction is inconsistent with the backward one for most videos. For instance, in Fig. 5, the scale of the actor always differs between the forward and backward predictions. However,

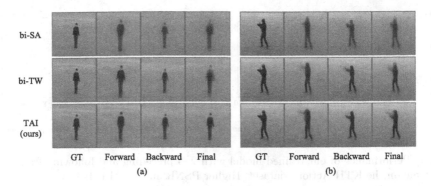

Fig. 5. Comparison of the forward, backward, and final predictions for the third middle frame (of ten) of two videos

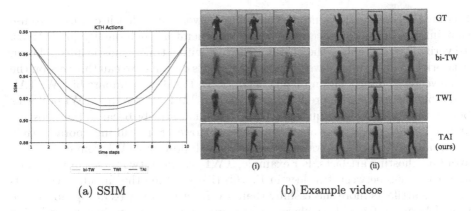

(a) SSIM   (b) Example videos

Fig. 6. Ablative comparison between bi-TW, TWI, and our full TAI model. Higher SSIM is better

the quality of the final prediction improves with the complexity of the blending strategy. For example, since bi-SA blends the two predictions evenly, we observe in the final prediction for Fig. 5a a blurry background and two outlines of the actor's body; in Fig. 5b, we see the outlines of two heads. bi-TW produces similar artifacts to bi-SA for both videos, but its final predictions are clearer. Finally, TAI reconciles the differences between the forward and backward predictions without introducing ghosting artifacts: in Fig. 5a, the final prediction compromises between the actor's sizes from the intermediate predictions, and in Fig. 5b, the difference in the actor's head position is resolved, resulting in a clean outline of the head. We conclude that even though all three methods generate inconsistent forward and backward predictions, TAI can successfully reconcile the differences to generate a crisp final prediction.

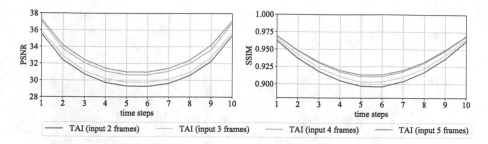

Fig. 7. Performance of our trained model with 2–5 preceding and following frames at test time on the KTH Actions dataset. Higher PSNR and SSIM is better

4.5   Ablation Studies

Feeding time information into the blending network such that it can *learn* to use that information most effectively is key to generating high-quality predictions. To verify this, we replace the blending module with a time-agnostic interpolation network and apply a time-weighted average to its outputs; we call this version the time-weighted interpolation (TWI) network. In Fig. 6, we compare bi-TW, TAI, and a bidirectional video prediction model with TWI. We see that TWI performs better than bi-TW both quantitatively and qualitatively because the ghosting artifacts in its predictions are less apparent. However, it still incorporates time information with a hand-crafted function, which prevents TWI from completely avoiding ghosting artifacts. For example, TWI generates two torsos in Fig. 6b (i) and a fake leg between two legs in Fig. 6b (ii). On the other hand, TAI avoids ghosting artifacts more successfully than TWI: for both videos in Fig. 6b, we see that TAI generates a clear, sharp outline around the actor without introducing artificial torsos or limbs.

4.6   Importance of Context Frames

In this section, we show our model's ability to leverage the context information from the preceding and the following sequences which, as argued in Sect. 1, is vital to performing well on the video frame inpainting task. In Fig. 7, we plot the quantitative performance of our trained model as we increase the number of available frames at test time from two to five (recall that we train our model on five preceding and following frames). Our model obtains progressively better PSNR and SSIM values as we increase the number of preceding and following frames; this shows that our model successfully leverages the increasing amount of context information to improve its predictions.

4.7   HMDB-51 and UCF-101

We conclude our experiments by demonstrating our model's ability to perform well on complex videos depicting challenging scenes and a wide variety of actions.

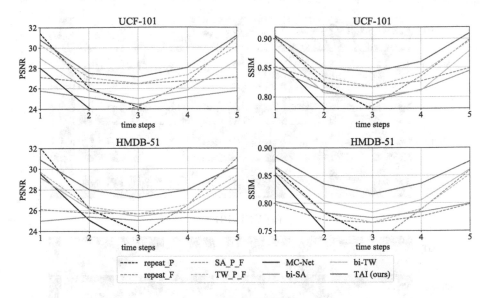

Fig. 8. Quantitative results on the UCF-101 and HMDB-51 datasets (higher PSNR and SSIM is better). We compare our method to the baselines described in Sect. 4.2

We do this by comparing our full TAI model to the baselines proposed in Sect. 4.2 on videos from HMDB-51 and UCF-101. We see from the quantitative results in Fig. 8 that none of the baselines outperform the others by a definitive margin. This contrasts with our findings in Sect. 4.3 where we found that for KTH Actions, bi-TW produces substantially better predictions than all the other baselines. We note that the biggest difference between KTH Actions and HMDB-51/UCF-101 is that the scenes in HMDB-51 and UCF-101 are far more complex than in KTH Actions; this suggests that bi-TW performs poorly when observing complex scenes. However, our model still outperforms all baselines on HMDB-51 and UCF-101, suggesting that it is best equipped for handling complex videos.

We present qualitative comparisons in Fig. 9. In Fig. 9a, we observe two contours of the girl's hair in the bi-SA prediction, and a blurry facial expression in the bi-TW prediction. On the other hand, our TAI model generates a unified contour of the hair and a clear facial expression. Moving on to Fig. 9b, we note that MC-Net distorts the background in the later middle frames, and that both bi-SA and bi-TW generate blurry patterns on the man's jacket and pants. However, TAI produces a clear white stripe on the man's pants, as well as a sharp outline around his jacket. Our results demonstrate that on video datasets containing complex scenes and a large number of action classes, TAI generates predictions that are more visually satisfying than several strong baselines.

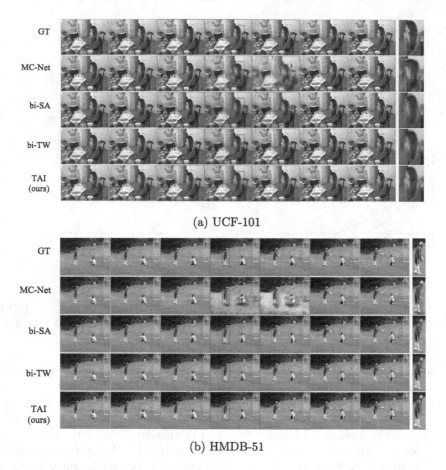

(a) UCF-101

(b) HMDB-51

Fig. 9. Comparison of predictions from our approach to baseline methods on the UCF-101 and HMDB-51 datasets. We visualize every second frame of the input and predicted sequences. Refer to the supplementary materials for more results

5 Conclusion

In this paper, we have tackled the video frame inpainting problem by generating two sets of intermediate predictions conditioned on the preceding and following frames respectively, and then blending them together with our novel TAI network. Our experiments on KTH Actions, HMDB-51, and UCF-101 show that our method generates more accurate and visually pleasing predictions than multiple strong baselines. Furthermore, our in-depth analysis has revealed that our TAI network successfully leverages time step information to reconcile inconsistencies in the intermediate predictions, and that it leverages the full context provided by the preceding and following frames. In future work, we aim to improve performance by exploiting semantic knowledge about the video content, e.g. by modeling human poses or the periodicity of certain actions. We also aim to explore models that can predict an even greater number of frames, i.e. several seconds of video instead of fractions of a second. To encourage innovations in deep learning for video frame inpainting, we have made our code publicly available at https://github.com/sunxm2357/TAI_video_frame_inpainting.

Acknowledgements. This work is partly supported by ARO W911NF-15-1-0354, DARPA FA8750-17-2-0112 and DARPA FA8750-16-C-0168. It reflects the opinions and conclusions of its authors, but not the funding agents.

References

1. Borzi, A., Ito, K., Kunisch, K.: Optimal control formulation for determining optical flow. SIAM J. Sci. Comput. **24**(3), 818–847 (2003)
2. Chen, K., Lorenz, D.A.: Image sequence interpolation using optimal control. J. Math. Imaging Vis. **41**(3), 222–238 (2011)
3. Cheung, V., Frey, B.J., Jojic, N.: Video epitomes. Int. J. Comput. Vis. **76**(2), 141–152 (2008)
4. Ebdelli, M., Le Meur, O., Guillemot, C.: Video inpainting with short-term windows: application to object removal and error concealment. IEEE Trans. Image Process. **24**(10), 3034–3047 (2015)
5. Granados, M., Kim, K.I., Tompkin, J., Kautz, J., Theobalt, C.: Background inpainting for videos with dynamic objects and a free-moving camera. In: Fitzgibbon, A., Lazebnik, S., Perona, P., Sato, Y., Schmid, C. (eds.) ECCV 2012. LNCS, vol. 7572, pp. 682–695. Springer, Heidelberg (2012). https://doi.org/10.1007/978-3-642-33718-5_49
6. Ioffe, S., Szegedy, C.: Batch normalization: accelerating deep network training by reducing internal covariate shift. In: International Conference on Machine Learning, pp. 448–456 (2015)
7. Jia, J., Tai-Pang, W., Tai, Y.W., Tang, C.K.: Video repairing: inference of foreground and background under severe occlusion. In: IEEE Conference on Computer Vision and Pattern Recognition (2004)
8. Jia, Y.T., Hu, S.M., Martin, R.R.: Video completion using tracking and fragment merging. Vis. Comput. **21**(8–10), 601–610 (2005)
9. Kalchbrenner, N., et al.: Video pixel networks. In: International Conference on Machine Learning (2017)
10. Kuehne, H., Jhuang, H., Garrote, E., Poggio, T., Serre, T.: HMDB: a large video database for human motion recognition. In: IEEE International Conference on Computer Vision, pp. 2556–2563 (2011)
11. Liu, Z., Yeh, R., Tang, X., Liu, Y., Agarwala, A.: Video frame synthesis using deep voxel flow. In: International Conference on Computer Vision (ICCV), vol. 2 (2017)
12. Long, G., Kneip, L., Alvarez, J.M., Li, H., Zhang, X., Yu, Q.: Learning image matching by simply watching video. In: Leibe, B., Matas, J., Sebe, N., Welling, M. (eds.) ECCV 2016. LNCS, vol. 9910, pp. 434–450. Springer, Cham (2016). https://doi.org/10.1007/978-3-319-46466-4_26
13. Lotter, W., Kreiman, G., Cox, D.: Deep predictive coding networks for video prediction and unsupervised learning. In: International Conference on Learning Representations (2017)
14. Mathieu, M., Couprie, C., LeCun, Y.: Deep multi-scale video prediction beyond mean square error. In: International Conference on Learning Representations (2016)

15. Miyato, T., Kataoka, T., Koyama, M., Yoshida, Y.: Spectral normalization for generative adversarial networks. In: International Conference on Learning Representations (2018)
16. Newson, A., Almansa, A., Fradet, M., Gousseau, Y., Pérez, P.: Video inpainting of complex scenes. SIAM J. Imaging Sci. **7**(4), 1993–2019 (2014)
17. Niklaus, S., Mai, L., Liu, F.: Video frame interpolation via adaptive separable convolution. In: IEEE Conference on Computer Vision and Pattern Recognition, pp. 261–270 (2017)
18. Patwardhan, K.A., Sapiro, G., Bertalmío, M.: Video inpainting under constrained camera motion. IEEE Trans. Image Process. **16**(2), 545–553 (2007)
19. Ranzato, M., Szlam, A., Bruna, J., Mathieu, M., Collobert, R., Chopra, S.: Video (language) modeling: a baseline for generative models of natural videos. arXiv preprint arXiv:1412.6604 (2014)
20. Schuldt, C., Laptev, I., Caputo, B.: Recognizing human actions: a local SVM approach. In: International Conference on Pattern Recognition, vol. 3, pp. 32–36 (2004)
21. Shen, Y., Lu, F., Cao, X., Foroosh, H.: Video completion for perspective camera under constrained motion. In: International Conference on Pattern Recognition, vol. 3, pp. 63–66 (2006)
22. Soomro, K., Zamir, A.R., Shah, M.: UCF101: a dataset of 101 human actions classes from videos in the wild. CRCV-TR-12-01 (2012)
23. Srivastava, N., Mansimov, E., Salakhudinov, R.: Unsupervised learning of video representations using LSTMs. In: International Conference On Machine Learning, pp. 843–852 (2015)
24. Villegas, R., Yang, J., Hong, S., Lin, X., Lee, H.: Decomposing motion and content for natural video sequence prediction. In: International Conference on Learning Representations (2017)
25. Wang, Z., Bovik, A.C., Sheikh, H.R., Simoncelli, E.P.: Image quality assessment: from error visibility to structural similarity. IEEE Trans. Image Process. **13**(4), 600–612 (2004)
26. Werlberger, M., Pock, T., Unger, M., Bischof, H.: Optical flow guided TV-L1 video interpolation and restoration. In: International Workshop on Energy Minimization Methods in Computer Vision and Pattern Recognition, pp. 273–286 (2011)
27. Wexler, Y., Shechtman, E., Irani, M.: Space-time video completion. In: IEEE Conference on Computer Vision and Pattern Recognition (2004)

Linear Solution to the Minimal Absolute Pose Rolling Shutter Problem

Zuzana Kukelova[1]([✉]), Cenek Albl[2], Akihiro Sugimoto[3], and Tomas Pajdla[2]

[1] Visual Recognition Group (VRG), FEE, Czech Technical University in Prague,
Prague, Czech Republic
kukelzuz@fel.cvut.cz
[2] Czech Institute of Informatics, Robotics and Cybernetics (CIIRC),
Czech Technical University in Prague, Prague, Czech Republic
[3] National Institute of Informatics, Tokyo, Japan

Abstract. This paper presents new efficient solutions to the rolling shutter camera absolute pose problem. Unlike the state-of-the-art polynomial solvers, we approach the problem using simple and fast linear solvers in an iterative scheme. We present several solutions based on fixing different sets of variables and investigate the performance of them thoroughly. We design a new alternation strategy that estimates all parameters in each iteration linearly by fixing just the non-linear terms. Our best 6-point solver, based on the new alternation technique, shows an identical or even better performance than the state-of-the-art R6P solver and is two orders of magnitude faster. In addition, a linear non-iterative solver is presented that requires a non-minimal number of 9 correspondences but provides even better results than the state-of-the-art R6P. Moreover, all proposed linear solvers provide a single solution while the state-of-the-art R6P provides up to 20 solutions which have to be pruned by expensive verification.

Keywords: Rolling shutter · Absolute pose · Minimal solvers

1 Introduction

Rolling shutter (RS) cameras are omnipresent. They can be found in smartphones, consumer, professional, and action cameras and even in self-driving cars. RS cameras are cheaper, and easier to produce, than global shutter cameras. They also posses other advantages over the global shutter cameras, such as higher achievable frame-rate or longer exposure times.

This work was supported by the European Regional Development Fund under the project IMPACT (reg. no. CZ.02.1.01/0.0/0.0/15_003/0000468), EC H2020-ICT-731970 LADIO project, ESI Fund, OP RDE programme under the project International Mobility of Researchers MSCA-IF at CTU No. CZ.02.2.69/0.0/0.0/17_050/0008025, and Grant-in-Aid for Scientific Research (Grant No. 16H02851) of the Ministry of Education, Culture, Sports, Science and Technology of Japan. A part of this work was done when Zuzana Kukelova was visiting the National Institute of Informatics (NII), Japan, funded in part by the NII MOU grant.

C. V. Jawahar et al. (Eds.): ACCV 2018, LNCS 11363, pp. 265–280, 2019.
https://doi.org/10.1007/978-3-030-20893-6_17

There is, however, a significant drawback when using them for computer vision applications. When the scene or the camera is moving during image capture, images produced by RS cameras will become distorted. The amount and type of distortion depends on the type and speed of camera motion and on the depth of the scene. It has been shown that RS image distortions can cause problems for standard computer vision methods such as Structure from Motion [1], visual SLAM [2] or multi-view dense stereo [3]. Therefore, having a special camera model for rolling shutter cameras is desirable.

The camera absolute pose computation is a fundamental problem in many computer vision tasks such as Structure from Motion, augmented reality, visual SLAM, and visual localization. The problem is to compute the camera pose from 3D points in the world and their 2D projections into an image. The minimal number of correspondences necessary to solve the absolute pose problem for a perspective calibrated camera is three. The first solution to this problem was introduced by Grunert [4] and since then it was many times revisited [5–7]. Other work has focused on computing the absolute pose from a larger than the minimal number of correspondences [8–12]. All of the previous work consider a perspective camera model, which is not suitable for dynamic RS cameras.

Recently, as RS cameras became more and more common, the focus turned to computing camera absolute pose from images containing RS effects. First, several RS camera motion models were introduced in [13]. A solution to RS absolute pose using non-minimal (eight and half) number of points was presented in [14]. It relied on a non-linear optimization and required a planar scene.

In [15], video sequences were exploited and the absolute camera pose was computed sequentially using a non-linear optimization starting from the previous camera pose. Another approach using video sequences was used for visual SLAM in [2] where the camera motion estimated from previous frames was used to compensate the RS distortion in the next frame prior to the optimization.

A polynomial solution that is globally optimal was presented in [16]. It uses Gloptipoly [17] solver to find a solution from 7 or more points. Authors show that the method provides better results than [14], but the runtime is in the order of seconds, making it impractical for typical applications such as RANSAC.

The first minimal solution to the rolling shutter camera absolute pose problem was presented in [18]. It uses the minimal number of six 2D to 3D point correspondences and the Gröbner basis method to generate an efficient solver. The proposed R6P is based on the constant linear and angular velocity model as in [1, 14, 16] but it uses the first order approximation to both the camera orientation and angular velocity, and, therefore, it requires an initialization of the camera orientation, e.g., from P3P [7]. Paper [18] has shown that R6P solver significantly outperforms perspective P3P solver in terms of camera pose precision and the number of inliers captured in the RANSAC loop.

1.1 Motivation

It has been demonstrated in the literature that RS camera absolute pose is beneficial and often necessary when dealing with RS images from moving camera or dynamic scene. Still, until now, all the presented solutions have significant drawbacks that make them impractical for general use.

The state-of-the-art solutions require a non-minimal or a larger number of points [14,16], planar scene [14], video sequences [1,2,15], are very slow [16] and provide too many solutions [18].

If one requires a practical algorithm similar to P3P, but working on RS images, the closest method available is R6P [18]. However, R6P still needs around 1.7 ms to compute the camera pose, compared to around 3 μs for P3P. Therefore, in typical applications where P3P is used, one would suffer a several orders of magnitude slowdown compared to P3P. This makes it hard to use for real-time applications such as augmented reality. In addition, R6P provides up to 20 real solutions, which need to be verified. This makes tasks like RANSAC, which uses hundreds or thousands of iterations and verifies all solutions, extremely slow compared to P3P. This motivates us to create a solution to RS absolute pose problem with similar performance to R6P [18] and runtime comparable to P3P.

1.2 Contribution

In this work we present solutions that remove previously mentioned drawbacks of the state-of-the-art methods and provide practical and fast rolling shutter camera absolute pose solvers. We take a different approach to formulating the problem and propose linear solutions to rolling shutter camera absolute pose. Specifically, we present the following RS absolute camera pose solvers:

- a 6-point linear iterative solver, which provides identical or even better solutions than R6P in 10 μs, which is up to 170× faster than R6P. This solver is based on a new alternating method;
- two 6-point linear iterative solvers that outperform R6P for purely translational motion;
- a 9-point linear non-iterative solver that provides more accurate camera pose estimates than R6P in 20 μs;

All solvers are easy to implement and they return a single solution. We formulate the problem of RS camera absolute pose in Sect. 2. Derivations of all new solvers are in Sect. 3. Section 4 contains experiments verifying the feasibility of the proposed solvers and it compares them against P3P and R6P [18].

2 Problem Formulation

For calibrated perspective cameras, the projection equation can be written as

$$\lambda_i \mathbf{x}_i = \mathbf{R}\mathbf{X}_i + \mathbf{C}, \tag{1}$$

where $\mathbf{R}$ and $\mathbf{C}$ are the rotation and translation bringing a 3D point $\mathbf{X}_i$ from a world coordinate system to the camera coordinate system with $\mathbf{x}_i = [r_i, c_i, 1]^\top$, and scalar $\lambda_i \in \mathbb{R}$. For RS cameras, every image row is captured at different time and hence at a different position when the camera is moving during the image capture. Camera rotation R and translation C are therefore functions of the image row r_i being captured

$$\lambda_i x_i = \lambda_i \begin{bmatrix} r_i \\ c_i \\ 1 \end{bmatrix} = R(r_i)X_i + C(r_i). \tag{2}$$

In recent work [1,3,13,14,16,18], it was shown that for the short time-span of a frame capture, the camera translation $C(r_i)$ can be approximated with a simple constant velocity model as

$$C(r_i) = C + (r_i - r_0)t, \tag{3}$$

where C is the camera center corresponding to the perspective case, i.e. when $r_i = r_0$, and t is the translational velocity.

The camera rotation $R(r_i)$ can be decomposed into two rotations to represent the camera initial orientation by R_v and the change of orientation during frame capture by $R_w(r_i - r_0)$.

In [16,18], it was observed that it is usually sufficient to linearize $R_w(r_i - r_0)$ around the initial rotation R_v using the first order Taylor expansion such that

$$\lambda_i \begin{bmatrix} r_i \\ c_i \\ 1 \end{bmatrix} = (I + (r_i - r_0)[w]_\times) R_v X_i + C + (r_i - r_0)t, \tag{4}$$

where $[w]_\times$ is a skew-symmetric matrix of vector w. The model (4), with linearized rolling shutter rotation, will deviate from the reality with increasing rolling shutter effect. Still, it is usually sufficient for most of the rolling shutter effects present in real situations.

In [18], a linear approximation to the camera orientation R_v was used to solve the rolling shutter absolute pose problem from a minimal number of six 2D-3D point correspondences. This model has the form

$$\lambda_i \begin{bmatrix} r_i \\ c_i \\ 1 \end{bmatrix} = (I + (r_i - r_0)[w]_\times)(I + [v]_\times) X_i + C + (r_i - r_0)t. \tag{5}$$

The drawback of the model (5) is that R_v is often not small and thus cannot be linearized. Therefore, the accuracy of the model is dependent on the initial orientation of the camera in the world frame. In [18], it was shown that the standard P3P algorithm [7] is able to estimate camera orientation with sufficient precision even for high camera rotation velocity and therefore P3P can be used to bring the camera rotation matrix R_v close to the identity, where (5) works reasonably.

The model (5) leads to a system of six quadratic equations in six unknowns. This system has 20 solutions and it was solved in [18] using the Gröbner basis method [19,20]. The Gröbner basis solver [18] for the R6P rolling shutter problem requires the G-J elimination of a 196×216 matrix and computing the eigenvectors of a 20×20 matrix. The R6P solver runs for about 1.7 ms and thus is too slow in many practical situations.

We will next show how to simplify this model by linearizing Eq. (5) and yet still obtaining a similar performance as the Gröbner basis R6P absolute pose solver [18] for the original model (5).

3 Linear Rolling Shutter Solvers

We present here several linear iterative solvers to the minimal absolute pose rolling shutter problem. All these solvers start with the model (5) and they use six 2D-3D image point correspondences to estimate 12 unknowns v, C, w, and t. The proposed solvers differ in the way how the system (5) is linearized. Additionally we propose a linear non-iterative 9 point absolute pose rolling shutter solver.

3.1 $R6P_{v,C}^{w,t}$ Solver

The $R6P_{v,C}^{w,t}$ solver is based on the idea of alternating between two linear solvers. The first $R6P_{v,C}$ solver fixes the rolling shutter parameters w and t in (5) and estimates only the camera parameters v and C. The second $R6P_{w,t}$ solver fixes the camera parameters v and C and estimates only the rolling shutter parameters w and t. Both these partial solvers results in 12 linear equations in 6 unknowns that can be solved in the least square sense. The motivation for this solver comes from the fact that even for larger rolling shutter speed, the camera parameters v and C can be estimated quite accurately.

The $R6P_{v,C}^{w,t}$ solver starts with $w_0 = 0$ and $t_0 = 0$ and, in the first iteration, uses linear $R6P_{v,C}$ solver to estimate v_1 and C_1. Using the estimated v_1 and C_1, the linear solver $R6P_{w,t}$ estimates w_1 and t_1. This process is repeated until the desired precision is obtained or a maximum number of iterations is reached.

The $R6P_{v,C}^{w,t}$ solver does not perform very well in our experiments, which we account to the fact that it never estimates the pose parameters v,C and the motion parameters w,t together in one step. Nevertheless, we present this solver as a logical first step when considering the iterative approach to RS absolute pose problem.

3.2 $R6P_{v,C,t}^{w}$ and $R6P_{v,C,t}^{w,t}$ Solver

To avoid problems of the $R6P_{v,C}^{w,t}$ solver, we introduce the $R6P_{v,C,t}^{w}$ solver. The $R6P_{v,C,t}^{w}$ solver alternates between two solvers, i.e. the linear $R6P_{v,C,t}$ solver, which fixes only the rolling shutter rotation w and estimates v, C and t, and the $R6P_{w}$ solver that estimates only the rolling shutter rotation w using the fixed v, C and t. The $R6P_{v,C,t}$ solver solves 12 linear equations in 9 unknowns and the $R6P_{w}$ solver solves 12 linear equations in 3 unknowns in the least square sense. Since the first $R6P_{v,C,t}$ solver assumes unknown rolling shutter translation, the camera parameters are estimated with better precision than in the case of the

R6P$_{v,C}$ solver. Moreover, in many applications, e.g. cameras on a car, cameras often undergo only a translation motion, and therefore w is negligible. In such situations, the first iteration of the R6P$_{v,C,t}$ solver already provides very precise estimates of the camera parameters.

Another approach is to use only the v and C estimated by R6P$_{v,C,t}$ solver and in the second step re-estimate the rolling shutter translation t together with the rolling shutter rotation w using the linear R6P$_{w,t}$ solver. The solver based on this strategy will be referred to as R6P$_{v,C,t}^{w,t}$.

The resulting solvers R6P$_{v,C,t}^{w}$ and R6P$_{v,C,t}^{w,t}$, again, alternate between the two linear solvers until the desired precision is obtained or a maximum number of iterations is reached. We show in the experiments that those solvers outperform R6P in the case of pure translational motion.

3.3 R6P$_{v,C,w,t}^{[v]\times}$ Solver

The R6P$_{v,C,w,t}^{[v]\times}$ solver estimates all unknown parameters v, C, w and t together in one step. To avoid non-linearity in (5), the solver fixes $[v]_\times$ that appears in the nonlinear term $[w]_\times [v]_\times$ in (5). Thus the solver solves equations

$$\lambda_i \begin{bmatrix} r_i \\ c_i \\ 1 \end{bmatrix} = (\mathbf{I} + (r_i - r_0)[w]_\times) \mathbf{X}_i + [v]_\times \mathbf{X}_i + (r_i - r_0)[w]_\times [\hat{v}]_\times \mathbf{X}_i + \mathbf{C} + (r_i - r_0)t, \quad (6)$$

where $\hat{v}$ is a fixed vector.

In the first iteration $\hat{v}$, is set to the zero vector and the term $(r_i - r_0)[w]_\times [\hat{v}]_\times \mathbf{X}_i$ in (6) disappears. This is usually a sufficient approximation. The explanation for this is as follows. After the initialization with P3P the camera rotation is already close to the identity and in real applications the rolling shutter rotation w during the capture is usually small. Therefore, the nonlinear term $[w]_\times [v]_\times$ is small, sometimes even negligible, and thus it can be considered to be zero in the first iteration.

In the remaining iterations we fix $\hat{v}$ in the $(r_i - r_0)[w]_\times [\hat{v}]_\times \mathbf{X}_i$ term to be equal to the v_i estimated in the previous iteration of the R6P$_{v,C,w,t}^{[v]\times}$ solver. Note that we fix only v that appears in the nonlinear term $[w]_\times [v]_\times$ and there is still another term with v in (6) from which a new v can be estimated. Therefore, all parameters are estimated at each step which is a novel alternating strategy. To our knowledge, all existing algorithms that are based on the alternating optimization approach completely fix a subset of the variables, meaning that they cannot estimate all the variables in one step.

The R6P$_{v,C,w,t}^{[v]\times}$ in each iteration solves only one system of 12 linear equations in 12 unknowns and is therefore very efficient. In experiments we will show that the R6P$_{v,C,w,t}^{[v]\times}$ provides very precise estimates already after 1 iteration and after 5 iterations it has virtually the same performance as the state-of-the-art R6P solver [18].

3.4 R9P

Our final solver is a non-iterative solver that uses a non-minimal number of nine 2D-3D point correspondences. We note that the projection Eq. (6) can be rewritten as

$$\lambda_i \begin{bmatrix} r_i \\ c_i \\ 1 \end{bmatrix} = (\mathtt{I} + [\mathtt{v}]_\times)\, \mathtt{X}_i + \mathtt{C} + (r_i - r_0)([\mathtt{w}]_\times(\mathtt{I} + [\hat{\mathtt{v}}]_\times)\mathtt{X}_i + \mathtt{t}). \tag{7}$$

We can substitute the term $[\mathtt{w}]_\times(\mathtt{I}+[\hat{\mathtt{v}}]_\times)$ in (7) with a 3×3 unknown matrix $\mathtt{R_{RS}}$. After eliminating the scalar values λ_i by multiplying Eq. (7) from the left by the skew symmetric matrix for vector $\begin{bmatrix} r_i & c_i & 1 \end{bmatrix}^\top$ and without considering the internal structure of the matrix $\mathtt{R_{RS}}$, we obtain three linear equations in 18 unknowns, i.e. $\mathtt{v}, \mathtt{C}, \mathtt{t}$, and 9 unknowns in $\mathtt{R_{RS}}$. Since only two from these tree equations are linearly independent we need nine 2D-3D point correspondences to solve this problem.

Note that the original formulation (5) was an approximation to the real rolling shutter camera model and therefore the formulation with a general 3×3 matrix $\mathtt{R_{RS}}$ is yet a different approximation to this model.

4 Experiments

We tested the proposed solvers on a variety of synthetic and real datasets and compared the results with the original R6P solver [18] as well as P3P. We followed the general pattern of experiments used in [18] in order to provide consistent comparison on the additional factor of experiments that are specific to our iterative solvers such as their convergence.

To analyze the accuracy of the estimated camera poses and velocities, we used synthetic data in the following setup. A random set of 3D points was generated in a cubic region with $x, y, z \in [-1; 1]$ and a camera with a distance $d \in [2; 3]$ from the origin and pointing towards the 3D points. The camera was set to be calibrated, i.e. $\mathtt{K} = \mathtt{I}$ and the field of view was set to 45°. Rolling shutter projections were created using a constant linear velocity and a constant angular velocity with various magnitudes.

Using the constant angular velocity model for generating the data ensures that our data is not generated with the same model as the one that is estimated by the solvers (linear approximation to a rotation). Although the used model is just an approximation of the real rolling shutter model and we could have chosen another one, e.g. constant angular acceleration, we consider the constant angular velocity model as a reasonable description of the camera motion during the short time period of frame capture.

We used 6 points for the original R6P and all proposed R6P iterative solvers. In order to provide P3P with the same data, we used all possible triplets from the 6 points used by R6P and then chose the best result. For R9P we used 9 points. Unless stated otherwise, all iterative solvers were run for maximum 5 iterations in the experiments.

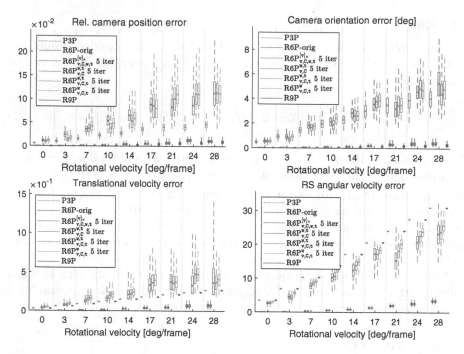

Fig. 1. Experiment on synthetic data focusing on the precision of estimated camera poses and velocities. Notice that the performance of $R6P_{v,C,w,t}^{[v]\times}$ is identical to R6P. In terms of camera pose these two solvers are slightly outperformed by R9P. Other linear solvers perform very poorly in all respects.

4.1 Synthetic Data

In the first experiment, we gradually increased the camera velocities during capture. The maximum translational velocity was 0.3 per frame and the maximum angular velocity was 30° per frame. Figure 1 shows the results, from which we can see how the increasing RS deformation affects the estimated camera pose and also estimated camera velocities in those solvers.

Rotational and Translational Motion: In agreement with [18], R6P provides much better results than P3P thanks to the RS camera model. The newly proposed solver $R6P_{v,C,w,t}^{[v]\times}$ provides almost identical results to R6P at much lower computation cost (cf. Table 1). The best estimates of the camera pose are provided by R9P at the cost of using more than minimal number of points. The other 6-point iterative solutions are performing really bad, often providing worse results than P3P. In the next experiment we tested the sensitivity of the proposed solvers to increasing levels of image noise. Figure 2 right shows that the new solvers have approximately the same noise sensitivity as R6P [18].

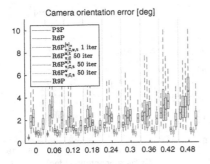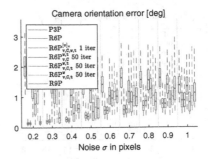

Fig. 2. (Left) Purely translational camera motion, increasing on the x axis. Image noise with σ 1pix. Notice that $\text{R6P}^{\text{w}}_{\text{v},\text{C},\text{t}}$ and $\text{R6P}^{\text{w},\text{t}}_{\text{v},\text{C},\text{t}}$ now outperform all the others. (Right) Performance on general camera motion with increasing image noise.

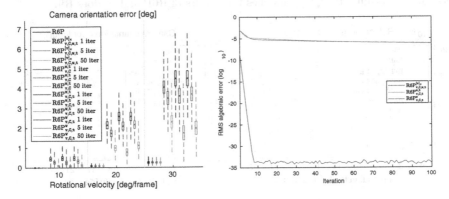

Fig. 3. Testing the convergence of the iterative solvers. All iterative solvers have been run with 1, 5 and 50 iterations on data with $\text{R} = \text{I}$ and increasing RS effect (left). Convergence of the algebraic error using the three viable iterative solvers (right).

Translational Motion Only: The advantage of solvers $\text{R6P}^{\text{w},\text{t}}_{\text{v},\text{C},\text{t}}$ and $\text{R6P}^{\text{w}}_{\text{v},\text{C},\text{t}}$ is when the motion of the camera is purely translational, or close to it, which is a common scenario in, e.g., a moving car or a moving train. In such cases, both original R6P and $\text{R6P}^{[\text{v}]\times}_{\text{v},\text{C},\text{w},\text{t}}$ provide significantly worse estimates of the camera pose. We explain this by the fact that $\text{R6P}^{\text{w},\text{t}}_{\text{v},\text{C},\text{t}}$ and $\text{R6P}^{\text{w}}_{\text{v},\text{C},\text{t}}$ are constrained to estimate only camera translation in the initial step, whereas R6P and $\text{R6P}^{[\text{v}]\times}_{\text{v},\text{C},\text{w},\text{t}}$ try to explain the image noise by the camera rotation. See Fig. 2 left. This fact can be used to create a "joined solver" that runs both $\text{R6P}^{\text{w}}_{\text{v},\text{C},\text{t}}$ and $\text{R6P}^{[\text{v}]\times}_{\text{v},\text{C},\text{w},\text{t}}$ and gives better performance than R6P [18] while still being significantly faster.

Convergence: For $\text{R6P}^{\text{w},\text{t}}_{\text{v},\text{C}}$, $\text{R6P}^{\text{w}}_{\text{v},\text{C},\text{t}}$, and $\text{R6P}^{\text{w},\text{t}}_{\text{v},\text{C},\text{t}}$, the maximum 5 iterations might not be enough to converge to a good solution, whereas $\text{R6P}^{[\text{v}]\times}_{\text{v},\text{C},\text{w},\text{t}}$ seems to perform at its best. We thus increased the maximum number of iterations. Figure 3 (left) shows that the performance of $\text{R6P}^{\text{w},\text{t}}_{\text{v},\text{C}}$, $\text{R6P}^{\text{w}}_{\text{v},\text{C},\text{t}}$, and $\text{R6P}^{\text{w},\text{t}}_{\text{v},\text{C},\text{t}}$ is

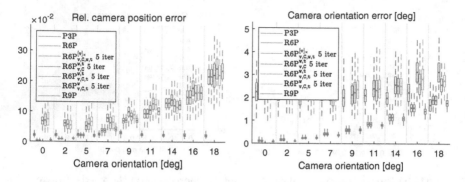

Fig. 4. Experiment showing the effect of the linearized camera pose which is present in all models. The further the camera orientation is from the linearization point, the worse are the results. $R6P_{v,C,w,t}^{[v]\times}$ matches the results of R6P and so does R9P.

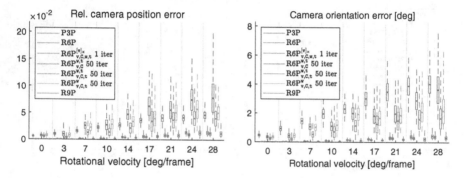

Fig. 5. Increasing the camera motion and estimating camera pose with all solvers being initialized with P3P. $R6P_{v,C,w,t}^{[v]\times}$ and R9P now provide consistently excellent results, comparable or outperforming those of R6P at a fraction of the computation cost. $R6P_{v,C}^{w,t}$, $R6P_{v,C,t}^{w}$ and $R6P_{v,C,t}^{w,t}$ with 50 iterations now perform better than P3P, but still not as good as the other RS solvers.

improved by increasing the maximum number of iterations to 50. However, it is still far below the performance of R6P, $R6P_{v,C,w,t}^{[v]\times}$, and R9P. $R6P_{v,C,w,t}^{[v]\times}$ performs as well as the R6P even with a single iteration, making it two orders of magnitude faster alternative. The algebraic error, evaluated on the Eq. (5), of the three viable solvers converges within 8 steps on average, see Fig. 3 (right).

The Effect of Linearized Camera Rotation Model: Since all the proposed solvers have a linearized form of the camera orientation, in the same way as R6P [18], we tested how being further from the linearization point affects the performance (Fig. 4). The camera orientation was set to be at a certain angle from $R = I$. The camera velocities were set to 0.15 per frame for the translation and 15° per frame for the rotation. In [18] the authors show that R6P outperforms P3P in terms of camera center estimation up to 6° away from the initial

Table 1. Average timings on 2.5 GHz i7 CPU per iteration for all used solvers.

Solver	P3P	R6P	$R6P^{[v]\times}_{v,C,w,t}$	$R6P^{w}_{v,C,t}$	$R6P^{w,t}_{v,C,t}$	$R6P^{w,t}_{v,C}$	R9P
Time per iteration	3 μs	1700 μs	10 μs	24 μs	30 μs	27 μs	20 μs
max # of solutions	4	20	1	1	1	1	1

R estimate and up to 15° away from R for the camera orientation estimate. Our results in Fig. 4 show similar behavior and identical results of R6P and $R6P^{[v]\times}_{v,C,w,t}$. R9P performs comparable to both, even slightly outperforming them in terms of camera orientation estimation.

Using P3P as Initial Estimate: Last synthetic experiment shows the performance of the solvers when using the initial estimate of R from the result of P3P. The camera orientation was randomly generated and the camera motion was increased as in the first experiment. P3P was computed first and the 3D scene was pre-rotated using R from P3P. This shows probably the most practical usage among all R6P solvers. To make the figure more informative, we chose the number of iterations for $R6P^{w,t}_{v,C}$, $R6P^{w}_{v,C,t}$, and $R6P^{w,t}_{v,C,t}$ to be 50 as the 5 iterations already proved to be insufficient, see Fig. 1. We also set the maximum number of iterations for $R6P^{[v]\times}_{v,C,w,t}$ to 1, to demonstrate the potential of this solver.

As seen in Fig. 5, $R6P^{[v]\times}_{v,C,w,t}$ provides at least as good, or even better, results than R6P after only a single iteration. This is a significant achievement since the computational cost of $R6P^{[v]\times}_{v,C,w,t}$ is two orders of magnitude less than of R6P. With 50 iterations the other iterative solvers perform better than P3P, but considering the computational cost of 50 iterations, which is even higher than that of a R6P, we cannot recommend using them in such a scenario.

Computation Time: The computation times for all the tested solvers are shown in Table 1. One iteration of $R6P^{[v]\times}_{v,C,w,t}$ is two orders of magnitude faster than R6P. According to the experiments, even one iteration of $R6P^{[v]\times}_{v,C,w,t}$ provides very good results, comparable with R6P and 5 iterations always match the results of R6P or even outperform them at 34× the speed. Note that R9P can be even faster than $R6P^{[v]\times}_{v,C,w,t}$ because it is non-iterative and runs only once and is therefore as fast as 2 iterations of $R6P^{[v]\times}_{v,C,w,t}$. One iteration of $R6P^{w,t}_{v,C}$, $R6P^{w}_{v,C,t}$ and $R6P^{w,t}_{v,C,t}$ is around three times slower than $R6P^{[v]\times}_{v,C,w,t}$ but still almost two orders of magnitude faster than R6P.

4.2 Real Data

We used the publicly available datasets from [1] and we show the results of the same frames shown in [18] (seq1, seq8, seq20 and seq22) in order to make a relevant comparison. We also added one more real dataset (House), containing high RS effects from a fast moving drone carrying a GoPro camera. The 3D-2D correspondences were obtained in the same way as in [18] by reconstructing the scene using global shutter images and then matching the 2D features from the RS images to the reconstructed 3D points.

We performed RANSAC with 1000 iterations for each solver to estimate the camera pose and calculated the number of inliers. The inlier threshold was set to 2 pixels in the case of the data from [1] which was captured by handheld iPhone at 720p and to 8 pixels for the GoPro footage which was recorder in 1080p. The higher threshold in the second case allowed to capture a reasonable number of inliers even for such fast camera motions. The results in Fig. 6 show the number of inliers captures over the sequences of images. We see that the performance of $R6P_{v,C,w,t}^{[v]\times}$ with 5 iterations is virtually identical to R6P. The results of $R6P_{v,C,t}^{w,t}$ and $R6P_{v,C,t}^{w}$ are also very similar and often outperform R6P and $R6P_{v,C,w,t}^{[v]\times}$, except for the most challenging images in the House dataset.

The performance of $R6P_{v,C}^{w,t}$ is unstable, sometimes performing comparable to or below P3P. In seq20 in particular, there is almost exclusively a fast translational camera motion. The drop in performance can therefore be explained by $R6P_{v,C}^{w,t}$ being the only solver that does not estimate the translational velocity t in the first step. R9P performs solidly across all the experiments and on the most challenging House dataset it even provides significantly better results.

To test another useful case of camera absolute pose, which is augmented reality, we created an environment filled with Aruco [21] markers in known positions. We set up the markers in such a way that they covered three perpendicular walls. The scene was recorded with a camera performing translational and rotational motion, similar to what a human does when looking around or shaking the head.

All solvers were used in RANSAC with 100 iterations to allow some robustness to outliers and noise. Note that 100 iterations of RANSAC would take at least 200 ms for R6P excluding the inlier verification. That makes R6P not valuable for real time purposes (in practice only less than 10 iterations of R6P would give realtime performance). On the other hand, 100 runs of $R6P_{v,C,w,t}^{[v]\times}$ with 5 iterations take around 5 ms (200 fps) and $R6P_{v,C,t}^{w}$ takes around 12.5 ms (80 fps). We did not test solvers $R6P_{v,C}^{w,t}$, $R6P_{v,C,t}^{w,t}$ and R9P in this experiment. This is because the performance of $R6P_{v,C}^{w,t}$ is unstable, the performance of $R6P_{v,C,t}^{w,t}$ is almost identical to $R6P_{v,C,t}^{w}$ and with R9P we do not have a way to extract the camera motion parameters and the reprojection without these parameters does not provide fair comparison.

We evaluated the reprojection error in each frame on all the detected markers. The results are shown in Fig. 7. All the rolling shutter solvers outperform P3P in terms of precision of the reprojections. $R6P_{v,C,w,t}^{[v]\times}$ again provides identical performance to R6P. $R6P_{v,C,t}^{w}$ has a slight edge over the others, which is interesting, considering its poor performance on the synthetic data.

Figure 7 gives a visualization of the estimated camera pose by reprojecting a cube in front of the camera. There is a significant misalignment between the cube and the scene during camera motion when using P3P pose estimate. In comparison, all the rolling shutter solvers keep the cube much more consistent with respect to the scene.

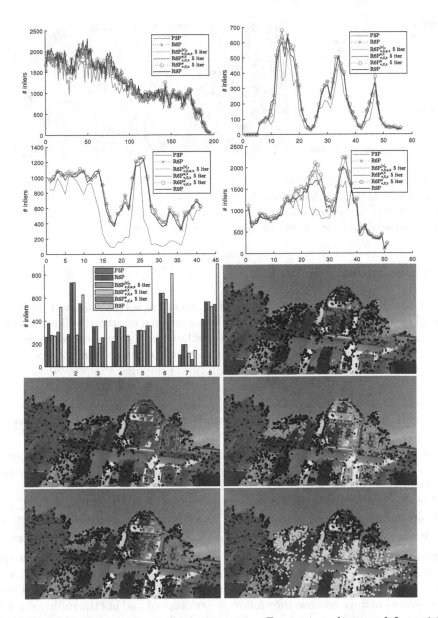

Fig. 6. Number of inliers on real data sequences. From top to bottom, left to right: seq01, seq08, seq20, seq22 and House. The x axis contains frame numbers. The bar graph for the House figure is used because there is no temporal relationship between adjacent frames so a line graph does not make sense. Following are sample images from the House dataset frame 6, containing a high amount of RS distortion. In this frame, R9P provided significantly more inliers than other methods. The results of R6P and $R6P_{v,C,w,t}^{[v]\times}$ are again identical, with the small exception of the first frame. The colored inliers in the sample images follow the same colors of algorithms as in the bar graph for House sequence. (Color figure online)

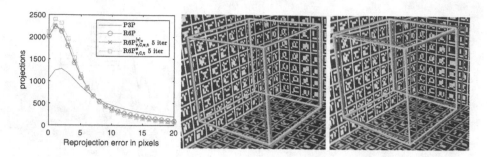

Fig. 7. Histogram of reprojection errors on the Aruco markers in the augmented reality experiment. The rolling shutter absolute pose solvers (R6P in magenta, $\text{R6P}^{[v]\times}_{v,C,w,t}$ in green, $\text{R6P}^w_{v,C,t}$ in cyan) keep the cube in place during camera motion whereas P3P (red) reprojects the cube all over the place. (Color figure online)

5   Conclusions

We revisited the problem of rolling shutter camera absolute pose and proposed several new practical solutions. The solutions are based on iterative linear solvers that improve the current state-of-the-art methods in terms of speed while providing the same precision or better. The practical benefit of our solvers is also the fact that they provide only a single solution, compared to up to 20 solutions of R6P [18].

The overall best performing $\text{R6P}^{[v]\times}_{v,C,w,t}$ solver needs only a single iteration to provide similar performance to R6P while being approximately 170x faster. At 5 iterations the performance of R6P is matched while the new $\text{R6P}^{[v]\times}_{v,C,w,t}$ solver is still approximately 34x faster than R6P. This allows for much broader applicability, especially in the area of augmented reality, visual SLAM and other real-time applications.

We also proposed 3 other iterative linear solvers ($\text{R6P}^{w,t}_{v,C}$, $\text{R6P}^{w,t}_{v,C,t}$, $\text{R6P}^w_{v,C,t}$) that alternate between estimating different camera pose and velocity parameters. These three solvers are slower than $\text{R6P}^{[v]\times}_{v,C,w,t}$ but still almost two orders of magnitude faster than R6P. While not as precise as R6P or $\text{R6P}^{[v]\times}_{v,C,w,t}$ in the synthetic experiments, they proved usefulness on the real data, providing more inliers and better reprojections than P3P and even R6P. We presented these three solvers mainly because they follow the concept of making the rolling shutter absolute pose equations linear by alternatively fixing some variables and then others. Although $\text{R6P}^{w,t}_{v,C,t}$ and $\text{R6P}^w_{v,C,t}$ do not offer the fastest and most precise results, they performed best in some of the experiments, especially for purely translational motion, and we think they are worth mentioning.

Last but not least we presented a non-iterative linear solver that uses 9 correspondences. This solver is as fast as 2 iterations of $\text{R6P}^{[v]\times}_{v,C,w,t}$ and proved to be the most precise in terms of estimated camera pose in the synthetic experiments and provided solid performance on the real data.

Altogether, this paper presents a big step forward in practical computation of rolling shutter camera absolute pose, making it more available in real world applications.

References

1. Hedborg, J., Forssén, P.E., Felsberg, M., Ringaby, E.: Rolling shutter bundle adjustment. In: CVPR, pp. 1434–1441 (2012)
2. Klein, G., Murray, D.: Parallel tracking and mapping on a camera phone. In: IEEE ISMAR, ISMAR 2009, pp.83–86 (2009)
3. Saurer, O., Koser, K., Bouguet, J.Y., Pollefeys, M.: Rolling shutter stereo. In: ICCV, pp. 465–472 (2013)
4. Grunert, J.A.: Das Pothenotische Problem in erweiterter Gestalt nebst über seine Anwendungen in der Geodäsie (1841)
5. Haralick, R., Lee, D., Ottenburg, K., Nolle, M.: Analysis and solutions of the three point perspective pose estimation problem. In: CVPR, pp. 592–598 (1991)
6. Ameller, M.A., Triggs, B., Quan, L.: Camera pose revisited: new linear algorithms. In: 14eme Congres Francophone de Reconnaissance des Formes et Intelligence Artificielle. Paper in French 2002 (2002)
7. Fischler, M.A., Bolles, R.C.: Random sample consensus: a paradigm for model fitting with applications to image analysis and automated cartography. Commun. ACM **24**, 381–395 (1981)
8. Lepetit, V., Moreno-Noguer, F., Fua, P.: EPnP: an accurate O(n) solution to the PnP problem. Int. J. Comput. Vis. **81**, 155–166 (2009)
9. Quan, L., Lan, Z.: Linear n-point camera pose determination. IEEE PAMI **21**, 774–780 (1999)
10. Triggs, B.: Camera pose and calibration from 4 or 5 known 3D points. In: ICCV, vol. 1, pp. 278–284 (1999)
11. Wu, Y., Hu, Z.: PnP problem revisited. J. Math. Imaging Vis. **24**, 131–141 (2006)
12. Zhi, L., Tang, J.: A complete linear 4-point algorithm for camera pose determination (2002)
13. Meingast, M., Geyer, C., Sastry, S.: Geometric models of rolling-shutter cameras. Computing Research Repository abs/cs/050 (2005)
14. Ait-Aider, O., Andreff, N., Lavest, J.M., Martinet, P.: Simultaneous object pose and velocity computation using a single view from a rolling shutter camera. In: Leonardis, A., Bischof, H., Pinz, A. (eds.) ECCV 2006. LNCS, vol. 3952, pp. 56–68. Springer, Heidelberg (2006). https://doi.org/10.1007/11744047_5
15. Hedborg, J., Ringaby, E., Forssen, P.E., Felsberg, M.: Structure and motion estimation from rolling shutter video. In: ICCV Workshops, pp. 17–23 (2011)
16. Magerand, L., Bartoli, A., Ait-Aider, O., Pizarro, D.: Global optimization of object pose and motion from a single rolling shutter image with automatic 2D-3D matching. In: Fitzgibbon, A., Lazebnik, S., Perona, P., Sato, Y., Schmid, C. (eds.) ECCV 2012. LNCS, vol. 7572, pp. 456–469. Springer, Heidelberg (2012). https://doi.org/10.1007/978-3-642-33718-5_33
17. Henrion, D., Lasserre, J.B., Lofberg, J.: GloptiPoly 3: moments, optimization and semidefinite programming. Optim. Methods Softw. **24**, 761–779 (2009)
18. Albl, C., Kukelova, Z., Pajdla, T.: R6P - rolling shutter absolute pose problem. In: CVPR, pp. 2292–2300 (2015)

19. Cox, D., Little, J., O'Shea, D.: Using Algebraic Geometry, 2nd edn. Springer, New York (2005). https://doi.org/10.1007/b138611
20. Kukelova, Z., Bujnak, M., Pajdla, T.: Automatic generator of minimal problem solvers. In: Forsyth, D., Torr, P., Zisserman, A. (eds.) ECCV 2008. LNCS, vol. 5304, pp. 302–315. Springer, Heidelberg (2008). https://doi.org/10.1007/978-3-540-88690-7_23
21. Garrido-Jurado, S., Muñoz-Salinas, R., Madrid-Cuevas, F., Marín-Jiménez, M.: Automatic generation and detection of highly reliable fiducial markers under occlusion. Pattern Recognit. **47**, 2280–2292 (2014)

Scale Estimation of Monocular SfM for a Multi-modal Stereo Camera

Shinya Sumikura[1]([✉]), Ken Sakurada[2], Nobuo Kawaguchi[1],
and Ryosuke Nakamura[2]

[1] Nagoya University, Nagoya, Japan
sumikura@ucl.nuee.nagoya-u.ac.jp, kawaguti@nagoya-u.jp
[2] National Institute of Advanced Industrial Science and Technology, Tokyo, Japan
{k.sakurada,r.nakamura}@aist.go.jp

Abstract. This paper proposes a novel method of estimating the absolute scale of monocular SfM for a multi-modal stereo camera. In the fields of computer vision and robotics, scale estimation for monocular SfM has been widely investigated in order to simplify systems. This paper addresses the scale estimation problem for a stereo camera system in which two cameras capture different spectral images (e.g., RGB and FIR), whose feature points are difficult to directly match using descriptors. Furthermore, the number of matching points between FIR images can be comparatively small, owing to the low resolution and lack of thermal scene texture. To cope with these difficulties, the proposed method estimates the scale parameter using batch optimization, based on the epipolar constraint of a small number of feature correspondences between the invisible light images. The accuracy and numerical stability of the proposed method are verified by synthetic and real image experiments.

1 Introduction

This paper addresses the problem of estimating the scale parameter of monocular Structure from Motion (SfM) for a multi-modal stereo camera system (Fig. 1). There has been growing interest in scene modeling with the development of mobile digital devices. In particular, researchers in the field of computer vision and robotics have exhaustively investigated scale estimation methods for monocular SfM to benefit from the simplicity of the camera system [5,14]. There are several ways to estimate the scale parameter—for example, integration with other sensors such as inertial measurement units (IMUs) [19] or navigation satellite systems (NSSs), such as the Global Positioning System (GPS). Also, some methods utilize the prior knowledge of the sensor setups [13,23]. In this paper, the scale parameter of monocular SfM is estimated by integrating the information of different spectral images, such as those taken by RGB and far-infrared

Electronic supplementary material The online version of this chapter (https://doi.org/10.1007/978-3-030-20893-6_18) contains supplementary material, which is available to authorized users.

(FIR) cameras in a stereo camera setup, whose feature points are difficult to directly match by using descriptors (e.g., SIFT [15], SURF [2], and ORB [22]).

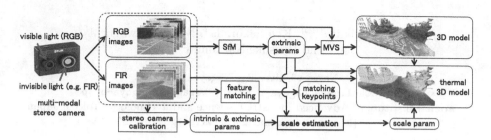

Fig. 1. Flowchart of the proposed scale estimation and the application example: thermal 3D reconstruction.

With the development of the production techniques of FIR cameras, they have been widely utilized for deriving the benefits of thermal information in the form of infrared radiation emitted by objects, such as infrastructure inspection [8,11,16,29,30], pedestrian detection in the dark [3], and monitoring volcanic activity [27]. Especially for unmanned aerial vehicles (UAVs), a stereo pair of RGB and FIR cameras, which we call a *multi-modal stereo camera*, is often mounted on the UAV for such inspection and monitoring. Although the multi-modal stereo camera can capture different spectral images simultaneously, for example, in the case of structural inspection, it is labor-intensive to compare a large number of image pairs. To improve the efficiency of the inspection, SfM [1,24] and Multi-View Stereo (MVS) [7,12,25] can be used for *thermal 3D reconstruction* (Fig. 1). The estimation of the absolute scale of the monocular SfM is needed in order to project FIR image information to the 3D model (Fig. 2a). However, it is difficult to match feature points between RGB and FIR images directly. Moreover, the number of matching points between FIR images is comparatively small due to the low resolution and the lack of thermal texture in a scene. Although machine learning methods, such as deep neural networks (DNNs) [6,9,31], can be used to match feature points between different types of images, the cost of dataset creation for every camera and scene is quite expensive.

To estimate the scale parameter from only the information of the multi-modal camera system, we leverage the stereo setup with a constant extrinsic parameter and a small number of feature correspondences between the same modal images other than the visible ones (Fig. 1). More concretely, the proposed method is based on a least-squares method of residuals by the epipolar constraint between the same modal images. The main contribution of this paper is threefold: first, the formulation of the scale estimation for a multi-modal stereo camera system; second, the verification of the effectiveness of the formulation through synthetic and real image experiments; and third, experimental thermal 3D mappings as one of the applications of the proposed method.

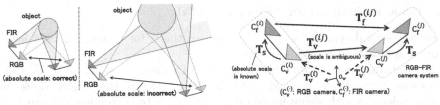

(a) Diagrams of thermal projection   (b) Definition of camera poses

Fig. 2. (a) Examples of projection when the absolute scale of RGB camera poses is correct (*left*) or incorrect (*right*). Green and red lines indicate the projection of the object in the RGB and FIR images, respectively. When the scale is incorrect, the reprojection of the FIR images is misaligned with the object. (b) Definition of camera poses for the ith and j^{th} viewpoints. $\mathbf{T}_v^{(\cdot)}$, $\mathbf{T}_f^{(\cdot)}$ and $\mathbf{T}_s$ represent the global poses of the RGB camera $C_v^{(\cdot)}$, FIR camera $C_f^{(\cdot)}$, and the relative pose between them, respectively. $\mathbf{T}_{(\cdot)}^{(ij)}$ represents the relative pose between the same type of cameras, $C_{(\cdot)}^{(i)}$ and $C_{(\cdot)}^{(j)}$. (Color figure online)

2 Related Work

2.1 Thermal 3D Reconstruction

The FIR camera is utilized with other types of sensors for thermal 3D reconstruction because the texture of FIR images is poorer than that of visible ones, especially for indoor scenes. Oreifej et al. [20] developed a fully automatic 3D thermal mapping system for building interiors using light detection and ranging (LiDAR) sensors to directly measure the depth of a scene. Additionally, depth image sensors are utilized to estimate the dense 3D model of a scene based on the Kinect Fusion algorithm [17] in the works of [16,29].

A combination of SfM and MVS is an alternative method for the 3D scene reconstruction. Ham et al. [8] developed a method to directly match feature points between RGB and FIR images, which works only in rich thermal-texture environments. Under similar conditions, the method proposed by Truong et al. [21] performs SfM using each of RGB and FIR images independently, aligning the two sparse point clouds.

Whereas the measurement range of the LiDAR sensor is longer than that of the depth image sensor, it has disadvantages in sensor size and weight, and is more expensive compared to RGB and depth cameras. Additionally, the depth image sensor can directly obtain dense 3D point clouds of a scene; however, it is unsuitable for wide-area measurement tasks because the measurement range is comparatively short. As mentioned, this study assumes thermal 3D reconstruction of wide areas for structural inspection by UAVs as an application. Thus, this paper proposes a scale estimation method of monocular SfM for a multi-modal stereo camera with the aim of thermal 3D reconstruction using an RGB–FIR camera system.

2.2 Scale Estimation for Monocular SfM

There are several types of scale estimation methods for monocular SfM based on other sensors and prior knowledge.

To estimate the absolute scale parameter of monocular SfM, an IMU is utilized as an internal sensor to integrate the information of the accelerations and angular velocities with vision-based estimation using the extended Kalman filter (EKF) [19]. As an external sensor, location information from NSSs (e.g., GPS) can be used to estimate the similarity transformation between the trajectories of monocular SfM and the GPS information based on a least-squares method.

Otherwise, prior knowledge of the sensor setups is utilized for scale estimation. Scaramuzza et al. [23] exploit the nonholonomic constraints of a vehicle on which a camera is mounted. The work by Kitt et al. [13] utilizes ground planar detection and the height from the ground of a camera.

The objective of this study is to estimate the scale parameter of monocular SfM from only multi-modal stereo camera images without other sensor information, for versatility. For example, in the case of structural inspection using UAVs, IMUs mounted on the drones suffer from vibration noise, and the GPS signal cannot be received owing to the structure. Additionally, assumptions of sensor setups restrain the application of scale estimation. Therefore, the proposed method utilizes only input image information and pre-calibration parameters.

As one of the scale estimation methods for a multi-modal stereo camera, which uses the information only from such a camera system, Truong et al. [21] proposed a method based on an alignment of RGB and FIR point clouds. This method requires the point cloud created only from FIR images. Thus, it is not applicable to scenes with non-rich thermal texture, such as indoor scenes. Otherwise, considering a multi-modal stereo camera as a multi-camera cluster with non-overlapping fields of view, we can theoretically apply scale estimation methods of monocular SfM for such a multi-camera cluster to a multi-modal stereo camera. The work by Clipp et al. [4] estimates the absolute scale of monocular SfM for a multi-camera cluster with non-overlapping fields of view by minimizing the residual based on the epipolar constraint between two viewpoints. This method does not perform the batch optimization, which utilizes multiple image pairs, and does not take the scale parameter into account when performing the bundle adjustment (BA) [28].

Thus, in this paper, we compare the proposed scale estimation method with the ones of Truong et al. [21] and by Clipp et al. [4].

3 Scale Estimation

3.1 Problem Formulation

In this section, we describe a novel method of estimating a scale parameter of reconstruction results from monocular SfM. Here we use a stereo system of RGB and FIR cameras (i.e., RGB–FIR) as an example of a multi-modal stereo camera system. Figure 2b expresses the global and relative transformation matrices of a system composed of two viewpoints with an RGB–FIR camera system.

We start with a given set of RGB images $\{I_v^{(1)}, I_v^{(2)}, \cdots, I_v^{(n)}\}$, and FIR images $\{I_f^{(1)}, I_f^{(2)}, \cdots, I_f^{(n)}\}$, whose k^{th} images, $I_v^{(k)}$ and $I_f^{(k)}$, are taken simultaneously using an RGB–FIR camera system whose constant extrinsic parameter is

$$T_s = \begin{bmatrix} R_s & t_s \\ 0^T & 1 \end{bmatrix}. \tag{1}$$

R_s and t_s represent the rotation matrix and the translation vector between the two cameras of the camera system, respectively. Those matrix and vector are estimated via calibration in advance. Additionally, we assume that the kth images, $I_v^{(k)}$ and $I_f^{(k)}$, are taken by the kth cameras, $C_v^{(k)}$(RGB) and $C_f^{(k)}$(FIR), with the global extrinsic parameters, $T_v^{(k)}$ and $T_f^{(k)}$, respectively. Note that $C_v^{(k)}$ and $C_f^{(k)}$ comprise the pair of cameras in the RGB–FIR camera system. $\{T_v^{(k)}\}$ can be estimated except for its absolute scale by monocular SfM of the RGB images.

Using $T_v^{(i)}$ and $T_v^{(j)}$, the relative transformation between $C_v^{(i)}$ and $C_v^{(j)}$ is computed by $T_v^{(j)}T_v^{(i)^{-1}}$. To solve the scale ambiguity, a scale parameter $s \in \mathbb{R}$ is introduced. Then, the relative transformation $T_v^{(ij)}$ between $C_v^{(i)}$ and $C_v^{(j)}$ including the scale parameter s is expressed by

$$T_v^{(ij)} = \begin{bmatrix} R_v^{(ij)} & s \cdot t_v^{(ij)} \\ 0^T & 1 \end{bmatrix}, \tag{2}$$

where $R_v^{(ij)}$ and $t_v^{(ij)}$ are the rotation matrix block and the translation vector block of $T_v^{(j)}T_v^{(i)^{-1}}$, respectively. The goal is to estimate the correct $s \in \mathbb{R}$.

3.2 Derivation of Scale Parameter s

With $T_v^{(ij)}$ and T_s, the relative transformation $T_f^{(ij)} = T_s T_v^{(ij)} T_s^{-1}$ between the two FIR cameras, $C_f^{(i)}$ and $C_f^{(j)}$, can be computed as

$$T_f^{(ij)} = \begin{bmatrix} R_s R_v^{(ij)} R_s^{-1} & s \cdot R_s t_v^{(ij)} + (I - R_s R_v^{(ij)} R_s^{-1}) t_s \\ 0^T & 1 \end{bmatrix} \tag{3}$$

$$= \begin{bmatrix} A^{(ij)} & s \cdot b^{(ij)} + c^{(ij)} \\ 0^T & 1 \end{bmatrix}, \tag{4}$$

where $A^{(ij)} = [a_1^{(ij)} | a_2^{(ij)} | a_3^{(ij)}] = R_s R_v^{(ij)} R_s^{-1}$, $b^{(ij)} = R_s t_v^{(ij)}$ and $c^{(ij)} = (I - R_s R_v^{(ij)} R_s^{-1}) t_s$. An essential matrix $E^{(ij)}$ between $C_f^{(i)}$ and $C_f^{(j)}$ can be derived from $T_f^{(ij)}$ and expressed as

$$E^{(ij)} = [sb^{(ij)} + c^{(ij)}]_\times A^{(ij)} \tag{5}$$

$$= s \cdot \left[\mathbf{b}^{(ij)} \times \mathbf{a}_1^{(ij)} \middle| \mathbf{b}^{(ij)} \times \mathbf{a}_2^{(ij)} \middle| \mathbf{b}^{(ij)} \times \mathbf{a}_3^{(ij)} \right]$$
$$+ \left[\mathbf{c}^{(ij)} \times \mathbf{a}_1^{(ij)} \middle| \mathbf{c}^{(ij)} \times \mathbf{a}_2^{(ij)} \middle| \mathbf{c}^{(ij)} \times \mathbf{a}_3^{(ij)} \right]. \tag{6}$$

The epipolar constraint between the two FIR images, $I_f^{(i)}$ and $I_f^{(j)}$, corresponding to the FIR cameras, $C_f^{(i)}$ and $C_f^{(j)}$, is formulated as

$$\mathbf{p}_k^{(j)^\mathsf{T}} \mathbf{E}^{(ij)} \mathbf{p}_k^{(i)} = 0, \tag{7}$$

where $\mathbf{p}_k^{(i)} = \left[x_k^{(i)}, y_k^{(i)}, 1 \right]^\mathsf{T}$ and $\mathbf{p}_k^{(j)} = \left[x_k^{(j)}, y_k^{(j)}, 1 \right]^\mathsf{T}$ are the kth corresponding feature points between $I_f^{(i)}$ and $I_f^{(j)}$, in the form of normalized image coordinates [10]. A normalized image point $\mathbf{p}_k^{(i)}$ is defined as

$$\mathbf{p}_k^{(i)} = \mathbf{K}_f^{-1} \left[u_k^{(i)}, v_k^{(i)}, 1 \right]^\mathsf{T} \quad \text{with} \quad \mathbf{K}_f = \begin{bmatrix} f_x & 0 & c_x \\ 0 & f_y & c_y \\ 0 & 0 & 1 \end{bmatrix}, \tag{8}$$

where $\mathbf{K}_f$ is the intrinsic parameter matrix of the FIR camera. $\left[u_k^{(i)}, v_k^{(i)} \right]$ is the feature point in pixels in $I_f^{(i)}$ and is the kth corresponding feature point with $\left[u_k^{(j)}, v_k^{(j)} \right]$ in $I_f^{(j)}$. Additionally, the normalized image point is also defined as

$$\mathbf{p}_k^{(i)} = \mathbf{X}_l^{(i)} \middle/ Z_l^{(i)}, \tag{9}$$

where $\mathbf{X}_l^{(i)} = [X_l^{(i)}, Y_l^{(i)}, Z_l^{(i)}]^\mathsf{T}$ is the lth 3D point in the coordinate system of the ith FIR camera $C_f^{(i)}$. Here, $\mathbf{X}_l^{(i)}$ corresponds to the feature point $\mathbf{p}_k^{(i)}$ on $I_f^{(i)}$.

The epipolar constraint of Eq. (7) can be expanded to

$$\mathbf{u}_k^{(ij)} \left(s \cdot \mathbf{f}^{(ij)} + \mathbf{g}^{(ij)} \right) = 0 \tag{10}$$

with

$$\mathbf{u}_k^{(ij)} = [x_k^{(i)} x_k^{(j)}, \ x_k^{(i)} y_k^{(j)}, \ x_k^{(i)}, \ y_k^{(i)} x_k^{(j)}, \ y_k^{(i)} y_k^{(j)}, \ y_k^{(i)}, \ x_k^{(j)}, \ y_k^{(j)}, \ 1], \tag{11}$$

$$\mathbf{f}^{(ij)} = \left[\left[\mathbf{b}^{(ij)} \times \mathbf{a}_1^{(ij)} \right]_1, \left[\mathbf{b}^{(ij)} \times \mathbf{a}_1^{(ij)} \right]_2, \cdots, \left[\mathbf{b}^{(ij)} \times \mathbf{a}_3^{(ij)} \right]_2, \left[\mathbf{b}^{(ij)} \times \mathbf{a}_3^{(ij)} \right]_3 \right]^\mathsf{T}, \tag{12}$$

$$\mathbf{g}^{(ij)} = \left[\left[\mathbf{c}^{(ij)} \times \mathbf{a}_1^{(ij)} \right]_1, \left[\mathbf{c}^{(ij)} \times \mathbf{a}_1^{(ij)} \right]_2, \cdots, \left[\mathbf{c}^{(ij)} \times \mathbf{a}_3^{(ij)} \right]_2, \left[\mathbf{c}^{(ij)} \times \mathbf{a}_3^{(ij)} \right]_3 \right]^\mathsf{T}. \tag{13}$$

If the coordinates of the feature points have no error, Eq. (10) is completely satisfied. However, in reality, the equation is not completely satisfied because coordinates of feature points usually have some error and the scale s is unknown. In such a case, the scalar residual $e_k^{(ij)}$ is defined as

$$e_k^{(ij)} = \mathbf{u}_k^{(ij)} \left(s \cdot \mathbf{f}^{(ij)} + \mathbf{g}^{(ij)} \right). \tag{14}$$

Likewise, the residual vector $\mathbf{e}^{(ij)}$ can be defined by

$$\mathbf{e}^{(ij)} = \mathbf{U}^{(ij)}\left(s \cdot \mathbf{f}^{(ij)} + \mathbf{g}^{(ij)}\right) \text{ with } \mathbf{U}^{(ij)} = \left[\, \mathbf{u}_1^{(ij)^\mathsf{T}} \mid \mathbf{u}_2^{(ij)^\mathsf{T}} \mid \cdots \mid \mathbf{u}_n^{(ij)^\mathsf{T}} \,\right]^\mathsf{T},$$

(15)

where n is the number of corresponding feature points between $\mathrm{I}_f^{(i)}$ and $\mathrm{I}_f^{(j)}$. Using a least-squares method, the scale parameter s can be estimated by

$$s = \arg\min_{s \in \mathbb{R}} \frac{1}{2} \sum_{i,j,i\neq j} \left\|\mathbf{e}^{(ij)}\right\|^2.$$

(16)

Collectively, the scale estimation problem comes down to determining s, such that the error function,

$$J(s) = \frac{1}{2} \sum_{i,j,i\neq j} \left\|\mathbf{U}^{(ij)}\left(s \cdot \mathbf{f}^{(ij)} + \mathbf{g}^{(ij)}\right)\right\|^2$$

(17)

is minimized. Thus, the scale parameter s is determined by solving the equation $\mathrm{d}J(s)/\mathrm{d}s = 0$ in terms of s. Therefore, the scale s is computed by

$$s = -\sum_{i,j,i\neq j} \left(\mathbf{f}^{(ij)^\mathsf{T}} \mathbf{U}^{(ij)^\mathsf{T}} \mathbf{U}^{(ij)} \mathbf{g}^{(ij)}\right) \Big/ \sum_{i,j,i\neq j} \left(\mathbf{f}^{(ij)^\mathsf{T}} \mathbf{U}^{(ij)^\mathsf{T}} \mathbf{U}^{(ij)} \mathbf{f}^{(ij)}\right).$$

(18)

3.3 Alternative Derivation

In Eq. (2), the scale parameter s and the relative translation vector $\mathbf{t}_v^{(ij)}$ between the two RGB cameras, $\mathrm{C}_f^{(i)}$ and $\mathrm{C}_f^{(j)}$, are multiplied. The scale parameter s can be alternatively applied to the translation vector $\mathbf{t}_s$ in $\mathbf{T}_s$, in contrast to Eqs. (1) and (2). This introduction of s is reasonable because multiplying $\mathbf{t}_s$ by s is geometrically equivalent to multiplying $\mathbf{t}_v^{(ij)}$ by $1/s$. Therefore, we can also estimate the scale parameter of monocular SfM, which has scale ambiguity, from

$$\mathbf{T}_v^{(ij)} = \begin{bmatrix} \mathbf{R}_v^{(ij)} & \mathbf{t}_v^{(ij)} \\ \mathbf{0}^\mathsf{T} & 1 \end{bmatrix} \quad \text{and} \quad \mathbf{T}_s = \begin{bmatrix} \mathbf{R}_s & s \cdot \mathbf{t}_s \\ \mathbf{0}^\mathsf{T} & 1 \end{bmatrix}.$$

(19)

When using Eq. (19) for scale estimation, the $\mathbf{A}^{(ij)}$, $\mathbf{b}^{(ij)}$ and $\mathbf{c}^{(ij)}$ in Eq. (4) are

$$\mathbf{A}^{(ij)} = \mathbf{R}_s \mathbf{R}_v^{(ij)} \mathbf{R}_s^{-1}, \quad \mathbf{b}^{(ij)} = (\mathbf{I} - \mathbf{R}_s \mathbf{R}_v^{(ij)} \mathbf{R}_s^{-1})\mathbf{t}_s \quad \text{and} \quad \mathbf{c}^{(ij)} = \mathbf{R}_s \mathbf{t}_v^{(ij)}.$$

(20)

The rest of the derivation procedure remains the same.

Hereinafter, the formula for the scale estimation based on Eqs. (1) and (2) is called Algorithm (1), whereas the formula based on Eq. (19) is called Algorithm (2).

3.4   Scale-Oriented Bundle Adjustment

After an initial estimation of the scale parameter by Eq. (18) of Algorithm (1) or (2), we perform the bundle adjustment (BA) [28]. Before the scale estimation, the camera poses of the RGB cameras are precisely estimated via monocular SfM, except for its absolute scale. Thus, our BA optimizes the scale parameter s rather than the translation vectors of the RGB cameras.

Using the scale parameter s, the reprojection error $\boldsymbol{\delta}_{k,l}^{(i)}$ of the lth FIR 3D point $\mathbf{X}_l = [X_l, Y_l, Z_l]^{\mathsf{T}}$ (in the world coordinate system) in the FIR image $\mathrm{I}_{\mathrm{f}}^{(i)}$ is defined as

$$\boldsymbol{\delta}_{k,l}^{(i)} = \mathbf{x}_k^{(i)} - \pi^{(i)}\left(s, \mathbf{X}_l\right), \tag{21}$$

where $\mathbf{x}_k^{(i)}$ represents the kth feature point in the ith FIR image $\mathrm{I}_{\mathrm{f}}^{(i)}$ and corresponds to $\mathbf{X}_l$. The projection function $\pi^{(i)}(\cdot)$ for the ith FIR camera is

$$\pi^{(i)}\left(s, \mathbf{X}_l\right) = \left[f_x X_l^{(i)}/Z_l^{(i)} + c_x,\ f_y Y_l^{(i)}/Z_l^{(i)} + c_y\right]^{\mathsf{T}}, \tag{22}$$

where $\mathbf{X}_l^{(i)} = [X_l^{(i)}, Y_l^{(i)}, Z_l^{(i)}]^{\mathsf{T}}$ is computed by

$$\mathbf{X}_l^{(i)} = \mathbf{R}_{\mathrm{s}}\mathbf{R}_{\mathrm{v}}^{(i)}\mathbf{X}_l + s \cdot \mathbf{R}_{\mathrm{s}}\mathbf{t}_{\mathrm{v}}^{(i)} + \mathbf{t}_{\mathrm{s}} \quad \text{(when using Algorithm (1))}, \tag{23}$$

$$\mathbf{X}_l^{(i)} = \mathbf{R}_{\mathrm{s}}\mathbf{R}_{\mathrm{v}}^{(i)}\mathbf{X}_l + \mathbf{R}_{\mathrm{s}}\mathbf{t}_{\mathrm{v}}^{(i)} + s \cdot \mathbf{t}_{\mathrm{s}} \quad \text{(when using Algorithm (2))}. \tag{24}$$

The cost function $\mathcal{L}(\cdot)$ composed of the reprojection errors is defined by

$$\mathcal{L}\left(s, \{\mathbf{X}_l\}, \mathbf{K}_{\mathrm{f}}; \{\mathbf{T}_{\mathrm{v}}^{(i)}\}, \mathbf{T}_{\mathrm{s}}\right) = \sum_{i,k,l} \rho_{\mathrm{h}}\left(\left\|\boldsymbol{\delta}_{k,l}^{(i)}\right\|^2 / \sigma_{\mathrm{r}}^2\right), \tag{25}$$

where $\rho_{\mathrm{h}}(\cdot)$ is the Huber loss function and σ_{r} is the standard deviation of the reprojection errors. The optimized scale parameter s is estimated as follows:

$$s = \underset{s \in \mathbb{R}, \{\mathbf{X}_l\}, \mathbf{K}_{\mathrm{f}}}{\arg\min}\ \mathcal{L}\left(s, \{\mathbf{X}_l\}, \mathbf{K}_{\mathrm{f}}; \{\mathbf{T}_{\mathrm{v}}^{(i)}\}, \mathbf{T}_{\mathrm{s}}\right). \tag{26}$$

Equation (26) is a non-convex optimization problem. Thus, it should be solved using iterative methods such as the Levenberg–Marquardt algorithm, for which an initial value is acquired by Eq. (18) of Algorithm (1) or (2). See the details of the derivation above in Sect. 1 of the supplementary material paper.

4   Synthetic Image Experiments

In Sect. 3, we described the two approaches of resolving scale ambiguity, with differences in the placement of the scale parameter s. In this section, we investigate, via simulation, the effect of noise given to feature points on scale estimation accuracy when varying the baseline length between the two cameras of the multi-modal stereo camera system.

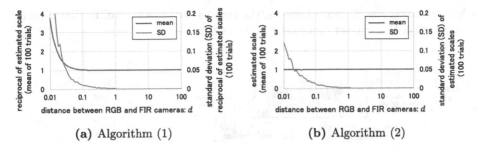

(a) Algorithm (1)   **(b) Algorithm (2)**

Fig. 3. Mean (left vertical axes) and standard deviation (right vertical axes) of a hundred estimated scales under feature point noise of $\sigma_n = 0.001$. Both horizontal axes represent the baseline length d between the two cameras of the RGB–FIR camera system, which is varied in the range of $[10^{-2}, 10^2]$. Note that the true value of the scale $s_{\text{true}} = 1.0$ here. The accuracy and stability of the estimated scales are different between (a) and (b), especially for $d < 0.1$.

The scale parameter is estimated in the synthetic environment with noise in both Algorithms (1) and (2). Preliminary experiments in the synthetic environment show that scale parameters can be estimated correctly using the proposed method when no noise is added to the feature points. See the details under the noise-free settings in Sect. 2 of the supplementary material paper.

4.1 Experimental Settings

The procedure for the synthetic image experiments is as follows:

1. Scatter 3D points $\mathbf{X}_i \in \mathbb{R}^3$ $(i = 1, 2, \cdots, n_p)$ randomly in a cubic space with a side length of D.
2. Arrange n_c RGB–FIR camera systems in the 3D space randomly. More concretely, a constant relative transformation of an RGB–FIR camera system $\mathbf{T}_s$ is given, and the absolute camera poses of the RGB cameras $\mathbf{T}_v^{(k)}$ $(k = 1, 2, \cdots, n_c)$ are set randomly. Then, the absolute camera poses of the FIR cameras $\mathbf{T}_f^{(k)}$ $(k = 1, 2, \cdots, n_c)$ are computed by $\mathbf{T}_f^{(k)} = \mathbf{T}_s \mathbf{T}_v^{(k)}$.
3. For all $k = 1, 2, \cdots, n_c$, reproject the 3D points $\mathbf{X}_1, \mathbf{X}_2, \cdots, \mathbf{X}_{n_p}$ to the kth FIR camera using $\mathbf{T}_f^{(k)}$. Then, determine the normalized image points $\mathbf{p}_i^{(k)}$ $(i = 1, 2, \cdots, n_p)$ using Eq. (9). Gaussian noise with a standard deviation $\sigma_n \geq 0$ can be added to all of the reprojected points.
4. Estimate the scale parameter s, using both Algorithms (1) and (2) with outlier rejection based on Eq. (14). Note that the true value of the scale parameter is 1.0 because the RGB camera positions are not scaled.

In this paper, we define $n_p = 1000$, $D = 2000$ and $n_c = 100$. In addition, the relative pose $\mathbf{T}_s$ between the two cameras of the camera system is set as

$$\mathbf{T}_s = \begin{bmatrix} \mathbf{R}_s & \mathbf{t}_s \\ \mathbf{0}^\mathsf{T} & 1 \end{bmatrix} \text{ with } \mathbf{R}_s = \mathbf{I} \text{ and } \mathbf{t}_s = \begin{bmatrix} d & 0 & 0 \end{bmatrix}^\mathsf{T}, \tag{27}$$

where $d > 0$ is the distance between the two cameras of the RGB–FIR camera system. d and σ_n are set depending on the simulation.

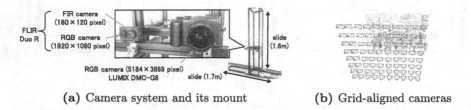

(a) Camera system and its mount   **(b)** Grid-aligned cameras

Fig. 4. (a) Camera system and its mount used in our experiment. The camera mount is used to capture images along the grid-aligned viewpoints. The stage, to which the camera system is fixed, can be moved in both vertical and horizontal directions. (b) Grid-aligned camera poses estimated by SfM. The images are captured using (a).

4.2 Effects of Feature Point Detection Error

We consider the effect of noise given to feature points on scale estimation accuracy when varying a baseline length of the stereo camera system. Setting $\sigma_n = 0.001$, we estimate scale parameters s 100 times and compute a mean and a standard deviation (SD) of $1/s$ (in Algorithm (1)) or s (in Algorithm (2)), with respect to each of the various baseline lengths d between the two cameras of the camera system. Figure 3 shows the relationship between d, the means and the SDs of the estimated scales for both Algorithms (1) and (2).

In Fig. 3b, the scale parameters are stably estimated in the region where d is relatively large $(0.1 < d)$ because the means are $s = s_{\text{true}} = 1.0$ and the SDs converge to 0.0. On the contrary, in the region where d is relatively small $(d < 0.1)$, the SD increases as d decreases but the means maintain the correct value of $s_{\text{true}} = 1.0$. Meanwhile, in Fig. 3a the means of the scale parameters are less accurate than the ones in Fig. 3b in the region where d is relatively small $(d < 0.1)$. In addition, the SDs in Fig. 3a are larger than the ones in Fig. 3b.

Hence, it is concluded that the estimated scales obtained by Algorithm (2) are more accurate and stable than the ones obtained by Algorithm (1). Additionally, the baseline length between the two cameras of a multi-modal stereo camera system should be as long as possible for scale estimation.

5 Real Image Experiments

5.1 Evaluation Method

We apply the proposed method to the experimental environment to verify that the method is capable of estimating the absolute scales of outputs from monocular SfM which uses a multi-modal stereo camera. For this verification, we need to prepare results of monocular SfM in which the actual distances between the cameras are already known. Therefore in this experiment, the multi-modal stereo camera system is fixed to the stage on the camera mount as shown in Fig. 4a, and we capture RGB and FIR images while moving the camera system on a grid of 100 [mm] intervals. The stage of the camera mount, where the camera system is fixed, can be moved in both vertical and horizontal directions. Figure 4b shows an example of grid-aligned camera poses estimated by SfM, whose images are captured using the camera mount shown in Fig. 4a.

Let $d^{(ij)}$ be the actual distance between the two RGB cameras $(C_v^{(i)}, C_v^{(j)})$ and $L^{(ij)}$ be the distance between $(C_v^{(i)}, C_v^{(j)})$ in the result of the monocular SfM, which has scale ambiguity. The estimated actual distance $\hat{d}^{(ij)}$ is computed by

$$\hat{d}^{(ij)} = s \cdot L^{(ij)} \,(\text{in Algorithm (1)}) \quad \text{and} \quad \hat{d}^{(ij)} = L^{(ij)}/s \,\big(\text{in Algorithm (2)}\big), \quad (28)$$

where s is the scale parameter in Eqs. (2) and (19), respectively. Additionally, the relative error $\epsilon^{(ij)}$ of $\hat{d}^{(ij)}$ can be defined as

$$\epsilon^{(ij)} = \frac{\hat{d}^{(ij)} - d^{(ij)}}{d^{(ij)}} \times 100[\%]. \quad (29)$$

The RGB–FIR camera system used in our experiment is shown in Fig. 4a. The RGB camera in the camera system is a LUMIX DMC–G8 (Panasonic Corp.) or the RGB camera part of a FLIR Duo R (FLIR Systems, Inc.), depending on the experimental setting of the baseline length. The FIR camera is the FIR camera part of the FLIR Duo R.

The procedure for the experiment is as follows:

1. Capture the RGB and FIR image pairs using the camera system and its mount shown in Fig. 4a. Additionally, some supplementary RGB and FIR images are added to stabilize the process of monocular SfM and scale estimation.
2. Perform a process of monocular SfM using the captured RGB images.
3. Compute feature point matches of the FIR images using SIFT [15] descriptor, whose outliers are rejected via RANdom SAmple Consensus (RANSAC) based on a five-point algorithm [18, 26].
4. Estimate the scale parameter by Algorithms (1) and (2).
5. Compute a mean of $\epsilon^{(ij)}$ with all the combinations, which is defined as

$$\bar{\epsilon} = \frac{1}{N(N-1)/2} \sum_{i<j} \epsilon^{(ij)}, \quad (30)$$

where N is the number of RGB images taken in a grid.

When detecting and describing feature points, FIR images are converted to gray-scaled images. FLIR Duo R outputs FIR images whose pixels contain values of radiation temperature. To convert them to gray-scaled images, a mean μ and a standard deviation σ_p of pixels for each image are computed, and then pixel values with a range of $[\mu - 2\sigma_p, \mu + 2\sigma_p]$ are mapped to $[0, 2^8 - 1]$.

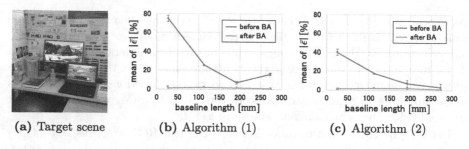

(a) Target scene   (b) Algorithm (1)   (c) Algorithm (2)

Fig. 5. (a) Target scene of evaluation. (b), (c) The means of $|\bar{\epsilon}|$ with 100 trials under various baseline setups $(26, 113, 192$ and $273\,[\mathrm{mm}])$, in both Algorithms (1) and (2). The error bars indicate the range of $\pm 1\sigma$ of $|\bar{\epsilon}|$. σ is a standard deviation of $|\bar{\epsilon}|$ with 100 trials. It is found that the means of $|\bar{\epsilon}|$ before BA decrease as the baseline length becomes larger in both (b) and (c). Additionally, the means of $|\bar{\epsilon}|$ in (b) are larger the ones in (c). On the contrary, after BA, the means of $|\bar{\epsilon}|$ approach nearly zero in both (b) and (c).

To confirm the effect of the difference in baseline lengths between the RGB and FIR cameras, datasets of RGB and FIR images are taken with each of the four baseline lengths of the camera system: $273\,[\mathrm{mm}]$, $192\,[\mathrm{mm}]$, $113\,[\mathrm{mm}]$ and $26\,[\mathrm{mm}]$. The systems with the first, second, and third baseline lengths use the LUMIX DMC–G8 as the RGB camera. The system with $26\,[\mathrm{mm}]$ uses the RGB camera equipped on the FLIR Duo R. Considering the randomness of RANSAC, for each of the four baseline lengths, the scale estimation and computation of $\bar{\epsilon}$ are performed 100 times. Then, a mean and a standard deviation of $|\bar{\epsilon}|$ are calculated.

Also, pre-calibration of an RGB–FIR stereo camera system is needed to perform the proposed scale estimation procedure. Thus, we adopt the stereo calibration method in which a planar pattern such as a chessboard is used [32]. See the details in Sect. 3 of the supplementary material paper.

5.2   Evaluation with a Real Scene

The experimental environment used in the evaluation is shown in Fig. 5a. The grid pattern along which the camera system is moved has 8 vertical × 10 horizontal grids. Thus, there are 80 RGB camera poses used for the evaluation. Additionally, 50 supplementary pairs of RGB and FIR images are included to stabilize the process of monocular SfM and scale estimation. Considering the randomness of RANSAC, we show the means and standard deviations of $|\bar{\epsilon}|$ with 100 trials of scale estimation. Figures 5b and c show the results when using Algorithms (1) and (2), respectively.

In both Figs. 5b and c, the means of $|\bar{\epsilon}|$ before BA decrease as the baseline length becomes larger. Additionally, the mean values in Fig. 5b are larger than the ones in Fig. 5c across the whole range of baseline length. Those results denote the same pattern as the experiments in the synthetic environment in Sect. 4. Consequently, without BA, it is evident that the smaller error of scale estimation

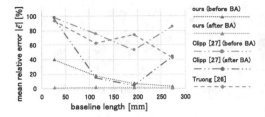

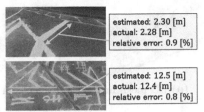

Fig. 6. The mean relative errors $|\bar{\epsilon}|$ acquired by Algorithm (2) of the proposed method (*ours*), [21] and [4]. *Ours* and [4] have randomness caused by RANSAC. Thus, we show the means of $|\bar{\epsilon}|$ with 100 trials for them.

Fig. 7. Evaluation of the practical result with road surface markings in the scene of Fig. 8a. High accuracy of the scale estimation is achieved as the relative errors are under 1.0[%].

occurs when using the camera system with the longer baseline as indicated by the simulation in Sect. 4. In addition, the difference in numerical stability of the proposed method occurs in experiments with both synthetic and real images.

On the contrary, after BA, the means of $|\bar{\epsilon}|$ approach nearly zero in both Figs. 5b and c, even though large error occurred before BA. Especially, at the 26 [mm] baseline length in Fig. 5b, the mean of $|\bar{\epsilon}|$ after BA is 1.64[%] whereas it is 74.9[%] before BA. Additionally, at the 273 [mm] baseline length after BA, high accuracy of the scale estimation is achieved as the means of $|\bar{\epsilon}|$ are 0.832[%] under Algorithm (1) and 0.876[%] under Algorithm (2). The SDs also decrease after BA compared to the ones before BA. Summarizing the above, we conclude that scale parameters estimated by both Algorithms (1) and (2) are suitable for an initial value of BA as well as that our BA effectively refines the scale parameters with respect to the accuracy and variance.

5.3 Comparison with the Existing Method

As mentioned in Sect. 2.2, we compare the proposed scale estimation method with the ones by Truong et al. [21] and by Clipp et al. [4]. We apply the two methods of [21] and [4] to the RGB–FIR image datasets used in Sect. 5.2, then evaluate the estimated scale parameter by calculating $\bar{\epsilon}$ accordingly. Figure 6 shows the comparison of the accuracies of the scale parameters estimated by Algorithm (2) of the proposed method, [21] and [4]. The results of the proposed method and [4] present the means of $|\bar{\epsilon}|$ with 100 trials both before and after BA. In result by [21], we adopt s_t computed by Eq. (6) in the paper of [21] as the scale parameter s.

As shown in Fig. 6, the $|\bar{\epsilon}|$ by [21] and [4] are much larger than the means of $|\bar{\epsilon}|$ by the proposed method throughout the whole range of baseline length. As for [21], the low accuracy mainly results from the erroneous 3D points reconstructed via SfM which uses only the FIR images. On the other hand, unlike our method, the method by [4] cannot deal with the epipolar residuals of multiple FIR image pairs. Thus, before BA, the means of $|\bar{\epsilon}|$ by [21] and [4] are much larger than the

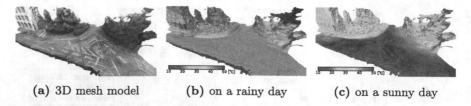

(a) 3D mesh model   (b) on a rainy day   (c) on a sunny day

Fig. 8. Examples of temporal thermal 3D modeling. The 3D mesh model reconstructed from RGB images is shown in (a). (b) and (c) show the thermal 3D reconstructions on a rainy day and on a sunny day, respectively. (Color figure online)

ones by the proposed method. Additionally, the BA in [4] does not optimize a scale parameter but rather rotations and translations. Thus, after BA, coupled with the poor initial estimation by [4], the BA is unstable as shown in Fig. 6.

5.4 Practical Examples

Figure 8 presents temporal thermal 3D mappings as a practical example of thermal 3D reconstruction. RGB and FIR images are captured by a smartphone-based RGB–FIR camera system, composed of a FLIR One (FLIR Systems, Inc.) and a smartphone. The baseline length of the camera system is 154 [mm].

A 3D mesh model shown in Fig. 8a is reconstructed from the RGB images using monocular SfM and MVS, and is then resized to the absolute scale estimated by the proposed method. The thermal 3D models shown in Figs. 8b and 8c are built by reprojecting FIR images to the 3D mesh model on a sunny day and on a rainy day, respectively. The thermal information is reprojected well as shown in Figs. 8b and c. In addition, as shown in Fig. 7, we measure the size of road surface markings in the 3D model (*estimated*) and in the real world (*actual*), as an evaluation of the estimated scales in practical scenes. The relative errors of the estimated size are approximately 0.8[%] in the scene in Fig. 8. See the additional results in Sect. 4 of the supplementary material paper.

6 Conclusion

In this paper, we have shown a novel method of estimating the scale parameter of monocular SfM for a multi-modal stereo camera system, which is composed of different spectral cameras (e.g., RGB and FIR) in a stereo camera setup. Owing to the difficulty of matching feature points directly between RGB and FIR images, we have leveraged a constant extrinsic parameter of the stereo setup and a small number of feature correspondences between the same modal images. Two types of formulae for scale parameter estimation, both of which are based on the epipolar constraint, were proposed in this paper. We have also verified the difference in scale estimation accuracy and stability between the two formulae in the synthetic and real image experiments. The cause for the difference in scale estimation stability requires further investigation.

Additionally, we have demonstrated a scale estimation of monocular SfM under the experimental environment using an RGB–FIR stereo camera, and we have verified its accuracy both before and after BA. The consequence shows that the proposed method can estimate an appropriate scale parameter and its accuracy depends on the baseline length between RGB and FIR cameras of a stereo camera system. Moreover, we have presented the thermal 3D modeling as an application of the proposed scale estimation method.

These results suggest that the proposed method is applicable to the construction of thermal 3D mappings using payload-limited vehicles, such as UAVs, on which an RGB–FIR camera system is mounted. Therefore, we conclude that the proposed method is suitable for scale estimation of monocular SfM.

Acknowledgements. This research is supported by the Hori Sciences & Arts Foundation, the New Energy and Industrial Technology Development Organization (NEDO) and JSPS KAKENHI Grant Number 18K18071.

References

1. Agarwal, S., Snavely, N., Simon, I., Seitz, S.M., Szeliski, R.: Building Rome in a day. In: International Conference on Computer Vision (ICCV), pp. 72–79 (2009)
2. Bay, H., Tuytelaars, T., Van Gool, L.: SURF: speeded up robust features. In: Leonardis, A., Bischof, H., Pinz, A. (eds.) ECCV 2006. LNCS, vol. 3951, pp. 404–417. Springer, Heidelberg (2006). https://doi.org/10.1007/11744023_32
3. Bertozzi, M., Broggi, A., Caraffi, C., Rose, M.D., Felisa, M., Vezzoni, G.: Pedestrian detection by means of far-infrared stereo vision. Comput. Vis. Image Underst. **106**(2), 194–204 (2007)
4. Clipp, B., Kim, J.H., Frahm, J.M., Pollefeys, M., Hartley, R.: Robust 6DOF motion estimation for non-overlapping, multi-camera systems. In: IEEE Workshop on Applications of Computer Vision (WACV) (2008)
5. Davison, A.J., Reid, I.D., Molton, N.D., Stasse, O.: MonoSLAM: real-time single camera SLAM. Trans. Pattern Anal. Mach. Intell. (TPAMI) **29**(6), 1052–1067 (2007)
6. DeTone, D., Malisiewicz, T., Rabinovich, A.: Toward geometric deep SLAM. arXiv preprint arXiv:1707.07410 (2017)
7. Furukawa, Y., Ponce, J.: Accurate, dense, and robust multi-view stereopsis. Trans. Pattern Anal. Mach. Intell. (TPAMI) **32**(8), 1362–1376 (2010)
8. Ham, Y., Golparvar-Fard, M.: An automated vision-based method for rapid 3D energy performance modeling of existing buildings using thermal and digital imagery. Adv. Eng. Inform. **27**(3), 395–409 (2013)
9. Han, X., Leung, T., Jia, Y., Sukthankar, R., Berg, A.C.: MatchNet: unifying feature and metric learning for patch-based matching. In: Conference on Computer Vision and Pattern Recognition (CVPR), pp. 3279–3286 (2015)
10. Hartley, R.I., Zisserman, A.: Multiple View Geometry in Computer Vision, 2nd edn. Cambridge University Press, Cambridge (2004). ISBN 0521540518
11. Iwaszczuk, D., Stilla, U.: Camera pose refinement by matching uncertain 3D building models with thermal infrared image sequences for high quality texture extraction. ISPRS J. Photogramm. Remote Sens. **132**, 33–47 (2017)

12. Jancosek, M., Pajdla, T.: Multi-view reconstruction preserving weakly-supported surfaces. In: Conference on Computer Vision and Pattern Recognition (CVPR), pp. 3121–3128 (2011)
13. Kitt, B.M., Rehder, J., Chambers, A.D., Schonbein, M., Lategahn, H., Singh, S.: Monocular visual odometry using a planar road model to solve scale ambiguity. In: European Conference on Mobile Robots (2011)
14. Klein, G., Murray, D.: Parallel tracking and mapping for small AR workspaces. In: International Symposium on Mixed and Augmented Reality (ISMAR), pp. 225–234 (2007)
15. Lowe, D.G.: Distinctive image features from scale-invariant keypoints. Int. J. Comput. Vis. (IJCV) **60**(2), 91–110 (2004)
16. Müller, A.O., Kroll, A.: Generating high fidelity 3-D thermograms with a handheld real-time thermal imaging system. IEEE Sens. J. **17**(3), 774–783 (2017)
17. Newcombe, R.A., et al.: KinectFusion: real-time dense surface mapping and tracking. In: International Symposium on Mixed and Augmented Reality (ISMAR), pp. 127–136 (2011)
18. Nistér, D.: An efficient solution to the five-point relative pose problem. IEEE Trans. Pattern Anal. Mach. Intell. **26**(6), 756–770 (2004)
19. Nützi, G., Weiss, S., Scaramuzza, D., Siegwart, R.: Fusion of IMU and vision for absolute scale estimation in monocular SLAM. J. Intell. Robot. Syst. **61**(1), 287–299 (2011)
20. Oreifej, O., Cramer, J., Zakhor, A.: Automatic generation of 3D thermal maps of building interiors. ASHRAE Trans. **120**, C1 (2014)
21. Phuc Truong, T., Yamaguchi, M., Mori, S., Nozick, V., Saito, H.: Registration of RGB and thermal point clouds generated by structure from motion. In: International Conference on Computer Vision Workshop (ICCVW) (2017)
22. Rublee, E., Rabaud, V., Konolige, K., Bradski, G.: ORB: an efficient alternative to SIFT or SURF. In: International Conference on Computer Vision (ICCV), pp. 2564–2571 (2011)
23. Scaramuzza, D., Fraundorfer, F., Pollefeys, M., Siegwart, R.: Absolute scale in structure from motion from a single vehicle mounted camera by exploiting non-holonomic constraints. In: International Conference on Computer Vision (ICCV), pp. 1413–1419 (2009)
24. Schönberger, J.L., Frahm, J.M.: Structure-from-motion revisited. In: Conference on Computer Vision and Pattern Recognition (CVPR), pp. 4104–4113 (2016)
25. Schönberger, J.L., Zheng, E., Frahm, J.-M., Pollefeys, M.: Pixelwise view selection for unstructured multi-view stereo. In: Leibe, B., Matas, J., Sebe, N., Welling, M. (eds.) ECCV 2016. LNCS, vol. 9907, pp. 501–518. Springer, Cham (2016). https://doi.org/10.1007/978-3-319-46487-9_31
26. Stewénius, H., Engels, C., Nistér, D.: Recent developments on direct relative orientation. ISPRS J. Photogramm. Remote Sens. **60**, 284–294 (2006)
27. Thiele, S.T., Varley, N., James, M.R.: Thermal photogrammetric imaging: a new technique for monitoring dome eruptions. J. Volcanol. Geotherm. Res. **337**(Suppl. C), 140–145 (2017)
28. Triggs, B., McLauchlan, P.F., Hartley, R.I., Fitzgibbon, A.W.: Bundle adjustment—a modern synthesis. In: Triggs, B., Zisserman, A., Szeliski, R. (eds.) IWVA 1999. LNCS, vol. 1883, pp. 298–372. Springer, Heidelberg (2000). https://doi.org/10.1007/3-540-44480-7_21
29. Vidas, S., Moghadam, P., Bosse, M.: 3D thermal mapping of building interiors using an RGB-D and thermal camera. In: International Conference on Robotics and Automation (ICRA), pp. 2311–2318 (2013)

30. Weinmann, M., Leitloff, J., Hoegner, L., Jutzi, B., Stilla, U., Hinz, S.: Thermal 3D mapping for object detection in dynamic scenes. ISPRS Ann. Photogramm. Remote. Sens. Spat. Inf. Sci. **2**(1), 53 (2014)
31. Zagoruyko, S., Komodakis, N.: Learning to compare image patches via convolutional neural networks. In: Conference on Computer Vision and Pattern Recognition (CVPR), pp. 4353–4361 (2015)
32. Zhang, Z.: A flexible new technique for camera calibration. IEEE Trans. Pattern Anal. Mach. Intell. (TPAMI) **22**, 1330–1334 (2000)

Geometry Meets Semantics
for Semi-supervised Monocular Depth
Estimation

Pierluigi Zama Ramirez$^{(\boxtimes)}$, Matteo Poggi, Fabio Tosi, Stefano Mattoccia,
and Luigi Di Stefano

University of Bologna, Viale del Risorgimento 2, Bologna, Italy
{pierluigi.zama,m.poggi,fabio.tosi5}@unibo.it

Abstract. Depth estimation from a single image represents a very excit-
ing challenge in computer vision. While other image-based depth sensing techniques leverage on the geometry between different viewpoints
(*e.g.*, stereo or structure from motion), the lack of these cues within
a single image renders ill-posed the monocular depth estimation task.
For inference, state-of-the-art encoder-decoder architectures for monocular depth estimation rely on effective feature representations learned
at training time. For unsupervised training of these models, geometry
has been effectively exploited by suitable images warping losses computed from views acquired by a stereo rig or a moving camera. In this
paper, we make a further step forward showing that learning semantic
information from images enables to improve effectively monocular depth
estimation as well. In particular, by leveraging on semantically labeled
images together with unsupervised signals gained by geometry through
an image warping loss, we propose a deep learning approach aimed at
joint semantic segmentation and depth estimation. Our overall learning
framework is semi-supervised, as we deploy groundtruth data only in
the semantic domain. At training time, our network learns a common
feature representation for both tasks and a novel cross-task loss function is proposed. The experimental findings show how, jointly tackling
depth prediction and semantic segmentation, allows to improve depth
estimation accuracy. In particular, on the KITTI dataset our network
outperforms state-of-the-art methods for monocular depth estimation.

1 Introduction

Depth sensing has always played an important role in computer vision because
of the increased reliability brought in by availability of 3D data in several key
tasks. In this context, dense depth estimation from images compares favorably
to active sensors, such as Time-of-Flight cameras or Lidars, due to the latter
either featuring short acquisition ranges or being cumbersome and much more
expensive. Although traditional image-based approaches rely on multiple acquisitions from different viewpoints, like in binocular or multi-view stereo, depth

© Springer Nature Switzerland AG 2019
C. V. Jawahar et al. (Eds.): ACCV 2018, LNCS 11363, pp. 298–313, 2019.
https://doi.org/10.1007/978-3-030-20893-6_19

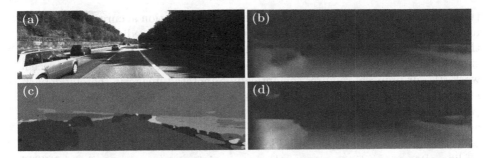

Fig. 1. Joint depth from mono and semantic segmentation. (a) Input image, (b) depth map by state-of-the-art method [1], (c) semantic and (d) depth maps obtained by our network.

estimation from a single image is receiving ever-increasing attention due to its unparalleled potential for seamless, cheap and widespread deployment. Recently proposed supervised learning frameworks based on Convolutional Neural Networks (CNNs) have achieved excellent results on this task, though they require massive amounts of training images labeled with per pixel groundtruth depth measurements. Obtaining these labels is particularly challenging and costly as it relies on expensive active sensors, such as high-end Lidars, which typically provide sparse and noisy measurements requiring further automatic or manual processing [2,3]. To address these issues, multiple acquisitions by a stereo rig [1] or a single moving camera [4] may be used to obtain supervision signals by warping different views according to the estimated depth and measuring the associated image re-projection error.

As for the depth-from-mono task, geometry cues are required at training time only. For inference, the depth estimation network is mainly driven by the learned global image context. Evidence of this can be gathered by running a monocular depth estimator, trained in either supervised or unsupervised manner, on imagery dealing with slightly different environments and observing how it may succeed in yielding reasonable results. These considerations suggest that the feature representation learned to predict depth from a single image is quite tightly linked to the *semantic* content of the scene, thus it leads us to conjecture that guiding the network through explicit knowledge about scene semantics may improve effectiveness in the depth-from-mono task. Moreover, the very recent work by Zamir, et al. [5], supports the argument that learning features from multiple tasks is beneficial to performance as there exist relevant dependencies between visual tasks. Although [5] is based on fully-supervised learning, we believe that the correlation between semantic segmentation and depth estimation can be exploited also within a semi-supervised learning framework, *i.e.* casting one of the two tasks in unsupervised manner.

Thus, in this paper, we propose to train a CNN architecture to perform both semantic segmentation and depth estimation from a single image. By optimizing our model jointly on the two tasks, we enable it to learn a more effective feature representation which yields improved depth estimation accuracy. We rely on unsupervised image re-projection loss [1] to pursue depth prediction whilst we let the network learn semantic information from the observed scene by supervision signals from pixel-level groundtruth semantic maps. Thus, with respect to recent work [1], our proposal requires semantically annotated imagery, thereby departing from a totally unsupervised towards a semi-supervised learning paradigm (*i.e.* unsupervised for depth and supervised for semantics). Yet, though manual annotation of per-pixel semantic labels is tedious, it is much less prohibitive than collecting groundtruth depths. Besides, while the former task may be performed off-line after acquisition, as recently proposed for some images of the KITTI dataset [6], one may very unlikely obtain depth labels out of already collected frames.

To the best of our knowledge, this paper is the first to propose integration of unsupervised monocular depth estimation with supervised semantic segmentation. By applying this novel paradigm, we improve a state-of-the-art encoder-decoder depth estimation architecture [1] according to two main contributions:

- we propose to introduce an additional decoder stream based on the same features as those deployed for depth estimation and trained for semantic segmentation; thereby, the overall architecture is trained to optimize both tasks jointly.
- we propose a novel loss term, the *cross-domain discontinuity* loss $\mathcal{L}_{cdd}$, aimed at enforcing spatial proximity between depth discontinuities and semantic contours.

Experimental results on the KITTI dataset prove that tackling the two tasks jointly does improve monocular depth estimation. For example, Fig. 1 suggests how recognizing objects like cars (c) can significantly ameliorate depth estimation (d) with respect to a depth-from-mono approach lacking any awareness about scene semantics (b). It is also worth highlighting that, unlike all previous unsupervised frameworks in this field, our proposal delivers not only the depth map (Fig. 1(d)) but also the semantic segmentation of the input image (Fig. 1, (c)) by an end-to-end training process.

2   Related Work

We review here the literature dealing with unsupervised monocular depth estimation and semantic segmentation, both relevant to our work.

Unsupervised Monocular Depth. Single view depth estimation [7–10] gained much more popularity in the last years thanks to the increasing availability of benchmarks [11,12]. Moreover, casting depth estimation as an image reconstruction task represents a very attractive way to overcome the need for expansive, groundtruth labels by using a large amount of unsupervised imagery. The work by Garg *et al.*[13] represents the first, pivotal step in this direction, proposing a network for monocular depth estimation by deploying, at training time, view reconstruction loss together with actual stereo pairs as supervision. Then, Godard et al.[1] introduced bilinear warping [14] alongside with more robust reconstruction losses, thereby achieving state-of-the-art performance for monocular depth estimation. This approach was extended to embedded systems [15], using a virtual trinocular setup at training time [16] or a GAN framework [17], Kuznietsov et al.[18] trained a network in a semi-supervised manner, by merging the unsupervised image reconstruction error together with the contribution from sparse depth groundtruth labels. While the above mentioned techniques require rectified stereo pairs at training time, Zhou et al.[4] proposed to train a network to infer depth from video sequences. This network computes a reconstruction loss between subsequent frames and, at the same time, predicts the relative poses between adjacent frames. Therefore, this method enables a fully-monocular setup whereby stereo pairs are no longer required for training. However, this strategy comes to a price in performance [4], delivering less accurate depth estimations compared to [1]. More recent works aimed at improving the single camera supervision approach because of its easiness of use, introducing 3D point-cloud alignment [19], differentiable visual odometry [20], joint optical flow estimation [21], or combining both stereo and video sequences supervision [20]. Nevertheless, none of them actually outperforms the synergy of stereo supervision and network model deployed by Godard et al. [1]. For this reason, in this paper we follow the guidelines of [1], currently the undisputed state-of-the-art for unsupervised monocular depth estimation.

Semantic Segmentation. While most early proposals relied on hand-crafted features and classifiers like Random Forests [22] or Support Vector Machines [23], nowadays pixel-level semantic segmentation approaches mainly exploit fully convolutional neural networks [24]. Compared to previous methods, the key advantage of the present-day strategy concerns the ability to *automatically* learn a better feature representation. Architectures for semantic segmentation focus on exploitation of contextual information and can be divided into five main groups. In the first, we find multi-scale prediction models [25–28], whereby the same architecture takes inputs at different scales so to extract features at different contextual levels. The second group consists of encoder-decoder architectures. The encoder is in charge of extracting low-resolution features from high-resolution inputs while the decoder should be able to recover fine object details from the feature representation so as to yield a high-resolution output map [24, 29–31]. The third group accounts for models which encode long range context information exploiting Conditional Random Fields either as a post processing module [27] or as an integral part of the network [32]. The fourth group includes models relying on spatial pyramid pooling to extract context information at different levels [27, 27, 33]. Finally, the fifth group deals with models deploying atrous-convolutions rather than the standard convolution operator to extract higher resolution features while keeping a large receptive field to capture long-range information [34, 35]. Our learning framework deploys an encoder-decoder architecture to fit with the monocular depth model in [1]. Thus, our semantic segmentation network may be thought of as belonging to the second group.

There exist also several works that, akin our paper, pursue joint estimation of depth and semantics from a single image. Ladicky et al. [36] combine depth regression with semantic classification deploying a bag-of-visual-words model and a boosting algorithm. Mousavian et al. [37] deploy a multi-scale CNN to estimate depth and used within a CRF to obtain semantic segmentation. Wang et al. [38] use local and global CNNs to extract pixels and regions potential which are fed to a CRF. More recent works, such as [39], demonstrate that jointly performing multiple task with adequate weighting of each task can be exploited to achieve better results. However, all these methods require groundtruth labels for both depth and semantics and are trained through multiple stages, whereas we propose to boost self-supervised depth estimation with easier to obtain semantic supervision only.

3   Proposed Method

In this section, we present our proposal for joint semantic segmentation and depth estimation from a single image. We first explain the main intuitions behind our work, then we describe the network architecture and the loss functions deployed in our deep learning framework.

Estimating the distance of objects from a camera through a single acquisition is an ill-posed problem. While other techniques can effectively measure depth based on features extracted from different view points (*e.g.*, binocular stereo allows for triangulating depth from point matches between two synchronized frames), monocular systems cannot rely on geometry constraints to infer distance unambiguously. Despite this lack of information, modern deep learning monocular frameworks achieved astounding results by learning effective feature representations from the observed environment. Common to latest work in this field [1,4,8,40] is the design of deep encoder-decoder architectures, with a first contractive portion progressively decimating image dimensions to reduce the computational load and increase the receptive field, followed by an expanding portion which restores the original input resolution. In particular, the encoding layers learn a high level feature representation crucial to infer depth. Although it is hard to tell what kind of information the network is actually learning at training time, we argue semantic to play an important role. Recent works like [1,4] somehow support this intuition. Indeed, although the authors trained and evaluated their depth estimators on the KITTI dataset [3], a preliminary training on CityScapes [41] turned out beneficial to achieve the best accuracy with both frameworks, despite the very different camera setup between the two datasets. Common to the datasets is, in fact, the kind of sensed environment and, thus, the overall semantics of the scenes under perception. This observation represents the main rationale underpinning our proposal. By explicitly training the network to learn the semantic context of the sensed environment we shall expect to enrich the feature representation resulting from the encoding module and thus

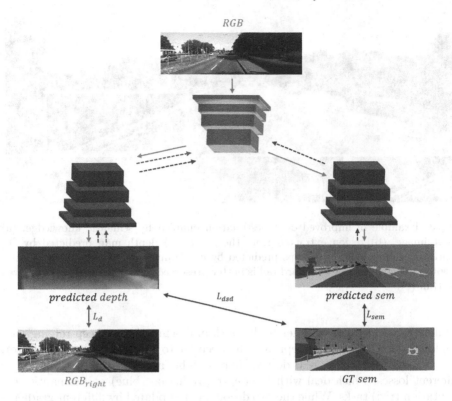

Fig. 2. Schematic representations of the proposed network architecture and semi-supervised learning framework. A single encoder (green) is shared between a depth (blue) and a semantic (red) decoder. The depth decoder is optimized to minimize $\mathcal{L}_d$ and $\mathcal{L}_{cdd}$, the semantic decoder to minimize $\mathcal{L}_s$. (Color figure online)

obtain a more accurate depth estimation. This may be realized by a deep model in which a single encoder is shared between two decoders in charge of providing, respectively, a depth map and a semantic segmentation map. Accordingly, minimization of the errors with respect to pixel-level semantic labels provides gradients that flow back into the encoder at training time, thereby learning a shared feature representation aware of both depth prediction as well as scene semantics. According to our claim, this should turn out conducive to better depth prediction.

Inspired by successful attempts to predict depth from a single image, we design a suitable encoder-decoder architecture for joint depth estimation and semantic segmentation. The encoder is in charge of learning a rich feature representation by increasing the receptive field of the network while reducing the input dimension and computational overhead. Popular encoders for this task are VGG [42] and ResNet50 [43]. The decoder restores the original input resolution by means of up-sampling operators followed by 3×3 convolutions linked by means of skip connections with the encoder at the corresponding resolution.

Fig. 3. Example of improved depth estimation enabled by semantic knowledge. (a) input image, (b) region extracted from the scene, (c) depth map predicted by [1], depth (d) and semantic (e) maps predicted by our framework. We can clearly notice how the the structure of the guard rail is better preserved by our method (e) compared to [1] in (c).

As illustrated in Fig. 2, to infer both depth and semantics we keep relying on a single encoder (green) and replicate the decoder to realize a second estimator. The two decoders (blue, red) do not share weights and are trained to minimize different losses, which deal with the depth prediction (blue) and semantic segmentation (red) tasks. While the two decoders are updated by different gradients flows, the shared encoder (green) is updated according to both flows, thereby learning a representation optimized jointly for the two tasks. We validate our approach by extending the architecture proposed by Godard *et al.*[1] for monocular depth estimation: the encoder produces two inverse depth (i.e., disparity) maps by processing the left image of a stereo pair. Then, the right image is used to obtain supervision signals by warping the left image according to the estimated disparities, as explained in the following section.

Figure 3 shows how the shared representation used to jointly tackle both tasks enables to reconstruct better shapes when estimating depth (e) thanks to the semantic context (d) learned by the network compared to standalone learning of depth (c) as in [1].

3.1 Loss Functions

To train the proposed architecture, we rely on the following multi-task loss function

$$\mathcal{L}_{tot} = \alpha_d \mathcal{L}_d + \alpha_s \mathcal{L}_s + \alpha_{cdd} \mathcal{L}_{cdd} \tag{1}$$

which consists in the weighted sum of three terms, namely the *depth* ($\mathcal{L}_d$), *semantic* ($\mathcal{L}_s$) and *cross-domain discontinuity* ($\mathcal{L}_{cdd}$) terms. As shown in Fig. 2, each term back-propagates gradients through a different decoder: in particular, $\mathcal{L}_d$ and $\mathcal{L}_{cdd}$ through the depth (blue) decoder whilst $\mathcal{L}_s$ through the semantic (red) decoder. All gradients then converge so to flow back into the shared (green) encoder.

Depth Term. The depth term, $\mathcal{L}_d$, in our multi-task loss is computed according to the unsupervised training paradigm proposed by Godard *et al.* [1]:

$$\mathcal{L}_d = \beta_{ap}(\mathcal{L}_{ap}^l + \mathcal{L}_{ap}^r) + \beta_{ds}(\mathcal{L}_{ds}^l + \mathcal{L}_{ds}^r) + \beta_{lr}(\mathcal{L}_{lr}^l + \mathcal{L}_{lr}^r) \qquad (2)$$

where the loss consists in the weighted sum of three terms, namely the *appearance*, *disparity smoothness* and *left-right consistency* terms. The first term measures the image re-projection error by means of the SSIM [44] and L1 difference between the original and warped images, I and $\tilde{I}$:

$$\mathcal{L}_{ap}^l = \frac{1}{N} \sum_{i,j} \gamma \frac{1 - SSIM(I_{i,j}^l, \tilde{I}_{i,j}^l)}{2} + (1 - \gamma)\|(I_{i,j}^l - \tilde{I}_{i,j}^l)\| \qquad (3)$$

The smoothness term penalizes large disparity differences between neighboring pixels along the x and y directions unless these occur in presence of strong intensity gradients in the reference image I

$$\mathcal{L}_{ds}^l = \frac{1}{N} \sum_{i,j} |\delta_x d_{i,j}^l| e^{-\|\delta_x I_{i,j}^l\|} + |\delta_y d_{i,j}^l| e^{-\|\delta_y I_{ij}^l\|} \qquad (4)$$

Finally, the left-right consistency enforces coherence between the predicted disparity maps, d^l and d^r, for left and right images:

$$\mathcal{L}_{lr}^l = \frac{1}{N} \sum_{i,j} |d_{i,j}^l - d_{i,j+d_{i,j}^l}^r| \qquad (5)$$

As proposed in [1], in our learning framework $\mathcal{L}_d$ is computed at four different scales.

Semantic Term. The semantic term $\mathcal{L}_s$ within our total loss is given by the standard cross-entropy between the predicted and groundtruth pixel-wise semantic labels:

$$\mathcal{L}_s = \mathcal{C}(p_t, \overline{p}_t) = H(p_t, \overline{p}_t) + KL(p_t, \overline{p}_t) \qquad (6)$$

where H denotes the entropy and KL the $KL-$divergence. The semantic term, $\mathcal{L}_s$, is computed at full resolution only.

Cross-Domain Discontinuity Term. We also introduce a novel cross-task loss term aimed at enforcing an explicit link between the two learning tasks by leveraging on the groundtruth pixel-wise semantic labels to improve depth prediction. We found that the most effective manner to realize this consists in deploying the observation that depth discontinuities are likely to co-occur with semantic boundaries. Accordingly, we have designed the following *cross-domain discontinuity*, $\mathcal{L}_{cdd}$, term:

$$\mathcal{L}_{cdd} = \frac{1}{N}\sum_{i,j} sgn(|\delta_x sem_{i,j}^l|)e^{-||\frac{\delta_x d_{i,j}^l}{d_{i,j}^l}||} + sgn(|\delta_y sem_{i,j}^l|)e^{-||\frac{\delta_y d_{i,j}^l}{d_{i,j}^l}||} \quad (7)$$

where sem denotes the groundtruth semantic map and d the predicted disparity map. Differently from the smoothness term $\mathcal{L}_{ds}^l$ in the disparity domain, the novel $\mathcal{L}_{cdd}$ term detects discontinuities between semantic labels encoded by the sign of the absolute value of the gradients in the semantic map. The idea behind this loss is that there should be a gradient peak between adjacent pixels belonging to different classes. Nevertheless, we do not care about its magnitude since the numeric labels do not have any mathematical meaning.

4   Experimental Results

In this section, we compare the performance of our semi-supervised joint depth estimation and semantic segmentation paradigm with respect to the proposal by Godard et al. [1], which represents nowadays the undisputed state-of-the-art for unsupervised monocular depth estimation. As discussed in Sect. 3, our method as well as the baseline used in our experiments, *i.e.* [1], require rectified stereo pairs at training time. Suitable datasets for this purpose are thus CityScapes [41] and KITTI [45], which provide a large number of training samples, *i.e.* about 23k and 29k rectified stereo pairs respectively. However, our method requires also pixel-wise groundtruth semantic labels at training time, which limits the actual amount of training samples available for our experiments. In particular, CityScapes includes about 3k finely annotated images, while the KITTI 2015 benchmark recently made available pixel-wise semantic groundtruths for about 200 images [6]. Therefore, to carry out a fair evaluation of the actual contribution provided by semantic information in the depth-from-mono task to the baseline fully unsupervised approach, we trained both methods based on the reduced datasets featuring stereo pairs alongside with semantically annotated left frames.

4.1   Implementation Details

Our proposal has been implemented in Tensorflow[1], starting from the source code made available by the authors of [1]. We adhere to the original training protocol by Godard et al., scheduling 50 epochs on the CityScapes dataset and 50 further on the KITTI 2015 images. For quantitative evaluation, we split the KITTI 2015 dataset into train and test sets, providing more details in the next section. We train on 256×512 images using a batch dimension of 2, we set the previously introduced hyper-parameters as follows: $\alpha_d = 1$, $\alpha_s = 0.1$, $\alpha_{cdd} = 0.1$,

---

[1] Source code and trained models are available at https://github.com/CVLAB-Unibo/Semantic-Mono-Depth.

$\beta_{ap} = 1$, $\beta_{lr} = 1$, $\beta_{ds} = \frac{1}{r}$ (being r the down-sampling factor at that resolution) and $\gamma = 0.85$. Models are trained using Adam optimizer [46], with $\beta_1 = 0.9$, $\beta_1 = 0.999$ and $\epsilon = 10^{-8}$. The initial learning rate is set to 10^{-4}, halved after 30 and 40 epochs. We perform data augmentation on input RGB images, in particular random gamma, brightness and color shifts sampled within the ranges [0.8,1.2] for gamma, [0.5,2.0] for brightness, and [0.8,1.2] for each color channel separately. Moreover we flip images horizontally with a probability of 50%. If the flip occurs, the right image in the stereo pair becomes the new reference image and we do not provide supervision signals from semantics (as right semantic maps are not available in the datasets). We implemented our network with both VGG and ResNet50 encoders, as in [1]. The semantic decoder adds about 20.5M parameters, resulting in nearly 50 and 79 million parameters for the two models (31 and 59, respectively, for [1]).

4.2 Monocular Depth Estimation: Evaluation on KITTI 2015

We quantitatively assess the effectiveness of our proposal on the KITTI 2015 training dataset for stereo [3]. It provides 200 synchronized pairs of images together with groundtruth disparity and semantic maps [6]. As already mentioned, to carry out a fair comparison between our approach and [1], we can use only these samples and thus the numerical results reported in our paper cannot be compared directly with those in [1]. Then, we randomly split the 200 pairs from KITTI into 160 training samples and 40 samples used only for evaluation[2]. We measure the accuracy of the predicted depth maps after training for 50 epochs on CityScapes and then fine-tuning for 50 more epochs on the samples selected from KITTI.

Table 1 reports quantitative results using VGG or ResNet50 as backbone encoder. Each model, one per row in the table, is trained with four different strategies:

- $\mathcal{L}_d$ uses only the depth term as loss (*i.e.*, equivalently to the baseline approach by Godard *et al.* [1]).
- $\mathcal{L}_d + \mathcal{L}_s$ adds the semantic term to the depth term.
- $\mathcal{L}_d + \mathcal{L}_s + \mathcal{L}_{cdd}$ minimizes our proposed total loss function (Eq. 1).
- $\mathcal{L}_d + \mathcal{L}_{cdd}$ minimizes only the losses dealing with the depth decoder.

The table provides results yielded by the four considered networks according to standard performance evaluation metrics [1] computed between estimated depth d and groundtruth D.

This ablation highlights how introducing the second decoder trained to infer semantic segmentation maps, significantly improves depth prediction according

---

[2] The testing samples, belonging to the KITTI 2015 dataset, are: 000001, 000003, 000004, 000019, 000032, 000033, 000035, 000038, 000039, 000042, 000048, 000064, 000067, 000072, 000087, 000089, 000093, 000095, 000105, 000106, 000111, 000116, 000119, 000123, 000125, 000127, 000128, 000129, 000134, 000138, 000150, 000160, 000161, 000167, 000174, 000175, 000178, 000184, 000185 and 000193.

Table 1. Ablation experiments on KITTI 2015 evaluation split, using different configurations of losses, encoders and post-processing (pp). Best setup highlighted in bold for each configuration.

	Encoder	pp	Abs Rel	Sq Rel	RMSE	RMSE log	δ_1	δ_2	δ_3
				Lower is better			Higher is better		
$\mathcal{L}_d$ [1]	VGG		0.160	2.707	7.220	0.239	0.837	0.928	0.966
$\mathcal{L}_d+\mathcal{L}_s$	VGG		0.155	2.511	6.968	**0.234**	0.841	**0.931**	**0.968**
$\mathcal{L}_d+\mathcal{L}_s+\mathcal{L}_{cdd}$	VGG		**0.154**	**2.453**	**6.949**	0.235	**0.844**	**0.931**	0.967
$\mathcal{L}_d+\mathcal{L}_{cdd}$	VGG		0.161	2.758	7.128	0.240	0.841	0.928	0.964
$\mathcal{L}_d$ [1]	VGG	✓	0.149	2.203	6.582	0.223	0.844	0.936	0.972
$\mathcal{L}_d+\mathcal{L}_s$	VGG	✓	0.147	2.229	6.583	0.223	0.847	**0.938**	0.972
$\mathcal{L}_d+\mathcal{L}_s+\mathcal{L}_{cdd}$	VGG	✓	**0.145**	**2.040**	**6.362**	**0.221**	**0.849**	**0.938**	0.971
$\mathcal{L}_d+\mathcal{L}_{cdd}$	VGG	✓	0.150	2.278	6.539	0.225	0.843	0.934	0.970
$\mathcal{L}_d$ [1]	ResNet		0.159	2.411	6.822	0.239	0.830	0.930	0.967
$\mathcal{L}_d+\mathcal{L}_s$	ResNet		0.152	2.385	6.775	0.231	0.843	0.934	0.970
$\mathcal{L}_d+\mathcal{L}_s+\mathcal{L}_{cdd}$	ResNet		**0.143**	**2.161**	**6.526**	**0.222**	**0.850**	**0.939**	**0.972**
$\mathcal{L}_d+\mathcal{L}_{cdd}$	ResNet		0.155	2.282	6.658	0.232	0.840	0.932	0.968
$\mathcal{L}_d$ [1]	ResNet	✓	0.148	2.104	6.439	0.224	0.839	0.936	0.972
$\mathcal{L}_d+\mathcal{L}_s$	ResNet	✓	0.144	2.050	6.351	0.220	0.849	0.938	0.972
$\mathcal{L}_d+\mathcal{L}_s+\mathcal{L}_{cdd}$	ResNet	✓	**0.136**	**1.872**	**6.127**	**0.210**	**0.854**	**0.945**	**0.976**
$\mathcal{L}_d+\mathcal{L}_{cdd}$	ResNet	✓	0.144	1.973	6.199	0.217	0.849	0.940	0.975

to all performance metrics for both type of encoder. Moreover, adding the cross-domain discontinuity term, $\mathcal{L}_{cdd}$, leads in most cases to further improvements. On the other hand, minimizing $\mathcal{L}_d$ and $\mathcal{L}_{cdd}$ alone leads to inferior performance compared to the baseline method. We obtain the best configuration according to all metrics using ResNet50 when both $\mathcal{L}_s$ and $\mathcal{L}_{cdd}$ are minimized alongside with the depth term $\mathcal{L}_d$.

Moreover, we also evaluated the output obtained by all models after performing the post-processing step proposed by [1], that consists in forwarding both the input image I and its horizontally flipped counterpart $\hat{I}$. This produces two depth maps d_I and $d_{\hat{I}}$, the latter is flipped back obtaining $\hat{d}_{\hat{I}}$ and averaged with the former, in order to reduce artifacts near occlusions. We can notice that the previous trend is confirmed. In particular, the full loss $\mathcal{L}_d + \mathcal{L}_s + \mathcal{L}_{cdd}$ leads to the best result on most scores. Furthermore, including the post-processing step allows the VGG model trained with our full loss to outperform the baseline ResNet50 architecture supervised by traditional depth losses only. This fact can be noticed in Table 1 comparing row 7 with row 13, observing that the former leads to better results except for δ_3 metric.

To further prove the effectiveness of our proposed method we compare it with other self-supervised approach as [4,19,21]. Thus, we have ran experiments with the source code available from [4,19,21] using the same testing data as for [1] and our method. Table 2 shows the outcome of this evaluation. We point out that we used the weights made available by the authors of [4,19,21], trained on a much

Table 2. Comparison with other self supervised method on KITTI 2015 evaluation split. Both [1] and our method use ResNet50 encoder.

	Lower is better				Higher is better		
	Abs Rel	Sq Rel	RMSE	RMSE log	δ_1	δ_2	δ_3
Zhou et al. [4]	0.286	7.009	8.377	0.320	0.691	0.854	0.929
Mahjourian et al. [19]	0.235	2.857	7.202	0.302	0.710	0.866	0.935
Yin et al. [21]	0.236	3.345	7.132	0.279	0.714	0.903	0.950
Godard et al. [1]	0.159	2.411	6.822	0.239	0.830	0.930	0.967
Ours	**0.143**	**2.161**	**6.526**	**0.222**	**0.850**	**0.939**	**0.972**

larger amount of data (i.e., the entire Cityscapes and KITTI sequences, some of them overlapping with the testing split as well) w.r.t. the much lower supervision provided to our network. Despite this fact, monocular supervised works [4,19,21] perform poorly compared to both [1] and our approach, confirming our semi-supervised framework to outperform them as well. We also point out that our test split relies on high-quality groundtruth labels for evaluation, available from KITTI 2015 stereo dataset, while the Eigen split used to validate [4,19,21] provides much worse quality depth measurements, as also argued by the authors of [1].

As our final test we also compare our method with the recent multi-task learning approach by Kendall et al. [39]. Differently from our approach, they jointly learn depth, semantic and instance segmentation in fully supervised manner. They run experiments Tiny Cityscapes, a split obtained by resizing the validation set of Cityscapes to 128 256 resolution. To compare our results to theirs we have taken our ResNet50 model trained on Cityscapes and validated it following the same protocol. Their depth-only model (trained supervised) achieves 0.640 inverse mean depth error, dropping to 0.522 when trained to tackle semantic and instance segmentation as well. Our ResNet50 network (trained unsupervised) starts with 1.705 error for depth-only, dropping to 1.488. Thus, the two approaches achieve 22% and 15 % improvement respectively. We point out that, besides relying on supervised learning for depth, [39] exploits both semantic and instance segmentation, requiring additional manually annotated labels, while we only enforce our cross-domain discontinuity loss.

Figure 4 depicts a qualitative comparison between the depth maps predicted by [1] and our semi-supervised framework. In the figure, from top to bottom, we consider images 000019 and 000095 belonging to our evaluation split. We can observe how explicitly learning the semantics of the scene helps to correct wrong depth estimations, especially on challenging objects. For example, we can notice how depth maps predicted by our frameworks provide better car shapes thanks to the contribution given by the semantic. This fact is particularly evident in correspondence of reflective or transparent surfaces like car windows as reported on image 000095. Moreover, the quality of thin structures like poles is improved as well, as clearly perceivable by looking at frame 000019.

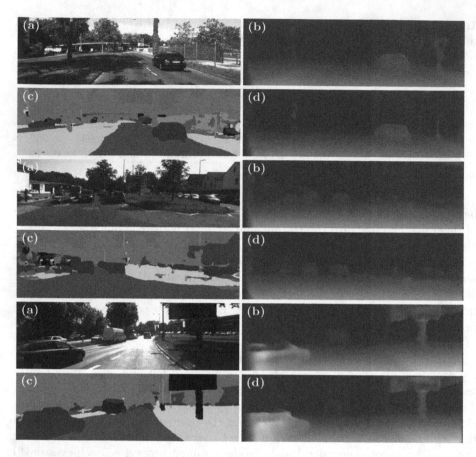

Fig. 4. Qualitative comparison between [1] and our proposal on KITTI 2015 evaluation split [3]. (a) Input image, (b) depth map by [1], (c) and (d) semantic and depth maps by our approach. Both models use Resnet50 as encoder. From top to bottom, results concerning images 000019, 000087 and 000095 belonging to our evaluation split.

4.3   Semantic Segmentation: Evaluation on KITTI 2015

Although our proposal is aimed at ameliorating depth prediction by learning richer features exploiting semantics, our network also delivers a semantic segmentation of the input image. To gather hints about the accuracy of this additional outcome of our network, we evaluated the semantic maps generated on the same KITTI evaluation split defined before. Differently from the monocular depth estimation task, results concerning semantic segmentation are quite far from the state-of-the-art. In particular, we obtain 88.51% and 88.19% per-pixel accuracy, respectively, with models based on VGG and ResNet50. We ascribe this to our architecture - inspired by [1] - being optimized for unsupervised depth prediction, whereas different design choices are often found in networks pursuing semantic segmentation (i.e., atrous convolutions, SPP layers ...). We also found that training the basic encoder-decoder for semantic segmentation only yields to 86.72% and 88.18% per-pixel accuracy with VGG and ResNet50, respectively. Thus, while semantics helps depth prediction inasmuch as to outperform the state-of-the-art within the proposed framework, the converse requires further studies as the observed improvements are indeed quite minor. Therefore, we plan to investigate on how to design a network architecture and associated semi-supervised learning framework whereby the synergy between monocular depth prediction and semantic segmentation may be exploited in order to significantly improve accuracy in both tasks.

5   Conclusion and Future Work

We have proposed a deep learning architecture to improve unsupervised monocular depth estimation by leveraging on semantic information. We have shown how training our architecture end-end to infer semantics and depth jointly enables us to outperform the state-of-the-art approach for unsupervised monocular depth estimation [1]. Our single-encoder/dual-decoder architecture is trained in a semi-supervised manner, *i.e.* using groundtruth labels only for the semantic segmentation task. Despite obtaining groundtruth labels for semantic is tedious and requires accurate and time-consuming manual annotation, it is still more feasible than depth labeling. In fact, this latter task requires expensive active sensors to be used at acquisition time and becomes almost unfeasible offline, on already captured frames. Thus, our method represents an attractive alternative to improve self-supervised training without adding more image samples. Future work will (i) explore single camera sequences as supervision [4,20,21] and (ii) dig into the semantic segmentation side of our framework, to reach top accuracy on this second task as well and to propose a state-of-the-art framework for joint depth and semantic estimation in a semi-supervised manner.

Acknowledgments. We gratefully acknowledge the support of NVIDIA Corporation with the donation of the Titan X GPU used for this research

References

1. Godard, C., Mac Aodha, O., Brostow, G.J.: Unsupervised monocular depth estimation with left-right consistency. In: CVPR (2017)
2. Geiger, A., Lenz, P., Urtasun, R.: Are we ready for autonomous driving? The kitti vision benchmark suite. In: CVPR, pp. 3354–3361. IEEE (2012)
3. Menze, M., Geiger, A.: Object scene flow for autonomous vehicles. In: Conference on Computer Vision and Pattern Recognition (CVPR) (2015)
4. Zhou, T., Brown, M., Snavely, N., Lowe, D.G.: Unsupervised learning of depth and ego-motion from video. In: CVPR, vol. 2, p. 7 (2017)
5. Zamir, A.R., Sax, A., Shen, W., Guibas, L., Malik, J., Savarese, S.: Taskonomy: disentangling task transfer learning. In: Proceedings of the IEEE Conference on Computer Vision and Pattern Recognition, pp. 3712–3722 (2018)

6. Alhaija, H.A., Mustikovela, S.K., Mescheder, L., Geiger, A., Rother, C.: Augmented reality meets deep learning for car instance segmentation in urban scenes. In: BMVC (2017)
7. Liu, F., Shen, C., Lin, G., Reid, I.: Learning depth from single monocular images using deep convolutional neural fields. TPAMI 38, 2024–2039 (2016)
8. Eigen, D., Puhrsch, C., Fergus, R.: Depth map prediction from a single image using a multi-scale deep network. In: Advances in Neural Information Processing Systems, pp. 2366–2374 (2014)
9. Wang, X., Fouhey, D., Gupta, A.: Designing deep networks for surface normal estimation. In: CVPR, pp. 539–547 (2015)
10. Cao, Y., Wu, Z., Shen, C.: Estimating depth from monocular images as classification using deep fully convolutional residual networks. IEEE Trans. Circuits Syst. Video Technol. 28, 3174–3182 (2017)
11. Saxena, A., Sun, M., Ng, A.Y.: Make3D: learning 3D scene structure from a single still image. TPAMI 31, 824–840 (2009)
12. Uhrig, J., Schneider, N., Schneider, L., Franke, U., Brox, T., Geiger, A.: Sparsity invariant CNNs. In: 3DV. (2017)
13. Garg, R., B.G., V.K., Carneiro, G., Reid, I.: Unsupervised CNN for single view depth estimation: geometry to the rescue. In: Leibe, B., Matas, J., Sebe, N., Welling, M. (eds.) ECCV 2016. LNCS, vol. 9912, pp. 740–756. Springer, Cham (2016). https://doi.org/10.1007/978-3-319-46484-8_45
14. Jaderberg, M., Simonyan, K., Zisserman, A., et al.: Spatial transformer networks. In: Advances in Neural Information Processing Systems, pp. 2017–2025 (2015)
15. Poggi, M., Aleotti, F., Tosi, F., Mattoccia, S.: Towards real-time unsupervised monocular depth estimation on CPU. In: IEEE/JRS Conference on Intelligent Robots and Systems (IROS) (2018)
16. Poggi, M., Tosi, F., Mattoccia, S.: Learning monocular depth estimation with unsupervised trinocular assumptions. In: 6th International Conference on 3D Vision (3DV) (2018)
17. Aleotti, F., Tosi, F., Poggi, M., Mattoccia, S.: Generative adversarial networks for unsupervised monocular depth prediction. In: Leal-Taixé, L., Roth, S. (eds.) ECCV 2018. LNCS, vol. 11129, pp. 337–354. Springer, Cham (2019). https://doi.org/10.1007/978-3-030-11009-3_20
18. Kuznietsov, Y., Stuckler, J., Leibe, B.: Semi-supervised deep learning for monocular depth map prediction. In: CVPR (2017)
19. Mahjourian, R., Wicke, M., Angelova, A.: Unsupervised learning of depth and ego-motion from monocular video using 3D geometric constraints. In: The IEEE Conference on Computer Vision and Pattern Recognition (CVPR) (2018)
20. Wang, C., Buenaposada, J.M., Zhu, R., Lucey, S.: Learning depth from monocular videos using direct methods. In: The IEEE Conference on Computer Vision and Pattern Recognition (CVPR) (2018)
21. Yin, Z., Shi, J.: GeoNet: unsupervised learning of dense depth, optical flow and camera pose. In: The IEEE Conference on Computer Vision and Pattern Recognition (CVPR) (2018)
22. Shotton, J., Johnson, M., Cipolla, R.: Semantic texton forests for image categorization and segmentation. In: CVPR, pp. 1–8. IEEE (2008)
23. Fulkerson, B., Vedaldi, A., Soatto, S.: Class segmentation and object localization with superpixel neighborhoods. In: ICCV, pp. 670–677. IEEE (2009)
24. Long, J., Shelhamer, E., Darrell, T.: Fully convolutional networks for semantic segmentation. In: CVPR, pp. 3431–3440 (2015)

25. Eigen, D., Fergus, R.: Predicting depth, surface normals and semantic labels with a common multi-scale convolutional architecture. In: ICCV, pp. 2650–2658 (2015)
26. Chen, L.C., Yang, Y., Wang, J., Xu, W., Yuille, A.L.: Attention to scale: scale-aware semantic image segmentation. In: CVPR, pp. 3640–3649 (2016)
27. Chen, L.C., Papandreou, G., Kokkinos, I., Murphy, K., Yuille, A.L.: DeepLab: semantic image segmentation with deep convolutional nets, atrous convolution, and fully connected CRFs. TPAMI **40**, 834–848 (2018)
28. Liang-Chieh, C., Papandreou, G., Kokkinos, I., Murphy, K., Yuille, A.: Semantic image segmentation with deep convolutional nets and fully connected CRFs. In: ICLR (2015)
29. Badrinarayanan, V., Kendall, A., Cipolla, R.: SegNet: a deep convolutional encoder-decoder architecture for image segmentation. TPAMI **39**, 2481–2495 (2017)
30. Ronneberger, O., Fischer, P., Brox, T.: U-Net: convolutional networks for biomedical image segmentation. In: Navab, N., Hornegger, J., Wells, W.M., Frangi, A.F. (eds.) MICCAI 2015. LNCS, vol. 9351, pp. 234–241. Springer, Cham (2015). https://doi.org/10.1007/978-3-319-24574-4_28
31. Lin, G., Milan, A., Shen, C., Reid, I.: RefineNet: multi-path refinement networks with identity mappings for high-resolution semantic segmentation. In: CVPR (2017)
32. Zheng, S., et al.: Conditional random fields as recurrent neural networks. In: ICCV, pp. 1529–1537 (2015)
33. Zhao, H., Shi, J., Qi, X., Wang, X., Jia, J.: Pyramid scene parsing network. In: CVPR, pp. 2881–2890 (2017)
34. Dai, J., et al.: Deformable convolutional networks. CoRR, abs/1703.06211 1, 3 (2017)
35. Wang, P., et al.: Understanding convolution for semantic segmentation. In: WACV (2018)
36. Ladicky, L., Shi, J., Pollefeys, M.: Pulling things out of perspective. In: CVPR, pp. 89–96 (2014)
37. Mousavian, A., Pirsiavash, H., Košecká, J.: Joint semantic segmentation and depth estimation with deep convolutional networks. In: 3DV, pp. 611–619. IEEE (2016)
38. Wang, P., Shen, X., Lin, Z., Cohen, S., Price, B., Yuille, A.L.: Towards unified depth and semantic prediction from a single image. In: CVPR, pp. 2800–2809 (2015)
39. Kendall, A., Gal, Y., Cipolla, R.: Multi-task learning using uncertainty to weigh losses for scene geometry and semantics (2018)
40. Laina, I., Rupprecht, C., Belagiannis, V., Tombari, F., Navab, N.: Deeper depth prediction with fully convolutional residual networks. In: 3DV, pp. 239–248 (2016)
41. Cordts, M., et al.: The cityscapes dataset for semantic urban scene understanding. In: CVPR, pp. 3213–3223 (2016)
42. Simonyan, K., Zisserman, A.: Very deep convolutional networks for large-scale image recognition (2015)
43. He, K., Zhang, X., Ren, S., Sun, J.: Deep residual learning for image recognition. In: CVPR, pp. 770–778 (2016)
44. Wang, Z., Bovik, A.C., Sheikh, H.R., Simoncelli, E.P.: Image quality assessment: from error visibility to structural similarity. IEEE Trans. Image Process. **13**, 600–612 (2004)
45. Geiger, A., Lenz, P., Stiller, C., Urtasun, R.: Vision meets robotics: the KITTI dataset. Int. J. Robot. Res. (IJRR) **32**, 1231–1237 (2013)
46. Kingma, D., Ba, J.: Adam: a method for stochastic optimization. arXiv preprint arXiv:1412.6980 (2014)

Deep Manifold Alignment for Mid-Grain Sketch Based Image Retrieval

Tu Bui[1]([✉]), Leonardo Ribeiro[2], Moacir Ponti[2], and John Collomosse[1,3]

[1] University of Surrey, Guildford, Surrey GU2 7XH, UK
{t.bui,j.collomosse}@surrey.ac.uk
[2] Universidade de São Paulo, São Carlos, SP 13566-590, Brazil
{leonardo.sampaio.ribeiro,ponti}@usp.br
[3] Creative Intelligence Lab, Adobe Research, San Jose, CA 95110, USA

Abstract. We present an algorithm for visually searching image collections using free-hand sketched queries. Prior sketch based image retrieval (SBIR) algorithms adopt either a category-level or fine-grain (instance-level) definition of cross-domain similarity—returning images that match the sketched object class (category-level SBIR), or a specific instance of that object (fine-grain SBIR). In this paper we take the middle-ground; proposing an SBIR algorithm that returns images sharing both the object category and key visual characteristics of the sketched query without assuming photo-approximate sketches from the user. We describe a deeply learned cross-domain embedding in which 'mid-grain' sketch-image similarity may be measured, reporting on the efficacy of unsupervised and semi-supervised manifold alignment techniques to encourage better intra-category (mid-grain) discrimination within that embedding. We propose a new mid-grain sketch-image dataset (MidGrain65c) and demonstrate not only mid-grain discrimination, but also improved category-level discrimination using our approach.

Keywords: SBIR · Manifold alignment · Visual search

1 Introduction

Free-hand sketch offers an intuitive and convenient query modality for visual search when a photographic sample of the desired content is unavailable. Yet, matching sketches and photographs is challenging; sketches are salient abstractions frequently drawn from canonical viewpoints, caricaturing objects, and introducing non-linear deformations [4,21]. Recently deep neural networks, in particular multi-branch (triplet) networks, have proven effective in learning a mapping across these two domains for sketch based image retrieval (SBIR). Such approaches typically fall into either of two camps according to granularity at which matching is performed: (1) category (object-level) SBIR in which a sketched query of a given object (e.g. a cat) should return images containing that object (e.g. cats) [1–3]; (2) fine-grain (instance-level) search in which a

© Springer Nature Switzerland AG 2019
C. V. Jawahar et al. (Eds.): ACCV 2018, LNCS 11363, pp. 314–329, 2019.
https://doi.org/10.1007/978-3-030-20893-6_20

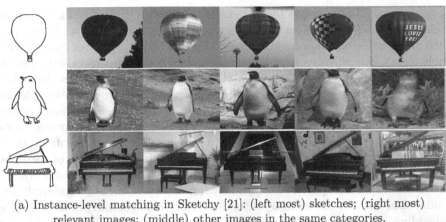

(a) Instance-level matching in Sketchy [21]: (left most) sketches; (right most) relevant images; (middle) other images in the same categories.

(b) Our MidGrain65c dataset.

Fig. 1. Mid-grain matching of sketches to photographs; retrieved images match both object class and exhibit key visual characteristics of the sketch without demanding fine-grain, instance-level matching of a specific sketched object (per [21,28]).

detailed sketch of a specific object (e.g. a shoe) should return only that specific shoe [16,21]. Whilst both bodies of work have made significant advances in cross-domain (sketch-photo) matching, arguably neither provides a model for practical SBIR. Category-level matching is analogous to sketched object classification, suggesting that the need for a sketch could be obviated simply by substituting a coarse-grain label (e.g. text keyword) as query. Conversely, instance-level search requires unrealistic photo-approximate recall of fine-grain object detail within the sketched query—unreasonable due to both the limitations of human visual recall and typical depictive skill of users [4]. Furthermore it is challenging to obtain large quantities of fine-grain annotated training data.

This paper proposes an intermediate level of granularity ('mid-grain') for cross-domain matching, in which the SBIR algorithm recalls images sharing both the object category and key visual characteristics of the sketched query (Fig. 1) but without requiring a precise sketch. For example, a sketch of an object in particular pose configuration returns similar objects in similar poses (e. g. front or side profiles of an elephant); or, a sketched sub-part of an object (e. g. piano keys) prioritizes recall of images dominated by that object part over images of the whole object. Specifically we explore unsupervised and semi-supervised manifold alignment techniques to enhance the ability to perform mid-grain discrimination in a metric space, using a novel pooled sampling to select training examples for a triplet-loss network, using only category level annotation. Refinement of this embedding for mid-grain discrimination is performed iteratively, through intra-category clustering and correspondence (in some experimental configurations, using a small amount of fine-grained annotation) enabling sampling of hard positive/negatives from these clusters to drive refinement of the triplet network. We demonstrate that this process significantly improves not only the mid-grain discrimination, but also the category-level discrimination capability of the resulting embedding. To evaluate the ability of the trained network to perform mid-grain SBIR we collected a mid-grain annotated test set (*MidGrain65c*), and release this as a secondary contribution to our work.

2   Related Work

Early sketch based image retrieval (SBIR) algorithms tackled sketch-image matching as an optimization; fitting the sketch as a deformable model to image content and deriving rankings from the support evidenced for the sketched structure. Scalable approaches to SBIR began to emerge in the late-2000s, adapting gradient feature and dictionary learning approaches (popularised in photographic visual search) to SBIR. Notably, the Bag of Visual Words (BovW) paradigm was extended to SBIR using the Gradient-Field HoG (GF-HoG) [10,11], Structure Tensor [7] and SHoG [6] descriptors all of which encode structure local to sparse key-points sampled from sketched strokes and Canny edge-pixels detected in images. Several BoVW indexing strategies were explored in [1,12] including those fusing additional modalities such as colour, or semantic object labels. Mindfinder [23] used Chamfer matching to match sketched strokes to edge-lets extracted from images under an efficient indexing scheme. Indexing of mid-level sparse features were also explored through HELO [19] and key-shapes [20]. Whilst performance enhancements were achieved e. g. by substituting more perceptually inspired edge detectors for Canny [15] in the preprocessing, recent years have seen more significant advances through the use of deep convolutional neural networks (CNNs) [13] to learn the search embedding. CNNs were initially explored in the context of sketched object classification [29] through Sketch-A-Net; a truncated form of AlexNet [13]. Although such models can serve as feature extractors for SBIR, significant improvements in accuracy can be delivered through use of multi-branch (contrastive- or triplet-loss) networks. Such networks learn a cross-domain embedding by bringing together matching sketch-image (positive) pairs and pushing apart non-matching (negative) pairs within the learned embedding. Fully siamese triplet networks were explored for fine-grain SBIR in [28], and perform well for instance-level retrieval

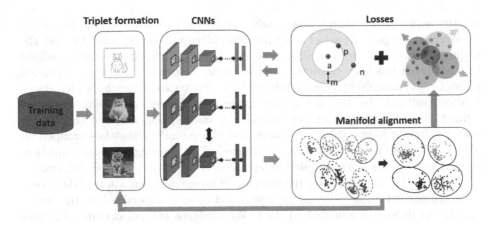

Fig. 2. An illustration of our mid-grain SBIR network.

on a dataset of single object class (e. g. shoes or chairs). Heterogeneous triplet i. e. partial weight sharing networks in which some (or none) of the weights are shared across the sketch (anchor) and image (positive/negative) branches of the triplet network enables independent functions to be learned in order to map the disparate sketch and image domains to a joint embedding for improved accuracy. Quadruplet networks [22] have also recently been explored, as have improved hard sampling strategies for triplet selection and assymetric feature matching [25]. Optimal weight sharing schemes and network architectures were studied extensively for category-level [2,3] and fine-grain [21] on the Flickr15k [11] and Sketchy benchmarks respectively. Under the latter, the test set is formed by presenting image to human participants and inviting them to sketch the content. During retrieval, the only image considered correct is that originally used to derive the sketch (instance-level search) [21]. To the best of our knowledge, no prior work explores the training or evaluation of models given a mid-grain definition of similarity.

3   Deep Representation for Mid-Grain Similarity

We learn a cross-domain embedding for sketch-image matching using a triplet CNN (convnet) adopting a high performing network architecture from the set of variants proposed in [3]. The network chosen is a fully unshared (heterogeneous) triplet network with GoogleNet Inception-v1 backbone, shown to achieve state of the art category-level SBIR performance (53.26% mAP on Flickr15k [11]). Our core contribution is a novel method for selecting exemplar triplets i. e. anchor (query sketch), positive (+) and negative (−) images to form training tuples using a novel pooled sampling approach that yields significant improvement not only in category-level SBIR but uniquely enables also mid-grain discrimination in SBIR ranking (Fig. 2). We first provide an overview of the sampling process, then detail each step in the Subsects. 3.1, 3.2, 3.3 and 3.4.

   Our training methodology is designed for the current scenario where very little instance-level data are available for training SBIR at fine-grain level. The positive and negative sketch-image pairs are therefore, be formed at class-level; however we propose to select only meaningful sketch-image pairs to feed the training network. First, two independently trained embeddings are initialized for the sketch (anchor) and image ($\pm$) branches respectively, using pre-trained (GoogLeNet/ImageNet) weights refined by a few training epochs under classification (softmax) for the sketch and image data. These embeddings form are refined over subsequent training epochs. For each epoch, a set of triplets are sampled from a joint dataset of images and corresponding sketches grouped by object class (see Sect. 4.1 for dataset details). The training set is the union of several smaller sets, each sampled independently per object class as follows.

First, the two manifolds for the sketch and image representation of the object class are aligned using either an unsupervised or semi-supervised (with a small amount of fine-grain annotation) data. We evaluate the performance of three alignment approaches for this purpose. Next, unsupervised clustering is performed over the aligned distributions to characterize the intra-category (mid-grain) variation by pooling similar content. An anchor sketch and positive image are sampled from one resultant pool, used a stochastic sampling technique (data closer to a cluster centre is more likely to be selected). A similar stochastic sampling is applied to choose a negative image from a completely different category that has undergone similar pooling. By successive selection of triplets in this manner and training under a variant of the magnet loss function, the network weights are refined, which then form the embeddings for subsequent alignment, pooling and training iterations. We now explain each of these alignment, pooling and training processes in greater detail.

3.1   Sketch-Image Manifold Alignment

Consider a training set $\mathcal{D}_C = \{X_C, Y_C\}$ for a single object class C compromising N_S sketches $X_C = \{x_1, x_2, ..., x_{N_S}\}$ and N_I images $Y_C = \{y_1, y_2, ..., y_{N_I}\}$ (for simplicity we drop C from now on in all subsequent math notations unless otherwise stated). Supposed a subset of the training data has instance-level labels i. e. correspondence. For simplicity of exposition we assume the correspondence is one-to-one although this need not to be the case (see Subsect. 3.1). Denote this subset $\mathcal{D}' = \{(x_i', y_i')\}_{i=1}^{M} \in \mathcal{D}$ where $M \ll \min(N_S, N_I)$. Denote $\mathcal{T} = \{f, g\}$ the parametrized embedding function that projects $\mathcal{D}$ into a P-dimensional embedding space – $U = f(X; \Theta_S) \in \mathbb{R}^{N_S \times P}$ and $V = g(Y; \Theta_I) \in \mathbb{R}^{N_I \times P}$ ($\mathcal{T}(.)$ is a triplet convnet in this work). We wish to align U with V in a common manifold for cross-domain similarity analysis to be implemented in the next step (Subsect. 3.2). Note that finding a common embedding is also the ultimate objective of $\mathcal{T}(.)$ and our goal is to assist the search for the best embedding through selection of appropriate data (positive/negative pairs) to feed to the network under our subsequent pooled sampling step. We consider three approaches:

Unsupervised Warping with PCA. This naive approach does not require any sketch-image correspondence (i. e. fine-grain annotation). The approach

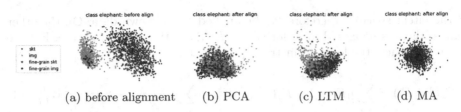

(a) before alignment   (b) PCA   (c) LTM   (d) MA

Fig. 3. Alignment of two distributions for a single category. Sketch and image embeddings were captured after the first training iteration. Embedding dimension is 256-D originally, visualized in 2-D using PCA.

assumes that sketches and images of a given category have the same distribution (mean, variance) in the latent (Mahalanobis) space. We employ PCA to derive Eigen decomposition for sketch and image representations, then warp the sketch representations U to have the same mean and variance as the image representations V.

$$u_i := (u_i - \mu_S)E_S \Sigma_S^{-1/2} \Sigma_I^{1/2} E_I^T + \mu_I, \quad i = 1, 2, ..., N_S \tag{1}$$

where (μ_S, E_S, Σ_S) and (μ_I, E_I, Σ_I) are the mean, eigenvectors and eigenvalues of the sketches and images respectively. Figure 3(b) shows the warping effects on an example category.

Learning a Transformation Matrix (LTM). We learn a linear transformation $\{W \in \mathbb{R}^{P \times P}, b \in \mathbb{R}^{1 \times P}\}$ to warp $U' \to V'$ then apply it on the larger set $U \to V$. Since the fine-grain training set $\mathcal{D}'$ is small, regularization on W is needed to combat overfitting. Concretely we wish to optimize:

$$\underset{W,b}{\arg\min} \frac{1}{2M} \sum_{i=1}^{M} ||u_i'W + b - v_i'||^2 + \frac{\lambda}{2} ||W - I||^2 \tag{2}$$

where λ is weight of the regularization term. W is forced closed to the identity matrix I since U and V are in a prospective joint embedding space. Note that we do not penalize the bias term b and tolerate free translation between the two distributions.

Equation 2 is solved using e. g. gradient descent. After learning (W, b), the sketch representations U is transformed to match with the images (Fig. 3(c)):

$$u_i := u_iW + b, \quad i = 1, 2, ..., N_S \tag{3}$$

Manifold Alignment (MA). Manifold alignment [26] assumes the two distributions have a similar underlining manifold. The approach aims to learn mapping functions $(F_S(.), F_I(.))$ to project the distributions (U, V) into a common space where not only correspondence but also local geometry are preserved. There are linear and non-linear approaches however we found the linear method more robust in our experiments. Additionally, the linear method produces explicit linear transformation matrices – $F(x) = x\mathcal{F}$, $\mathcal{F} \in \mathbb{R}^{P \times d}$ where d is the dimension of the latent space) – therefore can be applied on unknown data. On the other hands, there is no closed form for $(F_S(.), F_I(.))$ in the non-linear case. For the linear approach, the local geometry is preserved according to cost:

$$C_1(F_S, F_I) = \sum_{i,j}^{N_S} ||F_S(u_i) - F_S(u_j)||^2 W_{i,j}^S + \sum_{i,j}^{N_I} ||F_I(v_i) - F_I(v_j)||^2 W_{i,j}^I \quad (4)$$

where $W^S \in \mathbb{R}^{N_S \times N_S}$ and $W^I \in \mathbb{R}^{N_I \times N_I}$ are the pair-wise similarity matrices for sketch and image sets. An adjacency heat-map kernel defines W^S and W^I, e.g.:

$$W_{i,j}^S = \begin{cases} e^{-||u_i - u_j||^2} & \text{if } u_j \in \text{k nearest neighbour of } u_i \\ 0 & \text{otherwise} \end{cases} \quad (5)$$

The inter-domain correspondence is also preserved according to cost function:

$$C_2(F_S, F_I) = \sum_{i \in [1,N_S], j \in [1,N_I]} ||F_S(u_i) - F_I(v_j)||^2 W_{i,j}^{S,I} \quad (6)$$

where $W^{S,I} \in \mathbb{R}^{N_S \times N_I}$ is the inter-adjacency similarity matrix between the sketch and image sets. If a sketch-image pair is a known correspondence their similarity score is set to high, and low if their correspondence is unknown:

$$W_{i,j}^{S,I} = \begin{cases} 1 & \text{if } (u_i, v_j) \in \mathcal{D}' \\ 0 & \text{otherwise} \end{cases} \quad (7)$$

Note from the way Eq. 6 is formulated, manifold alignment does not explicitly require one-to-one correspondence. The final cost function integrates both intra- and inter-loss:

$$C(F^{(S)}, F^{(I)}) = C_1(.) + \alpha C_2(.) \quad (8)$$

We set $\alpha = 2.0$ to stress the importance of the fine-grain set in the total loss (the value of α is not so sensitive to performance as demonstrated empirically in Fig. 4c). We refer to [26] for the way to solve Eq. 8. Figure 3(d) visualizes a warping example for a representative category using this method.

3.2   Intra-category Clustering

Following the alignment of sketch and image domains for each category, the combined data is clustered into blobs of similar sketches and images. We experimented with four unsupervised clustering techniques considering their abilities to automatically select the number of clusters for each category.

k-means divides the sample set into K disjoint clusters, repeatedly update the clusters minimizing sum of square distance between samples and its centroids. We initialized the centroids using "kmeans++" and set number of clusters fixed at $K = 5$ (by inspection, based on typical number of human-separable appearance variants within each category).

Gaussian Mixtures (GMM). We followed the GMM fitting protocol of [18] to determine the number of clusters automatically by penalizing number of free parameters (thus number of clusters) in the mixture. This typically results in 3–4 clusters for each category.

Mean Shift. [5] widely used in clustering, segmentation and tracking applications. It is a recursive non-parametric technique for locating maxima of a density function that approximates the sample set.

DBSCAN. [8] locates data points with the highest neighbourhood density then expands clusters from them. The algorithm does not require prior knowledge of cluster number.

3.3 Magnet Loss

Softmax loss has been shown effective at sketch classification [29] and in [3,21,22] as a step in training SBIR embeddings. Yet we observe for mid-grain SBIR that softmax loss causes the intra-category sketch-time distribution to narrow, frustrating pooling. We adopt an approach similar to magnet clustering [17] but adapted to retrieval across domains rather than a single-domain classification. Magnet loss maintains a set of clusters within each category and minimizes the accumulated distance from the data points to their own centroids, as opposed to one single point in softmax loss.

$$\mathcal{L}(\Theta) = \frac{1}{N} \sum_{n=1}^{N} \{-\log \frac{e^{-\frac{1}{2\sigma^2}||z_n - \mu(z_n)||^2 - \beta}}{\sum_{c \neq C(z_n)} \sum_{k=1}^{K} e^{-\frac{1}{2\sigma^2}||z_n - \mu_k^c||^2}}\} + \qquad (9)$$

where μ_z is centroid of the cluster containing z, μ_k^c is centroid of cluster k in class c, $C(z)$ is category of z, σ^2 is variance of all sample z away from their respective centroid μ_z, $\beta \in \mathbb{R}$ is the threshold for acceptable distance between z and its centroid. The original magnet loss [17] is adapted for cross-domain retrieval as follows:

1. True cluster centroids μ_z and μ_k^c are used instead of approximating them within a mini-batch. Due to memory constraints the number of samples per cluster to be fed into each mini-batch is quite small. Therefore, approximating the centroids using just the samples in a mini-batch might lead to inaccurate results. Instead we pre-compute the centroids each time the clusters are updated, then feed them back to the training as fixed vectors (see Subsect. 3.4).
2. There is no constraint on the number of clusters per category. We used various clustering techniques (Subsect. 3.2), many of them with auto-selection of the cluster number, instead of just $k-$means with fixed k clusters [17].
3. If the clustering process is implemented on the data-aligned space, the cluster means (centroids) must be subsequently warped back to the embedding space. It is possible since the linear transformation of manifold alignment is reversible. In cases of warping using PCA or LTM, the sketch space is warped

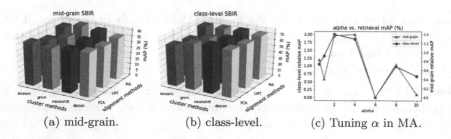

(a) mid-grain.   (b) class-level.   (c) Tuning α in MA.

Fig. 4. Comparing SBIR performance (mAP over MidGrain12c) for clustering and data alignment methods for (a) mid-grain and (b) category-level retrieval. (c) Effects of α in Eq. 8 on MA performance.

while the image space is kept fixed. In order to unify the cross-domain learning objectives we do not revert the centroids back to the sketch space.

3.4   Triplet Formation

Following data alignment (Subsect. 3.1) and clustering (Subsect. 3.1), we obtain a set of clusters (intra-category pools) along with their centroids for each class. The sketches and images of the same pool are candidates for positive pairs; whilst the ones in the nearest impostor pool are negative candidates. The list of centroids is used as the learning targets for magnet loss (Eq. 9) in the next training iteration.

Triplet is formed as follows:

1. Sample a seed class C as a uniform distribution.
2. Sample a cluster $l \sim p_c(l)$.
3. Sample a sketch $x^s \sim p_c^l(x^s)$ and a positive image $x_+^I \sim p_c^l(x_+^I)$.
4. Sample a negative image in the nearest impostor cluster $l' - x_-^I \sim p_c^{l'}(x_-^I)$.

where $p_c(l)$ is size of cluster l in class C. $p_c^l(x)$ is a function of probability that sample x belongs to cluster l. For example, if the clustering method is GMM, $p_c^l(x)$ is the probability density function of x given cluster l. In other cases, we used the distance heat map to represent $p_c^l(.)$.

Data Augmentation – We apply the following augmentation methods to enrich population of the training images and sketches: random crop (from 256×256 to 224×224), random rotation within a small range of $[-5,5]$ degrees and scaling with random ratio in range $[0.9,1.1]$. Random flip is not applied to preserve object viewpoint. Uniquely for sketches, we randomly discard up to 10% of stroke number. Data augmentation and sketch rendering are implemented on-the-fly in parallel with the main learning stream for speed efficiency.

4   Experiments

We first describe the training and test datasets in Subsect. 4.1, and evaluate algorithm configurations to determine our optimal models in Subsect. 4.2. Finally

Table 1. The Common65c dataset is formed using sketches and images from ImageNet, QuickDraw and Sketchy.

	QuickDraw [9]	ImageNet [13]	Sketchy [21]	Common65c- coarse	Common65c- fine
Class number	345	1000	125	65	65
# sketches	50M	0	75K	65K	4.7K
# images	0	1.2M	12.5K	65K	1.6K

Subsect. 4.3 shows performance of our proposed model in comparison with other approaches.

4.1 Datasets

As the *training* of our proposed approach involves clustering samples within the same categories, it is necessary to have large number of class-level sketches and images, plus (for LTM/MA) a small set of fine-grain data. QuickDraw [9] and ImageNet [13] are currently the largest datasets of sketches and images respectively, while Sketchy [21] is the largest instance-level SBIR dataset. We therefore intersect the category lists of these three datasets and obtain 65 common object categories from which we form a training set called Common65c. Specifically, Common65c consists of two subsets: a class-level subset, *Common65c-coarse*, and a instance-level subset, *Common65c-fine*. Common65c-coarse has 65k sketches from Quickdraw and 65k photo images from ImageNet, while Common65c-fine has 4680 sketches and 1560 images from Sketchy (Table 1). Note that we purposely restrict the size of the Common65c-fine set to just 24 images and 72 sketches per category (one image has 3 sketch correspondents) so that it is negligible against the Common65c-coarse. That would fit our original goal of building a semi-supervised mid-grain SBIR model.

A mid-grain *evaluation* dataset is also needed. To obtain the sketch set we sampled from QuickDraw 200 random sketches for each of the 65 categories, holding out data already used in the Common65c-coarse training set. A set of 138 sketches were sampled to form a balanced evaluation set manually selecting distinct views or sub-types of objects within each object class. Each sketch encodes a single mid-grain variant of an object.

To obtain the set of images corresponding to the sketch queries we scraped images through text keyword search for the 65 category names of Common65c on Adobe Stock image search. We chose this repository over Flickr, Google and Bing to avoid overlap with the ImageNet training set. Crowd annotation was used to select 1247 strong matches from the 500 images per category downloaded. We also added random 'distractor' images from Adobe Stock to form a 100k image corpus. This new dataset is called *MidGrain65c*. Several examples of sketch and corresponding images are shown Fig. 1.

We also created smaller datasets by sub-sampling 12 categories out of 65s, namely Common12c and MidGrain12c. These datasets were used to evaluate the clustering and alignment methods in the next section. All datasets are released as a further contribution.

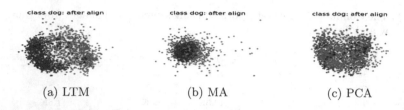

(a) LTM   (b) MA   (c) PCA

Fig. 5. A failure case of (a) LTM, as compared with (b) MA and (c) PCA.

4.2   Clustering and Alignment Methods

We experimented with the data alignment (PCA, LTM and MA) and clustering methods (k−means, GMM, Mean Shift, DBSCAN) of Subsects. 3.1 and 3.2. Training and evaluation were implemented on the Common12c and MidGrain12c sets respectively. Performance of these techniques is shown in Fig. 4(a-b). At mid-grain level (Fig. 4(a)), MA-GMM has the highest performance at 41.1% mAP, while LTM-KMeans performs the worst at 33.2%. At class-level (Fig. 4(b)), LTM-KMeans again under-performs the others at 61.9% but the highest accuracy is achieved with PCA-MeanShift at 76.3%. Other methods that rely on PCA alignment also obtain good results e. g. 74.2% for PCA-GMM, 75.9% for PCA-DBSCAN, thanks to its generic unbiased (and unsupervised) mechanism. It is opposite to the mid-grain case where MA dominantly outperforms others. Interestingly, the supervised LTM methods perform no better than PCA. Figure 5 shows a failed example of LTM where the fine-grain set is aligned but the majority of sketches and images are still separated. This is usually not the case for MA since it not only aligns correspondents but also respect local geometry.

Additionally, Fig. 4(a-b) indicates no correlation between mid-grain mAP and class-level mAP i. e. being the most superior at mid-grain level does not guarantee the same for category-level and vice versa. It is probably due to the trade off between discrimination (favoured in fine-grain SBIR) and generalization (preferred in category-level SBIR). This further encourages studies of mid-grain SBIR which comfortably sits between the two.

4.3   Baseline Comparison

We selected the best performing model in the previous experiments (**MA-GMM**) and trained it on the full dataset (Common65c). The following baselines were compared against:

SS-triplet-HM, standard triplet network with single staged training and hard-mining. The same network architecture as MA-GMM is employed (no-share 256-D InceptionV1) and the weight is initialized using the pretrained ImageNet model [24]. We implemented online hard-negative mining where the closest negative image within a mini-batch is selected for each anchor sketch. The whole Common65c dataset is used in training although the fine-grain labels of the subset Common65c-fine are not being used.

SS-contrast-HM, standard contrastive-loss network with single staged training and hard-mining. Otherwise identical to SS-triplet-HM.

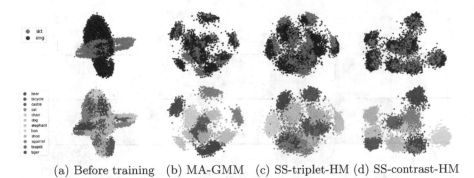

(a) Before training   (b) MA-GMM   (c) SS-triplet-HM (d) SS-contrast-HM

Fig. 6. PCA distribution of the Common12c data before and after training by domains (top row) and by categories (bottom row).

MS-reg-HM, multi-staged regression network with hard-mining proposed in Bui *et al.* [3]. The same architecture as MA-GMM is employed except the sketch and image branches are partially shared from block inception-4e.

Sketchy [21], fine-grain triplet-based network trained on the 75K Sketchy dataset. We used this publicly available model as a standard-alone baseline. Note we did not fine-tune it on Common65c since (i) it is a coarse-grain dataset and (ii) its 65 categories are a subset of the larger 125 Sketchy categories.

All other settings, unless specified otherwise, are kept the same.

Table 2 compares performance of these approaches on MidGrain65c at mid-grain and class-level. MS-REG-HM performs better than SS-triplet-HM which in turn is superior to SS-contrast-HM. The Sketchy model surprisingly has the lowest performance even though it was trained on a much more diverse and fine-grained dataset (we note that the sketch queries in MidGrain65c are originally from QuickDraw which is less clean than Sketchy due to the way QuickDraw was created). Sketchy also suffers a severe drop in performance when noisy distracting images are added to the benchmark, which shows its lack of generalization to "images in the wild". On top of that, our proposed approach MA-GMM outperforms the second-best by 6% and proves to be more robust in presence of distracting images. Note that MA-GMM needs just one training step as opposed to three stages in MS-reg-HM. It also employs a sub-optimal sharing configuration (no-share network) and does not directly use the fine-grain set to train its parameters. Figure 7 shows representative SBIR results.

Figure 6 visualizes the distributions of the training data Common12c before and after the networks were trained. Figure 6(a) was created after the third epoch in which sketches and images were being pre-trained separately using softmax loss (which serves as weight initialisation for MA-GMM). Intra-category pooling is visible however the two domains were inter-mixed due to a lack of cross-domain training. Contrastive loss makes the distribution for each category more compact, reducing intra-category discrimination (Fig. 6(d)). The more flexible triplet loss makes for wider distributions (Fig. 6(c)), however several distributions were mixed up probably due to strict hard-negative mining being less effective against

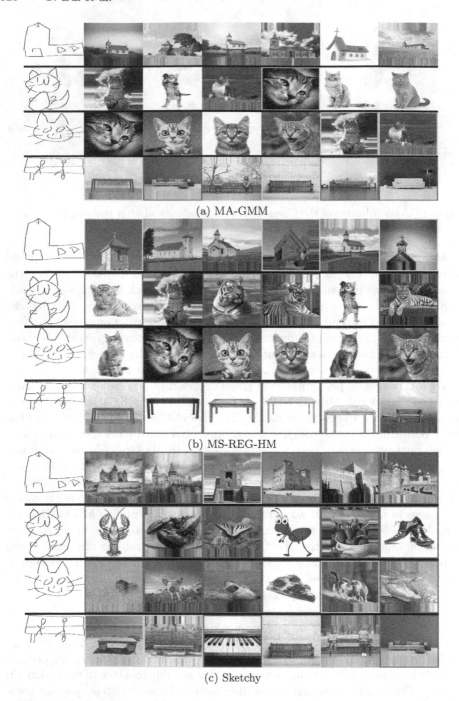

(a) MA-GMM

(b) MS-REG-HM

(c) Sketchy

Fig. 7. Mid-grain SBIR results of several representative queries (class "church", "cat" and "bench"), including failure cases. Red and yellow bounding boxes depict non-relevant images; the later indicates images of the same classes as the queries. (Color figure online)

Table 2. Mid-grain and class-level SBIRs of MA-GMM in comparison with other approaches, tested on MidGrain-65c with and without distracting images.

Methods	Mid-grain mAP (%)		Class-level mAP (%)	
	w. distract	w/o distract	w. distract	w/o distract
MA-GMM	**42.10**	**48.40**	**65.31**	**79.17**
MS-reg-HM [3]	36.08	45.58	53.52	74.01
SS-triplet-HM	32.13	43.39	45.85	69.35
SS-contrast-HM	22.34	42.65	31.64	66.82
Sketchy [21]	12.86	39.72	12.65	47.82

noisy data. MA-GMM brings more balance to the distributions, maintains the inter-category separation at the same time avoids squeezing the intra-category distance (Fig. 6(b)).

5   Conclusions

We report the first mid-grain SBIR algorithm; an unexplored topic fitting between object category and instance retrieval. We proposed a semi-supervised approach that utilizes mainly class-level datasets and a small quantity of fine-grain annotation combined with unsupervised intra-category clustering. We build upon the past success of triplet convnets for SBIR [3, 21] and the trend in visual search more broadly that targeted selection of triplets (e. g. hard-negative mining over conventional random sampling [25]) yields performance improvements. We go further, proposing a guided sampling scheme in which sketch-image representations within intra-category are aligned and pooled. We studied various data alignment and clustering strategies to determine the best combination (MA/GMM) for pooling. The whole process is integrated into a single staged end-to-end learning framework. We demonstrated our approach superior to other traditional methods on a newly created mid-grain dataset, MidGrain65c, by a 6% margin. Training time reduction is the main topic for future work. As manifold alignment and cluster updates are implemented on a regular basis, training needs to be frozen at the same frequency. Additionally, the requirement of a small amount of fine-grain training annotation (for best performance) is another limitation and an unsupervised approach that outperforms PCA is desirable. The need for this annotation narrows the diversity of our training set to 65 available categories. Another direction is developing attentive-models that focus on auto-detected regions of interest rather than the whole images. Recent work in this direction in broader image retrieval [14, 27] could be adapted.

Acknowledgments. This work was supported in part via an EPSRC doctoral training studentship (EP/M508160/1) and in part by UGPN/RCF 2017, FAPESP (grants 2016/16111-4, 2017/10068-2 and 2013/07375-0) and CNPq Fellowship (#307973/2017-4).

References

1. Bui, T., Collomosse, J.: Scalable sketch-based image retrieval using color gradient features. In: Proceedings of the IEEE International Conference on Computer Vision Workshops, pp. 1–8 (2015)
2. Bui, T., Ribeiro, L., Ponti, M., Collomosse, J.: Compact descriptors for sketch-based image retrieval using a triplet loss convolutional neural network. Comput. Vis. Image Underst. **164**, 27–37 (2017)
3. Bui, T., Ribeiro, L., Ponti, M., Collomosse, J.: Sketching out the details: sketch-based image retrieval using convolutional neural networks with multi-stage regression. Comput. Graph. **71**, 77–87 (2018)
4. Collomosse, J.P., McNeill, G., Watts, L.: Free-hand sketch grouping for video retrieval. In: International Conference on Pattern Recognition (ICPR) (2008)
5. Comaniciu, D., Meer, P.: Mean shift: a robust approach toward feature space analysis. IEEE Trans. Pattern Anal. Mach. Intell. **24**(5), 603–619 (2002)
6. Eitz, M., Hays, J., Alexa, M.: How do humans sketch objects? ACM Trans. Graph. **31**(4), 44:1–44:10 (2012). (Proceedings of SIGGRAPH)
7. Eitz, M., Hildebrand, K., Boubekeur, T., Alexa, M.: A descriptor for large scale image retrieval based on sketched feature lines. In: Proceedings of SBIM, pp. 29–36 (2009)
8. Ester, M., Kriegel, H.P., Sander, J., Xu, X., et al.: A density-based algorithm for discovering clusters in large spatial databases with noise. In: KDD, vol. 96, pp. 226–231 (1996)
9. Ha, D., Eck, D.: A neural representation of sketch drawings. arXiv preprint arXiv:1704.03477 (2017)
10. Hu, R., Barnard, M., Collomosse, J.P.: Gradient field descriptor for sketch based retrieval and localization. In: 2010 IEEE International Conference on Image Processing (ICIP), vol. 10, pp. 1025–1028 (2010)
11. Hu, R., Collomosse, J.: A performance evaluation of gradient field HOG descriptor for sketch based image retrieval. Comput. Vis. Image Underst. **117**(7), 790–806 (2013). https://doi.org/10.1016/j.cviu.2013.02.005
12. Hu, R., James, S., Wang, T., Collomosse, J.: Markov random fields for sketch based video retrieval. In: Proceedings of the 3rd ACM Conference on International Conference on Multimedia Retrieval, pp. 279–286. ACM (2013)
13. Krizhevsky, A., Sutskever, I., Hinton, G.: ImageNet classification with deep convolutional neural networks. In: Advances in Neural Information Processing Systems (2012)
14. Laskar, Z., Kannala, J.: Context aware query image representation for particular object retrieval. In: Sharma, P., Bianchi, F.M. (eds.) SCIA 2017. LNCS, vol. 10270, pp. 88–99. Springer, Cham (2017). https://doi.org/10.1007/978-3-319-59129-2_8
15. Qi, Y., et al.: Making better use of edges via perceptual grouping. In: Proceedings of the IEEE Conference on Computer Vision and Pattern Recognition (2015)
16. Qi, Y., Song, Y.Z., Zhang, H., Liu, J.: Sketch-based image retrieval via siamese convolutional neural network. In: 2016 IEEE International Conference on Image Processing (ICIP), pp. 2460–2464. IEEE (2016)
17. Rippel, O., Paluri, M., Dollar, P., Bourdev, L.: Metric learning with adaptive density discrimination. arXiv preprint arXiv:1511.05939 (2015)
18. Roberts, S.J., Husmeier, D., Rezek, I., Penny, W.: Bayesian approaches to Gaussian mixture modeling. IEEE Trans. Pattern Anal. Mach. Intell. **20**(11), 1133–1142 (1998)

19. Saavedra, J.M.: RST-SHELO: sketch-based image retrieval using sketch tokens and square root normalization. Multimed. Tools Appl. **76**(1), 931–951 (2017)
20. Saavedra, J.M., Barrios, J.M.: Sketch based image retrieval using learned keyshapes. In: Proceedings of the British Machine Vision Conference (2015)
21. Sangkloy, P., Burnell, N., Ham, C., Hays, J.: The sketchy database: learning to retrieve badly drawn bunnies. ACM Trans. Graph. (TOG) **35**(4), 119 (2016)
22. Seddati, O., Dupont, S., Mahmoudi, S.: Quadruplet networks for sketch-based image retrieval. In: Proceedings of the 2017 ACM on International Conference on Multimedia Retrieval, pp. 184–191. ACM (2017)
23. Sun, X., Wang, C., Xu, C., Zhang, L.: Indexing billions of images for sketch-based retrieval. In: Proceedings of the 21st ACM International Conference on Multimedia, pp. 233–242. ACM (2013)
24. Szegedy, C., et al.: Going deeper with convolutions. In: Proceedings of the IEEE Conference on Computer Vision and Pattern Recognition, pp. 1–9 (2015)
25. Tolias, G., Chum, O.: Asymmetric feature maps with application to sketch based retrieval. In: Proceedings of the IEEE Conference on Computer Vision and Pattern Recognition, vol. 1, p. 4 (2017)
26. Wang, C., Mahadevan, S.: A general framework for manifold alignment. In: AAAI Fall Symposium: Manifold Learning and its Applications, pp. 53–58 (2009)
27. Wei, X.S., Luo, J.H., Wu, J., Zhou, Z.H.: Selective convolutional descriptor aggregation for fine-grained image retrieval. IEEE Trans. Image Process. **26**(6), 2868–2881 (2017)
28. Yu, Q., Liu, F., Song, Y.Z., Xiang, T., Hospedales, T.M., Loy, C.C.: Sketch me that shoe. In: Proceedings of the IEEE Conference on Computer Vision and Pattern Recognition. IEEE (2016)
29. Yu, Q., Yang, Y., Song, Y.Z., Xiang, T., Hospedales, T.M.: Sketch-a-Net that beats humans. In: Proceedings of the British Machine Vision Conference. IEEE (2015)

Visual Graphs from Motion (VGfM): Scene Understanding with Object Geometry Reasoning

Paul Gay[1]([✉]), James Stuart[2], and Alessio Del Bue[1]

[1] Visual Geometry and Modelling (VGM) Lab, Istituto Italiano di Tecnologia (IIT),
Via Morego 30, 16163 Genova, Italy
{paul.gay,alessio.delbue}@iit.it
[2] Center for Cultural Heritage Technology, Istituto Italiano di Tecnologia (IIT),
Via Morego 30, 16163 Genova, Italy
stuart.james@iit.it

Abstract. Recent approaches on visual scene understanding attempt to build a scene graph – a computational representation of objects and their pairwise relationships. Such rich semantic representation is very appealing, yet difficult to obtain from a single image, especially when considering complex spatial arrangements in the scene. Differently, an image sequence conveys useful information using the multi-view geometric relations arising from camera motions. Indeed, object relationships are naturally related to the 3D scene structure. To this end, this paper proposes a system that first computes the geometrical location of objects in a generic scene and then efficiently constructs scene graphs from video by embedding such geometrical reasoning. Such compelling representation is obtained using a new model where geometric and visual features are merged using an RNN framework. We report results on a dataset we created for the task of 3D scene graph generation in multiple views.

Keywords: Scene graph · 3D object detection · Scene understanding

1 Introduction

The ability to automatically generate semantic relationships between objects in a scene is useful in numerous fields. As such, in recent years there has been a significant amount of research toward this goal [7,18,19,22,33] leading to the proposal of encoding relationships using a scene graph [13].

Common approaches for constructing scene graphs utilize visual appearance to guide the process, relying mainly on extracted Convolutional Neural Network (CNN) features. However, CNN visual features fail to encode spatial relationships

Electronic supplementary material The online version of this chapter (https://doi.org/10.1007/978-3-030-20893-6_21) contains supplementary material, which is available to authorized users.

© Springer Nature Switzerland AG 2019
C. V. Jawahar et al. (Eds.): ACCV 2018, LNCS 11363, pp. 330–346, 2019.
https://doi.org/10.1007/978-3-030-20893-6_21

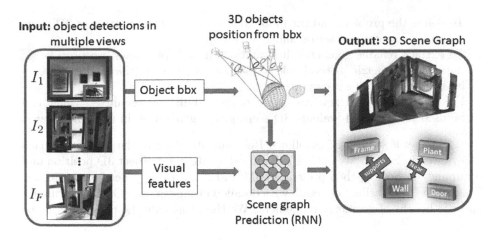

Fig. 1. Overview of the Visual Graphs from Motion (VGfM) approach for 3D scene graph generation from multiple views. As input, an object detector extracts and matches 2D bounding boxes from objects in multiple images. The 3D position and occupancy of each object are estimated and, in parallel, visual features are extracted from each bounding box. These elements are then used to predict a 3D graph where each edge defines the semantic relationship between a pair of ellipsoids

due to their invariance properties [25]. This is further compounded when considering complex 3D scenes where relationship predicates can become ambiguous and not easily solvable from a single view. This is exemplified in Fig. 1, considering the image I_2 the plant could be, '*near* the wall' or '*supported by* the wall'. This ambiguity can be rectified through the understanding provided by adjacent images, resolving for the camera pose and predicting the *near* predicate – 'plant *near* the wall', as the *support* predicate would be related to the shelf. In this paper we aim to encode the required information using the knowledge of the 3D geometry of the objects in the scene.

We therefore propose to combine the advantages of both visual and geometric information to efficiently predict spatial relations between objects as shown in Fig. 1. Given a set of 2D object bounding box detections matched across a sequence of images, using multi-view relations we compute the 3D locations and occupancies of objects described as a set of 3D ellipsoids. At the same time, we extract visual features from each object detection to model their visual appearance. These two representations are given as input to a Recurrent Neural Network (RNN) which has learned to predict a coherent scene graph where the objects are vertices and their relationships are edges. Overall, our Visual Graphs from Motion (VGfM) approach is appealing as it combines geometric and semantic understanding of an image, which has been a long term goal in computer vision [1,4,12,23,26,28,30]. We demonstrate the effectiveness of such a representation by creating a new dataset for 3D scene graph evaluation that is derived from the data provided in ScanNet [5]. To summarize, our contributions in this paper are:

- To define the problem and the model related to the computation of 3D scene graph representations across multiple views;
- To extract reliable geometric information in multiple views, we propose an improved geometric method able to estimate objects position and occupancy in 3D, modelled as a set of quadrics;
- Finally, to provide a new real world dataset, built over ScanNet, which can be used to learn and evaluate 3D scene graph generation in multiple views[1].

The paper is structured as follows. Relevant literature to the VGfM approach is reviewed in Sect. 2. We outline our refined strategy for object 3D position and occupancy in Sect. 3, then present VGfM and its learning procedure in Sect. 4. The dataset is described in Sect. 5 with detailed evaluation of VGfM performance and the benefit of geometry refinement. We then conclude the paper in Sect. 6.

2   Related Work

We now review the 3 topics related to our approach: scene graph generation from images, classification from videos and 3D object occupancy estimation.

Early works on visual relation detection were training classifiers to detect each relation in an image independently from each other [9,19]. However, a scene graph often contains chains of relationships for instance: *A man HOLDING a hand BELONGING TO a girl*. Intuitively, a model able to leverage on this fact should obtain more coherent scene graphs. To account for this, Xu *et al.* [31] proposed a model which explicitly defines a 2D scene graph. The framework naturally deals with chains of relations because inference is performed globally over all the objects and their potential relations. To this end, a message passing framework was developed using standard RNNs. This is in line with current approaches which combine the strengths of graphical models and neural networks [17,34]. Each object and relation represents a node in a two layer graph and is modelled by the hidden state of an RNN. The state of each node is refined by the messages sent from adjacent nodes. This architecture has the flexibility of graphical models and thus can be used to merge heterogeneous sources of information such as text and images [16]. We utilize this mechanism in our model while extending it to incorporate the 3D geometry. To the best of our knowledge, this is the first time that geometric reasoning is exploited for scene graph generation.

Object detection within a sequence (video) is largely still reliant on temporal confidence aggregation across image detections or applying RNN for temporal memory [29]. With the difficulty of predicting confidence within a CNN [21] these approaches rely on detection consistency. Alternatively, more advanced video tubelets in T-CNN [14] are optimized for the detection confidence. In a similar way, we exploit the multiple view information within our model by including a fusion mechanism based on message passing across images.

---

[1] Code and data can be found at: https://github.com/paulgay/VGfM.

Recently, new techniques have emerged to estimate the 3D spatial layout of the objects as well as their occupancy [2,10,24]. These techniques rely on the quality of deep learning object detectors [10,24] or the use of additional range data [2]. Similarly volumetric approaches have been used to construct the layout of objects in rooms, or construct objects and regress their positioning [30]. These strategies provide alternative representations for scene graph generation since they associate object labels to the 3D structure of the scene, but lack the relationships required to construct a scene graph. In particular the approach localization from Detection (LfD) [24] leverages 2D object detector information to obtain the 3D position and the occupancy of a set of objects represented through quadrics. Although ellipsoids are an approximation of the region occupied by an object, they provide the necessary support for spatial reasoning in a closed form which can be efficiently computed. However, in the current methods [11,24], there is no explicit constraint to enforce the quadric to be a valid ellipsoid. As a consequence, low baselines and inaccurate bounding boxes might result in degenerate quadrics. In the next section, we present an extension named LfD with Constraints (LfDC) which is based on linear constraints on the quadric centers. It has the advantage of being a fast closed-form solution while being more robust than LfD [24].

3   Robust Object Representation with 3D Quadrics

Even if they are an approximate representation of objects, a representation based on ellipsoids (or formally quadrics) can be embedded in the graph effectively with multiple views (as described in Sect. 4). In this section, we briefly consider the prior work for generating quadrics from multi-view images, then resolve for their limitations so making the approach more suitable for scene graph construction.

Let us consider a set of image frames $f = \{1 \dots F\}$ representing a 3D scene under different viewpoints. A set of $i = \{1 \dots N\}$ rigid objects is placed in arbitrary positions. We assume that each object is detected in at least 3 images. Each object i in each image frame f is given by a 3×3 symmetric matrix C_{if} which represents an ellipse inscribed in the bounding box as shown in Fig. 1 (left & top middle). The aim is to estimate the 4×4 matrix Q_i representing the 3D ellipsoid whose projection onto the image planes best fit the measured 2D ellipses C_{if}. The relationship between Q_i and their reprojected conics C_{if} is defined by the 3×4 perspective camera matrices P_f which are assumed to be known (i.e. the camera is calibrated). The LfD method described in [24] solves the problem in the dual space where it can be linearized as:

$$\beta_{if}c_{if} = G_f v_i, \tag{1}$$

where β_{if} is a scaling factor, the 6-vector c_{if} is the vectorised conic of the object i in image f, the 10-vector v_i is the vectorised quadric and the matrix G_f contains the elements of the camera projection matrix after linearization[2]. Then, stacking

---

[2] The supplemental material provides more mathematical details about this step.

(a)   (b)   (c)

Fig. 2. (a) are example ellipse reprojections of LfD [24] in red and LfDC in blue with cross and triangle respectively for the centers. (b, c) is the point cloud, 3D quadrics (using same color labelling), camera poses for two camera, the ground truth is shown in green. It can be seen that the proposed solution overcomes the limitation of [24]. (Color figure online)

column-wise Eq. (1) for $f = 1 \dots F$, with $F \geq 3$, we obtain:

$$M_i \mathbf{w}_i = \mathbf{0}_{6F}, \qquad (2)$$

where $\mathbf{0}_x$ denotes a column vector of zeros of length x, and the matrix $M_i \in \mathbb{R}^{6F \times (10+F)}$ and the vector $\mathbf{w}_i \in \mathbb{R}^{10+F}$ are defined as follow:

$$M_i = \begin{bmatrix} G_1 & -c_{i1} & \mathbf{0}_6 & \mathbf{0}_6 & \dots & \mathbf{0}_6 \\ G_2 & \mathbf{0}_2 & -c_{i2} & \mathbf{0}_2 & \dots & \mathbf{0}_2 \\ \vdots & & & & \ddots & \\ G_F & \mathbf{0}_2 & \mathbf{0}_2 & \mathbf{0}_2 & \dots & -c_{iF} \end{bmatrix}, \quad \mathbf{w}_i = \begin{bmatrix} \mathbf{v}_i \\ \boldsymbol{\beta}_i \end{bmatrix}, \qquad (3)$$

where $\boldsymbol{\beta}_i = [\beta_{i1}, \beta_{i2}, \cdots, \beta_{iF}]^{\top}$ contains the scale factors of the object i for the different frames.

Since the object detector can be inaccurate, it makes sense to find the quadric $\tilde{\mathbf{w}}_i$ by solving the following minimization problem:

$$\tilde{\mathbf{w}}_i = \arg\min_{\mathbf{w}} \|M_i \mathbf{w}\|_2^2, \quad s.t. \|\mathbf{w}\|_2^2 = 1, \qquad (4)$$

where the equality constraint $\|\mathbf{w}\|_2^2 = 1$ avoids the trivial zero solution. The solution of this problem consists in computing the SVD on the M_i matrix and taking the right singular vector associated to the minimum singular value.

However, the algebraic minimization in Eq. (4) does not enforce the obtained quadric to be a valid ellipsoid. As can be seen in Fig. 2, fitted ellipsoids can be inaccurate despite giving a reasonable 2D projection. The proposed LfDC solution generates ellipsoids as Fig. 2c, and in turn improves overall performance.

A common indication of the estimated quadric being degenerate can be fairly guessed by checking where the estimated ellipse center is located. If the center is outside the boundaries of the estimated ellipse contour, this clearly points out to a degenerate configuration. Given this last observation, rather than constraining directly the solution to lie in a valid ellipsoid parameter space, we include a set of equations imposing the reprojection of the center of the 3D ellipsoid being closer to the centers of the ellipses. This can be done by adding an additional set of rows in the matrix $\tilde{M}_i$ used in Eq. (2).

This constraint can be added by observing that the center parameters of the vectorised dual quadric $\mathbf{v}$ appear separately in linear terms[3] at position 4, 7 and 9 in the vector. The same fact holds for the vectorised conic $\mathbf{c}$ at positions 3 and 5 (we omit indexes to simplify the notation):

$$\mathbf{c}^* = \mathbf{c}_{3,5} = \begin{bmatrix} -t_1^c & -t_2^c \end{bmatrix}, \quad \mathbf{v}^* = \mathbf{v}_{4,7,9} = \begin{bmatrix} -t_1 & -t_2 & -t_3 \end{bmatrix}, \tag{5}$$

where $\mathbf{c}^*$ and $\mathbf{v}^*$ contain the centers of the ellipse and the ellipsoid respectively. We can use this fact to directly include the equations which enforce the ellipsoid center to be projected in the centers of the ellipses. Given a frame f and an object i, the constrained equations are:

$$G_f^c \mathbf{v}_i^* = \mathbf{c}_{if}^* \beta_{if}, \tag{6}$$

with the 2×10 matrix G_f^c defined as:

$$G_f^c = \begin{bmatrix} 0 & 0 & 0 & p_{11} & 0 & 0 & p_{12} & 0 & p_{13} & p_{14} \\ 0 & 0 & 0 & p_{21} & 0 & 0 & p_{22} & 0 & p_{23} & p_{24} \end{bmatrix}, \tag{7}$$

where each value p_{ij} corresponds to an element of the camera matrix P_f. These equations are included in the system of Eq. (2) by replacing the matrix M_i by $\tilde{M}_i$ such that:

$$\tilde{M}_i \mathbf{w}_i = 0_{8F}, \tag{8}$$

where the matrix $\tilde{M}_i \in \mathbb{R}^{8F \times (10+F)}$ is defined as follow:

$$\tilde{M}_i = \begin{bmatrix} G_1 & -\mathbf{c}_{i1} & 0_6 & 0_6 & \cdots & 0_6 \\ G_1^c & -\mathbf{c}_{i1}^* & 0_2 & 0_2 & \cdots & 0_2 \\ \vdots & & & & \ddots & \\ G_F & 0_6 & 0_6 & 0_6 & \cdots & -\mathbf{c}_{iF} \\ G_F^c & 0_2 & 0_2 & 0_2 & \cdots & -\mathbf{c}_{iF}^* \end{bmatrix}. \tag{9}$$

The solution of this new system can then be obtained with the SVD of the $\tilde{M}_i$ matrix as done for the minimization problem described in Eq. (4). This method, named LfDC, has both the effect of reducing the number of degenerated quadrics (i.e. to localize more objects in the scene) and to improve the quality of object localizations and occupancy estimation as it will be shown in the experimental section. For these reasons, LfDC also enables to improve the performances when estimating the scene graphs using multi-view relations.

---

[3] We refer to supplemental material for further mathematical details.

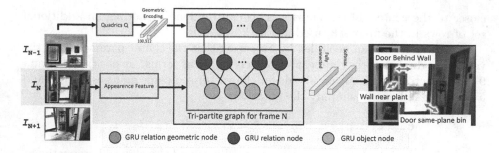

Fig. 3. Our scene graph generation algorithm takes as input a sequence of images with a set of object proposals (as ellipsoids). In addition, visual features are extracted for each of the bounding boxes, these features are then fed to initialise the GRU object and relation nodes. A tri-partite graph connects the object, relation and geometric nodes and iterative message passing updates the hidden states of the object and relation nodes. At the conclusion of the message passing the scene graph is predicted by the network and then the next image of the sequence is processed.

4   Scene Graphs from Multiple Images

The VGfM approach models the scene graph within a tri-partite graph which takes as input the features, both visual and geometric (from Sect. 3), and outputs the prediction of the object labels and predicates, as illustrated on Fig. 3. The graph merges geometric and visual information, as well as refining jointly the state of all the objects and their relationships. This process is performed iteratively over each of the F images of the sequence.

Therefore, let $G = (\vartheta, E)$ denotes the tri-partite graph of a current image. We define ϑ as the set of nodes that corresponds to attributes, defined as $\vartheta = \{\vartheta^g, \vartheta^o, \vartheta^r\}$ related to geometry, objects and relationships respectively, while E refers to pairwise edges which connect each object with its relation. The set of object nodes is denoted as $\vartheta^o = \{\vartheta_i^o, i = 1 \ldots O\}$ and models their semantic states. Similarly, ϑ^r models the semantic states of the relationships and is defined as $\vartheta^r = \{\vartheta_{i \to j}^r, i = 1 \ldots O, j = 1 \ldots O, i \neq j\}$. Finally, $\vartheta^g = \{\vartheta_{i \to j}^g, i = 1 \ldots O, j = 1 \ldots O, i \neq j\}$ is the set of geometric nodes constructed over the quadrics previously computed expressing the geometric state of each relation (see Sect. 4.1 for construction).

The states of the graph are then iteratively refined by message passing among the nodes, exchanging information about their respective hidden states (see Sect. 4.2). The hidden states $h_{i \to j}$ (resp. h_i) of each relation node $\vartheta_{i \to j}^r$ (and resp. object node ϑ_i^o) are modelled with Gated Recurrent Units [3] (GRU). This allows each node to refine its state by exploiting incoming messages from its neighbors. Differently from the object and relation nodes, each geometric node $\vartheta_{i \to j}^g$ is considered as an observation and its state $g_{i \to j}$ is fixed, this allows the reliability of the geometric information to be enforced. If the geometric nodes are removed from the graph, we obtain the framework of [31].

After K iterations of message passing the hidden states from the object and relation nodes are used to compute the classification decision, i.e. object and relation labels, as provided by the final fully connected layer. This layer takes as input the hidden state of a relation node and produces a distribution over the relation labels through a softmax, this step is performed to compute the object labels as well. We treat predicate labels as in the multi-label scenario where a predicate is detected for a given relation if the softmax score is higher than the label indicating its absence. We further outline the training specifics of the model in Sect. 4.4. With the creation of the scene graph the next image in the sequence is then processed.

As our goal is to share information between images, we can encourage sharing beyond object and relation nodes and pass messages between images within the sequence. This can be simply performed by connecting tri-partite graph nodes ϑ^r, ϑ^o among images and this process is explained in Sect. 4.3.

4.1   Construction of the Geometric Nodes

As described in Sect. 3, we obtain a set of ellipsoids $Q = \{Q_i, i = 1 \ldots O\}$ from the object detections. We then extract the 3D coordinates of the center of each quadric Q_i and the six points at the extremities of its main axis. Finally, the geometric encoder takes as input the coordinates extracted from the ellipsoids Q_i and Q_j in order to produce the state of the geometric node $\vartheta^g_{i \to j}$. This encoder consists of a multi-layer perceptron with two fully connected layers of sizes $100, 512$. These values were identified empirically to give enough capacity to the network to link both the quadric positions and occupancies and the given complexity of the final labels. We additionally experimented with a bag-of-word based encoding, proposed in [22], and found similar performances.

4.2   Message Passing Between Nodes

The refinement of the hidden states is carried out via message passing. At each inference iteration, messages are sent along the graph edges. Each relation node $\vartheta^r_{i \to j}$ is linked by undirected edges to the object state nodes ϑ^o_i, ϑ^o_j and the corresponding geometric node $\vartheta^g_{i \to j}$. We use the message pooling scheme proposed in [31].

At each iteration, the node ϑ^o_i receives the following message:

$$m_i = \sum_{j:i \to j} \sigma(\mathbf{a}_1[h_i, h_{i \to j}])h_{i \to j} + \sum_{j:j \to i} \sigma(\mathbf{a}_2[h_i, h_{j \to i}])h_{j \to i}, \tag{10}$$

where $[,]$ denotes the concatenation operator, σ is the sigmoid function, $\{j : i \to j\}$ is the set of all the relations where object j is present at the right of the predicate, and the weights $\mathbf{a}_1$ and $\mathbf{a}_2$ are learned. The relationship nodes are also updated, where each node $\vartheta^r_{i \to j}$ receives the following message:

$$m_{i \to j} = \sigma(\mathbf{b}_1[h_i, h_{i \to j}])h_i + \sigma(\mathbf{b}_2[h_j, h_{i \to j}])h_j + \sigma(\mathbf{b}_3[g_{i \to j}, h_{i \to j}])g_{i \to j}, \tag{11}$$

where b_1, b_2 and b_3 are learned parameters.

As with loopy belief propagation, this can be seen as an approximation of an exact global optimization, enabling the refinement of each hidden state based on its context. Conversely to a classic message passing scheme, the last inference decision on the label values is not performed within the tri-partite graph but by using a last fully connected layer. On average in our experiments, the inference time is 0.25 second per image on a Tesla K80.

4.3 Sharing Information Among Multiple Images

We now extend the proposed single image model to fuse information among the images of the sequence. In this case, the visual features can be shared where the network benefits from taking into account potential appearance changes as well as aiding consistency among the views. To this end, we rely on the message passing mechanism and include cross-image links which connect the tri-partite graphs for each image. As shown in Fig. 4, each relation node receives messages from all the nodes modelling the same relation in the other images. The same principle is applied for the object nodes.

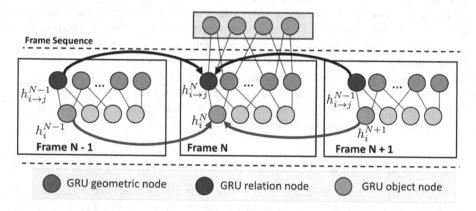

Fig. 4. This figure displays how the graphs operating on a single frame (same as shown on Fig. 3) are linked by the fusion mechanism.

We extend the notation so that it refers to nodes and messages image by image. Let us denote by $m_{i\to j}^f$ (resp. m_i^f) the message that the relation node $h_{i\to j}^f$ (resp. the object node h_i^f) appearing in the image f receives from the other images. Then, we compute the messages with the following equations:

$$m_{i\to j}^f = \sum_{l,f\neq l} \sigma(\mathbf{c}_1[h_{i\to j}^f, h_{i\to j}^l])h_{i\to j}^l, \tag{12}$$

$$m_i^f = \frac{1}{F} \sum_{l,f\neq l} \sigma(\mathbf{c}_2[h_i^f, h_i^l])h_i^l, \tag{13}$$

where c_1 and c_2 are learned weights. This formulation can be seen as weighted average of the visual features were the weights are learned as an attention mechanism. This new cross-image message is then added to the local one described in Sect. 4.3 to form the final message.

4.4 Learning

Our model is trained with cross-entropy loss. We also use similar hyperparameters to Xu et al. [31] with a learning rate of $1e^{-3}$ and $K = 2$ iterations of message passing. Batches of 8 images were used for the single image system. For the multi-image approach described in Sect. 4.3, each batch corresponds to one image sequence. We reduce the sequence to 10 images selected uniformly to save memory space. In contrast to [31], we retain all region proposals as we are considering the ellipsoid proposal that already prunes the per-frame object proposals. We extract visual features from VGG-16 [27] pretrained on MS-COCO and use the FC_7 layer to initialize the hidden states of the RNNs. The RNNs are trained while keeping the weights of the visual features fixed. Two sets of shared weights are optimized during training: one for the objects and one for the relations. The state of the GRU for both input and output has a dimension of 512.

5 Dataset Description and Experimental Evaluation

Prior datasets for the scene graph generation problem are based on singular images with relationship annotations, but in general they do not have multiview image sequences necessary to exploit the proposed model. We thus create GraphScanNet by manually extending and upgrading the ScanNet dataset [5] with relationships between the annotated objects. The ScanNet dataset provides 2.5 million views in more than 1500 scans annotated with semantic and instance level segmentation. 3D camera poses are also provided as estimated from an online 3D reconstruction pipeline (BundleFusion [6]) algorithm run on the RGB-D images. Since VGfM does not require depth, we also tried a visual SLAM algorithm [20], but we found that the results were not accurate enough.

Although one thousand object categories are present, we refine the list of objects to resolve for annotator errors and the frequency of object occurrences in sequences resulting in a refined list of 34 object categories. Our annotations are a set of 8762 view-independent compositional relationships between couples of 3D objects. Our proposed predicates are inspired by Visual Genome [15], but we opt for a concise set that is loosely aimed to encompass many relationships that can occur within the sequences. It can be seen from the ScanNet class labels that when annotators are given expressive freedom in labels, cultural or personal bias can make annotations implausible for learning systems where many objects are synonyms or localized vernaculars. Our predicates are as follows:

Part-of: A portion or division of a whole that is separate or distinct; piece, fragment, fraction, or section, e.g. shelf is *part-of* a bookcase.

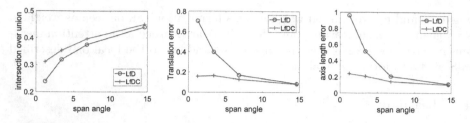

Fig. 5. Evaluation in terms of O_{3D} accuracy, translation and axes length errors for the LfD [24] method and our proposed approach LfDC.

Support: To bear or hold up (a load, mass, structure, part, etc.); serve as a foundation for. Where hypernyms could be considered support from *behind, below, hidden*; in our case 'below' is most prevalent.

Same-plane: Belonging to the same or near similar vertical plane in regards to the ground normal. As an example, a table might be *same-plan* as a chair.

Same-set: Belonging to a group with similar properties of function. The objects could define a region, e.g. in Fig. 6 the table, chair and plate belong to the same set whereas the shoes on the floor are separated. This is similar to the concept of scenario recently studied in [8], and where they proved this being a powerful clue for scene understanding.

As relationships are derived from images, there are differences in terms of number of instances for each predicate. *Same-set* and *Same-plane* appear about 30,000 times in the images, whereas *Support* 3,000 times and *Part-of* only 600 times. This has an impact on the performances as explained in the evaluation.

The 3D object segmentation enables us to construct a 3D ground-truth (GT) by fitting ellipsoids to each object mesh. Object bounding box in 2D are also computed by projecting each object point cloud into the image. Such bounding boxes are created by fitting a rectangle that encloses the set of 2D points. We then automatically extracted 2000 sequences coming from 700 different rooms with at least 4 objects in each of them. These sequences are challenging for 3D reconstruction, since the recording of the rooms was done by rotating the camera with limited translation motions. On average, the angle spanned by the camera trajectory is 4.3°.

5.1   Evaluation of the Quadric Estimation

We first evaluate how accurate are the quadrics obtained from the different methods. We run the original LfD method [24] on the extracted sequences and compared with the ones from our LfDC approach. On the 1979 sequences, we measured that only 48% of the quadrics estimated by LfD are valid ellipsoids. This number rises up to 60% when we use our LfDC method. This validates our initial hypothesis that the additional equations are useful to avoid non-valid quadrics. In the following, we evaluate the accuracy of the ellipsoids by considering only the ones who are found valid by all methods.

One of the main limitations of LfD is the sensibility when the image sequences have a short baseline (i.e. short camera path and/or very few image frames). To study this effect, the error and accuracy values are plotted in function of the maximum angle spanned by the camera during the sequence where the object is recorded. In Fig. 5, we compare the methods according to three metrics: O_{3D}, which is the intersection over union between the proposed and the GT quadrics, the translation and the axis length errors.

We can see that the LfDC outperforms the previous LfD method in terms of the three metrics: volume overlap, translation and axis length error. The constraints on the centers are beneficial to improve on these three aspects since the solution is still computed globally for all the quadric parameters. Secondly, we observe that, although relatively small in average, the improvements are important in case of a low baseline.

5.2   Evaluation on the Scene Graph Classification Task

We evaluate our systems on the tasks of object and relation classification i.e. given the bounding boxes of a pair of objects, the system must predict both the object classes and the predicate of their relation. These two tasks encompass the problem of scene graph generation when performed recursively over the image where annotations are performed in terms of multi-label fashion i.e. presence and absence. We selected 400 rooms for training, 150 as a validation set and 150 for testing.

We first study the influence of the quadric estimation algorithms. We run our VGfM and use as input the ellipsoids provided by LfD, LfDC and GT quadrics. Results are reported in Table 1. We can see that the differences between the different methods are relatively small, but still coherent with the accuracy reported in Fig. 5. The LfD obtains the worst results and the best performing method is LfDC. Overall, the use of GT quadrics brings an additional improvement, but the accuracy remains relatively close to the other methods.

Table 1. Comparison of the use of different quadrics to classify the scene graphs. The numbers in bold are related to the best results LfD and LfDC.

Object label	GT	LfD [24]	LfDC
	76%	75%	75%
Same-plane	75%	72%	**74%**
Same-set	62%	59%	**61%**
Support	69%	64%	**67%**
Part-of	69%	65%	**69%**

We now study the influence of the different components of the system in an ablation study in Table 2. The baseline [31] uses only visual appearance. The method VGfM-2D corresponds to a variation of our method without 3D information where we computed the geometric states from the coordinates of the 2D

Table 2. This table shows the accuracy for the prediction of each predicate and the object labels. The numbers in bold are the best performing methods.

Object label	[31]	VGfM-2D	Geometric encoder	VGfM	VGfM + Fusion
	74%	74%	58%	75%	**76%**
Same-plane	74%	74%	70%	74%	**78%**
Same-set	58%	59%	55%	61%	**62%**
Support	62%	64%	**85%**	67%	64%
Part-of	68%	69%	**80%**	69%	59%

bounding boxes instead of using the ellipsoids. To evaluate the potential of using geometry alone, we also report results while using only the geometric encoder described in Sect. 4.1. A softmax layer is appended to this encoder in order to use it as classifier. The resulting network is then trained from scratch for the tasks of predicting predicates and object labels. VGfM + Fusion corresponds to the addition of the fusion mechanism over multiple images described in Sect. 4.3. The results of the baseline method do not exceed 75% of accuracy, which suggests that this task is difficult especially for the high level *Same-set* predicate. As shown on the second column, augmenting the appearance with the 2D coordinates allows VGfM-2D to obtain an improvement of 1–2% as it is commonly observed in computer vision for this kind of feature augmentation.

The results of the geometric encoder shows large differences between the tasks. The low performance for the task of object classification is not surprising as a 3D bounding box alone carries little information about the object label. Regarding the results for the predicate prediction, we tested the same architecture but providing the GT ellipsoids and found only a difference of 1–5% depending on the predicates. It is thus possible that some errors are due to partly segmented objects in the annotations, resulting in inaccurate bounding boxes. We also observe that results are higher than any other method for the predicates *Support* and *Part-of*. One explanation is that these two predicates are less frequent in the dataset (respectively 3000 and 600 instances compared to around 30000 for the other classes). In these cases with less training data, having a more simple, shallower architecture with a reduced number of parameters helps. Unfortunately, standard data augmentation techniques such as cropping or shifting cannot be directly applied to augment the number of samples as they would introduce incoherences with the 3D geometry.

The proposed single image VGfM method has a better or similar accuracy than the methods which do not use 3D information. This suggests that the information contained in the ellipsoids is beneficial for predicting relationships and that our model is able to use it. We can draw similar conclusions for the fusion mechanism. Indeed the fusion mechanism shows improvements for the predicates which are common on the dataset. For these cases, the model successfully manages to leverage on the different sources of information to reach an improvement of accuracy of 4% with respect to the initial baseline. However, it fails to improve

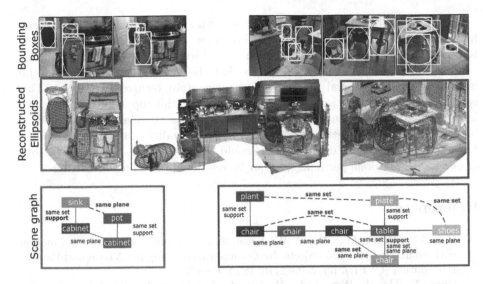

Fig. 6. The top row shows images extracted from two sequences together with the bounding box detections in yellow and in white the conics used to estimate the ellipsoids. The second row shows the resulting ellipsoids of these two sequences as well as the global object layout of the room. The third row shows the corresponding scene graphs obtained with our proposed approach. We did not display all the relations to ease the visualization. Predicates in bold brown font are miss-detections and bold green font with dashed line are false alarms (best viewed in color). (Color figure online)

for the ones which contain only a few training examples. This effect should be more important for the fusion mechanism since in this case, one training sample corresponds to a sequence of 10 images. Thus the number of instances in the training data is roughly divided by 10.

Figure 6 shows some qualitative results of two image sequences coming from the same room. On the left, the model successfully identified the two sets of objects, and it detects that the two cabinets are on the same plane. Since perspective effects are strong, this reasoning would be difficult with 2D features only. The right part is a complex scene with many overlapping objects. Although some errors are still present, leveraging over multiple views provides, as a 3D graph, a rich description of the scene which could enable further high level reasoning.

6   Conclusions

We addressed the problem of generating a 3D scene graph from multiple views of a scene. The VGfM approach leverages both geometry and visual appearance and it learns to refine globally the features and to merge the different sources of information through a message passing framework. We have evaluated on a new dataset which focuses on the relationships in 3D and show that our method outperforms a 2D baseline method.

The problem of creating a scene graph in both 2D and 3D from multiple views has been addressed for the first time in this paper, however there are many areas to be explored that can enhance performances. First, other sources of knowledge could be used. In particular, [32] shows that the manifold of the scene-graph is rather low dimensional as many of them contain recurrent patterns. This suggests that a strong prior could be built to encode this topology. Secondly, the knowledge about the visual appearance and the semantic relationships could be used to refine the geometric nodes by refining the quality of the ellipsoids. Last but not least, the case of dynamic scene could be investigated. As the predictions of our model are done per image, it can be readily applied on this setting.

References

1. Bao, S.Y., Bagra, M., Chao, Y.W., Savarese, S.: Semantic structure from motion with points, regions, and objects. In: Conference on Computer Vision and Pattern Recognition (CVPR), pp. 2703–2710. IEEE (2012)
2. Chen, X., Ma, H., Wan, J., Li, B., Xia, T.: Multi-view 3D object detection network for autonomous driving. In: Conference on Computer Vision and Pattern Recognition (CVPR), pp. 211–219. IEEE (2017)
3. Cho, K., Van Merriënboer, B., Bahdanau, D., Bengio, Y.: On the properties of neural machine translation: encoder-decoder approaches. arXiv preprint arXiv:1409.1259 (2014)
4. Choy, C.B., Xu, D., Gwak, J.Y., Chen, K., Savarese, S.: 3D-R2N2: a unified approach for single and multi-view 3D object reconstruction. In: Leibe, B., Matas, J., Sebe, N., Welling, M. (eds.) ECCV 2016. LNCS, vol. 9912, pp. 628–644. Springer, Cham (2016). https://doi.org/10.1007/978-3-319-46484-8_38
5. Dai, A., Chang, A.X., Savva, M., Halber, M., Funkhouser, T., Nießner, M.: Scannet: Richly-annotated 3D reconstructions of indoor scenes. In: Computer Vision and Pattern Recognition (CVPR), pp. 2075–2084. IEEE (2017)
6. Dai, A., Nießner, M., Zollöfer, M., Izadi, S., Theobalt, C.: BundleFusion: real-time globally consistent 3D reconstruction using on-the-fly surface re-integration. Trans. Graph. (TOG) **36**, 76a (2017)
7. Dai, B., Zhang, Y., Lin, D.: Detecting visual relationships with deep relational networks. In: Conference on Computer Vision and Pattern Recognition (CVPR), pp. 3298–3308 (2017)
8. Daniels, Z.A., Metaxas, D.N.: Scenarios: a new representation for complex scene understanding. arXiv preprint arXiv:1802.06117 (2018)
9. Desai, C., Ramanan, D., Fowlkes, C.: Discriminative models for static human-object interactions. In: Computer Vision and Pattern Recognition Workshops (CVPR), pp. 9–16. IEEE (2010)
10. Dong, J., Fei, X., Soatto, S.: Visual inertial semantic scene representation for 3D object detection. In: Conference on Computer Vision and Pattern Recognition (CVPR), pp. 782–790. IEEE (2017)
11. Gay, P., Rubino, C., Bansal, V., Del Bue, A.: Probabilistic structure from motion with objects (PSfMO). In: International Conference on Computer Vision (ICCV), pp. 3075–3084. IEEE (2017)
12. Hane, C., Zach, C., Cohen, A., Pollefeys, M.: Dense semantic 3D reconstruction. Pattern Anal. Mach. Intell. (PAMI) **39**(9), 1730–1743 (2017)

13. Johnson, J., et al.: Image retrieval using scene graphs. In: Conference on Computer Vision and Pattern Recognition (CVPR), pp. 3668–3678. IEEE (2015)
14. Kang, K., Ouyang, W., Li, H., Wang, X.: Object detection from video tubelets with convolutional neural networks. In: Conference on Computer Vision and Pattern Recognition (CVPR), pp. 1744–1756. IEEE (2016)
15. Krishna, R., et al.: Visual genome: connecting language and vision using crowd-sourced dense image annotations. Int. J. Comput. Vis. (IJCV) **123**(1), 32–73 (2017)
16. Li, Y., Ouyang, W., Zhou, B., Wang, K., Wang, X.: Scene graph generation from objects, phrases and region captions. In: Conference on Computer Vision and Pattern Recognition (CVPR), pp. 1261–1270. IEEE (2017)
17. Liang, X., Shen, X., Feng, J., Lin, L., Yan, S.: Semantic object parsing with graph LSTM. In: Leibe, B., Matas, J., Sebe, N., Welling, M. (eds.) ECCV 2016. LNCS, vol. 9905, pp. 125–143. Springer, Cham (2016). https://doi.org/10.1007/978-3-319-46448-0_8
18. Liao, W., Shuai, L., Rosenhahn, B., Yang, M.Y.: Natural language guided visual relationship detection. arXiv preprint arXiv:1711.06032 (2017)
19. Lu, C., Krishna, R., Bernstein, M., Fei-Fei, L.: Visual relationship detection with language priors. In: Leibe, B., Matas, J., Sebe, N., Welling, M. (eds.) ECCV 2016. LNCS, vol. 9905, pp. 852–869. Springer, Cham (2016). https://doi.org/10.1007/978-3-319-46448-0_51
20. Mur-Artal, R., Montiel, J.M.M., Tardos, J.D.: ORB-SLAM: a versatile and accurate monocular SLAM system. IEEE Trans. Rob. **31**(5), 1147–1163 (2015)
21. Nguyen, A., Yosinski, J., Clune, J.: Deep neural networks are easily fooled: high confidence predictions for unrecognizable images. In: Computer Vision and Pattern Recognition (CVPR), pp. 1544–1556. IEEE (2015)
22. Peyre, J., Laptev, I., Schmid, C., Sivic, J.: Weakly-supervised learning of visual relations. In: 2017 IEEE International Conference on Computer Vision (ICCV), pp. 5189–5198 (2017). https://doi.org/10.1109/ICCV.2017.554. ISSN 2380-7504
23. Reddy, N.D., Singhal, P., Chari, V., Krishna, K.M.: Dynamic body VSLAM with semantic constraints. In: International Conference on Intelligent Robots (ICIR), pp. 1897–1904. IEEE (2015)
24. Rubino, C., Crocco, M., Del Bue, A.: 3D object localisation from multi-view image detections. Pattern Anal. Mach. Intell. (PAMI) **40**(6), 1281–1294 (2018)
25. Sabour, S., Frosst, N., Hinton, G.E.: Dynamic routing between capsules. In: Neural Information Processing Systems NIPS, pp. 3856–3866 (2017)
26. Sengupta, S., Greveson, E., Shahrokni, A., Torr, P.H.S.: Urban 3D semantic modelling using stereo vision. In: International Conference on Robotics and Automation, pp. 580–585. IEEE (2013)
27. Simonyan, K., Zisserman, A.: Very deep convolutional networks for large-scale image recognition. arXiv preprint arXiv:1409.1556 (2014)
28. Sung, M., Kim, V.G., Angst, R., Guibas, L.: Data-driven structural priors for shape completion. ACM Trans. Graph. (TOG) **34**(6), 175 (2015)
29. Tripathi, S., Lipton, Z.C., Belongie, S.J., Nguyen, T.Q.: Context matters: refining object detection in video with recurrent neural networks. In: British Machine Vision Conference (BMVC), pp. 1723–1731. BMVA (2016)
30. Tulsiani, S., Gupta, S., Fouhey, D., Efros, A.A., Malik, J.: Factoring shape, pose, and layout from the 2D image of a 3D scene. In: Computer Vision and Pattern Regognition (CVPR). IEEE (2018)
31. Xu, D., Zhu, Y., Choy, C.B., Fei-Fei, L.: Scene graph generation by iterative message passing. In: 2017 IEEE Conference on Computer Vision and Pattern Recognition (CVPR), pp. 3097–3106. IEEE (2017)

32. Zellers, R., Yatskar, M., Thomson, S., Choi, Y.: Neural motifs: scene graph parsing with global context. In: Conference on Computer Vision and Pattern Recognition CVPR, pp. 3294–3304. IEEE (2018)
33. Zhang, H., Kyaw, Z., Chang, S.F., Chua, T.S.: Visual translation embedding network for visual relation detection. In: Conference on Computer Vision and Pattern Recognition (CVPR), pp. 4–12. IEEE (2017)
34. Zheng, S., et al.: Conditional random fields as recurrent neural networks. In: 2015 IEEE International Conference on Computer Vision (ICCV), pp. 1529–1537 (2015). https://doi.org/10.1109/ICCV.2015.179. ISSN 2380-7504

Deep Semantic Matching with Foreground Detection and Cycle-Consistency

Yun-Chun Chen[1,2]($\boxtimes$), Po-Hsiang Huang[2], Li-Yu Yu[2], Jia-Bin Huang[3],
Ming-Hsuan Yang[4,5], and Yen-Yu Lin[1]

[1] Academia Sinica, Taipei, Taiwan
ycchen918@citi.sinica.edu.tw
[2] National Taiwan University, Taipei, Taiwan
[3] Virginia Tech, Blacksburg, USA
[4] University of California, Merced, USA
[5] Google Cloud, Sunnyvale, USA

Abstract. Establishing dense semantic correspondences between object instances remains a challenging problem due to background clutter, significant scale and pose differences, and large intra-class variations. In this paper, we present an end-to-end trainable network for learning semantic correspondences using only matching image pairs without manual keypoint correspondence annotations. To facilitate network training with this weaker form of supervision, we (1) explicitly estimate the foreground regions to suppress the effect of background clutter and (2) develop cycle-consistent losses to enforce the predicted transformations across multiple images to be geometrically plausible and consistent. We train the proposed model using the PF-PASCAL dataset and evaluate the performance on the PF-PASCAL, PF-WILLOW, and TSS datasets. Extensive experimental results show that the proposed approach achieves favorably performance compared to the state-of-the-art. The code and model will be available at https://yunchunchen.github.io/WeakMatchNet/.

1 Introduction

Dense correspondence matching is an important and active research topic in computer vision. Optical flow estimation [1,2] and stereo matching [3,4] aim to estimate per-pixel correspondence to match across images depicting the same scene or object instance. While correspondence estimation has been extensively studied, there has been a growing trend to extend the idea of matching the same objects across images to matching images covering *different instances* of an object category. This progress not only attracts substantial attention but also facilitates many real-world applications ranging from object recognition [5], object co-segmentation [6–8], to 3D reconstruction [9]. However, due to the presence of background clutter, ambiguity induced by large intra-class variations, and the limited scalability of obtaining large-scale datasets with manually annotated correspondences, semantic matching remains challenging.

© Springer Nature Switzerland AG 2019
C. V. Jawahar et al. (Eds.): ACCV 2018, LNCS 11363, pp. 347–362, 2019.
https://doi.org/10.1007/978-3-030-20893-6_22

| Input | Rocco *et al.* [15] | Ours |

Fig. 1. Comparisons with the state-of-the-art semantic matching algorithm [15]. Existing semantic matching methods often suffer from background clutter during matching and may produce inconsistent matching results when swapping the source/target image. Through integrating foreground detection and cycle-consistent checking into semantic matching, our method produces more accurate and consistent matching results in both directions.

Conventional methods for semantic matching rely on hand-crafted descriptors such as SIFT [5] or HOG [10] as well as an effective geometric regularizer. However, these hand-crafted descriptors cannot be adapted to the given visual domains, leading to sub-optimal performance of semantic matching. Driven by the recent success of convolutional neural networks (CNNs), several learning-based approaches have been proposed for tackling the problem of semantic matching [11–15]. While promising results have been shown, these approaches still suffer from the following limitations. The methods in [11–14] require a vast amount of supervised data for training the network. Collecting a large-scale and diverse data, however, is expensive and labor-intensive. While weakly supervised methods such as Rocco *et al.* [15] have been recently proposed to relax the issue, these approaches implicitly enforce the background features from both images to be similar. Thus, they often suffer from the unfavorable effect of background clutter.

In this paper, we address these challenges by performing foreground detection and enforcing cycle consistency constraints in semantic matching. To suppress the negative impacts caused by background clutter, we develop a foreground detection module that allows the model to exclude background regions and focus on matching the detected foreground regions. As such, the effect of background clutter can be alleviated. To address the matching difficulties caused by complex appearance and large intra-class variations, we focus on filtering out correspondences with geometric inconsistency. Our key insight is that correct correspondence should be *cycle-consistent* meaning that when matching a particular point from one image to the other and then performing reverse matching, we should arrive at the same spot. To exploit this property, we introduce a cycle-consistency loss that provides additional supervisory signals for network training. We further extend this idea to explore transitivity consistency across multiple images. We build upon the model by Rocco et al. [15] for a weakly-supervised and end-to-end trainable network and evaluate the effectiveness of the proposed approach on three standard benchmarks. Experimental results demonstrate that our approach improves the baseline model [15], as shown in Fig. 1, and performs favorably against the state-of-the-art methods.

Our contributions are summarized as follows. First, we present a weakly-supervised learning framework that integrates foreground detection into semantic matching. With a module for explicit foreground detection, the proposed network suppresses the unfavorable effect of background clutter. Second, our model implicitly tackles the ambiguity induced by vast matching space by inferring bi-directional geometric transformations during matching. With these transformations, we explicitly enforce the inferred geometric transformations to be cycle-consistent by introducing the *forward-backward consistency loss*. In addition, we explore the property of transitivity consistency and introduce the *transitivity consistency loss* to further enhance the matching performance. We train our network with the image pairs of the PF-PASCAL dataset [16]. We then evaluate the proposed model on several standard benchmark datasets for semantic matching, including the PF-PASCAL [16], PF-WILLOW [16], and TSS [7] datasets. Extensive comparisons with existing semantic matching algorithms demonstrate that the proposed approach achieves the state-of-the-art performance.

2 Related Work

Semantic matching has been extensively studied in the literature. Here, we review several related topics.

Semantic Correspondence. Conventional methods to semantic matching [17–19] leverage hand-crafted descriptors such as SIFT [5] or HOG [10] along with geometric matching models. These methods find keypoint correspondences across images through energy minimization. The SIFT Flow [5] method aligns two images with SIFT features [5] using a similar formulation as an optical flow algorithm. Kim et al. [20] compute dense correspondence efficiently using the deformable spatial pyramid. Ham et al. [16] use the object proposals as the matching primitives and leverage the HOG descriptors to establish semantic correspondence. With the use of object proposals, the Proposal Flow method is robust to scaling and background clutter. Taniai et al. [7] propose a hierarchical Markov random field model to jointly recover object co-segmentation and dense correspondences. However, none of the aforementioned methods *learns* the descriptors for semantic matching.

Semantic Correspondence via Deep Learning. Convolutional neural networks have been successfully applied to semantic matching. Choy et al. [11] propose the universal correspondence network (UCN) and a correspondence contrastive loss for network training. The UCN method adopts a convolutional spatial transformer for feature transformations, making their method robust to scaling and rotations. Kim *et al.* [13] propose the fully convolutional self-similarity (FCSS) descriptor and integrate the descriptor into the Proposal Flow framework [16] for image matching. The SCNet [12] method learns a geometrically plausible model for semantic correspondence by incorporating geometric consistency constraints into its loss function. While the methods in [12,13] employ trainable descriptors for semantic correspondence, the feature matching is learned at the *object-proposal* level. Consequently, these methods are not end-to-end trainable since a fusion step is required to produce the final results. Rocco *et al.* [14] present an end-to-end trainable CNN architecture based on estimating parametric geometric transformations. While these methods [11–14,16] perform better than those based on hand-crafted features, the dependency of supervised data (in terms of manually labeled keypoint correspondence) for training limits the scalability.

Several recent CNN-based methods [15,21,22] have developed weakly supervised methods for semantic correspondence. The AnchorNet [21] learns a set of filters whose response is geometrically consistent across different object instances. The AnchorNet model, however, is not end-to-end trainable due to the use of the hand-crafted alignment model. The WarpNet [22] learns fine-grained image matching with small-scale and pose variations via aligning objects across images through known deformation. Inspired by the inlier scoring procedure of RANSAC, Rocco *et al.* [15] propose an end-to-end trainable alignment network which computes dense semantic correspondence while aligning two images.

Our proposed method differs from these methods [15,21] in two aspects. First, our approach further takes into account foreground detection. Our network learns feature embedding to enhance inter-image foreground similarity while alleviating the unfavorable effects caused by complex background. Second, our model simultaneously infers bi-directional transformations. We explicitly enforce cycle-consistent constraints on the predicted transformations, resulting in more accurate and consistent matching results.

Cycle Consistency. Exploiting cycle consistency property to regularize learning has been extensively studied. In the context of motion analysis, computing bi-directional optical flow has been shown to be useful to reason about occlusion for learning optical flow [23,24] and enforcing temporal consistency [25,26]. In the context of image-to-image translation, enforcing cycle consistency enables learning mapping between domains with unpaired data [27,28]. Several methods exploit the idea of cycle consistency for semantic matching. Zhou *et al.* [29] tackle the problem of matching multiple images by jointly optimizing feature matching and enforcing cycle consistency. The FlowWeb [30] method learns image alignment by establishing globally-consistent dense correspondences with cycle consistency constraints. However, these methods [29,30] employ hand-engineered descriptors which cannot adapt to an arbitrary object category given for matching. Zhou *et al.* [31] establish dense correspondences by using an additional 3D CAD model to form a cross-instance loop between synthetic data and real images. However, the cycle consistency loss in [31] requires four images at a time.

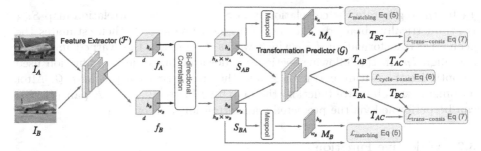

Fig. 2. Semantic matching network. Our model is composed of two CNN modules, including a feature extractor $\mathcal{F}$ for extracting features and a transformation predictor $\mathcal{G}$ for estimating the geometric transformations between a given image pair. We train the model with three loss functions, including the foreground-guided matching loss $\mathcal{L}_{\text{matching}}$, the forward-backward consistency loss $\mathcal{L}_{\text{cycle-consis}}$, and the transitivity consistency loss $\mathcal{L}_{\text{trans-consis}}$ (if given 3 input images).

In contrast, we develop two loss functions to enforce cycle consistency and do not need additional data to guide the training. Experimental results demonstrate that by exploiting cycle consistency constraints, the proposed method produces consistent matching results and improves the performance.

3   Proposed Algorithm

In this section, we first provide an overview of our approach. We then describe each loss in our objective function in detail and the implementation details.

3.1   Framework Overview

Let $\mathcal{D} = \{I_i\}_{i=1}^{N}$ denote a set of images consists of instances of the same object category, where I_i is the ith image and N is the number of images. Our goal is to learn a CNN-based model that can estimate the keypoint correspondences between each image pair (I_A, I_B) in $\mathcal{D}$ *without knowing the object class in advance*. Our formulation for semantic matching is *weakly-supervised* since training our model requires only weak image-level supervision in the form of training image pairs containing common objects. No ground truth keypoint correspondences are used.

To accomplish this task, we present an end-to-end trainable network which is composed of two modules: (1) the feature extractor $\mathcal{F}$ and (2) the transformation predictor $\mathcal{G}$. The feature extractor $\mathcal{F}$ extracts features for each image in a given image pair. The transformation predictor $\mathcal{G}$ predicts the transformation that warps an image so that the warped image can better align the other image.

As shown in Fig. 2, the proposed network architecture takes an image pair as input. For a given image pair (I_A, I_B), we use the feature extractor $\mathcal{F}$ to extract their feature maps f_A and f_B, respectively. We then compute correlation from

f_A to f_B to generate the correlation map S_{AB}. The other correlation map S_{BA} is symmetrically obtained. The transformation predictor $\mathcal{G}$ then estimates the geometric transformation T_{AB} which warps I_A so that the warped image $\tilde{I}_A$ can align I_B. In the following section, we describe our objective function used to optimize the feature extractor $\mathcal{F}$ and the transformation predictor $\mathcal{G}$. After optimizing the objective function, the matching between an image pair (I_A, I_B) can be performed via the predicted transformation T_{AB} or T_{BA}.

3.2   Objective Function

The overall training objective consists of three loss functions. First, the foreground-guided matching loss $\mathcal{L}_{\text{matching}}$ minimizes the distance between the corresponding features based on the estimated geometric transformations. Unlike existing semantic matching methods [14,15], our model predicts foreground masks to suppress the effect of background clutter by excluding background matching. Second, the forward-backward consistency loss $\mathcal{L}_{\text{cycle-consis}}$ and the transitivity consistency loss $\mathcal{L}_{\text{trans-consis}}$ enforce the predicted transformations across multiple images to be geometrically plausible and consistent. Both losses regularize the network training. Specifically, our training objective is

$$\mathcal{L} = \mathcal{L}_{\text{matching}} + \lambda_C \cdot \mathcal{L}_{\text{cycle-consis}} + \lambda_T \cdot \mathcal{L}_{\text{trans-consis}}, \tag{1}$$

where λ_C and λ_T are hyper-parameters used to control the relative importance of the respective loss functions. Below we outline the details of each loss function.

3.3   Foreground-Guided Matching Loss

To reduce the effect of background clutter and enforce only foreground regions to be similar, our model minimizes the foreground-guided matching loss $\mathcal{L}_{\text{matching}}$. Given an image pair (I_A, I_B), the feature extractor $\mathcal{F}$ extracts their respective feature maps $f_A \in \mathbb{R}^{h_A \times w_A \times d}$ and $f_B \in \mathbb{R}^{h_B \times w_B \times d}$, where d is the number of channels. We correlate f_A with f_B to generate the correlation map $S_{AB} \in \mathbb{R}^{h_A \times w_A \times h_B \times w_B}$. Each element $S_{AB}(i, j, s, t) = S_{AB}(\mathbf{p}, \mathbf{q})$ records the normalized inner product between the feature vectors stored at two spatial locations $\mathbf{p} = [i, j]^\top$ in f_A and $\mathbf{q} = [s, t]^\top$ in f_B. The other correlation map $S_{BA} \in \mathbb{R}^{h_B \times w_B \times h_A \times w_A}$ can be computed symmetrically. The correlation map S_{AB} is reshaped to a three-dimensional tensor with dimensions h_A, w_A, and $(h_B \times w_B)$, i.e., $S_{AB} \in \mathbb{R}^{h_A \times w_A \times (h_B \times w_B)}$. As such, the reshaped correlation map S_{AB} can be interpreted as a dense $h_A \times w_A$ grid with $(h_B \times w_B)$-dimensional local features. We apply the reshaping operation to S_{BA} as well. With the reshaped S_{AB}, we use the transformation predictor $\mathcal{G}$ [14] to estimate a geometric transformation T_{AB} which warps I_A to $\tilde{I}_A$ so that $\tilde{I}_A$ aligns well to I_B.

Since the correlation map $S_{AB}(\mathbf{p}, \mathbf{q})$ records the normalized inner product between two feature vectors located at $\mathbf{p}$ in f_A and $\mathbf{q}$ in f_B. Our model estimates the foreground mask $M_A \in \mathbb{R}^{h_A \times w_A}$ by

$$M_A(\mathbf{p}) = \max_{\mathbf{q}}(S_{AB}(\mathbf{p}, \mathbf{q})). \tag{2}$$

Note that both the correlation maps S_{AB} and S_{BA} are compiled through a rectified linear unit (ReLU) to eliminate negative matching values in advance. Therefore, the value of the estimated foreground masks at each pixel will be bounded between 0 and 1. Intuitively, the mask $M_A(\mathbf{p})$ has a low value (i.e., location $\mathbf{p}$ is likely to belong to background) if none of the feature vectors in f_B matches well with $f_A(\mathbf{p})$. The mask M_B can be obtained following a similar procedure.

With the estimated geometric transformation T_{AB}, we can identify and filter out geometrically inconsistent correspondences. Consider a correspondence with endpoints $(\mathbf{p} \in \mathcal{P}_A, \mathbf{q} \in \mathcal{P}_B)$, where $\mathcal{P}_A$ and $\mathcal{P}_B$ are the sets of all spatial coordinates of f_A and f_B, respectively. The distance $\|T_{AB}(\mathbf{p}) - \mathbf{q}\|$ represents the projection error of this correspondence with respect to transformation T_{AB}. Following Rocco *et al.* [15], we introduce a correspondence mask m_A to determine if the correspondences are geometrically consistent with transformation T_{AB}. Specifically, m_A is of the form

$$ m_A(\mathbf{p}, \mathbf{q}) = \begin{cases} 1, & \text{if } \|T_{AB}(\mathbf{p}) - \mathbf{q}\| \leq \varphi, \\ 0, & \text{otherwise.} \end{cases} \text{, for } \mathbf{p} \in \mathcal{P}_A \text{ and } \mathbf{q} \in \mathcal{P}_B, \qquad (3) $$

where $\varphi = 1$ is the number of pixels.

Given the geometric transformation T_{AB} and the correspondence mask m_A, we compute matching score of each spatial location $\mathbf{p} \in \mathcal{P}_A$ as

$$ s_A(\mathbf{p}) = \sum_{\mathbf{q} \in \mathcal{P}_B} m_A(\mathbf{p}, \mathbf{q}) \cdot S_{AB}(\mathbf{p}, \mathbf{q}). \qquad (4) $$

To suppress the effect of background clutter, we incorporate the estimated foreground masks to focus on matching the detected foreground regions. We define the foreground-guided matching loss $\mathcal{L}_{\text{matching}}$ as

$$ \mathcal{L}_{\text{matching}}(I_A, I_B; \mathcal{F}, \mathcal{G}) = -\left(\sum_{\mathbf{p} \in \mathcal{P}_A} s_A(\mathbf{p}) \cdot M_A(\mathbf{p}) + \sum_{\mathbf{q} \in \mathcal{P}_B} s_B(\mathbf{q}) \cdot M_B(\mathbf{q}) \right). \quad (5) $$

Note that the negative sign in (5) is used in the objective function, since maximizing the matching score corresponds to minimizing the foreground-guided matching loss $\mathcal{L}_{\text{matching}}$.

3.4   Cycle Consistency

For a pair of images I_A and I_B, the transformation predictor $\mathcal{G}$ estimates a geometric transformation T_{AB} which maps pixel coordinates from I_A to I_B. However, the large capacity of the transformation predictor $\mathcal{G}$ often leads to a circumstance where various transformations can warp I_A to $\tilde{I}_A$ such that $\tilde{I}_A$ aligns I_B very well. This phenomenon implies that using the foreground-guided matching loss $\mathcal{L}_{\text{matching}}$ alone is insufficient to reliably train the transformation predictor $\mathcal{G}$ in the weakly supervised setting since no ground truth correspondences are available to constrain the learning of predicting transformations. We address this issue by simultaneously estimating T_{AB} and T_{BA} and enforce the predicted transformations to be geometrically plausible and consistent across multiple images. As such, exploiting the cycle consistency constraint greatly reduces the feasible space of transformations and can serve as a regularization term in training the transformation predictor $\mathcal{G}$. To this end, we develop two loss functions where cycle-consistency checking is performed in conjunction with the proposed method such that the model is end-to-end trainable. The developed loss functions are described in the following.

Forward-Backward Consistency Loss. Consider the correlation maps S_{AB} and S_{BA} generated from images I_A and I_B. The forward consistency states that property $T_{BA}(T_{AB}(\mathbf{p})) \approx \mathbf{p}$ holds for any $\mathbf{p} \in \mathcal{P}_A$. By the same token, the backward consistency means $T_{AB}(T_{BA}(\mathbf{q})) \approx \mathbf{q}$ for any $\mathbf{q} \in \mathcal{P}_B$. The resultant forward-backward consistency loss $\mathcal{L}_{\text{cycle-consis}}$ is then defined by

$$\mathcal{L}_{\text{cycle-consis}}(I_A, I_B; \mathcal{F}, \mathcal{G}) = \sum_{\mathbf{p} \in \mathcal{P}_A} \|T_{BA}(T_{AB}(\mathbf{p})) - \mathbf{p}\| \\ + \sum_{\mathbf{q} \in \mathcal{P}_B} \|T_{AB}(T_{BA}(\mathbf{q})) - \mathbf{q}\|, \tag{6}$$

where $\|T_{BA}(T_{AB}(\mathbf{p})) - \mathbf{p}\|$ is the reprojection error between coordinate $\mathbf{p}$ and the reprojected coordinate $T_{BA}(T_{AB}(\mathbf{p}))$.

Transitivity Consistency Loss. We further extend the forward-backward consistency between a pair of images to the transitivity consistency across multiple images. Considering the case of three images I_A, I_B, and I_C, we first estimate three geometric transformations T_{AB}, T_{BC}, and T_{AC}. Transitivity consistency in this case states that the coordinate transformation from I_A to I_C should be path invariant. That is, for any coordinate $\mathbf{p} \in \mathcal{P}_A$, the property, $T_{BC}(T_{AB}(\mathbf{p})) \approx T_{AC}(\mathbf{p})$, holds. We can thus introduce the transitivity consistency loss $\mathcal{L}_{\text{trans-consis}}$ as

$$\mathcal{L}_{\text{trans-consis}}(I_A, I_B, I_C; \mathcal{F}, \mathcal{G}) = \sum_{\mathbf{p} \in \mathcal{P}_A} \|T_{BC}(T_{AB}(\mathbf{p})) - T_{AC}(\mathbf{p})\| \\ + \sum_{\mathbf{q} \in \mathcal{P}_B} \|T_{AC}(T_{BA}(\mathbf{p})) - T_{BC}(\mathbf{q})\|. \tag{7}$$

3.5 Network Selection and Initialization

We adopt the semantic matching network proposed by Rocco et al. [15] as our feature extractor $\mathcal{F}$ due to its state-of-the-art performance for image alignment. The network employs the ResNet-101 [32] model. The extracted features are those generated by layer conv4-23. For the transformation predictor $\mathcal{G}$, we use the same architecture as that in [14]. The transformation predictor $\mathcal{G}$ is a cascade of two modules predicting an affine transformation and a thin plate spline (TPS) transformation. Given an image pair, the model first estimates an affine transformation with 6 degrees of freedom to obtain a rough alignment. The model then performs a second-stage geometric estimation based on the roughly aligned image pair to predict TPS transformation for alignment refinement. Similar to Rocco *et al.* [14], we use a uniform 3×3 grid of control points for TPS, which corresponds to $3 \times 3 \times 2 = 18$ degrees of freedom. We initialize the feature extractor $\mathcal{F}$ and the transformation predictor $\mathcal{G}$ from the parameters pre-trained in [15] and fine-tune the feature extractor $\mathcal{F}$ and the transformation predictor $\mathcal{G}$ by using the proposed objective function. We note that there may exist degenerate solutions to the foreground-guided matching loss $\mathcal{L}_{\text{matching}}$ since no annotated correspondences are used to guide the network training. In this work, we build our model upon Rocco *et al.* [15], which is pre-trained on a large-scale synthetic dataset. The pre-trained model provides good enough initialization for predicting the geometric transformations, reducing the chance of falling into degenerate solutions. In addition, the foreground-guided matching loss $\mathcal{L}_{\text{matching}}$ and the cycle-consistency losses work jointly. The three adopted loss terms regularize the network training and avoid degenerate solutions.

4   Experimental Results

Experiments are conducted in this section. Here, we first describe the implementation details and the experimental setting. We evaluate and compare the proposed approach with the state-of-the-art, following analyzing the relative contributions of individual components in the proposed model.

4.1   Implementation Details

We implement our model using PyTorch. We use the training and validation image pairs from the PF-PASCAL dataset [16]. All images are resized to the resolution of 240×240. We perform data augmentation by horizontal flipping, random cropping the input images, and swapping the order of images in the image pair. We train our model using the ADAM optimizer [33] with an initial learning rate of 5×10^{-8}. For transitivity consistency loss, the input triplets are randomly selected within a mini-batch. We sample $10 \times 10 = 100$ spatial coordinates for computing the forward-backward consistency loss and the transitivity consistency loss. The training process takes about 2 h on a single NVIDIA GeForce GTX 1080 GPU.

4.2   Evaluation Metric and Datasets

We conduct the evaluation on the PF-PASCAL [16], PF-WILLOW [16], and TSS [7] benchmark datasets.

Table 1. Per-class PCK on the PF-PASCAL dataset with $\tau = 0.1$.

Method	aero	bike	bird	boat	bottle	bus	car	cat	chair	cow	d.table	dog	horse	moto	person	plant	sheep	sofa	train	tv	mean
HOG+PF-LOM [16]	73.3	74.4	54.4	50.9	49.6	73.8	72.9	63.6	46.1	79.8	42.5	48.0	68.3	66.3	42.1	62.1	65.2	57.1	64.4	58.0	62.5
UCN [11]	64.8	58.7	42.8	59.6	47.0	42.2	61.0	45.6	49.9	52.0	48.5	49.5	53.2	72.7	53.0	41.4	83.3	49.0	**73.0**	66.0	55.6
VGG-16+SCNet-A [12]	67.6	72.9	69.3	59.7	74.5	72.7	73.2	59.5	51.4	78.2	39.4	50.1	67.0	62.1	**69.3**	68.5	78.2	63.3	57.7	59.8	66.3
VGG-16+SCNet-AG [12]	83.9	81.4	70.6	62.5	60.6	81.3	81.2	59.5	53.1	81.2	**62.0**	58.7	65.5	73.3	51.2	58.3	60.0	69.3	61.5	**80.0**	69.7
VGG-16+SCNet-AG+ [12]	85.5	84.4	66.3	70.8	57.4	82.7	82.3	71.6	**54.3**	**95.8**	55.2	59.5	**68.6**	75.0	56.3	60.4	60.0	**73.7**	66.5	76.7	72.2
VGG-16+CNNGeo [14]	79.5	80.9	69.9	61.1	57.8	77.1	84.4	55.5	48.1	83.3	37.0	54.1	58.2	70.7	51.4	41.4	60.0	44.3	55.3	30.0	62.6
ResNet-101+CNNGeo(S) [14]	83.0	82.2	81.1	50.0	57.8	79.9	92.8	77.5	44.7	85.4	28.1	69.8	65.4	77.1	64.0	65.2	100.0	50.8	44.3	54.4	69.5
ResNet-101+CNNGeo(W) [15]	84.7	88.9	80.9	55.6	76.6	89.5	**93.9**	79.6	52.0	85.4	28.1	71.8	67.0	75.1	66.3	70.5	100.0	62.1	62.3	61.1	74.8
Ours	**85.6**	**89.6**	**82.1**	**83.3**	**85.9**	**92.5**	**93.9**	**80.2**	52.2	85.4	55.2	**75.2**	64.0	**77.9**	67.2	**73.8**	100.0	65.3	69.3	61.1	**78.0**

Evaluation Metric. We evaluate the performance of the proposed method on a semantic correspondence task. To assess the performance, we adopt the percentage of correct keypoints (PCK) metric [34] which measures the percentage of keypoints whose reprojection errors are below the given threshold. The reprojection error is the Euclidean distance $d(\phi(\mathbf{p}), \mathbf{p}^*)$ between the locations of the warped keypoint $\phi(\mathbf{p})$ and the ground truth keypoint $\mathbf{p}^*$. The threshold is defined as $\tau \cdot \max(h, w)$ where h and w are the height and width of the annotated object bounding box on the image, respectively.

PF-PASCAL [16]. The PF-PASCAL dataset is selected from the PASCAL 2011 keypoint annotations [35] containing 1,351 semantically related image pairs from 20 object categories. For images of a category, they contain different object instances of that category with similar poses but different appearances. In addition, the presence of background clutter makes it a challenging dataset on semantic matching. We divide the dataset into 735 pairs for training, 308 pairs for validation, and 308 pairs for testing. Manually annotated correspondences are provided for each image pairs. However, under the weakly supervised setting, we do not use the keypoint annotations for training. The annotations are used only for evaluation. We compute the PCK for each object category with τ equals to 0.1.

PF-WILLOW [16]. The PF-WILLOW dataset is composed of 100 images with 900 image pairs divided into four semantically related subsets: car, duck, motorbike, and wine bottle. Each subset contains images with large intra-class variations and background clutters. For each image, there are 10 keypoint annotations. We follow Han et al. [12] and compute the PCK at three different thresholds with τ equals to 0.05, 0.1, and 0.15, respectively.

TSS [7]. The TSS dataset comprises 400 semantically related image pairs divided into three groups, including FG3DCar, JODS, and PASCAL. FG3DCar contains 195 image pairs of automobiles. JODS is composed of 81 image pairs of airplanes, cars, and horses. There are 124 image pairs of trains, cars, buses, bikes, and motorbikes form the group of PASCAL. Ground truth flows for each image pair are provided. Following Taniai et al. [7], we compute the PCK over foreground object by setting τ to 0.05.

Table 2. Ablation experiments on PF-PASCAL with $\tau = 0.1$.

Method	Mean
Rocco *et al.* [15]	74.8
Rocco *et al.* [15] + $\mathcal{L}_{\text{matching}}$	75.5
Rocco *et al.* [15] + $\mathcal{L}_{\text{cycle-consis}}$	77.4
Rocco *et al.* [15] + $\mathcal{L}_{\text{trans-consis}}$	77.6
Ours	**78.0**

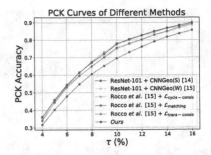

Fig. 3. PCK curves on the PF-PASCAL dataset.

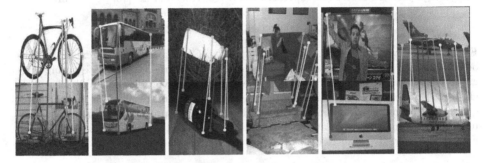

Fig. 4. Semantic correspondence results on the PF-PASCAL dataset. The matched coordinates are linked with color lines. (Color figure online)

4.3 Experimental Results on the PF-PASCAL Dataset

In the following, we compare the performance of the proposed method with the state-of-the-art approaches. Note that many of the existing methods require manually annotated correspondences while our model can be trained using only image-level supervision.

Performance Evaluation. We compare our method with the Proposal Flow [16], the UCN [11], different versions of the SCNet [12], the CNNGeo [14] with different feature extractors, and a weakly supervised approach proposed by Rocco *et al.* [15]. Table 1 presents the experimental results for the PF-PASCAL dataset. Our results show that the proposed approach compares favorably against state-of-the-art methods, achieving an overall PCK of 78.0% (outperforming the previous best method [15] by 3.2%). The advantage of incorporating foreground detection and enforcing cycle consistency constraints can be observed by comparing our method with ResNet-101+CNNGeo(W) [15] since both methods utilize the same feature descriptor and are trained with image-level supervision only.

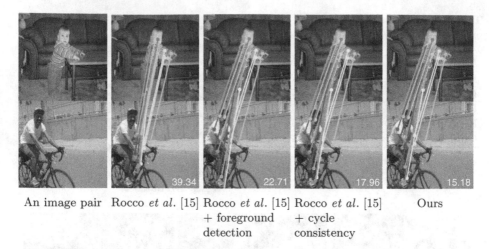

An image pair   Rocco *et al.* [15]   Rocco *et al.* [15]   Rocco *et al.* [15]   Ours
                                        + foreground   + cycle
                                        detection   consistency

Fig. 5. Visualization of the effect of each component. Given an image pair, existing methods often suffer from the negative impacts due to background clutter. Integrating foreground detection into semantic matching alleviates the unfavorable effects of background clutters. Enforcing cycle consistency improves the matching result. Our method integrates foreground detection and exploits cycle-consistency property in semantic matching, resulting in more accurate results. The bottom right corners display the errors, namely the average distances between the predicted keypoints and the ground truth.

Figure 4 presents the qualitative results of semantic correspondence on the PF-PASCAL dataset. To further highlight the importance of each component of the proposed method, we present an ablation study of our method.

Ablation Study. To analyze the importance of each loss function, we conduct ablation experiments on the PF-PASCAL [16] dataset. Table 2 presents the mean PCK value of the variants of our approach evaluated on the PF-PASCAL dataset with τ equals to 0.1. Our results show that both $\mathcal{L}_{\text{cycle}-\text{consis}}$ and $\mathcal{L}_{\text{trans}-\text{consis}}$ substantially improve the performance when comparing with Rocco *et al.* [15]. We visualize the effect of each component in Fig. 5. To demonstrate the effectiveness of forward-backward consistency property, we visualize an example in Fig. 7 where the red points indicate the key points and the green points represent the reprojected points. The length of the yellow line represents the distance (loss) between the corresponding points. We observe that enforcing cycle consistency effectively encourages the network to produce geometrically consistent predictions. However, the performance gain of using only the foreground-guided matching loss $\mathcal{L}_{\text{matching}}$ is modest. We believe that the reason is due to the evaluation protocol of datasets considers only the matching on the foreground region. Namely, matching a background pixel in the source image to a foreground pixel in the target image will not be penalized. To demonstrate the effect of foreground-guided matching loss $\mathcal{L}_{\text{matching}}$, we compute the percentage of correctly warped pixels (i.e., pixels in the foreground/background regions that are correctly warped into foreground/background region) over the entire dataset. As

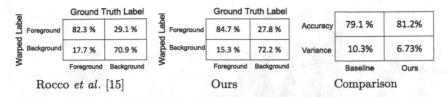

Fig. 6. Effect of using the foreground-guided matching loss $\mathcal{L}_{\text{matching}}$.

Table 3. Results on PF-WILLOW.

Method	$\tau = 0.05$	$\tau = 0.1$	$\tau = 0.15$
SIFT Flow [5]	0.247	0.380	0.504
DAISY w/SF [36]	0.324	0.456	0.555
DeepC w/SF [37]	0.212	0.364	0.518
LIFT w/SF [38]	0.224	0.346	0.489
VGG w/SF [39]	0.324	0.456	0.555
FCSS w/SF [13]	0.354	0.532	0.681
LOM HOG [16]	0.284	0.568	0.682
UCN [11]	0.291	0.417	0.513
DSFM [40]	-	0.680	-
SCNet-A [12]	0.390	0.725	0.873
SCNet-AG [12]	0.394	0.721	0.871
SCNet-AG+ [12]	0.386	0.704	0.853
ResNet-101+CNNGeo(S) [14]	0.448	0.777	0.899
ResNet-101+CNNGeo(W) [15]	0.477	0.812	0.917
Ours	**0.491**	**0.819**	**0.922**

Table 4. Results on TSS. Marker * indicates that the method uses extra images from the PASCAL VOC 2007 dataset.

Method	FG3DCar	JODS	PASCAL	Avg
HOG+PF-LOM [16]	0.786	0.653	0.531	0.657
HOG+TSS [7]	0.830	0.595	0.483	0.636
FCSS+SIFT Flow [13]	0.830	0.656	0.494	0.660
FCSS+PF-LOM [13]	0.839	0.635	0.582	0.685
HOG+OADSC [41]*	0.875	0.708	0.729	0.771
FCSS+DCTM [42]	0.891	0.721	**0.610**	0.740
VGG-16+CNNGeo [14]	0.835	0.656	0.527	0.673
ResNet-101+CNNGeo(S) [14]	0.886	0.758	0.560	0.735
ResNet-101+CNNGeo(W) [15]	0.892	0.758	0.562	0.737
Ours	**0.898**	**0.768**	0.560	**0.742**

shown in Fig. 6, our method effectively reduces the errors in matching pixels from foreground to background and vice versa. The improvement here is important in real-world applications but is not reflected in the metric used in the standard datasets. We also note that our method may not produce a clear figure-ground separation when the background contains visually similar regions to the foreground object in the other image. However, this case is also challenging for most methods.

The ablation study shows that all of the proposed components play crucial roles in producing accurate matching results. From Fig. 3, we observe that the proposed method outperforms the best competitor [15] with a significant margin at multiple thresholds.

4.4   Experimental Results on the PF-WILLOW and TSS Datasets

To evaluate the generalization capability, we apply the learned model trained on the PF-PASCAL dataset to test directly on the PF-WILLOW and TSS datasets without finetuning on these two datasets.

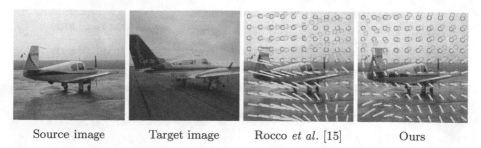

| Source image | Target image | Rocco *et al.* [15] | Ours |

Fig. 7. Cycle consistency property. We present the visualization that demonstrates the effect of forward-backward consistency loss where the red points indicate the keypoints while the green points denote the reprojected points. Yellow line represents the distance (loss) between the linked points. (Color figure online)

Results on the PF-WILLOW Dataset. Table 3 presents the quantitative results for the PF-WILLOW dataset. We compare the performance with several recent methods [11–15] as well as conventional approaches [5,36–39] using handcrafted features. The results are directly taken from [12] except [14,15]. For [14,15], we run the code provided by the authors to obtain the results. From Table 3, we observe that our model achieves the state-of-the-art performance with all three thresholds.

Results on the TSS Dataset. We also evaluate the performance on the TSS dataset. Table 4 presents the quantitative results. We observe that our method achieves the state-of-the-art performance on two of the three groups of the TSS dataset: FG3DCar and JODS. Our results are slightly worse than that in [41] in the PASCAL group. However, the method in [41] uses additional images from the PASCAL VOC 2007 dataset. We report their results for completeness. Under the same experimental settings, the proposed method performs favorably against existing approaches.

5   Conclusions

In this work, we present an effective approach to improve semantic matching. The core technical novelty of our approach lies in the explicit modeling of a *foreground detection* module to suppress the effect of background clutter and exploiting the *cycle consistency* constraints so that the predicted geometric transformations are geometrically plausible and consistent across multiple images. The network training requires only training image pairs with image-level supervision and thus significantly alleviates the cost of constructing and labeling large-scale training datasets. Experimental results demonstrate that our approach performs favorably against existing semantic matching algorithms on several standard benchmarks. Moving forward, we believe that the semantic matching network can be further integrated to other computer vision tasks, e.g., supporting 3D semantic object reconstruction and fine-grained visual recognition.

Acknowledgement. This work is supported in part by Ministry of Science and Technology under grants MOST 105-2221-E-001-030-MY2 and MOST 107-2628-E-001-005-MY3.

References

1. Horn, B.K.P., Schunck, B.G.: Determining optical flow. Artif. Intell. **17**(1–3), 185–203 (1981)
2. Lucas, B.D., Kanade, T., et al.: An iterative image registration technique with an application to stereo vision. In: IJCAI (1981)
3. Scharstein, D., Szeliski, R.: A taxonomy and evaluation of dense two-frame stereo correspondence algorithms. IJCV **47**, 7–42 (2002)
4. Wang, Z.-F., Zheng, Z.-G.: A region based stereo matching algorithm using cooperative optimization. In: CVPR (2008)
5. Liu, C., Yuen, J., Torralba, A.: SIFT Flow: dense correspondence across scenes and its applications. TPAMI **33**, 978–994 (2011)
6. Chen, H.-Y., Lin, Y.-Y., Chen, B.-Y.: Co-segmentation guided hough transform for robust feature matching. TPAMI **37**, 2388–2401 (2015)
7. Taniai, T., Sinha, S.N., Sato, Y.: Joint recovery of dense correspondence and cosegmentation in two images. In: CVPR (2016)
8. Hsu, K.-J., Lin, Y.-Y., Chuang, Y.-Y.: Co-attention CNNs for unsupervised object co-segmentation. In: IJCAI (2018)
9. Mustafa, A., Hilton, A.: Semantically coherent co-segmentation and reconstruction of dynamic scenes. In: CVPR (2017)
10. Dalal, N., Triggs, B.: Histograms of oriented gradients for human detection. In: CVPR (2005)
11. Choy, C.B., Gwak, J.Y., Savarese, S., Chandraker, M.: Universal correspondence network. In: NIPS (2016)
12. Han, K., et al.: SCNet: learning semantic correspondence. In: ICCV (2017)
13. Kim, S., Min, D., Ham, B., Jeon, S., Lin, S., Sohn, K.: FCSS: fully convolutional self-similarity for dense semantic correspondence. In: CVPR (2017)
14. Rocco, I., Arandjelović, R., Sivic, J.: Convolutional neural network architecture for geometric matching. In: CVPR (2017)
15. Rocco, I., Arandjelović, R., Sivic, J.: End-to-end weakly-supervised semantic alignment. In: CVPR (2018)
16. Ham, B., Cho, M., Schmid, C., Ponce, J.: Proposal flow: semantic correspondences from object proposals. TPAMI **40**, 1711–1725 (2017)
17. Hu, Y.-T., Lin, Y.-Y.: Progressive feature matching with alternate descriptor selection and correspondence enrichment. In: CVPR (2016)
18. Hu, Y.-T., Lin, Y.-Y., Chen, H.-Y., Hsu, K.-J., Chen, B.-Y.: Matching images with multiple descriptors: an unsupervised approach for locally adaptive descriptor selection. TIP **24**, 5995–6010 (2015)
19. Hsu, K.-J., Lin, Y.-Y., Chuang, Y.-Y., et al.: Robust image alignment with multiple feature descriptors and matching-guided neighborhoods. In: CVPR (2015)
20. Kim, J., Liu, C., Sha, F., Grauman, K.: Deformable spatial pyramid matching for fast dense correspondences. In: CVPR (2013)
21. Novotny, D., Larlus, D., Vedaldi, A.: AnchorNet: a weakly supervised network to learn geometry-sensitive features for semantic matching. In: CVPR (2017)
22. Kanazawa, A., Jacobs, D.W., Chandraker, M.: WarpNet: Weakly supervised matching for single-view reconstruction. In: CVPR (2016)

23. Meister, S., Hur, J., Roth, S.: UnFlow: unsupervised learning of optical flow with a bidirectional census loss. In: AAAI (2018)
24. Zou, Y., Luo, Z., Huang, J.-B.: DF-Net: unsupervised joint learning of depth and flow using cross-task consistency. In: Ferrari, V., Hebert, M., Sminchisescu, C., Weiss, Y. (eds.) ECCV 2018. LNCS, vol. 11209, pp. 38–55. Springer, Cham (2018). https://doi.org/10.1007/978-3-030-01228-1_3
25. Huang, J.-B., Kang, S.B., Ahuja, N., Kopf, J.: Temporally coherent completion of dynamic video. ACM Trans. Graph. (TOG) **35**(6), 196 (2016)
26. Lai, W.-S., Huang, J.-B., Wang, O., Shechtman, E., Yumer, E., Yang, M.-H.: Learning blind video temporal consistency. In: Ferrari, V., Hebert, M., Sminchisescu, C., Weiss, Y. (eds.) ECCV 2018. LNCS, vol. 11219, pp. 179–195. Springer, Cham (2018). https://doi.org/10.1007/978-3-030-01267-0_11
27. Zhu, J.-Y., Park, T., Isola, P., Efros, A.A.: Unpaired image-to-image translation using cycle-consistent adversarial networks. In: CVPR (2017)
28. Lee, H.-Y., Tseng, H.-Y., Huang, J.-B., Singh, M., Yang, M.-H.: Diverse image-to-image translation via disentangled representations. In: Ferrari, V., Hebert, M., Sminchisescu, C., Weiss, Y. (eds.) ECCV 2018. LNCS, vol. 11205, pp. 36–52. Springer, Cham (2018). https://doi.org/10.1007/978-3-030-01246-5_3
29. Zhou, X., Zhu, M., Daniilidis, K.: Multi-image matching via fast alternating minimization. In: ICCV (2015)
30. Zhou, T., Jae Lee, Y., Yu, S.X., Efros, A.A.: FlowWeb: joint image set alignment by weaving consistent, pixel-wise correspondences. In: CVPR (2015)
31. Zhou, T., Krahenbuhl, P., Aubry, M., Huang, Q., Efros, A.A.: Learning dense correspondence via 3D-guided cycle consistency. In: CVPR (2016)
32. He, K., Zhang, X., Ren, S., Sun, J.: Deep residual learning for image recognition. In: CVPR (2016)
33. Kingma, D.P., Ba, J.: Adam: A method for stochastic optimization. arXiv:1412.6980 (2014)
34. Yang, Y., Ramanan, D.: Articulated human detection with flexible mixtures of parts. TPAMI **35**, 2878–2890 (2013)
35. Bourdev, L., Malik, J.: Poselets: body part detectors trained using 3D human pose annotations. In: ICCV (2009)
36. Tola, E., Lepetit, V., Fua, P.: DAISY: An efficient dense descriptor applied to wide-baseline stereo. TPAMI **32**, 815–830 (2010)
37. Zagoruyko, S., Komodakis, N.: Learning to compare image patches via convolutional neural networks. In: CVPR (2015)
38. Yi, K.M., Trulls, E., Lepetit, V., Fua, P.: LIFT: Learned invariant feature transform. In: Leibe, B., Matas, J., Sebe, N., Welling, M. (eds.) ECCV 2016. LNCS, vol. 9910, pp. 467–483. Springer, Cham (2016). https://doi.org/10.1007/978-3-319-46466-4_28
39. Simonyan, K., Zisserman, A.: Very deep convolutional networks for large-scale image recognition. arXiv:1409.1556 (2014)
40. Ufer, N., Ommer, B.: Deep semantic feature matching. In: CVPR (2017)
41. Yang, F., Li, X., Cheng, H., Li, J., Chen, L.: Object-aware dense semantic correspondence. In: CVPR (2017)
42. Kim, S., Min, D., Lin, S., Sohn, K.: DCTM: Discrete-continuous transformation matching for semantic flow. In: CVPR (2017)

Hidden Two-Stream Convolutional Networks for Action Recognition

Yi Zhu[1][(✉)] [iD], Zhenzhong Lan[2] [iD], Shawn Newsam[1] [iD],
and Alexander Hauptmann[2] [iD]

[1] University of California at Merced, Merced, CA 95343, USA
{yzhu25,snewsam}@ucmerced.edu
[2] Carnegie Mellon University, Pittsburgh, PA 15213, USA
{lanzhzh,alex}@cs.cmu.edu

Abstract. Analyzing videos of human actions involves understanding the temporal relationships among video frames. State-of-the-art action recognition approaches rely on traditional optical flow estimation methods to pre-compute motion information for CNNs. Such a two-stage approach is computationally expensive, storage demanding, and not end-to-end trainable. In this paper, we present a novel CNN architecture that implicitly captures motion information between adjacent frames. We name our approach hidden two-stream CNNs because it only takes raw video frames as input and directly predicts action classes without explicitly computing optical flow. Our end-to-end approach is 10x faster than its two-stage baseline. Experimental results on four challenging action recognition datasets: UCF101, HMDB51, THUMOS14 and ActivityNet v1.2 show that our approach significantly outperforms the previous best real-time approaches.

Keywords: Action recognition · Optical flow · Unsupervised learning

1 Introduction

The field of human action recognition has advanced rapidly over the past few years. We have moved from manually designed features [3,23] to learned convolutional neural network (CNN) features [11,21]; from encoding appearance information to encoding motion information [19]; and from learning local features to learning global video features [13,25]. The performance has continued to soar higher as we incorporate more of the steps into an end-to-end learning framework. Nevertheless, current state-of-the-art CNN structures still have difficulty in capturing motion information directly from video frames. Instead, traditional local optical flow estimation methods are used to pre-compute motion information for the CNNs [19]. This two-stage pipeline, first compute optical flow

Electronic supplementary material The online version of this chapter (https://doi.org/10.1007/978-3-030-20893-6_23) contains supplementary material, which is available to authorized users.

© Springer Nature Switzerland AG 2019
C. V. Jawahar et al. (Eds.): ACCV 2018, LNCS 11363, pp. 363–378, 2019.
https://doi.org/10.1007/978-3-030-20893-6_23

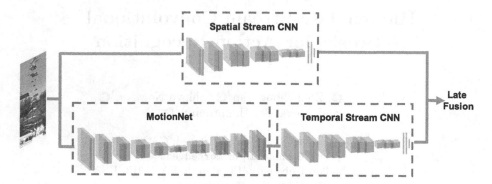

Fig. 1. Illustration of proposed hidden two-stream networks. MotionNet takes consecutive video frames as input and estimates motion. Then the temporal stream CNN learns to project the motion information to action labels. Late fusion is performed through the weighted averaging of the prediction scores of the temporal and spatial streams. Both streams are end-to-end trainable.

and then learn the mapping from optical flow to action labels, is sub-optimal for the following reasons:

- The pre-computation of optical flow is time consuming and storage demanding compared to the CNN step.
- Traditional optical flow estimation is completely independent of the final tasks like action recognition and is therefore potentially sub-optimal.

To solve the above problems, researchers have proposed various methods other than optical flow to capture motion information in videos. For example, new representations like motion vectors [27,33] and RGB image difference [25] or architectures like recurrent neural networks (RNN) [16] and 3D CNNs [17,21,22, 28]. However, most of these are not as effective as optical flow for human action recognition[1]. Therefore, in this paper, we aim to address the above mentioned problems in a more direct way. We adopt the end-to-end CNN approach to learn optical flow so that we can avoid costly computation and storage and obtain task-specific motion representations. However, we face many challenges to learn such a motion estimation model:

- We need to train the models without supervision. The ground truth flow required for supervised training is usually not available except for limited synthetic data [35,36].
- We need to train our optical flow estimation models from scratch. The models (filters) learned for optical flow estimation tasks are very different from models (filters) learned for other vision tasks [6,14,29].
- We cannot simply use the traditional optical flow estimation loss functions. We are concerned chiefly with how to learn an optimal motion representation for video action recognition.

---

[1] Detailed comparisons can be found in the supplementary material.

To address these challenges, we first train a CNN with the goal of generating optical flow from a set of consecutive frames. Through a set of specially designed operators and unsupervised loss functions, our new training step can generate optical flow that is similar to that generated by one of the best traditional methods [32]. As illustrated in the bottom of Fig. 1, we call this network MotionNet. Given the MotionNet, we concatenate it with a temporal stream CNN that maps the estimated optical flow to the target action labels. We then fine-tune this stacked temporal stream CNN in an end-to-end manner with the goal of predicting action classes for the input frames. We call our new approach hidden two-stream networks as it implicitly generates motion information for action recognition. Our contributions include:

- Our method is both computationally and storage efficient. It is around 10x faster than its two-stage baseline, and we do not need to store the pre-computed optical flow.
- Our method outperforms previous real-time approaches on four challenging action recognition datasets by a large margin.
- The proposed MotionNet is flexible in that it can be directly concatenated with other video action recognition frameworks [1,16,22,34] to improve their efficiency.
- We demonstrate the generalizability of our end-to-end learned optical flow by showing promising results on four optical flow benchmarks without fine-tuning.

2 Related Work

Significant advances in understanding human activities in video have been made over the past few years. Initially, traditional handcrafted features such as Improved Dense Trajectories (IDT) [23] dominated the field of video analysis for several years. Despite their superior performance, IDT and its improvements are computationally formidable for real applications. CNNs [11,21], which are often several orders of magnitude faster than IDTs, performed much worse than IDTs in the beginning. This inferior performance is mostly because CNNs have difficulty in capturing motion information among frames. Later on, two-stream CNNs [19] addressed this problem by pre-computing the optical flow using traditional optical flow estimation methods [32] and training a separate CNN to encode the pre-computed optical flow. This additional stream (a.k.a., the temporal stream) significantly improved the accuracy of CNNs and finally allowed them to outperform IDTs on several benchmarks. These accuracy improvements indicate the importance of temporal motion information for action recognition as well as the inability of existing CNNs to capture such information.

However, compared to the CNN, the optical flow calculation is computationally expensive. It is the major speed bottleneck of the current two-stream approaches. As an alternative, Zhang et al. [33] proposed to use motion vectors to replace the more precise optical flow. This simple improvement brought more than 20x speedup compared to the traditional two-stream approaches. However, this speed improvement came with an equally significant accuracy drop. The encoded motion vectors lack fine structures, and contain noisy and inaccurate motion patterns, leading to much worse accuracy compared to the more precise optical flow [32]. These weaknesses are fundamental and can not be improved. Another more promising approach is to learn to predict optical flow using supervised CNNs, which is closer to our approach. Ng *et al.* [15] used optical flow calculated by traditional methods as supervision to train a network to predict optical flow. This method avoids the pre-computation of optical flow at inference time and greatly speeds up the process. However, the quality of the optical flow calculated by this approach is limited by the quality of the traditional flow estimation, which again limits its potential on action recognition. Ilg *et al.* [8] use a network trained on synthetic data where ground truth flow exists. The ability of synthetic data to represent the complexity of real data is very limited. Ilg *et al.* [8] actually show that there is a domain gap between real data and synthetic data. To address this gap, they simply grow the synthetic data to narrow the gap. The problem with this solution is that it may not work for other datasets and it is not feasible to do this for all datasets. Our work addresses the optical flow estimation problem in a much more fundamental and promising way. We predict optical flow on-the-fly using CNNs, thus addressing the computation and storage problems. And we perform unsupervised pre-training on real data, thus addressing the domain gap problem.

Besides the computational problem, traditional optical flow estimation is completely independent of the high-level final tasks like action recognition and is therefore potentially sub-optimal. However, our approach is end-to-end optimized. It is important to distinguish between these two ways of introducing motion information to the encoding CNNs. Although optical flow is currently being used to represent the motion information in the videos, we do not know whether it is an optimal representation. There might be an underlying motion representation that is better than optical flow. In fact, a recent work [30] demonstrated that fixed flow estimation is not as good as task-oriented flow for general computer vision tasks. Hence, we believe that our end-to-end learning framework will help us extract better motion representations than traditional optical flow for action recognition. However, for notational convenience, we still refer our learned motion representation as optical flow.

3   Hidden Two-Stream Networks

In this section, we describe our proposed hidden two-stream networks in detail. We first introduce our unsupervised network for optical flow estimation along with employed good practices in Sect. 3.1. We name it MotionNet. In Sect. 3.2, we stack the temporal stream network upon MotionNet to allow end-to-end training. Finally, we introduce the hidden two-stream CNNs in Sect. 3.3 which combines our stacked temporal stream with a spatial stream.

3.1 Unsupervised Optical Flow Learning

We treat optical flow estimation as an image reconstruction problem [31]. Given a frame pair, we hope to generate the optical flow that allows us to reconstruct one frame from the other. Formally, taking a pair of adjacent frames I_1 and I_2 as input, our CNN generates a flow field V. Then using the predicted flow field V and I_2, we get the reconstructed frame I_1' using backward warping, i.e., $I_1' = \mathcal{T}[I_2, V]$, where $\mathcal{T}$ is the inverse warping function. Our goal is to minimize the photometric error between I_1 and I_1'. The intuition is that if the estimated flow and the next frame can be used to reconstruct the current frame, then the network should have learned useful representations of the underlying motions.

MotionNet. Our MotionNet is a fully convolutional network, consisting of a contracting part and an expanding part. The contracting part is a stack of convolutional layers and the expanding part is a chain of combined convolutional and deconvolutional layers. The details of our network can be seen in the supplementary material. We describe the challenges and proposed good practices to learn better motion representation for action recognition below.

First, we design a network that focuses on small displacement motion. For real data such as YouTube videos, we often encounter the problem that foreground motion (human actions of interest) is small, but the background motion (camera motion) is dominant. Thus, we adopt 3×3 kernels throughout the network to detect local, small motions. Besides, we keep the high frequency image details for later stages. Our first two convolutional layers do not use striding. We use strided convolution instead of pooling for image downsampling because pooling is shown to be harmful for dense per-pixel prediction tasks.

Second, our MotionNet computes multiple losses at multiple scales. Due to the skip connections between the contracting and expanding parts, the intermediate losses can regularize each other and guide earlier layers to converge faster to the final objective. We explore three loss functions that help us to generate better optical flow. These loss functions are as follows.

- A standard pixelwise reconstruction error function, which is calculated as:

$$L_{\text{pixel}} = \frac{1}{hw} \sum_i^h \sum_j^w \rho(I_1(i,j) - I_2(i + V_{i,j}^x, \ j + V_{i,j}^y)). \tag{1}$$

The V^x and V^y are the estimated optical flow in the horizontal and vertical directions. The inverse warping $\mathcal{T}$ is performed using a spatial transformer module [9]. Here we use a robust convex error function, the generalized Charbonnier penalty $\rho(x) = (x^2 + \epsilon^2)^\alpha$, to reduce the influence of outliers. h and w denote the height and width of images I_1 and I_2.
- A smoothness loss that addresses the aperture problem that causes ambiguity in estimating motions in non-textured regions. It is calculated as:

$$L_{\text{smooth}} = \rho(\nabla V_x^x) + \rho(\nabla V_y^x) + \rho(\nabla V_x^y) + \rho(\nabla V_y^y). \tag{2}$$

∇V_x^x and ∇V_y^x are the gradients of the estimated flow field V^x in each direction. Similarly, ∇V_x^y and ∇V_y^y are the gradients of V^y. The generalized Charbonnier penalty $\rho(x)$ is the same as in the pixelwise loss.

– A structural similarity (SSIM) loss function [26] that helps us to learn the structure of the frames. SSIM is a perceptual quality measure. Given two $K \times K$ image patches I_{p1} and I_{p2}, it is calculated as

$$\text{SSIM}(I_{p1}, I_{p2}) = \frac{(2\mu_{p1}\mu_{p2} + c_1)(2\sigma_{p1p2} + c_2)}{(\mu_{p1}^2 + \mu_{p2}^2 + c_1)(\sigma_{p1}^2 + \sigma_{p2}^2 + c_2)}. \tag{3}$$

Here, μ_{p1} and μ_{p2} are the mean of image patches I_{p1} and I_{p2}, σ_{p1} and σ_{p2} are the variance of image patches I_{p1} and I_{p2}, and σ_{p1p2} is the covariance of these two image patches. c_1 and c_2 are two constants to stabilize division by a small denominator. In our experiments, K is set to 8 and c_1 and c_2 are 0.0001 and 0.001, respectively.

In order to compare the similarity between two images I_1 and I_1', we adopt a sliding window approach to partition the images into local patches. The stride for the sliding window is set to 8 in both the horizontal and vertical directions. Hence, our SSIM loss function is defined as:

$$L_{\text{ssim}} = \frac{1}{N} \sum_n^N (1 - \text{SSIM}(I_{1n}, I_{1n}')). \tag{4}$$

where N is the number of patches we can extract from an image given the sliding stride of 8, n is the patch index. I_{1n} and I_{1n}' are two corresponding patches from original image I_1 and the reconstructed image I_1'. Our experiments show that this simple strategy significantly improves the quality of our estimated flows. It forces our MotionNet to produce flow fields with clear motion boundaries.

Hence, the loss at each scale s is a weighted sum of the pixelwise reconstruction loss, the piecewise smoothness loss, and the region-based SSIM loss,

$$L_s = \lambda_1 \cdot L_{\text{pixel}} + \lambda_2 \cdot L_{\text{smooth}} + \lambda_3 \cdot L_{\text{ssim}} \tag{5}$$

where λ_1, λ_2, and λ_3 weight the relative importance of the different metrics during training. Since we have predictions at five scales (flow2 to flow6) due to five expansions in the decoder, the overall loss of MotionNet is a weighted sum of loss L_s:

$$L_{\text{all}} = \sum_{s=1}^{5} \delta_s L_s \tag{6}$$

where the δ_s are set to balance the losses at each scale and are numerically of the same order. We describe how we determine the values of these weights in the supplementary materials.

Third, unsupervised learning of optical flow introduces artifacts in homogeneous regions because the brightness assumption is violated. We insert additional convolutional layers between deconvolutional layers in the expanding part to yield smoother motion estimation. We also explored other techniques in the literature, like adding flow confidence and multiplying by the original color images [8] during expanding. However, we did not observe any improvements.

In Sect. 5.1, we conduct an ablation study to demonstrate the contributions of each of these strategies. Though our network structure is similar to a concurrent work [8], MotionNet is fundamentally different from FlowNet2. First, we perform unsupervised learning while [8] performs supervised learning for optical flow prediction. Unsupervised learning allows us to avoid the domain gap between synthetic data and real data. Unsupervised learning also allows us to train the model for target tasks like action recognition in an end-to-end fashion even if the datasets of target applications do not have ground truth optical flow. Second, our network architecture is carefully designed to balance efficiency and accuracy. For example, MotionNet only has one network, while FlowNet2 has 5 similar subnetworks. The model footprints of MotionNet and FlowNet2 [8] are 170M and 654M, and the prediction speeds are 370 fps and 25 fps, respectively. We also present an architecture search in the supplementary materials to obtain deep insights in terms of the model trade-off between accuracy and efficiency.

3.2   Projecting Motion Features to Actions

Given that MotionNet and the temporal stream are both CNNs, we would like to combine these two modules into one stage and perform end-to-end training. There are multiple ways to design such a combination to project motion features to action labels. Here, we explore two ways, stacking and branching.

Stacking is the most straightforward approach and just places MotionNet in front of the temporal stream, treating MotionNet as an off-the-shelf flow estimator. Branching is more elegant in terms of architecture design. It uses a single network for both motion feature extraction and action classification. The convolutional features are shared between the two tasks. Due to space limitations, we show in the supplementary materials that stacking is more effective than branching. It achieves better action recognition performance while remaining complementary to the spatial stream. From now on, we choose stacking to project the motion features to action labels.

For stacking, we first need to normalize the estimated flows before feeding them to the encoding CNN. More specifically, as suggested in [19], we first clip the motions that are larger than 20 pixels to 20 pixels. Then we normalize and quantize the clipped flows to have a range between 0–255. We find such a normalization is important for good temporal stream performance and design a new normalization layer for it.

Second, we need to determine how to fine tune the network, including which loss to use during the fine tuning. We explored different settings. (a) Fixing MotionNet, which means that we do not use the action loss to fine-tune the optical flow estimator. (b) Both MotionNet and the temporal stream CNN are fine-tuned, but only the action categorical loss function is computed. No unsupervised objective (5) is involved. (c) Both MotionNet and the temporal stream

CNN are fine-tuned, and all the loss functions are computed. Since motion is largely related to action, we hope to learn better motion estimators by this multi-task way of learning. As will be demonstrated later in Sect. 4.2, model (c) achieves the best action recognition performance.

Third, we need to capture relatively long-term motion dependencies. We accomplish this by inputting a stack of multiple consecutive flow fields. Simonyan and Zisserman [19] found that a stack of 10 flow fields achieves a much higher accuracy than only using a single flow field. To make fair comparison, we also fix the length of our input to be 11 frames to allow us to generate 10 optical flows.

3.3   Hidden Two-Stream Networks

We also show the results of combining our stacked temporal stream with a spatial stream. These results are important as they are strong indicators of whether our stacked temporal stream indeed learns complementary motion information or just appearance information.

Following the testing scheme of [19,24], we evenly sample 25 frames/clips for each video. For each frame/clip, we perform 10x data augmentation by cropping the 4 corners and 1 center, flipping them horizontally and averaging the prediction scores (before softmax operation) over all crops of the samples. In the end, we fuse the two streams' scores with a spatial to temporal stream ratio of 1:1.5.

4   Experiments

4.1   Evaluation Datasets

We perform experiments on four widely used action recognition benchmarks, UCF101 [20], HMDB51 [12], THUMOS14 [5] and ActivityNet [7]. UCF101 is composed of realistic action videos from YouTube. It contains $13,320$ video clips distributed among 101 action classes. HMDB51 includes $6,766$ video clips of 51 actions extracted from a wide range of sources, such as online videos and movies. Both UCF101 and HMDB51 have a standard three-split evaluation protocol and we report the average recognition accuracies over the three splits. THUMOS14 and ActivityNet are large-scale video datasets for action recognition and detection, which contain long untrimmed videos. THUMOS14 has 101 action classes. It includes a training set, validation set, test set and background set. We don't use the background set in our experiments. We use 13,320 training and 1,010 validation videos for training and report the performance on 1,574 test videos. For ActivityNet, we use its 1.2 version which has 100 action classes. Following the standard evaluation split, 4,819 training and 2,383 validation videos are used for training and 2,480 videos for testing.

4.2   Results

In this section, we evaluate our proposed framework on the first split of UCF101. We report the accuracy as well as the processing speed of the inference step in

Table 1. Comparison of accuracy and efficiency. Top section: Two-stage temporal stream approaches. Middle Section: End-to-end temporal stream approaches. Bottom Section: Two-stream approaches.

Method	Accuracy (%)	fps
TV-L1 [32]	85.65	14.75
FlowNet [4]	55.27	52.08
FlowNet2 [8]	79.64	8.05
NextFlow [18]	72.2	42.02
Enhanced Motion Vectors [33]	79.3	390.7
MotionNet (2 frames)	84.09	48.54
ActionFlowNet (2 frames) [15]	70.0	200.0
ActionFlowNet (16 frames) [15]	83.9	–
Stacked Temporal Stream CNN (a)	83.76	169.49
Stacked Temporal Stream CNN (b)	84.04	169.49
Stacked Temporal Stream CNN (c)	84.88	169.49
Two-Stream CNNs [19]	88.0	14.3
Very Deep Two-Stream CNNs [24]	**90.9**	**12.8**
Hidden Two-Stream CNNs (a)	87.50	120.48
Hidden Two-Stream CNNs (b)	87.99	120.48
Hidden Two-Stream CNNs (c)	**89.82**	**120.48**

frames per second. The results are shown in Table 1. The implementation details are in the supplementary materials.

Top Section of Table 1: Here we compare the performance of two-stage approaches. By two-stage, we mean optical flow is pre-computed, cached, and then fed to a CNN classifier to project flow to action labels. For fair comparison, our MotionNet here is pre-trained on UCF101, but not fine-tuned using the action classification loss. It only takes frame pairs as input and outputs one flow estimate. The results show that our MotionNet achieves a good balance between accuracy and speed in this setting.

In terms of accuracy, our unsupervised MotionNet is competitive to TV-L1 while performing much better (4%–12% absolute improvement) than other methods of generating flows, including supervised training using synthetic data (FlowNet [4] and FlowNet2 [8]), and directly getting flows from compressed videos (Enhanced Motion Vectors [33]). These improvements are very significant in datasets like UCF101. In terms of speed, we are also among the best of the CNN based methods and much faster than TV-L1, which is one of the fastest traditional methods.

Middle Section of Table 1: Here we examine the performance of end-to-end CNN based approaches. None of these approaches store intermediate flow information and thus run much faster than the two-stage approaches. If we compare the average running time of these approaches to the two-stage ones, we can see that the time spent on writing and reading intermediate results is almost 3x as much as the time spent on all other steps. Therefore, from an efficiency perspective, it is important to do end-to-end training and predict optical flow on-the-fly.

ActionFlowNet [15] is what we denote as a branched temporal stream. It is a multi-task learning model to jointly estimate optical flow and recognize actions. The convolutional features are shared which leads to faster speeds. However, even the 16 frames ActionFlowNet performs 1% worse than our stacked temporal stream. Besides, ActionFlowNet uses optical flow from traditional methods as labels to perform supervised training. This indicates that during the training phase, it still needs to cache flow estimates which is computation and storage demanding for large-scale video datasets. Also the algorithm will mimic the failure cases of the classical approaches.

If we compare the way we fine-tune our stacked temporal stream CNNs, we can see that model (c) where we include all the loss functions to do end-to-end training, is better than the other models including fixing MotionNet weights (model (a)) and only using the action classification loss function (model (b)). These results show that both end-to-end fine-tuning and fine-tuning with unsupervised loss functions are important for stacked temporal stream CNN training.

Bottom Section of Table 1: Here we compare the performance of two-stream networks by fusing the prediction scores from the temporal stream CNN with the prediction scores from the spatial stream CNN. These comparisons are mainly used to show that stacked temporal stream CNNs indeed learn motion information that is complementary to what is learned in appearance streams.

The accuracy of the single stream spatial CNN is 80.97%. We observe from Table 1 that significant improvements are achieved by fusing a stacked temporal stream CNN with a spatial stream CNN to create a hidden two-stream CNN. These results show that our stacked temporal stream CNN is able to learn motion information directly from the frames and achieves much better accuracy than spatial stream CNN alone. This observation is true even in the case where we only use the action loss for fine-tuning the whole network (model (b)). This result is significant because it indicates that our unsupervised pre-training indeed finds a better path for CNNs to learn to recognize actions and this path will not be forgotten in the fine-tuning process. If we compare the hidden two-stream CNNs to the stacked temporal stream CNNs, we can see that the gap between model (c) and model (a)/(b) widens. The reason may be because, without the regularization of the unsupervised loss, the networks start to learn appearance information. Hence they become less complementary to the spatial CNNs.

Finally, we can see that our models achieve very similar accuracy to the original two-stream CNNs. Among the two representative works we show, Two-Stream CNNs [19] is the earliest two-stream work and Very Deep Two-Stream CNNs [24] is the one we improve upon. Therefore, Very Deep Two-Stream CNNs [24] is the most comparable work. We can see that our approach is about 1%

Table 2. Ablation study of good practices employed in MotionNet.

Method	Small Disp	SSIM	CDC	Smoothness	MultiScale	Accuracy (%)
MotionNet	×	×	×	×	×	77.79
MotionNet	✓	✓	✓	✓	×	80.63
MotionNet	✓	✓	✓	×	✓	80.14
MotionNet	✓	✓	×	✓	✓	81.25
MotionNet	✓	×	✓	✓	✓	81.58
MotionNet	×	✓	✓	✓	✓	82.22
MotionNet	✓	✓	✓	✓	✓	**82.71**

worse than Very Deep Two-Stream CNNs [24] in terms of accuracy but about 10x faster in terms of speed.

5 Discussion

5.1 Ablation Studies for MotionNet

Because of our specially designed loss functions and operators, our proposed MotionNet can produce high quality motion estimates, which allows us to achieve promising action recognition accuracy. Here, we run an ablation study to understand the contributions of these components. The results are shown in Table 2. *Small Disp* indicates using a network that focuses on small displacements. *CDC* means adding an extra convolution between deconvolutions in the expanding part of MotionNet. *MultiScale* indicates computing losses at multiple scales.

First, we examine the importance of using a network structure that focuses on small displacement motions. We keep the other aspects of the implementation the same, but use a larger kernel size and stride in the beginning of the network. The accuracy drops from 82.71% to 82.22%. This drop shows that using smaller kernels with a deeper network indeed helps to detect small motions.

Second, we examine the importance of adding the SSIM loss. Without SSIM, the action recognition accuracy drops to 81.58%. This more than 1% performance drop shows that it is important to focus on discovering the structure of frame pairs.

Third, we examine the effect of removing convolutions between the deconvolutions in the expanding part of MotionNet. This strategy is designed to smooth the motion estimation. As can be seen in Table 2, removing extra convolutions brings a significant performance drop from 82.71% to 81.25%.

Fourth, we examine the advantage of incorporating the smoothness objective. Without the smoothness loss, we obtain a much worse result of 80.14%. This result shows that our real-world data is very noisy. Adding smoothness regularization helps to generate smoother flow fields by suppressing noise. This suppression is important for the following temporal stream CNNs to learn better motion representations for action recognition.

Table 3. Evaluation of optical flow and action classification. For flow evaluation, lower error is better. For action recognition, higher accuracy is better.

Method	Sintel	KITTI2012	KITTI2015	Middlebury	UCF101
FlowNet2	**6.02**	**1.8**	**11.48**	0.52	81.97
TV-L1	10.46	14.6	47.64	**0.45**	**85.65**
MotionNet	11.93	7.5	30.65	0.91	84.88

Fifth, we examine the necessity of computing losses at multiple scales during deconvolution. Without the multi-scale scheme, the action recognition accuracy drops to 80.63%. The performance drop shows that it is important to regularize the output at each scale in order to produce the best flow estimation in the end. Otherwise, we found that the intermediate representations during deconvolution may drift to fit the action recognition task, and not predict optical flow.

Finally, we explore a model that does not employ any of these practices. As expected, the performance is the worst, which is 4.94% lower than our full MotionNet.

5.2   Learned Optical Flow

In this section, we systematically investigate the effects of different motion estimation models for action recognition, as well as their flow estimation quality. We also show some visual examples to discover possible directions for future improvement. Here, we compare three optical flow models: TV-L1, MotionNet and FlowNet2. To quantitatively evaluate the quality of learned flow, we test the three models on four well received benchmarks, MPI-Sintel, KITTI 2012, KITTI 2015 and Middlebury. For action recognition accuracy, we report their performance on UCF101 split1. The results can be seen in Table 3. We use EPE (endpoint error) to evaluate MPI-Sintel, KITTI 2012 and Middlebury with lower being better. We use Fl (percentage of optical flow outliers) to evaulate KITTI 2015 with lower being better. We use classification accuracy to evaluate UCF101 with higher being better.

For flow quality, FlowNet2 generally performs better, except on Middlebury because it mostly contains small displacements. Our MotionNet has similar performance to TV-L1 on Sintel and Middlebury, and outperforms TV-L1 on KITTI 2012 and KITTI 2015. The result is encouraging because the KITTI benchmark contains real data (not synthetic), which indicates that the flow estimation from our MotionNet is robust and generalizable. In addition, although FlowNet2 ranks higher on optical flow benchmarks, it performs the worst on action recognition tasks. This interesting observation means that lower EPE does not always lead to higher action recognition accuracy. This is because EPE is a very simple metric based on L2 distance, which does not consider motion boundary preservation or background motion removal. This is crucial, however, for recognizing complex human actions.

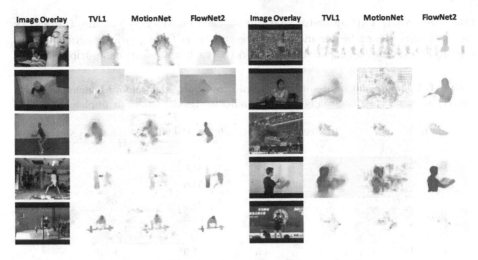

Fig. 2. Visual comparisons of estimated flow field from TV-L1, MotionNet and FlowNet2. Left: ApplyEyeMakeup, BabyCrawling, BodyWeightSquats, BoxingPunch-ingBag and CleanAndJerk. Right: Hammering, PlayingFlute, PommelHorse, Wall-Pushups and YoYo. This figure is best viewed in color. (Color figure online)

We also show some visual samples in Fig. 2 to help understand the effect of the quality of estimated flow fields for action recognition. The color scheme follows the standard flow field color coding in [8]. In general, the estimated flow fields from all three models look reasonable. MotionNet has lots of background noise compared to TV-L1 due to its global learning. This maybe the reason why it performs worse than TV-L1 for action recognition. FlowNet2 has very crisp motion boundaries, fine structures and smoothness in homogeneous regions. It is indeed a good flow estimator in terms of both EPE and visual inspection. However, it achieves much worse results for action recognition, 3.5% lower than TV-L1 and 2.9% lower than our MotionNet. Thus, which motion representation is best for action recognition remains an open question.

6   Comparison to State-of-the-Art Real-Time Approaches

In this section, we compare our proposed method to recent real-time state-of-the-art approaches as shown in Table 4[2]. Among all real-time methods, our hidden two-stream networks achieves the highest accuracy on the four benchmarks. We also show the flexibility of our MotionNet by concatenating it to temporal streams with different backbone CNN architectures, e.g., VGG16 [24], TSN [25] and I3D [1]. With deeper networks, we can achieve higher recognition accuracy and still be real-time. We are 6.1% better on UCF101, 14.2% better on HMDB51, 8.5% better on THUMOS14 and 7.8% better on ActivityNet than the previous

---

[2] In general, the requirement for real-time processing is 25 fps. We also compare to other non real-time approaches in the supplementary materials.

state-of-the-art. This indicates that our stacked end-to-end learning framework can implicitly learn better motion representations than motion vectors [10, 33] and RGB differences [25] with respect to the task of action recognition.

Table 4. Comparison to state-of-the-art real-time approaches on four benchmarks with respect to mean classification accuracy. * indicates results from our implementation.

Method	UCF101(%)	HMDB51(%)	THUMOS14(%)	ActivityNet(%)
MV + FV [10]	78.5	46.7	–	–
EMV [33]	80.2	–	41.6	–
C3D (1 Net) [21]	82.3	49.7*	54.6	74.1
ActionFlowNet [15]	83.9	56.4	51.3*	68.8*
RGB + EMV [33]	86.4	–	61.5	–
3DNet [2]	90.2	–	–	–
RGB Diff (TSN) [25]	91.0	64.5*	71.9*	83.0*
Ours (VGG16)	90.3	60.5	66.7	77.8
Ours (TSN)	93.2	66.8	74.5	87.9
Ours (I3D)	**97.1**	**78.7**	**80.6**	**91.2**

7   Conclusion

We have proposed a new framework called hidden two-stream networks to recognize human actions in video. It addresses the problem of capturing the temporal relationships among video frames which the current CNN architectures have difficulty with. Different from the current common practice of using traditional local optical flow estimation methods to pre-compute the motion information for CNNs, we use an unsupervised pre-training approach. Our MotionNet is computationally efficient and end-to-end trainable. It is flexible and can be directly applied in other frameworks for various video understanding applications. Experimental results on four challenging benchmarks demonstrate the effectiveness of our approach.

In the future, we would like to improve our hidden two-stream networks in the following directions. First, we would like to improve our optical flow prediction based on the observation that the smoothness loss has significant impact on the quality of the motion estimations for action recognition. Second, we would like to incorporate other best practices that improve the overall performance of the networks. For example, joint training of the two streams instead of a simple late fusion. Third, it would be interesting to see how addressing the false label assignment problem can help improve our overall performance. Finally, removing global camera motion and partial occlusion within the CNN framework would be helpful for both optical flow estimation and action recognition.

Acknowledgement. We gratefully acknowledge the support of NVIDIA Corporation through the donation of the Titan Xp GPUs used in this work.

References

1. Carreira, J., Zisserman, A.: Quo vadis, action recognition? A new model and the kinetics dataset. In: The IEEE Conference on Computer Vision and Pattern Recognition (CVPR) (2017)
2. Diba, A., Pazandeh, A.M., Van Gool, L.: Efficient two-stream motion and appearance 3D CNNs for video classification. In: European Conference on Computer Vision (ECCV) Workshops (2016)
3. Fernando, B., Gavves, E., Oramas, J.M., Ghodrati, A., Tuytelaars, T.: Modeling video evolution for action recognition. In: The IEEE Conference on Computer Vision and Pattern Recognition (CVPR) (2015)
4. Fischer, P., et al.: FlowNet: learning optical flow with convolutional networks. In: International Conference on Computer Vision (ICCV) (2015)
5. Gorban, A., et al.: THUMOS challenge: action recognition with a large number of classes (2015). http://www.thumos.info/
6. Gu, B., Xin, M., Huo, Z., Huang, H.: Asynchronous doubly stochastic sparse kernel learning. In: Association for the Advancement of Artificial Intelligence (AAAI) (2018)
7. Heilbron, F.C., Escorcia, V., Ghanem, B., Niebles, J.C.: ActivityNet: a large-scale video benchmark for human activity understanding. In: The IEEE Conference on Computer Vision and Pattern Recognition (CVPR) (2015)
8. Ilg, E., Mayer, N., Saikia, T., Keuper, M., Dosovitskiy, A., Brox, T.: FlowNet 2.0: evolution of optical flow estimation with deep networks. In: The IEEE Conference on Computer Vision and Pattern Recognition (CVPR) (2017)
9. Jaderberg, M., Simonyan, K., Zisserman, A., Kavukcuoglu, K.: Spatial transformer network. In: Neural Information Processing Systems (NIPS) (2015)
10. Kantorov, V., Laptev, I.: Efficient feature extraction, encoding and classification for action recognition. In: The IEEE Conference on Computer Vision and Pattern Recognition (CVPR) (2014)
11. Karpathy, A., Toderici, G., Shetty, S., Leung, T., Sukthankar, R., Fei-Fei, L.: Large-scale video classification with convolutional neural networks. In: The IEEE Conference on Computer Vision and Pattern Recognition (CVPR) (2014)
12. Kuehne, H., Jhuang, H., Garrote, E., Poggio, T., Serre, T.: HMDB: a large video database for human motion recognition. In: International Conference on Computer Vision (ICCV) (2011)
13. Lan, Z., Zhu, Y., Hauptmann, A.G., Newsam, S.: Deep local video feature for action recognition. In: The IEEE Conference on Computer Vision and Pattern Recognition (CVPR) (2017)
14. Miao, X., Zhen, X., Liu, X., Deng, C., Athitsos, V., Huang, H.: Direct shape regression networks for end-to-end face alignment. In: The IEEE Conference on Computer Vision and Pattern Recognition (CVPR) (2018)
15. Ng, J.Y.H., Choi, J., Neumann, J., Davis, L.S.: ActionFlowNet: learning motion representation for action recognition. In: IEEE Winter Conference on Applications of Computer Vision (WACV) (2018)
16. Ng, J.Y.H., Hausknecht, M., Vijay., S., Vinyals, O., Monga, R., Toderici, G.: Beyond short snippets: deep networks for video classification. In: The IEEE Conference on Computer Vision and Pattern Recognition (CVPR) (2015)
17. Qiu, Z., Yao, T., Mei, T.: Learning spatio-temporal representation with pseudo-3D residual networks. In: International Conference on Computer Vision (ICCV) (2017)

18. Sedaghat, N.: Next-flow: hybrid multi-tasking with next-frame prediction to boost optical-flow estimation in the wild. arXiv:1612.03777 (2016)
19. Simonyan, K., Zisserman, A.: Two-stream convolutional networks for action recognition in videos. In: Neural Information Processing Systems (NIPS) (2014)
20. Soomro, K., Zamir, A.R., Shah, M.: UCF101: a dataset of 101 human action classes from videos in the wild. In: CRCV-TR-12-01 (2012)
21. Tran, D., Bourdev, L., Fergus, R., Torresani, L., Paluri, M.: Learning spatiotemporal features with 3D convolutional networks. In: International Conference on Computer Vision (ICCV) (2015)
22. Tran, D., Wang, H., Torresani, L., Ray, J., LeCun, Y., Paluri, M.: A closer look at spatiotemporal convolutions for action recognition. In: The IEEE Conference on Computer Vision and Pattern Recognition (CVPR) (2018)
23. Wang, H., Schmid, C.: Action recognition with improved trajectories. In: International Conference on Computer Vision (ICCV) (2013)
24. Wang, L., Xiong, Y., Wang, Z., Qiao, Y.: Towards good practices for very deep two-stream ConvNets. arXiv:1507.02159 (2015)
25. Wang, L., et al.: Temporal segment networks: towards good practices for deep action recognition. In: Leibe, B., Matas, J., Sebe, N., Welling, M. (eds.) ECCV 2016. LNCS, vol. 9912, pp. 20–36. Springer, Cham (2016). https://doi.org/10.1007/978-3-319-46484-8_2
26. Wang, Z., Bovik, A.C., Sheikh, H.R., Simoncelli, E.P.: Image quality assessment: from error visibility to structural similarity. IEEE Trans. Image Process. **13**, 600–612 (2004)
27. Wu, C.Y., Zaheer, M., Hu, H., Manmatha, R., Smola, A.J., Krähenbühl, P.: Compressed video action recognition. arXiv:1712.00636 (2017)
28. Xie, S., Sun, C., Huang, J., Tu, Z., Murphy, K.: Rethinking spatiotemporal feature learning for video understanding. arXiv:1712.04851 (2017)
29. Xue, J., Zhang, H., Dana, K.: Deep texture manifold for ground terrain recognition. In: The IEEE Conference on Computer Vision and Pattern Recognition (CVPR) (2018)
30. Xue, T., Chen, B., Wu, J., Wei, D., Freeman, W.T.: Video enhancement with task-oriented flow. arXiv:1711.09078 (2017)
31. Yu, J.J., Harley, A.W., Derpanis, K.G.: Back to basics: unsupervised learning of optical flow via brightness constancy and motion smoothness. In: Hua, G., Jégou, H. (eds.) ECCV 2016. LNCS, vol. 9915, pp. 3–10. Springer, Cham (2016). https://doi.org/10.1007/978-3-319-49409-8_1
32. Zach, C., Pock, T., Bischof, H.: A duality based approach for realtime TV-L^1 optical flow. In: Hamprecht, F.A., Schnörr, C., Jähne, B. (eds.) DAGM 2007. LNCS, vol. 4713, pp. 214–223. Springer, Heidelberg (2007). https://doi.org/10.1007/978-3-540-74936-3_22
33. Zhang, B., Wang, L., Wang, Z., Qiao, Y., Wang, H.: Real-time action recognition with enhanced motion vector CNNs. In: The IEEE Conference on Computer Vision and Pattern Recognition (CVPR) (2016)
34. Zhu, Y., Long, Y., Guan, Y., Newsam, S., Shao, L.: Towards universal representation for unseen action recognition. In: The IEEE Conference on Computer Vision and Pattern Recognition (CVPR) (2018)
35. Zhu, Y., Newsam, S.: DenseNet for dense flow. In: IEEE International Conference on Image Processing (ICIP) (2017)
36. Zhu, Y., Newsam, S.: Learning optical flow via dilated networks and occlusion reasoning. In: IEEE International Conference on Image Processing (ICIP) (2018)

A Multi-purpose Convolutional Neural Network for Simultaneous Super-Resolution and High Dynamic Range Image Reconstruction

Soo Ye Kim and Munchurl Kim[✉]

Korea Advanced Institute of Science and Technology, Daejeon, Korea
{sooyekim,mkimee}@kaist.ac.kr

Abstract. High dynamic range (HDR) UHD-TVs are being rapidly deployed in consumer markets, offering a highly realistic experience to customers. However, these HDR UHD-TVs still need to handle the legacy low resolution (LR) video of standard dynamic range (SDR). In this paper, we propose a convolutional neural network based structure for the joint learning of super-resolution and inverse tone-mapping, which can be used for converting LR-SDR legacy video to high resolution (HR) HDR video. Our proposed structure is designed to perform three tasks: (i) SDR-to-HDR conversion of LR images, (ii) super-resolution of LR-SDR images to HR-SDR images and (iii) joint conversion from LR-SDR to HR-HDR images. We show the effectiveness of our proposed joint learning CNN architecture with extensive experiments.

Keywords: Super-resolution · High dynamic range · Multi-task learning

1 Introduction

Consumer displays such as TVs are evolving faster than ever, with the new theme being UHD TVs with *high dynamic range* (HDR) display capabilities. UHD displays boast the resolution of 3840×2160, which is four times the number of FHD pixels, and HDR displays render 10-bit pixels compared to the customary 8-bit pixels, allowing the user to enjoy more realistic visual experience. However in reality, it is unlikely to experience these new features at home due to the lack of received UHD-HDR video content. At the transmitting end, there is an abundance of the conventional HD, standard dynamic range (SDR) videos to send out. We first propose a convolutional neural network (CNN) structure that can directly reconstruct high-resolution HDR (HR-HDR) video frames from

This work was supported by Institute for Information & communications Technology Promotion (IITP) grant funded by the Korea government (MSIT) (No. 2017-0-00419, Intelligent High Realistic Visual Processing for Smart Broadcasting Media).

© Springer Nature Switzerland AG 2019
C. V. Jawahar et al. (Eds.): ACCV 2018, LNCS 11363, pp. 379–394, 2019.
https://doi.org/10.1007/978-3-030-20893-6_24

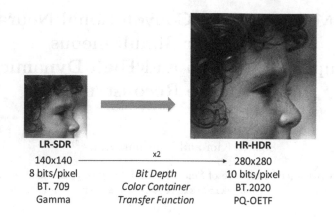

LR-SDR
140x140
8 bits/pixel
BT. 709
Gamma

x2

Bit Depth
Color Container
Transfer Function

HR-HDR
280x280
10 bits/pixel
BT.2020
PQ-OETF

Fig. 1. Conversion example from LR-SDR to HR-HDR

low-resolution SDR (LR-SDR) video frame inputs, which can be very helpful in converting LR-SDR legacy video to HR-HDR. Our proposed CNN architecture therefore handles two problems at the same time: (i) learning high frequency information in spatial regions and (ii) learning the contrast information in the signal amplitudes. Figure 1 shows a conversion example from LR-SDR to HR-HDR.

Topics related to this problem of going from LR-SDR to HR-HDR, are mainly super-resolution (SR) and inverse tone-mapping (ITM). SR methods up-scale LR images to HR images, and ITM methods map low dynamic range (LDR) images to HDR images. Although these two tasks may be performed in a cascaded structure (SR followed by ITM, or ITM followed by SR) for the conversion of LR-SDR to HR-HDR, simultaneous (joint) optimization of SR and ITM can generate higher quality output of HR-HDR frames. Moreover, our CNN-based model is also designed to perform the individual tasks in the same architecture with the joint optimization, which enhances the prediction accuracy and is useful in practice for various conversions (transformations) of video depending on target displays. Our network has three branches: SR, ITM and joint SR-ITM. Each branch produces the output after its corresponding conversion. Our main contributions in this paper are as follows:

- We first propose a CNN architecture that converts LR-SDR images to HR-HDR images in a jointly optimized manner.

- The proposed CNN architecture is designed to have a multi-purpose weight-sharing structure that produces HR-SDR, LR-HDR and HR-HDR frames from single LR-SDR input frames.

- We share its training strategy, and its structure is analyzed in depth.

2 Related Work

2.1 Super-Resolution

Super-resolution is a widely known low-level vision problem that aims to develop HR images from LR images. Deep-learning-based methods [4,17,20,30] showed superior performance compared to the traditional hand-crafted methods [7,32, 34] as in many other computer vision related fields. Since the first CNN-based method proposed by Dong *et al.* [4], CNN-based structures have been popular choices for SR although a powerful GAN-based SR model [20] was proposed later. Our problem of going from LR-SDR to HR-HDR is largely an SR problem although we map the LR-SDR images to the HDR space, which makes it different from the conventional SR problems. To enlarge the input LR images, we adopt the sub-pixel convolution introduced by Shi *et al.* [30] and our network predicts the HR residuals as proposed by Kim *et al.* [17] with residual learning.

2.2 Inverse Tone-Mapping

The visible dynamic range of the human eye is much wider than the display dynamic range for rendering digital images. Only a limited range of light can be represented on electric displays due to the limitations of optical and electrical sensors. In the computer graphics domain, ITM methods are used to map LDR images to the HDR space where they can be rendered with HDR graphics on professional HDR monitors. When these HDR images are tone-mapped back to the LDR domain, the resulting LDR images tend to look more realistic with enhanced contrast. Note that although LDR and SDR both refer to the same range of representation, the acronym *LDR* is used in the field of ITM and the acronym *SDR* is used to refer to consumer displays.

The first ITM method proposed by Banterle *et al.* [1] formulated the inverse of an existing tone-mapping operator [27] along with an expansion map. Other traditional methods employed edge enhancement in saturated regions [19,28] or aimed to find the global mapping function [24,25]. Huo *et al.* [12] considered the human retina response for ITM. CNN-based ITM methods [5,6,16,35] are relatively very recent including HDR imaging methods [6,16] that reconstruct one HDR image by merging multiple LDR images under diverse exposures. Autoencoder-based network models were also proposed in [5,35].

The advent of consumer HDR TVs opens up new possible applications of ITM methods: ITM can be used as a means to up-convert the existing SDR video to HDR video that may be directly displayed on HDR TVs. In this paper, we propose a joint SR-ITM method based CNNs, to directly up-convert a single LR-SDR image to an HR-HDR image for direct viewing on HDR TVs.

2.3 Multi-task Learning

The task of converting LR-SDR to HR-HDR is a joint problem of SR and ITM, where a CNN-based approach is firstly treated in this paper. In addition to this joint learning scheme, our network is also designed to perform the individual SR and ITM tasks in a unified CNN structure so that it gives three output images of HR-SDR, LR-HDR and HR-HDR, thus becoming a multi-task learning problem. The simplest way for multi-task learning would be to formulate additional losses from the individual tasks in the final loss function. With CNN-based structures, multi-task learning networks usually share the weights of layers across the multiple tasks [21,22,26]. This is known to increase performance and reduce the chance of overfitting. In more detail, Long et al. [21] proposed sharing the convolution layers among all tasks and modeling task-specific fully-connected layers that are separately trained; Lu et al. [22] proposed a model that groups similar tasks and gradually shares the features among the similar tasks; Misra et al. [26] used cross-stitch units between two networks to linearly combine the feature maps. The HR-HDR output branch of our network shares the weights of the early convolution layers of the two individual SR and ITM tasks. This enhances the performance of the joint task while being highly practical, which allows for separate individual applications in a unified network.

2.4   Joint Super-Resolution and Inverse Tone-Mapping

The earliest method that performs both SR and ITM was proposed by Gunturk et al. [10], which reconstructs an HR image from multiple input images of different exposures using a Bayesian model. Schubert et al. [29] reconstructed an HR-HDR image in two steps, where an HDR image is first obtained from two differently exposed images and SR is performed after. They also considered the camera response curve and implemented an iterative back projection method for SR [29]. However, methods requiring multiple input images of different exposures [10,29] cannot be applied for our problem since video contents for TVs are not available in multiple exposures. Focusing on the mathematical side, Bengtsson et al. [2] aimed to optimize SR and ITM problems in a perceptually uniform domain, and Traonmilin et al. [33] showed the lower bound of the number of required images and their corresponding exposure times that guarantee the recovery of HR-HDR images. Bengtsson et al. also proposed an SR method for HDR input images in [3]. In comparison, we propose the first method for *directly* reconstructing an HR-HDR image from a *single* LR-SDR image in a single step using a CNN model. Also, note that our method focuses on generating HDR videos to be viewed on HDR TVs, which had not been commercially deployed in the time that the previous methods were developed.

3   Proposed Method

We propose a CNN-based architecture for joint SR and ITM. Our network performs the individual tasks as well as the joint task, and the feature extraction layers for the individual SR and ITM tasks are shared with the SR-ITM joint learning. Consequently for the LR-SDR input, our proposed model produces the HR-HDR image for the joint task, and HR-SDR and LR-HDR images for the

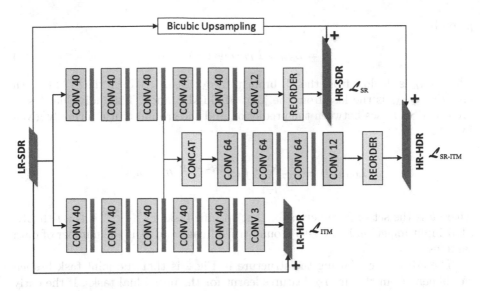

Fig. 2. Proposed multi-purpose CNN architecture with weight-sharing for the joint SR-ITM task. This structure generates three outputs: HR-SDR images from the SR branch (*light blue convolution layers*), LR-HDR images from the ITM branch *light green convolution layers*) and HR-HDR images from the joint SR-ITM branch (*light orange convolution layers*). The *grey rectangular boxes* after the convolution layers are ReLU activation functions (Color figure online)

individual tasks. The detailed architecture of our proposed CNN-based model is illustrated in Fig. 2. In Fig. 2, the *light blue* and *light green* convolution layers denote the SR and ITM branches, respectively, and the *light orange* convolution layers are those for the joint SR-ITM task. The number after *CONV*, denoted for convolution layer, indicates the number of its output channels. The feature maps from the third convolution layer of the individual SR and ITM tasks are concatenated at the *CONCAT* layer to be used for the joint task in producing the HR-HDR output.

3.1 Joint Task Learning

Unlike previous multi-task learning methods that usually share the early layers among all tasks (main and auxiliary), the proposed structure has separate feature extraction layers for the individual SR and ITM tasks that are only shared for the SR-ITM joint task, not among the individual SR and ITM tasks. This idea stems from the fact that our problem is a *joint task problem* where the main task is a combination of the individual tasks, not a multi-task problem with separate tasks to learn. The total number of convolution layers used for generating the HR-HDR images are thus 10 layers among which the first 3 layers are in parallel for the individual tasks with the same depth and the last four layers are cascaded to the final output. When training the whole network, the total loss term L is given by

$$L = L_{SR} + L_{ITM} + L_{SR-ITM} \tag{1}$$

where L_{SR} is the loss from the SR branch, L_{ITM} is the loss from the ITM branch and L_{SR-ITM} is the loss from the joint SR-ITM branch. The individual losses are the MSE losses between the prediction and the ground truth, formally given by

$$Loss\,(\theta) = \frac{1}{2N} \sum_{i=1}^{N} \| f\left(x_i^{LR-SDR}; \theta\right) - y_i \|^2 \tag{2}$$

where θ is the set of parameters for that specific task, x_i^{LR-SDR} is the i-th LR-SDR input image, y_i is the i-th ground truth image and N is the number of data samples.

The advantage of using the structure in Fig. 2 is that the joint task branch can benefit from the diverse features learnt for the individual tasks. If the early layers are shared among all the tasks, the learnt features would be averaged out. Another advantage is that this structure allows for intensive pre-training. Since there are separate branches (*light blue* and *light green* convolution layers in Fig. 2) for the individual tasks, the corresponding filter parameters can be pre-trained for the specific SR and ITM tasks before training them for the joint SR-ITM task, which highly aids the network to specialize for all tasks.

3.2 Multi-purpose Network

In addition to the joint SR-ITM task, our network performs the individual SR and ITM tasks. This is very practical since the outputs from the individual tasks can also be obtained from the same network. The input is a 3-channel YUV LR-SDR image for all tasks. For SR, this LR image is directly used as input without prior up-scaling, and the last layer produces 12 channels of image data, 4 for each channel of Y, U and V, which can be reordered to produce the HR output image, adopting the sub-pixel structure in [30]. For ITM, the input LR-SDR image is converted into an LR-HDR image after six convolution layers. Using all three channels is beneficial since the color container also changes when going from SDR to HDR.

Residual Learning. Residual learning in SR was first used in [17] for the accurate restoration of HR images with deeper convolution layers. It allows the network to focus on the high frequency details that are not present in the input by predicting the difference between the ground truth image and the input image. We adopt the residual learning for all three tasks, where the difference between the ground truth image and the bicubic-upscaled image is predicted for the tasks of SR and SR-ITM, and the difference between the ground truth image and the input image is predicted for the ITM task.

Table 1. Training data specifications

Video	No. of frames	Subimage sizes	Frame strides	Subimages/frame	No. of subimages
Mountain	9,659	180 × 180	50	10	1,480
Aquarium	7,360	180 × 180	50	10	1,220
Temple	5,580	180 × 180	30	10	1,210
Cuisine	7,377	180 × 180	30	10	1,700
Festival	7,500	180 × 180	30	10	2,570
Total no. of subimages					8,180

4 Experiments

4.1 Experiment Conditions

Data. A data sample for our network consists of an LR-SDR image for input and HR-SDR, LR-HDR and HR-HDR images for the labels of the three tasks (SR, ITM and SR-ITM, respectively). We collected five 3840 × 2160 HDR videos of 30 fps containing diverse scenes, namely *Mountain, Aquarium, Temple, Cuisine* and *Festival*, and their corresponding 3840 × 2160 SDR video pairs. These videos were professionally filmed and mastered by colorists. Both SDR and HDR video sets were down-scaled by 2 using the bicubic filter to create the LR-SDR and LR-HDR videos. All videos were converted to YUV 420, and all three channels were used for the input and the ground truth since the color container also changes when going from SDR to HDR. Then, 10 subimages of size 180 × 180 for HR videos, and 90 × 90 for LR videos were randomly cropped from each frame with a frame stride. The detailed specifications are given in Table 1.

Training Parameters. The learning rate was set to 5×10^{-5} for filters and 5×10^{-6} for biases. The weight decay was set to 5×10^{-4} for filters and 0 for biases. The mini-batch size was 32 and the network was trained using the Adam optimizer [18]. Every convolution layer except the last three layers (the last layer for each task) is followed by ReLU activation [9]. The loss function is given as the sum of the individual MSE losses for the three tasks as in Eqs. 1 and 2. The size of all convolution filters is 3 × 3 and the filter parameter values are initialized using the Xavier initialization [8].

4.2 Effect of Joint Learning

The simplest way to handle the joint SR-ITM task is performing the individual tasks in serial order: performing SR then ITM or ITM then SR. However, this may accumulate the errors since the final HR-HDR image has to be predicted on a prediction of HR-SDR or LR-HDR. To show that the direct reconstruction of the HR-HDR images results in more accurate images, we first perform experiments with three different methods illustrated in Fig. 3. In Fig. 3(a) and (b) show the serial methods and (c) is the integrated (joint) method, where the SR, ITM and SR-ITM blocks are simple 7-layer CNNs. We matched the total number of

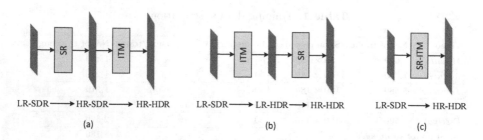

LR-SDR ⟶ HR-SDR ⟶ HR-HDR   LR-SDR ⟶ LR-HDR ⟶ HR-HDR   LR-SDR ⟶ HR-HDR

(a)   (b)   (c)

Fig. 3. Architecture comparison between serially performing the individual tasks and jointly performing both tasks. The SR, ITM and SR-ITM blocks (*light blue, light green* and *light orange* boxes) each consist of 7 convolution layers simply stacked one after another (Color figure online)

Table 2. Comparison between the serial methods and the joint method of Fig. 3

	Serial		Joint
Network	SR	ITM	SR-ITM
Output channels	46-46-46-46-46-46-12	46-46-46-46-46-46-3	64-64-64-64-64-64-12
Total parameters	199,701		193,356
Method	SR → ITM (a)	ITM → SR (b)	SR-ITM (c)
PSNR of Y (dB)	34.84	35.52	**35.73**
PSNR of YUV (dB)	38.19	38.80	**39.13**

parameters for all three methods by adjusting the number of filter channels. The depth of each block is matched to be seven. The performance results and the network specifications are given in Table 2. With a similar number of parameters, the joint SR-ITM network of Fig. 3. (c) outperforms the serial methods of Fig. 3(a) and (b) by at least 0.21 dB and 0.33 dB in PSNR for the Y channel only and the YUV channels, respectively, which supports our claim that joint learning is beneficial.

Multi-loss. With the joint learning structure in Fig. 3(c), we also experimented with auxiliary losses. Figure 3(c) was modelled to minimize the individual task losses as well as the joint loss. To calculate the loss between the produced HR-HDR image and the LR-HDR ground truth that is of a different size, the HR-HDR image was down-scaled using the bicubic filter. With auxiliary losses, the SR-ITM (*light orange block*) structure may be able to better generalize the task learning, or additional losses may help guide the network to perform the joint task more effectively. The losses were given by

$$L_1 = L_{SR-ITM} + \alpha L_{ITM} \tag{3}$$
$$L_2 = L_{SR-ITM} + \alpha L_{SR} \tag{4}$$

where L_{SR-ITM} is the loss for the joint task, and L_{SR} and L_{ITM} are the losses for the individual SR and ITM tasks, respectively. The α was set to 0.1. However, since the network structure has a single-branch, we found that naively adding the individual losses actually caused the network to defocus from the original SR-ITM task. The comparisons of using multiple loss functions are given in Table 3.

Table 3. Experiment on losses with structure Fig. 3(c)

Loss	L_1	L_2	L_{SR-ITM}
PSNR of Y (dB)	35.61	34.44	**35.73**
PSNR of YUV (dB)	38.95	37.30	**39.13**

4.3   Multi-purpose Architecture

Our proposed multi-purpose architecture is illustrated in Fig. 2. With this structure, the individual SR and ITM tasks are also performed and the feature maps produced from the individual tasks are stacked and fed into the network branch of the joint SR-ITM task. All filter parameters are trained at once using the joint loss given in Eq. 1. A detailed description of the network is given in Sect. 3. Compared to the simple 7-layer network of Fig. 3(c) (4th column in Table 2), this multi-purpose architecture shows up to 0.32 dB and 0.39 dB increase in PSNR for the Y channel only and the YUV channels, respectively, for the performance of the joint SR-ITM task. In addition to the benefit of producing the outputs for the individual tasks, the multi-purpose architecture also demonstrates its superiority in reconstructing the HR-HDR images. The comparison between the simple joint network and the multi-purpose architecture is given in Table 5. Note that the total number of parameters used for the joint SR-ITM task in the multi-purpose network (first three layers of the *light blue* and *light green* branches and all layers of the *light orange* branch in Fig. 2) is lower than the simple 7-layer network. Even with less parameters, the multi-purpose architecture generates more accurate HR-HDR images.

Another experiment was conducted depending on the positions of the concatenation layer in the multi-purpose network. For this experiment, the concatenation layer was positioned after the second, third and fourth convolution layers of the individual tasks. The number of parameters related to the SR-ITM task and the number of total parameters were matched for all three structures by adjusting the number of filter channels. The results are reported in Table 4. The performance difference between the different structures is marginal.

Pre-training. A decisive advantage of adopting the multi-purpose architecture is that the SR and ITM branches (*blue* and *green* in Fig. 2) can be pretrained independently prior to being used as parts of the whole architecture. Even if no additional data is used, a significantly higher performance could be obtained after pre-training the networks for individual tasks. Specifically, the SR branch is pretrained with the LR-SDR and HR-SDR pairs of the training data and the ITM

Table 4. Experiment on the position of the concatenation layer

Structure	Concat2			Concat3			Concat4		
Channels (input, output)	SR	SR-ITM	ITM	SR	SR-ITM	ITM	SR	SR-ITM	ITM
1	3,37	-	3,37	3,40	-	3,40	3,42	-	3,42
2	37,37	Concat	37,37	40,40	-	40,40	42,42	-	42,42
3	37,33	74,64	37,33	40,40	Concat	40,40	42,42	-	42,42
4	33,33	64,64	33,33	40,40	80,64	40,40	42,42	Concat	42,42
5	33,33	64,64	33,33	40,40	64,64	40,40	42,68	84,64	42,68
6	33,12	64,64	33,3	40,12	64,64	40,3	68,12	64,64	68,3
7	-	64,12	-	-	64,12	-	-	64,12	-
PSNR of Y (dB)	35.62	35.74	38.94	35.69	35.81	38.74	35.74	35.86	38.38
PSNR of YUV (dB)	40.03	39.21	41.41	40.30	39.25	40.63	40.39	39.29	40.90
Parameters for SR-ITM		187,184			186,924			190,160	
Total parameters		253,034			250,099			250,899	

Table 5. Comparison of the simple SR-ITM model and the multi-purpose architectures. The former is a simple 7-layer network and the multi-purpose model is illustrated in Fig. 2. Pre-training is highly beneficial for the multi-purpose network

Model		Simple SR-ITM	Multi-purpose	Multi-purpose (pre-train)
Parameters for SR-ITM		193,356	186,924	186,924
PSNR* (dB)	SR-ITM	35.73/39.13	35.81/39.25	**36.05/39.52**
	SR	-	35.69/40.30	**35.74/40.41**
	ITM	-	38.74/40.63	**39.75/42.04**

*PSNR of Y/PSNR of YUV

branch is pre-trained with the LR-SDR and LR-HDR pairs of the training data. After pre-training, the whole network is trained using the full data including the LR-SDR and HR-HDR pairs. Pre-training enhances the performance of the joint task by average 0.24 dB and 0.27 dB in PSNR for the Y channel only and the YUV channels, respectively. The performance regarding the individual tasks also increases, by 0.11 dB and 1.41 dB in PSNR for the Y channel on SR and ITM, respectively. The results are compared in Table 5.

Runtime Evaluation. The inference time of the proposed multi-purpose architecture is 308 ms for a FHD (1920×1080) input image to run through the whole network (all branches) with an NVIDIA TITAN Xp GPU.

4.4 Comparisons

Multi-task Learning. A common CNN structure for multi-task learning shares the early convolution layers among all the tasks as in Fig. 4 (The number after *CONV*, denoted for convolution layer, indicates the number of its output channels). In this case, all tasks must share the same early convolution layers. This model, designed for our purpose of performing SR, ITM and SR-ITM, employs the sub-pixel convolution for SR-related tasks and residual learning for all tasks

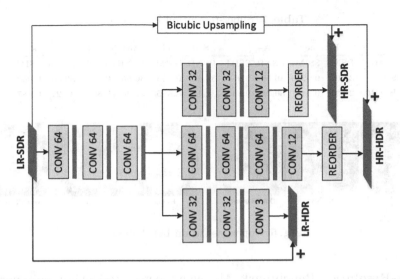

Fig. 4. Common multi-task learning architecture with early parameter-sharing. This is a multi-task learning model designed for SR, ITM and joint SR-ITM with residual learning

Table 6. Comparison of the multi-task model (Fig. 4) and the proposed multi-purpose model (Fig. 2)

Model		Multi-task	Multi-purpose	Multi-purpose (pre-train)
Parameters for SR-ITM		193,356	186,924	186,924
Total parameters		253,115	250,099	250,099
PSNR* (dB)	SR-ITM	35.69/38.97	35.81/39.25	**36.05/39.52**
	SR	35.70/40.32	35.69/40.30	**35.74/40.41**
	ITM	39.03/41.41	38.74/40.63	**39.75/42.04**

*PSNR of Y/PSNR of YUV

as with the proposed multi-purpose architecture. We compare its performance with the proposed architecture in Table 6.

The number of output channels of each convolution layer was adjusted so that the parameters related to the joint SR-ITM task, and the number of total parameters for the whole network became similar between both methods. Even with less parameters, the multi-purpose network outperformed the multi-task model by 0.36 dB and 0.55 dB in PSNR for the Y channel only and the YUV channels, respectively, in the joint SR-ITM task, thanks to the diverse feature extractions at the early layers. It was also able to better specialize in the individual task learning with the independent pre-training of the SR and ITM branches. A major advantage of our multi-purpose architecture is the effective pre-training process which is difficult to be realized in the conventional multi-task structure.

Table 7. Super-resolution benchmark

	Bicubic		A+ [32]		SelfEx [11]		SRCNN [4]		Ours	
Metric	PSNR	SSIM	PSNR	SSIM	PSNR	SSIM	PSNR	SSIM	PSNR	SSIM
Set5	33.66	0.9299	36.55	0.9544	36.49	0.9537	36.66	0.9542	36.55	0.9537
BSD100	29.31	0.8431	30.78	0.8863	31.18	0.8855	31.36	0.8879	31.21	0.8874

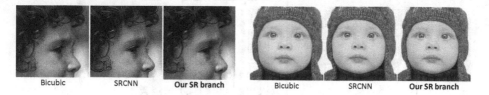

Bicubic   SRCNN   **Our SR branch**   Bicubic   SRCNN   **Our SR branch**

Fig. 5. Super-resolution benchmark

Super-Resolution Benchmark. Although the main task of our multi-purpose architecture is to infer the joint SR-ITM problem, it also generates the outputs for the individual SR and ITM tasks. We analyze the SR performance against other SR-dedicated methods [4,11,32] for Set5 and BSD100 datasets [23], which are commonly used for SR. PSNR and SSIM performance is given in Table 7 and the result images are shown in Fig. 5. The performance of the SR branch in our multi-purpose network is comparable to the performance of SRCNN [4] even when SR is an auxiliary task.

Inverse Tone-Mapping Benchmark. We also compare our ITM branch against other ITM methods [12,19,24,25,28] in Table 8. We tested on 15 different video frames collected from youtube, which is a different environment setting from our training dataset for fair comparison. For previous methods, the maximum brightness is set to $1,000\,cd/m^2$ and the expansion operator is applied in linear RGB space, after removing gamma correction [14]. After expansion, the color container is converted to RGB2020 [15], and PQ-OETF transfer function [31] is applied. Note that our ITM branch works directly in the pixel domain. Our ITM branch outperforms the previous methods by at least $0.34\,dB$.

Table 8. Inverse tone-mapping benchmark

	Kovaleski [19]	Meylan [25]	Rempel [28]	Masia [24]	Huo [12]	Our ITM branch
PSNR (dB)	19.14	20.46	20.65	20.71	25.72	26.06

Qualitative Analysis. Our method directly generates 3840×2160 UHD-HDR images from 1920×1080 HD-SDR input images. We examine the result images in Fig. 6. Our method increases contrast in saturated regions (1st, 5th row) while restoring the image details (2nd, 4th row) and enhancing edges (3rd row).

Fig. 6. Qualitative analysis of our method. Images in the 1st column are 1920 × 1080 SDR video frames that were used as input. On the 2nd and 3rd column are the image slices extracted from UHD frames generated by simple up-scaling using the bicubic filter (2nd column) and by our proposed method (3rd column)

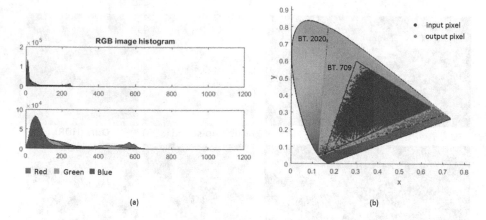

Fig. 7. Color distribution comparison between the input image and the generated output image. (a) is the RGB image histogram of the input (*top*) and output (*bottom*) and (b) shows the input (*black points*) and output (*light grey points*) pixels on the color gamut (Color figure online)

Color Gamut Expansion. When an LR-SDR input image is converted to an HR-HDR image, we directly map the color container from BT.709 [13] to BT.2020 [15]. For visualization, we have plotted the input pixels (Festival HD, *black points*) and the output pixels (*light grey points*) generated from our network in the xy-space in Fig. 7(b). The output has a much wider color gamut, where the inner and outer triangles are the color containers BT.709 and BT.2020, respectively. Figure 7(a) shows the RGB image histogram of the same input LR-SDR image (*top*) and the output HR-HDR image (*bottom*) produced from our network. The input LR-SDR image ranges from 0 to 255 and the output HR-HDR image from 0 to 1023 with four times as many pixels. The latter shows more variations in color.

5   Conclusion

The dynamic range and the resolution of TVs must increase continuously for electric displays to closely reproduce the real world, and converting LR-SDR videos to HR-HDR videos will become more important in the future. Although previous SR or ITM methods have not explored such applications yet, SR-ITM for creating HR-HDR video content is a promising direction. In this paper, we first proposed a CNN-based multi-purpose network that performs SR and ITM simultaneously as a joint task. Our multi-purpose network also conducts the individual SR and ITM tasks, thereby producing three outputs (HR-SDR, LR-HDR and HR-HDR). We analyzed different architectures designed for the joint learning purpose and provided extensive experiment results on our proposed CNN-based multi-purpose network for both the individual SR and ITM tasks, and the joint SR-ITM task.

References

1. Banterle, F., Ledda, P., Debattista, K., Chalmers, A., Bloj, M.: A framework for inverse tone mapping. Vis. Comput. **23**(7), 467–478 (2007)
2. Bengtsson, T., Gu, I.Y.H., Viberg, M., Lindström, K.: Regularized optimization for joint super-resolution and high dynamic range image reconstruction in a perceptually uniform domain. In: 2012 IEEE International Conference on Acoustics, Speech and Signal Processing (ICASSP), pp. 1097–1100. IEEE (2012)
3. Bengtsson, T., McKelvey, T., Gu, I.Y.H.: Super-resolution reconstruction of high dynamic range images with perceptual weighting of errors. In: 2013 IEEE International Conference on Acoustics, Speech and Signal Processing (ICASSP), pp. 2212–2216. IEEE (2013)
4. Dong, C., Loy, C.C., He, K., Tang, X.: Image super-resolution using deep convolutional networks. IEEE Trans. Pattern Anal. Mach. Intell. **38**(2), 295–307 (2016)
5. Eilertsen, G., Kronander, J., Denes, G., Mantiuk, R.K., Unger, J.: HDR image reconstruction from a single exposure using deep CNNs. ACM Trans. Graph. **36**(6), 178 (2017)
6. Endo, Y., Kanamori, Y., Mitani, J.: Deep reverse tone mapping. ACM Trans. Graph. **36**(6), 177 (2017)
7. Glasner, D., Bagon, S., Irani, M.: Super-resolution from a single image. In: Proceedings of the IEEE International Conference on Computer Vision, pp. 349–356. IEEE (2009)
8. Glorot, X., Bengio, Y.: Understanding the difficulty of training deep feedforward neural networks. In: Proceedings of the Thirteenth International Conference on Artificial Intelligence and Statistics, pp. 249–256 (2010)
9. Glorot, X., Bordes, A., Bengio, Y.: Deep sparse rectifier neural networks. In: Proceedings of the Fourteenth International Conference on Artificial Intelligence and Statistics, pp. 315–323 (2011)
10. Gunturk, B.K., Gevrekci, M.: High-resolution image reconstruction from multiple differently exposed images. IEEE Signal Process. Lett. **13**(4), 197–200 (2006)
11. Huang, J.B., Singh, A., Ahuja, N.: Single image super-resolution from transformed self-exemplars. In: Proceedings of the IEEE Conference on Computer Vision and Pattern Recognition, pp. 5197–5206 (2015)
12. Huo, Y., Yang, F., Dong, L., Brost, V.: Physiological inverse tone mapping based on retina response. Vis. Comput. **30**(5), 507–517 (2014)
13. ITU-R: Parameter values for the HDTV standards for production and international programme exchange. ITU-R Rec. BT.709-5 (2002). http://www.itu.int/rec/R-REC-BT.709
14. ITU-R: Reference electro-optical transfer function for flat panel displays used in HDTV studio production. ITU-R Rec. BT.1886 (2011)
15. ITU-R: Parameter values for ultra-high definition television systems for production and international programme exchange. Document ITU-R Rec. BT.2020-1 (2014). http://www.itu.int/rec/R-REC-BT.2020
16. Kalantari, N.K., Ramamoorthi, R.: Deep high dynamic range imaging of dynamic scenes. ACM Trans. Graph. **36**(4), 144 (2017)
17. Kim, J., Kwon Lee, J., Mu Lee, K.: Accurate image super-resolution using very deep convolutional networks. In: Proceedings of the IEEE Conference on Computer Vision and Pattern Recognition, pp. 1646–1654 (2016)
18. Kingma, D.P., Ba, J.: Adam: a method for stochastic optimization. In: Proceedings of the IEEE International Conference on Learning Representations (2015)

19. Kovaleski, R.P., Oliveira, M.M.: High-quality reverse tone mapping for a wide range of exposures. In: 2014 27th SIBGRAPI Conference on Graphics, Patterns and Images (SIBGRAPI), pp. 49–56. IEEE (2014)
20. Ledig, C., et al.: Photo-realistic single image super-resolution using a generative adversarial network. In: Proceedings of the IEEE Conference on Computer Vision and Pattern Recognition, pp. 4681–4690 (2017)
21. Long, M., Cao, Z., Wang, J., Philip, S.Y.: Learning multiple tasks with multilinear relationship networks. In: Advances in Neural Information Processing Systems, pp. 1593–1602 (2017)
22. Lu, Y., Kumar, A., Zhai, S., Cheng, Y., Javidi, T., Feris, R.: Fully-adaptive feature sharing in multi-task networks with applications in person attribute classification. In: Proceedings of the IEEE Conference on Computer Vision and Pattern Recognition, pp. 5334–5343 (2017)
23. Martin, D., Fowlkes, C., Tal, D., Malik, J.: A database of human segmented natural images and its application to evaluating segmentation algorithms and measuring ecological statistics. In: Proceedings of the IEEE International Conference on Computer Vision, vol. 2, pp. 416–423. IEEE (2001)
24. Masia, B., Serrano, A., Gutierrez, D.: Dynamic range expansion based on image statistics. Multimed. Tools Appl. $76(1)$, 631–648 (2017)
25. Meylan, L., Daly, S., Süsstrunk, S.: The reproduction of specular highlights on high dynamic range displays. In: Color and Imaging Conference, vol. 1, pp. 333–338. Society for Imaging Science and Technology (2006)
26. Misra, I., Shrivastava, A., Gupta, A., Hebert, M.: Cross-stitch networks for multi-task learning. In: Proceedings of the IEEE Conference on Computer Vision and Pattern Recognition, pp. 3994–4003 (2016)
27. Reinhard, E., Stark, M., Shirley, P., Ferwerda, J.: Photographic tone reproduction for digital images. ACM Trans. Graph. $21(3)$, 267–276 (2002)
28. Rempel, A.G., et al.: Ldr2Hdr: on-the-fly reverse tone mapping of legacy video and photographs. ACM Trans. Graph. $26(3)$, 39. ACM (2007)
29. Schubert, F., Schertler, K., Mikolajczyk, K.: A hands-on approach to high-dynamic-range and superresolution fusion. In: 2009 Workshop on Applications of Computer Vision (WACV), pp. 1–8. IEEE (2009)
30. Shi, W., et al.: Real-time single image and video super-resolution using an efficient sub-pixel convolutional neural network. In: Proceedings of the IEEE Conference on Computer Vision and Pattern Recognition, pp. 1874–1883 (2016)
31. SMPTE: High dynamic range electro-optical transfer function of mastering reference displays. SMPTE ST2084:2014 (2014)
32. Timofte, R., De Smet, V., Van Gool, L.: A+: adjusted anchored neighborhood regression for fast super-resolution. In: Cremers, D., Reid, I., Saito, H., Yang, M.-H. (eds.) ACCV 2014. LNCS, vol. 9006, pp. 111–126. Springer, Cham (2015). https://doi.org/10.1007/978-3-319-16817-3_8
33. Traonmilin, Y., Aguerrebere, C.: Simultaneous high dynamic range and super-resolution imaging without regularization. SIAM J. Imaging Sci. $7(3)$, 1624–1644 (2014)
34. Yang, J., Wright, J., Huang, T.S., Ma, Y.: Image super-resolution via sparse representation. IEEE Trans. Image Process. $19(11)$, 2861–2873 (2010)
35. Zhang, J., Lalonde, J.F.: Learning high dynamic range from outdoor panoramas. In: Proceedings of the IEEE International Conference on Computer Vision, pp. 4529–4538. IEEE (2017)

ITM-CNN: Learning the Inverse Tone Mapping from Low Dynamic Range Video to High Dynamic Range Displays Using Convolutional Neural Networks

Soo Ye Kim, Dae-Eun Kim, and Munchurl Kim$^{(\boxtimes)}$

Korea Advanced Institute of Science and Technology, Daejeon, Korea
{sooyekim,kimde,mkimee}@kaist.ac.kr

Abstract. While inverse tone mapping (ITM) was frequently used for graphics rendering in the high dynamic range (HDR) space, the advent of HDR TVs and the consequent need for HDR multimedia contents open up new horizons for the consumption of ultra-high quality video contents. Unfortunately, previous methods are not appropriate for HDR TVs, and their inverse-tone-mapped results are not visually pleasing with noise amplification or lack of details. In this paper, we first present the ITM problem for HDR TVs and propose a CNN-based architecture, called ITM-CNN, which restores lost details and local contrast with its training strategy for enhancing the performance based on image decomposition using the guided filter. We demonstrate the benefits of decomposing the image by experimenting with various architectures and also compare the performance for different training strategies. Our ITM-CNN is a powerful means to solve the lack of HDR video contents with legacy LDR videos.

Keywords: Inverse tone mapping · Convolutional neural network

1 Introduction

The human visual system perceives the world as much brighter, with stronger contrasts and more details than is typically presented in standard dynamic range (SDR) displays. In comparison, recently available high dynamic range (HDR) consumer displays allow users to enjoy videos closer to reality as seen by the naked eye, with the brightness of at least $1{,}000\,\mathrm{cd/m^2}$ (as opposed to $100\,\mathrm{cd/m^2}$ for SDR displays), higher contrast ratio, increased bit depth of 10 bits or more,

This work was supported by Institute for Information & communications Technology Promotion (IITP) grant funded by the Korea government (MSIT) (No. 2017-0-00419, Intelligent High Realistic Visual Processing for Smart Broadcasting Media).

Electronic supplementary material The online version of this chapter (https://doi.org/10.1007/978-3-030-20893-6_25) contains supplementary material, which is available to authorized users.

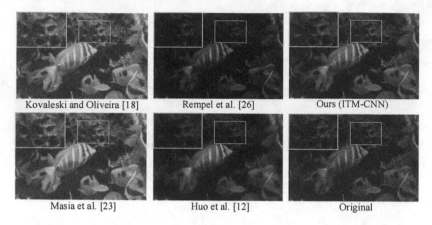

Fig. 1. Conventional ITM Methods. In the images shown in the 1st column, noise is amplified in the regions that should be dark, and the output HDR images in the 2nd column exhibit lack of details or contrast. Our approach reveals details without noise amplification while maximizing local contrast. It is subjectively and objectively the closest to the original HDR image and is suitable for viewing on consumer HDR displays

and wide color gamut (WCG). However, although HDR TVs are readily available in the market, there is a severe lack of HDR contents.

Inverse tone mapping (ITM), also referred to as reverse tone mapping, is a popular area of research in computer graphics that aims to predict HDR images from low dynamic range (LDR) images for better graphics rendering. Another field of research, HDR imaging, makes use of multiple LDR images of different exposures to create a single HDR image that contains details in the saturated regions. In the above two fields of research, the lighting calculations are conducted in the HDR domain with the belief that this would yield a more accurate representation of the graphic or natural scene on an SDR display. The HDR images are viewed on professional HDR monitors during rendering. Consequently, the HDR domain referred to in the above areas are not necessarily the same as the now available HDR consumer displays, and the resulting HDR images by the ITM methods for such purposes are not suitable for direct viewing on an HDR TV. When the conventional ITM methods are applied for an HDR TV with the maximum brightness of $1,000 \, cd/m^2$, they are not capable of fully utilizing the available HDR capacity due to their weakness in generating full contrast or/and details, or due to noise amplification as seen in Fig. 1. (Note that they are tone mapped for viewing on the paper.)

Therefore, we formulate a slightly different problem where we aim to generate HDR images that can be directly viewed on commercial HDR TVs. In this way, LDR legacy videos may be up-converted to be viewed on available HDR displays without additional information required. We propose an effective convolutional neural network (CNN) based structure and its learning strategy for up-converting a single LDR image of 8 bits/pixel, gamma-corrected [14], in the BT.709 color container [13], to an HDR image of 10 bits/pixel through the perceptual quantization (PQ) transfer function [27] in the BT.2020 color container [15], that may be directly viewed with commercial HDR TVs. Our contributions are three-fold:

- We raise the first ITM problem to readily available HDR consumer displays, and propose a CNN architecture designed for this purpose called ITM-CNN.
- Our architecture is a fully end-to-end CNN that is able to jointly optimize the LDR decomposition and HDR reconstruction phases.
- We propose its training strategy involving pre-training using guided filter decompositions.

2 Related Work

Tone mapping is a popular problem dealt in computer graphics and image processing. When graphics are rendered in the HDR domain for better representation of the scenes which have near-continuous brightness and high contrast in the real world, they have to be tone mapped somehow to the displayable range. ITM came later, to transfer the LDR domain images to the HDR domain. The term itself was first used by Banterle *et al.* in [2]. The previous ITM methods mainly focus on generating the expand map and revealing contrast in saturated regions. In this section, previous methods regarding ITM to the HDR domain will be reviewed. It should be noted that we address a slightly different problem in this paper than the previous methods, where our final goal is not viewing HDR rendered tone mapped images on SDR displays, nor viewing HDR images on a professional HDR monitor, but viewing generated HDR images directly on consumer HDR displays (e.g., HDR TVs).

ITM was first introduced in [2,3], where Banterle *et al.* formulated the inverse of Reinhard's tone mapping operator [25]. In addition to the inverse of the tone mapping operator, they also proposed an expand map, which specifies the amount of expansion for every pixel position. Two main purposes of the expand map is to reduce contouring artifacts resulting from quantization and to expand the bright regions in the LDR images. Similarly, Rempel *et al.* proposed a brightness enhancement function in [26]. The brightness enhancement function is derived from the blurred mask that indicates saturated pixel areas. With the edge stopping filter, the brightness enhancement function preserves edges with high contrast. Another related approach is [18,19] where Kovaleski and Oliveira used a bilateral grid to make an edge-preserving expand map.

There are also methods that find a global mapping function of the whole image instead of a pixel-wise mapping. In [24], Meylan *et al.* applied linear expansions with two different slopes depending on whether the pixel is classified as the diffuse region or the specular region. Pixels with values greater than a predefined threshold are classified into the specular region and all other pixels are classified into the diffuse region. The specular region is expanded with a steeper function than the diffuse region. The ITM algorithms presented above mainly classify pixels into two classes: pixels to be expanded more and pixels to be expanded less. Usually, the pixels in the bright regions tend to be expanded more.

Another method that investigates a global mapping function is [22]. In [22], Masia et al. evaluated a number of ITM algorithms and found that the performance of the algorithms decreased for overexposed input images. Based on this observation, they proposed an ITM curve based on the gamma curve, where the parameter gamma is a function of the statistics of the input image. Their following work [23] improves upon their previous work with a robust multilinear regression model. In [12], Huo et al. proposed an ITM algorithm imitating the characteristics of the human visual system and its retina response. This ITM algorithm enhances local contrast.

Recently, CNN-based structures have shown exceptional performance in modelling images to find a non-linear mapping, especially for classification problems [20] or regression problems [4,5]. There are very few ITM methods based on CNNs. One of them, proposed by Endo et al. [7] is an indirect approach where they use a combination of 2D and 3D CNNs to generate multiple LDR images (bracketed images) of different exposures from a single LDR image, and merge these bracketed images using the existing methods to obtain a final tone mapped HDR image. Kalantari et al. [17] proposed an HDR imaging method where they used a CNN for integrating the given multiple LDR images of different exposures to generate an HDR image which is tone mapped for viewing. Eilertsen et al. [6] and Zhang et al. [29] proposed encoder-decoder-based networks for HDR reconstruction which is also tone mapped for viewing.

However, the previous methods share an ultimate step of tone mapping the HDR-rendered images where the HDR domain referred to in their papers are that to be viewed on professional HDR monitors for rendering operations. Consequently, they have not considered transfer functions such as PQ-OETF [16,27] or Hybrid Log Gamma [16] and color containers related to SDR or HDR format. Even when the transfer function and the color container are converted manually, HDR images converted by the previous methods are not suitable for viewing on consumer HDR displays. In this paper, we propose an ITM method with ITM-CNN, by which the resulting HDR images can be directly viewed on commercial HDR TVs. The end-to-end CNN-based structure of our ITM-CNN benefits from image decomposition along with delicate training strategies.

3   Proposed Method

Our proposed ITM-CNN has an end-to-end CNN structure for the prediction of the HDR image from a single LDR image.

3.1   Network Architecture

In tone mapping, edge-preserving filters (e.g. bilateral filter) are frequently used on the HDR input to decompose the image into the base layer and detail layer

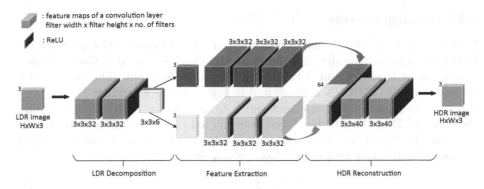

Fig. 2. Architecture of our ITM-CNN. Our ITM-CNN consist of three parts: LDR decomposition, feature extraction and HDR reconstruction. The first part is intended to decompose each LDR input image into two different sets of feature maps on which feature extraction, the second part, is performed in two separate branches. The last HDR reconstruction part concatenates the feature maps from both passes and aims to generate a single HDR output image

so that only the base layer is compressed while preserving the detail layer. The processed base and detail layers are then integrated to obtain a final LDR output image. In contrast, the purpose of an ITM algorithm is to predict lost details with an extended base layer to match the desired brightness to finally generate the output HDR image. If the image is decomposed into two parts with different characteristics, appropriate processing may be done for the individual branches for a more accurate prediction of the output image. Following from this idea, we explicitly model our CNN structure (ITM-CNN) as three parts: (i) LDR decomposition, (ii) feature extraction and (iii) HDR reconstruction, as illustrated in Fig. 2.

The first part of our ITM-CNN, LDR decomposition, consists of three convolution layers where the number of output channels for the last layer is six, intended to decompose each LDR input image into two different sets of feature maps, simply divided as the first three and the last three feature maps. Then, the convolution layers in the feature extraction part proceed individually for the two sets so that each of the two CNN branches are able to focus on the characteristics of the respective inputs for specialized feature extraction. Lastly, for HDR reconstruction, the extracted feature maps from the individual passes are concatenated and the network (HDR reconstruction part) learns to integrate the feature maps from the two passes to finally generate an HDR image. Our ITM-CNN jointly optimizes all the three steps of LDR decomposition, feature extraction and HDR reconstruction, but has to be trained delicately to fully benefit from the image filtering idea (decomposition of LDR input).

3.2   Training Strategy

First, we pre-train the feature extraction and HDR reconstruction parts of the ITM-CNN after setting the LDR decomposition part as a guided-filtering-based separation of the base and detail layers for the LDR input. The pre-training structure of the ITM-CNN is illustrated in Fig. 4. The guided filter [10,11] is an edge-preserving filter that does not suffer from gradient reversal artifacts like the bilateral filter [1]. The base layer is extracted using the self-guided filter as suggested in [10,11], and the detail layer is obtained by element-wise division of the input LDR image by the base layer, given as

$$I^{detail} = I^{LDR} \oslash I^{base} \tag{1}$$

where I^{LDR} is the LDR input, I^{detail} is the detail layer and I^{base} is the base layer. $\oslash$ in Eq. 1 denotes an element-wise division operator. An example of an image separated using the guided filter is given in Fig. 3.

After pre-training the feature extraction and HDR reconstruction parts using the pre-train structure with guided-filtering-separation, the guided filter is replaced with three convolution layers (LDR decomposition part in Fig. 2) allowing for the final fully convolutional architecture as given in Fig. 2. We pre-train the three layers in the new LDR decomposition part with the same data but without updating the weights of later layers by setting the learning rate to zero for those layers, so that the convolution layers learn to decompose the LDR input image into feature maps that lower the final loss, while utilizing the weights in later layers that were trained with guided filter separation.

LDR image   (a) Base layer   (b) Detail layer

Fig. 3. Image decomposition using the guided filter. The base layer is the result of self-guided filtering on the LDR image and the detail layer is the element-wise division of the LDR image by the base layer

When the pre-training is finished, the network (ITM-CNN) is finally trained end-to-end for joint optimization of all three parts. We observed a significant increase in performance by using this pre-training strategy.

4   Experiments

4.1   Experiment Conditions

Data. We collected 7,268 frames of 3840 × 2160 UHD resolution of the LDR-HDR data pairs containing diverse scenes. The specifications are given in Table 1.

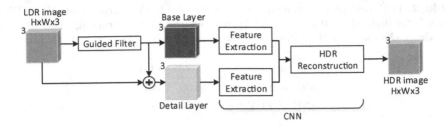

Fig. 4. Pre-train structure. Guided filter is used instead of the LDR decomposition part during the pre-training phase of feature extraction and HDR reconstruction parts

The HDR video is professionally filmed and mastered, and the LDR counterparts were generated through youtube, which we considered as most similar to commercially available data. Both the LDR and HDR data are normalized to be in the range [0, 1]. For the synthesis of training data, we randomly cropped 20 subimages of size 40×40 per frame with the frame stride of 30. This resulted in the total training data of size $40 \times 40 \times 3 \times 4860$. All videos were converted to the YUV color space and all three YUV channels were used for training. Although it is common to use Y channel only, using all three channels is more reasonable for our ITM problem since the color container also changes from BT.709 [13] to BT.2020 [15]. The quantitative benefit of using all three channels is shown in Table 2 when experimenting with a simple CNN structure. The large difference in the PSNR when measured for all three YUV channels is largely in part due to the color container and transfer function mismatch of LDR and HDR images if the U and V channels are not trained. Note that the Y channel benefits from the complementary information of U and V channels.

Table 1. Data specifications

Data type	Bit depth	Transfer function	Color container
LDR	8 bits/pixel	Gamma	BT.709
HDR	10 bits/pixel	PQ-OETF	BT.2020

For testing, we selected 14 UHD frames from six different scenes that are not included in the training set. The network was also tested on completely new type of video sequences that were filmed, mastered and rendered by different professionals. These three sequences - *Aquarium*, *Leaves* and *Cuisine* - each consists of 60 frames.

Training Parameters. The weight decay of the convolution filters were set to 5×10^{-4} with that of biases set to zero. The mini-batch size was 32 with the learning rate of 10^{-4} for filters and 10^{-5} for biases. All convolution filters are of

Table 2. ITM performance comparison of using single (Y) versus multiple (YUV) channels for input data. If all three YUV channels are used for training, the PSNR of only the Y channel as well as all channels increases significantly

Train data	Y only	YUV
PSNR of Y (dB)	44.36	46.36
PSNR of YUV (dB)	32.53	48.25

size 3×3 and the weights were initialized with the Xavier initialization [8] that draws the weights from a normal distribution with the variance expressed with both the number of input and output neurons. The loss function of the network (ITM-CNN) is given by

$$Loss\,(\theta) = \frac{1}{2n} \sum_{i=1}^{n} \left\| F\left(I_i^{LDR}; \theta\right) - I_i^{HDR} \right\|^2 \tag{2}$$

where θ is the set of model parameters, n is the number of training samples, I^{LDR} is the input LDR image, F is the non-linear mapping function of the ITM-CNN giving the prediction of the network as $F(I^{LDR}, \theta)$, and I^{HDR} is the ground truth HDR image. The activation function is the rectified linear unit (ReLU) [9] given by

$$ReLU = max(0, x) \tag{3}$$

All network models are implemented with the MatConvNet [28] package.

4.2   Input Decomposition

Decomposing the LDR input lets the feature extraction layers to concentrate on each of the decompositions. Specifically, we use the guided filter [10,11] for input decomposition. We compare three different architectures shown in Fig. 5 to observe the effect of decomposing the LDR input.

The first structure shown in Fig. 5(a) is a simple six-convolution-layer structure with residual learning. Since both the input LDR image with 8 bits/pixel and the ground truth HDR image with 10 bits/pixel are normalized to be in the range [0, 1], we can simply model the network (Fig. 5(a)) to learn the difference between the LDR and HDR image for a more accurate prediction. Although no decomposition is performed on the input LDR image, residual learning may be interpreted as an additive separation of the output that allows the CNN (Fig. 5(a)) to focus only on predicting the difference between LDR and HDR.

The second structure shown in Fig. 5(b) uses the guided filter for multiplicative input decomposition, and has two individual passes where one predicts the base layer and the other predicts the detail layer of the HDR image. The base and detail layer predictions are then multiplied element-wise to obtain the final HDR image. By providing the ground truth base and detail layers of the HDR

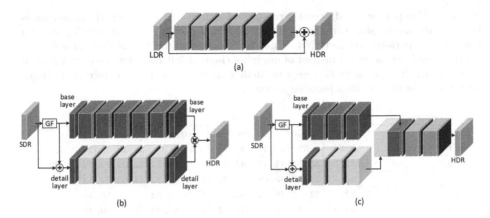

Fig. 5. Different architecture using image decompositions. Architecture (a) is a simple CNN with six layers and residual learning. For architecture (b), the guided filter separated image is fed into the network where the two individual CNN branches focus on the respective inputs, to predict the multiplicative guided filter separation of the HDR image. Instead of explicitly predicting the base and detail layers of the HDR image like in (b), architecture (c) allows convolution layers to learn to integrate the feature maps from the two passes after their concatenation

image, this second structure can fully concentrate on the decompositions for the final prediction.

The last structure shown in Fig. 5(c), also uses the guided filter for multiplicative input decomposition, but the feature maps from the individual passes are concatenated for direct prediction of the HDR image. This network learns the optimal integration operation that lowers the final loss through the last three convolutional layers, whereas for the structure in Fig. 5(b), we explicitly force the network to model the base and detail layers of the HDR image for an element-wise multiplicative integration. Note that this last structure is the same as the pre-train structure in Fig. 4.

The results of the experiment are given in Table 3 where (a), (b) and (c) denote the structures illustrated in Fig. 5. For fair comparison, we tune the number of filters in the hidden layers so that the total number of parameters for each of the structures are similar. We perform two additional experiments with structure (a) and (c) denoted by (a)* and (c)* where (a)* is the structure (a) without residual learning, and (c)* is the structure (c) with element-wise multiplication instead of concatenation for integrating the feature maps after the third convolution layer. We compare the structures in terms of PSNR measured only for the Y channel and for all three YUV channels.

Even with similar number of parameters, there is a maximum PSNR difference of 0.67 dB measured for Y channel only and 0.48 dB measured for YUV channels depending on whether input decomposition is used or not and how the decomposed inputs are treated. The highest performing structure is the structure (c), although (c)* shows comparable results for PSNR measured for YUV,

Table 3. Comparisons of different structures shown in Fig. 5. Even with similar number of parameters, structures using input decomposition by guided filtering show a much higher performance in PSNR. When the integration method is also learned using convolution layers as in (c) instead of implying the multiplicative nature of the decompositions at the end as in (b), we can further increase the performance. For simple structures like (a), residual learning is crucial

Structure	(a)*	(a)		(b)		(c)*		(c)	
Layer	Number of filter channels (input, output)								
1	3, 32	3, 32	3, 45	3, 32	3, 32	3, 32	3, 32	3, 32	3, 32
2	32, 32	32, 32	45, 45	32, 32	32, 32	32, 32	32, 32	32, 32	32, 32
3	32, 32	32, 32	45, 48	32, 32	32, 32	32, 32	32, 32	32, 32	32, 32
4	32, 32	32, 32	48, 45	32, 32	32, 32	32, 52		64, 40	
5	32, 32	32, 32	45, 45	32, 32	32, 32	52, 48		40, 40	
6	32, 3	32, 3	45, 3	32, 3	32, 3	48, 3		40, 3	
Total parameters	38,592	38,592	**77,760**	**77,184**		**77,328**		**77,112**	
PSNR of Y (dB)	45.46	46.36	46.36	46.84		46.73		**47.03**	
PSNR of YUV (dB)	47.28	48.25	48.39	48.65		**48.87**		**48.82**	

(a)*: (a) without residual learning
(c)*: (c) with element-wise multiplication after layer 3

Table 4. PSNR performance comparison between multiplicative and additive decompositions

	Additive	Multiplicative
PSNR of Y (dB)	46.70	47.03
PSNR of YUV (dB)	48.67	48.82
Total parameters	77,112	77,112

where the network has the freedom to learn the integration of two feature extraction passes. Comparing the structures (a) and (b), we confirm that the input decomposition using the guided filter is highly beneficial. Also, for the simple CNN architecture in the structure (a), it is crucial to use residual learning for improved prediction. Letting the convolution layers to focus on specific input decompositions with different characteristics, and learn to combine information generated by the different branches is important in reconstructing a high quality HDR image.

Multiplicative Separation. The motivation behind the multiplicative separation between the base and detail layers is that the multiplicative factors are of more importance than simple differences, as stated by the Weber's law. Our eye is more sensitive to the difference in darker environments than in lighter environments due to this reason. The experiment between additive and multiplicative separations when using the guided filter also support the multiplicative decomposition. The results between the two types of separations on the architecture of Fig. 5(c) are reported in Table 4.

Table 5. Results with different training procedures. There is at most 0.56 dB difference in PSNR depending on whether the network is pre-trained or not. The guided filter based pre-training is very effective

Procedure	(i)			(ii)			(iii)			(iv)		
Order	Decom.	Feat.	Recon.	Decom.	Feat.	Recon.	Decom.	Feat.	Recon.	Decom.	Feat.	Recon.
1st	-	-	-	-	-	-	-	-	-	-	▓	▓
2nd	-	-	-	-	▓	▓	-	▓	▓	▓	-	-
3rd	▓	▓	▓	▓	-	-	▓					
PSNR of Y	46.71			46.28			47.11			47.27		
PSNR of YUV	48.80			48.15			48.98			49.21		

Decom.: LDR decomposition part, Feat.: Feature extraction part, Recon.: HDR reconstruction part
▓▓▓▓ : guided filter based pre-training
▓▓▓▓ : simple training

4.3 Effect of Pre-training

We model a fully end-to-end CNN structure as illustrated in Fig. 2 by replacing the guided filter based separation in the structure (c) with three convolutional layers each with 32 filters of size 3 × 3. However, we find that pre-training the network is essential to fully utilize the three parts of the network (LDR decomposition, feature extraction and HDR reconstruction) as intended. Otherwise, the individual parts simply work as additional feature extraction layers for the whole network. Table 5 shows the results of the same network, the fully convolutional network in Fig. 2, with different training procedures. The first column indicates the training order. The second row denotes the three parts - LDR decomposition, feature extraction and HDR reconstruction - of ITM-CNN. A colored cell means that the specific part of the network was trained in the corresponding order, where only the layers of that part were trained in the n-th order, and the weights of other layers remained fixed. Orange colored cell means that the LDR decomposition part was replaced with the guided filter separation for the pre-training as in Fig. 4.

If the whole network is simply trained end-to-end without any pre-training (procedure (i)), it achieves 0.32 dB lower performance in PSNR of Y than the structure of Fig. 5(c), even though it has three more convolution layers or 11,808 more filter parameters. However, if the pre-trained filter values (of Figs. 4 or 5(c)) using the guided filter separation (instead of the LDR decomposition layers) are used to initialize the network before the end-to-end training (procedure (iii)), the resulting PSNR performance jumps with 0.4 dB and 0.18 dB for Y and YUV respectively, thus exceeding the best performing version in Table 3. The highest PSNR performance can be obtained by also pre-training the LDR decomposition layers in conjunction with the pre-training by the guided filter separation network and the end-to-end training at the end (procedure (iv)).

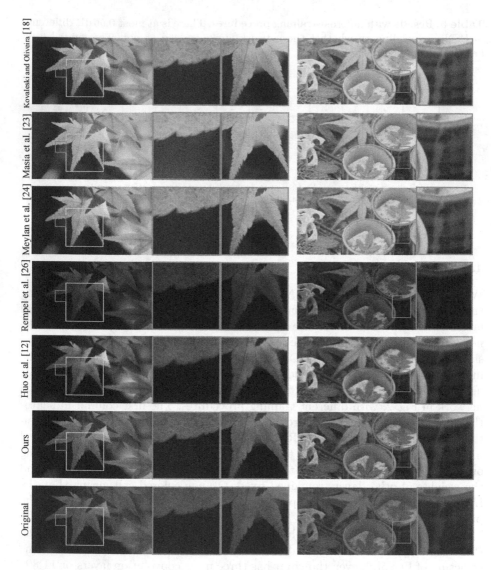

Fig. 6. Comparisons with previous methods [12, 18, 23, 24, 26]. Methods in the top three rows demonstrate obvious artifacts with amplified noise, especially in the regions that should be dark such as the background below the leaf (2nd column) and the shadowed glass cup (5th column). The result images of those methods are too bright overall, while the result of Rempel *et al.*s method in the 4th row is generally too dark with low contrast. Furthermore, as can be seen in the images in the 3rd column, the color of the leaf of other methods is irregular or unnatural when compared to the original image. Our ITM-CNN shows stable results with the color and intensity similar to the ground truth where dark regions are dark without noise amplification, while showing accurate details

Table 6. PSNR (dB) performance (*top*) and HDR-VDP-2.2.1 Q-score (*bottom*) comparison with previous ITM methods on three test sequences with 60 frames each. The result HDR images are compared to the ground truth HDR images that were intended for viewing on HDR TVs

Sequence	Banterle *et al.* [3]	Huo *et al.* [12]	Kovaleski *et al.* [18]	Masia *et al.* [23]	Meylan *et al.* [24]	Rempel *et al.* [26]	Ours (ITM-CNN)
Aquarium	20.78	28.57	23.24	23.96	23.59	24.80	**32.24**
	49.59	52.50	50.97	50.99	50.98	52.52	**66.19**
Leaves	19.53	29.47	23.48	19.64	23.05	25.13	**29.95**
	45.61	48.03	49.30	48.74	49.26	45.64	**61.30**
Cuisine	17.47	28.73	21.51	22.24	22.01	24.79	**31.07**
	53.46	56.01	54.88	54.95	54.91	54.72	**66.79**
Average	19.26	28.92	22.74	21.95	22.88	24.91	**31.09**
	49.56 ± 3.22	52.18±3.27	51.72 ± 2.35	51.56 ± 2.58	51.72 ± 2.37	50.96 ± 3.88	**64.76** ± 2.48

4.4 Comparisons with Conventional Methods

Since no previous method was explicitly trained for viewing with consumer HDR displays, fair comparison with our method is difficult. When comparing the previous ITM methods, we set the maximum brightness to $1,000 \, cd/m^2$, remove gamma correction and apply the expansion operator in the linear space. After the expansion, the color container is converted from BT.709 to BT.2020 and the PQ-OETF transfer function is applied for pixel values to be in the pixel domain. Note that our method works directly in the pixel domain without any conversion using the transfer function or color container.

Another complication is tone mapping for viewing on paper or SDR displays. All images in this paper were tone mapped using the madVR[1] renderer using the MPC-HC[2] player, heuristically found to be most similar as viewing with HDR consumer displays. Although this is not the exact application of our problem since our final goal is to view the output images on HDR TV, not to view the tone-mapped HDR images on SDR TV, the result images still support our approach to be valid and show that the existing methods are not directly applicable for viewing on HDR consumer displays. Previous methods are noticeably different from original HDR images with overall intensity variation, local dissimilarities and color discrepancies. The result images for subjective comparisons are given in Fig. 6. PSNR performance and HDR-VDP-2.2.1 [21] Q-score comparison is given in Table 6. We have also noted the standard deviation for average HDR-VDP scores. Our method outperforms previous methods in both PSNR and HDR-VDP. More comparisons can be found in the Supplementary Material.

5 Conclusion

Despite that high-end HDR TVs are readily available in the market, HDR video contents are scarce. This entails the need for a means to up-convert LDR legacy

---

[1] Available at http://madvr.com/.

[2] Available at https://mpc-hc.org/.

video to HDR video for the high-end HDR TVs. Although existing ITM methods share a similar goal of up-converting, their ultimate objective is not to render the inversely-tone-mapped HDR images on consumer HDR TV displays, but to transfer the LDR scenes to the HDR domain for better graphics rendering on professional HDR monitors. The resulting HDR images from previous ITM methods exhibit noise amplification in dark regions and lack of local contrast or unnatural colors when being viewed on consumer HDR TV displays.

In this paper, we first present the ITM problem for HDR consumer displays, where our CNN-based network, ITM-CNN, is trained to restore lost details and local contrast. For an accurate prediction of the HDR image, the different parts (LDR decomposition, feature extraction and HDR reconstruction) of ITM-CNN must be trained separately prior to end-to-end training. Specifically, we adopt the guided filter for LDR decomposition of the pre-training stage so that the later layers can focus on the individual decompositions with separate passes. The HDR reconstruction part of ITM-CNN learns to integrate the feature maps from the two passes. The resulting HDR images are artifact-free, restore local contrast and details, and are closest to the ground truth HDR images when compared to previous ITM methods. ITM-CNN is readily applicable to legacy LDR videos for their direct viewing as HDR videos on consumer HDR TV displays.

References

1. Aurich, V., Weule, J.: Non-linear Gaussian filters performing edge preserving diffusion. In: Sagerer, G., Posch, S., Kummert, F. (eds.) Mustererkennung 1995. INFORMAT, pp. 538–545. Springer, Heidelberg (1995). https://doi.org/10.1007/978-3-642-79980-8_63
2. Banterle, F., Ledda, P., Debattista, K., Chalmers, A.: Inverse tone mapping. In: Proceedings of the 4th International Conference on Computer Graphics and Interactive Techniques in Australasia and Southeast Asia, pp. 349–356. ACM (2006)
3. Banterle, F., Ledda, P., Debattista, K., Chalmers, A., Bloj, M.: A framework for inverse tone mapping. Vis. Comput. **23**(7), 467–478 (2007)
4. Dong, C., Loy, C.C., He, K., Tang, X.: Learning a deep convolutional network for image super-resolution. In: Fleet, D., Pajdla, T., Schiele, B., Tuytelaars, T. (eds.) ECCV 2014. LNCS, vol. 8692, pp. 184–199. Springer, Cham (2014). https://doi.org/10.1007/978-3-319-10593-2_13
5. Dong, C., Loy, C.C., He, K., Tang, X.: Image super-resolution using deep convolutional networks. IEEE Trans. Pattern Anal. Mach. Intell. **38**(2), 295–307 (2016)
6. Eilertsen, G., Kronander, J., Denes, G., Mantiuk, R.K., Unger, J.: HDR image reconstruction from a single exposure using deep CNNs. ACM Trans. Graph. **36**(6), 178 (2017)
7. Endo, Y., Kanamori, Y., Mitani, J.: Deep reverse tone mapping. ACM Trans. Graph. **36**(6), 177 (2017)
8. Glorot, X., Bengio, Y.: Understanding the difficulty of training deep feedforward neural networks. In: Proceedings of the Thirteenth International Conference on Artificial Intelligence and Statistics, pp. 249–256 (2010)
9. Glorot, X., Bordes, A., Bengio, Y.: Deep sparse rectifier neural networks. In: Proceedings of the Fourteenth International Conference on Artificial Intelligence and Statistics, pp. 315–323 (2011)

10. He, K., Sun, J., Tang, X.: Guided image filtering. In: Daniilidis, K., Maragos, P., Paragios, N. (eds.) ECCV 2010. LNCS, vol. 6311, pp. 1–14. Springer, Heidelberg (2010). https://doi.org/10.1007/978-3-642-15549-9_1

11. He, K., Sun, J., Tang, X.: Guided image filtering. IEEE Trans. Pattern Anal. Mach. Intell. **35**(6), 1397–1409 (2013)

12. Huo, Y., Yang, F., Dong, L., Brost, V.: Physiological inverse tone mapping based on retina response. Vis. Comput. **30**(5), 507–517 (2014)

13. ITU-R: Parameter values for the HDTV standards for production and international programme exchange. ITU-R Rec. BT.709-5 (2002). http://www.itu.int/rec/R-REC-BT.709

14. ITU-R: Reference electro-optical transfer function for flat panel displays used in HDTV studio production. ITU-R Rec. BT.1886 (2011)

15. ITU-R: Parameter values for ultra-high definition television systems for production and international programme exchange. Document ITU-R Rec. BT.2020-1 (2014). http://www.itu.int/rec/R-REC-BT.2020

16. ITU-R: Image parameter values for high dynamic range television systems for use in production and international programme exchange. ITU-R Rec. BT.2100-0 (2016). http://www.itu.int/rec/R-REC-BT.2100

17. Kalantari, N.K., Ramamoorthi, R.: Deep high dynamic range imaging of dynamic scenes. ACM Trans. Graph. **36**(4), 144 (2017)

18. Kovaleski, R.P., Oliveira, M.M.: High-quality reverse tone mapping for a wide range of exposures. In: 2014 27th SIBGRAPI Conference on Graphics, Patterns and Images (SIBGRAPI), pp. 49–56. IEEE (2014)

19. Kovaleski, R.P., Oliveira, M.M.: High-quality brightness enhancement functions for real-time reverse tone mapping. Vis. Comput. **25**(5–7), 539–547 (2009)

20. Krizhevsky, A., Sutskever, I., Hinton, G.E.: ImageNet classification with deep convolutional neural networks. In: Advances in Neural Information Processing Systems, pp. 1097–1105 (2012)

21. Mantiuk, R., Kim, K.J., Rempel, A.G., Heidrich, W.: HDR-VDP-2: a calibrated visual metric for visibility and quality predictions in all luminance conditions. ACM Trans. Graph. **30**(4), 40 (2011)

22. Masia, B., Agustin, S., Fleming, R.W., Sorkine, O., Gutierrez, D.: Evaluation of reverse tone mapping through varying exposure conditions. ACM Trans. Graph. **28**(5), 160 (2009)

23. Masia, B., Serrano, A., Gutierrez, D.: Dynamic range expansion based on image statistics. Multimed. Tools Appl. **76**(1), 631–648 (2017)

24. Meylan, L., Daly, S., Süsstrunk, S.: The reproduction of specular highlights on high dynamic range displays. In: Color and Imaging Conference, vol. 1, pp. 333–338. Society for Imaging Science and Technology (2006)

25. Reinhard, E., Stark, M., Shirley, P., Ferwerda, J.: Photographic tone reproduction for digital images. ACM Trans. Graph. **21**(3), 267–276 (2002)

26. Rempel, A.G., et al.: Ldr2Hdr: on-the-fly reverse tone mapping of legacy video and photographs. In: ACM Transactions on Graphics, vol. 26, p. 39. ACM (2007)

27. SMPTE: High dynamic range electro-optical transfer function of mastering reference displays. SMPTE ST2084:2014 (2014)

28. Vedaldi, A., Lenc, K.: MatConvNet: convolutional neural networks for MATLAB. In: Proceedings of the 23rd ACM International Conference on Multimedia, pp. 689–692. ACM (2015)

29. Zhang, J., Lalonde, J.F.: Learning high dynamic range from outdoor panoramas. In: Proceedings of the IEEE International Conference on Computer Vision (2017)

Structure Aware SLAM Using Quadrics and Planes

Mehdi Hosseinzadeh[1,3(✉)], Yasir Latif[1,3], Trung Pham[4], Niko Suenderhauf[2,3], and Ian Reid[1,3]

[1] The University of Adelaide, Adelaide, Australia
{mehdi.hosseinzadeh,yasir.latif,ian.reid}@adelaide.edu.au
[2] Queensland University of Technology, Brisbane, Australia
niko.suenderhauf@qut.edu.au
[3] Australian Centre for Robotic Vision, Brisbane, Australia
[4] NVIDIA, Santa Clara, CA 95051, USA
trungp@nvidia.com

Abstract. Simultaneous Localization And Mapping (SLAM) is a fundamental problem in mobile robotics. While point-based SLAM methods provide accurate camera localization, the generated maps lack semantic information. On the other hand, state of the art object detection methods provide rich information about entities present in the scene from a single image. This work marries the two and proposes a method for representing generic objects as quadrics which allows object detections to be seamlessly integrated in a SLAM framework. For scene coverage, additional dominant planar structures are modeled as infinite planes. Experiments show that the proposed points-planes-quadrics representation can easily incorporate Manhattan and object affordance constraints, greatly improving camera localization and leading to semantically meaningful maps.

Keywords: Visual semantic SLAM · Object SLAM · Planes · Quadrics

1 Introduction

Simultaneous Localization And Mapping (SLAM) is one of the fundamental problems in mobile robotics [2] and addresses the reconstruction of a previously unseen environment while simultaneously localizing a mobile robot with respect to it. While the representation of the robot pose depends on the degrees of

Supported by the ARC Fellowship FL130100102 to IR and the ACRV CE140100016.

Electronic supplementary material The online version of this chapter (https://doi.org/10.1007/978-3-030-20893-6_26) contains supplementary material, which is available to authorized users.

freedom of motion, the representation of the map depends on a multitude of factors including the available sensors, computational resources, intended high level task, and required precision. Many possible representations have been proposed.

For visual-SLAM, the simplest representation of the map is a collection of 3D points which correspond to salient image feature points. This representation is sparse and efficient to compute and update. Point based methods have been successfully used to map city-scale environments. However, this sparsity comes at a price: points-based maps lack semantic information and are not useful for high level task such as grasping and manipulation. Although methods to compute denser representations have been proposed [6,7,22–24] these representations remain equivalent to a collection of points and therefore carry no additional semantic information.

Man-made environments contain many objects that could potentially be used as landmarks in a SLAM map, encapsulating a higher level of information than a set of points. Previous object-based SLAM efforts have mostly relied on a database of predefined objects – which must be recognised and a precise 3D model fit to match the observation in the image to establish correspondence [29]. Other work [1] has admitted more general objects (and constraints) but only in a slow, offline structure-from-motion context. In contrast, we are concerned with live (real-time) SLAM, but we seek to represent a wide variety of objects. Like [1] we are not so concerned with high-fidelity reconstruction of individual objects, but rather to represent the location, orientation and rough shape of objects. A suitable representation is therefore potentially a quadric [10,31], which allows a compact representation of rough extent.

In addition to objects, much of the large-scale structure of a general scene (especially indoors) comprises dominant planar surfaces. Including planes in a SLAM map has also been explored before [15,28]. Planes are also a good representation for feature deprived regions, where they provide information complimentary to points and can represent significant portions of the environment with very few parameters, leading to a representation that can be constructed and updated online [15]. Pertinent to our purpose, such a representation also provides the potential for additional constraints for the points that lie on one of the planes and permits the introduction of useful affordance constraints between objects and their supporting planes, as we explain later in the paper. All these constraints lead to better estimate of the camera pose.

Modern SLAM is usually formulated as an unconstrained sparse nonlinear least-square problem [13]. The sparsity structure of the problem greatly effects the computation time of the systems. If planes and quadrics are to be introduced in a SLAM system, they should be represented in a way which is amenable to the non-linear least squares formulation and respects the sparsity pattern of the SLAM problem.

In this work, we propose a map representation that consists of points, and higher level geometric entities such as planes and objects as landmarks. Unlike previous work such as [1] we explicitly target real-time performance, and integrate within an online SLAM framework. Such performance would be impossible with uncritical choices of representation and to that end we propose a novel representation of objects based on quadrics that decomposes to permit clean, fast and effective real-time implementation. We show that this representation, along with point-plane, plane-plane (Manhattan), and plane-object (supporting) constraints, greatly reduces the error in the estimated camera trajectory without incurring great extra computational cost. Because of the higher-level primitives in the map, the representation remains compact, but carries crucial semantic information about the scene. To the best of authors' knowledge, this is the first *real-time* SLAM system proposed in literature that incorporates both higher level primitives of planes and previously unseen objects as landmarks.

The remainder of the paper is organized as follows. In the next section, we present the background for SLAM as the solution to a factor-graph, and explain how our proposal is integrated into such a framework. In particular, we give detailed descriptions of the mathematical representations of each landmark, and the factors they induce. Section 4 presents an overview of how the preceding section is integrated into an overall SLAM system. Experiments showing the efficacy and comparative performance of our system are presented in Sect. 5. We conclude with a summary and discussion of future research directions.

2   Related Work

SLAM is well studied problem in mobile robotics and many different solutions have been proposed for solving it. The most recent of these is the graph-based approach that formulates SLAM as a nonlinear least squares problem [13]. SLAM with cameras has also seen advancement in theory and good implementations that have lead to many real-time systems from sparse [6,20] to semi-dense [7,8] to fully dense [22–24].

Recently, there has been a lot of interest in extending the capability of a point-based representation by either applying the same techniques to other geometric primitives or fusing points with lines or planes to get better accuracy. Several methods have explored replacing points with lines [11,17]. However, lines present especial difficulty because of the lack of a good mathematical representation that is amenable to the least-squares framework. Some works have explored the possibility of using lines and points in the same framework [12,25] and have been more successful.

Recently, [15] proposed a representation for infinite planes that is amenable for use in a least-squares framework. Using this representation, they presented a method that work using just information of planes visible in the environment. Similarly, [35] use a monocular input to generate plane hypothesis using a Convolutional Neural Network (CNN) which is then refined over time using both the planes as well as points in the images. [33] proposed a method that fuses points and planes using an RGB-D sensor. In the latter works, they try to fuse the information of plane entities to increase the accuracy of depth inference.

Quadrics based representation was first proposed in [3] and later used in a structure from motion setup [10]. [32] presented a semantic mapping system that uses object detection coupled with RGB-D SLAM to reconstruct precise object models in the environment, however object models do not inform localization. [29] presented an object based SLAM system that uses pre-scanned object models as landmarks for SLAM but can not be generalized to unseen objects. [19] presented a system that fused multiple semantic predictions with a dense map reconstruction. SLAM is used as the backbone to establish multiple-view correspondences for fusion of semantic labels without informing the localization.

3 Landmark Representations

For object-oriented SLAM the map comprises not only points but higher-level entities representing landmarks which aim to be more semantically meaningful than sparse points. However to maintain real-time operation, there is a trade-off between complexity of the landmark representation and the computational cost of tracking and mapping.

In this work we consider two kinds of landmarks, which admit efficient implementation but can broadly capture the overall structure of many scenes, especially those captured indoors: (a) plane landmarks, whose role is to encapsulate high-level structure of regions; and (b) quadrics (more specifically ellipsoids) that serve as a general representation of objects in scene, capturing not detailed shape, but key properties such as size, extent, position and orientation. We introduce representations for both types of primitive that allow for efficient implementation in a SLAM framework, as well as admitting clean and effective constraints between primitives, such as supporting constraint between objects and planes.

3.1 Quadric Representation

As noted above, we represent general objects in a scene using an ellipsoid. Generally speaking, a quadric surface in 3D space can be represented by a homogeneous quadratic form defined on the 3D projective space $\mathbb{P}^3$ which satisfies $\mathbf{x}^T\mathbf{Q}\mathbf{x} = 0$, where $\mathbf{x} \in \mathbb{R}^4$ is the homogeneous 3D point and $\mathbf{Q} \in \mathbb{R}^{4\times4}$ is the symmetric matrix representing the quadric surface. However the relationship between a point-quadric and its projection into a camera (a conic) is not straightforward [14]. A widely accepted alternative is to make use of the dual space [3,10,31] in which a quadric is represented as the envelope of a set of tangent planes, viz:

$$\pi^T\mathbf{Q}^*\pi = 0 \tag{1}$$

This greatly simplifies the relationship between the quadric and its projection to a conic, however a further problem remains in the context of optimisation in a graph-SLAM framework. The issue is that an update of $\mathbf{Q}^*$, given an 9-dim error vector $\mathbf{e}$ in the tangent space of $\mathbf{Q}^*$, should be constrained to lie along a geodesic of the manifold. But finding these geodesics and updating with respect to them is computationally expensive, making a "straightforward" quadric representation intractable for incremental optimisation.

We seek to address both of these issues. For our object representation, we would like to restrict landmarks to belong to the set of bounded quadrics, namely ellipsoids. To do so requires imposing the constraint that $\mathbf{Q}^*$ must have 3 positive and 1 negative eigenvalues. Based on this restriction, the representation of dual ellipsoids $\mathbf{Q}^*$ can be decomposed as:

$$\mathbf{Q}^* = \mathbf{T}_Q \mathbf{Q}_c^* \mathbf{T}_Q^T = \begin{bmatrix} \mathbf{R} & \mathbf{t} \\ \mathbf{0}^T & 1 \end{bmatrix} \begin{bmatrix} a^2 & 0 & 0 & 0 \\ 0 & b^2 & 0 & 0 \\ 0 & 0 & c^2 & 0 \\ 0 & 0 & 0 & -1 \end{bmatrix} \begin{bmatrix} \mathbf{R}^T & \mathbf{0} \\ \mathbf{t}^T & 1 \end{bmatrix} \tag{2}$$

where $\mathbf{T}_Q \in \mathbf{SE(3)}$ transforms an axis-aligned (canonical) quadric at the origin, $\mathbf{Q}_c^*$, to a desired $\mathbf{SE(3)}$ pose, and a, b, c denote the scale of the canonical ellipsoid $\mathbf{Q}_c^*$ along its principal axes.

Optimizing on the space of quadrics must impose constraints on the eignevalues of $\mathbf{Q}^*$ to force the solution to be an ellipsoid. Recently [10,27] have parameterized ellipsoids to overcome this problem. They optimize on the space of ellipsoids, $\mathbb{E}$, to localise the quadric by their respective conic observations. However their representation requires solving a constrained least squares problem. While their parametrization is useful for observations of quadrics on camera frames as conics, it can not be used as generic constraints in the graph SLAM problem due to its constrained nature. The authors in [10] decompose the translation part of the representation, mainly for numerical stability in the optimisation because of the different scales of translation and the other parts of the representation, and impose some prior knowledge on the shape of the ellipsoids. For a more efficient representation of ellipsoids in graph-based SLAM, we exploit the underlying structure of $\mathbb{E}$ to represent the dual quadric as follows:

$$\mathbf{Q}^* = \mathbf{T}_Q \, \mathbf{Q}_c^* \, \mathbf{T}_Q^T = \begin{bmatrix} \mathbf{R} & \mathbf{t} \\ \mathbf{0}^T & 1 \end{bmatrix} \begin{bmatrix} \mathbf{LL}^T & \mathbf{0} \\ \mathbf{0} & -1 \end{bmatrix} \begin{bmatrix} \mathbf{R}^T & \mathbf{0} \\ \mathbf{t}^T & 1 \end{bmatrix} \quad \text{where} \quad \mathbf{L} = \begin{bmatrix} a & 0 & 0 \\ 0 & b & 0 \\ 0 & 0 & c \end{bmatrix} \tag{3}$$

with real numbers a, b and c, and so $\mathbf{LL}^T$ guarantees the required positive eigenvalues. We thus represent a dual ellipsoid $\mathbf{Q}^*$ using a tuple $(\mathbf{T}, \mathbf{L})$ where $\mathbf{T} \in \mathbf{SE(3)}$ and $\mathbf{L}$ lives in $\mathbf{D(3)}$ the space of real diagonal 3×3 matrices, i.e. an axis-aligned ellipsoid accompanied by a rigid transformation. This decomposition exploits the underlying $\mathbf{SE(3)} \times \mathbf{D(3)}$ structure of the manifold of $\mathbb{E}$, ensuring we remain in the space of ellipsoids without needing to solve a constrained optimisation problem.

We update the $\mathbf{Q}^* = (\mathbf{T}, \mathbf{L})$ separately in the underlying 6D space of $\mathbf{SE(3)}$ and 3D space of $\mathbf{D(3)}$, where both of them are Lie groups and can be updated efficiently by their respective Lie algebra. Thus the proposed update rule is:

$$\mathbf{Q}^* \oplus \Delta\mathbf{Q}^* = (\mathbf{T}, \mathbf{L}) \oplus (\Delta\mathbf{T}, \Delta\mathbf{L}) = (\mathbf{T} \cdot \Delta\mathbf{T}, \mathbf{L} + \Delta\mathbf{L}) \tag{4}$$

where $\oplus : \mathbb{E} \times \mathbb{E} \longmapsto \mathbb{E}$ is the mapping for updating ellipsoids, $\Delta\mathbf{L}$ is the update for $\mathbf{L}$ which comes from the first 3 elements of error vector $\mathbf{e}$ and applies in the

Euclidean space of $\mathbb{R}^3$ and ΔT is the update for T which comes from the last 6 elements of error vector e and applies in space of $\mathbf{SE(3)}$. This decoupled update is a good approximation given the incremental nature of evidence.

This proposed representation of ellipsoids is beneficial particularly when we want to impose constraints on different parts of this representation. For instance, this representation for $\mathbf{Q}^*$ makes it possible to apply prior knowledge for shapes and sizes of objects, using the $\mathbf{L}$ component, prior information about location and orientation of the object using the $\mathbf{T}$ component, and adjacency/supporting constraints (see Sect. 3.3).

3.2 Plane Representation

To represent planes as structural entities in the map, we represent an infinite plane π by its normalised homogeneous coordinates $\pi = [a\ b\ c\ d]^T$ where $\mathbf{n} = [a\ b\ c]^T$ is the normal vector and d is the distance to origin. The reason for considering normalised homogeneous vectors is inspired by [15] to have a minimal representation for planes to avoid rank-deficient information matrices in optimization. This representation of the planes is isomorphic to the northern hemisphere of $\mathcal{S}^3$, or equivalently the $\mathbf{SO}(3)$ Lie group, therefore the optimisation can be performed using three elements that represent an element of $\mathbf{SO}(3)$.

3.3 SLAM as a Factor-Graph

Following the seminal work of [4] it is now well known that SLAM can be represented as a factor graph $\mathcal{G}(\mathcal{V}, \mathcal{E})$ where the vertices $\mathcal{V}$ represent the variables that need to be estimated such as robot poses and points in 3D, and the edges $\mathcal{E}$ represent constraints or *factors* between the vertices.

In a traditional point-based SLAM system, factors exist between points and the camera that seek to minimize reprojection error:

$$f_r(\mathbf{x}_w, \mathbf{T}_c^w) = \| \mathbf{u}_c - \Pi(\mathbf{x}_w, \mathbf{T}_c^w) \|_{\Sigma_r} \tag{5}$$

where $\mathbf{x}_w$ represent a point in the world, $\mathbf{T}_c^w$ is the pose of the camera which takes a point in the current camera frame $(\mathbf{P}_c)$ to a point in the world frame $\mathbf{P}_w = \mathbf{T}_c^w \mathbf{P}_c$ that is observed at the pixel location $\mathbf{u}_c$, and $\Pi(.)$ is a function that projects a world point into the camera. $\| \mathbf{x} \|_{\Sigma}$ is the mahalanobis norm and equal to $\mathbf{x}^T \Sigma^{-1} \mathbf{x}$ where Σ is the covariance matrix associated with the factor. Likewise if odometry is known between two robot positions, a factor involving robot poses can be formulated as:

$$f_o(\mathbf{T}_c^w, \mathbf{T}_k^w) = \| \mathbf{T}_{c,odom}^k \ominus \mathbf{T}_c^k \|_{\Sigma_o} \tag{6}$$

The solution to the SLAM problem is a configuration of the vertices $\mathcal{V}^*$ that minimizes the error over all the involved factors.

In our proposed object-oriented SLAM representation, the vertices in the SLAM graph consists not only of points but potentially planes and/or general

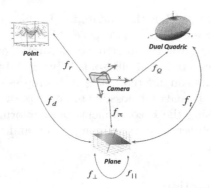

Fig. 1. The factor graph of our object-oriented SLAM system demonstrating all types of our landmark representations as nodes and observations and constraints as factors. For further details regarding these factors refer to Sect. 3.3

objects (represented by quadrics). Figure 1 shows the various factors involving cameras, points, planes, and quadric objects in our system. Below we describe in more detail how the new components of our SLAM system are introduced as additional factors in the graph.

Observations of Objects (Ellipsoids). A quadric $\mathbf{Q}^*$ in the scene projects to a conic $\mathbf{C}^*$ in an image [14]:

$$\mathbf{C}^* \sim \mathbf{P}\mathbf{Q}^*\mathbf{P}^\mathbf{T} \quad \text{and} \quad \mathbf{P} = \mathbf{K}\begin{bmatrix} I_{3\times3} & 0_{3\times3}\end{bmatrix}\mathbf{T}_\mathbf{c}^\mathbf{w} \tag{7}$$

where $\mathbf{P}$ is the projection matrix of the camera with calibration matrix $\mathbf{K}$ and $\mathbf{T}_\mathbf{c}^\mathbf{w}$ is the pose of the camera. For observed conic $\mathbf{C}^*_{obs}$, we consider the observation error for quadric $\mathbf{Q}^*$ as the Frobenius norm of the difference between normalized $\mathbf{C}^*_{obs}$ and normalized projected conic $\mathbf{C}^*$:

$$f_Q(\mathbf{Q}^*, \mathbf{T}_\mathbf{c}^\mathbf{w}) = \| \mathbf{C}^* - \mathbf{C}^*_{\mathbf{obs}} \|_\mathbf{F} = \sqrt{\mathbf{Tr}((\mathbf{C}^* - \mathbf{C}^*_{\mathbf{obs}})(\mathbf{C}^* - \mathbf{C}^*_{\mathbf{obs}})^\mathbf{T})} \tag{8}$$

which forms a factor between the quadric and the camera pose.

Observations of Planes. If we denote the observation of the plane π from a camera pose $\mathbf{T}_c^w$ by π_{obs}, we can measure the observation error by:

$$f_\pi(\pi, \mathbf{T}_\mathbf{c}^\mathbf{w}) = \| d(\mathbf{T}_c^{w-T}\pi, \pi_{obs}) \|_\Sigma^2 \tag{9}$$

where $\mathbf{T}_c^{w-T}\pi$ is the transformed plane to the camera coordinates frame and d is the distance function in the tangent space of the $\mathbf{SO}(3)$. For more details regarding plane updates and their corresponding exponential map refer to [15].

Point-Plane Constraints. If we believe that a point actually lies on a specific plane, it makes sense to impose a constraint between the point and the relevant plane landmark. To do so we introduce the following factor:

$$f_d(x, \pi) = \| \mathbf{n}^T(\mathbf{x} - \mathbf{x}_o) \|_\sigma^2 \tag{10}$$

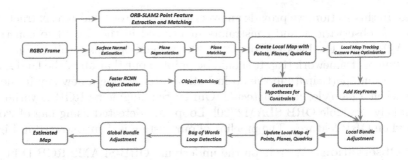

Fig. 2. The pipeline of our object-oriented SLAM system

which simply measures the orthogonal distance of the point **x** from the plane π with the unit normal vector **n**. $\mathbf{x}_o$ is an arbitrary point on the infinite plane.

Plane-Plane Constraints (Manhattan Assumption). Imposing constraints on relative plane orientations is simply a matter of introducing a factor on the plane surface normals. The most useful and common such constraints (especially indoors) are those associated with a Manhattan world in which planes are mostly mutually orthogonal or parallel. Constraints between planes π_1 and π_2 with unit normal vectors $\mathbf{n_1}$ and $\mathbf{n_2}$, respectively, are implemented as:

$$f_{\parallel}(\pi_1, \pi_2) = \| \, |\mathbf{n}_1^\top \mathbf{n}_2| - 1 \, \|_\sigma^2 \quad \text{for parallel planes} \tag{11}$$

$$f_{\perp}(\pi_1, \pi_2) = \| \, \mathbf{n}_1^\top \mathbf{n}_2 \, \|_\sigma^2 \quad \text{for perpendicular planes} \tag{12}$$

Supporting/Tangency Constraints. Almost all stable objects in the scene are supported by structural entities of the scene like planes; e.g. commonly objects are found on the floor or on a desk. Such an affordance relationship can be imposed between a quadric object and a structural infinite plane by introducing a geometric tangency constraint between them. To the best of our knowledge, this is the first time that such a constraint has been included in an online SLAM.

Although imposing a tangency constraint in the space of point quadrics could be tricky, in the dual space such a constraint takes a particularly simple form:

$$f_t(\pi, \mathbf{Q}^*) = \| \, \pi^T \mathbf{Q}^* \pi \, \|_\sigma^2 \tag{13}$$

where π is the normalised homogeneous plane that supports the quadric $\mathbf{Q}^*$.

4   System Implementation

Modern SLAM system can be divided into two functional parts: (**a**) a front-end: which deals with raw sensory input to initialize vertices and factors and (**b**) a back-end which optimizes the SLAM graph to create an updated estimate of the vertices. In this section, we provide an overview of our front-end that extracts the landmarks, observations and constraints mentioned in the Sect. 3 to construct the SLAM graph. The back-end of our SLAM system, optimises this graph using a least-squares framework [16]. It should be pointed out that all of the landmarks and constraints participate in the optimisation after adding a new key-frame, as well as when a loop closure is detected. Our system augments RGB-D variant of the publicly available ORB-SLAM2 [20]. Loops are detected using bag of words [9] based on ORB features. The pipeline of our system is demonstrated in Fig. 2.

Point Observations. We rely on the underlying ORB-SLAM2 RGB-D implementation for points; candidate features are extracted based on uniqueness and described using ORB features, with their depth initialized using the depth channel of the input. For data-association across frames, ORB features are matched in a coarse-to-fine pyramid in a local window around the previous observation.

Plane Observations. For planar landmarks, we are interested not only in the parameters of the infinite planes, but also their extent visible in the current image, so that points can be associated to the planes on which they are observed.

Most plane fitting models for RGB-D data use RANSAC which is extremely slow for the purpose of building a near real-time online SLAM framework. Our plane segmentation follows [34] which segments point clouds from RGB-D data in near real-time. For data-association across frames, we rely on the sparsity (few dominant planes in the scene) and inherent robustness (little variation frame-to-frame) of these landmarks. Using the difference between normals and the distance between planes, data-association is done in a nearest-neighbor fashion.

The plane segmentation and matching uses depth data, and is the only part of our system (other than ORB feature depth initialization) which relies on depth information. In the future we aim to remove even this requirement and make the system truly monocular by hypothesizing planes using single-view semantic segmentation, depth and normal estimation, as is now possible by deep nets [5].

Conic Observations. We use Faster-RCNN [26] with pre-trained model on COCO dataset [18] to detect the bounding boxes for objects of the scene. From the axis-aligned bounding boxes, the inscribed ellipsoid is computed as the conic projection of an observed quadric object. To avoid outliers and achieve robust detections we consider objects with 95% or more detection confidence.

For data-association across frames, we utilize the semantic labels and rely on the detection of the object to match the corresponding landmark. If more than one instance of a semantic class is found, we use nearest-neighbor matching in the feature space generated by the detector. This simple strategy is successful with high-confidence object detections, as shown in Sect. 5.

Note that the partial occlusions can result in an inconsistent observations of a same object from different viewpoints that can lead to inaccuracy in the trajectory and map. The following course of actions is employed in our system to mitigate the negative impact of partial occlusions: (a) we use robust kernels (Huber) to robustify against large error, (b) only consider objects with 95%

or more detection confidence. With these two recourses we have seen almost consistent observations of COCO objects in our experiments shown in Sect. 5.

Point-Plane Constraints. Finding association between points and planes is established during plane detection and segmentation. After detecting each plane and its finite boundary, its inlier points are determined to be those satisfying a threshold, th_{PP} distance, which we set as a function of the distance of the points from the camera, because further points have greater uncertainty.

Plane/Manhattan Constraints. The number of planes detected by our system is sufficiently small that we can consider all possible pairs, and introduce constraints with very little impact on overall speed of operation. At present we adopt the expedient of imposing a parallel constraint if the angle between the pair of planes is less than a threshold $th_M^{\parallel}$, and if the angle is within $th_M^{\perp}$ of 90° we introduce a perpendicular factor. For our experiments we have used $th_M^{\parallel} = 15°$ and $th_M^{\perp} = 75°$ in our system.

Manhattan constraints are imposed in a conservative manner with a large uncertainty and act as a prior on the relative orientation of the planes. Based on evidence gathered over image frames, they might end up being perpendicular or parallel but are not forced to be in that configuration if the data strongly favors an opposite interpretation.

Supporting/Tangency Constraints. A supporting/tangency constraint between a quadric and a plane is imposed based on the orthogonal distance of the centroid of the quadric and infinite plane. If this distance is less than th_S we enforce the tangency constraint. In our experiments this threshold depends on the size of the quadric $th_S = \max(20\,\text{cm}, a, b, c)$ where a, b, and c are half the length of the principal axes of the ellipsoid.

5   Experiments

We evaluate the performance of our SLAM system using the benchmarks RGB-D TUM dataset [30] and NYU-Depth V2 dataset [21]. These sequences have a wide range of conditions, from plane-rich scenes to scenes with little or no texture and also scenes with common objects such as those available in COCO dataset [18]. We show qualitative as well as quantitative results of our system using different combinations of the proposed landmarks and constraints and compare the accuracy in the estimated camera trajectory against the RGB-D variant of the state-of-the-art sparse mapping system, ORB-SLAM2 [20].

5.1   Qualitative Results

Some sequences in the TUM RGBD dataset contain little or no texture which makes it difficult for point-based SLAM systems to extract and track key-points. However these sequences have rich planar structures which are exploited by our SLAM system. The results for using planes with Manhattan constraints

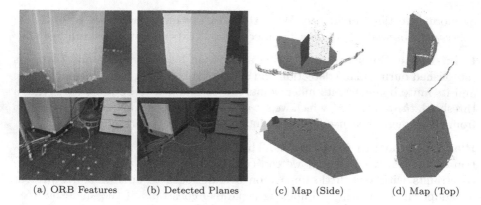

(a) ORB Features   (b) Detected Planes   (c) Map (Side)   (d) Map (Top)

Fig. 3. Qualitative results for 2 different TUM RGBD datasets with low texture object-less but rich planar structures

on `fr3/str_notex_far` and `fr1/floor` are given in Fig. 3. Results for more sequences are reported in the supplementary material. The figure depicts the image frame along with tracked features, detected and segmented planes, and the reconstructed map consisting of points and planes from two different viewpoints. For these sequences, ORB-SLAM2 is unable to detect features in the environment with the normal settings and loses track. Lowering the feature detection threshold in ORB-SLAM2 yields a greater number of features, but also results in more outliers leading to more inaccurate trajectories.

To show the quality of the mapping and tracking with planes and objects along with the Manhattan and supporting constraints, we use the sequences `fr1/xyz`, `fr2/desk` from TUM dataset, and `nyu/basement_1a`, `nyu/office_1` from NYU dataset. The reconstructions are shown in Fig. 4. The reconstructed map of `fr1/xyz` is depicted in column (c) and (d) of the first row. The planar structure of the map is consistent with the ground truth scene which consists of two planar monitors orthogonal to the green desk. Quadrics corresponding to objects on the desk have been reconstructed tangent to the desk, their supporting plane. Column (a) shows tracked ORB features and detected COCO objects with confidence of at least 0.95 at the corresponding frame. The red ellipses in column (a) are the projection of the reconstructed quadric objects. They closely fit the detected blue bounding boxes and their corresponding green computed ellipses.

We use `fr3/cabinet` to show the importance of using the Manhattan constraint. The sequence contains a loop around a cabinet. All the faces of this cabinet are parallel or perpendicular to each other. Figure 5 demonstrates the difference in the quality of the reconstruction of the cabinet's sides with and without Manhattan assumption in column (a) and column (b) respectively.

Figures 6(a, b) show the reconstructed quadric corresponding to the object on desk in the `fr1/xyz` before and after imposing the tangency constraint. Enforcing the tangency constraints makes sure that the quadric object is tangent to the supporting plane.

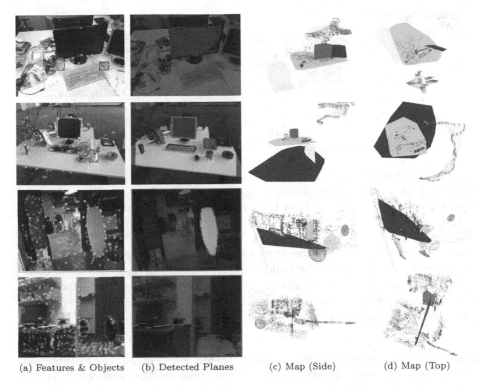

(a) Features & Objects   (b) Detected Planes   (c) Map (Side)   (d) Map (Top)

Fig. 4. Qualitative results for 2 different TUM RGBD and 2 different NYU-Depth-V2 datasets with rich planar structures and objects supported by planes

5.2 Quantitative Comparison

We compare the performance of the proposed SLAM system against the RGB-D variant of the state-of-the-art system ORB-SLAM2 for TUM RGBD dataset that the ground-truth trajectories are available. This baseline is a monocular

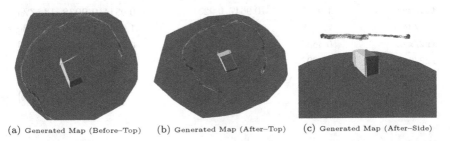

(a) Generated Map (Before–Top)   (b) Generated Map (After–Top)   (c) Generated Map (After–Side)

Fig. 5. Qualitative comparison of the reconstructed planes representing `cabinet` before and after imposing Manhattan assumption between the planes in the TUM `fr3/cabinet` dataset. Points and top-side plane of the cabinet have not been rendered for clarifying the difference in the map

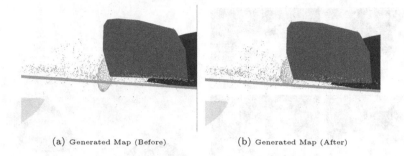

(a) Generated Map (Before)   (b) Generated Map (After)

Fig. 6. Qualitative comparison of the reconstructed quadric representing object `cup` before and after imposing supporting/tangency constraint between the quadric and plane representing `desk` in the TUM `fr1/xyz` dataset

point-based system that uses the depth information in the D-channel to initialize 3D points. Our implementation builds directly on their open-source C++ codebase, and we structure our results as an ablation study, considering the effects of introducing different landmarks and constraints. In each case, we report the RMSE Absolute Trajectory Error (ATE)[1] in Table 1.

Table 1. Comparison against RGB-D ORB-SLAM2. `PP`, `PP+M`, `PQ`, and `PPQ+MS` mean points-planes only, points-planes+Manhattan constraint, points-quadrics only, and all of the landmarks with Manhattan and supporting constraints, respectively. RMSE is reported for ATE in `cm` for 10 sequences in TUM RGBD datasets. Numbers in bold in each row represent the best performance for each sequence. Numbers in [ ] show the percentage of improvement over ORB-SLAM2.

Dataset	ORB-SLAM2	PP	PP+M	PQ	PPQ+MS
fr1/floor	1.4399	1.3798	**1.3246** [8.01%]	—	—
fr3/cabinet	7.9602	7.3724	**2.1675** [72.77%]	—	—
fr3/str_notex_near	1.6882	1.0883	**1.0648** [36.93%]	—	—
fr3/str_notex_far	2.0007	1.9092	**1.3722** [31.41%]	—	—
fr1/xyz	1.0457	0.9647	0.9231	0.9544	**0.9038** [13.57%]
fr1/desk	2.2668	1.5267	1.4831	1.9821	**1.4029** [38.11%]
fr2/xyz	0.3634	0.3301	0.3174	0.3453	**0.3097** [14.78%]
fr2/rpy	0.3207	0.3126	0.3011	0.3195	**0.2870** [10.51%]
fr2/desk	1.2962	1.2031	1.0186	1.1132	**0.8655** [33.23%]
fr3/long_office	1.5129	1.0601	0.9902	1.3644	**0.7403** [51.07%]

We first consider the case where points are augmented by the plane information (PP). This already improves the ATE in each case over the baseline,

---

[1] Comparison for RMSE of relative errors, RTE and RRE, as well as run-time analysis are reported in the supplementary material.

which improves even further by enforcing Manhattan constraints (PP+M). The Manhattan constraint significantly reduces the trajectory error when dominant structure is present in the scene.

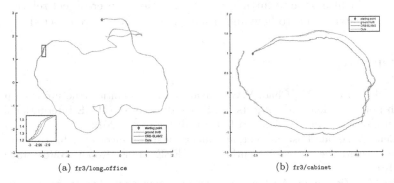

(a) fr3/long_office   (b) fr3/cabinet

Fig. 7. Comparison of estimated trajectories of ORB-SLAM2, our system, and ground truth: **(a)** for TUM `fr3/long_office` that has a large loop closure our trajectory is closer to the ground truth; **(b)** for TUM `fr3/cabinet` ORB-SLAM2 drifts significantly and loses track in this feature-poor sequence (~72% improvement in ATE)

Some sequences do not contain objects similar to the COCO dataset. For those that do, we investigate using the combination of points and quadrics (PQ) as landmarks. While this reduces the trajectory drift compared to baseline, the improvement is smaller compared with using PP+M. Finally, we report numbers for the full system (PPQ+MS) in which points, planes and quadrics are used as landmarks and Manhattan and support constraints are enforced. For `fr3/long_office` the improvement is significant (51.07%) because of the presence of a large loop in this sequence, where all of the points, planes and quadrics landmarks participate and are updated based on the loop closure.

Comparison of the estimated trajectories of our system against ground truth is presented in Fig. 7 for two example TUM sequences.

6   Conclusions

In this work, we have explored the effects of incorporating planes and quadrics as higher-level geometric entities in a sparse point-based SLAM framework. To do so we have introduced a new ellipsoid representation that is easily and effectively updated, and admits a simple method for imposing constraints between planes and objects. The improved performance due to using points and planes has been clearly shown by the experiments, most noticeably when there is dominant planar structure present. Of course in cases where enough planes are not present, the point based SLAM can still function as usual.

Currently, the method works with RGB-D input. As in "vanilla" ORB-SLAM2, 3D map points are initialized with depth obtained from the D-channel of the RGB-D camera. We also use the D-channel to initialise planes, and this is both a bottleneck in terms of computation and presents a limitation on the sensor. In future, we will explore methods that can provide plane estimate from monocular input, which will enable us to transition to a purely monocular implementation. We also hope to further explore additional inter-object relations and introduce greater rigour to how and when the constraints are effected.

References

1. Bao, S.Y., Bagra, M., Chao, Y.W., Savarese, S.: Semantic structure from motion with points, regions, and objects. In: Proceedings of the IEEE International Conference on Computer Vision and Pattern Recognition (2012)
2. Cadena, C., et al.: Past, present, and future of simultaneous localization and mapping: toward the robust-perception age. IEEE Trans. Robot. **32**(6), 1309–1332 (2016)
3. Cross, G., Zisserman, A.: Quadric reconstruction from dual-space geometry. In: 1998 Sixth International Conference on Computer Vision, pp. 25–31. IEEE (1998)
4. Dellaert, F., Kaess, M.: Factor graphs for robot perception. Found. Trends Robot. **6**(1–2), 1–139 (2017). https://doi.org/10.1561/2300000043
5. Eigen, D., Fergus, R.: Predicting depth, surface normals and semantic labels with a common multi-scale convolutional architecture. In: 2015 IEEE International Conference on Computer Vision, ICCV 2015, Santiago, Chile, 7–13 December 2015, pp. 2650–2658 (2015). https://doi.org/10.1109/ICCV.2015.304
6. Engel, J., Koltun, V., Cremers, D.: Direct sparse odometry. IEEE Trans. Pattern Anal. Mach. Intell. **40**, 611–625 (2017)
7. Engel, J., Schöps, T., Cremers, D.: LSD-SLAM: large-scale direct monocular SLAM. In: Fleet, D., Pajdla, T., Schiele, B., Tuytelaars, T. (eds.) ECCV 2014. LNCS, vol. 8690, pp. 834–849. Springer, Cham (2014). https://doi.org/10.1007/978-3-319-10605-2_54
8. Forster, C., Pizzoli, M., Scaramuzza, D.: SVO: fast semi-direct monocular visual odometry. In: 2014 IEEE International Conference on Robotics and Automation (ICRA), pp. 15–22. IEEE (2014)
9. Gálvez-López, D., Tardos, J.D.: Bags of binary words for fast place recognition in image sequences. IEEE Trans. Robot. **28**(5), 1188–1197 (2012)
10. Gay, P., Bansal, V., Rubino, C., Bue, A.D.: Probabilistic structure from motion with objects (PSfMO). In: 2017 IEEE International Conference on Computer Vision (ICCV), pp. 3094–3103, October 2017. https://doi.org/10.1109/ICCV.2017.334
11. Gee, A.P., Mayol-Cuevas, W.: Real-time model-based SLAM using line segments. In: Bebis, G., et al. (eds.) ISVC 2006. LNCS, vol. 4292, pp. 354–363. Springer, Heidelberg (2006). https://doi.org/10.1007/11919629_37
12. Gomez-Ojeda, R., Moreno, F.A., Scaramuzza, D., Gonzalez-Jimenez, J.: PL-SLAM: a stereo SLAM system through the combination of points and line segments. arXiv preprint arXiv:1705.09479 (2017)
13. Grisetti, G., Kummerle, R., Stachniss, C., Burgard, W.: A tutorial on graph-based SLAM. IEEE Intell. Transp. Syst. Mag. **2**(4), 31–43 (2010)
14. Hartley, R., Zisserman, A.: Multiple View Geometry in Computer Vision, 2nd edn. Cambridge University Press, New York (2003)

15. Kaess, M.: Simultaneous localization and mapping with infinite planes. In: 2015 IEEE International Conference on Robotics and Automation (ICRA), pp. 4605–4611. IEEE (2015)
16. Kümmerle, R., Grisetti, G., Strasdat, H., Konolige, K., Burgard, W.: g^2o: a general framework for graph optimization. In: 2011 IEEE International Conference on Robotics and Automation (ICRA), pp. 3607–3613. IEEE (2011)
17. Lemaire, T., Lacroix, S.: Monocular-vision based SLAM using line segments. In: 2007 IEEE International Conference on Robotics and Automation, pp. 2791–2796. IEEE (2007)
18. Lin, T.-Y., et al.: Microsoft COCO: common objects in context. In: Fleet, D., Pajdla, T., Schiele, B., Tuytelaars, T. (eds.) ECCV 2014. LNCS, vol. 8693, pp. 740–755. Springer, Cham (2014). https://doi.org/10.1007/978-3-319-10602-1_48
19. McCormac, J., Handa, A., Davison, A., Leutenegger, S.: SemanticFusion: dense 3D semantic mapping with convolutional neural networks. In: 2017 IEEE International Conference on Robotics and Automation (ICRA), pp. 4628–4635. IEEE (2017)
20. Mur-Artal, R., Montiel, J.M.M., Tardos, J.D.: ORB-SLAM: a versatile and accurate monocular slam system. IEEE Trans. Robot. **31**(5), 1147–1163 (2015)
21. Silberman, N., Hoiem, D., Kohli, P., Fergus, R.: Indoor segmentation and support inference from RGBD images. In: Fitzgibbon, A., Lazebnik, S., Perona, P., Sato, Y., Schmid, C. (eds.) ECCV 2012. LNCS, vol. 7576, pp. 746–760. Springer, Heidelberg (2012). https://doi.org/10.1007/978-3-642-33715-4_54
22. Newcombe, R.A., et al.: KinectFusion: real-time dense surface mapping and tracking. In: 2011 10th IEEE International Symposium on Mixed and Augmented Reality (ISMAR), pp. 127–136. IEEE (2011)
23. Newcombe, R.A., Lovegrove, S.J., Davison, A.J.: DTAM: dense tracking and mapping in real-time. In: 2011 IEEE International Conference on Computer Vision (ICCV), pp. 2320–2327. IEEE (2011)
24. Prisacariu, V.A., et al.: InfiniTAM v3: a framework for large-scale 3D reconstruction with loop closure. arXiv preprint arXiv:1708.00783 (2017)
25. Pumarola, A., Vakhitov, A., Agudo, A., Sanfeliu, A., Moreno-Noguer, F.: PL-SLAM: real-time monocular visual SLAM with points and lines. In: Proceedings of the International Conference on Robotics and Automation (ICRA). IEEE (2017)
26. Ren, S., He, K., Girshick, R., Sun, J.: Faster R-CNN: towards real-time object detection with region proposal networks. In: Advances in Neural Information Processing Systems (NIPS) (2015)
27. Rubino, C., Crocco, M., Bue, A.D.: 3D object localisation from multi-view image detections. IEEE Trans. Pattern Anal. Mach. Intell. **PP**(99), 1 (2018). https://doi.org/10.1109/TPAMI.2017.2701373
28. Salas-Moreno, R.F., Glocken, B., Kelly, P.H.J., Davison, A.J.: Dense planar SLAM. In: 2014 IEEE International Symposium on Mixed and Augmented Reality (ISMAR), pp. 157–164, September 2014. https://doi.org/10.1109/ISMAR.2014.6948422
29. Salas-Moreno, R.F., Newcombe, R.A., Strasdat, H., Kelly, P.H.J., Davison, A.J.: SLAM++: simultaneous localisation and mapping at the level of objects. In: 2013 IEEE Conference on Computer Vision and Pattern Recognition (CVPR) 2013, pp. 1352–1359 (2013). https://doi.org/10.1109/CVPR.2013.178
30. Sturm, J., Engelhard, N., Endres, F., Burgard, W., Cremers, D.: A benchmark for the evaluation of RGB-D SLAM systems. In: Proceedings of the International Conference on Intelligent Robot Systems (IROS), October 2012
31. Sünderhauf, N., Milford, M.: Dual quadrics from object detection boundingboxes as landmark representations in SLAM. Preprints arXiv:1708.00965, August 2017

32. Sünderhauf, N., Pham, T.T., Latif, Y., Milford, M., Reid, I.: Meaningful maps with object-oriented semantic mapping. In: 2017 IEEE/RSJ International Conference on Intelligent Robots and Systems (IROS), pp. 5079–5085. IEEE (2017)
33. Taguchi, Y., Jian, Y.D., Ramalingam, S., Feng, C.: Point-plane SLAM for handheld 3D sensors. In: 2013 IEEE International Conference on Robotics and Automation (ICRA), pp. 5182–5189. IEEE (2013)
34. Trevor, A., Gedikli, S., Rusu, R., Christensen, H.: Efficient organized point cloud segmentation with connected components. In: 3rd Workshop on Semantic Perception Mapping and Exploration (SPME), Karlsruhe, Germany (2013)
35. Yang, S., Song, Y., Kaess, M., Scherer, S.: Pop-up SLAM: semantic monocular plane SLAM for low-texture environments. In: 2016 IEEE/RSJ International Conference on Intelligent Robots and Systems (IROS), pp. 1222–1229. IEEE (2016)

Maintaining Natural Image Statistics
with the Contextual Loss

Roey Mechrez[✉], Itamar Talmi, Firas Shama, and Lihi Zelnik-Manor

Technion - Israel Institute of Technology, Haifa, Israel
{roey,titamar,lihi}@ee.technion.ac.il

Abstract. Maintaining natural image statistics is a crucial factor in restoration and generation of realistic looking images. When training CNNs, photorealism is usually attempted by adversarial training (GAN), that pushes the output images to lie on the manifold of natural images. GANs are very powerful, but not perfect. They are hard to train and the results still often suffer from artifacts. In this paper we propose a complementary approach, that could be applied with or without GAN, whose goal is to train a feed-forward CNN to maintain natural internal statistics. We look explicitly at the distribution of features in an image and train the network to generate images with natural feature distributions. Our approach reduces by orders of magnitude the number of images required for training and achieves state-of-the-art results on both single-image super-resolution, and high-resolution surface normal estimation. Project page: https://www.github.com/roimehrez/contextualLoss.

1 Introduction

"Facts are stubborn things, but statistics are pliable." — Mark Twain

Maintaining natural image statistics has been known for years as a key factor in the generation of natural looking images [22,31,32,42,45]. With the rise of CNNs, the utilization of explicit image priors was replaced by Generative Adversarial Networks (GAN) [15], where a corpus of images is used to train a network to generate images with natural characteristics, e.g., [3,18,20,30]. Despite the use of GANs within many different pipelines, results still sometimes suffer from artifacts, balanced training is difficult to achieve and depends on the architecture [3,34].

Well before the CNN era, natural image statistics were obtained by utilizing priors on the likelihood of the *patches* of the generated images [21,22,45]. Zoran and Weiss [45] showed that such statistical approaches, that harness priors on patches, lead in general to restoration of more natural looking images. A similar

---

R. Mechrez and I. Talmi—Contributed equally.

Electronic supplementary material The online version of this chapter (https://doi.org/10.1007/978-3-030-20893-6_27) contains supplementary material, which is available to authorized users.

Fig. 1. We demonstrate the advantages of using a statistical loss for training a CNN in: (left) single-image super resolution, and, (right) surface normal estimation. Our approach is easy to train and yields networks that generate images (or surfaces) that exhibit natural internal statistics.

concept is in the heart of sparse-coding where a dictionary of visual code-words is used to constrain the generated patches [2, 25]. The dictionary can be thought as a prior on the space of plausible image patches. A related approach is to constrain the generated image patches to the space of patches specific to the image to be restored [14, 16, 28, 44]. In this paper we want to build on these ideas in order to answer the following question: *Can we train a CNN to generate images that exhibit natural statistics?*

The approach we propose is a simple modification to the common practice. As typically done, we as well train CNNs on pairs of source-target images by minimizing an objective that measures the similarity between the generated image and the target. We extend on the common practice by proposing to use an objective that compares the *feature distributions* rather than just comparing the appearance. We show that by doing this the network learns to generate more natural looking images.

A key question is what makes a suitable objective for comparing distributions of features. The common divergence measures, such as Kullback-Leibler (KL), Earth-Movers-Distance and χ^2, all require estimating the distribution of features, which is typically done via Multivariate Kernel-Density-Estimation (MKDE). Since in our case the features are very high dimensional, and since we want a differentiable loss that can be computed efficiently, MKDE is not an option. Hence, we propose instead an approximation to KL that is both simple to compute and tractable. As it turns out, our approximation coincides with the recently proposed *Contextual loss* [27], that was designed for comparing images that are not spatially aligned. Since the Contextual is actually an approximation to KL, it could be useful as an objective also in applications where the images are aligned, and the goal is to generate natural looking images.

Fig. 2. Training with a statistical loss: To train a generator network G we compare the output image $G(s) \equiv x$ with the corresponding target image y via a statistical loss—the Contextual loss [27]—that compares their feature distributions.

Since all we propose is utilizing the Contextual loss during training, our approach is generic and can be adopted within many architectures and pipelines. In particular, it can be used in concert with GAN training. Hence, we chose super-resolution as a first test-case, where methods based on GANs are the current state-of-the-art. We show empirically, that using our statistical approach with GAN training outperforms previous methods, yielding images that are *perceptually* more realistic, while reducing the number of required training images by orders of magnitude.

Our second test-case further proves the generality of this approach to data that is not images, and shows the strength of the statistical approach without GAN. Maintaining natural internal statistics has been shown to be an important property also in the estimation of 3D surfaces [12,16,17]. Hence, we present experiments on surface normal estimation, where the network's input is a high-resolution image and its output is a map of normals. We successfully generate normal-maps that are more accurate than previous methods.

To summarize, the contributions we present are three-fold:

1. We show that the Contextual loss [27] can be viewed as an approximation to KL divergence. This makes it suitable for reconstruction problems.
2. We show that training with a statistical loss yields networks that maintain the natural internal statistics of images. This approach is easy to train and reduces significantly the training set size.
3. We present state-of-the-art results on both perceptual super-resolution and high-resolution surface normal estimation.

2   Training CNNs to Match Image Distributions

2.1   Setup

Our approach is very simple, as depicted in Fig. 2. To train a generator network G we use pairs of source s and target y images. The network outputs an image $G(s) \equiv x$, that should be as similar as possible to the target y. To measure the similarity we extract from both x and y dense features $X = \{x_i\}$ and $Y = \{y_j\}$, respectively, e.g., by using pretrained network or vectorized RGB patches. We denote by P_Y and P_X the probability distribution functions over Y and X, respectively. When the patch set X correctly models Y then the underlying probabilities P_Y and P_X are equal. Hence, we need to train G by minimizing an objective that measures the divergence between P_X and P_Y.

2.2   Review of the KL-divergence

There are many common measures for the divergence between two distributions, e.g., χ^2, Kullback-Leibler (KL), and Earth Movers Distance (EMD). We opted for the KL-divergence in this paper.

The KL-divergence between the two densities P_X and P_Y is defined as:

$$KL(P_X \| P_Y) = \int P_X \log \frac{P_X}{P_Y} \tag{1}$$

It computes the expectation of the logarithmic difference between the probabilities P_X and P_Y, where the expectation is taken using the probabilities P_X. We can rewrite this formula in terms of expectation:

$$KL(P_X \| P_Y) = E\big[\log P_X - \log P_Y\big] \tag{2}$$

This requires approximating the parametrized densities P_X, P_Y from the feature sets $X = \{x_i\}$ and $Y = \{y_j\}$. The most common method for doing this is to use Multivariate Kernel Density Estimation (MKDE), that estimates the probabilities $P_X(p_k)$ and $P_Y(p_k)$ as:

$$P_X(p_k) = \sum_{x_i \in X} K_H(p_k, x_i) \qquad P_Y(p_k) = \sum_{y_j \in Y} K_H(p_k, y_j) \tag{3}$$

Here $K_H(p_k, \xi)$ is an affinity measure (the kernel) between some point p_k and the samples ξ, typically taken as standard multivariate normal kernel $K_H(z) = (2\pi)^{-d/2}|H|^{-1/2} \exp(-\frac{1}{2}z^T H z)$, with $z = dist(p_k, \xi)$, d is the dimension and H is a $d \times d$ bandwidth matrix. We can now write the expectation of the KL-Divergence over the MKDE with uniform sample grid as follows:

$$KL(P_X \| P_Y) = \frac{1}{N} \sum_{p_k} \big[\log P_X(p_k) - \log P_Y(p_k)\big] \tag{4}$$

A common simplification that we adopt is to compute the MKDE not over a regular grid of $\{p_k\}$ but rather on the samples $\{x_i\}$ directly, i.e., we set $p_k = x_k$, which implies $K_H(p_k, x_i) = K_H(x_k, x_i)$ and $K_H(p_k, y_j) = K_H(x_k, y_j)$. Putting this together with Eq. (3) into Eq. (4) yields:

$$KL(P_X \| P_Y) = \frac{1}{N} \sum_k \left[\log \sum_{x_i \in X} K_H(x_k, x_i) - \log \sum_{y_j \in Y} K_H(x_k, y_j) \right] \quad (5)$$

To use Eq. (5) as a loss function we need to choose a kernel K_H. The most common choice of a standard multivariate normal kernel requires setting the bandwidth matrix H, which is non-trivial. Multivariate KDE is known to be sensitive to the optimal selection of the bandwidth matrix and the existing solutions for tuning it require solving an optimization problem which is not possible as part of a training process. Hence, we next propose an approximation, which is both practical and tractable.

2.3   Approximating the KL-divergence with the Contextual Loss

Our approximation is based on one further observation. It is insufficient to produce an image with the same distribution of features, but rather we want additionally that the samples will be similar. That is, we ask each point $x_i \in X$ to be close to a specific $y_j \in Y$.

To achieve this, while assuming that the number of samples is large, we set the MKDE kernel such that it approximates a delta function. When the kernel is a delta, the first log term of Eq. (5) becomes a constant since:

$$K_H(x_k, x_i) = \begin{cases} \approx 1 & \text{if } k = i \\ \approx 0 & \text{otherwise} \end{cases} \quad (6)$$

The kernel in the second log term of Eq. (5) becomes:

$$K_H(x_k, y_j) = \begin{cases} \approx 1 & \text{if } dist(x_k, y_j) \ll dist(x_k, y_l) \; \forall l \neq j \\ \approx 0 & \text{otherwise} \end{cases} \quad (7)$$

We can thus simplify the objective of Eq. (5):

$$E(x, y) = - \log \left(\frac{1}{N} \sum_j \max_i A_{ij} \right) \quad (8)$$

where we denote $A_{ij} = K_H(x_k, y_j)$. Next, we suggest two alternatives for the kernel A_{ij}, and show that one implies that the objective of Eq. (8) is equivalent to the Chamfer Distance [5], while the other implies it is equivalent to the Contextual loss of [27].

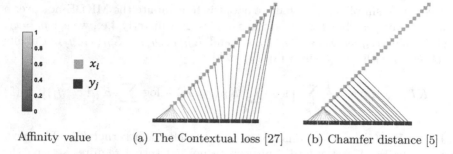

Affinity value   (a) The Contextual loss [27]   (b) Chamfer distance [5]

Fig. 3. The Contextual loss vs. Chamfer Distance: We demonstrate via a 2D example the difference between two approximations to the KL-divergence (a) The Contextual loss and (b) Chamfer Distance. Point sets Y and X are marked with blue and orange squares respectively. The colored lines connect each y_j with x_i with the largest affinity. The KL approximation of Eq. (8) sums over these affinities. It can be seen that the normalized affinities used by the Contextual loss lead to more diverse and meaningful matches between Y and X.

The Contextual Loss: As it turns out, the objective of Eq. (8) is identical to the Contextual loss recently proposed by [27]. Furthermore, they set the kernel A_{ij} to be close to a delta function, such that it fits Eq. (7). First the Cosine (or L2) distances $dist(x_i, y_j)$ are computed between all pairs x_i, y_j. The distances are then normalized: $\tilde{d}_{ij} = dist(x_i, y_j)/(\min_k dist(x_i, y_k) + \epsilon)$ (with $\epsilon = 1\mathrm{e}{-5}$), and finally the pairwise affinities $A_{ij} \in [0, 1]$ are defined as:

$$A_{ij} = \frac{\exp\left(1 - \tilde{d}_{ij}/h\right)}{\sum_l \exp\left(1 - \tilde{d}_{il}/h\right)} = \begin{cases} \approx 1 & \text{if } \tilde{d}_{ij} \ll \tilde{d}_{il} \ \ \forall l \neq j \\ \approx 0 & \text{otherwise} \end{cases} \tag{9}$$

where $h > 0$ is a scalar bandwidth parameter that we fix to $h = 0.1$, as proposed in [27]. When using these affinities our objective equals the Contextual loss of [27] and we denote $E(x, y) = \mathcal{L}_{\mathrm{CX}}(x, y)$.

The Chamfer Distance. A simpler way to set A_{ij} is to take a Gaussian kernel with a fixed $H = I$ s.t. $A_{ij} = exp(-dist(x_i, y_j))$. This choice implies that minimizing Eq. (8) is equivalent to minimizing the asymmetric Chamfer Distance [5] between X, Y defined as

$$\mathrm{CD}(X, Y) = \frac{1}{|X|} \sum_i \min_j dist(x_i, y_j) \tag{10}$$

CD has been previously used mainly for shape retrieval [36, 39] were the points are in $\mathbb{R}^3$. For each point in set X, CD finds the nearest point in the set Y and minimizes the sum of these distances. A downside of this choice for the kernel A_{ij} is that it does not satisfy the requirement in Eq. (7).

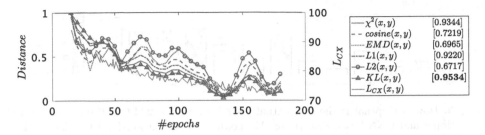

Fig. 4. Minimizing the KL-divergence: The curves represents seven measures of dissimilarity between the patch distribution of the target image y and that of the generated image x, during training a super-resolution network (details in supplementary) and using $\mathcal{L}_{CX}$ as the objective. The correlation between $\mathcal{L}_{CX}$ and all other measures, reported in square brackets, show highest correlation to the KL-divergence. It is evident that training with the Contextual loss results in minimizing also the KL-divergence.

The Contextual Loss vs. Chamfer Distance. To provide intuition on the difference between the two choices of affinity functions we present in Fig. 3 an illustration in 2D. Recall, that both the Contextual loss $\mathcal{L}_{CX}$ and the Chamfer distance CD find for each point in Y a single match in X, however, these matches are computed differently. CD selects the closet point, hence, we could get that multiple points in Y are matched to the same few points in X. Differently, $\mathcal{L}_{CX}$ computes normalized affinities, that consider the distances between every point x_i to all the points $y_j \in Y$. Therefore, it results in more diverse matches between the two sets of points, and provides a better measure of similarity between the two distributions. Additional example is presented in the supplementary.

Training with $\mathcal{L}_{CX}$ guides the network to match between the two point sets, and as a result the underlying distributions become closer. In contrast, training with CD, does not allow the two sets to get close. Indeed, we found empirically that training with CD does not converge, hence, we excluded it from our empirical reports.

3 Empirical Analysis

The Contextual loss has been proposed in [27] for measuring similarity between non-aligned images. It has therefore been used for applications such as style transfer, where the generated image and the target style image are very different. In the current study we assert that the Contextual loss can be viewed as a statistical loss between the distributions of features. We further assert that using such a loss during training would lead to generating images with realistic characteristics. This would make it a good candidate also for tasks where the training image pairs are aligned.

To support these claims we present in this section two experiments, and in the next section two real applications. The first experiment shows that minimizing the Contextual loss during training indeed implies also minimization of

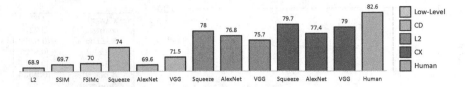

Fig. 5. How perceptual is the Contextual loss? Test on the 2AFC [43] data set with traditional and CNN-based distortions. We compare between low-level metrics (such as SSIM) and off-the-shelf deep networks trained with L2 distance, Chamfer distance (CD) and the Contextual loss ($\mathcal{L}_{CX}$). $\mathcal{L}_{CX}$ yields a performance boost across all three networks with the largest gain obtained for VGG – the most common loss network (i.e., perceptual loss).

the KL-divergence. The second experiment evaluates the relation between the Contextual loss and human perception of image quality.

Empirical Analysis of the Approximation. Since we are proposing to use the Contextual loss as an approximation to the KL-divergence, we next show empirically, that minimizing it during training also minimizes the KL-divergence.

To do this we chose a simplified super-resolution setup, based on SRRes-Net [20], and trained it with the Contextual loss as the objective. The details on the setup are provided in the supplementary. We compute during the training the Contextual loss, the KL-divergence, as well as five other common dissimilarity measures. To compute the KL-divergence, EMD and χ^2, we need to approximate the density of each image. As discussed in Sect. 2, it is not clear how the multivariate solution to KDE can be smoothly used here, therefore, instead, we generate a random projection of all 5×5 patches onto 2D and fit them using KDE with a Gaussian kernel in 2D [8]. This was repeated for 100 random projections and the scores were averaged over all projections (examples of projections are shown in the supplementary).

Figure 4 presents the values of all seven measures during the iterations of the training. It can be seen that all of them are minimized during the iterations. The KL-divergence minimization curve is the one most similar to that of the Contextual loss, suggesting that the Contextual loss forms a reasonable approximation.

Evaluating on Human Perceptual Judgment. Our ultimate goal is to train networks that generate images with high perceptual quality. The underlying hypothesis behind our approach is that training with an objective that maintains natural statistics will lead to this goal. To asses this hypothesis we repeated the evaluation procedure proposed in [43], for assessing the correlation between human judgment of similarity and loss functions based on deep features.

In [43] it was suggested to compute the similarity between two images by comparing their corresponding deep embeddings. For each image they obtained a deep embedding via a pre-trained network, normalized the activations and then computed the $L2$ distance. This was then averaged across spatial dimension and across all layers. We adopted the same procedure while replacing the $L2$ distance with the Contextual loss approximation to KL.

Our findings, as reported in Fig. 5 (the complete table is provided in the supplementary material), show the benefits of our proposed approach. The Contextual loss between deep features is more closely correlated with human judgment than $L2$ or Chamfer Distance between the same features. All of these perceptual measures are preferable over low-level similarity measures such as SSIM [41].

4   Applications

In this section we present two applications: single-image super-resolution, and high-resolution surface normal estimation. We chose the first to highlight the advantage of using our approach in concert with GAN. The second was selected since its output is not an image, but rather a surface of normals. This shows the generic nature of our approach to other domains apart from image generation, where GANs are not being used.

4.1   Single-Image Super-Resolution

To asses the contribution of our suggested framework for image restoration we experiment on single-image super-resolution. To place our efforts in context we start by briefly reviewing some of the recent works on super-resolution. A more comprehensive overview of the current trends can be found in [37].

Recent solutions based on CNNs can be categorized into two groups. The first group relies on the $L2$ or $L1$ losses [20,23,38], which lead to high PSNR and SSIM [41] at the price of low perceptual quality, as was recently shown in [7,43]. The second group of works aim at high perceptual quality. This is done by adopting perceptual loss functions [19], sometimes in combination with GAN [20] or by adding the Gram loss [13], which nicely captures textures [33].

Proposed Solution: Our main goal is to generate natural looking images, with natural internal statistics. At the same time, we do not want the structural similarity to be overly low (the trade-off between the two is nicely analyzed in [7,43]). Therefore, we propose an objective that considers both, with higher importance to perceptual quality. Specifically, we integrate three loss terms: (i) The Contextual loss – to make sure that the internal statistics of the generated image are similar to those of the ground-truth high-resolution image. (ii) The $L2$ loss, computed at **low** resolution – to drive the generated image to share the spatial structure of the target image. (iii) Finally, following [20] we add an adversarial term, which helps in pushing the generated image to look "real".

Given a low-resolution image s and a target high-resolution image y, our objective for training the network G is:

$$\mathcal{L}(G) = \lambda_{\text{CX}} \cdot \mathcal{L}_{\text{CX}}(G(s), y) + \lambda_{L2} \cdot ||G(s)^{\text{LF}} - y^{\text{LF}}||_2 + \lambda_{\text{GAN}} \cdot \mathcal{L}_{\text{GAN}}(G(s)) \quad (11)$$

Table 1. Super-resolution results: The table presents the mean scores obtained by our method and three others on BSD100 [26]. SSIM [41] measures structural similarity to the ground-truth, while NRQM [24] measures no-reference perceptual quality. Our approach provides an improvement on both scores, even though it required orders of magnitude fewer images for training. The table further provides an ablation test of the loss function to show that $\mathcal{L}_{CX}$ is a key ingredient in the quality of the results. L_P is the perceptual loss [19], L_T is the Gram loss [13], and both use VGG19 features.

Method	Loss function	Distortion SSIM [41]	Perceptual NRQM [24]	# Training images
Johnson [19]	L_P	0.631	7.800	10K
SRGAN [20]	$\mathcal{L}_{GAN} + L_P$	0.640	8.705	300K
EnhanceNet [33]	$\mathcal{L}_{GAN} + L_P + L_T$	0.624	8.719	200K
Ours **full**	$\mathcal{L}_{GAN} + \mathcal{L}_{CX} + L_2^{LF}$	0.643	**8.800**	800
Ours w/o L_2^{LF}	$\mathcal{L}_{GAN} + \mathcal{L}_{CX}$	**0.67**	8.53	800
Ours w/o $\mathcal{L}_{CX}$	$\mathcal{L}_{GAN} + L_2^{LF}$	0.510	8.411	800
SRGAN-MSE*	$\mathcal{L}_{GAN} + L_2$	0.643	8.4	800

*Our reimplementation

where in all our experiments $\lambda_{CX} = 0.1$, $\lambda_{GAN} = 1e-3$, and $\lambda_{L2} = 10$. The images $G(s)^{LF}, y^{LF}$ are low-frequencies obtained by convolution with a Gaussian kernel of width 21×21 and $\sigma = 3$. For the Contextual loss feature extraction we used layer $conv3\_4$ of VGG19 [35].

Implementation Details: We adopt the SRGAN architecture [20][1] and replace only the objective. We train it on just 800 images from the DIV2K dataset [1], for 1500 epochs. Our network is initialized by first training using only the $L2$ loss for 100 epochs.

Evaluation: Empirical evaluation was performed on the BSD100 dataset [26]. As suggested in [7] and PIRM challenge [6] we compute both structural similarity (SSIM [41]) to the ground-truth and perceptual quality (NRQM [24]). The "ideal" algorithm will have both scores high.

Table 1 compares our method with three recent solutions whose goal is high perceptual quality. It can be seen that our approach outperforms the state-of-the-art on both evaluation measures. This is especially satisfactory as we needed only 800 images for training, while previous methods had to train on tens or even hundreds of thousands of images. Note, that the values of the perceptual measure NRQM are not normalized and small changes are actually quite significant. For example the gap between [20] and [33] is only 0.014 yet visual inspection shows a significant difference. The gap between our results and [33] is 0.08, i.e., almost 6 times bigger, and visually it is significant. See supplementary for additional comparison on standard datasets.

---

[1] We used the implementation in https://github.com/tensorlayer/SRGAN.

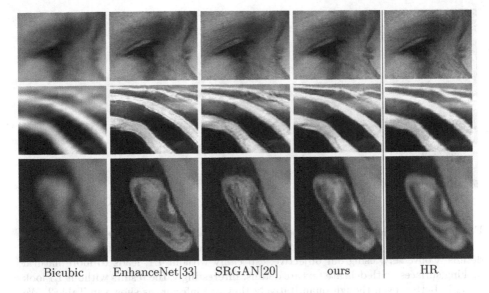

| Bicubic | EnhanceNet[33] | SRGAN[20] | ours | HR |

Fig. 6. Super-resolution qualitative evaluation: Training with GAN and a perceptual loss sometimes adds undesired textures, e.g., SRGAN added wrinkles to the girl's eyelid, unnatural colors to the zebra stripes, and arbitrary patterns to the ear. Our solution replaces the perceptual loss with the Contextual loss, thus getting rid of the unnatural patterns.

Figure 6 further presents a few qualitative results, that highlight the gap between our approach and previous ones. Both SRGAN [20] and EnhanceNet [33] rely on adversarial training (GAN) in order to achieve photo-realistic results. This tends to over-generate high-frequency details, which make the image look sharp, however, often these high-frequency components do not match those of the target image. The Contextual loss, when used in concert with GAN, reduces these artifacts, and results in natural looking image patches.

An interesting observation is that we achieve high perceptual quality while using for the Contextual loss features from a mid-layer of VGG19, namely *conv3_4*. This is in contrast to the reports in [20] that had to use for SRGAN the high-layer *conv5_4* for the perceptual loss (and failed when using low-layer such as *conv2_2*). Similarly, EnhanceNet required a mixture of *pool2* and *pool5*.

4.2 High-Resolution Surface Normal Estimation

The framework we propose is by no means limited to networks that generate images. It is a generic approach that could be useful for training networks for other tasks, where the natural statistics of the target should be exhibited in the network's output. To support this, we present a solution to the problem of surface normal estimation – an essential problem in computer vision, widely used for scene understanding and new-view synthesis.

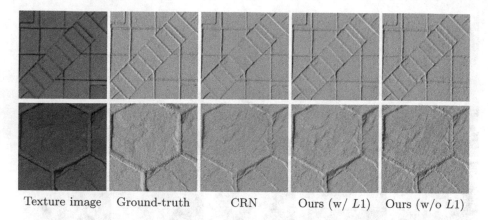

Texture image   Ground-truth   CRN   Ours (w/ $L1$)   Ours (w/o $L1$)

Fig. 7. Estimating surface normals: A visual comparison of our method with CRN [9]. CRN trains with $L1$ as loss, which leads to coarse reconstruction that misses many fine details. Conversely, using our objective, especially without $L1$, leads to more natural looking surfaces, with delicate texture details. Interestingly, the results without $L1$ look visually better, even though quantitatively they are inferior, as shown in Table 2. We believe this is due to the usage of structural evaluation measures rather than perceptual ones.

Data: The task we pose is to estimate the underlying normal map from a single monocular color image. Although this problem is ill-posed, recent CNN based approaches achieve satisfactory results [4,10,11,40] on the NYU-v2 dataset [29]. Thanks to its size, quality and variety, NYU-v2 is intensively used as a test-bed for predicting depth, normals, segmentation etc. However, due to the acquisition protocol, its data does not include the fine details of the scene and misses the underlying high frequency information, hence, it does not provide a detailed representation of natural surfaces.

Therefore, we built a new dataset of images of surfaces and their corresponding normal maps, where fine details play a major role in defining the surface structure. Examples are shown in Fig. 7. Our dataset is based on 182 different textures and their respective normal maps that were collected from the Internet[2], originally offered for usages of realistic interior home design, gaming, arts, etc. For each texture we obtained a high resolution color image (1024 × 1024) and a corresponding normal-map of a surface such that its underlying plane normal points towards the camera (see Fig. 7). Such image-normals pairs lack the effect of lighting, which plays an essential role in normal estimation. Hence, we used Blender[3], a 3D renderer, to simulate each texture under 10 different point-light locations. This resulted in a total of 1820 pairs of image-normals. The textures were split into 90% for training and 10% for testing, such that the test set includes all the 10 rendered pairs of each included texture.

---

[2] www.poliigon.com and www.textures.com.
[3] www.blender.org.

The collection offers a variety of materials including wood, stone, fabric, steel, sand, etc., with multiple patterns, colors and roughness levels, that capture the appearance of real-life surfaces. While some textures are synthetic, they look realistic and exhibit imperfections of real surfaces, which are translated into the fine-details of both the color image as well as its normal map.

Proposed Solution: We propose using an objective based on a combination of three loss terms: (i) The Contextual loss – to make sure that the internal statistics of the generated normal map match those of the target normal map. (ii) The $L2$ loss, computed at **low** resolution, and (iii) The $L1$ loss. Both drive the generated normal map to share the spatial layout of the target map. Our overall objective is:

$$\mathcal{L}(G) = \lambda_{\text{CX}} \cdot \mathcal{L}_{\text{CX}}(G(s), y) + \lambda_{L2} \cdot ||G(s)^{\text{LF}} - y^{\text{LF}}||_2 + \lambda_{L1} \cdot ||G(s) - y||_1 \quad (12)$$

where, $\lambda_{\text{CX}} = 1$, and $\lambda_{L2} = 0.1$. The normal-maps $G(s)^{\text{LF}}, y^{\text{LF}}$ are low-frequencies obtained by convolution with a Gaussian kernel of width 21×21 and $\sigma = 3$. We tested with both $\lambda_{L1} = 1$ and $\lambda_{L1} = 0$, which removes the third term.

Implementation Details: We chose as architecture the Cascaded Refinement Network (CRN) [9] originally suggested for label-to-image and was shown to yield great results in a variety of other tasks [27]. For the contextual loss we took as features 5×5 patches of the normal map (extracted with stride 2) and layers $conv1\_2, conv2\_2$ of VGG19. In our implementation we reduced memory consumption by random sampling of all three layers into 65×65 features.

Evaluation: Table 2 compares our results with previous solutions. We compare to the recently proposed PixelNet [4], that presented state-of-the-art results on NYU-v2. Since PixelNet was trained on NYU-v2, which lacks fine details, we also tried fine-tuning it on our dataset. In addition, we present results obtained with CRN [9]. While the original CRN was trained with both $L1$ and the perceptual loss [19], this combination provided poor results on normal estimation. Hence, we excluded the perceptual loss and report results with only $L1$ as the loss, or when using our objective of Eq. (12). It can be seen that CRN trained with our objective (with $L1$) leads to the best quantitative scores.

We would like to draw your attention to the inferior scores obtained when removing the $L1$ term from our objective (i.e., setting $\lambda_{L1} = 0$ in Eq. (12)). Interestingly, this contradicts what one sees when examining the results visually. Looking at the reconstructed surfaces reveals that they look more natural and more similar to the ground-truth without $L1$. A few examples illustrating this are provided in Figs. 7 and 8. This phenomena is actually not surprising at all. In fact, it is aligned with the recent trends in super-resolution, discussed in Sect. 4.1, where perceptual evaluation measures are becoming a common assessment tool. Unfortunately, such perceptual measures are not the common evaluation criteria for assessing reconstruction of surface normals.

Table 2. Quantitative evaluation of surface normal estimation (on our new high-resolution dataset). The table presents six evaluation statistics, previously suggested by [4,40], over the angular error between the predicted normals and ground-truth normals. For the first three criteria lower is better, while for the latter three higher is better. Our framework leads to the best results on all six measures.

Method	Mean (°)↓	Median (°)↓	RMSE (°)↓	11.25° (%)↑	22.5° (%)↑	30° (%)↑
PixelNet [4]	25.96	23.76	30.01	22.54	50.61	65.09
PixelNet [4] + FineTune	14.27	12.44	16.64	51.20	85.13	91.81
CRN [9]	8.73	6.57	11.74	74.03	90.96	95.28
Ours (without $L1$)	9.67	7.26	12.94	70.39	89.84	94.73
Ours (with $L1$)	**8.59**	**6.50**	**11.54**	**74.61**	**91.12**	**95.28**

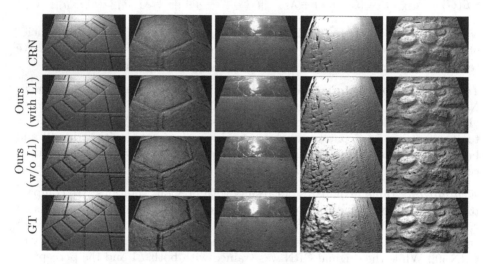

Fig. 8. Rendered images: To illustrate the benefits of our approach we render new view images using the estimated (or ground-truth) normal maps. Using our framework better maintains the statistics of the original surface and thus results with more natural looking images that are more similar to the ground-truth. Again, as was shown in Fig. 7, the results without $L1$ look more natural than those with $L1$.

Finally, we would like to emphasize, that our approach generalizes well to other textures outside our dataset. This can be seen from the results in Fig. 1 where two texture images, found online, were fed to our trained network. The reconstructed surface normals are highly detailed and look natural.

5   Conclusions

In this paper we proposed using loss functions based on a statistical comparison between the output and target for training generator networks. It was shown via multiple experiments that such an approach can produce high-quality and state-of-the-art results. While we suggest adopting the Contextual loss to measure the difference between distributions, other loss functions of a similar nature could (and should, may we add) be explored. We plan to delve into this in our future work.

Acknowledgements. This research was supported by the Israel Science Foundation under Grant 1089/16 and by the Ollendorf foundation.

References

1. Agustsson, E., Timofte, R.: Ntire 2017 challenge on single image super-resolution: dataset and study. In: CVPR Workshops, July 2017
2. Aharon, M., Elad, M., Bruckstein, A.: K-SVD: an algorithm for designing overcomplete dictionaries for sparse representation. IEEE Trans. Signal Process. **54**(11), 4311 (2006)
3. Arjovsky, M., Chintala, S., Bottou, L.: Wasserstein GAN. arXiv preprint arXiv:1701.07875 (2017)
4. Bansal, A., Chen, X., Russell, B., Ramanan, A.G., et al.: PixelNet: representation of the pixels, by the pixels, and for the pixels. In: CVPR (2016)
5. Barrow, H., Tenenbaum, J., Bolles, R., Wolf, H.: Parametric correspondence and chamfer matching: two new techniques for image matching. In: International Joint Conference on Artificial Intelligence (1977)
6. Blau, Y., Mechrez, R., Timofte, R., Michaeli, T., Zelnik-Manor, L.: 2018 PIRM challenge on perceptual image super-resolution. In: ECCVW (2018)
7. Blau, Y., Michaeli, T.: The perception-distortion tradeoff. In: CVPR (2018)
8. Botev, Z.I., Grotowski, J.F., Kroese, D.P., et al.: Kernel density estimation via diffusion. Ann. Stat. **38**(5), 2916–2957 (2010)
9. Chen, Q., Koltun, V.: Photographic image synthesis with cascaded refinement networks. In: ICCV (2017)
10. Chen, W., Xiang, D., Deng, J.: Surface normals in the wild. In: ICCV (2017)
11. Eigen, D., Fergus, R.: Predicting depth, surface normals and semantic labels with a common multi-scale convolutional architecture. In: Proceedings of the IEEE International Conference on Computer Vision, pp. 2650–2658 (2015)
12. Gal, R., Shamir, A., Hassner, T., Pauly, M., Cohen-Or, D.: Surface reconstruction using local shape priors. In: Symposium on Geometry Processing (2007)
13. Gatys, L.A., Ecker, A.S., Bethge, M.: Image style transfer using convolutional neural networks. In: CVPR (2016)
14. Glasner, D., Bagon, S., Irani, M.: Super-resolution from a single image. In: ICCV (2009)
15. Goodfellow, I., et al.: Generative adversarial nets. In: NIPS (2014)
16. Hassner, T., Basri, R.: Example based 3D reconstruction from single 2D images. In: CVPR Workshop (2006)
17. Huang, J., Lee, A.B., Mumford, D.: Statistics of range images. In: CVPR (2000)
18. Isola, P., Zhu, J.Y., Zhou, T., Efros, A.A.: Image-to-image translation with conditional adversarial networks. In: CVPR (2017)
19. Johnson, J., Alahi, A., Fei-Fei, L.: Perceptual losses for real-time style transfer and super-resolution. In: Leibe, B., Matas, J., Sebe, N., Welling, M. (eds.) ECCV 2016. LNCS, vol. 9906, pp. 694–711. Springer, Cham (2016). https://doi.org/10.1007/978-3-319-46475-6_43

20. Ledig, C., et al.: Photo-realistic single image super-resolution using a generative adversarial network. In: CVPR (2017)
21. Levin, A.: Blind motion deblurring using image statistics. In: Advances in Neural Information Processing Systems, pp. 841–848 (2007)
22. Levin, A., Zomet, A., Weiss, Y.: Learning how to inpaint from global image statistics. In: ICCV (2003)
23. Lim, B., Son, S., Kim, H., Nah, S., Lee, K.M.: Enhanced deep residual networks for single image super-resolution. In: CVPR Workshops (2017)
24. Ma, C., Yang, C.Y., Yang, X., Yang, M.H.: Learning a no-reference quality metric for single-image super-resolution. Comput. Vis. Image Underst. **158**, 1–16 (2017)
25. Mairal, J., Bach, F., Ponce, J., Sapiro, G.: Online learning for matrixfactorization and sparse coding. J. Mach. Learn. Res. **11**, 19–60 (2010)
26. Martin, D., Fowlkes, C., Tal, D., Malik, J.: A database of human segmented natural images and its application to evaluating segmentation algorithms and measuring ecological statistics. In: ICCV. IEEE (2001)
27. Mechrez, R., Talmi, I., Zelnik-Manor, L.: The contextual loss for image transformation with non-aligned data. In: Ferrari, V., Hebert, M., Sminchisescu, C., Weiss, Y. (eds.) Computer Vision – ECCV 2018. LNCS, vol. 11218, pp. 800–815. Springer, Cham (2018). https://doi.org/10.1007/978-3-030-01264-9_47
28. Michaeli, T., Irani, M.: Blind deblurring using internal patch recurrence. In: Fleet, D., Pajdla, T., Schiele, B., Tuytelaars, T. (eds.) ECCV 2014. LNCS, vol. 8691, pp. 783–798. Springer, Cham (2014). https://doi.org/10.1007/978-3-319-10578-9_51
29. Silberman, N., Hoiem, D., Kohli, P., Fergus, R.: Indoor segmentation and support inference from RGBD images. In: Fitzgibbon, A., Lazebnik, S., Perona, P., Sato, Y., Schmid, C. (eds.) ECCV 2012. LNCS, vol. 7576, pp. 746–760. Springer, Heidelberg (2012). https://doi.org/10.1007/978-3-642-33715-4_54
30. Radford, A., Metz, L., Chintala, S.: Unsupervised representation learning with deep convolutional generative adversarial networks. In: ICLR (2015)
31. Roth, S., Black, M.J.: Fields of experts. IJCV **82**, 205 (2009)
32. Ruderman, D.L.: The statistics of natural images. Netw.: Comput. Neural Syst. **5**(4), 517–548 (1994)
33. Sajjadi, M.S., Scholkopf, B., Hirsch, M.: EnhanceNet: single image super-resolution through automated texture synthesis. In: ICCV (2017)
34. Salimans, T., Goodfellow, I., Zaremba, W., Cheung, V., Radford, A., Chen, X.: Improved techniques for training GANs. In: NIPS (2016)
35. Simonyan, K., Zisserman, A.: Very deep convolutional networks for large-scale image recognition. arXiv preprint arXiv:1409.1556 (2014)
36. Sun, X., et al.: Pix3D: dataset and methods for single-image 3D shape modeling. In: CVPR (2018)
37. Timofte, R., Agustsson, E., Van Gool, L., Yang, M.H., Zhang, L., et al.: Ntire 2017 challenge on single image super-resolution: methods and results. In: CVPR Workshops, July 2017
38. Tong, T., Li, G., Liu, X., Gao, Q.: Image super-resolution using dense skip connections. In: CVPR (2017)
39. de Villiers, H.A., van Zijl, L., Niesler, T.R.: Vision-based hand pose estimation through similarity search using the earth mover's distance. IET Comput. Vis. **6**(4), 285–295 (2012)
40. Wang, X., Fouhey, D., Gupta, A.: Designing deep networks for surface normal estimation. In: CVPR (2015)

41. Wang, Z., Bovik, A.C., Sheikh, H.R., Simoncelli, E.P.: Image quality assessment: from error visibility to structural similarity. IEEE Trans. Image Process. **13**(4), 600–612 (2004)
42. Weiss, Y., Freeman, W.T.: What makes a good model of natural images? In: CVPR (2007)
43. Zhang, R., Isola, P., Efros, A.A., Shechtman, E., Wang, O.: The unreasonable effectiveness of deep features as a perceptual metric. In: CVPR (2018)
44. Zontak, M., Irani, M.: Internal statistics of a single natural image. In: CVPR (2011)
45. Zoran, D., Weiss, Y.: From learning models of natural image patches to whole image restoration. In: ICCV. IEEE (2011)

U-DADA: Unsupervised Deep Action Domain Adaptation

Arshad Jamal[1,2]([✉]), Vinay P. Namboodiri[2], Dipti Deodhare[1],
and K. S. Venkatesh[2]

[1] Centre for AI and Robotics, DRDO, Bangalore, India
arshad@iitk.ac.in
[2] Indian Institute of Technology, Kanpur, India

Abstract. The problem of domain adaptation has been extensively studied for object classification task. However, this problem has not been as well studied for recognizing actions. While, object recognition is well understood, the diverse variety of videos in action recognition make the task of addressing domain shift to be more challenging. We address this problem by proposing a new novel adaptation technique that we term as unsupervised deep action domain adaptation (U-DADA). The main concept that we propose is that of explicitly modeling density based adaptation and using them while adapting domains for recognizing actions. We show that these techniques work well both for domain adaptation through adversarial learning to obtain invariant features or explicitly reducing the domain shift between distributions. The method is shown to work well using existing benchmark datasets such as UCF50, UCF101, HMDB51 and Olympic Sports. As a pioneering effort in the area of deep action adaptation, we are presenting several benchmark results and techniques that could serve as baselines to guide future research in this area.

Keywords: Action recognition · Domain adaptation ·
Transfer learning

1 Introduction

When a camera network is deployed for surveillance and security applications, the biggest challenge is to effectively use the visual recognition (object and human activity/event) algorithms trained on the dataset available to the developers. Often, these algorithms fail due to the problem, commonly known as *domain shift* between the data in the development and the real environment. While, domain shift has been widely studied in the context of object adaptation, there are hardly any effort to address this problem for action/event classification. In this paper, we investigate the domain shift in action space.

Deep Networks have been shown to bridge the gap between the source and target domains and learn transferable features. However, they cannot completely

---

D. Deodhare—The author is a former scientist from CAIR, DRDO, Bangalore, India.

C. V. Jawahar et al. (Eds.): ACCV 2018, LNCS 11363, pp. 444–459, 2019.
https://doi.org/10.1007/978-3-030-20893-6_28

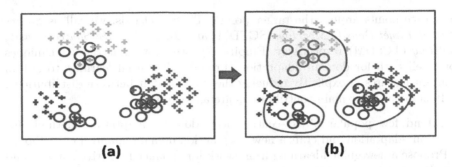

Fig. 1. Conceptual diagram of source sample selection to maximize positive transfer and minimize negative transfer. The samples of three classes from source domain are shown in three colors with '+' symbols. The unlabelled target domain samples are shown with 'o' symbol. Figure (b) shows the selected source samples. *Best viewed in color.* (Color figure online)

remove the gap between the two domains [11,32]. To overcome this, several methods [14,17–19,32] have been proposed which incorporate additional layers into the deep network to align the source and target domain distributions and reduce domain discrepancy. In addition, there are other class of methods [10,23,31] which leverages the concept of Generative Adversarial Network [13] and formulate the problem as minimax game to make the source and target feature representations indistinguishable through adversarial learning. However, all these methods have been proposed mainly for object adaptation task and they have been shown to perform well for the standard object adaptation datasets.

In this paper, we investigate an equally important, but under-explored problem of action domain adaptation, which is even more challenging due to the diverse variety of videos. Human Action Recognition has been widely studied in the standard setting of supervised classification [4,7,24,30,35]. However, there are no efforts to evaluate these methods in multi-domain setting or embed domain adaptation architectures. We built an action domain adaptation architecture on top of the popular 3D-CNN [30] and evaluate it using three multi-domain datasets.

All the deep domain adaptation methods, mentioned above, blindly use the source domain dataset to align it with the target domain. Intuitively, it seems reasonable to expect that certain source data points, which are close to the target data points in the learned feature space would have positive effect on the adaptation process. However, there could be many other samples in the source domain that can spoil the alignment process. In this paper, we propose to address the problem by maximizing the positive transfer and minimizing the negative transfer from the source to the target domain. This is achieved by explicitly modeling density based adaptation and using them while adapting domains for recognizing actions. The idea has been illustrated in Fig. 1 using a three class source and target dataset. We investigate two possibilities, one based on the density of the target points around each source point and another based on the density of the source points around the target points. These methods, we call as *Source Centred Target Density Modeling* (SCTDM) and *Target Centred Source Density Modeling* (TCSDM) respectively. Empirically, we show that these techniques work well both for domain adaptation through adversarial learning to obtain invariant features or explicitly reducing the domain shift between distributions.

In summary, our main contributions are as follows:

1. Extend few popular object-centric deep domain adaptation methods for action adaptation and craft a new deep action domain adaptation method.
2. Propose a new guided learning framework for enhanced positive transfer and reduced negative transfer between source and target domain.
3. Extensive evaluation using several action datasets.

2   Related Work

Activity/Event analysis has been a widely studied area and a large number of papers have been published. However, the literature review, here, mainly focuses on various domain adaptation methods, which is a popular field in the area of transfer learning [21]. In a recent survey paper [2], domain adaptation and transfer learning techniques have been comprehensively discussed with a specific view on visual applications. It covers the historical shallow methods, homogeneous and heterogeneous domain adaptation methods and the deep domain adaptation methods that integrate the adaptation within the deep architecture.

Recently, deep domain adaptation methods [9,17–19,23] have shown significant performance gains over the prior shallow transfer learning methods. Many of these methods learn a feature representation in a latent space shared by the source and target domains. A popular approach among them is to minimize Maximum Mean Discrepancy (MMD) or its variant to effectively align the two distributions. Where, MMD is a non-parametric metric that measures the distribution divergence between the mean embedding of the two distributions in Reproducing Kernel Hilbert Space (RKHS). For example, in Deep Domain Confusion (DDC) method [32], the MMD is used in last fully connected layer along with classification loss to learn representations that are both domain invariant and discriminative. In Deep Adaptation Network (DAN) [17], Multi-Kernel MMD is used to improve the transferability of the features from source to target domain. In Residual Transfer Network (RTN) [18], the assumption of shared classifier between source and target domain is relaxed. It combines MK-MMD with an adaptive classifier to further improve the performance. The classifier is adapted by learning a residual function with reference to the target classifier. In Joint Adaptation Network (JAN) [19], Joint-MMD (JMMD) is used to align the joint distributions of multiple domain-specific layers across two domains. In another approach, simple linear transformation is used to align the second-order statistics of the source and target distributions. This approach, called as correlation alignment (COROL) [28] was further extended in [29] with Deep COROL in which a non-linear transformation is learned to the correlations of layer activation.

Other class of methods [10,23,31] for domain adaptation leverages the concept of Generative Adversarial Network (GAN) [13] and formulate the problem as minimax game to learn a domain invariant feature representation. For example, in Domain Adversarial Neural Network (DANN) [10], gradient reversal layer is used for adversarial learning. In [31], a generic framework for adversarial adaptation is proposed in which the adversarial loss type with respect to the domain classifier and the weight sharing strategy can be chosen. In the adversarial learning methods, when the source and target features become completely indistinguishable, there are vanishing gradient problem. The Wasserstein Distance Guided Representation Learning (WDGRL) [23] method addresses the problem of vanishing distance.

All the domain adaptation methods discussed above are for image/object classification problem. The domain adaptation in videos has been highly underexplored. In fact, we could only find one subspace based method [15] on the video-to-video domain adaptation problem. There are few studies [3,16,26,34,36] on cross-view action recognition and a few on heterogeneous domain adaptation [5,6,33]. In that sense, to the best of our knowledge, this paper is one of the first few papers for the video-video domain adaptation.

3   Proposed Action Adaptation Approach

In this paper, the action domain adaptation networks are built on top of the feature embedding layers of a popular deep network architecture known as 3D-CNN [30]. This is either combined with the adversarial learning layer to obtain domain invariant features or distribution matching layer to explicitly reducing the domain shift between the distributions. The base convolutional layers of 3D-CNN learn mapping from the video input to a high-level feature space. The 3D-CNN network, when combined with the Gradient Reversal Layer (GRL), results in AGRL (Action GRL) and with Residual Transfer Network (RTN), it gives ARTN (Action RTN). We combine distribution matching and residual classifier learning with the GRL to create a unified adaptation framework named as unsupervised deep action domain adaptation (U-DADA), Further, we propose a density based adaptation approach, in which source samples are carefully selected to enhance positive transfer and reduce negative transfer between the two domains.

3.1   Problem Definition

Let's assume that the source domain consists of N_S labelled actions clips $\mathcal{D}_S = \{\mathbf{x}_S^i, y^i\}_{i=1}^{N_S}$, each having K-frames. Similarly, the target domain has N_T unlabelled action video clips, $\mathcal{D}_T = \{\mathbf{x}_T^i\}_{i=1}^{N_T}$, each having K-frames. The source and target domains are assumed to be sampled from different probability distributions p_S and p_T respectively, and $p_S \neq p_T$. The goal of this paper is to design a deep action domain adaptation network that learns feature embedding $\mathbf{f} = G_f(x)$ and transfer classifiers $y = G_y(f)$, such that the expected target risk

$Pr_{(x,y) \sim p_T}[G_y(G_f(x)) \neq y]$ can be bounded by leveraging the source domain labeled data.

3.2 Preliminaries

Maximum Mean Discrepancy: Let the source and target data be sampled from probability distributions p_S and p_T respectively. Maximum Mean Discrepancy (MMD) [14] is a kernel two-sample test which rejects or accepts the null hypothesis $p_S = p_T$ based on the observed samples. Formally, MMD is defined as,

$$D_{\mathcal{H}}(p_S, p_T) = \sup_{h \in \mathcal{H}} \left[\mathbb{E}_{\mathbf{X}_S}[h(\mathbf{X}_S)] - \mathbb{E}_{\mathbf{X}_T}[h(\mathbf{X}_T)] \right], \tag{1}$$

where $\mathcal{H}$ is a class of function lying in RKHS (Reproducing Kernel Hilbert Space), which can distinguish any two distribution. In this case, MMD is the distance between their mean embedding: $D_{\mathcal{H}}(p_S, p_T) = \|\mu_{\mathbf{X}_S}(p_S) - \mu_{\mathbf{X}_T}(p_T)\|^2_{\mathcal{H}}$. Theoretically, it has been shown [14] that $p_S = p_T$ if and only if $D_{\mathcal{H}}(p_S, p_T) = 0$. In practice, the MMD is estimated using the following equation:

$$
\begin{aligned}
\hat{D}_{\mathcal{H}}(p_S, p_T) = {} & \frac{1}{N_S^2} \sum_{i=1}^{N_S} \sum_{j=1}^{N_S} k(\mathbf{x}_S^i, \mathbf{x}_S^j) + \frac{1}{N_T^2} \sum_{i=1}^{N_T} \sum_{j=1}^{N_T} k(\mathbf{x}_T^i, \mathbf{x}_T^j) \\
& - \frac{2}{N_S N_T} \sum_{i=1}^{N_S} \sum_{j=1}^{N_T} k(\mathbf{x}_S^i, \mathbf{x}_T^j),
\end{aligned}
\tag{2}
$$

where, $\hat{D}_{\mathcal{H}}(p_S, p_T)$ is the unbiased estimate of $D_{\mathcal{H}}(p_S, p_T)$. The characteristic kernel $k(x^i, x^j) = e^{\|vec(x^i) - vec(x^j)\|^2/b}$ is the Gaussian kernel function defined on the vectorization of tensors x^i and x^j with bandwidth parameter b.

3.3   Deep Action Domain Adaptation (DADA)

In this paper, we craft a new action domain adaptation network, which is built on the popular deep network architecture known as 3D-CNN [30]. The proposed network, incorporates several popular choices from object adaptation space. This network, named as Deep Action Domain Adaptation (DADA), combines the adversarial learning and distribution matching ideas from the image adaptation literature. Our network architecture, shown in Fig. 2, includes seven layers of 3D-CNN for feature mapping $G_f(.; \theta_f)$, 3–5 layers of residual network for classifier adaptation $G_y(.; \theta_y)$, 1–3 layers of MK-MMD for feature distribution matching $D_{\mathcal{L}}(\mathcal{D}_S, \mathcal{D}_T)$, one layer for entropy of class-conditional distribution of target data $G_E(.; \theta_E)$ and three adversarial layers for domain alignment $G_d(.; \theta_d)$. In the network, the feature mapping layers share weight between source and target domains. Here, an adversarial game is played between a domain discriminator $G_d(.; \theta_d)$, which is trained to distinguish the source and target domain samples, and the feature extractor $G_f(.; \theta_f)$, which is fine-tuned simultaneously to confuse

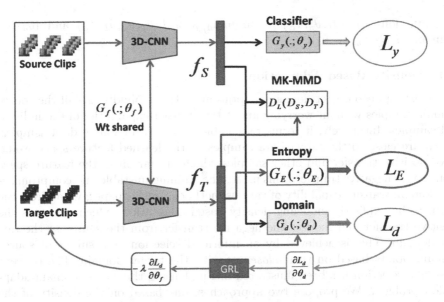

Fig. 2. Architecture of the proposed Deep Action Domain Adaptation (DADA) network. $G_f(.; \theta_f)$ is the feature mapping function, $G_y(.; \theta_y)$ is the class discriminator function, $G_E(.; \theta_E)$ is the entropy function and $G_d(.; \theta_d)$ is the domain discriminator function. L_y, L_E and L_d are the corresponding loss functions. $D_\mathcal{L}(\mathcal{D}_S, \mathcal{D}_T)$ is the distribution matching function. GRL is gradient reversal layer. Other back-propagation layers have been omitted for simplicity. *Best viewed in color.* (Color figure online)

the domain discriminator. Similarly, the other layers are fine-tuned to minimize the losses.

In the adversarial training, the parameters θ_f are learned by maximizing the domain discriminator loss L_d and the parameters θ_d are learned by minimizing the domain loss. In addition, the label prediction loss L_y, the MK-MMD loss $D(\mathcal{D}_S, \mathcal{D}_T)$ and target data entropy L_E are also minimized. The overall loss function for the DADA is:

$$L(\theta_f, \theta_y, \theta_E, \theta_d) = \frac{1}{N_s} \sum_{x_i \in \mathcal{D}_S} L_y(G_y(G_f(x_i)), y_i)$$
$$+ \gamma D_\mathcal{L}(\mathcal{D}_S, \mathcal{D}_T) + \frac{\mu}{N_T} \sum_{x_i \in \mathcal{D}_T} L_E(G_E(G_f(x_i))) \qquad (3)$$
$$- \frac{\lambda}{N_S + N_T} \sum_{x_i \in \mathcal{D}_S \cup \mathcal{D}_T} L_d(G_d(G_f(x_i)), d_i),$$

where γ, μ and λ are the trade-off parameters in the objective function (3) that shape the features during learning. L_y is the cross-entropy loss for label prediction, L_E is the entropy function of class-conditional distribution of the target features [18] and L_d is the domain classification loss [9]. At the end of the training, the parameters $\hat{\theta}_f$, $\hat{\theta}_y$, $\hat{\theta}_d$ will give the saddle point of the loss function (3): $(\hat{\theta}_f, \hat{\theta}_y, \hat{\theta_E}) = \text{argmin}_{\theta_f, \theta_E, \theta_y} L(\theta_f, \theta_y, \theta_E, \theta_d)$ and $(\hat{\theta}_d) = \text{argmax}_{\theta_d} L(\theta_f, \theta_y, \theta_E, \theta_d)$.

3.4 Density Based Adaptation

The existing deep object domain adaptation methods blindly use all the source domain samples without worrying about the transfer capabilities of the individual samples. Intuitively, it seems reasonable that certain source data samples, which are close to the target data samples in the learned feature space would have positive transfer and other samples which are far off in the feature space would have negative transfer. This makes the training unstable and compromises the domain transfer capability of various methods. In this paper, we address the problem by explicitly modeling density based adaptation, which enhances the positive transfer and reduces the negative transfer from the source to the target domain. This is achieved by an informed selection of a subset of source domain points based on their *closeness* with the target domain. The concept of source selection has been illustrated in Fig. 1 using three class domain adaptation problem. We propose two approaches, one based on the density of the target samples around each source sample and another based on the density of the source samples around the target samples. These methods, called as *Source Centred Target Density Modeling* (SCTDM) and *Target Centred Source Density Modeling* (TCSDM) are discussed below.

Source Centred Target Density Modeling (SCTDM): Let us define the number of target points around each source point as:

$$n_T(\mathbf{x}_S) = |\mathbf{x}_T|Sim(\mathbf{x}_S, \mathbf{x}_T) \geq \epsilon| \tag{4}$$

where, ϵ is the mean similarity between each source point and all the target points. The similarity measure, $Sim(\mathbf{x}_S, \mathbf{x}_T) = \mathbf{x}_S G \mathbf{x}_T'$, where G is a similarity kernel. There are several options available for G, which can be used as similarity kernel between source and target domain (e.g. Radial basis kernel). However, in this work, G is set to identity matrix. Further, we define the average target density for each class of the source data as,

$$\overline{n}_T^{(c)} = \frac{1}{N_S^c} \sum (n_T(\mathbf{x}_S)|\mathbf{y}_S = c) \tag{5}$$

where N_S^c is the number of source data points in class-c and $\mathbf{y}_S$ is the class label.

Given a source and target dataset $\mathbf{X}_S \in \mathbb{R}^{N_S \times D}$ and $\mathbf{X}_T \in \mathbb{R}^{N_T \times D}$, consisting of N_S and N_T D-dimensional feature vectors computed using the fine-tuned model. We compute the similarity $Sim(\mathbf{x}_S, \mathbf{x}_T)$ between the source and target domain and the average target density $\overline{n}_T^{(c)}$ for each class in the source domain and then select a balanced set of source samples having target density more than the $\overline{n}_T^{(c)}$ i.e. $\mathbf{X}_S' = \left\{ \mathbf{x}_S : n_T(\mathbf{x}_S) > \overline{n}_T^{(c)}, |\mathbf{X}_S'| < \alpha |\mathbf{X}_S| \right\}$. Here, α is a hyper parameter defining the fraction of the source data, the upper limit of which is fixed at 90% in all the experiments.

Target Centred Source Density Modeling (TCSDM): In the second approach, as illustrated in Fig. 1, we perform clustering of the target data, centred around which, we find a balanced set of samples from the source domain. If the number of classes in labelled source data is C, the target data is clustered into C-clusters. For each cluster $c \in C$, its radius R_c is found and also the distance between all the source points with C clusters are computed (a distance matrix $(N_S \times C)$. The distances are sorted to find the closest cluster for each source point. Now, for each class, the source points are examined in the order of their increasing distance from the cluster centre. The points are selected if they are within a distance of $R_c/2$ (empirically chosen based on the analysis of distances for the dataset) from the cluster centre and the total count of the particular source class is less than a predefined fraction. The percentage of source data to be selected is a hyper-parameter, whose upper limit is fixed at 90% in all the experiments.

4   Experiments

In this paper, our deep action domain adaptation method has been compared with two other deep adaptation methods, which are obtained by extending two object domain adaptation methods. They are adversarial learning based Gradient Reversal Layer (**AGRL** - Action GRL) method and feature distribution alignment method (**ARTN** - Action Residual Transfer Network). In addition, three baselines methods i.e. **3D-CNN**, **AGFK** (action variant of Geodesic Flow Kernel [12] method) and **ASA** (action variant of Subspace Alignment [8] method) have also been used in the experiments. Here, the first baseline provides the No Adaptation results. The details of the experimental setup including action datasets are discussed in the following subsections.

4.1   Setup

The action DA experiments require multiple distinct action datasets having the same action categories. Unfortunately, there are hardly any benchmark action datasets available for this experiment. We specifically created three multi-domain datasets, as described below, and evaluated the proposed approaches with them. Specifically, for the deep action adaptation methods, a larger eighteen class multi-domain dataset has been created from UCF101 dataset as one domain and a combination of Olympic Sports and HMDB51 datasets as the other domain. In all the cases, publicly available Sport 1M 3D-CNN model is fine-tuned using the source domain data, which is then used in the adaptation problems. The dataset details are as follows.

KTH, MSR Action II and SonyCam Datasets: Our first dataset collection, referred to as **KMS**, is a combination of three datasets, consisting of two benchmark datasets i.e. KTH [1] and MSR Action II [1] (denoted by **K** and **M** respectively) along with a six class dataset, referred to as SonyCam (denoted by **S**) captured using a **hand-held** Sony camera. In KTH and Sony-Cam datasets, there are six classes, namely, *Boxing, Handclapping, Handwaving, Jogging, Running* and *Walking*. MSR Action II dataset contains only the first three classes from the KTH dataset. For the **KMS** dataset collection, there are four adaptation problems (K → M, K → S, M → S and M → K). The SonyCam dataset is only used as target domain owing to its small size (180 clips across 6 action classes). In case of KTH dataset, we use training data partition of 1530 clips spread almost equally across six classes for source domains and testing data partition of 760 clips for target domain. In the MSR dataset, there are 202 clips for three classes (Boxing-80, Handclapping-51 and Handwaving-71).

UCF50 and Olympic Sports Datasets: The second dataset collection comprises a subset of six common classes from UCF50 [22] (denoted by **U**) and Olympic Sports [20] (denoted by **O**). The classes are *Basketball, Clean and Jerk, Diving, Pole Vault, Tennis* and *Discus Throw*. For UCF50 dataset, we use 70%–30% train-test split suggested in [27], which results into $432 - 168$ train/test action videos. Each of them are then segmented into 16-frames clips for training and testing. Similarly, for Olympic Sports dataset, the number of unsegmented videos in training and testing set are 260 and 55 respectively. In this case, **U → O** and **O → U** are the two adaptation problems being solved.

Olympic Sports, HMDB51 and UCF101 Datasets: In the third series of experiments, we combined the Olympic Sports and HMDB51 datasets (denoted by **OH**) to construct a much larger multi-domain dataset and used all the eighteen common classes between OH and UCF101 dataset. The eighteen common classes are *Basketball, Biking, Bowling, Clean and Jerk, Diving, Fencing, Golf Swing, Hammer Throw, High Jump, Horse Riding, Javelin Throw, Long Jump, Pole Vault, Pull-ups, Push-ups, Shot-put, Tennis Swing* and *Throw Discus*. The name of the classes varies slightly across the three datasets. For UCF101, the splits suggested in [25] has been used, which results in 2411 segmented videos of 32-frames distributed between train and test set of 1712 and 699 video clips. Similarly, for the **OH** combination, 70%–30% split has been used for training and testing, which results in 958 and 303 video clips for the two. In this case, **OH → UCF** and **UCF → OH** are the two DA problems.

4.2 Implementation Details

For the feature embedding, we used the 3D-CNN architecture [30]. All the subspace based domain adaptation experiments have been conducted using the 4096-dimensional *fc7* features computed for 16-frame clips, obtained by segmenting the action videos. The source and target domain points on the subspace are obtained by separately stacking all the features corresponding to the two domains and then computing the PCA of the resulting matrices.

In the case of deep action adaptation, we combine the feature mapping layers of the 3D-CNN with the layers of gradient reversal layer and distribution alignment layer to correspondingly obtain the **AGRL** and **ARTN** methods. Similarly, the proposed **DADA** network is built on top of the 3D-CNN model by incorporating all the components mentioned in Sect. 3.3. The inputs to the network are the mini-batch of the video clips. The classification is done using the softmax layer. We fine-tune all convolutional and pooling layers and train the classifier layer via back propagation. Since the classifier is trained from scratch, we set its learning rate to be 10 times that of the lower layers. We employ the mini-batch stochastic gradient descent (SGD) with momentum of 0.9 and the learning rate strategy implemented in RevGrad [9].

The proposed density based adaptation approach starts with computation of the feature vectors using the fine-tuned network. These features are then used to find a subset of source domain data samples using either of the two methods discussed in Sect. 3.4. Once, the source samples are selected, the end-to-end training is performed using the respective adaptation methods discussed above.

4.3   Results and Discussions

In this section, we first present the results of all the deep action adaptation methods for the three dataset collections. Then the effect of our proposed source subset selection approach is analyzed for these methods.

Domain Adaptation in Action Spaces: We have evaluated our action domain adaptation approaches for **UO, KMS** and **OH-UCF101** dataset collections. In majority of the cases, improvements have been observed over all the baselines. The two subspace based domain adaptation methods (i.e. AGFK and ASA) have been found to be generally better than 3D-CNN and the deep domain adaptation approaches substantially outperforms all the three baselines. In Table 1, results for the **KMS** and **UO** datasets have been given. It can be seen that the subspace based adaptation methods are better than the 3D-CNN No-Adaptation baseline, which was significantly improved by the **AGRL, ARTN** and **DADA** methods. In four out of six adaptation problems, the proposed DADA approach gives best results. In this table, all the three deep adaptation methods use TCSDM approach for source sample selection. In Table 2, the adaptation results for the **OH-UCF101** dataset has been given. There are substantial improvement over the three baseline, shown in the first three columns. The proposed DADA approach outperforms the other two deep adaptation methods for both the adaptation problems. Here, the three deep adaptation methods use SCTDM approach for source sample selection.

The results obtained for the action domain adaptation confirms the earlier findings of the object domain adaptation methods in [9,18]. The domain adaptation module, when integrated with the 3D-CNN, improves the domain adaptation performance. Moreover, the proposed adaptation network, incorporating the adversarial learning and multi-kernel two-sample matching, further improves the adaptation performance.

Table 1. Action Domain Adaptation results for the **KMS** and **UO** datasets. 4096-dimensional $fc7$ features are used for subspace based adaptation methods AGFK and ASA. All the deep methods (last three rows) use TCSDM approach for density based adaptation. The best results are shown in bold

Methods	K → S	K → M	M → S	M → K	U → O	O → U
3D-CNN [30]	61.11	49.8	70.22	71.89	82.13	83.16
AGFK	63.71	61.16	73.27	72.9	84.04	86.21
ASA	64.71	62.13	76.7	74.5	84.10	85.67
AGRL	70.44	73.2	77.33	86.85	88.65	91.6
ARTN	72.55	73.6	77.1	**97.38**	87.45	**92.58**
DADA	**73.11**	**76.6**	**77.78**	96.66	**93.01**	91.3

Table 2. Action Domain Adaptation results for the **OH-UCF101** datasets. 4096-dimensional $fc7$ features are used for subspace based adaptation methods AGFK and ASA. All the deep methods (last three columns) use SCTDM approach for density based adaptation. The best results are shown in bold

	3D-CNN [30]	AGFK	ASA	AGRL	ARTN	DADA
UCF → OH	72.24	72.31	70.57	76.37	**79.13**	**79.13**
OH → UCF	72.92	75.45	75.02	78.1	78.45	**80.17**

Analysis of Deep Action Domain Adaptation Learning: The performance of the three adaptation methods (3D-CNN, AGRL and DADA) across eighteen classes of OH-UCF101 dataset are shown in Fig. 3. For $OH \rightarrow UCF$ adaptation, the proposed DADA architecture outperforms the other methods for 12-classes and the AGRL method is best for other 6-classes. Similarly, for $UCF \rightarrow OH$ adaptation, our approach outperforms the other methods for 11-classes and the AGRL method is best for 5-classes and in other two classes 3D-CNN is best. In other experiments also, similar results were obtained.

The source sample selection methods (i.e. TCSDM and SCTDM) have been evaluated for the proposed DADA network using KMS and OH-UCF101 datasets. The results, as shown in Table 3, clearly demonstrates the positive effect of the informed source selection. In all the six adaptation problems, across the two datasets, the proposed density based adaptation improves the results over the full data training. Similarly, the improvements were also obtained for the other deep adaptation methods, the results for which are shown in Fig. 5.

The source samples not selected by the two methods were visually scrutinized to understand the reasons of their non-selection. There were three main observations: (i) the video clips were visually far away from the action class; (ii) the video clips had no action performed; (iii) the action are not visible due to clutter or only partially visible due to occlusion. Few example video clips, illustrating these observations, are shown in Fig. 4.

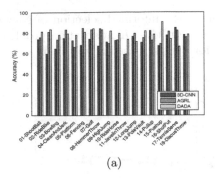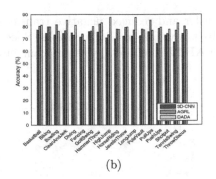

(a)   (b)

Fig. 3. Adaptation performance across eighteen classes of UCF101-OH datasets for **3D-CNN, AGRL, DADA** methods (a) $UCF101 \rightarrow OH$ (b) $OH \rightarrow UCF101$.

Table 3. Comparative analysis of the source selection methods for the **OH-UCF101** and **KMS** datasets. The best results are shown in bold

Methods	UCF →OH	OH → UCF	K → S	K → M	M → S	M → K
Full source data	**79.13**	78.45	71.33	73.2	77.3	89.1
SrcSel-TCSDM	78.96	79.78	73.11	**76.6**	**77.78**	**96.66**
SrcSel-SCTDM	**79.13**	**80.07**	**74.08**	74.91	76.89	87.76

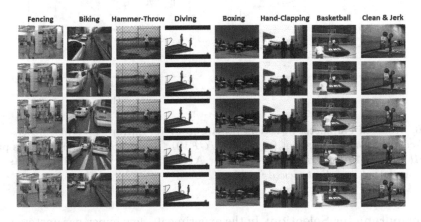

Fig. 4. Source video clips, not selected by the TCSDM method, for few classes in the KMS and OH-UCF101 dataset. Each column has 5 sampled frames of a video clip of the mentioned classes.

Effect of the Source Sample Selection on Training: The density based adaptation, discussed in Sect. 3.4 is evaluated using the KMS dataset for both **AGRL** and **ARTN** methods. The results are shown in Fig. 5. In each figure, two pair of graphs are shown, one for training using all the source data and the other for the proposed density based adaptation using a subset of source samples selected using the methods discussed in Sect. 3.4. The effect of enhanced positive transfer and reduced negative transfer due to the informed selection of source subset is visible in all the graphs. Specifically, for $M \rightarrow K$ adaptation problem, the **ARTN** method gave significant jump for density based adaptation.

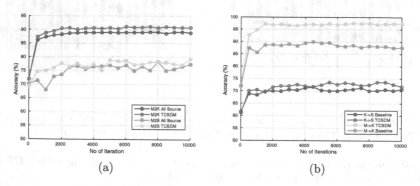

Fig. 5. Improvement due to guided learning: Accuracy vs. Iterations; (a) $K \rightarrow S$ and $M \rightarrow K$ for **AGRL** method (b) $M \rightarrow K$ and $M \rightarrow S$ for **ARTN** method.

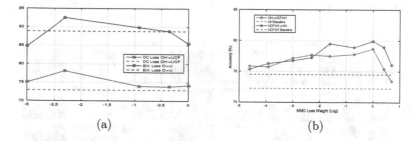

Fig. 6. Trade-off Parameter Selection: (a) Accuracy vs. Entropy Loss plot for $O \rightarrow U$ and Accuracy vs. DC Loss plot for $OH \rightarrow UCF101$ (b) Accuracy vs. MMD Loss plat for $OH \rightarrow UCF101$ and $UCF101 \rightarrow OH$ for **ARTN** method. All baseline results are shown as dotted line. *Best viewed in color*

Hyper-parameter Selection: In the experiments, few hyper-parameters have been chosen based on either the recommendations given in the respective papers or the specific experiments done in this paper. For example, the trade-off parameters μ, γ and λ in the optimization function (3) have been empirically selected based on the domain adaptation experiments. In order to minimize the search space of these individual parameters, greedy approach has been used. For example, the entropy loss parameter μ and MK-MMD parameter γ is selected by running the experiments for ARTN method, which is then used in Eq. (3) to selected λ.

The search space for λ and μ are $\{0.05, 0.1, 0.4, 0.7, 1.0\}$. The variation in the classification accuracy for these two parameters is shown in Fig. 6(a). The domain confusion parameter λ was found to be 0.1 and 0.4 for different adaptation problems and the entropy loss parameter was found to be 0.1. Similarly, the MK-MMD parameter γ is selected by running the experiments for the values of $\{0.01, 0.02, 0.05, 0.1, 0.2, 0.5, 1.0, 1.5, 2.0\}$. The variations in classification accuracy with MMD Loss weight for $OH \rightarrow UCF101$ and $UCF101 \rightarrow OH$ are shown in Fig. 6(a). The maximum accuracy was obtained for MMD Loss 1.0. In these experiments, as shown in Fig. 6, a bell-shaped curve is obtained as the accuracy first increases and then decreases with the variation in trade-off parameters.

The learning rate was another hyper-parameter, which was empirically selected. Experiments were done for learning rate between $0.01 - 0.0001$ using the **UO** dataset. The learning rate was reduced by a factor of $1/\sqrt{10}$. In this experiments, the maximum accuracy was obtained for 0.0001. For all other datasets, we have used the same learning rate.

5   Conclusions and Future Work

In this paper, we formulated the problem of domain adaptation for human action recognition and extended two popular approaches of object adaptation for deep action adaptation. We crafted a new deep domain adaptation network for action space. The methods have been comprehensively evaluated using three multi-domain dataset collections, one of which is a large eighteen class collection. We compare these methods with three baselines and show that our deep action domain adaptation method perform better then the baselines. Further, we proposed a new density based adaptation method to enhance the positive transfer and reduce the negative transfer between the source and target domains. Consistent and significant performance improvements have been obtained across various experiments. In this paper, several benchmark results and techniques have been proposed that could serve as baselines to guide future research in this area. In future, we would like to study the concept of continuous domain adaptation on the streaming action videos. In addition, we would like to study other deep learning frameworks for action domain adaptation.

Acknowledgment. The authors would like to thank the Director, Centre for AI & Robotics, Bangalore, India for supporting the research.

References

1. KTH and MSR action II dataset. http://www.cs.utexas.edu/~chaoyeh/web_action-_data/dataset_list.html
2. Csurka, G.: A comprehensive survey on domain adaptation for visual applications. In: Csurka, G. (ed.) Domain Adaptation in Computer Vision Applications. ACVPR, pp. 1–35. Springer, Cham (2017). https://doi.org/10.1007/978-3-319-58347-1_1

3. Davar, N.F., deCampos, T.E., Windridge, D., Kittler, J., Christmas, W.: Domain adaptation in the context of sport video action recognition. In: Domain Adaptation Workshop, in Conjunction with NIPS (2011)
4. Donahue, J., et al.: Long-term recurrent convolutional networks for visual recognition and description. In: CVPR (2015)
5. Duan, L., Xu, D., Tsang, I.W.: Domain adaptation from multiple sources: a domain-dependent regularization approach. IEEE Trans. Neural Netw. Learn. Syst. **23**(3), 504–518 (2012)
6. Duan, L., Xu, D., Tsang, I.W., Luo, J.: Visual event recognition in videos by learning from web data. PAMI **34**(9), 1667–1680 (2012)
7. Feichtenhofer, C., Pinz, A., Zisserman, A.: Convolutional two-stream network fusion for video action recognition. In: CVPR 2016, pp. 1933–1941 (2016)
8. Fernando, B., Habrard, A., Sebban, M., Tuytelaars, T.: Unsupervised visual domain adaptation using subspace alignment. In: ICCV 2013, pp. 2960–2967 (2013)
9. Ganin, Y., Lempitsky, V.S.: Unsupervised domain adaptation by backpropagation. In: Proceedings of the 32th International Conference on Machine Learning, ICML 2015, Lille, France, 6–11 July 2015, pp. 1180–1189 (2015)
10. Ganin, Y., et al.: Domain-adversarial training of neural networks. J. Mach. Learn. Res. **17**, 59:1–59:35 (2016)
11. Glorot, X., Bordes, A., Bengio, Y.: Domain adaptation for large-scale sentiment classification: a deep learning approach. In: Proceedings of the 28th International Conference on International Conference on Machine Learning, ICML 2011 (2011)
12. Gong, B., Shi, Y., Sha, F., Grauman, K.: Geodesic flow kernel for unsupervised domain adaptation. In: CVPR 2012, pp. 2066–2073 (2012)
13. Goodfellow, I.J., et al.: Generative adversarial networks. CoRR abs/1406.2661 (2014)
14. Gretton, A., Borgwardt, K.M., Rasch, M.J., Schölkopf, B., Smola, A.: A kernel two-sample test. J. Mach. Learn. Res. **13**(1), 723–773 (2012)
15. Jamal, A., Deodhare, D., Namboodiri, V., Venkatesh, K.S.: Eclectic domain mixing for effective adaptation in action spaces. Multimed. Tools Appl. **77**(22), 29949–29969 (2018). https://doi.org/10.1007/s11042-018-6179-y
16. Li, R.: Discriminative virtual views for cross-view action recognition. In: CVPR 2012, pp. 2855–2862 (2012)
17. Long, M., Cao, Y., Wang, J., Jordan, M.I.: Learning transferable features with deep adaptation networks. In: Proceedings of the 32th International Conference on Machine Learning, ICML 2015, Lille, France, 6–11 July 2015, pp. 97–105 (2015)
18. Long, M., Wang, J., Jordan, M.I.: Unsupervised domain adaptation with residual transfer networks. CoRR abs/1602.04433 http://arxiv.org/abs/1602.04433 (2016)
19. Long, M., Zhu, H., Wang, J., Jordan, M.I.: Deep transfer learning with joint adaptation networks. In: Proceedings of the 34th International Conference on Machine Learning, ICML 2017, Sydney, NSW, Australia, 6–11 August 2017, pp. 2208–2217 (2017)
20. Niebles, J.C., Chen, C.-W., Fei-Fei, L.: Modeling temporal structure of decomposable motion segments for activity classification. In: Daniilidis, K., Maragos, P., Paragios, N. (eds.) ECCV 2010. LNCS, vol. 6312, pp. 392–405. Springer, Heidelberg (2010). https://doi.org/10.1007/978-3-642-15552-9_29
21. Pan, S.J., Yang, Q.: A survey on transfer learning. IEEE Trans. Knowl. Data Eng. **22**(10), 1345–1359 (2010)
22. Reddy, K.K., Shah, M.: Recognizing 50 human action categories of web videos. Mach. Vis. Appl. **24**(5), 971–981 (2013)

23. Shen, J., Qu, Y., Zhang, W., Yu, Y.: Wasserstein distance guided representation learning for domain adaptation. In: AAAI. AAAI Press (2018)

24. Shou, Z., Wang, D., Chang, S.: Temporal action localization in untrimmed videos via multi-stage CNNs. In: CVPR, pp. 1049–1058. IEEE Computer Society (2016)

25. Soomro, K., Zamir, A.R., Shah, M., Soomro, K., Zamir, A.R., Shah, M.: Ucf101: a dataset of 101 human actions classes from videos in the wild. CoRR (2012)

26. Sui, W., Wu, X., Feng, Y., Jia, Y.: Heterogeneous discriminant analysis for cross-view action recognition. Neurocomputing **191**(C), 286–295 (2016). https://doi.org/10.1016/j.neucom.2016.01.051

27. Sultani, W., Saleemi, I.: Human action recognition across datasets by foreground-weighted histogram decomposition. In: CVPR 2014, Columbus, OH, USA, 23–28 June 2014, pp. 764–771 (2014)

28. Sun, B., Feng, J., Saenko, K.: Correlation alignment for unsupervised domain adaptation. CoRR abs/1612.01939 (2016)

29. Sun, B., Saenko, K.: Deep CORAL: correlation alignment for deep domain adaptation. In: Hua, G., Jégou, H. (eds.) ECCV 2016. LNCS, vol. 9915, pp. 443–450. Springer, Cham (2016). https://doi.org/10.1007/978-3-319-49409-8_35

30. Tran, D., Bourdev, L.D., Fergus, R., Torresani, L., Paluri, M.: Learning spatiotemporal features with 3d convolutional networks. In: ICCV 2015, Santiago, Chile, 7–13 December 2015, pp. 4489–4497 (2015)

31. Tzeng, E., Hoffman, J., Saenko, K., Darrell, T.: Adversarial discriminative domain adaptation. In: IEEE Conference on Computer Vision and Pattern Recognition, CVPR 2017, Honolulu, HI, USA, 21–26 July 2017, pp. 2962–2971 (2017)

32. Tzeng, E., Hoffman, J., Zhang, N., Saenko, K., Darrell, T.: Deep domain confusion: maximizing for domain invariance. CoRR abs/1412.3474, http://arxiv.org/abs/1412.3474 (2014)

33. Wang, H., Wu, X., Jia, Y.: Video annotation via image groups from the web. IEEE Trans. Multimed. **16**(5), 1282–1291 (2014)

34. Wu, X., Wang, H., Liu, C., Jia, Y.: Cross-view action recognition over heterogeneous feature spaces. In: IEEE International Conference on Computer Vision, pp. 609–616, December 2013. https://doi.org/10.1109/ICCV.2013.81

35. Xu, H., Das, A., Saenko, K.: R-c3d: region convolutional 3d network for temporal activity detection. In: 2017 IEEE International Conference on Computer Vision (ICCV), pp. 5794–5803 (2018)

36. Zhang, Z., Wang, C., Xiao, B., Zhou, W., Liu, S., Shi, C.: Cross-view action recognition via a continuous virtual path. In: CVPR 2013, Portland, OR, USA, 23–28 June 2013, pp. 2690–2697 (2013)

Artistic Object Recognition
by Unsupervised Style Adaptation

Christopher Thomas$^{(\boxtimes)}$ and Adriana Kovashka$^{(\boxtimes)}$

University of Pittsburgh, Pittsburgh, PA 15260, USA
{chris,kovashka}@cs.pitt.edu

Abstract. Computer vision systems currently lack the ability to reliably recognize artistically rendered objects, especially when such data is limited. In this paper, we propose a method for recognizing objects in artistic modalities (such as paintings, cartoons, or sketches), without requiring any labeled data from those modalities. Our method explicitly accounts for stylistic domain shifts between and within domains. To do so, we introduce a complementary training modality constructed to be similar in artistic style to the target domain, and enforce that the network learns features that are invariant between the two training modalities. We show how such artificial labeled source domains can be generated automatically through the use of style transfer techniques, using diverse target images to represent the style in the target domain. Unlike existing methods which require a large amount of unlabeled target data, our method can work with as few as ten unlabeled images. We evaluate it on a number of cross-domain object and scene classification tasks and on a new dataset we release. Our experiments show that our approach, though conceptually simple, significantly improves the accuracy that existing domain adaptation techniques obtain for artistic object recognition.

1 Introduction

Clever design of convolutional neural networks, and the availability of large-scale image datasets for training [23,29], have greatly increased the performance of object recognition systems. However, models trained on one dataset often do not perform well on another [28]. For example, training a model on photographs and applying it to an artistic modality such as cartoons is unlikely to yield acceptable results given the large differences in object appearance across domains [21], as illustrated in Fig. 1(a).

One possible solution to this problem is to obtain labeled training data from the domain that the model will be applied on (i.e. the *target* modality). Unfortunately, obtaining sufficient data for training today's deep convolutional networks on each modality of interest may be prohibitively expensive or impossible.

Electronic supplementary material The online version of this chapter (https://doi.org/10.1007/978-3-030-20893-6_29) contains supplementary material, which is available to authorized users.

C. V. Jawahar et al. (Eds.): ACCV 2018, LNCS 11363, pp. 460–476, 2019.
https://doi.org/10.1007/978-3-030-20893-6_29

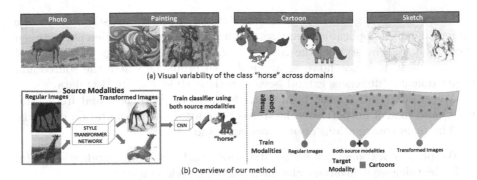

Fig. 1. (a) Illustration of the visual variation between instances of the same object across domains. (b) Overview of our method: We transform our training data so it resembles the style of the target domain. Left: We illustrate how we use style modification to create a synthetic source modality that looks like the target modality, causing the learned features to be more target-appropriate. Right: Training on any single modality causes learned features to be *too* domain specific, so we train on both domains.

In our scenario of recognition in artistic modalities, this problem is especially pronounced: a given artist usually does not produce limitless samples for a particular object class, yet each artist may have a unique style. This problem has led researchers to explore *domain adaptation* techniques: a model is trained on a domain where data is plentiful (the *source* domain) while ensuring that what the model learned can be applied to a disjoint *target* domain. Usually these approaches rely on a small amount of labeled data in the target domain [35] or on seeing some *unlabeled* target data and learning a feature space where the distributions on the source and target domains are similar [1,2,6,8,11,13,25,36].

In contrast to the more general domain adaptation methods above, we focus on a *specific type of domain difference*. We consider domains which exhibit differences due to artistic style [7,17,19], such as paintings, cartoons and sketches. Note that artistic domains often contain limited data—e.g. the PACS dataset of [21] contains on average less than 2,500 images per domain.

We propose two variants of our method, both of which learn style-invariant representations for recognition, one using as few as ten unlabeled target images. Our methods construct a new, *synthetic source modality* from a single photorealistic modality. The synthetic modality bears the *style* of the target modality, and is obtained for free (without human annotations) through the use of style transfer techniques [17,19]. We then train a network using both source modalities, ensuring that the features the model learns produce similar activations in the two source domains. Unlike existing methods which also create synthetic training data for domain adaptation [1,36], our method is easier to train, and requires orders of magnitude less target data (e.g. ten vs ten thousand). This translates to more accurate performance for domains where even unlabeled target data is sparse. We illustrate our method in Fig. 1(b).

Our method of generating synthetic data in the same artistic style as the target domain is applicable to any setting where the primary difference between the domains is the style of the content, e.g. cartoons, paintings, sketches, and line drawings. It is not however applicable to problems where the source and target domain differences extend beyond artistic style, e.g. RGB-D data.

We evaluate our approach on multiple datasets (both new and from prior work) and show it outperforms the state-of-the-art domain adaptation methods. The main contributions of our work are as follows:

- We propose a framework for constructing synthetic source modalities useful for learning style-invariant classifiers through style transfer.
- We develop a novel style selection component, which enables accurate adaptation with just ten target images.
- We release a new large dataset of photographs and artistic images across four domains: natural photographs, cartoons, paintings, and sketches. The dataset is available at http://www.cs.pitt.edu/~chris/artistic_objects/.
- The two versions of our approach outperform recent domain adaptation techniques on the challenging task of object recognition in artistic modalities, which exhibits larger domain shift than traditional adaptation scenarios.
- We conduct rich evaluation against many baselines in different settings (also see our supplementary file).

2   Related Work

Recognition on Artistic Modalities. There is limited work in performing object recognition on artistic modalities. [9] show that as paintings become more abstract, the performance of person detection degrades. [14,38] benchmark existing methods on artistic objects, but only propose improvements over older, non-convolutional techniques, which are greatly outperformed by neural networks. [37] provide a large dataset of artistic domains with per-image object annotations, but we found the labels were too coarse (due to multiple objects in the same image and no bounding box annotations) and the human annotations too sparse, to reliably perform recognition. [21] publish a dataset of objects in artistic modalities, and propose a domain *generalization* approach. We use this dataset but instead focus on domain *adaptation*, where we target a specific unlabeled modality, rather than attempting to do well on an unseen modality. Further, [21] require the availability of multiple original (non-synthetic) source modalities, while we only require one real modality.

Cross-Domain Retrieval. There has been interest in retrieving samples across domain boundaries, e.g. retrieving photographs that match a *sketch*. [31] find a joint embedding for sketches and photographs that ensures a paired sketch and photo are more similar in the learned space than a photo and sketch that are not paired. We utilize the dataset of [31] but perform recognition and not retrieval, and do not assume availability of labeled data from the target domain. [3] retrieve scene types across e.g. sketches and clipart. They propose a supervised approach (which we modify to an unsupervised setting for comparison) that encourages source and target neural activations to fit the same distribution.

Domain Adaptation. Domain adaptation techniques can be broadly divided into two categories: (1) semi-supervised [24,35] in which a limited amount of labeled target data is available, and (2) unsupervised techniques [1,6,8,11,25] (such as this paper) where only unlabeled target data is available. Older domain adaptation techniques either modify a classifier or ensure that the feature space in which we attempt to classify a novel modality are similar to the features for the source modality [11]. Recently, researchers have tackled the same problem in the context of training convolutional neural networks. [6,35] show how to learn domain-invariant features with CNNs by confusing domains, i.e. ensuring that a classifier cannot guess to which domain an image belongs based on its activations. Other approaches [2,8] train an autoencoder which captures features specific to the target domain, then train a classifier on the source and apply it to the target. While these approaches attempt to bring the *source and target* domains closer, we encourage feature invariance between our *two source* domains, while explicitly bringing the source and *target* closer via style transfer. We compare against a number of recent, state-of-the-art unsupervised domain adaptation approaches and find that our approach consistently outperforms them.

Several works use *multiple source domains* for domain adaptation but these assume multiple real human-labeled sources are available [13,21] or can be discovered in the given data [10]. Recent works [1,15,36] have tackled unsupervised domain adaptation using generative adversarial networks (GANs) [12] to generate synthetic target data. The networks are trained to produce novel data such that a discriminator network cannot tell it apart from the real target dataset. [15] extends the idea further by training a GAN which adapts source data at both the image and feature level. Our method has several important advantages over GAN-based approaches. We exploit the fact that our target modality's domain gap with respect to the source can be bridged by controlling for artistic style. Since we know we want to model style differences, we can explicitly extract and distill them, rather than requiring a GAN to learn these in an unsupervised way. This allows our method to use *orders of magnitude less target data*. The ability to leverage limited target data is essential in applications where target data is extremely limited, such as artistic domains [21]. Second, training generative adversarial networks is challenging [30] as the training is unstable and dataset-dependent. Our image translation networks are *easier to train* and require no tuning. Our approach outperforms [1] in experiments.

Other domain adaptation works have also attempted to model style. [40] propose a framework for handwriting recognition from different writers which projects each writer's writing into a "style-free" space and uses it to train a classifier. Another classic work [33] separates style and content using bilinear models and can generate a character in a certain writing style. Unlike our proposed methods, neither of these works use CNNs or perform object recognition.

Domain Generalization. Domain generalization methods [21,22,26,27,39] attempt to leverage knowledge from one or more source domains during training, and apply it on completely unseen target domains. [21] proposes a method of domain generalization on a dataset of paintings, cartoons, and sketches. In order to generalize to cartoons, for example, they assume data is available from all other modalities. In contrast, we perform adaptation towards a known, but unlabeled target modality, without requiring multiple source modalities.

Style Transfer. Style transfer methods [4,5,7,16,17,19] modify an image or video to have the style of some single target image. For example, we might modify a portrait to have the same artistic style as "Starry Night" by Van Gogh. [7] use a pixel-by-pixel loss, whereas [19] use a more holistic perceptual loss to ensure that both content and style are preserved while an input image is transformed. While [7] use a backpropagation technique to iteratively transform an image to another style, [19] train a CNN to directly perform the style transfer in a feed-forward network. More recently, [17] propose an encoder-decoder framework which allows mimicking the style of a target image without retraining a network. Earlier work [34] models style at the object part and scene level. We use [17,19] as the style transfer component of our framework. Importantly, the transformed data retains the classification labels from the photograph source data.

3   Approach

Our method explicitly controls for the stylistic gap between the source and target domains. While our method is based on existing style transfer approaches, its novelty is two-fold. First, we explicitly encourage variation in the styles towards which the source modality is modified, which we call *style selection*. In Sect. 4.3 and our supplementary file, we show that this novel style selection is crucial for attaining good performance in practice. Second, while other methods proposed to use synthetic data for adaptation, we apply our approach to a new problem: object recognition in *artistic* domains. This problem is characterized by larger domain shift compared to prior adaptation benchmarks, as shown in [21]; and by sparse unlabeled target data (see dataset sizes in Sect. 4.1).

The main intuition behind our approach is that we know a large part of the domain gap between photographs and our target modalities is their difference in artistic style. The key observation is that most of the images within an artistic modality exhibit one of a few "representative" styles. For example, some paintings may be cubist, expressionist, or photorealistic. Sketches may be different due to low-level detail, but look similar in terms of coarse visual appearance. Other unsupervised methods [1,8] require a large dataset of target images to learn this shared appearance. Because we specifically focus on artistic style variations, we can explicitly distill "representative" styles from clusters of artistically similar images, and then transfer those styles onto our labeled training data. We train on both original and transformed photos, and add a constraint to our method to encourage the features on both domains to be indistinguishable. Because the only difference between the real and synthetic domains is their style, this constraint, perforce, *factors out artistic style* from our feature representation and

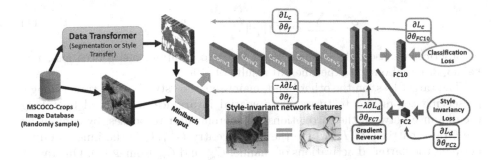

Fig. 2. Training with multiple modalities and style-invariance constraint. We train networks on real and synthetic data. We show an example of style transfer transforming photos into labeled synthetic cartoons. The style-invariance loss trains the FC2 layer to predict which modality the image came from. During backpropagation, we reverse its gradient before propagating it to the layers used by both classifiers. This encourages those layers to learn style-invariant features.

bridges the domain gap. Below we first describe how we obtain additional source modalities, and then how we learn style-invariant features during training.

Our approach automatically transforms photographs into the representative styles found in the target modality. Because the photos are labeled, the transformed photos retain their original labels. We consider two techniques for style transfer. While they are comparable in terms of perceptual quality overall, one [19] produces much higher-quality sketches (see the supplementary file), but is computationally less efficient, which limits the number of transformations we can create. We enable this method to produce rich, albeit few, transformations using a novel representative *style selection* technique (Sect. 3.1). The second style transfer technique [17] can be used to create more transformations as it is more efficient, but it produces less stable results.

3.1 Style Transfer via Johnson [19]

Johnson et al. [19] present an artistic style transfer technique which trains a feed-forward network to perform transfer towards *a single style*. Thus, performing transfer towards additional styles requires training multiple networks (which is computationally expensive). The style transformation network is trained to minimize two losses: the source loss $\mathcal{S}$, which preserves the content of a given source image, and the target loss $\mathcal{T}$, which preserves the style of a given (unlabeled) target image. Let $\Phi_i(I)$ be the neural activations of layer i of a pretrained VGG-16 [32] network on input image I. Let I_s denote a source domain image, I_t a target domain image, and $\widehat{I}_s$ a source domain image transformed by the style transfer network. The shape of $\Phi_i(I)$ is given by $C_i \times H_i \times W_i$, which represents the number of channels, height, and width of the activations of layer i respectively. The source loss $\mathcal{S}$ is thus given by:

$$S^{\Phi} = \sum_i \frac{1}{C_i H_i W_i} \left\| \Phi_i(\widehat{I_s}) - \Phi_i(I_s) \right\|_2^2 \tag{1}$$

In practice, we use only a single VGG layer to compute our source loss, $i =$ relu3_3, based on the experimental results of [19].

The target loss, on the other hand, maintains the "style" of the target image, preserving colors and textures. Style spatial invariance is achieved by taking the distance between the correlations of different filter responses, by computing the Gram matrix $G^{\Phi_i}(I)$, where the matrix entry $G^{\Phi_i}_{a,b}(I)$ is the inner product between the flattened activations of channel C_{i_a} and C_{i_b} from $\Phi_i(I)$. Our target loss is then just the normalized difference between the Gram matrices of the transformed source image and the target image:

$$T^{\Phi} = \sum_i \left\| G^{\Phi_i}(\widehat{I_s}) - G^{\Phi_i}(I_t) \right\|_F^2 \tag{2}$$

where F represents the Frobenius norm. Following [19]'s results, we use $i \in$ {relu1_2, relu2_2, relu3_3, relu4_3} for our target loss. The final loss formulation for our style transformation network is then $\mathcal{L} = \lambda_s S^{\Phi} + \lambda_t T^{\Phi}$, where $\lambda_s = 1$ and $\lambda_t = 5$. We omit the total variation regularizer term for simplicity.

Style Selection. In order to capture the artistic style variation *within* our target dataset, we choose a set of representative style images from our dataset to represent clusters with the same artistic style. We run the target data through layers in the style loss network that are used in computing the style reconstruction loss. We then compute the Gram matrix on the features to remove spatial information. Because of the high dimensionality of the features, we perform PCA and select the first thousand components. We cluster the resulting vectors using k-means, with $k = 10$. From each "style cluster" we select the image closest to its centroid as its style representative. We then train one style transfer network for each style representative, as described above.

3.2 Style Transfer via Huang [17]

Because style transfer via the previous approach requires training a network for every style representative, it is too computationally expensive for more than a few representative styles. We thus also explore a second, more recent style transfer technique by Huang and Belongie [17]. The model follows an hourglass, encoder-decoder architecture. The key takeaway of the approach is that style transfer can be performed on the output of the encoder (i.e. in feature space) by transferring channel-wise mean and variance across spatial locations. Using the same notation as above, style transfer is performed by transforming the encoder's output as follows, where $\widehat{\Phi_i(I_s)}$ represents the transformed source image features, and μ and σ represent the mean and variance across all spatial locations in the given feature map:

$$\widehat{\Phi_i(I_s)} = \sigma\left(\Phi_i(I_t)\right) \left(\frac{\Phi_i(I_s) - \mu\left(\Phi_i(I_s)\right)}{\sigma\left(\Phi_i(I_s)\right)} \right) + \mu\left(\Phi_i(I_t)\right) \tag{3}$$

Fig. 3. Examples of COCO images transformed towards two modalities: cartoons (left) and sketches (right). Background information is lost, which might be useful in non-photorealistic modalities such as cartoons that may not even have a background.

Notice that after training the decoder reconstruction network (the encoder is a pre-trained VGG network, as in Johnson [19]), performing style transfer towards any arbitrary image only requires one to compute $\Phi_i(I_s)$ and $\Phi_i(I_t)$, transform the source image features, and provide $\widehat{\Phi_i(I_s)}$ to the decoder to get the style-transferred image. This enables style transfer to be performed towards any arbitrary target image in a feedforward, efficient manner, without any retraining.

3.3 Creating the Synthetic Source Modality

Formally, let $\mathbf{I}_s = \left\{I_s^i, y_s^i\right\}_{i=1}^{N_s}$ denote the dataset of labeled source data and $\mathbf{I}_t = \left\{I_t^i\right\}_{i=1}^{N_t}$ the dataset of unlabeled target data, where N_s and N_t represent the number of images in each dataset. Our style transfer network $\Psi(I_s^i, \theta_t^j) \to \widehat{I}_s^i$, transforms each source domain image to a synthetic image $\widehat{I}_s^i$ which appears in the style of the single target image j captured by the parameters θ_t^j. In the case of Johnson's method [19], we train one style-transfer network for each of ten "style representatives," and apply each learned network to modify all source images. In the case of Huang's method [17], we randomly select ten target images *for each source image* I_s^i as our target styles. The transformed dataset is thus more stylistically diverse for our adaptation approach via Huang's method. For each target image sampled for either method, we obtain a transformed dataset in the style of that target, $\mathbf{I}_s^{I_t^j} = \left\{\Psi(\mathbf{I}_s, \theta_t^j), \mathbf{y}_s\right\}$, where $\mathbf{y}_s$ denote object labels from the source data. We emphasize the targets are only used for their style, *not their content* (i.e. not their object labels). Examples of style modification for cartoons and sketches are shown in Fig. 3.

3.4   Training with Two Modalities

We train convolutional neural networks which are exposed to two modalities of data. We modify the training procedure such that each minibatch passed to the network during training contains data from both real and synthetic domains. In order to explicitly control for style differences between the source and target domains in our learning process, we impose a style-invariance constraint on the network. The constraint causes the network to learn a feature representation such that it is difficult to predict which of the two source modalities an image came from, given the network's features. In other words, the network learns to *confuse or perform transfer between the source modalities.*

The key observation is that because we have deliberately constructed the synthetic modality such that it differs from the real modality *only in its artistic style*, in order to learn modality-indistinguishable features across both modalities, the network is forced to *factor-out* style from its representation and thus learn style-invariant features for recognition. A similar criterion is used in prior work [6,35] but to confuse the *source and target modalities.* This is an important distinction: because the source and target modalities may differ in several ways, learning modality-invariant features between them may cause the network to disable filters which ultimately are useful for classification on the target domain. In our case of source-to-source invariance, because our source domains contain the same images except in different styles, the network is only forced to disable filters which depend on artistic style. We illustrate our method in Fig. 2.

For each modality, we train a CNN using our source and transformed data to perform the following two classification tasks:

$$T\left(\left\{\mathbf{I}_s, \widehat{\mathbf{I}}_s\right\}; \theta_Y; \theta_F; \theta_D\right) \rightarrow \{\mathbf{y}, \mathbf{d}\} \tag{4}$$

where $\widehat{\mathbf{I}}_s$ denotes the collection of transformed data output by our style transfer networks. The first classification task (predicting $\mathbf{y}$) predicts the object class of the image using the parameters θ_Y. The second task is to predict from which modality a given image came from (denoted by $\mathbf{d}$) using the parameters θ_D. Both classifiers make their predictions using the intermediate network features θ_F. Thus, we seek the following parameters of the network: θ_F which *maximizes* the loss of the modality classifier while simultaneously minimizing the loss of the object classifier, θ_Y which *minimizes* the object classification loss, and θ_D which *minimizes* the modality classifier's loss. Our optimization process seeks the saddle point of the following adversarial functional:

$$\min_{\theta_F, \theta_Y} \max_{\theta_D} \alpha \mathcal{L}_d\left(\left\{\mathbf{I}_s, \widehat{\mathbf{I}}_s\right\}, \mathbf{d}\right) + \beta \mathcal{L}_y\left(\left\{\mathbf{I}_s, \widehat{\mathbf{I}}_s\right\}, \mathbf{y}\right) \tag{5}$$

where α and β are weighting parameters. In practice, we set α to be $1/10$ the value of β. We use a multinomial logistic loss to train both classifiers. $\mathcal{L}_d$ represents our domain classification loss, while $\mathcal{L}_y$ is the object classifier loss which trains our network to recognize the object categories of interest.

Implementation Details: We experiment exclusively with the AlexNet architecture in this paper, but we include results with ResNet in our supplementary. We train all CNNs using the Caffe [18] framework. We use a batch size of 256 for AlexNet and a learning rate of α =1e–4; higher learning rates caused training to diverge. We used SGD with momentum $\mu = 0.9$ and learning rate decay of $\gamma = 0.1$ every 25K iterations. We trained all networks for a maximum of 150K iterations, but found the loss typically converged much sooner.

4 Experimental Validation

4.1 Datasets

Most of our experiments focus on object recognition, using the **PACS** dataset of [21] and the **Sketchy Database** of [31] as our target domains. We complement these with our own dataset, described below. To test our method with a broader set of categories, we also test on **Castrejon** et al.'s [3] large dataset containing 205 scene categories in different modalities. Our method also uses a photorealistic modality as the original source modality; this is either the photo domain from the respective dataset, or COCO [23] (for our new dataset).

PACS [21] contains four domains, three artistic (sketches, cartoons, and paintings) and one photorealistic, which we use as the original, non-synthetic source domain. The dataset contains seven object categories (e.g. "dog", "elephant", "horse", "guitar") and 9,991 images in total. The authors demonstrate the much larger shift exhibited in PACS compared to prior adaptation datasets, by showing KL divergence and cross-domain accuracy loss statistics.

The Sketchy Database [31] contains 75,471 human-drawn sketches and accompanying photographs, from 125 common object categories in ImageNet.

Castrejon [3] extends the Places dataset [41] containing 205 scene categories by providing four new modalities: sketches, clipart, text descriptions, and spatial text images. We use the two *visual* modalities, sketches and clipart.

New Dataset: CASPA. Since the PACS dataset [21] is small, we complemented it by assembling images in the same three modalities as PACS. We use this additional dataset to test our conclusions on more test data. We call the dataset CASPA: (Cartoons, Sketches, Paintings). We assembled a dataset of 5,047 cartoons by querying Google Image Search with each of the ten animal categories from COCO: "bear", "bird", "cat", "cow", "dog", "elephant", "giraffe", "horse", "sheep", and "zebra". We chose these categories because sketch data of these animal classes was available. We also collected a new dataset of how different painters paint objects. We downloaded 1,391 paintings[1] which cover eight of our ten categories (except "giraffe" and "zebra"), and annotated these images with *2,834 bounding boxes*. Note that another painting dataset exists [14] but it only contains four of the ten classes we consider. To maintain the same set of domains as those used in PACS, we also include 12,008 sketches from

---

[1] from http://www.arab-painting.com/pic/Oil Painting Styles on Canvas/Animals.

the Sketchy Database [31]. PACS uses seven categories from [31], while we use twenty categories and collapse them down into coarser categories (i.e. different types of birds became the coarse category "bird"). In total, the dataset contains 18,446 images, almost twice more than PACS' 9,991. The dataset is available at http://www.cs.pitt.edu/~chris/artistic_objects/. As our photorealistic source domain, we use COCO [23]. Because images in COCO contain multiple objects, we use the provided bounding boxes to produce cropped images containing a single object, and eliminate crops which do not contain the ten animal categories listed above.

4.2 Baselines

We compare against several recent unsupervised domain adaptation methods; these do not require any labeled data on the target domain.

- GONG et al. [11] is a pre-CNN method which shows how statistical differences between features extracted from two domains can be corrected, by learning the geodesic flow between the two domains. We use FC7 features.
- GANIN and Lempitsky [6] make CNNs modality-invariant by learning features such that the CNN is unable to distinguish which modality the image came from, via a domain confusion loss. Since no labeled data is available from the target, we only use [6]'s domain confusion loss but not the classification loss.
- GHIFARY et al. [8] train an encoder-decoder architecture to compute the reconstruction loss with the target domain's data, and use the resulting features to train a classifier on the labeled source data.
- LONG et al. [25] propose to train separate classifiers for the source and target domain which differ only by a residual function. The source and target classifiers can still preserve domain-specific cues useful for classifying in that domain, but the source classifier is expressed as a residual function of the target classifier, and its residual layers capture the source-only features.
- CASTREJON et al. [3] learn a representation across scenes, by fixing the higher layers of the network while the lower layers are allowed to learn a domain-dependent representation. However, unlike [3], we cannot learn modality-specific lower-layer features without target labels. We train on ImageNet and fine-tune the higher layers on our photo labeled data, but we skip the second part of [3]'s "Method A" since we do not have labels on the modality data; we instead use generic pretrained ImageNet lower-level features.
- BOUSMALIS et al. [1] use a generative adversarial network (GAN) to transform labeled source data to appear as if it were target data. The generator adapts source images to fool the discriminator, while the discriminator attempts to distinguish between the generator's output and real target images. A classifier is jointly trained to classify the original and translated source images.

We also compare against PHOTO-ALEXNET, a standard AlexNet [20], trained on 1.3M ImageNet samples, fine-tuned on our photorealistic domain (COCO/Places, respectively). See our supplementary file for results using ResNet.

Note that we do not compare to the domain *generalization* approach in [21] since it assumes the availability of *multiple* human-labeled source modalities at training time, while we only require one. For BOUSMALIS et al. and GHIFARY et al. we use data generated by their methods instead of our style-transferred data, then proceed with training a network with two modalities and domain confusion loss. We found this made these methods more competitive.

Table 1. Our method outperforms all other domain adaptation techniques on average. The best method is in **bold** (excluding upper bound), and the second-best in *italics*.

Method	Target domain								Sketchy
	PACS				CASPA				
	Paint	Cart	Sketch	AVG	Paint	Cart	Sketch	AVG	Sketch
PHOTO-ALEXNET	0.560	0.276	0.328	0.388	0.663	0.222	0.398	0.428	0.093
GONG [11]	0.487	0.310	0.305	0.367	0.309	0.200	0.463	0.324	0.112
GANIN [6]	**0.624**	*0.638*	0.351	0.538	0.652	0.251	0.202	0.368	0.112
GHIFARY [8]	0.453	0.561	0.371	0.462	0.631	0.388	0.418	0.479	0.225
LONG [25]	0.614	**0.668**	0.417	0.566	0.628	*0.425*	0.497	0.517	*0.303*
CASTREJON [3]	0.580	0.293	0.328	0.400	0.628	0.231	0.458	0.439	0.085
BOUSMALIS [1]	0.609	0.472	0.559	0.547	0.666	0.408	0.482	0.519	0.284
OURS-JOHNSON	**0.624**	0.485	*0.653*	*0.587*	*0.677*	0.406	**0.625**	**0.569**	**0.326**
OURS-HUANG	0.619	0.480	**0.689**	**0.596**	**0.698**	**0.464**	*0.501*	*0.554*	0.234
UPPER BOUND	0.863	0.927	0.921	0.904	0.842	0.741	0.917	0.833	0.822

4.3 Results

In Table 1, we show the results of our comparison to state-of-the-art unsupervised domain adaptation methods. We first show the result of *not* performing any adaptation (PHOTO-ALEXNET). We then show the performance of six domain adaptation techniques (from 2012, 2015, 2016, and 2017). We next show the two versions of our method, using style transfer techniques from Johnson (Sect. 3.1) and Huang (Sect. 3.2). Finally, we show the performance of an UPPER BOUND method which "cheats" by having access to labeled target data at training time, which none of the baselines nor our methods see. We split the data from each modality into 90%/10% training/test sets (for the sake of the upper bound which requires target data). All results show top-1 accuracy.

Our Results. We see that one of our methods is always the best performer per dataset (average columns for **PACS** and **CASPA**, and the single column for **Sketchy**), and the other is second-best in two of three cases. For cartoons and paintings, OURS-HUANG is the stronger of our two methods, or our two methods perform similarly. On the full **Sketchy** dataset, which **PACS-Sketch** and **CASPA-Sketch** are subsets of, OURS-JOHNSON performs much better (by about 40%). This is because [17] and thus OURS-HUANG has trouble generating high-quality sketch transfer. This tendency holds for the subset chosen in

CASPA (as [19] is better than [17] by about 25%), but on the subset in **PACS**, [17] does somewhat better (6%). We believe this is due to the choice of categories in each sketch subset; we illustrate these results in our supplementary. Note **Sketchy** contains many more classes hence the lower performance overall.

While we observe *some* qualitative correlation between visual quality of the style transferred images and utility of the data for training our classifiers, we note that our key concern in this work is utility, not visual quality. We do observe, however, that in some cases loss of detail in synthetic sketches may be causing our classifiers trained on such data to struggle with classification, particularly for OURS-HUANG. We explore this problem in detail in our supplementary material.

Baseline Results. Our style transfer approach outperforms all other domain adaptation methods on all types of data except **PACS-Painting** (where it ties for best performance with GANIN), and on **PACS-Cartoon**. Our method outperforms the strongest baseline by 23% for **PACS-Sketch** (w.r.t. BOUSMALIS), 5% for **CASPA-Painting** (w.r.t. BOUSMALIS), 9% for **CASPA-Cartoon** (w.r.t. LONG), and 25% for **CASPA-Sketch** (w.r.t. LONG). On average, OURS-JOHNSON and OURS-HUANG outperform the best baseline by 4%/5% respectively on **PACS** (w.r.t. LONG), and 10%/7% on **CASPA** (w.r.t. LONG). OURS-JOHNSON outperforms LONG by 8% for **Sketchy**. To underscore the importance of style adaptation as opposed to naïve data transformations, we show using style transferred data outperforms edge maps (which are sketch-like) on sketches in our supp. file.

Interestingly, on **CASPA-Painting**, only three domain adaptation methods outperform the no-adaptation photo-only model, but our two are the only ones that do so by a significant margin. As shown in [21], paintings are closer to photographs than cartoons and sketches are, so it is not surprising that several domain adaptation methods fail to improve upon the source model's performance. By explicitly accounting for the style of the target modality, we improve the photo model's accuracy by 5%.

Data Requirements. Overall, the strongest baseline is LONG. The most recent method, BOUSMALIS [1], performs second-best. The performance of this GAN model is limited by the amount of training data available. While [1] uses all unlabeled target samples, that set of target samples is too limited to adequately train a full generative adversarial network. As a point of comparison, in their original work, [1] use 1000 *labeled* target images just to verify their hyperparameters. This is 100 times the amount of target data we use for domain adaptation in OURS-JOHNSON. This result underscores one of the key strengths of our approach: its ability to explicitly distill and control for style while requiring little target data. Notice that for all domain adaptation methods, there is still a large gap between the unsupervised recognition performance, and the supervised upper bound's performance.

Ablations. Our method is a framework for domain adaptation that explicitly accounts for the artistic style variations between domains. Within this framework, we show how to make the best use of limited target data, via the style selection technique in Sect. 3.1. In Sect. 3.4, we encourage style-invariant features to be learned, via a domain confusion loss over the source domains. We briefly demonstrate the benefit of these two techniques here; see the supplementary file for the full ablation study.

Style selection of ten diverse target style images has a great advantage over randomly choosing ten images for transfer. On **PACS-Sketches**, style selection achieves a 15% improvement over randomly choosing the style images (0.653 vs 0.569) and it achieves 14% improvement on **PACS-Cartoons** (0.485 vs 0.425). While style selection does require access to the target dataset to *choose* the representative styles from, our technique still significantly improves performance when a single set of ten images are selected at random (i.e. when the target data pool is limited to ten images); see our supp. for more details.

Encouraging style invariance via the domain confusion loss also boosts performance, by 28% (0.384 for style transfer using random targets and domain confusion loss, vs 0.299 without that loss) for **CASPA-Cartoons**, and 16% for **CASPA-Sketches** (0.594 vs 0.513).

Results on Castrejon's Dataset. In Table 2, we evaluate our methods against the two strongest baselines from Table 1, this time on the scene classification task in [3]'s dataset. Note that unlike [3], we do not train on target labels, and we only train with 250K Places images. Performance is low overall on this 205-way task. While our methods' performance is closely followed by BOUSMALIS, our methods perform best. In particular, OURS-JOHNSON outperforms both BOUSMALIS and LONG on both modalities. This experiment confirms our conclusions from Table 1 that explicitly controlling for style variation is key when the domain shift is caused by artistic style.

Table 2. Scene classification results using [3]'s data.

Method	Castrejon-Clipart	Castrejon-Sketches
PHOTO-ALEXNET	0.0689	0.0213
LONG [25]	0.0727	0.0402
BOUSMALIS [1]	0.0839	*0.0464*
OURS-JOHNSON	*0.0847*	**0.0479**
OURS-HUANG	**0.0885**	0.0456
UPPER BOUND	0.5937	0.3120

Supplementary File. Please see our supplementary for extensive additional experiments showing the performance of ablations of our method (comparing style selection vs. selecting random style images), methods that use a single source modality (including the synthetic modalities generated by our method), domain-agnostic style transfer using edge maps, a comparison of methods using the ResNet architecture, and a detailed exploration of the differences between the Huang [17] and Johnson [19] style transfer methods which help determine which method is appropriate for a given target domain.

5   Conclusion

We addressed the problem of training CNNs to recognize objects in unlabeled artistic modalities. We found the introduction of style-mimicking training modalities generated for free results in a domain-invariant representation. We confirm in extensive experiments that our method outperforms a variety of state-of-the-art and standard baselines. Compared to recent works which create synthetic training data, our method requires far less target data (as few as ten unlabeled target images) and is easier to train. We also release a large dataset in photographs and images showing objects across multiple artistic domains. Currently our method cannot handle large, exaggerated shape differences found in some cartoons or sketches. In future work, we will investigate making our domain adaptation method even more robust by performing more aggressive transformations, so we can recognize objects in even more abstract artistic renderings.

References

1. Bousmalis, K., Silberman, N., Dohan, D., Erhan, D., Krishnan, D.: Unsupervised pixel-level domain adaptation with generative adversarial networks. In: CVPR (IEEE) (2017)
2. Bousmalis, K., Trigeorgis, G., Silberman, N., Krishnan, D., Erhan, D.: Domain separation networks. In: NIPS (2016)
3. Castrejon, L., Aytar, Y., Vondrick, C., Pirsiavash, H., Torralba, A.: Learning aligned cross-modal representations from weakly aligned data. In: CVPR (IEEE) (2016)
4. Chen, D., Liao, J., Yuan, L., Yu, N., Hua, G.: Coherent online video style transfer. In: ICCV (IEEE) (2017)
5. Chen, D., Yuan, L., Liao, J., Yu, N., Hua, G.: StyleBank: an explicit representation for neural image style transfer. In: CVPR (IEEE) (2017)
6. Ganin, Y., Lempitsky, V.: Unsupervised domain adaptation by backpropagation. In: ICML (2015)
7. Gatys, L.A., Ecker, A.S., Bethge, M.: Image style transfer using convolutional neural networks. In: CVPR (IEEE) (2016)
8. Ghifary, M., Kleijn, W.B., Zhang, M., Balduzzi, D., Li, W.: Deep reconstruction-classification networks for unsupervised domain adaptation. In: Leibe, B., Matas, J., Sebe, N., Welling, M. (eds.) ECCV 2016. LNCS, vol. 9908, pp. 597–613. Springer, Cham (2016). https://doi.org/10.1007/978-3-319-46493-0_36
9. Ginosar, S., Haas, D., Brown, T., Malik, J.: Detecting people in Cubist art. In: Agapito, L., Bronstein, M.M., Rother, C. (eds.) ECCV 2014. LNCS, vol. 8925, pp. 101–116. Springer, Cham (2015). https://doi.org/10.1007/978-3-319-16178-5_7
10. Gong, B., Grauman, K., Sha, F.: Reshaping visual datasets for domain adaptation. In: NIPS (2013)

11. Gong, B., Shi, Y., Sha, F., Grauman, K.: Geodesic flow kernel for unsupervised domain adaptation. In: CVPR (IEEE) (2012)
12. Goodfellow, I., et al.: Generative adversarial nets. In: NIPS (2014)
13. Gupta, S., Hoffman, J., Malik, J.: Cross modal distillation for supervision transfer. In: CVPR (IEEE) (2016)
14. Hall, P., Cai, H., Wu, Q., Corradi, T.: Cross-depiction problem: recognition and synthesis of photographs and artwork. Comput. Vis. Media 1(2), 91–103 (2015)
15. Hoffman, J., et l.: Cycada: Cycle-consistent adversarial domain adaptation. In: ICML (2018)
16. Huang, H., et al.: Real-time neural style transfer for videos. In: CVPR (IEEE) (2017)
17. Huang, X., Belongie, S.: Arbitrary style transfer in real-time with adaptive instance normalization. In: ICCV (IEEE) (2017)
18. Jia, Y., et al.: Caffe: convolutional architecture for fast feature embedding. In: Proceedings of the ACM International Conference on Multimedia (2014)
19. Johnson, J., Alahi, A., Fei-Fei, L.: Perceptual losses for real-time style transfer and super-resolution. In: Leibe, B., Matas, J., Sebe, N., Welling, M. (eds.) ECCV 2016. LNCS, vol. 9906, pp. 694–711. Springer, Cham (2016). https://doi.org/10.1007/978-3-319-46475-6_43
20. Krizhevsky, A., Sutskever, I., Hinton, G.E.: ImageNet classification with deep convolutional neural networks. In: NIPS (2012)
21. Li, D., Yang, Y., Song, Y.Z., Hospedales, T.M.: Deeper, broader and artier domain generalization. In: ICCV (IEEE) (2017)
22. Li, W., Xu, Z., Xu, D., Dai, D., Van Gool, L.: Domain generalization andadaptation using low rank exemplar SVMs. IEEE Trans. Pattern Anal. Mach. Intell. 40, 1114–1127 (2017)
23. Lin, T.Y., et al.: Microsoft COCO: common objects in context. In: Fleet, D., Pajdla, T., Schiele, B., Tuytelaars, T. (eds.) ECCV 2014. LNCS, vol. 8693, pp. 740–755. Springer, Cham (2014). https://doi.org/10.1007/978-3-319-10602-1_48
24. Long, M., Cao, Y., Wang, J.: Learning transferable features with deep adaptation networks. In: ICML (2015)
25. Long, M., Zhu, H., Wang, J., Jordan, M.I.: Unsupervised domain adaptation with residual transfer networks. In: NIPS (2016)
26. Muandet, K., Balduzzi, D., Schölkopf, B.: Domain generalization via invariant feature representation. In: ICML (2013)
27. Niu, L., Li, W., Xu, D.: Visual recognition by learning from web data: a weakly supervised domain generalization approach. In: CVPR (IEEE) (2015)
28. Oquab, M., Bottou, L., Laptev, I., Sivic, J.: Learning and transferring mid-level image representations using convolutional neural networks. In: CVPR (IEEE) (2014)
29. Russakovsky, O., et al.: ImageNet large scale visual recognition challenge. Int. J. Comput. Vis. 115, 211–252 (2015)
30. Salimans, T., Goodfellow, I., Zaremba, W., Cheung, V., Radford, A., Chen, X.: Improved techniques for training GANs. In: NIPS (2016)
31. Sangkloy, P., Burnell, N., Ham, C., Hays, J.: The sketchy database: learning to retrieve badly drawn bunnies. ACM Trans. Graph. (TOG) 35(4), 119 (2016)
32. Simonyan, K., Zisserman, A.: Very deep convolutional networks for large-scale image recognition. In: ICLR (2015)
33. Tenenbaum, J.B., Freeman, W.T.: Separating style and content. In: NIPS (1997)
34. Thomas, C., Kovashka, A.: Seeing behind the camera: identifying the authorship of a photograph. In: CVPR (IEEE) (2016)

35. Tzeng, E., Hoffman, J., Darrell, T., Saenko, K.: Simultaneous deep transfer across domains and tasks. In: ICCV (IEEE) (2015)
36. Tzeng, E., Hoffman, J., Saenko, K., Darrell, T.: Adversarial discriminative domain adaptation. In: CVPR (IEEE) (2017)
37. Wilber, M.J., Fang, C., Jin, H., Hertzmann, A., Collomosse, J., Belongie, S.: BAM! the Behance artistic media dataset for recognition beyond photography. In: CVPR (IEEE) (2017)
38. Wu, Q., Cai, H., Hall, P.: Learning graphs to model visual objects across different depictive styles. In: Fleet, D., Pajdla, T., Schiele, B., Tuytelaars, T. (eds.) ECCV 2014. LNCS, vol. 8695, pp. 313–328. Springer, Cham (2014). https://doi.org/10. 1007/978-3-319-10584-0_21
39. Xu, Z., Li, W., Niu, L., Xu, D.: Exploiting low-rank structure from latent domains for domain generalization. In: Fleet, D., Pajdla, T., Schiele, B., Tuytelaars, T. (eds.) ECCV 2014. LNCS, vol. 8691, pp. 628–643. Springer, Cham (2014). https://doi. org/10.1007/978-3-319-10578-9_41
40. Zhang, X.Y., Liu, C.L.: Writer adaptation with style transfer mapping. IEEE Trans. Pattern Anal. Mach. Intell. **35**(7), 1773–1787 (2013)
41. Zhou, B., Lapedriza, A., Xiao, J., Torralba, A., Oliva, A.: Learning deep features for scene recognition using places database. In: NIPS (2014)

iPose: Instance-Aware 6D Pose Estimation of Partly Occluded Objects

Omid Hosseini Jafari[✉], Siva Karthik Mustikovela, Karl Pertsch,
Eric Brachmann, and Carsten Rother

Visual Learning Lab, Heidelberg University (HCI/IWR), Heidelberg, Germany
{omid.hosseini_jafari,siva.mustikovela}@iwr.uni-heidelberg.de

Abstract. We address the task of 6D pose estimation of known rigid
objects from single input images in scenarios where the objects are
partly occluded. Recent RGB-D-based methods are robust to moderate degrees of occlusion. For RGB inputs, no previous method works
well for partly occluded objects. Our main contribution is to present the
first deep learning-based system that estimates accurate poses for partly
occluded objects from RGB-D and RGB input. We achieve this with
a new instance-aware pipeline that decomposes 6D object pose estimation into a sequence of simpler steps, where each step removes specific
aspects of the problem. The first step localizes all known objects in the
image using an instance segmentation network, and hence eliminates
surrounding clutter and occluders. The second step densely maps pixels to 3D object surface positions, so called object coordinates, using an
encoder-decoder network, and hence eliminates object appearance. The
third, and final, step predicts the 6D pose using geometric optimization.
We demonstrate that we significantly outperform the state-of-the-art for
pose estimation of partly occluded objects for both RGB and RGB-D
input.

1 Introduction

Localization of object instances from single input images has been a long-
standing goal in computer vision. The task evolved from simple 2D detection
to full 6D pose estimation, *i.e.* estimating the 3D position and 3D orientation of
the object relative to the observing camera. Early approaches relied on objects
having sufficient texture to match feature points [30]. Later, with the advent of
consumer depth cameras, research focused on texture-less objects [15] in increasingly cluttered environments. Today, heavy occlusion of objects is the main performance benchmark for one-shot pose estimation methods.

O. Hosseini Jafari and S. K. Mustikovela—Equal contribution.

Electronic supplementary material The online version of this chapter (https://
doi.org/10.1007/978-3-030-20893-6_30) contains supplementary material, which is
available to authorized users.

C. V. Jawahar et al. (Eds.): ACCV 2018, LNCS 11363, pp. 477–492, 2019.
https://doi.org/10.1007/978-3-030-20893-6_30

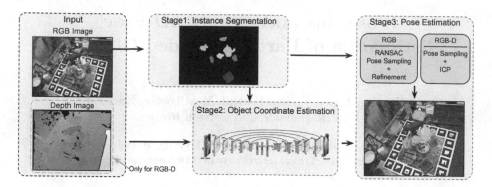

Fig. 1. Illustration of our modular, 3-stage pipeline for both RGB and RGB-D input images.

Recent RGB-D-based methods [16,31] are robust to moderate degrees of object occlusion. However, depth cameras fail under certain conditions, *e.g.* with intense sunlight, and RGB cameras are prevalent on many types of devices. Hence, RGB-based methods still have high practical relevance. In this work, we present a system for 6D pose estimation of rigid object instances with heavy occlusion, from single input images. Our method outperforms the state-of-the-art for both RGB and RGB-D input modalities.

During the last decade, computer vision has seen a large shift towards learning-based methods. In particular, deep learning has massively improved accuracy and robustness for many tasks. While 6D object pose estimation has also benefited from deep learning to some extent, with recent methods being able to estimate accurate poses in real time from single RGB images [20,33,38], the same does not hold when objects are partly occluded. In this case, aforementioned methods, despite being trained with partly occluded objects, either break down [20,38] or have to simplify the task by estimating poses from tight crops around the ground truth object position [33]. To the best of our knowledge, we are the first to show that deep learning can improve results considerably for objects that are moderately to heavily occluded, particularly for the difficult case of RGB input.

At the core, our method decomposes the 6D pose estimation problem into a sequence of three sub-tasks, or modules (see Fig. 1). We first detect the object in 2D, then we locally regress correspondences to the 3D object surface, and, finally, we estimate the 6D pose of the object. With each sub-task, we can remove specific aspects of the problem, such as object background and object appearance. In the first module, 2D detection is implemented by an instance segmentation network which estimates a tight mask for each object. Thus, we can separate the object from surrounding clutter and occluders, making the following steps invariant to the object environment, and allowing us to process each detected instance individually. In the second module, we present an encoder-decoder architecture for densely regressing so-called *object coordinates* [4], *i.e.* 3D points in the local coordinate frame of the object which define 2D-3D correspondences between the image and the object. The third module is a purely geometric pose optimization which is not learned from data because all aspects of object appearance have been removed in the previous steps. Since we estimate 6D poses successively from 2D instance segmentation, we call our approach *iPose*, short for "instance-aware pose estimation".

Our decomposition strategy is conceptually simple, but we show that it is considerably superior to other deep learning-based methods that try to reason about different aspects of these steps jointly. In particular, several recent works propose to extend state-of-the-art object detection networks to output 6D object poses directly. Kehl *et al.* [20] extend the SSD object detector [29] to recognize discretized view-points of specific objects, *i.e.* re-formulating pose regression as a classification problem. Similarly, Tekin *et al.* [38] extend the YOLO object detector [34] by letting image grid cells predict object presence, and simultaneously the 6D pose. Both approaches are highly sensitive to object occlusion, as we will show in the experimental evaluation. Directly predicting the 6D pose from observed object appearance is challenging, due to limited training data and innumerable occlusion possibilities.

We see three reasons for the success of our approach. Firstly, we exploit the massive progress in object detection and instance segmentation achieved by methods like MNC [6] and Mask R-CNN [12]. This is similar in spirit to the work of [20,38], but instead of extending the instance segmentation to predict 6D poses directly, we use it as a decoupled component within our step-by-step strategy. Secondly, the rich structural output of our dense object coordinate regression step allows for a geometric hypothesize-and-verify approach that can yield a good pose estimate even if parts of the prediction are incorrect, *e.g.* due to occlusion. Such a robust geometry-based step is missing in previous deep learning-based approaches [20,33,38]. Thirdly, we propose a new data augmentation scheme specifically designed for the task of 6D object pose estimation. Data augmentation is a common aspect of learning-based pose estimation methods, since training data is usually scarce. Previous works have placed objects at random 2D locations over arbitrary background images [3,20,33], which yields constellations where objects occlude each other in physically impossible ways. In contrast, our data augmentation scheme infers a common ground plane from ground truth poses and places additional objects in a physically plausible fashion. Hence, our data augmentation results in more realistic occlusion patterns which we found crucial for obtaining good results.

We summarize our main **contributions**:

- We propose *iPose*, a new deep learning architecture for 6D object pose estimation which is remarkably robust w.r.t. object occlusion, using a new three-step task decomposition approach.
- We are the first to surpass the state-of-the-art for partly occluded objects with a deep learning-based approach for both RGB-D and RGB inputs.

– We present a new data augmentation scheme for object pose estimation which generates physically plausible occlusion patterns, crucial for obtaining good results.

2   Related Work

Here, we give an overview of previous methods for 6D object pose estimation. Early pose estimation methods were based on matching sparse features [30] or templates [18]. Templates work well for texture-less objects where sparse feature detectors fail to identify salient points. Hinterstoisser *et al.* proposed the LINEMOD templates [15], which combine gradient and normal cues for robust object detection given RGB-D inputs. Annotating the template database with viewpoint information facilitates accurate 6D pose estimation [14,17,22,25,35]. An RGB version of LINEMOD [13] is less suited for pose estimation [3]. In general, template-based methods suffer from sensitivity to occlusion [4].

With a depth channel available, good results have been achieved by voting-based schemes [7,8,16,21,37,39]. In particular, Drost *et al.* [8] cast votes by matching point-pair features which combine normal and distance information. Recently, the method was considerably improved in [16] by a suitable sampling scheme, resulting in a purely geometric method that achieves state-of-the-art results for partly occluded objects given RGB-D inputs. Our deep learning-based pipeline achieves higher accuracy, and can also be applied to RGB images.

Recently, CNN-based methods have become increasingly popular for object pose estimation from RGB images. Rad *et al.* [33] presented the BB8 pipeline which resembles our decomposition philosophy to some extent. But their processing steps are more tightly coupled. For example, their initial detection stage does not segment the object, and can thus not remove object background. Also, they regress the 6D pose by estimating the 2D location of a sparse set of control points. We show that dense 3D object coordinate regression provides a richer output which is essential for robust geometric pose optimization. Rad *et al.* [33] evaluate BB8 on occluded objects but restrict pose prediction to image crops around the ground truth object position[1]. Our approach yields superior results for partly occluded objects *without* using prior knowledge about object position.

Direct regression of a 6D pose vector by a neural network, *e.g.* proposed by Kendall *et al.* for camera localization [23], exhibits low accuracy [5]. The works discussed in the introduction, *i.e.* Kehl *et al.* [20] and Tekin *et al.* [38], also regress object pose directly but make use of alternative pose parametrizations, namely discrete view point classification [20], or sparse control point regression [38] similar to BB8 [33]. We do *not* predict the 6D pose directly, but follow a step-by-step strategy to robustly obtain the 6D pose despite strong occlusions.

Object coordinates have been used previously for object pose estimation from RGB-D [4,26,31] or RGB inputs [3]. In these works, random forest matches image patches to 3D points in the local coordinate frame of the object, and

---

[1] Their experimental setup relies on ground truth crops and is not explicitly described in [33]. We verified this information via private email exchange with the authors.

the pose is recovered by robust, geometric optimization. Because few correct correspondences suffice for a pose estimate, these methods are inherently robust to object occlusion. In contrast to our work, they combine object coordinate prediction and object segmentation in a single module, using random forests. These two tasks are disentangled in our approach, with the clear advantage that each individual object mask is known for object coordinate regression. In this context, we are also the first to successfully train a neural network for object coordinate regression of known objects. Overall, we report superior pose accuracy for partly occluded objects using RGB and RGB-D inputs. Note that recently Behl *et al.* [2] have trained a network for object coordinate regression of vehicles (*i.e.* object class). However, our network, training procedure, and data augmentation scheme differ from [2].

To cope well with limited training data, we propose a new data augmentation scheme which generates physically plausible occlusion patterns. While plausible data augmentation is becoming common in object class detection works, see *e.g.* [1,9,28], our scheme is tailored specifically towards object instance pose estimation where previous works resorted to pasting 2D object crops on arbitrary RGB backgrounds [3,20,33]. We found physically plausible data augmentation to be crucial for obtaining good results for partly occluded objects.

To summarize, only few previous works have addressed the challenging task of pose estimation of partly occluded objects from single RGB or RGB-D inputs. We present the first viable deep learning approach for this scenario, improving state-of-the-art accuracy considerably for both input types.

3 Method

In this section, we describe our three-stage, instance-aware approach for 6D object pose estimation. The overall workflow of our method is illustrated in Fig. 1. Firstly, we obtain all object instances in a given image using an instance segmentation network (Sect. 3.1). Secondly, we estimate dense 3D object coordinates for each instance using an encoder-decoder network (Sect. 3.2). Thirdly, we use the pixel-wise correspondences between predicted object coordinates and the input image to sample 6D pose hypotheses, and further refine them using an iterative geometric optimization (Sect. 3.3). In Sect. 3.4, we describe our object-centric data augmentation procedure which we use to generate additional training data with realistic occlusions for the encoder-decoder network of step 2.

We denote the RGB input to our pipeline as I and RGB-D input as I-D. $\mathcal{K} = \{1, ..., K\}$ is a set of all known object classes, a subset of which could be present in the image. The goal of our method is to take an image I/I-D containing n objects $\mathcal{O} = \{O_1, ..., O_n\}$, each of which has a class from $\mathcal{K}$, and to estimate their 6D poses. Below, we describe each step of our pipeline in detail.

3.1 Stage 1: Instance Segmentation

The first step of our approach, instance segmentation, recognizes the identity of each object, and produces a fine grained mask. Thus we can separate the

RGB(-D) information pertaining only to a specific object from surrounding clutter and occluders. To achieve this, we utilize instance segmentation frameworks
such as [6,12]. Given an input I, the output of this network is a set of n instance
masks $\mathcal{M} = \{M_1, ..., M_n\}$ and an object class $k \in \mathcal{K}$ for each mask.

3.2 Stage 2: Object Coordinate Regression

An object coordinate denotes the 3D position of an object surface point in the
object's local coordinate frame. Thus given a pixel location p and its predicted
object coordinate C, a (p, C) pair defines a correspondence between an image I
and object O. Multiple such correspondences, at least three for RGB-D data and
four for RGB data, are required to recover the 6D object pose (see Sect. 3.3). In
order to regress pixelwise object coordinates C for each detected object, we use
a CNN with an encoder-decoder style architecture with skip connections. The
encoder consists of 5 convolutional layers with a stride of 2 in each layer, followed
by a set of 3 fully connected layers. The decoder has 5 deconvolutional layers
followed by the 3 layer output corresponding to 3-dimensional object coordinates.
Skip connections exist between symmetrically opposite conv-deconv layers. As
input for this network, we crop a detected object using its estimated mask M,
resize and pad the crop to a fixed size, and pass it through the object coordinate
network. The output of this network has 3 channels containing the pixelwise X,
Y and Z values of object coordinates C for mask M. We train separate networks
for RGB and RGB-D inputs.

3.3 Stage 3: Pose Estimation

In this section, we describe the geometric pose optimization step of our approach
for RGB-D and RGB inputs, respectively. This step is not learned from data,
but recovers the 6D object pose from the instance mask M of stage 1 and the
object coordinates C of stage 2.

RGB-D Setup. Our pose estimation is inspired by the original object coordinate framework of [4]. Compared to [4], we use a simplified scoring function to
rank pose hypotheses, and an Iterative Closest Point (ICP) refinement.

In detail, we use the depth channel and the mask M_O to calculate a 3D point
cloud P_O associated with object O w.r.t. the coordinate frame of the camera.
Also, stage 2 yields the pixelwise predicted object coordinates C_O. We seek the
6D pose H_O^* which relates object coordinates C_O with the point cloud P_O. For
ease of notation, we drop the subscript O, assuming that we are describing the
process for that particular object instance. We randomly sample three pixels
j_1, j_2, j_3 from mask M, from which we establish three 3D-3D correspondences
(P^{j_1}, C^{j_1}), (P^{j_2}, C^{j_2}), (P^{j_3}, C^{j_3}). We use the Kabsch algorithm [19] to compute
the pose hypothesis H_i from these correspondences. Using H_i, we transform C^{j_1},
C^{j_2}, C^{j_3} from the object coordinate frame to the camera coordinate frame. Let
these transformed points be T^j. We compute the Euclidean distance, $\|P^j, T^j\|$,
and if the distances of all three points are less than 10% of the object diameter,

we add H_i to our hypothesis pool. We repeat this process until we have collected 210 hypotheses. For each hypothesis H, we obtain a point cloud $P^*(H)$ in the camera coordinate system via rendering the object CAD model. This lets us score each hypothesis using

$$S_{\text{RGB-D}}(H) = \frac{\sum_{j \in M} \left[\|P^j - P^{*j}(H)\| < d/10 \right]}{|M|}, \tag{1}$$

where $[\cdot]$ returns 1 if the enclosed condition is true, and the sum is over pixels inside the mask M and normalized. The score $S_{\text{RGB-D}}(H)$ computes the average number the pixels inside the mask for which the rendered camera coordinates $P^{*j}(H)$ and the observed camera coordinates P^j agree, up to a tolerance of 10% of the object diameter d. From the initial pool of 210 hypotheses we select the top 20 according to the score $S_{\text{RGB-D}}(H)$. Finally, for each selected hypothesis, we perform ICP refinement with P as the target, the CAD model vertices as the source, and H_i as initialization. We choose the pose with the lowest ICP fitting error H_{ICP} for further refinement.

Rendering-Based Refinement. Under the assumption that the estimate H_{ICP} is already quite accurate, and using the instance mask M, we perform the following additional refinement: using H_{ICP}, we render the CAD model to obtain a point cloud P_r of the visible object surface. This is in contrast to the previous ICP refinement where all CAD model vertices were used. We fit P_r inside the mask M to the observed point cloud P via ICP, to obtain a refining transformation H_{ref}. This additional step pushes P_r towards the observed point cloud P, providing a further refinement to H_{ICP}. The final pose is thus obtained by $H^*_{\text{RGB-D}} = H_{\text{ICP}} * H_{\text{ref}}$.

Our instance-based approach is a clear advantage in both refinement steps, since we can use the estimated mask to precisely carve out the observed point cloud for ICP.

Fig. 2. Object centric data augmentation pipeline. (a) If the cropped object (Ape) is inserted within the red area, it can cause a physically plausible occlusion for the center object (Can). (b) shows the resulting augmented RGB image, and (c) shows the resulting augmented depth image. (Color figure online)

RGB Setup. Given RGB data, we follow Brachmann *et al.* [3] and estimate the pose of the objects through hypotheses sampling [4] and pre-emptive RANSAC

[36]. At this stage, the predicted object mask M and the predicted object coordinates C inside the mask are available. For each pixel j at the 2D position p_j inside M, the object coordinate network estimates a 3D point C^j in the local object coordinate system. Thus, we can sample 2D-3D correspondences between 2D points of the image and 3D object coordinate points from the area inside the object mask. Our goal is to search for a pose hypothesis H^* which maximizes the following score:

$$S_{\mathrm{RGB}}(H) = \sum_{j \in M} \left[\|p_j - AHC^j\|_2 < \tau_{\mathrm{in}} \right], \tag{2}$$

where A is the camera projection matrix, τ_{in} is a threshold, and $[\cdot]$ is 1 if the statement inside the bracket is true, otherwise 0. The score $S_{\mathrm{RGB}}(H)$ counts the number of pixel-residuals of re-projected object coordinate estimates which are below τ_{in}. We use pre-emptive RANSAC to maximize this objective function. We start by drawing four correspondences from the predicted mask M. Then, we solve the perspective-n-point problem (PnP) [10, 27] to obtain a pose hypothesis. If the re-projection error of the initial four correspondences is below threshold τ_{in} we keep the hypothesis. We repeat this process until 256 pose hypotheses have been collected. We score each hypothesis with $S_{\mathrm{RGB}}(H)$, but only using a sub-sampling of N pixels inside the mask for faster computation. We sort the hypotheses by score and discard the lower half. We refine the remaining hypotheses by re-solving PnP using their inlier pixels according to $S_{\mathrm{RGB}}(H)$. We repeat scoring with an increased pixel count N, discarding and refining hypotheses until only one hypothesis H_{RGB}^* remains as the final estimated pose.

3.4 Data Augmentation

Data augmentation is crucial for creating the amount of data necessary to train a CNN. Additionally, data augmentation can help to reduce dataset bias, and introduce novel examples for the network to train on. One possibility for data augmentation is to paste objects on a random background, where mutually overlapping objects occlude each other. This is done *e.g.* in [3, 20, 33] and we found this strategy sufficient for training our instance segmentation network in step 1. However, the resulting images and occlusion patterns are highly implausible, especially for RGB-D data where objects float in the scene, and occlude each other in physically impossible ways. Training the object coordinate network in step 2 with such implausible data made it difficult for the network to converge and also introduced bias towards impossible object occlusion configurations. In the following, we present an object-centric data augmentation strategy which generates plausible object occlusion patterns, and analyze its impact on the dataset. We assume that for each target object k in the set of all known objects $\mathcal{K}$, a sequence of images is available where the object is not occluded. For each image, we compute the ground plane on which the target object stands, as well as the distance between its base point and the camera. Then, as shown in Fig. 2(a) (red), a surface of interest is defined on the ground plane in front of the target

Fig. 3. Impact of our data augmentation. Top row illustrates the on-object occlusion distribution of the base training set before augmentation and the bottom row shows the same for augmented data using our object centric data augmentation. Red indicates that the part is often occluded and blue indicates rare occlusion in the dataset. (Color figure online)

object, representing a cone with an opening angle of 90°. Next, we search for images of other objects in $\mathcal{K}$, where the ground plane normal is close to that of the target object, and which are located in the defined surface of interest, based on their distance from the camera. Finally, by overlaying one or more of these chosen objects in front of the target object, we generate multiple augmented RGB and depth images ($c.f.$ Fig. 2(b, c)). Using this approach, the resulting occlusion looks physically correct for both the RGB and depth images.

To analyze the impact of our data augmentation scheme, we visualize the distribution of partial occlusion on the object surface in the following way: we first discretize the 3D bounding box surrounding each object into $20 \times 20 \times 20$ voxels. Using the ground truth 6D pose and the 3D CAD model, we can render the full mask of the object. Each pixel that lies inside the rendered mask but not inside the ground truth mask is occluded. We can look-up the ground truth object coordinate of each occluded pixel, and furthermore the associated bounding box voxel. We use the voxels as histogram bins and visualize the occlusion frequency as colors on the surface of the 3D CAD model.

The impact of our object-centric data augmentation for two objects of the LINEMOD dataset [14] is illustrated in Fig. 3. Firstly, by looking at the visualization (top row), we notice that the un-augmented data contains biased occlusion samples (irregular distribution of blue and red patches) which could induce overfitting on certain object parts, leading to reduced performance of the object coordinate network of step 2. In the second row, we see that the augmented data has a more regular distribution of occlusion. This visualization reveals the bias in the base training set, and demonstrates the efficacy of our object-centric data augmentation procedure in creating unbiased training data.

4   Experiments

In this section, we present various experiments quantifying the performance of our approach. In Sect. 4.1, we introduce the dataset which we use for evaluating our system. In Sect. 4.2, we compare the performance of our approach to existing RGB and RGB-D-based pose estimation approaches. In Sect. 4.2, we analyze the contribution of various modules of our approach to the final pose estimation performance. Finally, in Sects. 4.3 and 4.4, we discuss the performance of our instance segmentation and object coordinate estimation networks. Please see the supplemental materials for a complete list of parameter settings of our pipeline.

4.1 Datasets and Implementation

We evaluate our approach on *occludedLINEMOD*, a dataset published by Brachmann *et al.* [4]. It was created from the LINEMOD dataset [14] by annotating ground truth 6D poses for various objects in a sequence of 1214 RGB-D images. The objects are located on a table and embedded in dense clutter. Ground truth poses are provided for eight of these objects which, depending on the camera view, heavily occlude each other, making this dataset very challenging. We test both our RGB and RGB-D-based methods on this dataset.

To train our system, we use a separate sequence from the LINEMOD dataset which was annotated by Michel *et al.* [31]. For ease of reference we call this the LINEMOD-M dataset. LINEMOD-M comes with ground truth annotations of seven objects with mutual occlusion. One object of the test sequence, namely the Driller, is not present in this training sequence, so we do not report results for it. The training sequence is extremely limited in the amount of data it provides. Some objects are only seen from few viewpoints and with little occlusion, or occlusion affects only certain object parts.

Training Instance Segmentation. To train our instance segmentation network with a wide range of object viewpoints and diverse occlusion examples, we create synthetic images in the following way. We use RGB backgrounds from the NYUD dataset [32], and randomly overlay them with objects picked from the original LINEMOD dataset [14]. While this data is physically implausible, we found it sufficient for training the instance segmentation component of our pipeline. We combine these synthetic images with LINEMOD-M to obtain 9000 images with ground truth instance masks. We use Mask R-CNN [12] as our instance segmentation method. For training, we use a learning rate of $1e{-}3$, momentum of 0.9 and weight decay of $1e{-}4$. We initialize Mask R-CNN with weights trained on ImageNet, and finetune on our training set.

Training Object Coordinate Regression. For training the object coordinate estimation network, we found it important to utilize physically plausible data augmentation for best results. Therefore, we use the LINEMOD-M dataset along with the data obtained using our object-centric data augmentation pipeline described in Sect. 3.4. Note that the test sequence and our training data are strictly separated, *i.e.* we did not use parts of the test sequence for data augmentation. We trained our object coordinate network by minimizing a robust Huber loss function [11] using ADAM [24]. We train a separate network for each object. We rescale inputs and ground truth outputs for the network to 256×256 px patches.

Table 1. Results using RGB only. Comparison of our pose estimation accuracy for RGB inputs with competing methods. *Italic* numbers were generated using ground truth crops, thus they are not directly comparable.

	Acceptance Threshold: 5 px			Acceptance Threshold: 10 px					
	BB8 [33] (GT crops)	Brachmann [3]	Ours	BB8 [33] (GT crops)	Brachmann [3]	SSD-6D [20]	SSS-6D [38]	Ours
Ape	*28.5%*	**31.8%**	24.2%	*81.0%*	51.8%	0.5%	0%	**56.1%**
Can	*1.2%*	4.5%	**30.2%**	*27.8%*	19.1%	0.6%	0%	**72.4%**
Cat	*9.6%*	1.1%	**12.3%**	*61.8%*	7.1%	0.1%	0%	**39.7%**
Duck	*6.8%*	1.6%	**12.1%**	*41.3%*	6.4%	0%	5%	**50.1%**
Glue	*4.7%*	0.5%	**25.9%**	*37.7%*	6.4%	0%	0%	**55.1%**
HoleP.	*2.4%*	6.7%	**20.6%**	*45.4%*	2.6%	0.3%	1%	**61.2%**
Avg	*8.9%*	7.7%	**20.8%**	*49.2%*	17.1%	0.3%	0.01%	**56.0%**

4.2 Pose Estimation Accuracy

RGB Setup. We estimate object poses from RGB images ignoring the depth channel. We evaluate the performance using the *2D Projection* metric introduced by Brachmann *et al.* [3]. This metric measures the average re-projection error of 3D model vertices transformed by the ground truth pose and the estimated pose. A pose is accepted if the average re-projection error is less than a threshold.

In Table 1, we compare the performance of our pipeline to existing RGB-based methods using two different thresholds for the 2D projection metric. We see that our approach outperforms the previous works for most of the objects significantly. Our RGB only pipeline surpasses the state-of-the-art for a 5 pixel threshold by 13% and for a 10 pixel threshold by 39% on average. Note that the results of BB8 [33] were obtained from image crops around the ground truth object position. Similar to [33] and [38], we do not report results for *EggBox* since we could not get reasonable results for this extremely occluded object using RGB only. Note that SSD-6D [20] and SSS-6D [38] completely fail for partly occluded objects. We obtained the results of SSS-6D directly from [38], and of SSD-6D [20] using their publicly available source code and their pre-trained model. However, they did not release their pose refinement method, thus we report their performance without refinement. In the supplement, we show the accuracy of SSD-6D using different 2D re-projection thresholds. Most of the detections of SSD-6D are far off (see also their detection performance in Fig. 5, right), therefore we do not expect refinement to improve their results much. We show qualitative pose estimation results for the RGB setting in Fig. 4.

RGB-D Setup. Similar to the RGB setup, we measure accuracy as the percentage of correctly estimated poses. Following Hinterstoisser *et al.* [14], we accept a pose if the average 3D distance between object model vertices transformed using ground truth pose and predicted pose lies below 10% of the object diameter.

In Fig. 6, left, we compare the performance of our approach to Michel *et al.* [31] and Hinterstoisser *et al.* [16]. We significantly outperform the state-of-the-art on average by 6%, and show massive improvements for some objects. Figure 7

Input image   Ours   SSD-6D

Fig. 4. Qualitative results from the RGB setup. From left to right: input image, our results, results of SSD-6D [20].

Mask	Obj. Coord.	Pose Estimation	Accuracy
RF[16]	RF[16]	Brachmann [16]	52.9%
Ours (MNC)	RF[16]	Brachmann [16]	56.4%
Ours (MNC)	Ours (CNN)	Brachmann [16]	61.0%
Ours (MNC)	Ours (CNN)	Ours	75.7%
Ours (Mask R-CNN)	Ours (CNN)	Ours	**80.7%**

Method	MAP
Hinterstoisser [3]	0.21
Brachmann [17]	0.51
SSD-6D [14]	0.38
SSS-6D [15]	0.48
Ours	**0.84**

Fig. 5. Left. Pose estimation accuracies on the RGB-D dataset using various combinations of mask estimation, object coordinates estimation and pose estimation approaches. Right. Comparison of 2D detection performance.

shows qualitative results from our RGB-D pipeline and an illustration of the performance of our method on an object under increasing occlusion. Figure 6, right represents the percentage of correct poses as a function of occluded object surface. We see that for cases of mild occlusion, our method surpasses accuracy of 90% for all objects. For cases of heavy occlusion (above 60%) our method can still recover accurate poses.

Ablation Study. We investigate the contribution of each step of our method towards the final pose estimation accuracy for the RGB-D setup. As discussed before, our method consists of three steps, namely instance mask estimation, object coordinate regression and pose estimation. We compare to the method of Brachmann *et al.* [4] which has similar steps, namely soft segmentation (not instance-aware), object coordinate regression, and a final RANSAC-based pose estimation. The first two steps in [4] are implemented using a random forest, compared to two separate CNNs in our system. Figure 5, left shows the accuracy

Object	Michel et al. [4]	Hinterstoisser et al. [5]	Ours
Ape	80.7%	81.4%	**83.0%**
Can	88.5%	**94.7%**	89.6%
Cat	**57.8%**	55.2%	57.5%
Duck	74.4%	**79.7%**	76.6%
Eggbox	47.6%	65.5%	**82.1%**
Glue	73.8%	52.1%	**78.8%**
Holep.	96.3%	95.5%	**97.0%**
Avg.	74.2%	74.9%	**80.7%**

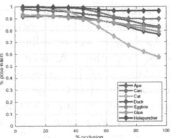

Fig. 6. Left. Comparison of our pose estimation accuracy (RGB-D) with competing methods. Right. The percentage of correctly estimated poses as a function of the level of occlusion.

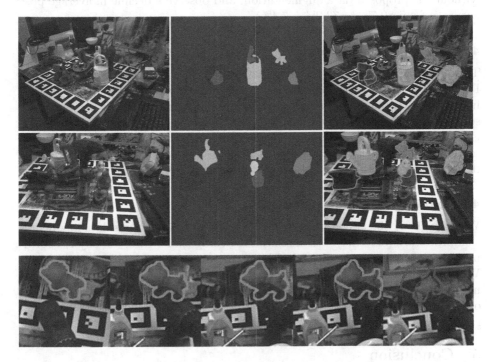

Fig. 7. Qualitative results from the RGB-D setup. Our approach reliably estimates poses for objects which are heavily occluded. (First two rows) The middle column shows estimated object masks of our instance segmentation step. (Last row) We show a sequence of estimated poses for the Cat object under increasing occlusion. We reliably estimate the correct pose until ca. 50% of the object is occluded.

for various re-combinations of these modules. The first row is the standard baseline approach of [4] which achieves an average accuracy of 52.9%. In the second row, we replace the soft segmentation estimated by [4] with an instance segmentation method, Multi-task Network Cascades (MNC) [6]. The instance masks effectively constrain the 2D search space which leads to better sampling of correspondences between depth points and object coordinate predictions. Next, we replace the object coordinate predictions of the random forest with our CNN-based predictions. Although we still perform the same pose optimization, this achieves a 4.6% performance boost, showing that our encoder-decoder network architecture predicts object coordinates more precisely. Next, we use the instance masks as above and object coordinates from our network with our geometric ICP-based refinement which further boosts the accuracy to 75.7%. Finally, in the last row, we use our full pipeline with masks from Mask R-CNN followed by our other modules to achieve state-of-the-art performance of 80.7%. The table clearly indicates that the accuracy of our pipeline as a whole improves when any of the modules improve. On the other hand, we trained our Obj.Coord. network without the proposed data augmentation, and observe a decline in average pose accuracy from 80.7% to 73.2% (−7.4%).

4.3   Instance Segmentation

The performance of instance segmentation is crucial for our overall accuracy. Figure 5, right shows the mean average precision of our method for a 2D bounding box IoU > 0.5 compared to other methods. Since our RGB only instance segmentation network is used for both, the RGB and RGB-D setting, the MAP is equal for both settings. We significantly outperform all other pose estimation methods, showing that our decoupled instance segmentation step can reliably detect objects, making the task for the following modules considerably easier.

4.4   Object Coordinate Estimation

We trained our object coordinate network with and without our data augmentation procedure (Sect. 3.4). We measure the average inlier rate, *i.e.* object coordinate estimates that are predicted within 2 cm of ground truth object coordinates. When the network is trained only using the LINEMOD-M dataset, the average inlier rate is 44% as compared to 52% when we use the data created using our object centric data augmentation procedure. A clear 8% increase in the inlier rate shows the importance of our proposed data augmentation.

5   Conclusion

We have presented *iPose*, a deep learning-based approach capable of estimating accurate poses of partly occluded objects. Our approach surpasses the state-of-the-art for both RGB and RGB-D inputs. We attribute the success of our method to our decomposition philosophy, and therefore the ability to leverage state-of-the-art instance segmentation networks. We are also the first to successfully train an encoder-decoder network for dense object coordinate regression, that facilitates our robust geometric pose optimization.

Acknowledgements. This project is funded by DFG grant COVMAP (RO 4804/2-1), Heidelberg Collaboratory for Image Processing (HCI), ERC grant No. 647769.

References

1. Alhaija, H.A., Mustikovela, S.K., Mescheder, L., Geiger, A., Rother, C.: Augmented reality meets deep learning for car instance segmentation in urban scenes. In: BMVC (2017)
2. Behl, A., Hosseini Jafari, O., Mustikovela, S.K., Alhaija, H.A., Rother, C., Geiger, A.: Bounding boxes, segmentations and object coordinates: how important is recognition for 3D scene flow estimation in autonomous driving scenarios? In: ICCV (2017)
3. Brachmann, E., Michel, F., Krull, A., Yang, M.Y., Gumhold, S., Rother, C.: Uncertainty-driven 6D pose estimation of objects and scenes from a single RGB image. In: CVPR (2016)
4. Brachmann, E., Krull, A., Michel, F., Gumhold, S., Shotton, J., Rother, C.: Learning 6D object pose estimation using 3D object coordinates. In: Fleet, D., Pajdla, T., Schiele, B., Tuytelaars, T. (eds.) ECCV 2014. LNCS, vol. 8690, pp. 536–551. Springer, Cham (2014). https://doi.org/10.1007/978-3-319-10605-2_35
5. Brachmann, E., et al.: DSAC-differentiable RANSAC for camera localization. In: CVPR (2017)
6. Dai, J., He, K., Sun, J.: Instance-aware semantic segmentation via multi-task network cascades. In: CVPR (2016)
7. Doumanoglou, A., Kouskouridas, R., Malassiotis, S., Kim, T.: 6D object detection and next-best-view prediction in the crowd. In: CVPR (2016)
8. Drost, B., Ulrich, M., Navab, N., Ilic, S.: Model globally, match locally: efficient and robust 3D object recognition. In: CVPR (2010)
9. Gaidon, A., Wang, Q., Cabon, Y., Vig, E.: Virtual worlds as proxy for multi-object tracking analysis. In: CVPR (2016)
10. Gao, X.S., Hou, X.R., Tang, J., Cheng, H.F.: Complete solution classification for the perspective-three-point problem. IEEE Trans. PAMI **25**, 930–943 (2003)
11. Girshick, R.: Fast R-CNN. In: ICCV (2015)
12. He, K., Gkioxari, G., Dollár, P., Girshick, R.: Mask R-CNN. In: ICCV (2017)
13. Hinterstoisser, S., et al.: Gradient response maps for real-time detection of textureless objects. IEEE Trans. PAMI **34**, 876–888 (2012)
14. Hinterstoisser, S., et al.: Model based training, detection and pose estimation of texture-less 3D objects in heavily cluttered scenes. In: Lee, K.M., Matsushita, Y., Rehg, J.M., Hu, Z. (eds.) ACCV 2012. LNCS, vol. 7724, pp. 548–562. Springer, Heidelberg (2013). https://doi.org/10.1007/978-3-642-37331-2_42
15. Hinterstoisser, S., et al.: Multimodal templates for real-time detection of textureless objects in heavily cluttered scenes. In: ICCV (2011)
16. Hinterstoisser, S., Lepetit, V., Rajkumar, N., Konolige, K.: Going further with point pair features. In: Leibe, B., Matas, J., Sebe, N., Welling, M. (eds.) ECCV 2016. LNCS, vol. 9907, pp. 834–848. Springer, Cham (2016). https://doi.org/10.1007/978-3-319-46487-9_51
17. Hodaň, T., Zabulis, X., Lourakis, M., Obdržálek, Š., Matas, J.: Detection and fine 3D pose estimation of texture-less objects in RGB-D images. In: IROS (2015)
18. Huttenlocher, D., Klanderman, G., Rucklidge, W.: Comparing images using the Hausdorff distance. IEEE Trans. PAMI **15**, 850–863 (1993)
19. Kabsch, W.: A solution for the best rotation to relate two sets of vectors. Acta Crystallogr. **32**, 922–923 (1976)
20. Kehl, W., Manhardt, F., Tombari, F., Ilic, S., Navab, N.: SSD-6D: making RGB-based 3D detection and 6D pose estimation great again. In: ICCV (2017)

21. Kehl, W., Milletari, F., Tombari, F., Ilic, S., Navab, N.: Deep learning of local RGB-D patches for 3D object detection and 6D pose estimation. In: Leibe, B., Matas, J., Sebe, N., Welling, M. (eds.) ECCV 2016. LNCS, vol. 9907, pp. 205–220. Springer, Cham (2016). https://doi.org/10.1007/978-3-319-46487-9_13

22. Kehl, W., Tombari, F., Navab, N., Ilic, S., Lepetit, V.: Hashmod: a hashing method for scalable 3D object detection. In: BMVC (2016)

23. Kendall, A., Grimes, M., Cipolla, R.: PoseNet: a convolutional network for real-time 6-DOF camera relocalization. In: ICCV (2015)

24. Kingma, D.P., Ba, J.: Adam: a method for stochastic optimization. In: ICLR (2015)

25. Konishi, Y., Hanzawa, Y., Kawade, M., Hashimoto, M.: Fast 6D pose estimation from a monocular image using hierarchical pose trees. In: Leibe, B., Matas, J., Sebe, N., Welling, M. (eds.) ECCV 2016. LNCS, vol. 9905, pp. 398–413. Springer, Cham (2016). https://doi.org/10.1007/978-3-319-46448-0_24

26. Krull, A., Brachmann, E., Michel, F., Yang, M.Y., Gumhold, S., Rother, C.: Learning analysis-by-synthesis for 6D pose estimation in RGB-D images. In: ICCV (2015)

27. Lepetit, V., Moreno-Noguer, F., Fua, P.: EPNP: An accurate $O(n)$ solution to the PnP problem. IJCV **81**, 155 (2009)

28. Li, C., Zia, M.Z., Tran, Q., Yu, X., Hager, G.D., Chandraker, M.: Deep supervision with shape concepts for occlusion-aware 3D object parsing. In: CVPR (2017)

29. Liu, W., et al.: SSD: single shot multibox detector. In: Leibe, B., Matas, J., Sebe, N., Welling, M. (eds.) ECCV 2016. LNCS, vol. 9905, pp. 21–37. Springer, Cham (2016). https://doi.org/10.1007/978-3-319-46448-0_2

30. Lowe, D.G.: Local feature view clustering for 3D object recognition. In: CVPR (2001)

31. Michel, F., et al.: Global hypothesis generation for 6D object pose estimation. In: CVPR (2017)

32. Silberman, N., Hoiem, D., Kohli, P., Fergus, R.: Indoor segmentation and support inference from RGBD images. In: Fitzgibbon, A., Lazebnik, S., Perona, P., Sato, Y., Schmid, C. (eds.) ECCV 2012. LNCS, vol. 7576, pp. 746–760. Springer, Heidelberg (2012). https://doi.org/10.1007/978-3-642-33715-4_54

33. Rad, M., Lepetit, V.: BB8: a scalable, accurate, robust to partial occlusion method for predicting the 3D poses of challenging objects without using depth. In: ICCV (2017)

34. Redmon, J., Divvala, S.K., Girshick, R.B., Farhadi, A.: You only look once: unified, real-time object detection. In: CVPR (2016)

35. Rios-Cabrera, R., Tuytelaars, T.: Discriminatively trained templates for 3D object detection: a real time scalable approach. In: ICCV (2013)

36. Shotton, J., Glocker, B., Zach, C., Izadi, S., Criminisi, A., Fitzgibbon, A.W.: Scene coordinate regression forests for camera relocalization in RGB-D images. In: CVPR (2013)

37. Tejani, A., Tang, D., Kouskouridas, R., Kim, T.-K.: Latent-class hough forests for 3D object detection and pose estimation. In: Fleet, D., Pajdla, T., Schiele, B., Tuytelaars, T. (eds.) ECCV 2014. LNCS, vol. 8694, pp. 462–477. Springer, Cham (2014). https://doi.org/10.1007/978-3-319-10599-4_30

38. Tekin, B., Sinha, S.N., Fua, P.: Real time seamless single shot 6D object pose prediction. In: CVPR (2018)

39. Zach, C., Penate-Sanchez, A., Pham, M.T.: A dynamic programming approach for fast and robust object pose recognition from range images. In: CVPR (2015)

Multi-Attribute Probabilistic Linear Discriminant Analysis for 3D Facial Shapes

Stylianos Moschoglou[1](✉), Stylianos Ploumpis[1], Mihalis A. Nicolaou[2], and Stefanos Zafeiriou[1]

[1] Imperial College London, London, UK
{s.moschoglou,s.ploumpis,s.zafeiriou}@imperial.ac.uk
[2] Computation-based Science and Technology Research Centre,
The Cyprus Institute, Nicosia, Cyprus
m.nicolaou@cyi.ac.cy

Abstract. Component Analysis (CA) consists of a set of statistical techniques that decompose data to appropriate latent components that are relevant to the task-at-hand (e.g., clustering, segmentation, classification). During the past years, an explosion of research in probabilistic CA has been witnessed, with the introduction of several novel methods (e.g., Probabilistic Principal Component Analysis, Probabilistic Linear Discriminant Analysis (PLDA), Probabilistic Canonical Correlation Analysis). A particular subset of CA methods such as PLDA, inspired by the classical Linear Discriminant Analysis, incorporate the knowledge of data labeled in terms of an attribute in order to extract a suitable discriminative subspace. Nevertheless, while many modern datasets incorporate labels with regards to multiple attributes (e.g., age, ethnicity, weight), existing CA methods can exploit at most a single attribute (i.e., one set of labels) per model. That is, in case multiple attributes are available, one needs to train a separate model per attribute, in effect not exploiting knowledge of other attributes for the task-at-hand. In this light, we propose the first, to the best of our knowledge, Multi-Attribute Probabilistic LDA (MAPLDA), that is able to jointly handle data annotated with multiple attributes. We demonstrate the performance of the proposed method on the analysis of 3D facial shapes, a task with increasing value due to the rising popularity of consumer-grade 3D sensors, on problems such as ethnicity, age, and weight identification, as well as 3D facial shape generation.

Keywords: Multi-Attribute · PLDA · Component Analysis · 3D shapes

Supported by an EPSRC DTA studentship from Imperial College London, EPSRC Project EP/N007743/1 (FACER2VM) and a Google Faculty Award.

Electronic supplementary material The online version of this chapter (https://doi.org/10.1007/978-3-030-20893-6_31) contains supplementary material, which is available to authorized users.

© Springer Nature Switzerland AG 2019
C. V. Jawahar et al. (Eds.): ACCV 2018, LNCS 11363, pp. 493–508, 2019.
https://doi.org/10.1007/978-3-030-20893-6_31

1   Introduction

Component Analysis (CA) techniques such as Principal Component Analysis (PCA) [10], Linear Discriminant Analysis (LDA) [23] and Canonical Correlation Analysis (CCA) [8] are among the most popular methods for feature extraction and dimensionality reduction, typically utilized in a wide range of applications in computer vision and machine learning. While CA methods such as PCA have been introduced in the literature more than a century ago, it was only during the last two decades that *probabilistic* interpretations of CA techniques have been introduced in the literature, with examples of such efforts including Probabilistic PCA (PPCA) [18,22,25], Probabilistic LDA (PLDA) [9,19,20,28–30] and Probabilistic CCA (PCCA) [3,12]. The rise in popularity of probabilistic CA methods can be attributed to several appealing properties, such as explicit variance modeling and inherent handling of missing data [2]. Furthermore, probabilistic CA models may be easily extended to mixture models [24] and Bayesian methodologies [13], while they can also be utilized as general density models [25].

While many CA methods such as PCA and CCA are typically considered to be unsupervised, methods such as LDA assume knowledge of labeled data in order to derive a discriminative subspace based on attribute values (labels), that can subsequently be utilized for predictive analysis e.g., classification of unlabeled data. Probabilistic LDA (PLDA) [14,20] constitutes one of the first attempts towards formulating a probabilistic generative CA model that incorporates information regarding data labels (e.g., the identity of a person in an image). In more detail, each datum is generated by two distinct subspaces: a subspace that incorporates information among instances belonging to the same class, and a subspace that models information that is unique to each datum. Put simply in the context of face recognition, all images of a specific subject share the same identity, while each image may carry its own particular variations (e.g., in terms of illumination, pose and so on).

Nevertheless, a feature of PLDA and other probabilistic LDA variants that can be disadvantageous is the *single-attribute* assumption. In other words, PLDA is limited to the knowledge of one attribute, effectively disregarding knowledge of any other attributes available for the data-at-hand that may prove beneficial for a given task. For example, it is reasonable to assume that knowledge of attributes such as *pose*, *expression* and *age* may be deemed beneficial in terms of determining the identity of a person in a facial image. By incorporating knowledge of multiple attributes, we would expect a generative model to better explain the observation variance, by decomposing the observation space into multiple components conditioned on the attributes at-hand. Figure 1 illustrates the more accurate representations we can obtain in this way.

In the past, PLDA was successfully applied to tasks such as face recognition and speaker verification [11,20]. The advent of Deep Convolutional Neural Networks (DCNNs) provided models that overperformed linear CA techniques with respect to feature extraction in computer vision applications that involve intensity images and video, mainly due to the complex variations introduced by the texture and the geometric transformations. Nevertheless, linear CA techniques

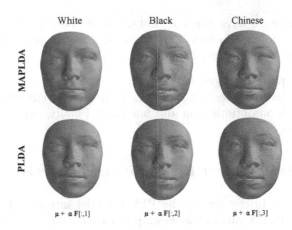

Fig. 1. Visualization of recovered components by MAPLDA as compared to PLDA, highlighting the improvement induced by explicitly accounting for multiple attributes. We denote with μ the global mean, and with $\mathbf{F}$ the learned subspace of the *ethnicity* attribute where $\alpha \geq 1$ is used to accentuate the component visualization. MAPLDA is trained by jointly taking into account the *ethnicity* and *age-group* attributes. As can be clearly seen, this leads to a more accurate representation of the *ethnicity attribute* in MAPLDA, which is more prominent for the *Black* class.

remain prominent and powerful techniques for tasks related to the analysis of 3D shapes, especially in case that dense correspondences have been established among them. Recently, very powerful frameworks have been proposed for establishing dense correspondences in large scale databases of 3D faces [6,16], 3D bodies [15] and 3D hands [21].

Given that several modern databases of 3D shapes are annotated in terms of multiple attributes, and further motivated by the aforementioned shortcomings of single-attribute methods, in this paper we propose a Multi-Attribute generative probabilistic variant of LDA, dubbed Multi-Attribute Probabilistic LDA (MAPLDA). The proposed MAPLDA is able to *jointly* model the influence of multiple attributes on observed data, thus effectively decomposing the observation space into a set of subspaces depending on multiple attribute instantiations. As shown via a set of experiments on age, ethnicity and age group identification, the joint multi-attribute modeling embedded in MAPLDA appears highly beneficial, outperforming other single-attribute approaches in an elegant probabilistic framework. In what follows, we briefly summarize the contributions of our paper.

- We present MAPLDA, the first, to the best of our knowledge, probabilistic variant of LDA that is *inherently* able to *jointly* model multiple attributes.
- We provide a probabilistic formulation and optimization procedure for training, as well as a flexible framework for performing inference on *any* subset of the multiple attributes available during training.

– We demonstrate the advantages of joint-attribute modelling by a set of experiments on the MeIn3D dataset [6], in terms of ethnicity, age and weight group identification, as well as facial shape generation.

The rest of the paper is organized as follows. In Sect. 2, we briefly introduce PLDA, a generative counterpart to LDA. MAPLDA is introduced in Sect. 3, along with details on optimization and inference. Finally, experimental evaluation is detailed in Sect. 4.

2   Probabilistic Linear Discriminant Analysis

In this section, we briefly review the PLDA model introduced in [14,20]. As aforementioned, PLDA carries the assumption that data are generated by two different subspaces: one that depends on the class and one that depends on the sample. That is, assuming we have a total of I classes, with each class i containing a total of J samples, then the j-th datum of the i-th class is defined as:

$$\mathbf{x}_{i,j} = \boldsymbol{\mu} + \mathbf{F}\mathbf{h}_i + \mathbf{G}\mathbf{w}_{i,j} + \boldsymbol{\epsilon}_{i,j} \tag{1}$$

where $\boldsymbol{\mu}$ denotes the global mean of the training set, $\mathbf{F}$ defines the subspace capturing the identity of every subject, with $\mathbf{h}_i$ being the latent identity variable representing the position in the particular subspace. Furthermore, $\mathbf{G}$ defines the subspace modeling variations among data, with $\mathbf{w}_{i,j}$ being the associated latent variable. Finally, $\boldsymbol{\epsilon}_{i,j}$ is a residual noise term which is Gaussian with diagonal covariance $\boldsymbol{\Sigma}$. Assuming zero-mean observations, the model in (1) can be described as:

$$P(\mathbf{x}_{i,j}|\mathbf{h}_i, \mathbf{w}_{i,j}, \boldsymbol{\theta}) = \mathcal{N}_{\mathbf{x}}(\mathbf{F}\mathbf{h}_i + \mathbf{G}\mathbf{w}_{i,j}, \boldsymbol{\Sigma}) \tag{2}$$
$$P(\mathbf{h}_i) = \mathcal{N}_{\mathbf{h}}(\mathbf{0}, \mathbf{I}) \tag{3}$$
$$P(\mathbf{w}_{i,j}) = \mathcal{N}_{\mathbf{w}}(\mathbf{0}, \mathbf{I}) \tag{4}$$

where the set of parameters $\boldsymbol{\theta} = \{\mathbf{F}, \mathbf{G}, \boldsymbol{\Sigma}\}$ is optimized during training via EM [7]. In the training process, EM is applied and the optimal set of parameters, $\boldsymbol{\theta} = \{\mathbf{F}, \mathbf{G}, \boldsymbol{\Sigma}\}$, is recovered.

3   Multi-Attribute PLDA (MAPLDA)

Let us consider a generalization of the single-attribute setting, as described in Sect. 2. In particular, let us assume that the data at-hand is labeled in terms of a total of N attributes, where each attribute may take K_i discrete instantiations (labels/classes), that is $a_i \in \{1, \cdots, K_i\}^1$. We further assume that a set of J data available during training for any distinct combination of attribute

---

[1] For brevity of notation, we denote $a_1, \ldots, a_N$ as $a_{1:N}$.

instantiations. The generative model for MAPLDA corresponding to the j-th observation (datum) can then be described as:

$$\mathbf{x}_{a_{1:N},j} = \boldsymbol{\mu} + \sum_{i=1}^{N} \mathbf{F}_i \mathbf{h}_{i,a_i} + \mathbf{G}\mathbf{w}_{a_{1:N},j} + \epsilon_{a_{1:N},j} \tag{5}$$

where $\boldsymbol{\mu}$ denotes the training set global mean, $\mathbf{F}_1, \ldots, \mathbf{F}_N$ are loadings that define the subspace bases for each particular attribute (e.g., $\mathbf{F}_1$ may be the basis for the attribute age-group, $\mathbf{F}_2$ the basis for the attribute ethnicity, etc.) and $\mathbf{h}_{1,a_1}, \ldots, \mathbf{h}_{N,a_N}$ are selectors that define the position in each subspace, respectively (e.g., selector $\mathbf{h}_{1,a_1}$ will render the distinct age-group instantiation with which each datum is annotated). Furthermore, matrix $\mathbf{G}$ defines a basis for the subspace that models the variations among the data and $\mathbf{w}_{a_{1:N},j}$ defines the position in that subspace for the j-th datum. Finally, random noise is captured through the term $\epsilon_{a_{1:N},j}$ which is specific for each datum and is set as a Gaussian with diagonal covariance $\boldsymbol{\Sigma}$. Note that from here on, to avoid cluttering the notation we omit dependence on attribute instantiations (unless specified otherwise), that is we denote $\mathbf{x}_{a_{1:N},j}$ as $\mathbf{x}_j$, $\mathbf{w}_{a_{1:N},j}$ as $\mathbf{w}_j$ and $\epsilon_{a_{1:N},j}$ as ϵ_j. Moreover, by assuming zero-mean observations, the model in (5) can be written more clearly as:

$$\mathbf{x}_j = \sum_{i=1}^{N} \mathbf{F}_i \mathbf{h}_{i,a_i} + \mathbf{G}\mathbf{w}_j + \epsilon_j \tag{6}$$

while the prior probabilities of (6) can be written as:

$$P\left(\mathbf{h}_{i,a_i}\right) = \mathcal{N}_{\mathbf{h}}\left(\mathbf{0}, \mathbf{I}\right), \quad \forall i \in \{1, \ldots, N\} \tag{7}$$
$$P\left(\mathbf{w}_j\right) = \mathcal{N}_{\mathbf{w}}\left(\mathbf{0}, \mathbf{I}\right) \tag{8}$$

and the posterior as:

$$P\left(\mathbf{x}_j | \mathbf{h}_{1,a_1}, \ldots, \mathbf{h}_{N,a_N}, \mathbf{w}_j, \boldsymbol{\theta}\right) = \mathcal{N}_{\mathbf{x}}\left(\sum_{i=1}^{N} \mathbf{F}_i \mathbf{h}_{i,a_i} + \mathbf{G}\mathbf{w}_j, \boldsymbol{\Sigma}\right) \tag{9}$$

where $\boldsymbol{\theta} = \{\mathbf{F}_1, \ldots, \mathbf{F}_N, \mathbf{G}, \boldsymbol{\Sigma}\}$ is the set of parameters. Having defined our model, in the next subsections we detail both the training and inference procedures of MAPLDA in the presence of multiple attributes. For further clarification, we note that the graphical model of MAPLDA is illustrated in Fig. 2.

3.1   Training with Multiple Attributes

In this section, we detail the estimation of both the latent variables and parameters involved in MAPLDA. We assume that we are interested in making predictions regarding a subset of available attributes. While any subset can be chosen, for purposes of clarity and without loss of generality, we assume this set consists of the first $N - 1$ attributes. That is, when given a test datum we can assign

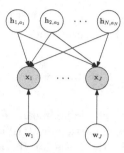

Fig. 2. Graphical model for J observed data of the training set (i.e., $\mathbf{x}_1, \ldots, \mathbf{x}_J$) for a distinct combination of attribute instantiations. The positions of the data in the subspaces $\mathbf{F}_1, \ldots, \mathbf{F}_N$ are given by the latent variables $\mathbf{h}_{1,a_1}, \ldots, \mathbf{h}_{N,a_N}$, respectively, while the position in subspace $\mathbf{G}$ is given by the latent variables $\mathbf{w}_1, \ldots, \mathbf{w}_J$, respectively.

any of the $N-1$ attributes to classes $a_i, i \in \{1, \ldots, K_i\}$, while exploiting the knowledge of the remaining attributes (e.g., by marginalization during inference). Furthermore, without loss of generality, assume that there is a total of M data for each distinct combination of the $N-1$ attributes instantiations. We denote $\mathbf{F} \doteq [\mathbf{F}_1\, \mathbf{F}_2 \ldots \mathbf{F}_{N-1}]$, and $\mathbf{h} \doteq \left[\mathbf{h}_{1,a_1}^T\, \mathbf{h}_{2,a_2}^T \ldots \mathbf{h}_{N-1,a_{N-1}}^T\right]^T$ the block matrices consisting of loadings and variables for the first N-1 attributes, and $\hat{\mathbf{h}}_N \doteq \left[\mathbf{h}_{N,1}^T\, \mathbf{h}_{N,2}^T \ldots \mathbf{h}_{N,K_N}^T\right]^T$ the latent variable block matrix for all attribute values of the N-th attribute. Following a block matrix formulation, we group the M data samples as follows,

$$
\begin{bmatrix} \mathbf{x}_1 \\ \mathbf{x}_2 \\ \vdots \\ \mathbf{x}_M \end{bmatrix} = \begin{bmatrix} \mathbf{F}\ e_{1,a_N} \otimes \mathbf{F}_N\ \mathbf{G}\ \mathbf{0}\ \ldots\ \mathbf{0} \\ \mathbf{F}\ e_{2,a_N} \otimes \mathbf{F}_N\ \mathbf{0}\ \mathbf{G}\ \ldots\ \mathbf{0} \\ \vdots\quad \vdots\qquad \vdots\ \ddots\ \vdots \\ \mathbf{F}\ e_{M,a_N} \otimes \mathbf{F}_N\ \mathbf{0}\ \mathbf{0}\ \ldots\ \mathbf{G} \end{bmatrix} \begin{bmatrix} \mathbf{h} \\ \hat{\mathbf{h}}_N \\ \mathbf{w}_1 \\ \vdots \\ \mathbf{w}_M \end{bmatrix} + \begin{bmatrix} \epsilon_1 \\ \vdots \\ \epsilon_M \end{bmatrix} \tag{10}
$$

where $\otimes$ denotes the Kronecker product, and $e_{i,a_N} \in \mathbb{R}^{1 \times K_N}$ is a one-hot embedding of the value of attribute a_N for datum $\mathbf{x}_i$ (recall that $a_N \in \{1, \ldots, K_N\}$). For example, assume that for $\mathbf{x}_1$, $a_N = K_N$. Then, $e_{1,N} = [0, \ldots, 0, 1] \in \mathbb{R}^{1 \times K_N}$ and $e_{1,N} \otimes \mathbf{F}_N = [\mathbf{0}, \ldots, \mathbf{0}, \mathbf{F}_N]$. Furthermore, (10) can be written compactly as:

$$
\mathbf{x}' = \mathbf{A}\mathbf{y} + \epsilon' \tag{11}
$$

where the prior and conditional probabilities of (11) can now be written as:

$$
P\left(\mathbf{x}'|\mathbf{y}, \boldsymbol{\theta}\right) = \mathcal{N}_{\mathbf{x}'}\left(\mathbf{A}\mathbf{y}, \boldsymbol{\Sigma}'\right) \tag{12}
$$
$$
P\left(\mathbf{y}\right) = \mathcal{N}_{\mathbf{y}}\left(\mathbf{0}, \mathbf{I}\right) \tag{13}
$$

where:

$$\Sigma' = \begin{bmatrix} \Sigma & 0 & \cdots & 0 \\ 0 & \Sigma & \cdots & 0 \\ \vdots & \vdots & \ddots & \vdots \\ 0 & 0 & \cdots & \Sigma \end{bmatrix} \tag{14}$$

Following EM and given an instantiation of the model parameters $\boldsymbol{\theta} = \{\mathbf{F}_1, \ldots, \mathbf{F}_N, \mathbf{G}, \boldsymbol{\Sigma}\}$, we need to estimate the sufficient statistics, that is the first and second moments of the posterior latent distribution $P(\mathbf{y}|\mathbf{x}', \boldsymbol{\theta})$. Since both (12) and (13) refer to Gaussian distributions, it can easily be shown [5] that the posterior also follows a Gaussian distribution:

$$P(\mathbf{y}|\mathbf{x}', \boldsymbol{\theta}) = \mathcal{N}_{\mathbf{y}}\left(\hat{\mathbf{A}}\mathbf{A}^T\boldsymbol{\Sigma}'^{-1}\mathbf{x}', \hat{\mathbf{A}}\right) \tag{15}$$

where $\hat{\mathbf{A}} \doteq \left(\mathbf{A}^T\boldsymbol{\Sigma}'^{-1}\mathbf{A} + \mathbf{I}\right)^{-1}$, and thus:

$$\mathbb{E}[\mathbf{y}] = \hat{\mathbf{A}}\mathbf{A}^T\boldsymbol{\Sigma}'^{-1}\mathbf{x}' \tag{16}$$

$$\mathbb{E}[\mathbf{y}\mathbf{y}^T] = \hat{\mathbf{A}} + \mathbb{E}[\mathbf{y}]\mathbb{E}[\mathbf{y}]^T \tag{17}$$

Having derived the sufficient statistics of MAPLDA, we carry on to the maximization step. In order to recover the parameter updates, we take the partial derivatives of the conditional (on the posterior) expectation of the complete-data log likelihood of MAPLDA with regards to parameters $\boldsymbol{\theta} = \{\mathbf{F}_1, \ldots, \mathbf{F}_N, \mathbf{G}, \boldsymbol{\Sigma}\}$. In order to do so, we firstly rewrite (6) as follows:

$$\mathbf{x}_j = \begin{bmatrix} \mathbf{F}_1 \cdots \mathbf{F}_N & \mathbf{G} \end{bmatrix} \begin{bmatrix} \mathbf{h}_{1,a_1} \\ \vdots \\ \mathbf{h}_{N,a_N} \\ \mathbf{w}_j \end{bmatrix} + \boldsymbol{\epsilon}_j \tag{18}$$

where (18) can be compactly written as:

$$\mathbf{x}_j = \mathbf{B}\mathbf{z}_j + \boldsymbol{\epsilon}_j. \tag{19}$$

By adopting the aforementioned grouping, our set of parameters is now denoted as $\boldsymbol{\theta} = \{\mathbf{B}, \boldsymbol{\Sigma}\}$, and the complete-data log likelihood conditioned on the posterior is formulated as:

$$\mathcal{Q}\left(\boldsymbol{\theta}, \boldsymbol{\theta}^{old}\right) = \sum_{\mathbf{Z}} P\left(\mathbf{Z}|\mathbf{X}, \boldsymbol{\theta}^{old}\right) \ln\left[P\left(\mathbf{X}, \mathbf{Z}|\boldsymbol{\theta}\right)\right] \tag{20}$$

where the joint can be decomposed as:

$$P(\mathbf{X}, \mathbf{Z}|\boldsymbol{\theta}) = \prod_{a_1=1}^{K_1} \cdots \prod_{a_N=1}^{K_N} \prod_{j=1}^{J} P\left(\mathbf{x}_{a_{1:N},j}|\mathbf{z}_{a_{1:N},j}\right) P\left(\mathbf{z}_{a_{1:N},j}\right) \tag{21}$$

It can be easily shown [5] that the updates are as follows:

$$\mathbf{B} = \left(\sum_{a_1=1}^{K_1} \cdots \sum_{a_N=1}^{K_N} \sum_{j=1}^{J} \mathbf{x}_{a_{1:N},j} \mathbb{E}\left[\mathbf{z}_{a_{1:N}}\right]^T \right) \left(\sum_{a_1=1}^{K_1} \cdots \sum_{a_N=1}^{K_N} \mathbb{E}\left[\mathbf{z}_{a_{1:N}} \mathbf{z}_{a_{1:N}}^T\right] \right)^{-1}$$

(22)

$$\Sigma = \frac{1}{\mathcal{K}J} \mathrm{Diag} \left(\mathbf{S}_t - \mathbf{B} \sum_{a_1=1}^{K_1} \cdots \sum_{a_N=1}^{K_N} \sum_{j=1}^{J} \mathbb{E}\left[\mathbf{z}_{a_{1:N}}\right] \mathbf{x}_{a_{1:N},j}^T \right),$$

(23)

with $\mathbf{S}_t = \sum_{a_1=1}^{K_1} \cdots \sum_{a_N=1}^{K_N} \sum_{j=1}^{J} \mathbf{x}_{a_{1:N},j} \mathbf{x}_{a_{1:N},j}^T$ being the total covariance matrix and

$$\mathcal{K} = \prod_{i=1}^{N} K_i.$$

3.2 Inference

Having completed the training process and derived the optimal MAPLDA parameters, we can proceed with inferences on unseen data on the first $N-1$ attributes. That is, given a datum (probe) from a test set, we aim to classify the datum into the appropriate classes for each of the corresponding $N-1$ attributes.

Since we do not have any prior knowledge of the conditions under which the data that belong to the test set may have been captured, it is very likely that the data may be perturbed by noise. Therefore, in order to determine the appropriate class, we compare the probe ($\mathbf{x}_p$) with a number of different data from a gallery in order to find the most likely match, in a similar manner to [20]. In essence, this boils down to maximum likelihood estimation under M (i.e., the total number of data in the gallery) different models. That is, for every model $m, m \in \{1, \ldots, M\}$, we calculate the log likelihood that the datum $\mathbf{x}_k$ in the gallery matches with the probe $\mathbf{x}_p$ and finally, we keep the pair that gives the largest log likelihood. This process falls under the so-called closed-set identification task, where a probe datum has to be matched with a gallery datum. The algorithm can be extended to cover other scenarios such as verification or open-set identification.

Without loss of generality, let us assume a gallery with M data, all of which are labeled with different instantiations per attribute. Our aim is to find the pair that produces the maximum likelihood between the probe datum and one of the M gallery data. More formally, this corresponds to:

$$M_v \equiv \underset{m \in \{1,\ldots,M\}}{\mathrm{argmax}} \ \{\ln P\left(\mathcal{M}_m | \mathbf{X}\right)\}$$

(24)

where $\mathbf{X} \doteq \left[\mathbf{x}_1^T, \ldots, \mathbf{x}_M^T, \mathbf{x}_p^T\right]^T$. The optimal set of instantiations is described by the model M_v. If we consider a uniform prior for the selection of each model (i.e.,

$P(\mathcal{M}_m)$ is a constant for all $m \in \{1, \ldots, M\}$), then the actual log likelihood in (24) can calculated using Bayes' theorem as follows:

$$P(\mathcal{M}_m | \mathbf{X}) = \frac{P(\mathbf{X}|\mathcal{M}_m)\,P(\mathcal{M}_m)}{\sum_{m=1}^{M} P(\mathbf{X}|\mathcal{M}_m)\,P(\mathcal{M}_m)} \qquad (25)$$

where the denominator is simply a normalizing constant, ensuring the probabilities sum to 1. Therefore, inference boils down to calculating:

$$\ln P(\mathbf{X}|\mathcal{M}_m) = \sum_{q=1, q \neq m}^{M} \ln P(\mathbf{x}_q) + \ln P(\mathbf{x}_p, \mathbf{x}_m) \qquad (26)$$

where for each model m, the probe is paired with the m-th datum in the gallery and an individual marginal is added for the rest of the gallery data.

As aforementioned, and without loss of generality, we assume that inference is conducted for the first $N - 1$ attributes. In order to perform inference without disregarding knowledge of attributes not required for inference, the sensible approach is to marginalize out the remaining N-th attribute. Then, following the process described above, we recover the optimal instantiations of attributes explained by model $\mathcal{M}_v$, utilizing (24), (25) and (26). The joint probabilities in (26) are Gaussians, and therefore, they can be estimated as:

$$P(\mathbf{x}_q) \sim \mathcal{N}_{\mathbf{x}_q}\left(\mathbf{0}, \mathbf{F}\mathbf{F}^T + \mathbf{F}_N\mathbf{F}_N^T + \mathbf{G}\mathbf{G}^T + \boldsymbol{\Sigma}\right) \qquad (27)$$

where $\mathbf{F} \doteq [\mathbf{F}_1\, \mathbf{F}_2 \ldots \mathbf{F}_{N-1}]$. By assigning $\mathbf{x}' \doteq [\mathbf{x}_p^T, \mathbf{x}_m^T]^T$ and using the "completing-the-square" method, the marginals can be estimated as:

$$P(\mathbf{x}') = \mathcal{N}_{\mathbf{x}'}\left(\mathbf{0}, \mathbf{A}\mathbf{A}^T + \boldsymbol{\Sigma}'\right) \qquad (28)$$

where:

$$\mathbf{A} = \begin{bmatrix} \mathbf{F} & \mathbf{G} & \mathbf{0} \\ \mathbf{F} & \mathbf{0} & \mathbf{G} \end{bmatrix}, \quad \boldsymbol{\Sigma}' = \begin{bmatrix} \boldsymbol{\Sigma} + \mathbf{F}_N\mathbf{F}_N^T & \mathbf{0} \\ \mathbf{0} & \boldsymbol{\Sigma} + \mathbf{F}_N\mathbf{F}_N^T \end{bmatrix} \qquad (29)$$

A graphical representation for this case can be found in Fig. 3.

Regarding the special case where inference about *only one* attribute is required, the marginals have the same form as in (27). The joint distribution, given that the attribute of interest is denoted as $i \in \{1, \ldots, N\}$, follows the form:

$$P(\mathbf{x}') \sim \mathcal{N}_{\mathbf{x}'}\left(\mathbf{0}, \mathbf{A}\mathbf{A}^T + \boldsymbol{\Sigma}'\right) \qquad (30)$$

where in this case:

$$\mathbf{A} = \begin{bmatrix} \mathbf{F}_i & \mathbf{G} & \mathbf{0} \\ \mathbf{F}_i & \mathbf{0} & \mathbf{G} \end{bmatrix}, \quad \boldsymbol{\Sigma}' = \begin{bmatrix} \boldsymbol{\Sigma} + \sum_{i=1, i \neq n}^{N} \mathbf{F}_i\mathbf{F}_i^T & \mathbf{0} \\ \mathbf{0} & \boldsymbol{\Sigma} + \sum_{i=1, i \neq n}^{N} \mathbf{F}_i\mathbf{F}_i^T \end{bmatrix} \qquad (31)$$

We finally note that MAPLDA is a generalization of PLDA; in the degenerate case where only one attribute is available during training, MAPLDA reduces to PLDA.

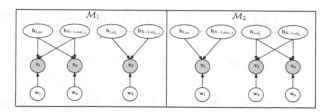

Fig. 3. Inference for *some* attributes (in this case, the first $N - 1$ attributes). For this particular case, only two data exist in the gallery, so the probe datum $\mathbf{x}_p$ can be matched with either datum $\mathbf{x}_1$ or datum $\mathbf{x}_2$. In case it does match with datum $\mathbf{x}_1$, then it is assigned labels $\{a_1, \ldots, a_{N-1}\}$ (model $\mathcal{M}_1$). Otherwise, it receives labels $\{a'_1, \ldots, a'_{N-1}\}$ (model $\mathcal{M}_2$).

3.3   3D Facial Shape Generation

We can exploit the generative property of MAPLDA, alongside the multi-attribute aspect of the model, to generate data with respect to different combinations of attribute values. Data generation can be accomplished as follows:

- Firstly, without loss of generality, we train a MAPLDA model with regards to two attributes we are interested in (e.g., attributes ethnicity and age, weight and age, etc.). After the training process, we recover the optimal $\mathbf{F}_1, \mathbf{F}_2, \mathbf{G}$ subspaces and noise diagonal covariance $\boldsymbol{\Sigma}$.
- Secondly, we pick the distinct instantiations of attributes we are interested in generating (e.g., *Chinese* ethnic group and *18–24* age group) and stack row-wise all the training data pertaining to these instantiations, creating a new vector $\mathbf{x}'$.
- Thirdly, if $\mathbf{h}_{i,a_i}$ and $\mathbf{h}_{j,a_j}$ are the selectors corresponding to the particular attributes, we stack them row-wise, i.e., $\mathbf{h}^T \doteq \begin{bmatrix} \mathbf{h}_{i,a_i} & \mathbf{h}_{j,a_j} \end{bmatrix}$, and calculate the posterior $\mathbb{E}\left[P\left(\mathbf{h}|\mathbf{x}'\right)\right]$ as

$$\mathbb{E}\left[P\left(\mathbf{h}|\mathbf{x}'\right)\right] = \mathbf{C}\mathbf{A}^T\mathbf{D}^{-1}\mathbf{x}', \tag{32}$$

where $\mathbf{A} = \begin{bmatrix} \mathbf{F}_1\,\mathbf{F}_2 \end{bmatrix}$, $\mathbf{C} = \left(\mathbf{I} + \mathbf{A}^T\mathbf{D}^{-1}\mathbf{A}\right)^{-1}$ and $\mathbf{D} = \left(\boldsymbol{\Sigma}' + \mathbf{G}'\mathbf{G}'^T\right)^{-1}$, where $\boldsymbol{\Sigma}'$ is defined as in (14), and $\mathbf{G}'$ is a block-diagonal matrix with copies of $\mathbf{G}$ on the diagonal.
- Finally, for selector $\mathbf{w}$, we choose a random vector from the multivariate normal distribution and the generated datum will be rendered as

$$\mathbf{x}_g = \mathbf{A}\mathbb{E}\left[P\left(\mathbf{h}|\mathbf{x}'\right)\right] + \mathbf{G}\mathbf{w}. \tag{33}$$

Examples of generated shapes are provided in the next section.

4   Experiments

Having described the training and inference procedure for MAPLDA, in this section we demonstrate the effectiveness of MAPLDA against PLDA [20], DS-LDA [27], Ioffe's PLDA variant [9], the Bayesian approach [17], LDA [4] and PCA

Table 1. *Ethnicity* identification. Average identification rates ± standard deviations per method. MAPLDA outperforms all of the compared methods.

Method	Mean	Std
MAPLDA	**0.990**	0.051
PLDA [20]	0.927	0.084
DS-LDA [27]	0.919	0.073
PLDA (Ioffe) [9]	0.917	0.089
Bayesian [17]	0.911	0.077
LDA [4]	0.878	0.079
PCA [26]	0.634	0.083

[26], by performing several experiments on facial shapes from MeIn3D dataset [6]. In these experiments we only take into account the 3D shape of the human face *without* any texture information.

MeIn3d Dataset

MeIn3D dataset [6] consists of $10,000$ raw facial scans that describe a large variation of the population. More specifically, MeIn3D dataset [6] consists of data annotated with multiple attributes (i.e., ethnicity, age, weight), thus it is highly appropriate for evaluating MAPLDA. Before performing any type of training or inference the scans are consistently re-parametrized into a form where the number of vertices, the triangulation and the anatomical meaning of each vertex are made consistent across all meshes. In this way all the training and the test meshes are brought into dense correspondence. In order to achieve this task we employ an optimal step non-rigid ICP algorithm [1]. We utilize the full spectrum of $10,000$ meshes where each mesh is labelled for a specific identity, age and ethnicity. The training and the inference is performed directly on the vectorized re-parametrized mesh of the form $\mathbb{R}^{3*N \times 1}$, where N is the distinct number of vertices.

4.1   Ethnicity Identification

In this experiment we identify the *ethnicity* attribute for a given 3D shape based on its shape features regardless of the *age-group* attribute (i.e., by marginalizing out the attribute *age-group*). We split the *ethnicity* attribute into three groups consisting of *White*, *Black* and *Asian* ethnic groups. We used 85% of the MeIn3D data for training and the rest for testing. Moreover, for each experiment, we used three random test data, with each test datum belonging in a different ethnic group. For the gallery we use the same set of distinct ethnic groups used in test samples from three random identities. We execute a total of 100 random experiments (i.e., we repeat the aforementioned process 100 times

Table 2. Confusion matrices of MAPLDA and PLDA for the *ethnicity* identification experiment. By incorporating the knowledge of the *age-group* attribute in the training phase, MAPLDA is able to better discriminate between the different ethnicities. In particular, MAPLDA classifies correctly all of the *Black* people in contrast with PLDA.

Actual	Predicted			Acc
	White	Black	Chinese	
White	**0.99**	0.00	0.01	0.99
Black	0.00	**1.00**	0.00	1.00
Chinese	0.02	0.00	**0.98**	0.98

(a) MAPLDA

Actual	Predicted			Acc
	White	Black	Chinese	
White	**0.97**	0.01	0.02	0.97
Black	0.04	**0.89**	0.07	0.89
Chinese	0.05	0.02	**0.93**	0.93

(b) PLDA [20]

Table 3. *Age-group* identification. Average identification rates ± standard deviations per method. MAPLDA outperforms all of the compared methods.

Method	Mean	Std
MAPLDA	**0.695**	0.063
PLDA [20]	0.540	0.079
PLDA (Ioffe) [9]	0.534	0.068
DS-LDA [27]	0.531	0.059
Bayesian [17]	0.529	0.071
LDA [4]	0.464	0.065
PCA [26]	0.327	0.074

for randomly chosen test data and galleries in every experiment). Average identification rates along with the corresponding standard deviations per setting are shown in Table 1. Confusion matrices for MAPLDA and PLDA are provided in Table 2. As can be seen, MAPLDA outperforms all of the compared methods, thus demonstrating the advantages of joint attribute modeling.

4.2 Age-group Identification

In this experiment we identify the *age-group* for a given datum regardless of the *ethnicity* attribute (i.e., by marginalizing out the *ethnicity* attribute). We split the *age-group* attribute into four groups consisting of under 18 years old (*<18*), *18–24*, *24–31* and *31–60* years old groups. We used 85% of the MeIn3D data for training and the rest for testing. Moreover, for each experiment we used four different random test data, with each test datum belonging in a different age group. For the gallery we use the same set of distinct age groups used in the test data from four random identities. We execute 100 random experiments per setting (i.e., we repeat the aforementioned process 100 times for randomly chosen probes and galleries in every experiment). Average identification rates along with the corresponding standard deviations per setting are shown in Table 3.

Table 4. Confusion matrices of MAPLDA and PLDA for the *age-group* identification experiment. By incorporating the knowledge of the *ethnicity* attribute in the training phase, MAPLDA is able to better discriminate between the different age-groups.

Actual	Predicted				Acc
	< 18	18-24	24-31	31-60	
< 18	**0.77**	0.18	0.05	0	0.77
18-24	0.14	**0.62**	0.23	0.01	0.62
24-31	0.02	0.20	**0.66**	0.12	0.66
31-60	0	0.06	0.19	**0.75**	0.75

(a) MAPLDA

Actual	Predicted				Acc
	< 18	18-24	24-31	31-60	
< 18	**0.59**	0.27	0.13	0.01	0.59
18-24	0.17	**0.48**	0.31	0.04	0.48
24-31	0.02	0.24	**0.52**	0.22	0.52
31-60	0.02	0.13	0.28	**0.57**	0.57

(b) PLDA [20]

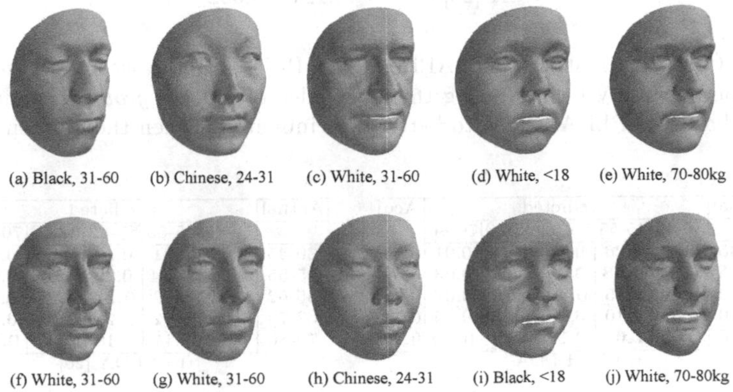

(a) Black, 31-60   (b) Chinese, 24-31   (c) White, 31-60   (d) White, <18   (e) White, 70-80kg

(f) White, 31-60   (g) White, 31-60   (h) Chinese, 24-31   (i) Black, <18   (j) White, 70-80kg

Fig. 4. 3D facial shapes generated via MAPLDA for different attribute combinations. (a–d) and (f–i) visualize different instantiations of attributes *ethnicity* and *age group*, while (e, j) of attributes *ethnicity* and *weight group*.

Confusion matrices for MAPLDA and PLDA are provided in Table 4. The identification rates are considerably lower compared to the *ethnicity* experiment and that demonstrates that the task of inferring the age of a certain face by the shape of it is a challenging one. Nevertheless, our proposed framework exhibits performance that outperforms all of the compared methods by a large margin.

4.3 Weight-group Identification

In this experiment we identify the *weight-group* attribute for a given datum regardless of *age-group* attribute (i.e., by marginalizing out the attribute *age-group*). We split the weight attribute into five groups consisting of *30–45* kg, *45–55* kg, *55–62* kg, *62–70* kg and *70–80* kg groups. We used 85% of the MeIn3D data for training and the rest for testing. Similarly to our previous experiments, we use five different random test data, with each test datum belonging in a different weight group. For the gallery we use the same set of distinct weight groups used in the test samples from five random identities. We execute 100 random experiments per setting (i.e., we repeat the aforementioned process 100

Table 5. *Weight-group* identification. Average identification rates ± standard deviations per method. MAPLDA outperforms all of the compared methods.

Method	Mean	Std
MAPLDA	**0.516**	0.051
PLDA [20]	0.380	0.084
PLDA (Ioffe) [9]	0.373	0.049
DS-LDA [27]	0.368	0.054
Bayesian [17]	0.364	0.071
LDA [4]	0.346	0.059
PCA [26]	0.197	0.062

Table 6. Confusion matrices of MAPLDA and PLDA for the *weight-group* identification experiment. By incorporating the knowledge of the *age-group* attribute in the training phase, MAPLDA is able to better discriminate between the different weight-groups.

Actual	Predicted					Acc
	30-45	45-55	55-62	62-70	70-80	
30-45	**0.55**	0.26	0.14	0.04	0.01	0.55
45-55	0.23	**0.58**	0.11	0.05	0.03	0.58
55-62	0.09	0.15	**0.46**	0.23	0.07	0.46
62-70	0.02	0.10	0.19	**0.53**	0.16	0.53
70-80	0.02	0.08	0.17	0.24	**0.49**	0.49

(a) MAPLDA

Actual	Predicted					Acc
	30-45	45-55	55-62	62-70	70-80	
30-45	**0.41**	0.31	0.19	0.06	0.03	0.41
45-55	0.26	**0.44**	0.20	0.07	0.03	0.44
55-62	0.10	0.22	**0.32**	0.28	0.08	0.32
62-70	0.04	0.12	0.25	**0.38**	0.21	0.38
70-80	0.06	0.11	0.18	0.30	**0.35**	0.35

(b) PLDA [20]

times for randomly chosen test data and galleries in every experiment). Average identification rates along with the corresponding standard deviations per setting are shown in Table 5. Confusion matrices for MAPLDA and PLDA are provided in Table 6. Weight identification is considered to be the most challenging experiment of all three, as predicting the correct *weight group* solely from 3D facial shapes without considering the scaling factor is a very difficult problem. Nevertheless, as it can be seen in Table 5, the top performance is given by MAPLDA which is 51.6%, outperforming the other methods by a large margin.

4.4   Generating Data

As thoroughly described in Sect. 3.3, the novel, multi-attribute nature of MAPLDA can be exploited to generate data with regards to a particular combination of attributes. By utilizing MeIn3D [6] dataset, we can train a multi-attribute model with regards to e.g., the *ethnicity* and *age-group* attributes and thus generate bespoke shapes that belong in a specific combination of attribute instantiations (e.g., ethnic group *Asian* and age group *24–31*). In Fig. 4, we visualize some examples of generated shapes belonging to a distinct combination of attributes such as *ethnicity* and *age-group* and *ethnicity* and *weight-group*.

5   Conclusions

In this paper, we introduced Multi-Attribute PLDA (MAPLDA), a novel component analysis method that is able to *jointly* model observations enriched with labels in terms of multiple attributes. We provide a probabilistic formulation and optimization procedure for training, as well as a flexible and efficient framework for inference on any subset of the attributes available during training. Evaluation is performed via several experiments on 3D facial shapes, namely ethnicity, age, and weight identification as well as 3D face generation under arbitrary instantiations of attributes. Results show that MAPLDA outperforms all compared methods, deeming the advantages of *joint* attribute modelling apparent.

References

1. Amberg, B., Romdhani, S., Vetter, T.: Optimal step nonrigid ICP algorithms for surface registration. In: Proceedings of the IEEE Conference on Computer Vision and Pattern Recognition, pp. 1–8. IEEE (2007)
2. Archambeau, C., Delannay, N., Verleysen, M.: Mixtures of robust probabilistic principal component analyzers. Neurocomputing **71**(7), 1274–1282 (2008)
3. Bach, F.R., Jordan, M.I.: A probabilistic interpretation of canonical correlation analysis (2005)
4. Belhumeur, P.N., Hespanha, J.P., Kriegman, D.J.: Eigenfaces vs. Fisherfaces: recognition using class specific linear projection. IEEE Trans. Pattern Anal. Mach. Intell. **19**(7), 711–720 (1997)
5. Bishop, C.M.: Pattern Recognition and Machine Learning. Springer, New York (2006)
6. Booth, J., Roussos, A., Zafeiriou, S., Ponniah, A., Dunaway, D.: A 3D morphable model learnt from 10,000 faces. In: Proceedings of the IEEE Conference on Computer Vision and Pattern Recognition, pp. 5543–5552 (2016)
7. Dempster, A.P., Laird, N.M., Rubin, D.B.: Maximum likelihood from incomplete data via the *EM* algorithm. J. Roy. Stat. Soc. Ser. B (Methodol.) 1–38 (1977)
8. Hardoon, D.R., Szedmak, S., Shawe-Taylor, J.: Canonical correlation analysis: an overview with application to learning methods. Neural Comput. **16**(12), 2639–2664 (2004)
9. Ioffe, S.: Probabilistic linear discriminant analysis. In: Leonardis, A., Bischof, H., Pinz, A. (eds.) ECCV 2006. LNCS, vol. 3954, pp. 531–542. Springer, Heidelberg (2006). https://doi.org/10.1007/11744085_41
10. Jolliffe, I.: Principal Component Analysis. Wiley, Hoboken (2002)
11. Kenny, P., Ouellet, P., Dehak, N., Gupta, V., Dumouchel, P.: A study of interspeaker variability in speaker verification. IEEE Trans. Audio Speech Lang. Process. **16**(5), 980–988 (2008)
12. Klami, A., Virtanen, S., Kaski, S.: Bayesian canonical correlation analysis. J. Mach. Learn. Res. **14**(1), 965–1003 (2013)
13. Lawrence, N.: Probabilistic non-linear principal component analysis with Gaussian process latent variable models. J. Mach. Learn. Res. **6**, 1783–1816 (2005)
14. Li, P., Fu, Y., Mohammed, U., Elder, J.H., Prince, S.J.: Probabilistic models for inference about identity. IEEE Trans. Pattern Anal. Mach. Intell. **34**(1), 144–157 (2012)

15. Loper, M., Mahmood, N., Romero, J., Pons-Moll, G., Black, M.J.: SMPL: a skinned multi-person linear model. ACM Trans. Graph. (TOG) **34**(6), 248 (2015)
16. Lüthi, M., Gerig, T., Jud, C., Vetter, T.: Gaussian process morphable models. IEEE Trans. Pattern Anal. Mach. Intell. **40**, 1860–1873 (2017)
17. Moghaddam, B., Jebara, T., Pentland, A.: Bayesian face recognition. Pattern Recogn. **33**(11), 1771–1782 (2000)
18. Moghaddam, B., Pentland, A.: Probabilistic visual learning for object representation. IEEE Trans. Pattern Anal. Mach. Intell. **19**(7), 696–710 (1997)
19. Nicolaou, M.A., Zafeiriou, S., Pantic, M.: A unified framework for probabilistic component analysis. In: Calders, T., Esposito, F., Hüllermeier, E., Meo, R. (eds.) ECML PKDD 2014. LNCS (LNAI), vol. 8725, pp. 469–484. Springer, Heidelberg (2014). https://doi.org/10.1007/978-3-662-44851-9_30
20. Prince, S.J., Elder, J.H.: Probabilistic linear discriminant analysis for inferences about identity. In: Proceedings of the IEEE International Conference on Computer Vision, pp. 1–8. IEEE (2007)
21. Romero, J., Tzionas, D., Black, M.J.: Embodied hands: modeling and capturing hands and bodies together. ACM Trans. Graph. (TOG) **36**(6), 245 (2017)
22. Roweis, S.: EM algorithms for PCA and SPCA. In: Advances in Neural Information Processing Systems, pp. 626–632 (1998)
23. Swets, D.L., Weng, J.J.: Using discriminant eigenfeatures for image retrieval. IEEE Trans. Pattern Anal. Mach. Intell. **8**, 831–836 (1996)
24. Tipping, M.E., Bishop, C.M.: Mixtures of probabilistic principal component analyzers. Neural Comput. **11**(2), 443–482 (1999)
25. Tipping, M.E., Bishop, C.M.: Probabilistic principal component analysis. J. Roy. Stat. Soc.: Ser. B (Stat. Methodol.) **61**(3), 611–622 (1999)
26. Turk, M.A., Pentland, A.P.: Face recognition using eigenfaces. In: Proceedings of the IEEE Conference on Computer Vision and Pattern Recognition, pp. 586–591. IEEE (1991)
27. Wang, X., Tang, X.: Dual-space linear discriminant analysis for face recognition. In: Proceedings of the IEEE Conference on Computer Vision and Pattern Recognition, vol. 2, pp. II-564–II-569. IEEE (2004)
28. Wibowo, M.E., Tjondronegoro, D., Zhang, L., Himawan, I.: Heteroscedastic probabilistic linear discriminant analysis for manifold learning in video-based face recognition. In: IEEE Workshop on Applications of Computer Vision (WACV), pp. 46–52. IEEE (2013)
29. Yu, S., Yu, K., Tresp, V., Kriegel, H.P., Wu, M.: Supervised probabilistic principal component analysis. In: Proceedings of the International Conference on Knowledge Discovery and Data Mining, pp. 464–473. ACM (2006)
30. Zhang, Y., Yeung, D.-Y.: Heteroscedastic probabilistic linear discriminant analysis with semi-supervised extension. In: Buntine, W., Grobelnik, M., Mladenić, D., Shawe-Taylor, J. (eds.) ECML PKDD 2009. LNCS (LNAI), vol. 5782, pp. 602–616. Springer, Heidelberg (2009). https://doi.org/10.1007/978-3-642-04174-7_39

Combination of Two Fully Convolutional Neural Networks for Robust Binarization

Romain Karpinski and Abdel Belaïd[⊠][iD]

Université de Lorraine-CNRS-LORIA, Campus scientifique,
54500 Vandoeuvre-Lès-Nancy, France
{romain.karpinski,abdel.belaid}@loria.fr
http://read.loria.fr/

Abstract. To be able to process historical documents, it is often required to first binarize the image (background and foreground separation) before applying the processing itself. Historical documents are challenging to binarize because of the numerous degradations they suffer such as bleed-through, illuminations, background degradations or ink drops. We present in this paper a new approach to tackle this task by a combination of two neural networks. Recently, the DIBCO binarization competition has seen a growing interest in the use of supervised methods to binarize challenging images. Inspired by the winner of the DIBCO 17 competition, which uses a fully convolutional neural network (FCN), we propose a combination of two FCNs to obtain better performance. While the two FCNs have the same architecture, they are trained on different representations of the input image. The first one uses downscaled image to capture the global context and the object locations. The second one works on patches of native resolution to help defining precisely the boundaries of the characters by capturing the local context. The final prediction is obtained by combining the results of the two FCNs. We show in the experiments that this strategy provides better results and outperforms the winner of the DIBCO17 competition.

Keywords: Historical documents · Binarization ·
Fully convolutional neural network

1 Introduction

Image binarization is the task of transforming an input image, whether in grayscale or color, into the binary space (0 or 1 values). The binary values represent whether a pixel belongs to the background or to the foreground (e.g. text pixels for textual documents). This type of image processing technique arises from the need to preprocess the information to simplify the next processing steps. These next processing steps can be for example text line detection [16], word spotting [9] or writer identification [11]. By first performing a binarization, one can expect an improvement of the pipeline because the image is easier to process. However, the binary image must be of highest quality so the next step is

© Springer Nature Switzerland AG 2019
C. V. Jawahar et al. (Eds.): ACCV 2018, LNCS 11363, pp. 509–524, 2019.
https://doi.org/10.1007/978-3-030-20893-6_32

not penalized. For example, if all pixels from a text character, are considered by the binarization algorithm as background, then the binary image will not contains this character. As a result, the required information can be missing from the input image thus resulting very likely in an error.

Obtaining good results in the context of historical documents can be tough because of the numerous degradations they suffer from. Historical documents are often very challenging since they can contain ink drops, bleed-through, stains, various illumination, etc. Nowadays, a huge number of techniques based on machine learning arises to handle this kind of documents. Machine learning approaches often equal or outperform classical methods thanks to their generalization capabilities. In this case, the binarization task is seen has a pixel labelling task called semantic segmentation. Semantic segmentation is the task of assigning a class probability for each pixel in an image (i.e. probability to be a text pixel for instance). The winner *Ilin et al.*, of the last DIBCO17 competition [22] on binarization, is a machine learning based method. It uses a special architecture of fully convolutional neural networks (FCN) [15] called U-net [23] which provide a high performance pixel labeling with only few labeled data. In this paper, we demonstrate on the DIBCO17 dataset that we can further improve the performance on the binarization task by combining the prediction of two FCNs.

The paper is organized as follow: in Sect. 2 we present the related work on binarization and fully convolutional neural networks. In Sect. 3, the proposed approach is described, then in Sect. 4, experiments are performed to demonstrate the effectiveness of our approach. Finally, conclusions and future work are drawn in Sect. 5.

2   Related Work

2.1   Binarization

The binary version of an image is obtain by thresholding the color or grayscale image. Generally, there are mainly two different kind of thresholding algorithms: local and global thresholding. Global thresholding approaches compute a single threshold for the whole image. In the context of historical documents global thresholding approaches such as Otsu [20] often has a suboptimal performance compared to local approaches. This is due to the fact that degradations can occur locally in an image such as illuminations, shadows or geometric deformations. On the other hand, local thresholding approaches are capable of adapting the binarization based on the local information of the image. However, they are often slower than global thresholding algorithm because of their need to compute statistics for each pixels to gather context from neighboring pixels. Local thresholding is usually done by using a small part of the image where statistics are computed to find the right threshold such as in Niblack et al. [18], Sauvola et al. [24] and Wolf et al. [27]. Other approaches such as Almeida et al. [4] employ bilateral filters on RGB images before applying the Otsu algorithm. Methods, such as Gatos et al. [8] and [28], use an estimation of the background and/or foreground to perform the binarization. Recently, the trend in binarization algorithm is to use machine learning approaches to perform the binarization. All these approaches mainly use convolutional neural networks (CNN) [14] such as the work of Pastor-Pellicer et al. [21]. The work of Calvo et al. [6] uses convolutional auto encoders to filter out the background and only keep the text pixels. Recently, Afzal et al. [3] and Westphal et al. [26] showed that recurrent neural networks can also be used to binarize patches. Tensmeyer et al. [25] used a fully convolutional neural network to perform the binarization. The next subsection will provide more details on fully convolutional neural networks as it is used in our proposed method.

2.2 Fully Convolutional Neural Networks

Usually, convolutional neural networks are composed of a series of convolutional layers followed by fully connected layers at the end. The use of the fully connected layers forces the input to be of a fixed size. Fully convolutional neural network originates from Long et al. [15] where the fully connected layers are replaced by upsampling and convolutional layers. One big advantage of this architecture is that it can process images of arbitrary sizes by using only convolutional layers and has very less weights in comparison. Generally, FCNs can be divided in two parts: the encoder part and the decoder part. The encoder part takes the input image and compresses it into a dense representation where the number of feature maps is high and the size is reduced. The decoder part has to decode the dense representation and upsample it to retrieve the original size. Therefore, a fully convolutional neural network outputs an image of the same size as the input. Also, it allows to perform semantic segmentation on full images which was not possible due to the complexity of the fully connected layers. Semantic segmentation is used in various areas such as baseline detection [7] or road line detection for autonomous driving [5].

Our approach combines the state of the art U-net with the module Squeeze and Excite (module SE) from Hu et al. [12] as it has shown to improve the performance of residual networks. Inspired from Grüning et al. [10] we use their architecture, called ARU-net, which has an attention mechanism to capture the information at different scales before performing the final classification. The proposed method does not only perform the binarization at patch level but also at the full image level to take advantage of the differences between these two scales. Results from the DIBCO17 competition indicate that combining local and global thresholding has better performances than using only one of those. Therefore, we decided to combine the outputs of two FCNs: one for a labeling with local context by using patches and one for a labeling with global context by using full resized images.

Our contribution to this paper is as follows:

1. We propose a new binarization method that combines the strength to suppress the weaknesses of two networks that work on different scales to produce state of the art results.

2. We show that these two networks alone have lower performances compared to their combination.
3. The effect of horizontal flipping as a data augmentation technique is studied in the context of binarization with FCNs and its interest shown.

3   Proposed Approach

An overview of the proposed approach can be found in Fig. 1. The method has two branches where each contains a neural network, more precisely two fully convolutional neural networks. The upper branch works on image patches without any rescaling. Then, the image is reconstructed from the patches by using a sliding window where only the center of each patch is kept for the final prediction. The centers of the patches are extracted to avoid border effects since the pixels that are close to the patch borders do not have a complete context to perform the prediction. The lower branch makes predictions on the whole rescaled image and labels all its pixels in one step. Then, the prediction is upsampled to retrieve the original image size. Finally, predictions from both branches are thresholded using a global threshold and combined using the pixel wise logical AND operator. Identical neural networks are employed for the two branches. The architecture is described in the next subsection.

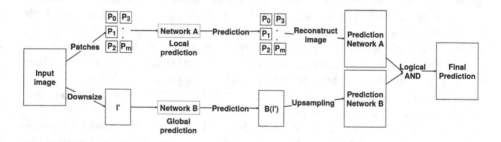

Fig. 1. Overview of the proposed approach.

3.1   The ARU-net

For the pixel labeling, we use a modified version of the ARU-net architecture of Grüning et al. [10] for both the local (patches) and global (full image) labeling. This architecture has been proven to provide better results on text baselines detection than a classical U-net with only a few addition of weights in the network. An overview of the ARU-net architecture can be seen in Fig. 2. It is composed of two neural networks: an Attention Network (AN) and a RU-net which is a U-net which has residual connections within its blocks. The U-net architecture will be described in Sect. 3.3 and the residual connections in 3.4. The ARU-net works by using the input image I plus n different scales S_n of the input image. For simplicity in the notations, we state that S_0 is I. The S_n scales are the successive downsampling of I by a factor of f, using average pooling. Therefore, the image size $S_n^{size} = S_n^{width} \times S_n^{height}$ relatively to I^{width} and I^{height} of I is computed by Eq. 1. Similarly, S_n^{height} is computed using the same equation but with I^{height} instead of I^{width}.

$$S_n^{width} = I^{width}/f^n \tag{1}$$

where f^n denotes the scaling factor.

All input images S_n are passed to the RU-net and the AN. The RU-net computes the features maps F_n which will be weighted and used to perform the pixel classification. The AN outputs the attention feature maps A_n that will be used to weight the F_n feature maps. As we have downsampled the images for $n > 0$, we need to perform the inverse operation of upsampling. Therefore, all F_n and A_n feature maps are upsampled using the nearest neighbour method to match the size of S_0. The number of different input image scales is called $Scale_{depth}$. Once all feature maps and attention maps have been computed for all the scales S_n, the attention maps A_n are concatenated and softmaxed pixelwise to distribute the weights along each scale giving AW_n feature maps. Then, all the feature maps F_n are weighted by their corresponding attention maps AW_n giving WF_n. Finally, all weighted feature maps WF_n are concatenated and a final convolutional layer performs the classification.

As said before, all S_n images are going through the same RU-net and AN. This makes the two networks more resilient to the scale variations that can occur between the different images. This is especially powerful when processing text images where the text size and annotations can have different shapes and scales.

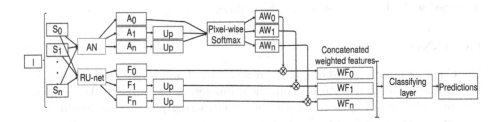

Fig. 2. ARU-net architecture overview. I is the input image. S_n is the scale of the image. AN is the attention network. RU-net is the network that extracts the features from the input image. A_n is the attention map. Boxes containing Up mean that the upsampling is done to match the size of S_0. AW_n is the softmaxed attention map. WF_n is the weighted features maps. Blue boxes are inputs, yellow are the neural networks, red are the attention maps and green, the feature maps. (Color figure online)

The architecture used for the attention network will be now defined.

3.2   Attention Network

The attention network designed in the original paper is a simple fully convolutional neural network. Its architecture can be best viewed in Table 1. The attention is computed with only 4 layers and a low number of filters with the final layer outputing one feature map. This single feature map will represent the attention of a given scale S_n. While this network is not suitable to perform the labelling, it has a sufficient number of filters to spot where the attention should be focused on. This attention mechanism will specialize all attention scales to spot one type of characteristics such as background, text or noise.

Table 1. Architecture of the Attention Network as described by Grüning et al. [10]

Input	#Filters	Kernel size	Activation
S_n			
Conv2D	12	4	Relu
MaxPooling 2×2			
Conv2D	16	4	Relu
MaxPooling 2×2			
Conv2D	32	4	Relu
MaxPooling 2×2			
Conv2D	1	4	Relu

The next subsection will detail the feature extractor RU-net by first describing the general principal of the U-net architecture, then the RU-net will be explained with the addition of the SE module.

3.3   U-Net

The U-net architecture was originaly proposed by Ronneberger et al. [23] to perform semantic segmentation of biomedical images. An example of U-net architecture is shown in Fig. 3. It consists of a contracting path which captures the context and an expanding path which retrieves the original image size. The contracting and expanding paths are both symetrical thus the architecture can be seen as close to the U shape (hence the name). A path consists of blocks of convolutions followed by max pooling for the contracting path and upsampling for the expanding path. To increase the resolution of the expanding path, skip connections are used between symetrical blocks of both paths. Skip connections consists in concatenating the upsampled block with the corresponding contracting block. Then, a convolution layer can be applied to this concatenation to learn to combine both contexts. Therefore, when the next upsampling is performed it has the context of the contracting block and the context from the previous expanding block. Moreover, the expanding path starts with a high number of filters which allow to take into consideration a lot of high level features. Also, it does not use fully connected layer and contains only pixel information so the spatial structure is kept. The advantage of the U-net is that it requires few images to have a good generalization [23].

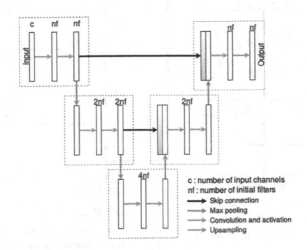

Fig. 3. Example of a U-net architecture with a depth of 3.

Now that the U-net architecture has been described, we need to define the blocks used to transform the U-net into a RU-net. Therefore, the next section describes the RU-net blocks.

3.4   RU-net

A RU-net is a U-net with residual connections within each blocks. It consists of two branches: the first one is the unactivated input, the second one is a classical chain of convolution layers followed by an activation function. The number of convolutions with activation block defines the depth of the residual connection. The last convolution layer is activated only after the unactivated input is summed to its unactivated output. The depth of the residual connection Res_{depth} corresponds to the number of convolution layers used. Figure 4(a) depicts the general principle of a residual connection of depth $Res_{depth} = 3$. To the residual modules we add the Squeeze and Excitation module which help to model an explicit relation between the feature maps (see Fig. 4(b)). First, the input feature maps are reduced to one feature by performing global average pooling. Then, two dense layers are applied to the feature maps to model the relation between them. Finally, the sigmoid activation is employed and its output is used to weight the original input feature maps. Compared to the original ARU-net architecture, we added the SE module to all residual blocks in the RU-net.

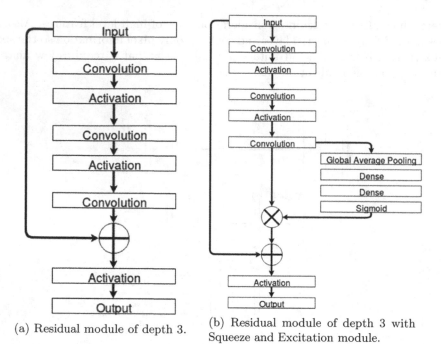

(a) Residual module of depth 3.

(b) Residual module of depth 3 with Squeeze and Excitation module.

Fig. 4. Residual module of depth 3 without and with SE module.

3.5   Full Image Binarizer

The goal of the full image binarizer is to detect the objects to binarize in the image. It means that it must find the approximate location of each object without detecting noises. In our case, the objects are the characters to binarize. Therefore, this network has the responsability to detect isolated noises such as bleed through, background degradations or ink drops. It aims to do so by capturing a large context of the image using the full image. Indeed, it is a lot easier to detect all these degradations when we can have the context of the full image. In fact, at a given pixel position, one may found bleed through very far from the closest main text making it hard to detect if we can only see bleed through. In the worst scenario, there is only bleed through in the image and the only thing that prevents the binarizer to falsely detect it is to have a global context.

One could employ this network to perform the binarization directly, but as it will be shown in the experiment section, this would greatly fail because of the downscaling which requires an upscaling step to match the original image size. In fact, this network will poorly detect the boundaries because of both the downsampling and the upsampling operations but will be stronger than patches to approximating the locations of characters.

3.6   Patch Image Binarizer

The goal of the patch image binarizer is to detect precisely the characters and especially their boundaries by using a local context on native resolution patches. We avoid, by using patches of the unresized images, the loss of precision due to the resizing made by the full image binarizer. However, this network can have trouble to identify noises that require a global context such as bleed through because of the constrained field of view on the local patch. Fortunately, these two networks have different complementary drawbacks and advantages that we can use by combining them to obtain a better prediction.

3.7   Prediction Combination

Before applying the predictions combination, predicted images are thresholded with the help of an analysis of the histogram. Therefore, a global threshold value is used to obtain for each binarizer a binary image. Then, the two predictions are simply passed through a bit-wise AND operator to get the final prediction. One could employ a more sofisticated mechanism to combine the predictions, however we choose in this paper to show that even a simple operation such as the bitwise AND operator improves the results.

4   Experiments

To verify the performance of the proposed approach, experiments are performed on the DIBCO competition on binarization. The next section describes the DIBCO competition and their metrics.

4.1   The DIBCO Competition

The DIBCO competition aims to evaluate the state of the art on the task of binarization. Documents are collected from two collections: IMPACT [1] for the printed and READ [2] for the handwritten images. We gathered training data from all the previous DIBCO competitions which gives us 87 training images. From those training images, 10 of them were randomly chosen for validation. The test consists in 10 printed and 10 handwritten images with several degradations such as bleed through, noises or holes in characters. The metrics used by the competitions are the FMeasure, the pseudo FMeasure, the PSNR and the DRD. The FMeasure defined by Eq. 2 is the harmonic mean between the precision and recall.

$$FM = \frac{2 \times Precision \times Recall}{Precision + Recall} \tag{2}$$

The pseudo FMeasure [19] is the weighted FMeasure by considering some pixels more important than others. It uses, similarly to the FMeasure, the Pseudo Recall and Pseudo Precision and take into consideration the distance to the contour of the ground truth. The PSNR, defined in Eq. 3, measures the pixel similarity between two images. The higher the value, the closer two images are from each others. Here C is the difference between foreground and background pixels, n the number of pixels in the image, y_i is the i-th pixel of the ground truth image and $\hat{y}_i$ is the i-th pixel of the predicted binary image.

$$PSNR = 10 \times \log(\frac{C^2}{MSE}) \tag{3}$$

where MSE is defined by Eq. 4

$$MSE = \frac{1}{n} \sum_{i=1}^{n} (y_i - \hat{y}_i)^2 \tag{4}$$

The Distance Reciprocal Distortion Metric or DRD [17], defined by Eq. 5, conveys the visual distortion as an human would see these distortions for binary images. It is defined in Eq. 5 where S is the number of wrongly classified pixels, $NUBN$ is the number of ground truth blocks of 8×8 which have at least one white and one black pixel. It uses, for each element in S, the DRD_k Eq. 6 which computes the distortion of a given pixel using a normalized weight matrix W_{Nm} of size 5×5. The ground truth block used to compute the distortion is centered around the k-th pixel at position (x, y) of the prediction y. The distortion is then the weighted sum of all pixels from the ground truth block that differs from the center pixels from y.

$$DRD = \frac{\sum_{k=1}^{S} DRD_k}{NUBN} \tag{5}$$

$$DRD_k = \sum_{i=-2}^{2} \sum_{j=-2}^{2} |y(i,j) - \hat{y}(x,y)| \times W_{Nm}(i,j) \tag{6}$$

4.2 Training Configuration

For the patch generation, random crops of fixed size are extracted from original images. Two patch sizes have been used for the experimentations: 512×512 and 1024×1024. Regarding full images, they are resized to have their maximum side to a maximum side MS. If the image maximum side $I_{side}^{max} = max(I^{width}, I^{height})$ is inferior to MS then the image is not resized. In other words, only images that are large, are resized while the others are left intact. Since the ARU-net requires the image to be divisible by a power of d and $d = 2$ in our case, we fixed $MS = 1024 = 2^{10}$. Remarkably, border padding is applied to images to rescaled images to make their size equal to $MS \times MS$ by adding zeros. This technique simplifies the U-net architecture as images will have the same size and therefore avoid the cropping of skip connections to fit the decoder size. This operation is summarized by Eq. 7. The RMSprop optimizer is used with an initial learning rate of 0.001 which is exponentially decayed over time by a factor $k = 0.03$. The loss function used to optimize the networks is the cross-entropy. Filters of size 3 are used for the U-net and filters of size 4 for the AN. A $Res_{depth} = 3$ is used in combination with $Scale_{depth} = 5$ for the ARU-net and the RU-net has a depth of 5 with an initial number of filters equal to 8. We train each network until convergence is reached.

$$I = \begin{cases} I & \text{if } I_{side}^{max} < MS \\ I^{size} * MS/I_{side}^{max} & \text{else} \end{cases} \tag{7}$$

4.3 Data Augmentation

To improve the performances of both our networks, we make use of data augmentation. Online data augmentation is performed to provide a large amount of different images. Data augmentation aims to add variability in the data by generally introducing noises or linear transforms. Online data augmentation produces augmented images during the training. The interest of doing it in an online way is that it is unlikely that we will submit twice the exact same image to the network. Also, to make our networks more resilient to bleed through, we decided to use the original images with synthetic bleed through using DocCreator [13]. This software allows to apply several different degradations such as holes, 3D deformations, bleed through or phantom characters. In our experiments, we only used the bleed through augmentation with a varying intensity scale $\gamma \in [0.2; 0.5]$. An example of synthetic bleed through image is provided in Fig. 5. Patches and image are then augmented using random rotations with an angle $\theta \in [-180; 180]^\circ$ and they can be horizontally flipped with Gaussian or salt and pepper noises.

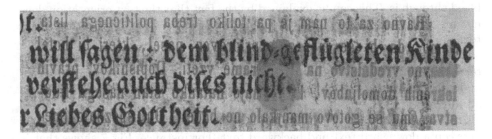

Fig. 5. Example of synthetic bleed through.

4.4 The Effect of Horizontal Flipping

We investigate the effect of horizontal flipping as one could think that it could confuse the network by having all the characters backwards compared to the bleed through. When there is no bleed through and the text does not have a lot more higher intensity than the background, if the image is horizontally flip it can be considered as a realistic bleed through. A small experiment has been conducted to verify whether the use of the transform confuses or not a neural network. To do so, patch binarizer has been trained for 50 epochs with and without horizontal flipping. Figure 6 shows the loss value after each epoch for the two strategies.

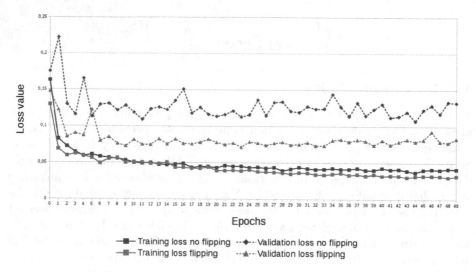

Fig. 6. The importance of horizontal flipping. Continuous lines represent training loss values and dashed lines, validation loss values.

Surprisingly, horizontal flipping is helping the network figuring out what the bleed through is. This can be explained by the fact that the text orientation does not matter so much but rather the relative pixel intensities between the main text and the bleed through. Usually, we can detect the bleed through by using only the text orientation (backwards characters) when there is only one kind of text. However, when we use random rotations, the text can be downward which makes it difficult for the network to distinguish downward from backward. Since all augmentation methods are independently performed on the image, we can also have both rotations and horizontal flips. Figures 7 and 8 show the differences between a downward text and backward text. For instance, Fig. 7 shows that is it not the text orientation that allows to distinguish the main text but only the pixels intensities. This is respected since we usually found ink of the same intensity in both recto and verso images. When the bleed through is present, the ink is overshadowed by the paper, thus making the bleed through lighter than the main text pixels.

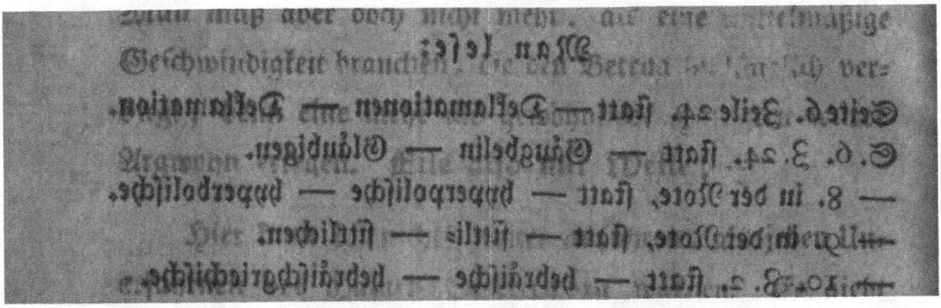

Fig. 7. Example of image flipped horizontally.

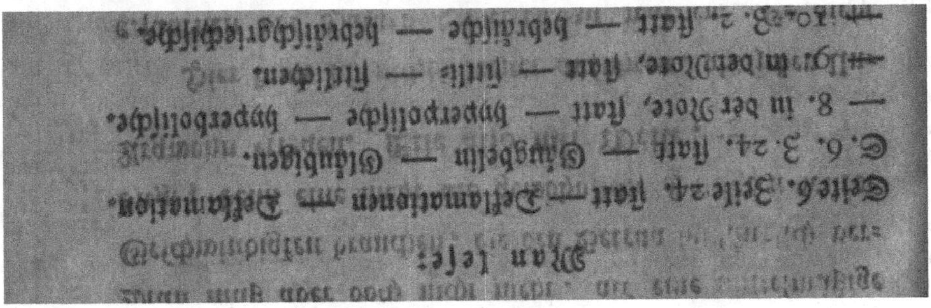

Fig. 8. Example of image rotated at 180°.

The only thing that remains to detect bleed through are the relative pixel intensities between the bleed through and the text pixels. The use of horizontal flipping improves the training because it helps the network learn this concept.

4.5 Results

Results of the experiments can be found in Table 2. One can see that not all methods improve the results compared to the state of the art. Those methods are the patch only with a patch size of 512 and the full image binarizer. While we know that the winner of DIBCO17 used patches, we do not know what size they used. However, when combining these two methods, we could obtain better results since they are complementary. To verify whether the patch context size influences the performance or not, we used patches of size 1024. The results shows that we obtained slightly better results but not for all metrics. Only the pseudo FMeasure did not improved, meaning that the errors made were more far from the ground truth (noises for example). When we combined the patches of size 1024 with the full image binarizer, we obtained again an improvement for all the metrics except for the pseudo FMeasure. Even if bigger patches improve the performances, using the full image binarizer, still helps to correct some mistakes even when using a simple combination of the prediction such as the logical AND operator.

Table 2. Results of our approach compared to the winner of DIBCO17.

DIBCO17 Test Set	FMeasure	Pseudo FMeasure	PSNR	DRD
Winner DIBCO17	91.04	92.86	18.28	3.4
Patch only 512	88.36	89.21	16.97	5.07
Patch only 1024	91.87	91.68	18.24	2.89
Image only	86.29	87.16	17.48	4.22
Combined patches 512	91.44	**93.05**	**18.519**	2.94
Combined patches 1024	**92.12**	92.49	18.516	**2.64**

4.6 Discussions

While the proposed approach outperforms the winning method of DIBCO17, it has the drawback of using two networks instead of one. Experiments showed that using big patches improves the results of the neural network. It suggests that if we could process images in their natural resolution it could further improve the state of the art. However, the results of the single neural network are still behind the combination of the two. Moreover, using the full rescaled image adds only little time, compared to the patch based network. Generally, most of the time used to compute the image prediction comes from the patch binarizer and not from the full image binarizer. The reason is simple: we need to label every pixel of the image at its original resolution with the patch binarizer in order to retrieve the prediction of the full image. For the full image binarizer, we have a lot less pixels to label because we predict on the downscaled images and upscale them after to obtain a prediction of the original size image. When using the big patches, the number of images to label is equal to $m + 1$ where m is the number of patches to label the whole image. Therefore, we can affirm that our approach adds only little execution time compared to other patch based methods when m is large (e.g. when processing large images).

5 Conclusion

We proposed in this paper a new robust method to binarize handwritten and printed document images. It consists in two fully convolutional neural networks with distincts objectives. The first one works on a reduced scale of the image and is precise to detect while the second woks globally. We show that these two networks alone are not capable of achieving better results. However, with a simple combination of the strength and weaknesses of the two FCNs, we were able to produce binarizations of very high quality. We showed that the proposed approach produces state of the art results on the DIBCO17 competition. While this technique works well, we still train the two networks independently. In future work, we plan on finding ways to add global image context to the patch binarizer so it can be trained end-to-end with a single neural network.

References

1. Impact project. http://www.impact-project.eu
2. Read project. http://read.transkribus.eu/
3. Afzal, M.Z., Pastor-Pellicer, J., Shafait, F., Breuel, T.M., Dengel, A., Liwicki, M.: Document image binarization using LSTM: a sequence learning approach. In: Proceedings of the 3rd International Workshop on Historical Document Imaging and Processing, pp. 79–84. ACM (2015)
4. Almeida, M., Lins, R.D., Bernardino, R., Jesus, D., Lima, B.: A new binarization algorithm for historical documents. J. Imaging 4(2), 27 (2018)
5. Alvarez, J.M., Gevers, T., LeCun, Y., Lopez, A.M.: Road scene segmentation from a single image. In: Fitzgibbon, A., Lazebnik, S., Perona, P., Sato, Y., Schmid, C. (eds.) ECCV 2012. LNCS, vol. 7578, pp. 376–389. Springer, Heidelberg (2012). https://doi.org/10.1007/978-3-642-33786-4_28
6. Calvo-Zaragoza, J., Gallego, A.J.: A selectional auto-encoder approach for document image binarization. arXiv preprint arXiv:1706.10241 (2017)
7. Fink, M., Layer, T., Mackenbrock, G., Sprinzl, M.: Baseline detection in historical documents using convolutional u-nets. In: 2018 13th IAPR International Workshop on Document Analysis Systems (DAS), pp. 37–42. IEEE (2018)
8. Gatos, B., Pratikakis, I., Perantonis, S.J.: Adaptive degraded document image binarization. Pattern Recogn. 39(3), 317–327 (2006)
9. Giotis, A.P., Sfikas, G., Gatos, B., Nikou, C.: A survey of document image word spotting techniques. Pattern Recogn. 68, 310–332 (2017)
10. Grüning, T., Leifert, G., Strauß, T., Labahn, R.: A Two-Stage Method for Text Line Detection in Historical Documents (2018). http://arxiv.org/abs/1802.03345
11. He, S., Wiering, M., Schomaker, L.: Junction detection in handwritten documents and its application to writer identification. Pattern Recogn. 48(12), 4036–4048 (2015)
12. Hu, J., Shen, L., Sun, G.: Squeeze-and-excitation networks. arXiv preprint arXiv:1709.01507 (2017)
13. Journet, N., Visani, M., Mansencal, B., Van-Cuong, K., Billy, A.: DocCreator: a new software for creating synthetic ground-truthed document images. J. Imaging 3(4), 62 (2017)
14. LeCun, Y., et al.: Backpropagation applied to handwritten zip code recognition. Neural Comput. 1(4), 541–551 (1989)
15. Long, J., Shelhamer, E., Darrell, T.: Fully convolutional networks for semantic segmentation. In: Proceedings of the IEEE Conference on Computer Vision and Pattern Recognition, pp. 3431–3440 (2015)
16. Louloudis, G., Gatos, B., Pratikakis, I., Halatsis, C.: Text line detection in handwritten documents. Pattern Recogn. 41(12), 3758–3772 (2008)
17. Lu, H., Kot, A.C., Shi, Y.Q.: Distance-reciprocal distortion measure for binary document images. IEEE Sig. Process. Lett. 11(2), 228–231 (2004)
18. Niblack, W.: An Introduction to Digital Image Processing. Prentice-Hall, Englewood Cliffs (1986)
19. Ntirogiannis, K., Gatos, B., Pratikakis, I.: Performance evaluation methodology for historical document image binarization. IEEE Trans. Image Process. 22(2), 595–609 (2013)
20. Otsu, N.: A threshold selection method from gray-level histograms. IEEE Trans. Syst. Man Cybern. 9(1), 62–66 (1979)

21. Pastor-Pellicer, J., España-Boquera, S., Zamora-Martínez, F., Afzal, M.Z., Castro-Bleda, M.J.: Insights on the use of convolutional neural networks for document image binarization. In: Rojas, I., Joya, G., Catala, A. (eds.) IWANN 2015. LNCS, vol. 9095, pp. 115–126. Springer, Cham (2015). https://doi.org/10.1007/978-3-319-19222-2_10

22. Pratikakis, I., Zagoris, K., Barlas, G., Gatos, B.: ICDAR 2017 competition on document image binarization (DIBCO 2017). In: 2017 14th IAPR International Conference on Document Analysis and Recognition (ICDAR), pp. 1395–1403. IEEE (2017)

23. Ronneberger, O., Fischer, P., Brox, T.: U-Net: convolutional networks for biomedical image segmentation. In: Navab, N., Hornegger, J., Wells, W.M., Frangi, A.F. (eds.) MICCAI 2015. LNCS, vol. 9351, pp. 234–241. Springer, Cham (2015). https://doi.org/10.1007/978-3-319-24574-4_28

24. Sauvola, J., Pietikäinen, M.: Adaptive document image binarization. Pattern Recogn. **33**(2), 225–236 (2000)

25. Tensmeyer, C., Martinez, T.: Document image binarization with fully convolutional neural networks. In: 2017 14th IAPR International Conference on Document Analysis and Recognition (ICDAR), vol. 1, pp. 99–104. IEEE (2017)

26. Westphal, F., Lavesson, N., Grahn, H.: Document image binarization using recurrent neural networks. In: 2018 13th IAPR International Workshop on Document Analysis Systems (DAS), pp. 263–268. IEEE (2018)

27. Wolf, C., Jolion, J.M., Chassaing, F.: Text localization, enhancement and binarization in multimedia documents. In: 2002 Proceedings of 16th International Conference on Pattern Recognition, vol. 2, pp. 1037–1040. IEEE (2002)

28. Afzal, M.Z., Krämer, M., Bukhari, S.S., Yousefi, M.R., Shafait, F., Breuel, T.M.: Robust binarization of stereo and monocular document images using percentile filter. In: Iwamura, M., Shafait, F. (eds.) CBDAR 2013. LNCS, vol. 8357, pp. 139–149. Springer, Cham (2014). https://doi.org/10.1007/978-3-319-05167-3_11

Deep Depth from Focus

Caner Hazirbas$^{(\boxtimes)}$, Sebastian Georg Soyer, Maximilian Christian Staab,
Laura Leal-Taixé, and Daniel Cremers

Technical University of Munich, Munich, Germany
{hazirbas,soyers,staab,leal.taixe,cremers}@cs.tum.edu

Abstract. Depth from focus (DFF) is one of the classical ill-posed
inverse problems in computer vision. Most approaches recover the depth
at each pixel based on the focal setting which exhibits maximal sharpness. Yet, it is not obvious how to reliably estimate the sharpness level,
particularly in low-textured areas. In this paper, we propose 'Deep Depth
From Focus (DDFF)' as the first end-to-end learning approach to this
problem. One of the main challenges we face is the hunger for data of
deep neural networks. In order to obtain a significant amount of focal
stacks with corresponding groundtruth depth, we propose to leverage
a light-field camera with a co-calibrated RGB-D sensor. This allows us
to digitally create focal stacks of varying sizes. Compared to existing
benchmarks our dataset is 25 times larger, enabling the use of machine
learning for this inverse problem. We compare our results with state-of-
the-art DFF methods and we also analyze the effect of several key deep
architectural components. These experiments show that our proposed
method 'DDFFNet' achieves state-of-the-art performance in all scenes,
reducing depth error by more than 75% compared to the classical DFF
methods.

Keywords: Depth from focus · Convolutional neural networks

1 Introduction

The goal of *depth from focus* (DFF) is to reconstruct a pixel-accurate disparity
map given a stack of images with gradually changing optical focus. The key
observation is that a pixel's sharpness is maximal when the object it belongs to
is in focus. Hence, most methods determine the depth at each pixel by finding
the focal distance at which the contrast measure is maximal. Nonetheless, DFF is
an ill-posed problem, since this assumption does not hold for all cases, especially
for textureless surfaces where sharpness cannot be determined. This is why most

This research was partially funded by the Humboldt Foundation through the Sofja
Kovalevskaja Award and ERC Consolidator Grant "3D Reloaded".

Electronic supplementary material The online version of this chapter (https://
doi.org/10.1007/978-3-030-20893-6_33) contains supplementary material, which is
available to authorized users.

C. V. Jawahar et al. (Eds.): ACCV 2018, LNCS 11363, pp. 525–541, 2019.
https://doi.org/10.1007/978-3-030-20893-6_33

methods rely on strong regularization to obtain meaningful depth maps which in turn leads to an often oversmoothed output.

Image	Disparity	VDFF	DDLF	PSP-LF	Lytro	PSPNet	Proposed

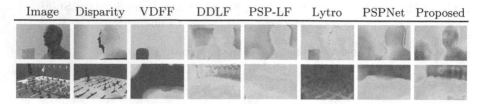

Fig. 1. Qualitative results of the DDFFNet versus state-of-the-art methods. Results are normalized by the maximum disparity, which the focal stacks are generated on (0.28 pixel). Warmer colors represent closer distances. Best viewed in color. (Color figure online)

While spatial smoothness is a rather primitive prior for depth reconstruction, with the advent of Convolutional Neural Networks (CNNs) we now have an alternative technique to resolve classical ill-posed problems such as semantic segmentation [3,14,29,34] or optical flow estimation [8]. The underlying expectation is that the rather naive and generic spatial smoothness assumption used in variational inference techniques is replaced with a more object-specific prior knowledge absorbed through huge amounts of training data.

A big strength of CNNs is their ability to extract meaningful image features, and correlate pixel information via convolutions. Our intuition is that a network will be able to find the image in the focal stack at which a pixel is maximally sharp, thereby correlating focus and depth. We therefore propose to tackle the task of depth from focus using end-to-end-learning. To that end, we create the first DFF dataset with real-world scenes and groundtruth measured depth. In order to obtain focal stacks in a reliable and fast way, we propose to use a light-field camera. Also called plenoptic camera, it allows us to obtain multi-view images of a scene with a single photographic exposure. All-in-focus images as well as focal stacks can be recovered digitally from a light-field image. Using this new dataset, we perform end-to-end learning of the disparity given a focal stack.

1.1   Contribution

We present *Deep Depth From Focus Network* (DDFFNet), an auto-encoder-style Convolutional Neural Network that outputs a disparity map from a focal stack. To train such a net, we create a dataset with 720 light-field images captured using a plenoptic camera, *i.e.* Lytro ILLUM, covering 12 indoor scenes. Given a light-field image, we can digitally generate a focal stack. Groundtruth depth is obtained from an RGB-D sensor which is calibrated to the light-field camera.

To the best of our knowledge, this is the largest dataset with groundtruth for the problem of DFF. We experimentally show that this amount of data is enough to successfully fine-tune a network. We compare our results with state-of-the-art DFF methods and provide a comprehensive study on the impact of different variations of the encoder-decoder type of network.

The contribution of this paper is three-fold:

- We propose DDFFNet, the first end-to-end learning method to compute depth maps from focal stacks.
- We introduce DDFF 12-Scene: a dataset with 720 light-field images and co-registered groundtruth depth maps recorded with an RGB-D sensor. We show that this data is enough to train a network for the task of DFF.
- We compare several state-of-the-art methods for DFF, as well as several variations of the encoder-decoder architecture, and show that our method outperforms the other methods by a large margin. It computes depth maps in 0.6 s on an NVidia Pascal Titan X GPU.

1.2   Related Work

Depth from Focus or Shape from Focus. Conventional methods aim at determining the depth of a pixel by measuring its sharpness or focus at different images of the focal stack [38]. Developing a discriminative measure for sharpness is non trivial, we refer the reader to [38] for an overview. Other works aim at filtering the contrast coefficients before determining depth values by windowed averaging [43] or non-linear filtering [31]. Another popular approach to obtain consistent results is to use total variation regularization. [30] proposed the first variational approach to tackle DFF while [32] defines an objective function composed of a smooth but nonconvex data term with a non-smooth but convex regularizer to obtain a robust (noise-free) depth map. Suwajanakorn *et al.* [42] computes DFF on mobile devices, focusing on compensating the motion between images of the focal stack. This results in a very involved model, that depends on optical flow results, and takes 20 min to obtain a depth map. Aforementioned methods heavily rely on priors/regularizers to increase the robustness of the algorithm, meaning their models may not generalize to all scenes. Interestingly, shape from focus was already tackled using neural networks in 1999 [2], showing their potential on synthetic experiments. The increasing power of deep architectures makes it now possible to move towards estimating depth of real-world scenarios.

Plenoptic or Light-Field Cameras. A light-field or plenoptic camera captures angular and spatial information on the distribution of light rays in space. In a single photographic exposure, these cameras are able to obtain multi-view images of a scene. The concept was first proposed in [1], and has recently gained interest from the computer vision community. These cameras have evolved from bulky devices [46] to hand-held cameras based on micro-lens arrays [33]. Several works focus on the calibration of these devices, either by using raw images and line features [4] or by decoding 2D lenslet images into 4D light-fields [6]. An analysis of the calibration pipeline is detailed in [5]. Light-field cameras are particularly interesting since depth and all-in-focus images can be computed directly from the 4D light-field [21,26,37]. Furthermore, focal stacks, *i.e.* images taken at different optical focuses, can be obtained from plenoptic cameras with a single photographic exposure. For this reason, we choose to capture our training dataset using these cameras, though any normal camera that captures images at different optical focuses can be used at test time.

To the best of our knowledge, there are only two light-field datasets with groundtruth depth maps [19,45]. While [45] provides 7 synthetic and only 6 real-scene light-fields, [19] generates a hand-crafted synthetic light-field benchmark composed of only 24 samples with groundtruth disparity maps. Our dataset is 25 times larger, composed of 12 indoor scenes, in total of 720 light-field samples with co-registered groundtruth depth obtained from an RGB-sensor, ranging from 0.5 to 7 m. In this work, we show that our data is enough to fine-tune a network for the specific task of predicting depth from focus.

Note that the Stanford Light-field dataset[1] has more samples than our dataset, but does not provide *groundtruth depth maps*. The depth maps in this dataset were produced by the standard Lytro toolbox which outputs lambda-scaled depth maps. Therefore, the maps are not in real distance metrics and there is no camera calibration provided. Furthermore, Lytro depth maps can be inaccurate as we will show in Sect. 4, and cannot be considered as groundtruth.

Deep Learning. Deep learning has had a large impact in computer vision since showing its excellent performance in the task of image classification [16,24,41]. A big part of its success has been the creation of very large annotated datasets such as ImageNet [39]. Of course, this can also be seen as a disadvantage, since creating such datasets with millions of annotations for each task would be impractical. Numerous recent works have shown that networks pre-trained on large datasets for seemingly unrelated tasks like image classification, can easily be fine-tuned to a new task for which there exists only a fairly small training dataset. This paradigm has been successfully applied to object detection [13], pixel-wise semantic segmentation [3,14,22,29,34,47], depth and normal estimation [12,25,27] or single image-based 3D localization [23,44], to name a few. Another alternative is to generate synthetic data to train very large networks, *e.g.*, for optical flow estimation [8]. Using synthetic data for training is not guaranteed to work, since the training data often does not capture the real challenge and noise distribution of real data. Several works use external sources of information to produce groundtruth. [11] uses sparse multi-view reconstruction results to train a CNN to predict surface normals, which are in turn used to improve the reconstruction. In [12], the authors aim at predicting depth from a single image, but create groundtruth depth data from matching stereo images. We propose to use an RGB-D sensor that can be registered to our light-field camera to obtain the groundtruth depth map. Even though an RGB-D sensor is not noise-free, we show that the network can properly learn to predict depth from focus even from imperfect data. We use the paradigm of fine-tuning a pre-

---

[1] http://lightfields.stanford.edu/.

trained network and show that this works even if the tasks of image classification and DFF seem relatively unrelated.

2   DDFF 12-Scene Benchmark

In this section we present our indoor DDFF 12-Scene dataset for *depth from focus*. This dataset is used for the training and evaluation of the proposed and several state-of-the-art methods. We first give the details on how we generate our data, namely the focal stack and groundtruth depth maps.

Why a 4D Light-Field Dataset for Depth from Focus? To determine the depth of a scene from focus, we first need to generate a focal stack obtainable by using any camera and changing the focal step manually to retrieve the refocused images. Nonetheless, this is a time-consuming task that would not allow us to collect a significant amount of data as it is required to train deep models. Given the time that it takes to change the focus on a camera, the illumination of the scene could have easily changed or several objects could have moved. We therefore propose to leverage a light-field camera as it has the following advantages: (i) only one image per scene needs to be taken, meaning all images will have the same photographic exposure and the capturing process will be efficient, (ii) refocusing can be performed digitally, which allows us to easily generate stacks with different focal steps, (iii) the dataset can be a benchmark not only for DFF, but also for other tasks such as depth from light-field or 3d reconstruction from light-field. Even though we do not intend to tackle these tasks in this work, we do show some comparative results on depth from light-Field in Sect. 4.

Light-Field Imaging. With light-field imaging technology, the original focus of the camera can be altered after the image is taken. Following this, we use a commercially available light-field camera, *i.e.* Lytro ILLUM[2], to collect data and then generate focal stacks. Plenoptic cameras capture a 4D light-field $L(u, v, x, y)$ which stores the light rays that intersect the image plane Ω at (x, y) and the focus or camera plane Π at (u, v). The pixel intensity $I(x, y)$ is then:

$$I(x, y) = \int_u \int_v L(u, v, x, y) \; \partial u \, \partial v . \tag{1}$$

Refocusing on an image corresponds to shifting and summing all sub-apertures, $I_{(u,v)}(x, y)$. Given the amount of shift, pixel intensities of a refocused image are computed as follows [7]:

$$I'(x, y) = \int_u \int_v L(u, v, x + \Delta_x(u), y + \Delta_y(v)) \, \partial u \, \partial v . \tag{2}$$

---

[2] Lytro ILLUM lightfield camera, `illum.lytro.com`, accessed: 2016-11-07.

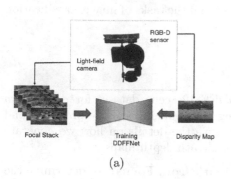 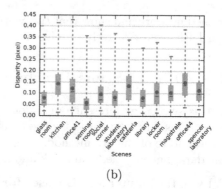

(a)   (b)

Fig. 2. (a) Experimental setup: we place an RGB-D sensor on top of a plenoptic camera in order to capture calibrated groundtruth depth maps and light-field images from which we then create focal stacks. These two inputs will be used to train the *DDFFNet*. (b) Whisker diagram of the disparity distribution for each scene. Circle and red line are the mean and median, respectively. Minimum disparity is 0.015 pixels (bottom orange lines), maximum disparity is 0.43 pixels (top orange lines). (Color figure online)

The shift (Δ_u, Δ_v) of each sub-aperture uv can be physically determined given an arbitrary depth Z in m, at which the camera is in-focus:

$$\begin{pmatrix} \Delta_x(u) \\ \Delta_y(v) \end{pmatrix} = \underbrace{\frac{\text{baseline} \cdot f}{Z}}_{\text{disparity}} \cdot \begin{pmatrix} u_{center} - u \\ v_{center} - v \end{pmatrix} , \tag{3}$$

where the baseline is the distance between adjacent sub-apertures in meter/pixel, f is the focal length of the microlenses in pixels and $(u, v)^T$ indicates the spatial position of the sub-aperture in the Π plane in pixels. Although shifting can be performed using bilinear or bicubic interpolation, to be able to perform subpixel accurate focusing on the images, following [21] we use the *phase shift algorithm* to observe the impact of subpixel shifts on the images:

$$\mathcal{F}\{I'(x + \Delta_x(u))\} = \mathcal{F}\{I(x)\} \cdot \exp^{2\pi i \Delta_x(u)} , \tag{4}$$

where $\mathcal{F}\{\cdot\}$ is the 2D discrete Fourier transform. We generate the focal stacks within a given disparity range, for which the focus shift on the images is clearly observable from close objects to far ones present in our dataset. Disparity values used in refocusing in Eq. 3 are sampled linearly in the given interval for a stack size of S, meaning that the focus plane equally shifts in-between the refocused images. Example refocused images for disparity $\in \{0.28, 0.17, 0.02\}$ are shown in Fig. 3. Note that we chose to use a light-field camera since it is easy to obtain a focal stack from it. Nonetheless, at test time, any imaging device could be used to take images at different optical focus.

Light-Field Camera Calibration. For consistent capturing over all scenes, we fix the focal length of the main lens to f=9.5 mm and lock the zoom. To increase

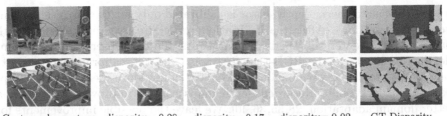

Center sub-aperture   disparity= 0.28   disparity= 0.17   disparity= 0.02   GT Disparity

Fig. 3. Example refocused images. *First column:* Center sub-aperture image. *Last column:* groundtruth disparity maps from the RGB-D sensor. *Middle columns:* Refocused images for varying disparity values in pixels, regions in focus are highlighted. Best viewed in color. (Color figure online)

the re-focusable range of the camera, we use the *hyperfocal mode*. Theoretically, we can then refocus from 27 cm distance to infinity. We set the white-balancing, ISO and shutter speed settings to *auto* mode. In order to estimate the intrinsic parameters of the light-field camera, we use the calibration toolbox by Bok *et al.* [4] with a chessboard pattern composed of 26.25 mm length squares. The radius of each microlens is set to 7 pixels as suggested in [4].

We can generate 9×9 undistorted sub-apertures, each of which has 383×552 image resolution. Estimated intrinsic parameters of the microlenses are: focal length $f = f_x = f_y = 521.4$, microlens optical center $(c_x, c_y)^T = (285.11, 187.83)^T$ and the baseline (distance between two adjacent sub-apertures in meter/pixel) is 27e$-$5. All estimated parameters can be found in the supplementary material.

Groundtruth Depth Maps from an RGB-D Sensor. Along with the light-field images, we also provide groundtruth depth maps. To this end, we use an RGB-D structure sensor, *i.e.* ASUS Xtion PRO LIVE, and mount it on the hot shoe of the light-field camera (see Fig. 2a). Since we only need the infrared camera of the RGB-D sensor, we align the main lens of Lytro ILLUM to the infrared image sensor as close as possible for a larger overlap on the field of views of both cameras. We save the 480×640 resolution depth maps in millimeters. RGB-D sensors are not accurate on glossy surfaces and might even produce a large amount of invalid/missing measurements. In order to reduce the number of missing values, we take nine consecutive frames and save the median depth of each pixel during recording/capturing.

Stereo Camera Calibration. We perform mono and stereo camera calibration to estimate the relative pose of the depth sensor with respect to the light-field camera. To this end, we use the publicly available *Camera Calibration Toolbox for Matlab*[3]. We use the same calibration pattern as for the light-field calibration. Stereo calibration is performed between the center sub-aperture $(u, v)^T = (5, 5)^T$ and the infrared camera image. While we fix the intrinsics

---

[3] www.vision.caltech.edu/bouguetj/calib_doc/.

of the light-field camera, depth sensor is calibrated only for the intrinsic parameters (no distortion). After the calibration procedure, we register the depth maps onto the center sub-aperture images. As one can observe in the examples in Fig. 3, due to the RGB-D sensor noise and the calibration procedure, some pixels around object boundaries do not contain depth measurements (represented in dark blue). Recorded depth maps can be improved further for a better domain adaptation [28,35,36,40]. We leave the possible improvements for future work. We convert depth to disparity to generalize the method to different cameras.

DDFF 12-Scene Benchmark. We collect the dataset in twelve different indoor environments: *glassroom, kitchen, office41, seminar room, social corner, student laboratory, cafeteria, library, locker room, magistrale, office44* and *spencer laboratory.* First six scenes are composed of 100 light-field images and depth pairs and the latter six scenes are composed of 20 pairs. Our scenes have at most 0.5 pixel disparity while the amount of measured disparity gradually decreases towards far distances. Fig. 2b plots the Whisker diagrams for each scene. Example center sub-aperture images for *office41* and *locker room* scenes and their corresponding disparity maps are shown in Fig. 3. Since the dataset consists mainly of indoor scenes, flat surfaces (wall, desk), textureless objects (monitor, door, cabinet) and glossy materials (screen, windows) are often present. Our dataset is therefore more challenging and 25 times larger than previous synthetic datasets [19,45]. DDFF 12-Scene dataset, consisting of the light-field images, generated focal stacks, registered depth maps and the source code of our method are publicly available on https://vision.cs.tum.edu/data/datasets/ddff12scene.

3   Depth from Focus Using Convolutional Neural Networks

This section describes our method for depth reconstruction from a focal stack. We formulate the problem as a minimization of a regression function, which is an end-to-end trained convolutional neural network.

Let S be a focal stack consisting of S refocused images $I \in \mathbb{R}^{H \times W \times C}$ and the corresponding target disparity map $D \in \mathbb{R}^{H \times W}$. We minimize the least square error between the estimated disparity $f(S)$ and the target D:

$$\mathcal{L} = \sum_{p}^{HW} \mathcal{M}(p) \cdot \left\| f_{\mathbf{W}}(S, p) - D(p) \right\|_2^2 + \lambda \| \mathbf{W} \|_2^2 . \tag{5}$$

Loss function $\mathcal{L}$ is summed over all valid pixels p where $D(p) > 0$, indicated by the mask $\mathcal{M}$ and $f : \mathbb{R}^{S \times H \times W \times C} \rightarrow \mathbb{R}^{H \times W}$ is a convolutional neural network. Weights, $\mathbf{W}$, are penalized with ℓ_2-norm. Depth/disparity maps captured by RGB-D sensors often have missing values, indicated with a value of 0. Therefore, we ignore the missing values during training in order to prevent networks from outputting artifacts.

Network Architecture. We propose an end-to-end trainable auto-encoder style convolutional neural network. CNNs designed for image classification are mostly encoder type networks which reduce the dimension of the input to a 1D vector [16,24,41]. This type of networks are very powerful at constructing descriptive hierarchical features later used for image classification. This is why for tasks which require a pixel-wise output, the encoder part is usually taken from these pre-trained networks [16,24,41] and a mirrored decoder part is created to upsample the output to image size. We follow this same paradigm of hierarchical feature learning for pixel-wise regression tasks [8,22,29,34] and design a convolutional auto-encoder network to generate a dense disparity map (see Fig. 1 in the supplementary material).

As a baseline for the encoder network, we use the VGG-16 net [41]. It consists of 13 convolutional layers, 5 poolings and 3 fully-connected layers. In order to reconstruct the input size, we remove the fully-connected layers and reconstruct the decoder part of the network by mirroring the encoder layers. We invert the 2×2 pooling operation with 4×4 upconvolution (deconvolution) [29] with a stride of 2 and initialize the weights of the upconvolution layers with bilinear interpolation, depicted as upsample (see supp. Fig. 1).

Similar to the encoder part, we use convolutions after upconvolution layers to further sharpen the activations. To accelerate the convergence, we add batch normalization [20] after each convolution and learn the scale and shift parameters during training. Batch normalization layers are followed by rectified linear unit (ReLU) activations. Moreover, after the 3rd, 4th and 5th poolings and before the corresponding upconvolutions, we apply dropout with a probability of 0.5 during training similar to [22]. In order to preserve the sharp object boundaries, we concatenate the feature maps of early convolutions conv1_2, conv2_2, conv3_3 with the decoder feature maps: outputs of the convolutions are concatenated with the outputs of corresponding upconvolutions (see supp. Figure 1).

We refer to this architecture as *DDFFNet*. There are several architectural choices that one can make that can significantly increase or decrease the performance of auto-encoder networks. Some of these changes are the way upsampling is done in the decoder part or the skip connections. For the problem of DFF, we study the performance of the followings variants:

- *DDFFNet-Upconv*: In the decoder part, we keep the upconvolutions.
- *DDFFNet-Unpool*: Upconvolutions are replaced by 2×2 unpooling operation [9].
- *DDFFNet-BL*: Upconvolutions are replaced by 2×2 bilinear interpolation (upsampling).
- *DDFFNet-CCx*: Here we study the effect of several concatenation connections, designed to obtain sharper edges in the depth maps.

Network Input. VGG-16 net takes the input size of $H \times W \times C$, precisely $224 \times 224 \times 3$. In contrast, we need to input the whole focal stack S into the network. Computing features per image I in the focal stack is a general way of incorporating sharpness into DFF approaches [32] and we make use of this

Image	Disparity	Unpool	BL	UpConv	CC1	CC2	CC3

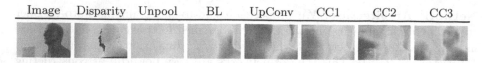

Fig. 4. Qualitative results of the variants of DDFFNet. While BL oversmooths the edges, CC1 and CC2 introduce artificial edges on the disparity map. Unpooling is not suitable well to recover the fine edges. Best viewed in color. (Color figure online)

intuition within our end-to-end trained CNN. Since the depth of a pixel is correlated with the sharpness level of that pixel and the convolutions are applied through input channels C, we consider the network as a feature extractor and therefore, we reshape our input to $(B \cdot S \times C \times H \times W)$ with a batch size of B. Hence, the network generates one feature map per image in the stack with a size of $(B \cdot S \times 1 \times H \times W)$. In order to train the network end-to-end, we reshape the output feature maps to $(B \times S \times H \times W)$ and apply 1×1 convolution as a regression layer through the stack, depicted as *Score* in supp. Figure 1.

4 Experimental Evaluation

We evaluate our method on the DDFF 12-Scene dataset proposed in Sect. 2. We first split the twelve scenes into training and test sets. We use the six scenes, *i.e. cafeteria, library, locker room, magistrale, office44, spencer laboratory* for testing as these scenes have in total 120 focal stacks and are also a good representation of the whole benchmark, as shown in Fig. 2b. The other six scenes are then used for training with a total of 600 focal stacks.

Evaluation Metrics. Following [10,12,19,27] we evaluate the resulting depth maps with eight different error metrics:

- MSE: $\frac{1}{|\mathcal{M}|} \sum_{p \in \mathcal{M}} \left\| f(\mathcal{S}_p) - D_p \right\|_2^2$
- RMS: $\sqrt{\frac{1}{|\mathcal{M}|} \sum_{p \in \mathcal{M}} \left\| f(\mathcal{S}_p) - D_p \right\|_2^2}$
- log RMS: $\sqrt{\frac{1}{|\mathcal{M}|} \sum_{p \in \mathcal{M}} \left\| \log f(\mathcal{S}_p) - \log D_p \right\|_2^2}$
- Absolute relative: $\frac{1}{|\mathcal{M}|} \sum_{p \in \mathcal{M}} \frac{|f(\mathcal{S}_p) - D_p|}{D_p}$
- Squared relative: $\frac{1}{|\mathcal{M}|} \sum_{p \in \mathcal{M}} \frac{\left\| f(\mathcal{S}_p) - D_p \right\|_2^2}{D_p}$
- Accuracy: % of D_p s.t max $\left(\frac{f(\mathcal{S}_p)}{D_p}, \frac{D_p}{f(\mathcal{S}_p)} \right) = \delta < thr$
- BadPix(τ): $\frac{|\{p \in \mathcal{M} : |f(\mathcal{S}_p) - D_p| > \tau\}|}{|\mathcal{M}|} \cdot 100$
- Bumpiness: $\frac{1}{|\mathcal{M}|} \sum_{p \in \mathcal{M}} \min(0.05, \|\mathrm{H}_\Delta(p)\|_F) \cdot 100$

where $\Delta = f(\mathcal{S}_p) - D_p$ and H is the Hessian matrix. The first five measures are standard error measures, therefore lower is better while for the Accuracy measure higher is better. BadPix(τ) quantifies the number of wrong pixels with a given threshold τ while Bumpiness metric focuses on the smoothness of the predicted depth maps [19].

Experimental Setup. For our experiments, we generate the focal stacks for $S = 10$ with disparities linearly sampled in $[0.28, 0.02]$ pixel (equivalent to $[0.5, 7]$ meters). We found this to be a good compromise between obtaining pixel sharpness at all depths and memory consumption and runtime, which heavily increases for larger focal stacks without bringing improved depth accuracy (see Fig. 5).

DDFF 12-Scene consists of 383×552 images, thus training on full resolution stacks is inefficient. One solution would be to downsample the images, however, interpolation could change the blur kernels, eventually affecting network performance. The solution we adopt is to train the network on $10 \times 224 \times 224 \times 3$ stack patches. To do so, we crop the training stacks and corresponding disparity maps with a patch size of 224 and a stride of 56, ensuring that cropped patches cover the whole image. Patches with more than 20% missing disparity values are removed from the training set. 20% of the training data is used as validation for model selection. At test time, results are computed on the full resolution 383×552 images.

We run all experiments on an NVidia Pascal Titan X GPU. Encoder part of the network is initialized from the pre-trained VGG-16 net, decoder part is initialized with variance scaling [15]. We use the SGD optimizer with momentum decay of 0.9. Batch size B is set to 2 and learning rate to 0.001. Every fourth epoch we exponentially reduce the learning rate by a factor of 0.9.

4.1 Ablation Studies

We first evaluate our architecture variations such as the three upsampling layers: unpooling, upconvolution and bilinear interpolation. We can see from Fig. 4, *Unpool* does not preserve the fine object edges while *BL* oversmooths them due to naive linear interpolation. These observations are also supported by the quantitative experiments in Table 1. Hence, we choose to use *UpConv* for the rest of architectural variations.

Within the tested concatenation schemes, *DDFFNet-CC1* and *DDFFNet-CC2* preserve too many edges as they benefit from larger feature maps. However, this produces incorrect depth and therefore achieving overall worse MSE compared to that of *DDFFNet-CC3*, see Table 1. On the other hand, *DDFFNet-CC3* preserves only the most important edges corresponding to object boundaries. Going deeper in the concat connections would not provide sufficiently fine structures, hence, we do not test connections after *CC3*.

We further plot the BadPix measure when changing the threshold τ in Fig. 5. In this plot, we compare our best architecture *DDFFNet-CC3* with focal stacks of varying sizes, $S \in \{5, 8, 10, 15\}$. Having light-field images allows us to digitally generate focal stacks of varying sizes, enabling us to find an optimal size. Even though increasing the stack size S should theoretically decrease the depth error, S-15 quickly overfits due to the fact that it was trained with a batch size of 1 to fit into the memory of a single GPU. We find that a focal stack of 10 images is the best memory-performance compromise, which is why all further experiments are done with $S = 10$.

Table 1. Quantitative results. *DDFFNet-CC3* is the best depth from focus method and provides also better results compared to Lytro, *i.e.* depth from light-field. Metrics are computed on the predicted and the groundtruth disparity maps.

Method		MSE ↓	RMS ↓	log RMS ↓	Abs. rel. ↓	Sqr. rel.↓	Accuracy ($\delta = 1.25$)			Bump. ↓
							δ ↑	δ^2 ↑	δ^3 ↑	
DDFFNet	Unpool	$2.9\,e^{-3}$	0.050	0.50	0.64	0.05	39.95	63.46	78.26	0.62
	BL	$2.1\,e^{-3}$	0.041	0.43	0.46	0.03	51.29	74.81	85.28	0.54
	UpConv	$1.4\,e^{-3}$	0.034	0.33	0.30	0.02	52.41	83.09	93.78	0.54
	CC1	$1.4\,e^{-3}$	0.033	0.33	0.37	0.02	60.38	82.11	90.63	0.75
	CC2	$1.8\,e^{-3}$	0.039	0.39	0.39	0.02	44.80	76.27	89.15	0.75
	CC3	$9.7\,e^{-4}$	0.029	0.32	0.29	0.01	61.95	85.14	92.99	0.59
PSPNet		$9.4\,e^{-4}$	0.030	0.29	0.27	0.01	62.66	85.90	94.42	0.55
Lytro		$2.1\,e^{-3}$	0.040	0.31	0.26	0.01	55.65	82.00	93.09	1.02
PSP-LF		$2.7\,e^{-3}$	0.046	0.45	0.46	0.03	39.70	65.56	82.46	0.54
DFLF		$4.8\,e^{-3}$	0.063	0.59	0.72	0.07	28.64	53.55	71.61	0.65
VDFF		$7.3\,e^{-3}$	0.080	1.39	0.62	0.05	8.42	19.95	32.68	0.79

4.2 Comparison to State-of-the-Art

We have implemented three baselines to compare our method with:

Variational DFF. We compare our results with the state-of-the-art variational method, VDFF [32], using their GPU code[4] and the same focal stacks as in our method. We run a grid search on several VDFF parameters and the results reported are for the best set of parameters. VDFF outputs a real valued index map. Each pixel is assigned to one of the stack images, where the pixel is in focus. Therefore, we directly interpolate these indices to their corresponding disparity values and compute our metrics on the mapped disparity output.

PSPNet for DFF. *Pyramid Scene Parsing Network* [47] is based on a deeper encoder (ResNet) and also capable of capturing global context information by aggregating different-region-based context through the pyramid pooling module. It is originally designed for semantic segmentation, however, we modified the network for depth from focus problem (input and output) and trained it end-to-end on our dataset. We also compare to PSPNet in order to observe the effects of significant architectural changes in terms of a deeper encoder (ResNet) with a recent decoder module for the problem of depth from focus.

Lytro Depth. For completion, we also compare with the depth computed from the light-field directly by the Lytro. Although this method technically does not compute DFF, we still think it is a valuable baseline to show the accuracy that depth from light-field methods can achieve. Lytro toolbox predicts depth in lambda units, thus the output is not directly comparable to our results. For this reason, we formulate the rescaling from Lytro depth to our groundtruth as an optimization problem that finds a unique scaling factor k^*. To do so, we minimize the least squares error between the resulting depth $\tilde{Z}_p$ and the groundtruth depth Z_p to find the best scaling factor k^*:

---

[4] https://github.com/adrelino/variational-depth-from-focus

$$k^* = \arg \min_k \sum_p \|k \cdot \tilde{Z}_p - Z_p\|_2^2, \tag{6}$$

where $k \in \mathbb{R}$. Note that this is the best possible mapping in terms of MSE to our groundtruth depth maps provided that the focal stack has uniform focal change, therefore, we are not penalizing during the conversion process. Evaluation metrics are then computed on $k^* \cdot \tilde{D}_p$ and D_p.

Depth from Light-Field. Even though we focus on the task of DFF, we want to provide a comparison to depth from light-field. For this purpose, we follow [17,18] and train our network (*DDFFNet-CC3*) as well as PSPNet with 11 sub-apertures from the light-field camera as input (see supp. Figure 3). We denote these models as DFLF and PSP-LF, respectively. To the best of our knowledge, there is no code for [17,18] to test their full pipeline on our dataset.

As we can see from Table 1, *DDFFNet-CC3* outperforms the other depth from focus method, *i.e.* VDFF [32], in all evaluation metrics, reducing depth error by more than 75%. The major reason for this is that VDFF proposes an optimization scheme that relies on precomputed hand-crafted features, which can handle the synthetic or clean high resolution images but fail in the realistic, challenging scenes of our dataset.

PSPNet performs on-par to *DDFFNet-CC3*, nevertheless, as shown in Fig. 1, pyramid pooling leads to oversmooth depth maps due to its upsampling strategy. Although this network is very efficient for semantic segmentation, we found that our decoder choice with skip connection CC3 yields more accurate, non-smooth depth maps.

Lytro, on the other hand, computes very inaccurate depth maps on flat surfaces (Fig. 1) while our *DDFFNet* estimates a smoother and also more accurate disparity maps. Note that Lytro depth is what is provided as groundtruth depth maps in the Stanford Light-field dataset, but this depth computation is relying on an algorithm that is not always accurate as we have shown. This is another advantage of the proposed dataset which provides groundtruth maps from an external RGB-D sensor.

As we can see in Table 1, our approach *DDFFNet-CC3* still performs better than depth from light-field (DFLF) with a similar number of images. Note that it would not be possible to fit all sub-aperture images provided by the light-field camera into GPU memory. In contrast to DFLF, our method is usable with any camera.

Moreover, we present the MSE and RMS error computed on the predicted depth maps in Table 2. *DDFFNet-CC3* achieves a much lower error when compared to VDFF or DFLF. *DDFFNet-UpConv* has a better depth error than *DDFFNet-CC3*, but, its badpix error is significantly larger than *DDFFNet-CC3*, demonstrated in Fig. 5.

Overall, experiments show that our method is more accurate by a large margin when compared to the classical variatonal DFF method [32] while also being orders of magnitude faster on a GPU. It is also more accurate than the Lytro

Table 2. Runtime and Depth error. DDFFNet is faster and more accurate than other state-of-the-art methods. For completeness, we also report the runtime of Lytro toolbox on CPU. VDFF performs worse as it requires many iterations of optimization during test.

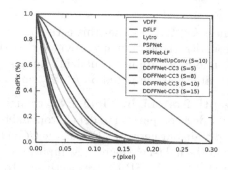

Method		Runtime (s.)	Depth (m.)
DDFFNet	Unpool	0.55	1.40
	BL	**0.43**	1.10
	UpConv	0.50	**0.58**
	CC1	0.60	0.79
	CC2	0.60	0.86
	CC3	0.58	0.86
DFLF		0.59	1.50
VDFF		2.83	8.90
Lytro		25.26 (CPU)	0.99

Fig. 5. Badpix(%) for DDFFNet-CC3 for $S \in \{5, 8, 10, 15\}$, DDFFNet-UpConv for $S = 10$, for Lytro, DFLF and VDFF. While τ increases BadPix error decreases. DDFFNet with stack size of 10 is better than VDFF and Lytro by a large margin.

predicted depth or a network trained for depth from light-field. Several network architectures were explored, and finally *CC3* was deemed the best with overall lowest disparity error while keeping object boundaries in the disparity map.

Is DDFFNet Generalizable to Other Cameras? To show the generality of our method, we capture focal stacks with an Android smartphone where the focus changes linearly from 0.1 to 4m and groundtruth depth maps with the depth camera of the smartphone. We present the results on this *mobile* depth from focus (mDFF) dataset in the supplementary material and share the dataset publicly on https://vision.cs.tum.edu/data/datasets/mdff.

5   Conclusions

Depth from focus (DFF) is a highly ill-posed inverse problem because the optimal focal distance is inferred from sharpness measures which fail in untextured areas. Existing variational solutions revert to spatial regularization to fill in the missing depth, which are not generalized to more complex geometric environments. In this work, we proposed 'Deep Depth From Focus' (DDFF) as the first deep learning solution to this classical inverse problem. To this end, we introduced a novel 25 times larger dataset with focal stacks from a light-field camera and groundtruth depth maps from an RGB-D camera. We devised suitable network architectures and demonstrated that DDFFNet outperforms existing approaches, reducing the depth error by more than 75% and predicting a disparity map in only 0.58 s.

References

1. Adelson, E., Wang, J.: Single lens stereo with a plenoptic camera. PAMI **1**(2), 99–106 (1992)
2. Asif, M., Choi, T.: Learning shape from focus using multilayer neural networks. In: SPIE, Vision Geometry VIII (1999)
3. Badrinarayanan, V., Kendall, A., Cipolla, R.: SegNet: a deep convolutional encoder-decoder architecture for image segmentation. PAMI **39**(12), 2481–2495 (2017)
4. Bok, Y., Jeon, H.G., Kweon, I.S.: Geometric calibration of micro-lens-based light field cameras using line features. PAMI **39**(2), 287–300 (2017)
5. Cho, D., Lee, M., Kim, S., Tai, Y.W.: Modeling the calibration pipeline of the lytro camera for high quality light-field image reconstruction. In: ICCV (2013)
6. Dansereau, D., Pizarro, O., Williams, B.: Decoding, calibration and rectification for lenselet-based plenoptic cameras. In: CVPR (2013)
7. Diebold, M., Goldluecke, B.: Epipolar plane image refocusing for improved depth estimation and occlusion handling. In: ICCV (2013)
8. Dosovitskiy, A., et al.: FlowNet: learning optical flow with convolutional networks. In: ICCV (2015)
9. Dosovitskiy, A., Tobias Springenberg, J., Brox, T.: Learning to generate chairs with convolutional neural networks. In: CVPR (2015)
10. Eigen, D., Puhrsch, C., Fergus, R.: Depth map prediction from a single image using a multi-scale deep network. In: NIPS (2014)
11. Galliani, S., Schindler, K.: Just look at the image: viewpoint-specific surface normal prediction for improved multi-view reconstruction. In: CVPR (2016)
12. Garg, R., B.G., V.K., Carneiro, G., Reid, I.: Unsupervised CNN for single view depth estimation: geometry to the rescue. In: Leibe, B., Matas, J., Sebe, N., Welling, M. (eds.) ECCV 2016. LNCS, vol. 9912, pp. 740–756. Springer, Cham (2016). https://doi.org/10.1007/978-3-319-46484-8_45
13. Girshick, R.: Fast R-CNN. In: ICCV (2015)
14. Hazirbas, C., Ma, L., Domokos, C., Cremers, D.: FuseNet: incorporating depth into semantic segmentation via fusion-based CNN architecture. In: Lai, S.-H., Lepetit, V., Nishino, K., Sato, Y. (eds.) ACCV 2016. LNCS, vol. 10111, pp. 213–228. Springer, Cham (2017). https://doi.org/10.1007/978-3-319-54181-5_14
15. He, K., Zhang, X., Ren, S., Sun, J.: Delving deep into rectifiers: surpassing human-level performance on imagenet classification. In: ICCV (2015)
16. He, K., Zhang, X., Ren, S., Sun, J.: Deep residual learning for image recognition. In: CVPR (2016)
17. Heber, S., Pock, T.: Convolutional networks for shape from light field. In: CVPR (2016)
18. Heber, S., Yu, W., Pock, T.: Neural EPI-volume networks for shape from light field. In: ICCV (2017)
19. Honauer, K., Johannsen, O., Kondermann, D., Goldluecke, B.: A dataset and evaluation methodology for depth estimation on 4D light fields. In: Lai, S.-H., Lepetit, V., Nishino, K., Sato, Y. (eds.) ACCV 2016. LNCS, vol. 10113, pp. 19–34. Springer, Cham (2017). https://doi.org/10.1007/978-3-319-54187-7_2
20. Ioffe, S., Szegedy, C.: Batch normalization: accelerating deep network training by reducing internal covariate shift. In: ICML (2015)
21. Jeon, H.G., et al.: Accurate depth map estimation from a lenslet light field camera. In: CVPR (2015)

22. Kendall, A., Badrinarayanan, V., Cipolla, R.: Bayesian SegNet: model uncertainty in deep convolutional encoder-decoder architectures for scene understanding. In: BMVC (2017)
23. Kendall, A., Grimes, M., Cipolla, R.: PoseNet: a convolutional network for real-time 6-DOF camera relocalization. In: ICCV (2015)
24. Krizhevsky, A., Sutskever, I., Hinton, G.E.: ImageNet classification with deep convolutional neural networks. In: NIPS (2012)
25. Li, B., Shen, C., Dai, Y., van den Hengel, A., He, M.: Depth and surface normal estimation from monocular images using regression on deep features and hierarchical CRFs. In: CVPR (2015)
26. Lin, H., Chen, C., Kang, S.B., Yu, J.: Depth recovery from light field using focal stack symmetry. In: ICCV (2015)
27. Liu, F., Shen, C., Lin, G., Reid, I.D.: Learning depth from single monocular images using deep convolutional neural fields. PAMI 38(10), 2024–2039 (2016)
28. Liu, M.Y., Tuzel, O., Taguchi, Y.: Joint geodesic upsampling of depth images. In: CVPR (2013)
29. Long, J., Shelhamer, E., Darrell, T.: Fully convolutional networks for semantic segmentation. In: CVPR (2015)
30. Mahmood, M.: Shape from focus by total variation. In: IVMSP Workshop (2013)
31. Mahmood, M., Choi, T.S.: Nonlinear approach for enhancement of image focus volume in shape from focus. TIP 21(5), 2866–2873 (2012)
32. Moeller, M., Benning, M., Schönlieb, C., Cremers, D.: Variational depth from focus reconstruction. TIP 24(12), 5369–5378 (2015)
33. Ng, R., Levoy, M., Brédif, M., Duval, G., Horowitz, M., Hanrahan, P.: Light field photography with a hand-held plenoptic camera. Technical report, Stanford University Computer Science Tech Report CSTR 2005-02 (2005)
34. Noh, H., Hong, S., Han, B.: Learning deconvolution network for semantic segmentation. In: ICCV (2015)
35. Park, J., Kim, H., Tai, Y.W., Brown, M.S., Kweon, I.: High quality depth map upsampling for 3D-TOF cameras. In: ICCV (2011)
36. Park, J., Kim, H., Tai, Y., Brown, M.S., Kweon, I.: High-quality depth map upsampling and completion for RGB-D cameras. TIP 23(12), 5559–5572 (2014)
37. Pérez-Nava, F., Lüke, J.P.: Simultaneous estimation of super-resolved depth and all-in-focus images from a plenoptic camera. In: 3DTV-CON (2009)
38. Pertuz, S., Puig, D., Garcia, M.A.: Analysis of focus measure operators for shape-from-focus. Pattern Recogn. 46(5), 1415–1432 (2013)
39. Russakovsky, O., et al.: ImageNet large scale visual recognition challenge. IJCV 115(3), 211–252 (2015)
40. Shen, J., Cheung, S.C.S.: Layer depth denoising and completion for structured-light RGB-D cameras. In: CVPR (2013)
41. Simonyan, K., Zisserman, A.: Very deep convolutional networks for large-scale image recognition. In: ICLR (2015)
42. Suwajanakorn, S., Hernandez, C., Seitz, S.M.: Depth from focus with your mobile phone. In: CVPR (2015)
43. Thelen, A., Frey, S., Hirsch, S., Hering, P.: Improvements in shape-from-focus for holographic reconstructions with regard to focus operators, neighborhood-size, and height value interpolation. TIP 18(1), 151–157 (2009)
44. Walch, F., Hazirbas, C., Leal-Taixe, L., Sattler, T., Hilsenbeck, S., Cremers, D.: Image-based localization using lstms for structured feature correlation. In: ICCV (2017)

45. Wanner, S., Meister, S., Goldlücke, B.: Datasets and benchmarks for densely sampled 4D light fields. In: VMV (2013)
46. Wilburn, B., et al.: High performance imaging using large camera arrays. In: TOG (2005)
47. Zhao, H., Shi, J., Qi, X., Wang, X., Jia, J.: Pyramid scene parsing network. In: CVPR (2017)

Random Temporal Skipping for Multirate Video Analysis

Yi Zhu$^{(\boxtimes)}$ ⓘ and Shawn Newsam ⓘ

University of California at Merced, Merced, CA 95343, USA
{yzhu25,snewsam}@ucmerced.edu

Abstract. Current state-of-the-art approaches to video understanding adopt temporal jittering to simulate analyzing the video at varying frame rates. However, this does not work well for multirate videos, in which actions or subactions occur at different speeds. The frame sampling rate should vary in accordance with the different motion speeds. In this work, we propose a simple yet effective strategy, termed random temporal skipping, to address this situation. This strategy effectively handles multirate videos by randomizing the sampling rate during training. It is an exhaustive approach, which can potentially cover all motion speed variations. Furthermore, due to the large temporal skipping, our network can see video clips that originally cover over 100 frames. Such a time range is enough to analyze most actions/events. We also introduce an occlusion-aware optical flow learning method that generates improved motion maps for human action recognition. Our framework is end-to-end trainable, runs in real-time, and achieves state-of-the-art performance on six widely adopted video benchmarks.

Keywords: Action recognition · Multirate video · Temporal modeling

1 Introduction

Significant progress has been made in video analysis during the last five years, including content-based video search, anomaly detection, human action recognition, object tracking and autonomous driving. Take human action recognition as an example. The performance on the challenging UCF101 dataset [18] was only 43.9% reported in the original; it now is 98.0%. Such great improvement is attributed to several factors, such as more complicated models (e.g., deep learning [1]), larger datasets (e.g., Kinetics [10]), better temporal analysis (e.g., two-stream networks [17,29]), etc.

However, there has been little work on varying frame-rate video analysis. For simplicity, we denote varying frame-rate as multirate throughout the paper. For real-world video applications, multirate handling is crucial. For surveillance video monitoring, communication package drops occur frequently due to bad internet connections. We may miss a chunk of frames, or miss the partial content of the frames. For activity/event analysis, the videos are multirate in nature. People

© Springer Nature Switzerland AG 2019
C. V. Jawahar et al. (Eds.): ACCV 2018, LNCS 11363, pp. 542–557, 2019.
https://doi.org/10.1007/978-3-030-20893-6_34

Fig. 1. Sample video frames of three actions: (a) playing guitar (b) wallpushup and (c) diving. (a) No temporal analysis is needed because context information dominates. (b) Temporal analysis would be helpful due to the regular movement pattern. (c) Only the last four frames have fast motion, so multirate temporal analysis is needed.

may perform the same action at different speeds. For video generation, we may manually interpolate frames or sample frames depending on the application. For the scenarios mentioned above, models pre-trained on fixed frame-rate videos may not generalize well to multirate ones. As shown in Fig. 1, for the action diving, there is no apparent motion in the first four frames, but fast motion exists in the last four frames. Dense sampling of every frame is redundant and results in large computational cost, while sparse sampling will lose information when fast motion occurs.

There are many ways to model the temporal information in a video, including trajectories [21], optical flow [17], temporal convolution [20], 3D CNNs [19] and recurrent neural networks (RNNs) [14]. However, none of these methods can directly handle multirate videos. Usually these methods need a fixed length input (a video clip) with a fixed sampling rate. A straightforward extension therefore is to train multiple such models, each corresponding to a different fixed frame-rate. This is similar to using image pyramids to handle the multi-scale problem in image analysis. But it is computational infeasible to train models for all the frame-rates. And, once the frame-rate differs, the system's performance may drop dramatically. Hence, it would be more desirable to use one model to handle multiple frame-rates.

In this work, we focus on human action recognition because action is closely related to frame-rate. Specifically, our contributions include the following. First, we propose a random temporal skipping strategy for effective multirate video analysis. It can simulate various motion speeds for better action modeling, and makes the training more robust. Second, we introduce an occlusion-aware optical flow learning method to generate better motion maps for human action recognition. Third, we adopt the "segment" idea [3,24] to reason about the temporal information of the entire video. By combining the local random skipping and global segments, our framework achieves state-of-the-art results on six large-scale video benchmarks. In addition, our model is robust under dramatic frame-rate changes, a scenario in which the previous best performing methods [1,3,24] fail.

2   Related Work

There is a large body of literature on video human action recognition. Here, we review only the most related work.

Deep Learning for Action Recognition. Initially, traditional handcrafted features such as Improved Dense Trajectories (IDT) [21] dominated the field of video analysis for several years. Despite their superior performance, IDT and its improvements [22] are computationally formidable for real-time applications. CNNs [9,19], which are often several orders of magnitude faster than IDTs, performed much worse than IDTs in the beginning. Later on, two-stream CNNs [17] addressed this problem by pre-computing optical flow and training a separate CNN to encode the pre-computed optical flow. This additional stream (a.k.a., the temporal stream) significantly improved the accuracy of CNNs and finally allowed them to outperform IDTs on several benchmark action recognition datasets. These accuracy improvements indicate the importance of temporal motion information for action recognition.

Modeling Temporal Information. However, compared to the CNN, the optical flow calculation is computationally expensive. It is thus the major speed bottleneck of the current two-stream approaches. There have been recent attempts to better model the temporal information. Tran et al. [19] pre-trained a deep 3D CNN network on a large-scale dataset, and use it as a general spatiotemporal feature extractor. The features generalize well to several tasks but are inferior to two-stream approaches. Ng et al. [14] reduced the dimension of each frame/clip using a CNN and aggregated frame-level information using Long Short Term Memory (LSTM) networks. Varol et al. [20] proposed to reduce the size of each frame and use longer clips (e.g., 60 vs 16 frames) as inputs. They managed to gain significant accuracy improvements compared to shorter clips with the same spatial size. Wang et al. [24] experimented with sparse sampling and jointly trained on the sparsely sampled frames/clips. In this way, they incorporate more temporal information while preserving the spatial resolution. Recent approaches [3,12] have evolved to end-to-end learning and are currently the best at incorporating global temporal information. However, none of them handle multirate video analysis effectively.

Multi-rate Video Analysis. To handle multirate videos, there are two widely adopted approaches. One is to train multiple models, each of them corresponding to a different fixed frame-rate. This is similar to using image pyramids to handle the multi-scale problem in image analysis. The other is to generate sliding windows of different lengths for each video (a.k.a, temporal jittering), with the hope of capturing temporal invariance. However, neither of these approaches is exhaustive, and they are both computationally intensive. [28] is the most similar work to ours since they deal with motion speed variance. However, our work differs in several aspects. First, we aim to explicitly learn the transitions between frames while [28] uses past and future neighboring video clips as the temporal context, and reconstruct the two temporal transitions. Their objective is considerably harder to optimize, which may lead to sub-optimal solutions. Second, our random skipping strategy is easy to implement without computational overhead whereas the image reconstruction of [28] will lead to significant computational burden. Third, their proposed multirate gated recurrent unit only works in RNNs, while our strategy is generally applicable.

In conclusion, to overcome the challenge that CNNs are incapable of capturing temporal information, we propose an occlusion-aware CNN to estimate accurate motion information for action recognition. To handle multirate video analysis, we introduce random temporal skipping to both capture short motion transitions and long temporal reasoning. Our framework is fast (real-time), end-to-end optimized and invariant to frame-rate.

3   Approach

There are two limitations to existing temporal modeling approaches: they require a fixed length input and a fixed sampling rate. For example, we usually adopt 16 frames to compute IDT and C3D features, 10 frames to compute optical flow for two-stream networks, and 30 frames for LSTM. These short durations do not allow reasoning on the entire video. In addition, a fixed sampling rate will either result in redundant information during slow movement or the loss of information during fast movement. The frame sampling rate should vary in accordance with different motion speeds. Hence, we propose random temporal skipping.

3.1   Random Temporal Skipping

In this section, we introduce random temporal skipping and illustrate its difference to traditional sliding window (fixed frame-rate) approaches. For easier understanding, we do not use temporal segments here.

Consider a video V with a total of T frames $[v_1, v_2, \ldots, v_T]$. In the situation of single-rate analysis, we randomly sample fixed length video clips from an entire video for training. Suppose the fixed length is N, then the input to our model will be a sequence of frames as

$$[v_t, v_{t+1}, \cdots, v_{t+N}]. \tag{1}$$

In order to learn a frame-rate invariant model, a straightforward way is using a sliding window. The process can be done either offline or online. The idea is to generate fixed length video clips with different temporal strides, thus covering more video frames. Much literature adopts such a strategy as data augmentation. Suppose we have a temporal stride of τ. The input now will be

$$[v_t, v_{t+\tau}, \cdots, v_{t+N\tau}]. \tag{2}$$

As shown in Fig. 1, a fixed sampling strategy does not work well for multirate videos. A single τ can not cover all temporal variations. The frame sampling rate should vary in accordance with different motion speeds. Motivated by this

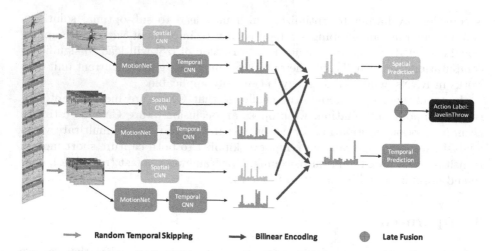

Fig. 2. Overview of our proposed framework. Our contributions are three fold: (a) random temporal skipping for temporal data augmentation; (b) occlusion-aware Motion-Net for better motion representation learning; (c) compact bilinear encoding for longer temporal context.

observation, we propose random temporal skipping. Instead of using a fixed temporal stride τ, we allow it vary randomly. The input now will be

$$[v_t, v_{t+\tau_1}, \cdots, v_{t+\tau_1+\tau_2+\cdots+\tau_N}]. \tag{3}$$

Here, τ_n, $n = 1, 2, \cdots, N$ are randomly sampled within the range of $[0, maxStride]$. $maxStride$ is a threshold value indicating the maximum distance we can skip in the temporal domain. Our proposed random temporal skipping represents an exhaustive solution. Given unlimited training iterations, we can model all possible combinations of motion speed, thus leading to the learning of frame-rate invariant features. In addition, this strategy can be easily integrated into existing frameworks with any model, and can be done on-the-fly during training.

3.2   Two-Stream Network Details

Since two-stream networks are the state-of-the-art [1,24] for several video benchmarks, we also build a two-stream model but with significant modifications. In this section, we first briefly recall temporal segment network (TSN) to illustrate the idea of segments. Then we describe our newly designed spatial and temporal streams, respectively.

Temporal Segment Network. With the goal of capturing long-range temporal structure for improved action recognition, Wang et al. proposed TSN [24] with a sparse sampling strategy. This allows an entire video to be analyzed with reasonable computational costs. TSN first divides a video evenly into three segments and one short snippet is randomly selected from each segment. Two-stream networks are then applied to the short snippets to obtain the initial action class prediction scores. The original TSN finally uses a segmental consensus function to combine the outputs from multiple short snippets to predict the action class probabilities for the video as a whole. Here, motivated by [3], we encode the features from different segments through compact bilinear models [4] as shown in Fig. 2.

Spatial Stream. A standard spatial stream takes a single video frame as input. Here, we extend this to multiple frames. Hence, our random temporal skipping also works for the spatial stream.

Temporal Stream. A standard temporal stream takes a stack of 10 optical flow images as input. However, the pre-computation of optical flow is time consuming, storage demanding and sub-optimal for action recognition. Motivated by [29], we propose to use a CNN to learn optical flow from video frames and directly feed the predictions to the temporal stream. We name this optical flow CNN MotionNet as shown in Fig. 2.

For the MotionNet, we treat optical flow estimation as an image reconstruction problem [32,33]. The intuition is that if we can use the predicted flow and the next frame to reconstruct the previous frame, our model has learned a useful representation of the underlying motion. Suppose we have two consecutive frames I_1 and I_2. Let us denote the reconstructed previous frame as I_1'. The goal then is to minimize the photometric error between the true previous frame I_1 and the reconstructed previous frame I_1':

$$L_{\text{reconst}} = \frac{1}{N} \sum_{i,j}^{N} \rho(I_1(i,j) - I_1'(i,j)). \tag{4}$$

N is the number of pixels. The reconstructed previous frame is computed from the true next frame using inverse warping, $I_1'(i,j) = I_2(i + U_{i,j}, j + V_{i,j})$, accomplished through spatial transformer modules [7] inside the CNN. U and V are the horizontal and vertical components of predicted optical flow. We use a robust convex error function, the generalized Charbonnier penalty $\rho(x) = (x^2 + \epsilon^2)^\alpha$, to reduce the influence of outliers. α is set to 0.45.

However, [29] is based on a simple brightness constancy assumption and does not incorporate reasoning about occlusion. This leads to noisier motion in the background and inconsistent flow around human boundaries. As we know, motion boundaries are important for human action recognition. Hence, we extend [29] by incorporating occlusion reasoning, hoping to learn better flow maps for action recognition.

In particular, our unsupervised learning framework should not employ the brightness constancy assumption to compute the loss when there is occlusion. Pixels that become occluded in the second frame should not contribute to the photometric error between the true and reconstructed first frames in Eq. 4. We therefore mask occluded pixels when computing the image reconstruction loss in order to avoid learning incorrect deformations to fill the occluded locations.

Our occlusion detection is based on a forward-backward consistency assumption. That is, for non-occluded pixels, the forward flow should be the inverse of the backward flow at the corresponding pixel in the second frame. We mark pixels as being occluded whenever the mismatch between these two flows is too large. Thus, for occlusion in the forward direction, we define the occlusion flag o^f be 1 whenever the constraint

$$|M^f + M^b_{M^f}|^2 < \alpha_1 \cdot (|M^f|^2 + |M^b_{M^f}|^2) + \alpha_2 \tag{5}$$

is violated, and 0 otherwise. o^b is defined in the same way, and M^f and M^b represent forward and backward flow. We set $\alpha_1 = 0.01$, $\alpha_2 = 0.5$ in all our experiments. Finally, the resulting occlusion-aware loss is represented as:

$$L = (1 - o^f) \cdot L^f_{\text{reconst}} + (1 - o^b) \cdot L^b_{\text{reconst}} \tag{6}$$

Once we learn a geometry-aware MotionNet to predict motions between consecutive frames, we can directly stack it to the original temporal CNN for action mapping. Hence, our whole temporal stream is now end-to-end optimized without the computational burden of calculating optical flow.

3.3 Compact Bilinear Encoding

In order to learn a compact feature for an entire video, we need to aggregate information from different segments. There are many ways to accomplish this goal, such as taking the maximum or average, bilinear pooling, Fisher Vector (FV) encoding [16], etc. Here, we choose compact bilinear pooling [4,5,13] due to its simplicity and good performance.

The classic bilinear model computes a global descriptor by calculating:

$$B = \phi(F \otimes F'). \tag{7}$$

Here, F are the feature maps from all channels in a specific layer, $\otimes$ denotes the outer product, ϕ is the model parameters we are going to learn and B is the bilinear feature. However, due to the many channels of feature maps and their large spatial resolution, the outer product will result in a prohibitively high dimensional feature representation.

For this reason, we use the Tensor Sketch algorithm as in [4] to avoid the computational intensive outer product by an approximate projection. Such approximation requires almost no parameter memory. We refer the readers to [4] for a detailed algorithm description.

After the approximate projection, we have compact bilinear features with very low feature dimension. Compact bilinear pooling can also significantly reduce the number of CNN model parameters since it can replace fully-connected layers, thus leading to less over-fitting. We will compare compact bilinear pooling to other feature encoding methods in later sections.

Table 1. Necessity of multirate analysis. RTS indicates random temporal skipping. Fixed sampling means we sample the video frames by a fixed length (numbers in the brackets, e.g., 1, 3, 5 frames apart). Random sampling indicates we sample the video frames by a random length of frames apart.

Method	Without RTS	With RTS
No sampling	95.6	96.4
Fixed sampling (1)	93.4	95.8
Fixed sampling (3)	91.5	94.9
Fixed sampling (5)	88.7	92.3
Random sampling	87.0	92.3

3.4 Spatio-Temporal Fusion

Following the testing scheme of [17, 23, 27], we evenly sample 25 frames/clips for each video. For each frame/clip, we perform 10x data augmentation by cropping the 4 corners and 1 center, flipping them horizontally and averaging the prediction scores (before softmax operation) over all crops of the samples. In the end, we obtain two predictions, one from each stream. We simply late fuse them by weighted averaging. The overview of our framework is shown in Fig. 2.

4 Experiments

Implementation Details. For the CNNs, we use the Caffe toolbox [8]. Our MotionNet is first pre-trained using Adam optimization with the default parameter values. It is a 25 layer CNN with an encoder-decoder architecture [29]. The initial learning rate is set to 3.2×10^{-5} and is divided in half every 100k iterations. We end our training at 400k iterations. Once MotionNet can estimate decent optical flow, we stack it to a temporal CNN for action prediction. Both the spatial CNN and the temporal CNN are BN-Inception networks pre-trained on ImageNet challenges [2]. We use stochastic gradient descent to train the networks, with a batch size of 128 and momentum of 0.9. We also use horizontal flipping, corner cropping and multi-scale cropping as data augmentation. Take UCF101 as an example. For the spatial stream CNN, the initial learning rate is set to 0.001, and divided by 10 every 4K iterations. We stop the training at 10K iterations. For the stacked temporal stream CNN, we set different initial learning rates for MotionNet and the temporal CNN, which are 10^{-6} and 10^{-3}, respectively. Then we divide the learning rates by 10 after 5K and 10K. The maximum iteration is set to 16K. Other datasets have the same learning process except the training iterations are different depending on the dataset size.

4.1 Trimmed Video

Dataset. In this section, we adopt three trimmed video datasets to evaluate our proposed method, UCF101 [18], HMDB51 [11] and Kinetics [10]. UCF101 is

Action	Diving	Hammer Throw	Shotput	Golf Swing	Throw Discus	Cricket Shot	Archery	Kayaking	Jump Rope	Billiards
Δ	7.2	6.8	6.6	6.1	5.7	5.4	5.2	4.6	3.9	3.4
Action	Sky Diving	Breast Stroke	Surfing	Playing Sita	Hula Hoop	Playing Violin	Playing Cello	Playing Guitar	Playing Flute	Drumming
Δ	0.5	0.4	0.4	0.4	0.3	0.2	0.2	0.1	0.0	-0.5

Fig. 3. Top-10 classes that benefit most (top) and least (bottom) in UCF101

composed of realistic action videos from YouTube. It contains 13, 320 video clips distributed among 101 action classes. HMDB51 includes 6, 766 video clips of 51 actions extracted from a wide range of sources, such as online videos and movies. Both UCF101 and HMDB51 have a standard three-split evaluation protocol and we report the average recognition accuracies over the three splits. Kinetics is similar to UCF101, but substantially larger. It consists of approximately 400, 000 video clips, and covers 400 human action classes.

Necessity of Multirate Analysis. First, we demonstrate the importance of multirate video analysis. We use UCF101 as the evaluation dataset. We show that a well-trained model with a fixed frame-rate does not work well when the frame-rate differs during testing. As shown in Table 1, no sampling means the dataset does not change. Fixed sampling means we manually sample the video frames by a fixed length (numbers in the brackets, e.g., 1, 3, 5 frames apart). Random sampling indicates we manually sample the video frames by a random length of frames apart. We set the maximum temporal stride to 5. "with RTS" and "without RTS" indicates the use of our proposed random temporal skipping strategy during model training or not. Here, all the samplings are performed for test videos, not training videos. This is used to simulate frame-rate changes between the source and target domains.

We make several observations. First, if we compare the left and right columns in Table 1, we can clearly see the advantage of using random temporal skipping and the importance of multirate analysis. Without RTS, the test accuracies are reduced dramatically when the frame-rate differs between the training and test videos. When RTS is adopted, the performance decrease becomes much less significant. Models with RTS perform 5% better than those without RTS on random sampling (last row). Second, in the situation that no sampling is performed (first row in Table 1), models with RTS perform better than those without RTS. This is because RTS helps to capture more temporal variation. It helps to regularize the model during training, acting like additional data augmentation. Third, if we change fixed sampling to random sampling (last two rows in Table 1), we can see that the recognition accuracy without RTS drops again, but the accuracy with RTS remains the same. This demonstrates that our proposed random temporal skipping captures frame-rate invariant features for human action recognition.

One interesting thing to note is that, with the increase of sampling rate, the performance of both approaches decrease. This maybe counter-intuitive because RTS should be able to handle the varying frame-rate. The reason for lower accuracy even when RTS is turned on is because videos in UCF101 are usually

Table 2. Comparison with various feature aggregation methods on UCF101 and HMDB51. Compact bilinear pooling achieves the best performance in terms of classification accuracy.

Method	UCF101	HMDB51
FC	94.9	69.7
BoVW	92.1	65.3
VLAD	94.3	66.8
FV	93.9	67.4
Compact bilinear pooling	**96.4**	**72.5**

short. Hence, we do not have as many training samples with large sampling rates as those with small sampling rates. We will show in the next section that when the videos are longer, models with RTS can be trained better.

Per-Class Breakdown. Here, we perform a per-class accuracy breakdown to obtain insights into why random temporal skipping works and how it helps. We choose the results from the last row in Table 1 to compare.

We list, in Fig. 3 below, the 10 classes in UCF101 that benefit the most from RTS and the 10 that benefit the least. The actions that benefit the most tend to exhibit varying motion speeds. The actions that benefit the least can either be considered still, and can thus be recognized by individual frames regardless of how they are sampled, or considered repetitive, and so a constant sampling rate is sufficient. Hence, our proposed random temporal skipping effectively handles different motion speeds.

Encoding Methods Comparison. In this section, we compare different feature encoding methods and show the effectiveness of compact bilinear encoding. In particular, we choose four widely adopted encoding approaches: Bag of Visual Words (BoVW), Vector of Locally Aggregated Descriptors (VLAD), Fisher Vector (FV) and Fully-Connected pooling (FC).

FC is the most widely adopted feature aggregation method in deep learning era, thus will be served as baseline. We put it between the last convolutional layer and the classification layer, and set its dimension to 4096. FC will be learned end-to-end during training. BoVW, VLAD and FV are clustering based methods. Although there are recent attempts to integrate them into CNN framework [12], for simplicity, we do not use them in an end-to-end network. We first extract features from a pre-trained model, and then encode the local features into global features by one of the above methods. Finally, we use support vector machines (SVM) to do the classification. To be specific, suppose we have N local features, BoVW quantizes each of the N local features as one of k codewords using a codebook generated through k-means clustering. VLAD is similar to BoVW but encodes the distance between each of the N local features and the assigned codewords. FV models the distribution of the local features using a Gaussian mixture model (GMM) with k components and computes the mean

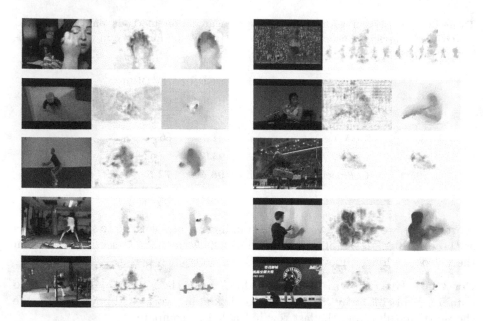

Fig. 4. Sample visualizations of UCF101 dataset to show the impact of reasoning occlusion during optical flow estimation. Left: overlapped image pairs. Middle: MotionNet without occlusion reasoning. Right: MotionNet with occlusion reasoning. The figure is best viewed in color. We can observe the clear improvement brought by occlusion reasoning. (Color figure online)

and standard deviation of the weighted difference between the N local features and these k components. In our experiments, we project each local feature into 256 dimensions using PCA and set the number of clusters (k) as 256. This is similar to what is suggested in [26] except we do not break the local features into multiple sub-features. For the bilinear models, we retain the convolutional layers of each network without the fully-connected layers. The convolutional feature maps extracted from the last convolutional layers (after the rectified activation) are fed as input into the bilinear models. Here, the convolutional feature maps for the last layer of BN-Inception produces an output of size $14 \times 14 \times 1024$, leading to bilinear features of size 1024×1024, and 8,196 features for compact bilinear models.

As can be seen in Table 2, our compact bilinear encoding achieves the best overall performance (two-stream network results). This observation is consistent with [3]. It is interesting that the more complicated encoding methods, BoVW, FV and VLAD, all perform much worse than baseline FC and compact bilinear pooling. We conjecture that this is because they are not end-to-end optimized.

Importance of Occlusion-Aware. One of our contributions in this work is introducing occlusion reasoning into the MotionNet [29] framework. Here, we show sample visualizations to demonstrate its effectiveness.

As can be seen in Fig. 4, optical flow estimates with occlusion reasoning are much better than those without. Occlusion reasoning can remove the background noise brought by invalid brightness constancy assumptions, reduce checkerboard artifacts, and generate flows with sharper boundaries due to awareness of disocclusion. Quantitatively, we use these two flow estimates as input to the temporal stream. Our network with occlusion reasoning performs 0.9% better than the baseline [29] on UCF101 (95.5 → 96.4). This makes sense because a clean background of optical flow should make it easier for the model to recognize the action itself than the context. We show that we can obtain both better optical flow and higher accuracy in action recognition by incorporating occlusion reasoning in an end-to-end network.

4.2 Untrimmed Video

Dataset. In this section, we adopt three untrimmed video datasets to evaluate our proposed method, ActivityNet [6], VIRAT 1.0 [15] and VIRAT 2.0 [15]. For ActivityNet, we use version 1.2 which has 100 action classes. Following the standard evaluation split, 4,819 training and 2,383 validation videos are used for training and 2,480 videos for testing. VIRAT 1.0 is a surveillance video dataset recorded in different scenes. Each video clip contains 1 to 20 instances of activities from 6 categories of person-vehicle interaction events including: loading an object to a vehicle, unloading an object from a vehicle, opening a vehicle trunk, closing a vehicle trunk, getting into a vehicle, and getting out of a vehicle. VIRAT 2.0 is an extended version of VIRAT 1.0. It includes 5 more events captured in more scenes: gesturing, carrying an object, running, entering a facility and exiting a facility. We follow the standard train/test split to report the performance.

Investigate Longer Temporal Context. In the previous section, we demonstrated that a well-trained model with a fixed frame-rate does not work well when frame-rate differs during testing. Here, we show that using a longer temporal context by random temporal skipping is useful for action recognition. We use ActivityNet as the evaluation dataset because most videos in ActivityNet are long (5 to 10 min) so that we can explore more speed variations.

Recall from Eq. 3 that *maxStride* is a threshold value indicating the maximum distance we can skip in the temporal domain. We set it from 0 frames to 9 frames apart, indicating no sampling to the longest temporal coverage. As shown in Fig. 5, we can see that the longer temporal context we utilize, the higher action recognition accuracy we obtain. One interesting observation is that the performance starts to saturate when *maxStride* is equal to 6. After that, longer temporal context does not help much. We think this may be due to the fact that the CNNs can not capture the transitions between frames that are so far away.

In addition, we investigate the impact of the number of sampled frames. We choose 5, 10, 15 and 20 frames as the length of the input video clip. As we can see in Fig. 5, more sampled frames always improves the action recognition accuracy. This demonstrates that longer temporal information benefits video understanding. With 20 input frames and a *maxStride* of 6, our method can have

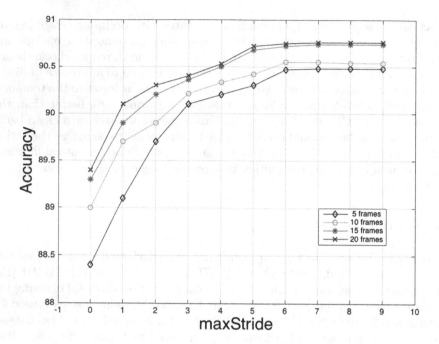

Fig. 5. Action recognition accuracy on ActivityNet. We observe that the longer temporal context we utilize, the better performance we obtain.

a temporal coverage of over 120 fames, which is about 5 s. Such a time duration is enough for analyzing most actions or events. For UCF101 and HMDB51 datasets, 5 s can cover the entire video.

4.3   Comparison to State-of-the-Art

We compare our method to recent state-of-the-art on the six video benchmarks. As shown in Table 3, our proposed random temporal skipping is an effective data augmentation technique, which leads to the top performance on all evaluation datasets.

For the trimmed video datasets, we obtain performance improvements of 0.8% on UCF101, 1.4% on HMDB51 and 1.4% on Kinetics. Because the videos are trimmed and short, we do not benefit much from learning longer temporal information. The improvement for UCF101 is smaller as the accuracy is already saturated on this dataset. Yet, our simple random temporal skipping strategy can improve it further.

For the three untrimmed video datasets, we obtain significant improvements, 1.8% on ActivityNet, 4.5% on VIRAT 1.0 and 3.0% on VIRAT 2.0. This demonstrates the importance of multirate video analysis in complex real-world applications, and the effectiveness of our method. We could adapt our approach to real-time action localization due to the precise temporal boundary modeling.

Table 3. Comparison to state-of-the-art approaches in accuracy (%).

Method	UCF101	HMDB51	Kinetics	ActivityNet	VIRAT 1.0	VIRAT 2.0
Two-stream [17]	88.0	59.4	62.2	71.9	80.4	92.6
C3D [19]	82.3	49.7	56.1	74.1	75.8	87.5
TDD [22]	90.3	63.2	–	–	86.6	93.2
LTC [20]	91.7	64.8	–	–	–	–
Depth2Action [31]	93.0	68.2	68.7	78.1	89.7	94.1
TSN [24]	94.0	68.5	73.9	89.0	–	–
TLE [3]	95.6	71.1	75.6	–	–	–
Ours	**96.4**	**72.5**	**77.0**	**91.1**	**94.2**	**97.1**

There is a recent work I3D [1] that reports higher accuracy on UCF101 (98.0%) and HMDB51 (80.7%). However, it uses additional training data ([10]) and the network is substantially deeper, which is not a fair comparison to the above approaches. In addition, we would like to note that our approach is real-time because no pre-computation of optical flow is needed. We are only about 1% worse than I3D, but 14 times faster.

5   Conclusion

In this work, we propose a simple yet effective strategy, termed random temporal skipping, to handle multirate videos. It can benefit the analysis of long untrimmed videos by capturing longer temporal contexts, and of short trimmed videos by providing extra temporal augmentation. The trained model using random temporal skipping is robust during inference time. We can use just one model to handle multiple frame-rates without further fine-tuning. We also introduce an occlusion-aware CNN to estimate better optical flow for action recognition on-the-fly. Our network can run in real-time and obtain state-of-the-art performance on six large-scale video benchmarks.

In the future, we would like to improve our framework in several directions. First, due to the inability of CNNs to learn large motions between distant frames, we will incorporate recurrent neural networks into our framework to handle even longer temporal contexts. Second, we will apply our method to online event detection since our model has a good trade-off between efficiency and accuracy. Third, we will study the fusion of two streams and compare to recent spatiotemporal feature learning work [25,30].

Acknowledgement. We gratefully acknowledge the support of NVIDIA Corporation through the donation of the Titan Xp GPUs used in this work.

References

1. Carreira, J., Zisserman, A.: Quo vadis, action recognition? a new model and the kinetics dataset. In: The IEEE Conference on Computer Vision and Pattern Recognition (CVPR) (2017)
2. Deng, J., Dong, W., Socher, R., Li, L.J., Li, K., Fei-Fei, L.: ImageNet: a large-scale hierarchical image database. In: The IEEE Conference on Computer Vision and Pattern Recognition (CVPR) (2009)
3. Diba, A., Sharma, V., Gool, L.V.: Deep temporal linear encoding networks. In: The IEEE Conference on Computer Vision and Pattern Recognition (CVPR) (2017)
4. Gao, Y., Beijbom, O., Zhang, N., Darrell, T.: Compact bilinear pooling. In: The IEEE Conference on Computer Vision and Pattern Recognition (CVPR) (2016)
5. Gu, B., Xin, M., Huo, Z., Huang, H.: Asynchronous doubly stochastic sparse kernel learning. In: Association for the Advancement of Artificial Intelligence (AAAI) (2018)
6. Heilbron, F.C., Escorcia, V., Ghanem, B., Niebles, J.C.: ActivityNet: a large-scale video benchmark for human activity understanding. In: The IEEE Conference on Computer Vision and Pattern Recognition (CVPR) (2015)
7. Jaderberg, M., Simonyan, K., Zisserman, A., Kavukcuoglu, K.: Spatial transformer network. In: Neural Information Processing Systems (NIPS) (2015)
8. Jia, Y., et al.: Caffe: Convolutional Architecture for Fast Feature Embedding. arXiv preprint arXiv:1408.5093 (2014)
9. Karpathy, A., Toderici, G., Shetty, S., Leung, T., Sukthankar, R., Fei-Fei, L.: Large-scale video classification with convolutional neural networks. In: The IEEE Conference on Computer Vision and Pattern Recognition (CVPR) (2014)
10. Kay, W., et al.: The Kinetics Human Action Video Dataset. arXiv preprint arXiv:1705.06950 (2017)
11. Kuehne, H., Jhuang, H., Garrote, E., Poggio, T., Serre, T.: HMDB: a large video database for human motion recognition. In: International Conference on Computer Vision (ICCV) (2011)
12. Lan, Z., Zhu, Y., Hauptmann, A.G., Newsam, S.: Deep local video feature for action recognition. In: The IEEE Conference on Computer Vision and Pattern Recognition (CVPR) (2017)
13. Miao, X., Zhen, X., Liu, X., Deng, C., Athitsos, V., Huang, H.: Direct shape regression networks for end-to-end face alignment. In: The IEEE Conference on Computer Vision and Pattern Recognition (CVPR) (2018)
14. Ng, J.Y.H., Hausknecht, M., Vijayanarasimhan, S., Vinyals, O., Monga, R., Toderici, G.: Beyond short snippets: deep networks for video classification. In: The IEEE Conference on Computer Vision and Pattern Recognition (CVPR) (2015)
15. Oh, S., et al.: A large-scale benchmark dataset for event recognition in surveillance video. In: The IEEE Conference on Computer Vision and Pattern Recognition (CVPR) (2011)
16. Perronnin, F., Sánchez, J., Mensink, T.: Improving the fisher kernel for large-scale image classification. In: Daniilidis, K., Maragos, P., Paragios, N. (eds.) ECCV 2010. LNCS, vol. 6314, pp. 143–156. Springer, Heidelberg (2010). https://doi.org/10.1007/978-3-642-15561-1_11
17. Simonyan, K., Zisserman, A.: Two-stream convolutional networks for action recognition in videos. In: Neural Information Processing Systems (NIPS) (2014)
18. Soomro, K., Zamir, A.R., Shah, M.: UCF101: a dataset of 101 human action classes from videos in the wild. In: CRCV-TR-12-01 (2012)

19. Tran, D., Bourdev, L., Fergus, R., Torresani, L., Paluri, M.: Learning spatiotemporal features with 3D convolutional networks. In: International Conference on Computer Vision (ICCV) (2015)
20. Varol, G., Laptev, I., Schmid, C.: Long-term temporal convolutions for action recognition. IEEE Trans. Pattern Anal. Mach. Intell. **40**(6), 1510–1517 (2017)
21. Wang, H., Schmid, C.: Action recognition with improved trajectories. In: International Conference on Computer Vision (ICCV) (2013)
22. Wang, L., Qiao, Y., Tang, X.: Action recognition with trajectory-pooled deep-convolutional descriptors. In: The IEEE Conference on Computer Vision and Pattern Recognition (CVPR) (2015)
23. Wang, L., Xiong, Y., Wang, Z., Qiao, Y.: Towards Good Practices for Very Deep Two-Stream ConvNets. arXiv preprint arXiv:1507.02159 (2015)
24. Wang, L., et al.: Temporal segment networks: towards good practices for deep action recognition. In: European Conference on Computer Vision (ECCV) (2016)
25. Xie, S., Sun, C., Huang, J., Tu, Z., Murphy, K.: Rethinking Spatiotemporal Feature Learning For Video Understanding. arXiv preprint arXiv:1712.04851 (2017)
26. Xu, Z., Yang, Y., Hauptmann, A.G.: A discriminative CNN video representation for event detection. In: The IEEE Conference on Computer Vision and Pattern Recognition (CVPR) (2015)
27. Xue, J., Zhang, H., Dana, K.: Deep texture manifold for ground terrain recognition. The IEEE Conference on Computer Vision and Pattern Recognition (CVPR) (2018)
28. Zhu, L., Xu, Z., Yang, Y.: Bidirectional multirate reconstruction for temporal modeling in videos. In: The IEEE Conference on Computer Vision and Pattern Recognition (CVPR) (2017)
29. Zhu, Y., Lan, Z., Newsam, S., Hauptmann, A.G.: Hidden two-stream convolutional networks for action recognition. In: Asian Conference on Computer Vision (ACCV) (2018)
30. Zhu, Y., Long, Y., Guan, Y., Newsam, S., Shao, L.: Towards universal representation for unseen action recognition. In: The IEEE Conference on Computer Vision and Pattern Recognition (CVPR) (2018)
31. Zhu, Y., Newsam, S.: Depth2Action: exploring embedded depth for large-scale action recognition. In: European Conference on Computer Vision (ECCV) (2016)
32. Zhu, Y., Newsam, S.: DenseNet for dense flow. In: IEEE International Conference on Image Processing (ICIP) (2017)
33. Zhu, Y., Newsam, S.: Learning optical flow via dilated networks and occlusion reasoning. In: IEEE International Conference on Image Processing (ICIP) (2018)

Tiny People Pose

Lukáš Neumann$^{(\boxtimes)}$ and Andrea Vedaldi

Department of Engineering Science,
University of Oxford, Oxford, UK
{lukas,vedaldi}@robots.ox.ac.uk

Abstract. While recent progress in pose recognition has been impressive, there remains ample margin for improvement, particularly in challenging scenarios such as low resolution images. In this paper, we consider the problem of recognizing pose from tiny images of people, down to 24px high. This is relevant when interpreting people at a distance, which is important in applications such as autonomous driving and surveillance in crowds. Addressing this challenge, which has received little attention so far, can inspire modifications of traditional deep learning approaches that are likely to be applicable well beyond the case of pose recognition.

Given the intrinsic ambiguity of recovering a person's pose from a small image, we propose to predict a posterior probability over pose configurations. In order to do so we: (1) define a new neural network architecture that explicitly expresses uncertainty; (2) train the network by explicitly minimizing a novel loss function based on the data log-likelihood; and (3) estimate posterior probability maps for all joints as a semi-dense sub-pixel Gaussian mixture model. We asses our method on downsampled versions of popular pose recognition benchmarks as well as on an additional newly-introduced testing dataset. Compared to state-of-the-art techniques, we show far superior performance at low resolution for both deterministic and probabilistic pose prediction.

1 Introduction

Interpreting images of people is an important problem in many applications of image understanding, and, as such, has received significant attention since the early days of computer vision research [7–9,30]. Deep learning has dramatically improved the performance of generic object detection and segmentation by methods such as Faster/Mask R-CNN [11,25], which, when applied to interpreting people in images, achieve good performance. However, models specialized for human pose recognition still perform better than such generic approaches [3,5,19], justifying research dedicated to this problem.

In this paper, we consider the problem of pose recognition, i.e. identifying in an image the location of landmark points of the human body, such as shoulders, wrists and hips. However, we do so in a setting that has not received much attention before, namely very small images of people (Fig. 1). Most approaches to pose recognition assume in fact that input images have a relatively large

© Springer Nature Switzerland AG 2019
C. V. Jawahar et al. (Eds.): ACCV 2018, LNCS 11363, pp. 558–574, 2019.
https://doi.org/10.1007/978-3-030-20893-6_35

Fig. 1. Human pose estimation at a distance. Given a small low-resolution patch of an image (detected by [13]), the proposed method estimates the joint probability distribution of all body parts, despite individual pixels' noise and ambiguities. Image taken from the *Tiny People* dataset

resolution, such that the apparent height of a person is in the order of a few hundred pixels. We consider instead the case in which a person's height is an order of magnitude smaller, down to 24 pixels high. These *tiny people* are very important in applications such as surveillance and autonomous driving, where understanding the action or intention of people at a distance can be critical.

Besides the interest in applications, the tiny people problem offers unique technical challenges which inspire significant modifications of traditional deep learning approaches to structured prediction, most of which extend well beyond the case of pose recognition.

First, since there are intrinsic limitations to how much information can be extracted from small images, one should not expect to always be able to infer pose with the same degree of certainty as in the high-resolution case. Instead, we start from the outset with the goal of estimating a probability distribution over possible poses, making this distribution as tight as possible given an observed image. Doing so requires to develop a network architecture that can explicitly *express uncertainty*, both in the training as well as the testing stage.

Our second contribution is revisiting the standard "sliding window" approach for human pose estimation, in which keypoint locations are found as maxima in a dense heat map [5,19], which can be interpreted as performing a sliding window search of body parts over all image locations. However, for small images of people the resulting heat maps may have fairly low resolution. Rather than artificially increasing the resolution of the image, we consider an alternative probabilistic approach where a low resolution feature map is used to generate a dense field of Gaussian blobs, resulting in a rich *continuous* mixture model which naturally allows sub-pixel accuracy in joint prediction without significantly increasing the computational burden.

The output of the method is a distribution over possible body joint configurations, estimated from a small image of a person. We assess the method on two standard benchmarks after reducing their resolution to approximate people seen at a distance. However, this approach cannot match *exactly* the statistics of people actually imaged at a distance. For this reason, we introduce a new specialized benchmark, *Tiny People*, containing small people instances that we manually collected and annotated. While this dataset is smaller than the other standard benchmarks that we also use for assessment, we show that it is statistically sufficiently large to reliably rank algorithms and thus to provide additional verification of the validity of our approach.

On both standard benchmarks and Tiny People, we compare our method against state-of-the-art pose recognition methods. Even after carefully tuning them to the low resolution settings in different ways, we show consistently better performance in low resolution pose recognition.

For measuring performance, we consider both traditional error metrics such as average landmark regression error, as well as the *model surprise*, namely the log-likelihood of the ground-truth labels under the posterior distribution predicted by the model. The latter allows us to properly asses the quality of the probabilistic predictions. In fact, the ability of our model to express a meaningful probability prediction sets it apart from models that share some superficial technical similarity, such as [21], which lack this capability.

2   Related Work

Human Pose Estimation. The problem of estimating position of human body parts has been extensively studied before. Early methods such as the Pictorial Structures (PS) of Fischler and Elschlager [9] or the Deformable Part Models of Felzenswalb *et al.* [8] explicitly decomposed people into parts, but with the current generation of models based on deep learning the concept of parts remains implicit. Among these, Toshev and Szegedy [30] use a CNN in an iterative manner to regress human keypoint position (x_i, y_i) directly, using a L^2 loss in their training. Thompson *et al.* [28,29] adapt the FCN [18] to predict a heat map for each keypoint independently, where the keypoint position is found as position of a maximal value in the corresponding heat map - this approach has become the standard representation for human pose estimation (see Sect. 3.1).

With the aim of improving the network architecture by having multiple downsample/up-sample stages, Newell *et al.* [19] introduced their Stacked Hourglass model, which is able to capture relationships at multiple scales. More recently, Chu *et al.* [5] extended Hourglass with context attention, improving its accuracy by 1 percent point on the standard MPII Human Pose dataset [1] and thus achieving the state-of-the-art result in a single person recognition.

Methods for pose estimation of **multiple people** can be divided into two subgroups: top-down and bottom-up. Top-down methods first detect bounding boxes of individual people and in a second stage a single human pose is inferred from the cropped region. Pishchulin *et al.* [24] use a model based on Pictorial

Structures. He *et al.* [11] introduced Mask R-CNN for object segmentation, which is also applied to human pose estimation by predicting an individual heat map for each keypoint. Papandreou *et al.* [21] employ a Faster R-CNN [25] with ResNet-101 backbone [12] as a person detector, and a separate ResNet-101 network to process the detected bounding box to infer a 3-dimensional "heat-map" for each keypoint. The heat map predicts whether given pixel is close to the keypoint as a binary classification, and a 2-dimensional vector encoding the distance of the current pixel to the keypoint. The final keypoint position is then given by taking an average of the 2-dimensional vector for all pixels classified positively by the binary classifier.

Bottom-up methods detect individual keypoints first and then associate these parts with human instances. Insafutdinov *et al.* [14] formulate the problem of associating detected parts to human instances as a linear program over a fully-connected graph, which is an NP-hard problem. More recently, Cao *et al.* [3] introduced Part Affinity Fields, where part confidence maps together with 2D vector fields that encode position and orientation of human limbs allow greedy inference of the associations, thus making the method run in real time.

Small Objects Recognition. Several authors have focused on the task of small object recognition in a classification setting. Efros *et al.* [7] use an optical-flow motion descriptor to recognize actions of people in sports videos using a k-nearest neighbor search in a annotated people action database. Park and Ramanan [22] used low-resolution people images as feature vectors for nearest neighbor search in a database of synthetically morphed trained images to infer human pose in video sequences.

Inspirational to our work, Hu and Ramanan [13] focused on detecting tiny human faces and proposed a cascade of face detectors to detect human faces of a wide range of scales, starting with faces of 20px in height. Their task however is a region binary classification problem (i.e. telling if a bounding box contains or not a face), whereas in our work we infer 16 keypoint positions within the region of a similar size.

Modeling Uncertainty. Probabilistic models have recently started to be applied in the context of deep learning as well. Gal and Ghahramani [10] studied a relationship between Dropout [27] and Gaussian processes. Kendall and Cipolla [15] estimate uncertainty in 6-DOF camera pose estimation by Monte Carlo sampling. Novotny *et al.* [20] explicitly model uncertainty as one of the network outputs in the task of 3D geometry prediction from videos in an unsupervised setup. Most recently, Kendall and Gal [16] model both aleatoric and epistemic uncertainty within one model for dense semantic segmentation, and Rupprecht *et al.* [26] introduced a meta-loss that allows a model to learn multiple hypotheses, but do not specify how to select the best one.

3   Method

We formulate *pose estimation* as the problem of learning a function Φ mapping an image $\mathbf{x} \in \mathbb{R}^{H \times W \times 3}$ to a set of K-landmark locations $\mathbf{u}_1, \ldots, \mathbf{u}_K \in \mathbb{R}^2$, corresponding to different body landmarks, such as the left hip, the right ankle, and so on.

We begin by discussing the typical formulation of pose estimation (Sect. 3.1) and then introduce our probabilistic formulation (Sect. 3.2), which is able to model uncertainties arising from estimating human pose from a low resolution image.

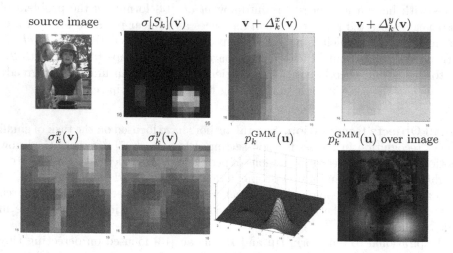

Fig. 2. The method emits a continuous Gaussian distribution $p_k^{\mathrm{GMM}}(\mathbf{u})$ for each keypoint k (*left elbow* shown above) by estimating Gaussian Mixture Model parameters using a coarse 16×16 feature map $\mathbf{v} \in \Omega_d$ generated over the whole image. Note that the resulting distribution has in principle infinite resolution, given only by the sampling step, and that it can also express multiple modes (second but smaller mode in the location of the right elbow in the above example)

3.1   Standard Formulation

The standard approach to implement a pose detector with a neural network is to express the landmark locations as maxima of a corresponding number of heat maps. To this end, let $\Phi : \mathbb{R}^{H \times W \times 3} \to \mathbb{R}^{\frac{H}{\delta} \times \frac{W}{\delta} \times K}$ where K is the number of body landmarks and $\delta \geq 1$ a downsampling factor (used for efficiency). Then a landmark's location is obtained as $\mathbf{u}_k = \mathrm{argmax}_{\mathbf{u} \in \Omega_\delta} S_k(\mathbf{u}; \Phi\mathbf{x})$, where $\Omega_\delta = \{1, 2, \ldots, H/\delta\} \times \{1, 2, \ldots, W/\delta\}$ is the downscaled version of the image domain and we extracted the k-th heat map $S_k(\mathbf{u}; \Phi\mathbf{x}) = [\Phi(\mathbf{x})]_{(\mathbf{u},k)}$ from the deep network's output. We implicitly assume that all landmarks coordinate are expressed relatively to that coordinate frame.

During training, the heat maps must be fitted to ground-truth data so that they strongly respond to the correct location of the landmarks. Very often this is done by direct L^2 regression of a manually-defined heat map shape. That is, if $\mathbf{u}_k^*$ is the ground truth location of a landmark, one minimizes the loss

$$\mathcal{L}_1(\Phi) = \sum_k \sum_{\mathbf{u} \in \Omega_\delta} w(\mathbf{u} - \mathbf{u}_k^*) \left(S_k(\mathbf{u}; \Phi\mathbf{x}) - g(\mathbf{u} - \mathbf{u}_k^*) \right)^2 \tag{1}$$

where g is a Gaussian-like kernel and w a weighting function which encourages g to be fitted well around its maximum (as otherwise the minimization would be dominated by the part of the domain far away from the peak, which occupy the majority of the image area).

Note that, while this method can successfully learn heat maps with maxima at the desired location, the choice of loss (1) and the Gaussian-like kernel g parameters is purely heuristic. Furthermore, the heat map does not convey any information beyond the location of its maximum. In the next section, we remedy this situation by introducing a probabilistic model instead, where heat maps become probability densities.

3.2   Probabilistic Formulation

It is possible to explicitly turn a heath map in *posterior probability over possible locations* of a certain landmark, for example by means of the softmax operator $\sigma[\cdot]$:

$$p_k(\mathbf{u}|\Phi\mathbf{x}) = \sigma[S_k](\mathbf{u}) = \frac{\exp S_k(\mathbf{u}; \Phi\mathbf{x})}{\sum_{\mathbf{v} \in \Omega} S_k(\mathbf{v}; \Phi\mathbf{x})}$$

The joint probability of combined landmark locations can then be written as the product:

$$p(\mathbf{u}_1, \ldots, \mathbf{u}_K|\Phi\mathbf{x}) = \prod_k p_k(\mathbf{v}_k|\Phi\mathbf{x}).$$

With this definition, loss (1) is replaced by the model likelihood, i.e. the probability of the observations $(\mathbf{u}_1^*, \ldots, \mathbf{u}_K^*)$ under the model:

$$\mathcal{L}_2(\Phi) = -\sum_k \log p_k(\mathbf{u}_k^*|\Phi\mathbf{x}). \tag{2}$$

This is a simple but powerful change because it allows the model to properly represent uncertainty in a landmark's location.

In order to efficiently encode high-resolution pose information, we consider a further extension of this architecture. We assume in particular that the feature map has fairly low resolution, so that it is efficient to compute. We also assume that the network estimates at each location $\mathbf{v} \in \Omega_\delta$ a displacement $\Delta_k(\mathbf{v}; \Phi\mathbf{x}) \in \mathbb{R}^2$ and a covariance matrix $\Sigma_k(\mathbf{v}; \Phi\mathbf{x}) \in \mathbb{S}_+^2$. In this manner, each feature map location *emits a Gaussian distribution* over possible landmark locations. This results in the mixture model:

$$\hat{p}_k(\mathbf{u}|\Phi\mathbf{x}) = \sum_{\mathbf{v} \in \Omega_d} \mathcal{N}(\mathbf{u}|\mathbf{v} + \Delta_k(\mathbf{v}; \Phi\mathbf{x}), \Sigma_k(\mathbf{v}; \Phi\mathbf{x})) \cdot p_k(\mathbf{v}|\Phi\mathbf{x}). \tag{3}$$

Table 1. Comparison of models' accuracy on the MPII Human Pose validation set with decreasing person height (PCKh @ 0.5)

Method	Input dimension	256px	128px	96px	64px	48px	32px	24px
HG [19]	256 × 256	**83.5**	**81.3**	80.2	72.4	59.4	32.8	14.1
HG-DOWNUP [19]	256 × 256	75.7	78.3	78.6	76.2	68.7	41.0	20.0
HG-64 [19]	64 × 64	77.6	77.5	76.7	74.3	65.9	45.2	18.9
Part Affinity Fields [3]	256 × 256	65.6	65.8	65.1	61.8	57.1	50.3	31.3
Our model	64 × 64	81.5	**81.3**	**80.5**	**79.7**	**75.0**	**61.8**	**48.0**

A key advantage of this model is that, while the summation is carried over a discrete (and coarse) domain, the resulting distribution p_k^{GMM} is continuous and thus has, in principle, infinite resolution. This can be interpreted as a probabilistic method to perform sub-pixel interpolation.

This probabilistic model is learned by maximizing the posterior logprobability of the ground-truth observations. Hence, given a training dataset $\left(\mathbf{x}_i, \mathbf{u}_1^{(i)}, \ldots, \mathbf{u}_K^{(i)}\right)$, one optimizes the loss

$$\mathcal{L}_3(\Phi) = -\frac{1}{N} \sum_{i=1}^{n} \log \prod_k \hat{p}_k^{(i)}(\mathbf{u}_k^{(i)} | \Phi \mathbf{x}_i), \qquad (4)$$

where $\mathbf{x}_i$ denotes the image and $\mathbf{u}_1^{(i)}, \ldots, \mathbf{u}_K^{(i)}$ denote the keypoint annotations for the i-th image. The loss (4) is differentiable w.r.t. $\Delta_k^{(i)}$, $\Sigma_k^{(i)}$ and $S_k^{(i)}$, so it can be minimized using standard gradient descent algorithms.

In our model, Φ is a fully convolutional neural network [18], which takes an input image $\mathbf{x}$ and outputs a 5-dimensional feature tensor for each keypoint k – the Gaussian mixture weights $S_k(\mathbf{v})$ and 4 Gaussian distribution parameters – means in x, y direction $\Delta_k(\mathbf{v})$ and a diagonal covariance matrix $\Sigma_k(\mathbf{v})$ for every $\mathbf{v}$ in the feature map Ω_d (see Fig. 2). We build on the Spatial ConvNet [23] architecture which is based on the popular VGG16 [4], by taking its first 8 convolutional layers and changing the input dimension to 64 × 64 pixels, which results in the output feature map resolution of 16 × 16 × 5K.

Discussion. Equation 3 might be reminiscent of the pose estimation in the wild method [21], which also regresses a dense displacement field in order to predict landmarks. The key difference is that our formulation estimates an actual joint probability distribution and, as shown in Eq. 4, optimizes over the label likelihood. While this might seem a minor difference, in reality it has a major effect. Instead of using heatmaps as a technical device to encode mere 2D positions as done in [21], our probability maps properly encode aleatoric uncertainty. By allowing the model to predict its own uncertainty we achieve more robust learning as well as a meaningful (verifiable) confidence score together that can be used in applications. In Sect. 4 we demonstrate both effects empirically in ablation studies.

4 Experiments

This section thoroughly evaluates our method against alternatives for low-resolution pose estimation. After discussing the learning setup (Sect. 4.1), the method is evaluated on two standard benchmarks—since the benchmarks do not contain small people, we scale images down in both datasets (Sect. 4.2). Additionally, we collected a new ad-hoc dataset of people seen at a distance, which is used only for testing the model (Sect. 4.3). We also show model performance in conjunction with a tiny people detector. An ablation study, which evaluates the main design choices of the proposed model, is presented in Sect. 4.4.

4.1 Training Details

In order to train our model, we combined the MPII Human Pose dataset [1] with the MS COCO dataset [17] and resized all instances of people using bilinear interpolation so that the resulting bounding box is 64 pixels in height (while we train the system at this resolution, we test it on much smaller images as well).

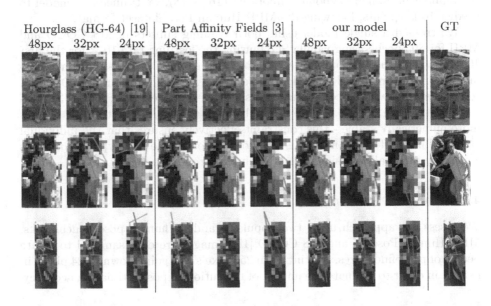

Fig. 3. Qualitative results on the **MPII Human Pose** validation set downsampled to 48, 32 and 24 pixels in height. Note that for Part Affinity Fields we only show the 12 keypoints consistent with MPII Human Pose annotation format. Note that *all methods were carefully optimized to give their best in the low-resolution setting* (see text). Best viewed zoomed in color (Color figure online)

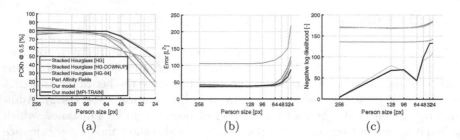

(a)   (b)   (c)

Fig. 4. Comparison of models' keypoint detection accuracy (a), regression error (b) and negative log-likelihood of the ground truth - "surprise" (c) on the **MPII Human Pose** validation set with decreasing person height

Since the testing set for the MPII Human Pose dataset is not publicly available, we split the MPII training set into training and validation subsets, following the data split published by Thompson *et al.* [29] and used elsewhere in the literature [2,31]. Note that because the MPII and COCO datasets slightly differ in the number of human keypoints annotated (16 vs 18), we trained our model to predict 16 keypoints, following the MPII Human Pose dataset format.

We trained a single model using both training subsets of MS COCO and MPII for 80 epochs using vanilla SGD, using the learning rate 10^{-5} for the first 40 epochs and then dropping the rate to a half every 10 epochs. For data augmentation, we only used a random scale augmentation in the range $(0.7, 1.3)$. In the training, we also constrain the displacement values $|\Delta(\mathbf{v}; \Phi\mathbf{x})| \leq 3$ (measured in the final 16×16 feature layer), because this makes the training process more numerically stable - this constraint effectively ensures that the individual elements in the feature map $\mathbf{v} \in \Omega_d$ do not contribute to keypoint locations which are physically outside of their individual receptive fields.

4.2   Standard Benchmarks

We assess our approach using two popular standard human pose benchmarks, MPII Human Pose [1] and MS COCO [17]. Images are downsampled to create people of predefined sizes, starting from 256 pixels and going down to 24 pixels in height, in order to evaluate the impact of resolution to pose estimation accuracy.

Baselines. We compare against two state-of-the-art methods for human pose estimation: Stacked Hourglass (HG) [19] and Part Affinity Fields [3]. We do our best to maximize the performance of these methods on our low-resolution data and test three approaches: naïve, retraining, and architecture editing. The **naïve** approach is to use off-the-shelf models trained by the respective authors and simply upscale the input using bilinear interpolation to the resolution expected by the model (256×256 pixels, which requires up to $8\times$ upsampling). By comparison, input images to our model area always down- or up-sampled to 64×64 pixels using the same mechanism. Since upsampling may change the image statistics, the second approach is to **retrain** the Stacked Hourglass model from scratch on the MPII dataset, using the training code and default parameters provided by the authors, on images first downsampled to 64×64 pixels and then upsampled to the expected resolution on 256×256 (HG-DOWNUP). The third approach is to **edit** the architecture to work directly on the same low-resolution data as ours. For Hourglass, we do so by removing the first two max-pooling layers to natively work on 64×64 input patches and retrain the model using the same protocol (HG-64). To make the comparison fair, we also include the results of our method when only trained on the MPII dataset (MPI-TRAIN).

Results. On the MPII Human Pose dataset (see Table 1 and Fig. 3), for people 128px high our method achieves competitive accuracy to the naïve Stacked Hourglass (HG) model [19], even though our effective input image size is in fact 64px, and outperforms Part Affinity Fields by a large margin. At 64px our model outperforms Stacked Hourglass by 10 and Part Affinity Fields (PAFs) by 20 percent points. Finally at 24px, our model has almost two times higher keypoint detection accuracy than PAFs and four times higher accuracy than Stacked Hourglass (see Fig. 4). Note that since PAFs output keypoints in the MS COCO format, we only evaluated the 12 keypoints which can mapped to the MPII annotations format. Also note, that retraining or editing the Hourglass architecture for the low resolution data does not bring a significant boost in performance for small people (see Fig. 4).

On the MS COCO dataset (using only the 12 keypoints for all methods), our method performs on par with Stacked Hourglass for larger people (128px), but with decreasing people size the margin grows in favor of our method, significantly outperforming both the Part Affinity Fields [3] and Stacked Hourglass for people sizes smaller than 48 pixels (see Fig. 5). Compared to MPII, accuracy on MS COCO is generally worse as the data is more challenging, particularly due to partial occlusions.

In all experiments, the standard PCKh@0.5 metric [1] was used to measure keypoint detection accuracy, which requires a detection to be within certain distance from the ground truth keypoint position, where the thresholding distance is given by 50% of the head segment length.

Additionally, we calculated the L^2 regression error as the distance between the detection and the ground truth normalized by the image height, and the negative log-likelihood of the ground truth, by taking the log-likelihood $-\log p(y_{gt}|x_{gt})$ of the probabilities for the ground truth keypoint locations produced by the model for the ground truth images. This is also known as "surprise" and is an indication of the quality of the probabilistic output of the model. Since the baseline models do not output probabilities, we assumed Gaussian distribution of their output, where the mean is the predicted landmark location and the variance is constant. The actual prediction variance value was calculated for

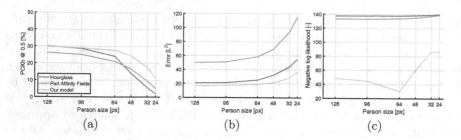

(a)   (b)   (c)

Fig. 5. Comparison of models' keypoint detection accuracy (a), regression error (b) and negative log-likelihood of the ground truth (model surprise) (c) on the **MS COCO** validation set with decreasing person size

each joint by comparing predictions to ground truth in the training set. In this case, the advantage of our probabilistic model is very significant at all resolution levels, indicating that meaningful probability maps are learned.

4.3   Tiny People

A limitation of the results in Sect. 4.2 is that images are resized synthetically. While this is simulates well the actual application scenario which is spotting people at a distance, we cannot guarantee that the image statistics match exactly.

For this reason, we introduce a new *Tiny People* dataset.[1] The dataset was collected by searching for 21 activity categories on Flickr (the category names were taken from the MPII Human Pose dataset [1]) and manually selecting images which contain small people. We intentionally chose manual image selection to avoid a bias towards a specific detection method, so that detection accuracy can also be also evaluated.

We collected 200 images with 585 people instances (see Fig. 6), where for each person instance we annotated 14 keypoints using the open source VGG Image Annotator tool [6]. We followed the annotation format of the MPII Human Pose dataset (16 keypoints), but we did not annotate the *lower neck* and *pelvis* keypoints as they cannot be realistically distinguished for small people. The average person height in the dataset is 51 pixels, which is significantly lower than the existing datasets (see Fig. 7).

Pose Estimation. We again compared our model to the two state-of-the-art methods (see Fig. 8) on Tiny People. We follow the same protocol as in the previous section with images being upsampled to 256 × 256 pixels by bilinear interpolation for the existing methods. Our method achieves the accuracy of almost 60% correctly localized keypoints (see Table 2), despite being trained only on the standard datasets, which is 17 percent points higher than Stacked Hourglass [19] and more than two times better than Part Affinity Fields [3].

---

[1] The dataset can be downloaded at http://www.robots.ox.ac.uk/vgg/data/tiny People/.

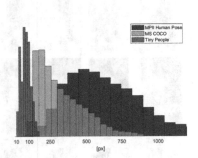

Fig. 6. Sample images from the Tiny People dataset

Fig. 7. Normalized histogram of people heights (as given by their bounding box annotation) in the standard datasets and in the newly introduced Tiny People dataset

Table 2. Comparison of models' accuracy on the Tiny People dataset

	PCKh @ 0.5	Avg. error [px]
Stacked Hourglass [19]	43.7	6.63
Part Affinity Fields [3]	25.5	18.99
Our model	**59.9**	**4.66**

The dataset is of course much smaller than other benchmarks, but its size is sufficient for evaluation purposes. In particular, with 585 pose instances, the measured error standard deviation $\frac{\sigma}{\sqrt{n}}$ is 0.3px vs the error differences between methods of > 2px, which is therefore well above significance (p-value 10^{-4}). Hence a dataset of this size is sufficient to reliably rank different algorithms.

The main failure mode is confusing left and right sides, which is given by intrinsic ambiguity of human body at a small scale—when the face is not distinguishable and there is not enough context in the image, it is not clear whether the person faces towards or away from the camera and it is thus not clear which arm (leg) is left or right.

Overall, these results further support the conclusion that our model performs better on small people than the state-of-the-art methods.

Tiny People Detection. In order to show, that the proposed pose estimation method can be easily incorporated into an end-to-end pipeline, we adapted the TinyFaces [13] detector for small people detection by modifying the expected aspect ratios and scales and trained it on the MS COCO training set, where every image was down-sampled by a factor of 4 resulting in an average person

| Hourglass | PAF | ours | GT | Hourglass | PAF | ours | GT |

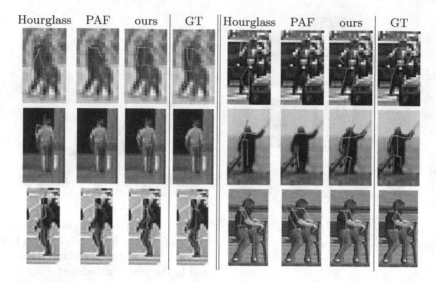

Fig. 8. Qualitative results on the **Tiny People** dataset, comparing our method against Hourglass (HG-64) [19] and PAF [3]. Note that *all methods were carefully optimized to give their best in the low-resolution setting* (see text). Best viewed zoomed in color. (Color figure online)

Fig. 9. Qualitative results of detection and pose estimation from the **Tiny People** dataset. Best viewed zoomed in color (Color figure online)

height of $\approx 50px$. After detection, patches are fed as input to our method for pose estimation (see Fig. 1).

Using the standard OKS keypoint evaluation metric, the pipeline achieved the average precision $AP^{OKS=0.50}$ of 24.5% on the four times downsampled COCO Validation set (evaluating only the 12 keypoints outputted by our model) and 53.5% on the newly introduced Tiny People dataset (see Fig. 9).

4.4   Ablation Study

In order to assess the impact of the newly introduced probabilistic formulation, we replace elements of our formulation with other choices common in the literature. We used the same network architecture backbone with the same input size

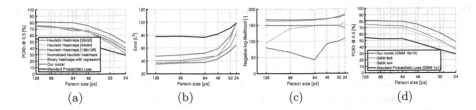

Fig. 10. Comparison of different representations for tiny human pose with decreasing person size, evaluated on the **MPII Human Pose** validation set - correctly detected keypoints (a), regression error (b) and negative log-likelihood of the ground truth (c). Keypoint detection accuracy as a function of the number of the Gaussian Mixture Model elements (d)

of 64×64 pixels and the same training data (Sect. 4.1) to train models with four different representations:

- **Heuristic heatmaps.** Dense $H \times H \times K$ heat maps ($H = 32, 64, 128$) are produced by adding additional de-convolution layers to the network. Predefined Gaussian-like kernels are used to produce heat maps around each keypoint location (Sect. 3.1) and a standard L^2 per-pixel loss is used in the training. This setting is analogous to stacked hourglass [19] and multi-context attention [5].
- **Normalized heuristic heatmaps.** The same $32 \times 32 \times K$ heat maps as above, but normalized at test time to create a probabilistic distribution over the image space.
- **Binary heatmaps with regression.** A $16 \times 16 \times 3K$ feature map with a binary heatmap around the each keypoint location combined with a 2-D vector which encodes keypoint offset in every location of the feature space. This representation can in principle produce sub-pixel accuracy because the offset is a real-valued parameter, but it does not capture uncertainty in the training nor the testing phase. This setting is analogous to pose estimation in the wild [21].
- **Standard probabilistic loss.** Directly predicting mean and variance of every keypoint from the whole image (see Eq. 2). This is equivalent to a Gaussian mixture model with only one element.

The ablation results (see Table 3 and Fig. 10) demonstrate that the proposed probabilistic representation outperforms the standard heatmap representations by a large margin, both in terms of the keypoint detection accuracy, as well as model surprise.

Furthermore, our continuous probabilistic distribution (inferred from a feature map of 16×16 and using Eq. 3) performs better than simply increasing the heat map resolution up to 128×128 pixels by means of deconvolutional layers. In fact, doing so makes the accuracy slightly worse, probably due to over-fitting.

Also note that taking the standard heatmap representation and normalizing it to create a "probability distribution" (*Normalized heuristic heatmaps*) reduces

Table 3. Comparison of different representations on the MPII Human Pose validation set with decreasing person height (PCKh @ 0.5)

Method	Output dimension	128px	96px	64px	48px	32px	24px
Heuristic heatmaps (32×32) [5,19]	$32 \times 32 \times K$	74.5	74.4	67.1	67.3	55.2	39.9
Heuristic heatmaps (64×64)	$64 \times 64 \times K$	74.1	72.8	70.1	65.2	50.8	36.1
Heuristic heatmaps (128×128)	$128 \times 128 \times K$	74.3	72.8	71.1	65.3	49.2	35.5
Normalized heuristic heatmaps	$32 \times 32 \times K$	74.5	74.4	67.1	67.3	55.2	39.9
Binary heatmaps [21]	$16 \times 16 \times 3K$	75.5	74.5	69.6	65.6	47.7	31.2
Our model (GMM 16×16)	$16 \times 16 \times 5K$	**81.3**	**80.5**	**79.7**	**75.0**	**61.8**	**48.0**
GMM 8×8	$8 \times 8 \times 5K$	75.5	73.8	72.5	65.3	50.4	36.9
GMM 4×4	$4 \times 4 \times 5K$	71.5	69.7	69.0	61.1	47.4	35.2
GMM 1×1	$4K$	54.7	52.8	52.8	46.0	35.6	28.8

the negative log-likelihood over assuming a Gaussian distribution (*Heuristic heatmaps* and *Binary heatmaps with regression*), but it is far inferior to the proposed approach (see Fig. 10c).

Finally, we show ablation experiments for the size of the feature map $\mathbf{v} \in \Omega_d$, i.e. the number of elements in the GMM (see Fig. 10d). The model becomes worse as the number of components is reduced and on contrary adding more than $16 \times 16 = 256$ components did not improve accuracy but made the computation slower (these lines are omitted for clarity as they overlap with the others).

5   Conclusion

We have shown that low-resolution pose recognition is significantly more ambiguous than its full-resolution counterpart and that modelling uncertainty explicitly in a deep network can significantly boosts recognition performance.

We have thoroughly validated this idea. We have tested standard benchmarks resized to low resolution and a new benchmark of people seen at a distance. We have conducted numerous ablation studies that emphasize the advantage of our probabilistic approach over other common modelling choices representative of state-of-the-art methods. We have also compared our approach to such methods directly, after thoroughly optimizing them for the low resolution setting in three different ways, to demonstrate that our approach is convincingly better in the low resolution setting, showing the usefulness of the probabilistic model.

Finally, on account of the small resolution, our model runs at 250 Hz on a single NVidia 1080Ti GPU, which is more than an order of magnitude faster than the existing methods, and which makes it suitable for integration to existing person detection pipelines.

Acknowledgement. We are very grateful to Continental Corporation for sponsoring this research.

References

1. Andriluka, M., Pishchulin, L., Gehler, P., Bernt, S.: 2D human pose estimation: new benchmark and state of the art analysis. In: IEEE Conference on Computer Vision and Pattern Recognition (CVPR), June 2014
2. Belagiannis, V., Zisserman, A.: Recurrent human pose estimation. In: 2017 12th IEEE International Conference on Automatic Face & Gesture Recognition (FG 2017), pp. 468–475. IEEE (2017)
3. Cao, Z., Simon, T., Wei, S.E., Sheikh, Y.: Realtime multi-person 2D pose estimation using part affinity fields. In: CVPR (2017)
4. Chatfield, K., Simonyan, K., Vedaldi, A., Zisserman, A.: Return of the devil in the details: delving deep into convolutional nets. arXiv preprint arXiv:1405.3531 (2014)
5. Chu, X., Yang, W., Ouyang, W., Ma, C., Yuille, A.L., Wang, X.: Multi-context attention for human pose estimation. In: The IEEE Conference on Computer Vision and Pattern Recognition (CVPR), July 2017
6. Dutta, A., Gupta, A., Zissermann, A.: VGG image annotator (VIA) (2016). http://www.robots.ox.ac.uk/vgg/software/via/. Accessed 14 Nov 2017
7. Efros, A.A., Berg, A.C., Mori, G., Malik, J.: Recognizing action at a distance. In: null. p. 726. IEEE (2003)
8. Felzenszwalb, P., McAllester, D., Ramanan, D.: A discriminatively trained, multiscale, deformable part model. In: IEEE Conference on Computer Vision and Pattern Recognition, 2008. CVPR 2008. pp. 1–8. IEEE (2008)
9. Fischler, M.A., Elschlager, R.A.: The representation and matching of pictorial structures. IEEE Trans. Comput. 100(1), 67–92 (1973)
10. Gal, Y., Ghahramani, Z.: Dropout as a bayesian approximation: representing model uncertainty in deep learning. In: International Conference on Machine Learning, pp. 1050–1059 (2016)
11. He, K., Gkioxari, G., Dollár, P., Girshick, R.: Mask R-CNN. In: The IEEE International Conference on Computer Vision (ICCV), October 2017
12. He, K., Zhang, X., Ren, S., Sun, J.: Deep residual learning for image recognition. In: Proceedings of the IEEE Conference on Computer Vision and Pattern Recognition, pp. 770–778 (2016)
13. Hu, P., Ramanan, D.: Finding tiny faces. In: The IEEE Conference on Computer Vision and Pattern Recognition (CVPR), July 2017
14. Insafutdinov, E., Pishchulin, L., Andres, B., Andriluka, M., Schiele, B.: DeeperCut: a deeper, stronger, and faster multi-person pose estimation model. In: Leibe, B., Matas, J., Sebe, N., Welling, M. (eds.) ECCV 2016. LNCS, vol. 9910, pp. 34–50. Springer, Cham (2016). https://doi.org/10.1007/978-3-319-46466-4_3
15. Kendall, A., Cipolla, R.: Modelling uncertainty in deep learning for camera relocalization. In: 2016 IEEE International Conference on Robotics and Automation (ICRA), pp. 4762–4769. IEEE (2016)
16. Kendall, A., Gal, Y.: What uncertainties do we need in bayesian deep learning for computer vision? arXiv preprint arXiv:1703.04977 (2017)
17. Lin, T.-Y., et al.: Microsoft coco: common objects in context. In: Fleet, D., Pajdla, T., Schiele, B., Tuytelaars, T. (eds.) ECCV 2014. LNCS, vol. 8693, pp. 740–755. Springer, Cham (2014). https://doi.org/10.1007/978-3-319-10602-1_48
18. Long, J., Shelhamer, E., Darrell, T.: Fully convolutional networks for semantic segmentation. In: Proceedings of the IEEE Conference on Computer Vision and Pattern Recognition, pp. 3431–3440 (2015)

19. Newell, A., Yang, K., Deng, J.: Stacked hourglass networks for human pose esti-mation. In: Leibe, B., Matas, J., Sebe, N., Welling, M. (eds.) ECCV 2016. LNCS, vol. 9912, pp. 483–499. Springer, Cham (2016). https://doi.org/10.1007/978-3-319-46484-8_29
20. Novotny, D., Larlus, D., Vedaldi, A.: Learning 3D object categories by looking around them. In: The IEEE International Conference on Computer Vision (ICCV), October 2017
21. Papandreou, G., et al.: Towards accurate multi-person pose estimation in the wild, July 2017
22. Park, D., Ramanan, D.: Articulated pose estimation with tiny synthetic videos. In: Proceedings of the IEEE Conference on Computer Vision and Pattern Recognition Workshops, pp. 58–66 (2015)
23. Pfister, T., Charles, J., Zisserman, A.: Flowing convnets for human pose estimation in videos. In: Proceedings of the IEEE International Conference on Computer Vision, pp. 1913–1921 (2015)
24. Pishchulin, L., Jain, A., Andriluka, M., Thormählen, T., Schiele, B.: Articulated people detection and pose estimation: reshaping the future. In: 2012 IEEE Confer-ence on Computer Vision and Pattern Recognition (CVPR), pp. 3178–3185. IEEE (2012)
25. Ren, S., He, K., Girshick, R., Sun, J.: Faster R-CNN: towards real-time object detection with region proposal networks. In: Advances in Neural Information Pro-cessing Systems, pp. 91–99 (2015)
26. Rupprecht, C., et al.: Learning in an uncertain world: representing ambiguity through multiple hypotheses. In: The IEEE International Conference on Computer Vision (ICCV), October 2017
27. Srivastava, N., Hinton, G.E., Krizhevsky, A., Sutskever, I., Salakhutdinov, R.: Dropout: a simple way to prevent neural networks from overfitting. J. Mach. Learn. Res. **15**(1), 1929–1958 (2014)
28. Tompson, J., Goroshin, R., Jain, A., LeCun, Y., Bregler, C.: Efficient object local-ization using convolutional networks. In: Proceedings of the IEEE Conference on Computer Vision and Pattern Recognition, pp. 648–656 (2015)
29. Tompson, J.J., Jain, A., LeCun, Y., Bregler, C.: Joint training of a convolutional network and a graphical model for human pose estimation. In: Advances in Neural Information Processing Systems, pp. 1799–1807 (2014)
30. Toshev, A., Szegedy, C.: Deeppose: human pose estimation via deep neural net-works. In: Proceedings of the IEEE Conference on Computer Vision and Pattern Recognition, pp. 1653–1660 (2014)
31. Wei, S.E., Ramakrishna, V., Kanade, T., Sheikh, Y.: Convolutional pose machines. In: Proceedings of the IEEE Conference on Computer Vision and Pattern Recog-nition, pp. 4724–4732 (2016)

Pose Estimation of a Single Circle Using Default Intrinsic Calibration

Damien Mariyanayagam[1](✉), Pierre Gurdjos[1], Sylvie Chambon[1],
Florent Brunet[2], and Vincent Charvillat[1]

[1] IRIT, INP-ENSEEIT, Toulouse, France
damien.mariyanayagam@alumni.enseeiht.fr
[2] Ubleam, Labège, France

Abstract. Circular markers are planar markers which offer great performances for detection and pose estimation. For an uncalibrated camera with rectangular pixels, the images of at least two coplanar circles in one view are generally required to recover the circle poses. Unfortunately, detecting more than one ellipse in the image is tricky and time-consuming, especially regarding concentric circles. On the other hand, when the camera is calibrated, the pose of one circle can be computed with its image alone but the solution is twofold and cannot be a priori disambiguated. Our contribution is to put beyond this limit (i) by dealing with the case of a calibrated camera with "default parameters" (e.g., using $2 \times 80\%$ of the image diagonal as focal length) that sees only one circle and (ii) by defining a theoretical framework where the pose ambiguity can be investigated. Regarding (i), we empirically show the surprising observation that default calibration leads to a circle pose estimation with accurate reprojection results which is quite satisfactory for augmented reality. As for (ii), we propose a new geometric formulation that enables to show how to detect geometric configurations in which the ambiguity can be removed.

Keywords: Circle pose estimation · Camera calibration · Circular marker

1 Introduction

The problem of estimating the pose of a camera (or dually of a 3D object) from a set of 2D projections in a single view has been widely studied in the computer vision literature [15]. The general case consists in solving a problem called PnP (Perspective n Point), using n correspondences of points 3D-2D with dedicated algorithms. The "minimal" problem i.e., which requires the minimal amount of information necessary, is known as the perspective-3-point-problem (P3P) and consists in recovering the pose of a calibrated camera from three correspondences. Many solutions are available for the general case when more information is available.

© Springer Nature Switzerland AG 2019
C. V. Jawahar et al. (Eds.): ACCV 2018, LNCS 11363, pp. 575–589, 2019.
https://doi.org/10.1007/978-3-030-20893-6_36

In a controlled environment, artificial features with known positions are very often deployed in the scene. They are used in a wide range of applications, especially when a reliable reference is needed to, e.g., in cluttered or texture-less environments. The most popular artificial features are probably coplanar features [4] whose layout in 2D space defines a so-called planar marker. The mapping between a planar marker and its image is a 2D projective transformation known as (world-to-image) homography and can be estimated from at least four world-to-image correspondences (the most simple planar marker is a square). Square markers are commonly used in this context [3,13,17]. Once the camera is calibrated, the decomposition of the homography matrix allows to recover the pose of the marker relative to the camera [14].

Other well-known artificial markers that have been recently investigated again are those consisting of coplanar circles [5,8,19]. The knowledge of at least two circle images (without any information on their parameters on the support plane) allows to compute a world-to-image homography without ambiguity for all the spatial configurations of two circles [5] (except when one circle encloses the other).

Given a single circle image, it is well-known that a twofold solution exists for the normal to the support plane (and so for the pose) *only if* the camera is calibrated [19]. In the case of a circular marker, we use the word pose to mention the pose of its external circle. We can notice that this is not directly equivalent to the camera pose which requires one more constraint to fix the additional degree of freedom embedded in the rotation of the circle around its axis. We propose to put beyond this limit by dealing with the case of a camera seeing one circle, for which we attach highly approximate values as camera parameters (for mobile phones, a distance equals to 2 times 70–100% of the diagonal of the image is an acceptable value). This is because, in this work, our goal is to be able to estimate the pose, for example, for augmented reality applications, as soon as one circle can be reliably detected in the image. Actually, our starting point came from the surprising observation, learned from empirical works, that very approximate calibration can lead to accurate results for augmented reality application. Our idea is to use these so-called "default intrinsics" by designing a generic camera model delivering a default focal length based on off-line calibration of several smartphone cameras.

The first contribution is to provide a new geometrical framework to state the pose problem in which the issue of how to remove the twofold ambiguity can be thoroughly investigated. Our first requirement was to provide a parametrization of the ambiguity problem that is both minimal and intuitive. Our second requirement was to define a removal test only depending on the minimal parameter set. Obviously if all the minimal parameters are known the ambiguity is always removed. Studying all the configurations is a possible work to do but required too much space to be developed in this article. We will focus on some remarkable configurations to illustrate our "theory".

The second contribution is to run extensive experiments that assesses how the inaccuracy of the calibration impacts the quality of the pose estimation.

We found out that exact calibration may not be required as small variations on the focal length do not affect the reprojection error of other reference coplanar points especially when the marker is far from the camera.

After reporting related works in Sect. 2, we remind the problem of recovering the pose from the projection of a circle, in Sect. 3, before introducing the solution proposed in Sect. 4. The idea is to introduce a new way of computing the vanishing line (dual to the vanishing point associated with the plane normal) from one circle image. Thanks to it, as the general method leads to two possible solutions, we show how under some assumptions about the geometric configuration we can recover the correct one. Then, as we suppose that we work with uncalibrated images, we explain how we select parameter values to obtain what we called default camera intrinsic parameters. Finally in Sect. 5, we evaluate our method in the context of augmented reality, before conclusions and perspectives, in Sect. 6.

2 Related Works

In the sequel, we assume a controlled environment which consists in features (or feature points) embedded in a planar structure. As recent efficient algorithms allow to detect ellipses precisely, circles become features worth of interest. We present in Fig. 1 some examples of existing circular markers and the marker used in this paper (c). The four projective and affine parameters of the world-to-image homography (the remaining four define a similarity on the world plane [6, p. 42]) can be recovered by detecting the images of two special points of the support plane, known as circular points (e.g., see [6, pp. 52–53]) which are common to all circles. Gurdjos et al. [5] relied on the notion of pencil of circle images to formulate the problem of detecting the images of the circular points as a problem of intersection of lines, obtained from the degenerate members of the pencil. Kim et al. [8] proposed algebraic and geometric solutions in the case of concentric circles. Calvet et al. [2] described a whole fiducial system using concentric circles which allows to accurately detect the position of the image of the circle common center under highly challenging conditions. In a same vein,

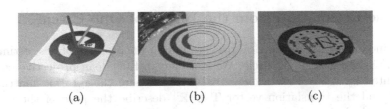

(a)   (b)   (c)

Fig. 1. Example of circular markers: (a) Pagani [11], (b) C2Tag [2] and (c) Bleam marker used in this paper.

Huang et al. [7] proposed to use the common self-polar triangle of concentric circles.

When using circular markers it is very common to simplify the model of the camera to only depend on a sole focal length parameter. The problem to solve contains, in addition to the ellipse parameters, the focal length. Chen et al. [18] autocalibrate the focal length using two or more coplanar circles. Then, the images of two circles are necessary to estimate the focal length. Based on the same method, Bergamasco et al. [1] designed a marker composed of small circles spread on the edge of two or more concentric rings. The image of each circle is used with a vote system to estimate the focal length and the image of the external rings.

Two circles on a planar marker (except if one encloses the other) is the minimum to fully estimate the homography without any other assumptions. However in some applications e.g., dealing with concentric circles, detecting the images of two or more circles can be tricky. First, the lack of points can induce an inaccurate estimation and, secondly it can be time consuming. When the camera has already been calibrated, it is possible to compute the homography from one circle image with two ambiguities. Zheng et al. [20] mentioned the existence of two algebraic solutions, corresponding to the indistinguishable geometric solutions but, unfortunately without providing clear understanding on how ambiguity can be raised. Pagani et al. [11] introduced a method quite similar to the solution proposed by Chen et al. [18], where the ambiguity is solved by minimizing a distance between the image of the marker rectified and the expected pattern on all possible poses.

In situations where the circle is observed from a distant camera (or equivalently when circle is small), Köser et al. [10] proposed to consider the local affine transformation (given by ellipse and circle correspondence) as the Jacobian of the perspectivity. We must point out that this work still uses a perspective camera model but considers the correspondence only as a local information providing only affine information. The same ambiguity obviously appears in the solution for the pose. In the next section, we introduce some geometrical background on the pose estimation of the circle in order to have a clear presentation of our contribution in Sect. 4.

3   Pose Estimation from the Image of One Circle

We remind here some geometrical background on the problem of pose estimation from the image of a single circle. We consider an Euclidean projective camera, represented by a 3×4-matrix $\mathsf{P} \sim \mathsf{KR} \left[\mathsf{I} \mid \mathbf{T}\right]$, where the rotation matrix $\mathsf{R} \in SO(3)^1$ and the translation vector $\mathbf{T} \in \mathbb{R}^3$ describe the pose of the camera, i.e., respectively its orientation and position in the object 3D frame. The upper triangular order-3 matrix K is the calibration matrix as defined in [6, p. 157].

Assume that $\mathcal{P}$ is a plane with equation $Z = 0$ in the world frame. The pose of $\mathcal{P}$ in the camera frame is given by the vector $[\mathbf{N} = \mathbf{r}_3, -d]^\top$, where $\mathbf{r}_3$, the

---

[1] $SO(3)$ refers to the 3D rotation group.

third column of R, defines the unit norm $\mathbf{N}$ of $\mathcal{P}$, and d is the orthogonal distance to $\mathcal{P}$. The restriction to $\mathcal{P}$ of the projection mapping is an homography whose matrix writes $\mathsf{H} \sim \mathsf{K}\mathsf{R}\left[\mathbf{e}_1 \mid \mathbf{e}_2 \mid \mathbf{T}\right]$, where $\mathbf{e}_1$ and $\mathbf{e}_2$ are the first two columns of I. In the projective plane, any conic can be represented in 2D homogeneous coordinates by a real symmetric order-3 matrix. Under perspective projection, any circle of $\mathcal{P}$, assuming its quasi-affine invariance [6, p. 515] i.e., that all its points lie in front of the camera, is mapped under the homography H to an ellipse by the projection equation $\mathsf{C} = \mathsf{H}^{-\top}\mathsf{Q}\mathsf{H}^{-1}$, where $\mathsf{Q} \in \mathrm{Sym}_3{}^2$ is the circle matrix and $\mathsf{C} \in \mathrm{Sym}_3$ is the ellipse matrix.

For reasons that will become clearer later, we want to parameterize the homography H, from only the knowledge of the circle image C and the vanishing line $\mathbf{v}_\infty$ of $\mathcal{P}$. Let $\mathsf{S}_\mathcal{P}$ be a similarity on the world plane that puts the circle Q into a unit circle centered at the origin and $\mathsf{S}_\mathcal{I}$ be a similarity on the image plane $\mathcal{P}$ that puts C into a canonical diagonal form $\mathsf{C}' = \mathrm{diag}(C'_{11}, C'_{22}, C'_{33})$. Using an approach similar to [2] with the notation $[u, v, 1]^\top \sim \mathsf{C}^{-1}\mathbf{v}_\infty$, it can be shown that, under the assumption of a camera with square pixels, we have $\mathsf{H} \sim \mathsf{S}_\mathcal{I}^{-1}\mathsf{M}\mathsf{S}_\mathcal{P}$ where

$$\mathsf{M} = \begin{bmatrix} -1 & C'_{22}uv & -u \\ 0 & -C'_{11}u^2 + 1 & -v \\ -C'_{11}u & C'_{22}v & 1 \end{bmatrix} \begin{bmatrix} r & 0 & 0 \\ 0 & -1 & 0 \\ 0 & 0 & s \end{bmatrix}$$

with $r = (-\dfrac{C'_{22}}{C'_{11}}(C'_{11}u^2 + C'_{22}v^2 + C'_{33}))^{1/2}$ and $s = \left(-C'_{22}(1 - C'_{11}u^2)\right)^{1/2}$

Note that the matrices $\mathsf{S}_\mathcal{P}$ and $\mathsf{S}_\mathcal{I}$ can be completely determined by the circle image C and M, except for an unknown 2D rotation around the circle centre on $\mathcal{P}$. Obviously, obtaining the pose of the camera from the circle pose requires this rotation. If needed, it is possible to place a visible mark on the contour to get it. This simple method proves to be efficient in many cases.

Our main task will be to recover the vanishing line $\mathbf{v}_\infty$ of the plane, as explained in the sequel. Note that the vector $\mathbf{x}_c = [u, v, 1]^\top$ defined above is that of the image of the circle centre which is the pole of $\mathbf{v}_\infty$ w.r.t. the dual ellipse of C whose matrix is C^{-1}.

4   Support Plane's Vanishing Line Estimation

We warn the reader that parts written in italics in this section requires a proof that is not provided due to lack of space. However all proofs which are not required for understanding will appear in an extended version of this paper.

4.1   A Twofold Solution in the Calibrated Case

In the case of calibrated image, an equivalent problem of computing the normal $\mathbf{N}$ of its support plane $\mathcal{P}$ is that of recovering the vanishing line $\mathbf{v}_\infty$ of $\mathcal{P}$ using

---

[2] Sym_3 refers to the space of order-3 real symmetric matrices.

relation $\mathbf{v}_\infty = \mathsf{K}^{-\top}\mathbf{N}$. In the following section, we propose a novel geometric framework which leads to a direct expression of the two solutions using pencil of conics. Then we will show using this framework that under certain conditions we can find geometric configurations where the "correct" solution can be recovered.

Let Q be the matrix of a circle on a plane $\mathcal{P}$, and $\psi = \mathsf{H}^\top\omega\mathsf{H}$ be that of the back-projection onto $\mathcal{P}$ of the image of the absolute conic [6, p. 81] given by $\omega = \mathsf{K}^{-\top}\mathsf{K}^{-1}$. It is easy to show that ψ represents a virtual[3] circle (as does ω).

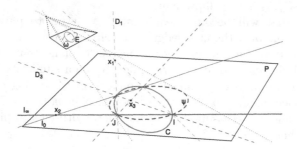

Fig. 2. Schematic representation of the degenerate conics in the plane $\mathcal{P}$

Let $\{\alpha_i\}_{i=1..3}$ denotes the set of generalized eigenvalues of the matrix-pair (Q, ψ), i.e., the three roots of the characteristic equation $\det(\mathsf{Q} - \alpha\psi) = 0$. The set of matrices $\{\mathsf{Q} - \alpha\psi\}_{\alpha\in\mathbb{R}\cup\{\infty\}}$ defines a conic pencil [5] which includes three degenerate conics with matrices $\mathsf{D}_i = \mathsf{Q} - \alpha_i\psi$. These rank-2 matrices represent line-pairs and have the form $\mathsf{D}_i = \mathbf{l}_a^i(\mathbf{l}_b^i)^\top + \mathbf{l}_b^i(\mathbf{l}_a^i)^\top$, where $\mathbf{l}_a^i$ and $\mathbf{l}_b^i$ are vectors of these lines. These line-pairs are represented in Fig. 2. Such line-pair matrix D_i can be easily decomposed and vectors of its lines recovered albeit it is impossible to distinguish $\mathbf{l}_a^i$ from $\mathbf{l}_b^i$. It can be shown that the projective signatures[4] of the three degenerate members always are $(1,1)$, $(2,0)$ and $(0,2)$. Assume, without loss of generality, that the degenerate conic D_2 is the one with signature $(1,1)$. **A first key result** is that D_2 is a pair of two distinct real lines, one of which being the line at infinity $\mathbf{l}_\infty = [0,0,1]^\top$; the other one being denoted by $\mathbf{l}_o$. The other two degenerate conics D_1 and D_3—with signatures $(2,0)$ and $(2,0)$—are pairs of two conjugate complex lines. In Fig. 2, we show the circles on their support plane and the degenerate conics. Consequently, the three (so-called) base points $\mathbf{x}_i$, where lines in a pair meet, are real. Moreover, their vectors are the generalized eigenvectors of (Q, ψ) and satisfy $\mathsf{D}_i\mathbf{x}_i = 0$.

Similarly, in the image plane, if C denotes the image of the circle Q, the set of matrices $\{\mathsf{C} - \lambda\omega\}_{\lambda\in\mathbb{R}\cup\{\infty\}}$ defines also a conic pencil whose members are the images of the pencil $\{\mathsf{Q} - \alpha\psi\}_{\alpha\in\mathbb{R}\cup\{\infty\}}$. Hence, the line-pair in $\{\mathsf{C} - \lambda\omega\}$ that

---

[3] Virtual conics have positive definite matrices, so, no real points on them.

[4] The signature of a conic is $\sigma(\mathsf{C}) = (\max(p,n), \min(p,n))$, where p and n count the positive and negative eigenvalues of its (real) matrix C. It is left unchanged by projective transformations.

includes the image of $\mathbf{l}_\infty$ i.e., the vanishing line $\mathbf{v}_\infty$, can always be identified since it is the only degenerate member with signature $(1,1)$. Nevertheless, at this step, it is impossible to distinguish $\mathbf{v}_\infty$ from the other line $\mathbf{v}_o$, image of $\mathbf{l}_o$.

Assume that all matrices Q, C, ψ and ω are normalized to have a unit determinant. It is known that, in this case, parameters in pencil satisfy $\alpha = \lambda$, so, the generalized eigenvalues of the matrix-pair (Q, ψ) are *exactly* the same as those of (C, ω).

It can be shown that the three generalized eigenvalues $\{\lambda_j\}_{j=1..3}$ *related to the conic pencil* $\{C - \lambda\omega\}_{\lambda \in \mathbb{R}\cup\{\infty\}}$ *can always be sorted such that* $\lambda_1 \geq \lambda_2 \geq \lambda_3$, *where* $L_2 = C - \lambda_2\omega$ *is the rank-2 conic with signature* $(1,1)$. Using Hermitian properties of E [9], we can compute:

$$\lambda_1 - \lambda_2 = \cos\alpha - \frac{\sqrt{3}}{3}\sin\alpha \quad \text{and} \quad \lambda_2 - \lambda_3 = 2\pi\frac{\sqrt{3}}{3}\sin\alpha \tag{1}$$

where

$$\alpha = \frac{1}{3}\arccos\left(\frac{1}{2}\frac{\operatorname{trace}(E)^3 - 9\,\operatorname{trace}(E)\,\operatorname{trace}(E^{-1}) + 27}{(\operatorname{trace}(E)^2 - 3\,\operatorname{trace}(E^{-1}))^{\frac{3}{2}}}\right) \quad \text{and } E = K^{-\top}CK^{-1}$$

Remind that L_2 is the conic which contains $\mathbf{v}_\infty$ plus $\mathbf{v}_o$, which are two *a priori* indistinguishable lines denoted by $\mathbf{v}_{1,2}$. Because the matrix L_2 is real, symmetric, rank-2 and order-3, *its generalized eigen-decomposition using the image of the base point vectors* $\mathbf{z}_1, \mathbf{z}_3 \in \mathbb{R}^3$ *writes as following:*

$$L_2 = \begin{bmatrix} \frac{\mathbf{z}_1}{\|\mathbf{z}_1\|} & \frac{\mathbf{z}_3}{\|\mathbf{z}_3\|} \end{bmatrix} \begin{bmatrix} \lambda_1 - \lambda_2 & 0 \\ 0 & \lambda_3 - \lambda_2 \end{bmatrix} \begin{bmatrix} \frac{\mathbf{z}_1^\top}{\|\mathbf{z}_1\|} \\ \frac{\mathbf{z}_3^\top}{\|\mathbf{z}_3\|} \end{bmatrix} \tag{2}$$

from which *it can be shown that*

$$\mathbf{v}_{1,2} = \sqrt{\lambda_1 - \lambda_2}\frac{\mathbf{z}_1}{\|\mathbf{z}_1\|} \pm \sqrt{\lambda_2 - \lambda_3}\frac{\mathbf{z}_3}{\|\mathbf{z}_3\|} \tag{3}$$

The two solutions to the normal to $\mathcal{P}$ are given by $N_{1,2} = K^\top\mathbf{v}_{1,2}$ in the camera frame, and (3) describes the known ambiguity in the plane pose, cf. [18].

4.2 About Removing the Twofold Ambiguity

We have seen that there are two solutions for the vanishing line (or the plane normal in the calibrated case) which are in general not distinguishable. In this section, we discuss whether known configurations allow the ambiguity to be removed. We extend the new theoretical framework proposed in Sect. 4.1 that involves the point $\mathbf{q}$ (on the support plane $\mathcal{P}$) where the optical axis cuts $\mathcal{P}$ plus the line $\mathcal{L}$ obtained by intersecting $\mathcal{P}$ and the principal plane[5] of the camera ($\mathcal{L}$ is orthogonal to the orthogonal projection of the optical axis onto $\mathcal{P}$). Now, let $\mathcal{L}'$ denotes the line parallel to $\mathcal{L}$ through the circle centre. Within this geometrical framework, we can claim, for instance, that *a sufficient condition for the ambiguity to be solved is given by the two following conditions:*

---

[5] The 3D plane through the camera centre and parallel to the image plane.

(i) $\mathbf{q}$ *and the orthogonal projection on* $\mathcal{P}$ *of the camera centre lie on the same side of* $\mathcal{L}'$;

(ii) *the point, intersection of the orthogonal projection on* $\mathcal{P}$ *of the optical axis and* $\mathcal{L}'$, *lies outside the circle centered at* $\mathbf{q}$ *with same radius as* Q.

Figure 3 illustrates this important result. We are convinced that future investigations using this framework can help to reveal more configurations in which the ambiguity can be removed. We are now giving more geometrical insights indicating how to determine such configurations, via three propositions. The first is the ***second key result*** which is the building brick of our approach:

Proposition 1 (second key result). *The line* $\mathbf{l_o}$ *in* D_2 *separates the two base points* $\mathbf{x_1}$ *and* $\mathbf{x_3}$. *Hence, denoting by* $\bar{\mathbf{x}}$ *the normalized vector* $\bar{\mathbf{x}} = \mathbf{x}/x_3$, *the following inequalities hold* $(\mathbf{l}_\infty^\top \bar{\mathbf{x}}_1)(\mathbf{l}_\infty^\top \bar{\mathbf{x}}_3) > 0$ *and* $(\mathbf{l_o}^\top \bar{\mathbf{x}}_1)(\mathbf{l_o}^\top \bar{\mathbf{x}}_3) < 0$.

These two inequalities hold under any affine transformation but not under a general projective transformation.

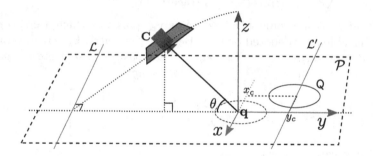

Fig. 3. Proposed parametrization for detecting the ambiguity.

How the conditions in Proposition 1 can be helpful in removing the plane pose ambiguity? Can we state a corollary saying that, in the image plane, under some known geometric configuration, we know which the line $\mathbf{v_o}$ in $\mathsf{C} - \lambda_2\omega$, image of $\mathbf{l_o}$, *always* separates points $\mathbf{z_1}$ and $\mathbf{z_3}$, images of base points $\mathbf{x_1}$ and $\mathbf{x_3}$, while the other does not? That is, if we a priori know the sign of $(\mathbf{v_o}^\top \bar{\mathbf{z}}_1)(\mathbf{v_o}^\top \bar{\mathbf{z}}_3)$ can we guarantee that $sign((\mathbf{v_o}^\top \bar{\mathbf{z}}_1)(\mathbf{v_o}^\top \bar{\mathbf{z}}_3)) = -sign((\mathbf{v_\infty}^\top \bar{\mathbf{z}}_1)(\mathbf{v_\infty}^\top \bar{\mathbf{z}}_3))$? If yes, since the vectors of the image of the base points $\{\mathbf{z_i}, i \in \{1,3\}\}$ are directly computable from the eigenvalues λ_j, $j \in \{1,3\}$ in Eq. (1), we could remove the ambiguity by choosing as vanishing line $\mathbf{v_\infty}$ the "correct" line in $\mathsf{C} - \lambda_2\omega$.

We claim the following proposition for this corollary to hold, *whose proof directly follows from the properties of quasi-affineness w.r.t. the base points* [6].

Proposition 2. *When* $\mathbf{x_1}$ *and* $\mathbf{x_3}$ *lie either both in front or both behind the camera i.e., on the same half-plane bounded by* $\mathcal{L}$, *we have* $(\mathbf{v_o}^\top \bar{\mathbf{z}}_1)(\mathbf{v_o}^\top \bar{\mathbf{z}}_3) < 0$ *and* $(\mathbf{v_\infty}^\top \bar{\mathbf{z}}_1)(\mathbf{v_\infty}^\top \bar{\mathbf{z}}_3) > 0$. *Otherwise* $(\mathbf{v_o}^\top \bar{\mathbf{z}}_1)(\mathbf{v_o}^\top \bar{\mathbf{z}}_3) > 0$ *and* $(\mathbf{v_\infty}^\top \bar{\mathbf{z}}_1)(\mathbf{v_\infty}^\top \bar{\mathbf{z}}_3) < 0$.

Now let us investigate a formal condition saying when $\mathbf{x_1}$ and $\mathbf{x_3}$ lie on the same half-plane bounded by $\mathcal{L}$. Consider an Euclidean representation of the projective world in which the origin is the point $\mathbf{q}$ at which the optical axis cuts the plane $\mathcal{P}$. Let the X-axis be parallel to the line $\mathcal{L}$ and the Y-axis is the orthogonal projection of the optical axis onto $\mathcal{P}$. Consequently, the Z-axis is directed by the normal to $\mathcal{P}$, as shown in Fig. 3. Let $\mathbf{C} = [0, -\cos\theta, \sin\theta]^\top$, $\theta \in [0, \frac{\pi}{2}]$, be the 3D cartesian coordinates of the camera centre, where $\pi - \theta$ is the angle between the Y-axis and the optical axis in the YZ-plane (note that we choose the scale such that the camera centre is at distance 1 from the origin). Therefore the direction of the optical axis is given by $-\mathbf{C}$.

In the 2D representation of the projective plane $\mathcal{P}$ (i.e., of the XZ-plane), let the circle have centre (x_c, y_c) and radius R. Let $\mathbf{d} = [0, 1, \cos\theta]^\top$ is the vector of line $\mathcal{L}$. It can be shown, using a symbolic software like MAPLE[6], that:

Proposition 3. *Base points $\mathbf{x_1}$ and $\mathbf{x_3}$ lie, in the world plane, on the same side of $\mathcal{L}$ if and only if*

$$\cos\theta(y_c^2 - R^2)(yc + cos\theta) + y_c cos\theta(1 + x_c^2) + x_c^2 + y_c^2 \leq 0 \qquad (4)$$

Since $\cos\theta > 0$, if $yc > 0$ and $y_c^2 - R^2 > 0$ then $\mathbf{x_1}$ and $\mathbf{x_3}$ lie on opposite sides of $\mathcal{L}$. The former inequality says that $\mathbf{q}$ must lie on the same side of $\mathcal{L}'$, the line parallel to $\mathcal{L}$ through the circle centre, as the orthogonal projection of the camera centre onto $\mathcal{P}$. The latter inequality says the point $(0, y_c)$ must lie outside the circle centered at $\mathbf{q}(0,0)$ with same radius R as Q. As we are in the "otherwise" part of Proposition 2, the vanishing line is given by the line that does not separate the image of the base points. Since $(0, y_c)$ represents the intersection of the orthogonal projection on $\mathcal{P}$ of the optical axis and $\mathcal{L}'$, this is the result announced at the beginning of this section.

This new parametrization is both minimal and intuitive. It can of course be extended to be used for further investigation in more applied areas. Moreover the ambiguity removal test introduced in this paper can be used in real applications. For instance, let the camera facing the ground where a circle is printed. The ambiguity is solved as long as the user tilts the camera downward until it targets a point (by checking the location of the principal point) distant from more than a radius of the circle center.

4.3 Defining Default Intrinsics for the Camera

In the previous section we have seen that, providing that the camera intrinsics are known, there is a twofold solution for the vanishing line. Having at one's disposal accurate intrinsics requires generally a calibration procedure. In many applications, the model of the camera can be simplified to reduce the number of parameters. A very common model is that of a camera with square pixels and principal point at the centre of the image plane. Consequently, the focal length is the sole unknown, e.g., for self-calibration purposes [12]. The focal length value

---

[6] https://fr.maplesoft.com/.

is sometimes available through EXIF data, stored in digital images or video files, through camera hardware on top level API (Android, iOS) or through data provided by manufacturer on websites. The focal length, denoted f, in pixels (what we need) can be obtained from this data if we find the field of view in angle or the focal length equivalent in 35 mm. However the focal length is very often given in millimeters without stipulating the sensor size, which is required to obtain the focal length in pixels.

We consider here the case where it is impossible to calibrate the camera by any of the methods mentioned above. So how to do? We propose to introduce a generic camera model delivering default intrinsics (i.e., focal length) and based on off-line calibration of several smartphone cameras. If a camera can generally take any focal length value, the optics and the sensor of smartphones are constrained by the device size and the desired field of view. Why doing that? We found out that surprisingly enough, that it is not necessary to have very accurate intrinsics to estimate the vanishing line given the image of a single circle. In fact, as shown in the experimental Sect. 5, this estimation is very robust to intrinsics fluctuation.

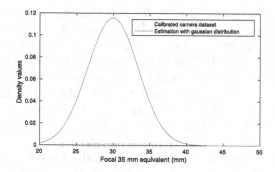

Fig. 4. Focal calibration of different camera parameters (Color figure online)

After calibrating a dozen of camera devices and obtaining data from manufacturers of twenty more smartphones, we estimate a gaussian model of the focal length equivalent in 35 mm, as shown in Fig. 4. In our case we obtained experimentally an average focal length of $f_{35} = 29.95$ mm with a variance of $\sigma_{f35}^2 = 11.86$. More precisely, we estimate a gaussian function (in blue) based of the focal values collected or estimated (in red) from different smartphone device brands.

One advantage of having a direct expression of the normal, using the closed-form of the previous section, is that we can express the normal with two differentiable functions $\mathbf{N_i} = g_i(f, \mathbf{C})$ with $i \in 1, 2$. Computing the distribution of $\mathbf{C}$ thanks to [16] and using the empiric distribution of f found with the devices, we can compute a first order approximation of the uncertainty on the normal.

Supposing that the ambiguity has been solved we can write:

$$\mathbf{N} = g(f_{35}, \mathbf{C}) \tag{5}$$

$$\Sigma_{\mathbf{N}} = \mathbf{J}_g(f_{35}, \mathbf{C})\sigma_{f35}^2\mathbf{J}_g(f_{35}, \mathbf{C})^{\top} \tag{6}$$

5 Experimental Results

5.1 Test Description

The goal of the tests presented in this section is to evaluate the proposed method to estimate the pose of a circle. We performed those tests on both synthetic and real images under the conditions illustrated in Fig. 5.

Fig. 5. Our setup consists of a reference chessboard and pose annotations.

In order not to test all the poses, we have simplified the problem to limit the trials to fewer parameters. First, we suppose that the camera is pointing at the centre of the marker, i.e. the principal axis of the camera passes through the centre of the marker, see Fig. 5, or at least it is close enough so that some pose parameters can be neglected. The angle γ is not important if we make the assumption that principal axis is orthogonal to the image plane. The angle β does not matter neither as we are only considering the pose of the circle (the rotation being recovered with groundtruth). The remaining variables whose variations are studied in our tests are the angle α and the distance r. Note that, in practice it is obvious that we have not constrained the camera to exactly point at the center of the marker. We have tried to aim the camera at some point close to the marker but not inside it, in order to allow us to use the sufficient condition exposed in Sect. 4.2, (the targeted point is more than one radius R from the marker center). We know that introducing generic camera parameter, as proposed in Sect. 4.3, should have a negative impact on the accuracy of the pose estimation. Consequently, one of the objectives of this experiment is to evaluate the sensitivity of the proposed method to inaccurate camera focal parameter. The observation of the distribution of focal length of various smartphone camera, see Fig. 4, reveals that all 35 mm focal equivalent are included in $[-30\%, +30\%]$ of the average value. So, five different values that span this range are used in the experiment: $\{0.7, 0.85, 1.0, 1.15, 1.3\}$. Any smartphones we have tested with focal parameters that fall in this range provide equivalent results. In this paper we only present the result obtain on real experiment with one smartphone. As the default focal have been shifted in our test, any focal value in this range (see in Fig. 4) can be represented with its corresponding focal modifier.

In order to generate synthetic images, we have simulated a synthetic camera using the same parameters as the real camera used in our test with resolution of 1280×720 pixels. The synthetic image have been sampled with a higher resolution before downsampling to avoid getting too much aliasing. To obtain real images, we have used the camera of a smartphone which have been calibrated with openCV library[7]. In both cases, we suppose that ellipses have been firstly detected in the images, i.e. contour points are first detected and then ellipses are estimated [16].

Finally, we evaluate the quality of the results obtained by using three different error measurements relative to the pose and the reprojection accuracy: error on the normal of the plane relative to the camera, error on the location of the marker and error of reprojection of 3D points close to the marker. Each curve illustrates the results obtained by applying a modifier on focal length used for pose estimation. The resulting errors are displayed as function of the distance r in the interval $[15 \times D, 45 \times D]$ where D is the diameter of the marker. This interval is related to the distances used for being able to detect and to recognize a marker for an augmented reality application, i.e. the distance where the marker occupies, at least 80 pixels. We also show results for three different angle values, $\alpha \in \{15, 30, 45\}$, displayed in three sub-figures.

5.2 Analysis of the Results

Results on synthetic images are presented in Fig. 6. We show the error of estimation for the orientation of the plane in Fig. 6a. We can see that in the calibrated case (black curve) the error slightly increases with the distance but decreases with the angle. This observation is in fact intuitive the more the circle is far, the more we lose accuracy on the ellipse detected and so is for the normal computed from it. When the circle is observed frontally (left figure with lower angle), the ellipse becomes more circular and the accuracy on the normal computed decreases as the solution approaches a degenerate case. These two observations are true for the error of reprojection in Fig. 6c and for real images in Fig. 7 as well.

The result we want to underline is that the error on the normal estimated with a wrong focal does not increase that much despite the rough modifier $[-30\%, +30\%]$ applied. Moreover we can see that the relative error with the calibrated case decreases with the distance. This observation is even more remarkable on the error of reprojection in Fig. 6c.

In Fig. 6b the result on the error of position is displayed, we can see that in the calibrated case the accuracy in position stays low and does not depend on the distance to the camera and the angles between the marker plane and

---

[7] https://opencv.org/.

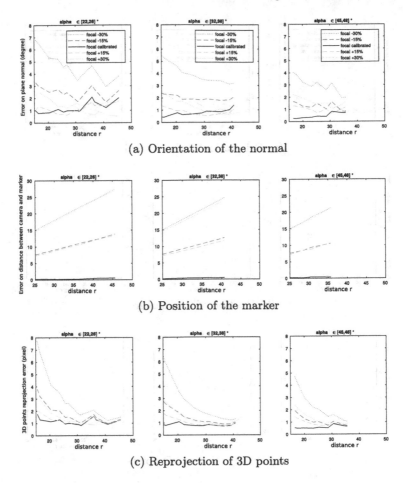

(a) Orientation of the normal

(b) Position of the marker

(c) Reprojection of 3D points

Fig. 6. Error with synthetic images.

the camera. In the uncalibrated cases, as expected the detection of the ellipses becomes less accurate when the distance increases and, consequently, the quality of the estimation of the marker position is also affected. In fact, the error in position increases linearly when the distance increases. This observation comes from the "vertigo effect". This is the real side effect of using a wrong focal, indeed the accurate location of the marker and especially its depth is largely affected. However the reprojection seen in Fig. 6c is actually good when the distance increases. It means that using generic parameter is not affecting the quality of the reprojection in a context where the marker is far from the camera.

Figure 7 allows us to present similar observations and conclusions on real images. The main differences are that the accuracy of the estimation seems to be more sensitive to the distance and so the size of the ellipse on the image. This is also not a big surprise as the detection of the ellipse is harder in real images.

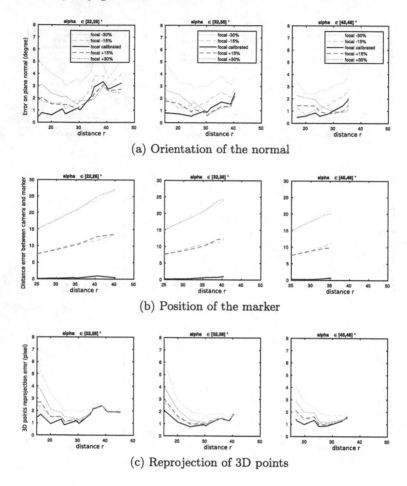

(a) Orientation of the normal

(b) Position of the marker

(c) Reprojection of 3D points

Fig. 7. Error with real images.

6   Conclusion

In this paper, we have introduced a method to estimate the pose of a circle (e.g. of a circular marker) from one image taken by a camera with "calibration by default". If, in general case, two solutions are found, we showed that some assumptions on geometric configuration can help to distinguish the correct pose. Moreover, we have demonstrated the interest of using these default camera parameters, in the context of augmented reality. In particular, the results presented showed that, in a case of a distant marker, the 3D reprojection errors is low and the error can be controlled with the uncertainties on the estimation. Future work would be to use more information in the marker environment to increase the stability of the detection of the marker to lead to a better pose estimation, for example by using points of interest outside the markers.

References

1. Bergamasco, F., Albarelli, A., Rodolà, E., Torsello, A.: RUNE-Tag: a high accuracy fiducial marker with strong occlusion resilience. In: CVPR (2011)
2. Calvet, L., Gurdjos, P., Griwodz, C., Gasparini, S.: Detection and accurate localization of circular fiducials under highly challenging conditions. In: CVPR (2016)
3. Fiala, M.: Artag, a fiducial marker system using digital techniques. In: CVPR (2005)
4. Fiala, M.: Designing highly reliable fiducial markers. PAMI **32**(7), 1317–1324 (2010)
5. Gurdjos, P., Sturm, P., Wu, Y.: Euclidean structure from $N \geq 2$ parallel circles: theory and algorithms. In: Leonardis, A., Bischof, H., Pinz, A. (eds.) ECCV 2006. LNCS, vol. 3951, pp. 238–252. Springer, Heidelberg (2006). https://doi.org/10.1007/11744023_19
6. Hartley, R., Zisserman, A.: Multiple View Geometry. Cambridge University Press, Cambridge (2003)
7. Huang, H., Zhang, H., Cheung, Y.M.: The common self-polar triangle of concentric circles and its application to camera calibration. In: CVPR (2015)
8. Kim, J.S., Gurdjos, P., Kweon, I.S.: Geometric and algebraic constraints of projected concentric circles and their applications to camera calibration. PAMI **27**(4), 637–642 (2005)
9. Kopp, J.: Efficient numerical diagonalization of hermitian 3x3 matrices. Int. J. Modern Phys. C **19**(03), 523–548 (2008)
10. Köser, K., Koch, R.: Differential spatial resection - pose estimation using a single local image feature. In: Forsyth, D., Torr, P., Zisserman, A. (eds.) ECCV 2008. LNCS, vol. 5305, pp. 312–325. Springer, Heidelberg (2008). https://doi.org/10.1007/978-3-540-88693-8_23
11. Pagani, A., Koehle, J., Stricker, D.: Circular Markers for camera pose estimation. In: Image Analysis for Multimedia Interactive Services (2011)
12. Pollefeys, M., Koch, R., Van Gool, L.: Self-calibration and metric reconstruction inspite of varying and unknown intrinsic camera parameters. IJCV **32**(1), 7–25 (1999)
13. Rekimoto, J.: Matrix: a realtime object identification and registration method for augmented reality. In: Asian Pacific Computer Human Interaction (1998)
14. Sturm, P.: Algorithms for plane-based pose estimation. In: CVPR (2000)
15. Szeliski, R.: Computer Vision: Algorithms and Applications. Springer, London (2010). https://doi.org/10.1007/978-1-84882-935-0
16. Szpak, Z.L., Chojnacki, W., van den Hengel, A.: Guaranteed ellipse fitting with a confidence region and an uncertainty measure for centre, axes, and orientation. JMIV **52**(2), 173–199 (2015)
17. Wagner, D., Schmalstieg, D.: Artoolkitplus for pose tracking on mobile devices. In: ISMAR (2007). https://doi.org/10.1.1.157.1879
18. Chen, Q., Wu, H., Wada, T.: Camera calibration with two arbitrary coplanar circles. In: Pajdla, T., Matas, J. (eds.) ECCV 2004. LNCS, vol. 3023, pp. 521–532. Springer, Heidelberg (2004). https://doi.org/10.1007/978-3-540-24672-5_41
19. Wu, H., Chen, Q., Wada, T.: Conic-based algorithm for visual line estimation from one image. In: Automatic Face and Gesture Recognition (2004)
20. Zheng, Y., Ma, W., Liu, Y.: Another way of looking at monocular circle pose estimation. In: ICIP (2008)

Deep Multi-instance Volumetric Image Classification with Extreme Value Distributions

Ruwan Tennakoon[1]([✉])[ID], Amirali K. Gostar[1][ID], Reza Hoseinnezhad[1][ID], Marleen de-Bruijne[2,3][ID], and Alireza Bab-Hadiashar[1][ID]

[1] School of Engineering, RMIT University, Melbourne, Australia
{ruwan.tennakoon,alireza.bab-hadiashar}@rmit.edu.au
[2] Biomedical Imaging Group Rotterdam, Erasmus MC,
Rotterdam, The Netherlands
[3] Department of Computer Science, University of Copenhagen,
Copenhagen, Denmark

Abstract. Predicting the presence of a disease in volumetric images is an essential task in medical imaging. The use of state-of-the-art techniques like deep convolutional neural networks (CNN) for such tasks is challenging due to limited supervised training data and high memory usage. This paper presents a weakly supervised solution that can be used in learning deep CNN features for volumetric image classification. In the proposed method, we use extreme value theory to model the feature distribution of the images without a pathology and use it to identify positive instances in an image that contains pathology. The experimental results show that the proposed method can learn classifiers that have similar performance to a fully supervised method and have significantly better performance in comparison with methods that use fixed number of instances from a positive image.

Keywords: Multiple instance learning · Weak supervision ·
Optical coherence tomography · OCT images ·
Retinal fluid classification · Macular Edema · ReTOUCH challenge ·
Intra-retinal fluid · Sub-retinal fluid · Pigment Epithelial Detachment ·
Learning (artificial intelligence) · Medical image processing

1 Introduction

Predicting the presence of a disease in volumetric (3D) images is an important task with many applications in medical imaging [13]. Due to high memory usage and limited availability of training data, applying state-of-the-art classification techniques such as deep convolutional neural networks (CNN) to volumetric image classification is challenging. A typical 3D medical image contains around $(512 \times 512 \times 100)$ voxels and feeding such images directly to a CNN would result in large memory usage and would require a network with very large set

© Springer Nature Switzerland AG 2019
C. V. Jawahar et al. (Eds.): ACCV 2018, LNCS 11363, pp. 590–604, 2019.
https://doi.org/10.1007/978-3-030-20893-6_37

of parameters (training of which requires large datasets). One option, as used in natural image classification, is to down-sample the image. The footprints of pathologies are often contained in a small area and down-sampling can easily obscure those instances.

A common approach to the above would be to partition the image into compact volumes (i.e. instances), and train a CNN using human expert annotation of each instance (analogous to object detection framework). At inference, the outputs of the instance CNN can then be aggregated according to some rule or using another classifier to generate image level predictions. The winning team of the "Data science Bowl 2017" [2] followed a variant of the above approach. However, in practice getting precise expert annotations is an expensive task and relying on those annotations excludes the use of medical image databases that already exist with only image level labels.

Another common approach is to consider the problem as a weakly-supervised classification problem. In this approach, an image is converted into a bag of instances and each bag has a label. A model can then be learned using multiple instance learning (MIL) assumption: At least one instance in a positive bag is positive and none of the instances in negative bags are positive. A recent survey of the use of multiple instance learning in medical imaging is presented in [15]. It is said that when a straightforward form of the above formulation is used for learning classifiers, utilised information is likely to be limited to one instance from a positive bag [22]. In medical image applications with limited training data, such behaviour is not desirable.

There have been several works that aim at including more than one instance from a positive bag during training. In simple-MIL approach [7,20] bag labels are propagated to instance labels and all the instances are used in training an instance classifier. Similarly, in mi-SVM [3], instance labels are initialised with bag labels and then updated iteratively in the training process using classifier output. State-of-the-art examples of formulations that use more than one instance from a positive bag in learning CNN features include: (1) MIL base whole mammogram classification [22]: This work proposed to use top-k instances from a positive bag as positive and the rest as negative. As the authors of the paper pointed out, defining a k that is appropriate for all images is challenging. As a possible solution, the authors proposed a soft method (i.e. sparse multi-instance learning), which adds sparsity constraint to the cost function. However, implementing such constraints is not feasible in problems where the full bag cannot be loaded to memory at once for back-propagation. (2) CNN based whole slide tissue image classification [11]: The method defines hidden variables to flag instances containing discriminative information and then uses an EM algorithm to infer both the hidden variable and CNN parameters, iteratively. Similarly, inferring the hidden variable requires a threshold and the authors note that using a simple thresholding scheme would ignore the useful instances that fall near the decision boundary. As such, they proposed an elaborate thresholding scheme consisting of two neural networks, spatial smoothing and image/class level thresholds (again require carefully tuned parameters) to improve the situation.

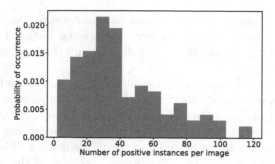

Fig. 1. The normalized histogram of positive instances per image of the OCT image classification dataset used in our experiments [1]. The number of positive instances per image in this dataset has a large variation and defining a fixed threshold is not realistic.

For many medical imaging applications defining thresholds indicating how many positive instances are likely to be in a given image, as required by the above-mentioned methods, is challenging. One such example is elaborated in Fig. 1 which shows the number of positive instances per image in a OCT image classification dataset [1]. The number of positive instances per image in this dataset has large variation and defining a fixed threshold is not realistic. In this paper, we propose to use extreme value theory (EVT) to model the maximum feature deviations (from the mean feature of negatives) of instances in the negative images and use this information to identify the probable positive instances in positive images. The proposed method eliminates the need for pre-defined thresholds (which are difficult to tune) and provides a mechanism for end-to-end training of CNN in a weakly supervised setting. While extreme value theory has been used in computer vision in the past for: SVM score calibration [16] and open-set classification [4,17], its use for training weakly supervised multi-instance learning classifiers has not yet been explored.

The rest of the paper is organized as follows: Sect. 2 provides a brief overview of EVT and volumetric image classification using learning methods. Section 3 describes the proposed method while Sect. 4 presents the experimental result on 3D-OCT image classification. Section 5 concludes the paper.

2   Background

2.1   Deep-Learning Based Volumetric Image Classification

Methods for deep-learning based volumetric image classification can be segmented into three categories: (1) Patch based detection, (2) Unsupervised or transfer learning based methods, (3) Multiple instance learning based methods.

In a typical patch based detection method, the training data consist of annotations of the pathology location and region. This information can be used to train CNN based classifiers that operate on smaller patches (eliminating the high memory requirement at training time) and at test time, all the patches in a test image are analysed for pathology. Such framework has been employed in detecting pulmonary nodules [18], colonic polyps [19], and cerebral micro-bleeds [9].

Another possible framework to avoid whole image based training is to use pretrained CNN or unsupervised learning techniques (such as auto-encoders) to learn feature representations of smaller patches and then aggregate them using a classifier to generate image level prediction [6]. Pre-trained networks might not be suitable for the special type of voxel information present in medical images and unsupervised learning might learn features that are not specialised (or discriminative) for the task at hand.

Multiple instance based deep learning methods [15] is a compromise between above two approaches that only use image level annotations at training time. These methods have been used for body part recognition [21], whole mammogram classification [22], etc.

2.2 Extreme Value Distribution

Extreme value theorem (EVT) [8], often used for modelling unusual events in weather and financial systems, is a counterpart of central limit theorem. While the central limit theorem describes the distribution of mean values, EVT describes the behaviour of extreme values sampled from any underlying distribution. To explain our proposed method, we first briefly explain the extreme value theorem [8]:

Theorem 1. *Let* $(X_1, X_2, \dots)$ *be a set of i.i.d. samples drawn from any distribution and* $M_n = \max(X_1, \dots, X_n)$. *If a sequence of real numbers* (a_n, b_n) *exist such that each* $a_n > 0$ *and*

$$\lim_{n \to \infty} P\left(\frac{M_n - b_n}{a_n} \leq x\right) = G(x). \tag{1}$$

If G *is a non-degenerate distribution function, then* G *belongs to one of the following families: Gumbel, Fréchet and Weibull.*

If samples are bounded from either side, the appropriate distribution of those extreme values will then be a *Weibull*. The i.i.d assumption in the above theorem was later relaxed to a weaker assumption of exchangeable random variables in [5].

The block maxima method of EVT is often used when there may be local dependencies that would play a role within blocks but not between blocks [10]. Our proposed modelling of negative instances fall into this category, where there might be some dependency between the instances from a given image but it is reasonable to assume independence between images themselves.

3   Proposed Method

Given a training dataset $\mathcal{X} = \left\{ \left(X^{(i)}, y^{(i)}\right) \right\}_{i=1}^{N}$ containing N volumetric images, $X^{(i)} \in \mathbb{R}^{h_i \times w_i \times z_i}$, and the corresponding expert annotations, $y^{(i)} \in \{0, 1\}$ (indicating whether a particular disease is present or not), our intention is to learn a model that can predict whether the particular disease is present in an unseen image $X^{(\cdot)}$.

The proposed method uses an iterative sampling based weakly supervised classification framework. In this approach each image is partitioned into a collection (bag) of smaller volumes (instances) $B^{(i)} := \{x_1^{(i)}, \ldots, x_{L_i}^{(i)}\}$; $x_l^{(i)} \subset X^{(i)}$ of size (h, w, d) and, the probability that a disease is present in a particular instance is modelled using a parametrized function, $f_\theta\left(x_j^{(i)}\right) \Leftrightarrow P\left(h_j^{(i)} = 1 \mid x_j^{(i)}\right)$. Here $h_j^{(i)}$ is the instance label, that indicates the presence of disease in instance j of image i. Using the MIL assumption, the disease presence probability for the overall image can be inferred as follows:

$$p\left(y^{(\cdot)} = 1 \mid X^{(\cdot)}\right) = \max\left(f_\theta\left(x_1^{(\cdot)}\right), \ldots, f_\theta\left(x_{L_i}^{(\cdot)}\right)\right). \tag{2}$$

Now, the challenge is to learn the model parameters, (θ) given only the bag labels. We consider the instance labels as hidden variables and use an expectation-minimization (EM) based framework, shown in Fig. 2, to learn the model parameters θ. The remainder of this section describes the two main steps in the proposed EM based method: (1) Learning the model that maps an image instance to instance label h and (2) Inferring the values of h using the EVT.

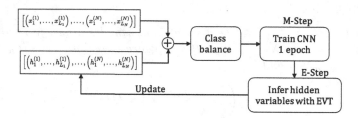

Fig. 2. The overall block diagram of the training phase.

3.1   Learning Deep CNN Model

In this paper the function f_θ is modelled using a CNN. The architecture of the CNN and the cost function used in the optimization are as follows:

CNN Architecture: The first five stages of the network (i.e. base model) has the same structure as the convolutional stages of the AlexNet architecture [12]. The output of the base model is connected to a two stage fully connected structure through a global average pooling layer as shown in Fig. 3. It should be noted that the proposed method is not restricted to the above architecture and one can select any suitable CNN architecture.

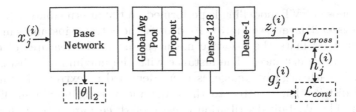

Fig. 3. Architecture of the proposed CNN.

Cost Function: The parameters of the overall network are obtained by optimizing a cost function consisting of three terms:

$$\theta^* = \arg\min_{\theta} \left\{ \mathcal{L}_{cr}(\hat{h}_j^{(i)}, h_j^{(i)}) + \lambda_1 \|\theta_b\|_2 + \lambda_2 \mathcal{L}_{ct}(\{g_j^{(i)}\}, \{h_j^{(i)}\}) \right\} \qquad (3)$$

where λ_1 and λ_2 are two hyper-parameters that balance the terms in the cost function, $\|\theta_b\|_2$ is the l2-norm of the base model parameters (acts as a regularizer), $\mathcal{L}_{cr}$ is binary cross-entropy and $\mathcal{L}_{ct}$ is the contrastive loss function.

The contrastive loss term, $\mathcal{L}_{ct}$, forces the features representation at dense-128 layer to have the following property: minimizes the distance distance between features of instances belonging to the same class while keeping the features of separate classes apart. This property is useful in the EVT fitting procedure explained in the next section. Instead of implementing the contrastive loss with a Siamese type architecture (which can be memory intensive) we used a simple trick where the contrastive loss is calculated between the adjacent instances of a batch as given by:

$$\mathcal{L}_{ct} = \sum_{\{j:0\leq j\leq N_b \wedge j/2\in\mathbb{N}\}} \left\{ \delta(h_j = h_{j+1}) \|g_j - g_{j+1}\|_2^2 \right.$$
$$\left. + \delta(h_j \neq h_{j+1}) \max\left(0, m - \|g_j - g_{j+1}\|_2\right)^2 \right\} \qquad (4)$$

where j index the instances in a batch with N_b elements, $g_j^{(d)}$ is the output feature at dense-128, m is just a margin (set to 1 in our experiments) and $\delta(\cdot)$ is 1 when the expression inside is true and zero otherwise.

3.2   Sampling Instance Labels with EVT

One of the main contributions of this paper is the way we assign labels to instances (infer the hidden variables). Instead of thresholding the CNN output ($\hat{h}_j^{(i)}$), as prescribed in [11], we propose to use the EVT to model extreme instances in the negative bags and then use that model to define the probability of being positive (i.e. positiveness) for instances in the positive bags. Using EVT provides a much sharper CDF and does not rely on making any assumptions about the shape of the underlying feature distribution.

Our proposed EVT modelling is performed on the intermediate CNN feature space at dense-128 layer (see Fig. 3). To identify the extreme instances in negative bags, we first estimate the negative mean (μ) using the features of correctly classified negative instances. The instance with the maximum l2-distance from the mean, in each negative image, is then identified as extreme instances and a Weibull distribution is fitted to those distances using maximum likelihood estimation. The Weibull distribution consist of three parameters: shape (k_w), scale (λ_w) and location (θ_w).

The CDF of the above estimated Weibull distribution can then be used to define the positiveness for all instance in positive bags as:

$$P\left(h_j^{(i)} = 1 \mid d_j^{(i)}, k_w, \lambda_w, \theta_w\right) = 1 - e^{-(\frac{d_j^{(i)} - \theta_w}{\lambda_w})^{k_w}} \tag{5}$$

where $d_j^{(i)} = \left\|g_j^{(i)} - \mu\right\|_2$. As mentioned before, the use of contrastive loss term make the l2-distance meaningful in this feature space (assumption that negative instances would have shorter distances to each other compared to positive instances is justified). As the above probability of positiveness is properly grounded, a simple threshold (we use $T_{evt} = 0.95$ in all our experiments) can be applied to infer the values of the hidden variables. This threshold is easy to tune and our experiments showed that the final result is not significantly affected by the value of this threshold. To make sure that each positive image has at least one positive instance, we always assign the corresponding hidden variable of the instance with maximum positive probability to one.

As it is likely to have more negative instances that positive ones, we sample equal amounts of those instances using the score $\hat{h}_j^{(i)}$ as the probability of selecting a given instance $x_j^{(i)}$. Such sampling strategy (hard negative mining) would increase the likelihood of including an incorrectly classified negative instance in the subsequent training iteration. The overall algorithm for sampling instance labels ($h_j^{(i)}$) is given in Algorithm 1. At the start of training the hidden variables are initialized with the respective bag labels. The image level predictions at the test time are determined using Eq. (2) on CNN output probabilities. The overall CNN training procedure is given in Algorithm 2.

4   Experimental Results

Dataset: We evaluated the proposed method on the 3D retinal OCT image classification task in ReTOUCH challenge [1]. OCT is an *in-vivo*, high resolution imaging technology that is capable of capturing a 3D volumetric image of the retinal and the sub-retinal layers, in addition to retinal pathology. Studies have shown that OCT signal have strong correlation with retinal histology and are extremely useful to diagnose Macular Edema (the swelling of the macular region of the eye, caused by fluid build-ups due to disruptions in blood-retinal barrier [14]) caused by different diseases. The objective is to classify OCT images

---

Algorithm 1. One iteration of inferring h with EVT.

Input: CNN features at dense-128 ($\{g_j^{(i)}\}$), CNN output ($\hat{h}_j^{(i)}$), image labels ($[y^{(i)}]_{i=1}^N$), EVT thresholds ($T_{evt} = 0.95$), EVT tail size β.

Output: $\{h_j^{(i)}\}$

1: $h_j^{(i)} \leftarrow -1 : \forall \, i = 1 \rightarrow N$ **and** $j = 1 \rightarrow L_i$
2: $g_{tn} \leftarrow$ Set of true-negative features.
3: $\mu = mean(g_{tn})$
4: $d_j^{(i)} = \|g_j^{(i)} - \mu\|_2 \; : \forall \, i = 1 \rightarrow N$ **and** $j = 1 \rightarrow L_i$
5: $M = \{M^{(i)} \leftarrow \max(d_1^{(i)}, \ldots, d_{L_i}^{(i)}) : \forall i = 1 \rightarrow N$ **if** $y^{(i)} = 0\}$
6: $[k_w, \lambda_w, \theta_w] \leftarrow FitWeibull(M, \beta)$
7: **for** $i = 1 \rightarrow N$ where $y^{(i)} = 1$, $j = 1 \rightarrow L_i$ **do**
8:     $w_j^{(i)} \leftarrow 1 - e^{-(\frac{-d_j^{(i)} - \theta_w}{\lambda_w})^{k_w}}$
9:     **if** $w_j^{(i)} > T_{evt} : h_j^{(i)} = 1$ **else if** $w_j^{(i)} < T_{evt} : h_j^{(i)} = 0$
10:    $h_{j*}^{(i)} = 1$ where $j* = argmax(w_1^{(i)}, \ldots, w_{L_i}^{(i)})$
11: **end for**
12: $n_p \leftarrow$ number of instances with $h_j^{(i)} = 1$
13: Sample n_p instances from negative images with acceptance probability $w_j^{(i)}$ and set corresponding $h_j^{(i)} \leftarrow 0$.

Algorithm 2. Training procedure for EVT-MIL.

Input: Image instances and bag labels $\{\{x_j^{(i)}\}_{j=1}^{L_i}, y^{(i)}\}_{i=1}^N$.

Output: Trained CNN model

1: $h_j^{(i)} \leftarrow y^{(i)} : \forall \, i = 1 \rightarrow N$ **and** $j = 1 \rightarrow L_i$
2: **for** $i = 1 \rightarrow \#epoch$ **do**
3:    Train CNN with $\{x_j^{(i)}, h_j^{(i)}\}_{i=1 \rightarrow N, \, j=1 \rightarrow L_i}$.
4:    $\{g_j^{(i)}\} \leftarrow$ Extract CNN Features at Dense-128.
5:    $\{h_{j*}^{(i)}\} \leftarrow$ Infer instance labels with Algorithm 1.
6: **end for**

---

according to the presence (or absence) of three types of fluids that cause Macular Edema: Intra-retinal fluid (IRF), Sub-retinal fluid (SRF) and Pigment Epithelial Detachment (PED) - although the name does not refer to a fluid, the detachment is marked by existence of excess fluid.

The ReTOUCH dataset consists of 112 volumetric OCT images. The images were captured using a variety of devices from three different manufacturers. A detailed description of the dataset is provided in Table 1. We have used the train/test split provided by the ReTOUCH organizers in our experiments (60% Train – 40% Test).

Table 1. Details of the ReTOUCH OCT image dataset.

	Spectralis	Cirrus	Topcon
Num images	38	38	36
Num positives (IRF/SRF/PED)	32/22/19	30/19/18	26/20/16
B-scans size	512×496	512×1024	$512 \times 885/650$
Num B-scans	49	128	128
Axial resolution	$3.9\,\mu m$	$2.0\,\mu m$	$2.6/3.5\,\mu m$

Implementation Details: The proposed method (EVT-MIL) was implemented using *keras* library with *tensor-flow* backend. For all methods, we extracted image patches with dimensions $512 \times 320 \times 1$ as instances. The cost balancing coefficients λ_1 and λ_2 of the proposed method was set to 0.001 and 0.0001, respectively. Network parameters was optimized for 100 epoch using "rmsprop" with learning rate 0.001 and decay $1e - 8$. The EVT tail size was set to the minimum of 30 or the number of negative training images. The code for the proposed method with those of competing methods used in this paper would be made publicly available once published.

We use area under ROC curve (AUC) for image level predictions as the metric in our evaluations.

Analysis of the Proposed Method: First, we use the SRF classification task of ReTOUCH dataset to evaluate the effectiveness of the proposed EVT based instance label sampling step. To this end, we replaced the EVT instance label sampling with: (1) Full-SUP: Uses ground-truth (or expert annotated) instance labels, (2) CNN-Th: Instance labels obtained by thresholding the CNN output probability. The ground truth instance labels were derived using the manually annotated segmentation masks provided with the ReTOUCH dataset The test-set AUC values for image level SRF classification task over 10 repeated runs of each method is shown in Fig. 4. As expected using the ground truth instance labels has resulted in the best performance which will provide an upper limit in our comparisons. The results obtained with the proposed EVT-MIL method is comparable to the fully supervised results showing the effectiveness of the proposed strategy. The figure also shows that using the proposed EVT based instance label sampling significantly improve the performance over using the CNN output probabilities. Similar behaviour was observed in PED and IRF classifications.

To gain an idea on the correlation between the instance labels predicted by proposed EVT based method and the ground truth instance labels, we have plotted the number of predicted positive instances against the number of true positive instances for each image (inferred using the ground truth annotations in the ReTOUCH dataset) at the last training epoch in Fig. 5. The figure shows that there is good correlation (R-squared score of 0.84 for SRF and 0.71 for PED) between the number of true and predicted positive instances in SRF and

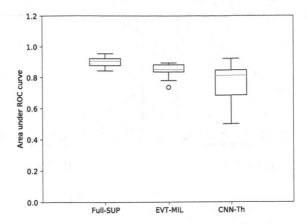

Fig. 4. The box-plot of test-set AUC values in image level Sub-retinal fluid (SRF) type classification task. The plot shows the variation of AUC over 10 repeated runs of each method. As expected using the ground truth instance labels has resulted in the best performance which will provide an upper limit in our comparisons. The results obtained with the proposed EVT-MIL method is comparable to the fully supervised results showing the effectiveness of the proposed strategy.

PED showing that our sampling scheme is effective for those cases. However, the correlation between true and predicted number of positive instances is lower for IRF. It should be noted that the number of true positive instances are calculated using manual annotations which may contain some errors specially around the pathology boundaries (annotations made by different annotators had an overall mean dice score agreement of 0.73).

EVT, given in Theorem 1. assumes that the number of samples n is large. However in practice the number of samples (which in our case is the number of negative images in the training dataset) can be limited. To understand how the number of negative images in the training set affect the performance of the proposed method, we varied the number of negative images during the training phase of the proposed algorithm and the results are shown in Fig. 6. The figure shows that the accuracy of the proposed method remains high upto (90%) and only reduces when the number of negative images are decreased beyond 90%.

Figure 7 shows the variation of test-set AUC value in image level SRF classification task with the EVT threshold. Those results show that AUC is not sensitive to large variation of EVT threshold.

Comparative Analysis: In this section, we compare the performance of EVT-MIL over three classification tasks (i.e. SRF, IRF, PED classification) with several competing methods: (1) Fully supervised classifier that uses expert annotated instance labels (Full-SUP), (2) Our implementation of top k positive instances (TOP-K) [22], (3) Infer h by thresholding the CNN output instead of using EVT (CNN-Th) and, (4) Use bag labels as instance labels (Simple-MIL).

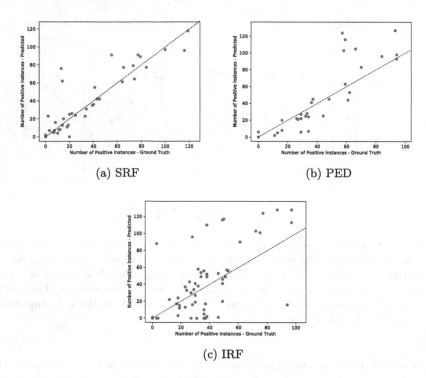

Fig. 5. Number of positive slices identified by the proposed method against the number of positive slices as per the ground truth segmentation masks.

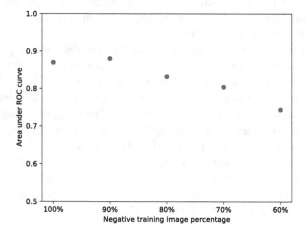

Fig. 6. The variation of test-set AUC value in image level SRF classification task with the percentage of negative images in the training phase.

Figure 8 show the mean and standard deviation of the test-set AUC value in image level fluid type classification over 10 repeated runs of each method. As expected, the figure shows that the Full-SUP method has been able to achieve the best AUC values across all three fluid types. The proposed method, trained without any instance level supervision signal, has also achieved comparable AUC values indicating that it is possible to learn a good image level predictor in a weakly supervised manner. The AUC archived by the proposed method is significantly better than that of TOP-K in SRF and PED which demonstrates the effectiveness of using adaptive number of positive instances in the proposed method compared to using fixed thresholds. The methods Simple-MIL and CNN-Th show comparative results to the proposed method in PED classification but their results in other two tasks are poor.

The results of the proposed method has the has the largest deviation form Full-SUP in IRF fluid type. This can be attributed to the limited number of negative samples present in IRF classification task compared to the other two fluid types. As shown in Table 1 the number of negative bags for IRF task is only 24 compared to 51 for SRF and 59 for PED. The empirical results in Fig. 6 also indicate that limiting number of negative bags at training time would affect EVT-MIL.

The top performing method in the Re-TOUCH challenge (i.e. SFU) produces AUC scores of 1.0 for all three fluid types. However, the above method uses expert annotated fluid segmentation masks for training and uses an independently formulated layer segmentation method. As such, their results are not directly comparable with our method, which only uses image level labels.

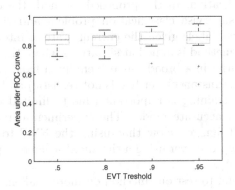

Fig. 7. The variation of test-set AUC value in image level SRF classification task with the EVT threshold.

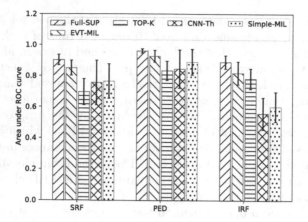

Fig. 8. The test-set AUC values in image level fluid type classification. The plots show the mean and the standard deviation of AUC values over 10 repeated runs for each method. Full-SUP: Fully supervised classifier trained using expert annotated instance labels, CNN-Th: Instance labels updated by thresholding CNN output at each epoch, Simple-MIL: Bag labels used as instance labels, TOP-K: K instances with highest CNN output in each positive bag labelled as positive and rest as negative and, EVT-MIL: proposed method.

5   Conclusion

The paper presents a novel method for training a deep neural network for volumetric image classification. In the proposed method, the original problem is posed as a weakly supervise classification problem and the EVT is used to infer the instance level labels given the current state of intermediate CNN features. The proposed method is aimed at situations where the number of positive instances in a bag varies in a broad range (defining a fixed threshold indicating the number of positive instances per bag is not realistic) and inclusion of all the positive instances in training is important (due to limited number of training bags) for learning an accurate model. The experimental results on fluid type classification in OCT images show that using the EVT to infer the instance labels significantly improve over using a threshold scheme as performed in state-of-the-art methods.

In future, we intend to test our method on more challenging problems (such as Emphysema detection in CT) that highlight the importance of using more than one instance from positive bag adaptively. We also intend to extend the algorithm to multi class classification problems.

References

1. Retinal oct fluid challenge. https://retouch.grand-challenge.org/home/
2. Solution of grt123 team. https://github.com/lfz/DSB2017/blob/master/solution-grt123-team.pdf
3. Andrews, S., Tsochantaridis, I., Hofmann, T.: Support vector machines for multiple-instance learning. In: Advances in Neural Information Processing Systems, pp. 577–584 (2003)
4. Bendale, A., Boult, T.E.: Towards open set deep networks. In: Proceedings of the IEEE Conference on Computer Vision and Pattern Recognition (CVPR), pp. 1563–1572 (2016)
5. Berman, S.M.: Limiting distribution of the maximum term in sequences of dependent random variables. Ann. Math. Stat. **33**(3), 894–908 (1962)
6. Chen, M., Shi, X., Zhang, Y., Wu, D., Guizani, M.: Deep features learning for medical image analysis with convolutional autoencoder neural network. IEEE Trans. Big Data **99**, 1–1 (2017)
7. Cheplygina, V., Sørensen, L., Tax, D.M., Pedersen, J.H., Loog, M., de Bruijne, M.: Classification of COPD with multiple instance learning. In: 22nd International Conference on Pattern Recognition (ICPR), pp. 1508–1513. IEEE (2014)
8. Coles, S.: An Introduction to Statistical Modeling of Extreme Values, vol. 208. Springer, Heidelberg (2001). https://doi.org/10.1007/978-1-4471-3675-0
9. Dou, Q., et al.: Automatic detection of cerebral microbleeds from mr images via 3D convolutional neural networks. IEEE Trans. Med. Imaging (TMI) **35**(5), 1182–1195 (2016)
10. Ferreira, A., De Haan, L., et al.: On the block maxima method in extreme value theory: PWM estimators. Ann. Stat. **43**(1), 276–298 (2015)
11. Hou, L., Samaras, D., Kurc, T.M., Gao, Y., Davis, J.E., Saltz, J.H.: Patch-based convolutional neural network for whole slide tissue image classification. In: Proceedings of the IEEE Conference on Computer Vision and Pattern Recognition (CVPR), pp. 2424–2433 (2016)
12. Krizhevsky, A., Sutskever, I., Hinton, G.E.: ImageNet classification with deep convolutional neural networks. In: Advances in Neural Information Processing Systems, pp. 1097–1105 (2012)
13. Litjens, G., et al.: A survey on deep learning in medical image analysis. Med. Image Anal. **42**(Suppl C), 60–88 (2017)
14. Marmor, M.F.: Mechanisms of fluid accumulation in retinal edema. In: Wolfensberger, T.J. (ed.) Macular Edema, pp. 35–45. Springer, Dordrecht (2000). https://doi.org/10.1007/978-94-011-4152-9_4
15. Quellec, G., Cazuguel, G., Cochener, B., Lamard, M.: Multiple-instance learning for medical image and video analysis. IEEE Rev. Biomed. Eng. **99**, 1–1 (2017)
16. Scheirer, W.J., Rocha, A., Micheals, R.J., Boult, T.E.: Meta-recognition: the theory and practice of recognition score analysis. IEEE Trans. Pattern Anal. Mach. Intell. (T-PAMI) **33**(8), 1689–1695 (2011)
17. Scheirer, W.J., Rocha, A., Sapkota, A., Boult, T.E.: Towards open set recognition. IEEE Trans. Pattern Anal. Mach. Intell. (T-PAMI) **35**(7), 1757–1772 (2013)
18. Setio, A.A.A., et al.: Pulmonary nodule detection in CT images: false positive reduction using multi-view convolutional networks. IEEE Trans. Med. Imaging (TMI) **35**(5), 1160–1169 (2016)
19. Shin, H.C., et al.: Deep convolutional neural networks for computer-aided detection: CNN architectures, dataset characteristics and transfer learning. IEEE Trans. Med. Imaging (TMI) **35**(5), 1285–1298 (2016)

20. Sorensen, L., Nielsen, M., Lo, P., Ashraf, H., Pedersen, J.H., De Bruijne, M.: Texture-based analysis of COPD: a data-driven approach. IEEE Trans. Med. imaging (TMI) **31**(1), 70–78 (2012)
21. Yan, Z., et al.: Multi-instance deep learning: discover discriminative local anatomies for body part recognition. IEEE Trans. Med. Imaging (TMI) **35**(5), 1332–1343 (2016)
22. Zhu, W., Lou, Q., Vang, Y.S., Xie, X.: Deep multi-instance networks with sparse label assignment for whole mammogram classification. In: Descoteaux, M., Maier-Hein, L., Franz, A., Jannin, P., Collins, D.L., Duchesne, S. (eds.) MICCAI 2017. LNCS, vol. 10435, pp. 603–611. Springer, Cham (2017). https://doi.org/10.1007/978-3-319-66179-7_69

Low-Resolution Face Recognition

Zhiyi Cheng[1($\boxtimes$)], Xiatian Zhu[2], and Shaogang Gong[1]

[1] School of Electronic Engineering and Computer Science,
Queen Mary University of London, London, UK
{z.cheng,s.gong}@qmul.ac.uk
[2] Vision Semantics Ltd., London, UK
eddy@visionsemantics.com

Abstract. Whilst recent face-recognition (FR) techniques have made significant progress on recognising constrained high-resolution web images, the same cannot be said on natively unconstrained low-resolution images at large scales. In this work, we examine systematically this under-studied FR problem, and introduce a novel Complement Super-Resolution and Identity (CSRI) joint deep learning method with a unified end-to-end network architecture. We further construct a new large-scale dataset *TinyFace* of native unconstrained low-resolution face images from selected public datasets, because none benchmark of this nature exists in the literature. With extensive experiments we show there is a significant gap between the reported FR performances on popular benchmarks and the results on TinyFace, and the advantages of the proposed CSRI over a variety of state-of-the-art FR and super-resolution deep models on solving this largely ignored FR scenario. The TinyFace dataset is released publicly at: https://qmul-tinyface.github.io/.

Keywords: Face recognition · Low-resolution · Super-resolution

1 Introduction

Face recognition (FR) models have made significant progress on constrained good-quality images, with reported 99.63% accuracy (1:1 verification) on the LFW benchmark [20] and 99.087% rank-1 rate (1:N identification with 1,000,000 distractors in the gallery) on the MegaFace challenge [22]. Surprisingly, in this work we show systematically that FR remains a significant challenge on *natively unconstrained low-resolution (LR)* images – *not artificially* down-sampled from high-resolution (HR) images, as typically captured in surveillance videos [9,47] and unconstrained (unposed) snapshots from a wide field of view at distance [44,46]. In particular, when tested against native low-resolution face images from a newly constructed tiny face dataset, we reveal that the performances of current state-of-the-art deep learning FR models degrade significantly. This is because the LR facial imagery lack sufficient visual information for current deep models to learn expressive feature representations, as compared to HR, good quality photo images under constrained (posed) viewing conditions (Fig. 1).

© Springer Nature Switzerland AG 2019
C. V. Jawahar et al. (Eds.): ACCV 2018, LNCS 11363, pp. 605–621, 2019.
https://doi.org/10.1007/978-3-030-20893-6_38

Fig. 1. Examples of (Left) **constrained high-resolution** web face images from five popular benchmarking FR datasets, and (Right) **native unconstrained low-resolution** web face images captured in typical natural scenes.

In general, unconstrained low-resolution FR (LRFR) is severely under-studied versus many FR models tested on popular benchmarks of HR images, mostly captured either under constrained viewing conditions or from "posed" photoshoots including passport photo verification for airport immigration control and identity check in e-banking. Another obstacle for enabling more studies on LRFR is the lack of large scale *native LR* face image data both for model training and testing, rather than artificially down-sampled synthetic data from HR images. To collect sufficient data for deep learning, it requires to process a large amount of public domain (e.g. from the web) video and image data generated from a wide range of sources such as social-media, e.g. the MegaFace dataset [22,28]. So far, this has only been available for HR and good quality (constrained) web face images, e.g. widely distributed celebrity images [20,27,30].

In this work, we investigate the largely neglected and practically significant LRFR problem. We make three contributions:

1. We propose a novel Super-Resolution and Identity joint learning approach to face recognition in native LR images, with a unified deep network architecture. Unlike most existing FR methods assuming constrained HR facial images in model training and test, the proposed approach is specially designed to improve the model generalisation for LRFR tasks by enhancing the compatibility of face enhancement and recognition. Compared to directly applying super-resolution algorithms to improve image details without jointly optimising for face discrimination, our method has been shown to be effective in reducing the negative effect of noisy fidelity for the LRFR task (Table 5).
2. We introduce a Complement Super-Resolution learning mechanism to overcome the inherent challenge of native LRFR concerning with the absence of HR facial images coupled with native LR faces, typically required for optimising image super-resolution models. This is realised by transferring the super-resolving knowledge from good-quality HR web images to the natively LR facial data subject to the face identity label constraints of native LR faces in every mini-batch training. Taken together with joint learning, we formulate a *Complement Super-Resolution and Identity joint learning* (**CSRI**) method.
3. We further create a large scale face recognition benchmark, named *Tiny-Face*, to facilitate the investigation of natively LRFR at large scales (large

gallery population sizes) in deep learning. The TinyFace dataset consists of 5,139 labelled facial identities given by 169,403 native LR face images (average 20×16 pixels) designed for 1:N recognition test. All the LR faces in TinyFace are collected from public web data across a large variety of imaging scenarios, captured under uncontrolled viewing conditions in pose, illumination, occlusion and background. Beyond artificially down-sampling HR facial images for LRFR performance test as in previous works, to our best knowledge, this is the first systematic study focusing specially on face recognition of native LR web images.

In the experiments, we benchmark the performance of four state-of-the-art deep learning FR models [26,30,36,42] and three super-resolution methods [11, 23,37] on the TinyFace dataset. We observe that the existing deep learning FR models suffer from significant performance degradation when evaluated on the TinyFace challenge. The results also show the superiority of the proposed CSRI model over the state-of-the-art methods on the LRFR tasks.

2   Related Work

Face Recognition. FR has achieved significant progress from hand-crafted feature based methods [1,4,8] to deep learning models [22,24,26,30,42]. One main driving force behind recent advances is the availability of large sized FR benchmarks and datasets. Earlier FR benchmarks are small, consisting of a limited number of identities and images [4,13,14,31,33,35]. Since 2007, the Labeled Faces in the Wild (LFW) [20] has shifted the FR community towards recognising more unconstrained celebrity faces at larger scales. Since then, a number of large FR training datasets and test evaluation benchmarks have been introduced, such as VGGFace [30], CASIA [45], CelebA [27], MS-Celeb-1M [16], MegaFace [22], and MegaFace2 [28]. Benefiting from large scale training data and deep learning techniques, the best FR model has achieved 99.087% on the current largest 1:N face identification evaluation (with 1,000,000 distractors) MegaFace[1].

Despite a great stride in FR on the HR web images, little attention has been paid to native LR face images. We found that state-of-the-art deep FR models trained on HR constrained face images do not generalise well to natively unconstrained LR face images (Table 3), but only generalise much better to synthetic LR data (Table 4). In this study, a newly created TinyFace benchmark provides for the first time a large scale native LRFR test for validating current deep learning FR models. TinyFace images were captured from real-world web social-media data. This complements the QMUL-SurvFace benchmark that is characterised by poor quality surveillance facial imagery captured from real-life security cameras deployed at open public spaces [9].

Low-Resolution Face Recognition. Existing LRFR methods can be summarised into two approaches: (1) Image super-resolution [12,15,18,41,48], and

---

[1]   http://megaface.cs.washington.edu/results/facescrub.html.

(2) resolution-invariant learning [2,6,10,17,25,34]. The first approach exploits two model optimisation criteria in model formulation: Pixel-level visual fidelity and face identity discrimination [15,40,41,48]. The second approach instead aims to learn resolution-invariant features [2,10,25] or learning a cross-resolution structure transformation [17,32,34,43]. All the existing LRFR methods share a number of limitations: (a) Considering only small gallery search pools (small scale) and/or artificially down-sampled LR face images; (b) Mostly relying on either hand-crafted features or without end-to-end model optimisation in deep learning; (c) Assuming the availability of labelled LR/HR image pairs for model training, which is unavailable in practice with native LR face imagery.

In terms of LRFR deployment, two typical settings exist. One is LR-to-HR which matches LR probe faces against HR gallery images such as passport photos [6,7,32,34]. The other is LR-to-LR where both probe and gallery are LR facial images [12,15,40,41,48]. Generally, LR-to-LR is a less stringent deployment scenario. This is because, real-world imagery data often contain a very large number of "joe public" without HR gallery images enrolled in the FR system. Besides, the two settings share the same challenge of how to synthesise discriminative facial appearance features missing in the original LR input data – one of the key challenges involved in solving the LRFR problem. The introduced TinyFace benchmark adopts the more general LR-to-LR setting.

Image Super-Recognition. Besides, image super-resolution (SR) deep learning techniques [11,23,37] have been significantly developed which may be beneficial for LRFR. At large, FR and SR studies advance independently. We discovered through our experiments that contemporary SR deep learning models bring about very marginal FR performance benefit on native LR unconstrained images, even after trained on large HR web face imagery. To address this problem, we design a novel deep neural network CSRI to improve the FR performance on unconstrained native LR face images.

3   Complement-Super-Resolution and Identity Joint Learning

For native LRFR, we need to extract identity discriminative feature representations from LR unconstrained images. To that end, we propose a deep neural network architecture for **Complement-Super-Resolution and Identity (CSRI)** joint learning. This approach is based on two considerations: (1) Joint learning of Super-Resolution (SR) and FR for maximising their compatibility and complementary advantages; (2) Complement-Super-Resolution learning for maximising the model discrimination on native LR face data at the absence of native HR counterparts in further SR-FR joint learning.

One major challenge in native LRFR is that we have no coupled HR images which are required for optimising the SR component. To address this problem, we consider knowledge transfer from auxiliary HR face data on which LR/HR pairs can be constructed by down-sampling.

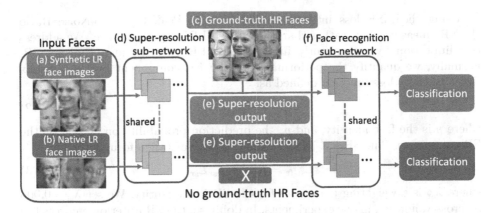

Fig. 2. Overview of the proposed Complement-Super-Resolution and Identity (CSRI) joint learning architecture. The CSRI contains two branches: (Orange): Synthetic LR SR-FR branch; (Blue): Native LR SR-FR branch. The two branches share parameters. (Color figure online)

CSRI Overview. Given the CSRI design above, we consider a multi-branch network architecture (Fig. 2). The CSRI contains two branches:

1. A *synthetic LR SR-FR* branch: For improving the compatibility and complementary advantages of SR and FR components by jointly learning auxiliary face data with artificially down-sampled LR/HR pairs (the top stream in Fig. 2);
2. A *native LR SR-FR* branch: For adapting super-resolving information of auxiliary LR/HR face pairs to the native LR facial imagery domain which lacks the corresponding HR faces by complement SR-FR learning (the bottom stream in Fig. 2).

In this study, we instantiate the CSRI by adopting the VDSR [23] for the SR component and the CentreFace [42] for the FR component. We detail these CSRI components as follows.

(I) Joint Learning of Super-Resolution and Face Recognition. To adapt the image SR ability for LRFR, we consider a SR-FR joint learning strategy by integrating the output of SR with the input of FR in the CSRI design so to exploit the intrinsic end-to-end deep learning advantage. To train this SR-FR joint network, we use both auxiliary training data with artificially down-sampled LR/HR face pairs $\{(I^{\mathrm{alr}}, I^{\mathrm{ahr}})\}$ and face identity labels $\{y\}$ (e.g. CelebA [27]). Formally, a SR model represents a non-linear mapping function between LR and HR face images. For SR component optimisation, we utilise the pixel-level Mean-Squared Error (MSE) minimisation criterion defined as

$$\mathcal{L}_{\mathrm{sr}} = \| I^{\mathrm{asr}} - I^{\mathrm{ahr}} \|_2^2 \qquad (1)$$

where I^{asr} denotes the super-resolved face image of I^{alr} (Fig. 2(a)), and I^{ahr} denotes the corresponding HR ground-truth image (Fig. 2(c)).

Using the MSE loss intrinsically favours the Peak Signal-to-Noise Ratio (PSNR) measurement, rather than the desired LRFR performance. We address this limitation by concurrently imposing the FR criterion in optimising SR. Formally, we quantify the performance of the FR component by the softmax Cross-Entropy loss function defined as:

$$\mathcal{L}_{\mathrm{fr}}^{\mathrm{syn}} = -\log(p_y) \tag{2}$$

where y is the face identity, and p_y the prediction probability on class y by the FR component. The SR-FR joint learning objective is then formulated as:

$$\mathcal{L}_{\mathrm{sr\text{-}fr}} = \mathcal{L}_{\mathrm{fr}}^{\mathrm{syn}} + \lambda_{\mathrm{sr}}\mathcal{L}_{\mathrm{sr}} \tag{3}$$

where λ_{sr} is a weighting parameter for the SR loss quantity. We set $\lambda_{\mathrm{sr}} = 0.003$ by cross-validation in our experiments. In doing so, the FR criterion enforces the SR learning to be identity discriminative simultaneously.

(II) Complement-Super-Resolution Learning. Given the SR-FR joint learning as above, the CSRI model learns to optimise the FR performance on the synthetic (artificially down-sampled) auxiliary LR face data. This model is likely to be sub-optimal for native LRFR due to the inherent visual appearance distribution discrepancy between synthetic and native LR face images (Fig. 6).

To overcome this limitation, we further constrain the SR-FR joint learning towards the native LR data by imposing the native LR face discrimination constraint into the SR component optimisation. Specifically, we jointly optimise the SR and FR components using both auxiliary (with LR/HR pairwise images) and native (with only LR images) training data for adapting the SR component learning towards native LR data. That is, we concurrently optimise the synthetic and native LR branches with the parameters shared in both SR and FR components. To enforce the discrimination of labelled native LR faces, we use the same Cross-Entropy loss formulation.

Overall Loss Function. After combining three complement SR-FR learning loss quantities, we obtain the final CSRI model objective as:

$$\mathcal{L}_{\mathrm{csrl}} = (\mathcal{L}_{\mathrm{fr}}^{\mathrm{syn}} + \mathcal{L}_{\mathrm{fr}}^{\mathrm{nat}}) + \lambda_{\mathrm{sr}}\mathcal{L}_{\mathrm{sr}} \tag{4}$$

where $\mathcal{L}_{\mathrm{fr}}^{\mathrm{nat}}$ and $\mathcal{L}_{\mathrm{fr}}^{\mathrm{syn}}$ measure the identity discrimination constraints on the native and synthetic LR training data, respectively. With such a joint multi-task (FR and SR) formulation, the SR optimisation is specifically guided to be more discriminative for the native LR facial imagery data.

Model Training and Deployment. The CSRI can be trained by the standard Stochastic Gradient Descent algorithm in an end-to-end manner. As the auxiliary and native LR data sets are highly imbalanced in size, we further propose to train the CSRI in two steps for improving the model convergence stability: (1) We first pre-train the *synthetic LR SR-FR* branch on a large auxiliary face data (CelebA [27]). (2) We then train the whole CSRI network on both auxiliary and native LR data.

In deployment, we utilise the *native LR SR-FR* branch to extract the feature vectors for face image matching with the Euclidean distance metric.

Fig. 3. Example TinyFace images auto-detected in unconstrained images.

4 TinyFace: Low-Resolution Face Recognition Benchmark

4.1 Dataset Construction

Low-Resolution Criterion. To create a native LR face dataset, we need an explicit LR criterion. As there is no existing standard in the literature, in this study we define LR faces as those $\leq 32 \times 32$ pixels by following the tiny object criterion [38]. Existing FR datasets are all $>100 \times 100$ pixels (Table 1).

Face Image Collection. The TinyFace dataset contains two parts, face images with *labelled* and *unlabelled* identities. The *labelled* TinyFace images were collected from the publicly available PIPA [46] and MegaFace2 [28] datasets, both of which provide unconstrained social-media web face images with large variety in facial expression/pose and imaging conditions. For the TinyFace to be realistic for LRFR test, we applied the state-of-the-art HR-ResNet101 model [19] for automatic face detection, rather than human cropping. Given the detection results, we removed those faces with spatial extent larger than 32×32 to ensure that all selected faces are of LR.

Face Image Filtering. To make a valid benchmark, it is necessary to remove the false face detections. We verified exhaustively every detection, which took approx. 280 person-hours, i.e. one labeller needs to manually verify detected tiny face images 8 hours/day consistently for a total of 35 days. Utilising multiple labellers introduces additional tasks of extra consistency checking across all the verified data by different labellers. After manual verification, all the remaining PIPA face images were then *labelled* using the identity classes available in the original data. As a result, we assembled 15,975 LR face images *with* 5,139 distinct identity labels, and 153,428 LR faces *without* identity labels. In total, we obtained 169,403 images of labelled and unlabelled faces. Figure 3 shows some examples randomly selected from TinyFace.

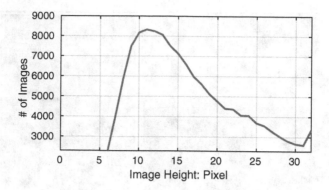

Fig. 4. Distribution of face image height in TinyFace.

Face Image Statistics. Table 1 summarises the face image statistics of Tiny-Face in comparison to 9 existing FR benchmarks. Figure 4 shows the distribution of TinyFace height resolution, ranging from 6 to 32 pixels with the average at 20. In comparison, existing benchmarks contain face images of ≥ 100 in average height, a $\geq 5\times$ higher resolution.

Table 1. Statistics of popular FR benchmarks.

Benchmark	Mean height	# Identity	# Image
LFW [20]	119	5,749	13,233
VGGFace [30]	138	2,622	2.6M
MegaFace [22]	352	530	1M
CASIA [45]	153	10,575	494,414
IJB-A [24]	307	500	5,712
CelebA [27]	212	10,177	202,599
UMDFaces [3]	>100	8,277	367,888
MS-Celeb-1M [16]	>100	99,892	**8,456,240**
MegaFace2 [28]	252	**672,057**	4,753,320
TinyFace (Ours)	**20**	5,139	169,403

4.2   Evaluation Protocol

Data Split. To establish an evaluation protocol on the TinyFace dataset, it is necessary to first define the training and test data partition. Given that both training and test data require labels with the former for model training and the latter for performance evaluation, we divided the 5,139 known identities into two halves: one (2,570) for training, the other (2,569) for test. All the unlabelled distractor face images are also used as test data (Table 2).

Table 2. Data partition and statistics of TinyFace.

Data	All	Training set	Test set		
			Probe	Gallery match	Gallery distractor
# Identity	5,139	2,570	2,569	2,569	Unknown
# Image	169,403	7,804	3,728	4,443	153,428

Face Recognition Task. In order to compare model performances on the MegaFace benchmark [28], we adopt the same face identification (1:N matching) protocol as the FR task for the TinyFace. Specifically, the task is to match a given probe face against a gallery set of enrolled face imagery with the best result being that the gallery image of a true-match is ranked at top-1 of the ranking list. For this protocol, we construct a probe and a gallery set from the test data as follows: (1) For each test face class of multiple identity labelled images, we randomly assigned half of the face images to the probe set, and the remaining to the gallery set. (2) We placed all the unlabelled disctractor images (with unknown identity) into the gallery set for enlarging the search space therefore presenting a more challenging task, similar to MegaFace [28]. The image and identity statistics of the probe and gallery sets are summarised in Table 2.

Performance Metrics. For FR performance evaluation, we adopt three metrics: the *Cumulative Matching Characteristic* (CMC) curve [24], the *Precision-Recall* (PR) curve [39], and mean Average Precision (mAP). Whilst CMC measures the proportion of test probes with the true match at rank k or better, PR quantifies a trade-off between precision and recall per probe with the aim to find all true matches in the gallery [21]. To summarise the overall performance, we adopt the *mean Average Precision* (mAP), i.e. the mean value of average precision of all per-probe PR curves.

4.3   Training vs Testing Data Size Comparison

To our knowledge, TinyFace is the largest native LR web face recognition benchmark (Table 1). It is a challenging test due to very LR face images ($5\times$ less than other benchmarks) with large variations in illumination, facial pose/expression, and background clutters. These factors represent more realistic real-world low-resolution face images for model robustness and effectiveness test.

In terms of training data size, TinyFace is smaller than some existing HR FR model *training* datasets, notably the MegaFace2 of 672,057 IDs. It is much more difficult to collect *natively* LR face images with label information. Unlike celebrities, there are much less facial images of known identity labels from the general public available for model training.

In terms of testing data size, on the other hand, the face identification *test* evaluation offered by the current largest benchmark MegaFace [22] contains *only 530 test face IDs* (from FaceScrub [29]) and 1 million gallery images, whilst TinyFace benchmark consists of 2,569 test IDs and 154,471 gallery images. Moreover, in comparison to LFW benchmark there are 5,749 face IDs in the LFW designed originally for 1:1 verification test [20], however a much smaller gallery set of 596 face IDs of LFW were adopted for 1:N matching test (open-set) with 10,090 probe images of which 596 true-matches (1-shot per ID) and 9,494 distractors [5]. Overall, TinyFace for 1:N test data has 3–4× more test IDs than MegaFace and LFW, and 15× more distractors than LFW 1:N test data.

5   Experiments

In this section, we presented experimental analysis on TinyFace, the *only* large scale native LRFR benchmark, by three sets of evaluations: **(1)** Evaluation of generic FR methods *without* considering the LR challenge. We adopted the state-of-the-art deep learning FR methods (Sect. 5.1); **(2)** Evaluation of LRFR methods. For this test, we applied super-resolution deep learning techniques in addition to the deep learning FR models (Sect. 5.2); **(3)** Component analysis of the proposed CSRI method (Sect. 5.3).

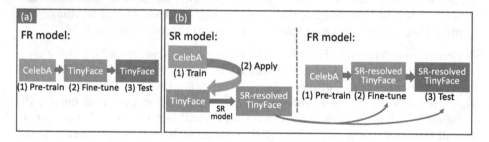

Fig. 5. Overview of training (a) generic FR models and (b) low-resolution FR models (Independent training of Super-Resulotion (SR) and FR models).

Table 3. *Generic* FR evaluation on TinyFace (Native LR face images).

Metric (%)	Rank-1	Rank-20	Rank-50	mAP
DeepID2 [36]	17.4	25.2	28.3	12.1
SphereFace [26]	22.3	35.5	40.5	16.2
VggFace [30]	30.4	40.4	42.7	23.1
CentreFace [42]	**32.1**	**44.5**	**48.4**	**24.6**

Table 4. Native (TinyFace) vs. synthetic (SynLR-MF2) LR face recognition.

FR model	Dataset	Rank-1	Rank-20	Rank-50	mAP
VggFace [30]	TinyFace	30.4	40.4	42.7	23.1
	SynLR-MF2	**34.8**	**46.8**	**49.4**	**26.0**
CentreFace [42]	TinyFace	32.1	44.5	48.4	24.6
	SynLR-MF2	**39.2**	**63.4**	**70.2**	**31.4**

5.1 Evaluation of Generic Face Resolution Methods

In this test, we evaluated four representative deep FR models including DeepID2 [36], VggFace [30], CentreFace [42] and SphereFace [26]. For model optimisation, we first trained a given FR model on the CelebA face data [27] before fine-tuning on the TinyFace training set[2] (see Fig. 5(a)). We adopted the parameter settings suggested by the original authors.

Results. Table 3 shows that the FR performance by any model is significantly inferior on TinyFace than on existing high-resolution FR benchmarks. For example, the best performer CentreFace yields Rank-1 32.1% on TinyFace *versus* 65.2% on MegaFace [22], i.e. more than half performance drop. This suggests that the FR problem is more challenging on natively unconstrained LR images.

Native vs Synthetic LR Face Images. For more in-depth understanding on *native* LRFR, we further compared with the FR performance on *synthetic* LR face images. For this purpose, we created a synthetic LR face dataset, which we call *SynLR-MF2*, using 169,403 HR MegaFace2 images [28]. Following the data distribution of TinyFace (Table 2), we randomly selected 15,975 images from 5,139 IDs as the labelled test images and further randomly selected 153,428 images from the remaining IDs as the unlabelled distractors. We down-sampled all selected MegaFace2 images to the average size (20×16) of TinyFace images. To enable a like-for-like comparison, we made a random data partition on SynLR-MF2 same as TinyFace (see Table 2).

Table 4 shows that FR on synthetic LR face images is a less challenging task than that of native LR images, with a Rank-20 model performance advantage of 6.4% (46.8–40.4) by VggFace and 18.9% (63.4–44.5) by CentreFace. This difference is also visually indicated in the comparison of native and synthetic LR face images in a variety of illumination/pose and imaging quality (Fig. 6). This demonstrates the importance of TinyFace as a native LRFR benchmark for testing more realistic real-world FR model performances.

5.2 Evaluation of Low-Resolution Face Resolution Methods

In this evaluation, we explored the potential of contemporary super-resolution (SR) methods in addressing the LRFR challenge. To compare with the proposed

---

[2] The SphereFace method fails to converge in fine-tuning on TinyFace even with careful parameter selection. We hence deployed the CelebA-trained SphereFace model.

Fig. 6. Comparison of (left) native LR face images from TinyFace and (right) synthetic LR face image from SynLR-MF2.

Table 5. Native *Low-Resolution* FR evaluation on TinyFace.

FR	Method		Rank-1	Rank-20	Rank-50	mAP
CentreFace	No		**32.1**	**44.5**	**48.4**	**24.6**
	SR	SRCNN [11]	28.8	38.6	42.3	21.7
		VDSR [23]	26.0	34.5	37.7	19.1
		DRRN [37]	29.4	39.4	43.0	22.2
VggFace	No		**30.4**	**40.4**	**42.7**	**23.1**
	SR	SRCNN [11]	29.6	39.2	41.4	22.7
		VDSR [23]	28.8	38.3	40.3	22.1
		DRRN [37]	29.4	39.8	41.9	22.4
RPCN [41]			18.6	25.3	27.4	12.9
CSRI (Ours)			44.8	60.4	65.1	36.2

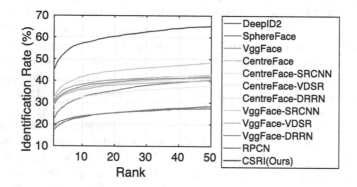

Fig. 7. Performance comparison of different methods in CMC curves on the TinyFace dataset.

CSRI model, we selected three representative deep learning generic-image SR models (SRCNN [11], VDSR [23] and DRRN [37]), and one LRFR deep model RPCN [41] (also using SR). We trained these SR models on the CelebA images [27] (202,599 LR/HR face pairs from 10,177 identities) with the authors suggested parameter settings for maximising their performance in the FR task

Fig. 8. Examples of super-resolved faces.

(see Fig. 5(b)). We adopted the CentreFace and VggFace (top-2 FR models, see Table 3) for performing FR model training and test on super-resolved faces generated by any SR model. Since the RPCN integrates SR with FR in design, we used both CelebA and TinyFace data to train the RPCN for a fair comparison.

Results. Table 5, Fig. 7 show that: (**1**) All SR methods *degrade* the performance of a deep learning FR model. The possible explanation is that the artifacts and noise introduced in super-resolution are likely to hurt the FR model generalisation (see Fig. 8). This suggests that applying SR as a separate process in a simplistic approach to enhancing LRFR not only does not offer any benefit, but also is more likely a hindrance. (**2**) The RPCN yields the worst performance although it was specially designed for LR face recognition. The possible reason is two-fold: (a) This method exploits the SR as model pre-training by design, which leads to insufficient FR supervision in the ID label guided model fine-tuning. (b) Adopting a weaker base network with 3 conv layers. These results suggest that existing methods are ineffective for face recognition on natively low-resolution images and when the test gallery population size becomes rather large. (**3**) The CSRI outperforms significantly all the competitors, e.g. the Rank-1 recognition performance gain by CSRI over CentreFace is significant at 12.7% (44.8–32.1). This shows the advantage of the CSRI model design in enabling FR on natively LR face images over existing generic FR models.

Table 6. Joint vs. independent learning of super-resolution and face recognition.

SR-FR	Rank-1	Rank-20	Rank-50	mAP
Independent learning	26.0	34.5	37.7	19.1
Joint learning	**36.1**	**49.8**	**54.5**	**28.2**

Table 7. Effect of complement super-resolution (CSR) learning.

CSR	Rank-1	Rank-20	Rank-50	mAP
✗	36.1	49.8	54.5	28.2
✓	**44.8**	**60.4**	**65.1**	**36.2**

5.3   Component Analysis of CSRI

To better understand the CSRI's performance advantage, we evaluated the individual model components on the TinyFace benchmark by incrementally introducing individual components of the CSRI model.

SR-FR joint learning was examined in comparison to SR-FR independent learning (same as in Sect. 5.2). For fair comparison, we used the VDSR [23] and CentreFace [42] which are adopted the components of CSRI. For SR-FR joint learning, we first trained the CSRI *synthetic LR SR-FR* branch on the CelebA data, followed by fine-tuning the FR part on TinyFace training data. Table 6 shows that SR-FR joint learning has a Rank-1 advantage of 10.1% (36.1–26.0) and 4.0% (36.1–32.1) over SR-FR independent learning and FR only (i.e. CentreFace in Table 3), respectively. This suggests the clear benefit of SR-FR joint learning due to the enhanced compatibility of SR and FR components obtained by end-to-end concurrent optimisation.

Complement SR learning was evaluated by comparing the full CSRI with the above SR-FR joint learning. Table 7 shows a Rank-1 boost of 8.7% (44.8–36.1), another significant benefit from the complement SR learning.

6   Conclusions

In this work, we presented for the first time a large scale *native* low-resolution face recognition (LRFR) study. This is realised by joint learning of Complement Super-Resolution and face Identity (CSRI) in an end-to-end trainable neural network architecture. By design, the proposed method differs significantly from most existing FR methods that assume high-resolution good quality facial imagery in both model training and testing, whereas ignoring the more challenging tasks in typical unconstrained low-resolution web imagery data. Furthermore, to enable a proper study of LRFR, we introduce a large LRFR benchmark TinyFace. Compared to previous FR datasets that focus on high-resolution face images, TinyFace is uniquely characterised by *natively low-resolution and unconstrained* face images, both for model training and testing. Our experiments show that TinyFace imposes a more challenging test to current deep learning face recognition models. For example, the CentreFace model yields 32.1% Rank-1 on Tiny-Face *versus* 65.2% on MegaFace, i.e. a 50+% performance degradation. Additionally, we demonstrate that synthetic (artificially down-sampled) LRFR is a relatively easier task than the native counterpart. We further show the performance advantage of the proposed CSRI approach to native LRFR. Extensive comparative evaluations show the superiority of CSRI over a range of state-of-the-art face recognition and super-resolution deep learning methods when tested on the newly introduced TinyFace benchmark. Our more detailed CSRI component analysis provides further insights on the CSRI model design.

Acknowledgement. This work was partially supported by the Royal Society Newton Advanced Fellowship Programme (NA150459), Innovate UK Industrial Challenge Project on Developing and Commercialising Intelligent Video Analytics Solutions for Public Safety (98111-571149), Vision Semantics Ltd, and SeeQuestor Ltd.

References

1. Ahonen, T., Hadid, A., Pietikainen, M.: Face description with local binary patterns: application to face recognition. IEEE TPAMI (2006)
2. Ahonen, T., Rahtu, E., Ojansivu, V., Heikkila, J.: Recognition of blurred faces using local phase quantization. In: ICPR (2008)
3. Bansal, A., Nanduri, A., Castillo, C., Ranjan, R., Chellappa, R.: UMDFaces: an annotated face dataset for training deep networks. arXiv (2016)
4. Belhumeur, P.N., Hespanha, J.P., Kriegman, D.J.: Eigenfaces vs. Fisherfaces: recognition using class specific linear projection. IEEE TPAMI (1997)
5. Best-Rowden, L., Han, H., Otto, C., Klare, B.F., Jain, A.K.: Unconstrained face recognition: identifying a person of interest from a media collection. IEEE Trans. Inf. Forensics Secur. **9**, 2144–2157 (2014)
6. Biswas, S., Bowyer, K.W., Flynn, P.J.: Multidimensional scaling for matching low-resolution facial images. In: BTAS (2010)
7. Biswas, S., Bowyer, K.W., Flynn, P.J.: Multidimensional scaling for matching low-resolution face images. IEEE TPAMI **34**, 2019–2030 (2012)
8. Chen, D., Cao, X., Wen, F., Sun, J.: Blessing of dimensionality: high-dimensional feature and its efficient compression for face verification. In: CVPR (2013)
9. Cheng, Z., Zhu, X., Gong, S.: Surveillance face recognition challenge. arXiv preprint arXiv:1804.09691 (2018)
10. Choi, J.Y., Ro, Y.M., Plataniotis, K.N.: Color face recognition for degraded face images. IEEE TSMC (Part B) **39**, 1217–1230 (2009)
11. Dong, C., Loy, C.C., He, K., Tang, X.: Learning a deep convolutional network for image super-resolution. In: Fleet, D., Pajdla, T., Schiele, B., Tuytelaars, T. (eds.) ECCV 2014. LNCS, vol. 8692, pp. 184–199. Springer, Cham (2014). https://doi.org/10.1007/978-3-319-10593-2_13
12. Fookes, C., Lin, F., Chandran, V., Sridharan, S.: Evaluation of image resolution and super-resolution on face recognition performance. J. Vis. Commun. Image Represent. **23**, 75–93 (2012)

13. Georghiades, A.S., Belhumeur, P.N., Kriegman, D.J.: From few to many: illumination cone models for face recognition under variable lighting and pose. IEEE TPAMI (2001)
14. Gross, R., Matthews, I., Cohn, J., Kanade, T., Baker, S.: Multi-pie. IVC **28**, 807–813 (2010)
15. Gunturk, B.K., Batur, A.U., Altunbasak, Y., Hayes, M.H., Mersereau, R.M.: Eigenface-domain super-resolution for face recognition. IEEE TIP **12**(5), 597–606 (2003)
16. Guo, Y., Zhang, L., Hu, Y., He, X., Gao, J.: MS-Celeb-1M: a dataset and benchmark for large-scale face recognition. In: Leibe, B., Matas, J., Sebe, N., Welling, M. (eds.) ECCV 2016. LNCS, vol. 9907, pp. 87–102. Springer, Cham (2016). https://doi.org/10.1007/978-3-319-46487-9_6
17. He, X., Cai, D., Yan, S., Zhang, H.J.: Neighborhood preserving embedding. In: ICCV (2005)
18. Hennings-Yeomans, P.H., Baker, S., Kumar, B.V.: Simultaneous super-resolution and feature extraction for recognition of low-resolution faces. In: CVPR (2008)
19. Hu, P., Ramanan, D.: Finding tiny faces. arXiv (2016)
20. Huang, G.B., Ramesh, M., Berg, T., Learned-Miller, E.: Labeled faces in the wild: a database for studying face recognition in unconstrained environments. University of Massachusetts, Technical report (2007)
21. Jegou, H., Douze, M., Schmid, C.: Product quantization for nearest neighbor search. IEEE TPAMI **33**(1), 117–128 (2011)
22. Kemelmacher-Shlizerman, I., Seitz, S.M., Miller, D., Brossard, E.: The MegaFace benchmark: 1 million faces for recognition at scale. In: CVPR (2016)
23. Kim, J., Kwon Lee, J., Mu Lee, K.: Accurate image super-resolution using very deep convolutional networks. In: CVPR (2016)
24. Klare, B.F., et al.: Pushing the frontiers of unconstrained face detection and recognition: IARPA Janus benchmark A. In: CVPR (2015)
25. Lei, Z., Ahonen, T., Pietikäinen, M., Li, S.Z.: Local frequency descriptor for low-resolution face recognition. In: FG (2011)
26. Liu, W., Wen, Y., Yu, Z., Li, M., Raj, B., Song, L.: SphereFace: deep hypersphere embedding for face recognition. arXiv (2017)
27. Liu, Z., Luo, P., Wang, X., Tang, X.: Deep learning face attributes in the wild. In: ICCV (2015)
28. Nech, A., Kemelmacher-Shlizerman, I.: Level playing field for million scale face recognition. arXiv preprint arXiv:1705.00393 (2017)
29. Ng, H.W., Winkler, S.: A data-driven approach to cleaning large face datasets. In: ICIP (2014)
30. Parkhi, O.M., Vedaldi, A., Zisserman, A.: Deep face recognition. In: BMVC (2015)
31. Phillips, P.J., et al.: FRVT 2006 and ICE 2006 large-scale experimental results. IEEE TPAMI **32**(5), 831–846 (2010)
32. Ren, C.X., Dai, D.Q., Yan, H.: Coupled kernel embedding for low-resolution face image recognition. IEEE TIP **21**(8), 3770–3783 (2012)
33. Samaria, F.S., Harter, A.C.: Parameterisation of a stochastic model for human face identification. In: IEEE Workshop on Applications of Computer Vision (1994)
34. Shekhar, S., Patel, V.M., Chellappa, R.: Synthesis-based recognition of low resolution faces. In: IJCB (2011)
35. Sim, T., Baker, S., Bsat, M.: The CMU pose, illumination, and expression (PIE) database. In: FG, pp. 53–58 (2002)
36. Sun, Y., Chen, Y., Wang, X., Tang, X.: Deep learning face representation by joint identification-verification. In: NIPS (2014)

37. Tai, Y., Yang, J., Liu, X.: Image super-resolution via deep recursive residual network. In: CVPR (2017)
38. Torralba, A., Fergus, R., Freeman, W.T.: 80 million tiny images: a large data set for nonparametric object and scene recognition. IEEE TPAMI **30**(11), 1958–1970 (2008)
39. Wang, D., Otto, C., Jain, A.K.: Face search at scale. IEEE TPAMI **39**, 1122–1136 (2016)
40. Wang, X., Tang, X.: Face hallucination and recognition. In: Kittler, J., Nixon, M.S. (eds.) AVBPA 2003. LNCS, vol. 2688, pp. 486–494. Springer, Heidelberg (2003). https://doi.org/10.1007/3-540-44887-X_58
41. Wang, Z., Chang, S., Yang, Y., Liu, D., Huang, T.S.: Studying very low resolution recognition using deep networks. In: CVPR (2016)
42. Wen, Y., Zhang, K., Li, Z., Qiao, Y.: A discriminative feature learning approach for deep face recognition. In: Leibe, B., Matas, J., Sebe, N., Welling, M. (eds.) ECCV 2016. LNCS, vol. 9911, pp. 499–515. Springer, Cham (2016). https://doi.org/10.1007/978-3-319-46478-7_31
43. Wong, Y., Sanderson, C., Mau, S., Lovell, B.C.: Dynamic amelioration of resolution mismatches for local feature based identity inference. In: ICPR (2010)
44. Yang, S., Luo, P., Loy, C.C., Tang, X.: WIDER FACE: a face detection benchmark. In: CVPR (2016)
45. Yi, D., Lei, Z., Liao, S., Li, S.Z.: Learning face representation from scratch. arXiv (2014)
46. Zhang, N., Paluri, M., Taigman, Y., Fergus, R., Bourdev, L.: Beyond frontal faces: improving person recognition using multiple cues. In: CVPR (2015)
47. Zhu, X.: Semantic structure discovery in surveillance videos. Ph.D. thesis, Queen Mary University of London (2016)
48. Zou, W.W., Yuen, P.C.: Very low resolution face recognition problem. IEEE TIP **21**(1), 327–340 (2012)

GANomaly: Semi-supervised Anomaly Detection via Adversarial Training

Samet Akcay[1]([⊠]), Amir Atapour-Abarghouei[1], and Toby P. Breckon[1,2]

[1] Department of Computer Science, Durham University, Durham, UK
{samet.akcay,amir.atapour-abarghouei,toby.breckon}@durham.ac.uk
[2] Department of Engineering, Durham University, Durham, UK

Abstract. Anomaly detection is a classical problem in computer vision, namely the determination of the *normal* from the *abnormal* when datasets are highly biased towards one class (normal) due to the insufficient sample size of the other class (abnormal). While this can be addressed as a supervised learning problem, a significantly more challenging problem is that of detecting the unknown/unseen anomaly case that takes us instead into the space of a one-class, semi-supervised learning paradigm. We introduce such a novel anomaly detection model, by using a conditional generative adversarial network that jointly learns the generation of high-dimensional image space and the inference of latent space. Employing encoder-decoder-encoder sub-networks in the generator network enables the model to map the input image to a lower dimension vector, which is then used to reconstruct the generated output image. The use of the additional encoder network maps this generated image to its latent representation. Minimizing the distance between these images and the latent vectors during training aids in learning the data distribution for the normal samples. As a result, a larger distance metric from this learned data distribution at inference time is indicative of an outlier from that distribution—*an anomaly*. Experimentation over several benchmark datasets, from varying domains, shows the model efficacy and superiority over previous state-of-the-art approaches.

Keywords: Anomaly detection · Semi-supervised learning · Generative Adversarial Networks · X-ray security imagery

1 Introduction

Despite yielding encouraging performance over various computer vision tasks, supervised approaches heavily depend on large, labeled datasets. In many of the real world problems, however, samples from the more unusual classes of interest are of insufficient sizes to be effectively modeled. Instead, the task of anomaly detection is to be able to identify such cases, by training only on samples considered to be *normal* and then identifying these unusual, insufficiently available samples (*abnormal*) that differ from the learned sample distribution

© Springer Nature Switzerland AG 2019
C. V. Jawahar et al. (Eds.): ACCV 2018, LNCS 11363, pp. 622–637, 2019.
https://doi.org/10.1007/978-3-030-20893-6_39

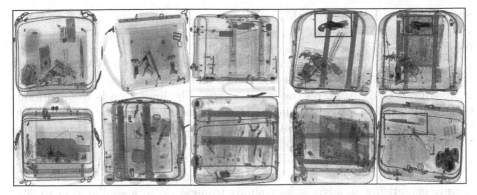

<table>
<tr><td>(a) Normal Data (X-ray Scans)</td><td>(b) Normal + Abnormal Data (X-ray Scans)</td></tr>
</table>

Fig. 1. Overview of our anomaly detection approach within the context of an X-ray security screening problem. Our model is trained on normal samples (a), and tested on normal and abnormal samples (b). Anomalies are detected when the output of the model is greater than a certain threshold $\mathcal{A}(x) > \phi$.

of normality. For example a tangible application, that is considered here within our evaluation, is that of X-ray screening for aviation or border security—where anomalous items posing a security threat are not commonly encountered, exemplary data of such can be difficult to obtain in any quantity, and the nature of any anomaly posing a potential threat may evolve due to a range of external factors. However, within this challenging context, human security operators are still competent and adaptable anomaly detectors against new and emerging anomalous threat signatures.

As illustrated in Fig. 1, a formal problem definition of the anomaly detection task is as follows: given a dataset $\mathcal{D}$ containing a large number of normal samples $\mathbf{X}$ for training, and relatively few abnormal examples $\hat{\mathbf{X}}$ for the test, a model f is optimized over its parameters θ. f learns the data distribution $p_{\mathbf{X}}$ of the normal samples during training while identifying abnormal samples as outliers during testing by outputting an anomaly score $\mathcal{A}(x)$, where x is a given test example. A Larger $\mathcal{A}(x)$ indicates possible abnormalities within the test image since f learns to minimize the output score during training. $\mathcal{A}(x)$ is general in that it can detect unseen anomalies as being non-conforming to $p_{\mathbf{X}}$.

There is a large volume of studies proposing anomaly detection models within various application domains [2–4, 23, 39]. Besides, a considerable amount of work taxonomized the approaches within the literature [9, 19, 28, 29, 33]. In parallel to the recent advances in this field, Generative Adversarial Networks (GAN) have emerged as a leading methodology across both unsupervised and semi-supervised problems. Goodfellow *et al.* [16] first proposed this approach by co-training a pair networks (generator and discriminator). The former network models high dimensional data from a latent vector to resemble the source data, while the latter distinguishes the modeled (i.e., approximated) and original data samples.

Several approaches followed this work to improve the training and inference stages [8,17]. As reviewed in [23], adversarial training has also been adopted by recent work within anomaly detection.

Schlegl *et al.* [39] hypothesize that the latent vector of a GAN represents the true distribution of the data and remap to the latent vector by optimizing a pre-trained GAN based on the latent vector. The limitation is the enormous computational complexity of remapping to this latent vector space. In a follow-up study, Zenati *et al.* [40] train a BiGAN model [14], which maps from image space to latent space jointly, and report statistically and computationally superior results albeit on the simplistic MNIST benchmark dataset [25].

Motivated by [6,39,40], here we propose a generic anomaly detection architecture comprising an adversarial training framework. In a similar vein to [39], we use single color images as the input to our approach drawn only from an example set of *normal* (non-anomalous) training examples. However, in contrast, our approach does not require two-stage training and is both efficient for model training and later inference (run-time testing). As with [40], we also learn image and latent vector spaces jointly. Our key novelty comes from the fact that we employ adversarial autoencoder within an encoder-decoder-encoder pipeline, capturing the training data distribution within both image and latent vector space. An adversarial training architecture such as this, practically based on only *normal* training data examples, produces superior performance over challenging benchmark problems. The main contributions of this paper are as follows:

- *semi-supervised anomaly detection*—a novel adversarial autoencoder within an encoder-decoder-encoder pipeline, capturing the training data distribution within both image and latent vector space, yielding superior results to contemporary GAN-based and traditional autoencoder-based approaches.
- *efficacy*—an efficient and novel approach to anomaly detection that yields both statistically and computationally better performance.
- *reproducibility*—simple and effective algorithm such that the results could be reproduced via the code[1] made publicly available.

2   Related Work

Anomaly detection has long been a question of great interest in a wide range of domains including but not limited to biomedical [39], financial [3] and security such as video surveillance [23], network systems [4] and fraud detection [2]. Besides, a considerable amount of work has been published to taxonomize the approaches in the literature [9,19,28,29,33]. The narrower scope of the review is primarily focused on reconstruction-based anomaly techniques.

The vast majority of the reconstruction-based approaches have been employed to investigate anomalies in video sequences. Sabokrou *et al.* [37] investigate the use of Gaussian classifiers on top of autoencoders (global) and nearest

---

[1] The code is available on https://github.com/samet-akcay/ganomaly.

neighbor similarity (local) feature descriptors to model non-overlapping video patches. A study by Medel and Savakis [30] employs convolutional long short-term memory networks for anomaly detection. Trained on normal samples only, the model predicts the future frame of possible standard example, which distinguishes the abnormality during the inference. In another study on the same task, Hasan et al. [18] considers a two-stage approach, using local features and fully connected autoencoder first, followed by fully convolutional autoencoder for end-to-end feature extraction and classification. Experiments yield competitive results on anomaly detection benchmarks. To determine the effects of adversarial training in anomaly detection in videos, Dimokranitou [13] uses adversarial autoencoders, producing a comparable performance on benchmarks.

More recent attention in the literature has been focused on the provision of adversarial training. The seminal work of Ravanbakhsh et al. [35] utilizes image to image translation [21] to examine the abnormality detection problem in crowded scenes and achieves state-of-the-art on the benchmarks. The approach is to train two conditional GANs. The first generator produces optical flow from frames, while the second generates frames from optical-flow.

The generalisability of the approach mentioned above is problematic since in many cases datasets do not have temporal features. One of the most influential accounts of anomaly detection using adversarial training comes from Schlegl et al. [39]. The authors hypothesize that the latent vector of the GAN represents the distribution of the data. However, mapping to the vector space of the GAN is not straightforward. To achieve this, the authors first train a generator and discriminator using only normal images. In the next stage, they utilize the pre-trained generator and discriminator by freezing the weights and remap to the latent vector by optimizing the GAN based on the z vector. During inference, the model pinpoints an anomaly by outputting a high anomaly score, reporting significant improvement over the previous work. The main limitation of this work is its computational complexity since the model employs a two-stage approach, and remapping the latent vector is extremely expensive. In a follow-up study, Zenati et al. [40] investigate the use of BiGAN [14] in an anomaly detection task, examining joint training to map from image space to latent space simultaneously, and vice-versa. Training the model via [39] yields superior results on the MNIST [25] dataset.

Overall prior work strongly supports the hypothesis that the use of autoencoders and GAN demonstrate promise in anomaly detection problems [23,39,40]. Motivated by the idea of GAN with inference studied in [39] and [40], we introduce a conditional adversarial network such that generator comprises encoder-decoder-encoder sub-networks, learning representations in both image and latent vector space jointly, and achieving state-of-the-art performance both statistically and computationally.

3   Our Approach: GANomaly

To explain our approach in detail, it is essential to briefly introduce the background of GAN.

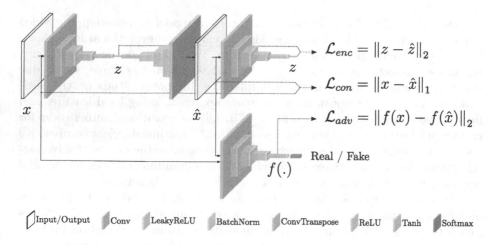

$$\mathcal{L}_{enc} = \|z - \hat{z}\|_2$$

$$\mathcal{L}_{con} = \|x - \hat{x}\|_1$$

$$\mathcal{L}_{adv} = \|f(x) - f(\hat{x})\|_2$$

Real / Fake

⬠ Input/Output ▮ Conv ▮ LeakyReLU ▮ BatchNorm ▮ ConvTranspose ▮ ReLU ▮ Tanh ▮ Softmax

Fig. 2. Pipeline of the proposed approach for anomaly detection.

Generative Adversarial Networks (GAN) are an unsupervised machine learning algorithm that was initially introduced by Goodfellow et al. [16]. The original primary goal of the work is to generate realistic images. The idea being that two networks (generator and discriminator) compete with each other during training such that the former tries to generate an image, while the latter decides whether the generated image is a real or a fake. The generator is a decoder-alike network that learns the distribution of input data from a latent space. The primary objective here is to model high dimensional data that captures the original real data distribution. The discriminator network usually has a classical classification architecture, reading an input image, and determining its validity (i.e., *real vs. fake*).

GAN have been intensively investigated recently due to their future potential [12]. To address training instability issues, several empirical methodologies have been proposed [7,38]. One well-known study that receives attention in the literature is Deep Convolutional GAN (DCGAN) by Radford and Chintala [34], who introduce a fully convolutional generative network by removing fully connected layers and using convolutional layers and batch-normalization [20] throughout the network. The training performance of GAN is improved further via the use of Wasserstein loss [8,17].

Adversarial Auto-Encoders (AAE) consist of two sub-networks, namely an encoder and a decoder. This structure maps the input to latent space and remaps back to input data space, known as reconstruction. Training autoencoders with adversarial setting enable not only better reconstruction but also control over latent space [12,27,31].

GAN with Inference are also used within discrimination tasks by exploiting latent space variables [10]. For instance, the research by [11] suggests that networks are capable of generating a similar latent representation for related high-dimensional image data. Lipton and Tripathi [26] also investigate the idea of inverse mapping by introducing a gradient-based approach, mapping images back to the latent space. This has also been explored in [15] with a specific focus on joint training of generator and inference networks. The former network maps from latent space to high-dimensional image space, while the latter maps from image to latent space. Another study by Donahue *et al.* [14] suggests that with the additional use of an encoder network mapping from image space to latent space, a vanilla GAN network is capable of learning inverse mapping.

3.1 Proposed Approach

Problem Definition. Our objective is to train an unsupervised network that detects anomalies using a dataset that is highly biased towards a particular class - i.e., comprising *normal* non-anomalous occurrences only for training. The formal definition of this problem is as follows:

We are given a large training dataset $\mathcal{D}$ comprising only M normal images, $\mathcal{D} = \{X_1, \ldots, X_M\}$, and a smaller testing dataset $\hat{\mathcal{D}}$ of N normal and abnormal images, $\hat{\mathcal{D}} = \{(\hat{X}_1, y_1), \ldots, (\hat{X}_N, y_N)\}$, where $y_i \in [0, 1]$ denotes the image label. In the practical setting, the training set is significantly larger than the test set such that $M \gg N$.

Given the dataset, our goal is first to model $\mathcal{D}$ to learn its manifold, then detect the abnormal samples in $\hat{\mathcal{D}}$ as outliers during the inference stage. The model f learns both the normal data distribution and minimizes the output anomaly score $\mathcal{A}(x)$. For a given test image $\hat{x}$, a high anomaly score of $\mathcal{A}(\hat{x})$ indicates possible anomalies within the image. The evaluation criteria for this is to threshold (ϕ) the score, where $\mathcal{A}(\hat{x}) > \phi$ indicates anomaly.

Ganomaly Pipeline. Figure 2 illustrates the overview of our approach, which contains two encoders, a decoder, and discriminator networks, employed within three sub-networks.

First sub-network is a bow tie autoencoder network behaving as the generator part of the model. The generator learns the input data representation and reconstructs the input image via the use of an encoder and a decoder network, respectively. The formal principle of the sub-network is the following: The generator G first reads an input image x, where $x \in \mathbb{R}^{w \times h \times c}$, and forward-passes it to its encoder network G_E. With the use of convolutional layers followed by batch-norm and leaky $ReLU()$ activation, respectively, G_E downscales x by compressing it to a vector z, where $z \in \mathbb{R}^d$. z is also known as the bottleneck features of G and hypothesized to have the smallest dimension containing the best representation of x. The decoder part G_D of the generator network G adopts the architecture of a DCGAN generator [34], using convolutional transpose layers, $ReLU()$ activation and batch-norm together with a tanh layer at the end. This approach upscales the vector z to reconstruct the image x as $\hat{x}$. Based on these, the generator network G generates image $\hat{x}$ via $\hat{x} = G_D(z)$, where $z = G_E(x)$.

The second sub-network is the encoder network E that compresses the image $\hat{x}$ that is reconstructed by the network G. With different parametrization, it has the same architectural details as G_E. E downscales $\hat{x}$ to find its feature representation $\hat{z} = E(\hat{x})$. The dimension of the vector $\hat{z}$ is the same as that of z for consistent comparison. This sub-network is one of the unique parts of the proposed approach. Unlike the prior autoencoder-based approaches, in which the minimization of the latent vectors is achieved via the bottleneck features, this sub-network E explicitly learns to minimize the distance with its parametrization. During the test time, moreover, the anomaly detection is performed with this minimization.

The third sub-network is the discriminator network D whose objective is to classify the input x and the output $\hat{x}$ as real or fake, respectively. This sub-network is the standard discriminator network introduced in DCGAN [34].

Having defined our overall multi-network architecture, as depicted in Fig. 2, we now move on to discuss how we formulate our objective for learning.

3.2   Model Training

We hypothesize that when an abnormal image is forward-passed into the network G, G_D is not able to reconstruct the abnormalities even though, G_E manages to map the input X to the latent vector z. This is because the network is modeled only on normal samples during training and its parametrization is not suitable for generating abnormal samples. An output $\hat{X}$ that has missed abnormalities can lead to the encoder network E mapping $\hat{X}$ to a vector $\hat{z}$ that has also missed abnormal feature representation, causing dissimilarity between z and $\hat{z}$. When there is such dissimilarity within latent vector space for an input image X, the model classifies X as an anomalous image. To validate this hypothesis, we formulate our objective function by combining three loss functions, each of which optimizes individual sub-networks.

Adversarial Loss. Following the current trend within the new anomaly detection approaches [39,40], we also use feature matching loss for adversarial learning. Proposed by Salimans *et al.* [38], feature matching is shown to reduce the instability of GAN training. Unlike the vanilla GAN where G is updated based on the output of D (*real/fake*), here we update G based on the internal representation of D. Formally, let f be a function that outputs an intermediate layer of the discriminator D for a given input x drawn from the input data distribution p_X, feature matching computes the $\mathcal{L}_2$ distance between the feature representation of the original and the generated images, respectively. Hence, our adversarial loss $\mathcal{L}_{adv}$ is defined as:

$$\mathcal{L}_{adv} = \mathbb{E}_{x \sim p_X} \| f(x) - \mathbb{E}_{x \sim p_X} f(G(x)) \|_2.$$ (1)

Contextual Loss. The adversarial loss $\mathcal{L}_{adv}$ is adequate to fool the discriminator D with generated samples. However, with only an adversarial loss, the generator is not optimized towards learning contextual information about the input data. It has been shown that penalizing the generator by measuring the distance between the input and the generated images remedies this issue [21]. Isola *et al.* [21] show that the use of $\mathcal{L}_1$ yields less blurry results than $\mathcal{L}_2$. Hence, we also penalize G by measuring the $\mathcal{L}_1$ distance between the original x and the generated images ($\hat{x} = G(x)$) using a contextual loss $\mathcal{L}_{con}$ defined as:

$$\mathcal{L}_{con} = \mathbb{E}_{x \sim p_{\mathbf{X}}} \| x - G(x) \|_1. \tag{2}$$

Encoder Loss. The two losses introduced above can enforce the generator to produce images that are not only realistic but also contextually sound. Moreover, we employ an additional encoder loss $\mathcal{L}_{enc}$ to minimize the distance between the bottleneck features of the input ($z = G_E(x)$) and the encoded features of the generated image ($\hat{z} = E(G(x))$). $\mathcal{L}_{enc}$ is formally defined as

$$\mathcal{L}_{enc} = \mathbb{E}_{x \sim p_{\mathbf{X}}} \| G_E(x) - E(G(x)) \|_2. \tag{3}$$

In so doing, the generator learns how to encode features of the generated image for normal samples. For anomalous inputs, however, it will fail to minimize the distance between the input and the generated images in the feature space since both G and E networks are optimized towards normal samples only.

Overall, our objective function for the generator becomes the following:

$$\mathcal{L} = w_{adv}\mathcal{L}_{adv} + w_{con}\mathcal{L}_{con} + w_{enc}\mathcal{L}_{enc} \tag{4}$$

where w_{adv}, w_{adv} and w_{adv} are the weighting parameters adjusting the impact of individual losses to the overall objective function.

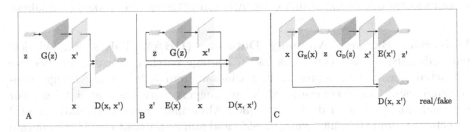

Fig. 3. Comparison of the three models. (A) AnoGAN [39], (B) Efficient-GAN-Anomaly [40], (C) Our Approach: GANomaly

3.3   Model Testing

During the test stage, the model uses $\mathcal{L}_{enc}$ given in Eq. 3 for scoring the abnormality of a given image. Hence, for a test sample $\hat{x}$, our anomaly score $\mathcal{A}(\hat{x})$ or $s_{\hat{x}}$ is defined as

$$\mathcal{A}(\hat{x}) = \|G_E(\hat{x}) - E(G(\hat{x}))\|_1. \tag{5}$$

To evaluate the overall anomaly performance, we compute the anomaly score for individual test sample $\hat{x}$ within the test set $\hat{\mathcal{D}}$, which in turn yields us a set of anomaly scores $\mathcal{S} = \{s_i : \mathcal{A}(\hat{x_i}), \hat{x_i} \in \hat{\mathcal{D}}\}$. We then apply feature scaling to have the anomaly scores within the probabilistic range of $[0, 1]$.

$$s_i' = \frac{s_i - min(\mathcal{S})}{max(\mathcal{S}) - min(\mathcal{S})} \tag{6}$$

The use of Eq. 6 ultimately yields an anomaly score vector $\mathcal{S}'$ for the final evaluation of the test set $\hat{\mathcal{D}}$.

4   Experimental Setup

To evaluate our anomaly detection framework, we use three types of dataset ranging from the simplistic benchmark of MNIST [25], the reference benchmark of CIFAR [24] and the operational context of anomaly detection within X-ray security screening [5].

MNIST. To replicate the results presented in [40], we first experiment on MNIST data [25] by treating one class being an anomaly, while the rest of the classes are considered as the normal class. In total, we have ten sets of data, each of which consider individual digits as the anomaly.

CIFAR10. Within our use of the CIFAR dataset, we again treat one class as abnormal and the rest as normal. We then detect the outlier anomalies as instances drawn from the former class by training the model on the latter labels.

University Baggage Anomaly Dataset—(UBA). This sliding window patched-based dataset comprises 230,275 image patches. Normal samples are extracted via an overlapping sliding window from a full X-ray image, constructed using single conventional X-ray imagery with associated false color materials mapping from dual-energy [36]. Abnormal classes $(122, 803)$ are of 3 sub-classes—knife $(63, 496)$, gun $(45, 855)$ and gun component $(13, 452)$—contain manually cropped threat objects together with sliding window patches whose intersection over union with the ground truth is greater than 0.3.

Full Firearm vs. Operational Benign—(FFOB). In addition to these datasets, we also use the UK government evaluation dataset [1], comprising both expertly concealed firearm (threat) items and operational benign (non-threat) imagery from commercial X-ray security screening operations (baggage/parcels). Denoted as FFOB, this dataset comprises $4, 680$ firearm full-weapons as full abnormal and $67, 672$ operational benign as full normal images, respectively.

The procedure for train and test set split for the above datasets is as follows: we split the normal samples such that 80% and 20% of the samples are considered as part of the train and test sets, respectively. We then resize MNIST to 32×32, DBA and FFOB to 64×64, respectively.

Following Schlegl et al. [39] (AnoGAN) and Zenati et al. [40] (EGBAD), our adversarial training is also based on the standard DCGAN approach [34] for a consistent comparison. As such, we aim to show the superiority of our multi-network architecture regardless of using any tricks to improve the GAN training. In addition, we also compare our method against the traditional variational autoencoder architecture [6] (VAE) to show the advantage of our multi-network architecture. We implement our approach in PyTorch [32] (v0.4.0 with Python 3.6.5) by optimizing the networks using Adam [22] with an initial learning rate $lr = 2e^{-3}$, and momentums $\beta_1 = 0.5$, $\beta_2 = 0.999$. Our model is optimized based on the weighted loss $\mathcal{L}$ (defined in Eq. 4) using the weight values $w_{bce} = 1$, $w_{rec} = 50$ and $w_{enc} = 1$, which were empirically chosen to yield optimum results. (Figure 5(b)). We train the model for 15, 25, 25 epochs for MNIST, UBA and FFOB datasets, respectively. Experimentation is performed using a dual-core Intel Xeon E5-2630 v4 processor and NVIDIA GTX Titan X GPU.

5 Results

We report results based on the area under the curve (AUC) of the Receiver Operating Characteristic (ROC), true positive rate (TPR) as a function of false positive rate (FPR) for different points, each of which is a TPR-FPR value for different thresholds.

Figure 4(a) presents the results obtained on MNIST data using 3 different random seeds, where we observe the clear superiority of our approach over previous contemporary models [6,39,40]. For each digit chosen as anomalous, our model achieves higher AUC than EGBAD [40], AnoGAN [39] and variational autoencoder pipeline VAE [6]. Due to showing its poor performance within relatively unchallenging dataset, we do not include VAE in the rest of experiments. Figure 4(b) shows the performance of the models trained on the CIFAR10 dataset. We see that our model achieves the best AUC performance for any of the class chosen as anomalous. The reason for getting relatively lower quantitative results within this dataset is that for a selected abnormal category, there exists a normal class that is similar to the abnormal (plane vs. bird, cat vs. dog, horse vs. deer and car vs. truck).

Table 1. AUC results for UBA and FFOB datasets

Method	UBA				FFOB
	Gun	Gun-parts	Knife	Overall	Full-weapon
AnoGAN [39]	0.598	0.511	**0.599**	0.569	0.703
EGBAD [40]	0.614	0.591	0.587	0.597	0.712
GANomaly	**0.747**	**0.662**	0.520	**0.643**	**0.882**

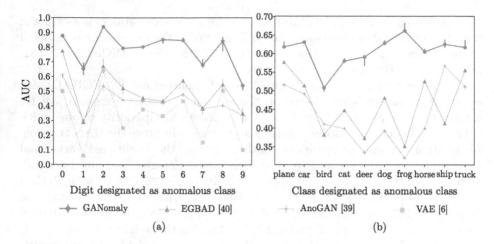

Fig. 4. Results for MNIST (a) and CIFAR (b) datasets. Variations due to the use of 3 different random seeds are depicted via error bars. All but GANomaly results in (a) were obtained from [40].

For UBA and FFOB datasets shown in Table 1, our model again outperforms other approaches excluding the case of the *knife*. In fact, the performance of the models for *knife* is comparable. Relatively lower performance of this class is its shape simplicity, causing an overfit and hence high false positives. For the overall performance, however, our approach surpasses the other models, yielding AUC of 0.666 and 0.882 on the UBA and FFOB datasets, respectively.

Figure 5 depicts how the choice of hyper-parameters ultimately affect the overall performance of the model. In Fig. 5(a), we see that the optimal performance is achieved when the size of the latent vector z is 100 for the MNIST

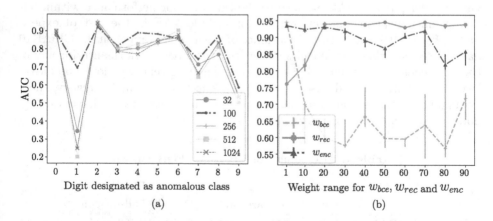

Fig. 5. (a) Overall performance of the model based on varying size of the latent vector z. (b) Impact of weighting the losses on the overall performance. Model is trained on MNIST dataset with an abnormal digit-2

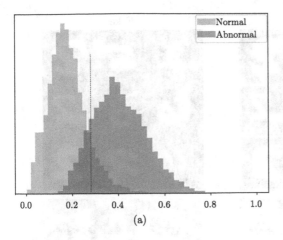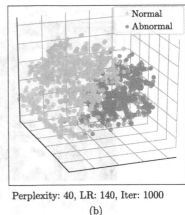

Perplexity: 40, LR: 140, Iter: 1000

(a)   (b)

Fig. 6. (a) Histogram of the scores for both normal and abnormal test samples. (b) t-SNE visualization of the features extracted from the last conv. layer $f(.)$ of the discriminator

dataset with an abnormal digit-2. Figure 5(b) demonstrates the impact of tuning the loss function in Eq. 4 on the overall performance. The model achieves the highest AUC when $w_{bce} = 1$, $w_{rec} = 50$ and $w_{enc} = 1$. We empirically observe the same tuning-pattern for the rest of datasets.

Figure 6 provides the histogram of the anomaly scores during the inference stage (a) and t-SNE visualization of the features extracted from the last convolutional layer of the discriminator network (b). Both of the figures demonstrate a clear separation within the latent vector z and feature $f(.)$ spaces.

Table 2 illustrates the runtime performance of the GAN-based models. Compared to the rest of the approaches, AnoGAN [39] is computationally rather expensive since optimization of the latent vector is needed for each example. For EGBAD [40], we report similar runtime performance to that of the original paper. Our approach, on the other hand, achieves the highest runtime performance. Runtime performance of both UBA and FFOB datasets are comparable to MNIST even though their image and network size are double than that of MNIST.

Table 2. Computational performance of the approaches. (Runtime in terms of millisecond)

Model	MNIST	CIFAR	DBA	FFOB
AnoGAN [39]	7120	7120	7110	7223
EGBAD [40]	8.92	8.71	8.88	8.87
GANomaly	**2.79**	**2.21**	**2.66**	**2.53**

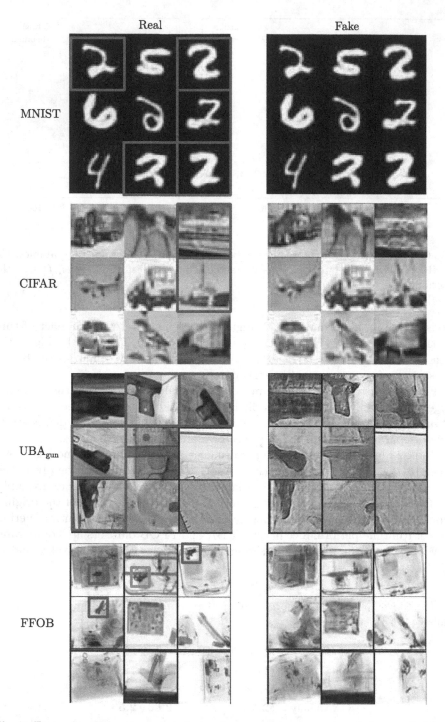

Fig. 7. Exemplar real and generated samples containing normal and abnormal objects in each dataset. The model fails to generate abnormal samples not being trained on.

A set of examples in Fig. 7 depict real and fake images that are respectively the input and output of our model. We expect the model to fail when generating anomalous samples. As can be seen in Fig. 7(a), this is not the case for the class of 2 in the MNIST data. This stems from the fact that MNIST dataset is relatively unchallenging, and the model learns sufficient information to be able to generate samples not seen during training. Another conclusion that could be drawn is that distance in the latent vector space provides adequate details for detecting anomalies even though the model cannot distinguish abnormalities in the image space. On the contrary to the MNIST experiments, this is not the case. Figures 7(b-c) illustrate that model is unable to produce abnormal objects.

Overall these results purport that our approach yields both statistically and computationally superior results than leading state-of-the-art approaches [39, 40].

6   Conclusion

We introduce a novel encoder-decoder-encoder architectural model for general anomaly detection enabled by an adversarial training framework. Experimentation across dataset benchmarks of varying complexity, and within the operational anomaly detection context of X-ray security screening, shows that the proposed method outperforms both contemporary state-of-the-art GAN-based and traditional autoencoder-based anomaly detection approaches with generalization ability to any anomaly detection task. Future work will consider employing emerging contemporary GAN optimizations [7,17,38], known to improve generalized adversarial training.

References

1. OSCT Borders X-ray Image Library: UK Home Office Centre for Applied Science and Technology (CAST). Publication Number: 146/16 (2016)
2. Abdallah, A., Maarof, M.A., Zainal, A.: Fraud detection system: a survey. J. Netw. Comput. Appl. **68**, 90–113 (2016). https://doi.org/10.1016/J.JNCA.2016.04.007. https://www.sciencedirect.com/science/article/pii/S1084804516300571
3. Ahmed, M., Mahmood, A.N., Islam, M.R.: A survey of anomaly detection techniques in financial domain. Future Gener. Comput. Syst. **55**, 278–288 (2016). https://doi.org/10.1016/J.FUTURE.2015.01.001. https://www.sciencedir ect.com/science/article/pii/S0167739X15000023
4. Ahmed, M., Naser Mahmood, A., Hu, J.: A survey of network anomaly detection techniques. J. Netw. Comput. Appl. **60**, 19–31 (2016). https://doi.org/ 10.1016/J.JNCA.2015.11.016. https://www.sciencedirect.com/science/article/pii/ S1084804515002891
5. Akcay, S., Kundegorski, M.E., Willcocks, C.G., Breckon, T.P.: Using deep convolutional neural network architectures for object classification and detection within X-ray baggage security imagery. IEEE Trans. Inf. Forensics Secur. **13**(9), 2203–2215 (2018). https://doi.org/10.1109/TIFS.2018.2812196
6. An, J., Cho, S.: Variational autoencoder based anomaly detection using reconstruction probability. Spec. Lect. IE **2**, 1–18 (2015)

7. Arjovsky, M., Bottou, L.: Towards principled methods for training generative adversarial networks. In: 2017 ICLR, April 2017. http://arxiv.org/abs/1701.04862
8. Arjovsky, M., Chintala, S., Bottou, L.: Wasserstein generative adversarial networks. In: Proceedings of the 34th International Conference on Machine Learning, pp. 214–223, Sydney, Australia, 06–11 August 2017. http://proceedings.mlr.press/v70/arjovsky17a.html
9. Chandola, V., Banerjee, A., Kumar, V.: Anomaly detection. ACM Comput. Surv. 41(3), 1–58 (2009). https://doi.org/10.1145/1541880.1541882
10. Chen, X., et al.: InfoGAN: interpretable representation learning by information maximizing generative adversarial nets. In: Advances in Neural Information Processing Systems, pp. 2172–2180 (2016)
11. Creswell, A., Bharath, A.A.: Inverting the generator of a generative adversarial network (II). arXiv preprint arXiv:1802.05701 (2018)
12. Creswell, A., White, T., Dumoulin, V., Arulkumaran, K., Sengupta, B., Bharath, A.A.: Generative adversarial networks: an overview. IEEE Signal Process. Mag. 35(1), 53–65 (2018)
13. Dimokranitou, A.: Adversarial autoencoders for anomalous event detection in images. Ph.D. thesis, Purdue University (2017)
14. Donahue, J., Krähenbühl, P., Darrell, T.: Adversarial feature learning. In: International Conference on Learning Representations (ICLR), Toulon, France, April 2017. http://arxiv.org/abs/1605.09782
15. Dumoulin, V., et al.: Adversarially learned inference. In: ICLR (2017)
16. Goodfellow, I., et al.: Generative adversarial nets. In: Advances in Neural Information Processing Systems, pp. 2672–2680 (2014)
17. Gulrajani, I., Ahmed, F., Arjovsky, M., Dumoulin, V., Courville, A.C.: Improved training of Wasserstein GANs. In: Advances in Neural Information Processing Systems, pp. 5767–5777 (2017)
18. Hasan, M., Choi, J., Neumann, J., Roy-Chowdhury, A.K., Davis, L.S.: Learning temporal regularity in video sequences. In: Proceedings of the IEEE Conference on Computer Vision and Pattern Recognition, pp. 733–742 (2016)
19. Hodge, V., Austin, J.: A survey of outlier detection methodologies. Artif. Intell. Rev. 22(2), 85–126 (2004). https://doi.org/10.1023/B:AIRE.0000045502.10941.a9
20. Ioffe, S., Szegedy, C.: Batch normalization: accelerating deep network training by reducing internal covariate shift. In: Proceedings of the 32nd International Conference on Machine Learning, pp. 448–456, Lille, France, 07–09 July 2015. http://proceedings.mlr.press/v37/ioffe15.html
21. Isola, P., Zhu, J., Zhou, T., Efros, A.A.: Image-to-image translation with conditional adversarial networks. In: 2017 IEEE Conference on Computer Vision and Pattern Recognition (CVPR), pp. 5967–5976, July 2017. https://doi.org/10.1109/CVPR.2017.632
22. Kinga, D., Adam, J.B.: Adam: a method for stochastic optimization. In: International Conference on Learning Representations (ICLR), vol. 5 (2015)
23. Kiran, B.R., Thomas, D.M., Parakkal, R.: An overview of deep learning based methods for unsupervised and semi-supervised anomaly detection in videos. J. Imaging 4(2), 36 (2018)
24. Krizhevsky, A., Hinton, G.: Learning multiple layers of features from tiny images. Technical report, Citeseer (2009)
25. LeCun, Y., Cortes, C.: MNIST handwritten digit database (2010). http://yann.lecun.com/exdb/mnist/
26. Lipton, Z.C., Tripathi, S.: Precise recovery of latent vectors from generative adversarial networks. In: ICLR Workshop (2017)

27. Makhzani, A., Shlens, J., Jaitly, N., Goodfellow, I., Frey, B.: Adversarial autoencoders. In: ICLR (2016)
28. Markou, M., Singh, S.: Novelty detection: a review-part 1: statistical approaches. Signal Process. **83**(12), 2481–2497 (2003). https://doi.org/10.1016/J.SIGPRO.2003.07.018. https://www.sciencedirect.com/science/article/pii/S016516840300 2020
29. Markou, M., Singh, S.: Novelty detection: a review-part 2: neural network based approaches. Signal Process. **83**(12), 2499–2521 (2003). https://doi.org/10.1016/J.SIGPRO.2003.07.019. https://www.sciencedirect.com/science/article/pii/S0165 168403002032
30. Medel, J.R., Savakis, A.: Anomaly detection in video using predictive convolutional long short-term memory networks. CoRR abs/1612.0 (2016)
31. Mirza, M., Osindero, S.: Conditional generative adversarial nets. arXiv preprint arXiv:1411.1784 (2014)
32. Paszke, A., et al.: Automatic differentiation in PyTorch (2017)
33. Pimentel, M.A., Clifton, D.A., Clifton, L., Tarassenko, L.: A review of novelty detection. Signal Process. **99**, 215–249 (2014)
34. Radford, A., Metz, L., Chintala, S.: Unsupervised representation learning with deep convolutional generative adversarial networks. In: ICLR (2016)
35. Ravanbakhsh, M., Sangineto, E., Nabi, M., Sebe, N.: Training adversarial discriminators for cross-channel abnormal event detection in crowds. CoRR abs/1706.0 (2017). http://arxiv.org/abs/1706.07680
36. Rogers, T.W., Jaccard, N., Morton, E.J., Griffin, L.D.: Automated X-ray image analysis for cargo security: critical review and future promise. J. X-Ray Sci. Technol. (Prepr.) **25**, 1–24 (2016)
37. Sabokrou, M., Fathy, M., Hoseini, M., Klette, R.: Real-time anomaly detection and localization in crowded scenes. In: 2015 IEEE Conference on Computer Vision and Pattern Recognition Workshops (CVPRW), pp. 56–62 (2015). https://doi.org/10.1109/CVPRW.2015.7301284, http://ieeexplore.ieee.org/document/7301284/
38. Salimans, T., Goodfellow, I., Zaremba, W., Cheung, V., Radford, A., Chen, X.: Improved techniques for training GANs. In: Advances in Neural Information Processing Systems, pp. 2234–2242 (2016)
39. Schlegl, T., Seeböck, P., Waldstein, S.M., Schmidt-Erfurth, U., Langs, G.: Unsupervised anomaly detection with generative adversarial networks to guide marker discovery. In: Niethammer, M., et al. (eds.) IPMI 2017. LNCS, vol. 10265, pp. 146–157. Springer, Cham (2017). https://doi.org/10.1007/978-3-319-59050-9_12
40. Zenati, H., Foo, C.S., Lecouat, B., Manek, G., Chandrasekhar, V.R.: Efficient GAN-based anomaly detection. arXiv preprint arXiv:1802.06222 (2018)

Deep Object Co-segmentation

Weihao Li[⊠], Omid Hosseini Jafari[⊠], and Carsten Rother

Visual Learning Lab, Heidelberg University (HCI/IWR), Heidelberg, Germany
{weihao.li,omid.hosseini_jafari,carsten.rother}@iwr.uni-heidelberg.de

Abstract. This work presents a deep object co-segmentation (DOCS) approach for segmenting common objects of the same class within a pair of images. This means that the method learns to ignore common, or uncommon, background *stuff* and focuses on common *objects*. If multiple object classes are presented in the image pair, they are jointly extracted as foreground. To address this task, we propose a CNN-based Siamese encoder-decoder architecture. The encoder extracts high-level semantic features of the foreground objects, a mutual correlation layer detects the common objects, and finally, the decoder generates the output foreground masks for each image. To train our model, we compile a large object co-segmentation dataset consisting of image pairs from the PASCAL dataset with common objects masks. We evaluate our approach on commonly used datasets for co-segmentation tasks and observe that our approach consistently outperforms competing methods, for both seen and unseen object classes.

1 Introduction

Object co-segmentation is the task of segmenting the common objects from a set of images. It is applied in various computer vision applications and beyond, such as browsing in photo collections [30], 3D reconstruction [21], semantic segmentation [33], object-based image retrieval [39], video object tracking and segmentation [30], and interactive image segmentation [30].

There are different challenges for object co-segmentation with varying level of difficulty: (1) Rother *et al.* [30] first proposed the term of *co-segmentation* as the task of segmenting the *common parts* of an image pair simultaneously. They showed that segmenting two images jointly achieves better accuracy in contrast to segmenting them independently. They assume that the common parts have similar appearance. However, the background in both images are significantly different, see Fig. 1(a). (2) Another challenge is to segment the same object instance or similar objects of the same class with low intra-class variation, even with similar background [2,39], see Fig. 1(b). (3) A more challenging task is to segment common objects from the same class with large variability in terms of scale, appearance, pose, viewpoint and background [31], see Fig. 1(c).

W. Li and O. Hosseini Jafari—Equal contribution.

© Springer Nature Switzerland AG 2019
C. V. Jawahar et al. (Eds.): ACCV 2018, LNCS 11363, pp. 638–653, 2019.
https://doi.org/10.1007/978-3-030-20893-6_40

(a) stone-pair   (b) panda   (c) car

(d) our object co-segmentation

Fig. 1. Different co-segmentation challenges: (a) segmenting common parts, in terms of small appearance deviation, with varying background [30], (b) segmenting common objects from the same class with low intra-class variation but similar background [2,38], (c) segmenting common objects from the same class with large variability in terms of scale, appearance, pose, viewpoint and background [31]. (d) segmenting common objects in images including more than one object from multiple classes. Second row shows our predicted co-segmentation of these challenging images.

All of the mentioned challenges assume that the image set contains only one common object and the common object should be salient within each image. In this work, we address a more general problem of co-segmentation without this assumption, *i.e.* multiple object classes can be presented within the images, see Fig. 1(d). As it is shown, the co-segmentation result for one specific image including multiple objects can be different when we pair it with different images. Additionally, we are interested in co-segmenting objects, *i.e. things* rather than *stuff*. The idea of object co-segmentation was introduced by Vicente *et al.* [39] to emphasize the resulting segmentation to be a *thing* such as a 'cat' or a 'monitor', which excludes common, or uncommon, *stuff* classes like 'sky' or 'sea'.

Segmenting objects in an image is one of the fundamental tasks in computer vision. While image segmentation has received great attention during the recent rise of deep learning [25,28,29,43,47], the related task of object co-segmentation remains largely unexplored by newly developed deep learning techniques. Most of the recently proposed object co-segmentation methods still rely on models without feature learning. This includes methods utilizing super-pixels, or proposal segments [36,39] to extract a set of object candidates, or methods which use a complex CRF model [22,28] with hand-crafted features [28] to find the segments with the highest similarity.

In this paper, we propose a simple yet powerful method for segmenting objects of a common semantic class from a pair of images using a convolutional encoder-decoder neural network. Our method uses a pair of Siamese encoder networks to extract semantic features for each image. The mutual correlation layer at the network's bottleneck computes localized correlations between the semantic features of the two images to highlight the heat-maps of common objects. Finally, the Siamese decoder networks combine the semantic features from each image with the correlation features to produce detailed segmentation masks through a series of deconvolutional layers. Our approach is trainable in an end-to-end manner and does not require any, potentially long runtime, CRF optimization procedure at evaluation time. We perform an extensive evaluation of our deep object co-segmentation and show that our model can achieve state-of-the-art performance on multiple common co-segmentation datasets. In summary, our main contributions are as follows:

- We propose a simple yet effective convolutional neural network (CNN) architecture for object co-segmentation that can be trained end-to-end. To the best of our knowledge, this is the first pure CNN framework for object co-segmentation, which does not depend on any hand-crafted features.
- We achieve state-of-the-art results on multiple object co-segmentation datasets, and introduce a challenging object co-segmentation dataset by adapting Pascal dataset for training and testing object co-segmentation models.

2   Related Work

We start by discussing object co-segmentation by roughly categorizing them into three branches: co-segmentation without explicit learning, co-segmentation with learning, and interactive co-segmentation. After that, we briefly discuss various image segmentation tasks and corresponding approaches based on CNNs.

Co-segmentation Without Explicit Learning. Rother et al. [30] proposed the problem of image co-segmentation for image pairs. They minimize an energy function that combines an MRF smoothness prior term with a histogram matching term. This forces the histogram statistic of common foreground regions to be similar. In a follow-up work, Mukherjee et al. [26] replace the l_1 norm in the cost function by an l_2 norm. In [14], Hochbaum and Singh used a reward model, in contrast to the penalty strategy of [30]. In [38], Vicente et al. studied various models and showed that a simple model based on Boykov-Jolly [3] works the best. Joulin et al. [19] formulated the co-segmentation problem in terms of a discriminative clustering task. Rubio et al. [32] proposed to match regions, which results from an over-segmentation algorithm, to establish correspondences between the common objects. Rubinstein et al. [31] combined a visual saliency and dense correspondences, using SIFT flow, to capture the sparsity and visual variability of the common object in a group of images. Fu et al. [12] formulated object co-segmentation for RGB-D input images as a fully-connected graph structure, together with mutex constraints. In contrast to these works, our method is a pure learning based approach.

Co-segmentation with Learning. In [39], Vicente et al. generated a pool of object-like proposal-segmentations using constrained parametric min-cut [4].

Then they trained a random forest classifier to score the similarity of a pair of segmentation proposals. Yuan *et al.* [45] introduced a deep dense conditional random field framework for object co-segmentation by inferring co-occurrence maps. These co-occurrence maps measure the objectness scores, as well as, similarity evidence for object proposals, which are generated using selective search [37]. Similar to the constrained parametric min-cut, selective search also uses hand-crafted SIFT and HOG features to generate object proposals. Therefore, the model of [45] cannot be trained end-to-end. In addition, [45] assume that there is a single common object in a given image set, which limits application in real-world scenarios. Recently, Quan *et al.* [28] proposed a manifold ranking algorithm for object co-segmentation by combining low-level appearance features and high-level semantic features. However, their semantic features are pre-trained on the ImageNet dataset. In contrast, our method is based on a pure CNN architecture, which is free of any hand-crafted features and object proposals and does not depend on any assumption about the existence of common objects.

Interactive Co-segmentation. Batra *et al.* [2] firstly presented an algorithm for interactive co-segmentation of a foreground object from a group of related images. They use users' scribbles to indicate the foreground. Collins *et al.* [7] used a random walker model to add consistency constraints between foreground regions within the interactive co-segmentation framework. However, their co-segmentation results are sensitive to the size and positions of users' scribbles. Dong *et al.* [9] proposed an interactive co-segmentation method which uses global and local energy optimization, whereby the energy function is based on scribbles, inter-image consistency, and a standard local smoothness prior. In contrast, our work is not a user-interactive co-segmentation approach.

Convolutional Neural Networks for Image Segmentation. In the last few years, CNNs have achieved great success for the tasks of image segmentation, such as semantic segmentation [24,25,27,43,44,46], interactive segmentation [42, 43], and salient object segmentation [15,23,41].

Semantic segmentation aims at assigning semantic labels to each pixel in an image. Fully convolutional networks (FCN) [25] became one of the first popular architectures for semantic segmentation. Noh *et al.* [27] proposed a deep deconvolutional network to learn the upsampling of low-resolution features. Both U-Net [29] and SegNet [1] proposed an encoder-decoder architecture, in which the decoder network consists of a hierarchy of decoders, each corresponding to an encoder. Yu *et al.* [44] and Chen *et al.* [5] proposed dilated convolutions to aggregate multi-scale contextual information, by considering larger receptive fields. Salient object segmentation aims at detecting and segmenting the salient objects in a given image. Recently, deep learning architectures have become popular for salient object segmentation [15,23,41]. Li and Yu [23] addressed salient object segmentation using a deep network which consists of a pixel-level multi-scale FCN and a segment scale spatial pooling stream. Wang *et al.* [41] proposed recurrent FCN to incorporate saliency prior knowledge for improved inference, utilizing a pre-training strategy based on semantic segmentation data.

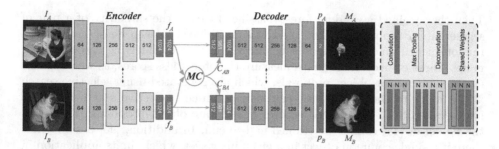

Fig. 2. Deep Object Co-segmentation. Our network includes three parts: (i) passing input images I_A and I_B through a Siamese encoder to extract feature maps f_A and f_B, (ii) using a mutual correlation network to perform feature matching to obtain correspondence maps C_{AB} and C_{BA}, (iii) passing concatenation of squeezed feature maps and correspondence maps through a Siamese decoder to get the common objects masks M_A and M_B.

Jain *et al.* [15] proposed to train a FCN to produce pixel-level masks of all "object-like" regions given a single input image.

Although CNNs play a central role in image segmentation tasks, there has been no prior work with a pure CNN architecture for object co-segmentation. To the best of our knowledge, our deep CNN architecture is the first of its kind for object co-segmentation.

3   Method

In this section, we introduce a new CNN architecture for segmenting the common objects from two input images. The architecture is end-to-end trainable for the object co-segmentation task. Figure 2 illustrates the overall structure of our architecture. Our network consists of three main parts: (1) Given two input images I_A and I_B, we use a Siamese encoder to extract high-level semantic feature maps f_A and f_B. (2) Then, we propose a mutual correlation layer to obtain correspondence maps C_{AB} and C_{BA} by matching feature maps f_A and f_B at pixel-level. (3) Finally, given the concatenation of the feature maps f_A and f_B and correspondence maps C_{AB} and C_{BA}, a Siamese decoder is used to obtain and refine the common object masks M_A and M_B.

In the following, we first describe each of the three parts of our architecture in detail. Then in Sect. 3.4, the loss function is introduced. Finally, in Sect. 3.5, we explain how to extend our approach to handle co-segmentation of a group of images, *i.e.* going beyond two images.

3.1   Siamese Encoder

The first part of our architecture is a Siamese encoder which consists of two identical feature extraction CNNs with shared parameters. We pass the input

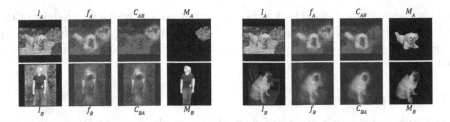

Fig. 3. The visualization of the heat-maps. Given a pair of input images I_A and I_B, after passing them through the Siamese encoder, we extract feature maps f_A and f_B. We use the mutual correlation layer to perform feature matching to obtain correspondence maps C_{AB} and C_{BA}. Then, using our Siamese decoder we predict the common objects masks M_A and M_B. As shown before correlation layer, the heat-maps are covering all the objects inside the images. After applying the correlation layer, the heat-maps on uncommon objects are filtered out. Therefore, we utilize the output of the correlation layer to guide the network for segmenting the common objects.

image pair I_A and I_B through the Siamese encoder network pair to extract feature maps f_A and f_B. More specifically, our encoder is based on the VGG16 network [35]. We keep the first 13 convolutional layers and replace $fc6$ and $fc7$ with two 3×3 convolutional layers $conv6\text{-}1$ and $conv6\text{-}2$ to produce feature maps which contain more spatial information. In total, our encoder network has 15 convolutional layers and 5 pooling layers to create a set of high-level semantic features f_A and f_B. The input to the Siamese encoder is two 512×512 images and the output of the encoder is two 1024-channel feature maps with a spatial size of 16×16.

3.2   Mutual Correlation

The second part of our architecture is a mutual correlation layer. The outputs of encoders f_A and f_B represent the high-level semantic content of the input images. When the two images contain objects that belong to a common class, they should contain similar features at the locations of the shared objects. Therefore, we propose a mutual correlation layer to compute the correlation between each pair of locations on the feature maps. The idea of utilizing the correlation layer is inspired by Flownet [10], in which the correlation layer is used to match feature points between frames for optical flow estimation. Our motivation of using the correlation layer is to filter the heat-maps (high-level features), which are generated separately for each input image, to highlight the heat-maps on the common objects (see Fig. 3). In detail, the mutual correlation layer performs a pixel-wise comparison between two feature maps f_A and f_B. Given a point (i, j) and a point (m, n) inside a patch around (i, j), the correlation between feature vectors $f_A(i, j)$ and $f_B(m, n)$ is defined as

$$C_{AB}(i, j, k) = \langle f_A(i, j), f_B(m, n) \rangle \tag{1}$$

where $k = (n - j)D + (m - i)$ and $D \times D$ is patch size. Since the common objects can locate at any place on the two input images, we set the patch size to $D = 2 * max(w - 1, h - 1) + 1$, where w and h are the width and height of the feature maps f_A and f_B. The output of the correlation layer is a feature map C_{AB} of size $w \times h \times D^2$. We use the same method to compute the correlation map C_{BA} between f_B and f_A.

3.3 Siamese Decoder

The Siamese decoder is the third part of our architecture, which predicts two foreground masks of the common objects. We squeeze the feature maps f_A and f_B and concatenate them with their correspondence maps C_{AB} and C_{BA} as the input to the Siamese decoder (Fig. 2). The same as the Siamese encoder, the decoder is also arranged in a Siamese structure with shared parameters. There are five blocks in our decoder, whereby each block has one deconvolutional layer and two convolutional layers. All the convolutional and deconvolutional layers in our Siamese decoder are followed by a ReLU activation function. By applying a Softmax function, the decoder produces two probability maps p_A and p_B. Each probability map has two channels, background and foreground, with the same size as the input images.

3.4 Loss Function

We define our object co-segmentation as a binary image labeling problem and use the standard cross entropy loss function to train our network. The full loss score $\mathcal{L}_{AB}$ is then estimated by $\mathcal{L}_{AB} = \mathcal{L}_A + \mathcal{L}_B$, where the $\mathcal{L}_A$ and the $\mathcal{L}_B$ are cross-entropy loss functions for the image A and the image B, respectively.

3.5 Group Co-segmentation

Although our architecture is trained for image pairs, our method can handle a group of images. Given a set of N images $\mathcal{I} = \{I_1, ..., I_N\}$, we pair each image with $K \leq N - 1$ other images from $\mathcal{I}$. Then, we use our DOCS network to predict the probability maps for the pairs, $\mathcal{P} = \{p_n^k : 1 \leq n \leq N, 1 \leq k \leq K\}$, where p_n^k is the predicted probability map for the kth pair of image I_n. Finally, we compute the final mask M_n for image I_n as

$$M_n(x, y) = \text{median}\{p_n^k(x, y)\} > \sigma. \tag{2}$$

where σ is the acceptance threshold. In this work, we set $\sigma = 0.5$. We use the median to make our approach more robust to groups with outliers.

4   Experiments

4.1 Datasets

Training a CNN requires a lot of data. However, existing co-segmentation datasets are either too small or have a limited number of object classes. The MSRC dataset [34] was first introduced for supervised semantic segmentation, then a subset was used for object co-segmentation [39]. This subset of MSRC only has 7 groups of images and each group has 10 images. The iCoseg dataset, introduced in [2], consists of several groups of images and is widely used to evaluate co-segmentation methods. However, each group contains images of the same object instance or very similar objects from the same class. The Internet dataset [31] contains thousands of images obtained from the Internet using image retrieval techniques. However, it only has three object classes: *car, horse* and *airplane*, where images of each class are mixed with other noise objects. In [11], Faktor and Irani use PASCAL dataset for object co-segmentation. They separate the images into 20 groups according to the object classes and assume that each group only has one object. However, this assumption is not common for natural images.

Inspired by [11], we create an object co-segmentation dataset by adapting the PASCAL dataset labeled by [13]. The original dataset consists of 20 foreground object classes and one background class. It contains $8,498$ training and $2,857$ validation pixel-level labeled images. From the training images, we sampled $161,229$ pairs of images, which have common objects, as a new co-segmentation training set. We used PASCAL validation images to sample $42,831$ validation pairs and $40,303$ test pairs. Since our goal is to segment the common objects from the pair of images, we discard the object class labels and instead we label the common objects as foreground. Figure 1(d) shows some examples of image pairs of our object co-segmentation dataset. In contrast to [11], our dataset consists of image pairs of one or more arbitrary common classes.

4.2   Implementation Details and Runtime

We use the Caffe framework [18] to design and train our network. We use our co-segmentation dataset for training. We did not use any images from the MSCR, Internet or iCoseg datasets to fine tune our model. The *conv1-conv5* layers of our Siamese encoder (VGG-16 net [35]) are initialized with weights trained on the Imagenet dataset [8]. We train our network on one GPU for 100K iterations using Adam solver [20]. We use small mini-batches of 10 image pairs, a momentum of 0.9, a learning rate of $1e-5$, and a weight decay of 0.0005.

Our method can handle a large set of images in linear time complexity $\mathcal{O}(N)$. As mentioned in Sect. 3.5 in order to co-segment an image, we pair it with K ($K \leq N-1$) other images. In our experiments, we used all possible pairs to make the evaluations comparable to other approaches. Although in this case our time complexity is quadratic $\mathcal{O}(N^2)$, our method is significantly faster than others.

Number of images	Others time	Our time
2	8 min [19]	0.1 s
30	4 to 9 h [19]	43.5 s
30	22.5 min [40]	43.5 s
418 (14 categories, $\sim$ 30 images per category)	29.2 h [11]	10.15 min
418 (14 categories, $\sim$ 30 images per category)	8.5 h [17]	10.15 min

To show the influence of number of pairs K, we validate our method on the Internet dataset w.r.t. K (Table 1). Each image is paired with K random images from the set. As shown, we achieve state-of-the-art performance even with $K = 10$. Therefore, the complexity of our approach is $\mathcal{O}(KN) = \mathcal{O}(N)$ which is linear with respect to the group size.

Table 1. Influence of number of pairs K.

Internet (N = 100)	K = 10		K = 20		K = 99 (all)	
	P	J	P	J	P	J
Car	93.93	82.89	93.91	82.85	93.90	82.81
Horse	92.31	69.12	92.35	69.17	92.45	69.44
Airplane	94.10	65.37	94.12	65.45	94.11	65.43
Average	93.45	72.46	93.46	72.49	93.49	72.56

4.3   Results

We report the performance of our approach on MSCR [34,38], Internet [31], and iCoseg [2] datasets, as well as our own co-segmentation dataset.

Metrics. For evaluating the co-segmentation performance, there are two common metrics. The first one is *Precision*, which is the percentage of correctly segmented pixels of both foreground and background masks. The second one is *Jaccard*, which is the intersection over union of the co-segmentation result and the ground truth foreground segmentation.

PASCAL Co-segmentation. As we mentioned in Sect. 4.1, our co-segmentation dataset consists of $40,303$ test image pairs. We evaluate the performance of our method on our co-segmentation test data. We also tried to obtain the common objects of same classes using a deep semantic segmentation model, here FCN8s [25]. First, we train FCN8s with the PASCAL dataset. Then, we obtain the common objects from two images by predicting the semantic labels using FCN8s and keeping the segments with common classes as foreground. Our co-segmentation method (**94.2%** for *Precision* and **64.5%** for *Jaccard*) outperforms FCN8s (**93.2%** for *Precision* and **55.2%** for *Jaccard*), which uses the same VGG encoder, and trained with the same training images. The improvement is probably due to the fact that our DOCS architecture is specifically designed for the object co-segmentation task, which FCN8s is designed for the semantic labeling problem. Another potential reason is that generating image pairs is a form of data augmentation. We would like to exploit these ideas in the future work. Figure 4 shows the qualitative results of our approach on the PASCAL

Fig. 4. Our qualitative results on PASCAL Co-segmentation dataset. (odd rows) the input images, (even rows) the corresponding object co-segmentation results.

co-segmentation dataset. We can see that our method successfully extracts different foreground objects for the left image when paired with a different image to the right.

MSRC. The MSRC subset has been used to evaluate the object co-segmentation performance by many previous methods [11,31,38,40]. For the fair comparison, we use the same subset as [38]. We use our group co-segmentation method to extract the foreground masks for each group. In Table 2, we show the quantitative results of our method as well as four state-of-the-art methods [11,31,39,40]. Our *Precision* and *Jaccard* show a significant improvement compared to previous methods. It is important to note that [39] and [40] are supervised methods, i.e. both use images of the MSRC dataset to train their models. We obtain the new state-of-the-art results on this dataset even without training or fine-tuning on any images from the MSRC dataset. Visual examples of object co-segmentation results on the subset of the MSRC dataset can be found in Fig. 5.

Internet. In our experiment, for the fair comparison, we followed [6,28,31,45] to use the subset of the Internet dataset to evaluate our method. In this subset, there are 100 images in each category. We compare our method with five previous approaches [6,19,28,31,45]. Table 3 shows the quantitative results of each object category with respect to *Precision* and *Jaccard*. We outperform most of the

Fig. 5. Our qualitative results on the MSRC dataset (seen classes). (odd rows) the input images, (even rows) the corresponding object co-segmentation results.

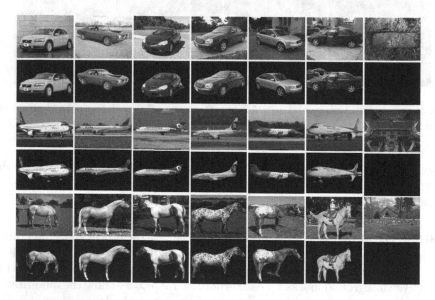

Fig. 6. Our qualitative results on the Internet dataset (seen classes). (odd rows) the input images, (even rows) the corresponding object co-segmentation results.

previous methods [6,19,28,31,45] in terms of *Precision* and *Jaccard*. Note that [45] is a supervised co-segmentation method, [6] trained a discriminative Latent-SVM detector and [28] used a CNN trained on the ImageNet to extract semantic features. Figure 6 shows some quantitative results of our method. It can be seen that even for the 'noise' images in each group, our method can successfully recognize them. We show the 'noise' images in the last column.

Table 2. Quantitative results on the MSRC dataset (seen classes). Quantitative comparison results of our DOCS approach with four state-of-the-art co-segmentation methods on the co-segmentation subset of the MSCR dataset.

MSCR	[39]	[31]	[40]	[11]	Ours
Precision	90.2	92.2	92.2	92.0	**95.4**
Jaccard	70.6	74.7	-	77.0	**82.9**

Table 3. Quantitative results on the Internet dataset (seen classes). Quantitative comparison of our DOCS approach with several state-of-the-art co-segmentation methods on the co-segmentation subset of the Internet dataset. 'P' is the *Precision*, and 'J' is the *Jaccard*.

Internet		[19]	[31]	[6]	[28]	[45]	Ours
Car	P	58.7	85.3	87.6	88.5	90.4	**93.9**
	J	37.1	64.4	64.9	66.8	72.0	**82.8**
Horse	P	63.8	82.8	86.2	89.3	90.2	**92.4**
	J	30.1	51.6	33.4	58.1	65.0	**69.4**
Airplane	P	49.2	88.0	90.3	92.6	91.0	**94.1**
	J	15.3	55.8	40.3	56.3	**66.0**	65.4
Average	P	57.2	85.4	88.0	89.6	91.1	**93.5**
	J	27.5	57.3	46.2	60.4	67.7	**72.6**

iCoseg. To show that our method can generalize on *unseen classes*, *i.e.* classes which are not part of the training data, we need to evaluate our method on *unseen classes*. Batra *et al.* [2] introduced the iCoseg dataset for the *interactive* co-segmentation task. In contrast to the MSRC and Internet datasets, there are multiple object classes in the iCoseg dataset which do not appear in PASCAL VOC dataset. Therefore, it is possible to use the iCoseg dataset to evaluate the generalization of our method on *unseen object classes*. We choose eight groups of images from the iCoseg dataset as our unseen object classes, which are *bear2, brown_bear, cheetah, elephant, helicopter, hotballoon, panda1* and *panda2*. There are two reasons for this choice: firstly, these object classes are not included in the PASCAL VOC dataset. Secondly, in order to focus on *objects*, in contrast to *stuff*, we ignore groups like *pyramid, stonehenge* and *taj-mahal*. We compare our method with four state-of-the-art approaches [11,16,17,31] on unseen objects of the iCoseg dataset. Table 4 shows the comparison results of each unseen object groups in terms of *Jaccard*. The results show that for 5 out of 8 object groups our method performs best, and it is also superior on average. Note that the results of [11,16,17,31] are taken from Table X in [17]. Figure 7 shows some qualitative results of our method. It can be seen that our object co-segmentation method can detect and segment the common objects of these unseen classes accurately.

Fig. 7. Our qualitative results on iCoseg dataset (unseen classes). Some results of our object co-segmentation method, with input image pairs in the odd rows and the corresponding object co-segmentation results in the even rows. For this dataset, the object classes were not known during training of our method (i.e. *unseen*).

Table 4. Quantitative results on the iCoseg dataset (unseen classes). Quantitative comparison of our DOCS approach with four state-of-the-art co-segmentation methods on some object classes of the iCoseg dataset, in terms of Jaccard. For this dataset, these object classes were not known during training of our method (i.e. *unseen*).

iCoseg	[31]	[16]	[11]	[17]	Ours
Bear2	65.3	70.1	72.0	67.5	**88.7**
Brownbear	73.6	66.2	**92.0**	72.5	91.5
Cheetah	69.7	75.4	67.0	**78.0**	71.5
Elephant	68.8	73.5	67.0	79.9	**85.1**
Helicopter	80.3	76.6	**82.0**	80.0	73.1
Hotballoon	65.7	76.3	88.0	80.2	**91.1**
Panda1	75.9	80.6	70.0	72.2	**87.5**
Panda2	62.5	71.8	55.0	61.4	**84.7**
Average	70.2	73.8	78.2	74.0	**84.2**

Furthermore to show the effect of number of PASCAL classes on the performance of our approach on unseen classes, we train our network on partial randomly picked PASCAL classes, *i.e.* $\{5, 10, 15\}$, and evaluate it on the iCoseg unseen classes. As it is shown in Table 5, our approach can generalize to unseen classes even when it is trained with only 10 classes from PASCAL.

Table 5. Analyzing the effect of number of training classes on unseen classes.

iCoseg	P(5)	P(10)	P(15)	P(20)
Average	75.5	83.9	83.7	84.2

4.4 Ablation Study

To show the impact of the mutual correlation layer in our network architecture, we design a baseline network *DOCS-Concat* without using mutual correlation layers. In detail, we removed the correlation layer and we concatenate f_A and f_B (instead of C_{AB}) for image I_A and concatenate f_B and f_A (instead of C_{BA}) for image I_B. In Table 6, we compare the performance of different network designs on multiple datasets. As shown, the mutual correlation layer in *DOCS-Corr* improved the performance significantly.

Table 6. Impact of mutual correlation layer.

	DOCS-Concat		DOCS-Corr	
	Precision	Jaccard	Precision	Jaccard
Pascal VOC	92.6	49.9	**94.2**	**64.5**
MSRC	92.6	72.0	**95.4**	**82.9**
Internet	91.8	62.7	**93.5**	**72.6**
iCoseg(unseen)	93.6	78.9	**95.1**	**84.2**

5 Conclusions

In this work, we presented a new and efficient CNN-based method for solving the problem of object class co-segmentation, which consists of jointly detecting and segmenting objects belonging to a common semantic class from a pair of images. Based on a simple encoder-decoder architecture, combined with the mutual correlation layer for matching semantic features, we achieve state-of-the-art performance on various datasets, and demonstrate good generalization performance on segmenting objects of new semantic classes, unseen during training. To train our model, we compile a large object co-segmentation dataset consisting of image pairs from PASCAL dataset with shared objects masks.

Acknowledgements. This work is funded by the DFG grant "COVMAP: Intelligente Karten mittels gemeinsamer GPS- und Videodatenanalyse" (RO 4804/2-1).

References

1. Badrinarayanan, V., Kendall, A., Cipolla, R.: SegNet: a deep convolutional encoder-decoder architecture for scene segmentation. TPAMI **39**, 2481–2495 (2017)
2. Batra, D., Kowdle, A., Parikh, D., Luo, J., Chen, T.: iCoseg: interactive co-segmentation with intelligent scribble guidance. In: CVPR (2010)
3. Boykov, Y.Y., Jolly, M.P.: Interactive graph cuts for optimal boundary & region segmentation of objects in ND images. In: ICCV (2001)
4. Carreira, J., Sminchisescu, C.: Constrained parametric min-cuts for automatic object segmentation. In: CVPR (2010)

5. Chen, L.C., Papandreou, G., Kokkinos, I., Murphy, K., Yuille, A.L.: Semantic image segmentation with deep convolutional nets and fully connected CRFs. In: ICLR (2015)
6. Chen, X., Shrivastava, A., Gupta, A.: Enriching visual knowledge bases via object discovery and segmentation. In: CVPR (2014)
7. Collins, M.D., Xu, J., Grady, L., Singh, V.: Random walks based multi-image segmentation: quasiconvexity results and GPU-based solutions. In: CVPR (2012)
8. Deng, J., Dong, W., Socher, R., Li, L.J., Li, K., Fei-Fei, L.: ImageNet: a large-scale hierarchical image database. In: CVPR (2009)
9. Dong, X., Shen, J., Shao, L., Yang, M.H.: Interactive cosegmentation using global and local energy optimization. IEEE Trans. Image Process. **24**, 3966–3977 (2015)
10. Dosovitskiy, A., et al.: FlowNet: learning optical flow with convolutional networks. In: ICCV (2015)
11. Faktor, A., Irani, M.: Co-segmentation by composition. In: ICCV (2013)
12. Fu, H., Xu, D., Lin, S., Liu, J.: Object-based RGBD image co-segmentation with mutex constraint. In: CVPR (2015)
13. Hariharan, B., Arbelaez, P., Bourdev, L., Maji, S., Malik, J.: Semantic contours from inverse detectors. In: ICCV (2011)
14. Hochbaum, D.S., Singh, V.: An efficient algorithm for co-segmentation. In: ICCV (2009)
15. Jain, S.D., Xiong, B., Grauman, K.: Pixel objectness. arXiv:1701.05349 (2017)
16. Jerripothula, K.R., Cai, J., Meng, F., Yuan, J.: Automatic image co-segmentation using geometric mean saliency. In: ICIP (2014)
17. Jerripothula, K.R., Cai, J., Yuan, J.: Image co-segmentation via saliency co-fusion. IEEE Trans. Multimedia **18**, 1896–1909 (2016)
18. Jia, Y., et al.: Caffe: convolutional architecture for fast feature embedding. In: ACM Multimedia (2014)
19. Joulin, A., Bach, F., Ponce, J.: Discriminative clustering for image co-segmentation. In: CVPR (2010)
20. Kingma, D., Ba, J.: Adam: a method for stochastic optimization. In: ICLR (2015)
21. Kowdle, A., Batra, D., Chen, W.-C., Chen, T.: iModel: interactive co-segmentation for object of interest 3D modeling. In: Kutulakos, K.N. (ed.) ECCV 2010. LNCS, vol. 6554, pp. 211–224. Springer, Heidelberg (2012). https://doi.org/10.1007/978-3-642-35740-4_17
22. Lee, C., Jang, W.D., Sim, J.Y., Kim, C.S.: Multiple random walkers and their application to image cosegmentation. In: CVPR (2015)
23. Li, G., Yu, Y.: Deep contrast learning for salient object detection. In: CVPR (2016)
24. Lin, G., Milan, A., Shen, C., Reid, I.: RefineNet: multi-path refinement networks for high-resolution semantic segmentation. In: CVPR (2017)
25. Long, J., Shelhamer, E., Darrell, T.: Fully convolutional networks for semantic segmentation. In: CVPR (2015)
26. Mukherjee, L., Singh, V., Dyer, C.R.: Half-integrality based algorithms for cosegmentation of images. In: CVPR (2009)
27. Noh, H., Hong, S., Han, B.: Learning deconvolution network for semantic segmentation. In: ICCV (2015)
28. Quan, R., Han, J., Zhang, D., Nie, F.: Object co-segmentation via graph optimized-flexible manifold ranking. In: CVPR (2016)
29. Ronneberger, O., Fischer, P., Brox, T.: U-Net: convolutional networks for biomedical image segmentation. In: Navab, N., Hornegger, J., Wells, W.M., Frangi, A.F. (eds.) MICCAI 2015. LNCS, vol. 9351, pp. 234–241. Springer, Cham (2015). https://doi.org/10.1007/978-3-319-24574-4_28

30. Rother, C., Minka, T., Blake, A., Kolmogorov, V.: Cosegmentation of image pairs by histogram matching-incorporating a global constraint into MRFs. In: CVPR (2006)
31. Rubinstein, M., Joulin, A., Kopf, J., Liu, C.: Unsupervised joint object discovery and segmentation in internet images. In: CVPR (2013)
32. Rubio, J.C., Serrat, J., López, A., Paragios, N.: Unsupervised co-segmentation through region matching. In: CVPR (2012)
33. Shen, T., Lin, G., Liu, L., Shen, C., Reid, I.: Weakly supervised semantic segmentation based on co-segmentation. In: BMVC (2017)
34. Shotton, J., Winn, J., Rother, C., Criminisi, A.: *TextonBoost*: joint appearance, shape and context modeling for multi-class object recognition and segmentation. In: Leonardis, A., Bischof, H., Pinz, A. (eds.) ECCV 2006. LNCS, vol. 3951, pp. 1–15. Springer, Heidelberg (2006). https://doi.org/10.1007/11744023_1
35. Simonyan, K., Zisserman, A.: Very deep convolutional networks for large-scale image recognition. In: ICLR (2015)
36. Taniai, T., Sinha, S.N., Sato, Y.: Joint recovery of dense correspondence and cosegmentation in two images. In: CVPR (2016)
37. Uijlings, J.R., Van De Sande, K.E., Gevers, T., Smeulders, A.W.: Selective search for object recognition. IJCV **104**, 154–171 (2013)
38. Vicente, S., Kolmogorov, V., Rother, C.: Cosegmentation revisited: models and optimization. In: Daniilidis, K., Maragos, P., Paragios, N. (eds.) ECCV 2010. LNCS, vol. 6312, pp. 465–479. Springer, Heidelberg (2010). https://doi.org/10.1007/978-3-642-15552-9_34
39. Vicente, S., Rother, C., Kolmogorov, V.: Object cosegmentation. In: CVPR (2011)
40. Wang, F., Huang, Q., Guibas, L.J.: Image co-segmentation via consistent functional maps. In: ICCV (2013)
41. Wang, L., Wang, L., Lu, H., Zhang, P., Ruan, X.: Saliency detection with recurrent fully convolutional networks. In: Leibe, B., Matas, J., Sebe, N., Welling, M. (eds.) ECCV 2016. LNCS, vol. 9908, pp. 825–841. Springer, Cham (2016). https://doi.org/10.1007/978-3-319-46493-0_50
42. Xu, N., Price, B., Cohen, S., Yang, J., Huang, T.: Deep GrabCut for object selection. In: BMVC (2017)
43. Xu, N., Price, B., Cohen, S., Yang, J., Huang, T.S.: Deep interactive object selection. In: CVPR (2016)
44. Yu, F., Koltun, V.: Multi-scale context aggregation by dilated convolutions. In: ICLR (2016)
45. Yuan, Z., Lu, T., Wu, Y.: Deep-dense conditional random fields for object cosegmentation. In: IJCAI (2017)
46. Zhao, H., Shi, J., Qi, X., Wang, X., Jia, J.: Pyramid scene parsing network. In: CVPR (2017)
47. Zheng, S., et al.: Conditional random fields as recurrent neural networks. In: ICCV (2015)

From Same Photo: Cheating on Visual Kinship Challenges

Mitchell Dawson[1]([⊠]) [iD], Andrew Zisserman[1] [iD], and Christoffer Nellåker[2] [iD]

[1] Visual Geometry Group (VGG), Department of Engineering Science,
University of Oxford, Oxford, UK
{mdawson,az}@robots.ox.ac.uk
[2] Nuffield Department of Women's & Reproductive Health, Big Data Institute,
IBME, University of Oxford, Oxford, UK
christoffer.nellaker@bdi.ox.ac.uk

Abstract. With the propensity for deep learning models to learn unintended signals from data sets there is always the possibility that the network can "cheat" in order to solve a task. In the instance of data sets for visual kinship verification, one such unintended signal could be that the faces are cropped from the same photograph, since faces from the same photograph are more likely to be from the same family. In this paper we investigate the influence of this artefactual data inference in published data sets for kinship verification.

To this end, we obtain a large data set, and train a CNN classifier to determine if two faces are from the same photograph or not. Using this classifier alone as a naive classifier of kinship, we demonstrate near state of the art results on five public benchmark data sets for kinship verification – achieving over 90% accuracy on one of them. Thus, we conclude that faces derived from the same photograph are a strong inadvertent signal in all the data sets we examined, and it is likely that the fraction of kinship explained by existing kinship models is small.

Keywords: Kinship verification · Data set bias · Deep learning · Convolutional neural network

1 Introduction

Kinship verification is the task of determining whether two or more people share a close family relation, using only photographs of their respective faces. Potential uses of kinship verification include being able to organise digital photo albums,

This research was financially supported by the EPSRC programme grant Seebibyte EP/M013774/1, the EPSRC Systems Biology DTC EP/G03706X/1, and the MRC Grant MR/M014568/1.

Electronic supplementary material The online version of this chapter (https://doi.org/10.1007/978-3-030-20893-6_41) contains supplementary material, which is available to authorized users.

C. V. Jawahar et al. (Eds.): ACCV 2018, LNCS 11363, pp. 654–668, 2019.
https://doi.org/10.1007/978-3-030-20893-6_41

Fig. 1. Representative examples of how cropping face images from the same original photo can make the kinship verification a trivial task. Confounding, non–kinship information includes camera specific noise, the background similarity (A, C), the historical era in which the photo was taken (B), image lighting and tone (A, B, C), and the relative age difference between parents and children (A, B, C).

detecting lost children using photos of the child's parents, and in distinguishing family traits from environmental or disease related changes in clinical research contexts.

Over the last few years, several kinship verification data sets have been developed for research groups to benchmark against. These data sets of images and videos have been produced by different groups, and each has its own unique characteristics including variations in the number of images, collection methods, and types of relation included.

In building these data sets for kinship verification, often different individuals' images have been cropped from larger family photos. While this is a good way to find people in the same family it also builds in another clue – a bias that people from the same photo are related. This has been overlooked as a potential issue, as it is far easier to identify whether two face images are from the same original photo than it is to determine if they are kin. As will be demonstrated, in some data sets, this 'from same photograph' (FSP) signal can be used to achieve results comparable to the state of the art (Fig. 1).

There are several cues that can be used to determine if two face images are cropped from the same photograph, and by inference are more likely to be kin. For example, common lighting and shadows, background, blur, resolution, tone, contrast, clothing, camera specific noise and exact regional overlap between crops. Another confounding signal, which is present when parent and child are cropped from the same photo, is that the age difference between the people shown in each crop will be roughly the same as the average age which parents give birth to children.

Deep neural networks are notorious for finding subtle data shortcuts to exploit in order to 'cheat' and thus not learn to solve the task in the desired manner; an example is the misuse of chromatic aberration in [6] to solve the relative-position task. Thus deep learning models are liable to pick up on these FSP cues to gain a boost in performance on kinship tasks.

This problem was raised by Lopez *et al.* [16], who recommended that the two KinFaceW data sets should no longer be used in kinship research. Their work showed that comparable results could be achieved on the data sets using a method with no understanding of kinship: classifying pairs of images based upon the distance between the chrominance averages of images in the Lab color space. Further to this work, Wu *et al.* [28] showed that results on kinship data sets can be improved by using colour images rather than grey-scale images. Although one might expect that skin colour could help to identify kinship relations, it also gives more information about the background and colour distribution of the image, a confounding variable which can be used to improve results on data sets containing images cropped from the same photo.

Other groups have attempted to avoid this issue by using images where each family member is cropped from different original photographs, such as the Family 101 [8] and UBKinFace [30] data sets. However, such images are expensive to find and so photographs of famous people and their children, who have many public images available, are frequently included, introducing a new bias into the data sets.

Many models have already reported on these data sets infected by the signal of pairs cropped from the same photo. Therefore, we would like to benchmark the extent to which these results could have used the 'from same photo' signal. This will provide a clear understanding of how much of the accuracy reported is based upon kinship signals, and how much could have been 'from same photo' signal.

In this paper we benchmark the accuracy which can be achieved on five popular kinship data sets, using only the signal of whether two face images are from the same photo. We achieve this by creating a new data set of 24,827 images, containing 145,618 faces, and 914,517 pairs of faces taken from non-familial group photos. We use this data set to train a CNN classifier to determine if two facial images are cropped from the same original photo or not. Crucially, this classifier has no understanding of kinship relations.

We present results on the KinFaceW-I [19], KinFaceW-II [19], Cornell Kin-Face [9], Families in the Wild (FIW) [24], and TSKinFace [23] data sets. We show that the 'from same photo' signal exists for all of these five data sets. For some, the signal is fairly weak, whereas for others it explains a large proportion of the state of the art results. In many cases we achieve comparable results with other submissions using only the 'from same photo' signal.

2   Training a Classifier to Detect Faces from the Same Photo

In this section, we describe our approach to train a CNN classifier to be able to determine whether two facial images are cropped from the same original photograph or not. For positive training data we use pairs of face images cropped from non-family group photographs. This was done to ensure the classifier could not learn kinship signals between faces. We evaluate the ability of our classifier to classify faces from the same photo on a held out test set.

Fig. 2. Examples of photos found using non-kin group search terms and the Bing Azure API [4]. Pairs of faces found in these images are used in creating the From Same Photo (FSP) data set.

2.1 Generating the FSP Data Set

We would like to build a data set of face images that were cropped from the same original photo, but crucially where the people shown in the face images do not share a kinship relation (Fig. 2).

We began by creating a list of 125 search terms that describe groups of people, who are unlikely to share a kinship relation. These include terms such as 'school students', 'business meeting', 'sport team photos' (the complete list of terms is given in the supplementary material). We then use the Bing Azure API [4] to find URLs of images related to these search terms. We ensure that the images returned are large enough to potentially contain high resolution faces, and that each URL is returned only once in an attempt to avoid duplicate images. These searches result in a list of 81,784 URLs: an average of 654 per search term. We download each image and, with some loss due to moved content and unusable file formats, obtain 76,450 images.

The Dlib face detector [10] is used to find faces within these images. For our purposes, a usable group photo is defined to be an image which contains at least two faces, where the height and width of both face detection regions is not less than 50 pixels. This results in a maximum usable positive data set of 24,827 group photos, which contains 145,618 face images and 914,517 possible pairs of face images. We partition this data set into training (70%), validation (10%) and testing (20%), as shown in Table 1.

Although the vast majority of pairs of faces in the positive FSP data set are correctly labelled, it was found that there are some cases of negative pairs making it through the processing pipeline. For example, some of the group images collected were composite collages of separate photos, and so the faces in the collages were not originally taken from the same photo. Another example which could lead to falsely labelled positive pairs comes from photographs of people standing next to portrait paintings or photographs which contain a face. These faces are also detected by Dlib, and so lead to pairs of faces being falsely labelled as positives. Furthermore, we can not exclude that some images will have true kin related people present in them. Overall, these examples make up a very tiny proportion of the data set, and so it is not expected that they skew our results significantly.

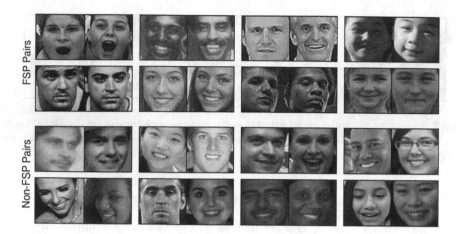

Fig. 3. Examples of pairs of faces used to train the From Same Photo (FSP) classifier. FSP pairs are cropped from the same non-kin group photo. Images in Non-FSP pairs are cropped from separate non-kin group photos.

Training the FSP classifier also requires creating a corresponding negative set of pairs of faces that are cropped from different original photographs. This is achieved by taking each image in the positive data set and randomly swapping one of the faces for another in the same training/validation/testing subset. This ensures that pairs of faces in the negative data set are not from the same photo, and that face photos do not leak across train, validation and testing splits. Furthermore, matching the total number of positive pairs and negative pairs in this way also helps to ensure that the FSP classifier does not learn a bias towards predicting a particular class (Fig. 3).

2.2   The FSP Classifier

In this section we describe the CNN classifier used to detect whether two facial photographs are cropped from the same original image. For training data we use the balanced FSP data set described above in Sect. 2.1. We evaluate the performance of the FSP classifier on a test set of images from the FSP data set, and analyse the results using the standard receiver operating characteristic (ROC) and precision-recall (PR) curves.

Architecture. The CNN architecture can be split into four distinct parts as shown in Fig. 4. The first part consists of two parallel copies of a pre-trained VGG-M-Face, up to the output from the fully connected FC6 layer. This architecture was first used in [2] and has been trained here for facial recognition on the VGGFace data set. The VGG-M-Face networks generate a 4096-dimensional feature vector for each face image of the input pair. Both feature vectors are then fed to a trainable fully connected layer to reduce their dimensionality. These reduced feature vectors are then stacked into a single vector and fed through

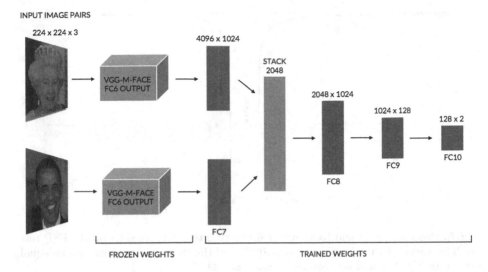

Fig. 4. The FSP network architecture.

three more fully connected layers and ReLU activation functions to produce a two-dimensional vector giving the probability that the pair belongs to the class 'from same photo' or 'not from same photo'. The network is implemented in the PyTorch framework, and the code (and data set) will be made publicly available.

Training. The FSP network was trained using stochastic gradient descent to minimise a softmax cross entropy loss function. During training we freeze the weights of the VGG-M-Face part of the model, but train all other layers. The initial learning rate was set to 0.1, and decreased by a factor of 0.5 every five epochs, until the classifier's performance on the validation set began to saturate. In training we use dropout with $p = 0.1$ between layers FC8 and FC9 to prevent overfitting. During training we augment our input images by resizing them up to 256×256 pixels and taking a random 224×224 pixel crop from the resulting image.

Testing. We evaluate the FSP network on a test set taken from the FSP data set that was not used in training or validation. The testing set consists of 323,236 pairs of face images, half of which are cropped from the same original photo.

Table 1. Summary of the number of pairs of face images in the data sets used to train, validate and test the FSP classifier. The area under receiver operating characteristic curve (ROC AUC) is reported for the FSP classifier on the test set of images

Data set	Train	Validation	Test	ROC AUC (%)
FSP	1,321,440	184,358	323,236	98.1

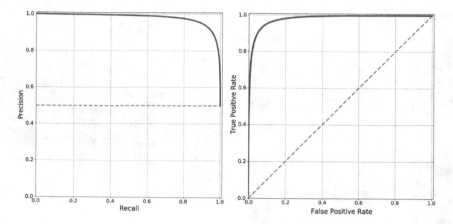

Fig. 5. Precision-recall and ROC curves for testing the FSP classifier on the FSP test set. The area under the ROC curve is 98.09%, and the classifier performs with an equal error rate of 6.97% and an average precision of 98.07%.

At test time we test a pair of images ten times using different permutations of region crops and horizontal flips. The result of these ten tests is then averaged to give the classifier score for a pair of images.

As can be seen in Fig. 5, the FSP classifier is able to tell whether two images are from the same photograph with very high accuracy. Testing resulted in an area under ROC curve of 98.09%, with an equal error rate of 6.97%.

3   Testing FSP Classifier on Kinship Data Sets

Kinship verification tasks have branched into three major challenges, consequently multiple different types of kinship verification data sets have been built. The first type of task is one-to-one kinship verification, where one wishes to determine whether two individuals are related. Alternatively, tri-subject kinship verification is where given a picture of a mother-father and a third person, we wish to determine if the third person is the biological child of the two parents. A final challenge is one-to-many family classification, where one wishes to know which family a person belongs to among a data set. We examined five popular data sets and the degree to which FSP is a biasing factor for the respective one-to-one kinship verification task challenges.

3.1   Kinship Verification Data Sets

KinFaceW-I & KinFaceW-II (Lu et al. [19]*).* These are two widely used kinship verification data sets introduced in 2014. They contain images of public figures paired with their parents or children. They are the most commonly tested on kinship data sets, but were also the first to receive criticism for using images cropped from the same photograph [16]. The KinFaceW-I data set contains pairs of images from the four main bi-subject kinship verification categories: mother-daughter (127 pairs), mother-son (116 pairs), father-daughter (134 pairs), father-son (156 pairs). The major differences between the two data sets are that KinFaceW-II is larger, and contains a greater number of photos cropped from the same original image compared to KinFaceW-I.

Typically these data sets are tested using five-fold cross validation, where both the positive and negative pairs are specified for each of the five folds. Here we collect all the positive and negative pairs across all five folds to create the balanced test set. The KinFaceW-I test set contains 1066 pairs of face images, and the KinFaceW-II test set contains 2000 pairs of face images, with 250 for each of the four major relations.

Cornell KinFace (Fang et al. [9]). This data set was published in 2010 and consists of parents and children of public figures and celebrities. It is the smallest data set among the five tested in this paper, consisting of only 144 positive pairs. Human level performance on this data set was benchmarked as 70.7%. For the negative set we randomly substitute a parent or child from the positive pair with a random parent or child from the remaining positive set. To avoid bias from choosing a particularly easy negative set we average over five different versions of the negative set, randomised uniquely each time.

Families in the Wild (FIW) (Robinson et al. [24]). Families in the wild is by far the largest of the data sets we test on. It contains 1000 families, 10,676 people and 30,725 face images. 418,060 pairs of images, heavily weighted towards over 37,000 pairs for each of the four major parent-child relationships, and over 75,000 for sibling-sibling relationships. The data set was made available as part of the 2018 Recognising Families in the Wild (RFIW) kinship verification challenge. Here we test on the 99,962 pairs of images in the challenge evaluation set.

TSKinFace (Qin et al. [23]). TSKinFace was introduced as an alternative to the growing number of bi-subject kinship verification data sets. For many of the use situations described for kinship verification, such as organising family photo albums or locating missing children, it is likely that pictures of both parents will be available. TSKinFace is the largest publicly available data set of triplet kinship images to date. The data set contains 787 images of 2589 individuals belonging to 1015 tri-subject kinship groups (father-mother-child). The images from TSKinFace are collected from family photographs.

TSKinFace specifies related triplets of father-mother-son and father-mother-daughter. For the negative set they randomly combine images of parents with an image of different child of the same gender as their own. To reduce the probability of reporting results on a particularly easy negative set, we repeated our experiments with a different set of permutations for the children and parents in the negative set each time. The data set is split by the gender of the child with 513 positive father-mother-son (FM-S) triplets and 502 positive father-mother-daughter (FM-D) triplets.

At test time we split each triplet into two pairs, father-child and mother-child. Each pair is then scored by the FSP classifier. We take the maximum of these two scores as the test score for a triplet. This corresponds to asking whether at least one of the parents is cropped from the same original photo as the child.

3.2 Implementation Details

We apply the FSP classifier to the kinship data sets naively, that is to say without further training for the intended kinship verification task. To achieve this we extract each image at three crop sizes. This is required as the Dlib face detector tends to propose tight square regions around the centre of a face, often cutting out chin, tops of heads and ears. However, the face images contained within two of the data sets we test on are more loosely cropped. We found that the greatest accuracy was achieved on KinFaceW-I, KinFaceW-II and FIW using the FSP classifier trained with images cropped to the standard Dlib size. Whereas on Cornell KinFace and TSKinFace, the best results were obtained by expanding the width and height of the images by 15%.

We report the accuracy our FSP classifier is able to obtain on each kinship test set. To determine the accuracy, we set the threshold of our FSP classifier using five-fold cross validation on the test sets. We determine the threshold which produces the maximum achievable accuracy for the FSP classifier on 80% of the test set, then calculate the accuracy on the remaining 20% of the test data for five splits. The mean accuracy across the splits is then reported.

4 Results

We show the results for the FSP classifier as a kinship classifier on the five data sets in Table 2. For each of the bi-subject kinship verification tasks we report high accuracies: KinFaceW-I 76.8%, KinFaceW-II 90.2%, FIW 58.6%, Cornell

Table 2. Results of using the FSP classifier to predict kinship on KinFaceW-I, KinFaceW-II, Cornell KinFace, FIW and TSKinFace data sets. Accuracy percentages are shown for the pair subsets of mother-daughter (MD), mother-son (MS), father-daughter (FD), and father-son (FS), and the triplet subsets of father-mother-daughter (FMD) and father-mother-son (FMS), as well as across the entire test set

Data set	MD	MS	FD	FS	FMD	FMS	All
KinFaceW-I	86.0	78.3	74.1	74.6			76.8
KinFaceW-II	94.8	90.3	84.5	92.3			90.2
FIW	60.3	59.3	59.0	57.5			58.6
TSKinFace					88.6	89.4	88.6
Cornell KinFace							76.7

Fig. 6. Examples found in kinship data sets which we predict are taken from the same photo. Each row corresponds to examples from one of the five analysed kinship data sets. Note the similarities in background, facial pose, lighting, and overall image tone between images cropped from the same original photo.

KinFace 76.7%. There is variance between the tasks depending on the gender of the parent and child in the image. In kinship verification tasks this could be interpreted as perhaps biases in facial similarities between genders, however this is not something we should expect from the FSP classifier. It is more likely to be due to biases in likelihood for various gender pairs of family members to show up together in photographs, or even just stochastic variance from data set sampling.

Table 3. Results of using the FSP classifier to predict kinship, and previously published kinship classifiers on all five kinship data sets. KinFaceW is abbreviated as KFW. Note the high accuracies achieved by using the FSP classifier as a kinship classifier on each data set, in comparison with the average and state-of-the-art maximum accuracies over results reported in previous publications. Also note the available human annotation benchmarks which are all exceeded by the FSP classifier model

Paper	Year	KFW-I	KFW-II	Cornell KF	FIW	TSKinFace
FSP classifier (ours)	2018	76.8	90.2	76.7	58.6	88.6
Mean accuracy[a]		78.3	82.0	79.2	67.2	85.7
Median accuracy[a]		78.8	82.8	79.0	68.8	87.2
Max accuracy		96.9	97.1	94.4	74.9	93.4
Human [9,23,35]		71.0	74.0	67.2		79.5
Aliradi et al. [1]	2018	80.6	88.6			
Moujahid et al. [21]	2018	88.2	88.2			
Lopez et al. [17]	2018	68.4	66.5			
Yan et al. [32]	2018	77.6	78.5			
Robinson et al. [25]	2018	82.4	86.6			
Kohli et al. [12]	2018	96.9	97.1	94.4		
Zhou et al. [36]	2018	82.8	85.7	81.4		
Mahpod et al. [20]	2018	79.8	87.0	76.6		
Zhao et al. [35]	2018	81.5	82.5	81.7		84.5
Wang et al. [26]	2018				69.5	
Xia et al. [29]	2018					90.7
Yang et al. [33]	2017	88.6	90.3			93.4
Chen et al. [3]	2017	83.3	84.3			
Lu et al. [18]	2017	83.5	84.3			
Patel et al. [22]	2017	78.7	80.6			
Kohli et al. [11]	2017	96.1	96.2	89.5		
Laiadi et al. [13]	2017			83.2	54.8	
Duan et al. [7]	2017				66.6	
Dahan et al. [5]	2017				65.0	
Li et al. [14]	2017				74.9	
Wang et al. [27]	2017				68.8	
Zhou et al. [37]	2016	78.8	75.7			
Xu et al. [31]	2016	77.9	77.1			
Liu et al. [15]	2016	77.9	81.4	75.9		
Zhang et al. [34]	2016					89.7
Robinson et al. [24]	2016				71.0	
Qin et al. [23]	2015					85.4
Lu et al [19]	2014	69.9	76.5	66.5		72.1
Fang et al. [9]	2010			70.7		

[a]Some results have been omitted due to page length constraints. These statistics are calculated using the full table of results, available in the Arxiv version of the paper.

Fig. 7. Examples of non-kinship pairs that the classifier incorrectly predicted as being from the same photo. Pairs shown, from left top right, are from the KinFaceW-I, Families in the Wild and Cornell KinFace data sets respectively.

In Table 3, we show summary statistics across a large number of published kinship verification models on the various data sets, and show that the FSP classifier performs kinship classification as well or better than most of them. We also achieve high accuracies for the tri-subject verification data set beating many published models and near the state-of-the-art published results (Table 3, TSKinFace 88.6%). In this instance there is no significant gender bias in accuracy of verification of kinship for the gender of the child. Finally, we can see that the FSP classifier consistently outperforms human classification of kinship. We can expect that the deep learning models will have inadvertently learnt the FSP signal as a means to solve the kinship verification task, but can only speculate if human classifiers uses the same type of information to simplify the task. Examples of positive kin pairs and triplets found by the FSP classifier are shown in Fig. 6. A selection of pairs the classifier falsely predicted as being from the same photo are displayed in Fig. 7.

5   Conclusions

In this work, we have applied a 'from same photograph' (FSP) classifier as a naive classifier of kinship to five data sets regularly used for kinship verification tasks, and thereby have estimated the degree to which the FSP signal contaminates these data sets. The FSP classifier performs amongst the best published kinship classifier models, despite not being trained for this primary task. It is likely that deep neural network models built with the intention to verify kinship, are instead primarily using this much easier to detect FSP signal. We have also obtained a new data set for training classifiers to detect facial crops from the same photograph to begin to address this problem.

Furthermore, it is important to note that there are many other spurious signals that one should expect in kinship verification data sets. For instance, deep learning kinship classifiers would also be expected to learn biases in distributions of age, gender and particularly ancestral backgrounds. Due to the way the FSP classifier has been trained it is blind to many of these other confounding non-kinship signals contained within existing kinship data sets.

We recommend that an FSP classifier should be an important part of kinship data set production pipelines: either to ensure the FSP signal is removed entirely, or is balanced between positive and negative kin pairs. It should be considered that inappropriate construction of negative sets can introduce biases by overly simplifying the task, such as generating father-father-child tri-subjects, mismatched ancestral backgrounds, and implausible age distributions (such as a child older than the parents). Kinship verification is a challenging task made more difficult by inherent biases in how data occurs in the wild. Sharing a photograph does not make us relatives, but we are likely to share a photograph if we are.

References

1. Aliradi, R., Belkhir, A., Ouamane, A., Elmaghraby, A.S.: DIEDA: discriminative information based on exponential discriminant analysis combined with local features representation for face and kinship verification. Multimedia Tools Appl. 1–18 (2018). https://link.springer.com/search?query=dieda&search-within=Journal& facet-journal-id=11042. https://link.springer.com/journal/11042/onlineFirst
2. Chatfield, K., Simonyan, K., Vedaldi, A., Zisserman, A.: Return of the devil in the details: delving deep into convolutional nets. arXiv preprint arXiv:1405.3531 (2014)
3. Chen, X., An, L., Yang, S., Wu, W.: Kinship verification in multi-linear coherent spaces. Multimedia Tools Appl. **76**(3), 4105–4122 (2017)
4. Corporation, M.: Bing Image Search API (2018). https://azure.microsoft.com/en-us/services/cognitive-services/bing-image-search-api/
5. Dahan, E., Keller, Y., Mahpod, S.: Kin-verification model on FIW dataset using multi-set learning and local features. In: Proceedings of the 2017 Workshop on Recognizing Families In the Wild, pp. 31–35. ACM (2017)
6. Doersch, C., Gupta, A., Efros, A.A.: Unsupervised visual representation learning by context prediction. In: International Conference on Computer Vision (ICCV) (2015)
7. Duan, Q., Zhang, L.: AdvNet: adversarial contrastive residual net for 1 million kinship recognition. In: Proceedings of the 2017 Workshop on Recognizing Families In the Wild, pp. 21–29. ACM (2017)
8. Fang, R., Gallagher, A.C., Chen, T., Loui, A.: Kinship classification by modeling facial feature heredity. In: 2013 20th IEEE International Conference on Image Processing (ICIP), pp. 2983–2987. IEEE (2013)
9. Fang, R., Tang, K.D., Snavely, N., Chen, T.: Towards computational models of kinship verification. In: 2010 17th IEEE International Conference on Image Processing (ICIP), pp. 1577–1580. IEEE (2010)
10. King, D.E.: Dlib-ml: a machine learning toolkit. J. Mach. Learn. Res. **10**, 1755–1758 (2009)
11. Kohli, N., Vatsa, M., Singh, R., Noore, A., Majumdar, A.: Hierarchical representation learning for kinship verification. IEEE Trans. Image Process. **26**(1), 289–302 (2017)
12. Kohli, N., Yadav, D., Vatsa, M., Singh, R., Noore, A.: Supervised mixed normautoencoder for kinship verification in unconstrained videos. IEEE Trans. Image Process. **28**(3), 1329–1341 (2018)
13. Laiadi, O., Ouamane, A., Benakcha, A., Taleb-Ahmed, A.: RFIW 2017: LPQ-SIEDA for large scale kinship verification. In: Proceedings of the 2017 Workshop on Recognizing Families In the Wild, pp. 37–39. ACM (2017)
14. Li, Y., et al.: KinNet: fine-to-coarse deep metric learning for kinship verification. In: Proceedings of the 2017 Workshop on Recognizing Families In the Wild, pp. 13–20. ACM (2017)

15. Liu, Q., Puthenputhussery, A., Liu, C.: A novel inheritable color space with application to kinship verification. In: 2016 IEEE Winter Conference on Applications of Computer Vision (WACV), pp. 1–9. IEEE (2016)
16. López, M.B., Boutellaa, E., Hadid, A.: Comments on the "kinship face in the wild" data sets. IEEE Trans. Pattern Anal. Mach. Intell. **38**(11), 2342–2344 (2016)
17. Lopez, M.B., Hadid, A., Boutellaa, E., Goncalves, J., Kostakos, V., Hosio, S.: Kinship verification from facial images and videos: human versus machine. Mach. Vis. Appl. **29**(5), 873–890 (2018)
18. Lu, J., Hu, J., Tan, Y.P.: Discriminative deep metric learning for face and kinship verification. IEEE Trans. Image Process. **26**(9), 4269–4282 (2017)
19. Lu, J., Zhou, X., Tan, Y.P., Shang, Y., Zhou, J.: Neighborhood repulsed metric learning for kinship verification. IEEE Trans. Pattern Anal. Mach. Intell. **36**(2), 331–345 (2014)
20. Mahpod, S., Keller, Y.: Kinship verification using multiview hybrid distancelearning. Comput. Vis. Image Underst. **167**, 28–36 (2017)
21. Moujahid, A., Dornaika, F.: A pyramid multi-level face descriptor: application to kinship verification. Multimedia Tools Appl. **78**(7), 9335–9354 (2019). https://doi.org/10.1007/s11042-018-6517-0
22. Patel, B., Maheshwari, R., Raman, B.: Evaluation of periocular features for kinship verification in the wild. Comput. Vis. Image Underst. **160**, 24–35 (2017)
23. Qin, X., Tan, X., Chen, S.: Tri-subject kinship verification: understanding the core of a family. IEEE Trans. Multimedia **17**(10), 1855–1867 (2015)
24. Robinson, J.P., Shao, M., Wu, Y., Fu, Y.: Families in the wild (FIW): large-scale kinship image database and benchmarks. In: Proceedings of the 2016 ACM on Multimedia Conference, pp. 242–246. ACM (2016)
25. Robinson, J.P., Shao, M., Wu, Y., Liu, H., Gillis, T., Fu, Y.: Visual kinshiprecognition of families in the wild. IEEE Trans. Pattern Anal. Mach. Intell. **40**(11), 2624–2637 (2018)
26. Wang, S., Ding, Z., Fu, Y.: Cross-generation kinship verification with sparsediscriminative metric. IEEE Trans. Pattern Anal. Mach. Intell. 1 (2018). https://ieeexplore.ieee.org/search/searchresult.jsp?newsearch=true&queryText=cross-generation&searchWithin=%22Publication%20Number%22:34
27. Wang, S., Robinson, J.P., Fu, Y.: Kinship verification on families in the wild with marginalized denoising metric learning. In: 2017 12th IEEE International Conference on Automatic Face & Gesture Recognition (FG 2017), pp. 216–221. IEEE (2017)
28. Wu, X., Boutellaa, E., López, M.B., Feng, X., Hadid, A.: On the usefulness of color for kinship verification from face images. In: 2016 IEEE International Workshop on Information Forensics and Security (WIFS), pp. 1–6. IEEE (2016)
29. Xia, C., Xia, S., Zhou, Y., Zhang, L., Shao, M.: Graph based family relationship recognition from a single image. In: Geng, X., Kang, B.-H. (eds.) PRICAI 2018. LNCS (LNAI), vol. 11012, pp. 310–320. Springer, Cham (2018). https://doi.org/10.1007/978-3-319-97304-3_24
30. Xia, S., Shao, M., Fu, Y.: Kinship verification through transfer learning. In: Proceedings of the Twenty-Second International Joint Conference on Artificial Intelligence - Volume Volume Three, IJCAI 2011, pp. 2539–2544. AAAI Press (2011)
31. Xu, M., Shang, Y.: Kinship verification using facial images by robust similarity learning. Math. Probl. Eng. **2016**, 8 p. (2016). Article ID 4072323. https://www.hindawi.com/journals/mpe/2016/4072323/cta/
32. Yan, H.: Learning discriminative compact binary face descriptor for kinship verification. Pattern Recogn. Lett. **117**, 146–152 (2018)

33. Yang, Y., Wu, Q.: A novel kinship verification method based on deep transfer learning and feature nonlinear mapping. DEStech Trans. Comput. Sci. Eng. AIEA (2017). http://dpi-proceedings.com/index.php/dtcse/issue/view/163/showToc. http://dpi-proceedings.com/index.php/dtcse/issue/view/163
34. Zhang, J., Xia, S., Pan, H., Qin, A.: A genetics-motivated unsupervised model for tri-subject kinship verification. In: 2016 IEEE International Conference on Image Processing (ICIP), pp. 2916–2920. IEEE (2016)
35. Zhao, Y.G., Song, Z., Zheng, F., Shao, L.: Learning a multiple kernel similarity metric for kinship verification. Inf. Sci. **430**, 247–260 (2018)
36. Zhou, X., Jin, K., Xu, M., Guo, G.: Learning deep compact similarity metric forkinship verification from face images. Inf. Fusion **48**, 84–94 (2018)
37. Zhou, X., Shang, Y., Yan, H., Guo, G.: Ensemble similarity learning for kinship verification from facial images in the wild. Inf. Fusion **32**, 40–48 (2016)

Class-Agnostic Counting

Erika Lu, Weidi Xie$^{(\boxtimes)}$, and Andrew Zisserman

Visual Geometry Group, University of Oxford, Oxford, UK
{erika,weidi,az}@robots.ox.ac.uk

Abstract. Nearly all existing counting methods are designed for a specific object class. Our work, however, aims to create a counting model able to count any class of object. To achieve this goal, we formulate counting as a matching problem, enabling us to exploit the image self-similarity property that naturally exists in object counting problems.

We make the following three contributions: *first*, a Generic Matching Network (GMN) architecture that can potentially count any object in a class-agnostic manner; *second*, by reformulating the counting problem as one of matching objects, we can take advantage of the abundance of video data labeled for tracking, which contains natural repetitions suitable for training a counting model. Such data enables us to train the GMN. *Third*, to customize the GMN to different user requirements, an adapter module is used to specialize the model with minimal effort, i.e. using a few labeled examples, and adapting only a small fraction of the trained parameters. This is a form of few-shot learning, which is practical for domains where labels are limited due to requiring expert knowledge (e.g. microbiology).

We demonstrate the flexibility of our method on a diverse set of existing counting benchmarks: specifically cells, cars, and human crowds. The model achieves competitive performance on cell and crowd counting datasets, and surpasses the state-of-the-art on the car dataset using only three training images. When training on the entire dataset, the proposed method outperforms all previous methods by a large margin.

Keywords: Category-agnostic object counting ·
Convolutional neural networks · Deep learning

1 Introduction

The objective of this paper is to count objects of interest in an image. In the literature, object counting methods are generally cast into two categories: detection-based counting [5,10,16] or regression-based counting [2,4,8,19,21,24,34]. The former relies on a visual object detector that can localize object instances in an image; this method, however, requires training individual detectors for different objects, and the detection problem remains challenging if only a small number of annotations are given. The latter avoids solving the hard detection problem – instead, methods are designed to learn either a mapping from global image features to a scalar (number of objects), or a mapping from dense image features

© Springer Nature Switzerland AG 2019
C. V. Jawahar et al. (Eds.): ACCV 2018, LNCS 11363, pp. 669–684, 2019.
https://doi.org/10.1007/978-3-030-20893-6_42

Fig. 1. The model (trained on tracking data) can count an object, e.g. windows or columns, specified as an exemplar patch (in red), without additional training. The heat maps indicate the localizations of the repeated objects. This image is unseen during training. (Color figure online)

to a density map, achieving better results on counting overlapping instances. However, previous methods for both categories of method (detection, regression) have only developed algorithms that can count a particular class of objects (e.g. cars, cells, penguins, people).

The objective of this paper is a class-agnostic counting network – one that is able to flexibly count object instances in an image by, for example, simply specifying an exemplar patch of interest as illustrated in Fig. 1. To achieve this, we build on a property of images that has been largely ignored explicitly in previous counting approaches – that of *image self-similarity*. At a simplistic level, an image is deemed self-similar if patches repeat to some approximation – for example if patches can be represented by other patches in the same image. Self-similarity has underpinned applications for many vision tasks, ranging from texture synthesis [11], to image denoising [7], to super-resolution [13].

Giving the observation of self-similarity, image counting can be recast as an image *matching* problem – counting instances is performed by matching (self-similar patches) within the same image. To this end we develop a *Generic Matching Network* (GMN) that learns a discriminative classifier to match instances of the exemplar. Furthermore, since matching variations of an object instance within an image is similar to matching variations of an object instance between images, we can take advantage of the abundance of video data labeled for tracking which contains natural repetitions, to train the GMN. This observation, that matching within an image can be thought of as tracking within an image, was previously made by Leung and Malik [22] for the case of repeated elements in an image.

Beyond generic counting, there is often a need to *specialize* matching to more restrictive or general requirements. For example, to count only red cars (rather than all cars) or to count cars at all orientations (which goes beyond simple similarity measures such as squared sum of differences), extending the intra-class variation for the object category of interest [14,18]. To this end, we include an adaptor module that enables fast domain adaptation [28] and few-shot learning [32,33], through the training of a small number of tunable parameters, using very few annotated data.

In the following sections, we begin by detailing the design and training procedure of the GMN in Sect. 2, and demonstrate its capabilities on a set of example counting tasks. In Sect. 3, we adapt the GMN to specialize on several counting benchmark datasets, including the VGG synthetic cells, HeLa cells, and cars captured by drones. During adaptation, only a small number of parameters (3% of the network size) are added and trained on the target domain. Using a very small number of training samples (as few as 3 images for the car dataset), the results achieved are either comparable to, or surpass the current state-of-the-art methods by a large margin. In Sect. 4, we further extend the counting-by-matching idea to a more challenging scenario: Shanghaitech crowd counting, and demonstrate promising results by matching image statistics on scenes where accurate instance-level localization is unobtainable.

2 Method

In this paper, we consider the problem of instance counting, where the objects to be counted in a single query are from the same category, such as the windows on a building, cars in a parking lot, or cells of a certain type.

To exploit the *self-similarity* property, the counting problem is reformalized as localizing and counting "repeated" instances by *matching*. We propose a novel architecture – GMN, and a counting approach which requires learning a comparison scheme for two given objects (patches) in a metric space. The structure of the model naturally accommodates class-agnostic counting, as it learns to search for repetitions of an exemplar patch containing the desired instance. Note that, the concept of *repetition* is defined in a very broad sense; in the following experiments, we show that objects with various shapes, overlaps, and complicated appearance changes can still be treated as "repeated" instances.

The entire GMN consists of three modules, namely, *embedding, matching*, and *adapting*, as illustrated in Fig. 2. In the *embedding* module, a two-stream network is used to encode the exemplar image patch and the full-resolution image into a feature vector and dense feature map, respectively. In the *matching* module, we learn a discriminative classifier to densely match the exemplar patch to instances in the image. Such learning overcomes within image variations such as illumination changes, small rotations, etc. The object locations and final count can then be acquired by simply taking the *local maximums* or *integration* over the output similarity maps, respectively. Empirically, integral-based counting shows better performance in scenarios where instances have significant overlap, while local max counting is preferred where objects are well-separated, and the positional information is of interest for further processing (e.g. seeds for segmentation).

To avoid the time-consuming collection of annotations for counting data, we use the observation that repetitions occur naturally in videos, as objects are seen under varying viewing conditions from frame to frame. Consequently, we can train the generic matching network with the extensive training data available for tracking (specifically the ILSVRC video dataset for object detection [31]). In total, the dataset contains nearly 4500 videos and over $1M$ annotated frames.

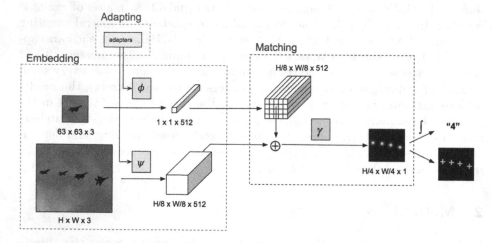

Fig. 2. The GMN architecture consists of three modules: embedding, matching, and adapting. The final count and detections are obtained by taking the integral and local maximums, respectively, over the output heatmap. The integral-based method is used for counting instances with significant overlap, while the local max is used where objects are well-separated and the positional information is of interest for further processing. The $\oplus$ represents channel-wise concatenation.

Given a trained matching model, several factors can prevent it from generalizing perfectly onto the target domain: for instance, the image statistics can be very different from the training set (e.g. natural images vs. microscopy images), or the user requirements can be different (e.g. counting cars vs. counting only red cars). Efficient domain adaptation requires a module that can change the network activations with minimal effort (that is, minimal number of trainable parameters and very few training data). Thus, for the *adapting* stage, we incorporate residual adapter modules [28] to specialize the GMN to such needs. Adapting to the new counting task then merely involves freezing the majority of parameters in the generic matching network, and training the adapters (a small number of extra parameters) on the target domain with only a few labeled examples.

2.1   Embedding

In this module, a two-stream network is defined for transforming raw RGB images into high-level feature encodings. The two streams are parametrized by separate functions for higher representation capacity:

$$v = \phi(z; \theta_1) \qquad f = \psi(x; \theta_2)$$

In detail, the function ϕ transforms an exemplar image patch $z \in R^{63 \times 63 \times 3}$ to a feature vector $v \in R^{1 \times 1 \times 512}$, and ψ maps the full image $x \in R^{H \times W \times 3}$ to a feature map $f \in R^{H/8 \times W/8 \times 512}$. Both the vector v and feature maps f are L2 normalized along the feature dimensions. In practice, our choices for $\phi(\cdot; \theta_1)$ and $\psi(\cdot; \theta_2)$ are ResNet-50 networks [15] truncated after the final conv3_x layer. The resulting feature map from the image patch is globally max-pooled into the feature vector v.

2.2 Matching

The relations between the resulting feature vector and maps are modeled by a trainable function $\gamma(\cdot; \theta_3)$ that takes the concatenation of v and f as input, and outputs a similarity heat map, as shown in Fig. 2. Before concatenation, v is broadcast to match the size of the feature maps to accommodate the fully convolutional feature, which allows for efficient modeling of the relations between the exemplar object and all other objects in the image. The similarity Sim is given by

$$Sim = \gamma([broadcast(v) : f]; \theta_3)$$

where ":" refers to concatenation, and $\gamma(\cdot; \theta_3)$ is parametrized by one 3×3 convolutional layer and one 3×3 convolutional transpose layer with stride 2 (for upsampling).

2.3 Training Generic Matching Networks

The generic matching network (consisting of embedding and matching modules) is trained on the ILSVRC video dataset. The ground truth label is a Gaussian placed at each instance location, multiplied by a scaling factor of 100, and a weighted MSE (Mean Squared Error) loss is used. Regressing a Gaussian allows the final count to be obtained by simply summing over the output similarity map, which in this sense doubles as a density map.

During training, the exemplar images are re-scaled to size 63×63 pixels, with the object of interest centered to fit the patch, and the larger 255×255 search image is taken as a crop centered around the scaled object (architecture details can be found in the arXiv version.) More precisely, we always scale the search image according to the bounding box (w,h) of the exemplar objects, where the scale factor is obtained by solving $s \times h \times w = 63^2$. The input data is augmented with horizontal flips and small ($<25°$) rotations and zooms, and we sample both positive and negative pairs. In all subsequent experiments, the network has been pre-trained as described here.

Once trained on the tracking data, the model can be directly applied for detecting repetitions within an image. We show a number of example predictions in Fig. 3. Note here, several interesting phenomena can be seen: *first*, as expected, the generic matching network has learned to match instances beyond a simplistic level; for instance, the animals are of different viewpoints, the bird in the fourth row is partially occluded, and the persons are not only partially occluded, but also in different shirts with substantial appearance variations; *second,* object overlaps can also be handled, as shown in the airplane cases; *third,* although the ImageNet training set is only composed of natural images, and none of the categories has a similar appearance or distribution to the HeLa cells, the generic matching network succeeds despite large appearance and shape variations which exist for cells. These results validate our idea of building a class-agnostic counting network. However, it is crucial to be able to easily *adapt* the pre-trained model to further specialize to new domains.

2.4   Adapting

The next objective is to specialize the network to new domains or new user requirements. We add *residual adapter modules* [28] implemented as 1×1 convolutions in parallel with the existing 3×3 convolutions in the embedding module of the network. During adaptation, we freeze all of the parameters in the pre-trained generic matching network, and train only the adapters and batch normalization layers. This results in 178K trainable parameters out of a total network size of 6.0M parameters, only 3% of the total.

2.5   Discussion and Relation to Prior Work

Object counting poses certain additional challenges that are less prominent or non-existent in tracking. First, rather than requiring a single maximum in a candidate window (that localizes the object), counting requires a clean output map to distinguish multiple matches from noise and false positives. Second, unlike the continuous variation of object shape and appearance in the tracking problem, object counting can have more challenging appearance changes, e.g. large degrees of rotation, and intra-class variation (in the case of cars, both color and shape). Thus, we find the approaches used in template matching (SSD or cross-correlation [6,9,22]) to be insufficient for our purposes (as will be shown in Table 3). To address these challenges, we learn a discriminative classifier $\gamma(\cdot; \theta_3)$ between the exemplar patch and search image, an idea that dates back to [23].

The residual adapters [28] are added only to the embedding module, but we train the batch normalization layers throughout the entire network. Marsden et al. [25] also use residual adapters to adapt a network for counting different objects. However, they place the modules in the final fully connected layers in order to regress a count, whereas we add them to the convolutional layers in the residual blocks of the embedding module, such that they are able to change the filter responses at every stage of the base model, providing more capacity for adaptation.

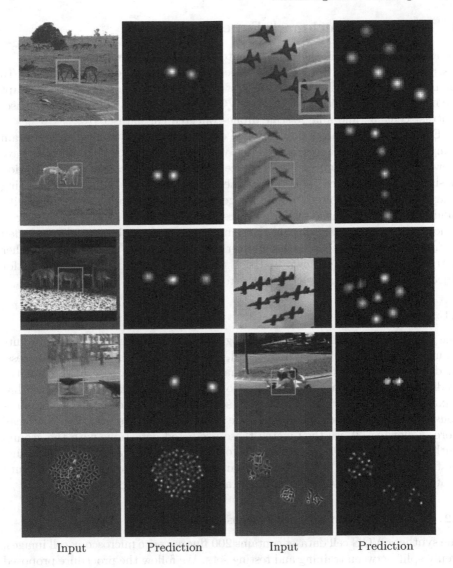

Input   Prediction   Input   Prediction

Fig. 3. Similarity predictions of the generic matching network on the video validation set, and on an *unseen* dataset of HeLa cells. The exemplar patch is marked with a red square. Images are padded with the mean value and the resolution has been changed for visualization purposes. As expected, the generic matching network has learned to match instances beyond a simplistic level; for instance, the animals are of different viewpoints, the matched bird in the fourth row is partially occluded, and the people are in different colored shirts. More interestingly, it acts as an excellent initialization for objects from unseen domains, even in the presence of large appearance and shape variation in the case of HeLa cells. (Color figure online)

3   Counting Benchmark Experiments

As a proof of concept, the generic matching network is visually validated as a strong initialization for counting objects from unseen domains (Fig. 3). To further demonstrate the effectiveness of the general-purpose GMN, we adapt the network to three different datasets: VGG synthetic cells [20,21], HeLa phase-contrast cells [3], and a large-scale drone-collected car dataset [16].

Each of these datasets poses unique challenges. The synthetic cells contain many overlapping instances, a condition where density estimation methods have shown strong performance. The HeLa cells exhibit significantly more variation in size and appearance than the synthetic cells, and the number of training images is extremely limited (only 11 images); thus, detection-based methods with handcrafted features have shown good results. In the car dataset, cars appear in various orientations, often within the same image, and can be partially occluded by trees and bridges; there is also clutter from motorbikes, buildings, and other distractors (Fig. 6). As shown in Hsieh et al. [16], state-of-the-art models for object detection produce a very high error rate.

3.1   Evaluation Metrics

The metrics we use for evaluation throughout this paper are the mean absolute counting error (MAE), precision, recall, and F_1 score. To determine successful detections, we first take the local maximums (above a threshold T) of the predicted similarity map as the detections. T is usually set as the value that maximizes the F_1 score on a validation set. Note that, since multiple combinations of recall and precision can give the same F_1 score, we prioritize the recall score. Following [3], we then match these predicted detections with the ground truth locations using the Hungarian algorithm, with the constraint that a successful detection must lie no further than a tolerance R from the ground truth location, where R is set as the average radius of each object.

3.2   Synthetic Fluorescence Microscopy

The synthetic VGG cell dataset contains 200 fluorescence microscopy cell images, evenly split between training and testing sets. We follow the procedure proposed by Lempitsky and Zisserman [21] of sampling 5 random splits of the training set with N training images and N validation images. Results in Table 1 and Fig. 4 show that our method is not restricted to detection-based counting, but also performs well on density estimation-type problems in a setting with high instance overlap. Note that, we compare with methods that are highly engineered for this dataset.

3.3   HeLa Cells on Phase Contrast Microscopy

The dataset contains 11 training and 11 testing images. We follow the training procedure of [3] and train in a leave-one-out fashion for selecting hyperparameters, e.g. detection threshold T. Results are shown in Table 2. As shown

Table 1. Results for the synthetic cell dataset. All methods are trained on the $N = 32$ split. Standard deviations are calculated using 5 random splits of training and validation sets and 5 randomly sampled exemplar patches per image. Note here, the exemplar patches are sampled from images in the training set, and different exemplar patches have negligible effect on performance.

Method	MAE	Precision	Recall	F_1-score
Xie et al. [34]	2.9 ± 0.2	-	-	-
Fiaschi et al. [12]	3.2 ± 0.1	-	-	-
Lempitsky and Zisserman [21]	3.5 ± 0.2	-	-	-
Barinova et al. [5]	6.0 ± 0.5	-	-	-
Singletons [3]	51.2 ± 0.8	98.87 ± 1.52	72.07 ± 0.85	83.37 ± 1.20
Full system w/o surface [3]	5.06 ± 0.2	95.00 ± 0.75	91.97 ± 0.43	93.46 ± 0.15
Ours	3.56 ± 0.27	99.43 ± 0.05	82.50 ± 0.15	90.18 ± 0.07

in Fig. 5, our method performs well in scenarios of large intra-class variations in shape and size, where SSD and cross-correlation would suffer. Overall, our GMN achieves comparable results to the conventional methods with hand-crafted features, despite the training dataset being extremely small for current deep learning standards.

Table 2. Results for the HeLa cell dataset. We calculate MAE using the detection counts, since the instances are well-separated. Our standard deviations are calculated using 5 randomly sampled exemplar patches per image. Note here, the 5 exemplar patches are sampled from images in the training set; different exemplar patches have negligible effect on performance.

Method	MAE	Precision	Recall	F_1-score
Correlation clustering [36]	-	-	-	95
Singletons [3]	2.36 ± 0.67	93.70 ± 0.20	91.94 ± 0.72	92.81 ± 0.35
Full system w/o surface [3]	3.84 ± 1.44	98.51 ± 1.16	95.76 ± 0.27	97.10 ± 0.27
Ours	3.53 ± 0.18	96.05 ± 0.04	94.22 ± 0.06	95.12 ± 0.05

3.4 Cars

We next demonstrate the GMN's performance on counting cars in aerial images. This drone-collected dataset (CARPK) consists of 989 training images and 459 testing images (nearly 90,000 instances of cars), where the images are taken from overhead shots of car parking lots. The training images are taken from three different parking lot scenes, and the test set is taken from a fourth scene. We compare our network to the region proposal and classification methods in Table 3.

In the experiments, we train two GMN models with augmentation: one on just three images (99 total cars) randomly sampled from the training scenes,

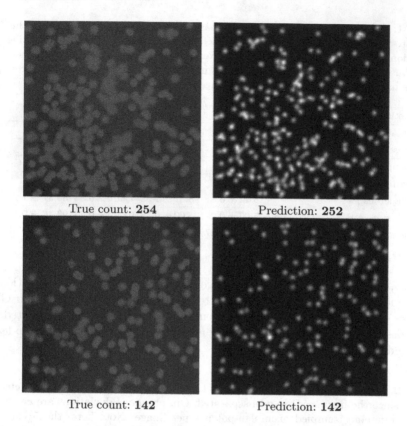

Fig. 4. Example of counting results on synthetic cell images. For each pair of images, left: original image, and right: the network's predicted heat map, which is *summed* to give the estimated count.

which achieves state-of-the-art results, and one on the full CARPK training set, which further boosts the performance by a large margin.

When determining counts based on local maximums, we note it is possible that our model outperforms the previous detection-based methods due to false positives and false negatives "canceling" each other, making the counting error very low. Thus, we investigate effects of the threshold T (as defined in Sect. 3.1) on selecting detections from candidate local maximums, and report results for several values of T. Note that, by varying this hyperparameter, we are able to explicitly control the precision-recall of our model. While calculating recall and precision, we consider a detection to be successful if it lies within 20 pixels (determined based on the mean car size) of the ground truth location. The recall reported for the region proposal methods in Table 3 is calculated by averaging across scores from using various IoU thresholds, as described in [16].

As shown in Table 3, the MAE is calculated with 5 randomly sampled exemplar patches per image, and the final counts are obtained by counting local max-

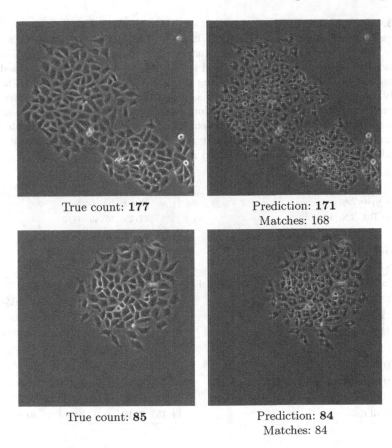

True count: **177**

Prediction: **171**
Matches: 168

True count: **85**

Prediction: **84**
Matches: 84

Fig. 5. Example detection results on the HeLa cell test set. Correct detections (based on Hungarian matching) are marked with a green '+', false positives with a red 'x', and missed detections with a yellow 'o'. (Color figure online)

imums (detection-based counting). Note here, the exemplar patches are sampled from images in the training set, and different exemplar patches have negligible effect on performance. We can see that even with a very high precision (model trained on the full dataset, with $T = 2.75$), our model can still outperform the previous state-of-the-art by a substantial margin (counting error: $MAE = 23.8$ vs $MAE = 19.7$). Further decreasing the threshold yields higher recall at the expense of precision, with our best model achieving a counting error of $MAE = 7.5$.

3.5 Discussion

From our experiments, the following phenomena can be observed:

First, in contrast to previous work, where different architectures are designed for density estimation in scenarios with significant instance overlap (e.g. VGG

Table 3. Mean Absolute Error (MAE), Root Mean Squared Error (RMSE), Recall and Precision comparisons on the CARPK dataset. The "*" indicates that the method has been fine tuned on the full dataset, and the "†" indicates that the method has been revised to fit the dataset, as described in [16]. We show our method trained on 3 images and on the full dataset, with varying thresholds T. We calculate MAE using 5 randomly sampled exemplar patches per image, and the final counts are obtained from local maximums (counting by detection). Note here, the exemplar patches are sampled from images in the training set, and different exemplar patches have negligible effect on performance. Standard deviation is not reported in this table, but can be easily computed following the previously reported manner.

Method	T	MAE	RMSE	Recall	Precision
*YOLO [16,29]	-	48.89	57.55	-	-
*Faster R-CNN [16,30]	-	47.45	57.39	-	-
*Faster R-CNN (RPN-small) [16,30]	-	24.32	37.62	-	-
†One-Look Regression [16,26]	-	59.46	66.84	-	-
*Spatially Regularized RPN [16]	-	23.80	36.79	57.5%	-
Template matching (Sum of Squared Distances)	-	49.8	59.7	20.0%	29.1%
Ours (3 images, 99 cars)	2.5	36.71	44.16	60.65%	93.91%
Ours (3 images, 99 cars)	2	22.32	28.72	71.32%	90.23%
Ours (3 images, 99 cars)	1.75	17.32	22.81	74.16%	87.87%
Ours (3 images, 99 cars)	1.5	13.38	18.03	76.1%	85.1%
Ours (full dataset)	2.75	19.66	25.12	78.61%	97.0%
Ours (full dataset)	2.5	14.36	19.01	83.2%	96.0%
Ours (full dataset)	2	8.38	11.55	87.46%	93.4%
Ours (full dataset)	1.75	**7.48**	**9.9**	88.4%	91.8%

synthetic cells) and for detection-based counting in scenarios with well-separated objects (e.g. HeLa cells and cars), the GMN has the flexibility to handle both scenarios. Based on the amount of instance overlap, the object counts can simply be obtained by taking either the integral in the former case, or the local maximum in the latter, or possibly even an ensemble of them [17].

Second, by training in a discriminative manner, the GMN is able to match instances beyond the simplistic level, making it more robust to large degrees of rotation and appearance variation than the baseline SSD-based template matching (as shown in Table 3).

Third, in the cases where training data is limited (11 images for HeLa cells, 3 for cars), the proposed model has consistently shown comparable or superior performance to the state-of-the-art methods, indicating the model's ease of adaptation, as well as verifying our observation that videos can be a natural data source for learning *self-similarity*.

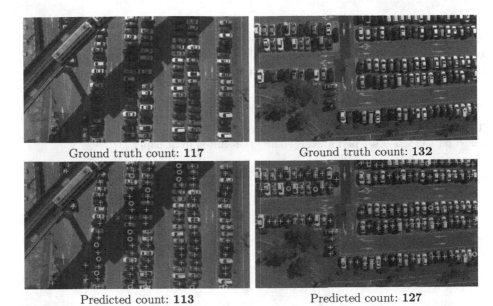

Ground truth count: **117**   Ground truth count: **132**

Predicted count: **113**   Predicted count: **127**

Fig. 6. Sample results on the CARPK dataset. Top row: original images. Bottom row: predicted detections. Correct detections are marked with a green '+', false positives with a red 'x', and missed detections with a yellow 'o'. Many of the missed detections are dark cars in shadow, which upon inspection are difficult for even a human eye to discern. (Color figure online)

4 Shanghaitech Crowd Counting

To further demonstrate the power and flexibility of counting-by-matching, we extend it to the Shanghaitech crowd counting dataset, which contains images of very large crowds of people from arbitrary camera perspectives, with individuals appearing at extremely varied scales due to perspective.

We carry out a preliminary implementation of our method on the Shanghaitech Part A crowd dataset. Inspired by the idea of crowd detection as repetitive textures [1], we conjecture that it is possible to ignore individual instances and match the statistics of patches instead; e.g. the statistics of patches with 10 people should be different from those with 20 people.

We take the following steps: (1) Using the ground truth dot annotations, we quantize 64×64 pixel patches into 10 different classes based on number of people, e.g. one class will be 0 people, another 5 people, etc. (See the arXiv version for more detail.) (2) Following the idea of counting-by-matching, we train the self-similarity architecture to embed the patches based on the number of people, i.e. if patches are sampled from the same class, the model must predict 1, otherwise 0. (3) We run the model on the test set using a sample of each class from the training set as the exemplar patch, with the final classification made by the maximum response.

Compared to other models that are specifically designed to count human crowds (e.g. CNNs with multiple branches), we aim for a method with the potential for low-shot category-agnostic counting. Our preliminary experiments show the possibility of scaling the counting-by-matching idea to human crowd datasets (Table 4).

Table 4. Preliminary results on Shanghaitech Part A (lower is better). Patches chosen based on validation set performance. The "†" result is from paper [37].

Method	MAE	RMSE
†Zhang et al. [35]	181.8	277.7
MCNN-CCR [37]	245.0	336.1
MCNN [37]	110.2	173.2
ic-CNN [27]	**69.8**	**117.3**
Ours	95.8	133.3

5 Conclusion

In this work, we recast counting as a matching problem, which offers several advantages over traditional counting methods. Namely, we make use of object detection video data that has not yet been utilized by the counting community, and we create a model that can flexibly adapt to various domains, which is a form of few-shot learning. We hope this unconventional structuring of the counting problem encourages further work towards an all-purpose counting model.

Several extensions are possible for future works: *first*, it would be interesting to consider counting in video sequences, rather than individual images or frames. Here the tracking analogue takes on an even greater significance as a counting model can take advantage of both within-frame and between-frame similarities, *second*, a carefully engineered scale-invariant network with more sophisticated feature fusion than the GMN could potentially improve the current results.

Acknowledgements. Funding for this research is provided by the Oxford-Google DeepMind Graduate Scholarship, and by the EPSRC Programme Grant Seebibyte EP/M013774/1.

References

1. Arandjelovic, O.: Crowd detection from still images. In: Proceedings of BMVC (2008)
2. Arteta, C., Lempitsky, V., Noble, J.A., Zisserman, A.: Interactive object counting. In: Fleet, D., Pajdla, T., Schiele, B., Tuytelaars, T. (eds.) ECCV 2014. LNCS, vol. 8691, pp. 504–518. Springer, Cham (2014). https://doi.org/10.1007/978-3-319-10578-9_33

3. Arteta, C., Lempitsky, V., Noble, J.A., Zisserman, A.: Detecting overlapping instances in microscopy images using extremal region trees. Med. Image Anal. **27**, 3–16 (2015)
4. Arteta, C., Lempitsky, V., Zisserman, A.: Counting in the wild. In: Leibe, B., Matas, J., Sebe, N., Welling, M. (eds.) ECCV 2016. LNCS, vol. 9911, pp. 483–498. Springer, Cham (2016). https://doi.org/10.1007/978-3-319-46478-7_30
5. Barinova, O., Lempitsky, V., Kohli, P.: On the detection of multiple object instances using Hough transforms. In: Proceedings of CVPR (2010)
6. Bertinetto, L., Valmadre, J., Henriques, J.F., Vedaldi, A., Torr, P.H.S.: Fully-convolutional siamese networks for object tracking. In: Hua, G., Jégou, H. (eds.) ECCV 2016. LNCS, vol. 9914, pp. 850–865. Springer, Cham (2016). https://doi.org/10.1007/978-3-319-48881-3_56
7. Buades, A., Coll, B., Morel, J.M.: A non-local algorithm for image denoising. In: Proceedings of CVPR, pp. 60–65 (2005)
8. Cho, S., Chow, T., Leung, C.: A neural-based crowd estimation by hybrid global learning algorithm. IEEE Trans. Syst. Man Cybern. Part B (Cybern.) **29**(4), 535–541 (2009)
9. Dekel, T., Oron, S., Rubinstein, M., Avidan, S., Freeman, W.: Best-buddies similarity for robust template matching. In: Proceedings of CVPR (2015)
10. Desai, C., Ramanan, D., Fowlkes, C.: Discriminative models for multi-class object layout. In: Proceedings of ICCV (2009)
11. Efros, A., Leung, T.: Texture synthesis by non-parametric sampling. In: Proceedings of ICCV, pp. 1039–1046, September 1999
12. Fiaschi, L., Nair, R., Köethe, U., Hamprecht, F.: Learning to count with regression forest and structured labels. In: Proceedings of ICPR (2012)
13. Glasner, D., Bagon, S., Irani, M.: Super-resolution from a single image. In: Proceedings of ICCV (2009)
14. Han, X., Leung, T., Jia, Y., Sukthankar, R., Berg, A.: Matchnet: unifying feature and metric learning for patch-based matching. In: Proceedings of CVPR (2015)
15. He, K., Zhang, X., Ren, S., Sun, J.: Deep residual learning for image recognition. In: Proceedings of CVPR (2016)
16. Hsieh, M., Lin, Y., Hsu, W.: Drone-based object counting by spatially regularized regional proposal networks. In: Proceedings of ICCV (2017)
17. Idrees, H., et al.: Composition loss for counting, density map estimation and localization in dense crowds. In: Ferrari, V., Hebert, M., Sminchisescu, C., Weiss, Y. (eds.) ECCV 2018. LNCS, vol. 11206, pp. 544–559. Springer, Cham (2018). https://doi.org/10.1007/978-3-030-01216-8_33
18. Koch, G., Zemel, R., Salakhutdinov, R.: Siamese neural networks for one-shot image recognition. In: ICML 2015 Deep Learning Workshop (2015)
19. Kong, D., Gray, D., Tao, H.: A viewpoint invariant approach for crowd counting. In: Proceedings of ICPR, vol. 3, pp. 1187–1190. IEEE (2006)
20. Lehmussola, A., Ruusuvuori, P., Selinummi, J., Huttunen, H., Yli-Harja, O.: Computational framework for simulating fluorescence microscope images with cell populations. IEEE Trans. Med. Imaging **26**(7), 1010–1016 (2007)
21. Lempitsky, V., Zisserman, A.: Learning to count objects in images. In: NIPS (2010)
22. Leung, T., Malik, J.: Detecting, localizing and grouping repeated scene elements from an image. In: Buxton, B., Cipolla, R. (eds.) ECCV 1996. LNCS, vol. 1064, pp. 546–555. Springer, Heidelberg (1996). https://doi.org/10.1007/BFb0015565
23. Malisiewicz, T., Gupta, A., Efros, A.A.: Ensemble of exemplar-SVMs for object detection and beyond. In: Proceedings of ICCV (2011)

24. Marana, A., Velastin, S., Costa, L., Lotufo, R.: Estimation of crowd density using image processing. In: Image Processing for Security Applications, p. 11/1 (1997)
25. Marsden, M., McGuinness, K., Little, S., Keogh, C.E., O'Connor, N.E.: People, penguins and petri dishes: adapting object counting models to new visual domains and object types without forgetting. In: Proceedings of CVPR (2018)
26. Mundhenk, T.N., Konjevod, G., Sakla, W.A., Boakye, K.: A large contextual dataset for classification, detection and counting of cars with deep learning. In: Leibe, B., Matas, J., Sebe, N., Welling, M. (eds.) ECCV 2016. LNCS, vol. 9907, pp. 785–800. Springer, Cham (2016). https://doi.org/10.1007/978-3-319-46487-9_48
27. Ranjan, V., Le, H., Hoai, M.: Iterative crowd counting. In: Ferrari, V., Hebert, M., Sminchisescu, C., Weiss, Y. (eds.) ECCV 2018. LNCS, vol. 11211, pp. 278–293. Springer, Cham (2018). https://doi.org/10.1007/978-3-030-01234-2_17
28. Rebuffi, S.A., Bilen, H., Vedaldi, A.: Efficient parametrization of multi-domain deep neural networks. In: Proceedings of CVPR (2018)
29. Redmon, J., Divvala, S.K., Girshick, R.B., Farhadi, A.: You only look once: unified, real-time object detection. In: Proceedings of CVPR (2016)
30. Ren, S., He, K., Girshick, R., Sun, J.: Faster R-CNN: towards real-time object detection with region proposal networks. In: NIPS (2016)
31. Russakovsky, O., et al.: Imagenet large scale visual recognition challenge. IJCV 115(3), 211–252 (2015)
32. Sung, F., Yang, Y., Zhang, L., Xiang, T., Torr, P.H.S., Hospedales, T.: Learning to compare: relation network for few-shot learning. In: Proceedings of CVPR (2018)
33. Vinyals, O., Blundell, C., Lillicrap, T., Kavukcuoglu, K., Wierstra, D.: Matching networks for one shot learning. In: NIPS (2016)
34. Xie, W., Noble, J.A., Zisserman, A.: Microscopy cell counting with fully convolutional regression networks. In: MICCAI 1st Workshop on Deep Learning in Medical Image Analysis (2015)
35. Zhang, C., Li, X., Wang, X., Yang, X.: Cross-scene crowd counting via deep convolutional neural networks. In: Proceedings of CVPR (2015)
36. Zhang, C., Yarkony, J., Hamprecht, F.A.: Cell detection and segmentation using correlation clustering. In: Golland, P., Hata, N., Barillot, C., Hornegger, J., Howe, R. (eds.) MICCAI 2014. LNCS, vol. 8673, pp. 9–16. Springer, Cham (2014). https://doi.org/10.1007/978-3-319-10404-1_2
37. Zhang, Y., Zhou, D., Chen, S., Gao, S., Ma, Y.: Single-image crowd counting via multi-column convolutional neural network. In: Proceedings of CVPR (2016)

A Computational Camera with Programmable Optics for Snapshot High-Resolution Multispectral Imaging

Jieen Chen[1]($\boxtimes$), Michael Hirsch[2], Bernhard Eberhardt[3],
and Hendrik P. A. Lensch[1]

[1] Eberhard-Karls-University Tuebingen, Tuebingen, Germany
{jieen.chen,hendrik.lensch}@uni-tuebingen.de
[2] Amazon Research, Tuebingen, Germany
hirsch@amazon.com
[3] Stuttgart Media University, Stuttgart, Germany
eberhardt@hdm-stuttgart.de

Abstract. Spectral imaging has many uses in the field of conservation of cultural heritage, medical imaging, etc. It collects spectral information at each location of an image plane as an image cube. Among various approaches, snapshot multispectral imaging techniques measure the cube within one integration period. Previous work has addressed the issue of optical design, while recent developments have shifted the focus towards computation. In this paper, we present a snapshot multispectral imaging technique with a computational camera and a corresponding image restoration algorithm. The main characteristics are: (1) transferring spectral information to the spatial domain by engineering user-defined PSFs; (2) measuring spectral images by computationally inverting the image formation. The design of our computational camera is based on a phase-coded aperture technique to generate spatial and spectral variant PSFs. The corresponding algorithm is designed by adapting single-channel and cross-channel priors. We show experimentally the viability of our technique: it reconstructs high resolution multispectral images from a snapshot. We further validate that the role of PSF design is critical.

1 Introduction

Computational cameras use controllable optical systems followed by computational decoding to produce new types of images. Among computational photography applications, spectral imaging is a branch that captures the spectra

---

M. Hirsch—The scientific idea and a preliminary version of code were developed prior to joining Amazon.

Electronic supplementary material The online version of this chapter (https://doi.org/10.1007/978-3-030-20893-6_43) contains supplementary material, which is available to authorized users.

C. V. Jawahar et al. (Eds.): ACCV 2018, LNCS 11363, pp. 685–699, 2019.
https://doi.org/10.1007/978-3-030-20893-6_43

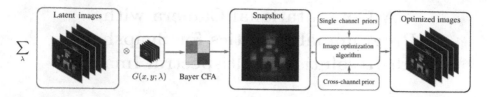

Fig. 1. Pipeline overview: PSF-engineering by computational camera and reconstruction of multispectral images.

at each location of the image plane as a 3D dataset. Conceptually, there are two approaches to acquire multispectral data: scanning and snapshot imaging. Scanning spectral imagers measure time-sequential 2D slices, e.g. using color filters. Snapshot spectral imagers measure all elements of the 3D dataset simultaneously and decode them in postprocessing. However, the optical design of snapshot imagers is typically of a rather high complexity in order to boost light collection capacity while guaranteeing a specific reconstruction quality. Various astronomical or biomedical applications [8] employ complicated setups with mirrors, fiber arrays, beam splitters, multiple color filters, etc.

Recent advances in computational imaging have shifted the workload from optics to algorithms. Image optimization algorithms have been explored for HDR, denoising, demosaicing, deconvolution, multispectral imaging, etc. In particular, deconvolution is related to optical design through Point Spread Function (PSF)-engineering. As the fingerprint of an imaging system, the PSF is the spatial response of a point light source. We address the problem of snapshot multispectral imaging by multiplexing spectral information to the spatial domain through wavelength-dependent PSFs. A linear disperser distributes colors along one dimension-which produces an overlap of spectra of neighboring pixels. Without a strong regularizer, this leads to error-prone restoration. However, by generating PSFs with two-dimensional color dispersion, the spectral information can be converted into a spatial code.

Computational cameras with wavelength-dependent PSFs for multispectral imaging have been developed in the past few years [18,21]. Current computational cameras do not provide flexibility to tune the spatial and spectral distribution of the PSFs.

In this paper, we aim to overcome the limitations of snapshot multispectral imaging by introducing a computational technique that combines a programmable optics device and a computational reconstruction pipeline. We employ an SLM as the programmable optics device to generate user-defined spatially and spectrally variant PSFs. Phase patterns are generated by a standard phase retrieval algorithm to encode the pupil function. An optimization pipeline is then implemented with TV, L2, and a cross-channel regularizer. An overview of our technique is shown in Fig. 1. The cross-channel regularizer enforces elimination of color fringing and properly locates edges across spectral bands. Our technique provides flexibility as a platform to computationally tune the PSF both spatially and spectrally. We examine the significance of appropriate PSF design in multispectral reconstruction. The technical contributions are as follows:

- Generating spatially and spectrally variant PSFs with a computational camera consisting of an off-the-shelf camera and a programmable optical device.
- A corresponding multispectral image reconstruction technique with Sobolev, TV, and cross-channel regularizers.

2   Related Work

Snapshot multispectral imaging is a technique to capture fine color spectrum information for each image pixel within a single shot. Compared to the scanning imaging spectrometer architectures, such as using a tunable filter camera [17], snapshot multispectral imaging allows light collection within a single integration time. An informative survey on snapshot multispectral imaging is presented in [8]. One of the common shortcomings in this area is the high setup complexity of the imaging system. Integral field spectrometry [2] uses prisms or glass plates to slice the optical beam into a long slit with multiple spectral images.

Coded Aperture Snapshot Spectral Imager (CASSI) [19] replaces the entrance slit with a coded aperture in order to measure the multispectral data cube. It takes advantage of compressive sensing theory to reconstruct data termed to be insufficiently sampled by the Nyquist limit. An over-complete dictionary learning for sparse reconstruction is presented in [13] based on CASSI. In [20], the authors investigated a dual-camera system constructed with one low frame rate CASSI camera and a panchromatic high frame rate camera to capture high-speed multispectral video. The method suffers from the complexity of an imaging setup with a prism, as well as the attenuation caused by the amplitude-coded aperture design. In contrast, our approach uses a phase-coded aperture setup for flexible design of PSFs which avoids this issue. A diffractive filter can also be produced following the experimental phase profile.

A multi-aperture filtered camera proposed in [12] measures the full spectral band using an array of imaging elements, such as a color-filtered lenslet array. Computational tomography-imaging spectrometry studied in [3,15] projects the spectral cube by a 2D dispersor at the aperture of the spectrometer. The main shortfall is the reduction of resolution due to angular projection. However, our approach enables full resolution reconstruction because of the convolution nature of PSF modulation.

A compact snapshot hyperspectral imaging system is proposed in [1], which equips an ordinary prism with a DSLR camera. With linear dispersion produced by the prism, the spectral information is estimated from sparse dispersion information especially from edges. Our approach, instead of linear dispersion, enhances spectral encoding by 2D dispersion. In [21], a diffractive filter is introduced; the authors build a diffractive filter to generate spatially, spectrally variant PSFs. Our approach provides more flexibility using an SLM which is able to generate arbitrary user-defined PSFs. Another technique that encodes color in the image by exploiting chromatic dispersion through a design of new phase masks is proposed in [18]. The phase masks produce controllable PSFs for different wavelengths. While this approach provides a multispectral imaging solution in microscopy, our method applies in the photography domain. A phase coded-aperture setup with programmable optics to control PSFs and refocus is presented in [5]. In this paper, we employ the phase coded-aperture setup to generate spectrally, spatially variant PSFs.

Image optimization finds the solution with minimal energy using optimization algorithms. Examples include both blind and non-blind deconvolution, demosaicing, image denoising, and inpainting. It is shown in [11] that a subset of low-level image processing problems can be solved through a single framework. This is presented in [9] as a domain-specific language and compiler for image optimization problems using proximal operators as fundamental building blocks that make it easy to experiment with different problem formulations and algorithm choices. In [14], the proximal operator of the regularization is replaced by a denoising neural network to solve image deconvolution and demosaicing problems. In this research, we employ demosaicing and non-blind deconvolution as a global optimization problem to reconstruct multispectral images.

3   Multispectral Imaging with PSF-Engineering

The principal advantage of our approach is the ability to measure spectral images from a snapshot with spectral information multiplexed in the spatial domain. The key ingredient is to modulate spectral-dependent PSFs which produce 2D dispersion.

This solution improves on traditional methods using linear gratings or prisms. An example of a comparison with a traditional prism is illustrated in Fig. 2. The PSFs of a linear dispersor smear across a fixed direction (Fig. 2(a)(c)). In particular, in spectral imaging, the spectrum is overlapped along the dispersion direction. However, with a 2D dispersion, each spectrum has a unique spatial distribution as a fingerprint. This is a cue for spectral image reconstruction. The phase images are optimized regarding one narrow band to generate PSFs with user-defined spatial distribution. The PSF-engineering becomes complete when

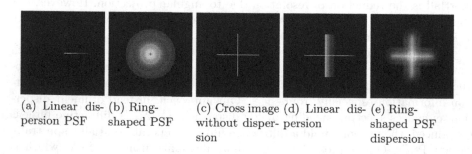

(a) Linear dispersion PSF   (b) Ring-shaped PSF   (c) Cross image without dispersion   (d) Linear dispersion   (e) Ring-shaped PSF dispersion

Fig. 2. Comparison of dispersion of prism and our approach.

the dispersive nature of the SLM helps to produce PSFs with different sizes for varying wavelengths. Once PSFs are measured, a reconstruction algorithm is modelled to invert the image formation.

3.1 Image Formation Model

The incoherent imaging process is modeled as the convolution of the latent image and the intensity PSF [7,16]. The PSFs are modulated in a wavelength-dependent fashion. Since a conventional RGB camera is used, the camera spectral response is also considered. Our spectral image formation is therefore modeled as,

$$I(x, y; c, \lambda) = \int_\lambda \Omega(c, \lambda)[i(x, y; \lambda) \otimes G(x, y; \lambda)] \, d\lambda \tag{1}$$

where $\otimes$ represents convolution; $i(x, y; \lambda)$ is the latent spectral image at wavelength λ; $G(x, y; \lambda)$ is the intensity PSF; $\Omega(c, \lambda)$ is the spectral response of each RGB pixel of the camera sensor ($c \in R, G, B$). With each spectral image, it is firstly convolved by its PSF and then filtered by mosaic patterns on the camera sensor.

3.2 Generating Spatially and Spectrally Variant PSFs with Programmable Optics

We introduce the design of spatial and spectral variant PSFs by the computational camera. The phase image is optimized under monochromatic conditions using the Gerchberg-Saxton algorithm [5,6] to produce PSFs with user-defined spatial distribution.

The SLM phase modulation varies with different wavelengths. Liquid crystal cells have a dispersion property which is caused by refractive indices of different wavelengths. With the SLM used in our setup, the phase shift ability is as follows: 633 nm has 5.4π, 532 nm has 6.7π and 452 nm has 9.0π. By exploiting the use of this property, we are able to generate spectral PSFs with different sizes. In Fig. 4, spatial and spectral variant PSFs are presented.

3.3 Design Spatial Distribution and Phase Profile of PSFs

We take advantage of the Fourier relation between the pupil function and the PSFs which assumes that the object is located at the far field. By the Gerchberg-Saxton phase retrieval algorithm in [6], the phase images for encoding programmable optics can be optimized. The spatial distribution of the PSF is defined by the user.

The PSF design problem can be phrased in terms of the strength of 2D dispersion, as well as the frequency coverage. This gives intuitive design cues for PSFs to be shapes such as spiral, spread dots, triangles, etc. Having the designed spatial distributions, we can optimize the phase profile to produce PSFs using a standard phase retrieval algorithm. Several example PSFs are shown in Fig. 4.

The example of a ring-shaped PSF is shown in Fig. 3(a). Its phase image is shown in Fig. 3(b). Due to the limited modulation depth, the optimized phase pattern has to be folded. Six monochromatic PSFs are shown in Fig. 3. One can clearly observe the PSF size variation with wavelength.

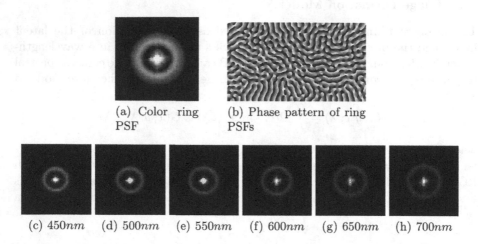

(a) Color ring PSF

(b) Phase pattern of ring PSFs

(c) 450nm   (d) 500nm   (e) 550nm   (f) 600nm   (g) 650nm   (h) 700nm

Fig. 3. Example of user-defined ring PSFs. Note the varying size for the different wavelengths.

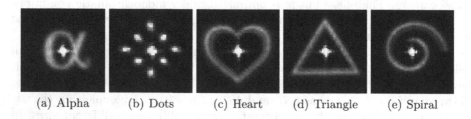

(a) Alpha   (b) Dots   (c) Heart   (d) Triangle   (e) Spiral

Fig. 4. Spatial and spectral variant PSFs captured by the computational camera.

4   Reconstruction of Spectral Images

In order to obtain multispectral images from a single PSF-modulated image, we introduce an inverse process with the knowledge of PSFs and the camera spectral response function. This problem can be outlined in terms of the image formation model. Combining our prior knowledge of hue consistency and image smoothness, we formulate an objective function with data fitting, single-channel, and cross-channel regularizers.

4.1   Image Formation Operation

Consider the multispectral latent images with resolution $X \times Y \times \Lambda$. The image formation can be discretized from Eq. 1 as,

$$I_0 = \sum_{n=1}^{N} \Omega_n G_n I_n \tag{2}$$

where Ω_n is the Bayer mosaicing operator at band n, G_n is a wavelength dependent convolution kernel, and N is the total number of spectral bands. I_0 is the single shot image captured by the computational camera with modulated PSFs. I_n is the latent spectral image at band n.

4.2   Reconstruction of Spectral Information

Our algorithm seeks the solution of the following objective function,

$$f = \arg\min_{I_n} \| \sum_{n=1}^{N} \Omega_n G_n I_n - I_0 \|_2^2 + \Gamma_n(I_n) + \Gamma_{crs}(I_n) \tag{3}$$

where the first term is a standard least-square data fitting term. The second and third terms are regularization terms where image priors are applied. We employ a non-blind deconvolution scheme with the prior knowledge of the modulated PSFs.

Although unique PSFs are produced for each spectral band, the inverse problem is highly ill-posed because of the multiplexing nature of the image formation. One advantage is the existence of the zeroth order diffraction–central peak in the PSFs, which preserves some amount of image edges. We enforce intraband and interband prior knowledge for spectral reconstruction. Through the use of single-channel image priors, homogeneous reconstruction with edges is enforced intraband. In addition, edge information is shared across different color bands through a cross-channel prior.

Two priors are chosen in order to recover intraband information: the Total Variation (TV) and Sobolev. The TV prior is capable of recovering blocky images from noisy data. The Sobolev prior is a quadratic term that preserves uniform smoothness. The single-channel regularization is thus formatted as,

$$\Gamma_n(I_n) = \sum_{n=1}^{N} \alpha \|\nabla I_n\|_2^2 + \beta \|\nabla I_n\|_1^1 \tag{4}$$

where α and β are weights of the priors.

The key part of regularization is a cross-channel prior which borrows edge information from other color channels to benefit the reconstruction. By producing PSFs with their size variation with wavelengths, we intentionally increase the chromatic aberration of the optical system, while traditionally, lens designers minimize it. During reconstruction, having cross-channel priors shares information between the individual reconstructed spectral images. We use the cross-channel regularizer employed by [10], which is based on the assumption that hue remains constant along edges. In other words, edges share the same location across all channels. This is formulated in an L1 fashion as follows,

$$\nabla I_k \cdot I_l \approx \nabla I_l \cdot I_k \tag{5}$$

where l and k represent two spectral bands. The cross-channel regularizer is described as,

$$\Gamma_{crs}(I_n) = \sum_{n=1}^{N} \sum_{n \neq i} \sigma_{ni} \|\nabla I_n \cdot I_i - \nabla I_i \cdot I_n\|_1 \tag{6}$$

where σ_{ni} is the weight for the prior. Having a strong cross-channel regularizer enables us to solve this highly ill-posed problem, because it emphasizes the inverse algorithm to search for regions that have constant hues, and rejects strong chromatic aberrations. However, we avoid using regularizer based on assumption of spectral smoothness.

5   Experimental Results and Discussion

To capture PSF-modulated snapshots, we build a computational camera with reference to [5]. Our computational camera shown in Fig. 5 is built in a phase coded-aperture fashion with an LCoS SLM.

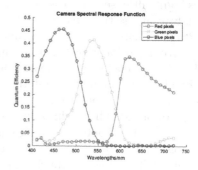

Fig. 5. Computational camera setup with a telephoto lens and SLM.

Fig. 6. Camera spectral response function

A 100 mm compact fixed focal lens is mounted on a conventional RGB camera. The small Field of View (FoV) of the telephoto lens makes the non-uniform phase coding caused by magnification negligible. The programmable optics we use in the setup is the PLUTO VIS-006-A (420–700 nm) HR version SLM by Holoeye, which offers 87% fill factor. All images are captured with a DVC4000C camera whose sensor has a Bayer color filter array. An HDR pipeline is selected for image acquisition. We insert a tunable VariSpec color filter (400–720 nm, bandwidth 10 nm) in front of a halogen light source Osram 64655 HLX to produce monochromatic illumination.

We measure the ground truth dataset by encoding a uniform gray image onto the SLM. Each scene is illuminated monochromatically while capturing the ground truth data. Similarly, monochromatic PSFs are measured by capturing images of a pinhole light source. A debayering algorithm is used to find the optimum of both the ground truth and PSF estimation. The optimization is formulated as,

$$f = \arg\min_{J_n} \| \Omega_n J_n^{gt} - J_n \|_2^2 + \gamma \| \nabla J_n^{gt} \|_2^2 \tag{7}$$

where J_n^{gt} is the captured image at band n, J_n is the latent image, and γ is the weight for the Sobolev regularizer. We access the camera spectral response function Ω_n from datasets provided by vendor shown in Fig. 6.

Due to our filtered monochromatic illumination, PSF-modulated snapshots and ground truth images are captured under different illumination spectra. In order to validate the multispectral images with the ground truths, we measure the scaling factor of the VariSpec filter using a Konica-Minolta CS2000A spectroradiometer.

Validation. The performance of our method is validated using both synthetic and real-world data with ground truth. For the synthetic images, we use the multispectral database from [22]. In Fig. 7, we show our results using a flower scene. The PSFs are designed to have 2D dispersion in ring shapes as are shown in Fig. 7(m). We opted for ring-shaped PSFs on the basis of their symmetric sampling. Six channels of PSFs are used during testing. The results show that without loss of resolution, our inverse approach is able to reconstruct all six multispectral images. The PSNRs of each image are 27.6, 28.9, 28.6, 28.4, 26.7 and 24.9 dB. Results show degrees of blur due to the parameter choices of the priors.

More interestingly, we show the real-world implementation. Multiple scenes are captured that contain a ColorChecker, plastic, organic and fabric materials. Three different designs of PSFs–ring, dots and spiral, are used and encoded with our computational camera in accordance with the optimized phase profiles. We successfully reconstruct six spectral bands with full resolution. Consequently, single RGB images are restored using these spectral images. We show our experimental results of a ColorChecker, when the ring PSFs are modulated in Fig. 8. The individual spectral images closely match the ground truth data. The image contrast within each band is faithfully restored. In the color images, the patches show clear spectral proximity to the ground truth. Please zoom-in to see more details. We further analyze reconstructions of images with other scenes. The RGB image results are displayed in Fig. 9. These tests reveal the reconstruction stability of our approach. Even with an organic object which has a low image gradient and homogeneous spectra, our method is still able to restore the spectral images. Inevitably, there are some discrepancies such as the highlight on the shoulder of the LEGO figure due to limited number of PSF bands.

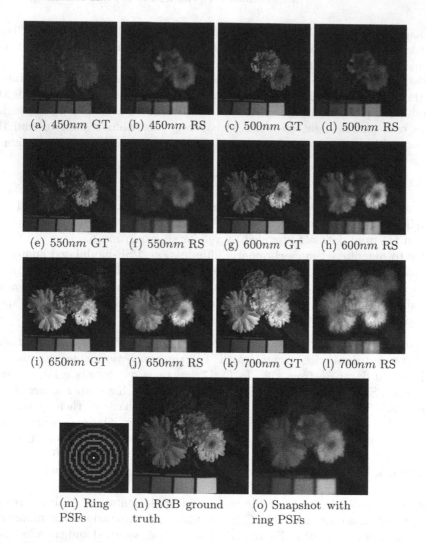

(a) 450nm GT (b) 450nm RS (c) 500nm GT (d) 500nm RS

(e) 550nm GT (f) 550nm RS (g) 600nm GT (h) 600nm RS

(i) 650nm GT (j) 650nm RS (k) 700nm GT (l) 700nm RS

(m) Ring PSFs (n) RGB ground truth (o) Snapshot with ring PSFs

Fig. 7. Synthetic results comparison using CAVE multispectral data. GT and RS stand for ground truth and results.

The image resolution of the ColorChecker, cloth, LEGO and lemon are 805×805, 805×805, 800×800 and 804×804. It is worth noting that all images are restored without compromising resolution. Please refer to the supplementary materials for results of diverse scenes using different PSFs (Table 1).

We run our image reconstruction experiments, as well as ground truth and PSF estimation with the L-BFGS-B optimizer. We use the MATLAB implementation in [4]. The real-world reconstruction parameters are empirically set to be $\alpha = 0.3 \times 10^{-2}$, $\beta = 0.8 \times 10^{-2}$, $\sigma_{ni} = 0.5$ and $\gamma = 1.0$. We employ strong

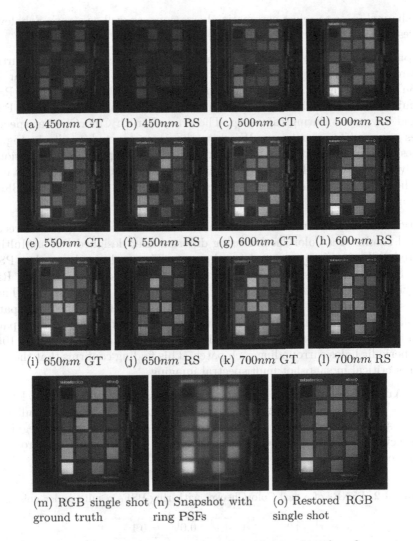

(a) 450nm GT   (b) 450nm RS   (c) 500nm GT   (d) 500nm RS

(e) 550nm GT   (f) 550nm RS   (g) 600nm GT   (h) 600nm RS

(i) 650nm GT   (j) 650nm RS   (k) 700nm GT   (l) 700nm RS

(m) RGB single shot (n) Snapshot with (o) Restored RGB
ground truth   ring PSFs   single shot

Fig. 8. Real-world ColorChecker scene comparison of ground truth and reconstruction. GT and RS stand for ground truth and results.

Table 1. PSNRs of real-world results

	ColorChecker			Lemon		
	Ring	Spiral	Dots	Ring	Spiral	Dots
Mean	21.5473	22.0312	22.2183	28.1851	21.7892	23.8086
	Lego			Cloth		
	Ring	Spiral	Dots	Ring	Spiral	Dots
Mean	22.9578	22.4835	21.3271	18.4300	19.0417	18.7232

cross-channel prior to reject chromatic aberrations, as well as strong Sobolev in PSF restoration for sharp spectral image reconstruction.

Comparison with Reconstruction from Linear Dispersion. We further compare results by designed PSFs and linear dispersion. PSFs with linear dispersion is shown in Fig. 11. A peak response is left in the center of the PSFs to mimic zeroth order diffraction. We synthesize the snapshot using these PSFs to avoid any noises during capturing. The ground truth ColorChecker spectral images are used for simulation. We show the reconstructed results in Fig. 11. The results indicate that multispectral imaging with simple linear dispersion is severely ill-posed. It is hardly usable for recovering multispectral images even with the strong cross-channel prior. It is verified that a 2D design of PSFs is necessary.

Comparison of Results with Different PSFs. We show in Fig. 10 the reconstructed results of a ColorChecker using different user-designed PSFs. Multiple captured PSFs in Fig. 4 are used for this test. The analysis shows that PSFs with different spatial distributions generate discrete levels of performance. Ring PSFs yield the best results compared to PSFs shaped as dots or spirals. There is a positive correlation between the specific halo artifact and the PSF spatial distribution. For example, in Fig. 10(c), asymmetric halos appear on each patch due to the particular non-uniform sampling of spiral PSFs. Similarly, Fig. 10(d) shows periodic halos surrounding each patch. This finding confirms that the PSF design is critical in snapshot multispectral imaging.

Noise Analysis. We evaluate reconstruction on real data with different level of Gaussian white noises added to the single shot input in Table 2. The influence of noise is reduced by the knowledge of the PSFs and the employed regularizers, especially the cross-channel regularizer shares edge information across less determined channels.

Table 2. PSNRs of a real ColorChecker with ring PSFs results under noise

σ^1	0	0.01	0.05	0.1
Ring	22.3361	22.3747	17.7970	14.7672

Limitations. We acknowledge that our research may have two limitations. The first is the number of spectral bands is still limited. It is possible that a trade-off exists between spatial and spectral resolution due to the ill-posed nature of this method. Careful investigation must be exercised regarding the maximal number of spectral bands. The second is the limited freedom in desiging 2D PSFs. Current PSF design is based-on optimizing phase profile of a single monochromatic band. However, it will be beneficial to design PSFs of each band separately. SLM-based color-multiplexing technique may be an interesting avenue to explore this design.

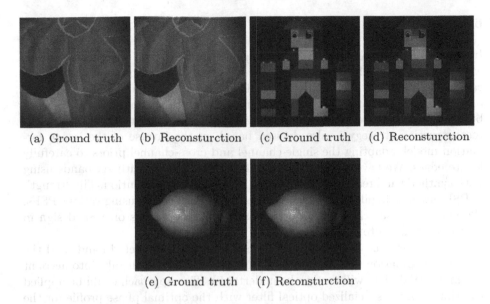

(a) Ground truth   (b) Reconsturction   (c) Ground truth   (d) Reconsturction

(e) Ground truth   (f) Reconsturction

Fig. 9. Reconstruction with diverse scenes using ring PSFs: cloth, LEGO and lemon.

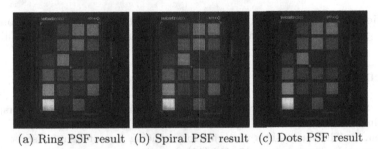

(a) Ring PSF result (b) Spiral PSF result (c) Dots PSF result

Fig. 10. Comparison of reconstruction from different PSFs.

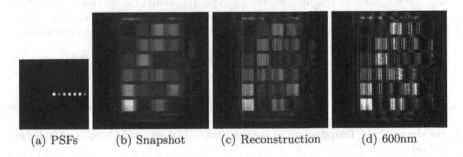

(a) PSFs   (b) Snapshot   (c) Reconstruction   (d) 600nm

Fig. 11. Reconstruction with linear dispersion. (a) Linear dispersion PSFs (b) Simulated snapshot (c) RGB image restored from reconstructed spectral image (d) Spectral image at 600 nm

6   Conclusion

In this paper, we presented a novel snapshot multispectral imaging technique with a computational camera, equiped with an SLM as the programmable optical device, enabling user-defined spatial and spectral variant PSFs. The 2D-dispersed PSFs thus multiplex spectral information to spatial domain. We have built up and calibrated the computational camera using off-the-shelf devices. A reconstruction strategy is also devised based on the inverse of the image formation model, adapting the single-channel and cross-channel priors to carefully locate edges. We have demonstrated multispectral results with six bands using both synthetic and real-world data without loss of image resolution. The strength of PSF design is highlighted by comparison of reconstruction using various PSFs. We hope our research will serve as a base for future studies on PSF design in computational photography.

The present study is limited by the number of reconstructed bands and the need for modulation of 2D dispersion. Further studies, which take into account optimal PSF design, will need to be undertaken. This approach could be applied to print a simple specialized optical filter with the optimal phase profile for the purpose of convenient low-cost snapshot multispectral imaging.

Acknowledgement. This work was partly supported by "Kooperatives Promotions-skolleg Digital Media" at Stuttgart Media University and the University of Tübingen.

References

1. Baek, S.H., Kim, I., Gutierrez, D., Kim, M.H.: Compact single-shot hyperspectral imaging using a prism. ACM Trans. Graph. (TOG) **36**(6), 217 (2017)
2. Bowen, I.: The image-slicer a device for reducing loss of light at slit of stellar spectrograph. Astrophys. J. **88**, 113 (1938)
3. Bulygin, T.V., Vishnyakov, G.N.: Spectrotomography: a new method of obtaining spectrograms of two-dimensional objects. In: Analytical Methods for Optical Tomography, pp. 315–322. International Society for Optics and Photonics (1992)
4. Carbonetto, P.: A MATLAB interface for L-BFGS-B (2014). https://github.com/pcarbo/lbfgsb-matlab
5. Chen, J., Hirsch, M., Heintzmann, R., Eberhardt, B., Lensch, H.P.A.: A phase-coded aperture camera with programmable optics. Electron. Imaging **2017**, 70–75 (2017)
6. Gerchberg, R.W.: A practical algorithm for the determination of phase from image and diffraction plane pictures. Optik **35**, 237 (1972)
7. Goodman, J.W.: Introduction to Fourier optics. Roberts and Company Publishers (2005)
8. Hagen, N., Kudenov, M.W.: Review of snapshot spectral imaging technologies. Opt. Eng. **52**(9), 090901–090901 (2013)
9. Heide, F., Diamond, S., Nießner, M., Ragan-Kelley, J., Heidrich, W., Wetzstein, G.: ProxImaL: efficient image optimization using proximal algorithms. ACM Trans. Graph. (TOG) **35**(4), 84 (2016)

10. Heide, F., Rouf, M., Hullin, M.B., Labitzke, B., Heidrich, W., Kolb, A.: High-quality computational imaging through simple lenses. ACM Trans. Graph. (TOG) **32**(5), 149 (2013)

11. Heide, F., Steinberger, M., Tsai, Y.T., Rouf, M., Pająk, D., Reddy, D., Gallo, O., Liu, J., Heidrich, W., Egiazarian, K., et al.: FlexISP: a flexible camera image processing framework. ACM Trans. Graph. (TOG) **33**(6), 231 (2014)

12. Hirai, A., Inoue, T., Itoh, K., Ichioka, Y.: Application of measurement multiple-image fourier of fast phenomena transform spectral imaging to measurement of fast phenomena. Opt. Rev. **1**(2), 205–207 (1994)

13. Lin, X., Liu, Y., Wu, J., Dai, Q.: Spatial-spectral encoded compressive hyperspectral imaging. ACM Trans. Graph. (TOG) **33**(6), 233 (2014)

14. Meinhardt, T., Möller, M., Hazirbas, C., Cremers, D.: Learning proximal operators: Using denoising networks for regularizing inverse imaging problems. arXiv e-prints, April 2017

15. Okamoto, T., Takahashi, A., Yamaguchi, I.: Simultaneous acquisition of spectral and spatial intensity distribution. Appl. Spectro. **47**(8), 1198–1202 (1993)

16. Peng, Y., Fu, Q., Heide, F., Heidrich, W.: The diffractive achromat full spectrum computational imaging with diffractive optics. In: SIGGRAPH ASIA 2016 Virtual Reality meets Physical Reality: Modelling and Simulating Virtual Humans and Environments, p. 4. ACM (2016)

17. Poger, S., Angelopoulou, E.: Multispectral sensors in computer vision. Stevens Institute of Technology Technical Report CS Report 2001, vol. 3 (2001)

18. Shechtman, Y., Weiss, L.E., Backer, A.S., Lee, M.Y., Moerner, W.: Multi-colour localization microscopy by point-spread-function engineering. Nat. Photonics **10**(9), 590 (2016)

19. Wagadarikar, A., John, R., Willett, R., Brady, D.: Single disperser design for coded aperture snapshot spectral imaging. Appl. Opt. **47**(10), B44–B51 (2008)

20. Wang, L., Xiong, Z., Gao, D., Shi, G., Zeng, W., Wu, F.: High-speed hyperspectral video acquisition with a dual-camera architecture. In: Proceedings of the IEEE Conference on Computer Vision and Pattern Recognition, pp. 4942–4950 (2015)

21. Wang, P., Shafran, E., Vasquez, F.G., Menon, R.: Snapshot high-resolution hyperspectral imager based on an ultra-thin diffractive filter. In: Imaging Systems and Applications, pp. IW1E-1. Optical Society of America (2016)

22. Yasuma, F., Mitsunaga, T., Iso, D., Nayar, S.K.: Generalized assorted pixel camera: postcapture control of resolution, dynamic range, and spectrum. IEEE Trans. Image Process. **19**(9), 2241–2253 (2010)

Unsupervised Intuitive Physics
from Visual Observations

Sebastien Ehrhardt[1]([✉]) [ID], Aron Monszpart[2,3] [ID], Niloy Mitra[2] [ID],
and Andrea Vedaldi[1] [ID]

[1] University of Oxford, Oxford, UK
{hyenal,vedaldi}@robots.ox.ac.uk
[2] University College London, London, UK
{a.monszpart,n.mitra}@cs.ucl.ac.uk
[3] Niantic, San Fransisco, USA
aron@nianticlabs.com

Abstract. While learning models of *intuitive physics* is an active area
of research, current approaches fall short of natural intelligences in one
important regard: they require external supervision, such as explicit
access to physical states, at training and sometimes even at test time.
Some approaches sidestep these requirements by building models on top
of handcrafted physical simulators. In both cases, however, methods
cannot learn automatically new physical environments and their laws
as humans do. In this work, we successfully demonstrate, for the first
time, learning unsupervised predictors of physical states, such as the
position of objects in an environment, *directly from raw visual observations and without relying on simulators.* We do so in two steps: (i) we
learn to track dynamically-salient objects in videos using causality and
equivariance, two non-generative unsupervised learning principles that
do not require manual or external supervision. (ii) we demonstrate
that the extracted positions are sufficient to successfully train visual
motion predictors that can take the underlying environment into account.
We validate our predictors on synthetic datasets; then, we introduce
a new dataset, ROLL4REAL, consisting of real objects rolling on complex terrains (pool table, elliptical bowl, and random height-field). We
show that it is possible to learn reliable object trajectory extrapolators
from raw videos alone, without any external supervision and with no
more prior knowledge than the choice of a convolutional neural network
architecture.

Keywords: Unsupervised learning · Motion · Convolution networks

1 Introduction

A striking property of natural intelligences is their ability to perform accurate
and rapid predictions of physical phenomena using only noisy sensory inputs.

S. Ehrhardt and A. Monszpart—Contributed equally.

© Springer Nature Switzerland AG 2019
C. V. Jawahar et al. (Eds.): ACCV 2018, LNCS 11363, pp. 700–716, 2019.
https://doi.org/10.1007/978-3-030-20893-6_44

Even more remarkable is the fact that such predictors are learned without explicit supervision; rather, natural intelligences induce their internal representation of physics automatically from experience.

Several authors have recently looked into the problem of learning physical predictors using deep neural networks in order to partially mimic this functionality. Early attempts predicted trajectories in hand-crafted spaces of physical parameters, such as positions and velocities, assuming that the ground-truth values of such parameters are fully observable during training. Others have considered performing predictions from visual observations, but used full supervision for training. Furthermore, while several papers [3,7] make use of simulators as a way to generate the required supervisory signals, limited work has been done in transferring such models to real data.

In this paper, we also investigate learning *physical predictors* using deep neural network. However, we do so in a **fully unsupervised manner**, learning from observations of unlabelled video sequences. In contrast to approaches such as the recent de-animation method of [39], we do not require synthetic data, nor do we rely on any handcrafted physical simulator for prediction. Our models are built directly from real data and learn intuitive physics models that empirically outperform more principled, but more brittle, models based on physical parameters [31].

Importantly, our goal is not to merely predict future frames in a video, a problem addressed before by several authors [19]. While we also predict future dynamics from a video stream, our goal is *not* to estimate appearance changes, but physical quantities such as object positions and velocities. So, where future frame prediction generates an image, our goal is to extract meaningful and actionable physical parameters from the data.

As a working example, we consider video footage of balls rolling on various surfaces, such as pool tables, bowls and random height-fields. Balls interact with the underlying environment (e.g., roll around obstacles) and among themselves (e.g., collide with each other). For rigorous assessment, in addition to considering several synthetic datasets, we also contribute **a new public dataset**, ROLL4REAL, containing a large number of such sequences captured in real-life. Methodologically, we make two contributions. First, inspired by [23], we show that an object **detector** can be learned in an **unsupervised manner** by tuning a convolutional detector to extract tracks that are maximally characteristic of the natural, causal ordering of the frames in a video. Second, we use these trajectories to learn **visual predictors** that automatically learn an internal representation of physics and can extrapolate the trajectory of the balls more reliably than even supervised approaches such as Interaction Networks (IN) [3] that use direct measurements of physical parameters.

Note that our goal, similar to other papers in this area, is not to come up with the best possible method for physical prediction. A handcrafted solution heavily engineered to use supervision, off-the-shelf trackers, and/or physical simulators may do better in raw predictive performance (although the task is in fact not simple, particularly as our terrains are complex and somewhat deformable).

Rather, we focus on developing machines that can learn such physical predictors from raw input.

Empirically, we show that vision-based models more gracefully handle observation noise compared to approaches such as [3,7] that are learned using physical ground-truth parameters extracted from simulated scenarios. We also show that the Visual Interaction Network (VIN) of [22], which also propose a vision-based physical predictor, fails to account for the interaction of the objects and their environment, whereas more distributed tensor based approach succeeds.

The rest of the paper is organized as follows. We discuss related work in Sect. 2. We then present the technical details of our approach in Sect. 3. Next, we introduce the new ROLL4REAL data in Sect. 4 and use the latter as well as several existing synthetic datasets to evaluate the approach in Sect. 5. We summarise our findings in Sect. 6.

2   Related Work

Existing work in learning physics can be organised according to several axes.

Nature of the Representation of Physics: A natural way to represent physics is to manually encode every object parameters and physical properties (mass, velocity, positions, etc.). From the earliest approaches [4] this has been widely used to represent physics and propagate it [3,7,26,32]. Some focusing on representing a small subset of physical parameters such as positions and velocities [37,38]. However, other approaches try to learn an implicit representation of physics, inspired by the success of implicit representation of dynamics [5,8,28,29]. Implicit physics are usually represented as activations in a deep neural network [10,20,36].

Hand-Crafted vs Learned Dynamics: Some approaches [37], including simulation-based ones [4,40], use physics by explicitly integrating parameters such as velocities. While this generally require extensive knowledge of the environment and object properties, other methods [3,7,10,26,32], integrate parameters of the scenarios through recurrent learnable predictors to make physical long term predictions.

Physical vs Visual Observations: Many approaches [3,7] assume direct access to physical quantities such as positions and velocities for prediction. If this first approach enable to make very accurate predictions it is however unlikely that such accuracy can be reached in the real-world. Others [4,13,17,20,21,33,36,40] take as input one or several frames of a scene to deduce physical properties (intuitive or explicit) or predict the next state of a system.

Qualitative vs Quantitative Predictions: While most of the papers discussed above consider *quantitative* predictions such as extrapolating trajectory, others have considered *qualitative* predictions focusing on *intuitive* physics, such as the stability of stacks of objects [4,20,21], the likelihood of a scenario [30] or the forces acting behind a scene [40]. Other papers are in between, and learn *plausible if not accurate physical predictions* [18,24,35], often for 3D computer graphics.

Nature of the Supervision: Most approaches are *passive and supervised*, as they are passive observer of physical scenarios and use ground truth information about key physical parameters (positions, velocities, stability) during training. While this approaches require an expensive annotation of data, some work tried to learn from unsupervised data either through active manipulation [2,9] or using the laws of physics [33].

Scenarios: Two favorite scenarios in such experiments are bouncing balls, including billard-like environment [14], and block towers [20]. As a variant, [36] consider balls subject to gravitational pulls, ignoring harder-to-model collisions. Most papers make use of simulated data, with limited validation on real data. A different approach [25] is to predict qualitative object forces and trajectories in fully-unconstrained natural images. The approach of [2] considers instead learning from active poking using a real-life robot. In most cases experiments are done on synthetic data. However, approaches such as [21,37,38] also used real data; [38] also contributed a dataset of videos of short physical experiments called *Phys-101*.

We relate to such previous work in that we also make physical predictions of the trajectory of ball-like objects. However, we differ in two significant ways. First, our approach, while using only passive observations, is *fully unsupervised*, and yet competitive if not more accurate than supervised counterparts. In particular, while [33,40] also do not use image labels, they use *a-priori* knowledge of physics for training (a fully-fledged simulator and renderer in the case of [40]). Second, we systematically test on *several real-life scenarios*, both in training and testing, using our new ROLL4REAL dataset. Compared to datasets such as *Phys-101*, ours allows testing long-term ball-rolling prediction in complex scenarios.

3 Method

Our goal is to construct a machine that can, given only raw videos and no supervision, learn physical parameters such as the position of the objects in the videos as well as proxies to physical laws that allow to predict the evolution of such parameters over time. For this, predicting appearance changes is not sufficient; instead, we decompose the problem in two steps. The first one is a method to discover and learn to extract object positions using as cue the fact that they should have a non-trivial causal dynamics (Sect. 3.1). This tracker scales well to large datasets and is able to detect different type of objects without any further specification. Then, we use the resulting object trajectories to learn visual predictors that can extrapolate the object positions through time, embodying a proxy to the laws of mechanics (Sect. 3.2).

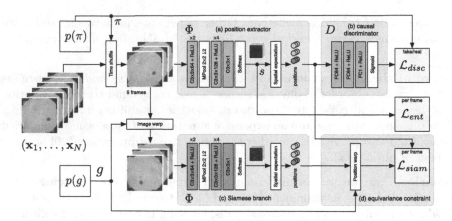

Fig. 1. Overview of our unsupervised object tracker. Each training point consists of a sequence of five video frames. Top: the sequence is randomly permuted with probability 50%. The position extractor (a) computes a probability map s for the object location, whose entropy is penalised by $\mathcal{L}_{ent}$. The reconstructed trajectory is then fed to a causal/non-causal discriminator network (b) that determines whether the sequence is causal or not, encouraged by $\mathcal{L}_{disc}$. The bottom Siamese branch (c) of the architecture takes a randomly warped version of the video and is expected by $\mathcal{L}_{siam}$ to extract correspondingly-warped positions in (d). Blue and green blocks contain learnable weights and green blocks are siamese shared ones. At test time only Φ is retained. (Color figure online)

3.1 Unsupervised Detection and Tracking of Dynamic Objects

Single-Object Detection. Let $\mathbf{x}_t \in \mathbb{R}^{H \times W \times 3}$ be a RGB video frame and assume we are given video sequences $\mathcal{X} = (\mathbf{x}_1, \ldots, \mathbf{x}_N)$, initially containing a single object moving in an environment, such as a rolling ball. Our goal is to learn a detector function $\Phi(\mathbf{x}_t) = u_t \in \mathbb{R}^2$ that extracts the 2D position u_t of the moving object at any given time (Fig. 1). The challenge is to do so *without* access to any label for supervision or any a-priori information about object shape.

We start by implementing $\Phi(\mathbf{x}_t)$ as a shallow Convolutional Neural Network (CNN) that extracts a scalar score $f_v \in \mathbb{R}$ for each image pixel $v \in \Omega = \{1, \ldots, H\} \times \{1, \ldots, W\}$, resulting in a heat map. This is then normalised to a probability distribution using the softmax operator $s_v = e^{f_v} / \sum_{z \in \Omega} e^{f_z}$ and the location u of the object is obtained as the expected value $u = \sum_v v s_v$ [13].

We learn Φ by combining two learning principles. The first one is **causality**. Applied to a video sequence, the detector produces a trajectory $\Phi(\mathcal{X}) = (\Phi(\mathbf{x}_1), \ldots, \Phi(\mathbf{x}_N))$. We expect that, when the detector locks properly on the rolling object, the trajectory is physically plausible (e.g., causal/smooth); at the same time, if the frames are shuffled by a random permutation π, the resulting trajectory should *not* be plausible anymore. We incorporate this constraint by learning a discriminator network $D(\Phi(\mathbf{x}_{\pi_1}), \ldots, \Phi(\mathbf{x}_{\pi_5}))$ that, for a subsequence, can distinguish between the natural ordering of the frames and a random shuffle (top row of Fig. 1). The permutation π is sampled with 50% probability as a consecutive sequence of 5 frames ($\pi_{i+1} = \pi_i + 1$, $i = 1, \ldots, 4$) and with 50% uniformly at random. The discriminator is a 3 layers multi-layer perceptron followed by a sigmoid and the loss

$$\mathcal{L}_{disc}(D, \pi) = \begin{cases} -\log D, & \pi_{i+1} = \pi_i + 1, \ i = 1, \ldots, 4, \\ -\log(1 - D), & \text{otherwise.} \end{cases}$$

The second learning principle is **equivariance** (cf., [27,34]). This principle suggests that, if a transformation g is applied to a frame $\mathbf{x}_t$ (e.g., a $\pm\pi/2$ rotation), then the output of the detector should change accordingly: $\Phi(g\mathbf{x}_t) = g\Phi(\mathbf{x}_t)$. This is implemented as a Siamese branch (bottom row in Fig. 1) extracting 2D positions $\Phi(g\mathcal{X}) = (\Phi(g\mathbf{x}_1), \ldots, \Phi(g\mathbf{x}_N))$ from the rotated frames and comparing them to the rotated 2D positions extracted from the original frames using the L^2 loss: $\mathcal{L}_{siam} = \frac{1}{N} \sum_t \|g^{-1}\Phi(g\mathbf{x}_t) - \Phi(\mathbf{x}_t)\|^2$.

Finally, in order to encourage the softmax operator to produce peaky distributions, we minimise the entropy of the resulting distribution $\mathcal{L}_{ent} = -\sum_{v \in \Omega} s_v \log(s_v)$. The final loss is therefore $\mathcal{L} = \lambda_d \mathcal{L}_{disc} + \lambda_e \mathcal{L}_{ent} + \lambda_s \mathcal{L}_{siam}$. In our experiment, $\lambda_d = 1$, $\lambda_e = 0.01$, and $\lambda_s = 0.001$.

Multi-object Tracking. We now extend the method from detection of single objects to tracking of multiple objects. In order to do so, the network is fine-tuned to videos containing two or more moving objects of different appearance.

Since the network produces only a single pair of coordinates, it can formally estimate the location of a single object in the image. However, when multiple objects are present, the unsupervised learning process could still converge to an undesirable result, such as predicting the center of mass of several objects combined, or randomly jumping between objects over time. The first is discouraged by the entropy loss which prefers sharp heat map. The second is discouraged by the causality loss, as discontinuous trajectories would not look plausibly ordered and consistent.

In practice, our model learns to track consistently a single object selected at random among the visible ones. Once this is done, in the next iteration, a second object is detected by suppressing (setting to zero) a circular region of radius r around the first object location in the activations f_v immediately preceding the softmax operator, and the process is repeated for further object occurrences. Before the suppression we also add a positive bias to the activations f_v in order to consider the previously detected objects as zero probabilities in the new heatmap. Note that we consider the number of objects as given since it is in itself already a very challenging task that is under active research [12].

3.2   Trajectory Extrapolation Networks

We consider existing network modules for physical prediction. While these modules use external supervision in the original papers, here we apply them to the output of the unsupervised tracker of Sect. 3.1, hence training such physical extrapolators in a *fully unsupervised* manner for the first time.

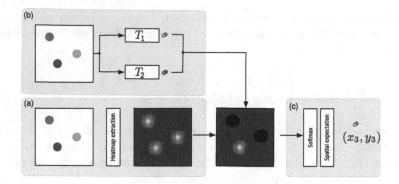

Fig. 2. Multiple object unsupervised tracker. (a) We first extract an object heatmap with the method described in Sect. 3.1. (b) Then we mask the objects detected by previously trained tracker (T_1 and T_2) on the heatmap by zeroing out the values around a circular area around their center. (c) Finally we extract position from this last heatmap with masked values.

We experiment in particular with *PosNet*, *DispNet*, and *ProbNet* from [11], configuring them to take as input the first four frames of a sequence and to produce as output the prediction of future object positions. These models learn an implicit representation of physics, which is extrapolated automatically by a recurrent propagation layer and used to extract estimates of the object positions. The difference between the models is that *PosNet* regresses positions from state, while *DispNet* and *ProbNet* regress displacements from state. Furthermore, *ProbNet* produces a probability estimate over trajectories (Fig. 2).

We also consider the *Visual Interaction Network* (VIN) module and its variant *Interaction Network from State* (IFS) [36]. While VIN uses only visual inputs for prediction just like the other networks, IFS works with an explicit state vector of physical parameters, which we set as the stacking of the 2D positions for four past frames which starts with positions extracted from our tracker. Additionally, in the synthetic experiments (first part of Table 2), IFS uses velocity and in BOWLS experiments the ground-truth ellipsoid axes parameters are appended to the state to inform the model of the shape of the ground. IFS and VIN are trained following [11]; in particular, this means that VIN uses the same setting as the original paper (32×32 pixels images).

We also note that while VIN and models from [11] have essentially the same core concepts (they consist of a first feature extractor module to extract implicit physical state, a recurrent propagation module to propagate the state, and an extractor module to get desired physical parameters from the state) their main difference resides in the structure of the propagated state. While VIN used a vector state representation, each of *PosNet*, *DispNet*, and *ProbNet* use a tensor representation.

All such models are trained by showing the network four initial frames of a sequence and the output of the unsupervised tracker up to time $T_{\text{train}} \in \{15, 20\}$ frames. At test time, the networks, which are recurrent, are used to extrapolate

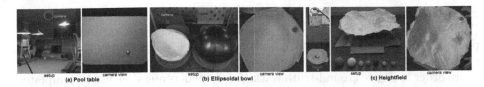

Fig. 3. Physical setup. In each of the three real-world scenarios (POOLR, BOWLR, HEIGHTR), we show the experimental setup (left) and a sample data frame (right).

the trajectory up to an arbitrary time T, also starting from four video frames. We test in particular $T = T_{train}$ and $T \gg T_{train}$ to assess the generalization capabilities of the models learned by the network.

In addition, for some experiments on single object we also consider *linear* and *quadratic* extrapolators as baselines. In both cases we fit a first (respectively second) order polynomial to the 10 first positions given as input (hence with a significant advantage compared to the networks which only observe four frames).

4 ROLL4REAL: A New Benchmark Dataset

In the absence of a suitable real-world dataset to evaluate intuitive physics on objects rolling on complex terrains, we created a new benchmark, ROLL4REAL (R4R).

Dataset Content. R4R consists of 1118 short 256×256 videos containing one or two balls rolling on three types of terrains (Fig. 3): a flat pool table (POOLR), a large ellipsoidal 'bowl' (BOWLR), and an irregular height-field (HEIGHTR). More specifically, there are 151 videos (avg. 99 frames/video) for the POOLR dataset with one ball; 216 videos (522 frames/video) for the BOWLR dataset with one ball; 543 videos (356 frames/video) for the HEIGHTR dataset with one ball; and 208 videos (206 frames/video) for the HEIGHTR dataset with two balls. We rolled a total of 7 differently colored balls for the HEIGHTR and BOWLR datasets, varying from 3.5 cm to 7 cm in diameter. The height-field surface fits into a $70 \times 70 \times 28$ cm^3 bounding box, with 76 cm diameter. The bowl was created using a 70 cm diameter ball, and is 60 cm high. Videos were randomly split into *train*, *validation*, and *test* sets. Ground-truth annotations are provided for the test split.

Dataset Collection. Both the bowl and height-field terrains were modeled using paper mâché on scaffolds, using a large inflatable ball and a custom-made wire-mesh frame, respectively. For the POOLR dataset, balls were rolled on the table, while for the other settings, balls were manually dropped from a small height and allowed to roll on. The setup was imaged using a fixed camera (Samsung Galaxy S8) from the top. The POOLR dataset was captured at 30 fps (due to low light), while all the others at 240 fps in order to reduce motion blur and later downsampled to 80 fps. Videos were cropped to only focus on the scenario of interest, i.e., ball(s) and terrain, and trimmed to retain the portion of the video containing motion. We rolled a total of 7 different balls: a pink foam ball (7 cm diameter), a fluorescent yellow tennis ball (6.8 cm), a blue and an orange ping-pong ball (4 cm), a black squash ball wit two yellow dots (4 cm), and a green and a brown cork ball (3.5 cm).

In order to create ground-truth tracks for the ball centers, we used a template-based tracker using zero-normalized cross-correlation in the LAB color space, and tracked each frame along with a smoothness term over time. The setup was manually initiated by providing suitable template. The raw results were then manually inspected, corrected, and saved as ground-truth. We found that due to environment jitter (the ball rolling on the different terrains often created vibration or deformation in the BOWLR and HEIGHTR datasets), differences in lighting across some experiments and different ball colors, the template-based tracker was not perfect and manual inspection was required.

It is worth noting that, while this process was enough to produce ground truth annotations for the test set, the method does not scale due to the need for manual verification and correction. While our aim here is to show the feasibility of learning physics in an unsupervised manner, such problems show that our deep tracker also has an applicative advantage compared to these traditional handcrafted approaches.

5   Results and Discussion

Implementation Details. For all networks trained on every dataset, weights were initialised using Xavier initialization [15]. The learning rate was initially set to 10^{-4} and was progressively decreased by a factor of 10 when no improvements were found over K epochs ($K = 100$ for the synthetic datasets). Training was stopped when the loss did not decrease for $2K$ consecutive epochs. Before processing images, we resized all dataset images to 128×128 pixels to fit in the GPU memory. We used TensorFlow [1] on a single NVIDIA Titan X GPU for all the experiments.

5.1   Unsupervised Tracker

We first evaluate our unsupervised object detector and tracker and compare against currently state-of-the-art trackers. We report results in Table 1 against the following trackers: 1. Optical Flow Lucas-Kanade (OFLK) from OpenCV [6] library; 2a. Flownet2-simple, which computes pairwise flowfields using FlowNet2 [16] and follows the velocity vectors; 2b. Flownet2-blob, where we after computing the flowfields from FlowNet2 [16], update the positions as the center of the blobs found in the flowfield. If no blob was detected, we updated the position according to 2a; 3. LAB: a template tracker similar to Sect. 4 without any manual corrections. Note that these methods need manual initialization at the objects positions (expect for LAB) or templating which needs more work with growing object count and/or variety. In addition to POOLR, BOWLR, and HEIGHTR from ROLL4REAL, we also consider two synthetic datasets from [11]

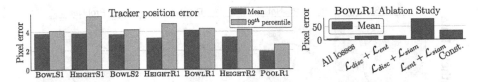

Fig. 4. Tracker errors and Ablation study. Left: Tracker errors on different dataset. The errors are consistently small across dataset and show that our tracker can perform well on a different range of real situations. Right: Ablation study. We try different combination of tracker losses on the BowLR dataset. 'Const.' indicates that we are predicting a constant point at the center of the image for reference. For left and right, position errors are reported in pixels. The number of balls in the datasets is appended to the name of the dataset.

Table 1. Tracker results across real datasets. The reported numbers are the average (left) and the variance (right) of the pixel error. All numbers refer to 128×128 images.

	PoolR		BowLR		HeightR		HeightR 2B.	
1. Optical Flow Lucas-Kanade	23.3	965	5.6	275	**2.7**	12.9	**2.0**	5.3
2a. FlowNet2-simple	41.4	767	30.4	715	16.6	206	-	-
2b. FlowNet2-blob	3.9	12.1	**2.2**	4.8	4.6	28.7	-	-
3. LAB w/o manual correction	**0.3**	**0.1**	16.4	247	8.3	104	21.7	102
4. Ours	1.9	0.2	4.1	**0.5**	3.3	**0.5**	3.4	**1.2**

in Fig. 4: BowLS for the ellipsoidal bowl with one or two balls and HeightS for the random height-fields. Figure 4-left reports the mean and 99th percentile pixel error of the extracted object positions against ground-truth averaged over multiple runs of our experiments. Even though the trackers perform well in practice, they suffer from *large variance*. For example, OFLK went off-track 15% of the time on the BowLR dataset, 10% for the HeightR, and 30% for PoolR. In contrast, ours never loses track of the object. The 99th percentile reported in Fig. 4 shows that the offset is almost constant generally due to the detection occurring on the edge of the objects. Overall, our method learns to track objects robustly in a diverse range of complex scenarios.

Importantly, since our tracker does not use any manual annotations it scales easily to larger synthetic datasets, multiple objects, and different object appearances within the same dataset by just providing more example data.

We also conducted an ablation study on the BowLR dataset to measure the impact of each loss term. Figure 4-right shows that, while each loss contributes to the final results, the best performance is obtained when all the terms are combined.

5.2   Unsupervised Physics Extrapolation

Supervised vs Unsupervised (Single Ball Synthetic Datasets). We now compare training predictors using either ground-truth object positions or the out-

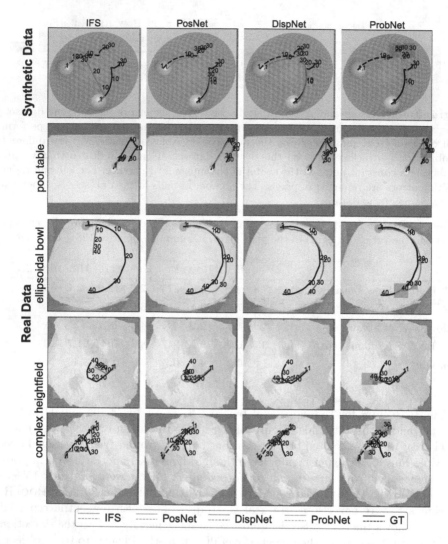

Fig. 5. Qualitative performance comparison for the various methods against ground-truth trajectories. Top-to-bottom: two balls colliding on an ellipsoidal bowl; single ball colliding against the walls of a pool table; single ball rolling on an ellipsoidal bow; single ball rolling on complex height-field; and two balls rolling on complex height-field. The top row is on synthetic data, while the other rows are on real-data. The green ellipsoids in the last column show the variance of the predictions estimated by *ProbNet* at selected locations. (Color figure online)

put of the unsupervised tracker. All predictors observe only $T_0 = 4$ frames as input (either positions or video frames) except VIN which uses $T_0 = 6$ and the least squares baselines which use $T_0 = 10$. All the networks were trained to predict T_{train} positions. Table 3 reports the average errors at time T_{train} and $2T_{train}$ to measure the ability of predictors to generalise beyond the training regime.

Table 2. Long term predictions compared on synthetic datasets with model trained with ground-truth from simulator. All the models (except VIN, Linear, and Quadratic) are given $T_0 = 4$ frames as input and train to predict first T_{train} positions. We report the average pixel error and perplexity for *PosNet* model at two different times. Perplexity, shown in bracket, is defined as $2^{-E[\log_2(p(x))]}$ where p is the estimated posterior distribution. *State* shows either the carried forward state is a physical quantity (Exp.), or an implicit vector or tensor (Imp.)

Method	Input	State	BowlS-$T_{train}=20$		HeightS-$T_{train}=20$	
			$T=T_{train}$	$2{\times}T_{train}$	T_{train}	$2{\times}T_{train}$
Method	Input	State	With positions from simulator			
Linear	2D pos.	Exp.	61.9	20.1	21.3	61.9
Quadratic	2D pos.	Exp.	11.7	93.1	26.7	126.0
IFS	2D pos.	Exp.	3.3	**8.9**	10.4	27.6
VIN	Visual	Imp.	24.0	30.2	42.6	42.7
PosNet	Visual	Imp.	**1.6**	24.4	7.2	24.6
DispNet	Visual	Imp.	2.5	20.6	7.7	25.8
ProbNet	Visual	Imp.	2.9 (32.1)	21.8 (54.0)	**6.4** (9.5)	**22.5** (12.7)
Method	Input	State	With positions from *unsupervised* tracker			
IFS	2D pos.	Exp.	13.3	**23.6**	23.1	38.3
VIN	Visual	Imp.	24.7	30.3	45.8	48.0
PosNet	Visual	Imp.	4.3	29.9	**6.6**	25.6
DispNet	Visual	Imp.	**3.9**	25.6	6.8	**22.7**
ProbNet	Visual	Imp.	4.9 (6.3)	27.0 (20.6)	6.9 (8.3)	23.3 (13.4)

Table 3. Long term predictions using one ball and real data. The table has the same format as Table 2. All models are trained using the unsupervised tracker, input and state are the same as Table 2, and we report pixel error (perplexity) at T.

Method	PoolR-$T_{train} = 15$		HeightR- $T_{train} = 20$		BowlR- $T_{train} = 20$	
	$T = T_{train}$	$2{\times}T_{train}$	T_{train}	$2{\times}T_{train}$	T_{train}	$2{\times}T_{train}$
IFS	26.0	37.5	48.0	58.1	26.2	39.1
VIN	50.9	40.8	40.2	47.3	33.9	33.0
PosNet	4.6	21.4	**5.6**	29.0	**5.6**	23.0
DispNet	**3.8**	23.6	**5.6**	**28.5**	6.5	**22.6**
ProbNet	4.7 (6.3)	**16.3** (11.3)	5.7(5.8)	30.0(22.5)	6.8(6.8)	23.5(13.8)

We see that the *Net* models (*ProbNet, DispNet, PosNet*) perform well using ground-truth positions or the unsupervised tracker outputs (e.g. *PosNet* error for BowlS/HeightS is 2.9/6.4 supervised vs 4.9/6.9 unsupervised), whereas IFS does not handle the transition well (3.3/10.4 to 13.3/23.1) and Linear, Quadratic and VIN are not competitive. The latest result shows a clear advantage of tensor-based state representations compared to vector based one. This suggests that modelling objects positions is done better by a representation which is spatially

Table 4. Long term predictions using two balls on real and synthetic data. Table layout and measures are the same as Table 2. Models are trained with positions from tracker, input and state are the same as Table 2, and we report pixel error (perplexity) at T.

Method	BowlS 2b.-$T_{train} = 15$		HeightR 2b.-$T_{train} = 15$	
	$T = T_{train}$	$2 \times T_{train}$	T_{train}	$2 \times T_{train}$
IFS	18.4	30.0	15.6	26.6
VIN	41.3	45.8	45.9	39.8
PosNet	**5.0**	**13.4**	**5.4**	**12.5**
DispNet	5.5	24.7	6.2	15.4
ProbNet	5.6 (7.3)	20.6 (13.7)	6.8 (7.9)	16.9 (12.4)

distributed. IFS also seems very sensitive to defects in the supplied annotations, since its knowledge of the environment is very limited, error correction is very challenging for it.

The main weakness of the *Net* models is that their performance degrades as prediction extends beyond the training horizon $2T_{train}$, whereas IFS generalizes more. At least *ProbNet* explicitly indicates that the model is uncertain when this occurs.

Synthetic vs Real (One Ball Datasets). On real datasets (Table 3), the *Net* models uniformly outperform others at both T_{train} and $2T_{train}$, with errors comparable to the synthetic case. Note that the real datasets in Roll4Real are particularly challenging due to the non-idealities of the surface (e.g. the BowlR surface is slightly elastic and wobbles as the ball rolls).

One vs Multiple Balls (Real and Synthetic Datasets). Finally, we move to cases where the balls are interacting with the environment and with each others due to collisions. This is particularly challenging when no ground-truth is used as multiple object tracking is much harder to achieve in an unsupervised setting than tracking a single object.

As shown in Table 4, the *Net* models still perform well. Due to memory limitations, models were trained for a slightly shorter time span T_{train}; since the corresponding predictions are shorter term, their errors are a little lower than before. Overall, the results show that neither perfect ground-truth annotations nor a very large dataset is required to train a reliable physical extrapolator. Still, we noticed that collisions were difficult to predict in the HeightR dataset (see the bottom row of Fig. 5), probably because such events are rare during training. In contrast, this seems to be much better handled by the models in the synthetic dataset (First row of Fig. 5).

5.3 Unsupervised Physics Interpolation

As in [11], we also study the interpolation problem considering their *Interp-Net* configuration. We compare the latter to the extrapolation network *DispNet*

Table 5. Extrapolation vs interpolation: one ball datasets. One ball datasets synthetic and real. Models are trained with positions from tracker. Pixel error at different time T.

T	PoolR $T_{train}=30$			BowlS $T_{train}=40$				HeightS $T_{train}=40$				BowlR $T_{train}=40$				HeightR $T_{train}=40$			
	10	20	30	10	20	30	40	10	20	30	40	10	20	30	40	10	20	30	40
DispNet	3.1	5.6	10.1	3.8	4.0	4.2	4.2	5.2	8.2	13.2	19.1	4.1	5.0	5.5	6.9	4.3	6.6	9.4	12.7
InterpNet	4.5	5.6	3.1	3.8	4.2	4.0	3.8	4.5	6.4	6.5	4.2	6.3	6.5	4.8	3.7	4.0	5.0	4.8	4.3

Table 6. Extrapolation vs interpolation: two balls datasets. Two balls datasets synthetic and real. Models are trained with positions from tracker. Pixel error at different time T.

T	BowlS 2b $T_{train}=30$			HeightR 2b $T_{train}=30$		
	10	20	30	10	20	30
DispNet	4.3	6.9	9.7	5.2	8.9	13.4
InterpNet	4.2	5.0	4.1	6.5	6.9	7.6

trained over a longer horizon $T_{train} = \{30, 40\}$. *InterpNet* has the same architecture has *DispNet* with the difference that, in addition to the first T_0 frames of the sequence, *InterpNet* additionally takes as input the last video frame as well. The first extracted state is used to regress the first T_0 positions as well as the positions at time T_{train}, so that this state is explicitly encouraged to encode information about the last position of the object as well. In Tables 5 and 6 we see that *InterpNet* managed to reduce the error in most cases. However in this case, compared to results in [11] *InterpNet* performs poorer on synthetic dataset and estimation of the intermediate states seems to be more challenging. Our interpretation is that the imperfect nature of the training data creates several possible path that this model in unable to solve. Finally we also noticed that the heightfield datasets seem to be very challenging as training for longer horizons didn't reduce the error as much as it does on the 'bowl'.

6 Conclusions

We presented a method that can learn to track physical objects such as balls rolling on complex terrains using only raw video sequences and no supervision. Combined with recent neural networks that can learn an implicit representation of physics, such a system is able to extrapolate object trajectories over time while accounting for object-environment and object-object interactions. To the best of our knowledge, this is the first time that learning long-term physics extrapolation without access to supervision or handcrafted simulators has been demonstrated. Through an extensive benchmark we also demonstrated the superiority of tensor-based state representation that were able to produce satisfactory results on real data without the need of large datasets.

We also contributed a new dataset, ROLL4REAL, of real-life video sequences for complex scenarios such as ball rollings on pool tables, bowls, and height-field, showing that all such methods are applicable to the real world. This data will be made publicly available.

In this work we used different colored objects to make them distinguishable, which in practice is one of the main limitation of our work. We plan to address this issue by using same colored objects and build a tracker that would be trained to detect all objects at once removing the need for iterative training.

Finally, we also plan to train the tracker and the extrapolator end-to-end, further improving tracking of multiple objects. We also aim at improving the generalisation of the predictors beyond the training regime; we believe that the key is to factor knowledge about the environment and the object dynamics to allow the models to remember the first better over longer time spans.

Acknowledgements. The authors would like to gratefully acknowledge the support of ERC 677195-IDIU and ERC SmartGeometry StG-2013-335373 grants.

References

1. Abadi, M., et al.: TensorFlow: large-scale machine learning on heterogeneous systems (2015). tensorflow.org
2. Agrawal, P., et al.: Learning to poke by poking: experiential learning of intuitive physics. In: Proceedings of NIPS, pp. 5074–5082 (2016)
3. Battaglia, P., et al.: Interaction networks for learning about objects, relations and physics. In: Proceedings of NIPS, pp. 4502–4510 (2016)
4. Battaglia, P., Hamrick, J., Tenenbaum, J.: Simulation as an engine of physical scene understanding. PNAS **110**(45), 18327–18332 (2013)
5. Bhattacharyya, A., et al.: Long-term image boundary prediction. In: Thirty-Second AAAI Conference on Artificial Intelligence. AAAI (2018)
6. Bradski, G.: The OpenCV library. Dr. Dobb's J. Softw. Tools **120**, 122–125 (2000)
7. Chang, M.B., et al.: A compositional object-based approach to learning physical dynamics. In: Proceedings of ICLR (2017)
8. Chiappa, S., et al.: Recurrent environment simulators (2017)
9. Denil, M., et al.: Learning to perform physics experiments via deep reinforcement learning. In: Deep Reinforcement Learning Workshop, NIPS (2016)
10. Ehrhardt, S., et al.: Learning A Physical Long-term Predictor. arXiv e-prints arXiv:1703.00247, March 2017
11. Ehrhardt, S., et al.: Learning to Represent Mechanics via Long-term Extrapolation and Interpolation. arXiv preprint arXiv:1706.02179, June 2017
12. Eslami, S.A., et al.: Attend, infer, repeat: fast scene understanding with generative models. In: Advances in Neural Information Processing Systems, pp. 3225–3233 (2016)
13. Finn, C., et al.: Deep spatial autoencoders for visuomotor learning. In: 2016 IEEE International Conference on Robotics and Automation (ICRA), pp. 512–519. IEEE (2016)
14. Fragkiadaki, K., et al.: Learning visual predictive models of physics for playing billiards. In: Proceedings of NIPS (2016)

15. Glorot, X., Bengio, Y.: Understanding the difficulty of training deep feedforward neural networks. In: Proceedings of the Thirteenth International Conference on Artificial Intelligence and Statistics, pp. 249–256 (2010)

16. Ilg, E., Mayer, N., Saikia, T., Keuper, M., Dosovitskiy, A., Brox, T.: Flownet 2.0: evolution of optical flow estimation with deep networks (2017)

17. Kansky, K., et al.: Schema networks: zero-shot transfer with a generative causal model of intuitive physics. In: International Conference on Machine Learning, pp. 1809–1818 (2017)

18. Ladický, L., et al.: Data-driven fluid simulations using regression forests. ACM Trans. Graph. (TOG) **34**(6), 199 (2015)

19. Lee, A.X., et al.: Stochastic adversarial video prediction. arXiv preprint arXiv:1804.01523 (2018)

20. Lerer, A., Gross, S., Fergus, R.: Learning physical intuition of block towers by example. In: Proceedings of the 33rd International Conference on International Conference on Machine Learning, vol. 48, pp. 430–438 (2016)

21. Li, W., Leonardis, A., Fritz, M.: Visual stability prediction and its application to manipulation. In: AAAI (2017)

22. Luc, P., Neverova, N., Couprie, C., Verbeek, J., LeCun, Y.: Predicting deeper into the future of semantic segmentation. In: ICCV (2017)

23. Misra, I., Zitnick, C.L., Hebert, M.: Shuffle and learn: unsupervised learning using temporal order verification. In: Leibe, B., Matas, J., Sebe, N., Welling, M. (eds.) ECCV 2016. LNCS, vol. 9905, pp. 527–544. Springer, Cham (2016). https://doi.org/10.1007/978-3-319-46448-0_32

24. Monszpart, A., Thuerey, N., Mitra, N.: SMASH: physics-guided reconstruction of collisions from videos. ACM Trans. Graph. (TOG) **35**(6), 1–14 (2016)

25. Mottaghi, R., et al.: Newtonian scene understanding: unfolding the dynamics of objects in static images. In: IEEE CVPR (2016)

26. Mrowca, D., et al.: Flexible Neural Representation for Physics Prediction. arXiv e-prints (2018)

27. Novotny, D., et al.: Self-supervised learning of geometrically stable features through probabilistic introspection (2018)

28. Oh, J., et al.: Action-conditional video prediction using deep networks in atari games. In: Advances in Neural Information Processing Systems, pp. 2863–2871 (2015)

29. Ondruska, P., Posner, I.: Deep tracking: seeing beyond seeing using recurrent neural networks. In: Proceedings of AAAI (2016)

30. Riochet, R., et al.: IntPhys: A Framework and Benchmark for Visual Intuitive Physics Reasoning. arXiv e-prints (2018)

31. Sanborn, A.N., Mansinghka, V.K., Griffiths, T.L.: Reconciling intuitive physics and newtonian mechanics for colliding objects. Psychol. Rev. **120**(2), 411 (2013)

32. Sanchez-Gonzalez, A., et al.: Graph networks as learnable physics engines for inference and control (2018)

33. Stewart, R., Ermon, S.: Label-free supervision of neural networks with physics and domain knowledge. In: AAAI, pp. 2576–2582 (2017)

34. Thewlis, J., Bilen, H., Vedaldi, A.: Unsupervised learning of object frames by dense equivariant image labelling. In: Advances in Neural Information Processing Systems (NIPS), pp. 844–855 (2017)

35. Tompson, J., et al.: Accelerating Eulerian Fluid Simulation With Convolutional Networks. arXiv e-print arXiv:1607.03597 (2016)

36. Watters, N., et al.: Visual interaction networks: learning a physics simulator from video. In: Guyon, I., Luxburg, U.V., Bengio, S., Wallach, H., Fergus, R., Vishwanathan, S., Garnett, R. (eds.) Advances in Neural Information Processing Systems 30, pp. 4542–4550. Curran Associates, Inc. (2017)
37. Wu, J., et al.: Galileo: perceiving physical object properties by integrating a physics engine with deep learning. In: Proceedings of NIPS, pp. 127–135 (2015)
38. Wu, J., et al.: Physics 101: learning physical object properties from unlabeled videos. In: Proceedings of BMVC (2016)
39. Wu, J., et al.: Learning to see physics via visual de-animation. In: Guyon, I., et al. (eds.) Advances in Neural Information Processing Systems (NIPS) 30, pp. 153–164. Curran Associates, Inc. (2017)
40. Wu, J., et al.: Learning to see physics via visual de-animation. In: Proceedings of NIPS (2017)

Deep Mixture of MRFs for Human Pose Estimation

Ioannis Marras[1,2(✉)], Petar Palasek[1,3], and Ioannis Patras[1]

[1] School of Electronic Engineering and Computer Science,
Queen Mary University of London, London, UK
{i.marras,p.palasek,i.patras}@qmul.ac.uk
[2] Huawei Noah's Ark Lab, London, UK
ioannis.marras@huawei.com
[3] MindVisionLabs Ltd, London, UK
petar.palasek@mindvisionlabs.com

Abstract. In this paper, we propose a new geometric model based on mixture of Markov Random Fields (MRFs) for human pose estimation. We build on previous work that expresses the global constraints on the relative locations of the body joints using an auto-encoder ConvNet which performs dimensionality reduction on the heat maps, and recovers in this manner a low dimensional manifold on which the global pose of the human body lies. To address the shortcomings of this architecture, and obtain more meaningful vectors that span the low dimensional pose space, we propose to replace the auto-encoder network layer with a layer that implements a Gaussian mixture model (GMM) that provides a soft clustering of the human pose predictions in an online fashion. We show that: (a) a large number of meaningful global poses is feasible, this way preserving the underlying structure of informative body poses; (b) the clustering helps to properly initialize the MRF filters of each different global pose, (c) a body joint masking data augmentation procedure can be better exploited and that (d) the system stability is significantly improved. To the best of our knowledge, this is the first time that a clustering algorithm like GMM is used in an online fashion for the problem of 2D human pose estimation. The efficacy of our framework has been demonstrated through extensive experiments on widely used public benchmarks.

Keywords: Human pose estimation · Deep learning ·
Markov Random Fields

1 Introduction

The problem of precise localization of important landmarks of the human body has received substantial attention in the Computer Vision community, since such

I. Marras and P. Palasek—This work was done while the authors were at Queen Mary University of London.

information is very important in understanding human activity in images and videos (i.e. gaming, video analysis, action and gesture recognition). Especially Deep Neural Networks (DNN), and more specifically Convolutional Neural Networks (ConvNets) [6,19,38] have demonstrated remarkable performance in this task. A key ingredient for the success of state-of-the-art deep learning models is the availability of large amounts of training data [1,20,34].

The enforcement of constraints between different outputs, that is the enforcement of geometric constraints on the relative locations of the body joints, is a central issue in human pose estimation. This is typically modeled at the later layers of a ConvNet. Recent methods introduce explicit geometric constraints in the form of a MRF (e.g. [37]) where pairwise relations between different joints are encoded in a single ConvNet layer. The use of a single filter to model all of the pairwise relations is a major drawback with such an approach. In the case of small pose variations this works well and therefore the conditional probabilities have a few distinct modes. However, for more complex poses the conditionals become more uninformative as they attempt to model pairwise relations under a wide variety of poses. In the same spirit, in [4] an implicit modeling of the geometric constraints in the latest layers of the network was performed imposing pairwise constraints encoded in a single filter. To deal with this problem, a recent approach in [26], improving the model in [36], showed that the idea of using global constraints, such as global poses, in order to build constrained MRF-based models is a way for simple geometric models to handle complex body poses.

The framework in [26] comprises of: (a) a coarse ConvNet that provides coarse low resolution heat-maps for the joint locations, (b) a part-based constrained MRF model, and (c) a refinement ConvNet, that refines the estimation within windows around the peaks of the coarse heat-maps. The coarse and the refinement models are reminiscent of recent works [28] that reuse early layers at the later stages of the architecture. The MRF-based spatial ConvNet between the coarse and the refinement model introduces geometric constraints between joints, where: (a) the dynamic filters that implement the message passing in the inference are factored in a way that constrains them by a low dimensional pose manifold, the projection to which is estimated by a side auto-encoder ConvNet that is jointly trained with the other two ConvNets, and (b) the strengths of the pairwise joint constraints are modeled by weights that are jointly estimated by the other parameters of the network. The geometric model expresses message-passing as convolution operations that can be implemented using ConvNets (the filters expressing conditional dependencies between the locations of different joints). Each of the filters is assumed to be a linear combination of K filters. The weights of this linear combination are the projection of the heat-maps into a K dimensional manifold that encodes global constraints related to the K global poses. The parameters of the whole architecture are learned by optimizing a cost function that combines both the generative term that comes from the auto-encoder ConvNet, and the discriminative term that comes from the heat-map prediction. This approach achieved significant improvement over

[36], although there are same major drawbacks. As it is reported in [26], choosing more than four global poses ($K > 4$) drops the pose estimation accuracy since meaningless poses were produced. The auto-encoder is used for performing mainly dimensionality reduction and not pure pose clustering since it is not able to determine what information is relevant (body pose structure understanding). As the body pose space is divided in a very small number of not very informative global poses, the variation of the learned global poses cannot be high. Another drawback is that the filters for all the different global poses are initialized with exactly the same information based on the empirical histograms of joint displacements provided by the coarse ConvNet, which negatively affects the performance/stability of the spatial model. Convergence to a global optimum is not guaranteed since the spatial model used [37] is not tree structured and at the same time the number of global poses is limited. Also, due to the Argmax function this cascade of ConvNets is not fully differentiable, and as the whole system cannot be fine-tuned properly the regression function is frequently sub-optimal. This has a negative effect especially on the geometric model training.

In this paper, we significantly improve the idea in [26] by modifying its MRF-part based spatial model network. More specifically, we propose to replace the auto-encoder ConvNet with a layer which implements a GMM [3] on the heat maps of human joint predictions in an online fashion – the goal is to define meaningful and informative global poses that correspond to the means of the extracted Gaussians. This approach allows estimating a larger number of global poses in comparison to [26], and leads to more accurate human joint localization. The underlying spatial model is a mixture of MRFs, where each mixture component is a simple MRF-part based geometric model that encodes the relative position of pairs of joints. An initial clustering of the heatmaps initilizes the mixture means and the MRF filters for a specific cluster (global pose) is based on the empirical histograms of joint displacements, for samples belonging to the specific cluster (global pose). In this way, the performance/stability of the geometric model is improved, and the providing better estimates for the refinement network to give a more accurate prediction within a window that contains high resolution image information. Based on the bibliography, in the case of challenging scenarios (i.e. occlusions) the solution to a successful pose estimation must rely on some sort of structural inference or knowledge – this is why body joint masking data augmentation schemes were adopted in works like [22]. Our spatial model explicitly learns a different meaningful joint inter-connectivity for each global body pose, enforcing global pose consistency, and can benefit more from these interesting ideas for data augmentation. Our cascade model is trained in an end-to-end fashion to minimize the weighted sum of the costs of each of the three ConvNets. To do that, we used the Soft-Argmax function [25] to convert heat-maps directly to joint coordinates and consequently allow detection methods to be transformed into regression methods. We show experimentally that our system provides state-of-the-art results on very challenging benchmarks. To the best of our knowledge, this is the first time that a soft clustering algorithm like GMM is used in an online fashion for the problem of 2D human pose estimation.

2   Related Work

Some approaches aim to model higher-order part relationships. Methods using Pictorial Structures, such as [13], made this approach tractable with so called Deformable Part Models (DPM). Following the Poselets approach, the Armlets approach in [14] employs a semi-global classifier for part configuration and shows good performance on real-world data. A cascade of body part detectors to obtain more discriminative templates was employed in [21]. Algorithms which model more complex joint relationships, such as [42], use a flexible mixture of templates modeled by linear SVMs. All these approaches use hand crafted features (i.e. edges, contours, HoG features and color histograms), which have been shown to have poor generalization performance.

A DNN to directly regress the 2D coordinates of joints was used in [38]. Recently, in [41] the use of very deep sequential convolution-deconvolution architecture with large receptive fields to directly perform pose matching on the heat-maps was proposed. The hourglass module proposed in [28] is an extension of [41] with the addition of residual connections between the convolution-deconvolution sub-modules. The hourglass module can effectively capture and combine features across scales. In [6], an image dependent spatial model indicating the likely location of a neighboring joint is combined with neural networks to improve the pose estimation accuracy. The Iterative Error Feedback (IEF) by injecting the prediction error back to the input space, improving estimations recursively is presented in [5]. In [7], a conditional adversarial network for pose estimation, termed Adversarial PoseNet, which trains a multi-task pose generator with two discriminator networks was proposed. The two discriminators function like an expert who distinguishes reasonable poses from unreasonable ones. In [8], the incorporation of convolutional neural networks with a multi-context attention mechanism into an end-to-end framework was proposed. In [18], together with extremely deep body part detectors, efficient image-conditioned pairwise terms were introduced between body parts that allow performing multi-people pose estimation based on an incremental optimization strategy. In [15], it is presented how chained predictions can lead to a powerful tool for structured vision tasks. Chain models allow to sidestep assumptions about the joint distribution of the output variables, other than the capacity of a neural network to model conditional distributions. In [17], it is shown that hierarchical Rectified Gaussian models can be optimized with rectified neural networks. Bottom-up baselines based on multi-scale prediction which consistently improve upon the results with top-down feedback are introduced. In [24], an approach where each location in the image votes for the position of each joint using a ConvNet is proposed. The voting scheme allows the use of information from the whole image, rather than relying on a sparse set of joint locations. Using dense, multi-target votes, enables the computation of image-dependent joint probabilities by looking at consensus voting. In [33], DeepCut, a graph cutting algorithm that relies on body parts detected by DeepPose [38] is proposed. In [16], a method for tackling the task of dense human pose estimation using discriminative trained models is presented. A Parsing Induced Learner (PIL) to assist human pose estimation by effectively exploiting parsing information is proposed in [29]. PIL learns to predict certain pose model parameters from parsing features and adapts the pose model to extracting complementary useful features. A method to jointly optimize data augmentation and network training is presented in [31]. An augmentation network is designed to generate adversarial data augmentations in order to improve the training of a target network.

A multi-scale regression network jointly optimizes the global body structure configuration via determining connectivity among body keypoints based on the mutli-scale features. In [36] heat-maps are generated by running an image through multiple resolution banks in parallel to simultaneously capture features at a variety of scales. In [26,37], multiple branches of convolutional networks fused the features from an image pyramid, and used MRFs for post-processing. A multi-scale structure-aware approach which works hand-in-hand with the structure-aware loss design, to infer high-order structural matching of detected body keypoints is presented in [22].

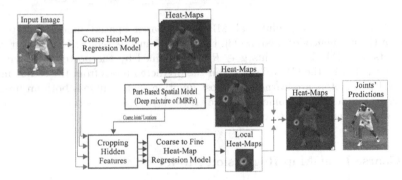

Fig. 1. The big picture of our unified learning framework is similar to [26]. The modified part is in the core of the framework and depicted with a red box. (Color figure online)

As it was shown in the bibliography, a GMM layer can be integrated into a deep neural network framework through a generalized softmax layer [39,40]. By estimating state posterior probabilities directly, the hybrid approach has shown enormous gains over old-fashioned GMMs. GMMs can be improved when trained on the output or a hidden layer of a neural network. The idea of a GMM layer has been used extensively in many computer vision and machine learning problems, i.e. action recognition [30], anomaly detection [43], clustering [11].

3 The Architecture of Our Framework

The outline of our unified learning framework is similar to [26] and it is shown in Fig. 1. It consists of a coarse heat-map regression model, a module for sampling and cropping the convolutional feature maps at a specified location for each joint, a fine heat-map regression (coarse to fine) model, and our proposed spatial geometric model.

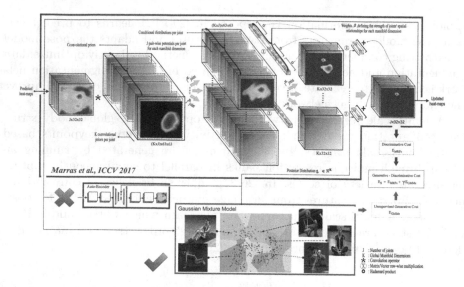

Fig. 2. The proposed convolutional MRF-part based spatial model architecture. Instead of the auto-encoder used in [26], the lower branch is replaced by a layer which implements a GMM. The weights $\mathbf{g} \in R^K$ are defined by the posterior distribution (Eq. 4) calculated by the GMM layer given the predicted poses from the coarse model. The GMM parameters are learned by a cost function that combines both an unsupervised generative term that comes from the GMM layer and a discriminative cost that comes from the heat-map prediction.

3.1   Coarse Heat-Map Regression Model

The same coarse heat-map regression model used in [26] is also used in our system. A ten layer multi-resolution ConvNet takes as input an RGB Gaussian pyramid of three levels, and for each body joint outputs a 32×32 pixel heat-map at a lower resolution than the input image due to the presence of pooling. Each output heat-map corresponds to a per-pixel likelihood for key joint locations on the human skeleton. A local contrast normalization (LCN) filtering using the same filter kernel in each of the three resolution inputs is performed by the first network layer. Please refer to [26] for more details.

3.2   Coarse-to-Fine Heat-Map Regression Model

Due to pooling, the coarse regression model loses spatial accuracy. To counteract this, an additional coarse-to-fine regression model is used to refine the localization result of the unified coarse model. The fine regression ConvNet proposed in [36] and used in [26] is also used in our framework. Its goal is to estimate the joint offset location within a region of the image extracted around the estimates of the coarse model by reusing existing convolution features from the coarse model. Cropping windows of varying sizes are used to define regions of interest, this way reducing the number of trainable parameters in the cascade. The output of this network is a high resolution per-pixel heat-map corresponding to the area selected by the cropping window. Please refer to [36] for more details.

3.3   Part-Based Spatial Model

The coarse model has difficulties learning an implicit model of the constraints of the body parts for the full range of possible body poses. Thus, the use of a higher-level spatial model to constrain the joint inter-connectivity and enforce a global pose consistency is of great importance. Our part-based spatial model, depicted in Fig. 2, improves the MRF-based spatial model proposed in [26], which formulates deep globally constrained tree-structured MRFs implemented as a specialized layer in a ConvNet. The expectation of this stage is not to improve the performance of detections that are already close to the ground-truth pose, but to remove false positive outliers that are anatomically incorrect. A short introduction of the model proposed in [26] is provided bellow. Afterwards, we describe in detail our part-based spatial model, based on a mixture of MRFs.

The model in [26] is an extension of the work in [37]. More informative conditionals are estimated as they model pairwise relations under specific global constraints. The message passing used in inference is expressed using convolutional filtering operations and the filters that produce the unary and the pairwise potentials of each MRF model can be learned by supervised training. It is important that the sizes of the convolution kernels are adjusted in a way that the largest joint displacement is covered within the convolution window. Since a 32×32 pixel heat-map is the input to this model, this results in large 63×63 convolution kernels that are able to account for a joint displacement radius restricted within the input heat-map. In this network, each of the filters, denoted by $f_{a|c}$, is a linear combination of K filters $f_{a|c}^k$, where the weights $\mathbf{g} \in R^K$ of this linear combination are determined by the projection of the heat-maps into a K dimensional manifold that encodes global constraints, such as the global pose. For the kth global pose, $f_{a|c}^k$ is the function of the conditional probability $e_{a|c}^k$ of the location of joint a, given the location of another joint c. That is:

$$f_{a|c} = \sum_{k=1}^{K} \mathbf{g}_k * f_{a|c}^k, \tag{1}$$

where $f_{a|c}^k = SoftPlus(e_{a|c}^k)$ (please refer to [26] for more details). The projection of the heat-map volume to the low dimensional manifold, that is the calculation of the weights $\mathbf{g}$, is performed by a separate branch of the network that performs dimensionality reduction on the heat-maps. The weights $\mathbf{g}$ are learned by a cost function that combines both a generative term that comes from the auto-encoder ConvNet and a discriminative cost that comes from the heat-map prediction. For each of the K dimensions of the pose manifold, a weighting scheme that determines the strength of the joints' spatial relationships is used. That is, it is allowed that, conditioned on a global pose, some pairwise relations between different joints are more informative that others. This is expressed as a filtering operation with weights $\beta_{a|c}^k, (1 \leq k \leq K)$ that are learned jointly with the other parameters of the network using back-propagation. That is:

$$\bar{e}_a = exp\left(\sum_{c \in V} \left[\sum_{k=1}^{K} \beta_{a|c}^k \log \left[\mathbf{g}_k * f_{a|c}^k * ReLU(e_c) + SoftPlus(b_{a|c}) \right] \right] \right). \quad (2)$$

The filtering steps of Eq. 2 are applied in an iterative manner updating the same $f_{a|c}$, $b_{a|c}$ and $\beta_{a|c}$ parameters.

4   The Proposed Deep Mixture of MRFs

A drawback of [26] is that the global poses of the spatial model depend on the auto-encoder that performs dimensionality reduction and not on a clustering algorithm which would preserve the underlying structure of meaningful body poses. As it is reported in that work, by choosing more than four global poses ($K > 4$) drops the pose estimation accuracy since not meaningful poses were produced – this means that the variation of the learned global poses is limited. In our work we show how a clustering method could be used to avoid this. More specifically, in the proposed spatial geometric model, we have replaced the auto-encoder ConvNet with a layer which implements a GMM with the goal of defining the global poses by clustering the pose predictions from the coarse ConvNet. The GMM procedure is implemented as a specialized layer in a ConvNet. The weights $\mathbf{g} \in R^K$ are defined by the posterior distribution calculated by the GMM layer, given the predicted poses from the coarse model. The GMM parameters are learned by a cost function that combines both the unsupervised generative term that comes from the GMM layer and the discriminative cost that comes from the heat-map prediction (Fig. 2).

Another reason that the global poses estimated in [26] are not very informative is the model initialization strategy. There is no initial estimation of the K-dimensional manifold, i.e. no initial clustering of the pose predictions is performed. Instead, K random perturbations of the empirical histograms of joint displacements, created based on all the pose predictions, are used to initialize each $f_{a|c}^k, (1 \leq k \leq K)$. This is a major drawback, since a good initialization improves the learning performance, decreases training time and improves the optimization stability. In our spatial geometric model, the initial clustering of the predicted poses makes it feasible to initialize $f_{a|c}^k$ using the corresponding empirical histograms of joint displacements created from only the pose predictions which belong to the kth global pose. We also present a way for training the GMM layer when the training data is not available all at once, but it is arriving in mini-batches, i.e. we show how to fit the GMM in an online fashion.

Regarding the optimization stability, the convergence to a global optimum is not guaranteed in [26] given that its spatial model is not tree structured and the number of global poses is limited. In our case, the creation of many informative global poses together with our model initialization technique improves the system performance even in case of complex body poses.

Gaussian Mixture Model Layer. A GMM is defined as a weighted sum of K components, which is the number of the global poses in our case:

$$u_\lambda(\boldsymbol{x}) = \sum_{k=1}^{K} w_k u_k(\boldsymbol{x}), \tag{3}$$

where w_k is a component weight and $u_k(\boldsymbol{x})$ is a probability density function of the Gaussian distribution. Every GMM can be described by the parameter set $\lambda = \{w_k, \boldsymbol{\mu}_k, \boldsymbol{\Sigma}_k, k = 1, ..., K\}$, where w_k is the k-th component weight, $\boldsymbol{\mu}_k$ is its mean vector and $\boldsymbol{\Sigma}_k$ its covariance matrix. The mixture coefficients $\{w_k\}$ are constrained to be positive and to sum to one which can be easily enforced using a softmax function as it was done in [23]. For each sample $\boldsymbol{x}_t$, the K posteriors describing the responsibility of each component for generating the sample can be found as:

$$\gamma_t(k) = \frac{w_k u_k(\boldsymbol{x}_t)}{\sum_l^K w_l u_l(\boldsymbol{x}_t)}. \tag{4}$$

When viewing the GMM as a neural network layer, we treat the sample $\boldsymbol{x}_t$ as the input to the layer and the posteriors $\{\gamma_t(k), k = 1, \ldots, K\}$ as its output.

Gaussian Mixture Model Training. Finding the $\boldsymbol{\theta}$ which maximizes $L(\boldsymbol{\theta}) = \log p(\boldsymbol{x}|\boldsymbol{\theta})$, i.e. estimating the parameters $\boldsymbol{\theta}$ of a Gaussian mixture model of a probability distribution of a random variable X, $p(\boldsymbol{x}|\boldsymbol{\theta}) = \sum_z p(\boldsymbol{x}, z|\boldsymbol{\theta})$, is done using the iterative expectation-maximization (EM) algorithm [10]. Starting from some initial estimate of the parameters $\boldsymbol{\theta}_0$, the EM algorithm iteratively performs two steps at each time step t; the E-step which determines the posterior distribution $\tilde{p}_t(z) = p(z|\boldsymbol{x}, \boldsymbol{\theta}_{t-1})$ using the parameter estimates from the previous time step $\boldsymbol{\theta}_{t-1}$, and the M-step which finds new estimates of the parameters $\boldsymbol{\theta}_t$ as the ones that maximize the expected value of the log likelihood $L(\boldsymbol{\theta})$ under the estimated posterior distribution from the E-step, $\tilde{p}_t$. That is, $\boldsymbol{\theta}_t$ is set to the $\boldsymbol{\theta}$ that maximizes $E_{\tilde{p}_t}[\log p(\boldsymbol{x}, z|\boldsymbol{\theta})]$. This procedure is guaranteed to never worsen the log likelihood of the data [10]. Following the work of [27], we can define a function $F(\tilde{p}, \boldsymbol{\theta})$ whose value is maximized or at least increased by both the E-step and the M-step of the EM algorithm as

$$F(\tilde{p}, \boldsymbol{\theta}) = E_{\tilde{p}}[\log p(\boldsymbol{x}, z|\boldsymbol{\theta})] + H(\tilde{p}) \quad \text{with} \quad H(\tilde{p}) = -E_{\tilde{p}}[\log \tilde{p}(\boldsymbol{x})]. \tag{5}$$

This function can also be written in terms of a Kullback-Liebler divergence between $\tilde{p}(z)$ and $p_\theta(z) = p(z|\boldsymbol{x}, \boldsymbol{\theta})$ as

$$F(\tilde{p}, \boldsymbol{\theta}) = -D(\tilde{p}||p_\theta) + L(\boldsymbol{\theta}) \quad \text{where} \quad D(\tilde{p}||p_\theta) = \sum_z \tilde{p}(z) \log \frac{\tilde{p}(z)}{p_\theta(z)} \tag{6}$$

is the KL divergence and $L(\boldsymbol{\theta})$ is the log-likelihood, $L(\boldsymbol{\theta}) = \log p(\boldsymbol{x}|\boldsymbol{\theta})$. The local and global maxima of $F(\tilde{p}, \boldsymbol{\theta})$ and $L(\boldsymbol{\theta})$ are equivalent [27], so maximizing $F(\tilde{p}, \boldsymbol{\theta})$ also leads to the maximum likelihood estimate parameters $\boldsymbol{\theta}$. When the objective function is defined as in Eq. 5 the E-step of the EM algorithm maximizes $F(\tilde{p}, \boldsymbol{\theta})$ with respect to $\tilde{p}$ and the M-step maximizes it with respect to $\boldsymbol{\theta}$. The unsupervised objective function whose goal is to fit a GMM to the given data can be written as

$$F(\boldsymbol{x}, \tilde{p}, \boldsymbol{\theta}) = - \sum_z \tilde{p}(z) \log \frac{\tilde{p}(z)}{p_\theta(z)} + \log p(\boldsymbol{x}|\boldsymbol{\theta}). \tag{7}$$

Online Gaussian Mixture Model Training. In the case when the expression $E_{\tilde{p}_t} \left[\log p(\boldsymbol{x}, z | \boldsymbol{\theta}) \right]$ which we wish to optimize in the M-step of the EM algorithm is not completely maximized, but only moved towards its maximum, the procedure will still result in improvements of the data likelihood [10]. As our goal is to train the GMM implemented as a neural network layer, we want to be able to use the usual, gradient based optimization methods for learning the GMM's parameters. We implement the M-step by calculating the gradients of the function defined in Eq. 6 with respect to all of the GMM parameters and performing a number of gradient ascent steps to move the value of $F(\tilde{p}, \boldsymbol{\theta})$ toward its maximum.

The steps of the generalized mini-batch EM algorithm which we use in this work are presented bellow. Given a mini-batch of training samples, i.e. only a small subset of the available training data, with t denoting the iteration of the algorithm, we can summarize the algorithm as follows:

- E-step: Maximize $F(\tilde{p}_t, \boldsymbol{\theta}_{t-1})$ with respect to $\tilde{p}_t$ by setting $\tilde{p}_t(z_k) \leftarrow \gamma_{t-1}(k)$, where $\gamma_{t-1}(k)$ is the posterior distribution over all the samples in the current mini-batch, calculated using the parameters $\boldsymbol{\theta}_{t-1}$ from time step $t-1$.
- M-step: Repeat n_M times:
  - Calculate the gradients of $F(\tilde{p}_t, \boldsymbol{\theta}_{t-1})$ with respect to each of the parameters θ_{t-1} in $\boldsymbol{\theta}_{t-1}$; $\nabla_{\theta_{t-1}} F(\tilde{p}_t, \boldsymbol{\theta}_{t-1})$.
  - Update each θ_t in $\boldsymbol{\theta}_t$ using a gradient based method, e.g.
    $\theta_t \leftarrow \theta_{t-1} + \lambda \nabla_{\theta_{t-1}} F(\tilde{p}_t, \boldsymbol{\theta}_{t-1})$.

Here we denoted the set of GMM parameters at iteration t as $\boldsymbol{\theta}_t$. Note that the gradient based optimization method used in the M step is not limited to gradient ascent, but other methods such as Adagrad [12] or RMSProp [35] could be used too. The weights $\mathbf{g} \in R^K$ are defined by the posterior distribution (Eq. 4) calculated by the GMM layer given the predicted poses from the coarse model.

Parameter Initialization. We use the k-means++ algorithm [2] to initialize the means μ_k for each of the Gaussians in our mixture model. We initialize each of the K component weights w_k to $1/K$ and set the standard deviations σ_k to values estimated from the data used for initialization. After, we find the closest mean, i.e. cluster center, for each of the predicted poses which are the input to the GMM layer and we initialize the filters $f_{a|c}^k$ using the corresponding empirical histograms of joint displacements created from the pose predictions which belong to the kth cluster (k^{th} global pose).

5   Evaluation

In the case of multi-person scenarios, more than one possible body joints can co-exist in the view. In an occluded case, no joint can be observed. To tackle these challenging scenarios, we used the joint masking data augmentation scheme introduced in [22] and increase the relevant training data to fine-tune the ConvNets. Occluded body joint training samples and samples with artificially inserted joints are generated in [22], in order to effectively improve the learning of the presented framework for extreme cases. More specifically, a background patch is copied and put onto a joint to cover it and simulate a joint occlusion, or a body joint patch is copied onto a nearby background to simulate multiple existing joints, the case that mostly occurs in multi-person scenarios. Since this data augmentation results in multiple identical joint patches, the solution to a successful pose estimation must rely on some sort of structural inference or knowledge. As our spatial model explicitly learns a different joint inter-connectivity for each meaningful global body pose, this way enforcing global pose consistency, such kind of interesting ideas for data augmentation are ideal for our system.

The curriculum learning strategy and the joint training strategy adopted in [26] were used in our system. One heat-map [32,38] for each of the joint positions is estimated. At training time, the ground truth labels for all ConvNets are heat-maps that are constructed for each joint separately by placing a 2D Gaussian with fixed variance at the ground truth position of the corresponding joint. Lets denote as E_C, $E_S = E_{MRF} + \beta E_{GMMs}$ and E_F the objective functions for each of our three ConvNets: Coarse, Spatial and Coarse-to-Fine model. E_{GMMs} denotes the objective function for the GMM ConvNet, while β is a constant used to provide a trade-off between the relative importance of the two sub-tasks. Also, let us denote by (I_i, N_i) the i-th training example, where $N_i \in R^{2J}$ denote the coordinates of the J joints in the image I_i. Given a training dataset $D = \{(I_i, N_i)\}$ and the ConvNet regressor ρ, we train all our ConvNets by estimating the network weights w that minimize the same objective function:

$$E_{\{C,MRF,F\}} = \sum_{(I,N)\in D} \sum_{m,n,j} \|G_{m,n,j}(N_j) - \rho_{m,n,j}(I, w)\|^2, \qquad (8)$$

where $G_{m,n,j}(N_j)$ is a Gaussian centred at N_j with σ fixed. The limitation of the regression methods in [26,37] is that the regression function is frequently suboptimal. In our case, we used the Soft-Argmax function [25] to convert heat-maps directly to joint coordinates and consequently allow detection methods to be transformed into regression methods. The main advantage of regression methods over detection ones is that they often are fully differentiable. This means that the output of the pose estimation can be used in further processing and the whole system can be fine-tuned.

We evaluate the proposed method on two widely used benchmarks on pose estimation: extended Leeds Sports Poses (LSP) [21] and MPII Human Pose [1]. The LSP dataset is composed by 2K annotated poses with up to 14 joint locations. The images were gathered from Flickr with sports people. The MPII dataset consists of images taken from a wide range of real-world activities with

Fig. 3. MPII dataset: visual results of human pose estimation on sample images by our system.

full-body pose annotations. It is composed of about 25K images of which 15K are training samples, 3K are validation samples and 7K are testing samples. The images are taken from YouTube videos covering 410 different human activities and the poses are manually annotated with 16 joints. The training protocol adopted in [37] was used. In case of severely occluded joints we used a ground truth heat-map of all zeros for supervision. Training the coarse heat-map regression model took around 4 days, the part-based spatial model took 3 days and the coarse to fine heat-map regression model took approximately 3 days on a 12 GB Nvidia Titan X GPU. A forward-pass for a single image through the whole architecture for $K = 15$ takes around 122 ms: 75 ms for the coarse ConvNet, 34 ms for the GMM-MRF ConvNet and 13 ms for the refinement ConvNet. For comparison purposes, in case of $K = 5$ the time for the GMM-MRF ConvNet is 20 ms.

5.1   Experimental Results

We performed quantitative evaluations of the 2D pose estimation using the probability of correct keypoints measure with respect to the head size (PCKh) as well as the standard percentage of correct keypoints (PCK) metric [9] which reports the percentage of keypoint detection falling within a normalized distance of the ground-truth. Figure 3 depicts some examples of human pose estimation results produced by our system. Our system performs very well even in the case of very challenging scenarios, i.e. occlusions, complex body poses.

The error per joint for the MPII and LSP datasets is reported in Tables 1 and 2. As reported in [26], it is hard to make the model in [26] converge to a good solution, especially for more than four global poses ($K > 4$). A reason for that is because the auto-encoder ConvNet performs mainly dimensionality reduction, not pure clustering. Even when the low-dimensional latent model converges, there is no guarantee that the learned global poses' structures are different and meaningful at the same time, which is critical for the performance of MRF model. Especially in the case of MPII, which is the most diverse dataset, this is a major drawback. This is the reason why a "Curriculum Learning Strategy" and a very small number of $K(= 4)$ were adopted in [26]. Once the low dimensional space is defined using the easy training samples, the learning rate is significantly decreased and the difficult cases cannot significantly change the low dimensional manifold. In our case, the GMM layer directly learns from the underlying meaningful pose structures. Even without the "Curriculum Learning Strategy", our system always converges for a much larger ($K = 15$) value, and leads to a

Table 1. Comparison with state-of-the-arts on MPII dataset.

Methods	PCKh @ 0.15								PCKh @ 0.5							
	Head	Sho.	Elb.	Wri.	Hip	Knee	Ank.	F.Body	Head	Sho.	Elb.	Wri.	Hip	Knee	Ank.	F.Body
Tompson et al., NIPS 2014 [37]	63.1	57.5	47.2	41.7	44.8	36.5	30.1	46.8	95.8	90.3	80.5	74.3	77.6	69.7	62.8	79.6
Carreira et al., CVPR 2016 [5]	62.3	58.8	48.4	39.6	49.9	40.2	33.5	48.3	95.7	91.7	81.7	72.4	82.8	73.2	66.4	81.3
Tompson et al., CVPR 2015 [36]	63.3	58.4	51.1	45.1	47.3	38.9	31.3	48.9	96.1	91.9	83.9	77.8	80.9	72.3	64.8	82.0
Pishchulin et al., CVPR 2016 [33]	61.2	57.4	50.6	43.9	49.3	42.9	35.3	49.4	94.1	90.2	83.4	77.3	82.6	75.7	68.6	82.4
Hu et al., CVPR 2016 [17]	-	-	-	-	-	-	-	-	95.0	91.6	83.0	76.6	81.9	74.5	69.5	82.4
Lifshitz et al., ECCV 2016 [24]	-	-	-	-	-	-	-	-	97.8	93.3	85.7	80.4	85.3	76.6	70.2	85.0
Gkioxari et al., ECCV 2016 [15]	-	-	-	-	-	-	-	-	96.2	93.1	86.7	82.1	85.2	81.4	74.1	86.1
Insafutdinov et al., ECCV 2016 [18]	-	-	-	-	-	-	-	-	96.8	95.2	89.3	84.4	88.4	83.4	78.0	88.5
Wei et al., CVPR 2016 [41]	64.6	62.1	55.8	50.5	55.0	49.7	46.5	55.4	97.8	95.0	88.7	84.0	88.4	82.8	79.4	88.9
Bulat et al., ECCV 2016 [4]	64.7	61.8	56.9	52.3	56.0	52.3	49.1	55.4	97.8	95.1	89.9	85.3	89.4	85.7	81.9	89.6
Newell et al., ECCV 2016 [28]	65.2	62.9	58.4	53.8	56.9	53.8	50.6	57.3	98.2	96.3	91.2	87.1	90.1	87.4	83.6	90.9
Chu et al., CVPR 2017 [8]	-	-	-	-	-	-	-	-	98.5	96.3	91.9	88.1	90.6	88.0	85.0	91.5
Peng et al., CVPR 2018 [31]	-	-	-	-	-	-	-	-	98.1	96.6	92.5	88.4	90.7	87.7	83.5	91.5
Chen et al., ICCV 2017 [7]	-	-	-	-	-	-	-	-	98.1	96.5	92.5	88.5	90.2	89.6	86.0	91.9
Ke et al., ECCV 2018 [22]	-	-	-	-	-	-	-	-	98.5	96.8	92.7	88.4	90.6	89.3	86.3	92.1
Marras et al., ICCV 2017 [26]	65.8	63.7	58.9	54.7	57.9	54.4	51.9	58.2	99.1	97.2	93.3	88.9	91.9	88.4	86.1	92.1
Nie et al., CVPR 2018 [29]	-	-	-	-	-	-	-	-	98.6	96.9	93.0	89.1	91.7	89.0	86.2	92.4
Ours - only k-means++	64.5	61.5	56.8	52.0	55.7	52.1	49.0	55.2	98.4	96.0	91.5	87.7	90.2	87.6	84.7	91.1
Ours (K=5)	64.8	62.5	57.8	53.5	56.3	53.1	49.9	56.7	98.4	96.8	92.9	89.2	91.6	88.9	86.3	92.3
Ours (K=10)	66.3	64.3	59.3	55.1	58.5	54.9	53.0	58.7	99.0	97.4	94.4	90.5	93.0	89.7	87.6	93.1
Ours (K=15) - No JMDA	66.4	64.5	59.5	55.4	58.7	55.0	53.3	58.9	99.0	97.5	94.5	90.6	93.1	89.8	87.8	93.2
Ours (K=15)	**66.6**	**64.7**	**59.9**	**55.8**	**59.0**	**55.3**	**53.6**	**59.2**	**99.1**	**97.8**	**94.8**	**91.0**	**93.3**	**90.0**	**88.1**	**93.5**

Table 2. Comparison with state-of-the-arts: PCK@0.2 on the LSP dataset.

Methods	Head	Sho.	Elb.	Wri.	Hip	Knee	Ank.	F.Body
Tompson et al., NIPS 2014 [37]	90.6	79.2	67.9	63.4	69.5	71.0	64.2	72.3
Carreira et al., CVPR 2016 [5]	90.5	81.8	65.8	59.8	81.6	70.6	62.0	73.1
Lifshitz et al., ECCV 2016 [24]	96.8	89.07	82.7	79.1	90.9	86.0	82.5	86.7
Pishchulin et al., CVPR 2016 [33]	97.0	91.0	83.8	78.1	91.0	86.7	82.0	87.1
Insafutdinov et al., ECCV 2016 [18]	97.4	92.7	87.5	84.4	91.5	89.9	87.2	90.1
Wei et al., CVPR 2016 [41]	97.8	92.5	87.0	83.9	91.5	90.8	89.9	90.5
Bulat et al., ECCV 2016 [4]	96.3	92.2	88.2	85.2	92.2	91.5	88.6	90.7
Marras et al., ICCV 2017 [26]	97.9	93.6	90.1	87.1	94.2	93.2	90.5	92.4
Chen et al., ICCV 2017 [7]	98.5	94.0	89.8	87.5	93.9	94.1	93.0	93.1
Peng et al., CVPR 2018 [31]	98.6	95.3	92.8	90.0	94.8	95.3	94.5	94.5
Ours - only k-means++	96.5	92.9	87.5	85.7	92.9	92.1	89.3	91.3
Ours (K=5)	98.2	94.4	91.6	89.1	94.0	94.1	93.4	93.7
Ours (K=10)	98.7	95.2	92.4	90.0	94.7	95.0	94.4	94.5
Ours (K=15) - No JMDA	98.8	95.4	92.7	90.2	94.9	95.2	94.6	94.7
Ours (K=15)	**99.0**	**95.5**	**93.1**	**90.6**	**95.2**	**95.5**	**95.0**	**95.0**

performance gain of around 1.1% over [26]. This way meaningful body pose structures are defined, allowing meaningful filters expressing the conditional dependencies between the location of different joints being estimated by the MRF procedure. By placing the GMM-MRF layer after any ConvNet which performs coarse body pose estimation and training them together, the coarse model is forced to estimate anatomically correct body poses. No experiments were conducted in the case of $K > 15$ due to the very large capacity of the network. For comparison purposes, we are providing results when a smaller number of global poses was used. Also, results without the joint masking data augmentation scheme (JMDA) are provided. Since this data augmentation results in multiple identical joint patches, the solution to a successful pose estimation must rely on some sort of structural inference or knowledge. As our spatial model explicitly learns a different joint inter-connectivity for each meaningful global body pose, this way enforcing global pose consistency, such kind of interesting ideas for data augmentation are ideal for our MRF-part based spatial model.

We used the k-means++ algorithm to initialize the means for each of the Gaussians in our mixture model. To gain insights on how the proposed online pose clustering accomplishes the goal of setting the pose estimations within the geometric constraints, in Fig. 4 we visualize the $\boldsymbol{\mu}_k$ (center of the kth global pose) for each of the 15 Gaussians generated for the MPII database from both the GMM layer trained in an online fashion and the k-means++ initialization algorithm. Also, the pose estimation accuracy when the global poses in our framework are generated only by the k-means++ algorithm in an offline fashion is reported as well. Furthermore, we provide our system performance without the masking augmentation procedure mentioned before. This technique contributes 0.3% PCKh, three times more than in the original work in [22]. This is also an evidence that our geometric model enforces global pose consistency. For both benchmarks, our system achieved the best results among all regression-based approaches, especially for wrists and angles that exhibit larger variations in their motion, because of which they are among the joints that are hard to get localized. The influence of our contribution is significant, while our high-level part-based spatial model helped a quite small and simple network perform even better than more sophisticated and larger systems in the bibliography.

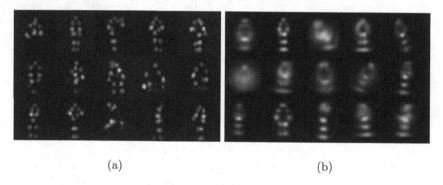

(a)   (b)

Fig. 4. Visualization of $\boldsymbol{\mu}_k$ (center of the kth global pose) for each of the $K = 15$ Gaussians generated for the MPII database from (a) k-means++ algorithm (initialization) and (b) GMM as a network layer used in an online fashion.

6   Conclusions

In this paper, we significantly improved the spatial model in [26] for 2D human pose estimation by proposing an MRF architecture in which the global constraints on the relative locations of the body joints, such as the global poses, are defined by a network layer which implements GMM in an online fashion with the goal of defining the global poses by clustering the human pose predictions. In this case a larger number of meaningful global poses can be estimated by performing clustering using a GMM, keeping the underlying structure of meaningful body poses preserved. Also, a better model initializations is feasible. The cascaded architecture achieved state-of-the-art results on challenging datasets.

References

1. Andriluka, M., Pishchulin, L., Gehler, P., Bernt, S.: 2D human pose estimation: new benchmark and state of the art analysis. In: CVPR, pp. 3686–3693, June 2014
2. Arthur, D., Vassilvitskii, S.: k-means++: the advantages of careful seeding. In: Proceedings of the Eighteenth Annual ACM-SIAM Symposium on Discrete Algorithms, pp. 1027–1035. Society for Industrial and Applied Mathematics (2007)
3. Bishop, C.M.: Pattern Recognition and Machine Learning. Springer, New York (2006)
4. Bulat, A., Tzimiropoulos, G.: Human pose estimation via convolutional part heatmap regression. In: Leibe, B., Matas, J., Sebe, N., Welling, M. (eds.) ECCV 2016. LNCS, vol. 9911, pp. 717–732. Springer, Cham (2016). https://doi.org/10.1007/978-3-319-46478-7_44
5. Carreira, J., Agrawal, P., Fragkiadaki, K., Malik, J.: Human pose estimation with iterative error feedback. In: CVPR, pp. 4733–4742 (2016)
6. Chen, X., Yuille, A.L.: Articulated pose estimation by a graphical model with image dependent pairwise relations. In: NIPS, pp. 1736–1744 (2014)
7. Chen, Y., Shen, C., Wei, X., Liu, L., Yang, J.: Adversarial PoseNet: a structure-aware convolutional network for human pose estimation. In: ICCV, pp. 1212–1221 (2017)
8. Chu, X., Yang, W., Ouyang, W., Ma, C., Yuille, A.L., Wang, X.: Multi-context attention for human pose estimation. In: CVPR, pp. 1831–1840 (2017)
9. Dantone, M., Gall, J., Leistner, C., Van Gool, L.: Body parts dependent joint regressors for human pose estimation in still images. PAMI 36, 2131–2143 (2014)
10. Dempster, A.P., Laird, N.M., Rubin, D.B.: Maximum likelihood from incomplete data via the EM algorithm. J. R. Stat. Soc. Ser. B (Methodol.) 39, 1–38 (1977)
11. Dilokthanakul, N., et al.: Deep unsupervised clustering with Gaussian mixture variational autoencoders. arXiv preprint arXiv:1611.02648 (2016)
12. Duchi, J., Hazan, E., Singer, Y.: Adaptive subgradient methods for online learning and stochastic optimization. JMLR 12, 2121–2159 (2011)
13. Felzenszwalb, P., McAllester, D., Ramanan, D.: A discriminatively trained, multi-scale, deformable part model. In: CVPR, pp. 1–8 (2008)
14. Gkioxari, G., Arbeláez, P., Bourdev, L., Malik, J.: Articulated pose estimation using discriminative armlet classifiers. In: CVPR, pp. 3342–3349 (2013)
15. Gkioxari, G., Toshev, A., Jaitly, N.: Chained predictions using convolutional neural networks. In: Leibe, B., Matas, J., Sebe, N., Welling, M. (eds.) ECCV 2016. LNCS, vol. 9908, pp. 728–743. Springer, Cham (2016). https://doi.org/10.1007/978-3-319-46493-0_44
16. Güler, R., Neverova, N., Kokkinos, I.: Densepose: dense human pose estimation in the wild. In: CVPR (2018)
17. Hu, P., Ramanan, D.: Bottom-up and top-down reasoning with convolutional latent-variable models. In: CVPR, pp. 5600–5609 (2016)
18. Insafutdinov, E., Pishchulin, L., Andres, B., Andriluka, M., Schiele, B.: DeeperCut: a deeper, stronger, and faster multi-person pose estimation model. In: Leibe, B., Matas, J., Sebe, N., Welling, M. (eds.) ECCV 2016. LNCS, vol. 9910, pp. 34–50. Springer, Cham (2016). https://doi.org/10.1007/978-3-319-46466-4_3
19. Jain, A., Tompson, J., LeCun, Y., Bregler, C.: MoDeep: a deep learning framework using motion features for human pose estimation. In: Cremers, D., Reid, I., Saito, H., Yang, M.-H. (eds.) ACCV 2014. LNCS, vol. 9004, pp. 302–315. Springer, Cham (2015). https://doi.org/10.1007/978-3-319-16808-1_21

20. Johnson, S., Everingham, M.: Clustered pose and nonlinear appearance models for human pose estimation. In: BMVC, pp. 12.1–12.11 (2010)
21. Johnson, S., Everingham, M.: Learning effective human pose estimation from inaccurate annotation. In: CVPR, pp. 1465–1472 (2011)
22. Ke, L., Chang, M.-C., Qi, H., Lyu, S.: Multi-scale structure-aware network for human pose estimation. In: Ferrari, V., Hebert, M., Sminchisescu, C., Weiss, Y. (eds.) ECCV 2018. LNCS, vol. 11206, pp. 731–746. Springer, Cham (2018). https://doi.org/10.1007/978-3-030-01216-8_44
23. Krapac, J., Verbeek, J., Jurie, F.: Modeling spatial layout with Fisher vectors for image categorization. In: ICCV, pp. 1487–1494. IEEE (2011)
24. Lifshitz, I., Fetaya, E., Ullman, S.: Human pose estimation using deep consensus voting. In: Leibe, B., Matas, J., Sebe, N., Welling, M. (eds.) ECCV 2016. LNCS, vol. 9906, pp. 246–260. Springer, Cham (2016). https://doi.org/10.1007/978-3-319-46475-6_16
25. Luvizon, D.C., Tabia, H., Picard, D.: Human pose regression by combining indirect part detection and contextual information. CoRR (2017)
26. Marras, I., Palasek, P., Patras, I.: Deep globally constrained MRFs for human pose estimation. In: ICCV, pp. 3466–3475 (2017)
27. Neal, R.M., Hinton, G.E.: A view of the EM algorithm that justifies incremental, sparse, and other variants. In: Jordan, M.I. (ed.) Learning in Graphical Models, pp. 355–368. Springer, Dordrecht (1998). https://doi.org/10.1007/978-94-011-5014-9_12
28. Newell, A., Yang, K., Deng, J.: Stacked hourglass networks for human pose estimation. In: Leibe, B., Matas, J., Sebe, N., Welling, M. (eds.) ECCV 2016. LNCS, vol. 9912, pp. 483–499. Springer, Cham (2016). https://doi.org/10.1007/978-3-319-46484-8_29
29. Nie, X., Feng, J., Zuo, Y., Yan, S.: Human pose estimation with parsing induced learner. In: CVPR, pp. 2100–2108 (2018)
30. Palasek, P., Patras, I.: Discriminative convolutional Fisher vector network for action recognition. arXiv preprint arXiv:1707.06119 (2017)
31. Peng, X., Tang, Z., Yang, F., Feris, R.S., Metaxas, D.: Jointly optimize data augmentation and network training: adversarial data augmentation in human pose estimation. In: CVPR, pp. 2226–2234 (2018)
32. Pfister, T., Simonyan, K., Charles, J., Zisserman, A.: Deep convolutional neural networks for efficient pose estimation in gesture videos. In: Cremers, D., Reid, I., Saito, H., Yang, M.-H. (eds.) ACCV 2014. LNCS, vol. 9003, pp. 538–552. Springer, Cham (2015). https://doi.org/10.1007/978-3-319-16865-4_35
33. Pishchulin, L., et al.: Deepcut: joint subset partition and labeling for multi person pose estimation. In: CVPR, pp. 4929–4937 (2016)
34. Sapp, B., Taskar, B.: Modec: multimodal decomposable models for human pose estimation. In: CVPR, pp. 3674–3681 (2013)
35. Tieleman, T., Hinton, G.: Lecture 6.5-rmsprop: divide the gradient by a running average of its recent magnitude. COURSERA: Neural Netw. Mach. Learn. 4(2), 26–31 (2012)
36. Tompson, J., Goroshin, R., Jain, A., LeCun, Y., Bregler, C.: Efficient object localization using convolutional networks. In: CVPR, pp. 648–656 (2015)
37. Tompson, J., Jain, A., LeCun, Y., Bregler, C.: Joint training of a convolutional network and a graphical model for human pose estimation. In: NIPS, pp. 1799–1807 (2014)
38. Toshev, A., Szegedy, C.: Deeppose: human pose estimation via deep neural networks. In: CVPR, pp. 1653–1660 (2014)

39. Tüske, Z., Tahir, M.A., Schlüter, R., Ney, H.: Integrating Gaussian mixtures into deep neural networks: softmax layer with hidden variables. In: ICASSP, pp. 4285–4289 (2015)
40. Variani, E., McDermott, E., Heigold, G.: A Gaussian mixture model layer jointly optimized with discriminative features within a deep neural network architecture. In: ICASSP, pp. 4270–4274 (2015)
41. Wei, S.E., Ramakrishna, V., Kanade, T., Sheikh, Y.: Convolutional pose machines. In: CVPR, pp. 4724–4732 (2016)
42. Yang, Y., Ramanan, D.: Articulated human detection with flexible mixtures of parts. PAMI **35**(12), 2878–2890 (2013)
43. Zong, B., et al.: Deep autoencoding Gaussian mixture model for unsupervised anomaly detection. In: ICLR (2018)

Author Index

Printed in the United States
By Bookmasters